D0110952

COLLINS
POCKET
GERMAN
DICTIONARY

GERMAN·ENGLISH ENGLISH·GERMAN

COLLINS
POCKET
GERMAN
DICTIONARY

GERMAN·ENGLISH ENGLISH·GERMAN

HarperCollins*Publishers*

First published in this edition 1990

© William Collins Sons & Co. Ltd. 1990

Latest reprint 1993

ISBN 0 00 433248 2 (vinyl)
ISBN 0 00 470106 2 (hardback)

Veronika Calderwood-Schnorr
Ute Nicol, Peter Terrell
Helga Holtkamp, Horst Kopleck
John Whitlam

editorial staff/Manuskriptbearbeitung
Elspeth Anderson, Val McNulty

supplement/Nachtrag
Roy Simon
*reproduced by kind permission of
Tayside Region Education Department*

---

*Printed in Great Britain by
HarperCollins Manufacturing, Glasgow*

INTRODUCTION

Produced for today's learner and user of German, this is a dictionary adapted to the requirements of the 1990's.

The new colour format introduces a more user-friendly approach to word search, and a wealth of modern and idiomatic phrases not normally found in a volume this size.

In addition, the supplement contains a variety of entertaining ways to improve your dictionary skills, and to help you to get the most out of the bilingual dictionary.

We hope you will enjoy using it and that it will significantly enhance your language studies.

ABKÜRZUNGEN		ABBREVIATIONS
Abkürzung	**abk, abbr**	abbreviation
Akkusativ	**acc**	accusative
Adjektiv	**adj**	adjective
Adverb	**adv**	adverb
Landwirtschaft	**AGR**	agriculture
Akkusativ	**akk**	accusative
Anatomie	**ANAT**	anatomy
Architektur	**ARCHIT**	architecture
Astrologie	**ASTROL**	astrology
Astronomie	**ASTRON**	astronomy
attributiv	**attrib**	attributive
Kraftfahrzeuge	**AUT**	automobiles
Hilfsverb	**aux**	auxiliary
Luftfahrt	**AVIAT**	aviation
besonders	**bes**	especially
Biologie	**BIOL**	biology
Botanik	**BOT**	botany
britisch	**BRIT**	British
Chemie	**CHEM**	chemistry
Film	**CINE**	cinema
Handel	**COMM**	commerce
Komparativ	**compar**	comparative
Computer	**COMPUT**	computing
Konjunktion	**conj**	conjunction
Kochen und Backen	**COOK**	cooking
zusammengesetztes Wort	**cpd**	compound
Dativ	**dat**	dative
bestimmter Artikel	**def art**	definite article
Diminutiv	**dimin**	diminutive
kirchlich	**ECCL**	ecclesiastical
Eisenbahn	**EISENB**	railways
Elektrizität	**ELEK, ELEC**	electricity
besonders	**esp**	especially
und so weiter	**etc**	et cetera
etwas	**etw**	something
Euphemismus, Hüllwort	**euph**	euphemism
Interjektion, Ausruf	**excl**	exclamation
Femininum	**f**	feminine
übertragen	**fig**	figurative
Finanzwesen	**FIN**	finance
nicht getrennt gebraucht	**fus**	(phrasal verb) inseparable

ABKÜRZUNGEN

ABBREVIATIONS

Genitiv	**gen**	genitive
Geographie	**GEOG**	geography
Geologie	**GEOL**	geology
Grammatik	**GRAM**	grammar
Geschichte	**HIST**	history
unpersönlich	**impers**	impersonal
unbestimmter Artikel	**indef art**	indefinite article
umgangssprachlich (! vulgär)	**inf(!)**	informal (! particularly offensive)
Infinitiv, Grundform	**infin**	infinitive
nicht getrennt gebraucht	**insep**	inseparable
unveränderlich	**inv**	invariable
unregelmäßig	**irreg**	irregular
jemand	**jd**	somebody
jemandem	**jdm**	(to) somebody
jemanden	**jdn**	somebody
jemandes	**jds**	somebody's
Rechtswesen	**JUR**	law
Kochen und Backen	**KOCH**	cooking
Komparativ	**kompar**	comparative
Konjunktion	**konj**	conjunction
Sprachwissenschaft	**LING**	linguistics
Literatur	**LITER**	of literature
Maskulinum	**m**	masculine
Mathematik	**MATH**	mathematics
Medizin	**MED**	medicine
Meteorologie	**MET**	meteorology
militärisch	**MIL**	military
Bergbau	**MIN**	mining
Musik	**MUS**	music
Substantiv, Hauptwort	**n**	noun
nautisch, Seefahrt	**NAUT**	nautical, naval
Nominativ	**nom**	nominative
Neutrum	**nt**	neuter
Zahlwort	**num**	numeral
Objekt	**obj**	object
oder	**od**	or
sich	**o.s.**	oneself
Parlament	**PARL**	parliament
abschätzig	**pej**	pejorative
Photographie	**PHOT**	photography
Physik	**PHYS**	physics

ABKÜRZUNGEN

ABBREVIATIONS

Plural	pl	plural
Politik	POL	politics
Partizip Perfekt	pp	past participle
Präposition	präp, prep	preposition
Typographie	PRINT	printing
Pronomen, Fürwort	pron	pronoun
Psychologie	PSYCH	psychology
1. Vergangenheit, Imperfekt	pt	past tense
Radio	RAD	radio
Eisenbahn	RAIL	railways
Religion	REL	religion
jemand(-en, -em)	sb	someone, somebody
Schulwesen	SCH	school
Naturwissenschaft	SCI	science
Singular, Einzahl	sg	singular
etwas	sth	something
Konjunktiv	sub	subjunctive
Subjekt	subj	(grammatical) subject
Superlativ	superl	superlative
Technik	TECH	technology
Nachrichtentechnik	TEL	telecommunications
Theater	THEAT	theatre
Fernsehen	TV	television
Typographie	TYP	printing
umgangssprachlich (! vulgär)	umg(!)	informal (! particularly offensive)
Hochschulwesen	UNIV	university
unpersönlich	unpers	impersonal
unregelmäßig	unreg	irregular
(nord)amerikanisch	US	(North) America
gewöhnlich	usu	usually
Verb	vb	verb
intransitives Verb	vi	intransitive verb
reflexives Verb	vr	reflexive verb
transitives Verb	vt	transitive verb
Zoologie	ZOOL	zoology
zusammengesetztes Wort	zW	compound
zwischen zwei Sprechern	-	change of speaker
ungefähre Entsprechung	≃	cultural equivalent
eingetragenes Warenzeichen	®	registered trademark

REGULAR GERMAN NOUN ENDINGS

nom		gen	pl
-ant	*m*	-anten	-anten
-anz	*f*	-anz	-anzen
-ar	*m*	-ar(e)s	-are
-chen	*nt*	-chens	-chen
-e	*f*	-e	-en
-ei	*f*	-ei	-eien
-elle	*f*	-elle	-ellen
-ent	*m*	-enten	enten
-enz	*f*	-enz	-enzen
-ette	*f*	-ette	-etten
-eur	*m*	-eurs	-eure
-euse	*f*	-euse	-eusen
-heit	*f*	-heit	-heiten
-ie	*f*	-ie	-ien
-ik	*f*	-ik	-iken
-in	*f*	-in	-innen
-ine	*f*	-ine	-inen
-ion	*f*	-ion	-ionen
-ist	*m*	-isten	-isten
-ium	*nt*	-iums	-ien
-ius	*m*	-ius	-iusse
-ive	*f*	-ive	-iven
-keit	*f*	-keit	-keiten
-lein	*nt*	-leins	-lein
-ling	*m*	-lings	-linge
-ment	*nt*	-ments	-mente
-mus	*m*	-mus	-men
-schaft	*f*	-schaft	-schaften
-tät	*f*	-tät	-täten
-tor	*m*	-tors	-toren
-ung	*f*	-ung	-ungen
-ur	*f*	-ur	-uren

PHONETIC SYMBOLS / LAUTSCHRIFT

[:] length mark/Längezeichen   *['] stress mark/Betonung*
['] glottal stop/Knacklaut

all vowel sounds are approximate only
alle Vokallaute sind nur ungefähre Entsprechungen

lie	[aɪ]	weit		day	[eɪ]		
now	[aʊ]	Haut		girl	[ɜː]		
above	[ə]	bitte		board	[ɔː]		
go	[əʊ]	oben		root	[uː]	Hut	
green	[iː]	viel		come	[ʌ]	Butler	
pity	[ɪ]	Bischof		salon	[õ]	Champignon	
rot	[ɒ,ɔ]	Post		avant (garde)	[ã]	Ensemble	
full	[ʊ]	Pult		fair	[ɛə]	mehr	
				beer	[ɪə]	Bier	
bet	[b]	Ball		toy	[ɔɪ]	Heu	
dim	[d]	dann		pure	[ʊə]		
face	[f]	Faß		wine	[w]		
go	[g]	Gast		thin	[θ]		
hit	[h]	Herr		this	[ð]		
you	[j]	ja					
cat	[k]	kalt		Hast	[a]	mash	
lick	[l]	Last		haben	[aː]		
must	[m]	Mast		Ensemble	[ã]	avant (garde)	
nut	[n]	Nuß		Metall	[e]	meths	
bang	[ŋ]	lang		häßlich	[ɛ]		
pepper	[p]	Pakt		Cousin	[ɛ̃]		
sit	[s]	Rasse		vital	[i]		
shame	[ʃ]	Schal		Moral	[o]		
tell	[t]	Tal		Champignon	[õ]	salon	
vine	[v]	was		ökonomisch	[ø]		
loch	[x]	Bach		gönnen	[œ]		
zero	[z]	Hase		Heu	[ɔʏ]	toy	
leisure	[ʒ]	Genie		kulant	[u]		
				physisch	[y]		
bat	[æ]			Müll	[ʏ]		
farm	[ɑː]	Bahn		ich	[ç]		
set	[e]	Kette					

[*]   r can be pronounced before a vowel; Bindungs-R

x

GERMAN IRREGULAR VERBS

*with 'sein'

infinitive	present indicative (2nd, 3rd sg.)	imperfect	past participle
aufschrecken*	schrickst auf, schrickt auf	schrak or schreckte auf	aufgeschreckt
ausbedingen	bedingst aus, bedingt aus	bedang or bedingte aus	ausbedungen
backen	bäckst, bäckt	backte or buk	gebacken
befehlen	befiehlst, befiehlt	befahl	befohlen
beginnen	beginnst, beginnt	begann	begonnen
beißen	beißt, beißt	biß	gebissen
bergen	birgst, birgt	barg	geborgen
bersten*	birst, birst	barst	geborsten
bescheißen*	bescheißt, bescheißt	beschiß	beschissen
bewegen	bewegst, bewegt	bewog	bewogen
biegen	biegst, biegt	bog	gebogen
bieten	bietest, bietet	bot	geboten
binden	bindest, bindet	band	gebunden
bitten	bittest, bittet	bat	gebeten
blasen	bläst, bläst	blies	geblasen
bleiben*	bleibst, bleibt	blieb	geblieben
braten	brätst, brät	briet	gebraten
brechen*	brichst, bricht	brach	gebrochen
brennen	brennst, brennt	brannte	gebrannt
bringen	bringst, bringt	brachte	gebracht
denken	denkst, denkt	dachte	gedacht
dreschen	drisch(e)st, drischt	drasch	gedroschen
dringen*	dringst, dringt	drang	gedrungen
dürfen	darfst, darf	durfte	gedurft
empfehlen	empfiehlst, empfiehlt	empfahl	empfohlen
erbleichen*	erbleichst, erbleicht	erbleichte	erblichen
erlöschen*	erlischst, erlischt	erlosch	erloschen
erschrecken*	erschrickst, erschrickt	erschrak	erschrocken
essen	ißt, ißt	aß	gegessen
fahren*	fährst, fährt	fuhr	gefahren
fallen*	fällst, fällt	fiel	gefallen
fangen	fängst, fängt	fing	gefangen
fechten	fichtst, ficht	focht	gefochten
finden	findest, findet	fand	gefunden
flechten	flichtst, flicht	flocht	geflochten
fliegen*	fliegst, fliegt	flog	geflogen
fliehen*	fliehst, flieht	floh	geflohen
fließen*	fließt, fließt	floß	geflossen
fressen	frißt, frißt	fraß	gefressen
frieren	frierst, friert	fror	gefroren
gären*	gärst, gärt	gor	gegoren
gebären	gebierst, gebiert	gebar	geboren
geben	gibst, gibt	gab	gegeben
gedeihen*	gedeihst, gedeiht	gedieh	gediehen
gehen*	gehst, geht	ging	gegangen

infinitive	present indicative (2nd, 3rd sg.)	imperfect	past participle
gelingen*	——, gelingt	gelang	gelungen
gelten	giltst, gilt	galt	gegolten
genesen*	gene(se)st, genest	genas	genesen
genießen	genießt, genießt	genoß	genossen
geraten*	gerätst, gerät	geriet	geraten
geschehen*	——, geschieht	geschah	geschehen
gewinnen	gewinnst, gewinnt	gewann	gewonnen
gießen	gießt, gießt	goß	gegossen
gleichen	gleichst, gleicht	glich	geglichen
gleiten*	gleitest, gleitet	glitt	geglitten
glimmen	glimmst, glimmt	glomm	geglommen
graben	gräbst, gräbt	grub	gegraben
greifen	greifst, greift	griff	gegriffen
haben	hast, hat	hatte	gehabt
halten	hältst, hält	hielt	gehalten
hängen	hängst, hängt	hing	gehangen
hauen	haust, haut	haute	gehauen
heben	hebst, hebt	hob	gehoben
heißen	heißt, heißt	hieß	geheißen
helfen	hilfst, hilft	half	geholfen
kennen	kennst, kennt	kannte	gekannt
klimmen*	klimmst, klimmt	klomm	geklommen
klingen	klingst, klingt	klang	geklungen
kneifen	kneifst, kneift	kniff	gekniffen
kommen*	kommst, kommt	kam	gekommen
können	kannst, kann	konnte	gekonnt
kriechen*	kriechst, kriecht	kroch	gekrochen
laden	lädst, lädt	lud	geladen
lassen	läßt, läßt	ließ	gelassen
laufen*	läufst, läuft	lief	gelaufen
leiden	leidest, leidet	litt	gelitten
leihen	leihst, leiht	lieh	geliehen
lesen	liest, liest	las	gelesen
liegen*	liegst, liegt	lag	gelegen
lügen	lügst, lügt	log	gelogen
mahlen	mahlst, mahlt	mahlte	gemahlen
meiden	meidest, meidet	mied	gemieden
melken	melkst, melkt	melkte	gemolken
messen	mißt, mißt	maß	gemessen
mißlingen*	——, mißlingt	mißlang	mißlungen
mögen	magst, mag	mochte	gemocht
müssen	mußt, muß	mußte	gemußt
nehmen	nimmst, nimmt	nahm	genommen
nennen	nennst, nennt	nannte	genannt
pfeifen	pfeifst, pfeift	pfiff	gepfiffen
preisen	preist, preist	pries	gepriesen
quellen*	quillst, quillt	quoll	gequollen
raten	rätst, rät	riet	geraten
reiben	reibst, reibt	rieb	gerieben
reißen*	reißt, reißt	riß	gerissen

infinitive	present indicative (2nd, 3rd sg.)	imperfect	past participle
reiten*	reitest, reitet	ritt	geritten
rennen*	rennst, rennt	rannte	gerannt
riechen	riechst, riecht	roch	gerochen
ringen	ringst, ringt	rang	gerungen
rinnen*	rinnst, rinnt	rann	geronnen
rufen	rufst, ruft	rief	gerufen
salzen	salzt, salzt	salzte	gesalzen
saufen	säufst, säuft	soff	gesoffen
saugen	saugst, saugt	sog	gesogen
schaffen	schaffst, schafft	schuf	geschaffen
scheiden	scheidest, scheidet	schied	geschieden
scheinen	scheinst, scheint	schien	geschienen
schelten	schiltst, schilt	schalt	gescholten
scheren	scherst, schert	schor	geschoren
schieben	schiebst, schiebt	schob	geschoben
schießen	schießt, schießt	schoß	geschossen
schinden	schindest, schindet	schindete	geschunden
schlafen	schläfst, schläft	schlief	geschlafen
schlagen	schlägst, schlägt	schlug	geschlagen
schleichen*	schleichst, schleicht	schlich	geschlichen
schleifen	schleifst, schleift	schliff	geschliffen
schließen	schließt, schließt	schloß	geschlossen
schlingen	schlingst, schlingt	schlang	geschlungen
schmeißen	schmeißt, schmeißt	schmiß	geschmissen
schmelzen*	schmilzt, schmilzt	schmolz	geschmolzen
schneiden	schneidest, schneidet	schnitt	geschnitten
schreiben	schreibst, schreibt	schrieb	geschrieben
schreien	schreist, schreit	schrie	geschrie(e)n
schreiten*	schreitest, schreitet	schritt	geschritten
schweigen	schweigst, schweigt	schwieg	geschwiegen
schwellen*	schwillst, schwillt	schwoll	geschwollen
schwimmen*	schwimmst, schwimmt	schwamm	geschwommen
schwinden*	schwindest, schwindet	schwand	geschwunden
schwingen	schwingst, schwingt	schwang	geschwungen
schwören	schwörst, schwört	schwor	geschworen
sehen	siehst, sieht	sah	gesehen
sein*	bist, ist	war	gewesen
senden	sendest, sendet	sandte	gesandt
singen	singst, singt	sang	gesungen
sinken*	sinkst, sinkt	sank	gesunken
sinnen	sinnst, sinnt	sann	gesonnen
sitzen*	sitzt, sitzt	saß	gesessen
sollen	sollst, soll	sollte	gesollt
speien	speist, speit	spie	gespie(e)n
spinnen	spinnst, spinnt	spann	gesponnen
sprechen	sprichst, spricht	sprach	gesprochen
sprießen*	sprießt, sprießt	sproß	gesprossen
springen*	springst, springt	sprang	gesprungen
stechen	stichst, sticht	stach	gestochen
stecken	steckst, steckt	steckte or stak	gesteckt

infinitive	present indicative (2nd, 3rd sg.)	imperfect	past participle
stehen	stehst, steht	stand	gestanden
stehlen	stiehlst, stiehlt	stahl	gestohlen
steigen*	steigst, steigt	stieg	gestiegen
sterben*	stirbst, stirbt	starb	gestorben
stinken	stinkst, stinkt	stank	gestunken
stoßen	stößt, stößt	stieß	gestoßen
streichen	streichst, streicht	strich	gestrichen
streiten*	streitest, streitet	stritt	gestritten
tragen	trägst, trägt	trug	getragen
treffen	triffst, trifft	traf	getroffen
treiben*	treibst, treibt	trieb	getrieben
treten*	trittst, tritt	trat	getreten
trinken	trinkst, trinkt	trank	getrunken
trügen	trügst, trügt	trog	getrogen
tun	tust, tut	tat	getan
verderben	verdirbst, verdirbt	verdarb	verdorben
verdrießen	verdrießt, verdrießt	verdroß	verdrossen
vergessen	vergißt, vergißt	vergaß	vergessen
verlieren	verlierst, verliert	verlor	verloren
verschleißen	verschleißt, verschleißt	verschliß	verschlissen
wachsen*	wächst, wächst	wuchs	gewachsen
wägen	wägst, wägt	wog	gewogen
waschen	wäschst, wäscht	wusch	gewaschen
weben	webst, webt	webte *or* wob	gewoben
weichen*	weichst, weicht	wich	gewichen
weisen	weist, weist	wies	gewiesen
wenden	wendest, wendet	wandte	gewandt
werben	wirbst, wirbt	warb	geworben
werden*	wirst, wird	wurde	geworden
werfen	wirfst, wirft	warf	geworfen
wiegen	wiegst, wiegt	wog	gewogen
winden	windest, windet	wand	gewunden
wissen	weißt, weiß	wußte	gewußt
wollen	willst, will	wollte	gewollt
wringen	wringst, wringt	wrang	gewrungen
zeihen	zeihst, zeiht	zieh	geziehen
ziehen*	ziehst, zieht	zog	gezogen
zwingen	zwingst, zwingt	zwang	gezwungen

UNREGELMÄSSIGE ENGLISCHE VERBEN

present	pt	pp	present	pt	pp
arise	arose	arisen	**feed**	fed	fed
awake	awoke	awaked	**feel**	felt	felt
be (am, is,	was, were	been	**fight**	fought	fought
are; being)			**find**	found	found
bear	bore	born(e)	**flee**	fled	fled
beat	beat	beaten	**fling**	flung	flung
become	became	become	**fly (flies)**	flew	flown
begin	began	begun	**forbid**	forbade	forbidden
behold	beheld	beheld	**forecast**	forecast	forecast
bend	bent	bent	**forego**	forewent	foregone
beseech	besought	besought	**foresee**	foresaw	foreseen
beset	beset	beset	**foretell**	foretold	foretold
bet	bet, betted	bet, betted	**forget**	forgot	forgotten
bid	bid, bade	bid, bidden	**forgive**	forgave	forgiven
bind	bound	bound	**forsake**	forsook	forsaken
bite	bit	bitten	**freeze**	froze	frozen
bleed	bled	bled	**get**	got	got, (*US*) gotten
blow	blew	blown	**give**	gave	given
break	broke	broken	**go (goes)**	went	gone
breed	bred	bred	**grind**	ground	ground
bring	brought	brought	**grow**	grew	grown
build	built	built	**hang**	hung,	hung, hanged
burn	burnt,	burnt, burned		hanged	
	burned		**have (has;**	had	had
burst	burst	burst	**having)**		
buy	bought	bought	**hear**	heard	heard
can	could	(been able)	**hide**	hid	hidden
cast	cast	cast	**hit**	hit	hit
catch	caught	caught	**hold**	held	held
choose	chose	chosen	**hurt**	hurt	hurt
cling	clung	clung	**keep**	kept	kept
come	came	come	**kneel**	knelt,	knelt, kneeled
cost	cost	cost		kneeled	
creep	crept	crept	**know**	knew	known
cut	cut	cut	**lay**	laid	laid
deal	dealt	dealt	**lead**	led	led
dig	dug	dug	**lean**	leant, leaned	leant, leaned
do (3rd	did	done	**leap**	leapt, leaped	leapt, leaped
person: he/			**learn**	learnt,	learnt, learned
she/it does)				learned	
draw	drew	drawn	**leave**	left	left
dream	dreamed,	dreamed, dreamt	**lend**	lent	lent
	dreamt		**let**	let	let
drink	drank	drunk	**lie (lying)**	lay	lain
drive	drove	driven	**light**	lit, lighted	lit, lighted
dwell	dwelt	dwelt	**lose**	lost	lost
eat	ate	eaten	**make**	made	made
fall	fell	fallen	**may**	might	—

present	pt	pp	present	pt	pp
mean	meant	meant	spend	spent	spent
meet	met	met	spill	spilt, spilled	spilt, spilled
mistake	mistook	mistaken	spin	spun	spun
mow	mowed	mown, mowed	spit	spat	spat
must	(had to)	(had to)	split	split	split
pay	paid	paid	spoil	spoiled, spoilt	spoiled, spoilt
put	put	put			
quit	quit, quitted	quit, quitted	spread	spread	spread
read	read	read	spring	sprang	sprung
rid	rid	rid	stand	stood	stood
ride	rode	ridden	steal	stole	stolen
ring	rang	rung	stick	stuck	stuck
rise	rose	risen	sting	stung	stung
run	ran	run	stink	stank	stunk
saw	sawed	sawn	stride	strode	stridden
say	said	said	strike	struck	struck, stricken
see	saw	seen	strive	strove	striven
seek	sought	sought	swear	swore	sworn
sell	sold	sold	sweep	swept	swept
send	sent	sent	swell	swelled	swollen, swelled
set	set	set	swim	swam	swum
shake	shook	shaken	swing	swung	swung
shall	should	—	take	took	taken
shear	sheared	shorn, sheared	teach	taught	taught
shed	shed	shed	tear	tore	torn
shine	shone	shone	tell	told	told
shoot	shot	shot	think	thought	thought
show	showed	shown	throw	threw	thrown
shrink	shrank	shrunk	thrust	thrust	thrust
shut	shut	shut	tread	trod	trodden
sing	sang	sung	wake	woke, waked	woken, waked
sink	sank	sunk			
sit	sat	sat	waylay	waylaid	waylaid
slay	slew	slain	wear	wore	worn
sleep	slept	slept	weave	wove, weaved	woven, weaved
slide	slid	slid			
sling	slung	slung	wed	wedded, wed	wedded, wed
slit	slit	slit			
smell	smelt, smelled	smelt, smelled	weep	wept	wept
			win	won	won
sow	sowed	sown, sowed	wind	wound	wound
speak	spoke	spoken	withdraw	withdrew	withdrawn
speed	sped, speeded	sped, speeded	withhold	withheld	withheld
			withstand	withstood	withstood
spell	spelt, spelled	spelt, spelled	wring	wrung	wrung
			write	wrote	written

infinitive	present indicative (2nd, 3rd sg.)	imperfect	past participle
stehen	stehst, steht	stand	gestanden
stehlen	stiehlst, stiehlt	stahl	gestohlen
steigen*	steigst, steigt	stieg	gestiegen
sterben*	stirbst, stirbt	starb	gestorben
stinken	stinkst, stinkt	stank	gestunken
stoßen	stößt, stößt	stieß	gestoßen
streichen	streichst, streicht	strich	gestrichen
streiten*	streitest, streitet	stritt	gestritten
tragen	trägst, trägt	trug	getragen
treffen	triffst, trifft	traf	getroffen
treiben*	treibst, treibt	trieb	getrieben
treten*	trittst, tritt	trat	getreten
trinken	trinkst, trinkt	trank	getrunken
trügen	trügst, trügt	trog	getrogen
tun	tust, tut	tat	getan
verderben	verdirbst, verdirbt	verdarb	verdorben
verdrießen	verdrießt, verdrießt	verdroß	verdrossen
vergessen	vergißt, vergißt	vergaß	vergessen
verlieren	verlierst, verliert	verlor	verloren
verschleißen	verschleißt, verschleißt	verschliß	verschlissen
wachsen*	wächst, wächst	wuchs	gewachsen
wägen	wägst, wägt	wog	gewogen
waschen	wäschst, wäscht	wusch	gewaschen
weben	webst, webt	webte or wob	gewoben
weichen*	weichst, weicht	wich	gewichen
weisen	weist, weist	wies	gewiesen
wenden	wendest, wendet	wandte	gewandt
werben	wirbst, wirbt	warb	geworben
werden*	wirst, wird	wurde	geworden
werfen	wirfst, wirft	warf	geworfen
wiegen	wiegst, wiegt	wog	gewogen
winden	windest, windet	wand	gewunden
wissen	weißt, weiß	wußte	gewußt
wollen	willst, will	wollte	gewollt
wringen	wringst, wringt	wrang	gewrungen
zeihen	zeihst, zeiht	zieh	geziehen
ziehen*	ziehst, zieht	zog	gezogen
zwingen	zwingst, zwingt	zwang	gezwungen

present	pt	pp	present	pt	pp
arise	arose	arisen	feed	fed	fed
awake	awoke	awaked	feel	felt	felt
be (am, is, are; being)	was, were	been	fight	fought	fought
			find	found	found
bear	bore	born(e)	flee	fled	fled
beat	beat	beaten	fling	flung	flung
become	became	become	fly (flies)	flew	flown
begin	began	begun	forbid	forbade	forbidden
behold	beheld	beheld	forecast	forecast	forecast
bend	bent	bent	forego	forewent	foregone
beseech	besought	besought	foresee	foresaw	foreseen
beset	beset	beset	foretell	foretold	foretold
bet	bet, betted	bet, betted	forget	forgot	forgotten
bid	bid, bade	bid, bidden	forgive	forgave	forgiven
bind	bound	bound	forsake	forsook	forsaken
bite	bit	bitten	freeze	froze	frozen
bleed	bled	bled	get	got	got, (US) gotten
blow	blew	blown	give	gave	given
break	broke	broken	go (goes)	went	gone
breed	bred	bred	grind	ground	ground
bring	brought	brought	grow	grew	grown
build	built	built	hang	hung, hanged	hung, hanged
burn	burnt, burned	burnt, burned			
			have (has; having)	had	had
burst	burst	burst	hear	heard	heard
buy	bought	bought	hide	hid	hidden
can	could	(been able)	hit	hit	hit
cast	cast	cast	hold	held	held
catch	caught	caught	hurt	hurt	hurt
choose	chose	chosen	keep	kept	kept
cling	clung	clung	kneel	knelt, kneeled	knelt, kneeled
come	came	come			
cost	cost	cost	know	knew	known
creep	crept	crept	lay	laid	laid
cut	cut	cut	lead	led	led
deal	dealt	dealt	lean	leant, leaned	leant, leaned
dig	dug	dug	leap	leapt, leaped	leapt, leaped
do (3rd person: he/she/it does)	did	done	learn	learnt, learned	learnt, learned
draw	drew	drawn	leave	left	left
dream	dreamed, dreamt	dreamed, dreamt	lend	lent	lent
			let	let	let
drink	drank	drunk	lie (lying)	lay	lain
drive	drove	driven	light	lit, lighted	lit, lighted
dwell	dwelt	dwelt	lose	lost	lost
eat	ate	eaten	make	made	made
fall	fell	fallen	may	might	—

NUMMER   # NUMBERS

ein(s)	1	one	
zwei	2	two	
drei	3	three	
vier	4	four	
fünf	5	five	
sechs	6	six	
sieben	7	seven	
acht	8	eight	
neun	9	nine	
zehn	10	ten	
elf	11	eleven	
zwölf	12	twelve	
dreizehn	13	thirteen	
vierzehn	14	fourteen	
fünfzehn	15	fifteen	
sechzehn	16	sixteen	
siebzehn	17	seventeen	
achtzehn	18	eighteen	
neunzehn	19	nineteen	
zwanzig	20	twenty	
einundzwanzig	21	twenty-one	
zweiundzwanzig	22	twenty-two	
dreißig	30	thirty	
vierzig	40	forty	
fünfzig	50	fifty	
sechzig	60	sixty	
siebzig	70	seventy	
achtzig	80	eighty	
neunzig	90	ninety	
hundert	100	a hundred	
hunderteins	101	a hundred and one	
zweihundert	200	two hundred	
zweihunderteins	201	two hundred and one	
dreihundert	300	three hundred	
dreihunderteins	301	three hundred and one	
tausend	1000	a thousand	
tausend(und)eins	1001	a thousand and one	
fünftausend	5000	five thousand	
eine Million	1000000	a million	

erste(r,s)	1.	first	1st
zweite(r,s)	2.	second	2nd
dritte(r,s)	3.	third	3rd
vierte(r,s)	4.	fourth	4th
fünfte(r,s)	5.	fifth	5th
sechste(r,s)	6.	sixth	6th
siebte(r,s)	7.	seventh	7th
achte(r,s)	8.	eighth	8th
neunte(r,s)	9.	ninth	9th
zehnte(r,s)	10.	tenth	10th

NUMMER

NUMBERS

elfte (r,s)	11.	eleventh	11th
zwölfte (r,s)	12.	twelfth	12th
dreizehnte (r,s)	13.	thirteenth	13th
vierzehnte (r,s)	14.	fourteenth	14th
fünfzehnte (r,s)	15.	fifteenth	15th
sechzehnte (r,s)	16.	sixteenth	16th
siebzehnte (r,s)	17.	seventeenth	17th
achtzehnte (r,s)	18.	eighteenth	18th
neunzehnte (r,s)	19.	nineteenth	19th
zwanzigste (r,s)	20.	twentieth	20th
einundzwanzigste (r,s)	21.	twenty-first	21st
dreißigste (r,s)	30.	thirtieth	30th
hundertste (r,s)	100.	hundredth	100th
hunderterste (r,s)	101.	hundred-and-first	101st
tausendste (r,s)	1000.	thousandth	1000th

Brüche usw.

Fractions etc.

ein Halb	½	a half	
ein Drittel	⅓	a third	
ein Viertel	¼	a quarter	
ein Fünftel	⅕	a fifth	
null Komma fünf	0,5	(nought) point five	0.5
drei Komma vier	3,4	three point four	3.4
sechs Komma acht neun	6,89	six point eight nine	6.89
zehn Prozent	10%	ten per cent	
hundert Prozent	100%	a hundred per cent	

Beispiele

Examples

er wohnt in Nummer 10 — he lives at number 10
es steht in Kapitel 7 — it's in chapter 7
auf Seite 7 — on page 7
er wohnt im 7. Stock — he lives on the 7th floor
er wurde 7. — he came in 7th
im Maßstab eins zu zwanzigtausend — scale one to twenty thousand

UHRZEIT

wieviel Uhr ist es?, wie spät
ist es?
es ist ...

Mitternacht, zwölf Uhr nachts
ein Uhr (morgens *or* früh)

fünf nach eins, ein Uhr fünf
zehn nach eins, ein Uhr zehn
viertel nach eins, ein Uhr fünfzehn
fünf vor halb zwei, ein Uhr
   fünfundzwanzig
halb zwei, ein Uhr dreißig
fünf nach halb zwei, ein Uhr
   fünfunddreißig
zwanzig vor zwei, ein Uhr vierzig
viertel vor zwei, ein Uhr
   fünfundvierzig
zehn vor zwei, ein Uhr fünfzig
zwölf Uhr (mittags), Mittag
halb eins (mittags *or* nachmittags),
   zwölf Uhr dreißig
zwei Uhr (nachmittags)

halb acht (abends)

um wieviel Uhr?
um Mitternacht
um sieben Uhr

in zwanzig Minuten
vor fünfzehn Minuten

THE TIME

what time is it?

it's ...

midnight, twelve p.m.
one o'clock (in the morning), one
   (a.m.)
five past one
ten past one
a quarter past one, one fifteen
twenty-five past one, one twenty-five

half past one, one thirty
twenty-five to two, one thirty-five

twenty to two, one forty
a quarter to two, one forty-five

ten to two, one fifty
twelve o'clock, midday, noon
half past twelve, twelve thirty (p.m.)

two o'clock (in the afternoon), two
   (p.m.)
half past seven (in the evening),
   seven thirty (p.m.)

at what time?
at midnight
at seven o'clock

in twenty minutes
fifteen minutes ago

DEUTSCH - ENGLISCH
GERMAN - ENGLISH

A

à [a] *präp* at
Aal [aːl] (-(e)s, -e) *m* eel
Aas [aːs] (-es, -e *od* Äser) *nt* carrion;
~**geier** *m* vulture

SCHLÜSSELWORT
---

ab [ap] *präp* +*dat* from; **Kinder ab 12
Jahren** children from the age of 12; **ab
morgen** from tomorrow; **ab sofort** as of
now
♦ *adv* **1** off; **links ab** to the left; **der
Knopf ist ab** the button has come off;
ab nach Hause! off you go home
2 (*zeitlich*): **von da ab** from then on;
von heute ab from today, as of today
3 (*auf Fahrplänen*): **München ab 12.20**
leaving Munich 12.20
4: **ab und zu** *od* **an** now and then *od*
again

Abänderung [ˈapˈɛndəruŋ] *f* alteration
Abart [ˈapˈaːrt] *f* (*BIOL*) variety; **a~ig**
adj abnormal
Abbau [ˈapbau] (-(e)s) *m* (+*gen*) dis-
mantling; (*Verminderung*) reduction
(in); (*Verfall*) decline (in); (*MIN*)
mining, quarrying; (*CHEM*) decomposi-
tion; **a~en** *vt* to dismantle; (*MIN*) to
mine; to quarry; (*verringern*) to reduce; (*CHEM*) to break down
abbeißen [ˈapbaisən] (*unreg*) *vt* to bite
off
Abberufung [ˈapbəruːfuŋ] *f* recall
abbestellen [ˈapbəʃtɛlən] *vt* to cancel
abbezahlen [ˈapbətsaːlən] *vt* to pay off
abbiegen [ˈapbiːgən] (*unreg*) *vi* to turn
off; (*Straße*) to bend ♦ *vt* to bend;
(*verhindern*) to ward off
Abbild [ˈapbɪlt] *nt* portrayal; (*einer
Person*) image, likeness; **a~en**
[ˈapbɪldən] *vt* to portray; ~**ung** *f*
illustration

Abbitte [ˈapbɪtə] *f*: (**bei jdm**) ~ **leisten**
od **tun** to make one's apologies (to sb)
abblenden [ˈapblɛndən] *vt*, *vi* (*AUT*) to
dip (*BRIT*), to dim (*US*)
Abblendlicht *nt* dipped (*BRIT*) *od*
dimmed (*US*) headlights *pl*
abbrechen [ˈapbrɛçən] (*unreg*) *vt*, *vi* to
break off; (*Gebäude*) to pull down;
(*Zelt*) to take down; (*aufhören*) to stop;
(*COMPUT*) to abort
abbrennen [ˈapbrɛnən] (*unreg*) *vt* to
burn off; (*Feuerwerk*) to let off ♦ *vi*
(*aux sein*) to burn down
abbringen [ˈapbrɪŋən] (*unreg*) *vt*: **jdn
von etw** ~ to dissuade sb from sth; **jdn
vom Weg** ~ to divert sb
abbröckeln [ˈapbrœkəln] *vt*, *vi* to
crumble off *od* away
Abbruch [ˈapbrux] *m* (*von Verhandlun-
gen etc*) breaking off; (*von Haus*)
demolition; **jdm/etw** ~ **tun** to harm sb/
sth; **a~reif** *adj* only fit for demolition
abbrühen [ˈapbryːən] *vt* to scald; **abge-
brüht** (*umg*) hard-boiled
abbuchen [ˈapbuːxən] *vt* to debit
abbürsten [ˈapbyrstən] *vt* to brush off
abdanken [ˈapdaŋkən] *vi* to resign;
(*König*) to abdicate
Abdankung *f* resignation; abdication
abdecken [ˈapdɛkən] *vt* to uncover;
(*Tisch*) to clear; (*Loch*) to cover
abdichten [ˈapdɪçtən] *vt* to seal; (*NAUT*)
to caulk
abdrehen [ˈapdreːən] *vt* (*Gas*) to turn
off; (*Licht*) to switch off; (*Film*) to
shoot ♦ *vi* (*Schiff*) to change course
Abdruck [ˈapdruk] *m* (*Nachdrucken*) re-
printing; (*Gedrucktes*) reprint; (*Gips~,
Wachs~*) impression; (*Finger~*) print;
a~en *vt* to print, to publish
abdrücken [ˈapdrykən] *vt* (*Waffe*) to
fire; (*Person*) to hug, to squeeze

Abend ['a:bənt] (-s, -e) *m* evening; guten ~ good evening; zu ~ essen to have dinner *od* supper; **a~** *adv*: **heute a~** this evening; **~brot** *nt* supper; **~essen** *nt* supper; **~kasse** *f* box office; **~kurs** *m* evening classes *pl*; **~land** *nt* (*Europa*) West; **a~lich** *adj* evening; **~mahl** *nt* Holy Communion; **~rot** *nt* sunset; **abends** *adv* in the evening

Abenteuer ['a:bəntɔyər] (-s, -) *nt* adventure; **a~lich** *adj* adventurous

Abenteurer (-s, -) *m* adventurer; **~in** *f* adventuress

aber ['a:bər] *konj* but; (*jedoch*) however ♦ *adv*: **tausend und ~ tausend** thousands upon thousands; **das ist ~ schön** that's really nice; **nun ist ~ Schluß!** now that's enough!; **vielen Dank -- ~ bitte!** thanks a lot — you're welcome; **A~glaube** *m* superstition; **~gläubisch** *adj* superstitious

aberkennen ['ap'ɛrkɛnən] (*unreg*) *vt* (*JUR*): **jdm etw ~** to deprive sb of sth, to take sth (away) from sb

Aberkennung *f* taking away

abermals ['a:bərma:ls] *adv* once again

Abf. *abk* (= *Abfahrt*) dep.

abfahren ['apfa:rən] (*unreg*) *vi* to leave, to depart ♦ *vt* to take *od* cart away; (*Strecke*) to drive; (*Reifen*) to wear; (*Fahrkarte*) to use

Abfahrt ['apfa:rt] *f* departure; (*SKI*) descent; (*Piste*) run; **~slauf** *m* (*SKI*) descent, run down; **~szeit** *f* departure time

Abfall ['apfal] *m* waste; (*von Speisen etc*) rubbish (*BRIT*), garbage (*US*); (*Neigung*) slope; (*Verschlechterung*) decline; **~eimer** *m* rubbish bin (*BRIT*), garbage can (*US*); **a~en** (*unreg*) *vi* (*auch fig*) to fall *od* drop off; (*POL, vom Glauben*) to break away; (*sich neigen*) to fall *od* drop away

abfällig ['apfɛlıç] *adj* disparaging, deprecatory

abfangen ['apfaŋən] (*unreg*) *vt* to intercept; (*Person*) to catch; (*unter Kontrolle bringen*) to check

abfärben ['apfɛrbən] *vi* to lose its colour; (*Wäsche*) to run; (*fig*) to rub off

abfassen ['apfasən] *vt* to write, to draft

abfertigen ['apfɛrtıgən] *vt* to prepare for dispatch, to process; (*an der Grenze*) to clear; (*Kundschaft*) to attend to

Abfertigung *f* preparing for dispatch, processing; clearance

abfeuern ['apfɔyərn] *vt* to fire

abfinden ['apfındən] (*unreg*) *vt* to pay off ♦ *vr* to come to terms; **sich mit jdm ~/nicht ~** to put up with/not get on with sb

Abfindung *f* (*von Gläubigern*) payment; (*Geld*) sum in settlement

abflauen ['apflauən] *vi* (*Wind, Erregung*) to die away, to subside; (*Nachfrage, Geschäft*) to fall *od* drop off

abfliegen ['apfli:gən] (*unreg*) *vi* (*Flugzeug*) to take off; (*Passagier auch*) to fly ♦ *vt* (*Gebiet*) to fly over

abfließen ['apfli:sən] (*unreg*) *vi* to drain away

Abflug ['apflu:k] *m* departure; (*Start*) take-off; **~zeit** *f* departure time

Abfluß ['apflus] *m* draining away; (*Öffnung*) outlet

Abfuhr ['apfu:r] (-, -en) *f* removal; (*fig*) snub, rebuff

abführen ['apfy:rən] *vt* to lead away; (*Gelder, Steuern*) to pay ♦ *vi* (*MED*) to have a laxative effect

Abführmittel ['apfy:rmıtəl] *nt* laxative, purgative

abfüllen ['apfylən] *vt* to draw off; (*in Flaschen*) to bottle

Abgabe ['apga:bə] *f* handing in; (*von Ball*) pass; (*Steuer*) tax; (*eines Amtes*) giving up; (*einer Erklärung*) giving

Abgang ['apgaŋ] *m* (*von Schule*) leaving; (*THEAT*) exit; (*MED: Ausscheiden*) passing; (: *Fehlgeburt*) miscarriage; (*Abfahrt*) departure; (*der Post, von Waren*) dispatch

Abgas ['apga:s] *nt* waste gas; (*AUT*) exhaust

abgeben ['apge:bən] (*unreg*) *vt* (*Gegenstand*) to hand *od* give in; (*Ball*) to pass; (*Wärme*) to give off; (*Amt*) to hand over; (*Schuß*) to fire; (*Erklärung,*

Urteil) to give; (*darstellen, sein*) to make ♦ *vr*: **sich mit jdm/etw ~ to** associate with sb/bother with sth; **jdm etw ~** (*überlassen*) to let sb have sth

abgehen ['apgeːən] (*unreg*) *vi* to go away, to leave; (*THEAT*) to exit; (*Baby*) to be aborted; (*Knopf etc*) to come off; (*abgezogen werden*) to be taken off; (*Straße*) to branch off ♦ *vt* (*Strecke*) to go *od* walk along; **etw geht jdm ab** (*fehlt*) sb lacks sth

abgelegen ['apgəleːgən] *adj* remote

abgemacht ['apgəmaxt] *adj* fixed; **~!** done!

abgeneigt ['apgənaɪkt] *adj* disinclined

Abgeordnete(r) ['apgəˈɔrdnətə(r)] *mf* member of parliament; elected representative

abgeschmackt ['apgəʃmakt] *adj* tasteless

abgesehen ['apgəzeːən] *adj*: **es auf jdn/ etw ~ haben** to be after sb/sth; **~ von** ... apart from ...

abgespannt ['apgəʃpant] *adj* tired out

abgestanden ['apgəʃtandən] *adj* stale; (*Bier auch*) flat

abgestorben ['apgəʃtɔrbən] *adj* numb; (*BIOL, MED*) dead

abgetragen ['apgətraːgən] *adj* shabby, worn out

abgewinnen ['apgəvɪnən] (*unreg*) *vt*: **einer Sache etw/Geschmack ~** to get sth/pleasure from sth

abgewöhnen ['apgəvøːnən] *vt*: **jdm/sich etw ~** to cure sb of sth/give sth up

abgleiten ['apglaɪtən] (*unreg*) *vi* to slip, to slide

Abgott ['apgɔt] *m* idol

abgöttisch ['apgœtɪʃ] *adj*: **~ lieben** to idolize

abgrenzen ['apgrɛntsən] *vt* (*auch fig*) to mark off; to fence off

Abgrund ['apgrʊnt] *m* (*auch fig*) abyss

abhacken ['aphakən] *vt* to chop off

abhalten ['aphaltən] (*unreg*) *vt* (*Versammlung*) to hold; **jdn von etw ~** (*fernhalten*) to keep sb away from sth; (*hindern*) to keep sb from sth

abhanden [apˈhandən] *adj*: **~ kommen** to get lost

Abhandlung ['aphandlʊŋ] *f* treatise, discourse

Abhang ['aphaŋ] *m* slope

abhängen ['aphɛŋən] *vt* (*Bild*) to take down; (*Anhänger*) to uncouple; (*Verfolger*) to shake off ♦ *vi* (*unreg*: *Fleisch*) to hang; **von jdm/etw ~** to depend on sb/sth

abhängig ['aphɛŋɪç] *adj*: **~ (von)** dependent (on); **A~keit** *f*: **A~keit (von)** dependence (on)

abhärten ['aphɛrtən] *vt, vr* to toughen (o.s.) up; **sich gegen etw ~** to inure o.s. to sth

abhauen ['aphauən] (*unreg*) *vt* to cut off; (*Baum*) to cut down ♦ *vi* (*umg*) to clear off *od* out

abheben ['apheːbən] (*unreg*) *vt* to lift (up); (*Karten*) to cut; (*Masche*) to slip; (*Geld*) to withdraw, to take out ♦ *vi* (*Flugzeug*) to take off; (*Rakete*) to lift off; (*KARTEN*) to cut ♦ *vr* to stand out

abhelfen ['aphɛlfən] (*unreg*) *vi* +*dat* to remedy

abhetzen ['aphɛtsən] *vr* to wear *od* tire o.s. out

Abhilfe ['aphɪlfə] *f* remedy; **~ schaffen** to put things right

abholen ['aphoːlən] *vt* (*Gegenstand*) to fetch, to collect; (*Person*) to call for; (*am Bahnhof etc*) to pick up, to meet

abhören ['aphøːrən] *vt* (*Vokabeln*) to test; (*Telefongespräch*) to tap; (*Tonband etc*) to listen to

Abhörgerät *nt* bug

Abitur [abiˈtuːr] *nt* (**-s**, **-e**) *nt* German school-leaving examination; **Abituri'ent(in)** *m(f)* candidate for school-leaving certificate

Abk. *abk* (= *Abkürzung*) abbr.

abkanzeln ['apkantsəln] (*umg*) *vt* to bawl out

abkapseln ['apkapsəln] *vr* to shut *od* cut o.s. off

abkaufen ['apkaufən] *vt*: **jdm etw ~** (*auch fig*) to buy sth from sb

abkehren ['apkeːrən] *vt* (*Blick*) to avert, to turn away ♦ *vr* to turn away

abklingen ['apklɪŋən] (*unreg*) *vi* to die

away; (*Radio*) to fade out

abknöpfen ['apknœpfən] *vt* to unbutton; jdm etw ~ (*umg*) to get sth off sb

abkochen ['apkɔxən] *vt* to boil

abkommen ['apkɔmən] (*unreg*) *vi* to get away; **von der Straße/von einem Plan** ~ to leave the road/give up a plan; **A**~ (-s, -) *nt* agreement

abkömmlich ['apkœmlıç] *adj* available, free

abkratzen ['apkratsən] *vt* to scrape off ♦ *vi* (*umg*) to kick the bucket

abkühlen ['apky:lən] *vt* to cool down ♦ *vr* (*Mensch*) to cool down *od* off; (*Wetter*) to get cool; (*Zuneigung*) to cool

abkürzen ['apkʏrtsən] *vt* to shorten; (*Wort auch*) to abbreviate; **den Weg** ~ to take a short cut

Abkürzung *f* (*Wort*) abbreviation; (*Weg*) short cut

abladen ['apla:dən] (*unreg*) *vt* to unload

Ablage ['apla:gə] *f* (*für Akten*) tray; (*für Kleider*) cloakroom

ablassen ['aplasən] (*unreg*) *vt* (*Wasser, Dampf*) to let off; (*vom Preis*) to knock off ♦ *vi*: **von etw** ~ to give sth up, to abandon sth

Ablauf ['aplauf] *m* (*Abfluß*) drain; (*von Ereignissen*) course; (*einer Frist, Zeit*) expiry (*BRIT*), expiration (*US*); **a**~**en** (*unreg*) *vi* (*abfließen*) to drain away; (*Ereignisse*) to happen; (*Frist, Zeit, Paß*) to expire ♦ *vt* (*Sohlen*) to wear (down *od* out)

ablegen ['aple:gən] *vt* to put *od* lay down; (*Kleider*) to take off; (*Gewohnheit*) to get rid of; (*Prüfung*) to take, to sit; (*Zeugnis*) to give

Ableger (-s, -) *m* layer; (*fig*) branch, offshoot

ablehnen ['aple:nən] *vt* to reject; (*Einladung*) to decline, to refuse ♦ *vi* to decline, to refuse

Ablehnung *f* rejection; refusal

ableiten ['aplaıtən] *vt* (*Wasser*) to divert; (*deduzieren*) to deduce; (*Wort*) to derive

Ableitung *f* diversion; deduction; derivation; (*Wort*) derivative

ablenken ['aplɛŋkən] *vt* to turn away, to deflect; (*zerstreuen*) to distract ♦ *vi* to change the subject

Ablenkung *f* distraction

ablesen ['aple:zən] (*unreg*) *vt* to read out; (*Meßgeräte*) to read

abliefern ['apli:fərn] *vt* to deliver; **etw bei jdm/einer Dienststelle** ~ to hand sth over to sb/in at an office

Ablieferung *f* delivery

abliegen ['apli:gən] (*unreg*) *vi* to be some distance away; (*fig*) to be far removed

ablösen ['aplø:zən] *vt* (*abtrennen*) to take off, to remove; (*in Amt*) to take over from; (*Wache*) to relieve

Ablösung *f* removal; relieving

abmachen ['apmaxən] *vt* to take off; (*vereinbaren*) to agree

Abmachung *f* agreement

abmagern ['apma:gərn] *vi* to get thinner

Abmagerungskur *f* diet; **eine** ~ **machen** to go on a diet

Abmarsch ['apmarʃ] *m* departure

abmelden ['apmɛldən] *vt* (*Zeitungen*) to cancel; (*Auto*) to take off the road ♦ *vr* to give notice of one's departure; (*im Hotel*) to check out; **jdn bei der Polizei** ~ to register sb's departure with the police

abmessen ['apmɛsən] (*unreg*) *vt* to measure

Abmessung *f* measurement

abmontieren ['apmɔnti:rən] *vt* to take off

abmühen ['apmy:ən] *vr* to wear o.s. out

Abnahme ['apna:mə] *f* (+*gen*) removal; (*COMM*) buying; (*Verringerung*) decrease (in)

abnehmen ['apne:mən] (*unreg*) *vt* to take off, to remove; (*Führerschein*) to take away; (*Prüfung*) to hold; (*Maschen*) to decrease ♦ *vi* to decrease; (*schlanker werden*) to lose weight; (**jdm**) **etw** ~ (*Geld*) to get sth (out of sb); (*kaufen, umg: glauben*) to buy sth (from sb); **jdm Arbeit** ~ to take work off sb's shoulders

Abnehmer (-s, -) *m* purchaser, customer

Abneigung ['apnaɪgʊŋ] *f* aversion, dislike

abnorm [ap'nɔrm] *adj* abnormal

abnutzen ['apnʊtsən] *vt* to wear out

Abnutzung *f* wear (and tear)

Abonnement [abɔn(ə)'mãː] (-s, -s) *nt* subscription

Abonnent(in) [abɔ'nɛnt(ɪn)] *m(f)* subscriber

abonnieren [abɔ'niːrən] *vt* to subscribe to

Abordnung [ap'ɔrdnʊŋ] *f* delegation

Abort [a'bɔrt] (-(e)s, -e) *m* lavatory

abpacken ['appakən] *vt* to pack

abpassen ['appasən] *vt* (*Person, Gelegenheit*) to wait for; (*in Größe: Stoff etc*) to adjust

abpfeifen ['appfaɪfən] (*unreg*) *vt, vi* (*SPORT*): (**das Spiel**) ~ to blow the whistle (for the end of the game)

Abpfiff ['appfɪf] *m* final whistle

abplagen ['appla:gən] *vr* to wear o.s. out

Abprall ['appral] *m* rebound; (*von Kugel*) ricochet; **a~en** *vi* to bounce off; to ricochet

abputzen ['apputsən] *vt* to clean

abraten ['apra:tən] (*unreg*) *vi*: **jdm von etw** ~ to advise sb against sth, to warn sb against sth

abräumen ['aprɔʏmən] *vt* to clear up *od* away

abreagieren ['aprɛagiːrən] *vt*: **seinen Zorn (an jdm/etw)** ~ to work one's anger off (on sb/sth) ♦ *vr* to calm down

abrechnen ['aprɛçnən] *vt* to deduct, to take off ♦ *vi* to settle up; (*fig*) to get even

Abrechnung *f* settlement; (*Rechnung*) bill

Abrede ['apre:də] *f*: **etw in** ~ **stellen** to deny *od* dispute sth

abregen ['apre:gən] (*umg*) *vr* to calm *od* cool down

Abreise ['apraɪzə] *nf* departure; **a~n** *vi* to leave, to set off

abreißen ['apraɪsən] (*unreg*) *vt* (*Haus*) to tear down; (*Blatt*) to tear off

abrichten ['aprɪçtən] *vt* to train

abriegeln ['apri:gəln] *vt* (*Tür*) to bolt; (*Straße, Gebiet*) to seal off

Abriß ['aprɪs] (-sses, -sse) *m* (*Übersicht*) outline

Abruf ['apru:f] *m*: **auf** ~ on call; **a~en** (*unreg*) *vt* (*Mensch*) to call away; (*COMM: Ware*) to request delivery of

abrunden ['aprʊndən] *vt* to round off

abrüsten ['aprʏstən] *vi* to disarm

Abrüstung *f* disarmament

abrutschen ['aprʊtʃən] *vi* to slip; (*AVIAT*) to sideslip

Abs. *abk* (= *Absender*) sender, from

Absage ['apza:gə] *f* refusal; **a~n** *vt* to cancel, to call off; (*Einladung*) to turn down ♦ *vi* to cry off; (*ablehnen*) to decline

absägen ['apzɛ:gən] *vt* to saw off

Absatz ['apzats] *m* (*COMM*) sales *pl*; (*Bodensatz*) deposit; (*neuer Abschnitt*) paragraph; (*Treppen~*) landing; (*Schuh~*) heel; **~gebiet** *nt* (*COMM*) market

abschaben ['apʃa:bən] *vt* to scrape off; (*Möhren*) to scrape

abschaffen ['apʃafən] *vt* to abolish, to do away with

Abschaffung *f* abolition

abschalten ['apʃaltən] *vt, vi* (*auch umg*) to switch off

abschätzen ['apʃɛtsən] *vt* to estimate; (*Lage*) to assess; (*Person*) to size up

abschätzig ['apʃɛtsɪç] *adj* disparaging, derogatory

Abschaum ['apʃaʊm] (-(e)s) *m* scum

Abscheu ['apʃɔʏ] (-(e)s) *m* loathing, repugnance; **a~erregend** *adj* repulsive, loathsome; **a~lich** [ap'ʃɔʏlɪç] *adj* abominable

abschicken ['apʃɪkən] *vt* to send off

abschieben ['apʃi:bən] (*unreg*) *vt* to push away; (*Person*) to pack off; (: *POL*) to deport

Abschied ['apʃi:t] (-(e)s, -e) *m* parting; (*von Armee*) discharge; (**von jdm**) ~ **nehmen** to say goodbye (to sb), to take one's leave (of sb); **seinen** ~ **nehmen** (*MIL*) to apply for discharge; **Abschiedsbrief** *m* farewell letter

abschießen ['apʃi:sən] (*unreg*) *vt* (*Flugzeug*) to shoot down; (*Geschoß*) to fire; (*umg: Minister*) to get rid of

abschirmen ['apʃɪrmən] vt to screen
abschlagen ['apʃlaːgən] (unreg) vt (abhacken, COMM) to knock off; (ablehnen) to refuse; (MIL) to repel
abschlägig ['apʃlɛːgɪç] adj negative
Abschlagszahlung f interim payment
abschleifen ['apʃlaɪfən] (unreg) vt to grind down; (Rost) to polish off ♦ vr to wear off
Abschlepp- ['apʃlɛp] zW: ~**dienst** m (AUT) breakdown service (BRIT), towing company (US); **a~en** vt to (take in) tow; ~**seil** nt towrope
abschließen ['apʃliːsən] (unreg) vt (Tür) to lock; (beenden) to conclude, to finish; (Vertrag, Handel) to conclude ♦ vr (sich isolieren) to cut o.s. off
Abschluß ['apʃlʊs] m (Beendigung) close, conclusion; (COMM: Bilanz) balancing; (von Vertrag, Handel) conclusion; **zum** ~ in conclusion; ~**prüfung** f final exam
abschmieren ['apʃmiːrən] vt (AUT) to grease, to lubricate
abschneiden ['apʃnaɪdən] (unreg) vt to cut off ♦ vi to do, to come off
Abschnitt ['apʃnɪt] m section; (MIL) sector; (Kontroll~) counterfoil; (MATH) segment; (Zeit~) period
abschnüren ['apʃnyːrən] vt to constrict
abschöpfen ['apʃœpfən] vt to skim off
abschrauben ['apʃraubən] vt to unscrew
abschrecken ['apʃrɛkən] vt to deter, to put off; (mit kaltem Wasser) to plunge in cold water; ~**d** adj deterrent; ~**des Beispiel** warning
abschreiben ['apʃraɪbən] (unreg) vt to copy; (verlorengeben) to write off; (COMM) to deduct
Abschrift ['apʃrɪft] f copy
Abschuß ['apʃʊs] m (eines Geschützes) firing; (Herunterschießen) shooting down; (Tötung) shooting
abschüssig ['apʃʏsɪç] adj steep
abschütteln ['apʃʏtəln] vt to shake off
abschwächen ['apʃvɛçən] vt to lessen; (Behauptung, Kritik) to tone down ♦ vr to lessen
abschweifen ['apʃvaɪfən] vi to wander
Abschweifung f digression

abschwellen ['apʃvɛlən] (unreg) vi (Geschwulst) to go down; (Lärm) to die down
abschwören ['apʃvøːrən] vi (+dat) to renounce
absehbar adj foreseeable; **in** ~**er Zeit** in the foreseeable future; **das Ende ist** ~ **the end is in sight**
absehen ['apzeːən] (unreg) vt (Ende, Folgen) to foresee ♦ vi: **von etw** ~ to refrain from sth; (nicht berücksichtigen) to leave sth out of consideration
abseits ['apzaɪts] adv out of the way ♦ präp +gen away from; **A~** nt (SPORT) offside
Absend- ['apzɛnd] zW: **a~en** (unreg) vt to send off, to dispatch; ~**er** (-s, -) m sender; ~**ung** f dispatch
absetzen ['apzɛtsən] vt (niederstellen, aussteigen lassen) to put down; (abnehmen) to take off; (COMM: verkaufen) to sell; (FIN: abziehen) to deduct; (entlassen) to dismiss; (König) to depose; (streichen) to drop; (hervorheben) to pick out ♦ vr (sich entfernen) to clear off; (sich ablagern) to be deposited
Absetzung f (FIN: Abzug) deduction; (Entlassung) dismissal; (von König) deposing; (Streichung) dropping
absichern ['apzɪçərn] vt to make safe; (schützen) to safeguard ♦ vr to protect o.s.
Absicht ['apzɪçt] f intention; **mit** ~ on purpose; **a~lich** adj intentional, deliberate
absinken ['apzɪŋkən] (unreg) vi to sink; (Temperatur, Geschwindigkeit) to decrease
absitzen ['apzɪtsən] (unreg) vi to dismount ♦ vt (Strafe) to serve
absolut [apzo'luːt] adj absolute; **A~ismus** [-'tɪsmʊs] m absolutism
absolvieren [apzɔl'viːrən] vt (SCH) to complete
absonder- ['apzɔndər] zW: ~**lich** [ap'zɔndərlɪç] adj odd, strange; ~**n** vt to separate; (ausscheiden) to give off, to secrete ♦ vr to cut o.s. off; **A~ung** f separation; (MED) secretion
abspalten ['apʃpaltən] vt to split off

abspeisen ['apʃpaizən] vt (fig) to fob off

abspenstig ['apʃpɛnstiç] adj: (jdm) ~ machen to lure away (from sb)

absperren ['apʃpɛrən] vt to block od close off; (Tür) to lock

Absperrung f (Vorgang) blocking od closing off; (Sperre) barricade

abspielen ['apʃpiːlən] vt (Platte, Tonband) to play; (SPORT: Ball) to pass ♦ vr to happen

absplittern ['apʃplɪtɐn] vt to chip off

Absprache ['apʃpraːxə] f arrangement

absprechen ['apʃprɛçən] (unreg) vt (vereinbaren) to arrange; **jdm etw** ~ to deny sb sth

abspringen ['apʃprɪŋən] (unreg) vi to jump down/off; (Farbe, Lack) to flake off; (AVIAT) to bale out; (sich distanzieren) to back out

Absprung ['apʃprʊŋ] m jump

abspülen ['apʃpyːlən] vt to rinse; (Geschirr) to wash up

abstammen ['apʃtamən] vi to be descended; (Wort) to be derived

Abstammung f descent; derivation

Abstand ['apʃtant] m distance; (zeitlich) interval; **davon** ~ **nehmen, etw zu tun** to refrain from doing sth; ~ **halten** (AUT) to keep one's distance; **mit** ~ **der beste** by far the best

abstatten ['apʃtatən] vt (Dank) to give; (Besuch) to pay

abstauben ['apʃtaubən] vt, vi to dust; (umg: stehlen) to pinch; (: schnorren) to scrounge

Abstecher ['apʃtɛçɐ] (-s, -) m detour

abstehen ['apʃteːən] (unreg) vi (Ohren, Haare) to stick out; (entfernt sein) to stand away

absteigen ['apʃtaigən] (unreg) vi (vom Rad etc) to get off, to dismount; **in einem Gasthof** ~ to put up at an inn; (in die zweite Liga) ~ to be relegated (to the second division)

abstellen ['apʃtɛlən] vt (niederstellen) to put down; (entfernt stellen) to pull out; (hinstellen: Auto) to park; (ausschalten) to turn od switch off; (Mißstand, Unsitte) to stop; (ausrichten): ~ **auf** +akk to gear to

Abstellgleis nt siding

abstempeln ['apʃtɛmpəln] vt to stamp

absterben ['apʃtɛrbən] (unreg) vi to die; (Körperteil) to go numb

Abstieg ['apʃtiːk] (-(e)s, -e) m descent; (SPORT) relegation; (fig) decline

abstimmen ['apʃtɪmən] vi to vote ♦ vt: ~ **(auf** +akk) (Instrument) to tune (to); (Interessen) to match (with); (Termine, Ziele) to fit in (with) ♦ vr to agree

Abstimmung f vote

Abstinenz [apsti'nɛnts] f abstinence; **teetotalism;** ~**ler(in)** (-s, -) m(f) teetotaller

abstoßen ['apʃtoːsən] (unreg) vt to push off od away; (verkaufen) to unload; (anekeln) to repel, to repulse; ~**d** adj repulsive

abstrakt [ap'strakt] adj abstract ♦ adv abstractly, in the abstract

abstreiten ['apʃtraitən] (unreg) vt to deny

Abstrich ['apʃtrɪç] m (Abzug) cut; (MED) smear; ~**e machen** to lower one's sights

abstufen ['apʃtuːfən] vt (Hang) to terrace; (Farben) to shade; (Gehälter) to grade

abstumpfen ['apʃtumpfən] vt (auch fig) to dull, to blunt ♦ vi to become dulled

Absturz ['apʃtʊrts] m fall; (AVIAT) crash

abstürzen ['apʃtʏrtsən] vi to fall; (AVIAT) to crash

absuchen ['apzuːxən] vt to scour, to search

absurd [ap'zʊrt] adj absurd

Abszeß [aps'tsɛs] (-sses, -sse) m abscess

Abt [apt] (-(e)s, -̈e) m abbot

Abt. abk (= Abteilung) dept.

abtasten ['aptastən] vt to feel, to probe

abtauen ['aptauən] vt, vi to thaw

Abtei [ap'tai] (-, -en) f abbey

Abteil [ap'tail] (-(e)s, -e) nt compartment; '**a~en** vt to divide up; (abtrennen) to divide off; ~**ung** f (in Firma, Kaufhaus) department; (in Krankenhaus) section; (MIL) unit

abtönen ['aptøːnən] vt (PHOT) to tone down

abtransportieren [ˈaptranspɔrtiːrən] *vt*
to take away, to remove
abtreiben [ˈaptraɪbən] (*unreg*) *vt* (*Boot, Flugzeug*) to drive off course; (*Kind*) to abort ♦ *vi* to be driven off course; to abort
Abtreibung *f* abortion
abtrennen [ˈaptrɛnən] *vt* (*lostrennen*) to detach; (*entfernen*) to take off; (*abteilen*) to separate off
abtreten [ˈaptreːtən] (*unreg*) *vt* to wear out; (*überlassen*) to hand over, to cede ♦ *vi* to go off; (*zurücktreten*) to step down
Abtritt [ˈaptrɪt] *m* resignation
abtrocknen [ˈaptrɔknən] *vt*, *vi* to dry
abtun [ˈaptuːn] (*unreg*) *vt* to take off; (*Gewohnheit*) to give up; (*fig*) to dismiss
abverlangen [ˈapfɛrlaŋən] *vt*: **jdm etw ~ to demand sth from sb**
abwägen [ˈapvɛːgən] (*unreg*) *vt* to weigh up
abwandeln [ˈapvandəln] *vt* to adapt
abwandern [ˈapvandərn] *vi* to move away; (*FIN*) to be transferred
abwarten [ˈapvartən] *vt* to wait for ♦ *vi* to wait
abwärts [ˈapvɛrts] *adv* down
Abwasch [ˈapvaʃ] (*-(e)s*) *m* washing-up; **a~en** (*unreg*) *vt* (*Schmutz*) to wash off; (*Geschirr*) to wash (up)
Abwasser [ˈapvasər] (*-s, -wässer*) *nt* sewage
abwechseln [ˈapvɛksəln] *vi, vr* to alternate; (*Personen*) to take turns; **~d** *adj* alternate
Abwechslung *f* change
Abweg [ˈapveːk] *m*: **auf ~e geraten/führen** to go/lead astray; **a~ig** [ˈapveːgɪç] *adj* wrong
Abwehr [ˈapveːr] (*-*) *f* defence; (*Schutz*) protection; (*~dienst*) counterintelligence (service); **a~en** *vt* to ward off; (*Ball*) to stop
abweichen [ˈapvaɪçən] (*unreg*) *vi* to deviate; (*Meinung*) to differ; **~d** *adj* deviant; differing
abweisen [ˈapvaɪzən] (*unreg*) *vt* to turn away; (*Antrag*) to turn down; **~d** *adj*

(*Haltung*) cold
abwenden [ˈapvɛndən] (*unreg*) *vt* to avert ♦ *vr* to turn away
abwerfen [ˈapvɛrfən] (*unreg*) *vt* to throw off; (*Profit*) to yield; (*aus Flugzeug*) to drop; (*Spielkarte*) to discard
abwerten [ˈapveːrtən] *vt* (*FIN*) to devalue
abwesend [ˈapveːzənt] *adj* absent
Abwesenheit [ˈapveːzənhaɪt] *f* absence
abwickeln [ˈapvɪkəln] *vt* to unwind; (*Geschäft*) to wind up
abwiegen [ˈapviːgən] (*unreg*) *vt* to weigh out
abwischen [ˈapvɪʃən] *vt* to wipe off *od* away; (*putzen*) to wipe
Abwurf [ˈapvʊrf] *m* throwing off; (*von Bomben etc*) dropping; (*von Reiter, SPORT*) throw
abwürgen [ˈapvʏrgən] (*umg*) *vt* to scotch; (*Motor*) to stall
abzahlen [ˈaptsaːlən] *vt* to pay off
abzählen [ˈaptsɛːlən] *vt, vi* to count (up)
Abzahlung *f* repayment; **auf ~ kaufen** to buy on hire purchase
abzapfen [ˈaptsapfən] *vt* to draw off; **jdm Blut ~** to take blood from sb
abzäunen [ˈaptsɔʏnən] *vt* to fence off
Abzeichen [ˈaptsaɪçən] *nt* badge; (*Orden*) decoration
abzeichnen [ˈaptsaɪçnən] *vt* to draw, to copy; (*Dokument*) to initial ♦ *vr* to stand out; (*fig: bevorstehen*) to loom
Abziehbild *nt* transfer
abziehen [ˈaptsiːən] (*unreg*) *vt* to take off; (*Tier*) to skin; (*Bett*) to strip; (*Truppen*) to withdraw; (*subtrahieren*) to take away, to subtract; (*kopieren*) to run off ♦ *vi* to go away; (*Truppen*) to withdraw
abzielen [ˈaptsiːlən] *vi*: **~ auf +akk** to be aimed at
Abzug [ˈaptsuːk] *m* departure; (*von Truppen*) withdrawal; (*Kopie*) copy; (*Subtraktion*) subtraction; (*Betrag*) deduction; (*Rauch~*) flue; (*von Waffen*) trigger
abzüglich [ˈaptsyːklɪç] *präp +gen* less
abzweigen [ˈaptsvaɪgən] *vi* to branch off

♦ *vt* to set aside

Abzweigung *f* junction

ach [ax] *excl* oh; ~ **ja!** (oh) yes; ~ **so!** I see; **mit A~ und Krach** by the skin of one's teeth

Achse ['aksə] *f* axis; (*AUT*) axle

Achsel ['aksəl] (-, -n) *f* shoulder; ~**höhle** *f* armpit; ~**zucken** *nt* shrug (of one's shoulders)

acht [axt] *num* eight; ~ **Tage** a week; **sich in** ~ **nehmen** (**vor** +*dat*) to be careful (of), to watch out (for); **etw außer** ~ **lassen** to disregard sth; ~**bar** *adj* worthy; ~**e(r, s)** *adj* eighth; ~**el** *num* eighth; ~**en** *vt* to respect ♦ *vi:* ~**en** (**auf** +*akk*) to pay attention (to); **darauf** ~**en, daß** ... to be careful that ...

ächten ['ɛçtən] *vt* to outlaw, to ban

Achterbahn ['axtər-] *f* roller coaster

Achterdeck *nt* (*NAUT*) afterdeck

acht- *zW:* ~**fach** *adj* eightfold; ~**geben** (*unreg*) *vi:* ~**geben** (**auf** +*akk*) to pay attention (to); ~**los** *adj* careless; ~**mal** *adv* eight times; ~**sam** *adj* attentive

Achtung ['axtʊŋ] *f* attention; (*Ehrfurcht*) respect ♦ *excl* look out!; (*MIL*) attention!; **alle** ~**!** good for you/ him *etc*

achtzehn *num* eighteen

achtzig *num* eighty

ächzen ['ɛçtsən] *vi* to groan

Acker ['akər] (-s, ⁼) *m* field; ~**bau** *m* agriculture; **a~n** *vt*, *vi* to plough; (*umg*) to slog away

ADAC [a:de:'a:tse:] *abk* (= *Allgemeiner Deutscher Automobil-Club*) ≈ AA, RAC

addieren [a'di:rən] *vt* to add (up)

Addition [aditsi'o:n] *f* addition

Adel ['a:dəl] (-s) *m* nobility; **a~ig** *adj* noble

Ader ['a:dər] (-, -n) *f* vein

Adler ['a:dlər] (-s, -) *m* eagle

adlig *adj* noble

Admiral [atmi'ra:l] (-s, -e) *m* admiral; ~**i'tät** *f* admiralty

Adopt- *zW:* **a~ieren** [adɔp'ti:rən] *vt* to adopt; ~**ion** [adɔptsi'o:n] *f* adoption; ~**iveltern** [adɔp'ti:f-] *pl* adoptive parents; ~**ivkind** *nt* adopted child

Adress- *zW:* ~**ant** [adrɛ'sant] *m* sender;

~**at** [adrɛ'sa:t] (-en, -en) *m* addressee; ~**e** [a'drɛsə] *f* address; **a~ieren** [adrɛ'si:rən] *vt:* **a~ieren** (**an** +*akk*) to address (to)

Adria ['a:dria] (-) *f* Adriatic

Advent [at'vɛnt] (-(e)s, -e) *m* Advent; **Adventskranz** *m* Advent wreath

aero- [aero] *präfix* aero-

Aerobic [ae'ro:bɪk] *nt* aerobics *sg*

Affäre [a'fɛːrə] *f* affair

Affe ['afə] (-n, -n) *m* monkey

affektiert [afɛk'ti:rt] *adj* affected

Affen- *zW:* **a~artig** *adj* like a monkey; **mit a~artiger Geschwindigkeit** like a flash; ~**hitze** (*umg*) *f* incredible heat; ~**schande** (*umg*) *f* crying shame

affig ['afɪç] *adj* affected

Afrika ['a:frika] (-s) *nt* Africa; ~**ner(in)** [-'ka:nər(ɪn)] (-s, -) *m(f)* African; **a~nisch** [-'ka:nɪʃ] *adj* African

After ['aftər] (-s, -) *m* anus

AG [a:'ge:] *abk* (= *Aktiengesellschaft*) ≈ Ltd. (*BRIT*); ≈ Inc. (*US*)

ägäisch [ɛ'gɛːɪʃ] *adj:* ~**es Meer** Aegean (Sea)

Agent [a'gɛnt] *m* agent; ~**ur** [agɛn'tu:r] *f* agency

Aggregat [agre'ga:t] (-(e)s, -e) *nt* aggregate; (*TECH*) unit; ~**zustand** *m* (*PHYS*) state

Aggress- *zW:* ~**ion** [agrɛsi'o:n] *f* aggression; **a~iv** [agrɛ'si:f] *adj* aggressive; ~**ivität** [agrɛsivi'tɛ:t] *f* aggressiveness

Agitation [agitatsi'o:n] *f* agitation

Agrarpolitik [a'gra:r-] *f* agricultural policy

Agrarstaat *m* agrarian state

Ägypt- [ɛ'gʏpt] *zW:* ~**en** (-s) *nt* Egypt; ~**er(in)** (-s, -) *m(f)* Egyptian; **ä~isch** *adj* Egyptian

ah [a:] *excl* ah

aha [a'ha:] *excl* aha

Ahn [a:n] (-en, -en) *m* forebear

ähneln ['ɛ:nəln] *vi* +*dat* to be like, to resemble ♦ *vr* to be alike *od* similar

ahnen ['a:nən] *vt* to suspect; (*Tod, Gefahr*) to have a presentiment of

ähnlich ['ɛ:nlɪç] *adj* (+*dat*) similar (to); **Ä~keit** *f* similarity

Ahnung ['a:nʊŋ] *f* idea, suspicion; pre-

sentiment; **a~slos** *adj* unsuspecting
Ahorn [ˈaːhɔrn] (-s, -e) *m* maple
Ähre [ˈɛːrə] *f* ear
Aids [eːdz] *nt* AIDS *sg*
Akademie [akadeˈmiː] *f* academy
Akademiker(in) [akaˈdeːmikər(ɪn)] (-s, -) *m(f)* university graduate
akademisch *adj* academic
akklimatisieren [aklimatiˈziːrən] *vr* to become acclimatized
Akkord [aˈkɔrt] (-(e)s, -e) ~m (MUS) chord; **im ~ arbeiten** to do piecework; **~arbeit** *f* piecework
Akkordeon [aˈkɔrdeɔn] (-s, -s) *nt* accordion
Akrobat(in) [akroˈbaːt(ɪn)] (-en, -en) *m(f)* acrobat
Akt [akt] (-(e)s, -e) *m* act; (KUNST) nude
Akte [ˈaktə] *f* file; **aktenkundig** *adj* on the files; **Aktenschrank** *m* filing cabinet; **Aktentasche** *f* briefcase
Aktie [ˈaktsiə] *f* share
Aktien- *zW*: **~emission** *f* share issue; **~gesellschaft** *f* joint-stock company; **~kurs** *m* share price
Aktion [aktsiˈoːn] *f* campaign; (Polizei~, Such~) action; **~är** [-ˈnɛːr] (-s, -e) *m* shareholder
aktiv [akˈtiːf] *adj* active; (MIL) regular; **~ieren** [-ˈviːrən] *vt* to activate; **A~iˈtät** *f* activity
Aktualität [aktualiˈtɛːt] *f* topicality; (einer Mode) up-to-dateness
aktuell [aktuˈel] *adj* topical; up-to-date
Akustik [aˈkustɪk] *f* acoustics *pl*
akut [aˈkuːt] *adj* acute
AKW [aːkaːˈveː] *nt abk* = **Atomkraftwerk**
Akzent [akˈtsɛnt] *m* accent; (Betonung) stress
akzeptieren [aktsɛpˈtiːrən] *vt* to accept
Alarm [aˈlarm] (-(e)s, -e) *m* alarm; **a~bereit** *adj* standing by; **~bereitschaft** *f* stand-by; **a~ieren** [-ˈmiːrən] *vt* to alarm
Alban- [alˈbaːn] *zW*: **~ien** (-s) *nt* Albania; **~ier(in)** (-s, -) *m(f)* Albanian; **a~isch** *adj* Albanian
albern [ˈalbərn] *adj* silly
Album [ˈalbʊm] (-s, **Alben**) *nt* album
Algebra [ˈalgebra] (-) *f* algebra

Alger- [alˈgeːr] *zW*: **~ien** (-s) *nt* Algeria; **~ier(in)** (-s, -) *m(f)* Algerian; **a~isch** *adj* Algerian
alias [ˈaːlias] *adv* alias
Alibi [ˈaːlibi] (-s, -s) *nt* alibi
Alimente [aliˈmɛntə] *pl* alimony *sg*
Alkohol [ˈalkohoːl] (-s, -e) *m* alcohol; **a~frei** *adj* non-alcoholic; **~iker(in)** [alkoˈhoːlikər(ɪn)] (-s, -) *m(f)* alcoholic; **a~isch** *adj* alcoholic; **~verbot** *nt* ban on alcohol
All [al] (-s) *nt* universe; **a~'abendlich** *adj* every evening; **'a~bekannt** *adj* universally known

alle(r, s) [ˈalə(r, s)] *adj* **1** (sämtliche) all; **wir alle** all of us; **alle Kinder waren da** all the children were there; **alle Kinder mögen ... all** children like ...; **alle beide** both of us/them; **sie kamen alle** they all came; **alles Gute** all the best; **alles in allem** all in all
2 (mit Zeit- oder Maßangaben) every; **alle vier Jahre** every four years; **alle fünf Meter** every five metres
♦ *pron* everything; **alles was er sagt** everything he says, all that he says
♦ *adv* (zu Ende, aufgebraucht) finished; **die Milch ist alle** the milk's all gone, there's no milk left; **etw alle machen** to finish sth up

Allee [aˈleː] *f* avenue
allein [aˈlaɪn] *adv* alone; (ohne Hilfe) on one's own, by oneself ♦ *konj* but, only; **nicht ~** (nicht nur) not only; **A~erziehende(r)** *mf* single parent; **A~gang** *m*: **im A~gang** on one's own; **A~herrscher** *m* autocrat; **~stehend** *adj* single
allemal [aləˈmaːl] *adv* (jedesmal) always; (ohne weiteres) with no bother; **ein für ~** once and for all
allenfalls [ˈalənfals] *adv* at all events; (höchstens) at most
aller- [ˈalər] *zW*: **~beste(r, s)** *adj* very best; **~dings** *adv* (zwar) admittedly; (gewiß) certainly
Allergie [alerˈgiː] *f* allergy; **allergisch**

[a'lergɪʃ] *adj* allergic

aller- *zW:* ~**hand** (*umg*) *adj inv* all sorts of; **das ist doch** ~**hand!** that's a bit much; ~**hand!** (*lobend*) good show!; **A~'heiligen** *nt* All Saints' Day; ~**höchstens** *adv* at the very most; ~**lei** *adj inv* all sorts of; ~**letzte(r, s)** *adj* very last; ~**seits** *adv* on all sides; **prost** ~**seits!** cheers everyone!; ~**wenigste(r, s)** *adj* very least

alles *pron* everything; ~ **in allem** all in all; ~ **Gute!** all the best!

allgemein ['algə'maɪn] *adj* general; **im** ~**en** in general; ~**gültig** *adj* generally accepted; **A~heit** *f* (*Menschen*) general public; **A~heiten** *pl* (*Redensarten*) general remarks

Alliierte(r) [ali'i:rtə(r)] *m* ally

all- *zW:* ~**jährlich** *adj* annual; ~**mählich** *adj* gradual; **A~tag** *m* everyday life; ~**täglich** *adj, adv* daily; (*gewöhnlich*) commonplace; ~**tags** *adv* on weekdays; ~**'wissend** *adj* omniscient; ~**zu** *adv* all too; ~**zuoft** *adv* all too often; ~**zuviel** *adv* too much

Almosen ['almo:zən] (-s, -) *nt* alms *pl*

Alpen ['alpən] *pl* Alps

Alphabet [alfa'be:t] (-(e)s, -e) *nt* alphabet; **a~isch** *adj* alphabetical

Alptraum ['alptraom] *m* nightmare

als [als] *konj* **1** (*zeitlich*) when; (*gleichzeitig*) as; **damals, als ...** (in the days) when ...; **gerade, als ...** just as ... **2** (*in der Eigenschaft*) than; **als Antwort** as an answer; **als Kind** as a child **3** (*bei Vergleichen*) than; **ich kam später als er** I came later than he (did) *od* later than him; **lieber ... als** rather ... than; **nichts als Ärger** nothing but trouble **4**: **als ob/wenn** as if

also ['alzo:] *konj* so; (*folglich*) therefore; ~ **gut** *od* **schön!** okay then; ~**, so was!** well really!; **na** ~! there you are then!

Alt [alt] (-s, -e) *m* (*MUS*) alto

alt *adj* old; **alles beim** ~**en lassen** to leave everything as it was

Altar [al'ta:r] (-(e)s, -äre) *m* altar

altbekannt *adj* long-known

Alt'eisen *nt* scrap iron

Alter ['altər] (-s, -) *nt* age; (*hohes*) old age; **im** ~ **von** at the age of; **a~n** *vi* to grow old, to age

Alternativ- [alterna'ti:f] *in zW* alternative; ~**e** *f* alternative

Alters- *zW:* ~**grenze** *f* age limit; ~**heim** *nt* old people's home; ~**versorgung** *f* old age pension

Altertum *nt* antiquity

alt- *zW:* **A~glascontainer** *m* bottle bank; ~**hergebracht** *adj* traditional; ~**klug** *adj* precocious; ~**modisch** *adj* old-fashioned; **A~papier** *nt* waste paper; **A~stadt** *f* old town

Aluminium [alu'mi:nium] (-s) *nt* aluminium, aluminum (*US*); ~**folie** *f* tinfoil

am [am] = **an dem**; ~ **Schlafen** (*umg*) sleeping; ~ **15. März** on March 15th; ~ **besten/schönsten** best/most beautiful

Amateur [ama'tø:r] *m* amateur

Amboß ['ambɔs] (-sses, -sse) *m* anvil

ambulant [ambu'lant] *adj* outpatient

Ambulanz [ambu'lants] *f* outpatients *sg*

Ameise ['a:maɪzə] *f* ant

Amerika [a'me:rika] (-s) *nt* America; ~**ner(in)** [-'ka:nər(ɪn)] (-s, -) *m(f)* American; **a~nisch** [-'ka:nɪʃ] *adj* American

Ampel ['ampəl] (-, -n) *f* traffic lights *pl*

amputieren [ampu'ti:rən] *vt* to amputate

Amsel ['amzəl] (-, -n) *f* blackbird

Amt [amt] (-(e)s, -er) *nt* office; (*Pflicht*) duty; (*TEL*) exchange; **a~ieren** [am'ti:rən] *vi* to hold office; **a~lich** *adj* official

Amts- *zW:* ~**person** *f* official; ~**richter** *m* district judge; ~**stunden** *pl* office hours; ~**zeit** *f* period of office

amüsant [amy'zant] *adj* amusing

amüsieren [amy'zi:rən] *vt* to amuse ♦ *vr* to enjoy o.s.

an [an] *präp +dat* **1** (*räumlich: wo?*) at; (*auf, bei*) on; (*nahe bei*) near; **an**

diesem Ort at this place; **an der Wand** on the wall; **zu nahe an etw** too near to sth; **unten am Fluß** down by the river; **Köln liegt am Rhein** Cologne is on the Rhine

2 (*zeitlich: wann?*) on; **an diesem Tag** on this day; **an Ostern** at Easter **3**: **arm an Fett** low in fat; **an etw sterben** to die of sth; **an (und für) sich** actually

♦ *präp +akk* **1** (*räumlich: wohin?*) to; **er ging ans Fenster** he went (over) to the window; **etw an die Wand hängen/schreiben** to hang/write sth on the wall **2** (*zeitlich: woran?*): **an etw denken** to think of sth

3 (*gerichtet an*) to; **ein Gruß/eine Frage an dich** greetings/a question to you

♦ *adv* **1** (*ungefähr*) about; **an die hundert** about a hundred

2 (*auf Fahrplänen*): **Frankfurt an 18.30** arriving Frankfurt 18.30

3 (*ab*): **von dort/heute an** from there/today onwards

4 (*angeschaltet, angezogen*) on; **das Licht ist an** the light is on; **ohne etwas an** with nothing on; *siehe auch* **am**

analog [ana'lo:k] *adj* analogous; **A~ie** [-'gi:] *f* analogy
Analyse [ana'ly:zə] *f* analysis
analysieren [analy'zi:rən] *vt* to analyse
Ananas ['ananas] (*-, - od -se*) *f* pineapple
Anarchie [anar'çi:] *f* anarchy
Anatomie [anato'mi:] *f* anatomy
anbahnen ['anba:nən] *vt, vr* to open up
Anbau ['anbau] *m* (*AGR*) cultivation; (*Gebäude*) extension; **a~en** *vt* (*AGR*) to cultivate; (*Gebäudeteil*) to build on
anbehalten ['anbəhaltən] (*unreg*) *vt* to keep on
anbei [an'bai] *adv* enclosed
anbeißen ['anbaisən] (*unreg*) *vt* to bite into ♦ *vi* to bite; (*fig*) to swallow the bait; **zum A~** (*umg*) good enough to eat
anbelangen ['anbəlaŋən] *vt* to concern; **was mich anbelangt** as far as I am concerned
anbeten ['anbe:tən] *vt* to worship

Anbetracht ['anbətraxt] *m*: **in ~ +***gen* in view of
anbiedern ['anbi:dərn] *vr*: **sich ~ (bei)** to make up (to)
anbieten ['anbi:tən] (*unreg*) *vt* to offer ♦ *vr* to volunteer
anbinden ['anbindən] (*unreg*) *vt* to tie up; **kurz angebunden** (*fig*) curt
Anblick ['anblik] *m* sight; **a~en** *vt* to look at
anbrechen ['anbrɛçən] (*unreg*) *vt* to start; (*Vorräte*) to break into ♦ *vi* to start; (*Tag*) to break; (*Nacht*) to fall
anbrennen ['anbrenən] (*unreg*) *vi* to catch fire; (*KOCH*) to burn
anbringen ['anbriŋən] (*unreg*) *vt* to bring; (*Ware*) to sell; (*festmachen*) to fasten
Anbruch ['anbrox] *m* beginning; **~ des Tages/der Nacht** dawn/nightfall
anbrüllen ['anbrylən] *vt* to roar at
Andacht ['andaxt] (*-, -en*) *f* devotion; (*Gottesdienst*) prayers *pl*
andächtig ['andɛçtiç] *adj* devout
andauern ['andauərn] *vi* to last, to go on; **~d** *adj* continual
Anden ['andən] *pl* Andes
Andenken ['andɛŋkən] (*-s, -*) *nt* memory; souvenir
andere(r, s) ['andərə(r, s)] *adj* other; (*verschieden*) different; **ein ~s Mal** another time; **kein ~r** nobody else; **von etw ~m sprechen** to talk about something else; **andererseits** *adv* on the other hand
ändern ['ɛndərn] *vt* to alter, to change ♦ *vr* to change
andernfalls ['andərnfals] *adv* otherwise
anders ['andərs] *adv*: **~ (als)** differently (from); **wer ~?** who else?; **jd/irgendwo ~** sb/somewhere else; **~ aussehen/klingen** to look/sound different; **~artig** *adj* different; **~farbig** *adj* of a different colour; **~herum** adv the other way round; **~wo** *adv* somewhere else; **~woher** *adv* from somewhere else
anderthalb ['andərt'halp] *adj* one and a half
Änderung ['ɛndəruŋ] *f* alteration, change

anderweitig ['andər'vaitiç] *adj* other ♦ *adv* otherwise; *(anderswo)* elsewhere

andeuten ['andɔytən] *vt* to indicate; *(Wink geben)* to hint at

Andeutung *f* indication; hint

Andrang ['andraŋ] *m* crush

andrehen ['andre:ən] *vt* to turn *od* switch on; jdm etw ~ *(umg)* to unload sth onto sb

androhen ['andro:ən] *vt:* jdm etw ~ to threaten sb with sth

aneignen ['an'aignən] *vt:* sich *dat* etw ~ to acquire sth; *(widerrechtlich)* to appropriate sth

aneinander [an'ai'nandər] *adv* at/on/to *etc* one another *od* each other; ~**fügen** *vt* to put together; ~**geraten** *(unreg)* *vi* to clash

anekeln ['an'e:kəln] *vt* to disgust

Anemone [ane'mo:nə] *f* anemone

anerkannt ['an'ɛrkant] *adj* recognized, acknowledged

anerkennen ['an'ɛrkɛnən] *(unreg)* *vt* to recognize, to acknowledge; *(würdigen)* to appreciate; ~**d** *adj* appreciative; ~**swert** *adj* praiseworthy

Anerkennung *f* recognition, acknowledgement; appreciation

anfachen ['anfaxən] *vt* to fan into flame; *(fig)* to kindle

anfahren ['anfa:rən] *(unreg)* *vt* to deliver; *(fahren gegen)* to hit; *(Hafen)* to put into; *(fig)* to bawl out ♦ *vi* to drive up; *(losfahren)* to drive off

Anfall ['anfal] *m (MED)* attack; **a~en** *(unreg)* *vt* to attack; *(fig)* to overcome ♦ *vi (Arbeit)* to come up; *(Produkt)* to be obtained

anfällig ['anfɛlıç] *adj* delicate; ~ **für etw** prone to sth

Anfang ['anfaŋ] *m* (-(e)s, -fänge) beginning, start; **von ~ an** right from the beginning; **zu ~** at the beginning; ~ **Mai** at the beginning of May; **a~en** *(unreg)* *vt, vi* to begin, to start; *(machen)* to do

Anfänger(in) ['anfɛŋər(ın)] (-s, -) *m(f)* beginner

anfänglich ['anfɛŋlıç] *adj* initial

anfangs *adv* at first; **A~buchstabe** *m* initial *od* first letter; **A~stadium** *nt* initial stages *pl*

anfassen ['anfasən] *vt* to handle; *(berühren)* to touch ♦ *vi* to lend a hand ♦ *vr* to feel

anfechten ['anfɛçtən] *(unreg)* *vt* to dispute; *(beunruhigen)* to trouble

anfertigen ['anfɛrtıgən] *vt* to make

anfeuern ['anfɔyərn] *vt (fig)* to spur on

anflehen ['anfle:ən] *vt* to implore

anfliegen ['anfli:gən] *(unreg)* *vt* to fly to

Anflug ['anflu:k] *m (AVIAT)* approach; *(Spur)* trace

anfordern ['anfɔrdərn] *vt* to demand; *(COMM)* to requisition

Anforderung *f* (+*gen*) demand (for)

Anfrage ['anfra:gə] *f* inquiry; **a~n** *vi* to inquire

anfreunden ['anfrɔyndən] *vr* to make friends

anfügen ['anfy:gən] *vt* to add; *(beifügen)* to enclose

anfühlen ['anfy:lən] *vt, vr* to feel

anführen ['anfy:rən] *vt* to lead; *(zitieren)* to quote; *(umg: betrügen)* to lead up the garden path

Anführer *m* leader

Anführung *f* leadership; *(Zitat)* quotation; **Anführungszeichen** *pl* quotation marks, inverted commas

Angabe ['anga:bə] *f* statement; *(TECH)* specification; *(umg: Prahlerei)* boasting; *(SPORT)* service; ~**n** *pl (Auskunft)* particulars

angeben ['ange:bən] *(unreg)* *vt* to give; *(anzeigen)* to inform on; *(bestimmen)* to set ♦ *vi (umg)* to boast; *(SPORT)* to serve

Angeber (-s, -; *umg)* *m* show-off; **Angebe'rei** *(umg)* *f* showing off

angeblich ['ange:plıç] *adj* alleged

angeboren ['angəbo:rən] *adj* inborn, innate

Angebot ['angəbo:t] *nt* offer; ~ **(an** +*dat)* *(COMM)* supply (of)

angebracht ['angəbraxt] *adj* appropriate, in order

angegriffen ['angəgrıfən] *adj* exhausted

angeheitert ['angəhaitərt] *adj* tipsy

angehen ['ange:ən] *(unreg)* *vt* to con-

cern; (angreifen) to attack; (bitten):
jdn ~ (um) to approach sb (for) ♦ vi
(Feuer) to light; (umg: beginnen) to
begin; ~d adj prospective
angehören ['angəhø:rən] vi to belong
Angehörige(r) mf relative
Angeklagte(r) ['angəkla:ktə(r)] mf
accused
Angel ['aŋəl] (-, -n) f fishing rod;
(Tür~) hinge
Angelegenheit ['angəle:gənhaɪt] f affair,
matter
Angel- zW: ~**haken** m fish hook; **a~n**
vt to catch ♦ vi to fish; ~**n** (-s) nt
angling, fishing; ~**rute** f fishing rod
angemessen ['angəmɛsən] adj
appropriate, suitable
angenehm ['angəne:m] adj pleasant; ~!
(bei Vorstellung) pleased to meet you
angenommen ['angənɔmən] adj
assumed; ~, wir ... assuming we ...
angesehen ['angəze:ən] adj respected
angesichts ['angəzɪçts] präp +gen in
view of, considering
angespannt ['angəʃpant] adj (Aufmerksamkeit) close; (Arbeit) hard
Angestellte(r) ['angəʃtɛltə(r)] mf
employee
angetan ['angəta:n] adj: **von jdm/etw ~
sein** to be impressed by sb/sth; **es jdm
~ haben** to appeal to sb
angewiesen ['angəvi:zən] adj: **auf jdn/
etw ~ sein** to be dependent on sb/sth
angewöhnen ['angəvø:nən] vt: **jdm/sich
etw ~** to get sb/become accustomed to
sth
Angewohnheit ['angəvo:nhaɪt] f habit
angleichen ['anglaɪçən] (unreg) vt, vr to
adjust
Angler ['aŋlər] (-s, -) m angler
angreifen ['angraɪfən] (unreg) vt to
attack; (anfassen) to touch; (Arbeit) to
tackle; (beschädigen) to damage
Angreifer (-s, -) m attacker
Angriff ['angrɪf] m attack; **etw in ~
nehmen** to make a start on sth
Angst [aŋst] (-, ⁼e) f fear; **jdm ist a~** sb
is afraid od scared; **~ haben (vor**
+dat) to be afraid od scared (of); **~
haben um jdn/etw** to be worried about

sb/sth; **jdm a~ machen** to scare sb;
~**hase** (umg) m chicken, scaredy-cat
ängst- ['ɛŋst] zW: ~**igen** vt to frighten
♦ vr: **sich ~igen (vor** +dat od **um)** to
worry (o.s.) (about); ~**lich** adj
nervous; (besorgt) worried; **Ä~lichkeit**
f nervousness
anhaben ['anha:bən] (unreg) vt to have
on; **er kann mir nichts ~** he can't hurt
me
anhalt- ['anhalt] zW: ~**en** (unreg) vt to
stop ♦ vi to stop; (andauern) to persist;
(jdm) **etw ~en** to hold sth up (against
sb); **jdn zur Arbeit/Höflichkeit ~en** to
make sb work/be polite; ~**end** adj
persistent; **A~er** (-s, -) m hitch-hiker;
per A~er fahren to hitch-hike; **An-
haltepunkt** m clue
anhand [an'hant] präp +gen with
Anhang ['anhaŋ] m appendix; (Leute)
family; supporters pl
anhäng- ['anhɛŋ] zW: ~**en** (unreg) vt to
hang up; (Wagen) to couple up;
(Zusatz) to add (on); **A~er** (-s, -) m
supporter; (AUT) trailer; (am Koffer)
tag; (Schmuck) pendant; **A~erschaft** f
supporters pl; ~**lich** adj devoted;
A~lichkeit f devotion; **A~sel** (-s, -) nt
appendage
Anhäufung ['anhɔʏfʊŋ] f accumulation
anheben ['anhe:bən] (unreg) vt to lift
up; (Preise) to raise
Anhieb ['anhi:b] m: **auf ~** at the very
first go; (kurz entschlossen) on the spur
of the moment
Anhöhe ['anhø:ə] f hill
anhören ['anhø:rən] vt to listen to;
(anmerken) to hear ♦ vr to sound
animieren [ani'mi:rən] vt to encourage,
to urge on
Anis [a'ni:s] (-es, -e) m aniseed
Ank. abk (= Ankunft) arr.
ankaufen ['ankaʊfən] vt to purchase, to
buy
Anker ['aŋkər] (-s, -) m anchor; **vor ~
gehen** to drop anchor; **a~n** vt, vi to
anchor; ~**platz** m anchorage
Anklage ['ankla:gə] f accusation; (JUR)
charge; ~**bank** f dock; **a~n** vt to
accuse; **jdn (eines Verbrechens) a~n**

(*JUR*) to charge sb (with a crime)
Ankläger ['anklɛːgər] *m* accuser
Anklang ['anklaŋ] *m*: **bei jdm ~ finden** to meet with sb's approval
Ankleidekabine *f* changing cubicle
ankleiden ['anklaɪdən] *vt, vr* to dress
anklopfen ['anklɔpfən] *vi* to knock
anknüpfen ['anknʏpfən] *vt* to fasten *od* tie on; (*fig*) to start ♦ *vi* (*anschließen*): **~ an** +*akk* to refer to
ankommen ['ankɔmən] (*unreg*) *vi* to arrive; (*näherkommen*) to approach; (*Anklang finden*): **bei jdm (gut) ~** to go down well with sb; **es kommt darauf an** it depends; (*wichtig sein*) that (is what) matters; **es darauf ~ lassen** to let things take their course; **gegen jdn/ etw ~** to cope with sb/sth; **bei jdm schlecht ~** to go down badly with sb
ankündigen ['ankʏndɪgən] *vt* to announce
Ankündigung *f* announcement
Ankunft ['ankʊnft] (-, **-künfte**) *f* arrival; **~szeit** *f* time of arrival
ankurbeln ['ankʊrbəln] *vt* (*AUT*) to crank; (*fig*) to boost
Anlage ['anlaːgə] *f* disposition; (*Begabung*) talent; (*Park*) gardens *pl*; (*Beilage*) enclosure; (*TECH*) plant; (*FIN*) investment; (*Entwurf*) layout
Anlaß ['anlas] (**-sses, -lässe**) *m*: **~ (zu)** cause (for); (*Ereignis*) occasion; **aus ~** +*gen* on the occasion of; **~ zu etw geben** to give rise to sth; **etw zum ~ nehmen** to take the opportunity of sth
anlassen (*unreg*) *vt* to leave on; (*Motor*) to start ♦ *vr* (*umg*) to start off
Anlasser (-s, -) *m* (*AUT*) starter
anläßlich ['anlɛslɪç] *präp* +*gen* on the occasion of
Anlauf ['anlaʊf] *m* run-up; **a~en** (*unreg*) *vi* to begin; (*neuer Film*) to show; (*SPORT*) to run up; (*Fenster*) to mist up; (*Metall*) to tarnish ♦ *vt* to call at; **rot a~en** to blush; **angelaufen kommen** to come running up
anlegen ['anleːgən] *vt* to put; (*anziehen*) to put on; (*gestalten*) to lay out; (*Geld*) to invest ♦ *vi* to dock; **etw an etw** *akk* **~** to put sth against *od* on sth; **ein**

Gewehr ~ (auf +*akk*) to aim a weapon (at); **es auf etw** *akk* **~** to be out for sth/to do sth; **sich mit jdm ~** (*umg*) to quarrel with sb
Anlegestelle *f* landing place
anlehnen ['anleːnən] *vt* to lean; (*Tür*) to leave ajar; **(sich) an etw** *akk* **~** to lean on/against sth
anleiten ['anlaɪtən] *vt* to instruct
Anleitung *f* instructions *pl*
anlernen ['anlɛrnən] *vt* to teach, to instruct
anliegen ['anliːgən] (*unreg*) *vi* (*Kleidung*) to cling; **A~** (-s, -) *nt* matter; (*Wunsch*) wish; **~d** *adj* adjacent; (*beigefügt*) enclosed
Anlieger (-s, -) *m* resident; „**~ frei**" "residents only"
anlügen ['anlyːgən] (*unreg*) *vt* to lie to
anmachen ['anmaxən] *vt* to attach; (*Elektrisches*) to put on; (*Zigarette*) to light; (*Salat*) to dress
anmaßen ['anmaːsən] *vt*: **sich** *dat* **etw ~** (*Recht*) to lay claim to sth; **~d** *adj* arrogant
Anmaßung *f* presumption
anmelden ['anmɛldən] *vt* to announce ♦ *vr* (*sich ankündigen*) to make an appointment; (*polizeilich, für Kurs etc*) to register
Anmeldung *f* announcement; appointment; registration
anmerken ['anmɛrkən] *vt* to observe; (*anstreichen*) to mark; **sich** *dat* **nichts ~ lassen** to not give anything away
Anmerkung *f* note
Anmut ['anmuːt] (-) *f* grace; **a~en** *vt* to give a feeling; **a~ig** *adj* charming
annähern ['annɛːərn] *vr* to get closer; **~d** *adj* approximate
Annäherung *f* approach; **Annäherungsversuch** *m* advances *pl*
Annahme ['annaːmə] *f* acceptance; (*Vermutung*) assumption
annehm- ['anneːm] *zW*: **~bar** *adj* acceptable; **~en** (*unreg*) *vt* to accept; (*Namen*) to take; (*Kind*) to adopt; (*vermuten*) to suppose, to assume ♦ *vr* (+*gen*) to take care (of); **A~lichkeit** *f* comfort

Annonce [a'nõ:sə] f advertisement
annoncieren [anõ'si:rən] vt, vi to advertise
annullieren [anʊ'li:rən] vt to annul
anöden ['an'ø:dən] (umg) vt to bore stiff
anonym [ano'ny:m] adj anonymous
Anorak ['anorak] (-s, -s) m anorak
anordnen ['an'ɔrdnən] vt to arrange; (befehlen) to order
Anordnung f arrangement; order
anpacken ['anpakən] vt to grasp; (fig) to tackle; **mit ~** to lend a hand
anpassen ['anpasən] vt: (jdm) ~ to fit (on sb); (fig) to adapt ♦ vr to adapt
Anpassung f fitting; adaptation; a~sfähig adj adaptable
Anpfiff ['anpfɪf] m (SPORT) (starting) whistle; kick-off; (umg) rocket
anprallen ['anpralən] vi: ~ (gegen od an +akk) to collide (with)
anprangern ['anpraŋərn] vt to denounce
anpreisen ['anpraɪzən] (unreg) vt to extol
Anprobe ['anpro:bə] f trying on
anprobieren ['anprobi:rən] vt to try on
anrechnen ['anrɛçnən] vt to charge; (fig) to count; **jdm etw hoch ~** to value sb's sth greatly
Anrecht ['anrɛçt] nt: ~ **(auf** +akk) right (to)
Anrede ['anre:də] f form of address; a~n vt to address; (belästigen) to accost
anregen ['anre:gən] vt to stimulate; **angeregte Unterhaltung** lively discussion; ~d adj stimulating
Anregung f stimulation; (Vorschlag) suggestion
anreichern ['anraɪçərn] vt to enrich
Anreise ['anraɪzə] f journey; a~n vi to arrive
Anreiz ['anraɪts] m incentive
Anrichte ['anrɪçtə] f sideboard; a~n vt to serve up; **Unheil a~n** to make mischief
anrüchig ['anryçɪç] adj dubious
anrücken ['anrykən] vi to approach; (MIL) to advance
Anruf ['anru:f] m call; a~en (unreg) vt

to call out to; (bitten) to call on; (TEL) to ring up, to phone, to call
ans [ans] = **an das**
Ansage ['anza:gə] f announcement; a~n vt to announce ♦ vr to say one will come; **Ansager(in)** (-s, -) m(f) announcer
Ansammlung f collection; (Leute) crowd
ansässig ['anzɛsɪç] adj resident
Ansatz ['anzats] m start; (Haar~) hairline; (Hals~) base; (Verlängerungsstück) extension; (Veranschlagung) estimate; ~**punkt** m starting point
anschaffen ['anʃafən] vt to buy, to purchase
Anschaffung f purchase
anschalten ['anʃaltən] vt to switch on
anschau- ['anʃaʊ] zW: ~**en** vt to look at; ~**lich** adj illustrative; **A~ung** f (Meinung) view; **aus eigener A~ung** from one's own experience
Anschein ['anʃaɪn] m appearance; **allem ~ nach** to all appearances; **den ~ haben** to seem, to appear; a~**end** adj apparent
Anschlag ['anʃla:k] m notice; (Attentat) attack; (COMM) estimate; (auf Klavier) touch; (Schreibmaschine) character; a~**en** ['anʃla:gən] (unreg) vt to put up; (beschädigen) to chip; (Akkord) to strike; (Kosten) to estimate ♦ vi to hit; (wirken) to have an effect; (Glocke) to ring; (Hund) to bark; **an etw** akk a~**en** to hit against sth
anschließen ['anʃli:sən] (unreg) vt to connect up; (Sender) to link up ♦ vi: **an etw** akk ~ to adjoin sth; (zeitlich) to follow sth ♦ vr: **sich jdm/etw ~** to join sb/sth; (beipflichten) to agree with sb/ sth; **sich an etw** akk ~ to adjoin sth; ~**d** adj adjacent; (zeitlich) subsequent ♦ adv afterwards
Anschluß ['anʃlʊs] m (ELEK, EISENB) connection; (von Wasser etc) supply; **im ~ an** +akk following; ~ **finden** to make friends
anschmiegsam ['anʃmi:kza:m] adj affectionate
anschnallen ['anʃnalən] vt to buckle on

♦ *vr* to fasten one's seat belt
anschneiden ['anʃnaɪdən] *(unreg) vt* to cut into; *(Thema)* to introduce
anschreiben ['anʃraɪbən] *(unreg) vt* to write (up); *(COMM)* to charge up; *(benachrichtigen)* to write to
anschreien ['anʃraɪən] *(unreg) vt* to shout at
Anschrift ['anʃrɪft] *f* address
Anschuldigung ['anʃʊldɪgʊŋ] *f* accusation
anschwellen ['anʃvɛlən] *(unreg) vi* to swell (up)
anschwemmen ['anʃvɛmən] *vt* to wash ashore
anschwindeln ['anʃvɪndəln] *vt* to lie to
ansehen ['anzeːən] *(unreg) vt* to look at; **A~** **(-s)** *nt* respect; *(Ruf)* reputation; **jdm etw ~** to see sth (from sb's face); **jdn/etw als etw ~** to look on sb/sth as sth; **~ für** to consider
ansehnlich ['anzeːnlɪç] *adj* fine-looking; *(beträchtlich)* considerable
ansetzen ['anzɛtsən] *vt (festlegen)* to fix; *(entwickeln)* to develop; *(Fett)* to put on; *(Blätter)* to grow; *(zubereiten)* to prepare ♦ *vi (anfangen)* to start, to begin; *(Entwicklung)* to set in; *(dick werden)* to put on weight ♦ *vr (Rost etc)* to start to develop; **~ an** *+akk (anfügen)* to fix on to; *(anlegen, an Mund etc)* to put to
Ansicht ['anzɪçt] *f (Anblick)* sight; *(Meinung)* view, opinion; **zur ~** on approval; **meiner ~ nach** in my opinion; **Ansichtskarte** *f* picture postcard; **Ansichtssache** *f* matter of opinion
anspannen ['anʃpanən] *vt* to harness; *(Muskel)* to strain
Anspannung *f* strain
Anspiel ['anʃpiːl] *nt (SPORT)* start; **a~en** *vi (SPORT)* to start play; **auf etw** *akk* **a~en** to refer *od* allude to sth; **~ung** *f*: **~ung (auf** *+akk)* reference (to), allusion (to)
Ansporn ['anʃpɔrn] **(-(e)s)** *m* incentive
Ansprache ['anʃpraːxə] *f* address
ansprechen ['anʃprɛçən] *(unreg) vt* to speak to; *(bitten, gefallen)* to appeal to

♦ *vi:* **(auf etw** *akk)* **~** to react (to sth); **jdn auf etw** *akk* **(hin) ~** to ask sb about sth; **~d** *adj* attractive
anspringen ['anʃprɪŋən] *(unreg) vi (AUT)* to start ♦ *vt* to jump at
Anspruch ['anʃprʊx] *m (Recht):* **~ (auf** *+akk)* claim (to); **hohe Ansprüche stellen/haben** to demand/expect a lot; **jdn/etw in ~ nehmen** to occupy sb/take up sth; **a~slos** *adj* undemanding; **a~svoll** *adj* demanding
anstacheln ['anʃtaxəln] *vt* to spur on
Anstalt ['anʃtalt] **(-, -en)** *f* institution; **~en machen, etw zu tun** to prepare to do sth
Anstand ['anʃtant] *m* decency
anständig ['anʃtɛndɪç] *adj* decent; *(umg)* proper; *(groß)* considerable
anstandslos *adv* without any ado
anstarren ['anʃtarən] *vt* to stare at
anstatt [an'ʃtat] *präp +gen* instead of ♦ *konj:* **~ etw zu tun** instead of doing sth
Ansteck- ['anʃtɛk] *zW:* **a~en** *vt* to pin on; *(MED)* to infect; *(Pfeife)* to light; *(Haus)* to set fire to ♦ *vr:* **ich habe mich bei ihm angesteckt** I caught it from him ♦ *vi (fig)* to be infectious; **a~end** *adj* infectious; **~ung** *f* infection
anstehen ['anʃteːən] *(unreg) vi* to queue (up) *(BRIT)*, to line up *(US)*
anstelle [an'ʃtɛlə] *präp +gen* in place of; **~n** [an'-] *vt (einschalten)* to turn on; *(Arbeit geben)* to employ; *(machen)* to do ♦ *vr* to queue (up) *(BRIT)*, to line up *(US)*; *(umg)* to act
Anstellung *f* employment; *(Posten)* post, position
Anstieg ['anʃtiːk] **(-(e)s, -e)** *m (+gen)* climb; *(fig: von Preisen etc)* increase (in)
anstiften ['anʃtɪftən] *vt (Unglück)* to cause; **jdn zu etw ~** to put sb up to sth
Anstifter **(-s, -)** *m* instigator
anstimmen ['anʃtɪmən] *vt (Lied)* to strike up with; *(Geschrei)* to set up
Anstoß ['anʃtoːs] *m* impetus; *(Ärgernis)* offence; *(SPORT)* kick-off; **der erste ~** the initiative; **~ nehmen an** *+dat* to take offence at; **a~en** *(unreg) vt* to push; *(mit Fuß)* to kick ♦ *vi* to knock,

to bump; (*mit der Zunge*) to lisp; (*mit Gläsern*): **a~en** (**auf** +*akk*) to drink (to), to drink a toast (to)

anstößig ['anʃtøːsɪç] *adj* offensive, indecent; **A~keit** *f* indecency, offensiveness

anstreichen ['anʃtraɪçən] (*unreg*) *vt* to paint

Anstreicher (-s, -) *m* painter

anstrengen ['anʃtrɛŋən] *vt* to strain; (*JUR*) to bring ♦ *vr* to make an effort; **angestrengt** *adv* as hard as one can; **~d** *adj* tiring

Anstrengung *f* effort

Anstrich ['anʃtrɪç] *m* coat of paint

Ansturm ['anʃtʊrm] *m* rush; (*MIL*) attack

Antarktis [ant'ʔarktɪs] (-) *f* Antarctic

antasten ['antastən] *vt* to touch; (*Recht*) to infringe upon; (*Ehre*) to question

Anteil ['antaɪl] (-s, -e) *m* share; (*Mitgefühl*) sympathy; **~ nehmen an** +*dat* to share in; (*sich interessieren*) to take an interest in; **~nahme** (-) *f* sympathy

Antenne [an'tɛnə] *f* aerial

Anti- ['anti] *in zW* anti; **~alko'holiker** *m* teetotaller; **a~autori'tär** *adj* antiauthoritarian; **~biotikum** [antibi'oːtikʊm] (-s, **-ka**) *nt* antibiotic

antik [an'tiːk] *adj* antique; **A~e** *f* (*Zeitalter*) ancient world; (*Kunstgegenstand*) antique

Antilope [anti'loːpə] *f* antelope

Antipathie [antipa'tiː] *f* antipathy

Antiquariat [antikvari'aːt] (-(e)s, -e) *nt* secondhand bookshop

Antiquitäten [antikvi'tɛːtən] *pl* antiques; **~händler** *m* antique dealer

Antrag ['antraːk] (-(e)s, **-träge**) *m* proposal; (*PARL*) motion; (*Gesuch*) application

antreffen ['antrɛfən] (*unreg*) *vt* to meet

antreiben ['antraɪbən] (*unreg*) *vt* to drive on; (*Motor*) to drive; (*anschwemmen*) to wash up ♦ *vi* to be washed up

antreten ['antreːtən] (*unreg*) *vt* (*Amt*) to take up; (*Erbschaft*) to come into; (*Beweis*) to offer; (*Reise*) to start, to begin ♦ *vi* (*MIL*) to fall in; (*SPORT*) to

line up; **gegen jdn ~** to play/fight (against) sb

Antrieb ['antriːp] *m* (*auch fig*) drive; **aus eigenem ~** of one's own accord

antrinken ['antrɪŋkən] (*unreg*) *vt* (*Flasche, Glas*) to start to drink from; **sich** *dat* **Mut/einen Rausch ~** to give o.s. Dutch courage/get drunk; **angetrunken sein** to be tipsy

Antritt ['antrɪt] *m* beginning, commencement; (*eines Amts*) taking up

antun ['antuːn] (*unreg*) *vt*: **jdm etw ~** to do sth to sb; **sich** *dat* **Zwang ~** to force o.s.; **sich** *dat* **etwas ~** to (try to) take one's own life

Antwort ['antvɔrt] (-, -en) *f* answer, reply; **a~en** *vi* to answer, to reply

anvertrauen ['anfertrauən] *vt*: **jdm etw ~** to entrust sb with sth; **sich jdm ~** to confide in sb

anwachsen ['anvaksən] (*unreg*) *vi* to grow; (*Pflanze*) to take root

Anwalt ['anvalt] (-(e)s, **-wälte**) *m* solicitor; lawyer; (*fig*) champion

Anwältin ['anvɛltɪn] *f siehe* **Anwalt**

Anwärter ['anvɛrtər] *m* candidate

anweisen ['anvaɪzən] (*unreg*) *vt* to instruct; (*zuteilen*) to assign

Anweisung *f* instruction; (*COMM*) remittance; (*Post~, Zahlungs~*) money order

anwend- ['anvɛnd] *zW*: **~bar** ['anvɛnt-] *adj* practicable, applicable; **~en** (*unreg*) *vt* to use, to employ; (*Gesetz, Regel*) to apply; **A~ung** *f* use; application

anwesend ['anveːzənt] *adj* present; **die A~en** those present

Anwesenheit *f* presence

anwidern ['anviːdərn] *vt* to disgust

Anzahl ['antsaːl] *f*: **~** (**an** +*dat*) number (of); **a~en** *vt* to pay on account; **~ung** *f* deposit, payment on account

Anzeichen ['antsaɪçən] *nt* sign, indication

Anzeige ['antsaɪgə] *f* (*Zeitungs~*) announcement; (*Werbung*) advertisement; (*bei Polizei*) report; **~ erstatten gegen jdn** to report sb (to the police); **a~n** *vt* (*zu erkennen geben*) to show; (*bekanntgeben*) to announce; (*bei*

Polizei) to report; ~r *m* indicator
anziehen ['antsi:ən] *(unreg)* *vt* to
attract; *(Kleidung)* to put on; *(Mensch)*
to dress; *(Seil)* to pull tight;
(Schraube) to tighten; *(Knie)* to draw
up; *(Feuchtigkeit)* to absorb ♦ *vr* to get
dressed; ~d *adj* attractive
Anziehung *f* *(Reiz)* attraction; **An-**
ziehungskraft *f* power of attraction;
(PHYS) force of gravitation
Anzug ['antsu:k] *m* suit; *(Herankom-*
men): **im ~ sein** to be approaching
anzüglich ['antsy:klıç] *adj* personal;
(anstößig) offensive; **A~keit** *f*
offensiveness; *(Bemerkung)* personal
remark
anzünden ['antsyndən] *vt* to light
Anzünder *m* lighter
anzweifeln ['antsvaıfəln] *vt* to doubt
Apathie [apa'ti:] *f* apathy
apathisch [a'pa:tıʃ] *adj* apathetic
Apfel ['apfəl] (-s, ⸚) *m* apple; ~**saft** *m*
apple juice; ~**sine** [apfəl'zi:nə] *f* orange;
~**wein** *m* cider
Apostel [a'pɔstəl] (-s, -) *m* apostle
Apostroph [apo'stro:f] (-s, -e) *m*
apostrophe
Apotheke [apo'te:kə] *f* chemist's (shop),
drugstore *(US)*; **Apotheker(in)** (-s, -)
m(f) chemist, druggist *(US)*
Apparat [apa'ra:t] (-(e)s, -e) *m* piece of
apparatus; camera; telephone; *(RADIO,*
TV) set; **am ~!** speaking!; ~**ur** [-'tu:r] *f*
apparatus
Appartement [apartə'mã:] (-s, -s) *nt* flat
Appell [a'pɛl] (-s, -e) *m* *(MIL)* muster,
parade; *(fig)* appeal; **a~ieren**
[apɛ'li:rən] *vi*: **a~ieren (an** +*akk)* to
appeal (to)
Appetit [ape'ti:t] (-(e)s, -e) *m* appetite;
guten ~ enjoy your meal; **a~lich** *adj*
appetizing; ~**losigkeit** *f* lack of appetite
Applaus [ap'laus] (-es, -e) *m* applause
Aprikose [apri'ko:zə] *f* apricot
April [a'prıl] (-(s), -e) *m* April
Aquarell [akva'rɛl] (-s, -e) *nt* water-
colour
Aquarium [a'kva:riʊm] *nt* aquarium
Äquator [ɛ'kva:tɔr] (-s) *m* equator
Arab- ['arab] *zW:* ~**er(in)** (-s, -) *m(f)*

Arab; ~**ien** [a'ra:biən] (-s) *nt* Arabia;
a~isch [a'ra:bıʃ] *adj* Arabian
Arbeit ['arbaıt] (-, -en) *f* work *no art;*
(Stelle) job; *(Erzeugnis)* piece of work;
(wissenschaftliche) dissertation;
(Klassen~) test; **das war eine ~** that
was a hard job; **a~en** *vi* to work ♦ *vt*
to work, to make; ~**er(in)** (-s, -) *m(f)*
worker; *(ungelernt)* labourer; ~**er-**
schaft *f* workers *pl*, labour force;
~**geber** (-s, -) *m* employer; ~**nehmer**
(-s, -) *m* employee
Arbeits- *in zW* labour; **arbeitsam** *adj*
industrious; ~**amt** *nt* employment
exchange; **a~fähig** *adj* fit for work,
able-bodied; ~**gang** *m* operation;
~**gericht** *nt* industrial tribunal; ~**kräfte**
pl workers, labour *sg*; **a~los** *adj* unemployed, out-of-work; ~**losigkeit** *f* unemployment; ~**platz** *m* job; place of
work; *(Großraumbüro)* workstation;
a~scheu *adj* work-shy; ~**tag** *m*
work(ing) day; **a~unfähig** *adj* unfit for
work; ~**zeit** *f* working hours *pl*
Archäologe [arçɛo'lo:gə] (-n, -n) *m*
archaeologist
Architekt(in) [arçi'tɛkt(ın)] (-en, -en)
m(f) architect; ~**ur** [-'tu:r] *f*
architecture
Archiv [ar'çi:f] (-s, -e) *nt* archive
arg [ark] *adj* bad, awful ♦ *adv* awfully,
very
Argentin- [argen'ti:n] *zW:* ~**ien** (-s) *nt*
Argentina, the Argentine; ~**ier(in)** (-s,
-) *m(f)* Argentinian; **a~isch** *adj*
Argentinian
Ärger ['ɛrgər] (-s) *m* *(Wut)* anger; *(Un-*
annehmlichkeit) trouble; **ä~lich** *adj*
(zornig) angry; *(lästig)* annoying, ag-
gravating; **ä~n** *vt* to annoy ♦ *vr* to get
annoyed; ~**nis** (-ses, -se) *nt* annoyance
arg- *zW:* ~**listig** *adj* cunning, insidious;
~**los** *adj* guileless, innocent;
A~losigkeit *f* guilelessness, innocence
Argument [argu'mɛnt] *nt* argument
Argwohn *m* suspicion
argwöhnisch *adj* suspicious
Arie ['a:riə] *f* aria
Aristokrat [arısto'kra:t] (-en, -en) *m*
aristocrat; ~**ie** [-'ti:] *f* aristocracy;

adj aristocratic
Arktis ['arktɪs] (-) *f* Arctic
Arm [arm] (-(e)s, -e) *m* arm; *(Fluß~)* branch
arm *adj* poor
Armatur [arma'tu:r] *f (ELEK)* armature; **~enbrett** *nt* instrument panel; *(AUT)* dashboard
Armband *nt* bracelet; **~uhr** *f* (wrist) watch
Arme(r) *mf* poor man(woman); **die ~n** the poor
Armee [ar'me:] *f* army
Ärmel ['ɛrməl] (-s, -) *m* sleeve; **etw aus dem ~ schütteln** *(fig)* to produce sth just like that; **~kanal** *m* English Channel
ärmlich ['ɛrmlɪç] *adj* poor
armselig *adj* wretched, miserable
Armut ['armu:t] (-) *f* poverty
Aroma [a'ro:ma] (-s, Aromen) *nt* aroma; **a~tisch** [aro'ma:tɪʃ] *adj* aromatic
arrangieren [arã'ʒi:rən] *vt* to arrange ♦ *vr* to come to an arrangement
Arrest [a'rɛst] (-(e)s, -e) *m* detention
arrogant [aro'gant] *adj* arrogant
Arroganz *f* arrogance
Arsch [arʃ] (-es, ⁼e; *umg!*) *m* arse *(BRIT!)*, ass *(US!)*
Art [a:rt] (-, -en) *f (Weise)* way; *(Sorte)* kind, sort; *(BIOL)* species; **eine ~ (von) Frucht** a kind of fruit; **Häuser aller ~** houses of all kinds; **es ist nicht seine ~, das zu tun** it's not like him to do that; **ich mache das auf meine ~** I do that my (own) way
Arterie [ar'te:riə] *f* artery; **Arterienverkalkung** *f* arteriosclerosis
artig ['a:rtɪç] *adj* good, well-behaved
Artikel [ar'ti:kəl] (-s, -) *m* article
Artillerie [artɪlə'ri:] *f* artillery
Arznei [a:rts'naɪ] *f* medicine; **~mittel** *nt* medicine, medicament
Arzt [a:rtst] (-es, ⁼e) *m* doctor
Ärztin ['ɛ:rtstɪn] *f* doctor
ärztlich ['ɛ:rtstlɪç] *adj* medical
As [as] (-ses, -se) *nt* ace
Asbest [as'bɛst] (-(e)s, -e) *m* asbestos
Asche ['aʃə] *f* ash, cinder; **Aschenbahn** *f* cinder track; **Aschenbecher** *m* ash-

tray; **Aschermittwoch** *m* Ash Wednesday
Äser ['ɛ:zər] *pl von* Aas
Asi- ['a:zi] *zW:* **~en** (-s) *nt* Asia; **~at(in)** [azi'a:t(ɪn)] (-en, -en) *m(f)* Asian; **a~atisch** [-'a:tɪʃ] *adj* Asian
asozial ['azotsia:l] *adj* antisocial; *(Familien)* asocial
Aspekt [as'pɛkt] (-(e)s, -e) *m* aspect
Asphalt [as'falt] (-(e)s, -e) *m* asphalt; **a~ieren** [-'ti:rən] *vt* to asphalt
aß *etc* [a:s] *vb siehe* essen
Asse ['asə] *pl von* As
Assistent(in) [asɪs'tɛnt(ɪn)] *m(f)* assistant
Assoziation [asotsiatsi'o:n] *f* association
Ast [ast] (-(e)s, ⁼e) *m* bough, branch
Aster (-, -n) *f* aster
ästhetisch [ɛs'te:tɪʃ] *adj* aesthetic
Asthma ['astma] (-s) *nt* asthma; **~tiker(in)** [ast'ma:tikər(ɪn)] (-s, -) *m(f)* asthmatic
Astro- [astro] *zW:* **~'loge** (-n, -n) *m* astrologer; **~lo'gie** *f* astrology; **~'naut** (-en, -en) *m* astronaut; **~'nom** (-en, -en) *m* astronomer; **~no'mie** *f* astronomy
Asyl [a'zy:l] (-s, -e) *nt* asylum; *(Heim)* home; *(Obdachlosen~)* shelter
Atelier [atəli'e:] (-s, -s) *nt* studio
Atem ['a:təm] (-s) *m* breath; **den ~ anhalten** to hold one's breath; **außer ~** out of breath; **a~beraubend** *adj* breathtaking; **a~los** *adj* breathless; **~pause** *f* breather; **~zug** *m* breath
Atheismus [ate'ɪsmus] *m* atheism
Atheist *m* atheist; **a~isch** *adj* atheistic
Athen [a'te:n] (-s) *nt* Athens; **~er(in)** (-s, -) *m(f)* Athenian; **a~isch** *adj* Athenian
Äther ['ɛ:tər] (-s, -) *m* ether
Äthiop- [ɛti'o:p] *zW:* **~ien** (-s) *nt* Ethiopia; **~ier(in)** (-s, -) *m(f)* Ethiopian; **ä~isch** *adj* Ethiopian
Athlet [at'le:t] (-en, -en) *m* athlete
Atlantik (-s) *m* Atlantic (Ocean)
atlantisch *adj* Atlantic
Atlas ['atlas] (- *od* -ses, -se *od* Atlanten) *m* atlas
atmen ['a:tmən] *vt, vi* to breathe

Atmosphäre [atmo'sfɛːrə] *f* atmosphere
atmosphärisch *adj* atmospheric
Atmung ['aːtmʊŋ] *f* respiration
Atom [a'toːm] (-s, -e) *nt* atom; **a~ar**
[ato'maːr] *adj* atomic; **~bombe** *f* atom
bomb; **~energie** *f* atomic *od* nuclear
energy; **~kraftgegner** *m* opponent of
nuclear power; **~kraftwerk** *nt* nuclear
power station; **~krieg** *m* nuclear *od*
atomic war; **~macht** *f* nuclear *od*
atomic power; **~müll** *m* atomic waste;
~sperrvertrag *m* (*POL*) nuclear non-
proliferation treaty; **~strom** *m* (electricity generated by) nuclear power;
~versuch *m* atomic test; **~waffen** *pl*
atomic weapons; **a~waffenfrei** *adj*
nuclear-free; **~zeitalter** *nt* atomic age
Attentat ['atəntaːt] (-(e)s, -e) *nt*: ~ (auf
+*akk*) (attempted) assassination (of)
Attentäter ['atəntɛːtər] *m* (would-be)
assassin
Attest [a'tɛst] (-(e)s, -e) *nt* certificate
attraktiv [atrak'tiːf] *adj* attractive
Attrappe [a'trapə] *f* dummy
Attribut [atri'buːt] (-(e)s, -e) *nt* (*GRAM*)
attribute
ätzen ['ɛtsən] *vi* to be caustic
au [au] *excl* ouch!; ~ **ja!** oh yes!

auch [aux] *adv* **1** (*ebenfalls*) also, too,
as well; **das ist auch schön** that's nice
too *od* as well; **er kommt - ich auch**
he's coming - so am I, me too; **auch
nicht** not ... either; **ich auch nicht** nor I,
me neither; **oder auch** or; **auch das
noch!** not that as well!
2 (*selbst, sogar*) even; **auch wenn das
Wetter schlecht ist** even if the weather
is bad; **ohne auch nur zu fragen** without
even asking
3 (*wirklich*) really; **du siehst müde aus
- bin ich auch** you look tired - (so) I
am; **so sieht es auch aus** it looks like it
too
4 (*auch immer*): **wer auch** whoever;
was auch whatever; **wie dem auch sei**
be that as it may; **wie sehr er sich
auch bemühte** however much he tried

auf [auf] *präp* +*dat* (*wo?*) on; **auf dem
Tisch** on the table; **auf der Reise** on the
way; **auf der Post/dem Fest** at the post
office/party; **auf der Straße** on the
road; **auf dem Land/der ganzen Welt** in
the country/the whole world
♦ *präp* +*akk* **1** (*wohin?*) on(to); **auf
den Tisch** on(to) the table; **auf die Post
gehen** go to the post office; **auf das
Land** into the country; **etw auf einen
Zettel schreiben** to write sth on a piece
of paper
2: **auf deutsch** in German; **auf Lebens-
zeit** for my/his lifetime; **bis auf ihn**
except for him; **auf einmal** at once; **auf
seinen Vorschlag (hin)** at his suggestion
♦ *adv* **1** (*offen*) open; **das Fenster ist
auf** the window is open
2 (*hinauf*) up; **auf und ab** up and
down; **auf und davon** up and away;
auf! (*los!*) come on!
3 (*aufgestanden*) up; **ist er schon auf?**
is he up yet?
♦ *konj*: **auf daß** (so) that

aufatmen ['auf'aːtmən] *vi* to heave a
sigh of relief
aufbahren ['aufbaːrən] *vt* to lay out
Aufbau ['aufbau] *m* (*Bauen*) building,
construction; (*Struktur*) structure;
(*aufgebautes Teil*) superstructure;
a~en *vt* to erect, to build (up);
(*Existenz*) to make; (*gestalten*) to construct; **a~en (auf** +*dat*) (*gründen*) to
found *od* base (on)
aufbauschen ['aufbauʃən] *vt* to puff
out; (*fig*) to exaggerate
aufbekommen ['aufbəkɔmən] (*unreg*)
vt (*öffnen*) to get open; (*Hausaufgaben*) to be given
aufbessern ['aufbɛsərn] *vt* (*Gehalt*) to
increase
aufbewahren ['aufbəvaːrən] *vt* to keep;
(*Gepäck*) to put in the left-luggage
office (*BRIT*) *od* baggage check (*US*)
Aufbewahrung *f* (safe)keeping;
(*Gepäck~*) left-luggage office (*BRIT*),
baggage check (*US*)

aufbieten ['aʊfbiːtən] (unreg) vt (Kraft) to summon (up); (Armee, Polizei) to mobilize; (Brautpaar) to publish the banns of

aufblasen ['aʊfblaːzən] (unreg) vt to blow up, to inflate ♦ vr (umg) to become big-headed

aufbleiben ['aʊfblaɪbən] (unreg) vi (Laden) to remain open; (Person) to stay up

aufblicken ['aʊfblɪkən] vi to look up; ~ zu to look up at; (fig) to look up to

aufblühen ['aʊfblyːən] vi to blossom, to flourish

aufbrauchen ['aʊfbraʊxən] vt to use up

aufbrausen ['aʊfbraʊzən] vi (fig) to flare up; ~d adj hot-tempered

aufbrechen ['aʊfbrɛçən] (unreg) vt to break òd prise (BRIT) open ♦ vi to burst open; (gehen) to start, to set off

aufbringen ['aʊfbrɪŋən] (unreg) vt (öffnen) to open; (in Mode) to bring into fashion; (beschaffen) to procure; (FIN) to raise; (ärgern) to irritate; **Verständnis für etw** ~ to be able to understand sth

Aufbruch ['aʊfbrʊx] m departure

aufbrühen ['aʊfbryːən] vt (Tee) to make

aufbürden ['aʊfbʏrdən] vt: **jdm etw** ~ to burden sb with sth

aufdecken ['aʊfdɛkən] vt to uncover

aufdringlich ['aʊfdrɪŋlɪç] adj pushy

aufeinander [aʊfaɪ'nandər] adv on top of each other; (schießen) at each other; (vertrauen) each other; ~**folgen** vi to follow one another; ~**folgend** adj consecutive; ~**legen** vt to lay on top of one another; ~**prallen** vi to hit one another

Aufenthalt ['aʊfɛnthalt] m stay; (Verzögerung) delay; (EISENB: Halten) stop; (Ort) haunt; **Aufenthaltsgenehmigung** f residence permit

auferlegen ['aʊfɛrleːgən] vt: **(jdm)** ~ to impose (upon sb)

Auferstehung ['aʊfˈɛrʃteːʊŋ] f resurrection

aufessen ['aʊfɛsən] (unreg) vt to eat up

auffahr- ['aʊffaːr] zW: ~**en** (unreg) vi (herankommen) to draw up; (hochfahren) to jump up; (wütend

werden) to flare up; (in den Himmel) to ascend ♦ vt (Kanonen, Geschütz) to bring up; ~**en auf** +akk (Auto) to run od crash into; ~**end** adj hot-tempered; **A~t** f (Hausauffahrt) drive; (Autobahnauffahrt) slip road (BRIT), (freeway) entrance (US); **A~unfall** m pile-up

auffallen ['aʊffalən] (unreg) vi to be noticeable; **jdm** ~ to strike sb; ~**d** adj striking

auffällig ['aʊffɛlɪç] adj conspicuous, striking

auffangen ['aʊffaŋən] (unreg) vt to catch; (Funkspruch) to intercept; (Preise) to peg

auffassen ['aʊffasən] vt to understand, to comprehend; (auslegen) to see, to view

Auffassung f (Meinung) opinion; (Auslegung) view, concept; (auch: Auffassungsgabe) grasp

auffindbar ['aʊffɪntbaːr] adj to be found

auffordern ['aʊffordərn] vt (befehlen) to call upon, to order; (bitten) to ask

Aufforderung f (Befehl) order; (Einladung) invitation

auffrischen ['aʊffrɪʃən] vt to freshen up; (Kenntnisse) to brush up; (Erinnerungen) to reawaken ♦ vi (Wind) to freshen

aufführen ['aʊffyːrən] vt (THEAT) to perform; (in einem Verzeichnis) to list, to specify ♦ vr (sich benehmen) to behave

Aufführung f (THEAT) performance; (Liste) specification

Aufgabe ['aʊfgaːbə] f task; (SCH) exercise; (Haus~) homework; (Verzicht) giving up; (von Gepäck) registration; (von Post) posting; (von Inserat) insertion

Aufgang ['aʊfgaŋ] m ascent; (Sonnen~) rise; (Treppe) staircase

aufgeben ['aʊfgeːbən] (unreg) vt (verzichten) to give up; (Paket) to send, to post; (Gepäck) to register; (Bestellung) to give; (Inserat) to insert; (Rätsel, Problem) to set ♦ vi to give up

Aufgebot ['aʊfgəboːt] nt supply; (Ehe~) banns pl

aufgedunsen [ˈaufgedʊnzən] *adj* swollen, puffed up

aufgehen [ˈaufgeːən] *(unreg) vi (Sonne, Teig)* to rise; *(sich öffnen)* to open; *(klarwerden)* to become clear; *(MATH)* to come out exactly; ~ **(in** +*dat)* *(sich widmen)* to be absorbed (in); in **Rauch/Flammen** ~ to go up in smoke/flames

aufgelegt [ˈaufgəleːkt] *adj:* **gut/schlecht** ~ **sein** to be in a good/bad mood; **zu etw** ~ **sein** to be in the mood for sth

aufgeregt [ˈaufgəreːkt] *adj* excited

aufgeschlossen [ˈaufgəflɔsən] *adj* open, open-minded

aufgeweckt [ˈaufgəvɛkt] *adj* bright, intelligent

aufgießen [ˈaufgiːsən] *(unreg) vt (Wasser)* to pour over; *(Tee)* to infuse

aufgreifen [ˈaufgraɪfən] *(unreg) vt (Thema)* to take up; *(Verdächtige)* to pick up, to seize

aufgrund [aufˈgrʊnt] *präp* +*gen* on the basis of; *(wegen)* because of

aufhaben [ˈaufhaːbən] *(unreg) vt* to have on; *(Arbeit)* to have to do

aufhalsen [ˈaufhalzən] *(umg) vt:* **jdm etw** ~ to saddle *od* lumber sb with sth

aufhalten [ˈaufhaltən] *(unreg) vt (Person)* to detain; *(Entwicklung)* to check; *(Tür, Hand)* to hold open; *(Augen)* to keep open ♦ *vr (wohnen)* to live; *(bleiben)* to stay; **sich mit etw** ~ to waste time over sth

aufhängen [ˈaufhɛŋən] *(unreg) vt (Wäsche)* to hang up; *(Menschen)* to hang ♦ *vr* to hang o.s.

Aufhänger (**-s, -**) *m (am Mantel)* loop; *(fig)* peg

aufheben [ˈaufheːbən] *(unreg) vt (hochheben)* to raise, to lift; *(Sitzung)* to wind up; *(Urteil)* to annul; *(Gesetz)* to repeal, to abolish; *(aufbewahren)* to keep ♦ *vr* to cancel itself out; **bei jdm gut aufgehoben sein** to be well looked after at sb's; **viel A~(s) machen (von)** to make a fuss about

aufheitern [ˈaufhaɪtərn] *vt, vr (Himmel, Miene)* to brighten; *(Mensch)* to cheer up

aufhellen [ˈaufhɛlən] *vt, vr* to clear up; *(Farbe, Haare)* to lighten

aufhetzen [ˈaufhɛtsən] *vt* to stir up

aufholen [ˈaufhoːlən] *vt* to make up ♦ *vi* to catch up

aufhorchen [ˈaufhɔrçən] *vi* to prick up one's ears

aufhören [ˈaufhøːrən] *vi* to stop; ~, **etw zu tun** to stop doing sth

aufklappen [ˈaufklapən] *vt* to open

aufklären [ˈaufklɛːrən] *vt (Geheimnis etc)* to clear up; *(Person)* to enlighten; *(sexuell)* to tell the facts of life to; *(MIL)* to reconnoitre ♦ *vr* to clear up

Aufklärung *f (von Geheimnis)* clearing up; *(Unterrichtung, Zeitalter)* enlightenment; *(sexuell)* sex education; *(MIL, AVIAT)* reconnaissance

aufkleben [ˈaufkleːbən] *vt* to stick on

Aufkleber (**-s, -**) *m* sticker

aufknöpfen [ˈaufknœpfən] *vt* to unbutton

aufkommen [ˈaufkɔmən] *(unreg) vi (Wind)* to come up; *(Zweifel, Gefühl)* to arise; *(Mode)* to start; **für jdn/etw** ~ to be liable *od* responsible for sb/sth

aufladen [ˈauflaːdən] *(unreg) vt* to load

Auflage [ˈauflaːgə] *f* edition; *(Zeitung)* circulation; *(Bedingung)* condition; **jdm etw zur** ~ **machen** to make sth a condition for sb

auflassen [ˈauflasən] *(unreg) vt (offen)* to leave open; *(aufgesetzt)* to leave on

auflauern [ˈauflauərn] *vi:* **jdm** ~ to lie in wait for sb

Auflauf [ˈauflauf] *m (KOCH)* pudding; *(Menschen~)* crowd

auflegen [ˈaufleːgən] *vt* to put on; *(Telefon)* to hang up; *(TYP)* to print

auflehnen [ˈaufleːnən] *vt* to lean on ♦ *vr* to rebel

Auflehnung *f* rebellion

auflesen [ˈaufleːzən] *(unreg) vt* to pick up

aufleuchten [ˈauflɔyçtən] *vi* to light up

auflockern [ˈauflɔkərn] *vt* to loosen; *(fig: Eintönigkeit etc)* to liven up

auflösen [ˈaufløːzən] *vt* to dissolve; *(Haare etc)* to loosen; *(Mißverständnis)* to sort out ♦ *vr* to dissolve; to come undone; to be resolved; **(in Tränen)** auf-

gelöst sein to be in tears
Auflösung f dissolving; (fig) solution
aufmachen ['aufmaxən] vt to open; (Kleidung) to undo; (zurechtmachen) to do up ♦ vr to set out
Aufmachung f (Kleidung) outfit, get-up; (Gestaltung) format
aufmerksam ['aufmɛrkza:m] adj attentive; **jdn auf etw** akk **~ machen** to point sth out to sb; **A~keit** f attention, attentiveness
aufmuntern ['aufmuntərn] vt (ermutigen) to encourage; (erheitern) to cheer up
Aufnahme ['aufna:mə] f reception; (Beginn) beginning; (in Verein etc) admission; (in Liste etc) inclusion; (Notieren) taking down; (PHOT) shot; (auf Tonband etc) recording; **a~fähig** adj receptive; **~prüfung** f entrance test
aufnehmen ['aufne:mən] (unreg) vt to receive; (hochheben) to pick up; (beginnen) to take up; (in Verein etc) to admit; (in Liste etc) to include; (fassen) to hold; (notieren) to take down; (fotografieren) to photograph; (auf Tonband, Platte) to record; (FIN: leihen) to take out; **es mit jdm ~ können** to be able to compete with sb
aufopfern ['aufɔpfərn] vt, vr to sacrifice; **~d** adj selfless
aufpassen ['aufpasən] vi (aufmerksam sein) to pay attention; **auf jdn/etw ~** to look after od watch sb/sth; **aufgepaßt!** look out!
Aufprall ['aufpral] (-s, -e) m impact; **a~en** vi to hit, to strike
Aufpreis ['aufprais] m extra charge
aufpumpen ['aufpumpən] vt to pump up
aufraffen ['aufrafən] vr to rouse o.s.
aufräumen ['aufrɔymən] vt, vi (Dinge) to clear away; (Zimmer) to tidy up
aufrecht ['aufrɛçt] adj (auch fig) upright; **~erhalten** (unreg) vt to maintain
aufreg- ['aufre:g] zW: **~en** vt to excite ♦ vr to get excited; **~end** adj exciting; **A~ung** f excitement
aufreibend ['aufraibənt] adj strenuous
aufreißen ['aufraisən] (unreg) vt (Umschlag) to tear open; (Augen) to open wide; (Tür) to throw open; (Straße) to take up
aufreizen ['aufraitsən] vt to incite, to stir up; **~d** adj exciting, stimulating
aufrichten ['aufrçtən] vt to put up, to erect; (moralisch) to console ♦ vr to rise; (moralisch): **sich ~ (an** +dat) to take heart (from); **aufrichtig** ['aufrçtç] adj sincere, honest; **Aufrichtigkeit** f sincerity
aufrücken ['aufrykən] vi to move up; (beruflich) to be promoted
Aufruf ['aufru:f] m summons; (zur Hilfe) call; (des Namens) calling out; **a~en** (unreg) vt (Namen) to call out; (auffordern): **jdn a~en (zu)** to call upon sb (for)
Aufruhr ['aufru:r] (-(e)s, -e) m uprising, revolt
aufrührerisch ['aufry:rərɪʃ] adj rebellious
aufrunden ['aufrundən] vt (Summe) to round up
Aufrüstung ['aufrystuŋ] f rearmament
aufrütteln ['aufrytəln] vt (auch fig) to shake up
aufs [aufs] = **auf das**
aufsagen ['aufza:gən] vt (Gedicht) to recite
aufsammeln ['aufzaməln] vt to gather up
aufsässig ['aufzɛsɪç] adj rebellious
Aufsatz ['aufzats] m (Geschriebenes) essay; (auf Schrank etc) top
aufsaugen ['aufzaugən] (unreg) vt to soak up
aufschauen ['auffauən] vi to look up
aufscheuchen ['aufʃɔyçən] vt to scare od frighten away
aufschieben ['aufʃi:bən] (unreg) vt to push open; (verzögern) to put off, to postpone
Aufschlag ['aufʃla:k] m (Ärmel~) cuff; (Jacken~) lapel; (Hosen~) turn-up; (Aufprall) impact; (Preis~) surcharge; (Tennis) service; **a~en** [-gən] (unreg) vt (öffnen) to open; (verwunden) to cut; (hochschlagen) to turn up; (aufbauen: Zelt, Lager) to pitch, to

erect; (*Wohnsitz*) to take up ♦ *vi*
(*aufprallen*) to hit; (*teurer werden*) to
go up; (*Tennis*) to serve
aufschließen ['aʊfʃliːsən] (*unreg*) *vt* to
open up, to unlock ♦ *vi* (*aufrücken*) to
close up
Aufschluß ['aʊfʃlʊs] *m* information;
a~reich *adj* informative, illuminating
aufschnappen ['aʊfʃnapən] *vt* (*umg*) to
pick up ♦ *vi* to fly open
aufschneiden ['aʊfʃnaɪdən] (*unreg*) *vt*
(*Geschwür*) to cut open; (*Brot*) to cut
up; (*MED*) to lance ♦ *vi* to brag
Aufschneider (-s, -) *m* boaster,
braggart
Aufschnitt ['aʊfʃnɪt] *m* (slices of) cold
meat
aufschrecken ['aʊfʃrɛkən] *vt* to startle ♦
vi (*unreg*) to start up
Aufschrei ['aʊfʃraɪ] *m* cry
aufschreiben ['aʊfʃraɪbən] (*unreg*) *vt* to
write down
aufschreien ['aʊfʃraɪən] (*unreg*) *vi* to
cry out
Aufschrift ['aʊfʃrɪft] *f* (*Inschrift*) inscription; (*auf Etikett*) label
Aufschub ['aʊfʃuːp] (-(e)s, -schübe) *m*
delay, postponement
Aufschwung ['aʊfʃvʊŋ] *m* (*Elan*) boost
♦ *nt* (*wirtschaftlich*) upturn, boom;
(*SPORT*) circle
Aufsehen ['aʊfzeːən] (-s) *nt* sensation,
stir
aufsehen (*unreg*) *vi* to look up; ~ zu
to look up at; (*fig*) to look up to
aufsehenerregend *adj* sensational
Aufseher(in) (-s, -) *m(f)* guard; (*im
Betrieb*) supervisor; (*Museums~*)
attendant; (*Park~*) keeper
aufsetzen ['aʊfzɛtsən] *vt* to put on;
(*Flugzeug*) to put down; (*Dokument*) to
draw up ♦ *vr* to sit up(right) ♦ *vi*
(*Flugzeug*) to touch down
Aufsicht ['aʊfzɪçt] *f* supervision; **die ~
haben** to be in charge
aufsitzen ['aʊfzɪtsən] (*unreg*) *vi* (*aufrecht hinsitzen*) to sit up; (*aufs Pferd,
Motorrad*) to mount, to get on; (*Schiff*)
to run aground; **jdm ~** (*umg*) to be
taken in by sb

aufsparen ['aʊfʃpaːrən] *vt* to save (up)
aufsperren ['aʊfʃpɛrən] *vt* to unlock;
(*Mund*) to open wide
aufspielen ['aʊfʃpiːlən] *vr* to show off
aufspießen ['aʊfʃpiːsən] *vt* to spear
aufspringen ['aʊfʃprɪŋən] (*unreg*) *vi*
(*hochspringen*) to jump up; (*sich
öffnen*) to spring open; (*Hände, Lippen*)
to become chapped; **auf etw** *akk* ~ to
jump onto sth
aufspüren ['aʊfʃpyːrən] *vt* to track
down, to trace
aufstacheln ['aʊfʃtaxəln] *vt* to incite
Aufstand ['aʊfʃtant] *m* insurrection, rebellion
aufständisch ['aʊfʃtɛndɪʃ] *adj* rebellious, mutinous
aufstecken ['aʊfʃtɛkən] *vt* to stick on, to
pin up; (*umg*) to give up
aufstehen ['aʊfʃteːən] (*unreg*) *vi* to get
up; (*Tür*) to be open
aufsteigen ['aʊfʃtaɪgən] (*unreg*) *vi*
(*hochsteigen*) to climb; (*Rauch*) to
rise; **auf etw** *akk* ~ to get onto sth
aufstellen ['aʊfʃtɛlən] *vt* (*aufrecht
stellen*) to put up; (*aufreihen*) to line
up; (*nominieren*) to nominate; (*formulieren: Programm etc*) to draw up;
(*leisten: Rekord*) to set up
Aufstellung *f* (*SPORT*) line-up; (*Liste*)
list
Aufstieg ['aʊfʃtiːk] (-(e)s, -e) *m* (*auf
Berg*) ascent; (*Fortschritt*) rise;
(*beruflich, SPORT*) promotion
aufstoßen ['aʊfʃtoːsən] (*unreg*) *vt* to
push open ♦ *vi* to belch
aufstützen ['aʊfʃtʏtsən] *vt* (*Körperteil*)
to prop, to lean; (*Person*) to prop up ♦
vr: **sich auf etw** *akk* ~ to lean on sth
aufsuchen ['aʊfzuːxən] *vt* (*besuchen*) to
visit; (*konsultieren*) to consult
Auftakt ['aʊftakt] *m* (*MUS*) upbeat; (*fig*)
prelude
auftanken ['aʊftaŋkən] *vi* to get petrol
(*BRIT*) *od* gas (*US*) ♦ *vt* to refuel
auftauchen ['aʊftaʊxən] *vi* to appear;
(*aus Wasser etc*) to emerge; (*U-Boot*)
to surface; (*Zweifel*) to arise
auftauen ['aʊftaʊən] *vt* to thaw ♦ *vi* to
thaw; (*fig*) to relax

aufteilen ['aʊftaɪlən] vt to divide up; (Raum) to partition

Aufteilung f division; partition

Auftrag ['aʊftraːk] (-(e)s, -träge) m order; (Anweisung) commission; (Aufgabe) mission; **im ~ von** on behalf of; **a~en** [-gən] (unreg) vt (Essen) to serve; (Farbe) to put on; (Kleidung) to wear out; **jdm etw a~en** to tell sb sth; **dick a~en** (fig) to exaggerate; **~geber** (-s, -) m (COMM) purchaser, customer

auftreiben ['aʊftraɪbən] (unreg) vt (umg: beschaffen) to raise

auftreten ['aʊftreːtən] (unreg) vt to kick open ♦ vi to appear; (mit Füßen) to tread; (sich verhalten) to behave; **A~** (-s) nt (Vorkommen) appearance; (Benehmen) behaviour

Auftrieb ['aʊftriːp] m (PHYS) buoyancy, lift; (fig) impetus

Auftritt ['aʊftrɪt] m (des Schauspielers) entrance; (Szene: auch fig) scene

auftun ['aʊftuːn] (unreg) vt to open ♦ vr to open up

aufwachen ['aʊfvaxən] vi to wake up

aufwachsen ['aʊfvaksən] (unreg) vi to grow up

Aufwand ['aʊfvant] (-(e)s) m expenditure; (Kosten auch) expense; (Luxus) show

aufwärmen ['aʊfvɛrmən] vt to warm up; (alte Geschichten) to rake up

aufwärts ['aʊfvɛrts] adv upwards; **A~entwicklung** f upward trend

aufwecken ['aʊfvɛkən] vt to wake up, to waken up

aufweisen ['aʊfvaɪzən] (unreg) vt to show

aufwenden ['aʊfvɛndən] (unreg) vt to expend; (Geld) to spend; (Sorgfalt) to devote

aufwendig adj costly

aufwerfen ['aʊfvɛrfən] (unreg) vt (Fenster etc) to throw open; (Probleme) to throw up, to raise

aufwerten ['aʊfveːrtən] vt (FIN) to revalue; (fig) to raise in value

aufwiegeln ['aʊfviːgəln] vt to stir up, to incite

aufwiegen ['aʊfviːgən] (unreg) vt to make up for

Aufwind ['aʊfvɪnt] m up-current

aufwirbeln ['aʊfvɪrbəln] vt to whirl up; **Staub ~** (fig) to create a stir

aufwischen ['aʊfvɪʃən] vt to wipe up

aufzählen ['aʊftsɛːlən] vt to list

aufzeichnen ['aʊftsaɪçnən] vt to sketch; (schriftlich) to jot down; (auf Band) to record

Aufzeichnung f (schriftlich) note; (Tonband~) recording; (Film~) record

aufzeigen ['aʊftsaɪgən] vt to show, to demonstrate

aufziehen ['aʊftsiːən] (unreg) vt (hochziehen) to raise, to draw up; (öffnen) to pull open; (Uhr) to wind; (umg: necken) to tease; (großziehen: Kinder) to raise, to bring up; (Tiere) to rear

Aufzug ['aʊftsuːk] m (Fahrstuhl) lift, elevator; (Aufmarsch) procession, parade; (Kleidung) get-up; (THEAT) act

aufzwingen ['aʊftsvɪŋən] (unreg) vt: **jdm etw ~** to force sth upon sb

Augapfel m eyeball; (fig) apple of one's eye

Auge ['aʊgə] (-s, -n) nt eye; (Fett~) globule of fat; **unter vier ~n** in private

Augen- zW: **~blick** m moment; **im ~blick** at the moment; **a~blicklich** adj (sofort) instantaneous; (gegenwärtig) present; **~braue** f eyebrow; **~weide** f sight for sore eyes; **~zeuge** m eye witness

August [aʊ'gʊst] (-(e)s od -, -e) m August

Auktion [aʊktsi'oːn] f auction

Aula ['aʊla] (-, **Aulen** od -s) f assembly hall

SCHLÜSSELWORT

aus [aʊs] präp +dat **1** (räumlich) out of; (von ... her) from; **er ist aus Berlin** he's from Berlin; **aus dem Fenster** out of the window

2 (gemacht/hergestellt aus) made of; **ein Herz aus Stein** a heart of stone

3 (auf Ursache deutend) out of; **aus Mitleid** out of sympathy; **aus Erfahrung** from experience; **aus Spaß** for fun

4: aus ihr wird nie etwas she'll never get anywhere
♦ adv **1** (*zu Ende*) finished, over; **aus und vorbei** over and done with
2 (*ausgeschaltet, ausgezogen*) out; (*Aufschrift an Geräten*) off; **Licht aus!** lights out!
3 (*in Verbindung mit von*): **von Rom aus** from Rome; **vom Fenster aus** out of the window; **von sich aus** (*selbständig*) of one's own accord; **von ihm aus** as far as he's concerned

ausarbeiten ['aʊs'arbaɪtən] vt to work out
ausarten ['aʊs'artən] vi to degenerate; (*Kind*) to become overexcited
ausatmen ['aʊs'a:tmən] vi to breathe out
ausbaden ['aʊsba:dən] (*umg*) vt: **etw ~ müssen** to carry the can for sth
Ausbau ['aʊsbaʊ] m extension, expansion; removal; **a~en** vt to extend, to expand; (*herausnehmen*) to take out, to remove; **a~fähig** adj (*fig*) worth developing
ausbessern ['aʊsbɛsərn] vt to mend, to repair
ausbeulen ['aʊsbɔʏlən] vt to beat out
Ausbeute ['aʊsbɔʏtə] f yield; (*Fische*) catch; **a~n** vt to exploit; (*MIN*) to work
ausbild- ['aʊsbɪld] zW: **~en** vt to educate; (*Lehrling, Soldat*) to instruct, to train; (*Fähigkeiten*) to develop; (*Geschmack*) to cultivate; **A~er** (-s, -) m instructor; **A~ung** f education; training, instruction; development; cultivation
ausbleiben ['aʊsblaɪbən] (*unreg*) vi (*Personen*) to stay away, not to come; (*Ereignisse*) to fail to happen, not to happen
Ausblick ['aʊsblɪk] m (*auch fig*) prospect (*lit, fig*), outlook, view
ausbrechen ['aʊsbrɛçən] (*unreg*) vi to break out ♦ vt to break off; **in Tränen/Gelächter ~** to burst into tears/out laughing
ausbreiten ['aʊsbraɪtən] vt to spread (out); (*Arme*) to stretch out ♦ vr to spread; **sich über ein Thema ~** to

expand *od* enlarge on a topic
ausbrennen ['aʊsbrɛnən] (*unreg*) vt to scorch; (*Wunde*) to cauterize ♦ vi to burn out
Ausbruch ['aʊsbrʊx] m outbreak; (*von Vulkan*) eruption; (*Gefühls~*) outburst; (*von Gefangenen*) escape
ausbrüten ['aʊsbry:tən] vt (*auch fig*) to hatch
Ausdauer ['aʊsdaʊər] f perseverance, stamina; **ausdauernd** adj persevering
ausdehnen ['aʊsde:nən] vt, vr (*räumlich*) to expand; (*zeitlich, auch Gummi*) to stretch; (*Nebel, fig: Macht*) to extend
ausdenken ['aʊsdɛŋkən] (*unreg*) vt: **sich dat etw ~** to think sth up
Ausdruck ['aʊsdrʊk] m expression, phrase; (*Kundgabe, Gesichts~*) expression; (*COMPUT*) print-out, hard copy; **a~en** vt (*COMPUT*) to print out
ausdrücken ['aʊsdrʏkən] vt (*auch vr: formulieren, zeigen*) to express; (*Zigarette*) to put out; (*Zitrone*) to squeeze
ausdrücklich adj express, explicit
ausdrucks- zW: **~los** adj expressionless, blank; **~voll** adj expressive; **A~weise** f mode of expression
auseinander [aʊs'aɪ'nandər] adv (*getrennt*) apart; **~ schreiben** to write as separate words; **~bringen** (*unreg*) vt to separate; **~fallen** (*unreg*) vi to fall apart; **~gehen** (*unreg*) vi (*Menschen*) to separate; (*Meinungen*) to differ; (*Gegenstand*) to fall apart; (*umg: dick werden*) to put on weight; **~halten** (*unreg*) vt to tell apart; **~nehmen** (*unreg*) vt to take to pieces, to dismantle; **~setzen** vt (*erklären*) to set forth, to explain ♦ vr (*sich verständigen*) to come to terms, to settle; (*sich befassen*) to concern o.s.; **A~setzung** f argument
auserlesen ['aʊs'ɛrle:zən] adj select, choice
Ausfahrt ['aʊsfa:rt] f (*des Zuges etc*) leaving, departure; (*Autobahn~*) exit; (*Garagen~ etc*) exit, way out; (*Spazierfahrt*) drive, excursion
Ausfall ['aʊsfal] m loss; (*Nicht-

stattfinden) cancellation; (*MIL*) sortie; (*Fechten*) lunge; (*radioaktiv*) fall-out; **a~en** (*unreg*) *vi* (*Zähne, Haare*) to fall *od* come out; (*nicht stattfinden*) to be cancelled; (*wegbleiben*) to be omitted; (*Person*) to drop out; (*Lohn*) to be stopped; (*nicht funktionieren*) to break down; (*Resultat haben*) to turn out; **a~end** *adj* impertinent; **~straße** *f* arterial road

Ausfertigung ['ausfɛrtɪguŋ] *f* drawing up; making out; (*Exemplar*) copy

ausfindig ['ausfɪndɪç] *adj*: ~ **machen** to discover

ausflippen ['ausflɪpən] (*umg*) *vi* to freak out

Ausflucht ['ausfluxt] (-, **-flüchte**) *f* excuse

Ausflug ['ausfluːk] *m* excursion, outing

Ausflügler ['ausflyːklər] (-s, -) *m* tripper

Ausfluß ['ausflʊs] *m* outlet; (*MED*) discharge

ausfragen ['ausfraːgən] *vt* to interrogate, to question

ausfressen ['ausfrɛsən] (*unreg*) *vt* to eat up; (*aushöhlen*) to corrode; (*umg: anstellen*) to be up to

Ausfuhr ['ausfuːr] (-, **-en**) *f* export, exportation ♦ *in zW* export

ausführ- ['ausfyːr] *zW*: **~en** *vt* (*verwirklichen*) to carry out; (*Person*) to take out; (*Hund*) to take for a walk; (*COMM*) to export; (*erklären*) to give details of; **~lich** *adj* detailed ♦ *adv* in detail; **A~lichkeit** *f* detail; **A~ung** *f* execution, performance; (*Durchführung*) completion; (*Herstellungsart*) version; (*Erklärung*) explanation

ausfüllen ['ausfʏlən] *vt* to fill up; (*Fragebogen etc*) to fill in; (*Beruf*) to be fulfilling for

Ausgabe ['ausgaːbə] *f* (*Geld*) expenditure, outlay; (*Aushändigung*) giving out; (*Gepäck~*) left-luggage office; (*Buch*) edition; (*Nummer*) issue; (*COMPUT*) output

Ausgang ['ausgaŋ] *m* way out, exit; (*Ende*) end; (*Ausgangspunkt*) starting point; (*Ergebnis*) result; (*Ausgehtag*) free time, time off; **kein** ~ no exit

Ausgangs- *zW*: **~basis** *f* starting point; **~punkt** *m* starting point; **~sperre** *f* curfew

ausgeben ['ausgeːbən] (*unreg*) *vt* (*Geld*) to spend; (*austeilen*) to issue, to distribute ♦ *vr*: **sich für etw/jdn** ~ to pass o.s. off as sth/sb

ausgedient ['ausgədiːnt] *adj* (*Soldat*) discharged; (*verbraucht*) no longer in use; ~ **haben** to have done good service

ausgefallen ['ausgəfalən] *adj* (*ungewöhnlich*) exceptional

ausgeglichen ['ausgəglɪçən] *adj* (well-)balanced; **A~heit** *f* balance; (*von Mensch*) even-temperedness

ausgehen ['ausgeːən] (*unreg*) *vi* to go out; (*zu Ende gehen*) to come to an end; (*Benzin*) to run out; (*Haare, Zähne*) to fall *od* come out; (*Feuer, Ofen, Licht*) to go out; (*Strom*) to go off; (*Resultat haben*) to turn out; **mir ging das Benzin aus** I ran out of petrol (*BRIT*) *od* gas (*US*); **auf etw** *akk* ~ to aim at sth; **von etw** ~ (*wegführen*) to lead away from sth; (*herrühren*) to come from sth; (*zugrunde legen*) to proceed from sth; **wir können davon** ~, **daß** ... we can take as our starting point that ...; **leer** ~ to get nothing; **schlecht** ~ to turn out badly

Ausgehverbot *nt* curfew

ausgelassen ['ausgəlasən] *adj* boisterous, high-spirited; **A~heit** *f* boisterousness, high spirits *pl*, exuberance

ausgelastet ['ausgəlastət] *adj* fully occupied

ausgelernt ['ausgəlɛrnt] *adj* trained, qualified

ausgemacht ['ausgəmaxt] *adj* settled; (*umg: Dummkopf etc*) out-and-out, downright; **es war eine ~e Sache, daß** ... it was a foregone conclusion that ...

ausgenommen ['ausgənɔmən] *präp* +*gen* except ♦ *konj* except; **Anwesende sind** ~ present company excepted

ausgeprägt ['ausgəprɛːkt] *adj* distinct

ausgerechnet ['ausgərɛçnət] *adv* just, precisely; ~ **du/heute** you of all people/today of all days

ausgeschlossen ['ausgəʃlɔsən] *adj* (*un-*

möglich) impossible, out of the question
ausgeschnitten ['aʊsgəʃnɪtən] *adj*
(*Kleid*) low-necked
ausgesprochen ['aʊsgəʃprɔxən] *adj*
(*Faulheit, Lüge etc*) out-and-out; (*unverkennbar*) marked ♦ *adv* decidedly
ausgezeichnet ['aʊsgətsaɪçnət] *adj*
excellent
ausgiebig ['aʊsgi:bɪç] *adj* (*Gebrauch*)
thorough, good; (*Essen*) generous, lavish; ~ **schlafen** to have a good sleep
Ausgleich ['aʊsglaɪç] (-(e)s, -e) *m*
balance; (*Vermittlung*) reconciliation;
(*SPORT*) equalization; **zum ~ einer Sache** *gen* in order to offset sth; **a~en**
(*unreg*) *vt* to balance (out); to reconcile; (*Höhe*) to even up ♦ *vi* (*SPORT*)
to equalize
ausgraben ['aʊsgra:bən] (*unreg*) *vt* to
dig up; (*Leichen*) to exhume; (*fig*) to
unearth
Ausgrabung *f* excavation; (*Ausgraben
auch*) digging up
Ausguß ['aʊsgʊs] *m* (*Spüle*) sink;
(*Abfluß*) outlet; (*Tülle*) spout
aushalten ['aʊshaltən] (*unreg*) *vt* to
bear, to stand; (*Geliebte*) to keep ♦ *vi*
to hold out; **das ist nicht zum A~** that
is unbearable
aushandeln ['aʊshandəln] *vt* to negotiate
aushändigen ['aʊshɛndɪgən] *vt*: **jdm
etw ~** to hand sth over to sb
Aushang ['aʊshaŋ] *m* notice
aushängen ['aʊshɛŋən] (*unreg*) *vt*
(*Meldung*) to put up; (*Fenster*) to take
off its hinges ♦ *vi* to be displayed ♦ *vr*
to hang out
ausharren ['aʊsharən] *vi* to hold out
ausheben ['aʊshe:bən] (*unreg*) *vt*
(*Erde*) to lift out; (*Grube*) to hollow
out; (*Tür*) to take off its hinges;
(*Diebesnest*) to clear out; (*MIL*) to enlist
aushelfen ['aʊshɛlfən] (*unreg*) *vi*: **jdm
~** to help sb out
Aushilfe ['aʊshɪlfə] *f* help, assistance;
(*Person*) (temporary) worker
Aushilfskraft *f* temporary worker
aushilfsweise *adv* temporarily, as a
stopgap

ausholen ['aʊsho:lən] *vi* to swing one's
arm back; (*zur Ohrfeige*) to raise one's
hand; (*beim Gehen*) to take long
strides; **weit ~** (*fig*) to be expansive
aushorchen ['aʊshɔrçən] *vt* to sound
out, to pump
aushungern ['aʊshʊŋərn] *vt* to starve
out
auskennen ['aʊskɛnən] (*unreg*) *vr* to
know a lot; (*an einem Ort*) to know
one's way about; (*in Fragen etc*) to be
knowledgeable
Ausklang ['aʊsklaŋ] *m* end
auskleiden ['aʊsklaɪdən] *vr* to undress ♦
vt (*Wand*) to line
ausklingen ['aʊsklɪŋən] (*unreg*) *vi* (*Ton,
Lied*) to die away; (*Fest*) to peter out
ausklopfen ['aʊsklɔpfən] *vt* (*Teppich*) to
beat; (*Pfeife*) to knock out
auskochen ['aʊskɔxən] *vt* to boil; (*MED*)
to sterilize; **ausgekocht** (*fig*) out-and-out
Auskommen ['aʊskɔmən] (-s) *nt*: **sein
~ haben** to have a regular income; **a~**
(*unreg*) *vi*: **mit jdm a~** to get on with
sb; **mit etw a~** to get by with sth
auskosten ['aʊskɔstən] *vt* to enjoy to the
full
auskundschaften ['aʊskʊntʃaftən] *vt* to
spy out; (*Gebiet*) to reconnoitre
Auskunft ['aʊskʊnft] (-, -**künfte**) *f* information; (*nähere*) details *pl*,
particulars *pl*; (*Stelle*) information
office; (*TEL*) directory inquiries *sg*
auslachen ['aʊslaxən] *vt* to laugh at, to
mock
ausladen ['aʊsla:dən] (*unreg*) *vt* to unload; (*umg: Gäste*) to cancel an invitation to
Auslage ['aʊsla:gə] *f* shop window (display); **~n** *pl* (*Ausgabe*) expenditure *sg*
Ausland ['aʊslant] *nt* foreign countries
pl; **im ~** abroad; **ins ~** abroad
Ausländer(in) ['aʊslɛndər(ɪn)] (-s, -)
m(f) foreigner
ausländisch *adj* foreign
Auslands- *zW*: **~gespräch** *nt* international call; **~korrespondent(in)** *m(f)*
foreign correspondent; **~reise** *f* trip
abroad
auslassen ['aʊslasən] (*unreg*) *vt* to leave

out; (*Wort etc auch*) to omit; (*Fett*) to melt; (*Kleidungsstück*) to let out ♦ *vr:* **sich über etw** *akk* ~ to speak one's mind about sth; **seine Wut** *etc* **an jdm** ~ to vent one's rage *etc* on sb

Auslassung *f* omission

Auslauf ['auslauf] *m* (*für Tiere*) run; (*Ausfluß*) outflow, outlet; **a~en** (*unreg*) *vi* to run out; (*Behälter*) to leak; (*NAUT*) to put out (to sea); (*langsam aufhören*) to run down

Ausläufer ['auslɔyfər] *m* (*von Gebirge*) spur; (*Pflanze*) runner; (*MET: von Hoch*) ridge; (: *von Tief*) trough

ausleeren ['ausle:rən] *vt* to empty

auslegen ['ausle:gən] *vt* (*Waren*) to lay out; (*Köder*) to put down; (*Geld*) to lend; (*bedecken*) to cover; (*Text etc*) to interpret

Auslegung *f* interpretation

Ausleihe ['auslaiə] *f* issuing; (*Stelle*) issue desk; **a~n** (*unreg*) *vt* (*verleihen*) to lend; **sich** *dat* **etw a~n** to borrow sth

Auslese ['ausle:zə] *f* selection; (*Elite*) elite; (*Wein*) choice wine; **a~n** (*unreg*) *vt* to select; (*umg: zu Ende lesen*) to finish

ausliefern ['ausli:fərn] *vt* to deliver (up), to hand over; (*COMM*) to deliver; **jdm/etw ausgeliefert sein** to be at the mercy of sb/sth

auslöschen ['auslœʃən] *vt* to extinguish; (*fig*) to wipe out, to obliterate

auslosen ['auslo:zən] *vt* to draw lots for

auslösen ['auslø:zən] *vt* (*Explosion, Schuß*) to set off; (*hervorrufen*) to cause, to produce; (*Gefangene*) to ransom; (*Pfand*) to redeem

Auslöser (**-s, -**) *m* (*PHOT*) release

ausmachen ['ausmaxən] *vt* (*Licht, Radio*) to turn off; (*Feuer*) to put out; (*entdecken*) to make out; (*vereinbaren*) to agree; (*beilegen*) to settle; (*Anteil darstellen, betragen*) to represent; (*bedeuten*) to matter; **macht es Ihnen etwas aus, wenn ...?** would you mind if ...?

ausmalen ['ausma:lən] *vt* to paint; (*fig*) to describe; **sich** *dat* **etw** ~ to imagine sth

Ausmaß ['ausma:s] *nt* dimension; (*fig auch*) scale

ausmerzen ['ausmɛrtsən] *vt* to eliminate

ausmessen ['ausmɛsən] (*unreg*) *vt* to measure

Ausnahme ['ausna:mə] *f* exception; **~fall** *m* exceptional case; **~zustand** *m* state of emergency

ausnahmslos *adv* without exception

ausnahmsweise *adv* by way of exception, for once

ausnehmen ['ausne:mən] (*unreg*) *vt* to take out, to remove; (*Tier*) to gut; (*Nest*) to rob; (*umg: Geld abnehmen*) to clean out; (*ausschließen*) to make an exception of ♦ *vr* to look, to appear; **~d** *adj* exceptional

ausnützen ['ausnytsən] *vt* (*Zeit, Gelegenheit*) to use, to turn to good account; (*Einfluß*) to use; (*Mensch, Gutmütigkeit*) to exploit

auspacken ['auspakən] *vt* to unpack

auspfeifen ['auspfaifən] (*unreg*) *vt* to hiss/boo at

ausplaudern ['ausplaudərn] *vt* (*Geheimnis*) to blab

ausprobieren ['ausprobi:rən] *vt* to try (out)

Auspuff ['auspuf] (**-(e)s, -e**) *m* (*TECH*) exhaust; **~rohr** *nt* exhaust (pipe); **~topf** *m* (*AUT*) silencer

ausradieren ['ausradi:rən] *vt* to erase, to rub out; (*fig*) to annihilate

ausrangieren ['ausrãʒi:rən] (*umg*) *vt* to chuck out

ausrauben ['ausraubən] *vt* to rob

ausräumen ['ausrɔymən] *vt* (*Dinge*) to clear away; (*Schrank, Zimmer*) to empty; (*Bedenken*) to dispel

ausrechnen ['ausrɛçnən] *vt* to calculate, to reckon

Ausrede ['ausre:də] *f* excuse; **a~n** *vi* to have one's say ♦ *vt:* **jdm etw a~n** to talk sb out of sth

ausreichen ['ausraiçən] *vi* to suffice, to be enough; **~d** *adj* sufficient, adequate; (*SCH*) adequate

Ausreise ['ausraizə] *f* departure; **bei der** ~ when leaving the country; **~erlaubnis** *f* exit visa; **a~n** *vi* to leave

the country
ausreißen ['aʊsraɪsn̩] (*unreg*) *vt* to tear *od* pull out ♦ *vi* (*Riß bekommen*) to tear; (*umg*) to make off, to scram
ausrenken ['aʊsrɛŋkən] *vt* to dislocate
ausrichten ['aʊsrɪçtən] *vt* (*Botschaft*) to deliver; (*Gruß*) to pass on; (*Hochzeit etc*) to arrange; (*in gerade Linie bringen*) to get in a straight line; (*angleichen*) to bring into line; (*TYP*) to justify; **ich werde es ihm ~** I'll tell him; **etwas/nichts bei jdm ~** to get somewhere/nowhere with sb
ausrotten ['aʊsrɔtən] *vt* to stamp out, to exterminate
ausrücken ['aʊsrʏkən] *vi* (*MIL*) to move off; (*Feuerwehr, Polizei*) to be called out; (*umg: weglaufen*) to run away
Ausruf ['aʊsruːf] *m* (*Schrei*) cry, exclamation; (*Bekanntmachung*) proclamation; **a~en** (*unreg*) *vt* to cry out, to exclaim; to call out; **~ezeichen** *nt* exclamation mark
ausruhen ['aʊsruːən] *vt, vr* to rest
ausrüsten ['aʊsrʏstən] *vt* to equip, to fit out
Ausrüstung *f* equipment
ausrutschen ['aʊsrʊtʃən] *vi* to slip
Aussage ['aʊszaːgə] *f* (*JUR*) statement; **a~n** *vt* to say, to state ♦ *vi* (*JUR*) to give evidence
ausschalten ['aʊsʃaltən] *vt* to switch off; (*fig*) to eliminate
Ausschank ['aʊsʃaŋk] (-(e)s, -schänke) *m* dispensing, giving out; (*COMM*) selling; (*Theke*) bar
Ausschau ['aʊsʃaʊ] *f*: **~ halten (nach)** to look out (for), to watch (for); **a~en** *vi*: **a~en (nach)** to look out (for), to be on the look-out (for)
ausscheiden ['aʊsʃaɪdən] (*unreg*) *vt* to take out; (*MED*) to secrete ♦ *vi*: **~ (aus)** to leave; (*SPORT*) to be eliminated (from) *od* knocked out (of)
Ausscheidung *f* separation; secretion; elimination; (*aus Amt*) retirement
ausschimpfen ['aʊsʃɪmpfən] *vt* to scold, to tell off
ausschlafen ['aʊsʃlaːfən] (*unreg*) *vi, vr* to have a good sleep ♦ *vt* to sleep off;

ich bin nicht ausgeschlafen I didn't have *od* get enough sleep
Ausschlag ['aʊsʃlaːk] *m* (*MED*) rash; (*Pendel~*) swing; (*Nadel~*) deflection; **den ~ geben** (*fig*) to tip the balance; **a~en** [-gən] (*unreg*) *vt* to knock out; (*auskleiden*) to deck out; (*verweigern*) to decline ♦ *vi* (*Pferd*) to kick out; (*BOT*) to sprout; **a~gebend** *adj* decisive
ausschließen ['aʊsʃliːsən] (*unreg*) *vt* to shut *od* lock out; (*fig*) to exclude
ausschließlich *adj* exclusive ♦ *adv* exclusively ♦ *präp* +*gen* exclusive of, excluding
Ausschluß ['aʊsʃlʊs] *m* exclusion
ausschmücken ['aʊsʃmʏkən] *vt* to decorate; (*fig*) to embellish
ausschneiden ['aʊsʃnaɪdən] (*unreg*) *vt* to cut out; (*Büsche*) to trim
Ausschnitt ['aʊsʃnɪt] *m* (*Teil*) section; (*von Kleid*) neckline; (*Zeitungs~*) cutting; (*aus Film etc*) excerpt
ausschreiben ['aʊsʃraɪbən] (*unreg*) *vt* (*ganz schreiben*) to write out (in full); (*ausstellen*) to write (out); (*Stelle, Wettbewerb etc*) to announce, to advertise
Ausschreitung ['aʊsʃraɪtʊŋ] *f* (*usu pl*) riot
Ausschuß ['aʊsʃʊs] *m* committee, board; (*Abfall*) waste, scraps *pl*; (*COMM: auch: ~ware f*) reject
ausschütten ['aʊsʃʏtən] *vt* to pour out; (*Eimer*) to empty; (*Geld*) to pay ♦ *vr* to shake (with laughter)
ausschweifend ['aʊsʃvaɪfənt] *adj* (*Leben*) dissipated, debauched; (*Phantasie*) extravagant
Ausschweifung *f* excess
aussehen ['aʊszeːən] (*unreg*) *vi* to look; **es sieht nach Regen aus** it looks like rain; **es sieht schlecht aus** things look bad; **A~** (-s) *nt* appearance
außen ['aʊsən] *adv* outside; (*nach ~*) outwards; **~ ist es rot** it's red (on the) outside
Außen- *zW*: **~bordmotor** *m* outboard motor; **~dienst** *m*: **im ~dienst sein** to work outside the office; **~handel** *m* foreign trade; **~minister** *m* foreign

minister; ~**ministerium** *nt* foreign office; ~**politik** *f* foreign policy; ~**seite** *f* outside; ~**seiter** (-s, -) *m* outsider; ~**welt** *f* outside world

außer ['ausər] *präp +dat* (*räumlich*) out of; (*abgesehen von*) except ♦ *konj* (*ausgenommen*) except; ~ **Gefahr** out of danger; ~ **Zweifel** beyond any doubt; ~ **Betrieb** out of order; ~ **Dienst** retired; ~ **Landes** abroad; ~ **sich** *dat* **sein** to be beside o.s.; ~ **sich** *akk* **geraten** to go wild; ~ **wenn** unless; ~ **daß** except; ~**dem** *konj* besides, in addition

äußere(r, s) ['ɔʏsərə(r, s)] *adj* outer, external

außer- *zW*: ~**ehelich** *adj* extramarital; ~**gewöhnlich** *adj* unusual; ~**halb** *präp +gen* outside ♦ *adv* outside

äußerlich *adj* external

äußern *vt* to utter, to express; (*zeigen*) to show ♦ *vr* to give one's opinion; (*Krankheit etc*) to show itself

außer- *zW*: ~**ordentlich** *adj* extraordinary; ~**planmäßig** *adj* unscheduled; ~'**stande** *adv* not in a position, unable

äußerst ['ɔʏsərst] *adv* extremely, most; ~**e(r, s)** *adj* utmost; (*räumlich*) farthest; (*Termin*) last possible; (*Preis*) highest

aussetzen ['auszɛtsən] *vt* (*Kind, Tier*) to abandon; (*Boote*) to lower; (*Belohnung*) to offer; (*Urteil, Verfahren*) to postpone ♦ *vi* (*aufhören*) to stop; (*Pause machen*) to have a break; **jdm/etw ausgesetzt sein** to be exposed to sb/sth; **an jdm/etw etwas ~** to find fault with sb/sth

Aussicht ['auszɪçt] *f* view; (*in Zukunft*) prospect; **etw in ~ haben** to have sth in view

Aussichts- *zW*: **a~los** *adj* hopeless; ~**punkt** *m* viewpoint; **a~reich** *adj* promising; ~**turm** *m* observation tower

aussöhnen ['auszø:nən] *vt* to reconcile ♦ *vr* to reconcile o.s., to become reconciled

Aussöhnung *f* reconciliation

aussondern ['auszɔndərn] *vt* to separate, to select

aussortieren ['auszɔrti:rən] *vt* to sort out

ausspannen ['ausʃpanən] *vt* to spread od stretch out; (*Pferd*) to unharness; (*umg: Mädchen*): **(jdm) jdn ~** to steal sb (from sb) ♦ *vi* to relax

aussperren ['ausʃpɛrən] *vt* to lock out

Aussperrung *f* lock-out

ausspielen ['ausʃpi:lən] *vt* (*Karte*) to lead; (*Geldprämie*) to offer as a prize ♦ *vi* (*KARTEN*) to lead; **jdn gegen jdn ~** to play sb off against sb; **ausgespielt haben** to be finished

Aussprache ['ausʃpra:xə] *f* pronunciation; (*Unterredung*) (frank) discussion

aussprechen ['ausʃprɛçən] (*unreg*) *vt* to pronounce; (*äußern*) to say, to express ♦ *vr* (*sich äußern*): **sich ~ (über +akk)** to speak (about); (*sich anvertrauen*) to unburden o.s. (about od on); (*diskutieren*) to discuss ♦ *vi* (*zu Ende sprechen*) to finish speaking

Ausspruch ['ausʃprux] *m* saying, remark

ausspülen ['ausʃpy:lən] *vt* to wash out; (*Mund*) to rinse

Ausstand ['ausʃtant] *m* strike; **in den ~ treten** to go on strike

ausstatten ['ausʃtatən] *vt* (*Zimmer etc*) to furnish; (*Person*) to equip, to kit out

Ausstattung *f* (*Ausstatten*) provision; (*Kleidung*) outfit; (*Aussteuer*) dowry; (*Aufmachung*) make-up; (*Einrichtung*) furnishing

ausstechen ['ausʃtɛçən] (*unreg*) *vt* (*Augen, Rasen, Graben*) to dig out; (*Kekse*) to cut out; (*übertreffen*) to outshine

ausstehen ['ausʃte:ən] (*unreg*) *vt* to stand, to endure ♦ *vi* (*noch nicht dasein*) to be outstanding

aussteigen ['ausʃtaigən] (*unreg*) *vi* to get out, to alight

ausstellen ['ausʃtɛlən] *vt* to exhibit, to display; (*umg: ausschalten*) to switch off; (*Rechnung etc*) to make out; (*Paß, Zeugnis*) to issue

Ausstellung *f* exhibition; (*FIN*) drawing up; (*einer Rechnung*) making out; (*eines Passes etc*) issuing

aussterben ['aʊsʃtɛrbən] (*unreg*) *vi* to die out

Aussteuer ['aʊsʃtɔʏər] *f* dowry

Ausstieg ['aʊsʃtiːk] (-(e)s, -e) *m* exit

ausstopfen ['aʊsʃtɔpfən] *vt* to stuff

ausstoßen ['aʊsʃtoːsən] (*unreg*) *vt* (*Luft, Rauch*) to give off, to emit; (*aus Verein etc*) to expel, to exclude; (*Auge*) to poke out

ausstrahlen ['aʊsʃtraːlən] *vt*, *vi* to radiate; (*RADIO*) to broadcast

Ausstrahlung *f* radiation; (*fig*) charisma

ausstrecken ['aʊsʃtrɛkən] *vt*, *vr* to stretch out

ausstreichen ['aʊsʃtraɪçən] (*unreg*) *vt* to cross out; (*glätten*) to smooth (out)

ausströmen ['aʊsʃtrøːmən] *vi* (*Gas*) to pour out, to escape ♦ *vt* to give off; (*fig*) to radiate

aussuchen ['aʊszuːxən] *vt* to select, to pick out

Austausch ['aʊstaʊʃ] *m* exchange; **a~bar** *adj* exchangeable; **a~en** *vt* to exchange, to swap; **~motor** *m* reconditioned engine

austeilen ['aʊstaɪlən] *vt* to distribute, to give out

Auster ['aʊstər] (-, -n) *f* oyster

austoben ['aʊstoːbən] *vr* (*Kind*) to run wild; (*Erwachsene*) to sow one's wild oats

austragen ['aʊstraːgən] (*unreg*) *vt* (*Post*) to deliver; (*Streit etc*) to decide; (*Wettkämpfe*) to hold

Australien [aʊsˈtraːliən] (-s) *nt* Australia

Australier(in) (-s, -) *m(f)* Australian

australisch *adj* Australian

austreiben ['aʊstraɪbən] (*unreg*) *vt* to drive out, to expel; (*Geister*) to exorcize

austreten ['aʊstreːtən] (*unreg*) *vi* (*zur Toilette*) to be excused ♦ *vt* (*Feuer*) to tread out, to trample; (*Schuhe*) to wear out; (*Treppe*) to wear down; **aus etw ~** to leave sth

austrinken ['aʊstrɪŋkən] (*unreg*) *vt* (*Glas*) to drain; (*Getränk*) to drink up ♦ *vi* to finish one's drink, to drink up

Austritt ['aʊstrɪt] *m* emission; (*aus Ver-*) *ein, Partei etc*) retirement, withdrawal

austrocknen ['aʊstrɔknən] *vt*, *vi* to dry up

ausüben ['aʊsʔyːbən] *vt* (*Beruf*) to practise, to carry out; (*Funktion*) to perform; (*Einfluß*) to exert; **einen Reiz auf jdn ~** to hold an attraction for sb; **eine Wirkung auf jdn ~** to have an effect on sb

Ausverkauf ['aʊsfɛrkaʊf] *m* sale; **a~en** *vt* to sell out; (*Geschäft*) to sell up; **a~t** *adj* (*Karten, Artikel*) sold out; (*THEAT: Haus*) full

Auswahl ['aʊsvaːl] *f*: **eine ~ (an +***dat*) a selection (of), a choice (of)

auswählen ['aʊsvɛːlən] *vt* to select, to choose

Auswander- ['aʊsvandər] *zW*: **~er** *m* emigrant; **a~n** *vi* to emigrate; **~ung** *f* emigration

auswärtig ['aʊsvɛrtɪç] *adj* (*nicht am/vom Ort*) out-of-town; (*ausländisch*) foreign

auswärts ['aʊsvɛrts] *adv* outside; (*nach außen*) outwards; **~ essen** to eat out; **A~spiel** *nt* away game

auswechseln ['aʊsvɛksəln] *vt* to change, to substitute

Ausweg ['aʊsveːk] *m* way out; **a~los** *adj* hopeless

ausweichen ['aʊsvaɪçən] (*unreg*) *vi*: **jdm/etw ~** to move aside *od* make way for sb/sth; (*fig*) to side-step sb/sth; **~d** *adj* evasive

ausweinen ['aʊsvaɪnən] *vr* to have a (good) cry

Ausweis ['aʊsvaɪs] (-es, -e) *m* identity card; passport; (*Mitglieds~, Bibliotheks~ etc*) card; **a~en** (*unreg*) *vt* to expel, to banish ♦ *vr* to prove one's identity; **~papiere** *pl* identity papers; **~ung** *f* expulsion

ausweiten ['aʊsvaɪtən] *vt* to stretch

auswendig ['aʊsvɛndɪç] *adv* by heart; **~ lernen** to learn by heart

auswerten ['aʊsvɛrtən] *vt* to evaluate

Auswertung *f* evaluation, analysis; (*Nutzung*) utilization

auswirken ['aʊsvɪrkən] *vr* to have an effect

Auswirkung f effect
auswischen ['ausvɪʃən] vt to wipe out;
jdm eins ~ (umg) to put one over on sb
Auswuchs ['ausvuːks] m (out)growth;
(fig) product
auswuchten ['ausvuxtən] vt (AUT) to
balance
auszahlen ['austsaːlən] vt (Lohn,
Summe) to pay out; (Arbeiter) to pay
off; (Miterbe) to buy out ♦ vr (sich
lohnen) to pay
auszählen ['austsɛːlən] vt (Stimmen) to
count; (BOXEN) to count out
auszeichnen ['austsaɪçnən] vt to honour;
(MIL) to decorate; (COMM) to price ♦ vr
to distinguish o.s.
Auszeichnung f distinction; (COMM)
pricing; (Ehrung) awarding of decoration; (Ehre) honour; (Orden) decoration; mit ~ with distinction
ausziehen ['austsiːən] (unreg) vt
(Kleidung) to take off; (Haare, Zähne,
Tisch etc) to pull out; (nachmalen) to
trace ♦ vr to undress ♦ vi (aufbrechen)
to leave; (aus Wohnung) to move out
Auszug ['austsuːk] m (aus Wohnung) removal; (aus Buch etc) extract;
(Konto~) statement; (Ausmarsch)
departure
Auto ['auto] (-s, -s) nt (motor-)car; ~
fahren to drive; ~**bahn** f motorway;
~**bahndreieck** nt motorway junction;
~**bahnkreuz** nt motorway intersection;
~**fähre** f car ferry; ~**fahrer(in)** m(f)
motorist, driver; ~**fahrt** f drive; a~**gen**
[-'geːn] adj autogenous; ~'**gramm** nt
autograph; ~'**mat** (-en, -en) m
machine; a~'**matisch** adj automatic;
a~**nom** [-'noːm] adj autonomous
Autor(in) ['autor, au'toːrɪn, pl -'toːrən]
(-s, -en) m(f) author
Auto- zW: ~**radio** nt car radio; ~**reifen**
m car tyre; ~**rennen** nt motor racing
autoritär [autori'tɛːr] adj authoritarian
Autorität f authority
Auto- zW: ~**stopp** m: per ~**stopp**
fahren to hitch-hike; ~**unfall** m car od
motor accident; ~**verleih** m car hire
(BRIT) od rental (US); ~**wäsche** f car
wash

Axt [akst] (-, ⁼e) f axe

B

Baby ['beːbi] (-s, -s) nt baby; ~**ausstat-**
tung f layette; ~**sitter** ['beːbizɪtər] (-s, -)
m baby-sitter
Bach [bax] (-(e)s, ⁼e) m stream, brook
Backbord (-(e)s, -e) nt (NAUT) port
Backe ['bakə] f cheek
backen (unreg) vt, vi to bake
Backenbart m sideboards pl
Backenzahn m molar
Bäcker ['bɛkər] (-s, -) m baker; ~**ei** f
bakery; (~**laden**) baker's (shop)
Back- zW: ~**obst** nt dried fruit; ~**ofen**
m oven; ~**pflaume** f prune; ~**pulver** nt
baking powder; ~**stein** m brick
Bad [baːt] (-(e)s, ⁼er) nt bath; (Schwimmen) bathe; (Ort) spa
Bade- ['baːdə] zW: ~**anstalt** f (swimming) baths pl; ~**anzug** m bathing
suit; ~**hose** f bathing od swimming
trunks pl; ~**kappe** f bathing cap;
~**mantel** m bath(ing) robe; ~**meister**
m baths attendant; ~**mütze** f bathing
cap; b~**n** vi to bathe, to have a bath ♦
vt to bath; ~**ort** m spa; ~**tuch** nt bath
towel; ~**wanne** f bath (tub); ~**zimmer**
nt bathroom
Bagatelle [baga'tɛlə] f trifle
Bagger ['bagər] (-s, -) m excavator;
(NAUT) dredger; b~**n** vt, vi to
excavate; to dredge
Bahn [baːn] (-, -en) f railway, railroad
(US); (Weg) road, way; (Spur) lane;
(Renn~) track; (ASTRON) orbit;
(Stoff~) length; b~**brechend** adj
pioneering; ~**damm** m railway
embankment; b~**en** vt: sich/jdm einen
Weg b~**en** to clear a way/a way for sb;
~**fahrt** f railway journey; ~**hof** m
station; auf dem ~**hof** at the station;
~**hofsvorsteher** m station-master;
~**linie** f (railway) line; ~**steig** m platform; ~**steigkarte** f platform ticket;
~**strecke** f (railway) line; ~**übergang**
m level crossing, grade crossing (US);
~**wärter** m signalman

Bahre ['ba:rə] f stretcher
Bajonett [bajo'nɛt] (-(e)s, -e) nt bayonet
Bakterien [bak'te:riən] pl bacteria pl
Balance [ba'lɑ̃:sə] f balance, equilibrium
balan'cieren vt, vi to balance
bald [balt] adv (zeitlich) soon; (beinahe) almost; ~**ig** ['baldɪç] adj early, speedy; ~**möglichst** adv as soon as possible
Baldrian ['baldria:n] (-s, -e) m valerian
Balkan ['balka:n] (-s) m: **der** ~ the Balkans pl
Balken ['balkən] (-s, -) m beam; (Trag~) girder; (Stütz~) prop
Balkon [bal'kõ:] (-s, -s od -e) m balcony; (THEAT) (dress) circle
Ball [bal] (-(e)s, ⁻e) m ball; (Tanz) dance, ball
Ballade [ba'la:də] f ballad
Ballast ['balast] (-(e)s, -e) m ballast; (fig) weight, burden
Ballen ['balən] (-s, -) m bale; (ANAT) ball; **b~** vt (formen) to make into a ball; (Faust) to clench ♦ vr (Wolken etc) to build up; (Menschen) to gather
Ballett [ba'lɛt] (-(e)s, -e) nt ballet
Ballkleid nt evening dress
Ballon [ba'lõ:] (-s, -s od -e) m balloon
Ballspiel nt ball game
Bambus ['bambʊs] (-ses, -se) m bamboo; ~**rohr** nt bamboo cane
banal [ba'na:l] adj banal
Banane [ba'na:nə] f banana
Band¹ [bant] (-(e)s, ⁻e) m (Buch~) volume
Band² (-(e)s, ⁻er) nt (Stoff~) ribbon, tape; (Fließ~) production line; (Faß~) hoop; (Ton~) tape; (ANAT) ligament; **etw auf** ~ **aufnehmen** to tape sth; **am laufenden** ~ (umg) non-stop
Band³ (-(e)s, -e) nt (Freundschafts~ etc) bond
Band⁴ [bɛnt] (-, -s) f band, group
band etc vb siehe **binden** ·
Bandage [ban'da:ʒə] f bandage
banda'gieren vt to bandage
Bande ['bandə] f band; (Straßen~) gang
bändigen ['bɛndɪgən] vt (Tier) to tame; (Trieb, Leidenschaft) to control, to restrain
Bandit [ban'di:t] (-en, -en) m bandit

Band- zW: ~**maß** nt tape measure; ~**scheibe** f (ANAT) disc; ~**wurm** m tapeworm
bange ['baŋə] adj scared; (besorgt) anxious; **jdm wird es** ~ sb is becoming scared; **jdm** ~ **machen** to scare sb; ~**n** vi: **um jdn/etw** ~**n** to be anxious od worried about sb/sth
Banjo ['banjo, 'bɛndʒo] (-s, -s) nt banjo
Bank¹ [baŋk] (-, ⁻e) f (Sitz~) bench; (Sand~ etc) (sand)bank, (sand)bar
Bank² (-, -en) f (Geld~) bank
Bankanweisung f banker's order
Bankbeamte(r) m bank clerk
Bankett [baŋ'kɛt] (-(e)s, -e) nt (Essen) banquet; (Straßenrand) verge (BRIT), shoulder (US); ~**e** f verge (BRIT), shoulder (US)
Bankier [baŋki'e:] (-s, -s) m banker
Bank- zW: ~**konto** nt bank account; ~**note** f banknote; ~**raub** m bank robbery
Bankrott [baŋ'krɔt] (-(e)s, -e) m bankruptcy; ~ **machen** to go bankrupt; **b~** adj bankrupt
Bann [ban] (-(e)s, -e) m (HIST) ban; (Kirchen~) excommunication; (fig: Zauber) spell; **b~en** vt (Geister) to exorcise; (Gefahr) to avert; (bezaubern) to enchant; (HIST) to banish
Banner (-s, -) nt banner, flag
Bar (-, -s) f bar
bar [ba:r] adj (+gen) (unbedeckt) bare; (frei von) lacking (in); (offenkundig) utter, sheer; ~**e(s) Geld** cash; **etw (in)** ~ **bezahlen** to pay sth (in) cash; **etw für ~e Münze nehmen** (fig) to take sth at its face value
Bär [bɛ:r] (-en, -en) m bear
Baracke [ba'rakə] f hut
barbarisch [bar'ba:rɪʃ] adj barbaric, barbarous
Bar- zW: **b~fuß** adj barefoot; ~**geld** nt cash, ready money; **b~geldlos** adj non-cash
Barhocker m bar stool
Barkauf m cash purchase
Barkeeper ['ba:rki:pər] (-s, -) m barman, bartender

barmherzig [barm'hɛrtsɪç] *adj* merciful, compassionate; **B~keit** *f* mercy, compassion

Barometer [baro'meːtər] (**-s**, **-**) *nt* barometer

Baron [ba'roːn] (**-s**, **-e**) *m* baron; **~esse** [baro'nɛsə] *f* daughter of a baron; **~in** *f* baroness

Barren ['barən] (**-s**, **-**) *m* parallel bars *pl*; (*Gold~*) ingot

Barriere [bari'ɛːrə] *f* barrier

Barrikade [bari'kaːdə] *f* barricade

Barsch [barʃ] (**-(e)s**, **-e**) *m* perch

barsch *adj* brusque, gruff

Barschaft *f* ready money

Barscheck *m* open *od* uncrossed cheque (*BRIT*), open check (*US*)

Bart [baːrt] (**-(e)s**, **ːe**) *m* beard; (*Schlüssel~*) bit

bärtig ['bɛːrtɪç] *adj* bearded

Barzahlung *f* cash payment

Base ['baːzə] *f* (*CHEM*) base; (*Kusine*) cousin

Basel ['baːzəl] *nt* Basle

Basen *pl von* **Base**; **Basis**

BASIC ['beːsik] *nt* (*COMPUT*) BASIC

basieren [ba'ziːrən] *vt* to base ♦ *vi* to be based

Basis ['baːzɪs] (**-**, **Basen**) *f* basis

Baß [bas] (**Basses**, **Bässe**) *m* bass

Bassin [ba'sɛ̃ː] (**-s**, **-s**) *nt* pool

Bassist [ba'sɪst] *m* bass

Baßstimme *f* bass voice

Bast [bast] (**-(e)s**, **-e**) *m* raffia

basteln *vt* to make ♦ *vi* to do handicrafts

bat *etc* [baːt] *vb siehe* **bitten**

Bataillon [batal'joːn] (**-s**, **-e**) *nt* battalion

Batist [ba'tɪst] (**-(e)s**, **-e**) *m* batiste

Batterie [batə'riː] *f* battery

Bau [baʊ] (**-(e)s**) *m* (*Bauen*) building, construction; (*Aufbau*) structure; (*Körper~*) frame; (*~stelle*) building site; (*pl Baue: Tier~*) hole, burrow; (: *MIN*) working(s); (*pl Bauten: Gebäude*) building; **sich im ~ befinden** to be under construction; **~arbeiter** *m* building worker

Bauch [baʊx] (**-(e)s**, **Bäuche**) *m* belly; (*ANAT auch*) stomach, abdomen; **~fell**

nt peritoneum; **b~ig** *adj* bulbous; **~redner** *m* ventriloquist; **~schmerzen** *pl* stomach-ache; **~tanz** *m* belly dance; belly dancing; **~weh** *nt* stomach-ache

bauen ['baʊən] *vt*, *vi* to build; (*TECH*) to construct; **auf jdn/etw ~** to depend *od* count upon sb/sth

Bauer¹ ['baʊər] (**-n** *od* **-s**, **-n**) *m* farmer; (*Schach*) pawn

Bauer² (**-s**, **-**) *nt od m* (bird-)cage

Bäuerin ['bɔʏərɪn] *f* farmer; (*Frau des Bauers*) farmer's wife

bäuerlich *adj* rustic

Bauern- *zW:* **~fänge'rei** *f* deception; **~haus** *nt* farmhouse; **~hof** *m* farm(yard)

Bau- *zW:* **b~fällig** *adj* dilapidated; **~fälligkeit** *f* dilapidation; **~gelände** *f* building site; **~genehmigung** *f* building permit; **~herr** *m* purchaser; **~kasten** *m* box of bricks; **~kosten** *pl* construction costs; **~land** *nt* building land; **b~lich** *adj* structural

Baum [baʊm] (**-(e)s**, **Bäume**) *m* tree

baumeln ['baʊməln] *vi* to dangle

bäumen ['bɔʏmən] *vr* to rear (up)

Baum- *zW:* **~schule** *f* nursery; **~stamm** *m* tree trunk; **~stumpf** *m* tree stump; **~wolle** *f* cotton

Bau- *zW:* **~plan** *m* architect's plan; **~platz** *m* building site; **~sparkasse** *f* building society; **~stein** *m* building stone, freestone; **~stelle** *f* building site; **~teil** *nt* prefabricated part (of building); **~ten** *pl von* **Bau**; **~unternehmer** *m* contractor, builder; **~weise** *f* (method of) construction; **~werk** *nt* building; **~zaun** *m* hoarding

Bayer(in) ['baɪər(ɪn)] *m(f)* Bavarian

Bayern ['baɪərn] *nt* Bavaria

bayrisch ['baɪrɪʃ] *adj* Bavarian

Bazillus [ba'tsɪlʊs] (**-**, **Bazillen**) *m* bacillus

beabsichtigen [bə''apzɪçtɪgən] *vt* to intend

beachten [bə''axtən] *vt* to take note of; (*Vorschrift*) to obey; (*Vorfahrt*) to observe

beachtlich *adj* considerable

Beachtung *f* notice, attention, observa-

tion
Beamte(r) [bə'amtə(r)] (-n, -n) *m* official; (*Staats~*) civil servant; (*Bank~ etc*) employee
Beamtin *f siehe* Beamte(r)
beängstigend [bə'ɛŋstɪgənt] *adj* alarming
beanspruchen [bə'anʃpruxən] *vt* to claim; (*Zeit, Platz*) to take up, to occupy; **jdn ~** to take up sb's time
beanstanden [bə'anʃtandən] *vt* to complain about, to object to
Beanstandung *f* complaint
beantragen [bə'antra:gən] *vt* to apply for, to ask for
beantworten [bə'antvɔrtən] *vt* to answer
Beantwortung *f* (+*gen*) reply (to)
bearbeiten [bə'arbaɪtən] *vt* to work; (*Material*) to process; (*Thema*) to deal with; (*Land*) to cultivate; (*CHEM*) to treat; (*Buch*) to revise; (*umg: beeinflussen wollen*) to work on
Bearbeitung *f* processing; cultivation; treatment; revision
Beatmung [bə'a:tmʊŋ] *f* respiration
beaufsichtigen [bə'aʊfzɪçtɪgən] *vt* to supervise
Beaufsichtigung *f* supervision
beauftragen [bə'aʊftra:gən] *vt* to instruct; **jdn mit etw ~** to entrust sb with sth
bebauen [bə'baʊən] *vt* to build on; (*AGR*) to cultivate
beben ['be:bən] *vi* to tremble, to shake; **B~** (-s, -) *nt* earthquake
Becher ['bɛçər] (-s, -) *m* mug; (*ohne Henkel*) tumbler
Becken ['bɛkən] (-s, -) *nt* basin; (*MUS*) cymbal; (*ANAT*) pelvis
bedacht [bə'daxt] *adj* thoughtful, careful; **auf etw** *akk* **~ sein** to be concerned about sth
bedächtig [bə'dɛçtɪç] *adj* (*umsichtig*) thoughtful, reflective; (*langsam*) slow, deliberate
bedanken [bə'daŋkən] *vr*: **sich (bei jdm) ~** to say thank you (to sb)
Bedarf [bə'darf] (-(e)s) *m* need, requirement; (*COMM*) demand; **je nach ~**

according to demand; **bei ~** if necessary; **~ an etw** *dat* **haben** to be in need of sth
Bedarfs- *zW*: **~artikel** *m* requisite; **~fall** *m* case of need; **~haltestelle** *f* request stop
bedauerlich [bə'daʊərlɪç] *adj* regrettable
bedauern [bə'daʊərn] *vt* to be sorry for; (*bemitleiden*) to pity; **B~** (-s) *nt* regret; **bedauernswert** *adj* (*Zustände*) regrettable; (*Mensch*) pitiable, unfortunate
bedecken [bə'dɛkən] *vt* to cover
bedeckt *adj* covered; (*Himmel*) overcast
bedenken [bə'dɛŋkən] (*unreg*) *vt* to think over, to consider; **B~** (-s, -) *nt* (*Überlegen*) consideration; (*Zweifel*) doubt; (*Skrupel*) scruple
bedenklich *adj* doubtful; (*bedrohlich*) dangerous, risky
bedeuten [bə'dɔytən] *vt* to mean; to signify; (*wichtig sein*) to be of importance; **~d** *adj* important; (*beträchtlich*) considerable
Bedeutung *f* meaning; significance; (*Wichtigkeit*) importance; **bedeutungslos** *adj* insignificant, unimportant; **bedeutungsvoll** *adj* momentous, significant
bedienen [bə'di:nən] *vt* to serve; (*Maschine*) to work, to operate ♦ *vr* (*beim Essen*) to help o.s.; **sich jds/einer Sache ~** to make use of sb/sth
Bedienung *f* service; (*Kellnerin*) waitress; (*Verkäuferin*) shop assistant; (*Zuschlag*) service (charge)
Bedingung *f* condition; (*Voraussetzung*) stipulation; **bedingungslos** *adj* unconditional
bedrängen [bə'drɛŋən] *vt* to pester, to harass
bedrohen [bə'dro:ən] *vt* to threaten
bedrohlich *adj* ominous, threatening
Bedrohung *f* threat, menace
bedrücken [bədrykən] *vt* to oppress, to trouble
bedürf- [bə'dyrf] *zW*: **~en** (*unreg*) *vi* +*gen* to need, to require; **B~nis** (-ses, -se) *nt* need; **B~nisanstalt** *f* public con-

venience, comfort station (US); ~**tig** adj in need, poor, needy

beeilen [bə''aɪlən] vr to hurry

beeindrucken [bə''aɪndrʊkən] vt to impress, to make an impression on

beeinflussen [bə''aɪnflʊsən] vt to influence

beeinträchtigen [bə''aɪntrɛçtɪgən] vt to affect adversely; (Freiheit) to infringe upon

beend(ig)en [bə''ɛnd(ɪg)ən] vt to end, to finish, to terminate

beengen [bə''ɛŋən] vt to cramp; (fig) to hamper, to oppress

beerben [bə''ɛrbən] vt: **jdn** ~ to inherit from sb

beerdigen [bə''e:rdɪgən] vt to bury

Beerdigung f funeral, burial; **Beerdigungsunternehmer** m undertaker

Beere ['be:rə] f berry; (Trauben~) grape

Beet [be:t] (-(e)s, -e) nt bed

befähigen [bə'fɛ:ɪgən] vt to enable

befähigt adj (begabt) talented; ~ (für) (fähig) capable (of)

Befähigung f capability; (Begabung) talent, aptitude

befahrbar [bə'fa:rba:r] adj passable; (NAUT) navigable

befahren [bə'fa:rən] (unreg) vt to use, to drive over; (NAUT) to navigate ♦ adj used

befallen [bə'falən] (unreg) vt to come over

befangen [bə'faŋən] adj (schüchtern) shy, self-conscious; (voreingenommen) biased; **B~heit** f shyness; bias

befassen [bə'fasən] vr to concern o.s.

Befehl [bə'fe:l] (-(e)s, -e) m command, order; **b~en** (unreg) vt to order ♦ vi to give orders; **jdm etw b~en** to order sb to do sth; **Befehlshaber** (-s, -) m commanding officer; **Befehlsverweigerung** f insubordination

befestigen [bə'fɛstɪgən] vt to fasten; (stärken) to strengthen; (MIL) to fortify; ~ **an** +dat to fasten to

Befestigung f fastening; strengthening; (MIL) fortification

befeuchten [bə'fɔʏçtən] vt to damp(en), to moisten

befinden [bə'fɪndən] (unreg) vr to be; (sich fühlen) to feel ♦ vt: **jdn/etw für als etw** ~ to deem sb/sth to be sth ♦ vi: ~ (**über** +akk) to decide (on), to adjudicate (on); **B~** (-s) nt health, condition; (Meinung) view, opinion

befolgen [bə'fɔlgən] vt to comply with, to follow

befördern [bə'fœrdərn] vt (senden) to transport, to send; (beruflich) to promote

Beförderung f transport; promotion

befragen [bə'fra:gən] vt to question

befreien [bə'fraɪən] vt to set free; (erlassen) to exempt

Befreier (-s, -) m liberator

Befreiung f liberation, release; (Erlassen) exemption

befremden [bə'frɛmdən] vt to surprise, to disturb; **B~** (-s) nt surprise, astonishment

befreunden [bə'frɔʏndən] vr to make friends; (mit Idee etc) to acquaint o.s.

befreundet adj friendly

befriedigen [bə'fri:dɪgən] vt to satisfy; ~**d** adj satisfactory

Befriedigung f satisfaction, gratification

befristet [bə'frɪstət] adj limited

befruchten [bə'frʊxtən] vt to fertilize; (fig) to stimulate

Befruchtung f: **künstliche** ~ artificial insemination

Befugnis [bə'fu:knɪs] (-, -se) f authorization, powers pl

befugt adj authorized, entitled

Befund [bə'fʊnt] (-(e)s, -e) m findings pl; (MED) diagnosis

befürchten [bə'fʏrçtən] vt to fear

Befürchtung f fear, apprehension

befürworten [bə'fy:rvɔrtən] vt to support, to speak in favour of

Befürworter (-s, -) m supporter, advocate

begabt [bə'ga:pt] adj gifted

Begabung [bə'ga:bʊŋ] f talent, gift

begann etc [bə'gan] vb siehe **beginnen**

begeben [bə'ge:bən] (unreg) vr (gehen)

to betake o.s.; (*geschehen*) to occur; **sich ~ nach** *od* **zu** to proceed to(wards); **B~heit** *f* occurrence

begegnen [bə'ge:gnən] *vi*: **jdm ~** to meet sb; (*behandeln*) to treat sb; **einer Sache** *dat* **~** to meet with sth

Begegnung *f* meeting

begehen [bə'ge:ən] (*unreg*) *vt* (*Straftat*) to commit; (*abschreiten*) to cover; (*Straße*) to use, to negotiate; (*Feier*) to celebrate

begehren [bə'ge:rən] *vt* to desire; **begehrenswert** *adj* desirable

begehrt *adj* in demand; (*Junggeselle*) eligible

begeistern [bə'gaɪstərn] *vt* to fill with enthusiasm, to inspire ♦ *vr*: **sich für etw ~** to get enthusiastic about sth

begeistert *adj* enthusiastic

Begeisterung *f* enthusiasm

Begierde [bə'gi:rdə] *f* desire, passion

begierig [bə'gi:rɪç] *adj* eager, keen

begießen [bə'gi:sən] (*unreg*) *vt* to water; (*mit Alkohol*) to drink to

Beginn [bə'gɪn] (*-(e)s*) *m* beginning; **zu ~** at the beginning; **b~en** (*unreg*) *vt*, *vi* to start, to begin

beglaubigen [bə'glaʊbɪgən] *vt* to countersign

Beglaubigung *f* countersignature

begleichen [bə'glaɪçən] (*unreg*) *vt* to settle, to pay

Begleit- [bə'glaɪt] *zW*: **b~en** *vt* to accompany; (*MIL*) to escort; **~er** (*-s, -*) *m* companion; (*Freund*) escort; (*MUS*) accompanist; **~erscheinung** *f* concomitant (occurrence); **~schreiben** *nt* covering letter; **~umstände** *pl* concomitant circumstances; **~ung** *f* company; (*MIL*) escort; (*MUS*) accompaniment

beglücken [bə'glʏkən] *vt* to make happy, to delight

beglückwünschen [bə'glʏkvʏnʃən] *vt*: **~ (zu)** to congratulate (on)

begnadigen [bə'gna:dɪgən] *vt* to pardon

Begnadigung *f* pardon, amnesty

begnügen [bə'gny:gən] *vr* to be satisfied, to content o.s.

Begonie [bə'go:niə] *f* begonia

begonnen [bə'gɔnən] *vb siehe* **beginnen**

begraben [bə'gra:bən] (*unreg*) *vt* to bury

Begräbnis [bə'grɛ:pnɪs] (*-ses, -se*) *nt* burial, funeral

begreifen [bə'graɪfən] (*unreg*) *vt* to understand, to comprehend

begreiflich [bə'graɪflɪç] *adj* understandable

Begrenztheit [bə'grɛntsthaɪt] *f* limitation, restriction; (*fig*) narrowness

Begriff [bə'grɪf] (*-(e)s, -e*) *m* concept, idea; **im ~ sein, etw zu tun** to be about to do sth; **schwer von ~** (*umg*) slow, dense; **begriffsstutzig** *adj* slow, dense

begründ- [bə'grʏnd] *zW*: **~en** *vt* (*Gründe geben*) to justify; **~et** *adj* well-founded, justified; **B~ung** *f* justification, reason

begrüßen [bə'gry:sən] *vt* to greet, to welcome

Begrüßung *f* greeting, welcome

begünstigen [bə'gʏnstɪgən] *vt* (*Person*) to favour; (*Sache*) to further, to promote

begutachten [bə'gu:t'axtən] *vt* to assess

begütert [bə'gy:tərt] *adj* wealthy, well-to-do

behaart [bə'ha:rt] *adj* hairy

behäbig [bə'hɛ:bɪç] *adj* (*dick*) portly, stout; (*geruhsam*) comfortable

behagen [bə'ha:gən] *vi*: **das behagt ihm nicht** he does not like it; **B~** (*-s*) *nt* comfort, ease

behaglich [bə'ha:klɪç] *adj* comfortable, cosy; **B~keit** *f* comfort, cosiness

behalten [bə'haltən] (*unreg*) *vt* to keep, to retain; (*im Gedächtnis*) to remember

Behälter [bə'hɛltər] (*-s, -*) *m* container, receptacle

behandeln [bə'handəln] *vt* to treat; (*Thema*) to deal with; (*Maschine*) to handle

Behandlung *f* treatment; (*von Maschine*) handling

beharren [bə'harən] *vi*: **auf etw** *dat* **~** to stick *od* keep to sth

beharrlich [bə'harlɪç] *adj* (*ausdauernd*) steadfast, unwavering; (*hartnäckig*) tenacious, dogged; **B~keit** *f* steadfast-ness; tenacity

behaupten [bə'haʊptən] *vt* to claim, to assert, to maintain; (*sein Recht*) to defend ♦ *vr* to assert o.s.

Behauptung *f* claim, assertion

beheizen [bə'haɪtsən] *vt* to heat

behelfen [bə'hɛlfən] (*unreg*) *vr*: **sich mit etw ~** to make do with sth

behelfsmäßig *adj* improvised, makeshift; (*vorübergehend*) temporary

behelligen [bə'hɛlɪgən] *vt* to trouble, to bother

beherbergen [bə'hɛrbɛrgən] *vt* to put up, to house

beherrschen [bə'hɛrʃən] *vt* (*Volk*) to rule, to govern; (*Situation*) to control; (*Sprache, Gefühle*) to master ♦ *vr* to control o.s.

beherrscht *adj* controlled

Beherrschung *f* rule; control; mastery

beherzigen [bə'hɛrtsɪgən] *vt* to take to heart

beherzt *adj* courageous, brave

behilflich [bə'hɪlflɪç] *adj* helpful; **jdm ~ sein (bei)** to help sb (with)

behindern [bə'hɪndərn] *vt* to hinder, to impede

Behinderte(r) *mf* disabled person

Behinderung *f* hindrance; (*Körper~*) handicap

Behörde [bə'hø:rdə] *f* (*auch pl*) author-ities *pl*

behördlich [bə'hø:rtlɪç] *adj* official

behüten [bə'hy:tən] *vt* to guard; **jdn vor etw *dat* ~** to preserve sb from sth

behutsam [bə'hu:tza:m] *adj* cautious, careful; **B~keit** *f* caution, carefulness

---

SCHLÜSSELWORT

bei [baɪ] *präp +dat* **1** (*nahe bei*) near; (*zum Aufenthalt*) at, with; (*unter, zwischen*) among; **bei München** near Munich; **bei uns** at our place; **beim Friseur** at the hairdresser's; **bei seinen Eltern wohnen** to live with one's par-ents; **bei einer Firma arbeiten** to work for a firm; **etw bei sich haben** to have sth on one; **jdn bei sich haben** to have sb with one; **bei Goethe** in Goethe;

beim Militär in the army

2 (*zeitlich*) at, on; (*während*) during; (*Zustand, Umstand*) in; **bei Nacht** at night; **bei Nebel** in fog; **bei Regen** if it rains; **bei solcher Hitze** in such heat; **bei meiner Ankuft** on my arrival; **bei der Arbeit** when I'm *etc* working; **beim Fahren** while driving

---

beibehalten ['baɪbəhaltən] (*unreg*) *vt* to keep, to retain

beibringen ['baɪbrɪŋən] (*unreg*) *vt* (*Beweis, Zeugen*) to bring forward; (*Gründe*) to adduce; **jdm etw ~** (*lehren*) to teach sb sth; (*zu verstehen geben*) to make sb understand sth; (*zufügen*) to inflict sth on sb

Beichte ['baɪçtə] *f* confession; **b~n** *vt* to confess ♦ *vi* to go to confession

Beichtstuhl *m* confessional

beide(s) ['baɪdə(s)] *pron, adj* both; **meine ~n Brüder** my two brothers, both my brothers; **die ersten ~n** the first two; **wir ~** we two; **einer von ~n** one of the two; **alles ~s** both (of them)

beider- ['baɪdər] *zW*: **~lei** *adj inv* of both; **~seitig** *adj* mutual, reciprocal; **~seits** *adv* mutually ♦ *präp +gen* on both sides of

beieinander [baɪʔaɪ'nandər] *adv* together

Beifahrer ['baɪfa:rər] *m* passenger; **~sitz** *m* passenger seat

Beifall ['baɪfal] (**-(e)s**) *m* applause; (*Zustimmung*) approval

beifällig ['baɪfɛlɪç] *adj* approving; (*Kommentar*) favourable

beifügen ['baɪfy:gən] *vt* to enclose

beige ['be:ʒə] *adj* beige, fawn

beigeben ['baɪge:bən] (*unreg*) *vt* (*zufügen*) to add; (*mitgeben*) to give ♦ *vi* (*nachgeben*) to give in

Beigeschmack ['baɪgəʃmak] *m* after-taste

Beihilfe ['baɪhɪlfə] *f* aid, assistance; (*Studien~*) grant; (*JUR*) aiding and abetting

beikommen ['baɪkɔmən] (*unreg*) *vi* **+dat** to get at; (*einem Problem*) to deal with

Beil [baɪl] (**-(e)s, -e**) *nt* axe, hatchet

Beilage ['baɪlaːgə] f (Buch~ etc) supplement; (KOCH) vegetables and potatoes pl

beiläufig ['baɪlɔyfɪç] adj casual, incidental ♦ adv casually, by the way

beilegen ['baɪleːgən] vt (hinzufügen) to enclose, to add; (beimessen) to attribute, to ascribe; (Streit) to settle

Beileid ['baɪlaɪt] nt condolence, sympathy; **herzliches ~** deepest sympathy

beiliegend ['baɪliːgənt] adj (COMM) enclosed

beim [baɪm] = **bei dem**

beimessen ['baɪmesən] (unreg) vt (+ dat) to attribute (to), to ascribe (to)

Bein [baɪn] (-(e)s, -e) nt leg

beinah(e) ['baɪnaː(ə)] adv almost, nearly

Beinbruch m fracture of the leg

beinhalten [bə'ʔɪnhaltən] vt to contain

beipflichten ['baɪpflɪçtən] vi: **jdm/etw ~** to agree with sb/sth

beirren [bə'ʔɪrən] vt to confuse, to muddle; **sich nicht ~ lassen** not to let o.s. be confused

beisammen [baɪ'zamən] adv together; **B~sein** (-s) nt get-together

Beischlaf ['baɪʃlaːf] m sexual intercourse

Beisein ['baɪzaɪn] (-s) nt presence

beiseite [baɪ'zaɪtə] adv to one side, aside; (stehen) on one side, aside; **etw ~ legen** (sparen) to put sth by; **jdn/etw ~ schaffen** to put sb/get sth out of the way

beisetzen ['baɪzɛtsən] vt to bury

Beisetzung f funeral

Beisitzer ['baɪzɪtsər] (-s, -) m (bei Prüfung) assessor

Beispiel ['baɪʃpiːl] (-(e)s, -e) nt example; **sich an jdm ein ~ nehmen** to take sb as an example; **zum ~ for** example; **b~haft** adj exemplary; **b~los** adj unprecedented; **beispielsweise** adv for instance od example

beißen ['baɪsən] (unreg) vt, vi to bite; (stechen: Rauch, Säure) to burn ♦ vr (Farben) to clash; **~d** adj biting, caustic; (fig auch) sarcastic

Beistand ['baɪʃtant] (-(e)s, =e) m sup-

port, help; (JUR) adviser

beistehen ['baɪʃteːən] (unreg) vi: **jdm ~** to stand by sb

beisteuern ['baɪʃtɔyərn] vt to contribute

beistimmen ['baɪʃtɪmən] vi +dat to agree with

Beitrag ['baɪtraːk] (-(e)s, =e) m contribution; (Zahlung) fee, subscription; (Versicherungs~) premium; **b~en** ['baɪtraːgən] (unreg) vt, vi: **b~en (zu)** to contribute (to); (mithelfen) to help (with)

beitreten ['baɪtreːtən] (unreg) vi +dat to join

Beitritt ['baɪtrɪt] m joining, membership

beiwohnen ['baɪvoːnən] vi: **einer Sache dat ~** to attend od be present at sth

Beize ['baɪtsə] f (Holz~) stain; (KOCH) marinade

beizeiten [baɪ'tsaɪtən] adv in time

bejahen [bə'jaːən] vt (Frage) to say yes to, to answer in the affirmative; (gutheißen) to agree with

bejahrt [bə'jaːrt] adj aged, elderly

bekämpfen [bə'kɛmpfən] vt (Gegner) to fight; (Seuche) to combat ♦ vr to fight

Bekämpfung f fight, struggle

bekannt [bə'kant] adj (well-)known; (nicht fremd) familiar; **mit jdm ~ sein** to know sb; **jdn mit jdm ~ machen** to introduce sb to sb; **das ist mir ~** I know that; **es/sie kommt mir ~ vor** it/ she seems familiar; **B~e(r)** mf acquaintance; friend; **B~enkreis** m circle of friends; **B~gabe** f announcement; **~geben** (unreg) vt to announce publicly; **~lich** adv as is well known, as you know; **~machen** vt to announce; **B~machung** f publication; announcement; **B~schaft** f acquaintance

bekehren [bə'keːrən] vt to convert ♦ vr to be od become converted

bekennen [bə'kɛnən] (unreg) vt to confess; (Glauben) to profess; **Farbe ~** (umg) to show where one stands

Bekenntnis [bə'kɛntnɪs] (-ses, -se) nt admission, confession; (Religion) confession, denomination

beklagen [bə'klaːgən] vt to deplore, to lament ♦ vr to complain; **be-**

klagenswert *adj* lamentable, pathetic
bekleiden [bə'klaɪdən] *vt* to clothe; (*Amt*) to occupy, to fill
Bekleidung *f* clothing
beklemmen [bə'klɛmən] *vt* to oppress
beklommen [bə'klɔmən] *adj* anxious, uneasy; **B~heit** *f* anxiety, uneasiness
bekommen [bə'kɔmən] (*unreg*) *vt* to get, to receive; (*Kind*) to have; (*Zug*) to catch, to get ♦ *vi*: **jdm ~** to agree with sb
bekömmlich [bə'kœmlɪç] *adj* easily digestible
bekräftigen [bə'krɛftɪgən] *vt* to confirm, to corroborate
Bekräftigung *f* corroboration
bekreuzigen [bə'krɔʏtsɪgən] *vr* to cross o.s.
bekümmern [bə'kʏmərn] *vt* to worry, to trouble
bekunden [bə'kʊndən] *vt* (*sagen*) to state; (*zeigen*) to show
belächeln [bə'lɛçəln] *vt* to laugh at
beladen [bə'laːdən] (*unreg*) *vt* to load
Belag [bə'laːk] (-(e)s, ⸚e) *m* covering, coating; (*Brot~*) spread; (*Zahn~*) tartar; (*auf Zunge*) fur; (*Brems~*) lining
belagern [bə'laːgərn] *vt* to besiege
Belagerung *f* siege
Belang [bə'laŋ] (-(e)s) *m* importance; **~e** *pl* (*Interessen*) interests, concerns; **b~en** *vt* (*JUR*) to take to court; **b~los** *adj* trivial, unimportant; **~losigkeit** *f* triviality
belassen [bə'lasən] (*unreg*) *vt* (*in Zustand, Glauben*) to leave; (*in Stellung*) to retain
belasten [bə'lastən] *vt* to burden; (*fig: bedrücken*) to trouble, to worry; (*COMM: Konto*) to debit; (*JUR*) to incriminate ♦ *vr* to weigh o.s. down; (*JUR*) to incriminate o.s.; **~d** *adj* (*JUR*) incriminating
belästigen [bə'lɛstɪgən] *vt* to annoy, to pester
Belästigung *f* annoyance, pestering
Belastung [bə'lastʊŋ] *f* load; (*fig: Sorge etc*) weight; (*COMM*) charge, debit(ing); (*JUR*) incriminatory evi-

dence; **Belastungsprobe** *f* capacity test; (*fig*) test; **Belastungszeuge** *m* witness for prosecution
belaufen [bə'laʊfən] (*unreg*) *vr*: **sich ~ auf** +*akk* to amount to
belebt [bə'leːpt] *adj* (*Straße*) busy
Beleg [bə'leːk] (-(e)s, -e) *m* (*COMM*) receipt; (*Beweis*) documentary evidence, proof; (*Beispiel*) example; **b~en** [bə'leːgən] *vt* to cover; (*Kuchen, Brot*) to spread; (*Platz*) to reserve, to book; (*Kurs, Vorlesung*) to register for; (*beweisen*) to verify, to prove; (*MIL: mit Bomben*) to bomb; **~schaft** *f* personnel, staff; **belegt** *adj*: **belegtes Brot** open sandwich
belehren [bə'leːrən] *vt* to instruct, to teach
Belehrung *f* instruction
beleibt [bə'laɪpt] *adj* stout, corpulent
beleidigen [bə'laɪdɪgən] *vt* to insult, to offend
Beleidigung *f* insult; (*JUR*) slander; libel
belesen [bə'leːzən] *adj* well-read
beleuchten [bə'lɔʏçtən] *vt* to light, to illuminate; (*fig*) to throw light on
Beleuchtung *f* lighting, illumination
Belgien ['bɛlgiən] *nt* Belgium; **Belgier(in)** *m(f)* Belgian; **belgisch** *adj* Belgian
belichten [bə'lɪçtən] *vt* to expose
Belichtung *f* exposure; **Belichtungsmesser** *m* exposure meter
Belieben [bə'liːbən] *nt*: (**ganz**) **nach ~** (just) as you wish
beliebig [bə'liːbɪç] *adj* any you like ♦ *adv* as you like; **ein ~es Thema** any subject you like *od* want; **~ viel/viele** as much/many as you like
beliebt [bə'liːpt] *adj* popular; **sich bei jdm ~ machen** to make o.s. popular with sb; **B~heit** *f* popularity
beliefern [bə'liːfərn] *vt* to supply
bellen ['bɛlən] *vi* to bark
Belletristik [bele'trɪstɪk] *f* fiction and poetry
belohnen [bə'loːnən] *vt* to reward
Belohnung *f* reward
belügen [bə'lyːgən] (*unreg*) *vt* to lie to,

to deceive
belustigen [bə'lʊstɪgən] *vt* to amuse
Belustigung *f* amusement
bemalen [bə'ma:lən] *vt* to paint
bemängeln [bə'mɛŋəln] *vt* to criticize
bemannen [bə'manən] *vt* to man
bemerk- [bə'mɛrk] *zW*: ~**bar** *adj* perceptible, noticeable; **sich ~bar machen** (*Person*) to make *od* get o.s. noticed; (*Unruhe*) to become noticeable; ~**en** *vt* (*wahrnehmen*) to notice, to observe; (*sagen*) to say, to mention; ~**enswert** *adj* remarkable, noteworthy; **B~ung** *f* remark; (*schriftlich auch*) note
bemitleiden [bə'mɪtlaɪdən] *vt* to pity
bemühen [bə'my:ən] *vr* to take trouble *od* pains
Bemühung *f* trouble, pains *pl*, effort
benachbart [bə'naxba:rt] *adj* neighbouring
benachrichtigen [bə'na:xrɪçtɪgən] *vt* to inform
Benachrichtigung *f* notification, information
benachteiligen [bə'na:xtaɪlɪgən] *vt* to put at a disadvantage; to victimize
benehmen [bə'ne:mən] (*unreg*) *vr* to behave; **B~** (-s) *nt* behaviour
beneiden [bə'naɪdən] *vt* to envy; **beneidenswert** *adj* enviable
benennen [bə'nɛnən] (*unreg*) *vt* to name
Bengel ['bɛŋəl] (-s, -) *m* (little) rascal *od* rogue
benommen [bə'nɔmən] *adj* dazed
benötigen [bə'nø:tɪgən] *vt* to need
benutzen [bə'nʊtsən] *vt* to use
benützen [bə'nʏtsən] *vt* to use
Benutzer (-s, -) *m* user; **b~freundlich** *adj* user-friendly
Benutzung *f* utilization, use
Benzin [bɛnt'si:n] (-s, -e) *nt* (*AUT*) petrol (*BRIT*), gas(oline) (*US*); ~**kanister** *m* petrol (*BRIT*) *od* gas (*US*) can; ~**tank** *m* petrol tank (*BRIT*), gas tank (*US*); ~**uhr** *f* petrol (*BRIT*) *od* gas (*US*) gauge
beobachten [bə'o:baxtən] *vt* to observe; **Beobachter** (-s, -) *m* observer; (*eines Unfalls*) witness;

(*PRESSE, TV*) correspondent; **Beobachtung** *f* observation
bepacken [bə'pakən] *vt* to load, to pack
bequem [bə'kve:m] *adj* comfortable; (*Ausrede*) convenient; (*Person*) lazy, indolent; ~**en** *vr*: **sich ~en(, etw zu tun)** to condescend (to do sth); **B~lichkeit** *f* convenience, comfort; (*Faulheit*) laziness, indolence
beraten [bə'ra:tən] (*unreg*) *vt* to advise; (*besprechen*) to discuss, to debate ♦ *vr* to consult; **gut/schlecht ~ sein** to be well/ill advised; **sich ~ lassen** to get advice
Berater (-s, -) *m* adviser
Beratung *f* advice; (*Besprechung*) consultation; **Beratungsstelle** *f* advice centre
berauben [bə'raʊbən] *vt* to rob
berechenbar [bə'rɛçənba:r] *adj* calculable
berechnen [bə'rɛçnən] *vt* to calculate; (*COMM: anrechnen*) to charge; ~**d** *adj* (*Mensch*) calculating, scheming
Berechnung *f* calculation; (*COMM*) charge
berechtigen [bə'rɛçtɪgən] *vt* to entitle; to authorize; (*fig*) to justify
berechtigt [bə'rɛçtɪçt] *adj* justifiable, justified
Berechtigung *f* authorization; (*fig*) justification
bereden [bə're:dən] *vt* (*besprechen*) to discuss; (*überreden*) to persuade ♦ *vr* to discuss
Bereich [bə'raɪç] (-(e)s, -e) *m* (*Bezirk*) area; (*PHYS*) range; (*Ressort, Gebiet*) sphere
bereichern [bə'raɪçərn] *vt* to enrich ♦ *vr* to get rich
bereinigen [bə'raɪnɪgən] *vt* to settle
bereit [bə'raɪt] *adj* ready, prepared; **zu etw ~ sein** to be ready for sth; **sich ~ erklären** to declare o.s. willing; ~**en** *vt* to prepare, to make ready; (*Kummer, Freude*) to cause; ~**halten** (*unreg*) *vt* to keep in readiness; ~**legen** *vt* to lay out; ~**machen** *vt, vr* to prepare, to get ready; ~**s** *adv* already; **B~schaft** *f* readiness; (*Polizei*) alert; **B~schafts-**

dienst *m* emergency service; **~stehen**
(*unreg*) *vi* (*Person*) to be prepared;
(*Ding*) to be ready; **~stellen** *vt*
(*Kisten, Pakete etc*) to put ready;
(*Geld etc*) to make available;
(*Truppen, Maschinen*) to put at the
ready; **~willig** *adj* willing, ready;
B~willigkeit *f* willingness, readiness
bereuen [bə'rɔʏən] *vt* to regret
Berg [bɛrk] (-(e)s, -e) *m* mountain; hill;
b~ab *adv* downhill; **~arbeiter** *m*
miner; **b~auf** *adv* uphill; **~bahn** *f*
mountain railway; **~bau** *m* mining
bergen ['bɛrgən] (*unreg*) *vt* (*retten*) to
rescue; (*Ladung*) to salvage; (*enthalten*) to contain
Berg- führer *m* mountain guide;
b~ig ['bɛrgɪç] *adj* mountainous; hilly;
~kette *f* mountain range; **~mann** (*pl*
~leute) *m* miner; **~rutsch** *m* landslide;
~steigen *nt* mountaineering; **~stei-
ger(in)** (-s, -) *m(f)* mountaineer, climber
Bergung ['bɛrgʊŋ] *f* (*von Menschen*)
rescue; (*von Material*) recovery;
(*NAUT*) salvage
Bergwacht *f* mountain rescue service
Bergwerk *nt* mine
Bericht [bə'rɪçt] (-(e)s, -e) *m* report,
account; **b~en** *vt, vi* to report; **~er-
statter** (-s, -) *m* reporter; (newspaper)
correspondent
berichtigen [bə'rɪçtɪgən] *vt* to correct
Berichtigung *f* correction
Bernstein ['bɛrnʃtaɪn] *m* amber
bersten ['bɛrstən] (*unreg*) *vi* to burst, to
split
berüchtigt [bə'rʏçtɪçt] *adj* notorious, infamous
berücksichtigen [bə'rʏkzɪçtɪgən] *vt* to
consider, to bear in mind
Berücksichtigung *f* consideration
Beruf [bə'ru:f] (-(e)s, -e) *m* occupation,
profession; (*Gewerbe*) trade; **b~en**
(*unreg*) *vt*: **b~en zu** to appoint to ♦ *vr*:
sich auf jdn/etw b~en to refer *od*
appeal to sb/sth ♦ *adj* competent,
qualified; **b~lich** *adj* professional
Berufs- *zW*: **~berater** *m* careers
adviser; **~beratung** *f* vocational

guidance; **~geheimnis** *nt* professional
secret; **~leben** *nt* professional life;
b~mäßig *adj* professional; **~schule** *f*
vocational *od* trade school; **~sportler**
m professional (sportsman); **b~tätig**
adj employed; **~verkehr** *m* rush-hour
traffic
Berufung *f* vocation, calling;
(*Ernennung*) appointment; (*JUR*)
appeal; **~ einlegen** to appeal
beruhen [bə'ru:ən] *vi*: **auf etw** *dat* **~** to
be based on sth; **etw auf sich ~ lassen**
to leave sth at that
beruhigen [bə'ru:ɪgən] *vt* to calm, to
pacify, to soothe ♦ *vr* (*Mensch*) to calm
(o.s.) down; (*Situation*) to calm down
Beruhigung *f* soothing; (*der Nerven*)
calming; **zu jds ~** (in order) to reassure sb; **Beruhigungsmittel** *nt* sedative
berühmt [bə'ry:mt] *adj* famous; **B~heit**
f (*Ruf*) fame; (*Mensch*) celebrity
berühren [bə'ry:rən] *vt* to touch;
(*gefühlsmäßig bewegen*) to affect;
(*flüchtig erwähnen*) to mention, to
touch on ♦ *vr* to meet, to touch
Berührung *f* contact
besagen [bə'za:gən] *vt* to mean
besagt *adj* (*Tag etc*) said
besänftigen *vt* to soothe, to calm: **~d**
adj soothing; **Besänftigung** *f* soothing,
calming
Besatz [bə'zats] (-es, -̈e) *m* trimming,
edging
Besatzung *f* garrison; (*NAUT, AVIAT*)
crew; **Besatzungsmacht** *f* occupying
power
beschädigen [bə'ʃɛ:dɪgən] *vt* to damage; **Beschädigung** *f* damage; (*Stelle*)
damaged spot
beschaffen [bə'ʃafən] *vt* to get, to
acquire ♦ *adj*: **das ist so ~, daß** that is
such that; **B~heit** *f* (*von Mensch*) constitution, nature
Beschaffung *f* acquisition
beschäftigen [bə'ʃɛftɪgən] *vt* to occupy;
(*beruflich*) to employ ♦ *vr* to occupy *od*
concern o.s.
beschäftigt *adj* busy, occupied
Beschäftigung *f* (*Beruf*) employment;

(Tätigkeit) occupation; *(Befassen)* concern

beschämen [bə'ʃɛ:mən] *vt* to put to shame; **~d** *adj* shameful; *(Hilfsbereitschaft)* shaming

beschämt *adj* ashamed

beschatten [bə'ʃatən] *vt* to shade; *(Verdächtige)* to shadow

Bescheid [bə'ʃaɪt] (-(e)s, -e) *m* information; *(Weisung)* directions *pl*; **~ wissen (uber** +*akk*) to be well-informed (about); **ich weiß ~** I know; **jdm ~ geben** *od* **sagen** to let sb know

bescheiden [bə'ʃaɪdən] *(unreg)* *vr* to content o.s. ♦ *adj* modest; **B~heit** *f* modesty

bescheinen [bə'ʃaɪnən] *(unreg)* *vt* to shine on

bescheinigen [bə'ʃaɪnɪɡən] *vt* to certify; *(bestätigen)* to acknowledge

Bescheinigung *f* certificate; *(Quittung)* receipt

bescheren [bə'ʃe:rən] *vt*: **jdm etw ~** to give sb sth as a Christmas present; **jdn ~** to give Christmas presents to sb

Bescherung *f* giving of Christmas presents; *(umg)* mess

beschildern [bə'ʃɪldərn] *vt* to put signs/a sign on

beschimpfen [bə'ʃɪmpfən] *vt* to abuse

Beschimpfung *f* abuse; insult

Beschlag [bə'ʃla:k] (-(e)s, -̈e) *m* *(Metallband)* fitting; *(auf Fenster)* condensation; *(auf Metall)* tarnish; finish; *(Hufeisen)* horseshoe; **jdn/etw in ~ nehmen** *od* **mit ~ belegen** to monopolize sb/sth; **b~en** [bə'ʃla:gən] *(unreg)* *vt* to cover; *(Pferd)* to shoe ♦ *vi, vr (Fenster etc)* to mist over; **b~en sein (in** *od* **auf** +*dat)* to be well versed (in); **b~nahmen** *vt* to seize, to confiscate; to requisition; **~nahmung** *f* confiscation, sequestration

beschleunigen [bə'ʃlɔynɪɡən] *vt* to accelerate, to speed up ♦ *vi (AUT)* to accelerate

Beschleunigung *f* acceleration

beschließen [bə'ʃli:sən] *(unreg)* *vt* to decide on; *(beenden)* to end, to close

Beschluß [bə'ʃlʊs] (-sses, -̈sse) *m* deci-

sion, conclusion; *(Ende)* conclusion, end

beschmutzen [bə'ʃmʊtsən] *vt* to dirty, to soil

beschönigen [bə'ʃø:nɪɡən] *vt* to gloss over

beschränken [bə'ʃrɛŋkən] *vt, vr:* **(sich) ~ (auf** +*akk*) to limit *od* restrict (o.s.) (to)

beschränk- *zW:* **~t** *adj* confined, restricted; *(Mensch)* limited, narrow-minded; **Beschränktheit** *f* restriction; **B~ung** *f* limitation

beschreiben [bə'ʃraɪbən] *(unreg)* *vt* to describe; *(Papier)* to write on

Beschreibung *f* description

beschriften [bə'ʃrɪftən] *vt* to mark, to label

Beschriftung *f* lettering

beschuldigen [bə'ʃʊldɪɡən] *vt* to accuse

Beschuldigung *f* accusation

beschützen [bə'ʃytsən] *vt:* **~ (vor** +*dat)* to protect (from); **Beschützer** (-s, -) *m* protector

Beschwerde [bə'ʃve:rdə] *f* complaint; *(Mühe)* hardship; **~n** *pl (Leiden)* trouble

beschweren [bə'ʃve:rən] *vt* to weight down; *(fig)* to burden ♦ *vr* to complain

beschwerlich *adj* tiring, exhausting

beschwichtigen [bə'ʃvɪçtɪɡən] *vt* to soothe, to pacify

beschwindeln [bə'ʃvɪndəln] *vt* *(betrügen)* to cheat; *(belügen)* to fib to

beschwingt [bə'ʃvɪŋt] *adj* in high spirits

beschwören [bə'ʃvø:rən] *(unreg)* *vt* *(Aussage)* to swear to; *(anflehen)* to implore; *(Geister)* to conjure up

beseitigen [bə'zaɪtɪɡən] *vt* to remove

Beseitigung *f* removal

Besen ['be:zən] (-s, -) *m* broom; **~stiel** *m* broomstick

besessen [bə'zɛsən] *adj* possessed

besetz- [bə'zɛts] *zW:* **~en** *vt (Haus, Land)* to occupy; *(Platz)* to take, to fill; *(Posten)* to fill; *(Rolle)* to cast; *(mit Edelsteinen)* to set; **~t** *adj* full; *(TEL)* engaged, busy; *(Platz)* taken; *(WC)* engaged; **Besetztzeichen** *nt* engaged tone; **B~ung** f occupation; filling; (von Rolle) casting; (die Schauspieler) cast

besichtigen [bə'zɪçtɪgən] vt to visit, to have a look at

Besichtigung f visit

Besied(e)lung [bə'ziːd(ə)lʊŋ] f population

besiegen [bə'ziːgən] vt to defeat, to overcome

besinnen [bə'zɪnən] (unreg) vr (nachdenken) to think, to reflect; (erinnern) to remember; **sich anders ~** to change one's mind

besinnlich adj contemplative

Besinnung f consciousness; **zur ~ kommen** to recover consciousness; (fig) to come to one's senses; **besinnungslos** adj unconscious

Besitz [bə'zɪts] (-es) m possession; (Eigentum) property; **b~en** (unreg) vt to possess, to own; (Eigenschaft) to have; **~er(in)** (-s, -) m(f) owner, proprietor; **~ergreifung** f occupation, seizure

besoffen [bə'zɔfən] (umg) adj drunk, stoned

besohlen [bə'zoːlən] vt to sole

Besoldung [bə'zɔldʊŋ] f salary, pay

besondere(r, s) [bə'zɔndərə(r, s)] adj special; (eigen) particular; (gesondert) separate; (eigentümlich) peculiar

Besonderheit [bə'zɔndərhaɪt] f peculiarity

besonders [bə'zɔndərs] adv especially, particularly; (getrennt) separately

besonnen [bə'zɔnən] adj sensible, level-headed; **B~heit** f prudence

besorg- [bə'zɔrg] zW: **~en** vt (beschaffen) to acquire; (kaufen auch) to purchase; (erledigen: Geschäfte) to deal with; (sich kümmern um) to take care of; **B~nis** (-, -se) f anxiety, concern; **~t** [bə'zɔrçt] adj anxious, worried; **Besorgtheit** f anxiety, worry; **B~ung** f acquisition; (Kauf) purchase

bespielen [bə'ʃpiːlən] vt to record

bespitzeln [bə'ʃpɪtsəln] vt to spy on

besprechen [bə'ʃprɛçən] (unreg) vt to discuss; (Tonband etc) to record, to speak onto; (Buch) to review ♦ vr to

discuss, to consult

Besprechung f meeting, discussion; (von Buch) review

besser ['bɛsər] adj better; **~n** vt to make better, to improve ♦ vr to improve; (Menschen) to reform; **B~ung** f improvement; **gute B~ung!** get well soon!; **B~wisser** (-s, -) m know-all

Bestand [bə'ʃtant] (-(e)s, ⁼e) m (Fortbestehen) duration, stability; (Kassen~) amount, balance; (Vorrat) stock; **~ haben, von ~ sein** to last long, to endure

beständig [bə'ʃtɛndɪç] adj (ausdauernd: auch fig) constant; (Wetter) settled; (Stoffe) resistant; (Klagen etc) continual

Bestandsaufnahme f stocktaking

Bestandteil m part, component; (Zutat) ingredient

bestärken [bə'ʃtɛrkən] vt: **jdn in etw** dat **~** to strengthen od confirm sb in sth

bestätigen [bə'ʃtɛːtɪgən] vt to confirm; (anerkennen, COMM) to acknowledge

Bestätigung f confirmation; acknowledgement

bestatt- [bə'ʃtat] zW: **~en** vt to bury; **B~er** (-s, -) m undertaker; **B~ung** f funeral

beste(r, s) ['bɛstə(r, s)] adj best; **so ist es am ~n** it's best that way; **am ~n gehst du gleich** you'd better go at once; **jdn zum ~n haben** to pull sb's leg; **einen Witz etc zum ~n geben** to tell a joke etc; **aufs ~** in the best possible way; **zu jds B~n** for the benefit of sb

bestechen [bə'ʃtɛçən] (unreg) vt to bribe

bestechlich adj corruptible

Bestechung f bribery, corruption

Besteck [bə'ʃtɛk] (-(e)s, -e) nt knife, fork and spoon, cutlery; (MED) set of instruments

bestehen [bə'ʃteːən] (unreg) vi to be; to exist; (andauern) to last ♦ vt (Kampf, Probe, Prüfung) to pass; **~ auf** +dat to insist on; **~ aus** to consist of

bestehlen [bə'ʃteːlən] (unreg) vt: **jdn (um etw) ~** to rob sb (of sth)

besteigen [bə'ʃtaɪɡən] (*unreg*) *vt* to climb, to ascend; (*Pferd*) to mount; (*Thron*) to ascend

Bestell- [bə'ʃtɛl] *zW:* ~**buch** *nt* order book: **b**~**en** *vt* to order; (*kommen lassen*) to arrange to see; (*nominieren*) to name; (*Acker*) to cultivate; (*Grüße, Auftrag*) to pass on; ~**schein** *m* order coupon; ~**ung** *f* (*COMM*) order; (*Bestellen*) ordering

bestenfalls ['bɛstən'fals] *adv* at best

bestens ['bɛstəns] *adv* very well

Bestie ['bɛstiə] *f* (*auch fig*) beast

bestimm- [bə'ʃtɪm] *zW:* ~**en** *vt* (*Regeln*) to lay down; (*Tag, Ort*) to fix; (*beherrschen*) to characterize; (*vorsehen*) to mean; (*ernennen*) to appoint; (*definieren*) to define; (*veranlassen*) to induce; ~**t** *adj* (*entschlossen*) firm; (*gewiß*) certain, definite; (*Artikel*) definite ♦ *adv* (*gewiß*) definitely, for sure; **suchen Sie etwas B~tes?** are you looking for something in particular?; **B~theit** *f* firmness; certainty; **B~ung** *f* (*Verordnung*) regulation; (*Festsetzen*) determining; (*Verwendungszweck*) purpose; (*Schicksal*) fate; (*Definition*) definition; **B~ungsort** *m* destination

Bestleistung *f* best performance

bestmöglich *adj* best possible

bestrafen [bə'ʃtraːfən] *vt* to punish

Bestrafung *f* punishment

bestrahlen [bə'ʃtraːlən] *vt* to shine on; (*MED*) to treat with X-rays

Bestrahlung *f* (*MED*) X-ray treatment, radiotherapy

Bestreben [bə'ʃtreːbən] (-s) *nt* endeavour, effort

bestreichen [bə'ʃtraɪçən] (*unreg*) *vt* (*Brot*) to spread

bestreiten [bə'ʃtraɪtən] (*unreg*) *vt* (*abstreiten*) to dispute; (*finanzieren*) to pay for, to finance

bestreuen [bə'ʃtrɔʏən] *vt* to sprinkle, to dust; (*Straße*) to grit

bestürmen [bə'ʃtʏrmən] *vt* (*mit Fragen, Bitten etc*) to overwhelm, to swamp

bestürzt [bə'ʃtʏrtst] *adj* dismayed

Bestürzung *f* consternation

Besuch [bə'zuːx] (-(e)s, -e) *m* visit; (*Person*) visitor; **einen ~ machen bei jdm** to pay sb a visit *od* call; ~ **haben** to have visitors; **bei jdm auf od zu ~ sein** to be visiting sb; **b~en** *vt* to visit; (*SCH etc*) to attend; **gut b~t** well-attended; ~**er(in)** (-s, -) *m(f)* visitor, guest; **Besuchszeit** *f* visiting hours *pl*

betagt [bə'taːkt] *adj* aged

betätigen [bə'tɛːtɪɡən] *vt* (*bedienen*) to work, to operate ♦ *vr* to involve o.s.; **sich als etw ~** to work as sth

Betätigung *f* activity; (*beruflich*) occupation; (*TECH*) operation

betäuben [bə'tɔʏbən] *vt* to stun; (*fig: Gewissen*) to still; (*MED*) to anaesthetize

Betäubungsmittel *nt* anaesthetic

Bete ['beːtə] *f*: **rote ~** beetroot (*BRIT*), beet (*US*)

beteiligen [bə'taɪlɪɡən] *vr*: **sich ~ (an** +*dat*) to take part (in), to participate (in), to share (in); (*an Geschäft: finanziell*) to have a share (in) ♦ *vt*: **jdn ~ (an** +*dat*) to give sb a share *od* interest (in)

Beteiligung *f* participation; (*Anteil*) share, interest; (*Besucherzahl*) attendance

beten ['beːtən] *vt, vi* to pray

beteuern [bə'tɔʏərn] *vt* to assert; (*Unschuld*) to protest

Beteuerung *f* assertion; protestation; assurance

Beton [be'tɔ̃ː] (-s, -s) *m* concrete

betonen [bə'toːnən] *vt* to stress

betonieren [beto'niːrən] *vt* to concrete

Betonung *f* stress, emphasis

betören [bə'tøːrən] *vt* to beguile

Betr. *abk* (= *betrifft*) re

Betracht [bə'traxt] *m*: **in ~ kommen** to be considered *od* relevant; **etw in ~ ziehen** to take sth into consideration; **außer ~ bleiben** not to be considered; **b~en** *vt* to look at; (*fig*) to look at, to consider; ~**er(in)** (-s, -) *m(f)* observer

beträchtlich [bə'trɛçtlɪç] *adj* considerable

Betrachtung *f* (*Ansehen*) examination; (*Erwägung*) consideration

Betrag [bə'traːk] (-(e)s, ⁼e) m amount; **b~en** [bə'traːgən] (unreg) vt to amount to ♦ vr to behave; **~en** (-s) nt behaviour

betreffen [bə'trɛfən] (unreg) vt to concern, to affect; **was mich betrifft** as for me; **~d** adj relevant, in question

betreffs [bə'trɛfs] präp +gen concerning, regarding; (COMM) re

betreiben [bə'traibən] (unreg) vt (ausüben) to practise; (Politik) to follow; (Studien) to pursue; (vorantreiben) to push ahead; (TECH: antreiben) to drive

betreten [bə'treːtən] (unreg) vt to enter; (Bühne etc) to step onto ♦ adj embarrassed; **B~ verboten** keep off/out

Betrieb [bə'triːp] (-(e)s, -e) m (Firma) firm, concern; (Anlage) plant; (Tätigkeit) operation; (Treiben) traffic; **außer ~ sein** to be out of order; **in ~ sein** to be in operation

Betriebs- zW: **b~fähig** adj in working order; **~ferien** pl company holidays (BRIT), company vacation sg (US); **~klima** nt (working) atmosphere; **~kosten** pl running costs; **~rat** m workers' council; **b~sicher** adj safe (to operate); **~störung** f breakdown; **~unfall** m industrial accident; **~wirtschaft** f economics

betrinken [bə'trɪŋkən] (unreg) vr to get drunk

betroffen [bə'trɔfən] adj (bestürzt) full of consternation; **von etw ~ werden** od **sein** to be affected by sth

betrüben [bə'tryːbən] vt to grieve

betrübt [bə'tryːpt] adj sorrowful, grieved

Betrug [bə'truːk] (-(e)s) m deception; (JUR) fraud

betrügen [bə'tryːgən] (unreg) vt to cheat; (JUR) to defraud; (Ehepartner) to be unfaithful to ♦ vr to deceive o.s.

Betrüger (-s, -) m cheat, deceiver; **b~isch** adj deceitful; (JUR) fraudulent

betrunken [bə'trʊŋkən] adj drunk

Bett [bɛt] (-(e)s, -en) nt bed; **ins** od **zu ~ gehen** to go to bed; **~bezug** m duvet cover; **~decke** f blanket; (Daunen~)

quilt; (Überwurf) bedspread

Bettel- ['bɛtəl] zW: **b~arm** adj very poor, destitute; **~ei** [bɛtə'lai] f begging; **b~n** vi to beg

bettlägerig ['bɛtlɛːgərɪç] adj bedridden

Bettlaken nt sheet

Bettler(in) ['bɛtlər(ɪn)] (-s, -) m(f) beggar

Bett- zW: **~(t)uch** nt sheet; **~vorleger** m bedside rug; **~wäsche** f bed linen; **~zeug** nt bedlinen pl

beugen ['bɔygən] vt to bend; (GRAM) to inflect ♦ vr (sich fügen) to bow

Beule ['bɔylə] f bump, swelling

beunruhigen [bə'ʊnruːɪgən] vt to disturb, to alarm ♦ vr to become worried

Beunruhigung f worry, alarm

beurlauben [bə'uːrlaubən] vt to give leave od a holiday to (BRIT), to grant vacation time to (US)

beurteilen [bə'ʊrtailən] vt to judge; (Buch etc) to review

Beurteilung f judgement; review; (Note) mark

Beute ['bɔytə] (-) f booty, loot

Beutel (-s, -) m bag; (Geld~) purse; (Tabak~) pouch

Bevölkerung [bə'fœlkərʊŋ] f population

bevollmächtigen [bə'fɔlmɛçtɪgən] vt to authorize

Bevollmächtigte(r) mf authorized agent

bevor [bə'foːr] konj before; **~munden** vt insep to treat like a child; **~stehen** (unreg) vi: (jdm) **~stehen** to be in store (for sb); **~stehend** adj imminent, approaching; **~zugen** vt insep to prefer; **B~zugung** f preference

bewachen [bə'vaxən] vt to watch, to guard

Bewachung f (Bewachen) guarding; (Leute) guard, watch

bewaffnen [bə'vafnən] vt to arm

Bewaffnung f (Vorgang) arming; (Ausrüstung) armament, arms pl

bewahren [bə'vaːrən] vt to keep; **jdn vor jdm/etw ~** to save sb from sb/sth

bewähren [bə've:rən] vr to prove o.s.; (Maschine) to prove its worth

bewahrheiten [bə'va:rhaitən] vr to

come true
bewährt adj reliable
Bewährung f (JUR) probation;
Bewährungsfrist f (period of) probation
bewältigen [bə'vɛltɪgən] vt to overcome; (Arbeit) to finish; (Portion) to manage
bewandert [bə'vandərt] adj expert, knowledgeable
bewässern [bə'vɛsərn] vt to irrigate
Bewässerung f irrigation
bewegen [bə've:gən] vt, vr to move;
jdn zu etw ~ to induce sb to do sth
Beweg- [bə've:k] zW: ~**grund** m motive; **b~lich** adj movable, mobile;
(flink) quick; **b~t** adj (Leben) eventful; (Meer) rough; (ergriffen) touched
Bewegung f movement, motion; (innere) emotion; (körperlich) exercise;
Bewegungsfreiheit f freedom of movement; (fig) freedom of action;
bewegungslos adj motionless
Beweis [bə'vaɪs] (-es, -e) m proof;
(Zeichen) sign; **b~bar** [bə'vaɪz-] adj provable; **b~en** (unreg) vt to prove;
(zeigen) to show; ~**mittel** nt evidence
Bewerb- [bə'vɛrb] zW: **b~en** (unreg) vr: sich **b~en** (um) to apply (for);
~**er(in)** (-s, -) m(f) applicant; ~**ung** f application
bewerkstelligen [bə'vɛrkʃtɛlɪgən] vt to manage, to accomplish
bewerten [bə've:rtən] vt to assess
bewilligen [bə'vɪlɪgən] vt to grant, to allow
Bewilligung f granting
bewir•en [bə'vɪrkən] vt to cause, to bring about
bewirten [bə'vɪrtən] vt to feed, to entertain (to a meal)
bewirtschaften [bə'vɪrtʃaftən] vt to manage
Bewirtung f hospitality
bewog etc [bə'vo:k] vb siehe **bewegen**
bewohn- [bə'vo:n] zW: ~**bar** adj habitable; ~**en** vt to inhabit, to live in;
B~er(in) (-s, -) m(f) inhabitant; (von Haus) resident
bewölkt [bə'vœlkt] adj cloudy, overcast
Bewölkung f clouds pl

Bewunder- [bə'vʊndər] zW: ~**er** (-s, -) m admirer; **b~n** vt to admire;
bewundernswert adj admirable, wonderful; ~**ung** f admiration
bewußt [bə'vʊst] adj conscious;
(absichtlich) deliberate; **sich** dat **einer Sache** gen ~ **sein** to be aware of sth;
~**los** adj unconscious; **B~losigkeit** f unconsciousness; **B~sein** nt consciousness; **bei B~sein** conscious
bezahlen [bə'tsa:lən] vt to pay; to pay for
Bezahlung f payment
bezaubern [bə'tsaʊbərn] vt to enchant, to charm
bezeichnen [bə'tsaɪçnən] vt (kennzeichnen) to mark; (nennen) to call; (beschreiben) to describe; (zeigen) to show, to indicate; ~**d** adj: ~**d** (für) characteristic (of), typical (of)
Bezeichnung f (Zeichen) mark, sign;
(Beschreibung) description
Bezichtigung [bə'tsɪçtɪgʊŋ] f accusation
beziehen [bə'tsi:ən] (unreg) vt (mit Überzug) to cover; (Bett) to make;
(Haus, Position) to move into;
(Standpunkt) to take up; (erhalten) to receive; (Zeitung) to subscribe to, to take ♦ vr (Himmel) to cloud over; etw auf jdn/etw ~ to relate sth to sb/sth;
sich ~ auf + akk to refer to
Beziehung f (Verbindung) connection;
(Zusammenhang) relation; (Verhältnis) relationship; (Hinsicht) respect; ~**en haben** (vorteilhaft) to have connections od contacts; **beziehungsweise** adv or;
(genauer gesagt auch) that is, or rather
Bezirk [bə'tsɪrk] (-(e)s, -e) m district
Bezug [bə'tsu:k] (-(e)s, -e) m (Hülle) covering; (COMM) ordering; (Gehalt) income, salary; (Beziehung): ~ (zu) relation(ship) (to); **in b~ auf** +akk with reference to; ~ **nehmen auf** +akk to refer to
bezüglich [bə'tsy:klɪç] präp +gen concerning, referring to ♦ adj (GRAM) relative; **auf etw** akk ~ relating to sth
bezwecken [bə'tsvɛkən] vt to aim at
bezweifeln [bə'tsvaɪfəln] vt to doubt, to query

Bhf. *abk* (= *Bahnhof*) station
Bibel ['biːbəl] (-, -n) *f* Bible
Biber ['biːbər] (-s, -) *m* beaver
Biblio- [biblio] *zW:* ~**graphie** [-gra'fiː] *f* bibliography; ~**thek** [-'teːk] (-, -en) *f* library; ~**thekar(in)** [-te'kaːr(ɪn)] (-s, -e) *m(f)* librarian
biblisch ['biːblɪʃ] *adj* biblical
bieder ['biːdər] *adj* upright, worthy; (*Kleid etc*) plain
bieg- ['biːg] *zW:* ~**en** (*unreg*) *vt, vr* to bend ♦ *vi* to turn; ~**sam** ['biːk-] *adj* flexible; **B~ung** *f* bend, curve
Biene ['biːnə] *f* bee
Bienenhonig *m* honey
Bier [biːr] (-(e)s, -e) *nt* beer; ~**deckel** *m* beer mat; ~**krug** *m* beer mug
bieten ['biːtən] (*unreg*) *vt* to offer; (*bei Versteigerung*) to bid ♦ *vr* (*Gelegenheit*): **sich jdm ~** to present itself to sb; **sich** *dat* **etw ~ lassen** to put up with sth
Bikini [bi'kiːni] (-s, -s) *m* bikini
Bilanz [bi'lants] *f* balance; (*fig*) outcome; ~ **ziehen (aus)** to take stock (of)
Bild [bɪlt] (-(e)s, -er) *nt* (*auch fig*) picture; photo; (*Spiegel~*) reflection; ~**bericht** *m* photographic report
bilden ['bɪldən] *vt* to form; (*erziehen*) to educate; (*ausmachen*) to constitute ♦ *vr* to arise; (*erziehen*) to educate o.s.
Bilderbuch *nt* picture book
Bilderrahmen *m* picture frame
Bild- *zW:* ~**fläche** *f* screen; (*fig*) scene; ~**hauer** (-s, -) *m* sculptor; **b~hübsch** *adj* lovely, pretty as a picture; **b~lich** *adj* figurative; pictorial; ~**schirm** *m* television screen; (*COMPUT*) monitor; **b~schön** *adj* lovely; ~**sichtgerät** *nt* visual display unit, VDU; ~**ung** *f* formation; (*Wissen, Benehmen*) education; ~**ungslücke** *f* gap in one's education; ~**ungspolitik** *f* educational policy
Billard ['bɪljart] (-s, -e) *nt* billiards *sg*; ~**kugel** *f* billiard ball
billig ['bɪlɪç] *adj* cheap; (*gerecht*) fair, reasonable; ~**en** ['bɪlɪgən] *vt* to approve of; **B~laden** (*umg*) *m* discount store; **B~ung** *f* approval
Billion [bɪli'oːn] *f* billion, trillion (*US*)

Binde ['bɪndə] *f* bandage; (*Arm~*) band; (*MED*) sanitary towel; ~**glied** *nt* connecting link; **b~n** (*unreg*) *vt* to bind, to tie; ~**strich** *m* hyphen; ~**wort** *nt* conjunction
Bindfaden *m* string
Bindung *f* bond, tie; (*Ski~*) binding
binnen ['bɪnən] *präp* (+*dat od gen*) within; **B~hafen** *m* river port; **B~handel** *m* internal trade
Binse ['bɪnzə] *f* rush, reed; **Binsenwahrheit** *f* truism
Bio- [bio] *in zW* bio-; ~**graphie** [-gra'fiː] *f* biography; ~**loge** [-'loːgə] (-n, -n) *m* biologist; ~**logie** [-lo'giː] *f* biology; **b~logisch** [-'loːgɪʃ] *adj* biological
Birke ['bɪrkə] *f* birch
Birma ['bɪrma] *nt* Burma
Birnbaum *m* pear tree
Birne ['bɪrnə] *f* pear; (*ELEK*) (light) bulb

| SCHLÜSSELWORT |
---

bis [bɪs] *präp* +*akk, adv* **1** (*zeitlich*) till, until; (*bis spätestens*) by; **Sie haben bis Dienstag Zeit** you have until *od* till Tuesday; **bis Dienstag muß es fertig sein** it must be ready by Tuesday; **bis auf weiteres** until further notice; **bis in die Nacht** into the night; **bis bald/gleich** see you later/soon
2 (*räumlich*) (up) to; **ich fahre bis Köln** I'm going to *od* I'm going as far as Cologne; **bis an unser Grundstück** (right *od* up) to our plot; **bis hierher** this far
3 (*bei Zahlen*) up to; **bis zu** up to
4: **bis auf etw** *akk* (*außer*) except sth; (*einschließlich*) including sth
♦ *konj* **1** (*mit Zahlen*) to; **10 bis 20** 10 to 20
2 (*zeitlich*) till, until; **bis es dunkel wird** till *od* until it gets dark; **von ... bis ... from ... to ...**

Bischof ['bɪʃɔf] (-s, ⁼e) *m* bishop
bischöflich ['bɪʃøːflɪç] *adj* episcopal
bisher [bɪs'heːr] *adv* till now, hitherto; ~**ig** *adj* till now
Biskuit [bɪs'kviːt] (-(e)s, -s *od* -e) *m od nt* (fatless) sponge; ~**teig** *m* sponge

mixture

Biß [bɪs] (-sses, -sse) *m* bite

biß *etc vb siehe* **beißen**

bißchen ['bɪsçən] *adj, adv* bit

Bissen ['bɪsən] (-s, -) *m* bite, morsel

bissig ['bɪsɪç] *adj* (*Hund*) snappy; (*Bemerkung*) cutting, biting

bist [bɪst] *vb siehe* **sein**

bisweilen [bɪs'vaɪlən] *adv* at times, occasionally

Bit [bɪt] *nt* (*COMPUT*) bit

Bitte ['bɪtə] *f* request; **b~** *excl* please; (*wie b~?*) (I beg your) pardon?; (*als Antwort auf Dank*) you're welcome; **darf ich?** -- **aber b~!** may I? — please do; **b~ schön!** it was a pleasure; **b~n** (*unreg*) *vt, vi:* **b~n** (**um**) to ask (for); **b~nd** *adj* pleading, imploring

bitter ['bɪtər] *adj* bitter; **~böse** *adj* very angry; **B~keit** *f* bitterness; **~lich** *adj* bitter

Blähungen ['blɛːʊŋən] *pl* (*MED*) wind *sg*

blamabel [bla'maːbəl] *adj* disgraceful

Blamage [bla'maːʒə] *f* disgrace

blamieren [bla'miːrən] *vr* to make a fool of o.s., to disgrace o.s. ♦ *vt* to let down, to disgrace

blank [blaŋk] *adj* bright; (*unbedeckt*) bare; (*sauber*) clean, polished; (*umg: ohne Geld*) broke; (*offensichtlich*) blatant

blanko ['blaŋko] *adv* blank; **B~scheck** *m* blank cheque

Bläschen ['blɛːsçən] *nt* bubble; (*MED*) (small) blister

Blase ['blaːzə] *f* bubble; (*MED*) blister; (*ANAT*) bladder; **~balg** (-(e)s, -bälge) *m* bellows *pl*; **b~n** (*unreg*) *vt, vi* to blow

Blas- ['blaːs] *zW:* **~instrument** *nt* wind instrument; **~kapelle** *f* brass band; **~musik** *f* brass band music

blaß [blas] *adj* pale

Blässe ['blɛsə] (-) *f* paleness, pallor

Blatt [blat] (-(e)s, ‐er) *nt* leaf; (*von Papier*) sheet; (*Zeitung*) newspaper; (*KARTEN*) hand

blättern ['blɛtərn] *vi:* **in etw** *dat* **~** to leaf through sth

Blätterteig *m* flaky *od* puff pastry

blau [blaʊ] *adj* blue; (*umg*) drunk, stoned; (*KOCH*) boiled; (*Auge*) black; **~er Fleck** bruise; **Fahrt ins B~e** mystery tour; **~äugig** *adj* blue-eyed; **B~licht** *nt* flashing blue light; **~machen** (*umg*) *vi* to skive off work

Blech [blɛç] (-(e)s, -e) *nt* tin, sheet metal; (*Back~*) baking tray; **~büchse** *f* tin, can; **~dose** *f* tin, can; **b~en** (*umg*) *vt, vi* to fork out; **~schaden** *m* (*AUT*) damage to bodywork

Blei [blaɪ] (-(e)s, -e) *nt* lead

Bleibe ['blaɪbə] *f* roof over one's head; **b~n** (*unreg*) *vi* to stay, to remain; **b~nlassen** (*unreg*) *vt* to leave (alone)

bleich [blaɪç] *adj* faded, pale; **~en** *vt* to bleach

Blei- *zW:* **b~ern** *adj* leaden; **b~frei** *adj* (*Benzin*) lead-free; **~stift** *m* pencil; **~stiftspitzer** *m* pencil sharpener

Blende ['blɛndə] *f* (*PHOT*) aperture; **b~n** *vt* to blind, to dazzle; (*fig*) to hoodwink; **b~nd** (*umg*) *adj* grand; **b~nd aussehen** to look smashing

Blick [blɪk] (-(e)s, -e) *m* (*kurz*) glance, glimpse; (*Anschauen*) look; (*Aussicht*) view; **b~en** *vi* to look; **sich b~en lassen** to put in an appearance; **~fang** *m* eye-catcher; **~feld** *nt* (*auch fig*) range of vision

blieb *etc* [bliːp] *vb siehe* **bleiben**

blind [blɪnt] *adj* blind; (*Glas etc*) dull; **~er Passagier** stowaway; **B~darm** *m* appendix; **B~darmentzündung** *f* appendicitis; **B~enschrift** ['blɪndən-] *f* braille; **B~heit** *f* blindness; **~lings** *adv* blindly; **B~schleiche** *f* slow worm

blinken ['blɪŋkən] *vi* to twinkle, to sparkle; (*Licht*) to flash, to signal; (*AUT*) to indicate ♦ *vt* to flash, to signal

Blinker (-s, -) *m* (*AUT*) indicator

blinzeln ['blɪntsəln] *vi* to blink, to wink

Blitz [blɪts] (-es, -e) *m* (flash of) lightning; **~ableiter** *m* lightning conductor; **b~en** *vi* (*aufleuchten*) to flash, to sparkle; **es b~t** (*MET*) there's a flash of lightning; **~licht** *nt* flashlight; **b~schnell** *adj* lightning ♦ *adv* (as) quick as a flash

Block [blɔk] (-(e)s, ‐e) *m* block; (*von*

Papier) pad; **Blockade** [blɔˈkaːdə] *f* blockade; **~flöte** *f* recorder; **b~frei** *adj* (*POL*) unaligned; **b~ieren** [blɔˈkiːrən] *vt* to block ♦ *vi* (*Räder*) to jam; **~schrift** *f* block letters *pl*
blöd [bløːt] *adj* silly, stupid; **B~sinn** *m* nonsense; **~sinnig** *adj* silly, idiotic
blond [blɔnt] *adj* blond, fair-haired

SCHLÜSSELWORT

bloß [bloːs] *adj* **1** (*unbedeckt*) bare; (*nackt*) naked; **mit der bloßen Hand** with one's bare hand; **mit bloßem Auge** with the naked eye
2 (*alleinig,. nur*) mere; **der bloße Gedanke** the very thought; **bloßer Neid** sheer envy
♦ *adv* only, merely; **laß das bloß!** just don't do that!; **wie ist das bloß passiert?** how on earth did that happen?

Blöße [ˈbløːsə] *f* bareness; nakedness; (*fig*) weakness
bloßlegen *vt* to expose
bloßstellen *vt* to show up
blühen [ˈblyːən] *vi* to bloom (*lit*), to be in bloom; (*fig*) to flourish
Blume [ˈbluːmə] *f* flower; (*von Wein*) bouquet; **Blumenkohl** *m* cauliflower; **Blumentopf** *m* flowerpot; **Blumenzwiebel** *f* bulb
Bluse [ˈbluːzə] *f* blouse
Blut [bluːt] (-(e)s) *nt* blood; **b~arm** *adj* anaemic; (*fig*) penniless; **b~befleckt** *adj* bloodstained; **~druck** *m* blood pressure
Blüte [ˈblyːtə] *f* blossom; (*fig*) prime
Blutegel *m* leech
bluten *vi* to bleed
Blütenstaub *m* pollen
Bluter *m* (*MED*) haemophiliac
Bluterguß *m* haemorrhage; (*auf Haut*) bruise
Blütezeit *f* flowering period; (*fig*) prime
Blut- *zW*: **~gruppe** *f* blood group; **b~ig** *adj* bloody; **b~jung** *adj* very young; **~probe** *f* blood test; **~spender** *m* blood donor; **~übertragung** *f* blood transfu-

sion; **~ung** *f* bleeding, haemorrhage; **~vergiftung** *f* blood poisoning; **~wurst** *f* black pudding
Bö [bøː] (-, -en) *f* squall
Bock [bɔk] (-(e)s, ⁼e) *m* buck, ram; (*Gestell*) trestle, support; (*SPORT*) buck; **~wurst** *f* type of pork sausage
Boden [ˈboːdən] (-s, ⁼) *m* ground; (*Fuß~*) floor; (*Meeres~, Faß~*) bottom; (*Speicher*) attic; **b~los** *adj* bottomless; (*umg*) incredible; **~schätze** *pl* mineral resources; **~see** *m*: **der ~see** Lake Constance; **~turnen** *nt* floor exercises *pl*
Böe [ˈbøːə] *f* squall
Bogen [ˈboːgən] (-s, -) *m* (*Biegung*) curve; (*ARCHIT*) arch; (*Waffe, MUS*) bow; (*Papier*) sheet; **~gang** *m* arcade
Bohle [ˈboːlə] *f* plank
Bohne [ˈboːnə] *f* bean; **Bohnenkaffee** *m* pure coffee
bohnern *vt* to wax, to polish
Bohnerwachs *nt* floor polish
Bohr- [boːr] *zW*: **b~en** *vt* to bore; **~er** (-s, -) *m* drill; **~insel** *f* oil rig; **~maschine** *f* drill; **~turm** *m* derrick
Boje [ˈboːjə] *f* buoy
Bolivien [boˈliːviən] *nt* Bolivia
Bolzen [ˈbɔltsən] (-s, -) *m* bolt
bombardieren [bɔmbarˈdiːrən] *vt* to bombard; (*aus der Luft*) to bomb
Bombe [ˈbɔmbə] *f* bomb
Bombenangriff *m* bombing raid
Bombenerfolg (*umg*) *m* smash hit
Bonbon [bõˈbõ] (-s, -s) *m od nt* sweet
Boot [boːt] (-(e)s, -e) *nt* boat
Bord [bɔrt] (-(e)s, -e) *m* (*AVIAT, NAUT*) board ♦ *nt* (*Brett*) shelf; **an ~** on board
Bordell [bɔrˈdɛl] (-s, -e) *nt* brothel
Bordstein *m* kerb(stone)
borgen [ˈbɔrgən] *vt* to borrow; **jdm etw ~** to lend sb sth
borniert [bɔrˈniːrt] *adj* narrow-minded
Börse [ˈbøːrzə] *f* stock exchange; (*Geld~*) purse
Borste [ˈbɔrstə] *f* bristle
Borte [ˈbɔrtə] *f* edging; (*Band*) trimming
bös [bøːs] *adj* = böse
bösartig [ˈbøːs-] *adj* malicious

Böschung ['bœʃʊŋ] f slope; (*Ufer~ etc*) embankment

böse ['bø:zə] *adj* bad, evil; (*zornig*) angry

boshaft ['bo:shaft] *adj* malicious, spiteful

Bosheit f malice, spite

böswillig ['bø:svɪlɪç] *adj* malicious

bot *etc* [bo:t] *vb siehe* **bieten**

Botanik [bo'ta:nɪk] f botany

botanisch [bo'ta:nɪʃ] *adj* botanical

Bot- ['bo:t] *zW*: ~**e** (-**n**, -**n**) *m* messenger; ~**schaft** f message, news; (*POL*) embassy; ~**schafter** (-**s**, -) *m* ambassador

Bottich ['bɔtɪç] (-(**e**)**s**, -**e**) *m* vat, tub

Bouillon [bʊl'jõ:] (-, -**s**) f consommé

Bowle ['bo:lə] f punch

Box- ['bɔks] *zW*: **b~en** *vi* to box; ~**er** (-**s**, -) *m* boxer; ~**handschuh** *m* boxing glove; ~**kampf** *m* boxing match

boykottieren [bɔykɔ'ti:rən] *vt* to boycott

brach *etc* [bra:x] *vb siehe* **brechen**

brachte *etc* ['braxtə] *vb siehe* **bringen**

Branche ['brã:ʃə] f line of business; **Branchenverzeichnis** *nt* yellow pages *pl*

Brand [brant] (-(**e**)**s**, -**e**) *m* fire; (*MED*) gangrene; **b~en** ['brandən] *vi* to surge; (*Meer*) to break; **b~marken** *vt* to brand; (*fig*) to stigmatize; ~**salbe** f ointment for burns; ~**stifter** *m* arsonist, fire-raiser; ~**stiftung** f arson; ~**ung** f surf; ~**wunde** f burn

Branntwein ['brantvaɪn] *m* brandy

Brasil- [bra'zi:l] *zW*: ~**ien** [-iən] *nt* Brazil; ~**ianer(in)** [-i'a:nər(ɪn)] *m(f)* Brazilian; **b~ianisch** *adj* Brazilian

Brat- ['bra:t] *zW*: ~**apfel** *m* baked apple; **b~en** (*unreg*) *vt* to roast; to fry; ~**en** (-**s**, -**e**) *m* roast, joint; ~**hähnchen** *nt* roast chicken; ~**huhn** *nt* roast chicken; ~**kartoffeln** *pl* fried *od* roast potatoes; ~**pfanne** f frying pan

Bratsche ['bra:tʃə] f viola

Bratspieß *m* spit

Bratwurst f grilled/fried sausage

Brauch [braʊx] (-(**e**)**s**, **Bräuche**) *m* custom; **b~bar** *adj* usable, serviceable; (*Person*) capable; **b~en** *vt* (*bedürfen*) to need; (*müssen*) to have to; (*inf:*

verwenden) to use

Braue ['braʊə] f brow

brauen *vt* to brew

Braue'rei f brewery

braun [braʊn] *adj* brown; (*von Sonne auch*) tanned

Bräune ['brɔʏnə] (-) f brownness; (*Sonnen~*) tan; **b~n** *vt* to make brown; (*Sonne*) to tan

braungebrannt *adj* tanned

Brause ['braʊzə] f shower bath; (*von Gießkanne*) rose; (*Getränk*) lemonade; **b~n** *vi* to roar; (*auch vr:* duschen) to take a shower

Braut [braʊt] (-, **Bräute**) f bride; (*Verlobte*) fiancée

Bräutigam ['brɔʏtɪgam] (-**s**, -**e**) *m* bridegroom; fiancé

Brautpaar *nt* bride and (bride)groom, bridal pair

brav [bra:f] *adj* (*artig*) good; (*ehrenhaft*) worthy, honest

bravo ['bra:vo] *excl* well done

BRD [be:'ʔɛr'de:] (-) f *abk* = **Bundesrepublik Deutschland**

Brech- ['brɛç] *zW*: ~**eisen** *nt* crowbar; **b~en** (*unreg*) *vt*, *vi* to break; (*Licht*) to refract; (*fig: Mensch*) to crush; (*speien*) to vomit; ~**reiz** *m* nausea, retching

Brei [braɪ] (-(**e**)**s**, -**e**) *m* (*Masse*) pulp; (*KOCH*) gruel; (*Hafer~*) porridge

breit [braɪt] *adj* wide, broad; **B~e** f width; (*esp bei Maßangaben*) breadth; (*GEOG*) latitude; ~**en** *vt*: etw über etw *akk* ~**en** to spread sth over sth; **B~engrad** *m* degree of latitude; ~**machen** *vr* to spread o.s. out; ~**treten** (*unreg; umg*) *vt* to go on about

Brems- ['brɛms] *zW*: ~**belag** *m* brake lining; ~**e** [-zə] f brake; (*ZOOL*) horsefly; **b~en** [-zən] *vi* to brake ♦ *vt* (*Auto*) to brake; (*fig*) to slow down; ~**licht** *nt* brake light; ~**pedal** *nt* brake pedal; ~**spur** f skid mark(s *pl*); ~**weg** *m* braking distance

Brenn- ['brɛn] *zW*: **b~bar** *adj* inflammable; **b~en** (*unreg*) *vi* to burn, to be on fire; (*Licht, Kerze etc*) to burn ♦ *vt* (*Holz etc*) to burn; (*Ziegel, Ton*) to

fire; (*Kaffee*) to roast; **darauf b~en,
etw zu tun** to be dying to do sth;
~(n)essel *f* stinging nettle; **~spiritus** *m*
methylated spirits; **~stoff** *m* fuel
brenzlig ['brɛntslıç] *adj* (*fig*) precarious
Brett [brɛt] (-(e)s, -er) *nt* board, plank;
(*Bord*) shelf; (*Spiel~*) board; **~er** *pl*
(*SKI*) skis; (*THEAT*) boards;
Schwarze(s) ~ notice board; **~erzaun**
m wooden fence
Brezel ['breːtsəl] (-, -n) *f* pretzel
brichst *etc* ['brıçst] *vb siehe* **brechen**
Brief [briːf] (-(e)s, -e) *m* letter; **~freund**
m penfriend; **~kasten** *m* letterbox;
~kopf *m* letterhead; **b~lich** *adj, adv*
by letter; **~marke** *f* (postage) stamp;
~öffner *m* letter opener; **~papier** *nt*
notepaper; **~tasche** *f* wallet; **~träger**
m postman; **~umschlag** *m* envelope;
~wechsel *m* correspondence
briet *etc* [briːt] *vb siehe* **braten**
Brikett [bri'kɛt] (-s, -s) *nt* briquette
brillant [bril'jant] *adj* (*fig*) brilliant; **B~**
(-en, -en) *m* brilliant, diamond
Brille ['brılə] *f* spectacles *pl*; (*Schutz~*)
goggles *pl*; (*Toiletten~*) (toilet) seat
bringen ['brıŋən] (*unreg*) *vt* to bring;
(*mitnehmen, begleiten*) to take; (*einbringen*: *Profit*) to bring in; (*veröffentlichen*) to publish; (*THEAT, CINE*)
to show; (*RADIO, TV*) to broadcast; (*in
einen Zustand versetzen*) to get; (*umg*:
tun können) to manage; **jdn dazu ~,
etw zu tun** to make sb do sth; **jdn nach
Hause ~** to take sb home; **jdn um etw
~** to make sb lose sth; **jdn auf eine
Idee ~** to give sb an idea
Brise ['briːzə] *f* breeze
Brit- ['briːt] *zW*: **~e** *m* Briton; **~in** *f*
Briton; **b~isch** *adj* British
bröckelig ['brœkəlıç] *adj* crumbly
Brocken ['brɔkən] (-s, -) *m* piece, bit;
(*Fels~*) lump of rock
brodeln ['broːdəln] *vi* to bubble
Brokat [bro'kaːt] (-(e)s, -e) *m* brocade
Brombeere ['brɔmbeːrə] *f* blackberry,
bramble (*BRIT*)
Bronchien ['brɔnçiən] *pl* bronchia(l
tubes) *pl*
Bronze ['brõːsə] *f* bronze

Brosche ['brɔʃə] *f* brooch
Broschüre [brɔ'ʃyːrə] *f* pamphlet
Brot [broːt] (-(e)s, -e) *nt* bread; (*Laib*)
loaf
Brötchen ['brøːtçən] *nt* roll
Bruch [brʊx] (-(e)s, ⁻e) *m* breakage;
(*zerbrochene Stelle*) break; (*fig*) split,
breach; (*MED*: *Eingeweide~*) rupture,
hernia; (*Bein~ etc*) fracture; (*MATH*)
fraction
brüchig ['brʊçıç] *adj* brittle, fragile;
(*Haus*) dilapidated
Bruch- *zW*: **~landung** *f* crash landing;
~strich *m* (*MATH*) line; **~stück** *nt* fragment; **~teil** *m* fraction
Brücke ['brʊkə] *f* bridge; (*Teppich*) rug
Bruder ['bruːdər] (-s, ⁻) *m* brother
brüderlich ['bryːdərlıç] *adj* brotherly
Brühe ['bryːə] *f* broth, stock; (*pej*)
muck
brüllen ['brʊlən] *vi* to bellow, to roar
brummen ['brʊmən] *vi* (*Bär, Mensch
etc*) to growl; (*Insekt*) to buzz; (*Moto-
ren*) to roar; (*murren*) to grumble ♦ *vt*
to growl
brünett [bry'nɛt] *adj* brunette, dark-
haired
Brunnen ['brʊnən] (-s, -) *m* fountain;
(*tief*) well; (*natürlich*) spring
brüsk [brʏsk] *adj* abrupt, brusque
Brüssel ['brʏsəl] *nt* Brussels
Brust [brʊst] (-, ⁻e) *f* breast; (*Männer~*)
chest
brüsten ['brʏstən] *vr* to boast
Brust- *zW*: **~fellentzündung** *f* pleurisy;
~kasten *m* chest; **~schwimmen** *nt*
breast-stroke
Brüstung ['brʏstʊŋ] *f* parapet
Brustwarze *f* nipple
Brut [bruːt] (-, -en) *f* brood; (*Brüten*)
hatching
brutal [bru'taːl] *adj* brutal; **B~i'tät** *f*
brutality
brüten ['bryːtən] *vi* (*auch fig*) to brood
Brutkasten *m* incubator
brutto ['brʊto] *adv* gross;
B~einkommen *nt* gross salary;
B~gehalt *nt* gross salary; **B~gewicht**
nt gross weight; **B~lohn** *m* gross
wages *pl*

Bube ['bu:bə] (-n, -n) m (*Schurke*) rogue; (*KARTEN*) jack

Buch [bu:x] (-(e)s, ̈-er) nt book; (*COMM*) account book; ~**binder** m bookbinder; ~**drucker** m printer

Buche f beech tree

buchen vt to book; (*Betrag*) to enter

Bücher- ['by:çər] zW: ~**brett** nt bookshelf; ~**ei** [-'raɪ] f library; ~**regal** nt bookshelves pl, bookcase; ~**schrank** m bookcase

Buch- zW: ~**fink** m chaffinch; ~**führung** f book-keeping, accounting; ~**halter(in)** (-s, -) m(f) book-keeper; ~**handel** m book trade; ~**händler(in)** m(f) bookseller; ~**handlung** f bookshop

Büchse ['byksə] f tin, can; (*Holz~*) box; (*Gewehr*) rifle; **Büchsenfleisch** nt tinned meat; **Büchsenöffner** m tin od can opener

Buch- zW: ~**stabe** ['bu:xʃta:bə] (-ns, -n) m letter (of the alphabet); **b~stabieren** [bu:xʃta'bi:rən] vt to spell; **b~stäblich** ['bu:xʃtɛːplıç] adj literal

Bucht ['buxt] (-, -en) f bay

Buchung ['bu:xʊŋ] f booking; (*COMM*) entry

Buckel ['bʊkəl] (-s, -) m hump

bücken ['bykən] vr to bend

Bückling ['byklıŋ] m (*Fisch*) kipper; (*Verbeugung*) bow

Bude ['bu:də] f booth, stall; (*umg*) digs pl (*BRIT*)

Büfett [by'fe:] (-s, -s) nt (*Anrichte*) sideboard; (*Geschirrschrank*) dresser; **kaltes** ~ cold buffet

Büffel ['byfəl] (-s, -) m buffalo

Bug [bu:k] (-(e)s, -e) m (*NAUT*) bow; (*AVIAT*) nose

Bügel ['by:gəl] (-s, -) m (*Kleider~*) hanger; (*Steig~*) stirrup; (*Brillen~*) arm; ~**brett** nt ironing board; ~**eisen** nt iron; ~**falte** f crease; **b~n** vt, vi to iron

Bühne ['by:nə] f stage; **Bühnenbild** nt set, scenery

Buhruf ['bu:ru:f] m boo

buk etc [bu:k] vb siehe **backen**

Bulgarien [bʊl'ga:riən] nt Bulgaria

Bull- ['bʊl] zW: ~**dogge** f bulldog; ~**dozer** ['bʊldo:zər] (-s, -) m bulldozer; ~**e** (-n, -n) m bull

Bummel ['bʊməl] (-s, -) m stroll; (*Schaufenster~*) window-shopping; ~**ant** [-'lant] m slowcoach; ~**ei** [-'laɪ] f wandering; dawdling; skiving; **b~n** vi to wander, to stroll; (*trödeln*) to dawdle; (*faulenzen*) to skive, to loaf around; ~**streik** m go-slow; ~**zug** m slow train

Bund¹ [bʊnt] (-(e)s, ̈-e) m (*Freundschafts~ etc*) bond; (*Organisation*) union; (*POL*) confederacy; (*Hosen~, Rock~*) waistband

Bund² (-(e)s, -e) nt bunch; (*Stroh~*) bundle

Bündel ['byndəl] (-s, -) nt bundle, bale; **b~n** vt to bundle

Bundes- ['bʊndəs] in zW Federal (*bes West German*); ~**bahn** f Federal Railways pl; ~**hauptstadt** f Federal capital; ~**kanzler** m Federal Chancellor; ~**land** nt Land; ~**liga** f football league; ~**präsident** m Federal President; ~**rat** m upper house of West German Parliament; ~**republik** f Federal Republic (of West Germany); ~**staat** m Federal state; ~**tag** m West German Parliament; ~**verfassungsgericht** nt Federal Constitutional Court; ~**wehr** f West German Armed Forces pl

bündig adj (*kurz*) concise

Bündnis (-ses, -se) nt alliance

Bunker ['bʊŋkər] (-s, -) m bunker

bunt [bʊnt] adj coloured; (*gemischt*) mixed; **jdm wird es zu** ~ it's getting too much for sb; **B~stift** m coloured pencil, crayon

Burg [bʊrk] (-, -en) f castle, fort

Bürge ['byrgə] (-n, -n) m guarantor; **b~n** vi: **b~n für** to vouch for

Bürger(in) ['byrgər(ın)] (-s, -) m(f) citizen; member of the middle class; ~**krieg** m civil war; **b~lich** adj (*Rechte*) civil; (*Klasse*) middle-class; (*pej*) bourgeois; ~**meister** m mayor; ~**recht** nt civil rights pl; ~**schaft** f population, citizens pl; ~**steig** m pavement; ~**tum** nt citizens pl

Bürgschaft f surety; ~ **leisten** to give security

Büro [by'ro:] (-s, -s) nt office; ~**angestellte(r)** mf office worker; ~**automatisierung** f office automation; ~**klammer** f paper clip; ~**krat** [byro'kra:t] (-en, -en) m bureaucrat; ~**kra'tie** f bureaucracy; **b~'kratisch** adj bureaucratic; ~**schluß** m office closing time

Bursch (-en, -en) m = **Bursche**

Bursche ['burʃə] (-n, -n) m lad, fellow; (Diener) servant

Bürste ['byrstə] f brush; **b~n** vt to brush

Bus [bus] (-ses, -se) m bus

Busch [buʃ] (-(e)s, ːe) m bush, shrub

Büschel ['byʃəl] (-s, -) nt tuft

buschig adj bushy

Busen ['bu:zən] (-s, -) m bosom; (Meer~) inlet, bay

Buße ['bu:sə] f atonement, penance; (Geld) fine

büßen ['by:sən] vi to do penance, to atone ♦ vt to do penance for, to atone for

Bußgeld ['bu:sgɛlt] nt fine

Büste ['bystə] f bust; **Büstenhalter** m bra

Butter ['butər] (-) f butter; ~**blume** f buttercup; ~**brot** nt (piece of) bread and butter; (umg) sandwich; ~**brotpapier** nt greaseproof paper; ~**dose** f butter dish; **b~weich** adj soft as butter; (fig, umg) soft

b.w. abk (= bitte wenden) p.t.o.

Byte [bait] (-s) nt byte

bzgl. abk (= bezüglich) re

bzw. abk = beziehungsweise

C

(siehe auch **K**, **Z**; für **CH** siehe auch **SCH**)

ca. abk (= circa) approx.

Café [ka'fe:] (-s, -s) nt café

Cafeteria [kafete'ri:a] (-, -s) f cafeteria

Camp- ['kɛmp] zW: **c~en** vi to camp;

~**er(in)** (-s, -) m(f) camper; ~**ing** (-s) nt camping; ~**ingkocher** m camping stove; ~**ingplatz** m camp(ing) site

CDU [tse:de:'u:] (-) f abk (= Christlich-Demokratische Union) Christian Democratic Union

Cellist [tʃɛ'lɪst] m cellist

Cello ['tʃɛlo] (-s, -s od Celli) nt cello

Chamäleon [ka'mɛ:leɔn] (-s, -s) nt chameleon

Champagner [ʃam'panjər] (-s, -) m champagne

Champignon ['ʃampɪnjõ] (-s, -s) m button mushroom

Chance ['ʃã:s(ə)] f chance, opportunity

Chaos ['ka:ɔs] (-, -) nt chaos

chaotisch [ka'o:tɪʃ] adj chaotic

Charakter [ka'raktər, pl karak'te:rə] (-s, -e) m character; **c~fest** adj of firm character, strong; **c~i'sieren** vt to characterize; **c~istisch** [karakte'rɪstɪʃ] adj: **c~istisch (für)** characteristic (of), typical (of); **c~los** adj unprincipled; ~**losigkeit** f lack of principle; ~**schwäche** f weakness of character; ~**stärke** f strength of character; ~**zug** m characteristic, trait

charmant [ʃar'mant] adj charming

Charme [ʃarm] (-s) m charm

Charterflug ['(t)ʃa:rtərflu:k] m charter flight

Chassis [ʃa'si:] (-, -) nt chassis

Chauffeur [ʃɔ'fø:r] m chauffeur

Chauvinist [ʃovi'nɪst] m chauvinist, jingoist

Chef [ʃɛf] (-s, -s) m head; (umg) boss; ~**arzt** m senior consultant; ~**in** (umg) f boss

Chemie [çe'mi:] (-) f chemistry; ~**faser** f man-made fibre

Chemikalie [çemi'ka:liə] f chemical

Chemiker(in) ['çe:mikər(ɪn)] (-s, -) m(f) (industrial) chemist

chemisch ['çe:mɪʃ] adj chemical; ~**e Reinigung** dry cleaning

Chiffre ['ʃɪfrə] f (Geheimzeichen) cipher; (in Zeitung) box number

Chile ['çi:le, 'tʃi:le] nt Chile; ~**ne** [-'le:nə] m Chilean; ~**nin** f Chilean; **c~nisch** adj Chilean

Chin- [ˈçiːn] *zW*: ~**a** *nt* China; ~**ese** [-ˈneːzə] *m* Chinese; ~**esin** *f* Chinese; **c~esisch** *adj* Chinese
Chips [tʃɪps] *pl* crisps, chips (*US*)
Chirurg [çiˈrʊrk] (**-en, -en**) *m* surgeon; ~**ie** [-ˈgiː] *f* surgery; **c~isch** *adj* surgical
Chlor [kloːr] (**-s**) *nt* chlorine; ~**o'form** (**-s**) *nt* chloroform
Cholera [ˈkoːlera] (**-**) *f* cholera
cholerisch [koˈleːrɪʃ] *adj* choleric
Chor [koːr] (**-(e)s, ⁼e**) *m* choir; (*Musik-stück, THEAT*) chorus; ~**al** [koˈraːl] (**-s, -äle**) *m* chorale
Choreograph [koreoˈgraːf] (**-en, -en**) *m* choreographer; ~**ie** [-ˈfiː] *f* choreography
Chorknabe *m* choirboy
Christ [krɪst] (**-en, -en**) *m* Christian; ~**baum** *m* Christmas tree; ~**entum** *nt* Christianity; ~**in** *f* Christian; ~**kind** *nt* ≈ Father Christmas; (*Jesus*) baby Jesus; **c~lich** *adj* Christian; ~**us** (**-**) *m* Christ
Chrom [kroːm] (**-s**) *nt* (*CHEM*) chromium; chrome
Chron- [ˈkroːn] *zW*: ~**ik** *f* chronicle; **c~isch** *adj* chronic; **c~ologisch** [-oˈloːgɪʃ] *adj* chronological
Chrysantheme [kryzanˈteːmə] *f* chrysanthemum
circa [ˈtsɪrka] *adv* about, approximately
Clown [klaʊn] (**-s, -s**) *m* clown
cm *abk* = **Zentimeter**
COBOL [ˈkoːbɔl] *nt* (*COMPUT*) COBOL
Cola [ˈkoːla] (**-, -s**) *f* Coke (®)
Computer [kɔmˈpjuːtər] (**-s, -**) *m* computer
Conférencier [kõferãsiˈeː] (**-s, -s**) *m* compère
Coupé [kuˈpeː] (**-s, -s**) *nt* (*AUT*) coupé, sports version
Coupon [kuˈpõː] (**-s, -s**) *m* coupon; (*Stoff~*) length of cloth
Cousin [kuˈzɛ̃ː] (**-s, -s**) *m* cousin; ~**e** [kuˈziːnə] *f* cousin
Creme [krɛːm] (**-, -s**) *f* cream; (*Schuh~*) polish; (*Zahn~*) paste; (*KOCH*) mousse; **c~farben** *adj* cream(-coloured)
CSU [tseːˈʔɛsˈʔuː] (**-**) *f abk* (= *Christlich-*

Soziale Union) Christian Social Union
Curry [ˈkœri] (**-s**) *m od nt* curry powder; ~**pulver** *nt* curry powder
Cursor [ˈkœrsər] *m* cursor
Cutter(in) [ˈkatər(ɪn)] (**-s, -**) *m(f)* (*CINE*) editor

D

da [daː] *adv* **1** (*örtlich*) there; (*hier*) here; **da draußen** out there; **da bin ich** here I am; **da, wo** where; **ist noch Milch da?** is there any milk left?
2 (*zeitlich*) then; (*folglich*) so
3: **da haben wir Glück gehabt** we were lucky there; **da kann man nichts machen** nothing can be done about it
♦ *konj* (*weil*) as, since

dabehalten (*unreg*) *vt* to keep
dabei [daˈbaɪ] *adv* (*räumlich*) close to it; (*noch dazu*) besides; (*zusammen mit*) with them; (*zeitlich*) during this; (*obwohl doch*) but, however; **was ist schon ~?** what of it?; **es ist doch nichts ~, wenn ...** it doesn't matter if ...; **bleiben wir ~** let's leave it at that; **es bleibt ~** that's settled; **das Dumme/Schwierige ~** the stupid/difficult part of it; **er war gerade ~, zu gehen** he was just leaving; ~**sein** (*unreg*) *vi* (*anwesend*) to be present; (*beteiligt*) to be involved; ~**stehen** (*unreg*) *vi* to stand around
Dach [dax] (**-(e)s, ⁼er**) *nt* roof; ~**boden** *m* attic, loft; ~**decker** (**-s, -**) *m* slater, tiler; ~**fenster** *nt* skylight; ~**luke** *f* skylight; ~**pappe** *f* roofing felt; ~**rinne** *f* gutter
Dachs [daks] (**-es, -e**) *m* badger
dachte *etc* [ˈdaxtə] *vb siehe* **denken**
Dachziegel *m* roof tile
Dackel [ˈdakəl] (**-s, -**) *m* dachshund
dadurch [daˈdʊrç] *adv* (*räumlich*) through it; (*durch diesen Umstand*) thereby, in that way; (*deshalb*) because of that, for that reason ♦ *konj*: ~, **daß**

because

dafür [da'fy:r] *adv* for it; (*anstatt*) instead; **er kann nichts ~** he can't help it; **er ist bekannt ~** he is well-known for that; **was bekomme ich ~?** what will I get for it?

dagegen [da'ge:gən] *adv* against it; (*im Vergleich damit*) in comparison with it; (*bei Tausch*) for it/them ♦ *konj* however; **ich habe nichts ~** I don't mind; **ich war ~** I was against it; **~ kann man nichts tun** one can't do anything about it; **~halten** (*unreg*) *vt* (*vergleichen*) to compare with it; (*entgegnen*) to object to it

daheim [da'haɪm] *adv* at home; **D~** (**-s**) *nt* home

daher [da'he:r] *adv* (*räumlich*) from there; (*Ursache*) from that ♦ *konj* (*deshalb*) that's why

dahin [da'hɪn] *adv* (*räumlich*) there; (*zeitlich*) then; (*vergangen*) gone; **~gegen** *konj* on the other hand; **~gehend** *adv* on this matter; **~gestellt** *adv*: **~gestellt bleiben** to remain to be seen; **~gestellt sein lassen** to leave open *od* undecided

dahinten [da'hɪntən] *adv* over there

dahinter [da'hɪntər] *adv* behind it; **~kommen** (*unreg*) *vi* to get to the bottom of it

Dahlie ['da:liə] *f* dahlia

dalli ['dali] (*umg*) *adv* chop chop

damalig ['da:ma:lɪç] *adj* of that time, then

damals ['da:ma:ls] *adv* at that time, then

Damast [da'mast] (**-(e)s, -e**) *m* damask

Dame ['da:mə] *f* lady; (*SCHACH, KARTEN*) queen; (*Spiel*) draughts *sg*; **damenhaft** *adj* ladylike; **Damenwahl** *f* ladies' excuse-me

damit [da'mɪt] *adv* with it; (*begründend*) by that ♦ *konj* in order that, in order to; **was meint er ~?** what does he mean by that?; **genug ~!** that's enough!; **~ eilt es nicht** there's no hurry

dämlich ['dɛ:mlɪç] (*umg*) *adj* silly, stupid

Damm [dam] (**-(e)s, ꞊e**) *m* dyke; (*Stau~*) dam; (*Hafen~*) mole; (*Bahn~, Straßen~*) embankment

dämmen ['dɛmən] *vt* (*Wasser*) to dam up; (*Schmerzen*) to keep back

dämmer- *zW*: **~ig** *adj* dim, faint; **~n** *vi* (*Tag*) to dawn; (*Abend*) to fall; **D~ung** *f* twilight; (*Morgen~*) dawn; (*Abend~*) dusk

dämonisch [dɛ'mo:nɪʃ] *adj* demoniacal

Dampf [dampf] (**-(e)s, ꞊e**) *m* steam; (*Dunst*) vapour; **d~en** *vi* to steam

dämpfen ['dɛmpfən] *vt* (*KOCH*) to steam; (*bügeln*) to iron with a damp cloth; (*fig*) to dampen, to subdue

Dampf- *zW*: **~er** (**-s, -**) *m* steamer; **~kochtopf** *m* pressure cooker; **~schiff** *nt* steamship; **~walze** *f* steamroller

danach [da'na:x] *adv* after that; (*zeitlich*) after that, afterwards; (*gemäß*) according to; according to which; according to that; **er sieht ~ aus** he looks it

Däne (**-n, -n**) *m* Dane

daneben [da'ne:bən] *adv* beside it; (*im Vergleich*) in comparison; **~benehmen** (*unreg*) *vr* to misbehave; **~gehen** (*unreg*) *vi* to miss; (*Plan*) to fail

Dän- ['dɛ:n] *zW*: **~emark** *nt* Denmark; **~in** *f* Dane; **d~isch** *adj* Danish

Dank [daŋk] (**-(e)s**) *m* thanks *pl*; **d~** *präp* (+*dat od gen*) thanks to; **vielen** *od* **schönen ~** many thanks; **jdm ~ sagen** to thank sb; **d~bar** *adj* grateful; (*Aufgabe*) rewarding; **~barkeit** *f* gratitude; **d~e** *excl* thank you, thanks; **d~en** *vi* +*dat* to thank; **d~enswert** *adj* (*Arbeit*) worthwhile; rewarding; (*Bemühung*) kind; **d~sagen** *vi* to express one's thanks

dann [dan] *adv* then; **~ und wann** now and then

daran [da'ran] *adv* on it; (*stoßen*) against it; **es liegt ~, daß ...** the cause of it is that ...; **gut/schlecht ~ sein** to be well-/badly off; **das Beste/Dümmste ~** the best/stupidest thing about it; **ich war nahe ~, zu ...** I was on the point of ...; **er ist ~ gestorben** he died from it *od* of it; **~gehen** (*unreg*) *vi* to start;

~setzen vt to stake; **er hat alles ~gesetzt, von Glasgow wegzukommen** he has done his utmost to get away from Glasgow

darauf [da'rauf] adv (*räumlich*) on it; (*zielgerichtet*) towards it; (*danach*) afterwards; **es kommt ganz ~ an, ob ...** it depends whether ...; **die Tage ~** the days following od thereafter; **am Tag ~** the next day; **~folgend** adj (*Tag, Jahr*) next, following; **~legen** vt to lay od put on top

daraus [da'raus] adv from it; **was ist ~ geworden?** what became of it?; **~ geht hervor, daß ...** this means that ...

Darbietung ['da:rbi:tuŋ] f performance

darf etc [darf] vb siehe **dürfen**

darin [da'rɪn] adv in (there), in it

Dar- ['da:r] zW: **d~legen** vt to explain, to expound, to set forth; **~legung** f explanation; **~leh(e)n** (-s, -) nt loan

Darm [darm] (-(e)s, ˥e) m intestine; (*Wurst~*) skin; **~saite** f gut string

Darstell- ['da:rʃtɛl] zW: **d~en** vt (*abbilden, bedeuten*) to represent; (*THEAT*) to act; (*beschreiben*) to describe ♦ vr to appear to be; **~er(in)** (-s, -) m(f) actor(actress); **~ung** f portrayal, depiction

darüber [da'ry:bər] adv (*räumlich*) over it, above it; (*fahren*) over it; (*mehr*) more; (*wahrenddessen*) meanwhile; (*sprechen, streiten*) about it; **~ geht nichts** there's nothing like it

darum [da'rom] adv (*räumlich*) round it ♦ konj that's why; **er bittet ~** he is pleading for it; **es geht ~, daß ...** the thing is that ...; **er würde viel ~ geben, wenn ...** he would give a lot to ...; **ich tue es ~, weil ...** I am doing it because ...

darunter [da'rontər] adv (*räumlich*) under it; (*dazwischen*) among them; (*weniger*) less; **ein Stockwerk ~** one floor below (it); **was verstehen Sie ~?** what do you understand by that?

das [das] def art the ♦ pron that

Dasein ['da:zaɪn] (-s) nt (*Leben*) life; (*Anwesenheit*) presence; (*Bestehen*) existence

dasein (*unreg*) vi to be there

daß [das] konj that

dasselbe [das'zɛlbə] art, pron the same

dastehen ['da:ʃte:ən] (*unreg*) vi to stand there

Datei [da:'taɪ] f file

Datenbank ['da:tənbaŋk] f data base

Datensichtgerät nt visual display unit, VDU

datieren [da'ti:rən] vt to date

Dattel ['datəl] (-, -n) f date

Datum ['da:tom] (-s, **Daten**) nt date; **Daten** pl (*Angaben*) data pl

Dauer ['dauər] (-, -n) f duration; (*gewisse Zeitspanne*) length; (*Bestand, Fortbestehen*) permanence; **es war nur von kurzer ~** it didn't last long; **auf die ~** in the long run; (*auf längere Zeit*) indefinitely; **~auftrag** m standing order; **d~haft** adj lasting, durable; **~karte** f season ticket; **~lauf** m jog(ging); **d~n** vi to last; **es hat sehr lang ged~t, bis er ...** it took him a long time to ...; **dauernd** adj constant; **~welle** f perm, permanent wave; **~wurst** f German salami; **~zustand** m permanent condition

Daumen ['daumən] (-s, -) m thumb

Daune ['daunə] f down; **Daunendecke** f down duvet, down quilt

davon [da'fɔn] adv of it; (*räumlich*) away; (*weg von*) from it; (*Grund*) because of it; **das kommt ~!** that's what you get; **~ abgesehen** apart from that; **~ sprechen/wissen** to talk/know of od about it; **was habe ich ~?** what's the point?; **~gehen** (*unreg*) vi to leave, to go away; **~laufen** (*unreg*) vi to run away

davor [da'fo:r] adv (*räumlich*) in front of it; (*zeitlich*) before (that); **~ warnen** to warn about it

dazu [da'tsu:] adv (*legen, stellen*) by it; (*essen, singen*) with it; **und ~ noch** and in addition; **ein Beispiel/seine Gedanken ~** one example for/his thoughts on this; **wie komme ich denn ~?** why should I?; **~ fähig sein** to be capable of it; **sich ~ äußern** to say something on it; **~gehören** vi to belong to it; **~kommen**

(*unreg*) *vi* (*Ereignisse*) to happen too;
(*an einen Ort*) to come along
dazwischen [da'tsvɪʃən] *adv* in
between; ~**kommen** (*räumlich auch*) between
(them); (*zusammen mit*) among them;
der Unterschied ~ the difference
between them; ~**kommen** (*unreg*) *vi*
(*hineingeraten*) to get caught in it; **es
ist etwas** ~**gekommen** something
cropped up; ~**reden** *vi* (*unterbrechen*)
to interrupt; (*sich einmischen*) to interfere; ~**treten** (*unreg*) *vi* to intervene
DB (-) *f abk* (= *Deutsche Bundesbahn*)
Federal Railways
DDR [de:de:''ɛr] (-) *f abk* (= *Deutsche
Demokratische Republik*) GDR
Debatte [de'batə] *f* debate
Deck [dɛk] (-(e)s, -s *od* -e) *nt* deck; **an**
~ **gehen** to go on deck
Decke *f* cover; (*Bett*~) blanket;
(*Tisch*~) tablecloth; (*Zimmer*~) ceil-
ing; **unter einer** ~ **stecken** to be hand in
glove; **d~l** (-s, -) *m* lid; **d~n** *vt* to cover
♦ *vr* to coincide
Deckung *f* (*Schützen*) covering;
(*Schutz*) cover; (*SPORT*) defence;
(*Übereinstimmen*) agreement;
deckungsgleich *adj* congruent
Defekt [de'fɛkt] (-(e)s, -e) *m* fault,
defect; **d~** *adj* faulty
defensiv [defɛn'si:f] *adj* defensive
definieren [defi'ni:rən] *vt* to define
Definition [definitsi'o:n] *f* definition
Defizit ['de:fitsɪt] (-s, -e) *nt* deficit
deftig ['dɛftɪç] *adj* (*Essen*) large; (*Witz*)
coarse
Degen ['de:gən] (-s, -) *m* sword
degenerieren [degene'ri:rən] *vi* to
degenerate
Dehn- ['de:n] *zW:* **d~bar** *adj* elastic;
(*fig*: *Begriff*) loose; ~**barkeit** *f*
elasticity; looseness; **d~en** *vt, vr* to
stretch
Deich [daɪç] (-(e)s, -e) *m* dyke, dike
Deichsel ['daɪksəl] (-, -n) *f* shaft
deichseln (*umg*) *vt* (*fig*) to wangle
dein(e) [daɪn(e)] *adj* (*D~ in Briefen*)
your; ~**e(r, s)** *pron* yours; ~**er** (*gen
von du*) *pron* of you; ~**erseits** *adv* on
your part; ~**esgleichen** *pron* people

like you; ~**etwegen** *adv* (*für dich*) for
your sake; (*wegen dir*) on your
account; ~**etwillen** *adv:* **um** ~**etwillen**
= ~**etwegen**; ~**ige** *pron:* **der/die/das**
~**ige** yours
dekadent [deka'dɛnt] *adj* decadent
Dekadenz *f* decadence
Deklination [deklinatsi'o:n] *f* declension
deklinieren [dekli'ni:rən] *vt* to decline
Dekolleté [dekɔl'te:] (-s, -s) *nt* low neckline
Deko- [deko] *zW:* ~**rateur** [-ra'tø:r] *m*
window dresser; ~**ration** [-ratsi'o:n] *f*
decoration; (*in Laden*) window dressing; **d~rativ** [-ra'ti:f] *adj* decorative;
d~rieren [-'ri:rən] *vt* to decorate;
(*Schaufenster*) to dress
Delegation [delegatsi'o:n] *f* delegation
delikat [deli'ka:t] *adj* (*zart, heikel*)
delicate; (*köstlich*) delicious
Delikatesse [delika'tɛsə] *f* delicacy; ~**n**
pl (*Feinkost*) delicatessen food; ~**nge-
schäft** *nt* delicatessen
Delikt [de'lɪkt] (-(e)s, -e) *nt* (*JUR*)
offence
Delle ['dɛlə] (*umg*) *f* dent
Delphin [dɛl'fi:n] (-s, -e) *m* dolphin
dem [de(:)m] *art dat von* **der**
Demagoge [dema'go:gə] (-n, -n) *m*
demagogue
dementieren [demɛn'ti:rən] *vt* to deny
dem- *zW:* ~**gemäß** *adv* accordingly;
~**nach** *adv* accordingly; ~**nächst** *adv*
shortly
Demokrat [demo'kra:t] (-en, -en) *m*
democrat; ~**ie** [-'ti:] *f* democracy;
d~isch *adj* democratic; **d~isieren**
[-i'zi:rən] *vt* to democratize
demolieren [demo'li:rən] *vt* to demolish
Demon- [demɔn] *zW:* ~**strant(in)**
[-'strant(ɪn)] *m(f)* demonstrator;
~**stration** [-stratsi'o:n] *f* demonstration;
d~strativ [-stra'ti:f] *adj* demonstrative;
(*Protest*) pointed; **d~strieren** [-'stri:rən]
vt, vi to demonstrate
Demoskopie [demosko'pi:] *f* public
opinion research
Demut ['de:mu:t] (-) *f* humility
demütig ['de:my:tɪç] *adj* humble; ~**en**
['de:my:tɪgən] *vt* to humiliate; **D~ung** *f*

humiliation

demzufolge ['de:mtsu'fɔlgə] *adv* accordingly

den [de(:)n] *art akk von* **der**

denen ['de:nən] *pron (dat pl) von* **der**; **die**; **das**

Denk- ['dɛŋk] *zW:* **d~bar** *adj* conceivable; **~en** (-s) *nt* thinking; **d~en** (*unreg*) *vt, vi* to think; **~fähigkeit** *f* intelligence; **d~faul** *adj* lazy; **~fehler** *m* logical error; **~mal** (-s, ⁼er) *nt* monument; **d~würdig** *adj* memorable; **~zettel** *m*: **jdm einen ~zettel verpassen** to teach sb a lesson

denn [dɛn] *konj* for ♦ *adv* then; (*nach Komparativ*) than; **warum ~?** why?

dennoch ['dɛnɔx] *konj* nevertheless

Denunziant [denuntsi'ant] *m* informer

deponieren [depo'ni:rən] *vt* (*COMM*) to deposit

Depot [de'po:] (-s, -s) *nt* warehouse; (*Bus~, EISENB*) depot; (*Bank~*) strongroom, safe (*US*)

Depression [depresi'o:n] *f* depression

deprimieren [depri'mi:rən] *vt* to depress

SCHLÜSSELWORT

der [de:r] (*f* **die**, *nt* **das**, *gen* **des**, **der**, **des**, *dat* **dem**, **der**, **dem**, *akk* **den**, **die**, **das**, *pl* **die**) *def art* the; **der Rhein** the Rhine; **der Klaus** (*umg*) Klaus; **die Frau** (*im allgemeinen*) women; **der Tod/das Leben** death/life; **der Fuß des Berges** the foot of the hill; **gib es der Frau** give it to the woman; **er hat sich die Hand verletzt** he has hurt his hand

♦ *relativ pron* (*bei Menschen*) who, that; (*bei Tieren, Sachen*) which, that; **der Mann, den ich gesehen habe** the man who *od* whom *od* that I saw

♦ *demonstrativ pron* he/she/it; (*jener, dieser*) that; (*pl*) those; **der/die war es** it was him/her; **der mit der Brille** the one with glasses; **ich will den (da)** I want that one

---

derart ['de:r'ʔa:rt] *adv* so; (*solcher Art*) such; **~ig** *adj* such, this sort of

derb [dɛrp] *adj* sturdy; (*Kost*) solid; (*grob*) coarse; **D~heit** *f* sturdiness;

solidity; coarseness

der- *zW:* **'~gleichen** *pron* such; **'~jenige** *pron* he; she; it; the one (who); that (which); **'~maßen** *adv* to such an extent, so; **~'selbe** *art, pron* the same; **~'weil(en)** *adv* in the meantime; **'~zeitig** *adj* present, current; (*damalig*) then

des [dɛs] *art gen von* **der**

desertieren [dezɛr'ti:rən] *vi* to desert

desgleichen ['dɛs'glaiçən] *adv* likewise, also

deshalb ['dɛs'halp] *adv* therefore, that's why

Desinfektion [dezinfɛktsi'o:n] *f* disinfection; **~smittel** *nt* disinfectant

desinfizieren [dezinfi'tsi:rən] *vt* to disinfect

dessen ['dɛsən] *pron gen von* **der**; **das**; **~'ungeachtet** *adv* nevertheless, regardless

Dessert [dɛ'sɛːr] (-s, -s) *nt* dessert

destillieren [dɛsti'li:rən] *vt* to distil

desto ['dɛsto] *adv* all the, so much the; **~ besser** all the better

deswegen ['dɛs've:gən] *konj* therefore, hence

Detail [de'tai] (-s, -s) *nt* detail

Detektiv [detɛk'ti:f] (-s, -e) *m* detective

deut- ['dɔyt] *zW:* **~en** *vt* to interpret, to explain ♦ *vi:* **~en (auf** +*akk*) to point (to *od* at); **~lich** *adj* clear; (*Unterschied*) distinct; **D~lichkeit** *f* clarity; distinctness

Deutsch [dɔytʃ] *nt* German

deutsch *adj* German; **auf ~** in German; **D~e Demokratische Republik** German Democratic Republic, East Germany; **~es Beefsteak** ≈ hamburger; **D~e** *f* German; **D~er** *m* German; **ich bin D~er** I am German; **D~land** *nt* Germany

Devise [de'vi:zə] *f* motto, device; **~n** *pl* (*FIN*) foreign currency, foreign exchange

Dezember [de'tsɛmbər] (-s, -) *m* December

dezent [de'tsɛnt] *adj* discreet

dezimal [detsi'ma:l] *adj* decimal; **D~bruch** *m* decimal (fraction);

D~system *nt* decimal system
d.h. *abk* (= *das heißt*) i.e.
Dia ['di:a] (-s, -s) *nt* (*PHOT*) slide, transparency
Diabetes [dia'be:tɛs] (-, -) *m* (*MED*) diabetes
Diagnose [dia'gno:zə] *f* diagnosis
diagonal [diago'na:l] *adj* diagonal; **D~e** *f* diagonal
Dialekt [dia'lɛkt] (-(e)s, -e) *m* dialect; **d~isch** *adj* dialectal; (*Logik*) dialectical
Dialog [dia'lo:k] (-(e)s, -e) *m* dialogue
Diamant [dia'mant] *m* diamond
Diät [di'ɛ:t] (-, -en) *f* diet; **~en** *pl* (*POL*) allowance
dich [dıç] (*akk von* **du**) *pron* you; yourself
dicht [dıçt] *adj* dense; (*Nebel*) thick; (*Gewebe*) close; (*undurchlässig*) (water)tight; (*fig*) concise ♦ *adv:* ~ **an/bei** close to; **~bevölkert** *adj* densely *od* heavily populated; **D~e** *f* density; thickness; closeness; (water)tightness; (*fig*) conciseness; **~en** *vt* (*dicht machen*) to make watertight; to seal; (*NAUT*) to caulk; (*LITER*) to compose, to write ♦ *vi* (*LITER*) to compose, to write; **D~er(in)** (-s, -) *m(f)* poet; (*Autor*) writer; **~erisch** *adj* poetical; **~halten** (*unreg; umg*) *vi* to keep one's mouth shut; **D~ung** *f* (*TECH*) washer; (*AUT*) gasket; (*Gedichte*) poetry; (*Prosa*) (piece of) writing
dick [dık] *adj* thick; (*fett*) fat; **durch ~ und dünn** through thick and thin; **D~e** *f* thickness; fatness; **~flüssig** *adj* viscous; **D~icht** (-s, -e) *nt* thicket; **D~kopf** *m* mule; **D~milch** *f* soured milk
die [di:] *def art siehe* **der**
Dieb(in) [di:p, 'di:bın] (-(e)s, -e) *m(f)* thief; **d~isch** *adj* thieving; (*umg*) immense; **~stahl** (-(e)s, ⁼e) *m* theft
Diele ['di:lə] *f* (*Brett*) board; (*Flur*) hall, lobby
dienen ['di:nən] *vi:* (jdm) ~ to serve (sb)
Diener (-s, -) *m* servant; **~in** *f* (maid)servant; **~schaft** *f* servants *pl*

Dienst [di:nst] (-(e)s, -e) *m* service; **außer ~** retired; **~ haben** to be on duty
Dienstag ['di:nsta:k] *m* Tuesday; **d~s** *adv* on Tuesdays
Dienst- *zW:* **~geheimnis** *nt* official secret; **~gespräch** *nt* business call; **d~habend** *adj* (*Arzt*) on duty; **~leistungsgewerbe** *nt* service industries *pl*; **d~lich** *adj* official; **~mädchen** *nt* (house)maid; **~reise** *f* business trip; **~stelle** *f* office; **~vorschrift** *f* official regulations *pl*; **~weg** *m* official channels *pl*; **~zeit** *f* working hours *pl*; (*MIL*) period of service
dies- ['di:s] *zW:* **~bezüglich** *adj* (*Frage*) on this matter; **~e(r, s)** ['di:zə(r, s)] *pron* this (one); **dieselbe** [di:'zɛlbə] *pron, art* the same
Dieselöl ['di:zəl'ø:l] *nt* diesel oil
diesig ['di:zıç] *adj* drizzly
dies- *zW:* **~jährig** *adj* this year's; **~mal** *adv* this time; **~seits** *präp* +*gen* on this side; **D~seits** (-) *nt* this life
Dietrich ['di:trıç] (-s, -e) *m* picklock
differential [dıferɛntsi'a:l] *adj* differential; **D~getriebe** *nt* differential gear; **D~rechnung** *f* differential calculus
differenzieren [dıferɛn'tsi:rən] *vt* to make distinctions in; **differenziert** *adj* (*Mensch etc*) complex
Dikt- [dıkt] *zW:* **~aphon** [-a'fo:n] *nt* dictaphone; **~at** [-'ta:t] (-(e)s, -e) *nt* dictation; **~ator** [-'ta:tɔr] *m* dictator; **d~atorisch** [-a'to:rıʃ] *adj* dictatorial; **~atur** [-a'tu:r] *f* dictatorship; **d~ieren** [-'ti:rən] *vt* to dictate
Dilemma [di'lɛma] (-s, -s *od* -ta) *nt* dilemma
Dilettant [dile'tant] *m* dilettante, amateur; **d~isch** *adj* amateurish, dilettante
Dimension [dimɛnzi'o:n] *f* dimension
Ding [dıŋ] (-(e)s, -e) *nt* thing, object; **d~lich** *adj* real, concrete; **~s(bums)** ['dıŋks(bums)] (-; *umg*) *nt* thingummybob
Diözese [diø'tse:zə] *f* diocese
Diphtherie [dıfte'ri:] *f* diphtheria
Diplom [di'plo:m] (-(e)s, -e) *nt* diploma, certificate; **~at** [-'ma:t] (-en, -en) *m*

diplomat; **~atie** [-a'tiː] *f* diplomacy; **d~atisch** [-'matɪʃ] *adj* diplomatic; **~ingenieur** *m* qualified engineer

dir [diːr] *(dat von* **du)** *pron* (to) you

direkt [di'rɛkt] *adj* direct; **D~or** *m* director; *(SCH)* principal, headmaster; **D~übertragung** *f* live broadcast

Dirigent [diri'gɛnt] *m* conductor

dirigieren [diri'giːrən] *vt* to direct; *(MUS)* to conduct

Dirne ['dɪrnə] *f* prostitute

Diskette [dɪs'kɛtə] *f* diskette, floppy disk

Diskont [dɪs'kɔnt] (-s, -e) *m* discount; **~satz** *m* rate of discount

Diskothek [dɪsko'teːk] (-, -en) *f* disco(theque)

diskret [dɪs'kreːt] *adj* discreet; **D~ion** *f* discretion

Diskussion [dɪskusi'oːn] *f* discussion; debate; **zur ~ stehen** to be under discussion

diskutabel [dɪsku'taːbəl] *adj* debatable

diskutieren [dɪsku'tiːrən] *vt, vi* to discuss; to debate

Distanz [dɪs'tants] *f* distance

Distel ['dɪstəl] (-, -n) *f* thistle

Disziplin [dɪstsi'pliːn] *f* discipline

Dividende [divi'dɛndə] *f* dividend

dividieren [divi'diːrən] *vt*: **(durch etw) ~** to divide (by sth)

DM [deː"ɛm] *abk* (= *Deutsche Mark)* German Mark

D-Mark ['deːmark] *f* D Mark, German Mark

SCHLÜSSELWORT

doch [dɔx] *adv* **1** *(dennoch)* after all; *(sowieso)* anyway; **er kam doch noch** he came after all; **du weißt es ja doch besser** you know better than I do anyway; **und doch ... and yet ...**

2 *(als bejahende Antwort)* yes I do/it does *etc*; **das ist nicht wahr - doch!** that's not true - yes it is!

3 *(auffordernd)*: **komm doch** do come; **laß ihm doch** just leave him; **nicht doch!** oh no!

4: **sie ist doch noch so jung** but she's still so young; **Sie wissen doch, wie das ist** you know how it is(, don't you?);

wenn doch if only

♦ *konj (aber)* but; *(trotzdem)* all the same; **und doch hat er es getan** but still he did it

---

Docht [dɔxt] (-(e)s, -e) *m* wick

Dogge ['dɔgə] *f* bulldog

Dogma ['dɔgma] (-s, -men) *nt* dogma; **d~tisch** [dɔg'maːtɪʃ] *adj* dogmatic

Doktor ['dɔktɔr, *pl* -'toːrən] (-s, -en) *m* doctor; **~-and** [-'rant] (-en, -en) *m* candidate for a doctorate; **~arbeit** *f* doctoral thesis

Dokument [doku'mɛnt] *nt* document

Dokumentar- [dokumen'taːr] *zW*: **~bericht** *m* documentary; **~film** *m* documentary (film); **d~isch** *adj* documentary

Dolch [dɔlç] (-(e)s, -e) *m* dagger

dolmetschen ['dɔlmɛtʃən] *vt, vi* to interpret

Dolmetscher(in) (-s, -) *m(f)* interpreter

Dom [doːm] (-(e)s, -e) *m* cathedral

dominieren [domi'niːrən] *vt* to dominate ♦ *vi* to predominate

Dompfaff ['dɔmpfaf] *m* bullfinch

Donau ['doːnau] *f* Danube

Donner ['dɔnər] (-s, -) *m* thunder; **d~n** *vi unpers* to thunder

Donnerstag ['dɔnərstaːk] *m* Thursday

doof [doːf] *(umg) adj* daft, stupid

Doppel ['dɔpəl] (-s, -) *nt* duplicate; *(SPORT)* doubles; **~bett** *nt* double bed; **~fenster** *nt* double glazing; **~gänger** (-s, -) *m* double; **~haus** *nt* semi-detached house; **~punkt** *m* colon; **~stecker** *m* two-way adaptor; **d~t** *adj* double; **in d~ter Ausführung** in duplicate; **~zentner** *m* 100 kilograms; **~zimmer** *nt* double room

Dorf [dɔrf] (-(e)s, ⁼er) *nt* village; **~bewohner** *m* villager

Dorn¹ [dɔrn] (-(e)s, -en) *m* *(BOT)* thorn

Dorn² (-(e)s, -e) *m* *(Schnallen~)* tongue, pin

dornig *adj* thorny

dörren ['dœrən] *vt* to dry

Dörrobst ['dœr'oːpst] *nt* dried fruit

Dorsch [dɔrʃ] (-(e)s, -e) *m* cod

dort [dɔrt] *adv* there; ~ **drüben** over there; ~**her** *adv* from there; ~**hin** *adv* (to) there; ~**ig** *adj* of that place; in that town

Dose ['doːzə] *f* box; (*Blech~*) tin, can

Dosen *pl von* Dose; Dosis

Dosenöffner *m* tin *od* can opener

Dosis ['doːzɪs] (-, Dosen) *f* dose

Dotter ['dɔtər] (-s, -) *m* (egg) yolk

Dozent [do'tsɛnt] *m* university lecturer

Drache ['draxə] (-n, -n) *m* (*Tier*) dragon

Drachen (-s, -) *m* kite

Draht [draːt] (-(e)s, ⁻e) *m* wire; **auf** ~ **sein** to be on the ball; ~**gitter** *nt* wire grating; ~**seil** *nt* cable; ~**seilbahn** *f* cable railway, funicular; ~**zange** *f* pliers *pl*

Drama ['draːma] (-s, Dramen) *nt* drama, play; ~**tiker** [-'maːtikər] (-s, -) *m* dramatist; **d~tisch** [-'maːtɪʃ] *adj* dramatic

dran [dran] (*umg*) *adv:* **jetzt bin ich** ~ **!** it's my turn now; *siehe* **daran**

Drang [draŋ] (-(e)s, ⁻e) *m* (*Trieb*): ~ (**nach**) impulse (for), urge (for), desire (for); (*Druck*) pressure

drängeln ['drɛŋəln] *vt, vi* to push, to jostle

drängen ['drɛŋən] *vt* (*schieben*) to push, to press; (*antreiben*) to urge ♦ *vi* (*eilig sein*) to be urgent; (*Zeit*) to press; **auf etw** *akk* ~ to press for sth

drastisch ['drastɪʃ] *adj* drastic

drauf [drauf] (*umg*) *adv* = **darauf**; **D~gänger** (-s, -) *m* daredevil

draußen ['drausən] *adv* outside, out-of-doors

Dreck [drɛk] (-(e)s) *m* mud, dirt; **d~ig** *adj* dirty, filthy

Dreh- ['dreː] *zW:* ~**arbeiten** *pl* (*CINE*) shooting *sg*; ~**bank** *f* lathe; **d~bar** *adj* revolving; ~**buch** *nt* (*CINE*) script; **d~en** *vt* to turn, to rotate; (*Zigaretten*) to roll; (*Film*) to shoot ♦ *vi* to turn, to rotate ♦ *vr* to turn; (*handeln von*): **es d~t sich um ...** it's about ...; ~**orgel** *f* barrel organ; ~**tür** *f* revolving door; ~**ung** *f* (*Rotation*) rotation; (*Um~, Wendung*) turn; ~**zahl** *f* rate of revolutions; ~**zahlmesser** *m* rev(olution) counter

drei [draɪ] *num* three; **D~eck** *nt* triangle; ~**eckig** *adj* triangular; ~**einhalb** *num* three and a half; ~**erlei** *adj inv* of three kinds; ~**fach** *adj* triple, treble ♦ *adv* three times; ~**hundert** *num* three hundred; **D~königsfest** *nt* Epiphany; ~**mal** *adv* three times; ~**malig** *adj* three times

dreinreden ['draɪnreːdən] *vi:* **jdm** ~ (*dazwischenreden*) to interrupt sb; (*sich einmischen*) to interfere with sb

dreißig ['draɪsɪç] *num* thirty

dreist [draɪst] *adj* bold, audacious; **D~igkeit** *f* boldness, audacity

drei- *zW:* ~**viertel** *num* three-quarters; **D~viertelstunde** *f* three-quarters of an hour; ~**zehn** *num* thirteen

dressieren [drɛ'siːrən] *vt* to train

Drillbohrer *m* light drill

drillen ['drɪlən] *vt* (*bohren*) to drill, to bore; (*MIL*) to drill; (*fig*) to train

Drilling *m* triplet

drin [drɪn] (*umg*) *adv* = **darin**

dringen ['drɪŋən] (*unreg*) *vi* (*Wasser, Licht, Kälte*): ~ (**durch/in** +*akk*) to penetrate (through/into); **auf etw** *akk* ~ to insist on sth

dringend ['drɪŋənt] *adj* urgent

dringlich ['drɪŋlɪç] *adj* urgent

Dringlichkeit *f* urgency

drinnen ['drɪnən] *adv* inside, indoors

dritte(r, s) ['drɪtə(r, s)] *adj* third; ~ **Welt** Third World; **D~s Reich** Third Reich; **Drittel** (-s, -) *nt* third; **drittens** *adv* thirdly

droben ['droːbən] *adv* above, up there

Droge ['droːgə] *f* drug; **drogenabhängig** *adj* addicted to drugs; **Drogenhändler** *m* drug pedlar, pusher; **Drogerie** [droːgə'riː] *f* chemist's shop

Drogist [dro'gɪst] *m* pharmacist, chemist

drohen ['droːən] *vi:* (**jdm**) ~ to threaten (sb)

dröhnen ['drøːnən] *vi* (*Motor*) to roar; (*Stimme, Musik*) to ring, to resound

Drohung ['droːʊŋ] *f* threat

drollig ['drɔlɪç] *adj* droll

Drossel ['drɔsəl] (-, -n) *f* thrush

drüben ['dry:bən] *adv* over there, on the other side

drüber ['dry:bər] (*umg*) *adv* = **darüber**

Druck [druk] (-(e)s, -e) *m* (*PHYS, Zwang*) pressure; (*TYP: Vorgang*) printing; (*: Produkt*) print; (*fig: Belastung*) burden, weight; ~**buchstabe** *m* block letter

drücken ['drykən] *vt* (*Knopf, Hand*) to press; (*zu eng sein*) to pinch; (*fig: Preise*) to keep down; (*: belasten*) to oppress, to weigh down ♦ *vi* to press; to pinch ♦ *vr*: **sich vor etw** *dat* ~ **to get out of (doing) sth**; ~**d** *adj* oppressive

Drucker (-s, -) *m* printer

Drücker (-s, -) *m* button; (*Tür~*) handle; (*Gewehr~*) trigger

Druck- *zW*: ~**e'rei** *f* printing works, press; ~**erschwärze** *f* printer's ink; ~**fehler** *m* misprint; ~**knopf** *m* press stud, snap fastener; ~**sache** *f* printed matter; ~**schrift** *f* block *od* printed letters *pl*

drum [drum] (*umg*) *adv* = **darum**

drunten ['druntən] *adv* below, down there

Drüse ['dry:zə] *f* gland

Dschungel ['dʒuŋəl] (-s, -) *m* jungle

du [du:] (*nom*) *pron* (D~ *in Briefen*) you; **D~ sagen** = **duzen**

ducken ['dukən] *vt* (*Kopf, Person*) to duck; (*fig*) to take down a peg or two ♦ *vr* to duck

Duckmäuser ['dukmɔyzər] (-s, -) *m* yesman

Dudelsack ['du:dəlzak] *m* bagpipes *pl*

Duell [du'ɛl] (-s, -e) *nt* duel

Duett [du'ɛt] (-(e)s, -e) *nt* duet

Duft [duft] (-(e)s, ⁼e) *m* scent, odour; **d~en** *vi* to smell, to be fragrant; **d~ig** *adj* (*Stoff, Kleid*) delicate, diaphanous

dulden ['duldən] *vt* to suffer; (*zulassen*) to tolerate ♦ *vi* to suffer

duldsam *adj* tolerant

dumm [dum] *adj* stupid; (*ärgerlich*) annoying; **der D~e sein** to be the loser; ~**erweise** *adv* stupidly; **D~heit** *f* stupidity; (*Tat*) blunder, stupid mistake; **D~kopf** *m* blockhead

dumpf [dumpf] *adj* (*Ton*) hollow, dull;

(*Luft*) musty; (*Erinnerung, Schmerz*) vague; ~**ig** *adj* musty

Düne ['dy:nə] *f* dune

düngen ['dyŋən] *vt* to manure

Dünger (-s, -) *m* dung, manure; (*künstlich*) fertilizer

dunkel ['duŋkəl] *adj* dark; (*Stimme*) deep; (*Ahnung*) vague; (*rätselhaft*) obscure; (*verdächtig*) dubious, shady; **im** ~**n tappen** (*fig*) to grope in the dark

Dunkel- *zW*: ~**heit** *f* darkness; (*fig*) obscurity; ~**kammer** *f* (*PHOT*) dark room; **d~n** *vi unpers* to grow dark; ~**ziffer** *f* estimated number of unreported cases

dünn [dyn] *adj* thin; ~**flüssig** *adj* watery, thin

Dunst [dunst] (-es, ⁼e) *m* vapour; (*Wetter*) haze

dünsten ['dynstən] *vt* to steam

dunstig ['dunstıç] *adj* vaporous; (*Wetter*) hazy, misty

Duplikat [dupli'ka:t] (-(e)s, -e) *nt* duplicate

Dur [du:r] (-, -) *nt* (*MUS*) major

SCHLÜSSELWORT

durch [durç] *präp* +*akk* **1** (*hindurch*) through; **durch den Urwald** through the jungle; **die ganze Welt reisen** to travel all over the world

2 (*mittels*) through, by (means of); (*aufgrund*) to, owing to; **Tod durch Herzschlag/den Strang** death from a heart attack/by hanging; **durch die Post** by post; **durch seine Bemühungen** through his efforts

♦ *adv* **1** (*hindurch*) through; **die ganze Nacht durch** all through the night; **den Sommer durch** during the summer; **8 Uhr durch** past 8 o'clock; **durch und durch** completely

2 (*durchgebraten etc*): (**gut**) **durch** well-done

---

durch- *zW*: ~**arbeiten** *vt, vi* to work through ♦ *vr* to work one's way through; ~'**aus** *adv* completely; (*unbedingt*) definitely; ~**aus nicht** absolutely not; ~**blättern** *vt* to leaf

through
Durchblick ['dʊrçblɪk] *m* view; (*fig*)
comprehension; **d~en** *vi* to look
through; (*umg: verstehen*): **(bei etw)**
d~en to understand (sth); **etw d~en**
lassen (*fig*) to hint at sth
durchbrechen ['dʊrçbrɛçən] (*unreg*) *vt*,
vi to break; **durch'brechen** (*unreg*) *vt*
insep (*Schranken*) to break through;
(*Schallmauer*) to break; (*Gewohnheit*)
to break free from
durchbrennen ['dʊrçbrɛnən] (*unreg*) *vi*
(*Draht, Sicherung*) to burn through;
(*umg*) to run away
Durchbruch ['dʊrçbrʊx] *m* (*Öffnung*)
opening; (*MIL*) breach; (*von Gefühlen*
etc) eruption; (*der Zähne*) cutting;
(*fig*) breakthrough; **zum ~ kommen** to
break through
durch- *zW:* **D~dacht** [dʊrç'daxt] *adj* well
thought-out; **~'denken** (*unreg*) *vt* to
think out; **~drehen** *vt* (*Fleisch*) to
mince ♦ *vi* (*umg*) to crack up
durcheinander [dʊrçʔaɪ'nandər] *adv* in a
mess, in confusion; (*umg: verwirrt*)
confused; **~ trinken** to mix one's
drinks; **D~** (**-s**) *nt* (*Verwirrung*) confusion; (*Unordnung*) mess; **~bringen**
(*unreg*) *vt* to mess up; (*verwirren*) to
confuse; **~reden** *vi* to talk at the same
time
durch- *zW:* **D~fahrt** *f* transit; (*Ver-*
kehr) thoroughfare; **D~fall** *m* (*MED*) diarrhoea; **~fallen** (*unreg*) *vi* to fall
through; (*in Prüfung*) to fail; **~finden**
(*unreg*) *vr* to find one's way through;
~'forschen *vt* *insep* to explore;
~fragen *vr* to find one's way by asking
durchführ- ['dʊrçfyːr] *zW:* **~bar** *adj*
feasible, practicable; **~en** *vt* to carry
out; **D~ung** *f* execution, performance
Durchgang ['dʊrçgaŋ] *m* passage(way);
(*bei Produktion, Versuch*) run; (*SPORT*)
round; (*bei Wahl*) ballot; „**~ verboten**"
"no thoroughfare"
Durchgangs- *zW:* **~handel** *m* transit
trade; **~lager** *nt* transit camp; **~ver-**
kehr *m* through traffic
durchgefroren ['dʊrçgəfroːrən] *adj*
(*Mensch*) frozen stiff

durchgehen ['dʊrçgeːən] (*unreg*) *vt*
(*behandeln*) to go over ♦ *vi* to go
through; (*ausreißen: Pferd*) to break
loose; (*Mensch*) to run away; **mein**
Temperament ging mit mir durch my
temper got the better of me; **jdm etw ~**
lassen to let sb get away with sth; **~d**
adj (*Zug*) through; (*Öffnungszeiten*)
continuous
durch- *zW:* **~greifen** (*unreg*) *vi* to take
strong action; **~halten** (*unreg*) *vi* to
last out ♦ *vt* to keep up; **~kommen**
(*unreg*) *vi* to get through; (*überleben*)
to pull through
durch'kreuzen *vt* *insep* to thwart, to
frustrate
durch- *zW:* **~lassen** (*unreg*) *vt*
(*Person*) to let through; (*Wasser*) to let
in; **~lässig** *adj* leaky; **D~lauferhitzer**
(**-s, -**) *m* (hot water) geyser; **~'leben**
vt *insep* to live *od* go through, to experience; **~lesen** (*unreg*) *vt* to read
through; **~'leuchten** *vt* *insep* to X-ray;
~machen *vt* to go through; **die Nacht**
~machen to make a night of it
Durchmarsch *m* march through
Durchmesser (**-s, -**) *m* diameter
durch- *zW:* **~'nässen** *vt* *insep* to soak
(through); **~nehmen** (*unreg*) *vt* to go
over; **~numerieren** *vt* to number con-
secutively; **~queren** [dʊrç'kveːrən] *vt* in-
sep to cross; **D~reiche** *f* (serving)
hatch; **D~reise** *f* transit; **auf der**
D~reise passing through; (*Güter*) in
transit; **~ringen** (*unreg*) *vr* to reach a
decision after a long struggle; **~rosten**
vi to rust through
durchs [dʊrçs] = **durch das**
Durchsage ['dʊrçzaːgə] *f* intercom *od*
radio announcement
durchschauen ['dʊrçʃaʊən] *vi* to look *od*
see through; **durch'schauen** *vt* *insep*
(*Person, Lüge*) to see through
durchscheinen ['dʊrçʃaɪnən] (*unreg*) *vi*
to shine through; **~d** *adj* translucent
Durchschlag ['dʊrçʃlaːk] *m* (*Doppel*)
carbon copy; (*Sieb*) strainer; **d~en**
(*unreg*) *vt* (*entzweischlagen*) to split
(in two); (*sieben*) to sieve ♦ *vi* (*zum*
Vorschein kommen) to emerge, to come

out ♦ *vr* to get by; **d~end** *adj* resounding

durchschneiden ['dʊrçʃnaɪdən] (*unreg*) *vt* to cut through

Durchschnitt ['dʊrçʃnɪt] *m* (*Mittelwert*) average; **über/unter dem ~** above/below average; **im ~** on average; **d~lich** *adj* average ♦ *adv* on average

Durchschnitts- *zW*: **~geschwindigkeit** *f* average speed; **~mensch** *m* average man, man in the street; **~wert** *m* average

durch- *zW*: **D~schrift** *f* copy; **~sehen** (*unreg*) *vt* to look through; **~setzen** *vt* to enforce ♦ *vr* (*Erfolg haben*) to succeed; (*sich behaupten*) to get one's way; **seinen Kopf ~setzen** to get one's way; **~'setzen** *vt insep* to mix

Durchsicht ['dʊrçzɪçt] *f* looking through, checking; **d~ig** *adj* transparent; **~igkeit** *f* transparency

durch- *zW*: **~sprechen** (*unreg*) *vt* to talk over; **~stehen** (*unreg*) *vt* to live through; **~streichen** (*unreg*) *vt* to cross out; **~'suchen** *vt insep* to search; **D~'suchung** *f* search; **~trieben** [-'triːbən] *adj* cunning, wily; **~'wachsen** *adj* (*Speck*) streaky; (*fig: mittelmäßig*) so-so; **~weg** *adv* throughout, completely; **~ziehen** (*unreg*) *vt* (*Faden*) to draw through ♦ *vi* to pass through; **D~zug** *m* (*Luft*) draught; (*von Truppen, Vögeln*) passage

SCHLÜSSELWORT

dürfen ['dʏrfən] (*unreg*) *vi* **1** (*Erlaubnis haben*) to be allowed to; **ich darf das** I'm allowed to (do that); **darf ich?** may I?; **darf ich ins Kino?** can *od* may I go to the cinema?; **es darf geraucht werden** you may smoke

2 (*in Verneinungen*): **er darf das nicht** he's not allowed to (do that); **das darf nicht geschehen** that must not happen; **da darf sie sich nicht wundern** that shouldn't surprise her

3 (*in Höflichkeitsformeln*): **darf ich Sie bitten, das zu tun?** may *od* could I ask you to do that?; **was darf es sein?** what can I do for you?

4 (*können*): **das dürfen Sie mir glauben** you can believe me

5 (*Möglichkeit*): **das dürfte genug sein** that should be enough; **es dürfte Ihnen bekannt sein, daß** ... as you will probably know ...

dürftig ['dʏrftɪç] *adj* (*ärmlich*) needy, poor; (*unzulänglich*) inadequate

dürr [dʏr] *adj* dried-up; (*Land*) arid; (*mager*) skinny, gaunt; **D~e** *f* aridity; (*Zeit*) drought; (*Magerkeit*) skinniness

Durst [dʊrst] (-(e)s) *m* thirst; **~ haben** to be thirsty; **d~ig** *adj* thirsty

Dusche ['duːʃə] *f* shower; **d~n** *vi, vr* to have a shower

Düse ['dyːzə] *f* nozzle; (*Flugzeug~*) jet

Düsen- *zW*: **~antrieb** *m* jet propulsion; **~flugzeug** *nt* jet (plane); **~jäger** *m* jet fighter

Dussel ['dʊsəl] (-s, -; *umg*) *m* twit

düster ['dyːstər] *adj* dark; (*Gedanken, Zukunft*) gloomy

Dutzend ['dʊtsənt] (-s, -e) *nt* dozen; **d~(e)mal** *adv* a dozen times; **d~weise** *adv* by the dozen

duzen ['duːtsən] *vt*: (**jdn**) **~** to use the familiar form of address "du" (to *od* with sb)

Dynamik [dy'naːmɪk] *f* (*PHYS*) dynamics *sg*; (*fig: Schwung*) momentum; (*von Mensch*) dynamism

dynamisch [dy'naːmɪʃ] *adj* (*auch fig*) dynamic

Dynamit [dyna'miːt] (-s) *nt* dynamite

Dynamo [dy'naːmo] (-s, -s) *m* dynamo

D-Zug ['deːtsuːk] *m* through train

E

Ebbe ['ɛbə] *f* low tide

eben ['eːbən] *adj* level, flat; (*glatt*) smooth ♦ *adv* just; (*bestätigend*) exactly; **~ deswegen** just because of that; **~bürtig** *adj*: **jdm ~bürtig sein** to be sb's equal; **E~e** *f* plain; (*fig*) level; **~falls** *adv* likewise; **~so** *adv* just as; **~sogut** *adv* just as well; **~sooft** *adv* just as often; **~soweit** *adv* just as far;

~**sowenig** adv just as little

Eber ['e:bər] (-s, -) m boar; ~**esche** f mountain ash, rowan

ebnen ['e:bnən] vt to level

Echo ['ɛço] (-s, -s) nt echo

echt [ɛçt] adj genuine; (typisch) typical; **E~heit** f genuineness

Eck- ['ɛk] zW: ~**ball** m corner (kick); ~**e** f corner; (MATH) angle; **e~ig** adj angular; ~**zahn** m eye tooth

edel ['e:dəl] adj noble; **E~metall** nt rare metal; **E~stein** m precious stone

EDV [e:de:'fau] (-) f abk (= elektronische Datenverarbeitung) electronic data processing

Efeu ['e:fɔy] (-s) m ivy

Effekten [ɛ'fɛktən] pl stocks

effektiv [ɛfɛk'ti:f] adj effective, actual

EG ['e:'ge:] (-) f abk (= Europäische Gemeinschaft) European Community

egal [e'ga:l] adj all the same

Ego- [e:go] zW: ~**ismus** [-'ısmʊs] m selfishness, egoism; ~**ist** [-'ıst] m egoist; **e~istisch** adj selfish, egoistic

Ehe ['e:ə] f marriage

ehe konj before

Ehe- zW: ~**bruch** m adultery; ~**frau** f married woman; wife; ~**leute** pl married people; **e~lich** adj matrimonial; (Kind) legitimate

ehemalig adj former

ehemals adv formerly

Ehemann m married man; husband

Ehepaar nt married couple

eher ['e:ər] adv (früher) sooner; (lieber) rather, sooner; (mehr) more

eheste(r, s) ['e:əstə(r, s)] adj (früheste) first, earliest; **am ~n** (liebsten) soonest; (meist) most; (wahrscheinlichst) most probably

Ehr- ['e:r] zW: **e~bar** adj honourable, respectable; ~**e** f honour; **e~en** vt to honour

Ehren- ['e:rən] zW: ~**gast** m guest of honour; **e~haft** adj honourable; ~**runde** f lap of honour; ~**sache** f point of honour; **e~voll** adj honourable; ~**wort** nt word of honour

Ehr- zW: ~**furcht** f awe, deep respect; ~**gefühl** nt sense of honour; ~**geiz** m

ambition; **e~geizig** adj ambitious; **e~lich** adj honest; ~**lichkeit** f honesty; **e~los** adj dishonourable; ~**ung** f honour(ing); **e~würdig** adj venerable

Ei [aı] (-(e)s, -er) nt egg

ei excl well, well

Eichamt nt Office of Weights and Measures

Eiche ['aıçə] f oak (tree)

Eichel (-, -n) f acorn

eichen vt to standardize

Eichhörnchen nt squirrel

Eichmaß nt standard

Eid [aıt] (-(e)s, -e) m oath

Eidechse ['aıdɛksə] f lizard

eidesstattlich adj: **~e Erklärung** affidavit

Eidgenosse m Swiss

Eidotter ['aıdɔtər] nt egg yolk

Eier- zW: ~**becher** m eggcup; ~**kuchen** m omelette; pancake; ~**likör** m advocaat; ~**schale** f eggshell; ~**stock** m ovary; ~**uhr** f egg timer

Eifer ['aıfər] (-s) m zeal, enthusiasm; ~**sucht** f jealousy; **e~süchtig** adj: **e~süchtig (auf +akk)** jealous (of)

eifrig ['aıfrıç] adj zealous, enthusiastic

Eigelb ['aıgɛlp] (-(e)s, -) nt egg yolk

eigen ['aıgən] adj own; (~artig) peculiar; **mit der/dem ihm ~en ... ** with that ... peculiar to him; **sich** dat **etw zu ~ machen** to make sth one's own; **E~art** f peculiarity; characteristic; ~**artig** adj peculiar; ~**händig** adj with one's own hand; **E~heim** nt owner-occupied house; **E~heit** f peculiarity; ~**mächtig** adj high-handed; **E~name** m proper name; ~**s** adv expressly, on purpose; **E~schaft** f quality, property, attribute; **E~schaftswort** nt adjective; **E~sinn** m obstinacy; ~**sinnig** adj obstinate; **eigentlich** adj actual, real ♦ adv actually, really; **E~tor** nt own goal; **E~tum** nt property; **E~tümer(in)** (-s, -) m(f) owner, proprietor; ~**tümlich** adj peculiar; **E~tümlichkeit** f peculiarity; **E~tumswohnung** f freehold flat

eignen ['aıgnən] vr to be suited

Eignung f suitability

Eil- ['aɪl] *zW:* ~**bote** *m* courier; ~**brief** *m* express letter; ~**e** *f* haste; **es hat keine** ~**e** there's no hurry; **e~en** *vi* (*Mensch*) to hurry; (*dringend sein*) to be urgent; **e~ends** *adv* hastily; ~**gut** *nt* express goods *pl*, fast freight (*US*); **e~ig** *adj* hasty, hurried; (*dringlich*) urgent; **es e~ig haben** to be in a hurry; ~**zug** *m* semi-fast train, limited stop train

Eimer ['aɪmər] (-s, -) *m* bucket, pail

ein [aɪn] *adv:* **nicht** ~ **noch aus wissen** not to know what to do

ein(e) *num one* ♦ *indef art* a, an

einander [aɪ'nandər] *pron* one another, each other

einarbeiten ['aɪnarbaɪtən] *vt* to train ♦ *vr:* **sich in etw** *akk* ~ to familiarize o.s. with sth

einatmen ['aɪna:tmən] *vt, vi* to inhale, to breathe in

Einbahnstraße ['aɪnba:nʃtra:sə] *f* one-way street

Einband ['aɪnbant] *m* binding, cover

einbauen ['aɪnbaʊən] *vt* to build in; (*Motor*) to install, to fit

Einbaumöbel *pl* built-in furniture *sg*

einberufen ['aɪnbəru:fən] (*unreg*) *vt* to convene; (*MIL*) to call up

einbeziehen ['aɪnbətsi:ən] (*unreg*) *vt* to include

einbiegen ['aɪnbi:gən] (*unreg*) *vi* to turn

einbilden ['aɪnbɪldən] *vt:* **sich** *dat* **etw** ~ to imagine sth

Einbildung *f* imagination; (*Dünkel*) conceit; **Einbildungskraft** *f* imagination

Einblick ['aɪnblɪk] *m* insight

einbrechen ['aɪnbrɛçən] (*unreg*) *vi* (*in Haus*) to break in; (*Nacht*) to fall; (*Winter*) to set in; (*durchbrechen*) to break; ~ **in** +*akk* (*MIL*) to invade

Einbrecher (-s, -) *m* burglar

einbringen ['aɪnbrɪŋən] (*unreg*) *vt* to bring in; (*Geld, Vorteil*) to yield; (*mitbringen*) to contribute

Einbruch ['aɪnbrʊx] *m* (*Haus~*) break-in, burglary; (*Eindringen*) invasion; (*des Winters*) onset; (*Durchbrechen*) break; (*MET*) approach; (*MIL*) penetration; (**bei/vor**) ~ **der Nacht** (at/before)

nightfall; **einbruchssicher** *adj* burglar-proof

einbürgern ['aɪnbyrgərn] *vt* to naturalize ♦ *vr* to become adopted

Einbürgerung *f* naturalization

Einbuße ['aɪnbu:sə] *f* loss, forfeiture

einbüßen ['aɪnby:sən] *vt* to lose, to forfeit

einchecken ['aɪntʃɛkən] *vt, vi* to check in

eindecken ['aɪndɛkən] *vr:* **sich** (**mit etw**) ~ to lay in stocks (of sth); to stock up (with sth)

eindeutig ['aɪndɔʏtɪç] *adj* unequivocal

eindringen ['aɪndrɪŋən] (*unreg*) *vi:* ~ (**in** +*akk*) to force one's way in(to); (*in Haus*) to break in(to); (*in Land*) to invade; (*Gas, Wasser*) to penetrate; (**auf jdn**) ~ (*mit Bitten*) to pester (sb)

eindringlich *adj* forcible, urgent

Eindringling *m* intruder

Eindruck ['aɪndrʊk] *m* impression

eindrücken ['aɪndrʏkən] *vt* to press in

eindrucksvoll *adj* impressive

eine(r, s) *pron* one; (*jemand*) someone

eineiig ['aɪn'aɪç] *adj* (*Zwillinge*) identical

eineinhalb ['aɪn'aɪn'halp] *num* one and a half

einengen ['aɪn'ɛŋən] *vt* to confine, to restrict

einer- ['aɪnər] *zW:* '**E~'lei** (-s) *nt* sameness; '~'**lei** *adj* (*gleichartig*) the same kind of; **es ist mir** ~**lei** it is all the same to me; ~**seits** *adv* on the one hand

einfach ['aɪnfax] *adj* simple; (*nicht mehrfach*) single ♦ *adv* simply; **E~heit** *f* simplicity

einfahren ['aɪnfa:rən] (*unreg*) *vt* to bring in; (*Barriere*) to knock down; (*Auto*) to run in ♦ *vi* to drive in; (*Zug*) to pull in; (*MIN*) to go down

Einfahrt *f* (*Vorgang*) driving in; pulling in; (*MIN*) descent; (*Ort*) entrance

Einfall ['aɪnfal] *m* (*Idee*) idea, notion; (*Licht~*) incidence; (*MIL*) raid; **e~en** (*unreg*) *vi* (*Licht*) to fall; (*MIL*) to raid; (*einstürzen*) to fall in, to collapse; (*einstimmen*): (**in etw** *akk*) **e~en** to join in (with sth); **etw fällt jdm ein** sth occurs to sb; **das fällt mir gar nicht ein** I wouldn't dream of it; **sich** *dat* **etwas e~en lassen** to have a good idea

einfältig ['aɪnfɛltɪç] *adj* simple(-minded)

Einfamilienhaus [aɪnfaˈmiːliənhaus] *nt* detached house

einfarbig ['aɪnfarbɪç] *adj* all one colour; (*Stoff etc*) self-coloured

einfetten ['aɪnfɛtən] *vt* to grease

einfinden ['aɪnfɪndən] (*unreg*) *vr* to come, to turn up

einfließen ['aɪnfliːsən] (*unreg*) *vi* to flow in

einflößen ['aɪnfløːsən] *vt*: **jdm etw ~** to give sb sth; (*fig*) to instil sth in sb

Einfluß ['aɪnflʊs] *m* influence; **e~reich** *adj* influential

einförmig ['aɪnfœrmɪç] *adj* uniform; **E~keit** *f* uniformity

einfrieren ['aɪnfriːrən] (*unreg*) *vi* to freeze (in) ♦ *vt* to freeze

einfügen ['aɪnfyːgən] *vt* to fit in; (*zusätzlich*) to add

Einfuhr ['aɪnfuːr] (-) *f* import; **~artikel** *m* imported article

einführen ['aɪnfyːrən] *vt* to bring in; (*Mensch, Sitten*) to introduce; (*Ware*) to import

Einführung *f* introduction

Eingabe ['aɪngaːbə] *f* petition; (*COMPUT*) input

Eingang ['aɪngaŋ] *m* entrance; (*COMM: Ankunft*) arrival; (*Erhalt*) receipt; **e~s** *adv* at the outset ♦ *präp +gen* at the outset of

eingeben ['aɪngeːbən] (*unreg*) *vt* (*Arznei*) to give; (*Daten etc*) to enter

eingebildet ['aɪngəbɪldət] *adj* imaginary; (*eitel*) conceited

Eingeborene(r) ['aɪngəboːrənə(r)] *mf* native

Eingebung *f* inspiration

eingedenk ['aɪngədɛŋk] *präp +gen* bearing in mind

eingefroren ['aɪngəfroːrən] *adj* frozen

eingehen ['aɪngeːən] (*unreg*) *vi* (*Aufnahme finden*) to come in; (*Sendung, Geld*) to be received; (*Tier,*

Pflanze) to die; (*Firma*) to fold; (*schrumpfen*) to shrink ♦ *vt* to enter into; (*Wette*) to make; **auf etw** *akk* **~** to go into sth; **auf jdn ~** to respond to sb; **jdm ~** (*verständlich sein*) to be comprehensible to sb; **~d** *adj* exhaustive, thorough

Eingemachte(s) ['aɪngəmaxtə(s)] *nt* preserves *pl*

eingenommen ['aɪngənɔmən] *adj*: **~ (von)** fond (of), partial (to); **~ (gegen)** prejudiced (against)

eingeschrieben ['aɪngəʃriːbən] *adj* registered

eingespielt ['aɪngəʃpiːlt] *adj*: **aufeinander ~ sein** to be in tune with each other

Eingeständnis ['aɪngəʃtɛntnɪs] (**-ses, -se**) *nt* admission, confession

eingestehen ['aɪngəʃteːən] (*unreg*) *vt* to confess

eingetragen ['aɪngətraːgən] *adj* (*COMM*) registered

Eingeweide ['aɪngəwaɪdə] (**-s, -**) *nt* innards *pl*, intestines *pl*

Eingeweihte(r) ['aɪngəwaɪtə(r)] *mf* initiate

eingleisig ['aɪnglaɪzɪç] *adj* single-track

eingreifen ['aɪngraɪfən] (*unreg*) *vi* to intervene, to interfere; (*Zahnrad*) to mesh

Eingriff ['aɪngrɪf] *m* intervention, interference; (*Operation*) operation

einhaken ['aɪnhaːkən] *vt* to hook in ♦ *vr*: **sich bei jdm ~** to link arms with sb ♦ *vi* (*sich einmischen*) to intervene

Einhalt ['aɪnhalt] *m*: **~ gebieten** +*dat* to put a stop to; **e~en** (*unreg*) *vt* (*Regel*) to keep ♦ *vi* to stop

einhändigen ['aɪnhɛndɪgən] *vt* to hand in

einhängen ['aɪnhɛŋən] *vt* to hang; (*Telefon*) to hang up ♦ *vi* (*TEL*) to hang up; **sich bei jdm ~** to link arms with sb

einheimisch ['aɪnhaɪmɪʃ] *adj* native

Einheit ['aɪnhaɪt] *f* unity; (*Maß, MIL*) unit; **e~lich** *adj* uniform; **Einheitspreis** *m* standard price

einholen ['aɪnhoːlən] *vt* (*Tau*) to haul in; (*Fahne, Segel*) to lower; (*Vor-*

sprung aufholen) to catch up with; (*Verspätung*) to make up; (*Rat, Erlaubnis*) to ask ♦ *vi* (*einkaufen*) to shop

Einhorn ['aɪnhɔrn] *nt* unicorn

einhüllen ['aɪnhʏlən] *vt* to wrap up

einig ['aɪnɪç] *adj* (*vereint*) united; **sich** *dat* ~ **sein** to be in agreement; ~ **werden** to agree

einige(r, s) ['aɪnɪgə(r, s)] *adj, pron* some ♦ *pl* some; (*mehrere*) several; ~**mal** *adv* a few times; ~**n** *vt* to unite ♦ *vr:* **sich** ~**n** (**auf** +*akk*) to agree (on)

einigermaßen *adv* somewhat; (*leidlich*) reasonably

einiges *pron* something

einig- *zW:* ~**gehen** (*unreg*) *vi* to agree; **E~keit** *f* unity; (*Übereinstimmung*) agreement; **E~ung** *f* agreement; (*Vereinigung*) unification

einkalkulieren ['aɪnkalkuliːrən] *vt* to take into account, to allow for

Einkauf ['aɪnkaʊf] *m* purchase; **e~en** *vt* to buy ♦ *vi* to shop; **e~en gehen** to go shopping

Einkaufs- *zW:* ~**bummel** *m* shopping spree; ~**korb** *m* shopping basket; ~**netz** *nt* string bag; ~**preis** *m* cost price; ~**wagen** *m* shopping trolley; ~**zentrum** *nt* shopping centre

einklammern ['aɪnklamərn] *vt* to put in brackets, to bracket

Einklang ['aɪnklaŋ] *m* harmony

einklemmen ['aɪnklɛmən] *vt* to jam

einkochen ['aɪnkɔxən] *vt* to boil down; (*Obst*) to preserve, to bottle

Einkommen ['aɪnkɔmən] (-s, -) *nt* income; ~(s)**steuer** *f* income tax

Einkünfte ['aɪnkʏnftə] *pl* income *sg*, revenue *sg*

einladen ['aɪnlaːdən] (*unreg*) *vt* (*Person*) to invite; (*Gegenstände*) to load; **jdn ins Kino** ~ to take sb to the cinema

Einladung *f* invitation

Einlage ['aɪnlaːgə] *f* (*Programm*~) interlude; (*Spar*~) deposit; (*Schuh*~) insole; (*Fußstütze*) support; (*Zahn*~) temporary filling; (*KOCH*) noodles *pl*, vegetables *pl etc* in soup

einlagern *vt* to store

einlassen ['aɪnlasən] (*unreg*) *vt* to let in; (*einsetzen*) to set in ♦ *vr:* **sich mit jdm/auf etw** *akk* ~ to get involved with sb/sth

Einlauf ['aɪnlaʊf] *m* arrival; (*von Pferden*) finish; (*MED*) enema; **e~en** (*unreg*) *vi* to arrive, to come in; (*in Hafen*) to enter; (*SPORT*) to finish; (*Wasser*) to run in; (*Stoff*) to shrink ♦ *vt* (*Schuhe*) to break in ♦ *vr* (*SPORT*) to warm up; (*Motor, Maschine*) to run in; **jdm das Haus e~en** to invade sb's house

einleben ['aɪnleːbən] *vr* to settle down

einlegen ['aɪnleːgən] *vt* (*einfügen: Blatt, Sohle*) to insert; (*KOCH*) to pickle; (*Pause*) to have; (*Protest*) to make; (*Veto*) to use; (*Berufung*) to lodge; (*AUT: Gang*) to engage

einleiten ['aɪnlaɪtən] *vt* to introduce, to start; (*Geburt*) to induce

Einleitung *f* introduction; induction

einleuchten ['aɪnlɔʏçtən] *vi:* (**jdm**) ~ to be clear *od* evident (to sb); ~**d** *adj* clear

einliefern ['aɪnliːfərn] *vt:* ~ (**in** +*akk*) to take (into)

einlösen ['aɪnløːzən] *vt* (*Scheck*) to cash; (*Schuldschein, Pfand*) to redeem; (*Versprechen*) to keep

einmachen ['aɪnmaxən] *vt* to preserve

einmal ['aɪnmaːl] *adv* once; (*erstens*) first; (*zukünftig*) some time; **nehmen wir** ~ **an** just let's suppose; **noch** ~ once more; **nicht** ~ not even; **auf** ~ all at once; **es war** ~ once upon a time there was/were; **E~'eins** *nt* multiplication tables *pl*; ~**ig** *adj* unique; (*nur einmal erforderlich*) single; (*prima*) fantastic

Einmannbetrieb [aɪn'manbətriːp] *m* one-man business

Einmarsch ['aɪnmarʃ] *m* entry; (*MIL*) invasion; **e~ieren** *vi* to march in

einmischen ['aɪnmɪʃən] *vr:* **sich** ~ (**in** +*akk*) to interfere (with)

einmütig ['aɪnmyːtɪç] *adj* unanimous

Einnahme ['aɪnnaːmə] *f* (*von Medizin*) taking; (*MIL*) capture, taking; ~**n** *pl*

(*Geld*) takings, revenue *sg*; **~quelle** *f* source of income

einnehmen ['ainne:mən] (*unreg*) *vt* to take; (*Stellung, Raum*) to take up; ~ **für/gegen** to persuade in favour of/against; **~d** *adj* charming

Einöde ['ain'ø:də] *f* desert, wilderness

einordnen ['ain'ɔrdnən] *vt* to arrange, to fit in ♦ *vr* to adapt; (*AUT*) to get into lane

einpacken ['ainpakən] *vt* to pack (up)

einparken ['ainparkən] *vt* to park

einpendeln ['ainpɛndəln] *vr* to even out

einpflanzen ['ainpflantsən] *vt* to plant; (*MED*) to implant

einplanen ['ainpla:nən] *vt* to plan for

einprägen ['ainprɛ:gən] *vt* to impress, to imprint; (*beibringen*): (**jdm**) ~ to impress (on sb); **sich** *dat* **etw** ~ to memorize sth

einrahmen ['ainra:mən] *vt* to frame

einräumen ['ainrɔymən] *vt* (*ordnend*) to put away; (*überlassen: Platz*) to give up; (*zugestehen*) to admit, to concede

einreden ['ainre:dən] *vt*: **jdm/sich etw** ~ to talk sb/o.s. into believing sth

einreiben ['ainraibən] (*unreg*) *vt* to rub in

einreichen ['ainraiçən] *vt* to hand in; (*Antrag*) to submit

Einreise ['ainraizə] *f* entry; **~bestimmungen** *pl* entry regulations; **~erlaubnis** *f* entry permit; **~genehmigung** *f* entry permit; **e~n** *vi*: (**in ein Land**) **e~n** to enter (a country)

einrichten ['ainrıçtən] *vt* (*Haus*) to furnish; (*schaffen*) to establish, to set up; (*arrangieren*) to arrange; (*möglich machen*) to manage ♦ *vr* (*in Haus*) to furnish one's house; **sich** ~ (**auf** +*akk*) (*sich vorbereiten*) to prepare o.s. (for); (*sich anpassen*) to adapt to (to)

Einrichtung *f* (*Wohnungs~*) furnishings *pl*; (*öffentliche Anstalt*) organization; (*Dienste*) service

einrosten ['ainrɔstən] *vi* to get rusty

Eins [ains] (**-, -en**) *f* one; **e~** *num* one; **es ist mir alles e~** it's all one to me

einsam ['ainza:m] *adj* lonely, solitary;

E~keit *f* loneliness, solitude

einsammeln ['ainzaməln] *vt* to collect

Einsatz ['ainzats] *m* (*Teil*) inset; (*an Kleid*) insertion; (*Verwendung*) use, employment; (*Spiel~*) stake; (*Risiko*) risk; (*MIL*) operation; (*MUS*) entry; **im** ~ in action; **e~bereit** *adj* ready for action

einschalten ['ainʃaltən] *vt* (*einfügen*) to insert; (*Pause*) to make; (*ELEK*) to switch on; (*Anwalt*) to bring in ♦ *vr* (*dazwischentreten*) to intervene

einschätzen ['ainʃɛtsən] *vt* to estimate, to assess ♦ *vr* to rate o.s.

einschenken ['ainʃɛŋkən] *vt* to pour out

einschicken ['ainʃıkən] *vt* to send in

einschl. *abk* (= *einschließlich*) incl.

einschlafen ['ainʃla:fən] (*unreg*) *vi* to fall asleep, to go to sleep

einschläfernd ['ainʃlɛ:fərnt] *adj* (*MED*) soporific; (*langweilig*) boring; (*Stimme*) lulling

Einschlag ['ainʃla:k] *m* impact; (*fig: Beimischung*) touch, hint; **e~en** (*unreg*) *vt* to knock in; (*Fenster*) to smash, to break; (*Zähne, Schädel*) to smash in; (*AUT: Räder*) to turn; (*kürzer machen*) to take up; (*Ware*) to pack, to wrap up; (*Weg, Richtung*) to take ♦ *vi* to hit; (*sich einigen*) to agree; (*Anklang finden*) to work, to succeed; **in etw** *akk*/**auf jdn e~en** to hit sb/sth

einschlägig ['ainʃlɛ:gıç] *adj* relevant

einschließen ['ainʃli:sən] (*unreg*) *vt* (*Kind*) to lock in; (*Häftling*) to lock up; (*Gegenstand*) to lock away; (*Bergleute*) to cut off; (*umgeben*) to surround; (*MIL*) to encircle; (*fig*) to include, to comprise ♦ *vr* to lock o.s. in

einschließlich *adv* inclusive ♦ *präp* +*gen* inclusive of, including

einschmeicheln ['ainʃmaiçəln] *vr*: **sich** ~ (**bei**) to ingratiate o.s. (with)

einschnappen ['ainʃnapən] *vi* (*Tür*) to click to; (*fig*) to be touchy; **eingeschnappt sein** to be in a huff

einschneidend ['ainʃnaidənt] *adj* drastic

Einschnitt ['ainʃnıt] *m* cutting; (*MED*) incision; (*Ereignis*) decisive point

einschränken ['aɪnʃrɛŋkən] *vt* to limit, to restrict; (*Kosten*) to cut down, to reduce ♦ *vr* to cut down (on expenditure); ~**d** *adj* restrictive

Einschränkung *f* restriction, limitation; reduction; (*von Behauptung*) qualification

Einschreib- ['aɪnʃraɪb] *zW*: ~(**e)brief** *m* recorded delivery letter; **e~en** (*unreg*) *vt* to write in; (*Post*) to send recorded delivery ♦ *vr* to register; (*UNIV*) to enrol; ~**en** *nt* recorded delivery letter

einschreiten ['aɪnʃraɪtən] (*unreg*) *vi* to step in, to intervene; ~ **gegen** to take action against

einschüchtern ['aɪnʃʏçtərn] *vt* to intimidate

einschweißen ['aɪnʃvaɪsən] *vt* to shrinkwrap

einsehen ['aɪnzeːən] (*unreg*) *vt* (*hineinsehen in*) to realize; (*Akten*) to have a look at; (*verstehen*) to see; **E~** (**-s**) *nt* understanding; **ein E~ haben** to show understanding

einseitig ['aɪnzaɪtɪç] *adj* one-sided

Einsend- ['aɪnzɛnd] *zW*: **e~en** (*unreg*) *vt* to send in; ~**er** (**-s, -**) *m* sender, contributor; ~**ung** *f* sending in

einsetzen ['aɪnzɛtsən] *vt* to put (in); (*in Amt*) to appoint, to install; (*Geld*) to stake; (*verwenden*) to use; (*MIL*) to employ ♦ *vi* (*beginnen*) to set in; (*MUS*) to enter, to come in ♦ *vr* to work hard; **sich für jdn/etw** ~ to support sb/sth

Einsicht ['aɪnzɪçt] *f* insight; (*in Akten*) look, inspection; **zu der** ~ **kommen, daß** ... to come to the conclusion that ...; **e~ig** *adj* (*Mensch*) judicious; ~**nahme** *f* examination; **einsichtslos** *adj* unreasonable; **einsichtsvoll** *adj* understanding

Einsiedler ['aɪnziːdlər] *m* hermit

einsilbig ['aɪnzɪlbɪç] *adj* (*auch fig*) monosyllabic; (*Mensch*) uncommunicative

einsperren ['aɪnʃpɛrən] *vt* to lock up

einspielen ['aɪnʃpiːlən] *vr* (*SPORT*) to warm up ♦ *vt* (*Film: Geld*) to bring in; (*Instrument*) to play in; **sich aufeinander** ~ to become attuned to each

other; **gut eingespielt** running smoothly

einspringen ['aɪnʃprɪŋən] (*unreg*) *vi* (*aushelfen*) to help out, to step into the breach

Einspritzmotor ['aɪnʃprɪtsmoːtər] *m* fuel injection engine

Einspruch ['aɪnʃprʊx] *m* protest, objection; **Einspruchsrecht** *nt* veto

einspurig ['aɪnʃpuːrɪç] *adj* (*EISENB*) single-track; (*AUT*) single-lane

einst [aɪnst] *adv* once; (*zukünftig*) one day, some day

Einstand ['aɪnʃtant] *m* (*TENNIS*) deuce; (*Antritt*) entrance (to office)

einstecken ['aɪnʃtɛkən] *vt* to stick in, to insert; (*Brief*) to post; (*ELEK: Stecker*) to plug in; (*Geld*) to pocket; (*mitnehmen*) to take; (*überlegen sein*) to put in the shade; (*hinnehmen*) to swallow

einstehen ['aɪnʃteːən] (*unreg*) *vi*: **für jdn/etw** ~ to guarantee sb/sth; (*verantworten*): **für etw** ~ to answer for sth

einsteigen ['aɪnʃtaɪgən] (*unreg*) *vi* to get in *od* on; (*in Schiff*) to go on board; (*sich beteiligen*) to come in; (*hineinklettern*) to climb in

einstellen ['aɪnʃtɛlən] *vt* (*aufhören*) to stop; (*Geräte*) to adjust; (*Kamera etc*) to focus; (*Sender, Radio*) to tune in; (*unterstellen*) to put; (*in Firma*) to employ, to take on ♦ *vi* (*Firma*) to take on staff/workers ♦ *vr* (*anfangen*) to set in; (*kommen*) to arrive; **sich auf jdn** ~ to adapt to sb; **sich auf etw** *akk* ~ to prepare o.s. for sth

Einstellung *f* (*Aufhören*) suspension, cessation; adjustment; focusing; (*von Arbeiter etc*) appointment; (*Haltung*) attitude

Einstieg ['aɪnʃtiːk] (**-(e)s, -e**) *m* entry; (*fig*) approach

einstig ['aɪnstɪç] *adj* former

einstimmig ['aɪnʃtɪmɪç] *adj* unanimous; (*MUS*) for one voice

einstmalig ['aɪnstmaːlɪç] *adj* former

einstmals *adv* once, formerly

einstöckig ['aɪnʃtœkɪç] *adj* two-storeyed

Einsturz ['aɪnʃtʊrts] *m* collapse

einstürzen ['aɪnʃtʏrtsən] *vi* to fall in, to collapse

Einsturzgefahr f danger of collapse
einstweilen adv meanwhile; (vorläufig) temporarily, for the time being
einstweilig adj temporary
eintägig ['aɪntɛːgɪç] adj one-day
eintasten ['aɪntastən] vt to key (in)
eintauschen ['aɪntauʃən] vt: ~ (gegen od für) to exchange (for)
eintausend ['aɪn'tauzənt] num one thousand
einteilen ['aɪntaɪlən] vt (in Teile) to divide (up); (Menschen) to assign
einteilig adj one-piece
eintönig ['aɪntøːnɪç] adj monotonous; **E~keit** f monotony
Eintopf ['aɪntɔpf] m stew; **~gericht** nt stew
Eintracht ['aɪntraxt] (-) f concord, harmony
einträchtig ['aɪntrɛçtɪç] adj harmonious
Eintrag ['aɪntraːk] (-(e)s, ⁻e) m entry; **amtlicher ~** entry in the register; **e~en** (unreg) vt (in Buch) to enter; (Profit) to yield ♦ vr to put one's name down; **jdm etw e~en** to bring sb sth
einträglich ['aɪntrɛːklɪç] adj profitable
eintreffen ['aɪntrɛfən] (unreg) vi to happen; (ankommen) to arrive
eintreten ['aɪntreːtən] (unreg) vi to occur; (sich einsetzen) to intercede ♦ vt (Tür) to kick open; **~ in** +akk to enter; (in Club, Partei) to join
Eintritt ['aɪntrɪt] m (Betreten) entrance; (Anfang) commencement; (in Club etc) joining
Eintritts- zW: **~geld** nt admission charge; **~karte** f (admission) ticket; **~preis** m admission charge
einüben ['aɪn'yːbən] vt to practise
Einvernehmen ['aɪnfɛrneːmən] (-s, -) nt agreement, harmony
einverstanden ['aɪnfərʃtandən] excl agreed, okay ♦ adj: **~ sein** to agree, to be agreed
Einverständnis ['aɪnfərʃtɛntnɪs] nt understanding; (gleiche Meinung) agreement
Einwand ['aɪnvant] (-(e)s, ⁻e) m objection
Einwanderer ['aɪnvandərər] m immi-

grant
einwandern vi to immigrate
Einwanderung f immigration
einwandfrei adj perfect ♦ adv absolutely
Einwegflasche ['aɪnveːgflaʃə] f no-deposit bottle
einweichen ['aɪnvaɪçən] vt to soak
einweihen ['aɪnvaɪən] vt (Kirche) to consecrate; (Brücke) to open; (Gebäude) to inaugurate; **~ (in** +akk) (Person) to initiate (in)
Einweihung f consecration; opening; inauguration; initiation
einweisen ['aɪnvaɪzən] (unreg) vt (in Amt) to install; (in Arbeit) to introduce; (in Anstalt) to send
einwenden ['aɪnvɛndən] (unreg) vt: **etwas ~ gegen** to object to, to oppose
einwerfen ['aɪnvɛrfən] (unreg) vt to throw in; (Brief) to post; (Geld) to put in, to insert; (Fenster) to smash; (äußern) to interpose
einwickeln ['aɪnvɪkəln] vt to wrap up; (fig: umg) to outsmart
einwilligen ['aɪnvɪlɪgən] vi: **~ (in** +akk) to consent (to), to agree (to)
Einwilligung f consent
einwirken ['aɪnvɪrkən] vi: **auf jdn/etw ~** to influence sb/sth
Einwohner ['aɪnvoːnər] (-s, -) m inhabitant; **~'meldeamt** nt registration office; **~schaft** f population, inhabitants pl
Einwurf ['aɪnvʊrf] m (Öffnung) slot; (von Münze) insertion; (von Brief) posting; (Einwand) objection; (SPORT) throw-in
Einzahl ['aɪntsaːl] f singular; **e~en** vt to pay in; **~ung** f paying in
einzäunen ['aɪntsɔynən] vt to fence in
Einzel ['aɪntsəl] (-s, -) nt (TENNIS) singles; **~fall** m single instance, individual case; **~haft** f solitary confinement; **~handel** m retail trade; **~handelspreis** m retail price; **~heit** f particular, detail; **e~n** adj single; (vereinzelt) the odd ♦ adv singly; **e~n angeben** to specify; **der/die e~ne** the individual; **das e~ne** the particular; **ins**

e~ne gehen to go into detail(s); ~teil
nt component (part); ~zimmer nt
single room
einziehen ['aıntsiːən] (unreg) vt to draw
in, to take in; (Kopf) to duck; (Fühler,
Antenne, Fahrgestell) to retract;
(Steuern, Erkundigungen) to collect;
(MIL) to draft, to call up; (aus dem
Verkehr ziehen) to withdraw;
(konfiszieren) to confiscate ♦ vi to move
in; (Friede, Ruhe) to come;
(Flüssigkeit) to penetrate
einzig ['aıntsıç] adj only; (ohnegleichen)
unique; das ~e the only thing; der/die
~e the only one; ~artig adj unique
Einzug ['aıntsuːk] m entry, moving in
Eis [aıs] (-es, -) nt ice; (Speise~) ice
cream; ~bahn f ice od skating rink;
~bär m polar bear; ~becher m sun-
dae; ~bein nt pig's trotters pl; ~berg
m iceberg; ~decke f sheet of ice;
~diele f ice-cream parlour
Eisen ['aızən] (-s, -) nt iron
Eisenbahn f railway, railroad (US);
~er (-s, -) m railwayman, railway
employee, railroader (US); ~schaffner
m railway guard; ~wagen m railway
carriage
Eisenerz nt iron ore
eisenhaltig adj containing iron
eisern ['aızərn] adj iron; (Gesundheit)
robust; (Energie) unrelenting; (Reserve) emergency
Eis- zW: e~frei adj clear of ice;
~hockey nt ice hockey; e~ig ['aızıç] adj
icy; e~kalt adj icy cold; ~kunstlauf m
figure skating; ~laufen nt ice skating;
~läufer(in) m(f) ice-skater; ~pickel m
ice-axe; ~schießen nt ≈ curling;
~schrank m fridge, ice-box (US);
~zapfen m icicle; ~zeit f ice age
eitel ['aıtəl] adj vain; E~keit f vanity
Eiter ['aıtər] (-s) m pus; e~ig adj
suppurating; e~n vi to suppurate
Eiweiß (-es, -e) nt white of an egg;
(CHEM) protein
Eizelle f ovum
Ekel¹ ['eːkəl] (-s) m nausea, disgust
Ekel² (-s, -) nt (umg: Mensch) nauseating person

ekelerregend adj nauseating, disgusting
ekelhaft adj nauseating, disgusting
ekelig adj nauseating, disgusting
ekeln vt to disgust ♦ vr: sich ~ (vor
+dat) to loathe, to be disgusted (at); es
ekelt jdn od jdm sb is disgusted
eklig adj nauseating, disgusting
Ekstase [ɛk'staːzə] f ecstasy
Ekzem [ɛk'tseːm] (-s, -e) nt (MED)
eczema
Elan [e'laːn] (-s) m elan
elastisch [e'lastıʃ] adj elastic
Elastizität [elastıtsi'tɛːt] f elasticity
Elch [ɛlç] (-(e)s, -e) m elk
Elefant [ele'fant] m elephant
elegant [ele'gant] adj elegant
Eleganz [ele'gants] f elegance
Elek- [e'lɛk] zW: ~triker [-trikər] (-s, -)
m electrician; e~trisch [-trıʃ] adj electric; e~trisieren [-tri'ziːrən] vt (auch fig)
to electrify; (Mensch) to give an electric shock to ♦ vr to get an electric
shock; ~trizität [-tritsi'tɛːt] f electricity;
~trizitätswerk nt power station;
(Gesellschaft) electric power company
Elektro- [e'lɛktro] zW: ~de [-'troːdə] f
electrode; ~herd m electric cooker;
~n (-s, -en) nt electron; ~nen(ge)hirn
[-'troːnən-] nt electronic brain;
~nenrechner m computer; e~nisch adj
electronic; e~nische Post electronic
mail; e~nischer Briefkasten electronic
mailbox; ~rasierer m electric razor
Element [ele'mɛnt] (-s, -e) nt element;
(ELEK) cell, battery; e~ar [-'taːr] adj
elementary; (naturhaft) elemental
Elend ['eːlɛnt] (-(e)s) nt misery; e~ adj
miserable; Elendsviertel nt slum
elf [ɛlf] num eleven; E~ (-, -en) f
(SPORT) eleven
Elfe f elf
Elfenbein nt ivory
Elfmeter m (SPORT) penalty (kick)
Elite [e'liːtə] f elite
Elixier [elı'ksiːr] (-s, -e) nt elixir
Ellbogen m elbow
Elle ['ɛlə] f ell; (Maß) yard
Ellenbogen m elbow
Ellipse [ɛ'lıpsə] f ellipse

Elsaß ['ɛlzas] (- *od* -sses) *nt*: das ~ Alsace

Elster ['ɛlstər] (-, -n) *f* magpie

elterlich ['ɛltərlɪç] *adj* parental

Eltern ['ɛltərn] *pl* parents; ~**haus** *nt* home; **e~los** *adj* parentless

Email [e'maːj] (-s, -s) *nt* enamel; **e~lieren** [ema'jiːrən] *vt* to enamel

Emanzipation [emantsipatsi'oːn] *f* emancipation

emanzi'pieren *vt* to emancipate

Embryo ['ɛmbryo] (-s, -s *od* **Embryonen**) *m* embryo

Emigration [emigratsi'oːn] *f* emigration

emigrieren [-'griːrən] *vi* to emigrate

empfahl *etc* [ɛm'pfaːl] *vb siehe* **empfehlen**

Empfang [ɛm'pfaŋ] (-(e)s, ⸚e) *m* reception; (*Erhalten*) receipt; **in** ~ **nehmen** to receive; **e~en** (*unreg*) *vt* to receive ♦ *vi* (*schwanger werden*) to conceive

Empfäng- [ɛm'pfɛŋ] *zW*: ~**er** (-s, -) *m* receiver; (*COMM*) addressee, consignee; **e~lich** *adj* receptive, susceptible; ~**nis** (-, -se) *f* conception; ~**nisverhütung** *f* contraception

Empfangs- *zW*: ~**bestätigung** *f* acknowledgement; ~**dame** *f* receptionist; ~**schein** *m* receipt; ~**zimmer** *nt* reception room

empfehlen [ɛm'pfeːlən] (*unreg*) *vt* to recommend ♦ *vr* to take one's leave; **empfehlenswert** *adj* recommendable

Empfehlung *f* recommendation

empfiehlst *etc* [ɛm'pfiːlst] *vb siehe* **empfehlen**

empfind- [ɛm'pfɪnt] *zW*: ~**en** [-dən] (*unreg*) *vt* to feel; ~**lich** *adj* sensitive; (*Stelle*) sore; (*reizbar*) touchy; ~**sam** *adj* sentimental; **E~ung** [-dʊŋ] *f* feeling, sentiment

empfohlen [ɛm'pfoːlən] *vb siehe* **empfehlen**

empor [ɛm'poːr] *adv* up, upwards

empören [ɛm'pøːrən] *vt* to make indignant; to shock ♦ *vr* to become indignant; ~**d** *adj* outrageous

Emporkömmling [ɛm'poːrkœmlɪŋ] *m* upstart, parvenu

Empörung *f* indignation

emsig ['ɛmzɪç] *adj* diligent, busy

End- ['ɛnd] *in zW* final; ~**e** (-s, -n) *nt* end; **am** ~**e** at the end; (*schließlich*) in the end; **am** ~**e sein** to be at the end of one's tether; ~**e Dezember** at the end of December; **zu** ~**e sein** to be finished; **e~en** *vi* to end; **e~gültig** *adj* final, definite

Endivie [ɛn'diːviə] *f* endive

End- *zW*: **e~lich** *adj* final; (*MATH*) finite ♦ *adv* finally; **e~lich!** at last!; **komm e~lich!** come on!; **e~los** *adj* endless, infinite; ~**lospapier** *nt* continuous stationery; ~**spiel** *nt* final(s); ~**spurt** *m* (*SPORT*) final spurt; ~**station** *f* terminus; ~**ung** *f* ending

Energie [enɛr'giː] *f* energy; ~**einsparung** *f* energy saving; **e~los** *adj* lacking in energy, weak; ~**wirtschaft** *f* energy industry

energisch [e'nɛrgɪʃ] *adj* energetic

eng [ɛŋ] *adj* narrow; (*Kleidung*) tight; (*fig: Horizont*) narrow, limited; (*Freundschaft, Verhältnis*) close; ~ **an etw** *dat* close to sth

Engagement [ãgaʒə'mãː] (-s, -s) *nt* engagement; (*Verpflichtung*) commitment

engagieren [ãga'ʒiːrən] *vt* to engage ♦ *vr* to commit o.s.; **ein engagierter Schriftsteller** a committed writer

Enge ['ɛŋə] *f* (*auch fig*) narrowness; (*Land~*) defile; (*Meer~*) straits *pl*; **jdn in die** ~ **treiben** to drive sb into a corner

Engel ['ɛŋəl] (-s, -) *m* angel; **e~haft** *adj* angelic; ~**macher(in)** (-s, -; *umg*) *m(f)* backstreet abortionist

engherzig *adj* petty

England *nt* England

Engländer(in) *m(f)* Englishman (woman)

englisch *adj* English

Engpaß *m* defile, pass; (*fig, Verkehr*) bottleneck

en gros [ã'groː] *adv* wholesale

engstirnig ['ɛŋʃtɪrnɪç] *adj* narrow-minded

Enkel ['ɛŋkəl] (-s, -) *m* grandson; ~**in** *f* granddaughter

enorm [e'nɔrm] *adj* enormous

Ensemble [ã'sãbəl] (-s, -s) *nt* company, ensemble

entbehren [ɛnt'be:rən] *vt* to do without, to dispense with

entbehrlich *adj* superfluous

entbinden [ɛnt'bɪndən] (*unreg*) *vt* (+*gen*) to release (from); (*MED*) to deliver ♦ *vi* to give birth

Entbindung *f* release; (*MED*) confinement; **Entbindungsheim** *nt* maternity hospital

entdeck- [ɛnt'dɛk] *zW:* **~en** *vt* to discover; **E~er** (-s, -) *m* discoverer; **E~ung** *f* discovery

Ente ['ɛntə] *f* duck; (*fig*) canard, false report

enteignen [ɛnt''aɪgnən] *vt* to expropriate; (*Besitzer*) to dispossess

enteisen [ɛnt''aɪzən] *vt* to de-ice, to defrost

enterben [ɛnt''ɛrbən] *vt* to disinherit

entfallen [ɛnt'falən] (*unreg*) *vi* to drop, to fall; (*wegfallen*) to be dropped; **jdm ~** (*vergessen*) to slip sb's memory; **auf jdn ~** to be allotted to sb

entfalten [ɛnt'faltən] *vt* to unfold; (*Talente*) to develop ♦ *vr* to open; (*Mensch*) to develop one's potential

Entfaltung *f* unfolding; (*von Talenten*) development

entfern- [ɛnt'fɛrn] *zW:* **~en** *vt* to remove; (*hinauswerfen*) to expel ♦ *vr* to go away, to withdraw; **~t** *adj* distant; **weit davon ~t sein, etw zu tun** to be far from doing sth; **E~ung** *f* distance; (*Wegschaffen*) removal; **E~ungsmesser** (-s, -) *m* (*PHOT*) rangefinder

entfremden [ɛnt'frɛmdən] *vt* to estrange, to alienate

Entfremdung *f* alienation, estrangement

entfrosten [ɛnt'frɔstən] *vt* to defrost

Entfroster (-s, -) *m* (*AUT*) defroster

entführ- [ɛnt'fy:r] *zW:* **~en** *vt* to carry off, to abduct; to kidnap; **E~er** *m* kidnapper; **E~ung** *f* abduction; kidnapping

entgegen [ɛnt'ge:gən] *präp* +*dat* contrary to, against ♦ *adv* towards; **~bringen** (*unreg*) *vt* to bring; **jdm etw**

~bringen (*fig*) to show sb sth; **~gehen** (*unreg*) *vi* +*dat* to go to meet, to go towards; **~gesetzt** *adj* opposite; (*widersprechend*) opposed; **~halten** (*unreg*) *vt* (*fig*) to object; **E~kommen** *nt* obligingness; **~kommen** (*unreg*) *vi* +*dat* to approach; to meet; (*fig*) to accommodate; **~kommend** *adj* obliging; **~nehmen** (*unreg*) *vt* to receive, to accept; **~sehen** (*unreg*) *vi* +*dat* to await; **~setzen** *vt* to oppose; **~treten** (*unreg*) *vi* +*dat* to step up to; (*fig*) to oppose, to counter; **~wirken** *vi* +*dat* to counteract

entgegnen [ɛnt'ge:gnən] *vt* to reply, to retort

entgehen [ɛnt'ge:ən] (*unreg*) *vi* (*fig*): **jdm ~** to escape sb's notice; **sich** *dat* **etw ~ lassen** to miss sth

entgeistert [ɛnt'gaɪstərt] *adj* thunderstruck

Entgelt [ɛnt'gɛlt] (-(e)s, -e) *nt* compensation, remuneration

entgleisen [ɛnt'glaɪzən] *vi* (*EISENB*) to be derailed; (*fig: Person*) to misbehave; **~ lassen** to derail

entgräten [ɛnt'grɛ:tən] *vt* to fillet, to bone

Enthaarungsmittel [ɛnt'ha:rʊŋsmɪtəl] *nt* depilatory

enthalten [ɛnt'haltən] (*unreg*) *vt* to contain ♦ *vr:* **sich (von etw) ~** to abstain (from sth), to refrain (from sth)

enthaltsam [ɛnt'haltza:m] *adj* abstinent, abstemious; **E~keit** *f* abstinence

enthemmen [ɛnt'hɛmən] *vt:* **jdn ~** to free sb from his inhibitions

enthüllen [ɛnt'hʏlən] *vt* to reveal, to unveil

Enthusiasmus [ɛntuzi'asmʊs] *m* enthusiasm

entkommen [ɛnt'kɔmən] (*unreg*) *vi:* **~ (aus** *od* +*dat*) to get away (from), to escape (from)

entkräften [ɛnt'krɛftən] *vt* to weaken, to exhaust; (*Argument*) to refute

entladen [ɛnt'la:dən] (*unreg*) *vt* to unload; (*ELEK*) to discharge ♦ *vr* (*ELEK, Gewehr*) to discharge; (*Ärger etc*) to vent itself

entlang [ɛnt'laŋ] *präp* (+*akk od dat*)
along ♦ *adv* along; ~ **dem Fluß, den
Fluß** ~ along the river; **~gehen** (*unreg*) *vi* to walk along

entlarven [ɛnt'larfən] *vt* to unmask, to
expose

entlassen [ɛnt'lasən] (*unreg*) *vt* to discharge; (*Arbeiter*) to dismiss

Entlassung *f* discharge; dismissal;
Entlassungsabfindung *f* redundancy
payment

entlasten [ɛnt'lastən] *vt* to relieve;
(*Achse*) to relieve the load on;
(*Angeklagten*) to exonerate; (*Konto*) to
clear

Entlastung *f* relief; (*COMM*) crediting

entlegen [ɛnt'le:gən] *adj* remote

entlocken [ɛnt'lɔkən] *vt*: (**jdm etw**) ~
to elicit (sth from sb)

entmachten [ɛnt'maxtən] *vt* to deprive
of power

entmilitarisiert [ɛntmilitari'ziːrt] *adj*
demilitarized

entmündigen [ɛnt'myndɪgən] *vt* to
certify

entmutigen [ɛnt'muːtɪgən] *vt* to discourage

entnehmen [ɛnt'ne:mən] (*unreg*) *vt*
(+*dat*) to take out (of), to take (from);
(*folgern*) to infer (from)

entrahmen [ɛnt'ra:mən] *vt* to skim

entreißen [ɛnt'raɪsən] (*unreg*) *vt*: **jdm
etw** ~ to snatch sth (away) from sb

entrichten [ɛnt'rɪçtən] *vt* to pay

entrosten [ɛnt'rɔstən] *vt* to derust

entrüst- [ɛnt'rʏst] *zW*: **~en** *vt* to incense, to outrage ♦ *vr* to be filled with
indignation; **~et** *adj* indignant, out-
raged; **E~ung** *f* indignation

entschädigen [ɛnt'ʃɛːdɪgən] *vt* to
compensate

Entschädigung *f* compensation

entschärfen [ɛnt'ʃɛrfən] *vt* to defuse;
(*Kritik*) to tone down

Entscheid [ɛnt'ʃaɪt] (-(e)s, -e) *m* decision; **e~en** (*unreg*) *vt, vi, vr* to decide;
e~end *adj* decisive; (*Stimme*) casting;
~ung *f* decision

entschieden [ɛnt'ʃiːdən] *adj* decided;
(*entschlossen*) resolute; **E~heit** *f*

firmness, determination

entschließen [ɛnt'ʃliːsən] (*unreg*) *vr* to
decide

entschlossen [ɛnt'ʃlɔsən] *adj* deter-
mined, resolute; **E~heit** *f* determination

Entschluß [ɛnt'ʃlʊs] *m* decision;
e~freudig *adj* decisive; **~kraft** *f*
determination, decisiveness

entschuldigen [ɛnt'ʃʊldɪgən] *vt* to
excuse ♦ *vr* to apologize

Entschuldigung *f* apology; (*Grund*)
excuse; **jdn um** ~ **bitten** to apologize to
sb; **~!** excuse me; (*Verzeihung*) sorry

entsetz- [ɛnt'zɛts] *zW*: **~en** *vt* to
horrify; (*MIL*) to relieve ♦ *vr* to be
horrified *od* appalled; **E~en** (-s) *nt*
horror, dismay; **~lich** *adj* dreadful,
appalling; **~t** *adj* horrified

entsinnen [ɛnt'zɪnən] (*unreg*) *vr* +*gen*
to remember

entspannen [ɛnt'ʃpanən] *vt, vr*
(*Körper*) to relax; (*POL: Lage*) to ease

Entspannung *f* relaxation, rest; (*POL*)
détente; **Entspannungspolitik** *f* policy
of détente

entsprechen [ɛnt'ʃprɛçən] (*unreg*) *vi*
+*dat* to correspond to; (*Anforderungen,
Wünschen*) to meet, to comply with;
~d *adj* appropriate ♦ *adv* accordingly

entspringen [ɛnt'ʃprɪŋən] (*unreg*) *vi*
(+*dat*) to spring (from)

entstehen [ɛnt'ʃte:ən] (*unreg*) *vi*: ~
(**aus** *od* **durch**) to arise (from), to result (from)

Entstehung *f* genesis, origin

entstellen [ɛnt'ʃtɛlən] *vt* to disfigure;
(*Wahrheit*) to distort

entstören [ɛnt'ʃtøːrən] *vt* (*RADIO*) to
eliminate interference from; (*AUT*) to
suppress

enttäuschen [ɛnt'tɔʏʃən] *vt* to disappoint

Enttäuschung *f* disappointment

Entwarnung [ɛnt'varnʊŋ] *f* all clear
(signal)

entwässern [ɛnt'vɛsərn] *vt* to drain

entweder ['ɛntveːdər] *konj* either

entwenden [ɛnt'vɛndən] (*unreg*) *vt* to
purloin, to steal

entwerfen [ɛnt'vɛrfən] (*unreg*) *vt* (*Zeichnung*) to sketch; (*Modell*) to design; (*Vortrag, Gesetz etc*) to draft

entwerten [ɛnt'veːrtən] *vt* to devalue; (*stempeln*) to cancel

Entwerter (-s, -) *m* ticket punching machine

entwickeln [ɛnt'vɪkəln] *vt, vr* (*auch* PHOT) to develop; (*Mut, Energie*) to show (o.s.), to display (o.s.)

Entwickler (-s, -) *m* developer

Entwicklung [ɛnt'vɪklʊŋ] *f* development; (PHOT) developing

Entwicklungs- *zW:* ~**hilfe** *f* aid for developing countries; ~**jahre** *pl* adolescence *sg;* ~**land** *nt* developing country

entwöhnen [ɛnt'vøːnən] *vt* to wean; (*Süchtige*): (**einer Sache** *dat od* **von etw**) ~ to cure (of sth)

Entwöhnung *f* weaning; cure, curing

entwürdigend [ɛnt'vʏrdɪɡənt] *adj* degrading

Entwurf [ɛnt'vʊrf] *m* outline, design; (*Vertrags~, Konzept*) draft

entziehen [ɛnt'tsiːən] (*unreg*) *vt* (+*dat*) to withdraw (from), to take away (from); (*Flüssigkeit*) to draw (from), to extract (from) ♦ *vr* (+*dat*) to escape (from); (*jds Kenntnis*) to be outside *od* beyond; (*der Pflicht*) to shirk (from)

Entziehung *f* withdrawal; ~**sanstalt** *f* drug addiction/alcoholism treatment centre; ~**skur** *f* treatment for drug addiction/alcoholism

entziffern [ɛnt'tsɪfərn] *vt* to decipher; to decode

entzücken [ɛnt'tsʏkən] *vt* to delight; **E~** (-s) *nt* delight; ~**d** *adj* delightful, charming

entzünden [ɛnt'tsʏndən] *vt* to light, to set light to; (*fig,* MED) to inflame; (*Streit*) to spark off ♦ *vr* (*auch fig*) to catch fire; (*Streit*) to start; (MED) to become inflamed

Entzündung *f* (MED) inflammation

entzwei [ɛnt'tsvaɪ] *adv* broken; in two; ~**brechen** (*unreg*) *vt, vi* to break in two; ~**en** *vt* to set at odds ♦ *vr* to fall out; ~**gehen** (*unreg*) *vi* to break (in two)

Enzian ['ɛntsiaːn] (-s, -e) *m* gentian

Enzym [ɛn'tsyːm] (-s, -e) *nt* enzyme

Epidemie [epide'miː] *f* epidemic

Epilepsie [epile'psiː] *f* epilepsy

Episode [epi'zoːdə] *f* episode

Epoche [e'pɔxə] *f* epoch; **e~machend** *adj* epoch-making

Epos ['eːpɔs] (-s, **Epen**) *nt* epic (poem)

er [eːr] (*nom*) *pron* he; it

erachten [ɛr''axtən] *vt:* ~ **für** *od* **als** to consider (to be); **meines E~s** in my opinion

erarbeiten [ɛr''arbaɪtən] *vt* to work for, to acquire; (*Theorie*) to work out

erbarmen [ɛr'barmən] *vr* (+*gen*) to have pity *od* mercy (on); **E~** (-s) *nt* pity

erbärmlich [ɛr'bɛrmlɪç] *adj* wretched, pitiful; **E~keit** *f* wretchedness

erbarmungslos [ɛr'barmʊŋsloːs] *adj* pitiless, merciless

erbau- [ɛr'baʊ] *zW:* ~**en** *vt* to build, to erect; (*fig*) to edify; **E~er** (-s, -) *m* builder; ~**lich** *adj* edifying; **E~ung** *f* construction; (*fig*) edification

Erbe¹ ['ɛrbə] (-n, -n) *m* heir

Erbe² *nt* inheritance; (*fig*) heritage

erben *vt* to inherit

erbeuten [ɛr'bɔʏtən] *vt* to carry off; (MIL) to capture

Erb- [ɛrb] *zW:* ~**faktor** *m* gene; ~**folge** *f* (line of) succession; ~**in** *f* heiress

erbittern [ɛr'bɪtərn] *vt* to embitter; (*erzürnen*) to incense

erbittert [ɛr'bɪtərt] *adj* (*Kampf*) fierce, bitter

erblassen [ɛr'blasən] *vi* to (turn) pale

erbleichen [ɛr'blaɪçən] (*unreg*) *vi* to (turn) pale

erblich ['ɛrplɪç] *adj* hereditary

erbosen [ɛr'boːzən] *vt* to anger ♦ *vr* to grow angry

erbrechen [ɛr'brɛçən] (*unreg*) *vt, vr* to vomit

Erbschaft *f* inheritance, legacy

Erbse ['ɛrpsə] *f* pea

Erd- ['eːrd] *zW:* ~**achse** *f* earth's axis; ~**atmosphäre** *f* earth's atmosphere; ~**beben** *nt* earthquake; ~**beere** *f* strawberry; ~**boden** m ground; ~**e** f earth; **zu ebener** ~**e** at ground level; **e**~**en** vt (ELEK) to earth

erdenklich [ɛr'dɛŋklıç] adj conceivable

Erd- zW: ~**gas** nt natural gas; ~**ge-schoß** nt ground floor; ~**kunde** f geography; ~**nuß** f peanut; ~**oberfläche** f surface of the earth; ~**öl** nt (mineral) oil

erdrosseln [ɛr'drɔsəln] vt to strangle, to throttle

erdrücken [ɛr'drʏkən] vt to crush

Erdrutsch m landslide

Erdteil m continent

erdulden [ɛr'dʊldən] vt to endure, to suffer

ereifern [ɛr''aıfərn] vr to get excited

ereignen [ɛr''aıgnən] vr to happen

Ereignis [ɛr''aıgnıs] (-ses, -se) nt event; **e**~**reich** adj eventful

erfahren [ɛr'faːrən] (unreg) vt to learn, to find out; (erleben) to experience ♦ adj experienced

Erfahrung f experience; **erfah-rungsgemäß** adv according to experience

erfassen [ɛr'fasən] vt to seize; (fig: einbeziehen) to include, to register; (verstehen) to grasp

erfinden [ɛr'fınd] zW: ~**en** (unreg) vt to invent; **E**~**er** (-s, -) m inventor; ~**erisch** adj inventive; **E**~**ung** f invention

Erfolg [ɛr'fɔlk] (-(e)s, -e) m success; (Folge) result; **e**~**en** vi to follow; (sich ergeben) to result; (stattfinden) to take place; (Zahlung) to be effected; **e**~**los** adj unsuccessful; ~**losigkeit** f lack of success; **e**~**reich** adj successful; **e**~**versprechend** adj promising

erforderlich adj requisite, necessary

erfordern [ɛr'fɔrdərn] vt to require, to demand

erforschen [ɛr'fɔrʃən] vt (Land) to explore; (Problem) to investigate; (Gewissen) to search

Erforschung f exploration; investigation; searching

erfreuen [ɛr'frɔyən] vr: **sich** ~ **an** +dat to enjoy ♦ vt to delight; **sich einer Sa-**che gen ~ to enjoy sth

erfreulich [ɛr'frɔylıç] adj pleasing, gratifying; ~**erweise** adv happily, luckily

erfrieren [ɛr'friːrən] (unreg) vi to freeze (to death); (Glieder) to get frostbitten; (Pflanzen) to be killed by frost

erfrischen [ɛr'frıʃən] vt to refresh

Erfrischung f refreshment; **Erfri-schungsraum** m snack bar, cafeteria

erfüllen [ɛr'fʏlən] vt (Raum etc) to fill; (fig: Bitte etc) to fulfil ♦ vr to come true

ergänzen [ɛr'gɛntsən] vt to supplement, to complete ♦ vr to complement one another

Ergänzung f completion; (Zusatz) supplement

ergeben [ɛr'geːbən] (unreg) vt to yield, to produce ♦ vr to surrender; (folgen) to result ♦ adj devoted, humble; **sich etw** dat ~ (sich hingeben) to give o.s. up to sth, to yield to sth; **dem Trunk** ~ addicted to drink; **E**~**heit** f devotion, humility

Ergebnis [ɛr'geːpnıs] (-ses, -se) nt result; **e**~**los** adj without result, fruitless

ergehen [ɛr'geːən] (unreg) vi to be issued, to go out ♦ vi unpers: **es ergeht ihm gut/schlecht** he's faring od getting on well/badly ♦ vr: **sich in etw** dat ~ to indulge in sth; **etw über sich** ~ **lassen** to put up with sth

ergiebig [ɛr'giːbıç] adj productive

ergreifen [ɛr'graıfən] (unreg) vt (auch fig) to seize; (Beruf) to take up; (Maßnahmen) to resort to; (rühren) to move

ergriffen [ɛr'grıfən] adj deeply moved

Erguß [ɛr'gʊs] m discharge; (fig) outpouring, effusion

erhaben [ɛr'haːbən] adj raised, embossed; (fig) exalted, lofty; **über etw** akk ~ **sein** to be above sth

erhalten [ɛr'haltən] (unreg) vt to receive; (bewahren) to preserve, to maintain; **gut** ~ in good condition

erhältlich [ɛr'hɛltlıç] adj obtainable, available

Erhaltung f maintenance, preservation

erhärten [ɛr'hɛrtən] *vt* to harden; (*These*) to substantiate, to corroborate

erheben [ɛr'he:bən] (*unreg*) *vt* to raise; (*Protest, Forderungen*) to make; (*Fakten*) to ascertain, to establish ♦ *vr* to rise (up); **sich über etw** *akk* ~ to rise above sth

erheblich [ɛr'he:plɪç] *adj* considerable

erheitern [ɛr'haɪtərn] *vt* to amuse, to cheer (up)

Erheiterung *f* exhilaration; **zur allgemeinen** ~ to everybody's amusement

erhitzen [ɛr'hɪtsən] *vt* to heat ♦ *vr* to heat up; (*fig*) to become heated

erhoffen [ɛr'hɔfən] *vt* to hope for

erhöhen [ɛr'hø:ən] *vt* to raise; (*verstärken*) to increase

erhol- [ɛr'ho:l] *zW:* ~**en** *vr* to recover; (*entspannen*) to have a rest; ~**sam** *adj* restful; **E~ung** *f* recovery; relaxation, rest; ~**ungsbedürftig** *adj* in need of a rest, run-down; **E~ungsheim** *nt* convalescent/rest home

erhören [ɛr'hø:rən] *vt* (*Gebet etc*) to hear; (*Bitte etc*) to yield to

erinnern [ɛr'ɪnərn] *vt:* ~ (**an** +*akk*) to remind (of) ♦ *vr:* **sich** (**an** *akk* **etw**) ~ to remember (sth)

Erinnerung *f* memory; (*Andenken*) reminder

erkält- [ɛr'kɛlt] *zW:* ~**en** *vr* to catch cold; ~**et** *adj* with a cold; ~**et sein** to have a cold; **E~ung** *f* cold

erkennbar *adj* recognizable

erkennen [ɛr'kɛnən] (*unreg*) *vt* to recognize; (*sehen, verstehen*) to see

erkennt- *zW:* ~**lich** *adj:* **sich** ~**lich zeigen** to show one's appreciation; **E~lichkeit** *f* gratitude; (*Geschenk*) token of one's gratitude; **E~nis** (-, -se) *f* knowledge; (*das Erkennen*) recognition; (*Einsicht*) insight; **zur E~nis kommen** to realize

Erkennung *f* recognition

Erker ['ɛrkər] (-s, -) *m* bay; ~**fenster** *nt* bay window

erklär- [ɛr'klɛ:r] *zW:* ~**bar** *adj* explicable; ~**en** *vt* to explain; ~**lich** *adj* explicable; (*verständlich*) understandable; **E~ung** *f* explanation; (*Aussage*) declaration

erkranken [ɛr'kraŋkən] *vi* to fall ill

Erkrankung *f* illness

erkund- [ɛr'kʊnd] *zW:* ~**en** *vt* to find out, to ascertain; (*bes MIL*) to reconnoitre, to scout; ~**igen** *vr:* **sich** ~**igen** (**nach**) to inquire (about); **E~igung** *f* inquiry; **E~ung** *f* reconnaissance, scouting

erlahmen [ɛr'la:mən] *vi* to tire; (*nachlassen*) to flag, to wane

erlangen [ɛr'laŋən] *vt* to attain, to achieve

Erlaß [ɛr'las] (-sses, -lässe) *m* decree; (*Aufhebung*) remission

erlassen (*unreg*) *vt* (*Verfügung*) to issue; (*Gesetz*) to enact; (*Strafe*) to remit; **jdm etw** ~ to release sb from sth

erlauben [ɛr'laubən] *vt:* (**jdm etw**) ~ to allow *od* permit (sb (to do) sth) ♦ *vr* to permit o.s., to venture

Erlaubnis [ɛr'laupnɪs] (-, -se) *f* permission; (*Schriftstück*) permit

erläutern [ɛr'lɔʏtərn] *vt* to explain

Erläuterung *f* explanation

Erle ['ɛrlə] *f* alder

erleben [ɛr'le:bən] *vt* to experience; (*Zeit*) to live through; (*mit~*) to witness; (*noch mit~*) to live to see

Erlebnis [ɛr'le:pnɪs] (-ses, -se) *nt* experience

erledigen [ɛr'le:dɪgən] *vt* to take care of, to deal with; (*Antrag etc*) to process; (*umg: erschöpfen*) to wear out; (: *ruinieren*) to finish; (: *umbringen*) to do in

erleichter- [ɛr'laɪçtər] *zW:* ~**n** *vt* to make easier; (*fig: Last*) to lighten; (*lindern, beruhigen*) to relieve; ~**t** *adj* relieved; **E~ung** *f* facilitation; lightening; relief

erleiden [ɛr'laɪdən] (*unreg*) *vt* to suffer, to endure

erlernen [ɛr'lɛrnən] *vt* to learn, to acquire

erlesen [ɛr'le:zən] *adj* select, choice

erleuchten [ɛr'lɔʏçtən] *vt* to illuminate; (*fig*) to inspire

Erleuchtung *f* (*Einfall*) inspiration

Erlös [ɛr'løːs] (-es, -e) *m* proceeds *pl*

erlösen [ɛr'løːzən] *vt* to redeem, to save

Erlösung *f* release; (*REL*) redemption

ermächtigen [ɛr'mɛçtɪgən] *vt* to authorize, to empower

Ermächtigung *f* authorization, authority

ermahnen [ɛr'maːnən] *vt* to exhort, to admonish

Ermahnung *f* admonition, exhortation

ermäßigen [ɛr'mɛːsɪgən] *vt* to reduce

Ermäßigung *f* reduction

ermessen [ɛr'mɛsən] (*unreg*) *vt* to estimate, to gauge; **E~** (-s) *nt* estimation; discretion; **in jds E~ liegen** to lie within sb's discretion

ermitteln [ɛr'mɪtəln] *vt* to determine; (*Täter*) to trace ♦ *vi*: **gegen jdn ~** to investigate sb

Ermittlung [ɛr'mɪtlʊŋ] *f* determination; (*Polizei~*) investigation

ermöglichen [ɛr'møːklɪçən] *vt* (+*dat*) to make possible (for)

ermorden [ɛr'mɔrdən] *vt* to murder

Ermordung *f* murder

ermüden [ɛr'myːdən] *vt, vi* to tire; (*TECH*) to fatigue; **Ermüdungd** *adj* tiring; (*fig*) wearisome

Ermüdung *f* fatigue; **Ermüdungserscheinung** *f* sign of fatigue

ermutigen [ɛr'muːtɪgən] *vt* to encourage

ernähr- [ɛr'nɛːr] *zW*: **~en** *vt* to feed, to nourish; (*Familie*) to support ♦ *vr* to support o.s., to earn a living; **sich ~en von** to live on; **E~er** (-s, -) *m* breadwinner; **E~ung** *f* nourishment; nutrition; (*Unterhalt*) maintenance

ernennen [ɛr'nɛnən] (*unreg*) *vt* to appoint

Ernennung *f* appointment

erneu- [ɛr'nɔy] *zW*: **~ern** *vt* to renew; to restore; to renovate; **E~erung** *f* renewal; restoration; renovation; **~t** *adj* renewed, fresh ♦ *adv* once more

ernst [ɛrnst] *adj* serious; **E~** (-es) *m* seriousness; **das ist mein E~** I'm quite serious; **im E~** in earnest; **E~ machen mit etw** to put sth into practice; **E~fall** *m* emergency; **~gemeint** *adj* meant in earnest, serious; **~haft** *adj* serious;

E~haftigkeit *f* seriousness; **~lich** *adj* serious

Ernte ['ɛrntə] *f* harvest; **e~n** *vt* to harvest; (*Lob etc*) to earn

ernüchtern [ɛr'nʏçtərn] *vt* to sober up; (*fig*) to bring down to earth

Erober- [ɛr'oːbər] *zW*: **~er** (-s, -) *m* conqueror; **e~n** *vt* to conquer; **~ung** *f* conquest

eröffnen [ɛr''œfnən] *vt* to open ♦ *vr* to present itself; **jdm etw ~** to disclose sth to sb

Eröffnung *f* opening

erörtern [ɛr''œrtərn] *vt* to discuss

Erörterung *f* discussion

Erotik [e'roːtɪk] *f* eroticism

erotisch *adj* erotic

erpress- [ɛr'prɛs] *zW*: **~en** *vt* (*Geld etc*) to extort; (*Mensch*) to blackmail; **E~er** (-s, -) *m* blackmailer; **E~ung** *f* extortion; blackmail

erraten [ɛr'raːtən] (*unreg*) *vt* to guess

erreg- [ɛr'reːg] *zW*: **~en** *vt* to excite; (*ärgern*) to infuriate; (*hervorrufen*) to arouse, to provoke ♦ *vr* to get excited *od* worked up; **E~er** (-s, -) *m* causative agent; **E~ung** *f* excitement

erreichbar *adj* accessible, within reach

erreichen [ɛr'raiçən] *vt* to reach; (*Zweck*) to achieve; (*Zug*) to catch

errichten [ɛr'rɪçtən] *vt* to erect, to put up; (*gründen*) to establish, to set up

erringen [ɛr'rɪŋən] (*unreg*) *vt* to gain, to win

erröten [ɛr'røːtən] *vi* to blush, to flush

Errungenschaft [ɛr'rʊŋənʃaft] *f* achievement; (*umg: Anschaffung*) acquisition

Ersatz [ɛr'zats] (-es) *m* substitute; replacement; (*Schaden~*) compensation; (*MIL*) reinforcements *pl*; **~dienst** *m* (*MIL*) alternative service; **~reifen** *m* (*AUT*) spare tyre; **~teil** *nt* spare (part)

erschaffen [ɛr'ʃafən] (*unreg*) *vt* to create

erscheinen [ɛr'ʃainən] (*unreg*) *vi* to appear

Erscheinung *f* appearance; (*Geist*) apparition; (*Gegebenheit*) phenomenon; (*Gestalt*) figure

erschießen [ɛr'ʃiːsən] (*unreg*) *vt* to

shoot (dead)
erschlagen [ɛr'ʃlaːgən] (*unreg*) *vt* to strike dead
erschöpf- [ɛr'ʃœpf] *zW:* ~**en** *vt* to exhaust; ~**end** *adj* exhaustive, thorough; ~**t** *adj* exhausted; **E**~**ung** *f* exhaustion
erschrecken [ɛr'ʃrɛkən] *vt* to startle, to frighten ♦ *vi* to be frightened *od* startled; ~**d** *adj* alarming, frightening
erschrocken [ɛr'ʃrɔkən] *adj* frightened, startled
erschüttern [ɛr'ʃytərn] *vt* to shake; (*fig*) to move deeply
Erschütterung *f* shaking; shock
erschweren [ɛr'ʃveːrən] *vt* to complicate
erschwingen [ɛr'ʃvɪŋən] (*unreg*) *vt* to afford
erschwinglich *adj* within one's means
ersehen [ɛr'zeːən] (*unreg*) *vt:* **aus etw** ~, **daß** to gather from sth that
ersetzen [ɛr'zɛtsən] *vt* to replace; **jdm Unkosten** *etc* ~ to pay sb's expenses *etc*
ersichtlich [ɛr'zɪçtlɪç] *adj* evident, obvious
ersparen [ɛr'ʃpaːrən] *vt* (*Ärger etc*) to spare; (*Geld*) to save
Ersparnis (-, -se) *f* saving

SCHLÜSSELWORT

erst [eːrst] *adv* **1** first; **mach erst mal die Arbeit fertig** finish your work first; **wenn du das erst mal hinter dir hast** once you've got that behind you
2 (*nicht früher als, nur*) only; (*nicht bis*) not till; **erst gestern** only yesterday; **erst morgen** not until tomorrow; **erst als** only when, not until; **wir fahren erst später** we're not going until later; **er ist (gerade) erst angekommen** he's only just arrived
3: **wäre er doch erst zurück!** if only he were back!

---

erstatten [ɛr'ʃtatən] *vt* (*Kosten*) to (re)pay; **Anzeige** *etc* **gegen jdn** ~ to report sb; **Bericht** ~ to make a report
Erstaufführung ['eːrst'aʊffyːrʊŋ] *f* first performance

erstaunen [ɛr'ʃtaʊnən] *vt* to astonish ♦ *vi* to be astonished; **E**~ (-s) *nt* astonishment
erstaunlich *adj* astonishing
erst- ['eːrst] *zW:* **E**~**ausgabe** *f* first edition; ~**beste(r, s)** *adj* first that comes along; ~**e(r, s)** *adj* first
erstechen [ɛr'ʃtɛçən] (*unreg*) *vt* to stab (to death)
erstehen [ɛr'ʃteːən] (*unreg*) *vt* to buy ♦ *vi* to (a)rise
erstens ['eːrstəns] *adv* firstly, in the first place
ersticken [ɛr'ʃtɪkən] *vt* (*auch fig*) to stifle; (*Mensch*) to suffocate; (*Flammen*) to smother ♦ *vi* (*Mensch*) to suffocate; (*Feuer*) to be smothered; **in Arbeit** ~ to be snowed under with work
erst- *zW:* ~**klassig** *adj* first-class; **E**~**kommunion** *f* first communion; ~**malig** *adj* first; ~**mals** *adv* for the first time
erstrebenswert [ɛr'ʃtreːbənsveːrt] *adj* desirable, worthwhile
erstrecken [ɛr'ʃtrɛkən] *vr* to extend, to stretch
ersuchen [ɛr'zuːxən] *vt* to request
ertappen [ɛr'tapən] *vt* to catch, to detect
erteilen [ɛr'taɪlən] *vt* to give
Ertrag [ɛr'traːk] (-(e)s, ̈e) *m* yield; (*Gewinn*) proceeds *pl*
ertragen (*unreg*) *vt* to bear, to stand
erträglich [ɛr'trɛːklɪç] *adj* tolerable, bearable
ertrinken [ɛr'trɪŋkən] (*unreg*) *vi* to drown; **E**~ (-s) *nt* drowning
erübrigen [ɛr'yːbrɪgən] *vt* to spare ♦ *vr* to be unnecessary
erwachen [ɛr'vaxən] *vi* to awake
erwachsen [ɛr'vaksən] *adj* grown-up; **E**~**e(r)** *mf* adult; **E**~**enbildung** *f* adult education
erwägen [ɛr'vɛːgən] (*unreg*) *vt* to consider
Erwägung *f* consideration
erwähn- [ɛr'vɛːn] *zW:* ~**en** *vt* to mention; ~**enswert** *adj* worth mentioning; **E**~**ung** *f* mention
erwärmen [ɛr'vɛrmən] *vt* to warm, to

heat ♦ *vr* to get warm, to warm up; sich ~ **für** to warm to

erwarten [ɛrˈvartən] *vt* to expect; (*warten auf*) to wait for; **etw kaum ~ können** to be hardly able to wait for sth

Erwartung *f* expectation; **erwartungsgemäß** *adv* as expected; **erwartungsvoll** *adj* expectant

erwecken [ɛrˈvɛkən] *vt* to rouse, to awake; **den Anschein ~** to give the impression

Erweis [ɛrˈvaɪs] (-es, -e) *m* proof; **e~en** (*unreg*) *vt* to prove ♦ *vr*: **sich e~en** (**als**) to prove (to be); **jdm einen Gefallen/Dienst e~en** to do sb a favour/service

Erwerb [ɛrˈvɛrp] (-(e)s, -e) *m* acquisition; (*Beruf*) trade; **e~en** (*unreg*) *vt* to acquire

erwerbs- *zW:* **~los** *adj* unemployed; **E~quelle** *f* source of income; **~tätig** *adj* (gainfully) employed; **~unfähig** *adj* unable to work

erwidern [ɛrˈviːdərn] *vt* to reply; (*vergelten*) to return

erwiesen [ɛrˈviːzən] *adj* proven

erwischen [ɛrˈvɪʃən] (*umg*) *vt* to catch, to get

erwünscht [ɛrˈvʏnʃt] *adj* desired

erwürgen [ɛrˈvʏrgən] *vt* to strangle

Erz [ɛːrts] (-es, -e) *nt* ore

erzähl- [ɛrˈtsɛːl] *zW:* **~en** *vt* to tell ♦ *vi*: **sie kann gut ~en** she's a good storyteller; **E~er** (-s, -) *m* narrator; **E~ung** *f* story, tale

Erzbischof *m* archbishop

Erzengel *m* archangel

erzeug- [ɛrˈtsɔʏɡ] *zW:* **~en** *vt* to produce; (*Strom*) to generate; **E~nis** (-ses, -se) *nt* product, produce; **E~ung** *f* production; generation

erziehen [ɛrˈtsiːən] (*unreg*) *vt* to bring up; (*bilden*) to educate, to train

Erziehung *f* bringing up; (*Bildung*) education

Erziehungs- *zW:* **~beihilfe** *f* educational grant; **~berechtigte(r)** *mf* parent; guardian; **~heim** *nt* approved school

erzielen [ɛrˈtsiːlən] *vt* to achieve, to

obtain; (*Tor*) to score

erzwingen [ɛrˈtsvɪŋən] (*unreg*) *vt* to force, to obtain by force

es [ɛs] (*nom*, *akk*) *pron* it

Esche [ˈɛʃə] *f* ash

Esel [ˈeːzəl] (-s, -) *m* donkey, ass

Eskalation [ɛskalatsiˈoːn] *f* escalation

eßbar [ˈɛsbaːr] *adj* eatable, edible

essen [ˈɛsən] (*unreg*) *vt*, *vi* to eat; **E~** (-s, -) *nt* meal; food

Essenszeit *f* mealtime; dinner time

Essig [ˈɛsɪç] (-s, -e) *m* vinegar; **~gurke** *f* gherkin

Eß- [ˈɛs] *zW:* **~kastanie** *f* sweet chestnut; **~löffel** *m* tablespoon; **~tisch** *m* dining table; **~waren** *pl* foodstuffs, provisions; **~zimmer** *nt* dining room

etablieren [etaˈbliːrən] *vr* to become established; to set up in business

Etage [eˈtaːʒə] *f* floor, storey; **Etagenbetten** *pl* bunk beds; **Etagenwohnung** *f* flat

Etappe [eˈtapə] *f* stage

Etat [eˈtaː] (-s, -s) *m* budget

etepetete [eːtəpeˈteːtə] (*umg*) *adj* fussy

Ethik [ˈeːtɪk] *f* ethics *sg*

ethisch [ˈeːtɪʃ] *adj* ethical

Etikett [etiˈkɛt] (-(e)s, -e) *nt* label; tag; **~e** *f* etiquette, manners *pl*; **e~ieren** [-ˈtiːrən] *vt* to label; to tag

etliche [ˈɛtlɪçə] *pron pl* some, quite a few

etliches *pron* a thing or two

Etui [ɛtˈviː] (-s, -s) *nt* case

etwa [ˈɛtva] *adv* (*ungefähr*) about; (*vielleicht*) perhaps; (*beispielsweise*) for instance; **nicht ~** by no means; **~ig** [ˈɛtvaɪç] *adj* possible

etwas *pron* something; anything; (*ein wenig*) a little ♦ *adv* a little

euch [ɔʏç] *pron* (*akk von ihr*) you; yourselves; (*dat von ihr*) (to) you

euer [ˈɔʏər] *pron* (*gen von ihr*) of you ♦ *adj* your

Eule [ˈɔʏlə] *f* owl

eure *adj* *f siehe* **euer**

eure(r, s) [ˈɔʏrə(r, s)] *pron* yours; **eurerseits** *adv* on your part; **eures** *adj nt siehe* **euer**; **euresgleichen** *pron* people like you; **euretwegen** *adv* (*für* *euch*) for your sakes; (*wegen euch*) on your account; **euretwillen** *adv*: um euretwillen = euretwegen

eurige ['ɔyrɪgə] *pron*: der/die/das ~ yours

Euro- *zW*: ~**pa** [ɔy'roːpa] *nt* Europe; ~**päer(in)** [ɔyro'pɛːər(ɪn)] *mf* European; **e~päisch** *adj* European; ~**pameister** [ɔy'roːpa-] *m* European champion

Euter ['ɔytər] (-**s**, -) *nt* udder

ev. *abk* = evangelisch

evakuieren [evaku'iːrən] *vt* to evacuate

evangelisch [evaŋ'geːlɪʃ] *adj* Protestant

Evangelium [evaŋ'geːliʊm] *nt* gospel

eventuell [eventu'ɛl] *adj* possible ♦ *adv* possibly, perhaps

evtl. *abk* = eventuell

EWG [eːveː'geː] (-) *f abk* (= *Europäische Wirtschaftsgemeinschaft*) EEC, Common Market

ewig ['eːvɪç] *adj* eternal; **E~keit** *f* eternity

Ex- [ɛks] *in zW* ex-

exakt [ɛ'ksakt] *adj* exact

Examen [ɛ'ksaːmən] (-**s**, - *od* **Examina**) *nt* examination

Exemplar [ɛksɛm'plaːr] (-**s**, -**e**) *nt* specimen; (*Buch~*) copy; **e~isch** *adj* exemplary

exerzieren [ɛksɛr'tsiːrən] *vi* to drill

Exil [ɛ'ksiːl] (-**s**, -**e**) *nt* exile

Existenz [ɛksɪs'tɛnts] *f* existence; (*Unterhalt*) livelihood, living; (*pej: Mensch*) character; ~**kampf** *m* struggle for existence; ~**minimum** (-**s**) *nt* subsistence level

existieren [ɛksɪs'tiːrən] *vi* to exist

exklusiv [ɛksklu'ziːf] *adj* exclusive; ~**e** [-'ziːvə] *adv* exclusive of, not including ♦ *präp +gen* exclusive of, not including

exotisch [ɛ'ksoːtɪʃ] *adj* exotic

Expedition [ɛkspeditsi'oːn] *f* expedition

Experiment [ɛksperi'ment] *nt* experiment; **e~ell** [-'tɛl] *adj* experimental; **e~ieren** [-'tiːrən] *vi* to experiment

Experte [ɛks'pɛrtə] (-**n**, -**n**) *m* expert, specialist

Expertin *f* expert, specialist

explo- [ɛksplo] *zW*: ~**dieren** [-'diːrən] *vi* to explode; **E~sion** [-zi'oːn] *f* explosion;

~**siv** [-'ziːf] *adj* explosive

Export [ɛks'pɔrt] (-(**e**)**s**, -**e**) *m* export; ~**eur** [-'tøːr] *m* exporter; ~**handel** *m* export trade; **e~ieren** [-'tiːrən] *vt* to export; ~**land** *nt* exporting country

Expreßgut [ɛks'prɛs-] *nt* express goods *pl*, express freight

Expreßzug *m* express (train)

extra ['ɛkstra] *adj inv* (*umg: gesondert*) separate; (*besondere*) extra ♦ *adv* (*gesondert*) separately; (*speziell*) specially; (*absichtlich*) on purpose; (*vor Adjektiven, zusätzlich*) extra; **E~** (-**s**, -**s**) *nt* extra; **E~ausgabe** *f* special edition; **E~blatt** *nt* special edition

Extrakt [ɛks'trakt] (-(**e**)**s**, -**e**) *m* extract

extrem [ɛks'treːm] *adj* extreme; ~**istisch** [-'mɪstɪʃ] *adj* (*POL*) extremist; **E~itäten** [-'tɛːtən] *pl* extremities

exzentrisch [ɛks'tsɛntrɪʃ] *adj* eccentric

Exzeß [ɛks'tsɛs] (-**sses**, -**sse**) *m* excess

F

Fa. *abk* (= *Firma*) firm; (*in Briefen*) Messrs

Fabel ['faːbəl] (-, -**n**) *f* fable; **f~haft** *adj* fabulous, marvellous

Fabrik [fa'briːk] *f* factory; ~**ant** [-'kant] *m* (*Hersteller*) manufacturer; (*Besitzer*) industrialist; ~**arbeiter** *m* factory worker; ~**at** [-'kaːt] (-(**e**)**s**, -**e**) *nt* manufacture, product; ~**ation** [-atsi'oːn] *f* manufacture, production; ~**gelände** *nt* factory site

Fach [fax] (-(**e**)**s**, -**er**) *nt* compartment; (*Sachgebiet*) subject; ein Mann vom ~ an expert; ~**arbeiter** *m* skilled worker; ~**arzt** *m* (medical) specialist; ~**ausdruck** *m* technical term

Fächer ['fɛçər] (-**s**, -) *m* fan

Fach- *zW*: ~**hochschule** *f* ≈ technical college; **f~kundig** *adj* expert, specialist; **f~lich** *adj* professional; expert; ~**mann** (*pl* -**leute**) *m* specialist; **f~männisch** *adj* professional; ~**schule** *f* technical college; **f~simpeln** *vi* to talk shop; ~**werk** *nt* timber frame

Fackel ['fakəl] (-, -**n**) *f* torch

fad(e) [faːt, 'faːdə] *adj* insipid; (*langweilig*) dull

Faden ['faːdən] (-s, ⸗) *m* thread; f~scheinig *adj* (*auch fig*) threadbare

fähig ['fɛːɪç] *adj*: ~ (zu *od* +*gen*) capable (of); able (to); Γ~ keit *f* ability

fahnden ['faːndən] *vi*: ~ nach to search for

Fahndung *f* search; **Fahndungsliste** *f* list of wanted criminals, wanted list

Fahne ['faːnə] *f* flag, standard; **eine ~ haben** (*umg*) to smell of drink; **Fahnenflucht** *f* desertion

Fahrausweis *m* ticket

Fahrbahn *f* carriageway (*BRIT*), roadway

Fähre ['fɛːrə] *f* ferry

fahren ['faːrən] (*unreg*) *vt* to drive; (*Rad*) to ride; (*befördern*) to drive, to take; (*Rennen*) to drive in ♦ *vi* (*sich bewegen*) to go; (*Schiff*) to sail; (*abfahren*) to leave; **mit dem Auto/Zug ~** to go *od* travel by car/train; **mit der Hand ~ über** +*akk* to pass one's hand over

Fahr- *zW*: ~er(in) (-s, -) *m(f)* driver; ~erflucht *f* hit-and-run; ~gast *m* passenger; ~geld *nt* fare; ~gestell *nt* chassis; (*AVIAT*) undercarriage; ~karte *f* ticket; ~kartenausgabe *f* ticket office; ~kartenschalter *m* ticket office; f~lässig *adj* negligent; **f~lässige Tötung** manslaughter; ~lässigkeit *f* negligence; ~lehrer *m* driving instructor; ~plan *m* timetable; f~planmäßig *adj* scheduled; ~preis *m* fare; ~prüfung *f* driving test; ~rad *nt* bicycle; ~schein *m* ticket; ~schule *f* driving school; ~stuhl *m* lift (*BRIT*), elevator (*US*)

Fahrt [faːrt] (-, -en) *f* journey; (*kurz*) trip; (*AUT*) drive; (*Geschwindigkeit*) speed; **gute ~!** have a good journey

Fährte ['fɛːrtə] *f* track, trail

Fahrtkosten *pl* travelling expenses

Fahrtrichtung *f* course, direction

Fahrzeug *nt* vehicle; ~halter (-s, -) *m* owner of a vehicle

Faksimile [fak'ziːmile] *nt* facsimile

Fakten *pl von* **Faktum**

Faktor ['faktɔr] *m* factor

Faktum ['faktʊm] (-s, -ten) *nt* fact

Fakultät [fakʊl'tɛːt] *f* faculty

Falke ['falkə] (-n, -n) *m* falcon

Fall [fal] (-(e)s, ⸗e) *m* (*Sturz*) fall; (*Sachverhalt*, JUR, GRAM) case; **auf jeden ~**, **auf alle Fälle** in any case; (*bestimmt*) definitely; **auf keinen ~!** no way!; ~e *f* trap; f~en (*unreg*) *vi* to fall; **etw f~en lassen** to drop sth

fällen ['fɛlən] *vt* (*Baum*) to fell; (*Urteil*) to pass

fallenlassen (*unreg*) *vt* (*Bemerkung*) to make; (*Plan*) to abandon, to drop

fällig ['fɛlɪç] *adj* due

falls [fals] *adv* in case, if

Fallschirm *m* parachute; ~jäger *pl* paratroops; ~springer *m* parachutist

falsch [falʃ] *adj* false; (*unrichtig*) wrong

fälschen ['fɛlʃən] *vt* to forge

Falschgeld *nt* counterfeit money

fälsch- *zW*: ~lich *adj* false; ~licherweise *adv* mistakenly; F~ung *f* forgery

Falte ['faltə] *f* (*Knick*) fold, crease; (*Haut~*) wrinkle; (*Rock~*) pleat; f~n *vt* to fold; (*Stirn*) to wrinkle

familiär [famili'ɛːr] *adj* familiar

Familie [fa'miːliə] *f* family

Familien- *zW*: ~kreis *m* family circle; ~name *m* surname; ~stand *m* marital status

Fanatiker [fa'naːtikər] (-s, -) *m* fanatic

fanatisch *adj* fanatical

Fanatismus [fana'tɪsmʊs] *m* fanaticism

fand *etc* [fant] *vb siehe* **finden**

Fang [faŋ] (-(e)s, ⸗e) *m* catch; (*Jagen*) hunting; (*Kralle*) talon, claw; f~en (*unreg*) *vt* to catch ♦ *vr* to get caught; (*Flugzeug*) to level out; (*Mensch: nicht fallen*) to steady o.s.; (*fig*) to compose o.s.; (*in Leistung*) to get back on form

Farb- ['farb] *zW*: ~aufnahme *f* colour photograph; ~band *m* typewriter ribbon; ~e *f* colour; (*zum Malen etc*) paint; (*Stoffarbe*) dye; f~echt *adj* colourfast

färben ['fɛrbən] *vt* to colour; (*Stoff, Haar*) to dye

farbenblind ['farbən-] *adj* colour-blind

farbenfroh adj colourful, gay

Farb- zW: ~**fernsehen** nt colour television; ~**film** m colour film; ~**foto** nt colour photograph; **f~ig** adj coloured; ~**ige(r)** mf coloured (person); ~**kasten** m paintbox; **f~los** adj colourless; ~**stift** m coloured pencil; ~**stoff** m dye; ~**ton** m hue, tone

Färbung ['fɛrbʊŋ] f colouring; (Tendenz) bias

Farn [farn] (-(e)s, -e) m fern; bracken

Farnkraut nt = **Farn**

Fasan [fa'zaːn] (-(e)s, -e(n)) m pheasant

Fasching ['faʃɪŋ] (-s, -e od -s) m carnival

Faschismus [fa'ʃɪsmʊs] m fascism

Faschist m fascist

Faser ['faːzər] (-, -n) f fibre; **f~n** vi to fray

Faß [fas] (-sses, Fässer) nt vat, barrel; (für Öl) drum; **Bier vom** ~ draught beer

Fassade [fa'saːdə] f façade

faßbar ['fasbaːr] adj comprehensible

fassen ['fasən] vt (ergreifen) to grasp, to take; (inhaltlich) to hold; (Entschluß etc) to take; (verstehen) to understand; (Ring etc) to set; (formulieren) to formulate, to phrase ♦ vr to calm down; **nicht zu** ~ unbelievable

Fassung ['fasʊŋ] f (Umrahmung) mounting; (Lampen~) socket; (Wortlaut) version; (Beherrschung) composure; **jdn aus der** ~ **bringen** to upset sb; **fassungslos** adj speechless

fast [fast] adv almost, nearly

fasten ['fastən] vi to fast; **F~zeit** f Lent

Fastnacht f Shrove Tuesday; carnival

fatal [fa'taːl] adj fatal; (peinlich) embarrassing

faul [faʊl] adj rotten; (Person) lazy; (Ausreden) lame; **daran ist etwas** ~ there's something fishy about it; ~**en** vi to rot; **faulenzen** vi to idle; **Faulenzer** (-s, -) m idler, loafer; **F~heit** f laziness; ~**ig** adj putrid

Fäulnis ['fɔʏlnɪs] (-) f decay, putrefaction

Faust ['faʊst] (-, Fäuste) f fist; **auf eigene** ~ off one's own bat; ~**hand-**schuh** m mitten

Favorit [favo'riːt] (-en, -en) m favourite

FDP [ɛfdeː'peː] (-) f abk (= Freie Demokratische Partei) Free Democratic Party

Februar ['feːbruaːr] (-(s), -e) m February

fechten ['fɛçtən] (unreg) vi to fence

Feder ['feːdər] (-, -n) f feather; (Schreib~) pen nib; (TECH) spring; ~**ball** m shuttlecock; ~**bett** nt continental quilt; ~**halter** m penholder, pen; **f~leicht** adj light as a feather; **f~n** vi (nachgeben) to be springy; (sich bewegen) to bounce ♦ vt to spring; ~**ung** f (AUT) suspension

Fegefeuer nt purgatory

fegen ['feːgən] vt to sweep

fehl [feːl] adj: ~ **am Platz** od **Ort** out of place; ~**en** vi to be wanting od missing; (abwesend sein) to be absent; **etw** ~**t jdm** sb lacks sth; **du** ~**st mir** I miss you; **was** ~**t ihm?** what's wrong with him?; **F~er** (-s, -) m mistake, error; (Mangel, Schwäche) fault; ~**erfrei** adj faultless; without any mistakes; ~**erhaft** adj incorrect; faulty; **F~geburt** f miscarriage; ~**gehen** (unreg) vi to go astray; **F~griff** m blunder; **F~konstruktion** f badly designed thing; **F~schlag** m failure; ~**schlagen** (unreg) vi to fail; **F~start** m (SPORT) false start; **F~zündung** f (AUT) misfire, backfire

Feier ['faɪər] (-, -n) f celebration; ~**abend** m time to stop work; ~**abend machen** to stop, to knock off; **jetzt ist** ~**abend!** that's enough!; **f~lich** adj solemn; ~**lichkeit** f solemnity; ~**lichkeiten** pl (Veranstaltungen) festivities; **f~n** vt, vi to celebrate; ~**tag** m holiday

feig(e) ['faɪg(ə)] adj cowardly

Feige f fig

Feigheit f cowardice

Feigling m coward

Feile ['faɪlə] f file

feilschen vi to haggle

fein [faɪn] adj fine; (vornehm) refined; (Gehör etc) keen; ~**!** great!

Feind [faɪnt] (-(e)s, -e) *m* enemy; **f~lich** *adj* hostile; **~schaft** *f* enmity; **f~selig** *adj* hostile; **~seligkeit** *f* hostility

Fein- *zW*: **f~fühlend** *adj* sensitive; **f~fühlig** *adj* sensitive; **~gefühl** *nt* delicacy, tact; **~heit** *f* fineness; refinement; keenness; **~kostgeschäft** *nt* delicatessen (shop); **~schmecker** (-s, -) *m* gourmet

Feld [fɛlt] (-(e)s, -er) *nt* field; (*SCHACH*) square; (*SPORT*) pitch; **~herr** *m* commander; **~stecher** (-s, -) *m* binoculars *pl*; **~webel** (-s, -) *m* sergeant; **~weg** *m* path

Felge ['fɛlgə] *f* (wheel) rim

Fell [fɛl] (-(e)s, -e) *nt* fur; coat; (*von Schaf*) fleece; (*von toten Tieren*) skin

Fels [fɛls] (-en, -en) *m* rock; (*Klippe*) cliff

Felsen ['fɛlzən] (-s, -) *m* = **Fels**; **f~fest** *adj* firm; **~vorsprung** *m* ledge

felsig *adj* rocky

Felsspalte *f* crevice

feminin [femi'ni:n] *adj* feminine; (*pej*) effeminate

Fenster ['fɛnstər] (-s, -) *nt* window; **~brett** *nt* windowsill; **~platz** *m* window seat; **~putzer** (-s, -) *m* window cleaner; **~scheibe** *f* windowpane; **~sims** *m* windowsill

Ferien ['fe:riən] *pl* holidays, vacation *sg* (*US*); **~ haben** to be on holiday; **~kurs** *m* holiday course; **~reise** *f* holiday; **~zeit** *f* holiday period

Ferkel ['fɛrkəl] (-s, -) *nt* piglet

fern [fɛrn] *adj, adv* far-off, distant; **~ von hier** a long way (away) from here; **der F~e Osten** the Far East; **F~amt** *nt* (*TEL*) exchange; **F~bedienung** *f* remote control; **F~e** *f* distance; **~er** *adj* further ♦ *adv* further; (*weiterhin*) in future; **F~gespräch** *nt* trunk call; **F~glas** *nt* binoculars *pl*; **~halten** (*unreg*) *vt, vr* to keep away; **F~lenkung** *f* remote control; **F~meldeamt** *nt* international exchange; **F~rohr** *nt* telescope; **F~schreiben** *nt* telex; **F~sehapparat** *m* television set; **F~sehen** (-s) *nt* television; **im F~sehen** on television; **~sehen** (*unreg*) *vi* to watch television; **F~seher** *m* television; **F~sehüberwachungsanlage** *f* closed-circuit television; **F~sprecher** *m* telephone; **F~sprechzelle** *f* telephone box *od* booth (*US*)

Ferse ['fɛrzə] *f* heel

fertig ['fɛrtɪç] *adj* (*bereit*) ready; (*beendet*) finished; (*gebrauchs~*) ready-made; **F~bau** *m* prefab(ricated house); **F~keit** *f* skill; **~machen** *vt* (*beenden*) to finish; (*umg*: *Person*) to finish; (: *körperlich*) to exhaust; (: *moralisch*) to get down ♦ *vr* to get ready; **~stellen** *vt* to complete

Fessel ['fɛsəl] (-, -n) *f* fetter; **f~n** *vt* to bind; (*mit Fesseln*) to fetter; (*fig*) to spellbind; **f~nd** *adj* fascinating, captivating

Fest (-(e)s, -e) *nt* party; festival; **frohes ~!** Happy Christmas!

fest [fɛst] *adj* firm; (*Nahrung*) solid; (*Gehalt*) regular ♦ *adv* (*schlafen*) soundly; **~e Kosten** fixed cost; **~angestellt** *adj* permanently employed; **~binden** (*unreg*) *vt* to tie, to fasten; **~bleiben** (*unreg*) *vi* to stand firm; **F~essen** *nt* banquet; **~halten** (*unreg*) *vt* to seize, to hold fast; (*Ereignis*) to record ♦ *vr*: **sich ~halten (an** +*dat*) to hold on (to); **~igen** *vt* to strengthen; **F~igkeit** *f* strength; **F~ival** ['fɛstɪval] (-s, -s) *nt* festival; **F~land** *nt* mainland; **~legen** *vt* to fix ♦ *vr* to commit o.s.; **~lich** *adj* festive; **~machen** *vt* to fasten; (*Termin etc*) to fix; **F~nahme** *f* arrest; **~nehmen** (*unreg*) *vt* to arrest; **F~rede** *f* address; **~setzen** *vt* to fix, to settle; **F~spiel** *nt* festival; **F~spiele** *pl* (*Veranstaltung*) festival *sg*; **~stehen** (*unreg*) *vi* to be certain; **~stellen** *vt* to establish; (*sagen*) to remark; **F~ung** *f* fortress; **F~wochen** *pl* festival *sg*

Fett [fɛt] (-(e)s, -e) *nt* fat, grease

fett *adj* fat; (*Essen etc*) greasy; (*TYP*) bold; **~arm** *adj* low fat; **~en** *vt* to grease; **~ig** *adj* greasy, fatty; **F~näpfchen** *nt*: **ins F~näpfchen treten** to put one's foot in it

Fetzen ['fɛtsən] (-s, -) *m* scrap

feucht [fɔʏçt] *adj* damp; (*Luft*) humid;

F~**igkeit** f dampness; humidity

Feuer ['fɔyər] (-s, -) nt fire; (zum Rauchen) a light; (fig: Schwung) spirit; ~**alarm** nt fire alarm; ~**eifer** m zeal; f~**fest** adj fireproof; ~**gefahr** f danger of fire; f~**gefährlich** adj inflammable; ~**leiter** f fire escape ladder; ~**löscher** (-s, -) m fire extinguisher; ~**melder** (-s, -) m fire alarm; f~**n** vt, vi (auch fig) to fire; ~**stein** m flint; ~**wehr** (-, -en) f fire brigade; ~**wehrwagen** m fire engine; ~**werk** nt fireworks pl; ~**zeug** nt (cigarette) lighter

Fichte ['fıçtə] f spruce, pine

Fieber ['fiːbər] (-s, -) nt fever, temperature; f~**haft** adj feverish; ~**messer** m thermometer; ~**thermometer** nt thermometer

fiel etc [fiːl] vb siehe **fallen**

fies [fiːs] (umg) adj nasty

Figur [fi'guːr] (-, -en) f figure; (Schach~) chessman, chess piece

Filiale [fili'aːlə] f (COMM) branch

Film [fɪlm] (-(e)s, -e) m film; ~**aufnahme** f shooting; f~**en** vt, vi to film; ~**kamera** f cine-camera

Filter ['fɪltər] (-s, -) m filter; f~**n** vt to filter; ~**papier** nt filter paper; ~**zigarette** f tipped cigarette

Filz [fɪlts] (-es, -e) m felt; f~**en** vt (umg) to frisk ♦ vi (Wolle) to mat; ~**stift** m felt-tip pen

Finale [fi'naːlə] (-s, -(s)) nt finale; (SPORT) final(s)

Finanz [fi'nants] f finance; ~**amt** nt Inland Revenue Office; ~**beamte(r)** m revenue officer; f~**iell** [-tsi'ɛl] adj financial; f~**ieren** [-'tsiːrən] vt to finance; ~**minister** m Chancellor of the Exchequer (BRIT), Minister of Finance

Find- ['fɪnd] zW: f~**en** (unreg) vt to find; (meinen) to think ♦ vr to be (found); (sich fassen) to compose o.s.; **ich f~e nichts dabei, wenn ...** I don't see what's wrong if ...; **das wird sich f~en** things will work out; ~**er** (-s, -) m finder; f~**ig** adj resourceful

fing etc [fɪŋ] vb siehe **fangen**

Finger ['fɪŋər] (-s, -) m finger; ~**ab-**

druck m fingerprint; ~**hut** m thimble; (BOT) foxglove; ~**nagel** m fingernail; ~**spitze** f fingertip

fingieren [fɪŋ'giːrən] vt to feign

fingiert adj made-up, fictitious

Fink [fɪŋk] (-en, -en) m finch

Finn- [fɪn] zW: ~**e** (-n, -n) m Finn; ~**in** f Finn; f~**isch** adj Finnish; ~**land** nt Finland

finster ['fɪnstər] adj dark, gloomy; (verdächtig) dubious; (verdrossen) grim; (Gedanke) dark; **F~nis** (-) f darkness, gloom

Finte ['fɪntə] f feint, trick

Firma ['fɪrma] (-, -men) f firm

Firmen- ['fɪrmən] zW: ~**inhaber** m owner of firm; ~**schild** nt (shop) sign; ~**zeichen** nt trademark

Firnis ['fɪrnɪs] (-ses, -se) m varnish

Fisch [fɪʃ] (-(e)s, -e) m fish; ~**e** pl (ASTROL) Pisces sg; f~**en** vt, vi to fish; ~**er** (-s, -) m fisherman; ~**e'rei** f fishing, fishery; ~**fang** m fishing; ~**geschäft** nt fishmonger's (shop); ~**gräte** f fishbone

fix [fɪks] adj fixed; (Person) alert, smart; ~ **und fertig** finished; (erschöpft) done in; ~**ieren** [fi'ksiːrən] vt to fix; (anstarren) to stare at

flach [flax] adj flat; (Gefäß) shallow

Fläche ['flɛçə] f area; (Ober~) surface; ~**ninhalt** m surface area

Flachland nt lowland

flackern ['flakərn] vi to flare, to flicker

Flagge ['flagə] f flag

Flamme ['flamə] f flame

Flanell [fla'nɛl] (-s, -e) m flannel

Flanke ['flaŋkə] f flank; (SPORT: Seite) wing

Flasche ['flaʃə] f bottle; (umg: Versager) wash-out

Flaschen- zW: ~**bier** nt bottled beer; ~**öffner** m bottle opener; ~**zug** m pulley

flatterhaft adj flighty, fickle

flattern ['flatərn] vi to flutter

flau [flau] adj weak, listless; (Nachfrage) slack; **jdm ist ~** sb feels queasy

Flaum [flaum] (-(e)s) m (Feder) down; (Haare) fluff

flauschig ['flauʃɪç] *adj* fluffy
Flausen ['flauzən] *pl* silly ideas;
(*Ausflüchte*) weak excuses
Flaute ['flautə] *f* calm; (*COMM*) reces-
sion
Flechte ['flɛçtə] *f* plait; (*MED*) dry scab;
(*BOT*) lichen; **f~n** (*unreg*) *vt* to plait;
(*Kranz*) to twine
Fleck [flɛk] (-(e)s, -e) *m* spot;
(*Schmutz~*) stain; (*Stoff~*) patch;
(*Makel*) blemish; **nicht vom ~ kommen**
(*auch fig*) not to get any further; **vom
~ weg** straight away
Flecken (-s, -) *m* = **Fleck**; **f~los** *adj*
spotless; **~mittel** *nt* stain remover;
~wasser *nt* stain remover
fleckig *adj* spotted; stained
Fledermaus ['fle:dərmaus] *f* bat
Flegel ['fle:gəl] (-s, -) *m* (*Mensch*) lout;
f~haft *adj* loutish, unmannerly; **~jahre**
pl adolescence *sg*
flehen ['fle:ən] *vi* to implore; **flehentlich**
adj imploring
Fleisch [flaɪʃ] (-(e)s) *nt* flesh; (*Essen*)
meat; **~brühe** *f* beef tea, meat stock;
~er (-s, -) *m* butcher; **~e'rei** *f*
butcher's (shop); **~wolf** *m* mincer;
~wunde *f* flesh wound
Fleiß [flaɪs] (-es) *m* diligence, industry;
f~ig *adj* diligent, industrious
fletschen ['flɛtʃən] *vt* (*Zähne*) to show
flexibel [flɛ'ksi:bəl] *adj* flexible
Flicken ['flɪkən] (-s, -) *m* patch; **f~** *vt* to
mend
Flieder ['fli:dər] (-s, -) *m* lilac
Fliege ['fli:gə] *f* fly; (*Kleidung*) bow tie;
f~n (*unreg*) *vt, vi* to fly; **auf jdn/etw
f~n** (*umg*) to be mad about sb/sth;
Fliegenpilz *m* toadstool; **~r** (-s, -) *m*
flier, airman
fliehen ['fli:ən] (*unreg*) *vi* to flee
Fliese ['fli:zə] *f* tile
Fließ- ['fli:s] *zW*: **~band** *nt* production
od assembly line; **f~en** (*unreg*) *vi* to
flow; **f~end** *adj* flowing; (*Rede,
Deutsch*) fluent; (*Übergänge*) smooth
flimmern ['flɪmərn] *vi* to glimmer
flink [flɪŋk] *adj* nimble, lively
Flinte ['flɪntə] *f* rifle; shotgun
Flitter ['flɪtər] (-s, -) *m* spangle, tinsel;

~wochen *pl* honeymoon *sg*
flitzen ['flɪtsən] *vi* to flit
Flocke ['flɔkə] *f* flake
flog *etc* [flo:k] *vb siehe* **fliegen**
Floh [flo:] (-(e)s, ᵆe) *m* flea; **~markt** *m*
flea market
florieren [flo'ri:rən] *vi* to flourish
Floskel ['flɔskəl] (-, -n) *f* set phrase
Floß [flo:s] (-es, ᵆe) *nt* raft, float
floß *etc vb siehe* **fließen**
Flosse ['flɔsə] *f* fin
Flöte ['flø:tə] *f* flute; (*Block~*) recorder
Flötist(in) [flø'tɪst(ɪn)] *m(f)* flautist
flott [flɔt] *adj* lively; (*elegant*) smart;
(*NAUT*) afloat; **F~e** *f* fleet, navy
Fluch [flu:x] (-(e)s, ᵆe) *m* curse; **f~en** *vi*
to curse, to swear
Flucht [fluxt] (-, -en) *f* flight;
(*Fenster~*) row; (*Zimmer~*) suite;
f~artig *adj* hasty
flücht- ['flʏçt] *zW*: **~en** *vi, vr* to flee, to
escape; **~ig** *adj* fugitive; (*vergänglich*)
transitory; (*oberflächlich*) superficial;
(*eilig*) fleeting; **F~igkeit** *f* transitoriness; superficiality; **F~igkeitsfehler** *m*
careless slip; **F~ling** *m* fugitive, refugee
Flug [flu:k] (-(e)s, ᵆe) *m* flight; **im ~** air-
borne, in flight; **~blatt** *nt* pamphlet
Flügel ['fly:gəl] (-s, -) *m* wing; (*MUS*)
grand piano
Fluggast *m* airline passenger
flügge ['flʏgə] *adj* (fully-)fledged
Flug- *zW*: **~geschwindigkeit** *f* flying *od*
air speed; **~gesellschaft** *f* airline
(company); **~hafen** *m* airport; **~höhe**
f altitude (of flight); **~plan** *m* flight
schedule; **~platz** *m* airport; (*klein*) air-
field; **~schein** *m* plane ticket; **~ver-
kehr** *m* air traffic; **~zeug** *nt*
(aero)plane, airplane (*US*); **~zeugent-
führung** *f* hijacking of a plane;
~zeughalle *f* hangar; **~zeugträger** *m*
aircraft carrier
Flunder ['flundər] (-, -n) *f* flounder
flunkern ['fluŋkərn] *vi* to fib, to tell sto-
ries
Fluor ['flu:ɔr] (-s) *nt* fluorine
Flur [flu:r] (-(e)s, -e) *m* hall;
(*Treppen~*) staircase

Fluß [flʊs] (-sses, ⸗sse) *m* river; (*Fließen*) flow; **im ~ sein** (*fig*) to be in a state of flux

flüssig ['flʏsɪç] *adj* liquid; **F~keit** *f* liquid; (*Zustand*) liquidity; **~machen** *vt* (*Geld*) to make available

flüstern ['flʏstərn] *vt, vi* to whisper

Flut [fluːt] (-, -en) *f* (*auch fig*) flood; (*Gezeiten*) high tide; **f~en** *vi* to flood; **⸗licht** *nt* floodlight

Fohlen ['foːlən] (-s, -) *nt* foal

Föhre ['føːrə] *f* Scots pine

Folge ['fɔlgə] *f* series, sequence; (*Fortsetzung*) instalment; (*Auswirkung*) result; **in rascher ~** in quick succession; **etw zur ~ haben** to result in sth; **~n haben** to have consequences; **einer Sache** *dat* **~ leisten** to comply with sth; **f~n** *vi* +*dat* to follow; (*gehorchen*) to obey; **jdm f~n können** (*fig*) to follow *od* understand sb; **f~nd** *adj* following; **f~ndermaßen** *adv* as follows, in the following way; **f~nschwer** *adj* momentous; **f~rn** *vt*: **f~rn (aus)** to conclude (from); **~rung** *f* conclusion

folglich *adv* consequently

folgsam *adj* obedient

Folie ['foːliə] *f* foil

Folter ['fɔltər] (-, -n) *f* torture; (*Gerät*) rack; **f~n** *vt* to torture

Fön [føːn] (-(e)s, -e; ®) *m* hair-dryer; **f~en** *vt* to (blow) dry

Fontäne [fɔn'tɛːnə] *f* fountain

Förder- ['fœrdər] *zW*: **~band** *nt* conveyor belt; **~korb** *m* pit cage; **f~lich** *adj* beneficial

fordern ['fɔrdərn] *vt* to demand

fördern *vt* to promote; (*unterstützen*) to help; (*Kohle*) to extract

Förderung *f* promotion; help; extraction

Forderung ['fɔrdərʊŋ] *f* demand

Forelle [fo'rɛlə] *f* trout

Form [fɔrm] (-, -en) *f* shape; (*Gestaltung*) form; (*Guß~*) mould; (*Back~*) baking tin; **in ~ sein** to be in good form *od* shape; **in ~ von** in the shape of

Formali'tät *f* formality

Format [fɔr'maːt] (-(e)s, -e) *nt* format;

(*fig*) distinction; **f~ieren** [-'tiːrən] *vt* to format

Formati'on *f* formation

formbar *adj* malleable

Formel (-, -n) *f* formula

formell [fɔr'mɛl] *adj* formal

formen *vt* to form, to shape

Formfehler *m* faux-pas, gaffe; (*JUR*) irregularity

formieren [-'miːrən] *vt* to form ♦ *vr* to form up

förmlich ['fœrmlɪç] *adj* formal; (*umg*) real; **F~keit** *f* formality

formlos *adj* shapeless; (*Benehmen etc*) informal

Formu'lar (-s, -e) *nt* form

formu'lieren *vt* to formulate

forsch [fɔrʃ] *adj* energetic, vigorous

forschen *vi*: **~ (nach)** to search (for); (*wissenschaftlich*) to (do) research; **~d** *adj* searching

Forscher (-s, -) *m* research scientist; (*Natur~*) explorer

Forschung ['fɔrʃʊŋ] *f* research; **Forschungsreise** *f* scientific expedition

Forst [fɔrst] (-(e)s, -e) *m* forest

Förster ['fœrstər] (-s, -) *m* forester; (*für Wild*) gamekeeper

fort [fɔrt] *adv* away; (*verschwunden*) gone; (*vorwärts*) on; **und so ~** and so on; **in einem ~** on and on; **~bestehen** (*unreg*) *vi* to survive; **~bewegen** *vt, vr* to move away; **~bilden** *vr* to continue one's education; **~bleiben** (*unreg*) *vi* to stay away; **F~dauer** *f* continuance; **~fahren** (*unreg*) *vi* to depart; (*fortsetzen*) to go on, to continue; **~führen** *vt* to continue, to carry on; **~gehen** (*unreg*) *vi* to go away; **~geschritten** *adj* advanced; **~müssen** (*unreg*) *vi* to have to go; **~pflanzen** *vr* to reproduce; **F~pflanzung** *f* reproduction

Forts. *abk* (= *Fortsetzung*) cont(d).

fortschaffen *vt* to remove

fortschreiten (*unreg*) *vi* to advance

Fortschritt ['fɔrtʃrɪt] *m* advance; **~e machen** to make progress; **f~lich** *adj* progressive

fort- *zW*: **~setzen** *vt* to continue; **F~setzung** *f* continuation; (*folgender*

Teil) instalment; **F~setzung folgt** to be continued; **~während** *adj* incessant, continual

Foto ['fo:to] (-s, -s) *nt* photo(graph); **~apparat** *m* camera; **~'graf** *m* photographer, **gra'fie** *f* photography; (*Bild*) photograph; **f~gra'fieren** *vt* to photograph; **~graph ♦** *vi* to take photographs; **~kopie** *f* photocopy; **f~kopieren** *vt* to photocopy

Foul [faul] (-s, -s) *nt* foul

Fr. *abk* (= *Frau*) Mrs, Ms

Fracht [fraxt] (-, -en) *f* freight; (*NAUT*) cargo; (*Preis*) carriage; **~ zahlt Empfänger** (*COMM*) carriage forward; **~er** (-s, -) *m* freighter, cargo boat; **~gut** *nt* freight

Frack [frak] (-(e)s, ⁻e) *m* tails *pl*

Frage ['fra:gə] *f* question; **etw in ~ stellen** to question sth; **jdm eine ~ stellen** to ask sb a question, to put a question to sb; **nicht in ~ kommen** to be out of the question; **~bogen** *m* questionnaire; **f~n** *vt*, *vi* to ask; **~zeichen** *nt* question mark

fraglich *adj* questionable, doubtful

fraglos *adv* unquestionably

Fragment [fra'gment] *nt* fragment

fragwürdig ['fra:kvʏrdɪç] *adj* questionable, dubious

Fraktion [fraktsi'o:n] *f* parliamentary party

frankieren [fraŋ'ki:rən] *vt* to stamp, to frank

Frankiermaschine *f* franking machine

franko ['fraŋko] *adv* post-paid; carriage paid

Frankreich ['fraŋkraɪç] (-s) *nt* France

Franse ['franzə] *f* fringe

Franzose [fran'tso:zə] *m* Frenchman

Französin [fran'tsø:zɪn] *f* Frenchwoman

französisch *adj* French

fraß *etc* [fras] *vb siehe* **fressen**

Fratze ['fratsə] *f* grimace

Frau [frau] (-, -en) *f* woman; (*Ehe~*) wife; (*Anrede*) Mrs, Ms; **~ Doktor** Doctor; **~enarzt** *m* gynaecologist; **~enbewegung** *f* feminist movement; **f~enfeindlich** *adj* anti-women; **~enzimmer** *nt* female, broad (*US*)

Fräulein ['frɔʏlaɪn] *nt* young lady; (*Anrede*) Miss, Ms

fraulich ['fraulɪç] *adj* womanly

frech [frɛç] *adj* cheeky, impudent; **F~dachs** *m* cheeky monkey; **F~heit** *f* cheek, impudence

Fregatte [fre'gatə] *f* frigate

frei [fraɪ] *adj* free; (*Stelle, Sitzplatz*) free, vacant; (*Mitarbeiter*) freelance; (*unbekleidet*) bare; **sich dat einen Tag ~ nehmen** to take a day off; **von etw ~ sein** to be free of sth; **im F~en** in the open air; **~ sprechen** to talk without notes; **~ Haus** (*COMM*) carriage paid; **~er Wettbewerb** fair/open competition; **F~bad** *nt* open-air swimming pool; **~bekommen** (*unreg*) *vt*: **jdn ~bekommen** to get sb freed; **einen Tag ~bekommen** to get a day off; **~gebig** *adj* generous; **~halten** (*unreg*) *vt* to keep free; **~händig** *adv* (*fahren*) with no hands; **F~heit** *f* freedom; **~heitlich** *adj* liberal; **F~heitsstrafe** *f* prison sentence; **F~karte** *f* free ticket; **~lassen** (*unreg*) *vt* to (set) free; **~legen** *vt* to expose; **~lich** *adv* certainly, admittedly; **ja ~lich** yes of course; **F~lichtbühne** *f* open-air theatre; **~machen** *vt* (*Post*) to frank ♦ *vr* to arrange to be free; (*entkleiden*) to undress; **Tage ~machen** to take days off; **~sprechen** (*unreg*) *vt*: **~sprechen (von)** to acquit (of); **F~spruch** *m* acquittal; **~stellen** *vt*: **jdm etw ~stellen** to leave sth (up) to sb; **F~stoß** *m* free kick

Freitag *m* Friday; **f~s** *adv* on Fridays

frei- *zW*: **~willig** *adj* voluntary; **F~zeit** *f* spare od free time; **F~zeitbeschäftigung** *f* leisure pursuit; **~zügig** *adj* liberal, broad-minded; (*mit Geld*) generous

fremd [frɛmt] *adj* (*unvertraut*) strange; (*ausländisch*) foreign; (*nicht eigen*) someone else's; **etw ist jdm ~** sth is foreign to sb; **~artig** *adj* strange; **F~e(r)** ['frɛmdə(r)] *mf* stranger; (*Ausländer*) foreigner; **F~enführer** *m* (tourist) guide; **F~enlegion** *f* foreign legion; **F~enverkehr** *m* tourism;

F~**enzimmer** nt guest room; F~**körper** m foreign body; ~**ländisch** adj foreign; F~**ling** m stranger; F~**sprache** f foreign language; F~**wort** nt foreign od loan word

Frequenz [fre'kvɛnts] f (RAD) frequency

fressen ['frɛsən] (unreg) vt, vi to eat

Freude ['frɔydə] f joy, delight

freudig adj joyful, happy

freuen ['frɔyən] vt unpers to make happy od pleased ♦ vr to be glad od happy; **freut mich!** pleased to meet you; **sich auf etw** akk ~ to look forward to sth; **sich über etw** akk ~ to be pleased about sth

Freund [frɔynt] (-(e)s, -e) m friend; boyfriend; ~**in** [-dɪn] f friend; girlfriend; f~**lich** adj kind, friendly; f~**licherweise** adv kindly; ~**lichkeit** f friendliness, kindness; ~**schaft** f friendship; f~**schaftlich** adj friendly

Frieden ['fri:dən] (-s, -) m peace; **im** ~ in peacetime

Friedens- zW: ~**schluß** m peace agreement; ~**vertrag** m peace treaty; ~**zeit** f peacetime

fried- zW: ~**fertig** adj peaceable; F~**hof** m cemetery; ~**lich** adj peaceful

frieren ['fri:rən] (unreg) vt, vi to freeze; **ich friere, es friert mich** I'm freezing, I'm cold

Fries [fri:s] (-es, -e) m (ARCHIT) frieze

frigid(e) [fri'gi:t, fri'gi:də] adj frigid

Frikadelle [frika'dɛlə] f rissole

frisch [frɪʃ] adj fresh; (lebhaft) lively; ~ **gestrichen!** wet paint!; **sich** ~ **machen** (o.s.) up; F~**e** f freshness; liveliness

Friseur [fri'zø:r] m hairdresser

Friseuse [fri'zø:zə] f hairdresser

Frisier- [fri'zi:r] zW: f~**en** vt to do; (fig: Abrechnung) to fiddle, to doctor ♦ vr to do one's hair; ~**salon** m hairdressing salon; ~**tisch** m dressing table

frißt etc [frɪst] vb siehe **fressen**

Frist [frɪst] (-, -en) f period; (Termin) deadline; f~**los** adj (Entlassung) instant

Frisur [fri'zu:r] f hairdo, hairstyle

frivol [fri'vo:l] adj frivolous

froh [fro:] adj happy, cheerful; **ich bin** ~, **daß** ... I'm glad that ...

fröhlich ['frø:lɪç] adj merry, happy; F~**keit** f merriness, gaiety

Frohsinn m cheerfulness

fromm [frɔm] adj pious, good; (Wunsch) idle

Frömmigkeit ['frœmɪçkaɪt] f piety

Fronleichnam [fro:n'laɪçna:m] (-(e)s) m Corpus Christi

Front [frɔnt] (-, -en) f front; f~**al** [frɔn'ta:l] adj frontal

fror etc [fro:r] vb siehe **frieren**

Frosch [frɔʃ] (-(e)s, =e) m frog; (Feuerwerk) squib; ~**mann** m frogman; ~**schenkel** m frog's leg

Frost [frɔst] (-(e)s, =e) m frost; ~**beule** f chilblain

frösteln ['frœstəln] vi to shiver

Frost- zW: ~**gefahr** f danger of frost; f~**ig** adj frosty; ~**schutzmittel** nt antifreeze

Frottee [frɔ'te:] (-(s), -s) nt od m towelling

Frottier(hand)tuch [frɔ'ti:r(hant)tu:x] nt towel

Frucht [frʊxt] (-, =e) f (auch fig) fruit; (Getreide) corn; f~**bar** adj fruitful, fertile; ~**barkeit** f fertility; f~**en** vi to be of use; f~**los** adj fruitless; ~**saft** m fruit juice

früh [fry:] adj, adv early; **heute** ~ this morning; F~**aufsteher** (-s, -) m early riser; F~**e** f early morning; ~**er** adj earlier; (ehemalig) former ♦ adv formerly; ~**er war das anders** that used to be different; ~**estens** adv at the earliest; F~**geburt** f premature birth/baby; F~**jahr** nt spring; F~**ling** m spring; ~**reif** adj precocious; F~**stück** nt breakfast; ~**stücken** vi to (have) breakfast; ~**zeitig** adj early; (pej) untimely

frustrieren [frʊs'tri:rən] vt to frustrate

Fuchs [fʊks] (-es, =e) m fox

fuchsen (umg) vt to rile, to annoy

Füchsin ['fʏksɪn] f vixen

fuchsteufelswild adj hopping mad

fuchteln ['fʊxtəln] vi to gesticulate wildly

Fuge ['fu:gə] f joint; (MUS) fugue

fügen ['fy:gən] *vt* to place, to join ♦ *vr:* **sich ~** (**in** +*dat*) to be obedient (to); (*anpassen*) to adapt oneself (to) ♦ *vr unpers* to happen

fügsam ['fy:kza:m] *adj* obedient

fühl- ['fy:l] *zW:* **~bar** *adj* perceptible, noticeable; **~en** *vt, vi, vr* to feel; **F~er** (-s, -) *m* feeler

fuhr *etc* [fu:r] *vb siehe* **fahren**

führen ['fy:rən] *vt* to lead; (*Geschäft*) to run; (*Name*) to bear; (*Buch*) to keep ♦ *vi* to lead ♦ *vr* to behave

Führer ['fy:rər] (-s, -) *m* leader; (*Fremden~*) guide; **~schein** *m* driving licence

Führung ['fy:rʊŋ] *f* leadership; (*eines Unternehmens*) management; (*MIL*) command; (*Benehmen*) conduct; (*Museums~*) conducted tour; **Führungskraft** *f* executive; **Führungszeugnis** *nt* certificate of good conduct

Fülle ['fylə] *f* wealth, abundance; **f~n** *vt* to fill; (*KOCH*) to stuff ♦ *vr* to fill (up)

Füllen (-s, -) *nt* foal

Füller (-s, -) *m* fountain pen

Füllfederhalter *m* fountain pen

Füllung *f* filling; (*Holz~*) panel

fummeln ['fʊməln] (*umg*) *vi* to fumble

Fund [fʊnt] (-(e)s, -e) *m* find

Fundament [-da'mɛnt] *nt* foundation; **fundamen'tal** *adj* fundamental

Fundbüro *nt* lost property office, lost and found (*US*)

Fundgrube *f* (*fig*) treasure trove

fundieren [-'di:rən] *vt* to back up

fundiert *adj* sound

fünf [fynf] *num* five; **~hundert** *num* five hundred; **F~kampf** *m* pentathlon; **~te(r, s)** *adj* fifth; **F~tel** (-s, -) *nt* fifth; **~zehn** *num* fifteen; **~zig** *num* fifty

Funk [fʊŋk] (-s) *m* radio, wireless; **~e** (-ns, -n) *m* (*auch fig*) spark; **f~eln** *vi* to sparkle; **~en** (-s, e) *m* (*auch fig*) spark; **~er** (-s, -) *m* radio operator; **~gerät** *nt* radio set; **~spruch** *m* radio signal; **~station** *f* radio station; **~streife** *f* police radio patrol

Funktion [fʊŋktsi'o:n] *f* function; **f~ieren** [-'ni:rən] *vi* to work, to function

für [fy:r] *präp* +*akk* for; **was ~** what kind *od* sort of; **das F~ und Wider** the pros and cons *pl*; **Schritt ~ Schritt** step by step; **F~bitte** *f* intercession

Furche ['fʊrçə] *f* furrow

Furcht [fʊrçt] ( ) *f* fear; **f~bar** *adj* terrible, frightful

fürchten ['fyrçtən] *vt* to be afraid of, to fear ♦ *vr:* **sich ~** (**vor** +*dat*) to be afraid (of)

fürchterlich *adj* awful

furchtlos *adj* fearless

furchtsam *adj* timid

füreinander [fy:r'aɪ'nandər] *adv* for each other

Furnier [fʊr'ni:r] (-s, -e) *nt* veneer

fürs [fy:rs] = **für das**

Fürsorge ['fy:rzɔrgə] *f* care; (*Sozial~*) welfare; **~r(in)** (-s, -) *m(f)* welfare worker; **~unterstützung** *f* social security, welfare benefit (*US*)

Fürsprache *f* recommendation; (*um Gnade*) intercession

Fürsprecher *m* advocate

Fürst [fyrst] (-en, -en) *m* prince; **~en-tum** *nt* principality; **~in** *f* princess; **f~lich** *adj* princely

Fusion [fuzi'o:n] *f* merger

Fuß [fu:s] (-es, ꞓe) *m* foot; (*von Glas, Säule etc*) base; (*von Möbel*) leg; **zu ~** on foot; **~ball** *m* football; **~ballplatz** *m* football pitch; **~ballspiel** *nt* football match; **~ballspieler** *m* footballer; **~boden** *m* floor; **~bremse** *f* (*AUT*) footbrake; **~ende** *nt* foot; **~gänger(in)** (-s, -) *m(f)* pedestrian; **~gängerzone** *f* pedestrian precinct; **~note** *f* footnote; **~spur** *f* footprint; **~tritt** *m* kick; (*Spur*) footstep; **~weg** *m* footpath

Futter ['fʊtər] (-s, -) *nt* fodder, feed; (*Stoff*) lining; **~al** [-'ra:l] (-s, -e) *nt* case

füttern ['fytərn] *vt* to feed; (*Kleidung*) to line

Futur [fu'tu:r] (-s, -e) *nt* future

G

g *abk* = **Gramm**

gab *etc* [ga:p] *vb siehe* **geben**

Gabe ['gɑːbə] f gift
Gabel ['gɑːbəl] (-, -n) f fork; ~**ung** f fork
gackern ['gakərn] vi to cackle
gaffen ['gafən] vi to gape
Gage ['gɑːʒə] f fee; salary
gähnen ['gɛːnən] vi to yawn
galant [ga'lant] adj gallant
Galerie [galə'riː] f gallery
Galgen ['galgən] (-s, -) m gallows sg; ~**frist** f respite; ~**humor** m macabre humour
Galle ['galə] f gall; (Organ) gall-bladder
Galopp [ga'lɔp] (-s, -s od -e) m gallop; g~**ieren** [-'piːrən] vi to gallop
Gamasche [ga'maʃə] f gaiter; (kurz) spat
gammeln ['gaməln] (umg) vi to bum around
Gang [gaŋ] (-(e)s, ⁼e) m walk; (Boten~) errand; (~art) gait; (Abschnitt eines Vorgangs) operation; (Essens~, Ablauf) course; (Flur etc) corridor; (Durch~) passage; (TECH) gear; **in** ~ **bringen** to start up; (fig) to get off the ground; **in** ~ **sein** to be in operation; (fig) to be under way
gang adj: ~ **und gäbe** usual, normal
gängig ['gɛŋɪç] adj common, current; (Ware) in demand, selling well
Ganove [ga'noːvə] (-n, -n; umg) m crook
Gans [gans] (-, ⁼e) f goose
Gänse- ['gɛnzə] zW: ~**blümchen** nt daisy; ~**braten** m roast goose; ~**haut** f goose pimples pl; ~**marsch** m: **im** ~**marsch** in single file; ~**rich** (-s, -e) m gander
ganz [gants] adj whole; (vollständig) complete ♦ adv quite; (völlig) completely; ~ **Europa** all Europe; **sein** ~**es Geld** all his money; ~ **und gar nicht** not at all; **es sieht** ~ **so aus it** really looks like it; **aufs G~e gehen** to go for the lot
gänzlich ['gɛntslɪç] adj complete, entire ♦ adv completely, entirely
gar [gɑːr] adj cooked, done ♦ adv quite; ~ **nicht/nichts/keiner** not/nothing/nobody at all; ~ **nicht schlecht** not bad at all

Garage [ga'rɑːʒə] f garage
Garantie [garan'tiː] f guarantee; g~**ren** vt to guarantee; **er kommt garantiert** he's guaranteed to come
Garbe ['garbə] f sheaf; (MIL) burst of fire
Garderobe [gardə'roːbə] f wardrobe; (Abgabe) cloakroom; **Garderobenfrau** f cloakroom attendant; **Garderobenständer** m hallstand
Gardine [gar'diːnə] f curtain
garen ['gɑːrən] vt, vi to cook
gären ['gɛːrən] (unreg) vi to ferment
Garn [garn] (-(e)s, -e) nt thread; yarn (auch fig)
Garnele [gar'neːlə] f shrimp, prawn
garnieren [gar'niːrən] vt to decorate; (Speisen, fig) to garnish
Garnitur [garni'tuːr] f (Satz) set; (Unterwäsche) set of (matching) underwear; **erste** ~ (fig) top rank; **zweite** ~ second rate
garstig ['garstɪç] adj nasty, horrid
Garten ['gartən] (-s, ⁼) m garden; ~**arbeit** f gardening; ~**gerät** nt gardening tool; ~**schere** f pruning shears pl; ~**tür** f garden gate
Gärtner(in) ['gɛrtnər(ɪn)] (-s, -) m(f) gardener; ~**ei** [-'raɪ] f nursery; (Gemüse~) market garden (BRIT), truck farm (US)
Gärung ['gɛːrʊŋ] f fermentation
Gas [gɑːs] (-es, -e) nt gas; ~ **geben** (AUT) to accelerate, to step on the gas; ~**herd** m gas cooker; ~**kocher** m gas cooker; ~**leitung** f gas pipe; ~**maske** f gasmask; ~**pedal** nt accelerator, gas pedal
Gasse ['gasə] f lane, alley; **Gassenjunge** m street urchin
Gast [gast] (-es, ⁼e) m guest; (in Lokal) patron; **bei jdm zu** ~ **sein** to be sb's guest; ~**arbeiter(in)** m(f) foreign worker
Gästebuch ['gɛstəbuːx] nt visitors' book, guest book
Gast- zW: g~**freundlich** adj hospitable; ~**geber** (-s, -) m host; ~**geberin** f hostess; ~**haus** nt hotel, inn; ~**hof** m hotel, inn; g~**ieren** [-'tiːrən] vi (THEAT)

to (appear as a) guest; **g~lich** *adj*
hospitable; **~rolle** *f* guest role
gastronomisch [gastro'no:mɪʃ] *adj*
gastronomic (al)
Gast- *zW*: **~spiel** *nt* (*THEAT*) guest
performance; **~stätte** *f* restaurant;
pub; **~wirt** *m* innkeeper; **~wirtschaft** *f*
hotel, inn; **~zimmer** *nt* (guest) room
Gas- *zW*: **~vergiftung** *f* gas poisoning;
~werk *nt* gasworks *sg*; **~zähler** *m* gas
meter
Gatte ['gatə] (**-n, -n**) *m* husband, spouse
Gatter ['gatər] (**-s, -**) *nt* railing, grating;
(*Eingang*) gate
Gattin *f* wife, spouse
Gattung ['gatʊŋ] *f* genus; kind
Gaul [gaʊl] (**-(e)s, Gäule**) *m* horse; nag
Gaumen ['gaʊmən] (**-s, -**) *m* palate
Gauner ['gaʊnər] (**-s, -**) *m* rogue; **~ei**
[-'raɪ] *f* swindle
Gaze ['ga:zə] *f* gauze
geb. *abk* = **geboren**
Gebäck [gə'bɛk] (**-(e)s, -e**) *nt* pastry
gebacken [gə'bakən] *adj* baked; (*ge-
braten*) fried
Gebälk [gə'bɛlk] (**-(e)s**) *nt* timberwork
Gebärde [gə'bɛ:rdə] *f* gesture; **g~n** *vr*
to behave
gebären [gə'bɛ:rən] (*unreg*) *vt* to give
birth to, to bear
Gebärmutter *f* uterus, womb
Gebäude [gə'bɔʏdə] (**-s, -**) *nt* building;
~komplex *m* (building) complex
Gebell [gə'bɛl] (**-(e)s**) *nt* barking
geben ['ge:bən] (*unreg*) *vt, vi* to give;
(*Karten*) to deal ♦ *vb unpers*: **es gibt**
there is/are; there will be ♦ *vr* (*sich
verhalten*) to behave, to act; (*aufhören*)
to abate; **jdm etw ~** to give sb sth *od*
sth to sb; **ein Wort gab das andere** one
angry word led to another; **was gibt's?**
what's up?; **was gibt es im Kino?**
what's on at the cinema?; **sich geschlagen ~** to admit defeat; **das wird
sich schon ~** that'll soon sort itself out
Gebet [gə'be:t] (**-(e)s, -e**) *nt* prayer
gebeten *vb siehe* **bitten**
Gebiet [gə'bi:t] (**-(e)s, -e**) *nt* area;
(*Hoheits~*) territory; (*fig*) field; **g~en**
(*unreg*) *vt* to command, to demand;

g~erisch *adj* imperious
Gebilde [gə'bɪldə] (**-s, -**) *nt* object
gebildet *adj* cultured, educated
Gebirge [gə'bɪrgə] (**-s, -**) *nt* mountain
chain
Gebiß [gə'bɪs] (**-sses, -sse**) *nt* teeth *pl*;
(*künstlich*) dentures *pl*
gebissen *vb siehe* **beißen**
geblieben [gə'bli:bən] *vb siehe* **bleiben**
geboren [gə'bo:rən] *adj* born; (*Frau*)
née
geborgen [gə'bɔrgən] *adj* secure, safe
Gebot [gə'bo:t] (**-(e)s, -e**) *nt* command;
(*REL*) commandment; (*bei Auktion*) bid
geboten *vb siehe* **bieten**
Gebr. *abk* (= *Gebrüder*) Bros.
gebracht [gə'braxt] *vb siehe* **bringen**
gebraten [gə'bra:tən] *adj* fried
Gebrauch [gə'braʊx] (**-(e)s, Gebräuche**)
m use; (*Sitte*) custom; **g~en** *vt* to use
gebräuchlich [gə'brɔʏçlɪç] *adj* usual,
customary
Gebrauchs- *zW*: **~anweisung** *f* directions *pl* for use; **~artikel** *m* article of
everyday use; **g~fertig** *adj* ready for
use; **~gegenstand** *m* commodity
gebraucht [gə'braʊxt] *adj* used;
G~wagen *m* secondhand *od* used car
gebrechlich [gə'brɛçlɪç] *adj* frail
gebrochen [gə'brɔxən] *adj* broken
Gebrüder [gə'bry:dər] *pl* brothers
Gebrüll [gə'brʏl] (**-(e)s**) *nt* roaring
Gebühr [gə'by:r] (**-, -en**) *f* charge, fee;
nach ~ fittingly; **über ~** unduly; **g~en**
vi: **jdm g~en** to be sb's due *od* due to
sb ♦ *vr* to be fitting; **g~end** *adj* fitting,
appropriate ♦ *adv* fittingly, appropri-
ately
Gebühren- *zW*: **~erlaß** *m* remission
of fees; **~ermäßigung** *f* reduction of
fees; **g~frei** *adj* free of charge;
g~pflichtig *adj* subject to a charge
gebunden [gə'bʊndən] *vb siehe* **binden**
Geburt [gə'bu:rt] (**-, -en**) *f* birth
Geburten- *zW*: **~beschränkung** *f* birth
control; **~kontrolle** *f* birth control;
~reglung *f* birth control; **~ziffer** *f*
birth-rate
gebürtig [gə'bʏrtɪç] *adj* born in, native
of; **~e Schweizerin** native of Switzer-

land
Geburts- zW: ~**anzeige** f birth notice;
~**datum** nt date of birth; ~**jahr** nt year
of birth; ~**ort** m birthplace; ~**tag** m
birthday; ~**urkunde** f birth certificate
Gebüsch [gə'byʃ] (-(e)s, -e) nt bushes pl
gedacht [gə'daxt] vb siehe **denken**
Gedächtnis [gə'dɛçtnɪs] (-ses, -se) nt
memory; ~**feier** f commemoration
Gedanke [gə'daŋkə] (-ns, -n) m thought;
sich über etw akk ~**n machen** to think
about sth
Gedanken- zW: ~**austausch** m
exchange of ideas; **g~los** adj thoughtless; ~**losigkeit** f thoughtlessness;
~**strich** m dash; ~**übertragung** f
thought transference, telepathy; **g~voll**
adj thoughtful
Gedeck [gə'dɛk] (-(e)s, -e) nt
cover(ing); (Speisenfolge) menu; **ein ~**
auflegen to lay a place
gedeihen [gə'daɪən] (unreg) vi to
thrive, to prosper
gedenken [gə'dɛŋkən] (unreg) vi +gen
(sich erinnern) to remember;
(beabsichtigen) to intend
Gedenk- zW: ~**feier** f commemoration;
~**minute** f minute's silence; ~**tag** m
remembrance day
Gedicht [gə'dɪçt] (-(e)s, -e) nt poem
gediegen [gə'di:gən] adj (good) quality;
(Mensch) reliable, honest
Gedränge [gə'drɛŋə] (-s) nt crush,
crowd; **ins ~ kommen** (fig) to get into
difficulties
gedrängt adj compressed; ~ **voll**
packed
gedrungen [gə'drʊŋən] adj thickset,
stocky
Geduld [gə'dʊlt] f patience; **g~en**
[gə'dʊldən] vr to be patient; **g~ig** adj
patient, forbearing; **Geduldsprobe** f
trial of (one's) patience
gedurft [gə'dʊrft] vb siehe **dürfen**
geehrt [gə'e:rt] adj: **Sehr ~e Frau X!**
Dear Mrs X
geeignet [gə''aɪgnət] adj suitable
Gefahr [gə'fa:r] (-, -en) f danger; ~
laufen, etw zu tun to run the risk of
doing sth; **auf eigene ~** at one's own

risk
gefährden [gə'fɛ:rdən] vt to endanger
Gefahrenquelle f source of danger
Gefahrenzulage f danger money
gefährlich [gə'fɛ:rlɪç] adj dangerous
Gefälle [gə'fɛlə] (-s, -) nt gradient, incline
Gefallen¹ [gə'falən] (-s, -) m favour
Gefallen² (-s) nt pleasure; **an etw** dat
~ **finden** to derive pleasure from sth
gefallen pp von **fallen** ♦ vi (unreg):
jdm ~ to please sb; **er/es gefällt mir** I
like him/it; **das gefällt mir an ihm**
that's one thing I like about him; **sich**
dat **etw ~ lassen** to put up with sth
gefällig [gə'fɛlɪç] adj (hilfsbereit)
obliging; (erfreulich) pleasant; **G~keit**
f favour; helpfulness; **etw aus G~keit**
tun to do sth out of the goodness of
one's heart
gefälligst adv kindly
gefangen [gə'faŋən] adj captured; (fig)
captivated; **G~e(r)** m(f) prisoner, captive; ~**halten** (unreg) vt to keep
prisoner; **G~nahme** f capture;
~**nehmen** (unreg) vt to take prisoner;
G~schaft f captivity
Gefängnis [gə'fɛŋnɪs] (-ses, -se) nt
prison; ~**strafe** f prison sentence;
~**wärter** m prison warder
Gefäß [gə'fɛ:s] (-es, -e) nt vessel (auch
ANAT), container
gefaßt [gə'fast] adj composed, calm; **auf**
etw akk ~ **sein** to be prepared od ready
for sth
Gefecht [gə'fɛçt] (-(e)s, -e) nt fight;
(MIL) engagement
Gefieder [gə'fi:dər] (-s, -) nt plumage,
feathers pl
gefleckt [gə'flɛkt] adj spotted, mottled
geflogen [gə'flo:gən] vb siehe **fliegen**
geflossen [gə'flɔsən] vb siehe **fließen**
Geflügel [gə'fly:gəl] (-s) nt poultry
Gefolge [gə'fɔlgə] (-s, -) nt retinue
Gefolgschaft f following
gefragt [gə'fra:kt] adj in demand
gefräßig [gə'frɛ:sɪç] adj voracious
Gefreite(r) [gə'fraɪtə(r)] m lance corporal; (NAUT) able seaman; (AVIAT) air-
craftman

gefrieren [gə'fri:rən] (unreg) vi to freeze
Gefrier- zW: ~**fach** nt icebox; ~**fleisch** nt frozen meat; **g~getrocknet** adj freeze-dried; ~**punkt** m freezing point; ~**schutzmittel** nt antifreeze; ~**truhe** f deep-freeze
gefroren [gə'fro:rən] vb siehe **frieren**
gefügig [gə'fy:gɪç] adj pliant; (Mensch) obedient
Gefühl [gə'fy:l] (-(e)s, -e) nt feeling; **etw im ~ haben** to have a feel for sth; **g~los** adj unfeeling
gefühls- zW: ~**betont** adj emotional; **G~duselei** [-du:zə'laɪ] f over-sentimentality; ~**mäßig** adj instinctive
gefunden [gə'fʊndən] vb siehe **finden**
gegangen [gə'gaŋən] vb siehe **gehen**
gegeben [gə'ge:bən] vb siehe **geben** ♦ adj given; **zu ~er Zeit** in good time
gegebenenfalls [gə'ge:bənənfals] adv if need be

┌─────────────────────┐
│ *SCHLÜSSELWORT* │
└─────────────────────┘

gegen ['ge:gən] präp +akk **1** against; **nichts gegen jdn haben** to have nothing against sb; **X gegen Y** (SPORT, JUR) X versus Y; **ein Mittel gegen Schnupfen** something for colds
2 (in Richtung auf) towards; **gegen Osten** to(wards) the east; **gegen Abend** towards evening; **gegen einen Baum fahren** to drive into a tree
3 (ungefähr) round about; **gegen 3 Uhr** around 3 o'clock
4 (gegenüber) towards; (ungefähr) around; **gerecht gegen alle** fair to all
5 (im Austausch für) for; **gegen bar** for cash; **gegen Quittung** against a receipt
6 (verglichen mit) compared with

Gegenangriff m counter-attack
Gegenbeweis m counter-evidence
Gegend ['ge:gənt] (-, -en) f area, district
Gegen- zW: **g~ei'nander** adv against one another; ~**fahrbahn** f oncoming carriageway; ~**frage** f counter-question; ~**gewicht** nt counterbalance; ~**gift** nt antidote; ~**leistung** f service in return; ~**satz** m contrast; ~**sätze überbrücken** to overcome differences;

g~sätzlich adj contrary, opposite; (widersprüchlich) contradictory; **g~seitig** adj mutual, reciprocal; **sich g~seitig helfen** to help each other; ~**seitigkeit** f reciprocity; ~**spieler** m opponent; ~**stand** m object; **g~ständlich** adj objective, concrete; ~**stimme** f vote against; ~**stoß** m counterblow; ~**stück** nt counterpart; ~**teil** nt opposite; **im ~teil** on the contrary; **g~teilig** adj opposite, contrary
gegenüber [ge:gən'y:bər] präp +dat opposite; (zu) to(wards); (angesichts) in the face of ♦ adv opposite; **G~** (-s, -) nt person opposite; ~**liegen** (unreg) vr to face each other; ~**stehen** (unreg) vr to be opposed (to each other); ~**stellen** vt to confront; (fig) to contrast; **G~stellung** f confrontation; (fig) contrast; ~**treten** (unreg) vi +dat to face
Gegen- zW: ~**verkehr** m oncoming traffic; ~**vorschlag** m counterproposal; ~**wart** f present; **g~wärtig** adj present ♦ adv at present; **das ist mir nicht mehr g~wärtig** that has slipped my mind; ~**wert** m equivalent; ~**wind** m headwind; **g~zeichnen** vt, vi to countersign
gegessen [gə'gɛsən] vb siehe **essen**
Gegner ['ge:gnər] (-s, -) m opponent; **g~isch** adj opposing; ~**schaft** f opposition
gegrillt [gə'grɪlt] adj grilled
Gehackte(s) [gə'haktə(s)] nt mince(d meat)
Gehalt¹ [gə'halt] (-(e)s, -e) m content
Gehalt² (-(e)s, ⁼er) nt salary
Gehalts- zW: ~**empfänger** m salary earner; ~**erhöhung** f salary increase; ~**zulage** f salary increment
gehaltvoll adj (nahrhaft) nutritious
gehässig [gə'hɛsɪç] adj spiteful, nasty; **G~keit** f spite(fulness)
Gehäuse [gə'hɔyzə] (-s, -) nt case; casing; (von Apfel etc) core
geheim [gə'haɪm] adj secret; **G~dienst** m secret service, intelligence service; ~**halten** (unreg) vt to keep secret; **G~nis** (-ses, -se) nt secret; mystery; ~**nisvoll** adj mysterious; **G~nummer** f

(*TEL*) secret number; **G~polizei** *f* secret police

gehen ['ge:ən] (*unreg*) *vt, vi* to go; (*zu Fuß* ~) to walk ♦ *vb unpers*: **wie geht es (dir)**? how are you *od* things?; ~ **nach** (*Fenster*) to face; **mir/ihm geht es gut** I'm/he's (doing) fine; **geht das**? is that possible?; **geht's noch**? can you manage?; **es geht** not too bad, O.K.; **das geht nicht** that's not on; **es geht um etw** sth is concerned, it's about sth

geheuer [gə'hɔyər] *adj*: **nicht** ~ eerie; (*fragwürdig*) dubious

Gehilfe [gə'hɪlfə] (**-n, -n**) *m* assistant

Gehilfin *f* assistant

Gehirn [gə'hɪrn] (**-(e)s, -e**) *nt* brain; ~**erschütterung** *f* concussion; ~**wäsche** *f* brainwashing

geholfen *vb siehe* **helfen**

Gehör [gə'hø:r] (**-(e)s**) *nt* hearing; **musikalisches** ~ ear; ~ **finden** to gain a hearing; **jdm** ~ **schenken** to give sb a hearing

gehorchen [gə'hɔrçən] *vi* +*dat* to obey

gehören [gə'hø:rən] *vi* to belong ♦ *vr unpers* to be right *od* proper

gehörig *adj* proper; ~ **zu** *od* +*dat* belonging to; part of

gehorsam [gə'ho:rza:m] *adj* obedient; **G~** (**-s**) *m* obedience

Gehsteig ['ge:ʃtaik] *m* pavement, sidewalk (*US*)

Gehweg ['ge:ve:k] *m* pavement, sidewalk (*US*)

Geier ['gaiər] (**-s, -**) *m* vulture

Geige ['gaigə] *f* violin

Geiger (**-s, -**) *m* violinist

Geigerzähler *m* geiger counter

geil [gail] *adj* randy (*BRIT*), horny (*US*)

Geisel ['gaizəl] (**-, -n**) *f* hostage

Geist [gaist] (**-(e)s, -er**) *m* spirit; (*Gespenst*) ghost; (*Verstand*) mind

geisterhaft *adj* ghostly

Geistes- *zW*: **g~abwesend** *adj* absentminded; ~**blitz** *m* brainwave; ~**gegenwart** *f* presence of mind; **g~krank** *adj* mentally ill; ~**kranke(r)** *mf* mentally ill person; ~**krankheit** *f* mental illness; ~**zustand** *m* state of mind

geist- *zW*: ~**ig** *adj* intellectual; mental;

(*Getränke*) alcoholic; ~**ig behindert** mentally handicapped; ~**lich** *adj* spiritual, religious; clerical; **G~liche(r)** *m* clergyman; **G~lichkeit** *f* clergy; ~**los** *adj* uninspired, dull; ~**reich** *adj* clever; witty; ~**voll** *adj* intellectual; (*weise*) wise

Geiz [gaits] (**-es**) *m* miserliness, meanness; **g~en** *vi* to be miserly; ~**hals** *m* miser; **g~ig** *adj* miserly, mean; ~**kragen** *m* miser

gekannt [gə'kant] *vb siehe* **kennen**

geknickt [gə'knɪkt] *adj* (*fig*) dejected

gekocht [gə'kɔxt] *adj* boiled

gekonnt [gə'kɔnt] *adj* skilful ♦ *vb siehe* **können**

Gekritzel [gə'krɪtsəl] (**-s**) *nt* scrawl, scribble

gekünstelt [gə'kʏnstəlt] *adj* artificial, affected

Gelächter [gə'lɛçtər] (**-s, -**) *nt* laughter

geladen [gə'la:dən] *adj* loaded; (*ELEK*) live; (*fig*) furious

gelähmt [gə'lɛ:mt] *adj* paralysed

Gelände [gə'lɛndə] (**-s, -**) *nt* land, terrain; (*von Fabrik, Sport~*) grounds *pl*; (*Bau~*) site; ~**lauf** *m* cross-country race

Geländer [gə'lɛndər] (**-s, -**) *nt* railing; (*Treppen~*) banister(s)

gelangen [gə'laŋən] *vi*: ~ (**an** +*akk od* **zu**) to reach; (*erwerben*) to attain; **in jds Besitz** ~ to come into sb's possession

gelassen [gə'lasən] *adj* calm, composed; **G~heit** *f* calmness, composure

Gelatine [ʒela'ti:nə] *f* gelatine

geläufig [gə'lɔyfɪç] *adj* (*üblich*) common; **das ist mir nicht** ~ I'm not familiar with that

gelaunt [gə'launt] *adj*: **schlecht/gut** ~ in a bad/good mood; **wie ist er** ~? what sort of mood is he in?

gelb [gɛlp] *adj* yellow; (*Ampellicht*) amber; ~**lich** *adj* yellowish; **G~sucht** *f* jaundice

Geld [gɛlt] (**-(e)s, -er**) *nt* money; **etw zu** ~ **machen** to sell sth off; ~**anlage** *f* investment; ~**automat** *m* cash dispenser; ~**beutel** *m* purse; ~**börse** *f*

purse; **~geber** (-s, -) *m* financial backer; **g~gierig** *adj* avaricious; **~schein** *m* banknote; **~schrank** *m* safe, strongbox; **~strafe** *f* fine; **~stück** *nt* coin; **~wechsel** *m* exchange (of money)

Gelee [ʒə'leː] (-s, -s) *nt od m* jelly

gelegen [gə'leːgən] *adj* situated; (*passend*) convenient, opportune ♦ *vb siehe* **liegen**; **etw kommt jdm ~** sth is convenient for sb

Gelegenheit [gə'leːgənhaɪt] *f* opportunity; (*Anlaß*) occasion; **bei jeder ~** at every opportunity

Gelegenheits- *zW:* **~arbeit** *f* casual work; **~arbeiter** *m* casual worker; **~kauf** *m* bargain

gelegentlich [gə'leːgəntlɪç] *adj* occasional ♦ *adv* occasionally; (*bei Gelegenheit*) some time (or other) ♦ *präp* +*gen* on the occasion of

gelehrt [gə'leːrt] *adj* learned; **G~e(r)** *mf* scholar; **G~heit** *f* scholarliness

Geleise [gə'laɪzə] (-s, -) *nt* = **Gleis**

Geleit [gə'laɪt] (-(e)s, -e) *nt* escort; **g~en** *vt* to escort; **~schutz** *m* escort

Gelenk [gə'lɛŋk] (-(e)s, -e) *nt* joint; **g~ig** *adj* supple

gelernt [gə'lɛrnt] *adj* skilled

Geliebte(r) [gə'liːptə(r)] *mf* sweetheart, beloved

geliehen *vb siehe* **leihen**

gelind(e) [gə'lɪnt, gə'lɪndə] *adj* mild, light; (*fig: Wut*) fierce; **gelinde gesagt** to put it mildly

gelingen [gə'lɪŋən] (*unreg*) *vi* to succeed; **es ist mir gelungen, etw zu tun** I succeeded in doing sth

gell [gɛl] *excl* isn't it?; aren't you? *etc*

geloben [gə'loːbən] *vt*, *vi* to vow, to swear

gelten ['gɛltən] (*unreg*) *vt* (*wert sein*) to be worth ♦ *vi* (*gültig sein*) to be valid; (*erlaubt sein*) to be allowed ♦ *vb unpers:* **es gilt, etw zu tun** it is necessary to do sth; **jdm viel/wenig ~** to mean a lot/not to mean much to sb; **was gilt die Wette?** what do you bet?; **jdm ~** (*gemünzt sein auf*) to be meant for *od* aimed at sb; **etw ~ lassen** to accept sth; **als** *od* **für etw ~** to be considered to be sth; **jdm** *od* **für jdn ~** (*betreffen*) to apply to *od* for sb; **~d** *adj* prevailing; **etw ~d machen** to assert sth; **sich ~d machen** to make itself/o.s. felt

Geltung ['gɛltʊŋ] *f:* **~ haben** to have validity; **sich/etw** *dat* **~ verschaffen** to establish one's position/the position of sth; **etw zur ~ bringen** to show sth to its best advantage; **zur ~ kommen** to be seen/heard *etc* to its best advantage

Geltungsbedürfnis *nt* desire for admiration

Gelübde [gə'lʏpdə] (-s, -) *nt* vow

gelungen [gə'lʊŋən] *adj* successful

gem. *abk* = **gemischt**

gemächlich [gə'mɛːçlɪç] *adj* leisurely

Gemahl [gə'maːl] (-(e)s, -e) *m* husband; **~in** *f* wife

Gemälde [gə'mɛːldə] (-s, -) *nt* picture, painting

gemäß [gə'mɛːs] *präp* +*dat* in accordance with ♦ *adj* (+*dat*) appropriate (to)

gemäßigt *adj* moderate; (*Klima*) temperate

gemein [gə'maɪn] *adj* common; (*niederträchtig*) mean; **etw ~ haben** (**mit**) to have sth in common (with)

Gemeinde [gə'maɪndə] *f* district, community; (*Pfarr~*) parish; (*Kirchen~*) congregation; **~steuer** *f* local rates *pl*; **~verwaltung** *f* local administration; **~wahl** *f* local election

Gemein- *zW:* **g~gefährlich** *adj* dangerous to the public; **~heit** *f* commonness; mean thing to do/to say; **~platz** *m* commonplace, platitude; **g~sam** *adj* joint, common (*auch MATH*) ♦ *adv* together, jointly; **g~same Sache mit jdm machen** to be in cahoots with sb; **etw g~sam haben** to have sth in common; **~samkeit** *f* community, having in common; **~schaft** *f* community; **in ~schaft mit** jointly *od* together with; **g~schaftlich** *adj* = **gemeinsam**; **~schaftsarbeit** *f* teamwork; team effort; **~sinn** *m* public spirit; **~wohl** *nt* common good

Gemenge [gə'mɛŋə] (-s, -) *nt* mixture; (*Hand~*) scuffle

gemessen [gə'mɛsən] *adj* measured

Gemetzel [gə'mɛtsəl] (-s, -) *nt* slaughter, carnage, butchery

Gemisch [gə'mɪʃ] (-es, -e) *nt* mixture; **g~t** *adj* mixed

gemocht [gə'mɔxt] *vb siehe* **mögen**

Gemse ['gɛmzə] *f* chamois

Gemunkel [gə'mʊŋkəl] (-s) *nt* gossip

Gemurmel [gə'mʊrməl] (-s) *nt* murmur(ing)

Gemüse [gə'my:zə] (-s, -) *nt* vegetables *pl*; **~garten** *m* vegetable garden; **~händler** *m* greengrocer

gemußt *vb siehe* **müssen**

Gemüt [gə'my:t] (-(e)s, -er) *nt* disposition, nature; person; **sich** *dat* **etw zu ~e führen** (*umg*) to indulge in sth; **die ~er erregen** to arouse strong feelings; **g~lich** *adj* comfortable, cosy; (*Person*) good-natured; **~lichkeit** *f* comfortableness, cosiness; amiability

Gemüts- *zW*: **~mensch** *m* sentimental person; **~ruhe** *f* composure; **~zustand** *m* state of mind

gemütvoll *adj* warm, tender

genannt [gə'nant] *vb siehe* **nennen**

genau [gə'nau] *adj* exact, precise ♦ *adv* exactly, precisely; **etw ~ nehmen** to take sth seriously; **~genommen** *adv* strictly speaking; **G~igkeit** *f* exactness, accuracy; **~so** *adv* just the same; **~so gut** just as good

genehm [gə'ne:m] *adj* agreeable, acceptable; **~igen** *vt* to approve, to authorize; **sich** *dat* **etw ~igen** to indulge in sth; **G~igung** *f* approval, authorization; (*Schriftstück*) permit

General [geneˈraːl] (-s, -e *od* ⸚e) *m* general; **~direktor** *m* director general; **~konsulat** *nt* consulate general; **~probe** *f* dress rehearsal; **~streik** *m* general strike; **g~überholen** *vt* to overhaul thoroughly

Generation [generatsiˈoːn] *f* generation

Generator [geneˈraːtɔr] *m* generator, dynamo

generell [genəˈrɛl] *adj* general

genesen [gəˈneːzən] (*unreg*) *vi* to convalesce, to recover

Genesung *f* recovery, convalescence

genetisch [geˈneːtɪʃ] *adj* genetic

Genf [genf] *nt* Geneva; **der ~er See** Lake Geneva

genial [geniˈaːl] *adj* brilliant; **G~iˈtät** *f* brilliance, genius

Genick [gəˈnɪk] (-(e)s, -e) *nt* (back of the) neck; **~starre** *f* stiff neck

Genie [ʒeˈniː] (-s, -s) *nt* genius

genieren [ʒeˈniːrən] *vt* to bother ♦ *vr* to feel awkward *od* self-conscious; **geniert es Sie, wenn ...?** do you mind if ...?

genießbar *adj* edible; drinkable

genießen [gəˈniːsən] (*unreg*) *vt* to enjoy; to eat; to drink

Genießer (-s, -) *m* epicure; pleasure lover; **g~isch** *adj* appreciative ♦ *adv* with relish

genommen *vb siehe* **nehmen**

Genosse [gəˈnɔsə] (-n, -n) *m* (*bes POL*) comrade, companion; **Genossenschaft** *f* cooperative (association)

Genossin *f* (*bes POL*) comrade, companion

genug [gəˈnuːk] *adv* enough

Genüge [gəˈnyːgə] *f*: **jdm/etw ~ tun** *od* **leisten** to satisfy sb/sth; **g~n** *vi* (+*dat*) to be enough (for); **g~nd** *adj* sufficient

genügsam [gəˈnyːkzaːm] *adj* modest, easily satisfied; **G~keit** *f* undemandingness

Genugtuung [gəˈnuːktuːʊŋ] *f* satisfaction

Genuß [gəˈnʊs] (-sses, ⸚sse) *m* pleasure; (*Zusichnehmen*) consumption; **in den ~ von etw kommen** to receive the benefit of sth

genüßlich [gəˈnʏslɪç] *adv* with relish

Genußmittel *pl* (semi-)luxury items

geöffnet [gəˈœfnət] *adj* open

Geograph [geoˈgraːf] (-en, -en) *m* geographer; **Geograˈphie** *f* geography; **g~isch** *adj* geographical

Geologe [geoˈloːgə] (-n, -n) *m* geologist; **Geoloˈgie** *f* geology

Geometrie [geomeˈtriː] *f* geometry

Gepäck [gəˈpɛk] (-(e)s) *nt* luggage, baggage; **~abfertigung** *f* luggage office; **~annahme** *f* luggage office; **~aufbewahrung** *f* left-luggage office (*BRIT*), baggage check (*US*); **~aufgabe**

f luggage office; **~ausgabe** *f* luggage office; **~netz** *nt* luggage-rack; **~rückgabe** *f* luggage office; **~träger** *m* porter; (*Fahrrad*) carrier; **~wagen** *m* luggage van (*BRIT*), baggage car (*US*)

gepflegt [gə'pfle:kt] *adj* well-groomed; (*Park etc*) well looked after

---
SCHLÜSSELWORT
---

gerade [gə'ra:də] *adj* straight; (*aufrecht*) upright; **eine gerade Zahl** an even number
♦ *adv* **1** (*genau*) just, exactly; (*speziell*) especially; **gerade deshalb** that's just *od* exactly why; **das ist es ja gerade!** that's just it!; **gerade du** you especially; **warum gerade ich?** why me (of all people)?; **jetzt gerade nicht!** not now!; **gerade neben** right next to
2 (*eben, soeben*) just; **er wollte gerade aufstehen** he was just about to get up; **gerade erst** only just; **gerade noch** (only) just

Gerade *f* straight line; **g~aus** *adv* straight ahead; **g~heraus** *adv* straight out, bluntly; **g~zu** *adv* (*beinahe*) virtually, almost

gerannt [gə'rant] *vb siehe* **rennen**

Gerät [gə're:t] (-(e)s, -e) *nt* device; (*Werkzeug*) tool; (*SPORT*) apparatus; (*Zubehör*) equipment *no pl*

geraten [gə'ra:tən] (*unreg*) *vi* (*gedeihen*) to thrive; (*gelingen*): (*jdm*) ~ to turn out well (for sb); **gut/schlecht** ~ to turn out well/badly; **an jdn** ~ to come across sb; **in etw** *akk* ~ to get into sth; **in Angst** ~ to get frightened; **nach jdm** ~ to take after sb

Geratewohl [gəra:tə'vo:l] *nt*: **aufs** ~ on the off chance; (*bei Wahl*) at random

geräumig [gə'rɔʏmɪç] *adj* roomy

Geräusch [gə'rɔʏʃ] (-(e)s, -e) *nt* sound, noise; **g~los** *adj* silent

gerben ['gɛrbən] *vt* to tan

gerecht [gə'rɛçt] *adj* just, fair; **jdm/etw** ~ **werden** to do justice to sb/sth; **G~igkeit** *f* justice, fairness

Gerede [gə're:də] (-s) *nt* talk, gossip

gereizt [gə'raɪtst] *adj* irritable; **G~heit** *f* irritation

Gericht [gə'rɪçt] (-(e)s, -e) *nt* court; (*Essen*) dish; **mit jdm ins** ~ **gehen** (*fig*) to judge sb harshly; **das Jüngste** ~ the Last Judgement; **g~lich** *adj* judicial, legal ♦ *adv* judicially, legally

Gerichts- *zW:* **~barkeit** *f* jurisdiction; **~hof** *m* court (of law); **~kosten** *pl* (legal) costs; **~saal** *m* courtroom; **~verfahren** *nt* legal proceedings *pl*; **~verhandlung** *f* trial; **~vollzieher** *m* bailiff

gerieben [gə'ri:bən] *adj* grated; (*umg: schlau*) smart, wily ♦ *vb siehe* **reiben**

gering [gə'rɪŋ] *adj* slight, small; (*niedrig*) low; (*Zeit*) short; **~fügig** *adj* slight, trivial; **~schätzig** *adj* disparaging

geringste(r, s) *adj* slightest, least; **geringstenfalls** *adv* at the very least

gerinnen [gə'rɪnən] (*unreg*) *vi* to congeal; (*Blut*) to clot; (*Milch*) to curdle

Gerippe [gə'rɪpə] (-s, -) *nt* skeleton

gerissen [gə'rɪsən] *adj* wily, smart

geritten [gə'rɪtən] *vb siehe* **reiten**

gern(e) ['gɛrn(ə)] *adv* willingly, gladly; **~(e) haben, ~(e) mögen** to like; **etwas ~(e) tun** to like doing something; **ich möchte ~(e) ...** I'd like ...; **ja, ~(e)** yes, please; yes, I'd like to; **~(e) geschehen** it's a pleasure

gerochen [gə'rɔxən] *vb siehe* **riechen**

Geröll [gə'rœl] (-(e)s, -e) *nt* scree

Gerste ['gɛrstə] *f* barley; **Gerstenkorn** *nt* (*im Auge*) stye

Geruch [gə'rʊx] (-(e)s, ⁼e) *m* smell, odour; **g~los** *adj* odourless

Gerücht [gə'rʏçt] (-(e)s, -e) *nt* rumour

geruchtilgend *adj* deodorant

geruhen [gə'ru:ən] *vi* to deign

Gerümpel [gə'rʏmpəl] (-s) *nt* junk

Gerüst [gə'rʏst] (-(e)s, -e) *nt* (*Bau~*) scaffold(ing); frame

gesamt [gə'zamt] *adj* whole, entire; (*Kosten*) total; (*Werke*) complete; **im ~en** all in all; **~deutsch** *adj* all-German; **G~eindruck** *m* general impression; **G~heit** *f* totality, whole; **G~schule** *f* ≈ comprehensive school

gesandt [gə'zant] *vb siehe* **senden**

Gesandte(r) _m_ envoy
Gesandtschaft [gə'zantʃaft] _f_ legation
Gesang [gə'zaŋ] (-(e)s, ˉe) _m_ song; (_Singen_) singing; ~**buch** _nt_ (_REL_) hymn book
Gesäß [gə'zɛːs] (-es, -e) _nt_ seat, bottom
Geschäft [gə'ʃɛft] (-(e)s, -e) _nt_ business; (_Laden_) shop; (~_sabschluß_) deal; **Geschäftemacher** (-s, -) _m_ wheeler-dealer; **g~ig** _adj_ active, busy; (_pej_) officious; **g~lich** _adj_ commercial ♦ _adv_ on business
Geschäfts- _zW:_ ~**bericht** _m_ financial report; ~**essen** _nt_ business lunch; ~**führer** _m_ manager; (_Klub_) secretary; ~**geheimnis** _nt_ trade secret; ~**jahr** _nt_ financial year; ~**lage** _f_ business conditions _pl_; ~**mann** _m_ businessman; **g~mäßig** _adj_ businesslike; ~**reise** _f_ business trip; ~**schluß** _m_ closing time; ~**stelle** _f_ office, place of business; **g~tüchtig** _adj_ business-minded; ~**viertel** _nt_ business quarter; shopping centre; ~**wagen** _m_ company car; ~**zeit** _f_ business hours
geschehen [gə'ʃeːən] (_unreg_) _vi_ to happen; **es war um ihn ~** that was the end of him
gescheit [gə'ʃait] _adj_ clever
Geschenk [gə'ʃɛŋk] (-(e)s, -e) _nt_ present, gift
Geschichte [gə'ʃiçtə] _f_ story; (_Sache_) affair; (_Historie_) history
geschichtlich _adj_ historical
Geschick [gə'ʃik] (-(e)s, -e) _nt_ aptitude; (_Schicksal_) fate; ~**lichkeit** _f_ skill, dexterity; **g~t** _adj_ skilful
geschieden [gə'ʃiːdən] _adj_ divorced
geschienen [gə'ʃiːnən] _vb siehe_ **scheinen**
Geschirr [gə'ʃir] (-(e)s, -e) _nt_ crockery; pots and pans _pl_; (_Pferd_) harness; ~**spülmaschine** _f_ dishwasher; ~**tuch** _nt_ dish cloth
Geschlecht [gə'ʃlɛçt] (-(e)s, -er) _nt_ sex; (_GRAM_) gender; (_Gattung_) race; family; **g~lich** _adj_ sexual
Geschlechts- _zW:_ ~**krankheit** _f_ venereal disease; ~**teil** _nt_ genitals _pl_; ~**verkehr** _m_ sexual intercourse

geschlossen [gə'ʃlɔsən] _adj_ shut ♦ _vb siehe_ **schließen**
Geschmack [gə'ʃmak] (-(e)s, ˉe) _m_ taste; **nach jds ~** to sb's taste; **~ finden an etw** _dat_ to (come to) like sth; **g~los** _adj_ tasteless; (_fig_) in bad taste; **Geschmackssache** _f_ matter of taste; **Geschmackssinn** _m_ sense of taste; **g~voll** _adj_ tasteful
geschmeidig [gə'ʃmaidiç] _adj_ supple; (_formbar_) malleable
geschnitten [gə'ʃnitən] _vb siehe_ **schneiden**
Geschöpf [gə'ʃœpf] (-(e)s, -e) _nt_ creature
Geschoß [gə'ʃɔs] (-sses, -sse) _nt_ (_MIL_) projectile, missile; (_Stockwerk_) floor
geschossen _vb siehe_ **schießen**
geschraubt [gə'ʃraupt] _adj_ stilted, artificial
Geschrei [gə'ʃrai] (-s) _nt_ cries _pl_, shouting; (_fig: Aufheben_) noise, fuss
geschrieben [gə'ʃriːbən] _vb siehe_ **schreiben**
Geschütz [gə'ʃyts] (-es, -e) _nt_ gun, cannon; **ein schweres ~ auffahren** (_fig_) to bring out the big guns; ~**feuer** _nt_ artillery fire, gunfire
geschützt _adj_ protected
Geschwader [gə'ʃvaːdər] (-s, -) _nt_ (_NAUT_) squadron; (_AVIAT_) group
Geschwafel [gə'ʃvaːfəl] (-s) _nt_ silly talk
Geschwätz [gə'ʃvɛts] (-es) _nt_ chatter, gossip; **g~ig** _adj_ talkative
geschweige [gə'ʃvaigə] _adv:_ ~ (**denn**) let alone, not to mention
geschwind [gə'ʃvint] _adj_ quick, swift; **G~igkeit** [-diçkait] _f_ speed, velocity; **G~igkeitsbegrenzung** _f_ speed limit; **G~igkeitsüberschreitung** _f_ exceeding the speed limit
Geschwister [gə'ʃvistər] _pl_ brothers and sisters
geschwollen [gə'ʃvɔlən] _adj_ pompous
geschwommen [gə'ʃvɔmən] _vb siehe_ **schwimmen**
Geschworene(r) [gə'ʃvoːrənə(r)] _mf_ juror; ~**n** _pl_ jury
Geschwulst [gə'ʃvulst] (-, ˉe) _f_ swelling; growth, tumour

Geschwür [gə'ʃvy:r] (-(e)s, -e) nt ulcer
Gesell- [gə'zɛl] zW: ~**e** (-n, -n) m fellow; (Handwerk~) journeyman; **g~ig** adj sociable; ~**igkeit** f sociability; ~**schaft** f society; (Begleitung, COMM) company; (Abendgesellschaft etc) party; **g~schaftlich** adj social; ~**schaftsordnung** f social structure; ~**schaftsschicht** f social stratum
gesessen [gə'zɛsən] vb siehe **sitzen**
Gesetz [gə'zɛts] (-es, -e) nt law; ~**buch** nt statute book; ~**entwurf** m bill; ~**esvorlage** f bill; **g~gebend** adj legislative; ~**gebung** f legislation; **g~lich** adj legal, lawful; ~**lichkeit** f legality, lawfulness; **g~los** adj lawless; **g~mäßig** adj lawful; **g~t** adj (Mensch) sedate; **g~widrig** adj illegal, unlawful
ges. gesch. abk (= gesetzlich geschützt) registered
Gesicht [gə'zɪçt] (-(e)s, -er) nt face; das zweite ~ second sight; das ist mir nie zu ~ gekommen I've never laid eyes on that
Gesichts- zW: ~**ausdruck** m (facial) expression; ~**farbe** f complexion; ~**punkt** m point of view; ~**züge** pl features
Gesindel [gə'zɪndəl] (-s) nt rabble
gesinnt [gə'zɪnt] adj disposed, minded
Gesinnung [gə'zɪnʊŋ] f disposition; (Ansicht) views pl; **Gesinnungswandel** m change of opinion, volte-face
gesittet [gə'zɪtət] adj well-mannered
Gespann [gə'ʃpan] (-(e)s, -e) nt team; (umg) couple
gespannt adj tense, strained; (begierig) eager; **ich bin ~, ob** I wonder if od whether; **auf etw/jdn ~ sein** to look forward to sth/meeting sb
Gespenst [gə'ʃpɛnst] (-(e)s, -er) nt ghost, spectre; **g~erhaft** adj ghostly
gesperrt [gə'ʃpɛrt] adj closed off
Gespött [gə'ʃpœt] (-(e)s) nt mockery; **zum ~ werden** to become a laughing stock
Gespräch [gə'ʃprɛ:ç] (-(e)s, -e) nt conversation; discussion(s); (Anruf) call; **g~ig** adj talkative; ~**igkeit** f talkative-

ness; **Gesprächsthema** nt subject od topic (of conversation)
gesprochen [gə'ʃprɔxən] vb siehe **sprechen**
gesprungen [gə'ʃprʊŋən] vb siehe **springen**
Gespür [gə'ʃpy:r] (-s) nt feeling
Gestalt [gə'ʃtalt] (-, -en) f form, shape; (Person) figure; **in ~ von** in the form of; ~ **annehmen** to take shape; **g~en** vt (formen) to shape, to form; (organisieren) to arrange, to organize ♦ vr: **sich g~en (zu)** to turn out (to be); ~**ung** f formation; organization
gestanden [gə'ʃtandən] vb siehe **stehen**
Geständnis [gə'ʃtɛntnɪs] (-ses, -se) nt confession
Gestank [gə'ʃtaŋk] (-(e)s) m stench
gestatten [gə'ʃtatən] vt to permit, to allow; ~ **Sie?** may I?; **sich dat ~, etw zu tun** to take the liberty of doing sth
Geste ['gɛstə] f gesture
gestehen [gə'ʃte:ən] (unreg) vt to confess
Gestein [gə'ʃtain] (-(e)s, -e) nt rock
Gestell [gə'ʃtɛl] (-(e)s, -e) nt frame; (Regal) rack, stand
gestern [gɛstərn] adv yesterday; ~ **abend/morgen** yesterday evening/ morning
Gestirn [gə'ʃtɪrn] (-(e)s, -e) nt star; (Sternbild) constellation
gestohlen [gə'ʃto:lən] vb siehe **stehlen**
gestorben [gə'ʃtɔrbən] vb siehe **sterben**
gestreift [gə'ʃtraift] adj striped
gestrichen [gə'ʃtrɪçən] adj cancelled
gestrig [gɛstrɪç] adj yesterday's
Gestrüpp [gə'ʃtryp] (-(e)s, -e) nt undergrowth
Gestüt [gə'ʃty:t] (-(e)s, -e) nt stud farm
Gesuch [gə'zu:x] (-(e)s, -e) nt petition; (Antrag) application; **g~t** adj (COMM) in demand; wanted; (fig) contrived
gesund [gə'zʊnt] adj healthy; **wieder ~ werden** to get better; **G~heit** f health(iness); **G~heit!** bless you!; ~**heitlich** adj health attrib, physical ♦ adv: **wie geht es Ihnen ~heitlich?** how's your health?; ~**heitsschädlich** adj unhealthy; **G~heitswesen** nt health

service; **G~heitszustand** *m* state of health

gesungen [gə'zʊŋən] *vb siehe* **singen**

getan [gə'ta:n] *vb siehe* **tun**

Getöse [gə'tø:zə] (-s) *nt* din, racket

Getränk [gə'trɛŋk] (-(e)s, -e) *nt* drink; **Getränkekarte** *f* wine list

getrauen [gə'trauən] *vr* to dare, to venture

Getreide [gə'traidə] (-s, -) *nt* cereals *pl*, grain; **~speicher** *m* granary

getrennt [gə'trɛnt] *adj* separate

Getriebe [gə'tri:bə] (-s, -) *nt* (*Leute*) bustle; (*AUT*) gearbox

getrieben *vb siehe* **treiben**

getroffen [gə'trɔfən] *vb siehe* **treffen**

getrost [gə'tro:st] *adv* without any bother

getrunken [gə'trʊŋkən] *vb siehe* **trinken**

Getue [gə'tu:ə] (-s) *nt* fuss

geübt [gə''y:pt] *adj* experienced

Gewächs [gə'vɛks] (-es, -e) *nt* growth; (*Pflanze*) plant

gewachsen [gə'vaksən] *adj*: **jdm/etw ~ sein** to be sb's equal/equal to sth

Gewächshaus *nt* greenhouse

gewagt [gə'va:kt] *adj* daring, risky

gewählt [gə'vɛ:lt] *adj* (*Sprache*) refined, elegant

Gewähr [gə'vɛ:r] (-) *f* guarantee; **keine ~ übernehmen für** to accept no responsibility for; **g~en** *vt* to grant; (*geben*) to provide; **g~leisten** *vt* to guarantee

Gewahrsam [gə'va:rza:m] (-s, -e) *m* safekeeping; (*Polizei~*) custody

Gewährsmann *m* informant, source

Gewährung *f* granting

Gewalt [gə'valt] (-, -en) *f* power; (*große Kraft*) force; (*~taten*) violence; **mit aller ~** with all one's might; **~anwendung** *f* use of force; **g~ig** *adj* tremendous; (*Irrtum*) huge; **~marsch** *m* forced march; **g~sam** *adj* forcible; **g~tätig** *adj* violent

gewandt [gə'vant] *adj* deft, skilful; (*erfahren*) experienced; **G~heit** *f* dexterity, skill

gewann *etc* [gə'van] *vb siehe* **gewinnen**

Gewässer [gə'vɛsər] (-s, -) *nt* waters *pl*

Gewebe [gə've:bə] (-s, -) *nt* (*Stoff*) fabric; (*BIOL*) tissue

Gewehr [gə'vɛ:r] (-(e)s, -e) *nt* gun; rifle; **~lauf** *m* rifle barrel

Geweih [gə'vai] (-(e)s, -e) *nt* antlers *pl*

Gewerb- [gə'vɛrb] *zW*: **~e** (-s, -) *nt* trade, occupation; **Handel und ~e** trade and industry; **Gewerbeschule** *f* technical school; **g~lich** *adj* industrial; trade (*attrib*); **gewerbsmäßig** *adj* professional; **Gewerbszweig** *m* line of trade

Gewerkschaft [gə'vɛrkʃaft] *f* trade union; **~ler** (-s, -) *m* trade unionist; **Gewerkschaftsbund** *m* trade unions federation

Gewicht [gə'vɪçt] (-(e)s, -e) *nt* weight; (*fig*) importance; **g~ig** *adj* weighty

gewieft [gə'vi:ft] *adj* shrewd, cunning

gewiegt [gə'vi:kt] *adj* shrewd, cunning

gewillt [gə'vɪlt] *adj* willing, prepared

Gewimmel [gə'vɪməl] (-s) *nt* swarm

Gewinde [gə'vɪndə] (-s, -) *nt* (*Kranz*) wreath; (*von Schraube*) thread

Gewinn [gə'vɪn] (-(e)s, -e) *m* profit; (*bei Spiel*) winnings *pl*; **etw mit ~ verkaufen** to sell sth at a profit; **~- und Verlustrechnung** (*COMM*) profit and loss account; **~beteiligung** *f* profit-sharing; **g~bringend** *adj* profitable; **g~en** (*unreg*) *vt* to win; (*erwerben*) to gain; (*Kohle, Öl*) to extract ♦ *vi* to win; (*profitieren*) to gain; **an etw** *dat* **g~en** to gain (in) sth; **~er(in)** (-s, -) *m(f)* winner; **~spanne** *f* profit margin; **~(n)ummer** *f* winning number; **~ung** *f* winning; gaining; (*von Kohle etc*) extraction

Gewirr [gə'vɪr] (-(e)s, -e) *nt* tangle; (*von Straßen*) maze

gewiß [gə'vɪs] *adj* certain ♦ *adv* certainly

Gewissen [gə'vɪsən] (-s, -) *nt* conscience; **g~haft** *adj* conscientious; **~haftigkeit** *f* conscientiousness; **g~los** *adj* unscrupulous

Gewissens- *zW*: **~bisse** *pl* pangs of conscience, qualms; **~frage** *f* matter of conscience; **~freiheit** *f* freedom of conscience; **~konflikt** *m* moral conflict

gewissermaßen [gəvɪsər'ma:sən] *adv*

more or less, in a way

Gewißheit [gə'vɪshaɪt] f certainty

Gewitter [gə'vɪtər] (-s, -) nt thunderstorm; **g~n** vi unpers: **es g~t** there's a thunderstorm

gewitzt [gə'vɪtst] adj shrewd, cunning

gewogen [gə'vo:gən] adj (+dat) well-disposed (towards)

gewöhnen [gə'vø:nən] vt: **jdn an etw akk ~** to accustom sb to sth; (erziehen zu) to teach sb sth ♦ vr: **sich an etw akk ~** to get used od accustomed to sth

Gewohnheit [gə'vo:nhaɪt] f habit; (Brauch) custom; **aus ~** from habit; **zur ~ werden** to become a habit

Gewohnheits- in zW habitual; **~mensch** m creature of habit; **~recht** nt common law

gewöhnlich [gə'vø:nlɪç] adj usual; ordinary; (pej) common; **wie ~** as usual

gewohnt [gə'vo:nt] adj usual; **etw ~ sein** to be used to sth

Gewöhnung f: **~ (an +akk)** getting accustomed (to)

Gewölbe [gə'vœlbə] (-s, -) nt vault

gewonnen [gə'vɔnən] vb siehe gewinnen

geworden [gə'vɔrdən] vb siehe werden

geworfen [gə'vɔrfən] vb siehe werfen

Gewühl [gə'vy:l] (-(e)s) nt throng

Gewürz [gə'vʏrts] (-es, -e) nt spice, seasoning; **~nelke** f clove; **g~t** adj spiced

gewußt [gə'vust] vb siehe wissen

Gezeiten [gə'tsaɪtən] pl tides

gezielt [gə'tsi:lt] adj with a particular aim in mind, purposeful; (Kritik) pointed

geziert [gə'tsi:rt] adj affected

gezogen [gə'tso:gən] vb siehe ziehen

Gezwitscher [gə'tsvɪtʃər] (-s) nt twitter(ing), chirping

gezwungen [gə'tsvuŋən] adj forced; **~ermaßen** adv of necessity

gibst etc [gɪpst] vb siehe geben

Gicht [gɪçt] (-) f gout; **g~isch** adj gouty

Giebel ['gi:bəl] (-s, -) m gable; **~dach** nt gable(d) roof; **~fenster** nt gable window

Gier [gi:r] (-) f greed; **g~ig** adj greedy

gießen ['gi:sən] (unreg) vt to pour; (Blumen) to water; (Metall) to cast; (Wachs) to mould

Gießkanne f watering can

Gift [gɪft] (-(e)s, -e) nt poison; **g~ig** adj poisonous; (fig: boshaft) venomous; **~zahn** m fang

ging etc vb siehe gehen

Ginster ['gɪnstər] (-s, -) m broom

Gipfel ['gɪpfəl] (-s, -) m summit, peak; (fig: Höhepunkt) height; **g~n** vi to culminate; **~treffen** nt summit (meeting)

Gips [gɪps] (-es, -e) m plaster; (MED) plaster (of Paris); **~abdruck** m plaster cast; **g~en** vt to plaster; **~verband** m plaster (cast)

Giraffe [gi'rafə] f giraffe

Girlande [gɪr'landə] f garland

Giro ['ʒi:ro] (-s, -s) nt giro; **~konto** nt current account

Gischt [gɪʃt] (-(e)s, -e) m spray

Gitarre [gi'tarə] f guitar

Gitter ['gɪtər] (-s, -) nt grating, bars pl; (für Pflanzen) trellis; (Zaun) railing(s); **~bett** nt cot; **~fenster** nt barred window; **~zaun** m railing(s)

Glacéhandschuh [gla'se:hantʃu:] m kid glove

Gladiole [gladi'o:lə] f gladiolus

Glanz [glants] (-es) m shine, lustre; (fig) splendour

glänzen ['glɛntsən] vi to shine (also fig), to gleam ♦ vt to polish; **~d** adj shining; (fig) brilliant

Glanz- zW: **~leistung** f brilliant achievement; **g~los** adj dull; **~zeit** f heyday

Glas [gla:s] (-es, ‑er) nt glass; **~bläser** (-s, -) m glass blower; **~er** (-s, -) m glazier; **~faser** f fibreglass; **g~ieren** [gla'zi:rən] vt to glaze; **g~ig** adj glassy; **~scheibe** f pane; **~ur** [gla'zu:r] f glaze; (KOCH) icing

glatt [glat] adj smooth; (rutschig) slippery; (Absage) flat; (Lüge) downright

Glätte ['glɛtə] f smoothness; slipperiness

Glatteis nt (black) ice; **jdn aufs ~**

führen (*fig*) to take sb for a ride
glätten *vt* to smooth out
Glatze ['glatsə] *f* bald head; **eine ~ bekommen** to go bald
Glaube ['glaubə] (-ns, -n) *m*: **~ (an** +*akk*) faith (in); belief (in); **g~n** *vt*, *vi* to believe; to think; **jdm g~n** to believe sb; **an etw** *akk* **g~n** to believe in sth; **daran g~n müssen** (*umg*) to be for it; **Glaubensbekenntnis** *nt* creed
glaubhaft ['glaubhaft] *adj* credible
gläubig ['glɔybɪç] *adj* (*REL*) devout; (*vertrauensvoll*) trustful; **G~e(r)** *mf* believer; **die G~en** the faithful; **G~er** (-s, -) *m* creditor
glaubwürdig ['glaubvʏrdɪç] *adj* credible; (*Mensch*) trustworthy; **G~keit** *f* credibility; trustworthiness
gleich [glaɪç] *adj* equal; (*identisch*) (the) same, identical ♦ *adv* equally; (*sofort*) straight away; (*bald*) in a minute; **es ist mir ~** it's all the same to me; **2 mal 2 ~ 4** 2 times 2 is *od* equals 4; **~ groß** the same size; **~ nach/an** right after/at; **~altrig** *adj* of the same age; **~artig** *adj* similar; **~bedeutend** *adj* synonymous; **~berechtigt** *adj* having equal rights; **G~berechtigung** *f* equal rights *pl*; **~bleibend** *adj* constant; **~en** (*unreg*) *vi*: **jdm/etw ~en** to be like sb/sth ♦ *vr* to be alike; **~falls** *adv* likewise; **danke ~falls!** the same to you; **G~förmigkeit** *f* uniformity; **~gesinnt** *adj* like-minded; **G~gewicht** *nt* equilibrium, balance; **~gültig** *adj* indifferent; (*unbedeutend*) unimportant; **G~gültigkeit** *f* indifference; **~heit** *f* equality; **~kommen** (*unreg*) *vi* +*dat* to be equal to; **~mäßig** *adj* even, equal; **G~mut** *m* equanimity; **G~nis** (-ses, -se) *nt* parable; **~sam** *adv* as it were; **G~strom** *m* (*ELEK*) direct current; **~tun** (*unreg*) *vi*: **es jdm ~tun** to match sb; **G~ung** *f* equation; **~viel** *adv* no matter; **~zeitig** *adj* simultaneous
Gleis [glaɪs] (-es, -e) *nt* track, rails *pl*; (*Bahnsteig*) platform
gleiten ['glaɪtən] (*unreg*) *vi* to glide; (*rutschen*) to slide
Gletscher ['glɛtʃər] (-s, -) *m* glacier;

~spalte *f* crevasse
Glied [gliːt] (-(e)s, -er) *nt* member; (*Arm, Bein*) limb; (*von Kette*) link; (*MIL*) rank(s); **g~ern** *vt* to organize, to structure; **~erung** *f* structure, organization; **~maßen** *pl* limbs
glimmen ['glɪmən] (*unreg*) *vi* to glow, to gleam
glimpflich ['glɪmpflɪç] *adj* mild, lenient; **~ davonkommen** to get off lightly
glitzern ['glɪtsərn] *vi* to glitter; to twinkle
Globus ['gloːbus] (- *od* -ses, Globen *od* -se) *m* globe
Glocke ['glɔkə] *f* bell; **etw an die große ~ hängen** (*fig*) to shout sth from the rooftops
Glocken- *zW*: **~geläut** *nt* peal of bells; **~spiel** *nt* chime(s); (*MUS*) glockenspiel; **~turm** *m* bell tower
Glosse ['glɔsə] *f* comment
glotzen ['glɔtsən] (*umg*) *vi* to stare
Glück [glʏk] (-(e)s) *nt* luck, fortune; (*Freude*) happiness; **~ haben** to be lucky; **viel ~!** good luck!; **zum ~** fortunately; **g~en** *vi* to succeed; **es g~te ihm, es zu bekommen** he succeeded in getting it
gluckern ['glukərn] *vi* to glug
Glück- *zW*: **g~lich** *adj* fortunate; (*froh*) happy; **g~licherweise** *adv* fortunately; **Glücksbringer** (-s, -) *m* lucky charm; **g~'selig** *adj* blissful
Glücks- *zW*: **~fall** *m* stroke of luck; **~kind** *nt* lucky person; **~sache** *f* matter of luck; **~spiel** *nt* game of chance
Glückwunsch *m* congratulations *pl*, best wishes *pl*
Glüh- ['glyː] *zW*: **~birne** *f* light bulb; **g~en** *vi* to glow; **~wein** *m* mulled wine; **~würmchen** *nt* glow-worm
Glut [gluːt] (-, -en) *f* (*Röte*) glow; (*Feuers~*) fire; (*Hitze*) heat; (*fig*) ardour
GmbH ['geːʔɛmbeːˈhaː] *f* *abk* (= *Gesellschaft mit beschränkter Haftung*) Ltd. (*BRIT*); Inc. (*US*)
Gnade ['gnaːdə] *f* (*Gunst*) favour; (*Erbarmen*) mercy; (*Milde*) clemency

Gnaden- *zW*: **~frist** *f* reprieve, respite; **g~los** *adj* merciless; **~stoß** *m* coup de grâce

gnädig ['gnɛːdɪç] *adj* gracious; (*voll Erbarmen*) merciful

Gold [gɔlt] (-(e)s) *nt* gold; **g~en** *adj* golden; **~fisch** *m* goldfish; **~grube** *f* goldmine; **~regen** *m* laburnum

Golf[1] [gɔlf] (-(e)s, -e) *m* gulf

Golf[2] (-s) *nt* golf; **~platz** *m* golf course; **~schläger** *m* golf club; **~spieler** *m* golfer

Golfstrom *m* Gulf Stream

Gondel ['gɔndəl] (-, -n) *f* gondola; (*Seilbahn*) cable-car

gönnen ['gœnən] *vt*: **jdm etw ~** not to begrudge sb sth; **sich** *dat* **etw ~** to allow o.s. sth

Gönner (-s, -) *m* patron; **g~haft** *adj* patronizing

Gosse ['gɔsə] *f* gutter

Gott [gɔt] (-es, -er) *m* god; **mein ~!** for heaven's sake!; **um ~es Willen!** for heaven's sake!; **grüß ~!** hello; **~ sei Dank!** thank God!; **~esdienst** *m* service; **~eslästerung** *f* blasphemy; **~heit** *f* deity

Göttin ['gœtɪn] *f* goddess

göttlich *adj* divine

gottlos *adj* godless

Götze ['gœtsə] (-n, -n) *m* idol

Grab [graːp] (-(e)s, -er) *nt* grave; **g~en** ['graːbən] (*unreg*) *vt* to dig; **~en** (-s, -) *m* ditch; (*MIL*) trench; **~stein** *m* gravestone

Grad [graːt] (-(e)s, -e) *m* degree; **~einteilung** *f* graduation

Graf [graːf] (-en, -en) *m* count, earl

Gräfin ['grɛːfɪn] *f* countess

Grafschaft *f* county

Gram [graːm] (-(e)s) *m* grief, sorrow

grämen ['grɛːmən] *vr* to grieve

Gramm [gram] (-s, -e) *nt* gram(me)

Grammatik [gra'matɪk] *f* grammar

grammatisch *adj* grammatical

Grammophon [gramo'foːn] (-s, -e) *nt* gramophone

Granat [gra'naːt] (-(e)s, -e) *m* (*Stein*) garnet

Granate *f* (*MIL*) shell; (*Hand~*) grenade

Granit [gra'niːt] (-s, -e) *m* granite

graphisch ['graːfɪʃ] *adj* graphic

Gras [graːs] (-es, -er) *nt* grass; **g~en** *vi* to graze; **~halm** *m* blade of grass

grassieren [gra'siːrən] *vi* to be rampant, to rage

gräßlich ['grɛslɪç] *adj* horrible

Grat [graːt] (-(e)s, -e) *m* ridge

Gräte ['grɛːtə] *f* fishbone

gratis ['graːtɪs] *adj*, *adv* free (of charge); **G~probe** *f* free sample

Gratulation [gratulatsi'oːn] *f* congratulation(s)

gratulieren [gratu'liːrən] *vi*: **jdm ~ (zu etw)** to congratulate sb (on sth); **(ich) gratuliere!** congratulations!

grau [grau] *adj* grey

Grauen (-s) *nt* horror; **g~** *vi unpers*: **es graut jdm vor etw** sb dreads sth, sb is afraid of sth ♦ *vr*: **sich g~ vor** to dread, to have a horror of; **g~haft** *adj* horrible

grauhaarig *adj* grey-haired

grausam ['grauzaːm] *adj* cruel; **G~keit** *f* cruelty

Grausen ['grauzən] (-s) *nt* horror; **g~** *vb* = **grauen**

gravieren [gra'viːrən] *vt* to engrave; **~d** *adj* grave

Grazie ['graːtsiə] *f* grace

graziös [gratsi'øːs] *adj* graceful

greifbar *adj* tangible, concrete; **in ~er Nähe** within reach

greifen ['graifən] (*unreg*) *vt* to seize; to grip; **nach etw ~** to reach for sth; **um sich ~** (*fig*) to spread; **zu etw ~** (*fig*) to turn to sth

Greis [grais] (-es, -e) *m* old man; **~enalter** *nt* old age; **g~enhaft** *adj* senile; **~in** *f* old woman

grell [grɛl] *adj* harsh

Grenz- ['grɛnts] *zW*: **~beamte(r)** *m* frontier official; **~e** *f* boundary; (*Staats~*) frontier; (*Schranke*) limit; **g~en** *vi*: **g~en (an** +*akk*) to border (on); **g~enlos** *adj* boundless; **~fall** *m* borderline case; **~übergang** *m* frontier crossing

Greuel ['grɔyəl] (-s, -) *m* horror, revul-

sion; **etw ist jdm ein ~** sb loathes sth;
~**tat** f atrocity
greulich ['grɔylɪç] adj horrible
Griech- ['gri:ç] zW: ~**e** (**-n, -n**) m
Greek; ~**enland** nt Greece; ~**in** f
Greek; **g~isch** adj Greek
griesgrämig ['gri:sgrɛːmɪç] adj grumpy
Grieß [gri:s] (**-es, -e**) m (KOCH)
semolina
Griff [grɪf] (**-(e)s, -e**) m grip;
(Vorrichtung) handle; **g~bereit** adj
handy
Grill [grɪl] m grill; ~**e** f cricket; **g~en**
vt to grill
Grimasse [gri'masə] f grimace
grimmig ['grɪmɪç] adj furious; (heftig)
fierce, severe
grinsen ['grɪnzən] vi to grin
Grippe ['grɪpə] f influenza, flu
grob [gro:p] adj coarse, gross; (Fehler,
Verstoß) gross; **G~heit** f coarseness;
coarse expression
Groll [grɔl] (**-(e)s**) m resentment; **g~en**
vi (Donner) to rumble; **g~en** (**mit** od
+dat) to bear ill will (towards)
Groschen ['grɔʃən] m 10 pfennig piece
groß [gro:s] adj big, large; (hoch) tall;
(fig) great ♦ adv greatly; **im ~en und
ganzen** on the whole; ~**artig** adj great,
splendid; **G~aufnahme** f (CINE) close-
up; **G~britannien** nt Great Britain
Größe ['grøːsə] f size; (Höhe) height;
(fig) greatness
Groß- zW: ~**einkauf** m bulk purchase;
~**eltern** pl grandparents; **g~enteils**
adv mostly
Größenwahn ['grøːsənvaːn] m mega-
lomania
Groß- zW: ~**format** nt large size;
~**handel** m wholesale trade; ~**händler**
m wholesaler; ~**macht** f great power;
~**maul** m braggart; **g~mütig** adj
magnanimous; ~**mutter** f grand-
mother; ~**rechner** m mainframe
(computer); **g~spurig** adj pompous;
~**stadt** f city, large town
größte(r, s) ['grøːstə(r, s)] adj superl von
groß; **größtenteils** adv for the most
part
Groß- zW: **g~tun** (unreg) vi to boast;

~**vater** m grandfather; **g~ziehen** (un-
reg) vt to raise; **g~zügig** adj generous;
(Planung) on a large scale
grotesk [gro'tɛsk] adj grotesque
Grotte ['grɔtə] f grotto
Grübchen ['gry:pçən] nt dimple
Grube ['gru:bə] f pit; mine
grübeln ['gry:bəln] vi to brood
Grubenarbeiter m miner
Grubengas nt firedamp
Gruft [gruft] (**-, ~e**) f tomb, vault
grün [gry:n] adj green; **G~anlage** f
park
Grund [grʊnt] (**-(e)s, ~e**) m ground;
(von See, Gefäß) bottom; (fig) reason;
im ~e genommen basically; ~**ausbildung** f basic training; ~**besitz** m
land(ed property), real estate; ~**buch**
nt land register
gründen ['grʏndən] vt to found ♦ vr:
sich ~ (**auf** +dat) to be based (on); ~
auf +akk to base on
Gründer (**-s, -**) m founder
Grund- zW: ~**gebühr** f basic charge;
~**gesetz** nt constitution; ~**lage** f
foundation; **g~legend** adj fundamental
gründlich adj thorough
Grund- zW: ~**los** adj groundless;
~**regel** f basic rule; ~**riß** m plan; (fig)
outline; ~**satz** m principle; **g~sätzlich**
adj fundamental; (Frage) of principle ♦
adv fundamentally; (prinzipiell) on
principle; ~**schule** f elementary school;
~**stein** m foundation stone; ~**stück** nt
estate; plot
Gründung f foundation
Grundzug m characteristic
Grünen pl (POL): **die ~** the Greens
Grün- zW: ~**kohl** m kale; ~**schnabel**
m greenhorn; ~**span** m verdigris;
~**streifen** m central reservation
grunzen ['grʊntsən] vi to grunt
Gruppe ['grʊpə] f group; **gruppenweise**
adv in groups
gruppieren [grʊ'piːrən] vt, vr to group
gruselig adj creepy
gruseln ['gru:zəln] vi unpers: **es gruselt
jdm vor etw** sth gives sb the creeps ♦
vr to have the creeps
Gruß [gru:s] (**-es, ~e**) m greeting; (MIL)

salute; **viele Grüße** best wishes; **mit freundlichen Grüßen** yours sincerely; **Grüße an** +*akk* regards to

grüßen ['gry:sən] *vt* to greet; (*MIL*) to salute; **jdn von jdm ~** to give sb sb's regards; **jdn · lassen** to send sb one's regards

gucken ['gʊkən] *vi* to look

Gulasch ['gu:laʃ] (-(e)s, -e) *nt* goulash

gültig ['gʏltɪç] *adj* valid; **G~keit** *f* validity

Gummi ['gʊmi] (-s, -s) *nt od m* rubber; (~*harze*) gum; ~**band** *nt* rubber *od* elastic band; (*Hosen~*) elastic; ~**baum** *m* rubber plant; **gummieren** [gʊ'mi:rən] *vt* to gum; ~**knüppel** *m* rubber truncheon; ~**strumpf** *m* elastic stocking

günstig ['gʏnstɪç] *adj* convenient; (*Gelegenheit*) favourable; **das habe ich ~ bekommen** it was a bargain

Gurgel ['gʊrgəl] (-, -n) *f* throat; **g~n** *vi* to gurgle; (*im Mund*) to gargle

Gurke ['gʊrkə] *f* cucumber; **saure ~** pickled cucumber, gherkin

Gurt [gʊrt] (-(e)s, -e) *m* belt

Gürtel ['gʏrtəl] (-s, -) *m* belt; (*GEOG*) zone; ~**reifen** *m* radial tyre

Guß [gʊs] (-sses, Güsse) *m* casting; (*Regen~*) downpour; (*KOCH*) glazing; ~**eisen** *nt* cast iron

---
SCHLÜSSELWORT
---

gut [gu:t] *adj* good; **alles Gute** all the best; **also gut** all right then
♦ *adv* well; **gut schmecken** to taste good; **gut, aber ...** OK, but ...; (*na gut*), **ich komme** all right, I'll come; **gut drei Stunden** a good three hours; **das kann gut sein** that may well be; **laß es gut sein** that'll do

---

Gut [gu:t] (-(e)s, -er) *nt* (*Besitz*) possession; **Güter** *pl* (*Waren*) goods; ~**achten** (-s, -) *nt* (expert) opinion; ~**achter** (-s, -) *m* expert; **g~artig** *adj* good-natured; (*MED*) benign; **g~bürgerlich** *adj* (*Küche*) (good) plain; ~**dünken** *nt*: **nach ~dünken** at one's discretion

Güte ['gy:tə] *f* goodness, kindness;

(*Qualität*) quality

Güter- *zW*: ~**abfertigung** *f* (*EISENB*) goods office; ~**bahnhof** *m* goods station; ~**wagen** *m* goods waggon (*BRIT*), freight car (*US*); ~**zug** *m* goods train (*BRIT*), freight train (*US*)

gut- *zW*: ~**gehen** (*unreg*) *vb unpers* to work, to come off; **es geht jdm ~** sb's doing fine; ~**gemeint** *adj* well meant; ~**gläubig** *adj* trusting; **G~haben** (-s) *nt* credit; ~**heißen** (*unreg*) *vt* to approve (of)

gütig ['gy:tɪç] *adj* kind

Gut- *zW*: **g~mütig** *adj* good-natured; ~**mütigkeit** *f* good nature; ~**schein** *m* voucher; **g~schreiben** (*unreg*) *vt* to credit; ~**schrift** *f* credit; **g~tun** (*unreg*) *vi*: **jdm g~tun** to do sb good; **g~willig** *adj* willing

Gymnasium [gʏm'na:ziʊm] *nt* grammar school (*BRIT*), high school (*US*)

Gymnastik [gʏm'nastɪk] *f* exercises *pl*, keep fit

H

Haag [ha:g] *m*: **Den ~** the Hague

Haar [ha:r] (-(e)s, -e) *nt* hair; **um ein ~** nearly; **an den ~en herbeigezogen** (*umg*: *Vergleich*) very far-fetched; ~**bürste** *f* hairbrush; **h~en** *vi*, *vr* to lose hair; ~**esbreite** *f*: **um ~esbreite** by a hair's-breadth; **h~genau** *adv* precisely; **h~ig** *adj* hairy; (*fig*) nasty; ~**klemme** *f* hair grip; ~**nadel** *f* hairpin; **h~scharf** *adv* (*beobachten*) very sharply; (*daneben*) by a hair's breadth; ~**schnitt** *m* haircut; ~**shampoo** *nt* shampoo; ~**spange** *f* hair slide; **h~sträubend** *adj* hair-raising; ~**teil** *nt* hairpiece; ~**waschmittel** *nt* shampoo

Habe ['ha:bə] (-) *f* property

haben ['ha:bən] (*unreg*) *vt*, *vb aux* to have; **Hunger/Angst ~** to be hungry/afraid; **woher hast du das?** where did you get that from?; **was hast du denn?** what's the matter (with you)?; **du hast zu schweigen** you're to be quiet; **ich hätte gern** I would like; **H~** (-s, -) *nt* credit

Habgier f avarice; **h~ig** adj avaricious

Habicht ['ha:bɪçt] (-s, -e) m hawk

Habseligkeiten pl belongings

Hachse ['haksə] f (KOCH) knuckle

Hacke ['hakə] f hoe; (Ferse) heel; **h~n** vt to hack, to chop; (Erde) to hoe

Hackfleisch nt mince, minced meat

Hafen ['ha:fən] (-s, ⸚) m harbour, port; **~arbeiter** m docker; **~damm** m jetty, mole; **~stadt** f port

Hafer ['ha:fər] (-s, -) m oats pl; **~flocken** pl rolled oats; **~schleim** m gruel

Haft [haft] (-) f custody; **h~bar** adj liable, responsible; **~befehl** m warrant (for arrest); **h~en** vi to stick, to cling; **h~en für** to be liable od responsible for; **h~enbleiben** (unreg) vi: **h~enbleiben (an** +dat) to stick (to); **~pflicht** f liability; **~pflichtversicherung** f (AUT) third party insurance; **~schalen** pl contact lenses; **~ung** f liability

Hagebutte ['ha:gəbutə] f rose hip

Hagedorn ['ha:gədɔ-] m hawthorn

Hagel ['ha:gəl] (-s) m hail; **h~n** vi unpers to hail

hager ['ha:gər] adj gaunt

Hahn [ha:n] (-(e)s, ⸚e) m cock; (Wasser~) tap, faucet (US)

Hähnchen ['hɛ:nçən] nt cockerel; (KOCH) chicken

Hai(fisch) ['hai(fɪʃ)] (-(e)s, -e) m shark

Häkchen ['hɛ:kçən] nt small hook

Häkel- ['hɛ:kəl] zW: **~arbeit** f crochet work; **h~n** vt to crochet; **~nadel** f crochet hook

Haken ['ha:kən] (-s, -) m hook; (fig) catch; **~kreuz** nt swastika; **~nase** f hooked nose

halb [halp] adj half; **~ eins** half past twelve; **ein ~es Dutzend** half a dozen; **H~dunkel** nt semi-darkness

halber ['halbər] präp +gen (wegen) on account of; (für) for the sake of

Halb- zW: **~heit** f half-measure; **h~ieren** vt to halve; **~insel** f peninsula; **h~jährlich** adj half-yearly; **~kreis** m semicircle; **~kugel** f hemisphere; **~leiter** m semiconductor;

~links (-, -) m (SPORT) inside left; **~mond** m half-moon; (fig) crescent; **h~offen** adj half-open; **~pension** f half-board; **~rechts** (-, -) m (SPORT) inside right; **~schuh** m shoe; **~tagsarbeit** f part-time work; **h~wegs** adv half-way; **h~wegs besser** more or less better; **~wertzeit** f half-life; **~wüchsige(r)** mf adolescent; **~zeit** f (SPORT) half; (Pause) half time

half etc [half] vb siehe helfen

Hälfte ['hɛlftə] f half

Halfter¹ ['halftər] (-s, -) m od nt (für Tiere) halter

Halfter² (-, -n od -s, -) f od nt (Pistolen~) holster

Halle ['halə] f hall; (AVIAT) hangar; **h~n** vi to echo, to resound; **~nbad** nt indoor swimming pool

hallo [ha'lo:] excl hello

Halluzination [halutsinatsi'o:n] f hallucination

Halm [halm] (-(e)s, -e) m blade; stalk

Hals [hals] (-es, ⸚e) m neck; (Kehle) throat; **~ über Kopf** in a rush; **~kette** f necklace; **~-Nasen-Ohren-Arzt** m ear, nose and throat specialist; **~schlagader** f carotid artery; **~schmerzen** pl sore throat sg; **~tuch** nt scarf; **~wirbel** m cervical vertebra

Halt [halt] (-(e)s, -e) m stop; (fester ~) hold; (innerer ~) stability; **h~** excl stop!, halt!; **h~bar** adj durable; (Lebensmittel) non-perishable; (MIL, fig) tenable; **~barkeit** f durability; (non-)perishability

halten ['haltən] (unreg) vt to keep; (fest~) to hold ♦ vi to hold; (frisch bleiben) to keep; (stoppen) to stop ♦ vr (frisch bleiben) to keep; (sich behaupten) to hold out; **~ für** to regard as; **~ von** to think of; **an sich ~** to restrain o.s.; **sich rechts/links ~** to keep to the right/left

Haltestelle f stop

Halteverbot nt: **hier ist ~** there's no waiting here

Halt- zW: **h~los** adj unstable; **h~machen** vi to stop; **~ung** f posture; (fig) attitude; (Selbstbeherrschung)

composure
Halunke [ha'lʊŋkə] (-n, -n) m rascal
hämisch ['hɛːmɪʃ] adj malicious
Hammel ['haməl] (-s, = od -) m wether;
~**fleisch** nt mutton
Hammer ['hamər] (-s, =) m hammer
hämmern ['hɛmərn] vt, vi to hammer
Hämorrhoiden [hɛmɔro'iːdən] pl
haemorrhoids
Hampelmann ['hampəlman] m (auch
fig) puppet
Hamster ['hamstər] (-s, -) m hamster;
~**ei** [-'raɪ] f hoarding; **h~n** vi to hoard
Hand [hant] (-, =e) f hand; ~**arbeit** f
manual work; (Nadelarbeit) needlework; ~**arbeiter** m manual worker;
~**bremse** f handbrake; ~**buch** nt hand-
book, manual
Händedruck ['hɛndədrʊk] m handshake
Handel ['handəl] (-s) m trade;
(Geschäft) transaction
Handeln ['handəln] (-s) nt action
handeln vi to trade; (agieren) to act ♦
vr unpers: **sich ~ um** to be a question
of, to be about; ~ **von** to be about
Handels- zW: ~**bilanz** f balance of
trade; ~**kammer** f chamber of
commerce; ~**name** m trade name;
~**reisende(r)** m commercial traveller;
~**schule** f business school; **h~üblich**
adj customary; (Preis) going attrib;
~**vertreter** m sales representative
Hand- zW: ~**feger** (-s, -) m handbrush;
h~fest adj hefty; **h~gearbeitet** adj
handmade; ~**gelenk** nt wrist;
~**gemenge** nt scuffle; ~**gepäck** nt
hand-luggage; **h~greiflich** adj palpable;
h~greiflich werden to become violent;
~**griff** m flick of the wrist; **h~haben** vt
insep to handle
Händler ['hɛndlər] (-s, -) m trader,
dealer
handlich ['hantlıç] adj handy
Handlung ['handlʊŋ] f act(ion); (in
Buch) plot; (Geschäft) shop; ~**sweise** f
behaviour
Hand- zW: ~**pflege** f manicure;
~**schelle** f handcuff; ~**schlag** m handshake; ~**schrift** f handwriting; (Text)
manuscript; ~**schuh** m glove; ~**tasche**

f handbag; ~**tuch** nt towel; ~**werk** nt
trade, craft; ~**werker** (-s, -) m crafts-
man, artisan; ~**werkzeug** nt tools pl
Hanf [hanf] (-(e)s) m hemp
Hang [haŋ] (-(e)s, =e) m inclination;
(Ab~) slope
Hänge- ['hɛŋə] in zW hanging; ~**brücke**
f suspension bridge; ~**matte** f
hammock
hängen ['hɛŋən] vi (unreg) to hang ♦
vt: **etw an etw** akk) ~ to hang sth (on
sth); ~ **an** +dat (fig) to be attached to;
sich ~ an +akk to hang on to, to cling
to; ~**bleiben** (unreg) vi to be caught;
(fig) to remain, to stick; ~**bleiben an**
+dat to catch od get caught on;
~**lassen** (unreg) vt (vergessen) to
leave; **den Kopf ~lassen** to get down-
hearted
Hannover [ha'noːfər] (-s) nt Hanover
hänseln ['hɛnzəln] vt to tease
hantieren [han'tiːrən] vi to work, to be
busy; **mit etw ~** to handle sth
hapern ['haːpərn] vi unpers: **es hapert
an etw** dat there is a lack of sth
Happen ['hapən] (-s, -) m mouthful
Hardware ['haːdweə] f hardware
Harfe ['harfə] f harp
Harke ['harkə] f rake; **h~n** vt, vi to
rake
harmlos ['harmloːs] adj harmless;
H~igkeit f harmlessness
Harmonie [harmo'niː] f harmony;
h~ren vi to harmonize
Harmonika [har'moːnika] (-, -s) f
(Zieh~) concertina
harmonisch [har'moːnɪʃ] adj harmonious
Harmonium [har'moːniʊm] (-s, -nien od
-s) nt harmonium
Harn [harn] (-(e)s, -e) m urine; ~**blase**
f bladder
Harpune [har'puːnə] f harpoon
harren ['harən] vi: ~ (**auf** +akk) to wait
(for)
hart [hart] adj hard; (fig) harsh
Härte ['hɛrtə] f hardness; (fig) harsh-
ness
hart- zW: ~**gekocht** adj hard-boiled;
~**herzig** adj hard-hearted; ~**näckig** adj

stubborn; **H~näckigkeit** f stubborn-
ness; **H~platte** f hard disk
Harz [haːrts] (**-es, -e**) nt resin
Haschee [ha'ʃeː] (**-s, -s**) nt hash
Haschisch ['haʃɪʃ] (**-**) nt hashish
Hase ['haːzə] (**-n, -n**) m hare
Haselnuß ['haːzəlnʊs] f hazelnut
Hasenfuß m coward
Hasenscharte f harelip
Haß [has] (**-sses**) m hate, hatred
hassen ['hasən] vt to hate
häßlich ['hɛslɪç] adj ugly; (gemein)
nasty; **H~keit** f ugliness; nastiness
Hast [hast] f haste
hast vb siehe **haben**
hasten vi to rush
hastig adj hasty
hat [hat] vb siehe **haben**
hatte etc ['hatə] vb siehe **haben**
Haube ['haubə] f hood; (Mütze) cap;
(AUT) bonnet, hood (US)
Hauch [haux] (**-(e)s, -e**) m breath;
(Luft~) breeze; (fig) trace; **h~dünn**
adj extremely thin; **h~en** vi to breathe
Haue ['hauə] f hoe; pick; (umg) hiding;
h~n (unreg) vt to hew, to cut; (umg)
to thrash
Haufen ['haufən] (**-s, -**) m heap; (Leute)
crowd; **ein ~ (x)** (umg) loads od a lot
(of x); **auf einem ~** in one heap
häufen ['hɔyfən] vt to pile up ♦ vr to
accumulate
haufenweise adv in heaps; in droves;
etw ~ haben to have piles of sth
häufig ['hɔyfɪç] adj frequent ♦ adv
frequently; **H~keit** f frequency
Haupt [haupt] (**-(e)s, Häupter**) nt head;
(Ober~) chief ♦ in zW main; **~bahnhof**
m central station; **h~beruflich** adv as
one's main occupation; **~darsteller(in)**
m(f) leading actor(actress); **~eingang**
m main entrance; **~film** m main film
Häuptling ['hɔyptlɪŋ] m chief(tain)
Haupt- zW: **~mann** (pl **-leute**) m (MIL)
captain; **~person** f central figure;
~quartier nt headquarters pl; **~rolle** f
leading part; **~sache** f main thing;
h~sächlich adj chief ♦ adv chiefly;
~satz m main clause; **~schlagader** f
aorta; **~schule** f ≈ secondary school;

~sendezeit f (TV) prime time; **~stadt**
f capital; **~straße** f main street;
~wort nt noun
Haus [haus] (**-es, Häuser**) nt house;
nach ~e home; **zu ~e** at home; **~ange-
stellte** f domestic servant; **~arbeit** f
housework; (SCH) homework; **~arzt** m
family doctor; **~aufgabe** f (SCH) homework; **~besitzer(in)** m(f) house-owner;
~eigentümer(in) m(f) house-owner
Häuserblock ['hɔyzərblɔk] m block (of
houses)
Häusermakler ['hɔyzər-] m estate agent
(BRIT), real estate agent (US)
Haus- zW: **~frau** f housewife;
h~gemacht adj home-made; **~halt** m
household; (POL) budget; **h~halten**
(unreg) vi (sparen) to economize;
~hälterin f housekeeper; **~haltsgeld** nt
housekeeping (money); **~haltsgerät** nt
domestic appliance; **~herr** m host;
(Vermieter) landlord; **h~hoch** adv:
h~hoch verlieren to lose by a mile
hausieren [hau'ziːrən] vi to peddle
Hausierer (**-s, -**) m peddlar
häuslich ['hɔyslɪç] adj domestic
Haus- zW: **~meister** m caretaker,
janitor; **~nummer** f street number;
~ordnung f house rules pl; **~putz** m
house cleaning; **~schlüssel** m front-
door key; **~schuh** m slipper; **~such-
ung** f police raid; **~tier** nt pet; **~wirt**
m landlord; **~wirtschaft** f domestic
science
Haut [haut] (**-, Häute**) f skin; (Tier~)
hide; **h~eng** adj skin-tight; **~farbe** f
complexion
Haxe ['haksə] f = **Hachse**
Hbf. abk = **Hauptbahnhof**
he [heː] excl hey
Hebamme ['heːpʔamə] f midwife
Hebel ['heːbəl] (**-s, -**) m lever
heben ['heːbən] (unreg) vt to raise, to
lift
Hecht [hɛçt] (**-(e)s, -e**) m pike
Heck [hɛk] (**-(e)s, -e**) nt stern; (von
Auto) rear
Hecke ['hɛkə] f hedge
Heckenrose f dog rose
Heckenschütze m sniper

Heer [heːr] (-(e)s, -e) *nt* army

Hefe ['heːfə] *f* yeast

Heft [hɛft] (-(e)s, -e) *nt* exercise book; (*Zeitschrift*) number; (*von Messer*) haft

heften *vt*: (**an** +*akk*) to fasten (to); (*nähen*) to tack ((on) to); **etw an etw** *akk* ~ to fasten sth to sth; **Hefter** (-s, -) *m* folder

heftig *adj* fierce, violent; **H~keit** *f* fierceness, violence

Heft- *zW*: ~**klammer** *f* paper clip; ~**maschine** *f* stapling machine; ~**pflaster** *nt* sticking plaster; ~**zwecke** *f* drawing pin

Hehl [heːl] *m od nt*: **kein(en)** ~ **aus etw machen** to make no secret of sth; ~**er** (-s, -) *m* receiver (of stolen goods), fence

Heide[1] ['haɪdə] *f* heath, moor; (~*kraut*) heather

Heide[2] (-n, -n) *m* heathen, pagan

Heidekraut *nt* heather

Heidelbeere *f* bilberry

Heidentum *nt* paganism

Heidin *f* heathen, pagan

heikel ['haɪkəl] *adj* awkward, thorny; (*wählerisch*) fussy

Heil [haɪl] (-(e)s) *nt* well-being; (*Seelen~*) salvation; **h~** *adj* in one piece, intact; ~**and** (-(e)s, -e) *m* saviour; **h~bar** *adj* curable; **h~en** *vt* to cure ♦ *vi* to heal; **h~froh** *adj* very relieved

heilig ['haɪlıç] *adj* holy; **H~abend** *m* Christmas Eve; **H~e(r)** *mf* saint; ~**en** *vt* to sanctify, to hallow; **H~enschein** *m* halo; **H~keit** *f* holiness; ~**sprechen** (*unreg*) *vt* to canonize; **H~tum** *nt* shrine; (*Gegenstand*) relic

Heil- *zW*: **h~los** *adj* unholy; (*fig*) hopeless; ~**mittel** *nt* remedy; **h~sam** *adj* (*fig*) salutary; **Heilsarmee** *f* Salvation Army; ~**ung** *f* cure

Heim [haɪm] (-(e)s, -e) *nt* home; **h~** *adv* home

Heimat ['haɪmaːt] (-, -en) *f* home (town/country *etc*); ~**land** *nt* homeland; **h~lich** *adj* native, home *attrib*; (*Gefühle*) nostalgic; **h~los** *adj* home-

less; ~**ort** *m* home town/area; ~**vertriebene(r)** *mf* displaced person

Heim- *zW*: ~**computer** *m* home computer; **h~fahren** (*unreg*) *vi* to drive home; ~**fahrt** *f* journey home; **h~gehen** (*unreg*) *vi* to go home; (*sterben*) to pass away; **h~isch** *adj* (*gebürtig*) native; **sich ~isch fühlen** to feel at home; ~**kehr** (-, -en) *f* homecoming; **h~kehren** *vi* to return home; **h~lich** *adj* secret; ~**lichkeit** *f* secrecy; ~**reise** *f* journey home; **h~suchen** *vt* to afflict; (*Geist*) to haunt; **h~tückisch** *adj* malicious; ~**weg** *m* way home; ~**weh** *nt* homesickness; ~**weh haben** to be homesick; **h~zahlen** *vt*: **jdm etw h~zahlen** to pay sb back for sth

Heirat ['haɪraːt] (-, -en) *f* marriage; **h~en** *vt* to marry ♦ *vi* to marry, to get married ♦ *vr* to get married

Heiratsantrag *m* proposal

heiser ['haɪzər] *adj* hoarse; **H~keit** *f* hoarseness

heiß [haɪs] *adj* hot; ~**e(r) Draht** hot line; ~**e(s) Eisen** (*umg*) hot potato; ~**blütig** *adj* hot-blooded

heißen ['haɪsən] (*unreg*) *vi* to be called; (*bedeuten*) to mean ♦ *vt* to command; (*nennen*) to name ♦ *vi unpers*: **es heißt** it says; it is said; **das heißt** that is (to say)

Heißhunger *m* ravenous hunger

heißlaufen (*unreg*) *vi, vr* to overheat

heiter ['haɪtər] *adj* cheerful; (*Wetter*) bright; **H~keit** *f* cheerfulness; (*Belustigung*) amusement

Heiz- ['haɪts] *zW*: **h~bar** *adj* heated; (*Raum*) with heating; ~**decke** *f* electric blanket; **h~en** *vt* to heat; ~**er** (-s, -) *m* stoker; ~**körper** *m* radiator; ~**öl** *nt* fuel oil; ~**sonne** *f* electric fire; ~**ung** *f* heating; ~**ungsanlage** *f* heating system

hektisch ['hɛktɪʃ] *adj* hectic

Held [hɛlt] (-en, -en) *m* hero; ~**in** *f* heroine

helfen ['hɛlfən] (*unreg*) *vi* to help; (*nützen*) to be of use ♦ *vb unpers*: **es hilft nichts, du mußt ... ** it's no use, you'll have to ...; **jdm (bei etw)** ~ to help sb (with sth); **sich** *dat* **zu ~ wissen** to be resourceful

Helfer (-s, -) *m* helper, assistant; **Helfershelfer** *m* accomplice

hell [hɛl] *adj* clear, bright; (*Farbe, Bier*) light; **~blau** *adj* light blue; **~blond** *adj* ash-blond; **H~e** (-) *f* clearness, brightness; **H~seher** *m* clairvoyant; **~wach** *adj* wide-awake

Helm [hɛlm] (-(e)s, -e) *m* (*auf Kopf*) helmet

Hemd [hɛmt] (-(e)s, -en) *nt* shirt; (*Unter~*) vest; **~bluse** *f* blouse

hemmen [ˈhɛmən] *vt* to check, to hold up; **gehemmt sein** to be inhibited

Hemmung *f* check; (*PSYCH*) inhibition; **hemmungslos** *adj* unrestrained, without restraint

Hengst [hɛŋst] (-es, -e) *m* stallion

Henkel [ˈhɛŋkəl] (-s, -) *m* handle

Henker (-s, -) *m* hangman

Henne [ˈhɛnə] *f* hen

SCHLÜSSELWORT

her [heːr] *adv* **1** (*Richtung*): **komm her zu mir** come here (to me); **von England her** from England; **von weit her** from a long way away; **her damit!** hand it over!; **wo hat er das her?** where did he get that from?
2 (*Blickpunkt*): **von der Form her** as far as the form is concerned
· **3** (*zeitlich*): **das ist 5 Jahre her** that was 5 years ago; **wo bist du her?** where do you come from?; **ich kenne ihn von früher her** I know him from before

---

herab [hɛˈrap] *adv* down(ward)s); **~hängen** (*unreg*) *vi* to hang down; **~lassen** (*unreg*) *vt* to let down ♦ *vr* to condescend; **~lassend** *adj* condescending; **~setzen** *vt* to lower, to reduce; (*fig*) to belittle, to disparage; **~würdigen** *vt* to belittle, to disparage

heran [hɛˈran] *adv*: **näher ~!** come up closer!; **~ zu mir!** come up to me!; **~bringen** (*unreg*) *vt*: **~bringen (an +akk)** to bring up (to); **~fahren** (*unreg*) *vi*: **~fahren (an +akk)** to drive up (to); **~kommen** (*unreg*) *vi*: (**an jdn/**

etw) ~kommen to approach (sb/sth), to come near (to sb/sth); **~machen** *vr*: **sich an jdn ~machen** to make up to sb; **~wachsen** (*unreg*) *vi* to grow up; **~ziehen** (*unreg*) *vt* to pull nearer; (*aufziehen*) to raise; (*ausbilden*) to train; **jdn zu etw ~ziehen** to call upon sb to help in sth

herauf [hɛˈrauf] *adv* up(ward(s)), up here; **~beschwören** (*unreg*) *vt* to conjure up, to evoke; **~bringen** (*unreg*) *vt* to bring up

heraus [hɛˈraus] *adv* out; **~bekommen** (*unreg*) *vt* to get out; (*fig*) to find *od* figure out; **~bringen** (*unreg*) *vt* to bring out; (*Geheimnis*) to elicit; **~finden** (*unreg*) *vt* to find out; **~fordern** *vt* to challenge; **H~forderung** *f* challenge; provocation; **~geben** (*unreg*) *vt* to hand over, to surrender; (*zurückgeben*) to give back; (*Buch*) to edit; (*veröffentlichen*) to publish; **H~geber** (-s, -) *m* editor; (*Verleger*) publisher; **~halten** (*unreg*) *vr*: **sich aus etw ~halten** to keep out of sth; **~hängen**[1] *vt* to hang out; **~hängen**[2] (*unreg*) *vi* to hang out; **~holen (aus)** to get out (of); **~kommen** (*unreg*) *vi* to come out; **dabei kommt nichts ~** nothing will come of it; **~reißen** (*unreg*) *vt* to tear out; to pull out; **~rücken** *vt* (*Geld*) to fork out, to hand over; **mit etw ~rücken** (*fig*) to come out with sth; **~stellen** *vr*: **sich ~stellen (als)** to turn out (to be); **~ziehen** (*unreg*) *vt* to pull out, to extract

herb [hɛrp] *adj* slightly bitter, acid; (*Wein*) dry; (*fig: schmerzlich*) bitter; (: *streng*) stern, austere

herbei [hɛrˈbai] *adv* (over) here; **~führen** *vt* to bring about; **~schaffen** *vt* to procure

herbemühen [ˈheːrbəmyːən] *vr* to take the trouble to come

Herberge [ˈhɛrbɛrgə] *f* shelter; hostel, inn

Herbergsmutter *f* warden

Herbergsvater *m* warden

herbitten (*unreg*) *vt* to ask to come

(here)

herbringen (*unreg*) *vt* to bring here

Herbst [hɛrpst] (-(e)s, -e) *m* autumn, fall (*US*); **h~lich** *adj* autumnal

Herd [heːrt] (-(e)s, -e) *m* cooker; (*fig, MED*) focus, centre

Herde ['heːrdə] *f* herd; (*Schaf~*) flock

herein [hɛ'raɪn] *adv* in (here), here; **~!** come in!; **~bitten** (*unreg*) *vt* to ask in; **~brechen** (*unreg*) *vi* to set in; **~bringen** (*unreg*) *vt* to bring in; **~dürfen** (*unreg*) *vi* to have permission to enter; **~fallen** (*unreg*) *vi* to be caught, to be taken in; **~fallen auf** +*akk* to fall for; **~kommen** (*unreg*) *vi* to come in; **~lassen** (*unreg*) *vt* to admit; **~legen** *vt*: **jdn ~legen** to take sb in

Her- *zW*: **~fahrt** *f* journey here; **h~fallen** (*unreg*) *vi*: **h~fallen über** +*akk* to fall upon; **~gang** *m* course of events; **h~geben** (*unreg*) *vt* to give, to hand (over); **sich zu etw h~geben** to lend one's name to sth; **h~gehen** (*unreg*) *vi*: **hinter jdm h~gehen** to follow sb; **es geht hoch h~** there are a lot of goings-on; **h~halten** (*unreg*) *vt* to hold out; **h~halten müssen** (*umg*) to have to suffer; **h~hören** *vi* to listen

Hering ['heːrɪŋ] (-s, -e) *m* herring

her- [hɛr] *zW*: **~kommen** (*unreg*) *vi* to come; **komm mal ~!** come here!; **~kömmlich** *adj* traditional; **H~kunft** (-, -künfte) *f* origin; **~laufen** (*unreg*) *vi*: **~laufen hinter** +*dat* to run after

Hermelin [hɛrmə'liːn] (-s, -e) *m od nt* ermine

hermetisch [hɛ'meːtɪʃ] *adj* hermetic ♦ *adv* hermetically

her'nach *adv* afterwards

her'nieder *adv* down

Herr [hɛr] (-(e)n, -en) *m* master; (*Mann*) gentleman; (*REL*) Lord; (*vor Namen*) Mr.; **mein ~!** sir!; **meine ~en!** gentlemen!; **~endoppel** *nt* men's doubles; **~eneinzel** *nt* men's singles; **~enhaus** *nt* mansion; **~enkonfektion** *f* menswear; **h~enlos** *adj* ownerless

herrichten ['heːrrɪçtən] *vt* to prepare

Herr- *zW*: **~in** *f* mistress; **h~isch** *adj* domineering; **h~lich** *adj* marvellous, splendid; **~lichkeit** *f* splendour, magnificence; **~schaft** *f* power, rule; (*Herr und Herrin*) master and mistress; **meine ~schaften!** ladies and gentlemen!

herrschen ['hɛrʃən] *vi* to rule; (*bestehen*) to prevail, to be

Herrscher(in) (-s, -) *m(f)* ruler

her- *zW*: **~rühren** *vi* to arise, to originate; **~sagen** *vt* to recite; **~stellen** *vt* to make, to manufacture; **H~steller** (-s, -) *m* manufacturer; **H~stellung** *f* manufacture

herüber [hɛ'ryːbər] *adv* over (here), across

herum [hɛ'rʊm] *adv* about, (a)round; **um etw ~** around sth; **~führen** *vt* to show around; **~gehen** (*unreg*) *vi* to walk about; **um etw ~gehen** to walk *od* go round sth; **~irren** *vi* to wander about; **~kriegen** (*umg*) *vt* to bring *od* talk around; **~sprechen** (*unreg*) *vr* to get around, to be spread; **~treiben** *vi, vr* to drift about; **~ziehen** *vi, vr* to wander about

herunter [hɛ'rʊntər] *adv* downward(s), down (there); **~gekommen** *adj* rundown; **~hängen** (*unreg*) *vi* to hang down; **~holen** *vt* to bring down; **~kommen** (*unreg*) *vi* to come down; (*fig*) to come down in the world; **~machen** *vt* to take down; (*schimpfen*) to have a go at

hervor [hɛr'foːr] *adv* out, forth; **~bringen** (*unreg*) *vt* to produce; (*Wort*) to utter; **~gehen** (*unreg*) *vi* to emerge, to result; **~heben** (*unreg*) *vt* to stress; (*als Kontrast*) to set off; **~ragend** *adj* (*fig*) excellent; **~rufen** (*unreg*) *vt* to cause, to give rise to

Herz [hɛrts] (-ens, -en) *nt* heart; (*KARTEN*) hearts *pl*; **~anfall** *m* heart attack; **~enslust** *f*: **nach ~enslust** to one's heart's content; **~fehler** *m* heart defect; **h~haft** *adj* hearty; **~infarkt** *m* heart attack; **~klopfen** *nt* palpitation; **h~lich** *adj* cordial; **h~lichen Glückwunsch** congratulations *pl*; **h~liche Grüße** best wishes; **h~los** *adj* heartless

Herzog ['hɛrtsoːk] (-(e)s, ⸚e) m duke; ~in f duchess; h~lich adj ducal; ~tum nt duchy

Herzschlag m heartbeat; (MED) heart attack

herzzerreißend adj heartrending

heterogen [hetero'geːn] adj heterogeneous

Hetze ['hɛtsə] f (Eile) rush; h~n vt to hunt; (verfolgen) to chase ♦ vi (eilen) to rush; jdn/etw auf jdn/etw h~n to set sb/sth on sb/sth; h~n gegen to stir up feeling against; h~n zu to agitate for; ~'rei f agitation; (Eile) rush

Heu [hɔy] (-(e)s) nt hay; **Geld wie ~** stacks of money; ~boden m hayloft

Heuchelei [hɔyçə'laɪ] f hypocrisy

heucheln ['hɔyçəln] vt to pretend, to feign ♦ vi to be hypocritical

Heuchler(in) ['hɔyçlər(ɪn)] (-s, -) m(f) hypocrite; h~isch adj hypocritical

heulen ['hɔylən] vi to howl; to cry; **das ~de Elend bekommen** to get the blues

Heuschnupfen m hay fever

Heuschrecke ['hɔyʃrɛkə] f grasshopper; locust

heute ['hɔytə] adv today; **~ abend/früh** this evening/morning

heutig ['hɔytɪç] adj today's

heutzutage ['hɔyttsutaːgə] adv nowadays

Hexe ['hɛksə] f witch; h~n vi to practise witchcraft; **ich kann doch nicht h~n** I can't work miracles; **Hexenkessel** m (auch fig) cauldron; **Hexenschuß** m lumbago; **Hexe'rei** f witchcraft

Hieb [hiːp] (-(e)s, -e) m blow; (Wunde) cut, gash; (Stichelei) cutting remark; **~e bekommen** to get a thrashing

hielt etc [hiːlt] vb siehe **halten**

hier [hiːr] adv here; **~auf** adv thereupon; (danach) after that; **~behalten** (unreg) vt to keep here; **~bei** adv herewith, enclosed; **~bleiben** (unreg) vi to stay here; **~durch** adv by this means; (örtlich) through here; **~her** adv this way, here; **~hin** adv here; **~lassen** (unreg) vt to leave here; **~mit** adv hereby; **~nach** adv hereafter; **~von** adv about this, hereof; **~zulande** adv in this country

hiesig ['hiːzɪç] adj of this place, local

hieß etc [hiːs] vb siehe **heißen**

Hilfe ['hɪlfə] f help; aid; **Erste ~** first aid; **~!** help!

Hilf- zW: h~los adj helpless; **~losigkeit** f helplessness; h~reich adj helpful

Hilfs- zW: **~arbeiter** m labourer; h~bedürftig adj needy; h~bereit adj ready to help; **~kraft** f assistant, helper; **~schule** f school for backward children

hilfst etc [hɪlfst] vb siehe **helfen**

Himbeere ['hɪmbeːrə] f raspberry

Himmel ['hɪməl] (-s, -) m sky; (REL, liter) heaven; h~blau adj sky-blue; **~fahrt** f Ascension; h~schreiend adj outrageous; **Himmelsrichtung** f direction

himmlisch ['hɪmlɪʃ] adj heavenly

SCHLÜSSELWORT

---

hin [hɪn] adv **1** (Richtung): **hin und zurück** there and back; **hin und her** to and fro; **bis zur Mauer hin** up to the wall; **wo ist er hin?** where has he gone?; **Geld hin, Geld her** money or no money

2 (auf ... hin): **auf meine Bitte hin** at my request; **auf seinen Rat hin** on the basis of his advice

3: **mein Glück ist hin** my happiness has gone

---

hinab [hɪ'nap] adv down; **~gehen** (unreg) vi to go down; **~sehen** (unreg) vi to look down

hinauf [hɪ'naʊf] adv up; **~arbeiten** vr to work one's way up; **~steigen** (unreg) vi to climb

hinaus [hɪ'naʊs] adv out; **~gehen** (unreg) vi to go out; **~gehen über** +akk to exceed; **~laufen** (unreg) vi to run out; **~laufen auf** +akk to come to, to amount to; **~lehnen** vr to lean out; **~schieben** (unreg) vt to put off, to postpone; **~wollen** vi to want to go out; **~wollen auf** +akk to drive at, to

get at
Hinblick ['hınblık] *m*: **in** *od* **im ~ auf**
+*akk* in view of
hinder- ['hındər] *zW*: **~lich** *adj*: **~lich**
sein to be a hindrance *od* nuisance; **~n**
vt to hinder, to hamper; **jdn an etw** *dat*
~n to prevent sb from doing sth; **H~nis**
(-ses, -se) *nt* obstacle; **H~nisrennen** *nt*
steeplechase
hindeuten ['hındɔʏtən] *vi*: **~ auf** +*akk*
to point to
hindurch [hın'dʊrç] *adv* through;
across; (*zeitlich*) through(out)
hinein [hı'naın] *adv* in; **~fallen** (*unreg*)
vi to fall in; **~fallen in** +*akk* to fall
into; **~gehen** (*unreg*) *vi* to go in;
~gehen in +*akk* to go into, to enter;
~geraten (*unreg*) *vi*: **~geraten in** +*akk*
to get into; **~passen** *vi* to fit in;
~passen in +*akk* to fit into; (*fig*) to fit
in with; **~steigern** *vr* to get worked up;
~versetzen *vr*: **sich ~versetzen in**
+*akk* to put o.s. in the position of
hin- ['hın] *zW*: **~fahren** (*unreg*) *vi* to
go; to drive ♦ *vt* to take; to drive;
H~fahrt *f* journey there; **~fallen** (*unreg*) *vi* to fall (down); **~fällig** *adj* frail; (*fig: ungültig*) invalid; **H~gabe** *f* devotion; **~geben** (*unreg*) *vr* +*dat* to give
o.s. up to, to devote o.s. to; **~gehen**
(*unreg*) *vi* to go; (*Zeit*) to pass;
~halten (*unreg*) *vt* to hold out;
(*warten lassen*) to put off, to stall
hinken ['hıŋkən] *vi* to limp; (*Vergleich*)
to be unconvincing
hin- ['hın] *zW*: **~legen** *vt* to put down ♦
vr to lie down; **~nehmen** (*unreg*) *vt*
(*fig*) to put up with, to take; **H~reise** *f*
journey out; **~reißen** (*unreg*) *vt* to
carry away, to enrapture; **sich ~reißen**
lassen, etw zu tun to get carried away
and do sth; **~richten** *vt* to execute;
H~richtung *f* execution; **~setzen** *vt* to
put down ♦ *vr* to sit down; **~sichtlich**
präp +*gen* with regard to; **H~spiel** *nt*
(*SPORT*) first leg; **~stellen** *vt* to put
(down) ♦ *vr* to place o.s.
hintanstellen [hınt''anʃtɛlən] *vt* (*fig*) to
ignore
hinten ['hıntən] *adv* at the back;

behind; **~herum** *adv* round the back;
(*fig*) secretly
hinter ['hıntər] *präp* (+*dat od akk*)
behind; (: *nach*) after; **~ jdm hersein**
to be after sb; **H~achse** *f* rear axle;
H~bliebene(r) *mf* surviving relative;
~e(r, s) *adj* rear, back; **~einander** *adv*
one after the other; **H~gedanke** *m*
ulterior motive; **~gehen** (*unreg*) *vt* to
deceive; **H~grund** *m* background;
H~halt *m* ambush; **~hältig** *adj* under-
hand, sneaky; **~her** *adv* afterwards,
after; **H~hof** *m* backyard; **H~kopf** *m*
back of one's head; **~lassen** (*unreg*) *vt*
to leave; **~'legen** *vt* to deposit; **H~list**
f cunning, trickery; (*Handlung*) trick,
dodge; **~listig** *adj* cunning, crafty;
H~mann (*pl* -männer) *m* person
behind; **H~rad** *nt* back wheel;
H~radantrieb *m* (*AUT*) rear wheel
drive; **~rücks** *adv* from behind; **H~tür**
f back door; (*fig: Ausweg*) loophole;
~'ziehen (*unreg*) *vt* (*Steuern*) to evade
hinüber [hı'nyːbər] *adv* across, over;
~gehen (*unreg*) *vi* to go over *od* across
hinunter [hı'nʊntər] *adv* down;
~bringen (*unreg*) *vt* to take down;
~schlucken *vt* (*auch fig*) to swallow;
~steigen (*unreg*) *vi* to descend
Hinweg ['hınveːk] *m* journey out
hinweghelfen [hın'vɛk-] (*unreg*) *vi*:
jdm über etw *akk* **~** to help sb to get
over sth
hinwegsetzen [hın'vɛk-] *vr*: **sich ~**
über +*akk* to disregard
hin- ['hın] *zW*: **H~weis** (-es, -e) *m*
(*Andeutung*) hint; (*Anweisung*) instruction; (*Verweis*) reference; **~weisen**
(*unreg*) *vi*: **~weisen auf** +*akk* (*anzeigen*) to point to; (*sagen*) to point out, to
refer to; **~werfen** (*unreg*) *vt* to throw
down; **~ziehen** (*unreg*) *vr* (*fig*) to drag
on
hinzu [hın'tsuː] *adv* in addition; **~fügen**
vt to add
Hirn [hırn] (-(e)s, -e) *nt* brain(s);
~gespinst (-(e)s, -e) *nt* fantasy;
h~verbrannt *adj* half-baked, crazy
Hirsch [hırʃ] (-(e)s, -e) *m* stag
Hirse ['hırzə] *f* millet

Hirt [hɪrt] (**-en, -en**) *m* herdsman; (*Schaf~, fig*) shepherd
hissen ['hɪsən] *vt* to hoist
Historiker [hɪs'toːrikər] (**-s, -**) *m* historian
historisch [hɪs'toːrɪʃ] *adj* historical
Hitze ['hɪtsə] (**-**) *f* heat; **h~beständig** *adj* heat-resistant; **h~frei** *adj*: **h~frei haben** to have time off school because of excessively hot weather; **~welle** *f* heat wave
hitzig ['hɪtsɪç] *adj* hot-tempered; (*Debatte*) heated
Hitz- *zW*: **~kopf** *m* hothead; **h~köpfig** *adj* fiery, hotheaded; **~schlag** *m* heatstroke
hm [(h)m] *excl* hm
Hobby ['hɔbɪ] *nt* hobby
Hobel ['hoːbəl] (**-s, -**) *m* plane; **~bank** *f* carpenter's bench; **h~n** *vt*, *vi* to plane; **~späne** *pl* wood shavings
Hoch (**-s, -s**) *nt* (*Ruf*) cheer; (*MET*) anticyclone
hoch [hoːx] (*attrib* **hohe(r, s)**) *adj* high; **~achten** *vt* to respect; **H~achtung** *f* respect, esteem; **~achtungsvoll** *adv* yours faithfully; **H~amt** *nt* high mass; **~begabt** *adj* extremely gifted; **H~betrieb** *m* intense activity; (*COMM*) peak time; **H~burg** *f* stronghold; **H~deutsch** *nt* High German; **~dotiert** *adj* highly paid; **H~druck** *m* high pressure; **H~ebene** *f* plateau; **~erfreut** *adj* highly delighted; **H~form** *f* top form; **~halten** (*unreg*) *vt* to hold up; (*fig*) to uphold, to cherish; **H~haus** *nt* multi-storey building; **~heben** (*unreg*) *vt* to lift (up); **H~konjunktur** *f* boom; **H~land** *nt* highlands *pl*; **~leben** *vi*: **jdn ~leben lassen** to give sb three cheers; **H~mut** *m* pride; **~mütig** *adj* proud, haughty; **~näsig** *adj* stuck-up, snooty; **H~ofen** *m* blast furnace; **~prozentig** *adj* (*Alkohol*) strong; **H~rechnung** *f* projection; **H~saison** *f* high season; **H~schätzung** *f* high esteem; **H~schule** *f* college; university; **H~sommer** *m* middle of summer; **H~spannung** *f* high tension; **H~sprung** *m* high jump
höchst [høːçst] *adv* highly, extremely

Hochstapler ['hoːxʃtaːplər] (**-s, -**) *m* swindler
höchste(r, s) *adj* highest; (*äußerste*) extreme
Höchst- *zW*: **h~ens** *adv* at the most; **~geschwindigkeit** *f* maximum speed; **h~persönlich** *adv* in person; **~preis** *m* maximum price; **h~wahrscheinlich** *adv* most probably
Hoch- *zW*: **~verrat** *m* high treason; **~wasser** *nt* high water; (*Überschwemmung*) floods *pl*; **~würden** *m* Reverend; **~zahl** *f* (*MATH*) exponent
Hochzeit ['hɔxtsaɪt] (**-, -en**) *f* wedding; **Hochzeitsreise** *f* honeymoon
hocken ['hɔkən] *vi*, *vr* to squat, to crouch
Hocker (**-s, -**) *m* stool
Höcker ['hœkər] (**-s, -**) *m* hump
Hoden ['hoːdən] (**-s, -**) *m* testicle
Hof [hoːf] (**-(e)s, ⁺e**) *m* (*Hinter~*) yard; (*Bauern~*) farm; (*Königs~*) court
hoffen ['hɔfən] *vi*: **~** (**auf** +*akk*) to hope (for)
hoffentlich ['hɔfəntlɪç] *adv* I hope, hopefully
Hoffnung ['hɔfnʊŋ] *f* hope
Hoffnungs- *zW*: **h~los** *adj* hopeless; **~losigkeit** *f* hopelessness; **~schimmer** *m* glimmer of hope; **h~voll** *adj* hopeful
höflich ['høːflɪç] *adj* polite, courteous; **H~keit** *f* courtesy, politeness
hohe(r, s) ['hoːə(r, s)] *adj attrib siehe* **hoch**
Höhe ['høːə] *f* height; (*An~*) hill
Hoheit ['hoːhaɪt] *f* (*POL*) sovereignty; (*Titel*) Highness
Hoheitsgebiet *nt* sovereign territory
Hoheitsgewässer *nt* territorial waters *pl*
Höhen- ['høːən] *zW*: **~angabe** *f* altitude reading; (*auf Karte*) height marking; **~messer** (**-s, -**) *m* altimeter; **~sonne** *f* sun lamp; **~unterschied** *m* difference in altitude
Höhepunkt *m* climax
höher *adj*, *adv* higher
hohl [hoːl] *adj* hollow
Höhle ['høːlə] *f* cave, hole; (*Mund~*) cavity; (*fig, ZOOL*) den

Hohlheit *f* hollowness
Hohlmaß *nt* measure of volume
Hohn [hoːn] (-(e)s) *m* scorn
höhnisch *adj* scornful, taunting
holen ['hoːlən] *vt* to get, to fetch; (*Atem*) to take; **jdn/etw ~ lassen** to send for sb/sth
Holland ['hɔlant] *nt* Holland; **Holländer(in)** ['hɔlɛndər(ın)] *m(f)* Dutchman(woman)
holländisch ['hɔlɛndıʃ] *adj* Dutch
Hölle ['hœlə] *f* hell
höllisch ['hœlıʃ] *adj* hellish, infernal
holperig ['hɔlpərıç] *adj* rough, bumpy
Holunder [ho'lundər] (-s, -) *m* elder
Holz [hɔlts] (-es, -er) *nt* wood
hölzern ['hœltsərn] *adj* (*auch fig*) wooden
Holz- *zW*: **~fäller** (-s, -) *m* lumberjack, woodcutter; **h~ig** *adj* woody; **~kohle** *f* charcoal; **~scheit** *nt* log; **~schuh** *m* clog; **~weg** *m* (*fig*) wrong track; **~wolle** *f* fine wood shavings *pl*
homosexuell [homozɛksu'ɛl] *adj* homosexual
Honig ['hoːnıç] (-s, -e) *m* honey; **~wabe** *f* honeycomb
Honorar [hono'raːr] (-s, -e) *nt* fee
honorieren [hono'riːrən] *vt* to remunerate; (*Scheck*) to honour
Hopfen ['hɔpfən] (-s, -) *m* hops *pl*
hopsen ['hɔpsən] *vi* to hop
Hörapparat *m* hearing aid
hörbar *adj* audible
horchen ['hɔrçən] *vi* to listen; (*pej*) to eavesdrop; **horch!** listen!
Horde ['hɔrdə] *f* horde
hören ['høːrən] *vt, vi* to hear; **Musik/Radio ~** to listen to music/the radio
Hörer (-s, -) *m* hearer; (*RADIO*) listener; (*UNIV*) student; (*Telefon~*) receiver
Horizont [hori'tsɔnt] (-(e)s, -e) *m* horizon; **h~al** [-'taːl] *adj* horizontal
Hormon [hɔr'moːn] (-s, -e) *nt* hormone
Hörmuschel *f* (*TEL*) earpiece
Horn [hɔrn] (-(e)s, -er) *nt* horn; **~haut** *f* horny skin
Hornisse [hɔr'nısə] *f* hornet
Horoskop [horo'skoːp] (-s, -e) *nt* horoscope

Hörsaal *m* lecture room
horten ['hɔrtən] *vt* to hoard
Hose ['hoːzə] *f* trousers *pl*, pants *pl* (*US*)
Hosen- *zW*: **~anzug** *m* trouser suit; **~rock** *m* culottes *pl*; **~tasche** *f* (trouser) pocket; **~träger** *m* braces *pl* (*BRIT*), suspenders *pl* (*US*)
Hostie ['hɔstiə] *f* (*REL*) host
Hotel [ho'tɛl] (-s, -s) *nt* hotel
Hotelier [hoteli'eː] (-s, -s) *m* hotelkeeper, hotelier
Hubraum ['huːp-] *m* (*AUT*) cubic capacity
hübsch [hypʃ] *adj* pretty, nice
Hubschrauber ['huːpʃraubər] (-s, -) *m* helicopter
Huf [huːf] (-(e)s, -e) *m* hoof; **~eisen** *nt* horseshoe; **~nagel** *m* horseshoe nail
Hüft- ['hyft] *zW*: **~e** *f* hip; **~gürtel** *m* girdle; **~halter** (-s, -) *m* girdle
Hügel ['hyːgəl] (-s, -) *m* hill; **h~ig** *adj* hilly
Huhn [huːn] (-(e)s, -er) *nt* hen; (*KOCH*) chicken
Hühnerauge ['hyːnər-] *nt* corn
Hühnerbrühe ['hyːnər-] *f* chicken broth
Hülle ['hylə] *f* cover(ing); wrapping; **in ~ und Fülle** galore; **h~n** *vt*: **h~n** (**in** +*akk*) to cover (with); to wrap (in)
Hülse ['hylzə] *f* husk, shell; **Hülsenfrucht** *f* pulse
human [hu'maːn] *adj* humane; **~i'tär** *adj* humanitarian; **H~i'tät** *f* humanity
Hummel ['huməl] (-, -n) *f* bumblebee
Hummer ['humər] (-s, -) *m* lobster
Humor [hu'moːr] (-s, -e) *m* humour; **~ haben** to have a sense of humour; **~ist** [-'rıst] *m* humorist; **h~istisch** *adj* humorous; **h~voll** *adj* humorous
humpeln ['humpəln] *vi* to hobble
Humpen ['humpən] (-s, -) *m* tankard
Hund [hunt] (-(e)s, -e) *m* dog
Hunde- ['hundə] *zW*: **~hütte** *f* (dog) kennel; **~kuchen** *m* dog biscuit; **h~müde** (*umg*) *adj* dog-tired
hundert ['hundərt] *num* hundred; **H~'jahrfeier** *f* centenary; **~prozentig** *adj, adv* one hundred per cent
Hündin ['hyndın] *f* bitch
Hunger ['huŋər] (-s) *m* hunger; **~ haben**

to be hungry; **h~n** *vi* to starve;
Hungersnot *f* famine; **~streik** *m*
hunger strike
hungrig ['huŋrɪç] *adj* hungry
Hupe ['hu:pə] *f* horn; **h~n** *vi* to hoot, to
sound one's horn
hüpfen ['hʏpfən] *vi* to hop; to jump
Hürde ['hʏrdə] *f* hurdle; *(für Schafe)*
pen; **Hürdenlauf** *m* hurdling
Hure ['hu:rə] *f* whore
hurra [hu'ra:] *excl* hooray!
hurtig ['hurtɪç] *adj* brisk, quick ♦ *adv*
briskly, quickly
huschen ['huʃən] *vi* to flit; to scurry
Husten ['hu:stən] (-s) *m* cough; **h~** *vi* to
cough; **~anfall** *m* coughing
fit; **~bonbon** *m od nt* cough drop; **~saft** *m*
cough mixture
Hut[1] [hu:t] (-(e)s, ⁼e) *m* hat
Hut[2] (-) *f* care; **auf der ~ sein** to be on
one's guard
hüten ['hy:tən] *vt* to guard ♦ *vr* to watch
out; **sich ~, zu** to take care not to; **sich
~ (vor)**, to beware (of), to be on one's
guard (against)
Hütte ['hʏtə] *f* hut; cottage; *(Eisen~)*
forge
Hyäne [hy'ɛ:nə] *f* hyena
Hyazinthe [hya'tsɪntə] *f* hyacinth
Hydrant [hy'drant] *m* hydrant
hydraulisch [hy'draulɪʃ] *adj* hydraulic
Hygiene [hygi'e:nə] (-) *f* hygiene
hygienisch [hygi'e:nɪʃ] *adj* hygienic
Hymne ['hʏmnə] *f* hymn; anthem
hyper- ['hʏpər] *präfix* hyper-
Hypno- [hʏp'no:] *zW:* **~se** *f* hypnosis;
h~tisch *adj* hypnotic; **~tiseur** [-ti'zø:r]
m hypnotist; **h~ti'sieren** *vt* to
hypnotize
Hypothek [hypo'te:k] (-, -en) *f* mortgage
Hypothese [hypo'te:zə] *f* hypothesis
hypothetisch [hypo'te:tɪʃ] *adj* hypo-
thetical
Hysterie [hʏste'ri:] *f* hysteria
hysterisch [hʏs'te:rɪʃ] *adj* hysterical

I

i.A. *abk* (= *im Auftrag*) for; *(in Briefen
auch)* p.p.
Ich (-(s), -(s)) *nt* self; *(PSYCH)* ego
ich [ɪç] *pron* I; **~ bin's!** it's me!
Ideal [ide'a:l] (-s, -e) *nt* ideal; **i~** *adj*
ideal; **~ist** [-'lɪst] *m* idealist; **i~istisch**
[-'lɪstɪʃ] *adj* idealistic
Idee [i'de:, *pl* i'de:ən] *f* idea
identifizieren [i'dentifi'tsi:rən] *vt* to
identify
identisch [i'dentɪʃ] *adj* identical
Identität [identi'tɛ:t] *f* identity
Ideo- [ideo] *zW:* **~loge** [-'lo:gə] (-n, -n)
m ideologist; **~logie** [-lo'gi:] *f* ideology;
i~logisch [-'lo:gɪʃ] *adj* ideological
Idiot [idi'o:t] (-en, -en) *m* idiot; **i~isch**
adj idiotic
idyllisch [i'dʏlɪʃ] *adj* idyllic
Igel ['i:gəl] (-s, -) *m* hedgehog
ignorieren [ɪgno'ri:rən] *vt* to ignore
ihm [i:m] *(dat von* **er, es)** *pron* (to)
him; (to) it
ihn [i:n] *(akk von* **er)** *pron* him; it; **~en**
(dat von **sie** *pl) pron* (to) them; **I~en**
(dat von **Sie** *pl) pron* (to) you

SCHLÜSSELWORT

ihr [i:r] *pron* **1** *(nom pl)* you; **ihr seid es**
it's you
2 *(dat von sie)* to her; **gib es ihr** give it
to her; **er steht neben ihr** he is standing
beside her
♦ *possessiv pron* **1** *(sg)* her; (*: bei
Tieren, Dingen)* its; **ihr Mann** her husband
2 *(pl)* their; **die Bäume und ihre
Blätter** the trees and their leaves

---

ihr(e) *adj (sg)* her; its; *(pl)* their; **I~(e)**
adj your
ihre(r, s) *pron (sg)* hers; its; *(pl)*
theirs; **I~(r, s)** *pron* yours; **~r** *(gen von
sie sg/pl) pron* of her/them; **I~r** *(sg/pl)
pron von* **Sie)** *pron* of you; **ihrerseits** *adv* for
her/their part; **ihresgleichen** *pron*
people like her/them; *(von Dingen)*

others like it; **ihretwegen** *adv* (*für sie*) for her/its/their sake; (*wegen ihr*) on her/its/their account; **ihretwillen** *adv*: **um ihretwillen** = **ihretwegen**

ihrige *pron*: **der/die/das ihrige** hers; its; theirs

illegal ['ɪlega:l] *adj* illegal

Illusion [ɪluzi'o:n] *f* illusion

illusorisch [ɪlu'zo:rɪʃ] *adj* illusory

illustrieren [ɪlʊs'tri:rən] *vt* to illustrate

Illustrierte *f* magazine

Iltis ['ɪltɪs] (-ses, -se) *m* polecat

im [ɪm] = **in dem**

Imbiß ['ɪmbɪs] (-sses, -sse) *m* snack; ~**halle** *f* snack bar; ~**stube** *f* snack bar

imitieren [ɪmi'ti:rən] *vt* to imitate

immatrikulieren [ɪmatriku'li:rən] *vi, vr* to register

immer ['ɪmər] *adv* always; ~ **wieder** again and again; ~ **noch** still; ~ **noch nicht** still not; **für** ~ forever; ~ **wenn ich ...** every time I ...; ~ **schöner/trauriger** more and more beautiful/sadder and sadder; **was/wer** (**auch**) ~ whatever/whoever; ~**hin** *adv* all the same; ~**zu** *adv* all the time

Immobilien [ɪmo'bi:liən] *pl* real estate *sg*

immun [ɪ'mu:n] *adj* immune; **I**~**ität** [-i'tɛ:t] *f* immunity

Imperfekt ['ɪmpɛrfɛkt] (-s, -e) *nt* imperfect (tense)

Impf- ['ɪmpf] *zW*: **i**~**en** *vt* to vaccinate; ~**stoff** *m* vaccine, serum; ~**ung** *f* vaccination; ~**zwang** *m* compulsory vaccination

imponieren [ɪmpo'ni:rən] *vi* +*dat* to impress

Import [ɪm'pɔrt] (-(e)s, -e) *m* import; **i**~**ieren** [-'ti:rən] *vt* to import

impotent ['ɪmpotɛnt] *adj* impotent

imprägnieren [ɪmprɛ'gni:rən] *vt* to (water)proof

improvisieren [ɪmprovi'zi:rən] *vt, vi* to improvize

Impuls [ɪm'pʊls] (-es, -e) *m* impulse; **i**~**iv** [-'zi:f] *adj* impulsive

imstande [ɪm'ʃtandə] *adj*: ~ **sein** to be in a position; (*fähig*) to be able

in [ɪn] *präp* +*akk* **1** (*räumlich: wohin?*) in, into; **in die Stadt** into town; **in die Schule gehen** to go to school

2 (*zeitlich*): **bis ins 20. Jahrhundert** into *od* up to the 20th century

♦ *präp* +*dat* **1** (*räumlich: wo*) in; **in der Stadt** in town; **in der Schule sein** to be at school

2 (*zeitlich: wann*): **in diesem Jahr** this year; (*in jenem Jahr*) in that year; **heute in zwei Wochen** two weeks today

Inanspruchnahme [ɪn'ʔanʃprʊxna:mə] *f* (+*gen*) demands *pl* (on)

Inbegriff ['ɪnbəgrɪf] *m* embodiment, personification; **i**~**en** *adv* included

indem [ɪn'de:m] *konj* while; ~ **man etw macht** (*dadurch*) by doing sth

Inder(in) ['ɪndər(ɪn)] *m(f)* Indian

Indianer(in) [ɪndi'a:nər(ɪn)] (-s, -) *m(f)* Red Indian

indianisch *adj* Red Indian

Indien ['ɪndiən] *nt* India

indirekt ['ɪndirɛkt] *adj* indirect

indisch ['ɪndɪʃ] *adj* Indian

indiskret ['ɪndɪskre:t] *adj* indiscreet

indiskutabel ['ɪndɪsku'ta:bəl] *adj* out of the question

Individu- [ɪndividu] *zW*: ~**alist** [-a'lɪst] *m* individualist; ~**alität** [-ali'tɛ:t] *f* individuality; **i**~**ell** [-'ɛl] *adj* individual; ~**um** [ɪndi'vi:duʊm] (-s, -en) *nt* individual

Indiz [ɪn'di:ts] (-es, -ien) *nt* (*JUR*) clue; ~ (**für**) sign (of)

Indonesien [ɪndo'ne:ziən] *nt* Indonesia

industrialisieren [ɪndʊstriali'zi:rən] *vt* to industrialize

Industrie [ɪndʊs'tri:] *f* industry ♦ *in zW* industrial; ~**gebiet** *nt* industrial area; ~**gelände** *nt* industrial *od* trading estate; **industriell** [ɪndʊstri'ɛl] *adj* industrial; ~**zweig** *m* branch of industry

ineinander [ɪn'aɪ'nandər] *adv* in(to) one another *od* each other

Infarkt [ɪn'farkt] (-(e)s, -e) *m* coronary (thrombosis)

Infektion [ɪnfɛktsi'o:n] *f* infection; ~**skrankheit** *f* infectious disease

Infinitiv [ˈɪnfiniːtiːf] (-s, -e) m infinitive
infizieren [ɪnfiˈtsiːrən] vt to infect ♦ vr:
  sich (bei jdm) ~ to be infected (by sb)
Inflation [ɪnflatsiˈoːn] f inflation
inflationär [ɪnflatsioˈnɛːr] adj inflationary
infolge [ɪnˈfɔlgə] präp +gen as a result
  of, owing to; ~**dessen** [-ˈdɛsən] adv consequently
Informatik [ɪnfɔrˈmaːtɪk] f information
  studies pl
Information [ɪnfɔrmatsiˈoːn] f information no pl
informieren [ɪnfɔrˈmiːrən] vt to inform ♦
  vr: **sich** ~ **(über** +akk) to find out
  (about)
Infusion [ɪnfuziˈoːn] f infusion
Ingenieur [ɪnʒeniˈøːr] m engineer;
  ~**schule** f school of engineering
Ingwer [ˈɪŋvər] (-s) m ginger
Inh. abk (= Inhaber) prop.; (= Inhalt)
  contents
Inhaber(in) [ˈɪnhaːbər(ɪn)] (-s, -) m(f)
  owner; (Haus~) occupier; (Lizenz~)
  licensee, holder; (FIN) bearer
inhalieren [ɪnhaˈliːrən] vt, vi to inhale
Inhalt [ˈɪnhalt] (-(e)s, -e) m contents pl;
  (eines Buchs etc) content; (MATH)
  area; volume; i~**lich** adj as regards
  content
Inhalts- zW: ~**angabe** f summary;
  i~**los** adj empty; ~**verzeichnis** nt table
  of contents
inhuman [ˈɪnhumaːn] adj inhuman
Initiative [initsiaˈtiːvə] f initiative
Injektion [ɪnjɛktsiˈoːn] f injection
inklusive [ɪnkluˈziːvə] präp +gen inclusive of ♦ adv inclusive
inkognito [ɪnˈkɔgnito] adv incognito
Inkrafttreten [ɪnˈkrafttreːtən] (-s) nt
  coming into force
Inland [ˈɪnlant] (-(e)s) nt (GEOG) inland;
  (POL, COMM) home (country)
inmitten [ɪnˈmɪtən] präp +gen in the
  middle of; ~ **von** amongst
innehaben [ˈɪnəhaːbən] (unreg) vt to
  hold
innen [ˈɪnən] adv inside; I~**architekt** m
  interior designer; I~**einrichtung** f
  (interior) furnishings pl; I~**minister** m
  minister of the interior, Home

Secretary (BRIT); I~**politik** f domestic
  policy; I~**stadt** f town/city centre
inner- [ˈɪnər] zW: ~**e(r, s)** adj inner;
  (im Körper, inländisch) internal; I~**e(s)**
  nt inside; (Mitte) centre; (fig) heart;
  I~**eien** [-ˈraɪən] pl innards; ~**halb** adv
  within; (räumlich) inside ♦ präp +gen
  within; inside; ~**lich** adj internal;
  (geistig) inward; ~**ste(r, s)** adj inner-
  most; I~**ste(s)** nt heart
inoffiziell [ˈɪnˈɔfitsiɛl] adj unofficial
ins [ɪns] = **in das**
Insasse [ˈɪnzasə] (-n, -n) m (Anstalt) inmate; (AUT) passenger
insbesondere [ɪnsbəˈzɔndərə] adv
  (e)specially
Inschrift [ˈɪnʃrɪft] f inscription
Insekt [ɪnˈzɛkt] (-(e)s, -en) nt insect
Insel [ˈɪnzəl] (-, -n) f island
Inser- zW: ~**at** [ɪnzeˈraːt] (-(e)s, -e) nt
  advertisement; ~**ent** [ɪnzeˈrɛnt] m
  advertiser; i~**ieren** [ɪnzeˈriːrən] vt, vi to
  advertise
insgeheim [ɪnsgəˈhaɪm] adv secretly
insgesamt [ɪnsgəˈzamt] adv altogether,
  all in all
insofern [ˈɪnzoˈfɛrn] adv in this respect
  ♦ konj if; (deshalb) (and) so; ~ **als** in
  so far as
insoweit [ˈɪnzoˈvaɪt] = **insofern**
Installateur [ɪnstalaˈtøːr] m electrician;
  plumber
Instandhaltung [ɪnˈʃtant-] f maintenance
Instandsetzung [ɪnˈʃtant-] f overhaul;
  (eines Gebäudes) restoration
Instanz [ɪnˈstants] f authority; (JUR)
  court; ~**enweg** m official channels pl
Instinkt [ɪnˈstɪŋkt] (-(e)s, -e) m instinct;
  i~**iv** [-ˈtiːf] adj instinctive
Institut [ɪnstiˈtuːt] (-(e)s, -e) nt institute
Instrument [ɪnstruˈmɛnt] nt instrument
Intell- [ɪntel] zW: i~**ektuell** [-ɛktuˈɛl] adj
  intellectual; i~**igent** [-iˈgɛnt] adj in-
  telligent; ~**igenz** [-iˈgɛnts] f intelligence;
  (Leute) intelligentsia pl
Intendant [ɪntɛnˈdant] m director
intensiv [ɪntɛnˈziːf] adj intensive
Interess- zW: i~**ant** [ɪntɛreˈsant] adj
  interesting; i~**anterweise** adv interest-

ingly enough; ~**e** [ɪntɛ'rɛsə] (-s, -n) *nt* interest; ~**e haben an** +*dat* to be interested in; ~**ent** [ɪntɛrɛ'sɛnt] *m* interested party; **i~ieren** [ɪntɛrɛ'siːrən] *vt* to interest ♦ *vr*: **sich i~ieren für** to be interested in

Internat [ɪntɛr'naːt] (-(e)s, -e) *nt* boarding school

inter- [ɪntɛr] *zW*: ~**national** [-natsio'naːl] *adj* international; ~**pretieren** [-pre'tiːrən] *vt* to interpret; **I~vall** [-'val] (-s, -e) *nt* interval; **I~view** ['-vjuː] (-s, -s) *nt* interview; ~**viewen** [-'vjuːən] *vt* to interview

intim [ɪn'tiːm] *adj* intimate; **I~ität** [ɪntimi'tɛːt] *f* intimacy

intolerant ['ɪntolerant] *adj* intolerant

intransitiv ['ɪntranzitiːf] *adj* (*GRAM*) intransitive

Intrige [ɪn'triːgə] *f* intrigue, plot

Invasion [ɪnvazi'oːn] *f* invasion

Inventar [ɪnvɛn'taːr] (-s, -e) *nt* inventory

Inventur [ɪnvɛn'tuːr] *f* stocktaking; ~**machen** to stocktake

investieren [ɪnvɛs'tiːrən] *vt* to invest

Investition [ɪnvɛstitsi'oːn] *f* investment

Investmentgesellschaft [ɪn'vɛstmɛntgəzɛlʃaft] *f* unit trust

inwiefern [ɪnvi'fɛrn] *adv* how far, to what extent

inwieweit [ɪnvi'vaɪt] *adv* how far, to what extent

inzwischen [ɪn'tsvɪʃən] *adv* meanwhile

Irak [i'raːk] (-s) *m*: **der** ~ Iraq; **i~isch** *adj* Iraqi

Iran [i'raːn] (-s) *m*: **der** ~ Iran; **i~isch** *adj* Iranian

irdisch ['ɪrdɪʃ] *adj* earthly

Ire ['iːrə] (-n, -n) *m* Irishman

irgend ['ɪrgənt] *adv* at all; **wann/was/wer** ~ whenever/whatever/whoever; ~**jemand/etwas** somebody/something; anybody/anything; ~**ein(e, s)** *adj* some, any; ~**einmal** *adv* sometime or other; (*fragend*) ever; ~**wann** *adv* sometime; ~**wie** *adv* somehow; ~**wo** *adv* somewhere; anywhere; ~**wohin** *adv* somewhere; anywhere

Irin ['iːrɪn] *f* Irishwoman

Irland ['ɪrlant] (-s) *nt* Ireland

Ironie [iro'niː] *f* irony

ironisch [i'roːnɪʃ] *adj* ironic(al)

irre ['ɪrə] *adj* crazy, mad; **I~(r)** *mf* lunatic; ~**führen** *vt* to mislead; ~**machen** *vt* to confuse; ~**n** *vi* to be mistaken; (*umherirren*) to wander, to stray ♦ *vr* to be mistaken; **I~nanstalt** *f* lunatic asylum

irrig ['ɪrɪç] *adj* incorrect, wrong

Irr- *zW*: **i~sinnig** *adj* mad, crazy; (*umg*) terrific; ~**tum** (-s, -tümer) *m* mistake, error; **i~tümlich** *adj* mistaken

Island ['iːslant] (-s) *nt* Iceland

Isolation [izolatsi'oːn] *f* isolation; (*ELEK*) insulation

Isolator [izo'laːtɔr] *m* insulator

Isolier- [izo'liːr] *zW*: ~**band** *nt* insulating tape; **i~en** *vt* to isolate; (*ELEK*) to insulate; ~**station** *f* (*MED*) isolation ward; ~**ung** *f* isolation; (*ELEK*) insulation

Israel ['ɪsraeːl] (-s) *nt* Israel; ~**i** [-'eːli] (-s, -s) *m* Israeli; **i~isch** *adj* Israeli

ißt [ɪst] *vb siehe* **essen**

ist [ɪst] *vb siehe* **sein**

Italien [i'taːliən] (-s) *nt* Italy; ~**er(in)** [-li'eːnər(ɪn)] (-s) *m(f)* Italian; **i~isch** *adj* Italian

i.V. *abk* = **in Vertretung**

J

ja [jaː] *adv* **1** yes; **haben Sie das gesehen? - ja** did you see it? - yes(, I did); **ich glaube ja** (yes) I think so

2 (*fragend*) really?; **ich habe gekündigt - ja?** I've quit - have you?; **du kommst, ja?** you're coming, aren't you?

3: **sei ja vorsichtig** do be careful; **Sie wissen ja, daß ...** as you know, ...; **tu das ja nicht!** don't do that!; **ich habe es ja gewußt** I just knew it; **ja, also ...** well you see ...

Jacht [jaxt] (-, -en) *f* yacht

Jacke ['jakə] *f* jacket; (*Woll~*) cardigan

Jackett [ʒa'kɛt] (-s, -s *od* -e) *nt* jacket

Jagd [jaːkt] (-, -en) *f* hunt; (*Jagen*)

hunting; **~beute** f kill; **~flugzeug** nt fighter; **~gewehr** nt sporting gun

jagen ['ja:gən] vi to hunt; (eilen) to race ♦ vt to hunt; (weg~) to drive (off); (verfolgen) to chase

Jäger ['jɛ:gər] (-s, -) m hunter

jäh [jɛ:] adj sudden, abrupt; (steil) steep, precipitous

Jahr [ja:r] (-(e)s, -e) nt year; **j~elang** adv for years

Jahres- zW: **~abonnement** nt annual subscription; **~abschluß** m end of the year; (COMM) annual statement of account; **~beitrag** m annual subscription; **~bericht** m annual report; **~hauptversammlung** f annual general meeting; **~tag** m anniversary; **~wechsel** m turn of the year; **~zahl** f date; year; **~zeit** f season

Jahr- zW: **~gang** m age group; (von Wein) vintage; **~'hundert** (-s, -e) nt century; **~'hundertfeier** f centenary

jährlich ['jɛ:rlɪç] adj, adv yearly

Jahrmarkt m fair

Jahr'zehnt nt decade

Jähzorn m sudden anger; hot temper; **j~ig** adj hot-tempered

Jalousie [ʒalu'zi:] f venetian blind

Jammer ['jamər] (-s) m misery; **es ist ein ~, daß ...** it is a crying shame that ...

jämmerlich ['jɛmərlɪç] adj wretched, pathetic

jammern vi to wail ♦ vt unpers: **es jammert jdn** it makes sb feel sorry

jammerschade adj: **es ist ~** it is a crying shame

Januar ['janua:r] (-(s), -e) m January

Japan ['ja:pan] (-s) nt Japan; **~er(in)** [-'pa:nər(ɪn)] (-s) m(f) Japanese; **j~isch** adj Japanese

Jargon [ʒar'gõ:] (-s, -s) m jargon

jäten ['jɛ:tən] vt: **Unkraut ~** to weed

jauchzen ['jauxtsən] vi to rejoice, to shout (with joy)

jaulen ['jaulən] vi to howl

jawohl [ja'vo:l] adv yes (of course)

Jawort ['ja:vɔrt] nt consent

Jazz [dʒɛs] (-) m jazz

---

je [je:] adv **1** (jemals) ever; **hast du so was je gesehen?** did you ever see anything like it?

2 (jeweils) every, each; **sie zahlten je 3 Mark** they paid 3 marks each

♦ konj **1**: **je nach** depending on; **je nachdem** it depends; **je nachdem, ob ...** depending on whether ...

2: **je eher, desto** od **um so besser** the sooner the better

---

Jeans [dʒi:nz] pl jeans

jede(r, s) ['je:də(r, s)] adj every, each ♦ pron everybody; (~ einzelne) each; **ohne ~ x** without any x

jedenfalls adv in any case

jedermann pron everyone

jederzeit adv at any time

jedesmal adv every time, each time

jedoch [je'dɔx] adv however

jemals ['je:ma:ls] adv ever

jemand ['je:mant] pron somebody; anybody

Jemen ['je:mən] (-s) m: **der ~** the Yemen

jene(r, s) ['je:nə(r, s)] adj that ♦ pron that one

jenseits ['je:nzaits] adv on the other side ♦ präp +gen on the other side of, beyond

Jenseits nt: **das ~** the hereafter, the beyond

jetzig ['jɛtsɪç] adj present

jetzt [jɛtst] adv now

jeweilig adj respective

jeweils adv: **~ zwei zusammen** two at a time; **zu ~ 5 DM** at 5 marks each; **~ das erste** the first each time

Jh. abk = **Jahrhundert**

Jockei ['dʒɔke] (-s, -s) m jockey

Jod [jo:t] (-(e)s) nt iodine

jodeln ['jo:dəln] vi to yodel

joggen ['dʒɔgən] vi to jog

Joghurt ['jo:gurt] (-s, -s) m od nt yogurt

Johannisbeere [jo'hanɪsbe:rə] f redcurrant; **schwarze ~** blackcurrant

johlen ['jo:lən] vi to yell

Jolle ['jɔlə] f dinghy

jonglieren [ʒõˈgliːrən] *vi* to juggle
Jordanien [jɔrˈdaːniən] (-s) *nt* Jordan
Journal- [ʒʊrnal] *zW:* ~**ismus** [-ˈlɪsmʊs] *m* journalism; ~**ist(in)** [-ˈlɪst(ɪn)] *m(f)* journalist; **journaˈlistisch** *adj* journalistic
Jubel [ˈjuːbəl] (-s) *m* rejoicing; **j**~**n** *vi* to rejoice
Jubiläum [jubiˈlɛːʊm] (-s, **Jubiläen**) *nt* anniversary; jubilee
jucken [ˈjʊkən] *vi* to itch ♦ *vt:* **es juckt mich am Arm** my arm is itching; **das juckt mich** that's itchy
Juckreiz [ˈjʊkraɪts] *m* itch
Jude [ˈjuːdə] (-n, -n) *m* Jew
Judentum (-) *nt* Judaism; Jewry
Judenverfolgung *f* persecution of the Jews
Jüdin [ˈjyːdɪn] *f* Jewess
jüdisch [ˈjyːdɪʃ] *adj* Jewish
Judo [ˈjuːdo] (-(s)) *nt* judo
Jugend [ˈjuːgənt] (-) *f* youth; ~**club** *m* youth club; ~**herberge** *f* youth hostel; ~**kriminalität** *f* juvenile crime; **j**~**lich** *adj* youthful; ~**liche(r)** *mf* teenager, young person
Jugoslaw- [jugoˈslaːv] *zW:* ~**e** *m* Yugoslavian; ~**ien** (-s) *nt* Yugoslavia; ~**in** *f* Yugoslavian; **j**~**isch** *adj* Yugoslavian
Juli [ˈjuːli] (-(s), -s) *m* July
jun. *abk* (= *junior*) jr.
jung [jʊŋ] *adj* young; **J**~**e** (-n, -n) *m* boy, lad; **J**~**e(s)** *nt* young animal; **J**~**en** *pl* (*von Tier*) young *pl*
Jünger [ˈjyŋər] (-s, -) *m* disciple
jünger *adj* younger
Jungfer [ˈjʊŋfər] (-, -n) *f:* **alte** ~ old maid
Jungfernfahrt *f* maiden voyage
Jung- *zW:* ~**frau** *f* virgin; (*ASTROL*) Virgo; ~**geselle** *m* bachelor; ~**gesellin** *f* unmarried woman
jüngst [jʊŋst] *adv* lately, recently; ~**e(r, s)** *adj* youngest; (*neueste*) latest
Juni [ˈjuːni] (-(s), -s) *m* June
Junior [ˈjuːniɔr, *pl* -ˈoːrən] (-s, -en) *m* junior
Jurist [juˈrɪst] *m* jurist, lawyer; **j**~**isch** *adj* legal

Justiz [jʊsˈtiːts] (-) *f* justice; ~**beamte(r)** *m* judicial officer; ~**irrtum** *m* miscarriage of justice
Juwel [juˈveːl] (-s, -en) *nt od m* jewel
Juwelier [juveˈliːr] (-s, -e) *m* jeweller; ~**geschäft** *nt* jeweller's (shop)
Jux [jʊks] (-es, -e) *m* joke, lark

K

Kabarett [kabaˈrɛt] (-s, -e *od* -s) *nt* cabaret; ~**ist** [-ˈtɪst] *m* cabaret artiste
Kabel [ˈkaːbəl] (-s, -) *nt* (*ELEK*) wire; (*stark*) cable; ~**fernsehen** *nt* cable television
Kabeljau [ˈkaːbəljaʊ] (-s, -e *od* -s) *m* cod
kabeln *vt, vi* to cable
Kabine [kaˈbiːnə] *f* cabin; (*Zelle*) cubicle
Kabinett [kabiˈnɛt] (-s, -e) *nt* (*POL*) cabinet
Kachel [ˈkaxəl] (-, -n) *f* tile; **k**~**n** *vt* to tile; ~**ofen** *m* tiled stove
Käfer [ˈkɛːfər] (-s, -) *m* beetle
Kaffee [ˈkafe] (-s, -s) *m* coffee; ~**kanne** *f* coffeepot; ~**klatsch** *m* hen party; coffee morning; ~**kränzchen** *nt* hen party; coffee morning; ~**löffel** *m* coffee spoon; ~**satz** *m* coffee grounds *pl*
Käfig [ˈkɛːfɪç] (-s, -e) *m* cage
kahl [kaːl] *adj* bald; ~**geschoren** *adj* shaven, shorn; **K**~**heit** *f* baldness; ~**köpfig** *adj* bald-headed
Kahn [kaːn] (-(e)s, ̈e) *m* boat, barge
Kai [kaɪ] (-s, -e *od* -s) *m* quay
Kaiser [ˈkaɪzər] (-s, -) *m* emperor; ~**in** *f* empress; **k**~**lich** *adj* imperial; ~**reich** *nt* empire; ~**schnitt** *m* (*MED*) Caesarian (section)
Kakao [kaˈkao] (-s, -s) *m* cocoa
Kaktee [kakˈteː(ə)] (-, -n) *f* cactus
Kaktus [ˈkaktʊs] (-, -teen) *m* cactus
Kalb [kalp] (-(e)s, ̈er) *nt* calf; **k**~**en** [ˈkalbən] *vi* to calve; ~**fleisch** *nt* veal; ~**sleder** *nt* calf(skin)
Kalender [kaˈlɛndər] (-s, -) *m* calendar; (*Taschen*~) diary
Kaliber [kaˈliːbər] (-s, -) *nt* (*auch fig*) calibre
Kalk [kalk] (-(e)s, -e) *m* lime; (*BIOL*)

calcium; ~**stein** *m* limestone

kalkulieren [kalku'li:rən] *vt* to calculate

Kalorie [kalo'ri:] *f* calorie

kalt [kalt] *adj* cold; **mir ist (es)** ~ I am cold; ~**bleiben** (*unreg*) *vi* to remain unmoved; ~**blütig** *adj* cold-blooded; (*ruhig*) cool

Kälte ['kɛltə] (-) *f* cold; coldness; ~**grad** *m* degree of frost *od* below zero; ~**welle** *f* cold spell

kalt- *zW:* ~**herzig** *adj* cold-hearted; ~**schnäuzig** *adj* cold, unfeeling; ~**stellen** *vt* to chill; (*fig*) to leave out in the cold

kam *etc* [ka:m] *vb siehe* **kommen**

Kamel [ka'me:l] (-(e)s, -e) *nt* camel

Kamera ['kamera] (-, -s) *f* camera

Kamerad [kamə'ra:t] (-en, -en) *m* comrade, friend; ~**schaft** *f* comradeship; **k~schaftlich** *adj* comradely

Kamille [ka'mɪlə] *f* camomile; ~**ntee** *m* camomile tea

Kamin [ka'mi:n] (-s, -e) *m* (*außen*) chimney; (*innen*) fireside, fireplace; ~**feger** (-s, -) *m* chimney sweep; ~**kehrer** (-s, -) *m* chimney sweep

Kamm [kam] (-(e)s, -e) *m* comb; (*Berg~*) ridge; (*Hahnen~*) crest

kämmen ['kɛmən] *vt* to comb ♦ *vr* to comb one's hair

Kammer ['kamər] (-, -n) *f* chamber; small bedroom; ~**diener** *m* valet

Kampagne [kam'panjə] *f* campaign

Kampf [kampf] (-(e)s, -e) *m* fight, battle; (*Wettbewerb*) contest; (*fig: Anstrengung*) struggle; **k~bereit** *adj* ready for action

kämpfen ['kɛmpfən] *vi* to fight

Kämpfer (-s, -) *m* fighter, combatant

Kampf- *zW:* ~**handlung** *f* action; **k~los** *adj* without a fight; ~**richter** *m* (*SPORT*) referee; (*TENNIS*) umpire

Kanada ['kanada] (-s) *nt* Canada

Kanadier(in) [ka'na:diər(ɪn)] (-s, -) *m(f)* Canadian

kanadisch [ka'na:dɪʃ] *adj* Canadian

Kanal [ka'na:l] (-s, **Kanäle**) *m* (*Fluß*) canal; (*Rinne, Ärmel~*) channel; (*für Abfluß*) drain; ~**inseln** *pl* Channel Islands; ~**isation** [-izatsi'o:n] *f* sewage

system

Kanarienvogel [ka'na:riənfo:gəl] *m* canary

kanarisch [ka'na:rɪʃ] *adj:* **K~e Inseln** Canary Islands, Canaries

Kandi- [kandi] *zW:* ~**dat** [-'da:t] (-en, -en) *m* candidate; ~**datur** [-da'tu:r] *f* candidature, candidacy; **k~dieren** [-'di:rən] *vi* to stand, to run

Kandis(zucker) ['kandɪs(tsʊkər)] (-) *m* candy

Känguruh ['kɛŋguru] (-s, -s) *nt* kangaroo

Kaninchen [ka'ni:nçən] *nt* rabbit

Kanister [ka'nɪstər] (-s, -) *m* can, canister

Kännchen ['kɛnçən] *nt* pot

Kanne ['kanə] *f* (*Krug*) jug; (*Kaffee~*) pot; (*Milch~*) churn; (*Gieß~*) can

kannst *etc* [kanst] *vb siehe* **können**

Kanon ['ka:nɔn] (-s, -s) *m* canon

Kanone [ka'no:nə] *f* gun; (*HIST*) cannon; (*fig: Mensch*) ace

Kantate [kan'ta:tə] *f* cantata

Kante ['kantə] *f* edge

Kantine [kan'ti:nə] *f* canteen

Kanu ['ka:nu] (-s, -s) *nt* canoe

Kanzel ['kantsəl] (-, -n) *f* pulpit

Kanzler ['kantslər] (-s, -) *m* chancellor

Kap [kap] (-s, -s) *nt* cape (*GEOG*); ~ **der Guten Hoffnung** Cape of Good Hope

Kapazität [kapatsi'tɛ:t] *f* capacity; (*Fachmann*) authority

Kapelle [ka'pɛlə] *f* (*Gebäude*) chapel; (*MUS*) band

kapieren [ka'pi:rən] (*umg*) *vt, vi* to get, to understand

Kapital [kapi'ta:l] (-s, -e *od* -ien) *nt* capital; ~**anlage** *f* investment; ~**ismus** [-'lɪsmʊs] *m* capitalism; ~**ist** [-'lɪst] *m* capitalist; **k~istisch** *adj* capitalist

Kapitän [kapi'tɛ:n] (-s, -e) *m* captain

Kapitel [ka'pɪtəl] (-s, -) *nt* chapter

Kapitulation [kapitulatsi'o:n] *f* capitulation

kapitulieren [kapitu'li:rən] *vi* to capitulate

Kaplan [ka'pla:n] (-s, **Kapläne**) *m* chaplain

Kappe ['kapə] *f* cap; (*Kapuze*) hood

kappen *vt* to cut

Kapsel ['kapsəl] (-, -n) *f* capsule

Kapstadt ['kapʃtat] (-s) *nt* Cape Town

kaputt [ka'put] (*umg*) *adj* kaput, broken; (*Person*) exhausted, finished; **am Auto ist etwas ~** there's something wrong with the car; **~gehen** (*unreg*) *vi* to break; (*Schuhe*) to fall apart; (*Firma*) to go bust; (*Stoff*) to wear out; (*sterben*) to cop it (*umg*); **~machen** *vt* to break; (*Mensch*) to exhaust, to wear out

Kapuze [ka'puːtsə] *f* hood

Karaffe [ka'rafə] *f* carafe; (*geschliffen*) decanter

Karamel [kara'mɛl] (-s) *m* caramel; **~bonbon** *m* toffee

Karat [ka'raːt] (-(e)s, -e) *nt* carat

Karate [ka'raːtə] (-s) *nt* karate

Karawane [kara'vaːnə] *f* caravan

Kardinal [kardi'naːl] (-s, **Kardinäle**) *m* cardinal; **~zahl** *f* cardinal number

Karfreitag [kaːr'fraɪtaːk] *m* Good Friday

kärglich ['kɛrklɪç] *adj* poor, scanty

karibisch [ka'riːbɪʃ] *adj*: **K~e Inseln** Caribbean Islands

kariert [ka'riːrt] *adj* (*Stoff*) checked; (*Papier*) squared

Karies ['kaːries] (-) *f* caries

Karikatur [karika'tuːr] *f* caricature; **~ist** [-'rɪst] *m* cartoonist

Karneval ['karnəval] (-s, -e *od* -s) *m* carnival

Karo ['kaːro] (-s, -s) *nt* square; (*KARTEN*) diamonds; **~-As** *nt* ace of diamonds

Karosserie [karɔsə'riː] *f* (*AUT*) body(work)

Karotte [ka'rɔtə] *f* carrot

Karpaten [kar'paːtən] *pl* Carpathians

Karpfen ['karpfən] (-s, -) *m* carp

Karre ['karə] *f* cart, barrow

Karren (-s, -) *m* cart, barrow

Karriere [kari'ɛːrə] *f* career; **~ machen** to get on, to get to the top; **~macher** (-s, -) *m* careerist

Karte ['kartə] *f* card; (*Land~*) map; (*Speise~*) menu; (*Eintritts~, Fahr~*) ticket; **alles auf eine ~ setzen** to put all one's eggs in one basket

Kartei [kar'taɪ] *f* card index; **~karte** *f* index card

Kartell [kar'tɛl] (-s, -e) *nt* cartel

Kartenspiel *nt* card game; pack of cards

Kartoffel [kar'tɔfəl] (-, -n) *f* potato; **~brei** *m* mashed potatoes *pl*; **~mus** *nt* mashed potatoes *pl*; **~püree** *nt* mashed potatoes *pl*; **~salat** *m* potato salad

Karton [kar'tõː] (-s, -s) *m* cardboard; (*Schachtel*) cardboard box; **k~iert** [karto'niːrt] *adj* hardback

Karussell [karʊ'sɛl] (-s, -s) *nt* roundabout (*BRIT*), merry-go-round

Karwoche ['kaːrvɔxə] *f* Holy Week

Käse ['kɛːzə] (-s, -) *m* cheese; **~blatt** (*umg*) *nt* (local) rag; **~kuchen** *m* cheesecake

Kaserne [ka'zɛrnə] *f* barracks *pl*; **Kasernenhof** *m* parade ground

Kasino [ka'ziːno] (-s, -s) *nt* club; (*MIL*) officers' mess; (*Spiel~*) casino

kaspisch ['kaspɪʃ] *adj*: **K~es Meer** Caspian Sea

Kasse ['kasə] *f* (*Geldkasten*) cashbox; (*in Geschäft*) till, cash register; cash desk, checkout; (*Kino~, Theater~* etc) box office; ticket office; (*Kranken~*) health insurance; (*Spar~*) savings bank; **~ machen** to count the money; **getrennte ~ führen** to pay separately; **an der ~** (*in Geschäft*) at the desk; **gut bei ~ sein** to be in the money

Kassen- *zW*: **~arzt** *m* panel doctor (*BRIT*); **~bestand** *m* cash balance; **~patient** *m* panel patient (*BRIT*); **~prüfung** *f* audit; **~sturz** *m*: **~sturz machen** to check one's money; **~zettel** *m* receipt

Kassette [ka'sɛtə] *f* small box; (*Tonband, PHOT*) cassette; (*Bücher~*) case

Kassettenrecorder (-s, -) *m* cassette recorder

kassieren [ka'siːrən] *vt* to take ♦ *vi*: **darf ich ~?** would you like to pay now?

Kassierer [ka'siːrər] (-s, -) *m* cashier; (*von Klub*) treasurer

Kastanie [kas'taːniə] *f* chestnut; (*Baum*) chestnut tree

Kasten ['kastən] (-s, -) *m* (*auch SPORT*)

box; case; (*Truhe*) chest; ~**wagen** *m* van

kastrieren [kas'triːrən] *vt* to castrate

Katalog [kata'loːk] (-(e)s, -e) *m* catalogue

Katalysator [kataly'zaːtɔr] *m* catalyst

Katarrh [ka'tar] (-s, -e) *m* catarrh

katastrophal [katastro'faːl] *adj* catastrophic

Katastrophe [kata'stroːfə] *f* catastrophe, disaster

Kat-Auto ['kat'auto] *n* car fitted with a catalytic converter

Kategorie [katego'riː] *f* category

kategorisch [kate'goːrɪʃ] *adj* categorical

Kater ['kaːtər] (-s, -) *m* tomcat; (*umg*) hangover

kath. *abk* (= *katholisch*) Cath.

Kathedrale [kate'draːlə] *f* cathedral

Kathode [ka'toːdə] *f* cathode

Katholik [kato'liːk] (-en, -en) *m* Catholic

katholisch [ka'toːlɪʃ] *adj* Catholic

Kätzchen ['kɛtsçən] *nt* kitten

Katze ['katsə] *f* cat; **für die Katz** (*umg*) in vain, for nothing

Katzen- *zW*: ~**auge** *nt* cat's eye; (*Fahrrad*) rear light; ~**jammer** (*umg*) *m* hangover; ~**sprung** (*umg*) *m* stone's throw; short journey

Kauderwelsch ['kaudərvɛlʃ] (-(s)) *nt* jargon; (*umg*) double Dutch

kauen ['kauən] *vt, vi* to chew

Kauf [kauf] (-(e)s, **Käufe**) *m* purchase, buy; (*Kaufen*) buying; **ein guter ~** a bargain; **etw in ~ nehmen** to put up with sth; **k~en** *vt* to buy

Käufer(in) ['kɔyfər(ɪn)] (-s, -) *m(f)* buyer

Kaufhaus *nt* department store

Kaufkraft *f* purchasing power

käuflich ['kɔyflɪç] *adj* purchasable, for sale; (*pej*) venal ♦ *adv*: ~ **erwerben** to purchase

Kauf- *zW*: **k~lustig** *adj* interested in buying; ~**mann** (*pl* -**leute**) *m* businessman; shopkeeper; **k~männisch** *adj* commercial; **k~männischer Angestellter** office worker

Kaugummi ['kaugumi] *m* chewing gum

Kaulquappe ['kaulkvapə] *f* tadpole

kaum [kaum] *adv* hardly, scarcely

Kaution [kautsi'oːn] *f* deposit; (*JUR*) bail

Kauz [kauts] (-es, **Käuze**) *m* owl; (*fig*) queer fellow

Kavalier [kava'liːr] (-s, -e) *m* gentleman, cavalier; **Kavaliersdelikt** *nt* peccadillo

Kaviar ['kaːviar] *m* caviar

keck [kɛk] *adj* daring, bold; **K~heit** *f* daring, boldness

Kegel ['keːgəl] (-s, -) *m* skittle; (*MATH*) cone; ~**bahn** *f* skittle alley; bowling alley; **k~n** *vi* to play skittles

Kehle ['keːlə] *f* throat

Kehlkopf *m* larynx

Kehre ['keːrə] *f* turn(ing), bend; **k~n** *vt, vi* (*wenden*) to turn; (*mit Besen*) to sweep; **sich an etw** *dat* **nicht k~n** not to heed sth

Kehricht ['keːrɪçt] (-s) *m* sweepings *pl*

Kehrmaschine *f* sweeper

Kehrseite *f* reverse, other side; wrong side; bad side

kehrtmachen *vi* to turn about, to about-turn

keifen ['kaifən] *vi* to scold, to nag

Keil [kail] (-(e)s, -e) *m* wedge; (*MIL*) arrowhead; ~**riemen** *m* (*AUT*) fan belt

Keim [kaim] (-(e)s, -e) *m* bud; (*MED, fig*) germ; **k~en** *vi* to germinate; **k~frei** *adj* sterile; ~**zelle** *f* (*fig*) nucleus

kein [kain] *adj* no, not ... any; ~**e(r, s)** *pron* no one, nobody; none

keinesfalls *adv* on no account

keineswegs *adv* by no means

keinmal *adv* not once

Keks [keːks] (-es, -e) *m od nt* biscuit

Kelch [kɛlç] (-(e)s, -e) *m* cup, goblet, chalice

Kelle ['kɛlə] *f* (*Suppen~*) ladle; (*Maurer~*) trowel

Keller ['kɛlər] (-s, -) *m* cellar; ~**assel** (-, -n) *f* woodlouse

Kellner(in) ['kɛlnər(ɪn)] (-s, -) *m(f)* waiter(tress)

keltern ['kɛltərn] *vt* to press

kennen ['kɛnən] (*unreg*) *vt* to know; ~**lernen** *vt* to get to know; **sich ~lernen** to get to know each other; (*zum ersten mal*) to meet

Kenner (-s, -) *m* connoisseur

kenntlich *adj* distinguishable, discernible; etw ~ **machen** to mark sth

Kenntnis (-, -se) *f* knowledge *no pl*; etw zur ~ **nehmen** to note sth; **von etw** ~ **nehmen** to take notice of sth; **jdn in** ~ **setzen** to inform sb

Kenn- *zW*: ~**zeichen** *nt* mark, characteristic; **k~zeichnen** *vt insep* to characterize; ~**ziffer** *f* reference number

kentern ['kɛntərn] *vi* to capsize

Keramik [ke'ra:mɪk] (-, -en) *f* ceramics *pl*, pottery

Kerb- ['kɛrb] *zW*: ~**e** *f* notch, groove; **k~n** *vt* to notch; ~**holz** *nt*: **etw auf dem ~holz haben** to have done sth wrong

Kerker ['kɛrkər] (-s, -) *m* prison

Kerl [kɛrl] (-s, -e) *m* chap, bloke (*BRIT*), guy; **sie ist ein netter** ~ she's a good sort

Kern [kɛrn] (-(e)s, -e) *m* (*Obst~*) pip, stone; (*Nuß~*) kernel; (*Atom~*) nucleus; (*fig*) heart, core; ~**energie** *f* nuclear energy; ~**forschung** *f* nuclear research; ~**frage** *f* central issue; **k~gesund** *adj* thoroughly healthy, fit as a fiddle; **k~ig** *adj* (*kraftvoll*) robust; (*Ausspruch*) pithy; ~**kraftwerk** *nt* nuclear power station; **k~los** *adj* seedless, pipless; ~**physik** *f* nuclear physics *sg*; ~**reaktion** *f* nuclear reaction; ~**schmelze** *f* meltdown; ~**spaltung** *f* nuclear fission; ~**waffen** *pl* nuclear weapons

Kerze ['kɛrtsə] *f* candle; (*Zünd~*) plug; **kerzengerade** *adj* straight as a die; **Kerzenständer** *m* candle holder

keß [kɛs] *adj* saucy

Kessel ['kɛsəl] (-s, -) *m* kettle; (*von Lokomotive etc*) boiler; (*GEOG*) depression; (*MIL*) encirclement

Kette ['kɛtə] *f* chain; **k~n** *vt* to chain

Ketten- *zW*: ~**laden** *m* chain store; ~**rauchen** *nt* chain smoking; ~**reaktion** *f* chain reaction

Ketzer ['kɛtsər] (-s, -) *m* heretic

keuchen ['kɔyçən] *vi* to pant, to gasp

Keuchhusten *m* whooping cough

Keule ['kɔylə] *f* club; (*KOCH*) leg

keusch [kɔyʃ] *adj* chaste; **K~heit** *f* chastity

kfm. *abk* = **kaufmännisch**

Kfz [ka:'ɛf'tsɛt] *abk* = **Kraftfahrzeug**

KG [ka:'ge:] (-, -s) *f* *abk* (= *Kommanditgesellschaft*) limited partnership

kg *abk* = **Kilogramm**

kichern ['kɪçərn] *vi* to giggle

kidnappen ['kɪdnɛpən] *vt* to kidnap

Kiefer[1] ['ki:fər] (-s, -) *m* jaw

Kiefer[2] (-, -n) *f* pine; **Kiefernzapfen** *m* pine cone

Kiel [ki:l] (-(e)s, -e) *m* (*Feder~*) quill; (*NAUT*) keel

Kieme ['ki:mə] *f* gill

Kies [ki:s] (-es, -e) *m* gravel; ~**elstein** *m* pebble

Kilo ['ki:lo] *nt* kilo; ~**gramm** [kilo'gram] *nt* kilogram; ~**meter** [kilo'me:tər] *m* kilometre; ~**meterzähler** *m* ≈ milometer

Kind [kɪnt] (-(e)s, -er) *nt* child; **von** ~ **auf** from childhood

Kinder- ['kɪndər] *zW*: ~**ei** *f* childishness; ~**garten** *m* nursery school, playgroup; ~**geld** *nt* child benefit (*BRIT*); ~**lähmung** *f* poliomyelitis; **k~leicht** *adj* childishly easy; **k~los** *adj* childless; ~**mädchen** *nt* nursemaid; **k~reich** *adj* with a lot of children; ~**spiel** *nt* (*fig*) child's play; ~**tagesstätte** *f* daynursery; ~**wagen** *m* pram, baby carriage (*US*)

Kind- *zW*: ~**heit** *f* childhood; **k~isch** *adj* childish; **k~lich** *adj* childlike

Kinn [kɪn] (-(e)s, -e) *nt* chin; ~**haken** *m* (*BOXEN*) uppercut; ~**lade** *f* jaw

Kino ['ki:no] (-s, -s) *nt* cinema; ~**besucher** *m* cinema-goer; ~**programm** *nt* film programme

Kiosk ['ki:ɔsk] (-(e)s, -e) *m* kiosk

Kippe ['kɪpə] *f* cigarette end; (*umg*) fag; **auf der** ~ **stehen** (*fig*) to be touch and go

kippen *vi* to topple over, to overturn ♦ *vt* to tilt

Kirch- ['kɪrç] *zW*: ~**e** *f* church; ~**enlied** *nt* hymn; ~**gänger** (-s, -) *m* churchgoer; ~**hof** *m* churchyard; **k~lich** *adj* ecclesiastical; ~**turm** *m* church tower,

steeple
Kirmes ['kɪrmɛs] (-, -sen) f fair
Kirsche ['kɪrʃə] f cherry
Kissen ['kɪsən] (-s, -) nt cushion; (Kopf~) pillow; ~**bezug** m pillowslip
Kiste ['kɪstə] f box; chest
Kitsch [kɪtʃ] (-(e)s) m kitsch; **k~ig** adj kitschy
Kitt [kɪt] (-(e)s, -e) m putty; ~**el** (-s, -) m overall, smock; **k~en** vt to putty; (fig: Ehe etc) to cement
Kitz [kɪts] (-es, -e) nt kid; (Reh~) fawn
kitzelig ['kɪtsəlɪç] adj (auch fig) ticklish
kitzeln vi to tickle
KKW [ka:ka:'ve:] nt abk = **Kernkraftwerk**
kläffen ['klɛfən] vi to yelp
Klage ['kla:gə] f complaint; (JUR) action; **k~n** vi (wehklagen) to lament, to wail; (sich beschweren) to complain; (JUR) to take legal action
Kläger(in) ['klɛ:gər(ɪn)] (-s, -) m(f) plaintiff
kläglich ['klɛ:klɪç] adj wretched
klamm [klam] adj (Finger) numb; (feucht) damp
Klammer ['klamər] (-, -n) f clamp; (in Text) bracket; (Büro~) clip; (Wäsche~) peg; (Zahn~) brace; **k~n** vr: **sich k~n an** +akk to cling to
Klang [klaŋ] (-(e)s, ¨e) m sound; **k~voll** adj sonorous
Klappe ['klapə] f valve; (Ofen~) damper; (umg: Mund) trap; **k~n** vi (Geräusch) to click; (Sitz etc) to tip ♦ vt (Sitz etc) to tip ♦ vb unpers to work; **Klappentext** m blurb
Klapper ['klapər] (-, -n) f rattle; **k~ig** adj run-down, worn-out; **k~n** vi to clatter, to rattle; ~**schlange** f rattlesnake; ~**storch** m stork
Klapp- zW: ~**messer** nt jack-knife; ~**rad** nt collapsible bicycle; ~**stuhl** m folding chair; ~**tisch** m folding table
klar [kla:r] adj clear; (NAUT) ready for sea; (MIL) ready for action; **sich** dat **im ~en sein über** +akk to be clear about; **ins ~e kommen** to get clear; **(na) ~!** of course!
Kläranlage f purification plant

klären ['klɛ:rən] vt (Flüssigkeit) to purify; (Probleme) to clarify ♦ vr to clear (itself) up
Klarheit f clarity
Klarinette [klari'nɛtə] f clarinet
klar- zW: ~**legen** vt to clear up, to explain; ~**machen** vt (Schiff) to get ready for sea; **jdm etw ~machen** to make sth clear to sb; ~**sehen** (unreg) vi to see clearly; **K~sichtfolie** f transparent film; ~**stellen** vt to clarify
Klärung ['klɛ:rʊŋ] f (von Flüssigkeit) purification; (von Probleme) clarification
Klasse ['klasə] f class; (SCH) class, form; **k~** (umg) adj smashing
Klassen- zW: ~**arbeit** f test; ~**bewußtsein** nt class consciousness; ~**gesellschaft** f class society; ~**kampf** m class conflict; ~**lehrer** m form master; **k~los** adj classless; ~**sprecher(in)** m(f) form prefect; ~**zimmer** nt classroom
klassifizieren [klasifi'tsi:rən] vt to classify
Klassik ['klasɪk] f (Zeit) classical period; (Stil) classicism; ~**er** (-s, -) m classic
klassisch adj (auch fig) classical
Klatsch [klatʃ] (-(e)s, -e) m smack, crack; (Gerede) gossip; ~**base** f gossip, scandalmonger; ~**e** (umg) f crib; **k~en** vi (Geräusch) to clash; (reden) to gossip; (applaudieren) to applaud, to clap ♦ vt: **jdm Beifall k~en** to applaud sb; ~**mohn** m (corn) poppy; **k~naß** adj soaking wet
Klaue ['klauə] f claw; (umg: Schrift) scrawl; **k~n** (umg) vt to pinch
Klausel ['klauzəl] (-, -n) f clause
Klausur [klau'zu:r] f seclusion; ~**arbeit** f examination paper
Klaviatur [klavia'tu:r] f keyboard
Klavier [kla'vi:r] (-s, -e) nt piano
Kleb- ['kle:b] zW: **k~en** vt, vi: **k~en (an** +akk) to stick (to); **k~rig** adj sticky; ~**stoff** m glue; ~**streifen** m adhesive tape
Klecks [klɛks] (-es, -e) m blot, stain; **k~en** vi to blot; (pej) to daub

Klee [kle:] (-s) *m* clover; ~**blatt** *nt* cloverleaf; (*fig*) trio

Kleid [klaɪt] (-(e)s, -er) *nt* garment; (*Frauen~*) dress; ~**er** *pl* (*Kleidung*) clothes; **k~en** ['klaɪdən] *vt* to clothe, to dress; to suit ♦ *vr* to dress

Kleider- ['klaɪdər] *zW*: ~**bügel** *m* coat hanger; ~**bürste** *f* clothes brush; ~**schrank** *m* wardrobe

Kleid- *zW*: **k~sam** *adj* flattering; ~**ung** *f* clothing; ~**ungsstück** *nt* garment

Kleie ['klaɪə] *f* bran

klein [klaɪn] *adj* little, small; **K~asien** *nt* Asia Minor; **K~e(r, s)** *mf* little one; **K~format** *nt* small size; **im K~format** small-scale; **K~geld** *nt* small change; ~**hacken** *vt* to chop up, to mince; **K~igkeit** *f* trifle; **K~kind** *nt* infant; **K~kram** *m* details *pl*; ~**laut** *adj* dejected, quiet; ~**lich** *adj* petty, paltry; **K~od** ['klaɪno:t] (-s, -odien) *nt* gem, jewel; treasure; ~**schneiden** (*unreg*) *vt* to chop up; ~**städtisch** *adj* provincial; **kleinstmöglich** *adj* smallest possible

Kleister ['klaɪstər] (-s, -) *m* paste; **k~n** *vt* to paste

Klemme ['klɛmə] *f* clip; (*MED*) clamp; (*fig*) jam; **k~n** *vt* (*festhalten*) to jam; (*quetschen*) to pinch, to nip ♦ *vr* to catch o.s.; (*sich hineinzwängen*) to squeeze o.s. ♦ *vi* (*Tür*) to stick, to jam; **sich hinter jdn/etw k~n** to get on to sb/ down to sth

Klempner ['klɛmpnər] (-s, -) *m* plumber

Kleptomanie [klɛptoma'ni:] *f* kleptomania

Klerus ['kle:rʊs] (-) *m* clergy

Klette ['klɛtə] *f* burr

Kletter- ['klɛtər] *zW*: ~**er** (-s, -) *m* climber; **k~n** *vi* to climb; ~**pflanze** *f* creeper

Klient(in) [kli'ɛnt(ɪn)] *m(f)* client

Klima ['kli:ma, *pl* kli'ma:tə] (-s, -s *od* -te) *nt* climate; ~**anlage** *f* air conditioning; ~**wechsel** *m* change of air

Klinge ['klɪŋə] *f* blade; sword

Klingel ['klɪŋəl] (-, -n) *f* bell; ~**beutel** *m* collection bag; **k~n** *vi* to ring

klingen ['klɪŋən] (*unreg*) *vi* to sound; (*Gläser*) to clink

Klinik ['kli:nɪk] *f* hospital, clinic

Klinke ['klɪŋkə] *f* handle

Klippe ['klɪpə] *f* cliff; (*im Meer*) reef; (*fig*) hurdle

klipp und klar ['klɪp'ʊntkla:r] *adj* clear and concise

Klips [klɪps] (-es, -e) *m* clip; (*Ohr~*) earring

klirren ['klɪrən] *vi* to clank, to jangle; (*Gläser*) to clink; ~**de Kälte** biting cold

Klischee [kli'ʃe:] (-s, -s) *nt* (*Druckplatte*) plate, block; (*fig*) cliché; ~**vorstellung** *f* stereotyped idea

Klo [klo:] (-s, -s; *umg*) *nt* loo (*BRIT*), john (*US*)

Kloake [klo'a:kə] *f* sewer

klobig ['klo:bɪç] *adj* clumsy

klopfen ['klɔpfən] *vi* to knock; (*Herz*) to thump ♦ *vt* to beat; **es klopft** somebody's knocking; **jdm auf die Schulter ~** to tap sb on the shoulder

Klopfer (-s, -) *m* (*Teppich~*) beater; (*Tür~*) knocker

Klops [klɔps] (-es, -e) *m* meatball

Klosett [klo'zɛt] (-s, -e *od* -s) *nt* lavatory, toilet; ~**papier** *nt* toilet paper

Kloß [klo:s] (-es, ⁼e) *m* (*im Hals*) lump; (*KOCH*) dumpling

Kloster ['klo:stər] (-s, ⁼) *nt* (*Männer~*) monastery; (*Frauen~*) convent

klösterlich ['klø:stərlɪç] *adj* monastic; convent *cpd*

Klotz [klɔts] (-es, ⁼e) *m* log; (*Hack~*) block; **ein ~ am Bein** (*fig*) a drag, a millstone round (sb's) neck

Klub [klʊp] (-s, -s) *m* club; ~**sessel** *m* easy chair

Kluft [klʊft] (-, ⁼e) *f* cleft, gap; (*GEOL*) gorge, chasm

klug [klu:k] *adj* clever, intelligent; **K~heit** *f* cleverness, intelligence

Klumpen ['klʊmpən] (-s, -) *m* (*Erd~*) clod; (*Blut~*) clot; (*Gold~*) nugget; (*KOCH*) lump; **k~** *vi* to go lumpy; to clot

km *abk* = **Kilometer**

km/h *abk* (= *Kilometer je Stunde*) kph, ≈ mph

knabbern ['knabərn] *vt, vi* to nibble

Knabe ['kna:bə] (-n, -n) *m* boy; **knaben-**

haft *adj* boyish
Knäckebrot ['knɛkəbroːt] *nt* crispbread
knacken ['knakən] *vt, vi (auch fig)* to crack
Knall [knal] (-(e)s, -e) *m* bang; *(Peitschen~)* crack; ~ **und Fall** *(umg)* unexpectedly; ~**bonbon** *nl* cracker; **k~en** *vi* to bang; to crack; **k~rot** *adj* bright red
knapp [knap] *adj* tight; *(Geld)* scarce; *(Sprache)* concise; **eine ~e Stunde** just under an hour; ~ **unter/neben** just under/by; ~**halten** *(unreg) vt*: **jdn (mit etw)** ~**halten** to keep sb short (of sth); **K~heit** *f* tightness; scarcity; conciseness
knarren ['knarən] *vi* to creak
knattern ['knatərn] *vi* to rattle; *(Maschinengewehr)* to chatter
Knäuel ['knɔʏəl] (-s, -) *m od nt (Woll~)* ball; *(Menschen~)* knot
Knauf [knaʊf] (-(e)s, **Knäufe**) *m* knob; *(Schwert~)* pommel
knautschen ['knaʊtʃən] *vt, vi* to crumple
Knebel ['kneːbəl] (-s, -) *m* gag; **k~n** *vt* to gag; *(NAUT)* to fasten
kneifen ['knaɪfən] *(unreg) vt* to pinch ♦ *vi* to pinch; *(sich drücken)* to back out; **vor etw** ~ to dodge sth
Kneipe ['knaɪpə] *(umg) f* pub
kneten ['kneːtən] *vt* to knead; *(Wachs)* to mould
Knick [knɪk] (-(e)s, -e) *m (Sprung)* crack; *(Kurve)* bend; *(Falte)* fold; **k~en** *vt, vi (springen)* to crack; *(brechen)* to break; *(Papier)* to fold; **geknickt sein** to be downcast
Knicks [knɪks] (-es, -e) *m* curtsey; **k~en** *vi* to curtsey
Knie [kniː] (-s, -) *nt* knee; ~**beuge** *f* knee bend; ~**fall** *m* genuflection; ~**gelenk** *nt* knee joint; ~**kehle** *f* back of the knee; **k~n** *vi* to kneel; ~**scheibe** *f* kneecap; ~**strumpf** *m* knee-length sock
Kniff [knɪf] (-(e)s, -e) *m (fig)* trick, knack; **k~elig** *adj* tricky
knipsen ['knɪpsən] *vt (Fahrkarte)* to punch; *(PHOT)* to take a snap of, to

snap ♦ *vi (PHOT)* to take a snap *od* snaps
Knirps [knɪrps] (-es, -e) *m* little chap; *(®: Schirm)* telescopic umbrella
knirschen ['knɪrʃən] *vi* to crunch; **mit den Zähnen** ~ to grind one's teeth
knistern ['knɪstərn] *vi* to crackle
Knitter- ['knɪtər] *zW.-* **falte** *f* crease; **k~frei** *adj* non-crease; **k~n** *vi* to crease
Knoblauch ['knoːplaʊx] (-(e)s) *m* garlic
Knöchel ['knœçəl] (-s, -) *m* knuckle; *(Fuß~)* ankle
Knochen ['knɔxən] (-s, -) *m* bone; ~**bau** *m* bone structure; ~**bruch** *m* fracture; ~**gerüst** *nt* skeleton
knöchern [knœçərn] *adj* bone
knochig ['knɔxɪç] *adj* bony
Knödel ['knøːdəl] (-s, -) *m* dumpling
Knolle ['knɔlə] *f* tuber
Knopf [knɔpf] (-(e)s, ᵋe) *m* button; *(Kragen~)* stud
knöpfen ['knœpfən] *vt* to button
Knopfloch *nt* buttonhole
Knorpel ['knɔrpəl] (-s, -) *m* cartilage, gristle; **k~ig** *adj* gristly
Knospe ['knɔspə] *f* bud
Knoten ['knoːtən] (-s, -) *m* knot; *(BOT)* node; *(MED)* lump; **k~** *vt* to knot; ~**punkt** *m* junction
Knüller ['knʏlər] (-s, -; *umg*) *m* hit; *(Reportage)* scoop
knüpfen ['knʏpfən] *vt* to tie; *(Teppich)* to knot; *(Freundschaft)* to form
Knüppel ['knʏpəl] (-s, -) *m* cudgel; *(Polizei~)* baton, truncheon; *(AVIAT)* (joy)stick; ~**schaltung** *f (AUT)* floor-mounted gear change
knurren ['knʊrən] *vi (Hund)* to snarl; to growl; *(Magen)* to rumble; *(Mensch)* to mutter
knusperig ['knʊspərɪç] *adj* crisp; *(Keks)* crunchy
k.o. [kaːˈoː] *adj* knocked out; *(fig)* done in
Koalition [koalitsiˈoːn] *f* coalition
Kobalt ['koːbalt] (-s) *nt* cobalt
Kobold ['koːbɔlt] (-(e)s, -e) *m* goblin, imp
Kobra ['koːbra] (-, -s) *f* cobra
Koch [kɔx] (-(e)s, ᵋe) *m* cook; ~**buch** *nt*

cook(ery) book; **k~en** vt, vi to cook; (Wasser) to boil; **~er** (-s, -) m stove, cooker

Köcher ['kœçər] (-s, -) m quiver

Kochgelegenheit ['kɔxgəle:gənhaɪt] f cooking facilities pl

Köchin ['kœçɪn] f cook

Koch- zW: **~löffel** m kitchen spoon; **~nische** f kitchenette; **~platte** f hotplate; **~salz** nt cooking salt; **~topf** m saucepan, pot

Köder ['kø:dər] (-s, -) m bait, lure

Koexistenz [koeksɪs'tɛnts] f coexistence

Koffein [kɔfe'i:n] (-s) nt caffeine; **k~frei** adj decaffeinated

Koffer ['kɔfər] (-s, -) m suitcase; (Schrank~) trunk; **~radio** nt portable radio; **~raum** m (AUT) boot (BRIT), trunk (US)

Kognak ['kɔnjak] (-s, -s) m brandy, cognac

Kohl [ko:l] (-(e)s, -e) m cabbage

Kohle ['ko:lə] f coal; (Holz~) charcoal; (CHEM) carbon; **~hydrat** (-(e)s, -e) nt carbohydrate

Kohlen- zW: **~dioxyd** (-(e)s, -e) nt carbon dioxide; **~händler** m coal merchant, coalman; **~säure** f carbon dioxide; **~stoff** m carbon

Kohlepapier nt carbon paper

Kohlrübe f turnip

Koje ['ko:jə] f cabin; (Bett) bunk

Kokain [koka'i:n] (-s) nt cocaine

kokett [ko'kɛt] adj coquettish, flirtatious

Kokosnuß ['ko:kɔsnʊs] f coconut

Koks [ko:ks] (-es, -e) m coke

Kolben ['kɔlbən] (-s, -) m (Gewehr~) rifle butt; (Keule) club; (CHEM) flask; (TECH) piston; (Mais~) cob

Kolchose [kɔl'ço:zə] f collective farm

Kolik ['ko:lɪk] f colic, the gripes pl

Kollaps [kɔ'laps] (-es, -e) m collapse

Kolleg [kɔl'e:k] (-s, -s od -ien) nt lecture course; **~e** [kɔ'le:gə] (-n, -n) m colleague; **~in** f colleague; **~ium** nt working party; (SCH) staff

Kollekte [kɔ'lɛktə] f (REL) collection

kollektiv [kɔlɛk'ti:f] adj collective

Kollision [kɔlizi'o:n] f collision; (zeitlich) clash

Köln [kœln] (-s) nt Cologne

Kolonie [kolo'ni:] f colony

kolonisieren [koloni'zi:rən] vt to colonize

Kolonne [ko'lɔnə] f column; (von Fahrzeugen) convoy

Koloß [ko'lɔs] (-sses, -sse) m colossus

kolossal [kolɔ'sa:l] adj colossal

Kombi- ['kɔmbi] zW: **~nation** [-natsi'o:n] f combination; (Vermutung) conjecture; (Hemdhose) combinations pl; **~nationsschloß** nt combination lock; **k~nieren** [-'ni:rən] vt to combine ♦ vi to deduce, to work out; (vermuten) to guess; **~wagen** m station wagon; **~zange** f (pair of) pliers pl

Komet [ko'me:t] (-en, -en) m comet

Komfort [kɔm'fo:r] (-s) m luxury

Komik ['ko:mɪk] f humour, comedy; **~er** (-s, -) m comedian

komisch ['ko:mɪʃ] adj funny

Komitee [komi'te:] (-s, -s) nt committee

Komma ['kɔma] (-s, -s od -ta) nt comma; 2 ~ 3 2 point 3

Kommand- [kɔ'mand] zW: **~ant** [-'dant] m commander, commanding officer; **~eur** [-'dø:r] m commanding officer; **k~ieren** [-'di:rən] vt, vi to command; **~o** (-s, -s) nt command, order; (Truppe) detachment, squad; **auf ~o** to order

kommen ['kɔmən] (unreg) vi to come; (näher~) to approach; (passieren) to happen; (gelangen, geraten) to get; (Blumen, Zähne, Tränen etc) to appear; (in die Schule, das Zuchthaus etc) to go; ~ **lassen** to send for; **das kommt in den Schrank** that goes in the cupboard; **zu sich ~** to come round od to; **zu etw ~** to acquire sth; **um etw ~** to lose sth; **nichts auf jdn/etw ~ lassen** to have nothing said against sb/sth; **jdm frech ~** to get cheeky with sb; **auf jeden vierten kommt ein Platz** there's one place for every fourth person; **wer kommt zuerst?** who's first?; **unter ein Auto ~** to be run over by a car; **wie hoch kommt das?** what does that cost?; **komm gut nach Hause!** safe journey (home); **~den Sonntag** next Sunday;

K~ (-s) *nt* coming
Kommentar [kɔmɛn'taːr] *m* commentary; **kein ~** no comment; **k~los** *adj* without comment
Kommentator [kɔmɛn'taːtɔr] *m* (*TV*) commentator
kommentieren [kɔmɛn'tiːrən] *vt* to comment on
kommerziell [kɔmɛrtsi'ɛl] *adj* commercial
Kommilitone [kɔmili'toːnə] (-n, -n) *m* fellow student
Kommissar [kɔmɪ'saːr] *m* police inspector
Kommission [kɔmɪsɪ'oːn] *f* (*COMM*) commission; (*Ausschuß*) committee
Kommode [kɔ'moːdə] *f* (chest of) drawers
Kommunalsteuer [kɔmu'naːlʃtɔyər] *f* rates *pl*; community charge (*BRIT*)
Kommune [kɔ'muːnə] *f* commune
Kommunikation [kɔmunɪkatsɪ'oːn] *f* communication
Kommunion [kɔmuni'oːn] *f* communion
Kommuniqué [kɔmyni'keː] (-s, -s) *nt* communiqué
Kommunismus [kɔmu'nɪsmʊs] *m* communism
Kommunist(in) [kɔmu'nɪst(ɪn)] *m(f)* communist; **k~isch** *adj* communist
kommunizieren [kɔmuni'tsiːrən] *vi* to communicate; (*REL*) to receive Communion
Komödie [ko'møːdiə] *f* comedy
Kompagnon [kɔmpan'jõː] (-s, -s) *m* (*COMM*) partner
kompakt [kɔm'pakt] *adj* compact
Kompanie [kɔmpa'niː] *f* company
Kompaß ['kɔmpas] (-sses, -sse) *m* compass
kompatibel [kɔmpa'tiːbəl] *adj* compatible
kompetent [kɔmpe'tɛnt] *adj* competent
Kompetenz *f* competence, authority
komplett [kɔm'plɛt] *adj* complete
Komplikation [kɔmplikatsɪ'oːn] *f* complication
Kompliment [kɔmpli'mɛnt] *nt* compliment
Komplize [kɔm'pliːtsə] (-n, -n) *m* accomplice
kompliziert [kɔmpli'tsiːrt] *adj* complicated
komponieren [kɔmpo'niːrən] *vt* to compose
Komponist [kɔmpo'nɪst] *m* composer
Komposition [kɔmpozitsɪ'oːn] *f* composition
Kompost [kɔm'pɔst] (-(e)s, -e) *m* compost
Kompott [kɔm'pɔt] (-(e)s, -e) *nt* stewed fruit
Kompromiß [kɔmpro'mɪs] (-sses, -sse) *m* compromise; **k~bereit** *adj* willing to compromise; **~lösung** *f* compromise solution
Kondens- [kɔn'dɛns] *zW*: **~ation** [kɔndɛnzatsɪ'oːn] *f* condensation; **~ator** [kɔndɛn'zaːtɔr] *m* condenser; **k~ieren** [kɔndɛn'ziːrən] *vt* to condense; **~milch** *f* condensed milk
Konditionstraining [kɔnditsɪ'oːnstrɛːnɪŋ] *nt* fitness training
Konditor [kɔn'diːtɔr] *m* pastrycook; **~ei** [kɔndito'raɪ] *f* café; cake shop
Kondom [kɔn'doːm] (-s, -e) *nt* condom
Konferenz [kɔnfe'rɛnts] *f* conference, meeting
Konfession [kɔnfesɪ'oːn] *f* (religious) denomination; **k~ell** [-'nɛl] *adj* denominational; **konfessionslos** *adj* non-denominational
Konfetti [kɔn'fɛti] (-(s)) *nt* confetti
Konfirmand [kɔnfɪr'mant] *m* candidate for confirmation
Konfirmation [kɔnfɪrmatsɪ'oːn] *f* (*REL*) confirmation
konfirmieren [kɔnfɪr'miːrən] *vt* to confirm
konfiszieren [kɔnfɪs'tsiːrən] *vt* to confiscate
Konfitüre [kɔnfi'tyːrə] *f* jam
Konflikt [kɔn'flɪkt] (-(e)s, -e) *m* conflict
konfrontieren [kɔnfrɔn'tiːrən] *vt* to confront
konfus [kɔn'fuːs] *adj* confused
Kongreß [kɔn'grɛs] (-sses, -sse) *m* congress
Kongruenz [kɔngru'ɛnts] *f* agreement, congruence

König ['kø:nɪç] (-(e)s, -e) *m* king; ~**in** ['kø:nɪgɪn] *f* queen; **k~lich** *adj* royal; ~**reich** *nt* kingdom; ~**tum** (-(e)s) *nt* kingship

Konjugation [kɔnjugatsi'o:n] *f* conjugation

konjugieren [kɔnju'gi:rən] *vt* to conjugate

Konjunktion [kɔnjʊŋktsi'o:n] *f* conjunction

Konjunktiv ['kɔnjʊŋkti:f] (-s, -e) *m* subjunctive

Konjunktur [kɔnjʊŋk'tu:r] *f* economic situation; (*Hoch~*) boom

konkav [kɔn'ka:f] *adj* concave

konkret [kɔn'kre:t] *adj* concrete

Konkurrent(in) [kɔnkʊ'rɛnt(ɪn)] *m(f)* competitor

Konkurrenz [kɔnkʊ'rɛnts] *f* competition; **k~fähig** *adj* competitive; ~**kampf** *m* competition; rivalry, competitive situation

konkurrieren [kɔnkʊ'ri:rən] *vi* to compete

Konkurs [kɔn'kʊrs] (-es, -e) *m* bankruptcy

SCHLÜSSELWORT

---

können ['kœnən] (*pt* **konnte**, *pp* **gekonnt** *od* (*als Hilfsverb*) **können**) *vt, vi* **1** to be able to; **ich kann es machen** I can do it, I am able to do it; **ich kann es nicht machen** I can't do it, I'm not able to do it; **ich kann nicht ...** I can't ..., I cannot ...; **ich kann nicht mehr** I can't go on

2 (*wissen, beherrschen*) to know; **können Sie Deutsch?** can you speak German?; **er kann gut Englisch** he speaks English well; **sie kann keine Mathematik** she can't do mathematics

3 (*dürfen*) to be allowed to; **kann ich gehen?** can I go?; **könnte ich ...?** could I ...?; **kann ich mit?** (*umg*) can I come with you?

4 (*möglich sein*): **Sie könnten recht haben** you may be right; **das kann sein** that's possible; **kann sein** maybe

---

Können (-s) *nt* ability

konnte *etc* ['kɔntə] *vb siehe* **können**

konsequent [kɔnze'kvɛnt] *adj* consistent

Konsequenz [kɔnze'kvɛnts] *f* consistency; (*Folgerung*) conclusion

Konserv- [kɔn'zɛrv] *zW*: **k~ativ** [-a'ti:f] *adj* conservative; ~**ative(r)** [-a'ti:və(r)] *mf* (*POL*) conservative; ~**e** *f* tinned food; ~**enbüchse** *f* tin, can; **k~ieren** [-'vi:rən] *vt* to preserve; ~**ierung** *f* preservation; ~**ierungsmittel** *nt* preservative

Konsonant [kɔnzo'nant] *m* consonant

konstant [kɔn'stant] *adj* constant

konstruieren [kɔnstru'i:rən] *vt* to construct

Konstrukteur [kɔnstrʊk'tø:r] *m* designer

Konstruktion [kɔnstrʊktsi'o:n] *f* construction

konstruktiv [kɔnstrʊk'ti:f] *adj* constructive

Konsul ['kɔnzʊl] (-s, -n) *m* consul; ~**at** [-'la:t] *nt* consulate

konsultieren [kɔnzʊl'ti:rən] *vt* to consult

Konsum [kɔn'zu:m] (-s) *m* consumption; ~**artikel** *m* consumer article; ~**ent** [-'mɛnt] *m* consumer; **k~ieren** [-'mi:rən] *vt* to consume

Kontakt [kɔn'takt] (-(e)s, -e) *m* contact; **k~arm** *adj* unsociable; **k~freudig** *adj* sociable; ~**linsen** *pl* contact lenses

kontern ['kɔntərn] *vt, vi* to counter

Kontinent ['kɔntinɛnt] *m* continent

Kontingent [kɔntɪŋ'gɛnt] (-(e)s, -e) *nt* quota; (*Truppen~*) contingent

kontinuierlich [kɔntinu'i:rlɪç] *adj* continuous

Konto ['kɔnto] (-s, **Konten**) *nt* account; ~**auszug** *m* statement (of account); ~**inhaber(in)** *m(f)* account holder; ~**stand** *m* balance

Kontra ['kɔntra] (-s, -s) *nt* (*KARTEN*) double; **jdm** ~ **geben** (*fig*) to contradict sb; ~**baß** *m* double bass; ~**hent** [-'hɛnt] *m* (*COMM*) contracting party; ~**punkt** *m* counterpoint

Kontrast [kɔn'trast] (-(e)s, -e) *m* contrast

Kontroll- [kɔn'trɔl] *zW*: ~**e** *f* control, supervision; (*Paß~*) passport control; ~**eur** [-'lø:r] *m* inspector; **k~ieren** [-'li:rən] *vt* to control, to supervise;

(*nachprüfen*) to check

Kontur [kɔn'tuːr] *f* contour

Konvention [kɔnvɛntsi'oːn] *f* convention; **k~ell** [-'nɛl] *adj* conventional

Konversation [kɔnvɛrzatsi'oːn] *f* conversation; **Konversationslexikon** *nt* encyclopaedia

konvex [kɔn'vɛks] *adj* convex

Konvoi ['kɔnvɔy] (-s, -s) *m* convoy

Konzentration [kɔntsɛntratsi'oːn] *f* concentration

konzentrieren [kɔntsɛn'triːrən] *vt, vr* to concentrate

konzentriert *adj* concentrated ♦ *adv* (*zuhören, arbeiten*) intently

Konzept [kɔn'tsɛpt] (-(e)s, -e) *nt* rough draft; **jdn aus dem ~ bringen** to confuse sb

Konzern [kɔn'tsɛrn] (-s, -e) *m* combine

Konzert [kɔn'tsɛrt] (-(e)s, -e) *nt* concert; (*Stück*) concerto; **~saal** *m* concert hall

Konzession [kɔntsesi'oːn] *f* licence; (*Zugeständnis*) concession

Konzil [kɔn'tsiːl] (-s, -e *od* -ien) *nt* council

kooperativ [koʼopera'tiːf] *adj* cooperative

koordinieren [koʼɔrdiʼniːrən] *vt* to coordinate

Kopf [kɔpf] (-(e)s, ̈e) *m* head; **~bedeckung** *f* headgear; **~haut** *f* scalp; **~hörer** *m* headphones *pl*; **~kissen** *nt* pillow; **k~los** *adj* panicstricken; **k~rechnen** *vi* to do mental arithmetic; **~salat** *m* lettuce; **~schmerzen** *pl* headache *sg*; **~sprung** *m* header, dive; **~tuch** *nt* headscarf; **~weh** *nt* headache; **~zerbrechen** *nt*: **jdm ~zerbrechen machen** to be a headache for sb

Kopie [koʼpiː] *f* copy; **k~ren** *vt* to copy

Koppel¹ ['kɔpəl] (-, -n) *f* (*Weide*) enclosure

Koppel² (-s, -) *nt* (*Gürtel*) belt

koppeln *vt* to couple

Koppelung *f* coupling

Koralle [koʼralə] *f* coral; **Korallenriff** *nt* coral reef

Korb [kɔrp] (-(e)s, ̈e) *m* basket; **jdm einen ~ geben** (*fig*) to turn sb down;

~ball *m* basketball; **~stuhl** *m* wicker chair

Kord [kɔrt] (-(e)s, -e) *m* corduroy

Kordel ['kɔrdəl] (-, -n) *f* cord, string

Kork [kɔrk] (-(e)s, -e) *m* cork; **~en** (-s, -) *m* stopper, cork; **~enzieher** (-s, -) *m* corkscrew

Korn [kɔrn] (-(e)s, ̈er) *nt* corn, grain; (*Gewehr*) sight; **~blume** *f* cornflower

Körper ['kœrpər] (-s, -) *m* body; **~bau** *m* build; **k~behindert** *adj* disabled; **~gewicht** *nt* weight; **~größe** *f* height; **k~lich** *adj* physical; **~pflege** *f* personal hygiene; **~schaft** *f* corporation; **~schaftssteuer** *f* corporation tax; **~teil** *m* part of the body

korpulent [kɔrpuʼlɛnt] *adj* corpulent

korrekt [kɔ'rɛkt] *adj* correct; **K~or** *m* proofreader; **K~ur** [-'tuːr] *f* (*eines Textes*) proofreading; (*Text*) proof; (*SCH*) marking, correction

Korrespond- [kɔrespɔnd] *zW*: **~ent(in)** [-'dɛnt(ın)] *m(f)* correspondent; **~enz** [-'dɛnts] *f* correspondence; **k~ieren** [-'diːrən] *vi* to correspond

Korridor ['kɔridɔːr] (-s, -e) *m* corridor

korrigieren [kɔriʼgiːrən] *vt* to correct

Korruption [kɔruptsi'oːn] *f* corruption

Korsett [kɔr'zɛt] (-(e)s, -e) *nt* corset

Kose- ['koːzə] *zW*: **~form** *f* pet form; **~name** *m* pet name; **~wort** *nt* term of endearment

Kosmetik [kɔs'meːtık] *f* cosmetics *pl*; **~erin** *f* beautician

kosmetisch *adj* cosmetic; (*Chirurgie*) plastic

kosmisch ['kɔsmıʃ] *adj* cosmic

Kosmo- [kɔsmo] *zW*: **~naut** [-'naut] (-en, -en) *m* cosmonaut; **~polit** [-po'liːt] (-en, -en) *m* cosmopolitan; **k~politisch** [-po'liːtıʃ] *adj* cosmopolitan; **Kosmos** ['kɔsmɔs] (-) *m* cosmos

Kost [kɔst] (-) *f* (*Nahrung*) food; (*Verpflegung*) board; **k~bar** *adj* precious; (*teuer*) costly, expensive; **~barkeit** *f* preciousness; costliness, expensiveness; (*Wertstück*) valuable

Kosten *pl* cost(s); (*Ausgaben*) expenses; **auf ~ von** at the expense of; **k~** *vt* to cost; (*versuchen*) to taste ♦ *vi*

to taste; **was kostet ...?** what does ... cost?, how much is ...?; **~anschlag** *m* estimate; **k~los** *adj* free (of charge)
köstlich ['kœstlɪç] *adj* precious; *(Einfall)* delightful; *(Essen)* delicious; **sich ~ amüsieren** to have a marvellous time
Kostprobe *f* taste; *(fig)* sample
kostspielig *adj* expensive
Kostüm [kɔs'tyːm] (**-s, -e**) *nt* costume; *(Damen~)* suit; **~fest** *nt* fancy-dress party; **k~ieren** [kɔsty'miːrən] *vt, vr* to dress up; **~verleih** *m* costume agency
Kot [koːt] (**-(e)s**) *m* excrement
Kotelett [kɔtə'lɛt] (**-(e)s, -e** *od* **-s**) *nt* cutlet, chop; **~en** *pl* *(Bart)* sideboards
Köter ['køːtər] (**-s, -**) *m* cur
Kotflügel *m* *(AUT)* wing
Krabbe ['krabə] *f* shrimp; **krabbeln** *vi* to crawl
Krach [krax] (**-(e)s, -s** *od* **-e**) *m* crash; *(andauernd)* noise; *(umg: Streit)* quarrel, argument; **k~en** *vi* to crash; *(beim Brechen)* to crack ♦ *vr* *(umg)* to argue, to quarrel
krächzen ['krɛçtsən] *vi* to croak
Kraft [kraft] (**-, ~e**) *f* strength; power; force; *(Arbeits~)* worker; **in ~ treten** to come into force; **k~** *präp* +*gen* by virtue of; **~fahrer** *m* (motor) driver; **~fahrzeug** *nt* motor vehicle; **~fahrzeugbrief** *m* logbook; **~fahrzeugsteuer** *f* ≈ road tax
kräftig ['krɛftɪç] *adj* strong; **~en** [krɛftɪgən] *vt* to strengthen
Kraft- *zW:* **k~los** *adj* weak; powerless; *(JUR)* invalid; **~probe** *f* trial of strength; **k~voll** *adj* vigorous; **~wagen** *m* motor vehicle; **~werk** *nt* power station
Kragen ['kraːgən] (**-s, -**) *m* collar; **~weite** *f* collar size
Krähe ['krɛːə] *f* crow; **k~n** *vi* to crow
Kralle ['kralə] *f* claw; *(Vogel~)* talon; **k~n** *vt* to clutch; *(krampfhaft)* to claw
Kram [kraːm] (**-(e)s**) *m* stuff, rubbish; **k~en** *vi* to rummage; **~laden** *(pej)* *m* small shop
Krampf [krampf] (**-(e)s, ~e**) *m* cramp; *(zuckend)* spasm; **~ader** *f* varicose vein; **k~haft** *adj* convulsive; *(fig:*

Versuche) desperate
Kran [kraːn] (**-(e)s, ~e**) *m* crane; *(Wasser~)* tap, faucet *(US)*
Kranich ['kraːnɪç] (**-s, -e**) *m* *(ZOOL)* crane
krank [krank] *adj* ill, sick; **K~e(r)** *mf* sick person, invalid; patient
kranken ['krankən] *vi:* **an etw** *dat* **~** *(fig)* to suffer from sth
kränken ['krɛŋkən] *vt* to hurt
Kranken- *zW:* **~bericht** *m* medical report; **~geld** *nt* sick pay; **~haus** *nt* hospital; **~kasse** *f* health insurance; **~pfleger** *m* nursing orderly; **~schein** *m* health insurance card; **~schwester** *f* nurse; **~versicherung** *f* health insurance; **~wagen** *m* ambulance
Krank- *zW:* **k~haft** *adj* diseased; *(Angst etc)* morbid; **~heit** *f* illness; disease; **~heitserreger** *m* disease-causing agent
kränklich *adj* sickly
Kränkung *f* insult, offence
Kranz [krants] (**-es, ~e**) *m* wreath, garland
kraß [kras] *adj* crass
Krater ['kraːtər] (**-s, -**) *m* crater
Kratz- [krats] *zW:* **~bürste** *f* *(fig)* crosspatch; **k~en** *vt, vi* to scratch; **~er** (**-s, -**) *m* scratch; *(Werkzeug)* scraper
Kraul [kraʊl] (**-s**) *nt* crawl; **~schwimmen** to do the crawl; **k~en** *vi* *(schwimmen)* to do the crawl ♦ *vt* *(streicheln)* to fondle
kraus [kraʊs] *adj* crinkly; *(Haar)* frizzy; *(Stirn)* wrinkled; **K~e** ['kraʊzə] *f* frill, ruffle
Kraut [kraʊt] (**-(e)s, Kräuter**) *nt* plant; *(Gewürz)* herb; *(Gemüse)* cabbage
Krawall [kra'val] (**-s, -e**) *m* row, uproar
Krawatte [kra'vatə] *f* tie
Krebs [kreːps] (**-es, -e**) *m* crab; *(MED, ASTROL)* cancer
Kredit [kre'diːt] (**-(e)s, -e**) *m* credit; **~karte** *f* credit card
Kreide ['kraɪdə] *f* chalk; **k~bleich** *adj* as white as a sheet
Kreis [kraɪs] (**-es, -e**) *m* circle; *(Stadt~ etc)* district; **im ~ gehen** *(auch fig)* to go round in circles

kreischen ['kraɪʃən] *vi* to shriek, to screech

Kreis- *zW*: ~**el** ['kraɪzəl] (-s, -) *m* top; (*Verkehrs~*) roundabout (*BRIT*), traffic circle (*US*); **k~en** ['kraɪzən] *vi* to spin; ~**lauf** *m* (*MED*) circulation; (*fig: der Natur etc*) cycle; ~**säge** *f* circular saw

Kreißsaal ['kraɪszaːl] *m* delivery room

Kreisstadt *f* county town

Kreisverkehr *m* roundabout traffic

Krematorium [krema'toːriʊm] *nt* crematorium

Kreml ['krɛm(ə)l] (-s) *m* Kremlin

krepieren [kre'piːrən] (*umg*) *vi* (*sterben*) to die, to kick the bucket

Krepp [krɛp] (-s, -s *od* -e) *m* crepe; ~**(p)apier** *nt* crepe paper; ~**sohle** *f* crepe sole

Kresse ['krɛsə] *f* cress

Kreta ['kreːta] (-s) *nt* Crete

Kreuz [krɔʏts] (-es, -e) *nt* cross; (*ANAT*) small of the back; (*KARTEN*) clubs; **k~en** *vt, vr* to cross ♦ *vi* (*NAUT*) to cruise; ~**er** (-s, -) *m* (*Schiff*) cruiser; ~**fahrt** *f* cruise; ~**gang** *m* cloisters *pl*; **k~igen** *vt* to crucify; ~**igung** *f* crucifixion; ~**otter** *f* adder; ~**ung** *f* (*Verkehrskreuzung*) crossing, junction; (*Züchten*) cross; ~**verhör** *nt* cross-examination; ~**weg** *m* crossroads; (*REL*) Way of the Cross; ~**worträtsel** *nt* crossword puzzle; ~**zug** *m* crusade

Kriech- ['kriːç] *zW*: **k~en** (*unreg*) *vi* to crawl, to creep; (*pej*) to grovel, to crawl; ~**er** (-s, -) *m* crawler; ~**spur** *f* crawler lane; ~**tier** *nt* reptile

Krieg [kriːk] (-(e)s, -e) *m* war

kriegen ['kriːgən] (*umg*) *vt* to get

Kriegs- *zW*: ~**dienstverweigerer** *m* conscientious objector; ~**erklärung** *f* declaration of war; ~**fuß** *m*: **mit jdm/ etw auf ~fuß stehen** to be at logger-heads with sb/to have difficulties with sth; ~**gefangene(r)** *m* prisoner of war; ~**gefangenschaft** *f* captivity; ~**gericht** *nt* court-martial; ~**schiff** *nt* warship; ~**verbrecher** *m* war criminal; ~**versehrte(r)** *m* person disabled in the war; ~**zustand** *m* state of war

Krim [krɪm] (-) *f* Crimea

Krimi ['kriːmi] (-s, -s; *umg*) *m* thriller

Kriminal- [krimi'naːl] *zW*: ~**beamte(r)** *m* detective; ~**i'tät** *f* criminality; ~**polizei** *f* ≈ Criminal Investigation Department (*BRIT*), Federal Bureau of Investigation (*US*); ~**roman** *m* detective story

kriminell [krimi'nɛl] *adj* criminal; **K~e(r)** *m* criminal

Krippe ['krɪpə] *f* manger, crib; (*Kinder~*) crèche

Krise ['kriːzə] *f* crisis; **k~ln** *vi*: **es k~lt** there's a crisis

Kristall [krɪs'tal] (-s, -e) *m* crystal ♦ *nt* (*Glas*) crystal

Kriterium [kri'teːriʊm] *nt* criterion

Kritik [kri'tiːk] *f* criticism; (*Zeitungs~*) review, write-up; ~**er** ['kriːtikər] (-s, -) *m* critic; **k~los** *adj* uncritical

kritisch ['kriːtiʃ] *adj* critical

kritisieren [kriti'ziːrən] *vt, vi* to criticize

kritzeln ['krɪtsəln] *vt, vi* to scribble, to scrawl

Krokodil [kroko'diːl] (-s, -e) *nt* crocodile

Krokus ['kroːkʊs] (-, - *od* -se) *m* crocus

Krone ['kroːnə] *f* crown; (*Baum~*) top

krönen ['krøːnən] *vt* to crown

Kron- *zW*: ~**korken** *m* bottle top; ~**leuchter** *m* chandelier; ~**prinz** *m* crown prince

Krönung ['krøːnʊŋ] *f* coronation

Kropf [krɔpf] (-(e)s, ⁼e) *m* (*MED*) goitre; (*von Vogel*) crop

Kröte ['krøːtə] *f* toad

Krücke ['krʏkə] *f* crutch

Krug [kruːk] (-(e)s, ⁼e) *m* jug; (*Bier~*) mug

Krümel ['kryːməl] (-s, -) *m* crumb; **k~n** *vt, vi* to crumble

krumm [krʊm] *adj* (*auch fig*) crooked; (*kurvig*) curved; ~**beinig** *adj* bandy-legged; ~**lachen** (*umg*) *vr* to laugh o.s. silly; ~**nehmen** (*unreg; umg*) *vt*: **jdm etw ~nehmen** to take sth amiss

Krümmung ['krʏmʊŋ] *f* bend, curve

Krüppel ['krʏpəl] (-s, -) *m* cripple

Kruste ['krʊstə] *f* crust

Kruzifix [krutsi'fɪks] (-es, -e) *nt* crucifix

Kübel ['kyːbəl] (-s, -) *m* tub; (*Eimer*) pail

Kubikmeter [ku'bi:kme:tər] *m* cubic metre

Küche ['kʏçə] *f* kitchen; (*Kochen*) cooking, cuisine

Kuchen ['ku:xən] (-s, -) *m* cake; ~**form** *f* baking tin; ~**gabel** *f* pastry fork

Küchen- *zW*: ~**herd** *m* cooker, stove; ~**schabe** *f* cockroach; ~**schrank** *m* kitchen cabinet

Kuckuck ['kʊkʊk] (-s, -e) *m* cuckoo; ~**suhr** *f* cuckoo clock

Kufe ['ku:fə] *f* (*Faß*) vat; (*Schlitten~*) runner; (*AVIAT*) skid

Kugel ['ku:gəl] (-, -n) *f* ball; (*MATH*) sphere; (*MIL*) bullet; (*Erd~*) globe; (*SPORT*) shot; **k~förmig** *adj* spherical; ~**kopf** *m* golf ball; ~**lager** *nt* ball bearing; **k~rund** *adj* (*Gegenstand*) round; (*umg: Person*) tubby; ~**schreiber** *m* ball-point (pen), biro (®); **k~sicher** *adj* bulletproof; ~**stoßen** (-s) *nt* shot-put

Kuh [ku:] (-, ⸚e) *f* cow

kühl [ky:l] *adj* (*auch fig*) cool; **K~anlage** *f* refrigeration plant; **K~e** (-) *f* coolness; ~**en** *vt* to cool; **K~er** (-s, -) *m* (*AUT*) radiator; **K~erhaube** *f* (*AUT*) bonnet (*BRIT*), hood (*US*); **K~raum** *m* cold-storage chamber; **K~schrank** *m* refrigerator; **K~truhe** *f* freezer; **K~ung** *f* cooling; **K~wasser** *nt* radiator water

kühn [ky:n] *adj* bold, daring; **K~heit** *f* boldness

Küken ['ky:kən] (-s, -) *nt* chicken

kulant [ku'lant] *adj* obliging

Kuli ['ku:li] (-s, -s) *m* coolie; (*umg: Kugelschreiber*) biro (®)

Kulisse [ku'lɪsə] *f* scenery

kullern ['kʊlərn] *vi* to roll

Kult [kʊlt] (-(e)s, -e) *m* worship, cult; **mit etw einen ~ treiben** to make a cult out of sth

kultivieren [-i'vi:rən] *vt* to cultivate

kultiviert *adj* cultivated, refined

Kultur [kʊl'tu:r] *f* culture; civilization; (*des Bodens*) cultivation; ~**banause** (*umg*) *m* philistine, low-brow; **k~ell** [-u'rɛl] *adj* cultural

Kümmel ['kʏməl] (-s, -) *m* caraway seed; (*Branntwein*) kümmel

Kummer ['kʊmər] (-s) *m* grief, sorrow

kümmerlich *adj* miserable, wretched

kümmern ['kʏmərn] *vt* to concern ♦ *vr*: **sich um jdn ~** to look after sb; **das kümmert mich nicht** that doesn't worry me; **sich um etw ~** to see to sth

Kumpel ['kʊmpəl] (-s, -; *umg*) *m* mate

kündbar ['kʏntba:r] *adj* redeemable, recallable; (*Vertrag*) terminable

Kunde[1] ['kʊndə] (-n, -n) *m* customer

Kunde[2] *f* (*Botschaft*) news

Kundendienst *m* after-sales service

Kundenkonto *nt* charge account

Kund- *zW*: ~**gabe** *f* announcement; **k~geben** (*unreg*) *vt* to announce; ~**gebung** *f* announcement; (*Versammlung*) rally

Künd- *zW*: **k~igen** *vi* to give in one's notice ♦ *vt* to cancel; **jdm k~igen** to give sb his notice; **die Stellung/ Wohnung k~igen** to give notice that one is leaving one's job/house; **jdm die Stellung/Wohnung k~igen** to give sb notice to leave his/her job/house; ~**igung** *f* notice; ~**igungsfrist** *f* period of notice

Kundin *f* customer

Kundschaft *f* customers *pl*, clientele

künftig ['kʏnftɪç] *adj* future ♦ *adv* in future

Kunst [kʊnst] (-, ⸚e) *f* art; (*Können*) skill; **das ist doch keine ~** it's easy; ~**dünger** *m* artificial manure; ~**faser** *f* synthetic fibre; ~**fertigkeit** *f* skilfulness; ~**geschichte** *f* history of art; ~**gewerbe** *nt* arts and crafts *pl*; ~**griff** *m* trick, knack; ~**händler** *m* art dealer

Künstler(in) ['kʏnstlər(ɪn)] (-s, -) *m(f)* artist; **k~isch** *adj* artistic; ~**name** *m* pseudonym

künstlich ['kʏnstlɪç] *adj* artificial

Kunst- *zW*: ~**sammler** (-s, -) *m* art collector; ~**seide** *f* artificial silk; ~**stoff** *m* synthetic material; ~**stück** *nt* trick; ~**turnen** *nt* gymnastics *sg*; **k~voll** *adj* artistic; ~**werk** *nt* work of art

kunterbunt ['kʊntərbʊnt] *adj* higgledy-piggledy

Kupfer ['kʊpfər] (-s) *nt* copper; ~**geld**

nt coppers *pl*; **k~n** *adj* copper
Kuppe ['kʊpə] *f* (*Berg~*) top; (*Finger~*) tip
Kupp- ['kʊp-] *zW:* **~e'lei** *f* (*JUR*) procuring; **k~eln** *vi* (*JUR*) to procure; (*AUT*) to declutch ♦ *vt* to join; **~lung** *f* coupling; (*AUT*) clutch
Kur [ku:r] (-, -en) *f* cure, treatment
Kür [ky:r] (-, -en) *f* (*SPORT*) free exercises *pl*
Kurbel ['kʊrbəl] (-, -n) *f* crank, winder; (*AUT*) starting handle; **~welle** *f* crankshaft
Kürbis ['kyrbɪs] (-ses, -se) *m* pumpkin; (*exotisch*) gourd
Kurgast *m* visitor (to a health resort)
kurieren [ku'ri:rən] *vt* to cure
kurios [kuri'o:s] *adj* curious, odd; **K~i'tät** *f* curiosity
Kurort *m* health resort
Kurpfuscher *m* quack
Kurs [kʊrs] (-es, -e) *m* course; (*FIN*) rate; **~buch** *nt* timetable; **k~ieren** [kʊr'zi:rən] *vi* to circulate; **k~iv** *adv* in italics; **~us** ['kʊrzʊs] (-, **Kurse**) *m* course; **~wagen** *m* (*EISENB*) through carriage
Kurve ['kʊrvə] *f* curve; (*Straßen~*) curve, bend; **kurvenreich** *adj* (*Straße*) bendy; **kurvig** *adj* (*Straße*) bendy
kurz [kʊrts] *adj* short; **~ gesagt** in short; **zu ~ kommen** to come off badly; **den kürzeren ziehen** to get the worst of it; **K~arbeit** *f* short-time work; **~ärm(e)lig** *adj* short-sleeved
Kürze ['kyrtsə] *f* shortness, brevity; **k~n** *vt* to cut short; (*in der Länge*) to shorten; (*Gehalt*) to reduce
kurz- *zW:* **~erhand** *adv* on the spot; **~fristig** *adj* short-term; **K~geschichte** *f* short story; **~halten** (*unreg*) *vt* to keep short; **~lebig** *adj* short-lived
kürzlich ['kyrtslɪç] *adv* lately, recently
Kurz- *zW:* **~schluß** *m* (*ELEK*) short circuit; **~schrift** *f* shorthand; **k~sichtig** *adj* short-sighted; **~welle** *f* shortwave
kuscheln ['kʊʃəln] *vr* to snuggle up
Kusine [ku'zi:nə] *f* cousin
Kuß [kʊs] (-sses, -̈sse) *m* kiss
küssen ['kʏsən] *vt, vr* to kiss

Küste ['kʏstə] *f* coast, shore; **Küstenwache** *f* coastguard (station)
Küster ['kʏstər] (-s, -) *m* sexton, verger
Kutsche ['kʊtʃə] *f* coach, carriage; **~r** (-s, -) *m* coachman
Kutte ['kʊtə] *f* habit
Kuvert [ku've:r] (-s, -e *od* -s) *nt* envelope, cover
Kybernetik [kybɛr'ne:tɪk] *f* cybernetics *sg*

L

l. *abk* = **Liter**
Labor [la'bo:r] (-s, -e *od* -s) *nt* lab; **~ant(in)** [labo'rant(ın)] *m(f)* lab(oratory) assistant; **~atorium** [labora'to:riʊm] *nt* laboratory
Labyrinth [laby'rınt] (-s, -e) *nt* labyrinth
lächeln ['lɛçəln] *vi* to smile; **L~** (-s) *nt* smile
lachen ['laxən] *vi* to laugh
lächerlich ['lɛçərlıç] *adj* ridiculous
Lachgas *nt* laughing gas
lachhaft *adj* laughable
Lachs [laks] (-es, -e) *m* salmon
Lack [lak] (-(e)s, -e) *m* lacquer, varnish; (*von Auto*) paint; **l~ieren** [la'ki:rən] *vt* to varnish; (*Auto*) to spray; **~ierer** [la'ki:rər] (-s, -) *m* varnisher
Lackmus ['lakmʊs] (-) *m od nt* litmus
Laden ['la:dən] (-s, -̈) *m* shop; (*Fenster~*) shutter
laden ['la:dən] (*unreg*) *vt* (*Lasten*) to load; (*JUR*) to summon; (*einladen*) to invite
Laden- *zW:* **~dieb** *m* shoplifter; **~diebstahl** *m* shoplifting; **~schluß** *m* closing time; **~tisch** *m* counter
Ladung ['la:dʊŋ] *f* (*Last*) cargo, load; (*Beladen*) loading; (*JUR*) summons; (*Einladung*) invitation; (*Spreng~*) charge
lag *etc* [la:k] *vb siehe* **liegen**
Lage ['la:gə] *f* position, situation; (*Schicht*) layer; **in der ~ sein** to be in a position
Lager ['la:gər] (-s, -) *nt* camp; (*COMM*) warehouse; (*Schlaf~*) bed; (*von Tier*)

lair; (*TECH*) bearing; ~**bestand** *m* stocks *pl*; ~**haus** *nt* warehouse, store

lagern ['la:gərn] *vi* (*Dinge*) to be stored; (*Menschen*) to camp ♦ *vt* to store; (*betten*) to lay down; (*Maschine*) to bed

Lagune [la'gu:nə] *f* lagoon

lahm [la:m] *adj* lame; ~**en** *vi* to be lame

lähmen ['lɛ:mən] *vt* to paralyse

lahmlegen *vt* to paralyse

Lähmung *f* paralysis

Laib [laip] (-s, -e) *m* loaf

Laie ['laiə] (-n, -n) *m* layman; **laienhaft** *adj* amateurish

Laken ['la:kən] (-s, -) *nt* sheet

Lakritze [la'krɪtsə] *f* liquorice

lallen ['lalən] *vt, vi* to slur; (*Baby*) to babble

Lamelle [la'mɛlə] *f* lamella; (*ELEK*) lamina; (*TECH*) plate

Lametta [la'mɛta] (-s) *nt* tinsel

Lamm [lam] (-(e)s, ∸er) *nt* lamb; ~**fell** *nt* lambskin

Lampe ['lampə] *f* lamp; **Lampenfieber** *nt* stage fright; **Lampenschirm** *m* lampshade

Lampion [lampi'õ:] (-s, -s) *m* Chinese lantern

Land [lant] (-(e)s, ∸er) *nt* land; (*Nation, nicht Stadt*) country; (*Bundes~*) state; **auf dem** ~**(e)** in the country; ~**besitz** *m* landed property; **Landebahn** *f* runway; **l~en** ['landən] *vt, vi* to land

Landes- ['landəs] *zW*: ~**farben** *pl* national colours; ~**innere(s)** *nt* inland region; ~**sprache** *f* national language; **l~üblich** *adj* customary; ~**verrat** *m* high treason; ~**währung** *f* national currency

Land- *zW*: ~**haus** *nt* country house; ~**karte** *f* map; ~**kreis** *m* administrative region; **l~läufig** *adj* customary

ländlich ['lɛntlɪç] *adj* rural

Land- *zW*: ~**schaft** *f* countryside; (*KUNST*) landscape; **l~schaftlich** *adj* scenic; regional; ~**straße** *f* country road; ~**streicher** (-s, -) *m* tramp; ~**strich** *m* region; ~**tag** *m* (*POL*) regional parliament

Landung ['landʊŋ] *f* landing

Landungs- *zW*: ~**boot** *nt* landing craft; ~**brücke** *f* jetty, pier; ~**stelle** *f* landing place

Land- *zW*: ~**wirt** *m* farmer; ~**wirtschaft** *f* agriculture; ~**zunge** *f* spit

lang [laŋ] *adj* long; (*Mensch*) tall; ~**atmig** *adj* long-winded; ~**e** *adv* for a long time; (*dauern, brauchen*) a long time

Länge ['lɛŋə] *f* length; (*GEOG*) longitude

langen ['laŋən] *vi* (*ausreichen*) to do, to suffice; (*fassen*): ~ (**nach**) to reach (for) ♦ *vt*: **jdm etw** ~ to hand *od* pass sb sth; **es langt mir** I've had enough

Längengrad *m* longitude

Längenmaß *nt* linear measure

lang- *zW*: **L~eweile** *f* boredom; ~**fristig** *adj* long-term; ~**lebig** *adj* long-lived

länglich *adj* longish

längs [lɛŋs] *präp* (+*gen od dat*) along ♦ *adv* lengthwise

lang- *zW*: ~**sam** *adj* slow; **L~samkeit** *f* slowness; **L~schläfer(in)** *m(f)* late riser; **L~spielplatte** *f* long-playing record

längst [lɛŋst] *adv*: **das ist** ~ **fertig** that was finished a long time ago, that has been finished for a long time; ~**e(r, s)** *adj* longest

lang- *zW*: ~**weilen** *vt* to bore ♦ *vr* to be bored; ~**weilig** *adj* boring, tedious; **L~welle** *f* long wave; ~**wierig** *adj* lengthy, long-drawn-out

Lanze ['lantsə] *f* lance

Lappalie [la'pa:liə] *f* trifle

Lappen ['lapən] (-s, -) *m* cloth, rag; (*ANAT*) lobe

läppisch ['lɛpɪʃ] *adj* foolish

Lappland ['laplant] (-s) *nt* Lapland

Lapsus ['lapsʊs] (-, -) *m* slip

Lärche ['lɛrçə] *f* larch

Lärm [lɛrm] (-(e)s) *m* noise; **l~en** *vi* to be noisy, to make a noise

Larve ['larfə] *f* (*BIOL*) larva

las *etc* [la:s] *vb siehe* **lesen**

lasch [laʃ] *adj* slack

Lasche ['laʃə] *f* (*Schuh~*) tongue

Laser ['le:izə] (-s, -) *m* laser

lassen ['lasən] (*pt* **ließ**, *pp* **gelassen** *od* (*als Hilfsverb*) **lassen**) *vt* **1** (*unterlassen*) to stop; (*momentan*) to leave; **laß das (sein)!** don't (do it)!; (*hör auf*) stop it!; **laß mich!** leave me alone; **lassen wir das!** let's leave it; **er kann das Trinken nicht lassen** he can't stop drinking
2 (*zurücklassen*) to leave; **etw lassen, wie es ist** to leave sth (just) as it is
3 (*überlassen*): **jdn ins Haus lassen** to let sb into the house
♦ *vi*: **laß mal, ich mache das schon** leave it, I'll do it
♦ *Hilfsverb* **1** (*veranlassen*): **etw machen lassen** to have *od* get sth done; **sich** *dat* **etw schicken lassen** to have sth sent (to one)
2 (*zulassen*): **jdn etw wissen lassen** to let sb know sth; **das Licht brennen lassen** to leave the light on; **jdn warten lassen** to keep sb waiting; **das läßt sich machen** that can be done
3: **laß uns gehen** let's go

lässig ['lɛsɪç] *adj* casual; **L~keit** *f* casualness
Last [last] (*-, -en*) *f* load, burden; (*NAUT, AVIAT*) cargo; (*meist pl: Gebühr*) charge; **jdm zur ~ fallen** to be a burden to sb; **l~en** *vi*: **l~en auf** +*dat* to weigh on
Laster ['lastər] (*-s, -*) *nt* vice
lästern ['lɛstərn] *vt, vi* (*Gott*) to blaspheme; (*schlecht sprechen*) to mock
Lästerung *f* jibe; (*Gottes~*) blasphemy
lästig ['lɛstɪç] *adj* troublesome, tiresome
Last- *zW*: **~kahn** *m* barge; **~kraftwagen** *m* heavy goods vehicle; **~schrift** *f* debit; **~wagen** *m* lorry, truck
Latein [la'taɪn] (*-s*) *nt* Latin; **~amerika** *nt* Latin America
latent [la'tɛnt] *adj* latent
Laterne [la'tɛrnə] *f* lantern; (*Straßen~*) lamp, light; **Laternenpfahl** *m* lamppost
latschen ['la:tʃən] (*umg*) *vi* (*gehen*) to

wander, to go; (*lässig*) to slouch
Latte ['latə] *f* lath; (*SPORT*) goalpost; (*quer*) crossbar
Latzhose ['latsho:zə] *f* dungarees *pl*
lau [lau] *adj* (*Nacht*) balmy; (*Wasser*) lukewarm
Laub [laup] (*-(e)s*) *nt* foliage; **~baum** *m* deciduous tree, **frosch** *m* tree frog; **~säge** *f* fretsaw
Lauch [laux] (*-(e)s, -e*) *m* leek
Lauer ['lauər] *f*: **auf der ~ sein** *od* **liegen** to lie in wait; **l~n** *vi* to lie in wait; (*Gefahr*) to lurk
Lauf [lauf] (*-(e)s, Läufe*) *m* run; (*Wett~*) race; (*Entwicklung, ASTRON*) course; (*Gewehr*) barrel; **einer Sache** *dat* **ihren ~ lassen** to let sth take its course; **~bahn** *f* career
laufen ['laufən] (*unreg*) *vt, vi* to run; (*umg: gehen*) to walk; **~d** *adj* running; (*Monat, Ausgaben*) current; **auf dem ~den sein/halten** to be/keep up to date; **am ~den Band** (*fig*) continuously
Läufer ['lɔyfər] (*-s, -*) *m* (*Teppich, SPORT*) runner; (*Fußball*) half-back; (*Schach*) bishop
Lauf- *zW*: **~masche** *f* run, ladder (*BRIT*); **~stall** *m* playpen; **~steg** *m* catwalk; **~werk** *nt* (*COMPUT*) disk drive; **~zettel** *m* circular
Lauge ['laugə] *f* soapy water; (*CHEM*) alkaline solution
Laune ['launə] *f* mood, humour; (*Einfall*) caprice; (*schlechte*) temper; **launenhaft** *adj* capricious, changeable
launisch *adj* moody; bad-tempered
Laus [laus] (*-, Läuse*) *f* louse; **~bub** *m* rascal, imp
lauschen ['lauʃən] *vi* to eavesdrop, to listen in
lauschig ['lauʃɪç] *adj* snug
laut [laut] *adj* loud ♦ *adv* loudly; (*lesen*) aloud ♦ *präp* (+*gen od dat*) according to; **L~** (*-(e)s, -e*) *m* sound
Laute ['lautə] *f* lute
lauten ['lautən] *vi* to say; (*Urteil*) to be
läuten ['lɔytən] *vt, vi* to ring, to sound
lauter ['lautər] *adj* (*Wasser*) clear, pure; (*Wahrheit, Charakter*) honest ♦ *adj inv* (*Freude, Dummheit etc*) sheer ♦ *adv*

nothing but, only
läutern ['lɔytərn] *vt* to purify
Läuterung *f* purification
laut- *zW:* ~**hals** *adv* at the top of one's voice; ~**los** *adj* noiseless, silent; **L~schrift** *f* phonetics *pl;* **l~sprecher** *m* loudspeaker; **L~sprecherwagen** *m* loudspeaker van; ~**stark** *adj* vociferous; **L~stärke** *f* (*RADIO*) volume
lauwarm ['lauvarm] *adj* (*auch fig*) lukewarm
Lava ['la:va] (-, **Laven**) *f* lava
Lavendel [la'vɛndəl] (-s, -) *m* lavender
Lawine [la'vi:nə] *f* avalanche; ~**ngefahr** *f* danger of avalanches
lax [laks] *adj* lax
Lazarett [latsa'rɛt] (-(e)s, -e) *nt* (*MIL*) hospital, infirmary
Leben (-s, -) *nt* life
leben ['le:bən] *vt, vi* to live; ~**d** *adj* living; **lebendig** [le'bɛndɪç] *adj* living, alive; (*lebhaft*) lively; **Lebendigkeit** *f* liveliness
Lebens- *zW:* ~**alter** *nt* age; ~**art** *f* way of life; ~**erwartung** *f* life expectancy; **l~fähig** *adj* able to live; ~**gefahr** *f:* ~**gefahr!** danger!; **in** ~**gefahr** dangerously ill; **l~gefährlich** *adj* dangerous; (*Verletzung*) critical; ~**haltungskosten** *pl* cost of living *sg;* ~**jahr** *nt* year of life; ~**lauf** *m* curriculum vitae; **l~lustig** *adj* cheerful, lively; ~**mittel** *pl* food *sg;* ~**mittelgeschäft** *nt* grocer's (shop); **l~müde** *adj* tired of life; ~**retter** *m* lifesaver; ~**standard** *m* standard of living; ~**unterhalt** *m* livelihood; ~**versicherung** *f* life insurance; ~**wandel** *m* way of life; ~**zeichen** *nt* sign of life
Leber ['le:bər] (-, -n) *f* liver; ~**fleck** *m* mole; ~**tran** *m* cod-liver oil; ~**wurst** *f* liver sausage
Lebewesen *nt* creature
Lebewohl *nt* farewell, goodbye
leb- ['le:p] *zW:* ~**haft** *adj* lively, vivacious; **L~kuchen** *m* gingerbread; ~**los** *adj* lifeless
Leck [lɛk] (-(e)s, -e) *nt* leak; **l~** *adj* leaky, leaking; **l~en** *vi* (*Loch haben*) to leak; (*schlecken*) to lick ♦ *vt* to lick

lecker ['lɛkər] *adj* delicious, tasty; **L~bissen** *m* dainty morsel
led. *abk* = **ledig**
Leder ['le:dər] (-s, -) *nt* leather; **l~n** *adj* leather; ~**waren** *pl* leather goods
ledig ['le:dɪç] *adj* single; **einer Sache** *gen* ~ **sein** to be free of sth; ~**lich** *adv* merely, solely
leer [le:r] *adj* empty; vacant; ~ **machen** to empty; **L~e** (-) *f* emptiness; ~**en** *vt, vr* to empty; **L~gewicht** *nt* weight when empty; **L~lauf** *m* neutral; ~**stehend** *adj* empty; **L~ung** *f* emptying; (*Post*) collection
legal [le'ga:l] *adj* legal, lawful; ~**i'sieren** *vt* to legalize; **L~i'tät** *f* legality
legen ['le:gən] *vt* to lay, to put, to place; (*Ei*) to lay ♦ *vr* to lie down; (*fig*) to subside
Legende [le'gɛndə] *f* legend
leger [le'ʒe:r] *adj* casual
legieren [le'gi:rən] *vt* to alloy
Legierung *f* alloy
Legislative [legɪsla'ti:və] *f* legislature
legitim [legi'ti:m] *adj* legitimate; **L~ation** [-atsi'o:n] *f* legitimation; ~**ieren** [-'mi:rən] *vt* to legitimate ♦ *vr* to prove one's identity
Lehm [le:m] (-(e)s, -e) *m* loam; **l~ig** *adj* loamy
Lehne ['le:nə] *f* arm; back; **l~n** *vt, vr* to lean
Lehnstuhl *m* armchair
Lehr- *zW:* ~**amt** *nt* teaching profession; ~**brief** *m* indentures *pl;* ~**buch** *nt* textbook
Lehre ['le:rə] *f* teaching, doctrine; (*beruflich*) apprenticeship; (*moralisch*) lesson; (*TECH*) gauge; **l~n** *vt* to teach; ~**r(in)** (-s, -) *m(f)* teacher; **Lehrerzimmer** *nt* staff room
Lehr- *zW:* ~**gang** *m* course; ~**jahre** *pl* apprenticeship *sg;* ~**ling** *m* apprentice; **l~reich** *adj* instructive; ~**stelle** *f* apprenticeship; ~**stuhl** *m* chair; ~**zeit** *f* apprenticeship
Leib [laip] (-(e)s, -er) *m* body; **halt ihn mir vom** ~**!** keep him away from me!; **l~haftig** *adj* personified; (*Teufel*) incarnate; **l~lich** *adj* bodily; (*Vater etc*)

own; ~**wache** f bodyguard
Leiche ['laɪçə] f corpse
Leichen- zW: ~**haus** nt mortuary;
~**träger** m bearer; ~**wagen** m hearse
Leichnam ['laɪçnaːm] (-(e)s, -e) m
corpse
leicht [laɪçt] adj light; (einfach) easy;
L~athletik f athletics sg; ~**fallen** (unreg) vi: jdm ~**fallen** to be easy for sb;
~**fertig** adj frivolous; ~**gläubig** adj
gullible, credulous; **L~gläubigkeit** f
gullibility, credulity; ~**hin** adv lightly;
L~igkeit f easiness; **mit L~igkeit** with
ease; ~**machen** vt: **es sich** dat ~**machen** to make things easy for o.s.;
L~sinn m carelessness; ~**sinnig** adj
careless
Leid [laɪt] (-(e)s) nt grief, sorrow; **l~**
adj: **etw l~ haben** od **sein** to be tired of
sth; **es tut mir/ihm l~** I am/he is sorry;
er/das tut mir l~ I am sorry for him/it;
l~en ['laɪdən] (unreg) vt to suffer;
(erlauben) to permit ♦ vi to suffer;
jdn/etw nicht l~en können not to be
able to stand sb/sth; ~**en** (-s, -) nt
suffering; (Krankheit) complaint; ~**enschaft** f passion; **l~enschaftlich** adj
passionate
leider ['laɪdər] adv unfortunately; **ja, ~**
yes, I'm afraid so; ~ **nicht** I'm afraid
not
Leidtragende(r) mf bereaved; (Benachteiligter) one who suffers
Leidwesen nt: **zu jds ~** to sb's disappointment
Leier ['laɪər] (-, -n) f lyre; (fig) old
story; ~**kasten** m barrel organ
Leihbibliothek f lending library
leihen ['laɪən] (unreg) vt to lend; **sich**
dat **etw ~** to borrow sth
Leih- zW: ~**gebühr** f hire charge;
~**haus** nt pawnshop; ~**schein** m pawn
ticket; (Buchleihschein etc) borrowing
slip; ~**wagen** m hired car
Leim [laɪm] (-(e)s, -e) m glue; **l~en** vt
to glue
Leine ['laɪnə] f line, cord; (Hunde~)
leash, lead
Leinen nt linen; **l~** adj linen
Leintuch nt (Bett~) sheet; linen cloth

Leinwand f (KUNST) canvas; (CINE)
screen
leise ['laɪzə] adj quiet; (sanft) soft,
gentle
Leiste ['laɪstə] f ledge; (Zier~) strip;
(ANAT) groin
leisten ['laɪstən] vt (Arbeit) to do;
(Gesellschaft) to keep; (Ersatz) to
supply; (vollbringen) to achieve; **sich**
dat **etw ~ können** to be able to afford
sth
Leistung f performance; (gute)
achievement
Leistungs- zW: ~**druck** m pressure;
l~fähig adj efficient; ~**fähigkeit** f
efficiency; ~**sport** m competitive sport;
~**zulage** f productivity bonus
Leitartikel m leading article
Leitbild nt model
leiten ['laɪtən] vt to lead; (Firma) to
manage; (in eine Richtung) to direct;
(ELEK) to conduct
Leiter¹ ['laɪtər] (-s, -) m leader, head;
(ELEK) conductor
Leiter² (-, -n) f ladder
Leit- zW: ~**faden** m guide; ~**motiv** nt
leitmotiv; ~**planke** f crash barrier
Leitung f (Führung) direction; (CINE,
THEAT etc) production; (von Firma)
management; directors pl; (Wasser~)
pipe; (Kabel) cable; **eine lange ~**
haben to be slow on the uptake
Leitungs- zW: ~**draht** m wire; ~**rohr**
nt pipe; ~**wasser** nt tap water
Lektion [lɛktsiˈoːn] f lesson
Lektüre [lɛkˈtyːrə] f (Lesen) reading;
(Lesestoff) reading matter
Lende ['lɛndə] f loin; **Lendenstück** nt
fillet
lenk- ['lɛŋk] zW: ~**bar** adj (Fahrzeug)
steerable; (Kind) manageable; ~**en** vt
to steer; (Kind) to guide; (Blick,
Aufmerksamkeit): ~**en** (**auf** +akk) to
direct (at); **L~rad** nt steering wheel;
L~stange f handlebars pl
Leopard [leoˈpart] (-en, -en) m leopard
Lepra ['leːpra] (-) f leprosy
Lerche ['lɛrçə] f lark
lernbegierig adj eager to learn
lernen ['lɛrnən] vt to learn

lesbar ['leːsbaːr] adj legible
Lesbierin ['lɛsbiərin] f lesbian
lesbisch ['lɛsbɪʃ] adj lesbian
Lese ['leːzə] f (Wein) harvest
Lesebuch nt reading book, reader
lesen (unreg) vt, vi to read; (ernten) to gather, to pick
Leser(in) (-s, -) m(f) reader; ~brief m reader's letter; l~lich adj legible
Lesung ['leːzʊŋ] f (PARL) reading
letzte(r, s) ['lɛtstə(r, s)] adj last; (neueste) latest; **zum ~nmal** for the last time; ~ns adv lately; ~re(r, s) adj latter
Leuchte ['lɔʏçtə] f lamp, light; l~n vi to shine, to gleam; ~r (-s, -) m candlestick
Leucht- zW: ~farbe f fluorescent colour; ~kugel f flare; ~rakete f flare; ~reklame f neon sign; ~röhre f strip light; ~turm m lighthouse; ~zifferblatt nt luminous dial
leugnen ['lɔʏgnən] vt to deny
Leugnung f denial
Leukämie [lɔʏkɛˈmiː] f leukaemia
Leukoplast [lɔʏkoˈplast] (®; -(e)s, -e) nt elastoplast ®
Leumund ['lɔʏmʊnt] (-(e)s, -e) m reputation
Leumundszeugnis nt character reference
Leute ['lɔʏtə] pl people pl
Leutnant ['lɔʏtnant] (-s, -s od -e) m lieutenant
Lexikon ['lɛksikɔn] (-s, Lexiken od Lexika) nt encyclop(a)edia
libanesisch [libaˈneːzɪʃ] adj Lebanese
Libanon ['liːbanɔn] (-s) m: (der) ~ the Lebanon
Libelle [liˈbɛlə] f dragonfly; (TECH) spirit level
liberal [libeˈraːl] adj liberal; L~e(r) mf liberal; L~ismus [liberaˈlɪsmʊs] m liberalism
Libero ['liːbero] (-s, -s) m (Fußball) sweeper
Libyen ['liːbiən] (-s) nt Libya
libysch ['liːbɪʃ] adj Libyan
Licht [lɪçt] (-(e)s, -er) nt light; ~bild nt photograph; (Dia) slide; ~blick m

cheering prospect; l~empfindlich adj sensitive to light; l~en vt to clear; (Anker) to weigh ♦ vr to clear up; (Haar) to thin; ~hupe f flashing of headlights; ~jahr nt light year; ~maschine f dynamo; ~schalter m light switch
Lichtung f clearing, glade
Lid [liːt] (-(e)s, -er) nt eyelid; ~schatten m eyeshadow
lieb [liːp] adj dear; **das ist ~ von dir** that's kind of you; ~äugeln vi insep: **mit etw ~äugeln** to have one's eye on sth; **mit dem Gedanken ~äugeln, etw zu tun** to toy with the idea of doing sth
Liebe ['liːbə] f love; l~bedürftig adj: l~bedürftig sein to need love; ~'lei f flirtation; l~n vt to love; to like
liebens- zW: ~wert adj loveable; ~würdig adj kind; ~würdigerweise adv kindly; L~würdigkeit f kindness
lieber ['liːbər] adv rather, preferably; **ich gehe ~ nicht** I'd rather not go; siehe auch gern; lieb
Liebes- zW: ~brief m love letter; ~kummer m: ~kummer haben to be lovesick; ~paar nt courting couple, lovers pl
liebevoll adj loving
lieb- zW: ~gewinnen (unreg) vt to get fond of; ~haben (unreg) vt to be fond of; L~haber (-s, -) m lover; L~habe'rei f hobby; ~kosen [liːpˈkoːzən] vt insep to caress; ~lich adj lovely, charming; L~ling m darling; L~lings- in zW favourite; ~los adj unloving; L~schaft f love affair; ~ste(r, s) adj favourite; **etw am ~sten mögen** to like sth best
Lied [liːt] (-(e)s, -er) nt song; (REL) hymn; ~erbuch nt songbook; hymn book
liederlich ['liːdərlıç] adj slovenly; (Lebenswandel) loose, immoral; L~keit f slovenliness; immorality
lief etc [liːf] vb siehe laufen
Lieferant [lifəˈrant] m supplier
liefern ['liːfərn] vt to deliver; (versorgen mit) to supply; (Beweis) to produce
Liefer- zW: ~schein m delivery note;

~**termin** *m* delivery date; ~**ung** *f* delivery; supply; ~**wagen** *m* van

Liege ['li:gə] *f* bed

liegen ['li:gən] (*unreg*) *vi* to lie; (*sich befinden*) to be; **mir liegt nichts/viel daran** it doesn't matter to me/it matters a lot to me; **es liegt bei Ihnen, ob ... it's** up to you whether ...; **Sprachen ~ mir nicht** languages are not my line; **woran liegt es?** what's the cause?; ~**bleiben** (*unreg*) *vi* (*im Bett*) to stay in bed; (*nicht aufstehen*) to stay lying down; (*vergessen werden*) to be left (behind); ~**lassen** (*unreg*) *vt* (*vergessen*) to leave behind

Liege- *zW:* ~**sitz** *m* (*AUT*) reclining seat; ~**stuhl** *m* deck chair; ~**wagen** *m* (*EISENB*) couchette

lieh *etc* [li:] *vb siehe* **leihen**

ließ *etc* [li:s] *vb siehe* **lassen**

liest *etc* [li:st] *vb siehe* **lesen**

Lift [lɪft] (-(e)s, -e *od* -s) *m* lift

Likör [li'kø:r] (-s, -e) *m* liqueur

lila ['li:la] *adj inv* purple, lilac; **L~** (-s, -s) *nt* (*Farbe*) purple, lilac

Lilie ['li:liə] *f* lily

Limonade [limo'na:də] *f* lemonade

Linde ['lɪndə] *f* lime tree, linden

lindern ['lɪndərn] *vt* to alleviate, to soothe

Linderung *f* alleviation

Lineal [line'a:l] (-s, -e) *nt* ruler

Linie ['li:niə] *f* line

Linien- *zW:* ~**blatt** *nt* ruled sheet; ~**flug** *m* scheduled flight; ~**richter** *m* linesman; **l~treu** *adj* (*POL*) loyal to the party line

linieren [lin'i:rən] *vt* to line

Linke ['lɪŋkə] *f* left side; left hand; (*POL*) left; **l~(r, s)** *adj* left; **ein l~r** (*POL*) a left-winger; **l~ Masche** purl

linkisch *adj* awkward, gauche

links [lɪŋks] *adv* left; to *od* on the left; ~ **von mir** on *od* to my left; **L~außen** [lɪŋks''ausən] (-s, -) *m* (*SPORT*) outside left; **L~händer(in)** (-s, -) *m(f)* left-handed person; **L~kurve** *f* left-hand bend; **L~verkehr** *m* driving on the left

Linoleum [li'no:leum] (-s) *nt* lino(leum)

Linse ['lɪnzə] *f* lentil; (*optisch*) lens *sg*

Lippe ['lɪpə] *f* lip; **Lippenstift** *m* lipstick

lispeln ['lɪspəln] *vi* to lisp

Lissabon ['lɪsabon] (-s) *nt* Lisbon

List [lɪst] *f* cunning; trick, ruse

Liste ['lɪstə] *f* list

listig ['lɪstɪç] *adj* cunning, sly

Litanei [lita'nai] *f* litany

Liter ['li:tər] (-s, -) *nt od m* litre

literarisch [litə'ra:rɪʃ] *adj* literary

Literatur [litera'tu:r] *f* literature

Litfaßsäule ['lɪtfaszɔylə] *f* advertising pillar

Lithographie [litogra'fi:] *f* lithography

Liturgie [litur'gi:] *f* liturgy

liturgisch [li'turgɪʃ] *adj* liturgical

Litze ['lɪtsə] *f* braid; (*ELEK*) flex

live [laɪf] *adv* (*RADIO, TV*) live

Livree [li'vre:] (-, -n) *f* livery

Lizenz [li'tsɛnts] *f* licence

Lkw [ɛlka:'ve:] (-(s), -(s)) *m abk* = **Lastkraftwagen**

Lob [lo:p] (-(e)s) *nt* praise

Lobby ['lɔbɪ] *f* lobby

loben ['lo:bən] *vt* to praise; **lobenswert** *adj* praiseworthy

löblich ['lø:plɪç] *adj* praiseworthy, laudable

Loch [lɔx] (-(e)s, ⁻er) *nt* hole; **l~en** *vt* to punch holes in; ~**er** (-s, -) *m* punch

löcherig ['lœçərɪç] *adj* full of holes

Lochkarte *f* punch card

Lochstreifen *m* punch tape

Locke ['lɔkə] *f* lock, curl; **l~n** *vt* to entice; (*Haare*) to curl; **Lockenwickler** (-s, -) *m* curler

locker ['lɔkər] *adj* loose; ~**lassen** (*unreg*) *vi*: **nicht ~lassen** not to let up; ~**n** *vt* to loosen

lockig ['lɔkɪç] *adj* curly

Lodenmantel ['lo:dənmantəl] *m* thick woollen coat

lodern ['lo:dərn] *vi* to blaze

Löffel ['lœfəl] (-s, -) *m* spoon

Logarithmus [loga'rɪtmus] *m* logarithm

Loge ['lo:ʒə] *f* (*THEAT*) box; (*Freimaurer*) (masonic) lodge; (*Pförtner~*) office

Logik ['lo:gɪk] *f* logic

logisch ['lo:gɪʃ] *adj* logical

Lohn [lo:n] (-(e)s, ⁻e) *m* reward; (*Arbeits~*) pay, wages *pl*; ~**büro** *nt* wages office; ~**empfänger** m wage earner

lohnen ['lo:nən] vr unpers to be worth it ♦ vt (liter): (jdm etw) ~ to reward (sb for sth); ~**d** adj worthwhile

Lohn- zW: ~**steuer** f income tax; ~**streifen** m pay slip; ~**tüte** f pay packet

Lokal [lo'ka:l] (-(e)s, -e) nt pub(lic house)

lokal adj local; ~**i'sieren** vt to localize

Lokomotive [lokomo'ti:və] f locomotive

Lokomotivführer m engine driver

Lorbeer ['lɔrbe:r] (-s, -en) m (auch fig) laurel; ~**blatt** nt (KOCH) bay leaf

Lore ['lo:rə] f (MIN) truck

Los [lo:s] (-es, -e) nt (Schicksal) lot, fate; (Lotterie~) lottery ticket

los [lo:s] adj (locker) loose; ~! go on!; etw ~ sein to be rid of sth; was ist ~? what's the matter?; dort ist nichts/viel ~ there's nothing/a lot going on there; etw ~ haben (umg) to be clever; ~**binden** (unreg) vt to untie

löschen ['lœʃən] vt (Feuer, Licht) to put out, to extinguish; (Durst) to quench; (COMM) to cancel; (COMPUT) delete; (Tonband) to erase; (Fracht) to unload ♦ vi (Feuerwehr) to put out a fire; (Tinte) to blot

Lösch- zW: ~**fahrzeug** nt fire engine; fire boat; ~**gerät** nt fire extinguisher; ~**papier** nt blotting paper

lose ['lo:zə] adj loose

Lösegeld nt ransom

losen ['lo:zən] vi to draw lots

lösen ['lø:zən] vt to loosen; (Rätsel etc) to solve; (Verlobung) to call off; (CHEM) to dissolve; (Partnerschaft) to break up; (Fahrkarte) to buy ♦ vr (aufgehen) to come loose; (Zucker etc) to dissolve; (Problem, Schwierigkeit) to (re)solve itself

los- zW: ~**fahren** (unreg) vi to leave; ~**gehen** (unreg) vi to set out; (anfangen) to start; (Bombe) to go off; auf jdn ~**gehen** to go for sb; ~**kaufen** vt (Gefangene, Geißeln) to pay ransom for; ~**kommen** (unreg) vi: von etw ~**kommen** to get away from sth;

~**lassen** (unreg) vt (Seil) to let go of; (Schimpfe) to let loose; ~**laufen** (unreg) vi to run off

löslich ['lø:slɪç] adj soluble; **L~keit** f solubility

los- zW: ~**lösen** vt: (sich) ~**lösen** to free (o.s.); ~**machen** vt to loosen; (Boot) to unmoor ♦ vr to get away; ~**schrauben** vt to unscrew; ~**sprechen** (unreg) vt to absolve

Losung ['lo:zʊŋ] f watchword, slogan

Lösung ['lø:zʊŋ] f (Lockermachen) loosening; (eines Rätsels, CHEM) solution; ~**smittel** nt solvent

loswerden (unreg) vt to get rid of

Lot [lo:t] (-(e)s, -e) nt plumbline; im ~ vertical; (fig) on an even keel

löten ['lø:tən] vt to solder

Lothringen ['lo:trɪŋən] (-s) nt Lorraine

Lötkolben m soldering iron

Lotse ['lo:tsə] (-n, -n) m pilot; (AVIAT) air traffic controller; **l~n** vt to pilot; (umg) to lure

Lotterie [lɔtə'ri:] f lottery

Löwe ['lø:və] (-n, -n) m lion; (ASTROL) Leo; **Löwenanteil** m lion's share; **Löwenzahn** m dandelion

loyal [loa'ja:l] adj loyal

lt. abk (= laut) according to

Luchs [lʊks] (-es, -e) m lynx

Lücke ['lʏkə] f gap; **Lückenbüßer** (-s, -) m stopgap; **lückenlos** adj complete

Luder ['lu:dər] (-s, -) nt (pej: Frau) hussy; (bedauernswert) poor wretch

Luft [lʊft] (-, -e) f air; (Atem) breath; in der ~ liegen to be in the air; jdn wie ~ behandeln to ignore sb; ~**angriff** m air raid; ~**ballon** m balloon; ~**blase** f air bubble; ~**dicht** adj airtight; ~**druck** m atmospheric pressure

lüften ['lʏftən] vt to air; (Hut) to lift, to raise ♦ vi to let some air in

Luft- zW: ~**fahrt** f aviation; **l~gekühlt** adj air-cooled; **l~ig** adj (Ort) breezy; (Raum) airy; (Kleider) summery; ~**kissenfahrzeug** nt hovercraft; ~**kurort** m health resort; **l~leer** adj: **l~leerer Raum** vacuum; ~**linie** f: in der ~**linie** as the crow flies; ~**loch** nt air-hole; (AVIAT) air-pocket; ~**matratze**

f lilo (®; *BRIT*), air mattress; **~pirat** *m* hijacker; **~post** *f* airmail; **~röhre** *f* (*ANAT*) windpipe; **~schlange** *f* streamer; **~schutzkeller** *m* air-raid shelter

Lüftung ['lʏftʊŋ] *f* ventilation

Luft- *zW*: **~verkehr** *m* air traffic; **~waffe** *f* air force; **~zug** *m* draught

Lüge ['lyːgə] *f* lie; **jdn/etw ~n strafen** to give the lie to sb/sth; **l~n** (*unreg*) *vi* to lie

Lügner(in) (-s, -) *m(f)* liar

Luke ['luːkə] *f* dormer window; hatch

Lümmel ['lʏml] (-s, -) *m* lout; **l~n** *vr* to lounge (about)

Lump [lʊmp] (-en, -en) *m* scamp, rascal

Lumpen ['lʊmpən] (-s, -) *m* rag

lumpen *vi*: **sich nicht ~ lassen** not to be mean

lumpig ['lʊmpɪç] *adj* shabby

Lunge ['lʊŋə] *f* lung; **Lungenentzündung** *f* pneumonia; **lungenkrank** *adj* consumptive

lungern ['lʊŋərn] *vi* to hang about

Lupe ['luːpə] *f* magnifying glass; **unter die ~ nehmen** (*fig*) to scrutinize

Lupine [lu'piːnə] *f* lupin

Lust [lʊst] (-, ⁼e) *f* joy, delight; (*Neigung*) desire; **~ haben zu** *od* **auf etw** *akk*/**etw zu tun** to feel like sth/doing sth

lüstern ['lʏstərn] *adj* lustful, lecherous

lustig ['lʊstɪç] *adj* (*komisch*) amusing, funny; (*fröhlich*) cheerful

Lüstling *m* lecher

Lust- *zW*: **l~los** *adj* unenthusiastic; **~mord** *m* sex(ual) murder; **~spiel** *nt* comedy

lutschen ['lʊtʃən] *vt, vi* to suck; **am Daumen ~** to suck one's thumb

Lutscher (-s, -) *m* lollipop

Luxemburg ['lʊksəmbʊrk] (-s) *nt* Luxembourg

luxuriös [lʊksuri'øːs] *adj* luxurious

Luxus ['lʊksʊs] (-) *m* luxury; **~artikel** *pl* luxury goods; **~hotel** *nt* luxury hotel

Lymphe ['lʏmfə] *f* lymph

lynchen ['lʏnçən] *vt* to lynch

Lyrik ['lyːrɪk] *f* lyric poetry; **~er** (-s, -) *m* lyric poet

lyrisch ['lyːrɪʃ] *adj* lyrical

M

m *abk* = **Meter**

Maas [maːs] (-) *f* Meuse

Mach- ['max] *zW*: **~art** *f* make; **m~bar** *adj* feasible; **~e** (-; *umg*) *f* show, sham

---
SCHLÜSSELWORT
---

machen ['maxən] *vt* **1** to do; (*herstellen, zubereiten*) to make; **was machst du da?** what are you doing (there)?; **das ist nicht zu machen** that can't be done; **das Radio leiser machen** to turn the radio down; **aus Holz gemacht** made of wood

2 (*verursachen, bewirken*) to make; **jdm Angst machen** to make sb afraid; **das macht die Kälte** it's the cold that does that

3 (*ausmachen*) to matter; **das macht nichts** that doesn't matter; **die Kälte macht mir nichts** I don't mind the cold

4 (*kosten, ergeben*) to make; **3 und 5 macht 8** 3 and 5 is *od* are 8; **was** *od* **wieviel macht das?** how much does that make?

5: **was macht die Arbeit?** how's the work going?; **was macht dein Bruder?** how is your brother doing?; **das Auto machen lassen** to have the car done; **mach's gut!** take care!; (*viel Glück*) good luck!

♦ *vi*: **mach schnell!** hurry up!; **Schluß machen** to finish (off); **mach schon!** come on!; **das macht müde** it makes you tired; **in etw** *dat* **machen** to be *od* deal in sth

♦ *vr* to come along (nicely); **sich an etw** *akk* **machen** to set about sth; **sich verständlich machen** to make o.s. understood; **sich** *dat* **viel aus jdm/etw machen** to like sb/sth

Macht [maxt] (-, ⁼e) *f* power; **~haber** (-s, -) *m* ruler

mächtig ['mɛçtɪç] *adj* powerful, mighty; (*umg*: *ungeheuer*) enormous

Macht- *zW:* **m~los** *adj* powerless;
~**probe** *f* trial of strength; ~**stellung** *f*
position of power; ~**wort** *nt:* **ein ~wort
sprechen** to excercise one's authority
Machwerk *nt* work; (*schlechte Arbeit*)
botched-up job
Mädchen ['mɛːtçən] *nt* girl; **m~haft** *adj*
girlish; ~**name** *m* maiden name
Made ['maːdə] *f* maggot
madig ['maːdɪç] *adj* maggoty; **jdm etw
~ machen** to spoil sth for sb
mag *etc* [maːk] *vb siehe* **mögen**
Magazin [maga'tsiːn] (-s, -e) *nt*
magazine
Magen ['maːgən] (-s, - *od* :) *m* stomach;
~**schmerzen** *pl* stomachache *sg*
mager ['maːgər] *adj* lean; (*dünn*) thin;
M~keit *f* leanness; thinness
Magie [ma'giː] *f* magic
Magier ['maːgiər] (-s, -) *m* magician
magisch ['maːgɪʃ] *adj* magical
Magnet [ma'gneːt] (-s *od* -en, -en) *m*
magnet; ~**band** *nt* magnetic tape;
m~isch *adj* magnetic; **m~i'sieren** *vt* to
magnetize; ~**nadel** *f* magnetic needle
Mahagoni [maha'goːni] (-s) *nt*
mahogany
mähen ['mɛːən] *vt, vi* to mow
Mahl [maːl] (-(e)s, -e) *nt* meal; **m~en**
(*unreg*) *vt* to grind; ~**zeit** *f* meal ♦ *excl*
enjoy your meal
Mahnbrief *m* reminder
Mähne ['mɛːnə] *f* mane
mahnen ['maːnən] *vt* to remind;
(*warnend*) to warn; (*wegen Schuld*) to
demand payment from
Mahnung *f* reminder; admonition,
warning
Mähren ['mɛːrən] (-s) *nt* Moravia
Mai [maɪ] (-(e)s, -e) *m* May;
~**glöckchen** *nt* lily of the valley;
~**käfer** *m* cockchafer
Mailand *nt* Milan
mailändisch *adj* Milanese
Mais [maɪs] (-es, -e) *m* maize, corn
(*US*); ~**kolben** *m* corncob
Majestät [majɛs'tɛːt] *f* majesty; **m~isch**
adj majestic
Major [ma'joːr] (-s, -e) *m* (*MIL*) major;
(*AVIAT*) squadron leader

Majoran [majo'raːn] (-s, -e) *m* marjo-
ram
makaber [ma'kaːbər] *adj* macabre
Makel ['maːkəl] (-s, -) *m* blemish;
(*moralisch*) stain; **m~los** *adj*
immaculate, spotless
mäkeln ['mɛːkəln] *vi* to find fault
Makkaroni [maka'roːni] *pl* macaroni *sg*
Makler(in) ['maːklər(ɪn)] (-s, -) *m(f)*
broker
Makrele [ma'kreːlə] *f* mackerel
Makrone [ma'kroːnə] *f* macaroon
Mal [maːl] (-(e)s, -e) *nt* mark, sign;
(*Zeitpunkt*) time; **m~** *adv* times;
(*umg*) *siehe* **einmal** ♦ *suffix:* -**m~**
-times
malen *vt, vi* to paint
Maler (-s, -) *m* painter
Male'rei *f* painting
malerisch *adj* picturesque
Malkasten *m* paintbox
Mallorca [ma'lɔrka] (-s) *nt* Majorca
malnehmen (*unreg*) *vt, vi* to multiply
Malz [malts] (-es) *nt* malt; ~**bonbon** *nt*
cough drop; ~**kaffee** *m* malt coffee
Mama ['mamaː] (-, -s; *umg*) *f* mum(my)
(*BRIT*), mom(my) (*US*)
Mami ['mami] (-, -s; *umg*) *f* mum(my)
(*BRIT*), mom(my) (*US*)
Mammut ['mamʊt] (-s, -e *od* -s) *nt*
mammoth
man [man] *pron* one, you; ~ **sagt, ...**
they *od* people say ...; **wie schreibt ~
das?** how do you write it?, how is it
written?
manche(r, s) ['mançə(r, s)] *adj* many a;
(*pl: einige*) a number of ♦ *pron* some
mancherlei *adj inv* various ♦ *pron inv*
a variety of things
manchmal *adv* sometimes
Mandant(in) [man'dant(ɪn)] *m(f)* (*JUR*)
client
Mandarine [manda'riːnə] *f* mandarin,
tangerine
Mandat [man'daːt] (-(e)s, -e) *nt*
mandate
Mandel ['mandəl] (-, -n) *f* almond;
(*ANAT*) tonsil
Manege [ma'nɛːʒə] *f* ring, arena
Mangel¹ ['maŋəl] (-, -n) *f* mangle

Mangel² (-s, ⸚) m lack; (*Knappheit*) shortage; (*Fehler*) defect, fault; ~ **an** +*dat* shortage of; ~**erscheinung** f deficiency symptom; m~**haft** *adj* poor; (*fehlerhaft*) defective, faulty; m~**n** *vi unpers*: es m~t jdm an etw *dat* sb lacks sth ♦ *vt* (*Wäsche*) to mangle; m~s *präp* +*gen* for lack of

Manie [ma'ni:] f mania

Manier [ma'ni:r] (-) f manner; style; (*pej*) mannerism; ~**en** *pl* (*Umgangsformen*) manners

Manifest [mani'fɛst] (-es, -e) nt manifesto

Maniküre [mani'ky:rə] f manicure; m~**n** *vt* to manicure

manipulieren [manipu'li:rən] *vt* to manipulate

Manko ['maŋko] (-s, -s) nt deficiency; (*COMM*) deficit

Mann [man] (-(e)s, ⸚er) m man; (*Ehe~*) husband; (*NAUT*) hand; **seinen ~ stehen** to hold one's own

Männchen ['mɛnçən] nt little man; (*Tier*) male

Mannequin [manə'kɛ̃:] (-s, -s) nt fashion model

männlich ['mɛnlɪç] *adj* (*BIOL*) male; (*fig, GRAM*) masculine

Mannschaft f (*SPORT, fig*) team; (*AVIAT, NAUT*) crew; (*MIL*) other ranks *pl*

Manöver [ma'nø:vər] (-s, -) nt manoeuvre

manövrieren [manø'vri:rən] *vt, vi* to manoeuvre

Mansarde [man'zardə] f attic

Manschette [man'ʃɛtə] f cuff; (*TECH*) collar; sleeve; **Manschettenknopf** m cufflink

Mantel ['mantəl] (-s, ⸚) m coat; (*TECH*) casing, jacket

Manuskript [manu'skrɪpt] (-(e)s, -e) nt manuscript

Mappe ['mapə] f briefcase; (*Akten~*) folder

Märchen ['mɛːrçən] nt fairy tale; m~**haft** *adj* fabulous; ~**prinz** m Prince Charming

Marder ['mardər] (-s, -) m marten

Margarine [marga'ri:nə] f margarine

Marienkäfer ['ma'ri:ɔnkɛːfər] m ladybird

Marine [ma'ri:nə] f navy; m~**blau** *adj* navy-blue

marinieren [mari'ni:rən] *vt* to marinate

Marionette [mario'nɛtə] f puppet

Mark¹ [mark] (-, -) f (*Münze*) mark

Mark² (-(e)s) nt (*Knochen~*) marrow; **jdm durch ~ und Bein gehen** to go right through sb

markant [mar'kant] *adj* striking

Marke ['markə] f mark; (*Warensorte*) brand; (*Fabrikat*) make; (*Rabatt~, Brief~*) stamp; (*Essens~*) ticket; (*aus Metall etc*) token, disc

markieren [mar'ki:rən] *vt* to mark; (*umg*) to act ♦ *vi* (*umg*) to act it

Markierung f marking

Markise [mar'ki:zə] f awning

Markstück nt one-mark piece

Markt [markt] (-(e)s, ⸚e) m market; ~**forschung** f market research; m~**gängig** *adj* marketable; ~**platz** m market place; ~**wirtschaft** f market economy

Marmelade [marmə'la:də] f jam

Marmor ['marmor] (-s, -e) m marble; m~**ieren** [-'ri:rən] *vt* to marble; m~**n** *adj* marble

Marokkaner(in) [maro'ka:nər(ın)] (-s, -) m(f) Moroccan

marok'kanisch *adj* Moroccan

Marokko [ma'rɔko] (-s) nt Morocco

Marone [ma'ro:nə] (-, -n *od* **Maroni**) f chestnut

Marotte [ma'rɔtə] f fad, quirk

Marsch¹ [marʃ] (-(e)s, ⸚e) m march ♦ *excl* march!

Marsch² (-, -en) f marsh

Marsch- *zW*: ~**befehl** m marching orders *pl*; m~**bereit** *adj* ready to move; m~**ieren** [mar'ʃi:rən] *vi* to march

Märtyrer(in) ['mɛrtyrər(ın)] (-s, -) m(f) martyr

März [mɛrts] (-(es), -e) m March

Marzipan [martsi'pa:n] (-s, -e) nt marzipan

Masche ['maʃə] f mesh; (*Strick~*) stitch; **das ist die neueste ~** that's the latest thing; **Maschendraht** m wire mesh; **maschenfest** adj runproof

Maschine [ma'ʃiːnə] f machine; (Motor) engine; (Schreib~) typewriter; **maschinell** [maʃi'nɛl] adj machine(-); mechanical

Maschinen- zW: **~bauer** m mechanical engineer; **~gewehr** nt machine gun; **~pistole** f submachine gun; **~schaden** m mechanical fault; **~schlosser** m fitter; **~schrift** f typescript

maschineschreiben (unreg) vi to type

Maschinist [maʃi'nɪst] m engineer

Maser ['maːzər] (-, -n) f (von Holz) grain; **~n** pl (MED) measles sg; **~ung** f grain(ing)

Maske ['maskə] f mask

Maskenball m fancy-dress ball

Maskerade [maskə'raːdə] f masquerade

maskieren [mas'kiːrən] vt to mask; (verkleiden) to dress up ♦ vr to disguise o.s.; to dress up

Maß¹ [maːs] (-es, -e) nt measure; (Mäßigung) moderation; (Grad) degree, extent

Maß² (-, -(e)) f litre of beer

Massage [ma'saːʒə] f massage

Maßanzug m made-to-measure suit

Maßarbeit f (fig) neat piece of work

Masse ['masə] f mass

Massen- zW: **~artikel** m mass-produced article; **~grab** nt mass grave; **m~haft** adj loads of; **~medien** pl mass media pl; **~veranstaltung** f mass meeting

Masseur [ma'søːr] m masseur

Masseurin f masseuse

maßgebend adj authoritative

maßhalten (unreg) vi to exercise moderation

massieren [ma'siːrən] vt to massage; (MIL) to mass

massig ['masɪç] adj massive; (umg) massive amount of

mäßig ['mɛːsɪç] adj moderate; **~en** ['mɛːsɪɡən] vt to restrain, to moderate; **M~keit** f moderation

Massiv (-s, -e) nt massif

massiv [ma'siːf] adj solid; (fig) heavy,

rough

Maß- zW: **~krug** m tankard; **m~los** adj extreme; **~nahme** f measure, step; **m~regeln** vt insep to reprimand; **~stab** m rule, measure; (fig) standard; (GEOG) scale; **m~voll** adj moderate

Mast [mast] (-(e)s, -e(n)) m mast; (ELEK) pylon

mästen ['mɛstən] vt to fatten

Material [materi'aːl] (-s, -ien) nt material(s); **~fehler** m material defect; **~ismus** [-'lɪsmʊs] m materialism; **~ist** [-'lɪst] m materialist; **m~istisch** [-'lɪstɪʃ] adj materialistic

Materie [ma'teːriə] f matter, substance

materiell [materi'ɛl] adj material

Mathematik [matema'tiːk] f mathematics sg; **~er(in)** [mate'maːtikər(ɪn)] (-s, -) m(f) mathematician

mathematisch [mate'maːtɪʃ] adj mathematical

Matratze [ma'tratsə] f mattress

Matrixdrucker ['maːtrɪksdrʊkər] m dot-matrix printer

Matrize [ma'triːtsə] f matrix; (zum Abziehen) stencil

Matrose [ma'troːzə] (-n, -n) m sailor

Matsch [matʃ] (-(e)s) m mud; (Schnee~) slush; **m~ig** adj muddy; slushy

matt [mat] adj weak; (glanzlos) dull; (PHOT) matt; (SCHACH) mate

Matte ['matə] f mat

Mattscheibe f (TV) screen; **~ haben** (umg) not to be quite with it

Mauer ['mauər] (-, -n) f wall; **m~n** vi to build; to lay bricks ♦ vt to build

Maul [maul] (-(e)s, **Mäuler**) nt mouth; **m~en** (umg) vi to grumble; **~esel** m mule; **~korb** m muzzle; **~sperre** f lockjaw; **~tier** nt mule; **~wurf** m mole

Maurer ['maurər] (-s, -) m bricklayer

Maus [maus] (-, **Mäuse**) f (auch COMPUT) mouse

Mause- ['mauzə] zW: **~falle** f mousetrap; **m~n** vi to catch mice ♦ vt (umg) to pinch; **m~tot** adj stone dead

maximal [maksi'maːl] adj maximum ♦ adv at most

Maximum ['maksimʊm] nt maximum

Maxi-Single ['maksi'sıŋgl] (-, -s) f 12-inch single

Mayonnaise [majɔ'nɛːzə] f mayonnaise

m.E. abk (= meines Erachtens) in my opinion

Mechan- [me'çaːn] zW: ~**ik** f mechanics sg; (Getriebe) mechanics pl; ~**iker** (-s, -) m mechanic, engineer; **m~isch** adj mechanical; ~**ismus** [meça'nısmʊs] m mechanism

meckern ['mɛkərn] vi to bleat; (umg) to moan

Medaille [me'daljə] f medal

Medaillon [medal'jõː] (-s, -s) nt (Schmuck) locket

Medikament [medika'mɛnt] nt medicine

meditieren [medi'tiːrən] vi to meditate

Medizin [medi'tsiːn] (-, -en) f medicine; **m~isch** adj medical

Meer [meːr] (-(e)s, -e) nt sea; ~**busen** m bay, gulf; ~**enge** f straits pl; ~**esspiegel** m sea level; ~**rettich** m horseradish; ~**schweinchen** nt guinea-pig

Megaphon [mega'foːn] (-s, -e) nt megaphone

Mehl [meːl] (-(e)s, -e) nt flour; **m~ig** adj floury

mehr [meːr] adj, adv more; ~**deutig** adj ambiguous; ~**ere** adj several; ~**eres** pron several things; ~**fach** adj multiple; (wiederholt) repeated; **M~heit** f majority; ~**malig** adj repeated; ~**mals** adv repeatedly; ~**stimmig** adj for several voices; ~**stimmig** **singen** to harmonize; **M~wertsteuer** f value added tax; **M~zahl** f majority; (GRAM) plural

meiden ['maidən] (unreg) vt to avoid

Meile ['mailə] f mile; **Meilenstein** m milestone; **meilenweit** adj for miles

mein(e) [main] adj my; ~**e(r, s)** pron mine

Meineid ['main'ait] m perjury

meinen ['mainən] vi to think ♦ vt to think; (sagen) to say; (sagen wollen) to mean; **das will ich ~** I should think so

mein- zW: ~**erseits** adv for my part; ~**esgleichen** pron people like me; ~**etwegen** adv (für mich) for my sake;

(wegen mir) on my account; (von mir aus) as far as I'm concerned; I don't care od mind; ~**etwillen** adv: um ~**etwillen** for my sake, on my account

Meinung ['mainʊŋ] f opinion; **ganz meine ~** I quite agree; **jdm die ~ sagen** to give sb a piece of one's mind

Meinungs- zW: ~**austausch** m exchange of views; ~**umfrage** f opinion poll; ~**verschiedenheit** f difference of opinion

Meise ['maizə] f tit(mouse)

Meißel ['maisəl] (-s, -) m chisel; **m~n** vt to chisel

meist [maist] adj most ♦ adv mostly; **am ~en** the most; ~**ens** adv generally, usually

Meister ['maistər] (-s, -) m master; (SPORT) champion; **m~haft** adj masterly; ~**schaft** f mastery; (SPORT) championship; ~**stück** nt masterpiece; ~**werk** nt masterpiece

Melancholie [melaŋko'liː] f melancholy

melancholisch [melaŋ'koːlɪʃ] adj melancholy

Melde- ['mɛldə] zW: ~**frist** f registration period; **m~n** vt to report ♦ vr to report; (SCH) to put one's hand up; (freiwillig) to volunteer; (auf etw, am Telefon) to answer; **sich m~n bei** to report to; to register with; **sich zu Wort m~n** to ask to speak; ~**pflicht** f obligation to register with the police; ~**stelle** f registration office

Meldung ['mɛldʊŋ] f announcement; (Bericht) report

meliert [me'liːrt] adj (Haar) greying; (Wolle) flecked

melken ['mɛlkən] (unreg) vt to milk

Melodie [melo'diː] f melody, tune

melodisch [me'loːdɪʃ] adj melodious, tuneful

Melone [me'loːnə] f melon; (Hut) bowler (hat)

Membran [mem'braːn] (-, -en) f (TECH) diaphragm

Membrane f (TECH) diaphragm

Memoiren [memo'aːrən] pl memoirs

Menge ['mɛŋə] f quantity; (Menschen~) crowd; (große Anzahl) lot (of); **m~n**

vt to mix ♦ *vr*: **sich m~n in** +*akk* to meddle with; **Mengenlehre** *f* (*MATH*) set theory; **Mengenrabatt** *m* bulk discount

Mensch [mɛnʃ] (**-en, -en**) *m* human being, man; person ♦ *excl* hey!; **kein ~** nobody

Menschen- *zW*: **~feind** *m* misanthrope; **m~freundlich** *adj* philanthropical; **~kenner** *m* judge of human nature; **m~möglich** *adj* humanly possible; **~rechte** *pl* human rights; **m~unwürdig** *adj* beneath human dignity; **~verstand** *m*: **gesunder ~verstand** common sense

Mensch- *zW*: **~heit** *f* humanity, mankind; **m~lich** *adj* human; (*human*) humane; **~lichkeit** *f* humanity

Menstruation [mɛnstruatsi'oːn] *f* menstruation

Mentalität [mɛntali'tɛːt] *f* mentality

Menü [me'nyː] (**-s, -s**) *nt* (*auch COMPUT*) menu

Merk- [mɛrk] *zW*: **~blatt** *nt* instruction sheet *od* leaflet; **m~en** *vt* to notice; **sich** *dat* **etw m~en** to remember sth; **m~lich** *adj* noticeable; **~mal** *nt* sign, characteristic; **m~würdig** *adj* odd

meßbar ['mɛsbaːr] *adj* measurable

Messe ['mɛsə] *f* fair; (*ECCL*) mass

messen (*unreg*) *vt* to measure ♦ *vr* to compete

Messer (**-s, -**) *nt* knife; **~spitze** *f* knife point; (*in Rezept*) pinch

Meßgerät *nt* measuring device, gauge

Messing ['mɛsɪŋ] (**-s**) *nt* brass

Metall [me'tal] (**-s, -e**) *nt* metal; **m~en** *adj* metallic; **m~isch** *adj* metallic

Meteor [mete'oːr] (**-s, -e**) *nt* meteor

Meter ['meːtər] (**-s, -**) *nt od m* metre; **~maß** *nt* tape measure

Methode [me'toːdə] *f* method

methodisch [me'toːdɪʃ] *adj* methodical

Metropole [metro'poːlə] *f* metropolis

Metzger ['mɛtsgər] (**-s, -**) *m* butcher; **~ei** [-'rai] *f* butcher's (shop)

Meuchelmord ['mɔʏçəlmɔrt] *m* assassination

Meute ['mɔʏtə] *f* pack; **~rei** *f* mutiny; **m~rn** *vi* to mutiny

miauen [mi'auən] *vi* to miaow

mich [mɪç] (*akk von* **ich**) *pron* me; myself

Miene ['miːnə] *f* look, expression

mies [miːs] (*umg*) *adj* lousy

Miet- ['miːt] *zW*: **~auto** *nt* hired car; **~e** *f* rent, **zur ~e wohnen** to live in rented accommodation; **m~en** *vt* to rent; (*Auto*) to hire; **~er(in)** (**-s, -**) *m(f)* tenant; **Mietshaus** *nt* tenement, block of (rented) flats; **~vertrag** *m* lease

Migräne [mi'grɛːnə] *f* migraine

Mikro- ['mikro] *zW*: **~computer** *m* microcomputer; **~fon** (**-s, -e**) *nt* microphone; **~phon** [-'foːn] (**-s, -e**) *nt* microphone; **~skop** [-'skoːp] (**-s, -e**) *nt* microscope; **m~skopisch** *adj* microscopic; **~wellenherd** *m* microwave (oven)

Milch [mɪlç] (**-**) *f* milk; **~glas** *nt* frosted glass; **m~ig** *adj* milky; **~kaffee** *m* white coffee; **~pulver** *nt* powdered milk; **~straße** *f* Milky Way; **~zahn** *m* milk tooth

mild [mɪlt] *adj* mild; (*Richter*) lenient; (*freundlich*) kind, charitable; **M~e** ['mɪldə] *f* mildness; leniency; **~ern** *vt* to mitigate, to soften; (*Schmerz*) to alleviate; **~ernde Umstände** extenuating circumstances

Milieu [mili'øː] (**-s, -s**) *nt* background, environment; **m~geschädigt** *adj* maladjusted

Mili- [mili] *zW*: **m~tant** [-'tant] *adj* militant; **~tär** [-'tɛːr] (**-s**) *nt* military, army; **~tärgericht** *nt* military court; **m~tärisch** *adj* military

Milli- ['mɪli] *zW*: **~ardär** [-ar'dɛːr] *m* multimillionaire; **~arde** [-'ardə] *f* milliard; billion (*bes US*); **~meter** *m* millimetre; **~on** [-'oːn] (**-, -en**) *f* million; **~onär** [-o'nɛːr] *m* millionaire

Milz [mɪlts] (**-, -en**) *f* spleen

Mimik ['miːmɪk] *f* mime

Mimose [mi'moːzə] *f* mimosa; (*fig*) sensitive person

minder ['mɪndər] *adj* inferior ♦ *adv* less; **M~heit** *f* minority; **~jährig** *adj* minor; **M~jährigkeit** *f* minority; **~n** *vt, vr* to decrease, to diminish; **M~ung** *f*

decrease; ~**wertig** *adj* inferior;
M~wertigkeitskomplex *m* inferiority
complex
Mindest- ['mɪndəst] *zW:* ~**alter** *nt* minimum age; ~**betrag** *m* minimum
amount; **m~e(r, s)** *adj* least; **zum**
m~en at least; **m~ens** *adv* at least;
~**lohn** *m* minimum wage; ~**maß** *nt*
minimum
Mine ['miːnə] *f* mine; (*Bleistift~*) lead;
(*Kugelschreiber~*) refill; **Minenfeld** *nt*
minefield
Mineral [mine'raːl] (-s, -e *od* -ien) *nt*
mineral; **m~isch** *adj* mineral;
~**wasser** *nt* mineral water
Miniatur [minia'tuːr] *f* miniature
minimal [mini'maːl] *adj* minimal
Minimum ['miːnimʊm] *nt* minimum
Minister [mi'nɪstər] (-s, -) *m* minister;
m~iell [mɪnɪsteri'ɛl] *adj* ministerial;
~**ium** [mɪnɪs'teːriʊm] *nt* ministry;
~**präsident** *m* prime minister
Minus ['miːnʊs] (-, -) *nt* deficit
minus *adv* minus; **M~pol** *m* negative
pole; **M~zeichen** *nt* minus sign
Minute [mi'nuːtə] *f* minute; **Minuten-**
zeiger *m* minute hand
Mio. *abk* (= *Million(en)*) million(s)
mir [miːr] (*dat von* **ich**) *pron* (to) me; ~
nichts, dir nichts just like that
Misch- ['mɪʃ] *zW:* ~**ehe** *f* mixed marriage; **m~en** *vt* to mix; ~**ling** *m* half-
caste; ~**ung** *f* mixture
Miß- ['mɪs] *zW:* **m~'achten** *vt insep* to
disregard; ~'**achtung** *f* disregard;
~**behagen** *nt* discomfort, uneasiness;
~**bildung** *f* deformity; **m~'billigen** *vt*
insep to disapprove of; ~**billigung** *f* disapproval; ~**brauch** *m* abuse; (*falscher*
Gebrauch) misuse; **m~'brauchen** *vt in-*
sep to abuse; **jdn zu** *od* **für etw**
m~brauchen to use sb for *od* to do sth;
~**erfolg** *m* failure; ~**fallen** (-s) *nt* displeasure; **m~'fallen** (*unreg*) *vi insep:*
jdm m~fallen to displease sb; ~**geburt**
f freak; (*fig*) abortion; ~**geschick** *nt*
misfortune; **m~glücken** [mɪs'glʏkən] *vi*
insep to fail; **jdm m~glückt etw** sb does
not succeed with sth; ~**griff** *m* mistake; ~**gunst** *f* envy; **m~günstig** *adj*

envious; **m~'handeln** *vt insep* to ill-
treat; ~'**handlung** *f* ill-treatment
Mission [mɪsi'oːn] *f* mission; ~**ar(in)**
[mɪsio'naːr(ɪn)] *m(f)* missionary
Miß- *zW:* ~**klang** *m* discord; ~**kredit**
m discredit; **m~lingen** [mɪs'lɪŋən] (*un-*
reg) *vi insep* to fail; ~**mut** *m* sullen-
ness; **m~mutig** *adj* sullen; **m~'raten**
(*unreg*) *vi insep* to turn out badly ♦ *adj*
ill-bred, ~**stand** *m* bad state of affairs;
abuse; ~**stimmung** *f* ill-humour, discord; **m~'trauen** *vi insep* to mistrust;
~**trauen** (-s) *nt* distrust, suspicion;
~**trauensantrag** *m* (*POL*) motion of no
confidence; ~**trauensvotum** (-s, -**voten**)
nt (*POL*) vote of no confidence;
m~trauisch *adj* distrustful, suspicious;
~**verhältnis** *nt* disproportion; ~**ver-**
ständnis *nt* misunderstanding; **m~'**
verstehen (*unreg*) *vt insep* to misunderstand
Mist [mɪst] (-(e)s) *m* dung; dirt; (*umg*)
rubbish
Mistel (-, -n) *f* mistletoe
Misthaufen *m* dungheap
mit [mɪt] *präp +dat* with; (*mittels*) by ♦
adv along, too; ~ **der Bahn** by train; ~
10 Jahren at the age of 10; **wollen Sie**
~? do you want to come along?
Mitarbeit ['mɪt'arbaɪt] *f* cooperation;
m~en *vi* to cooperate, to collaborate;
~**er(in)** *m(f)* collaborator; co-worker ♦
pl (*Personal*) staff
Mit- *zW:* ~**bestimmung** *f* participation
in decision-making; **m~bringen** (*un-*
reg) *vt* to bring along; ~**bürger(in)**
m(f) fellow citizen
miteinander [mɪt'aɪ'nandər] *adv*
together, with one another
miterleben *vt* to see, to witness
Mitesser ['mɪt'ɛsər] (-s, -) *m* blackhead
Mit- *zW:* **m~geben** (*unreg*) *vt* to give;
~**gefühl** *nt* sympathy; **m~gehen** (*un-*
reg) *vi* to go/come along; **m~ge-**
nommen *adj* done in, in a bad way;
~**gift** *f* dowry
Mitglied ['mɪtgliːt] *nt* member; **Mit-**
gliedsbeitrag *m* membership fee;
~**schaft** *f* membership
Mit- *zW:* **m~halten** (*unreg*) *vi* to keep

up; ~**hilfe** f help, assistance; **m~hören**
vt to listen in to; **m~kommen** (unreg)
vi to come along; (verstehen) to keep
up, to follow; ~**läufer** m hanger-on;
(POL) fellow-traveller

Mitleid nt sympathy; (Erbarmen)
compassion; ~**enschaft** f: in ~**enschaft
ziehen** to affect; **m~ig** adj sympathetic; **mitleidslos** adj pitiless, merciless

Mit- zW: **m~machen** vt to join in, to
take part in; ~**mensch** m fellow man;
m~nehmen (unreg) vt to take along/
away; (anstrengen) to wear out, to
exhaust; **zum ~nehmen** to take away

mitsamt [mɪt'zamt] präp +dat together
with

Mitschuld f complicity; **m~ig** adj:
m~ig (an +dat) implicated (in); (an
Unfall) partly responsible (for)

Mit- zW: ~**schüler(in)** m(f) schoolmate;
m~spielen vi to join in, to take part;
~**spieler(in)** m(f) partner; ~**spra-
cherecht** ['mɪtʃpraːxərɛçt] nt voice, say

Mittag ['mɪtaːk] (-(e)s, -e) m midday,
lunchtime; (zu) ~ **essen** to have lunch;
m~ adv at lunchtime od noon; ~**essen**
nt lunch, dinner

mittags adv at lunchtime od noon;
M~pause f lunch break; **M~schlaf** m
early afternoon nap, siesta

Mittäter(in) ['mɪtɛːtər(ɪn)] m(f)
accomplice

Mitte ['mɪtə] f middle; (POL) centre;
aus unserer ~ from our midst

mitteilen ['mɪttaɪlən] vt: **jdm etw ~** to
inform sb of sth, to communicate sth to
sb

Mitteilung f communication

Mittel ['mɪtəl] (-s, -) nt means; method;
(MATH) average; (MED) medicine; **ein
~ zum Zweck** a means to an end;
~**alter** nt Middle Ages pl; **m~alterlich**
adj mediaeval; ~**amerika** nt Central
America; **m~bar** adj indirect; ~**ding**
nt cross; ~**europa** nt Central Europe;
m~los adj without means; **m~mäßig**
adj mediocre, middling; ~**mäßigkeit** f
mediocrity; ~**meer** nt Mediterranean;
~**punkt** m centre; **m~s** präp +gen by
means of; ~**stand** m middle class;

~**streckenrakete** f medium-range missile; ~**streifen** m central reservation;
~**stürmer** m centre-forward; ~**weg** m
middle course; ~**welle** f (RADIO)
medium wave

mitten ['mɪtən] adv in the middle; ~ **auf
der Straße/in der Nacht** in the middle of
the street/night

Mitternacht ['mɪtərnaxt] f midnight

mittlere(r, s) ['mɪtlərə(r, s)] adj middle;
(durchschnittlich) medium, average

mittlerweile ['mɪtlər'vaɪlə] adv meanwhile

Mittwoch ['mɪtvɔx] (-(e)s, -e) m
Wednesday; **m~s** adv on Wednesdays

mitunter [mɪt''ʊntər] adv occasionally,
sometimes

Mit- zW: **m~verantwortlich** adj jointly
responsible; **m~wirken** vi: **m~wirken
(bei)** to contribute (to); (THEAT) to take
part (in); ~**wirkung** f contribution;
participation

Möbel ['møːbəl] pl furniture sg;
~**wagen** m furniture od removal van

mobil [mo'biːl] adj mobile; (MIL)
mobilized; **M~iar** [mobili'aːr] (-s, -e) nt
furnishings pl; **M~machung** f mobiliza-
tion

möblieren [møˈbliːrən] vt to furnish;
möbliert wohnen to live in furnished
accommodation

möchte etc ['mœçtə] vb siehe **mögen**

Mode ['moːdə] f fashion

Modell [mo'dɛl] (-s, -e) nt model;
m~ieren [-'liːrən] vt to model

Modenschau f fashion show

modern [mo'dɛrn] adj modern;
(modisch) fashionable; ~**isieren** vt to
modernize

Mode- zW: ~**schau** f fashion show;
~**schmuck** m fashion jewellery;
~**schöpfer(in)** m(f) fashion designer;
~**wort** nt fashionable word, buzz word

modisch ['moːdɪʃ] adj fashionable

Mofa ['moːfa] (-s, -s) nt small moped

mogeln ['moːgəln] (umg) vi to cheat

mögen ['møːgən] (pt **mochte**, pp
gemocht od (als Hilfsverb) **mögen**) vt,

vi to like; **magst du/mögen Sie ihn?** do you like him?; **ich möchte ...** I would like ..., I'd like ...; **er möchte in die Stadt** he'd like to go into town; **ich möchte nicht, daß du ...** I wouldn't like you to ...; **ich mag nicht mehr** I've had enough
♦ *Hilfsverb* to like to; (*wollen*) to want; **möchtest du etwas essen?** would you like something to eat?; **sie mag nicht bleiben** she doesn't want to stay; **das mag wohl sein** that may well be; **was mag das heißen?** what might that mean?; **Sie möchten zu Hause anrufen** could you please call home?

möglich ['mø:klıç] *adj* possible; **~erweise** *adv* possibly; **M~keit** *f* possibility; **nach M~keit** if possible; **~st** *adv* as ... as possible
Mohn [mo:n] (-(e)s, -e) *m* (*~blume*) poppy; (*~samen*) poppy seed
Möhre ['mø:rə] *f* carrot
Mohrrübe *f* carrot
mokieren [mo'ki:rən] *vr*: **sich ~ über** +*akk* to make fun of
Moldau ['mɔldau] (-) *f* Moldavia
Mole ['mo:lə] *f* (harbour) mole
Molekül [mole'ky:l] (-s, -e) *nt* molecule
Molkerei [mɔlkə'rai] *f* dairy
Moll [mɔl] (-, -) *nt* (MUS) minor (key)
mollig *adj* cosy; (*dicklich*) plump
Moment [mo'mɛnt] (-(e)s, -e) *m* moment ♦ *nt* factor; **im ~** at the moment; **~ (mal)!** just a moment; **m~an** [-'ta:n] *adj* momentary ♦ *adv* at the moment
Monarch [mo'narç] (-en, -en) *m* monarch; **~ie** [monar'çi:] *f* monarchy
Monat ['mo:nat] (-(e)s, -e) *m* month; **m~elang** *adv* for months; **m~lich** *adj* monthly; **~skarte** *f* monthly ticket
Mönch [mœnç] (-(e)s, -e) *nt* monk
Mond [mo:nt] (-(e)s, -e) *m* moon; **~finsternis** *f* eclipse of the moon; **m~hell** *adj* moonlit; **~landung** *f* moon landing; **~schein** *m* moonlight; **~sonde** *f* moon probe
Mono- [mono] *in zW* mono; **~log** [-'lo:k] (-s, -e) *m* monologue; **~pol** [-'po:l] (-s,

-e) *nt* monopoly; **m~polisieren** [-poli'zi:rən] *vt* to monopolize; **m~ton** [-'to:n] *adj* monotonous; **~tonie** [-to'ni:] *f* monotony
Monsun [mɔn'zu:n] (-s, -e) *m* monsoon
Montag ['mo:nta:k] (-(e)s, -e) *m* Monday
Montage ['mɔn'ta:ʒə] *f* (PHOT etc) montage; (TECH) assembly; (*Einbauen*) fitting
montags *adv* on Mondays
Monteur [mɔn'tø:r] *m* fitter
montieren [mɔn'ti:rən] *vt* to assemble
Monument [monu'mɛnt] *nt* monument; **m~al** *adj* monumental
Moor [mo:r] (-(e)s, -e) *nt* moor
Moos [mo:s] (-es, -e) *nt* moss
Moped ['mo:pet] (-s, -s) *nt* moped
Mops [mɔps] (-es, ⁼e) *m* pug
Moral [mo'ra:l] (-, -en) *f* morality; (*einer Geschichte*) moral; **m~isch** *adj* moral
Moräne [mo'rɛ:nə] *f* moraine
Morast [mo'rast] (-(e)s, -e) *m* morass, mire; **m~ig** *adj* boggy
Mord [mɔrt] (-(e)s, -e) *m* murder; **~anschlag** *m* murder attempt
Mörder(in) ['mœrdər(ın)] (-s, -) *m(f)* murderer(eress)
Mord- *zW*: **~kommission** *f* murder squad; **Mordsglück** (*umg*) *nt* amazing luck; **mordsmäßig** (*umg*) *adj* terrific, enormous; **Mordsschreck** (*umg*) *m* terrible fright; **~verdacht** *m* suspicion of murder; **~waffe** *f* murder weapon
morgen ['mɔrgən] *adv* tomorrow; **M~** (-s, -) *m* morning; **~ früh** tomorrow morning; **M~mantel** *m* dressing gown; **M~rock** *m* dressing gown; **M~röte** *f* dawn; **~s** *adv* in the morning
morgig ['mɔrgıç] *adj* tomorrow's; **der ~e Tag** tomorrow
Morphium ['mɔrfium] *nt* morphine
morsch [mɔrʃ] *adj* rotten
Morsealphabet ['mɔrzə-] *nt* Morse code
morsen *vi* to send a message by morse code
Mörtel ['mœrtəl] (-s, -) *m* mortar
Mosaik [moza'i:k] (-s, -en *od* -e) *nt* mosaic

Moschee [mɔ'ʃeː] (-, -n) f mosque
Moskau ['mɔskaʊ] (-s) nt Moscow; ~er
adj Muscovite
Moskito [mɔs'kiːto] (-s, -s) m mosquito
Most [mɔst] (-(e)s, -e) m (unfermented)
fruit juice; (Apfelwein) cider
Motel [mo'tɛl] (-s, -s) nt motel
Motiv [mo'tiːf] (-s, -e) nt motive; (MUS)
theme; m~ieren [moti'viːrən] vt to
motivate; ~ierung f motivation
Motor ['moːtɔr, pl mo'toːrən] (-s, -en) m
engine; (bes ELEK) motor; ~boot nt
motorboat; ~enöl nt motor oil;
m~isieren [motori'ziːrən] vt to motorize;
~rad nt motorcycle; ~schaden m
engine trouble od failure
Motte ['mɔtə] f moth; **Mottenkugel** f
mothball(s)
Motto ['mɔto] (-s, -s) nt motto
Möwe ['møːvə] f seagull
Mrd. abk (= Milliarde(n)) thousand
million(s), billion(s) (US)
Mücke ['mʏkə] f midge, gnat; **Mücken-
stich** m midge od gnat bite
müde ['myːdə] adj tired
Müdigkeit ['myːdɪçkaɪt] f tiredness
Muff [mʊf] (-(e)s, -e) m (Handwärmer)
muff
Muffel (-s, -; umg) m killjoy, sourpuss
muffig adj (Luft) musty
Mühe ['myːə] f trouble, pains pl; **mit
Müh und Not** with great difficulty; **sich
dat** ~ **geben** to go to a lot of trouble;
m~los adj without trouble, easy;
m~voll adj laborious, arduous
Mühle ['myːlə] f mill; (Kaffee~) grinder
Müh- zW: m~sal (-, -e) f tribulation;
m~sam adj arduous, troublesome;
m~selig adj arduous, laborious
Mulde ['mʊldə] f hollow, depression
Mull [mʊl] (-(e)s, -e) m thin muslin;
~binde f gauze bandage
Müll [mʏl] (-(e)s, -e) m refuse; ~abfuhr f
rubbish disposal; (Leute) dustmen pl;
~abladeplatz m rubbish dump; ~eimer
m dustbin, garbage can (US); ~haufen
m rubbish heap; ~schlucker (-s, -) m
garbage disposal unit; ~verbrennungs-
anlage f incinerator; ~wagen m
dustcart, garbage truck (US)

mulmig ['mʊlmɪç] adj rotten; (umg)
dodgy; **jdm ist** ~ sb feels funny
multiplizieren [mʊltipli'tsiːrən] vt to
multiply
Mumie ['muːmiə] f mummy
Mumm [mʊm] (-s; umg) m gumption,
nerve
München ['mʏnçən] (-s) nt Munich
Mund [mʊnt, pl 'mʏndər] (-(e)s, ⁼er) m
mouth; ~art f dialect
Mündel ['mʏndəl] (-s, -) nt ward
münden ['mʏndən] vi: ~ **in** +akk to
flow into
Mund- zW: m~faul adj taciturn;
~geruch m bad breath; ~harmonika f
mouth organ
mündig ['mʏndɪç] adj of age; **M~keit** f
majority
mündlich ['mʏntlɪç] adj oral
Mundstück nt mouthpiece; (Zigaret-
ten~) tip
Mündung ['mʏndʊŋ] f (von Fluß)
mouth; (Gewehr) muzzle
Mund- zW: ~wasser nt mouthwash;
~werk nt: **ein großes** ~werk **haben** to
have a big mouth; ~winkel m corner
of the mouth
Munition [munitsi'oːn] f ammunition;
Munitionslager nt ammunition dump
munkeln ['mʊŋkəln] vi to whisper, to
mutter
Münster ['mʏnstər] (-s, -) nt minster
munter ['mʊntər] adj lively; **M~keit** f
liveliness
Münze ['mʏntsə] f coin; m~n vt to coin,
to mint; **auf jdn gemünzt sein** to be
aimed at sb
Münzfernsprecher ['mʏntsfɛrnʃprɛçər]
m callbox (BRIT), pay phone
mürb(e) ['mʏrb(ə)] adj (Gestein)
crumbly; (Holz) rotten; (Gebäck)
crisp; **jdn** ~ **machen** to wear sb down;
M~teig m shortcrust pastry
murmeln ['mʊrməln] vt, vi to murmer,
to mutter
Murmeltier ['mʊrməltiːr] nt marmot
murren ['mʊrən] vi to grumble, to
grouse
mürrisch ['mʏrɪʃ] adj sullen
Mus [muːs] (-es, -e) nt purée

Muschel ['muʃəl] (-, -n) f mussel; (~schale) shell; (Telefon~) receiver
Muse ['mu:zə] f muse
Museum [mu'ze:um] (-s, Museen) nt museum
Musik [mu'zi:k] f music; (Kapelle) band; m~alisch [-'ka:lɪʃ] adj musical; ~box f jukebox; ~er ['mu:zikər] (-s, -) m musician; ~hochschule f college of music; ~instrument nt musical instrument; ~truhe f radiogram
musizieren [muzi'tsi:rən] vi to make music
Muskat [mus'ka:t] (-(e)s, -e) m nutmeg
Muskel ['muskəl] (-s, -n) m muscle; ~kater m: einen ~kater haben to be stiff
Muskulatur [muskula'tu:r] f muscular system
muskulös [musku'lø:s] adj muscular
Muß [mus] (-) nt necessity, must
Muße ['mu:sə] (-) f leisure

müssen ['mysən] (pt mußte, pp gemußt od (als Hilfsverb) müssen) vi 1 (Zwang) must (nur im Präsens), to have to; ich muß es tun I must do it, I have to do it; ich mußte es tun I had to do it; er muß es nicht tun he doesn't have to do it; muß ich? must I?, do I have to?; wann müßt ihr zur Schule? when do you have to go to school?; er hat gehen müssen he (has) had to go; muß das sein? is that really necessary?; ich muß mal (umg) I need the toilet
2 (sollen): das mußt du nicht tun! you oughtn't to od shouldn't do that; Sie hätten ihn fragen müssen you should have asked him
3: es muß geregnet haben it must have rained; es muß nicht wahr sein it needn't be true

müßig ['my:sɪç] adj idle; M~gang m idleness
Muster ['mustər] (-s, -) nt model; (Dessin) pattern; (Probe) sample; m~gültig adj exemplary; m~n vt

(Tapete) to pattern; (fig, MIL) to examine; (Truppen) to inspect; ~ung f (von Stoff) pattern; (MIL) inspection
Mut [mu:t] m courage; nur ~! cheer up!; jdm ~ machen to encourage sb; m~ig adj courageous; m~los adj discouraged, despondent
mutmaßlich ['mu:tma:slɪç] adj presumed ♦ adv probably
Mutter[1] ['mutər] (-, =) f mother
Mutter[2] (-, Muttern) f (Schrauben~) nut
Muttergesellschaft f parent company
mütterlich ['mʏtərlɪç] adj motherly; ~erseits adv on the mother's side
Mutter- zW: ~liebe f motherly love; ~mal nt Mehrwertsteuer; ~schaft f motherhood, maternity; ~schutz m maternity regulations; 'm~'seelena'llein adj all alone; ~sprache f native language; ~tag m Mother's Day
Mutti ['muti] (-, -s) f mum(my) (BRIT), mom(my) (US)
mutwillig ['mu:tvɪlɪç] adj malicious, deliberate
Mütze ['mʏtsə] f cap
MwSt abk (= Mehrwertsteuer) VAT
mysteriös [mʏsteri'ø:s] adj mysterious
Mythos ['my:tɔs] (-, Mythen) m myth

N

na [na] excl well; ~ gut okay then
Nabel ['na:bəl] (-s, -) m navel; ~schnur f umbilical cord

nach [na:x] präp +dat 1 (örtlich) to; nach Berlin to Berlin; nach links/rechts (to the) left/right; nach oben/hinten up/back
2 (zeitlich) after; einer nach dem anderen one after the other; nach Ihnen! after you!; zehn (Minuten) nach drei ten (minutes) past three
3 (gemäß) according to; nach dem Gesetz according to the law; dem Namen nach judging by his/her name; nach allem, was ich weiß as far as I

know

♦ *adv*: **ihm nach!** after him!; **nach und nach** gradually, little by little; **nach wie vor** still

---

nachahmen ['na:x'a:mən] *vt* to imitate

Nachahmung *f* imitation

Nachbar(in) ['na:xba:r(ɪn)] (**-s, -n**) *m(f)* neighbour; ~**haus** *nt*: **im** ~**haus** next door; **n~lich** *adj* neighbourly; ~**schaft** *f* neighbourhood; ~**staat** *m* neighbouring state

nach- *zW*: ~**bestellen** *vt*: **50 Stück** ~**bestellen** to order another 50; **N~bestellung** *f* (*COMM*) repeat order; ~**bilden** *vt* to copy; **N~bildung** *f* imitation, copy; ~**blicken** *vi* to gaze after; ~**datieren** *vt* to postdate

nachdem [na:x'de:m] *konj* after; (*weil*) since; **je ~** (**ob**) it depends (whether)

nach- *zW*: ~**denken** (*unreg*) *vi*: ~**denken über** +*akk* to think about; **N~denken** (**-s**) *nt* reflection, meditation; ~**denklich** *adj* thoughtful, pensive

Nachdruck ['na:xdrʊk] *m* emphasis; (*TYP*) reprint, reproduction

nachdrücklich ['na:xdrʏklɪç] *adj* emphatic

nacheinander [na:x'aɪ'nandər] *adv* one after the other

nachempfinden ['na:x'ɛmpfɪndən] (*unreg*) *vt*: **jdm etw ~** to feel sth with sb

Nacherzählung ['na:x'ɛrtsɛ:lʊŋ] *f* reproduction (of a story)

Nachfahr ['na:xfa:r] (**-s, -en**) *m* descendant

Nachfolge ['na:xfɔlgə] *f* succession; **n~n** *vi* +*dat* to follow; ~**r(in)** (**-s, -**) *m(f)* successor

nachforschen *vt, vi* to investigate

Nachforschung *f* investigation

Nachfrage ['na:xfra:gə] *f* inquiry; (*COMM*) demand; **n~n** *vi* to inquire

nach- *zW*: ~**fühlen** *vt* = ~**empfinden**; ~**füllen** *vt* to refill; ~**geben** (*unreg*) *vi* to give way, to yield; **N~gebühr** *f* (*POST*) excess postage; **N~geburt** *f* afterbirth

nachgehen ['na:xge:ən] (*unreg*) *vi* (+*dat*) to follow; (*erforschen*) to in-

quire (into); (*Uhr*) to be slow

Nachgeschmack ['na:xgəʃmak] *m* aftertaste

nachgiebig ['na:xgi:bɪç] *adj* soft, accommodating; **N~keit** *f* softness

nachhaltig ['na:xhaltɪç] *adj* lasting; (*Widerstand*) persistent

nachhelfen ['na:xhɛlfən] (*unreg*) *vi* +*dat* to assist (*jdm sb*), to help

nachher [na:x'he:r] *adv* afterwards

Nachhilfeunterricht ['na:xhɪlfəʊntərrɪçt] *m* extra tuition

nachholen ['na:xho:lən] *vt* to catch up with; (*Versäumtes*) to make up for

Nachkomme ['na:xkɔmə] (**-, -n**) *m* descendant

nachkommen (*unreg*) *vi* to follow; (*einer Verpflichtung*) to fulfil; **N~schaft** *f* descendants *pl*

Nachkriegs- ['na:xkri:ks] *in zW* postwar; ~**zeit** *f* postwar period

Nach- *zW*: ~**laß** (**-lasses, -lässe**) *m* (*COMM*) discount, rebate; . (*Erbe*) estate; **n~lassen** (*unreg*) *vt* (*Strafe*) to remit; (*Summe*) to take off; (*Schulden*) to cancel ♦ *vi* to decrease, to ease off; (*Sturm*) to die down, to ease off; (*schlechter werden*) to deteriorate; **er hat n~gelassen** he has got worse; **n~lässig** *adj* negligent, careless; ~**lässigkeit** *f* negligence, carelessness

nachlaufen ['na:xlaʊfən] (*unreg*) *vi* +*dat* to run after, to chase

nachmachen ['na:xmaxən] *vt* to imitate (*jdm etw sth from sb*), to copy; (*fälschen*) to counterfeit

Nachmittag ['na:xmɪta:k] *m* afternoon; **am ~** in the afternoon; **n~s** *adv* in the afternoon

Nach- *zW*: ~**nahme** *f* cash on delivery; **per** ~**nahme** C.O.D.; ~**name** *m* surname; ~**porto** *nt* excess postage

nachprüfen ['na:xpry:fən] *vt* to check, to verify

nachrechnen ['na:xrɛçnən] *vt* to check

Nachrede ['na:xre:də] *f*: **üble ~** libel; slander

Nachricht ['na:xrɪçt] (**-, -en**) *f* (piece of) news; (*Mitteilung*) message; ~**en** *pl* (*Neuigkeiten*) news; ~**enagentur** *f* news agency; **~endienst** m (*MIL*) intelligence service; **~ensprecher(in)** m(f) newsreader; **~entechnik** f telecommunications sg

Nachruf ['naːxruːf] m obituary

nachsagen ['naːxzaːgən] vt to repeat; **jdm etw** ~ to say sth of sb

nachschicken ['naːxʃɪkən] vt to forward

nachschlagen ['naːxʃlaːgən] (*unreg*) vt to look up

Nachschlagewerk nt reference book

Nachschlüssel m duplicate key

Nachschub m supplies pl; (*Truppen*) reinforcements pl

nachsehen ['naːxzeːən] (*unreg*) vt (*prüfen*) to check ♦ vi (*erforschen*) to look and see; **jdm etw** ~ to forgive sb sth; **das N~ haben** to come off worst

nachsenden ['naːxzɛndən] (*unreg*) vt to send on, to forward

Nachsicht ['naːxzɪçt] (-) f indulgence, leniency; **n~ig** adj indulgent, lenient

nachsitzen ['naːxzɪtsən] (*unreg*) vi: ~ (**müssen**) (*SCH*) to be kept in

Nachspeise ['naːxʃpaɪzə] f dessert, sweet, pudding

Nachspiel ['naːxʃpiːl] nt epilogue; (*fig*) sequel

nachsprechen ['naːxʃprɛçən] (*unreg*) vt: (**jdm**) ~ to repeat (after sb)

nächst [nɛːçst] präp +dat (*räumlich*) next to; (*außer*) apart from; **~beste(r, s)** adj first that comes along; (*zweitbeste*) next best; **N~e(r)** mf neighbour; **~e(r, s)** adj next; (*nächstgelegen*) nearest; **N~enliebe** f love for one's fellow men; **~ens** adv shortly, soon; **~liegend** adj nearest; (*fig*) obvious; **~möglich** adj next possible

nachsuchen ['naːxzuːxən] vi: **um etw** ~ to ask od apply for sth

Nacht [naxt] (-, ̈e) f night

Nachteil ['naːxtaɪl] m disadvantage; **n~ig** adj disadvantageous

Nachthemd nt (*Herren~*) nightshirt; (*Damen~*) nightdress

Nachtigall ['naxtɪgal] (-, -en) f nightingale

Nachtisch ['naːxtɪʃ] m = **Nachspeise**

Nachtklub m night club

nächtlich ['nɛçtlɪç] adj nightly

Nachtlokal nt night club

Nach- zW: **~trag** (-(e)s, -träge) m supplement; **n~tragen** (*unreg*) vt to carry; (*zufügen*) to add; **jdm etw n~tragen** to hold sth against sb; **n~träglich** adj later, subsequent; additional ♦ adv later, subsequently; additionally; **n~trauern** vi: **jdm/etw n~trauern** to mourn the loss of sb/sth

Nacht- zW: **~ruhe** f sleep; **n~s** adv at od by night; **~schicht** f nightshift; **nachtsüber** adv during the night; **~tarif** m off-peak tariff; **~tisch** m bedside table; **~wächter** m night watchman

Nach- zW: **~untersuchung** f checkup; **n~wachsen** (*unreg*) vi to grow again; **~wehen** pl afterpains; (*fig*) aftereffects

Nachweis ['naːxvaɪs] (-es, -e) m proof; **n~bar** adj provable, demonstrable; **n~en** (*unreg*) vt to prove; **jdm etw n~en** to point sth out to sb; **n~lich** adj evident, demonstrable

nach- zW: **~wirken** vi to have aftereffects; **N~wirkung** f after-effect; **N~wort** nt epilogue; **N~wuchs** m offspring; (*beruflich etc*) new recruits pl; **~zahlen** vt, vi to pay extra; **~zählen** vt to count again, to check; **N~zahlung** f additional payment; (*zurückdatiert*) back pay; **N~zügler** (-s, -) m straggler

Nacken ['nakən] (-s, -) m nape of the neck

nackt [nakt] adj naked; (*Tatsachen*) plain, bare; **N~heit** f nakedness

Nadel ['naːdəl] (-, -n) f needle; (*Steck~*) pin; **~kissen** nt pincushion; **~öhr** nt eye of a needle; **~wald** m coniferous forest

Nagel ['naːgəl] (-s, ̈) m nail; **~feile** f nailfile; **~haut** f cuticle; **~lack** m nail varnish od polish (*BRIT*); **n~n** vt, vi to nail; **n~neu** adj brand-new; **~schere** f nail scissors pl

nagen ['naːgən] vt, vi to gnaw

Nagetier ['naːgətiːr] nt rodent

nah(e) ['naː(ə)] adj (*räumlich*) near(by); (*Verwandte*) near; (*Freun-*

de) close; (*zeitlich*) near, close ♦ *adv*
near(by); near, close; (*verwandt*)
closely ♦ *präp* +*dat* near (to), close to;
der N~e Osten the Near East;
Nahaufnahme *f* close-up

Nähe ['nɛːə] (-) *f* nearness, proximity;
(*Umgebung*) vicinity; **in der ~** close
by; at hand; **aus der ~** from close to

nahe- *zW*: **~bei** *adv* nearby; **~gehen**
(*unreg*) *vi* +*dat* to grieve; **~kommen**
(*unreg*) *vi* (+*dat*) to get close (to);
~legen *vt*: **jdm etw ~legen** to suggest
sth to sb; **~liegen** (*unreg*) *vi* to be
obvious; **~liegend** *adj* obvious; **~n** *vi*,
vr to approach, to draw near

nähen ['nɛːən] *vt*, *vi* to sew

näher *adj*, *adv* nearer; (*Erklärung,
Erkundigung*) more detailed; **N~e(s)** *nt*
details *pl*, particulars *pl*

Näherei *f* sewing, needlework

Näherin *f* seamstress

näherkommen (*unreg*) *vi*, *vr* to get
closer

nähern *vr* to approach

nahe- *zW*: **~stehen** (*unreg*) *vi* (+*dat*)
to be close (to); **einer Sache ~stehen** to
sympathize with sth; **~stehend** *adj*
close; **~treten** (*unreg*) *vi*: **jdm** (**zu**)
~treten to offend sb; **~zu** *adv* nearly

Nähgarn *nt* thread

nahm *etc* [naːm] *vb siehe* **nehmen**

Nähmaschine *f* sewing machine

Nähnadel *f* needle

nähren ['nɛːrən] *vt* to feed ♦ *vr*
(*Person*) to feed o.s.; (*Tier*) to feed

nahrhaft ['naːrhaft] *adj* nourishing, nutritious

Nahrung ['naːrʊŋ] *f* food; (*fig auch*)
sustenance

Nahrungs- *zW*: **~mittel** *nt* foodstuffs
pl; **~mittelindustrie** *f* food industry;
~suche *f* search for food

Nährwert *m* nutritional value

Naht [naːt] (-, ⁻e) *f* seam; (*MED*) suture;
(*TECH*) join; **n~los** *adj* seamless; **n~los
ineinander übergehen** to follow without
a gap

Nah- *zW*: **~verkehr** *m* local traffic;
~verkehrszug *m* local train; **~ziel** *nt*
immediate objective

naiv [naˈiːf] *adj* naive; **N~ität** *f* naivety

Name ['naːmə] (-ns, -n) *m* name; **im ~n
von** on behalf of; **n~ns** *adv* by the
name of; **~nstag** *m* name day, saint's
day; **n~ntlich** *adj* by name ♦ *adv*
particularly, especially

namhaft ['naːmhaft] *adj* (*berühmt*)
famed, renowned; (*beträchtlich*) considerable; **~ machen** to name

nämlich ['nɛːmlɪç] *adv* that is to say,
namely; (*denn*) since

nannte *etc* ['nantə] *vb siehe* **nennen**

nanu [naˈnuː] *excl* well, well!

Napf [napf] (-(e)s, ⁻e) *m* bowl, dish

Narbe ['narbə] *f* scar

narbig ['narbɪç] *adj* scarred

Narkose [narˈkoːzə] *f* anaesthetic

Narr [nar] (-en, -en) *m* fool; **n~en** *vt* to
fool; **~heit** *f* foolishness

Närrin ['nɛrɪn] *f* fool

närrisch *adj* foolish, crazy

Narzisse [narˈtsɪsə] *f* narcissus; daffodil

naschen ['naʃən] *vt*, *vi* to nibble;
(*heimlich kosten*) to pinch a bit

naschhaft *adj* sweet-toothed

Nase ['naːzə] *f* nose

Nasen- *zW*: **~bluten** (-s) *nt* nosebleed;
~loch *nt* nostril; **~tropfen** *pl* nose
drops

naseweis *adj* pert, cheeky; (*neugierig*)
nosey

Nashorn ['naːshɔrn] *nt* rhinoceros

naß [nas] *adj* wet

Nässe ['nɛsə] (-) *f* wetness; **n~n** *vt* to
wet

naßkalt *adj* wet and cold

Naßrasur *f* wet shave

Nation [natsi'oːn] *f* nation

national [natsio'naːl] *adj* national;
N~hymne *f* national anthem; **~isieren**
[-i'ziːrən] *vt* to nationalize; **N~i'sierung** *f*
nationalization; **N~ismus** [-'lɪsmʊs] *m*
nationalism; **~istisch** [-'lɪstɪʃ] *adj*
nationalistic; **N~i'tät** *f* nationality;
N~mannschaft *f* national team;
N~sozialismus *m* national socialism

Natron ['naːtrɔn] (-s) *nt* soda

Natter ['natər] (-, -n) *f* adder

Natur [na'tuːr] *f* nature; (*körperlich*)
constitution; **~a'lismus** *m* naturalism;

~**erscheinung** f natural phenomenon od event; n~**farben** adj natural coloured; n~**gemäß** adj natural; ~**gesetz** nt law of nature; ~**katastrophe** f natural disaster

natürlich [na'tyːrlıç] adj natural ♦ adv naturally; **ja, ~!** yes, of course; **N~keit** f naturalness

Natur- zW: ~**produkt** nt natural product; n~**rein** adj natural, pure; ~**schutzgebiet** nt nature reserve; ~**wissenschaft** f natural science; ~**wissenschaftler(in)** m(f) scientist; ~**zustand** m natural state

nautisch ['naʊtıʃ] adj nautical

Nazi ['naːtsi] (-s, -s) m Nazi

n.Chr. abk (= nach Christus) A.D.

Neapel [ne'aːpəl] (-s) nt Naples

Nebel ['neːbəl] (-s, -) m fog, mist; n~**ig** adj foggy, misty; ~**scheinwerfer** m foglamp

neben ['neːbən] präp (+akk od dat) next to; (+dat: außer) apart from, besides; ~**an** [neːbən'an] adv next door; **N~anschluß** m (TEL) extension; ~**bei** [neːbən'baɪ] adv at the same time; (außerdem) additionally; (beiläufig) incidentally; **N~beschäftigung** f second job; **N~buhler(in)** (-s, -) m(f) rival; ~**einander** [neːbən'aɪ'nandər] adv side by side; ~**einanderlegen** vt to put next to each other; **N~eingang** m side entrance; ~**erscheinung** f side effect; **N~fach** nt subsidiary subject; **N~fluß** m tributary; **N~geräusch** nt (RADIO) atmospherics pl, interference; ~**her** [neːbən'heːr] adv (zusätzlich) besides; (gleichzeitig) at the same time; (daneben) alongside; ~**herfahren** (unreg) vi to drive alongside; **N~kosten** pl extra charges, extras; **N~produkt** nt by-product; **N~rolle** f minor part; **N~sache** f trifle, side issue; ~**sächlich** adj minor, peripheral; **N~straße** f side street

neblig ['neːblıç] adj foggy, misty

Necessaire [nesɛ'sɛːr] (-s, -s) nt (Näh~) needlework box; (Nagel~) manicure case

neck- ['nɛk] zW: ~**en** vt to tease;

N~e'rei f teasing; ~**isch** adj coy; (Einfall, Lied) amusing

Neffe ['nɛfə] (-n, -n) m nephew

negativ [nega'tiːf] adj negative; **N~** (-s, -e) nt (PHOT) negative

Neger ['neːgər] (-s, -) m negro; ~**in** f negress

nehmen ['neːmən] (unreg) vt to take; **jdn zu sich ~** to take sb in; **sich ernst ~** to take o.s. seriously; **nimm dir doch bitte** please help yourself

Neid [naɪt] (-(e)s) m envy; ~**er** (-s, -) m envier; n~**isch** adj envious, jealous

neigen ['naɪgən] vt to incline, to lean; (Kopf) to bow ♦ vi: **zu etw ~** to tend to sth

Neigung f (des Geländes) slope; (Tendenz) tendency, inclination; (Vorliebe) liking; (Zuneigung) affection

nein [naɪn] adv no

Nelke ['nɛlkə] f carnation, pink; (Gewürz) clove

Nenn- ['nɛn] zW: n~**en** (unreg) vt to name; (mit Namen) to call; **wie n~t man ...?** what do you call ...?; n~**enswert** adj worth mentioning; ~**er** (-s, -) m denominator; ~**wert** m nominal value; (COMM) par

Neon ['neːɔn] (-s) nt neon; ~**licht** nt neon light; ~**röhre** f neon tube

Nerv [nɛrf] (-s, -en) m nerve; **jdm auf die ~en gehen** to get on sb's nerves; n~**enaufreibend** adj nerve-racking; ~**enbündel** nt bundle of nerves; ~**enheilanstalt** f mental home; n~**enkrank** adj mentally ill; ~**enschwäche** f neurasthenia; ~**ensystem** nt nervous system; ~**enzusammenbruch** m nervous breakdown; n~**ös** [nɛr'vøːs] adj nervous; ~**osi'tät** f nervousness; n~**tötend** adj nerve-racking; (Arbeit) soul-destroying

Nerz [nɛrts] (-es, -e) m mink

Nessel ['nɛsəl] (-, -n) f nettle

Nest [nɛst] (-(e)s, -er) nt nest; (umg: Ort) dump

nett [nɛt] adj nice; (freundlich) nice, kind; ~**erweise** adv kindly

netto ['nɛtoː] adv net

Netz [nɛts] (-es, -e) nt net; (Gepäck~)

rack; (*Einkaufs~*) string bag; (*Spinnen~*) web; (*System*) network; **jdm ins ~ gehen** (*fig*) to fall into sb's trap; **~anschluß** *m* mains connection; **~haut** *f* retina

neu [nɔy] *adj* new; (*Sprache, Geschichte*) modern; **seit ~estem** (since) recently; **die ~esten Nachrichten** the latest news; **~ schreiben** to rewrite, to write again; **N~anschaffung** *f* new purchase *od* acquisition; **~artig** *adj* new kind of; **N~auflage** *f* new edition; **N~bau** *m* new building; **~erdings** *adv* (*kürzlich*) (since) recently; (*von neuem*) again; **N~erung** *f* innovation, new departure; **N~fundland** *nt* Newfoundland; **N~gier** *f* curiosity; **~gierig** *adj* curious; **N~guinea** *nt* New Guinea; **N~heit** *f* newness; novelty; **N~igkeit** *f* news *sg*; **N~jahr** *nt* New Year; **~lich** *adv* recently, the other day; **N~ling** *m* novice; **N~mond** *m* new moon

neun [nɔyn] *num* nine; **~zehn** *num* nineteen; **~zig** *num* ninety

neureich *adj* nouveau riche; **N~e(r)** *mf* nouveau riche

Neur- *zW*: **~ose** [nɔy'roːzə] *f* neurosis; **~otiker** [nɔy'roːtikər] (*-s, -*) *m* neurotic; **n~otisch** *adj* neurotic

Neu- *zW*: **~seeland** [nɔy'zeːlant] *nt* New Zealand; **~seeländer(in)** [nɔy'zeːlɛndər(ɪn)] *m(f)* New Zealander; **n~seeländisch** *adj* New Zealand *cpd*

neutral [nɔy'traːl] *adj* neutral; **~i'sieren** *vt* to neutralize; **N~i'tät** *f* neutrality

Neutron ['nɔytrɔn] (*-s, -en*) *nt* neutron

Neutrum ['nɔytrʊm] (*-s, -a od -en*) *nt* neuter

Neu- *zW*: **~wert** *m* purchase price; **~zeit** *f* modern age; **n~zeitlich** *adj* modern, recent

---

nicht [nɪçt] *adv* **1** (*Verneinung*) not; **er ist es nicht** it's not him, it isn't him; **er raucht nicht** (*gerade*) he isn't smoking; (*gewöhnlich*) he doesn't smoke; **ich kann das nicht - ich auch nicht** I can't do it - neither *od* nor can I; **es regnet nicht mehr** it's not raining any more

2 (*Bitte, Verbot*): **nicht!** don't!, no!; **nicht berühren!** do not touch!; **nicht doch!** don't!

3 (*rhetorisch*): **du bist müde, nicht (wahr)?** you're tired, aren't you?; **das ist schön, nicht (wahr)?** it's nice, isn't it?

4: **was du nicht sagst!** the things you say!

Nichtangriffspakt [nɪçt''angrɪfspakt] *m* non-aggression pact

Nichte ['nɪçtə] *f* niece

nichtig ['nɪçtɪç] *adj* (*ungültig*) null, void; (*wertlos*) futile; **N~keit** *f* nullity, invalidity; (*Sinnlosigkeit*) futility

Nichtraucher(in) *m(f)* non-smoker

nichtrostend *adj* stainless

nichts [nɪçts] *pron* nothing; **für ~ und wieder ~** for nothing at all; **N~ (-)** *nt* nothingness; (*pej: Person*) nonentity; **~desto'weniger** *adv* nevertheless; **N~nutz** (*-es, -e*) *m* good-for-nothing; **~nutzig** *adj* worthless, useless; **~sagend** *adj* meaningless; **N~tun** (*-s*) *nt* idleness

Nickel ['nɪkəl] (*-s*) *nt* nickel

nicken ['nɪkən] *vi* to nod

Nickerchen ['nɪkərçən] *nt* nap

nie [niː] *adv* never; **~ wieder** *od* **mehr** never again; **~ und nimmer** never ever

nieder ['niːdər] *adj* low; (*gering*) inferior ♦ *adv* down; **N~gang** *m* decline; **~gehen** (*unreg*) *vi* to descend; (*AVIAT*) to come down; (*Regen*) to fall; (*Boxer*) to go down; **~geschlagen** *adj* depressed, dejected; **N~geschlagenheit** *f* depression, dejection; **N~lage** *f* defeat; **N~lande** *pl* Netherlands; **N~länder(in)** *m(f)* Dutchman(woman); **~ländisch** *adj* Dutch; **~lassen** (*unreg*) *vr* (*sich setzen*) to sit down; (*an Ort*) to settle (down); (*Arzt, Rechtsanwalt*) to set up a practice; **N~lassung** *f* settlement; (*COMM*) branch; **~legen** *vt* to lay down; (*Arbeit*) to stop; (*Amt*) to resign; **N~rhein** *nt* Lower Rhine; **N~sachsen** *nt* Lower Saxony; **N~schlag** *m* (*MET*) precipitation; rainfall; **~schlagen** (*unreg*) *vt* (*Gegner*) to beat down; (*Gegenstand*) to knock down; (*Augen*) to lower; (*Aufstand*) to put down ♦ *vr* (*CHEM*) to precipitate; **N~schrift** *f* transcription; **~trächtig** *adj* base, mean; **N~trächtigkeit** *f* meanness, baseness; outrage; **N~ung** *f* (*GEOG*) depression; (*Mündungsgebiet*) flats *pl*

niedlich ['ni:tlɪç] *adj* sweet, cute
niedrig ['ni:drɪç] *adj* low; (*Stand*) lowly, humble; (*Gesinnung*) mean
niemals ['ni:ma:ls] *adv* never
niemand ['ni:mant] *pron* nobody, no one; **Niemandsland** *nt* no-man's land
Niere ['ni:rə] *f* kidney; **Nierenentzündung** *f* kidney infection
nieseln ['ni:zəln] *vi* to drizzle
niesen ['ni:zən] *vi* to sneeze
Niete ['ni:tə] *f* (*TECH*) rivet; (*Los*) blank; (*Reinfall*) flop; (*Mensch*) failure; **n~n** *vt* to rivet
Nikotin [niko'ti:n] (-s) *nt* nicotine
Nil [ni:l] *m* Nile; **~pferd** *nt* hippopotamus
Nimmersatt ['nɪmɐzat] (-(e)s, -e) *m* glutton
nimmst *etc* [nɪmst] *vb siehe* **nehmen**
nippen ['nɪpən] *vt, vi* to sip
nirgend- ['nɪrgənt] *zW:* **~s** *adv* nowhere; **~wo** *adv* nowhere; **~wohin** *adv* nowhere
Nische ['ni:ʃə] *f* niche
nisten ['nɪstən] *vi* to nest
Nitrat [ni'tra:t] (-(e)s, -e) *nt* nitrate
Niveau [ni'vo:] (-s, -s) *nt* level
Nixe ['nɪksə] *f* water nymph

SCHLÜSSELWORT

noch [nɔx] *adv* **1** (*weiterhin*) still; **noch nicht** not yet; **noch nie** never (yet); **noch immer** *od* **immer noch** still; **bleiben Sie doch noch** stay a bit longer
2 (*in Zukunft*) still, yet; **das kann noch passieren** that might still happen; **er wird noch kommen** he'll come (yet)
3 (*nicht später als*): **noch vor einer Woche** only a week ago; **noch am selben Tag** the very same day; **noch im 19. Jahrhundert** as late as the 19th century; **noch heute** today

4 (*zusätzlich*): **wer war noch da?** who else was there?; **noch einmal** once more, again; **noch dreimal** three more times; **noch einer** another one
5 (*bei Vergleichen*): **noch größer** even bigger; **das ist noch besser** that's better still; **und wenn es noch so schwer ist** however hard it is
6: **Geld noch und noch** heaps (and heaps) of money; **sie hat noch und noch versucht, ...** she tried again and again to ...
♦ *konj*: **weder A noch B** neither A nor B

noch- *zw:* **~mal** ['nɔxma:l] *adv* again, once more; **~malig** ['nɔxma:lɪç] *adj* repeated; **~mals** *adv* again, once more
Nominativ ['no:minati:f] (-s, -e) *m* nominative
nominell [nomi'nɛl] *adj* nominal
Nonne ['nɔnə] *f* nun
Nord(en) ['nɔrd(ən)] (-s) *m* north
Nord'irland *nt* Northern Ireland
nordisch *adj* northern
nördlich ['nœrtlɪç] *adj* northerly, northern ♦ *präp* +*gen* (to the) north of; **~ von** (to the) north of
Nord- *zW:* **~pol** *m* North Pole; **~rhein-Westfalen** *nt* North Rhine-Westphalia; **~see** *f* North Sea; **n~wärts** *adv* northwards
Nörg- ['nœrg] *zW:* **~elei** *f* grumbling; **n~eln** *vi* to grumble; **~ler** (-s, -) *m* grumbler
Norm [nɔrm] (-, -en) *f* norm; (*Größenvorschrift*) standard; **n~al** [nɔr'ma:l] *adj* normal; **n~alerweise** *adv* normally; **n~ali'sieren** *vt* to normalize ♦ *vr* to return to normal; **n~en** *vt* to standardize
Norweg- ['nɔrve:g] *zW:* **~en** *nt* Norway; **~er(in)** (-s, -) *m(f)* Norwegian; **n~isch** *adj* Norwegian
Not [no:t] (-, ⁻e) *f* need; (*Mangel*) want; (*Mühe*) trouble; (*Zwang*) necessity; **zur ~** if necessary; (*gerade noch*) just about
Notar [no'ta:r] (-s, -e) *m* notary; **n~i'ell** *adj* notarial
Not- *zW:* **~ausgang** *m* emergency exit;

~**behelf** (-s, -e) *m* makeshift; ~**bremse** *f* emergency brake; **n~dürftig** *adj* scanty; (*behelfsmäßig*) makeshift

Note ['noːtə] *f* note; (*SCH*) mark (*BRIT*), grade (*US*)

Noten- *zW*: ~**blatt** *nt* sheet of music; ~**schlüssel** *m* clef; ~**ständer** *m* music stand

Not- *zW*: ~**fall** *m* (case of) emergency; **n~falls** *adv* if need be; **n~gedrungen** *adj* necessary, unavoidable; **etw n~gedrungen machen** to be forced to do sth

notieren [no'tiːrən] *vt* to note; (*COMM*) to quote

Notierung *f* (*COMM*) quotation

nötig ['nøːtɪç] *adj* necessary; **etw ~ haben** to need sth; ~**en** *vt* to compel, to force; ~**enfalls** *adv* if necessary

Notiz [no'tiːts] (-, -en) *f* note; (*Zeitungs~*) item; ~ **nehmen** to take notice; ~**buch** *nt* notebook

Not- *zW*: ~**lage** *f* crisis, emergency; **n~landen** *vi* to make a forced *od* emergency landing; **n~leidend** *adj* needy; ~**lösung** *f* temporary solution; ~**lüge** *f* white lie

notorisch [no'toːrɪʃ] *adj* notorious

Not- *zW*: ~**ruf** *m* emergency call; ~**stand** *m* state of emergency; ~**unterkunft** *f* emergency accommodation; ~**verband** *m* emergency dressing; ~**wehr** (-) *f* self-defence; **n~wendig** *adj* necessary; ~**wendigkeit** *f* necessity; ~**zucht** *f* rape

Novelle [no'vɛlə] *f* short novel; (*JUR*) amendment

November [no'vɛmbər] (-s, -) *m* November

Nr. *abk* (= *Nummer*) no.

Nu [nuː] *m*: **im ~** in an instant

Nuance [ny'ãːsə] *f* nuance

nüchtern ['nʏçtərn] *adj* sober; (*Magen*) empty; (*Urteil*) prudent; **N~heit** *f* sobriety

Nudel ['nuːdəl] (-, -n) *f* noodle; ~**n** *pl* (*Teigwaren*) pasta *sg*; (*in Suppe*) noodles

Null [nʊl] (-, -en) *f* nought, zero; (*pej*: *Mensch*) washout; **n~** *num* zero;

(*Fehler*) no; **n~ Uhr** midnight; **n~ und nichtig** null and void; ~**punkt** *m* zero; **auf dem ~punkt** at zero

numerieren [nume'riːrən] *vt* to number

numerisch [nu'meːrɪʃ] *adj* numerical

Nummer ['nʊmər] (-, -n) *f* number; (*Größe*) size; **Nummernschild** *nt* (*AUT*) number *od* license (*US*) plate

nun [nuːn] *adv* now ♦ *excl* well; **das ist ~ mal** so that's the way it is

nur [nuːr] *adv* just, only; **wo bleibt er ~?** (just) where is he?

Nürnberg ['nʏrnbɛrk] (-s) *nt* Nuremberg

Nuß [nʊs] (-, **Nüsse**) *f* nut; ~**baum** *m* walnut tree; ~**knacker** (-s, -) *m* nutcracker

Nüster ['nyːstər] (-, -n) *f* nostril

Nutte ['nʊtə] (*umg*) *f* tart

nutz [nʊts] *adj*: **zu nichts ~ sein** to be no use for anything

nütze ['nʏtsə] *adj* = nutz

Nutzen (-s) *m* usefulness; (*Gewinn*) profit; **von ~** useful; **n~** *vi* to be of use ♦ *vt*: **etw zu etw n~** to use sth for sth; **was nutzt es?** what's the use?, what use is it?

nützen *vi*, *vt* = nutzen

nützlich ['nʏtslɪç] *adj* useful; **N~keit** *f* usefulness

Nutz- *zW*: **n~los** *adj* useless; ~**losigkeit** *f* uselessness; ~**nießer** (-s, -) *m* beneficiary

Nylon ['naɪlɔn] (-(s)) *nt* nylon

O

Oase [o'aːzə] *f* oasis

ob [ɔp] *konj* if, whether; ~ **das wohl wahr ist?** can that be true?; **und ~!** you bet!

Obdach ['ɔpdax] (-(e)s) *nt* shelter, lodging; **o~los** *adj* homeless; ~**lose(r)** *mf* homeless person

Obduktion [ɔpdʊktsi'oːn] *f* post-mortem

obduzieren [ɔpdu'tsiːrən] *vt* to do a post-mortem on

O-Beine ['oːbaɪnə] *pl* bow *od* bandy legs

oben ['oːbən] *adv* above; (*in Haus*) upstairs; **nach ~** up; **von ~** down; ~

ohne topless; **jdn von ~ bis unten ansehen** to look sb up and down; **Befehl von ~** orders from above; **~an** *adv* at the top; **~auf** *adv* up above, on the top ♦ *adj* (*munter*) in form; **~drein** *adv* into the bargain; **~erwähnt** *adj* abovementioned; **~genannt** *adj* abovementioned

Ober ['o:bər] (-s, -) *m* waiter; **die ~en** *pl* (*umg*) the bosses; (*ECCL*) the superiors; **~arm** *m* upper arm; **~arzt** *m* senior physician; **~aufsicht** *f* supervision; **~bayern** *nt* Upper Bavaria; **~befehl** *m* supreme command; **~befehlshaber** *m* commander-in-chief; **~bekleidung** *f* outer clothing; **~'bürgermeister** *m* lord mayor; **~deck** *nt* upper *od* top deck; **o~e(r, s)** *adj* upper; **~fläche** *f* surface; **o~flächlich** *adj* superficial; **~geschoß** *nt* upper storey; **o~halb** *adv* above ♦ *präp* +*gen* above; **~haupt** *nt* head, chief; **~haus** *nt* (*POL*) upper house, House of Lords (*BRIT*); **~hemd** *nt* shirt; **~herrschaft** *f* supremacy, sovereignty; **~in** *f* matron; (*ECCL*) Mother Superior; **~kellner** *m* head waiter; **~kiefer** *m* upper jaw; **~körper** *m* upper part of body; **~leitung** *f* direction; (*ELEK*) overhead cable; **~licht** *nt* skylight; **~lippe** *f* upper lip; **~schenkel** *m* thigh; **~schicht** *f* upper classes *pl*; **~schule** *f* grammar school (*BRIT*), high school (*US*); **~schwester** *f* (*MED*) matron

Oberst ['o:bərst] (-en *od* -s, -en *od* -e) *m* colonel; **o~e(r, s)** *adj* very top, topmost

Ober- *zW*: **~stufe** *f* upper school; **~teil** *nt* upper part; **~weite** *f* bust/chest measurement

obgleich [ɔp'glaiç] *konj* although

Obhut ['ɔphu:t] (-) *f* care, protection; **in jds ~ sein** to be in sb's care

obig ['o:biç] *adj* above

Objekt [ɔp'jɛkt] (-(e)s, -e) *nt* object; **~iv** [-'ti:f] (-s, -e) *nt* lens; **o~iv** *adj* objective; **~ivi'tät** *f* objectivity

Oblate [o'bla:tə] *f* (*Gebäck*) wafer; (*ECCL*) host

Obligation [ɔbligatsi'o:n] *f* bond

obligatorisch [ɔbliga'to:rɪʃ] *adj* compulsory, obligatory

Oboe [o'bo:ə] *f* oboe

Obrigkeit ['o:brɪçkait] *f* (*Behörden*) authorities *pl*, administration; (*Regierung*) government

obschon [ɔp'ʃo:n] *konj* although

Observatorium [ɔpzɛrva'to:riʊm] *nt* observatory

obskur [ɔps'ku:r] *adj* obscure; (*verdächtig*) dubious

Obst [o:pst] (-(e)s) *nt* fruit; **~baum** *m* fruit tree; **~garten** *m* orchard; **~händler** *m* fruiterer, fruit merchant; **~kuchen** *m* fruit tart

obszön [ɔps'tsø:n] *adj* obscene; **O~i'tät** *f* obscenity

obwohl [ɔp'vo:l] *konj* although

Ochse ['ɔksə] (-n, -n) *m* ox; **o~n** (*umg*) *vt, vi* to cram, to swot (*BRIT*); **Ochsenschwanzsuppe** *f* oxtail soup; **Ochsenzunge** *f* oxtongue

öd(e) ['ø:d(ə)] *adj* (*Land*) waste, barren; (*fig*) dull; **Öde** *f* desert, waste(land); (*fig*) tedium

oder ['o:dər] *konj* or; **das stimmt, ~?** that's right, isn't it?

Ofen ['o:fən] (-s, -̈) *m* oven; (*Heiz~*) fire, heater; (*Kohlen~*) stove; (*Hoch~*) furnace; (*Herd*) cooker, stove; **~rohr** *nt* stovepipe

offen ['ɔfən] *adj* open; (*aufrichtig*) frank; (*Stelle*) vacant; **~ gesagt** to be honest; **~bar** *adj* obvious; **~baren** [ɔfən'ba:rən] *vt* to reveal, to manifest; **O~'barung** *f* (*REL*) revelation; **~bleiben** (*unreg*) *vi* (*Fenster*) to stay open; (*Frage, Entscheidung*) to remain open; **~halten** (*unreg*) *vt* to keep open; **O~heit** *f* candour, frankness; **~herzig** *adj* candid, frank; (*Kleid*) revealing; **~kundig** *adj* well-known; (*klar*) evident; **~lassen** (*unreg*) *vt* to leave open; **~sichtlich** *adj* evident, obvious

offensiv [ɔfɛn'zi:f] *adj* offensive; **O~e** [-'zi:və] *f* offensive

offenstehen (*unreg*) *vi* to be open; (*Rechnung*) to be unpaid; **es steht Ihnen offen, es zu tun** you are at liberty to do it

öffentlich ['œfəntlıç] *adj* public; **Ö~keit**

f (Leute) public; *(einer Versammlung etc)* public nature; **in aller Ö~keit** in public; **an die Ö~keit dringen** to reach the public ear
offiziell [ɔfitsi'ɛl] *adj* official
Offizier [ɔfi'tsiːr] (-s, -e) *m* officer; **~skasino** *nt* officers' mess
öffnen ['œfnən] *vt, vr* to open; **jdm die Tür ~** to open the door for sb
Öffner ['œfnər] (-s, -) *m* opener
Öffnung ['œfnʊŋ] *f* opening; **Öffnungszeiten** *pl* opening times
oft [ɔft] *adv* often
öfter ['œftər] *adv* more often *od* frequently; **~s** *adv* often, frequently
oftmals *adv* often, frequently
oh [oː] *excl* oh; **~ je!** oh dear
OHG [oːha'geː] *abk* (= *Offene Handelsgesellschaft*) general partnership
ohne ['oːnə] *präp +akk* without ♦ *konj* without; **das ist nicht ~** *(umg)* it's not bad; **~ weiteres** without a second thought; *(sofort)* immediately; **~ zu fragen** without asking; **~ daß er es wußte** without him knowing it; **~dies** [oːnə'diːs] *adv* anyway; **~einander** [oːnə'ʔaɪ'nandər] *adv* without each other; **~gleichen** [oːnə'glaɪçən] *adj* unsurpassed, without equal; **~hin** [oːnə'hɪn] *adv* anyway, in any case
Ohnmacht ['oːnmaxt] *f* faint; *(fig)* impotence; **in ~ fallen** to faint
ohnmächtig ['oːnmɛçtɪç] *adj* in a faint, unconscious; *(fig)* weak, impotent; **sie ist ~** she has fainted
Ohr [oːr] (-(e)s, -en) *nt* ear; *(Gehör)* hearing
Öhr [øːr] (-(e)s, -e) *nt* eye
Ohren- *zW:* **~arzt** *m* ear specialist; **o~betäubend** *adj* deafening; **~schmalz** *nt* earwax; **~schmerzen** *pl* earache *sg*; **~schützer** (-s, -) *m* earmuff
Ohr- *zW:* **~feige** *f* slap on the face; box on the ears; **o~feigen** *vt:* **jdn o~feigen** to slap sb's face; to box sb's ears; **~läppchen** *nt* ear lobe; **~ring** *m* earring; **~wurm** *m* earwig; *(MUS)* catchy tune
ökonomisch [øko'noːmɪʃ] *adj* economical

Oktave [ɔk'taːvə] *f* octave
Oktober [ɔk'toːbər] (-s, -) *m* October
ökumenisch [øku'meːnɪʃ] *adj* ecumenical
Öl [øːl] (-(e)s, -e) *nt* oil; **~baum** *m* olive tree; **ö~en** *vt* to oil; *(TECH)* to lubricate; **~farbe** *f* oil paint; **~feld** *nt* oilfield; **~film** *m* film of oil; **~heizung** *f* oil-fired central heating; **ö~ig** *adj* oily
oliv [o'liːf] *adj* olive-green; **O~e** *f* olive
Öl- *zW:* **~meßstab** *m* dipstick; **~sardine** *f* sardine; **~standanzeiger** *m* (*AUT*) oil gauge; **~ung** *f* lubrication; oiling; *(ECCL)* anointment; **die Letzte ~ung** Extreme Unction; **~wechsel** *m* oil change; **~zeug** *nt* oilskins *pl*
Olymp- [o'lymp] *zW:* **~iade** [-i'aːdə] *f* Olympic Games *pl*; **~iasieger(in)** [-iaziː'gər(ɪn)] *m(f)* Olympic champion; **~iateilnehmer(in)** *m(f)* Olympic competitor; **o~isch** *adj* Olympic
Oma ['oːma] (-, -s; *umg*) *f* granny
Omelett [ɔm(ə)'lɛt] (-(e)s, -s) *nt* omelet(te)
Omen ['oːmɛn] (-s, -) *nt* omen
Omnibus ['ɔmnibʊs] *m* (omni)bus
Onanie [ona'niː] *f* masturbation; **o~ren** *vi* to masturbate
Onkel ['ɔŋkəl] (-s, -) *m* uncle
Opa ['oːpa] (-s, -s; *umg*) *m* grandpa
Opal [o'paːl] (-s, -e) *m* opal
Oper ['oːpər] (-, -n) *f* opera; opera house
Operation [operatsi'oːn] *f* operation; **~ssaal** *m* operating theatre
Operette [ope'rɛtə] *f* operetta
operieren [ope'riːrən] *vt* to operate on ♦ *vi* to operate
Opern- *zW:* **~glas** *nt* opera glasses *pl*; **~haus** *nt* opera house; **~sänger(in)** *m(f)* opera singer
Opfer ['ɔpfər] (-s, -) *nt* sacrifice; *(Mensch)* victim; **o~n** *vt* to sacrifice; **~stock** *m* (*ECCL*) offertory box; **~ung** *f* sacrifice
Opium ['oːpiʊm] (-s) *nt* opium
opponieren [ɔpo'niːrən] *vi:* **gegen jdn/etw ~** to oppose sb/sth
opportun [ɔpɔr'tuːn] *adj* opportune; **O~ist** [-'nɪst] *m* opportunist
Opposition [ɔpozitsi'oːn] *f* opposition;

o~ell [-'nɛl] *adj* opposing

Optik ['ɔptɪk] *f* optics *sg*; ~er (-s, -) *m* optician

optimal [ɔpti'maːl] *adj* optimal, optimum

Optimismus [ɔpti'mɪsmʊs] *m* optimism

Optimist [ɔpti'mɪst] *m* optimist; o~**isch** *adj* optimistic

optisch ['ɔptɪʃ] *adj* optical

Orakel [o'raːkəl] (-s, -) *nt* oracle

Orange [o'rãːʒə] *f* orange; o~ *adj* orange; **Orangeade** [orãˈʒaːdə] *f* orangeade; **Orangeat** [orãˈʒaːt] (-s, -e) *nt* candied peel; **Orangensaft** *m* orange juice

Orchester [ɔr'kɛstər] (-s, -) *nt* orchestra

Orchidee [ɔrçi'deːə] *f* orchid

Orden ['ɔrdən] (-s, -) *m* (ECCL) order; (MIL) decoration; **Ordensschwester** *f* nun

ordentlich ['ɔrdəntlɪç] *adj* (anständig) decent, respectable; (geordnet) tidy, neat; (umg: annehmbar) not bad; (: tüchtig) real, proper ♦ *adv* properly; ~er Professor (full) professor; O~**keit** *f* respectability; tidiness, neatness

ordinär [ɔrdiˈnɛːr] *adj* common, vulgar

ordnen ['ɔrdnən] *vt* to order, to put in order

Ordner (-s, -) *m* steward; (COMM) file

Ordnung *f* order; (Ordnen) ordering; (Geordnetsein) tidiness; ~ **machen** to tidy up; **in** ~! okay!

Ordnungs- *zW:* o~**gemäß** *adj* proper, according to the rules; o~**halber** *adv* as a matter of form; ~**strafe** *f* fine; o~**widrig** *adj* contrary to the rules, irregular; ~**zahl** *f* ordinal number

Organ [ɔr'gaːn] (-s, -e) *nt* organ; (Stimme) voice; ~**isation** [-izatsi'oːn] *f* organisation; ~**isator** [-i'zaːtɔr] *m* organizer; o~**isch** *adj* organic; o~**isieren** [-i'ziːrən] *vt* to organize, to arrange; (umg: beschaffen) to acquire ♦ *vr* to organize; ~**ismus** [-'nɪsmʊs] *m* organism; ~**ist** [-'nɪst] *m* organist

Orgasmus [ɔr'gasmʊs] *m* orgasm

Orgel ['ɔrgəl] (-, -n) *f* organ

Orgie ['ɔrgiə] *f* orgy

Orient ['oːriɛnt] (-s) *m* Orient, east;

~**ale** [-'taːlə] (-n, -n) *m* Oriental; o~**alisch** [-'taːlɪʃ] *adj* oriental

orientier- *zW:* ~**en** [-'tiːrən] *vt* (örtlich) to locate; (fig) to inform ♦ *vr* to find one's way *od* bearings; to inform o.s.; O~**ung** [-'tiːrʊŋ] *f* orientation; (fig) information; O~**ungssinn** *m* sense of direction

original [origi'naːl] *adj* original; O~ (-s, -e) *nt* original; O~**fassung** *f* original version; O~**i'tät** *f* originality

originell [origi'nɛl] *adj* original

Orkan [ɔr'kaːn] (-(e)s, -e) *m* hurricane

Ornament [ɔrna'mɛnt] *nt* decoration, ornament; o~**al** [-'taːl] *adj* decorative, ornamental

Ort [ɔrt] (-(e)s, -e *od* ⁻er) *m* place; **an** ~ **und Stelle** on the spot; o~**en** *vt* to locate

ortho- [ɔrto] *zW:* ~**dox** [-'dɔks] *adj* orthodox; O~**graphie** [-gra'fiː] *f* spelling, orthography; ~'**graphisch** *adj* orthographic; O~**päde** [-'pɛːdə] (-n, -n) *m* orthopaedic specialist, orthopaedist; O~**pädie** [-pɛ'diː] *f* orthopaedics *sg*; ~'**pädisch** *adj* orthopaedic

örtlich ['œrtlɪç] *adj* local; Ö~**keit** *f* locality

Ortschaft *f* village, small town

Orts- *zW:* o~**fremd** *adj* non-local; ~**gespräch** *nt* local (phone)call; ~**name** *m* place-name; ~**netz** *nt* (TEL) local telephone exchange area; ~**zeit** *f* local time

Ortung *f* locating

Öse ['øːzə] *f* loop, eye

Ost- ['ɔst] *zW:* ~'**asien** *nt* Eastern Asia; ~**block** *m* (POL) Eastern bloc; ~**en** (-s) *m* east

Ost'ende *nt* Ostend

Oster- ['oːstər] *zW:* ~**ei** *nt* Easter egg; ~**fest** *nt* Easter; ~**glocke** *f* daffodil; ~**hase** *m* Easter bunny; ~**montag** *m* Easter Monday; ~**n** (-s, -) *nt* Easter

Österreich ['øːstərraiç] (-s) *nt* Austria; ~**er(in)** (-s, -) *m(f)* Austrian; ö~**isch** *adj* Austrian

Ostersonntag *m* Easter Day *od* Sunday

östlich ['œstlɪç] *adj* eastern, easterly

Ost- *zW:* ~**see** *f* Baltic Sea; **o~wärts** *adv* eastwards; ~**wind** *m* east wind

Otter[1] ['ɔtər] (-s, -) *m* otter

Otter[2] (-, -n) *f* (*Schlange*) adder

Ouvertüre [uvɛr'tyːrə] *f* overture

oval [o'vaːl] *adj* oval

Ovation [ovatsi'oːn] *f* ovation

Ovulation [ovulatsi'oːn] *f* ovulation

Oxyd [ɔ'ksyːt] (-(e)s, -e) *nt* oxide; **o~ieren** [ɔksy'diːrən] *vt, vi* to oxidize; ~**ierung** *f* oxidization

Ozean ['oːtseaːn] (-s, -e) *m* ocean; ~**dampfer** *m* (ocean-going) liner

Ozon [o'tsoːn] (-s) *nt* ozone

P

Paar [paːr] (-(e)s, -e) *nt* pair; (*Ehe~*) couple; **ein p~** a few; **p~en** *vt, vr* to couple; (*Tiere*) to mate; ~**lauf** *m* pair skating; **p~mal** *adv:* **ein p~mal** a few times; ~**ung** *f* combination; mating; **p~weise** *adv* in pairs; in couples

Pacht [paxt] (-, -en) *f* lease; **p~en** *vt* to lease

Pächter ['pɛçtər] (-s, -) *m* leaseholder, tenant

Pack [pak] (-(e)s, -e *od* ⁼e) *m* bundle, pack ♦ *nt* (*pej*) mob, rabble

Päckchen ['pɛkçən] *nt* small package; (*Zigaretten*) packet; (*Post~*) small parcel

Pack- *zW:* **p~en** *vt* to pack; (*fassen*) to grasp, to seize; (*umg: schaffen*) to manage; (*fig: fesseln*) to grip; ~**en** (-s, -) *m* bundle; (*fig: Menge*) heaps of; ~**esel** *m* (*auch fig*) packhorse; ~**papier** *nt* brown paper, wrapping paper; ~**ung** *f* packet; (*Pralinenpackung*) box; (*MED*) compress

Pädagog- [pɛda'goːg] *zW:* ~**e** (-n, -n) *m* teacher; ~**ik** *f* education; **p~isch** *adj* educational, pedagogical

Paddel ['padəl] (-s, -) *nt* paddle; ~**boot** *nt* canoe; **p~n** *vi* to paddle

Page [pa:ʒə] (-n, -n) *m* page; **Pagenkopf** *m* pageboy (cut)

Paket [pa'keːt] (-(e)s, -e) *nt* packet; (*Post~*) parcel; ~**karte** *f* dispatch note;

~**post** *f* parcel post; ~**schalter** *m* parcels counter

Pakt [pakt] (-(e)s, -e) *m* pact

Palast [pa'last] (-es, **Paläste**) *m* palace

Palästin- [palɛs'tiːn] *zW:* ~**a** (-s) *nt* Palestine; ~**enser(in)** [palɛsti'nɛnzər(ɪn)] (-s, -) *m(f)* Palestinian; **p~'ensisch** *adj* Palestinian

Palme ['palmə] *f* palm (tree)

Palmsonntag *m* Palm Sunday

Pampelmuse ['pampəlmuːzə] *f* grapefruit

pampig ['pampɪç] (*umg*) *adj* (*frech*) fresh

panieren [pa'niːrən] *vt* (*KOCH*) to bread

Paniermehl [pa'niːrmeːl] *nt* breadcrumbs *pl*

Panik ['paːnɪk] *f* panic

panisch ['paːnɪʃ] *adj* panic-stricken

Panne ['panə] *f* (*AUT etc*) breakdown; (*Mißgeschick*) slip; **Pannenhilfe** *f* breakdown service

panschen ['panʃən] *vi* to splash about ♦ *vt* to water down

Panther ['pantər] (-s, -) *m* panther

Pantoffel [pan'tɔfəl] (-s, -n) *m* slipper; ~**held** (*umg*) *m* henpecked husband

Pantomime [panto'miːmə] *f* mime

Panzer ['pantsər] (-s, -) *m* armour; (*Platte*) armour plate; (*Fahrzeug*) tank; ~**glas** *nt* bulletproof glass; **p~n** *vt* to armour ♦ *vr* (*fig*) to arm o.s.

Papa [pa'paː] (-s, -s; *umg*) *m* dad, daddy

Papagei [papa'gaɪ] (-s, -en) *m* parrot

Papier [pa'piːr] (-s, -e) *nt* paper; (*Wert~*) security; ~**fabrik** *f* paper mill; ~**geld** *nt* paper money; ~**korb** *m* wastepaper basket; ~**tüte** *f* paper bag

Papp- ['pap] *zW:* ~**deckel** *m* cardboard; ~**e** *f* cardboard; ~**el** (-, -n) *f* poplar; **p~en** (*umg*) *vt, vi* to stick; **p~ig** *adj* sticky; ~**maché** [-ma'ʃeː] (-s, -s) *nt* papier-mâché

Paprika ['paprika] (-s, -s) *m* (*Gewürz*) paprika; (*~schote*) pepper

Papst [paːpst] (-(e)s, ⁼e) *m* pope

päpstlich ['pɛːpstlɪç] *adj* papal

Parabel [pa'raːbəl] (-, -n) *f* parable; (*MATH*) parabola

Parade [pa'ra:də] f (MIL) parade, re-view; (SPORT) parry; ~**marsch** m march-past; ~**schritt** m goose-step

Paradies [para'di:s] (-es, -e) nt paradise; p~**isch** adj heavenly

Paradox [para'dɔks] (-es, -e) nt paradox; p~ adj paradoxical

Paragraph [para'gra:f] (-en, -en) m paragraph; (JUR) section

parallel [para'le:l] adj parallel; P~**e** f parallel

Paranuß ['pa:ranʊs] f Brazil nut

Parasit [para'zi:t] (-en, -en) m (auch fig) parasite

parat [pa'ra:t] adj ready

Pärchen ['pɛːrçən] nt couple

Parfüm [par'fy:m] (-s, -s od -e) nt perfume; ~**erie** [-ə'ri:] f perfumery; ~**flasche** f scent bottle; p~**ieren** [-'mi:rən] vt to scent, to perfume

parieren [pa'ri:rən] vt to parry ♦ vi (umg) to obey

Paris [pa'ri:s] (-) nt Paris; ~**er** adj Parisian ♦ m Parisian; ~**erin** f Parisian

Park [park] (-s, -s) m park; ~**anlage** f park; (um Gebäude) grounds pl; p~**en** vt, vi to park; ~**ett** [par'kɛt] (-(e)s, -e) nt parquet (floor); (THEAT) stalls pl; ~**haus** nt multi-storey car park; ~**lücke** f parking space; ~**platz** m parking place; car park, parking lot (US); ~**scheibe** f parking disc; ~**uhr** f parking meter; ~**verbot** nt parking ban

Parlament [parla'mɛnt] nt parliament; ~**arier** [-'ta:riər] (-s, -) m parliamentarian; p~**arisch** [-'ta:rɪʃ] adj parliamentary

Parlaments- zW: ~**beschluß** m vote of parliament; ~**mitglied** nt member of parliament; ~**sitzung** f sitting (of parliament)

Parodie [paro'di:] f parody; p~**ren** vt to parody

Parole [pa'ro:lə] f password; (Wahlspruch) motto

Partei [par'tai] f party; ~ **ergreifen für jdn** to take sb's side; p~**isch** adj partial, bias(s)ed; ~**nahme** f: ~**nahme (für)** support (of od for), taking the part (of); ~**tag** m party conference

Parterre [par'tɛr(ə)] (-s, -s) nt ground floor; (THEAT) stalls pl

Partie [par'ti:] f part; (Spiel) game; (Ausflug) outing; (Mann, Frau) catch; (COMM) lot; **mit von der ~ sein** to join in

Partisan [parti'za:n] (-s od -en, -en) m partisan

Partitur [parti'tu:r] f (MUS) score

Partizip [parti'tsi:p] (-s, -ien) nt participle

Partner(in) ['partnər(ɪn)] (-s, -) m(f) partner; p~**schaftlich** adj as partners

Party ['pa:rti] (-, -s od **Parties**) f party

Paß [pas] (-sses, =sse) m pass; (Ausweis) passport

passabel [pa'sa:bəl] adj passable, reasonable

Passage [pa'sa:ʒə] f passage

Passagier [pasa'ʒi:r] (-s, -e) m passenger; ~**flugzeug** nt airliner

Paßamt nt passport office

Passant [pa'sant] m passer-by

Paßbild nt passport photograph

passen ['pasən] vi to fit; (Farbe) to go; (auf Frage, KARTEN, SPORT) to pass; **das paßt mir nicht** that doesn't suit me; ~ **zu** (Farbe, Kleider) to go with; **er paßt nicht zu dir** he's not right for you; ~**d** adj suitable; (zusammenpassend) matching; (angebracht) fitting; (Zeit) convenient

passier- [pa'si:r] zW: ~**bar** adj passable; ~**en** vt to pass; (durch Sieb) to strain ♦ vi to happen; P~**schein** m pass, permit

Passion [pasi'o:n] f passion; p~**iert** [-'ni:rt] adj enthusiastic, passionate; ~**sspiel** nt Passion Play

passiv ['pasi:f] adj passive; P~ (-s, -e) nt passive; P~**a** pl (COMM) liabilities; P~**i'tät** f passiveness

Paß- zW: ~**kontrolle** f passport control; ~**stelle** f passport office; ~**straße** f (mountain) pass

Paste ['pastə] f paste

Pastell [pas'tɛl] (-(e)s, -e) nt pastel

Pastete [pas'te:tə] f pie

pasteurisieren [pastøri'zi:rən] vt to pasteurize

Pastor ['pastɔr] *m* vicar; pastor, minister

Pate ['pa:tə] (**-n**, **-n**) *m* godfather; **~nkind** *nt* godchild

Patent [pa'tɛnt] (**-(e)s**, **-e**) *nt* patent; (*MIL*) commission; **p~** *adj* clever; **~amt** *nt* patent office; **p~ieren** [-'ti:rən] *vt* to patent; **~inhaber** *m* patentee

Pater ['pa:tər] (**-s**, **- *od* Patres**) *m* (*ECCL*) Father

pathetisch [pa'te:tɪʃ] *adj* emotional; bombastic

Pathologe [pato'lo:gə] (**-n**, **-n**) *m* pathologist

pathologisch *adj* pathological

Pathos ['pa:tɔs] (**-**) *nt* emotiveness, emotionalism

Patient(in) [patsi'ɛnt(ɪn)] *m(f)* patient

Patin ['pa:tɪn] *f* godmother

Patina ['pa:tina] (**-**) *f* patina

Patriot [patri'o:t] (**-en**, **-en**) *m* patriot; **p~isch** *adj* patriotic; **~ismus** [-'tɪsmʊs] *m* patriotism

Patrone [pa'tro:nə] *f* cartridge

patrouillieren [patrʊl'ji:rən] *vi* to patrol

patsch [patʃ] *excl* splash; **P~e** (*umg*) *f* (*Bedrängnis*) mess, jam; **~en** *vi* to smack, to slap; (*im Wasser*) to splash; **~naß** *adj* soaking wet

patzig ['patsɪç] (*umg*) *adj* cheeky, saucy

Pauke ['paʊkə] *f* kettledrum; **auf die ~ hauen** to live it up

pausbäckig ['paʊsbɛkɪç] *adj* chubby-cheeked

pauschal [paʊ'ʃa:l] *adj* (*Kosten*) inclusive; (*Urteil*) sweeping; **P~e** *f* flat rate; **P~gebühr** *f* flat rate; **P~preis** *m* all-in price; **P~reise** *f* package tour; **P~summe** *f* lump sum

Pause ['paʊzə] *f* break; (*THEAT*) interval; (*Innehalten*) pause; (*Kopie*) tracing

pausen *vt* to trace; **~los** *adj* non-stop; **P~zeichen** *nt* call sign; (*MUS*) rest

Pauspapier ['paʊspapi:r] *nt* tracing paper

Pavian ['pa:via:n] (**-s**, **-e**) *m* baboon

Pazif- [pa'tsi:f] *zW*: **~ik** (**-s**) *m* Pacific; **p~isch** *adj*: **der ~ische Ozean** the Pacific (Ocean); **~ist** [patsi'fɪst] *m*

pacifist; **p~istisch** *adj* pacifist

Pech [pɛç] (**-s**, **-e**) *nt* pitch; (*fig*) bad luck; **~ haben** to be unlucky; **p~schwarz** *adj* pitch-black; **~strähne** (*umg*) *m* unlucky patch; **~vogel** (*umg*) *m* unlucky person

Pedal [pe'da:l] (**-s**, **-e**) *nt* pedal

Pedant [pe'dant] *m* pedant; **~e'rie** *f* pedantry; **p~isch** *adj* pedantic

Pegel ['pe:gəl] (**-s**, **-**) *m* water gauge; **~stand** *m* water level

peilen ['paɪlən] *vt* to get a fix on

Pein [paɪn] (**-**) *f* agony, pain; **p~igen** *vt* to torture; (*plagen*) to torment; **p~lich** *adj* (*unangenehm*) embarrassing, awkward, painful; (*genau*) painstaking; **~lichkeit** *f* painfulness, awkwardness; scrupulousness

Peitsche ['paɪtʃə] *f* whip; **p~n** *vt* to whip; (*Regen*) to lash

Pelikan ['pe:lika:n] (**-s**, **-e**) *m* pelican

Pelle ['pɛlə] *f* skin; **p~n** *vt* to skin, to peel

Pellkartoffeln *pl* jacket potatoes

Pelz [pɛlts] (**-es**, **-e**) *m* fur

Pendel ['pɛndəl] (**-s**, **-**) *nt* pendulum; **~verkehr** *m* shuttle traffic; (*für Pendler*) commuter traffic

Pendler ['pɛndlər] (**-s**, **-**) *m* commuter

penetrant [pene'trant] *adj* sharp; (*Person*) pushing

Penis ['pe:nɪs] (**-**, **-se**) *m* penis

pennen ['pɛnən] (*umg*) *vi* to kip

Pension [pɛnzi'o:n] *f* (*Geld*) pension; (*Ruhestand*) retirement; (*für Gäste*) boarding *od* guest-house; **~är(in)** [-'nɛ:r(ɪn)] (**-s**, **-e**) *m(f)* pensioner; **~at** [-'na:t] (**-(e)s**, **-e**) *nt* boarding school; **p~ieren** [-'ni:rən] *vt* to pension off; **p~iert** *adj* retired; **~ierung** *f* retirement; **~sgast** *m* boarder, paying guest

Pensum ['pɛnzʊm] (**-s**, **Pensen**) *nt* quota; (*SCH*) curriculum

per [pɛr] *präp +akk* by, per; (*pro*) per; (*bis*) by

Perfekt ['pɛrfɛkt] (**-(e)s**, **-e**) *nt* perfect; **p~** [pɛr'fɛkt] *adj* perfect; **~ionismus** [pɛrfɛktsio'nɪsmʊs] *m* perfectionism

perforieren [pɛrfo'ri:rən] *vt* to perforate

Pergament [pɛrga'mɛnt] *nt* parchment;

~**papier** nt greaseproof paper

Periode [peri'o:də] f period

periodisch [peri'o:dɪʃ] adj periodic; (dezimal) recurring

peripher [peri'fe:r] adj peripheral; ~es Gerät peripheral

Perle ['pɛrlə] f (auch fig) pearl; **p~n** vi to sparkle; (Tropfen) to trickle

Perlmutt ['pɛrlmʊt] (-s) nt mother-of-pearl

perplex [pɛr'plɛks] adj dumbfounded

Pers- ['pɛrz] zW: ~**er(in)** (-s, -) m(f) Persian; ~**i'aner** (-s, -) m Persian lamb; ~**ien** [-iən] (-s) nt Persia; **p~isch** adj Persian

Person [pɛr'zo:n] (-, -en) f person; **ich für meine ~** speaking personally I

Personal [pɛrzo'na:l] (-s) nt personnel; (Bedienung) servants pl; ~**ausweis** m identity card; ~**computer** m personal computer; ~**ien** [-iən] pl particulars; ~**i'tät** f personality; ~**mangel** m undermanning; ~**pronomen** nt personal pronoun

Personen- zW: ~**aufzug** m lift, elevator (US); ~**gesellschaft** f partnership; ~**kraftwagen** m private motorcar; ~**schaden** m injury to persons; ~**zug** m stopping train; passenger train

personifizieren [pɛrzonifi'tsi:rən] vt to personify

persönlich [pɛr'zø:nlıç] adj personal ♦ adv in person; personally; **P~keit** f personality

Perspektive [pɛrspɛk'ti:və] f perspective

Perücke [pe'rʏkə] f wig

pervers [pɛr'vɛrs] adj perverse; **P~i'tät** f perversity

Pessimismus [pɛsi'mɪsmʊs] m pessimism

Pessimist [pɛsi'mɪst] m pessimist; **p~isch** adj pessimistic

Pest [pɛst] (-) f plague

Petersilie [petər'zi:liə] f parsley

Petroleum [pe'tro:leʊm] (-s) nt paraffin, kerosene (US)

Pfad [pfa:t] (-(e)s, -e) m path; ~**finder** (-s, -) m boy scout; ~**finderin** f girl guide

Pfahl [pfa:l] (-(e)s, ⁼e) m post, stake

Pfand [pfant] (-(e)s, ⁼er) nt pledge, security; (Flaschen~) deposit; (im Spiel) forfeit; ~**brief** m bond

pfänden ['pfɛndən] vt to seize, to distrain

Pfänderspiel nt game of forfeits

Pfandhaus nt pawnshop

Pfandschein m pawn ticket

Pfändung ['pfɛndʊŋ] f seizure, distraint

Pfanne ['pfanə] f (frying) pan

Pfannkuchen m pancake; (Berliner) doughnut

Pfarr- ['pfar] zW: ~**ei** [-'raɪ] f parish; ~**er** (-s, -) m priest; (evangelisch) vicar; minister; ~**haus** nt vicarage; manse

Pfau [pfaʊ] (-(e)s, -en) m peacock; ~**enauge** nt peacock butterfly

Pfeffer ['pfɛfər] (-s, -) m pepper; ~**korn** nt peppercorn; ~**kuchen** m gingerbread; ~**minz** (-es, -e) nt peppermint; ~**mühle** f pepper-mill; **p~n** vt to pepper; (umg: werfen) to fling; **gepfefferte Preise/Witze** steep prices/spicy jokes

Pfeife ['pfaɪfə] f whistle; (Tabak~, Orgel~) pipe; **p~n** (unreg) vt, vi to whistle; ~**r** (-s, -) m piper

Pfeil [pfaɪl] (-(e)s, -e) m arrow

Pfeiler ['pfaɪlər] (-s, -) m pillar, prop; (Brücken~) pier

Pfennig ['pfɛnıç] (-(e)s, -e) m pfennig (hundredth part of a mark)

Pferd [pfe:rt] (-(e)s, -e) nt horse

Pferde- ['pfe:rdə] zW: ~**rennen** nt horse-race; horse-racing; ~**schwanz** m (Frisur) ponytail; ~**stall** m stable

Pfiff [pfɪf] (-(e)s, -e) m whistle

Pfifferling ['pfıfərlıŋ] m yellow chanterelle (mushroom); **keinen ~ wert** not worth a thing

pfiffig adj sly, sharp

Pfingsten ['pfıŋstən] (-, -) nt Whitsun (BRIT), Pentecost

Pfingstrose ['pfıŋstro:zə] f peony

Pfirsich ['pfırzıç] (-s, -e) m peach

Pflanz- ['pflants] zW: ~**e** f plant; **p~en** vt to plant; ~**enfett** nt vegetable fat; **p~lich** adj vegetable; ~**ung** f plantation

Pflaster ['pflastər] (-s, -) *nt* plaster; (*Straße*) pavement; **p~n** *vt* to pave; **~stein** *m* paving stone

Pflaume ['pflaumə] *f* plum

Pflege ['pfle:gə] *f* care; (*von Idee*) cultivation; (*Kranken~*) nursing; **in ~ sein** (*Kind*) to be fostered out; **p~bedürftig** *adj* needing care; **~eltern** *pl* foster parents; **~kind** *nt* foster child; **p~leicht** *adj* easy-care; **~mutter** *f* foster mother; **p~n** *vt* to look after; (*Kranke*) to nurse; (*Beziehungen*) to foster; **~r** (-s, -) *m* orderly; male nurse; **~rin** *f* nurse, attendant; **~vater** *m* foster father

Pflicht [pflıçt] (-, -en) *f* duty; (*SPORT*) compulsory section; **p~bewußt** *adj* conscientious; **~fach** *nt* (*SCH*) compulsory subject; **~gefühl** *nt* sense of duty; **p~gemäß** *adj* dutiful ♦ *adv* as in duty bound; **~versicherung** *f* compulsory insurance

pflücken ['pflʏkən] *vt* to pick; (*Blumen*) to pick, to pluck

Pflug [pflu:k] (-(e)s, ⁻e) *m* plough

pflügen ['pfly:gən] *vt* to plough

Pforte ['pfɔrtə] *f* gate; door

Pförtner ['pfœrtnər] (-s, -) *m* porter, doorkeeper, doorman

Pfosten ['pfɔstən] (-s, -) *m* post

Pfote ['pfo:tə] *f* paw; (*umg: Schrift*) scrawl

Pfropfen ['pfrɔpfən] (-s, -) *m* (*Flaschen~*) stopper; (*Blut~*) clot; **p~** *vt* (*stopfen*) to cram; (*Baum*) to graft

pfui [pfʊi] *excl* ugh!

Pfund [pfʊnt] (-(e)s, -e) *nt* pound; **p~ig** *adj* (*umg*) great

pfuschen ['pfʊʃən] (*umg*) *vi* to be sloppy; **jdm ins Handwerk ~** to interfere in sb's business

Pfuscher ['pfʊʃər] (-s, -; *umg*) *m* sloppy worker; (*Kur~*) quack; **~ei** [-'raı] (*umg*) *f* sloppy work; quackery

Pfütze ['pfʏtsə] *f* puddle

Phänomen [fɛno'me:n] (-s, -e) *nt* phenomenon; **p~al** [-'na:l] *adj* phenomenal

Phantasie [fanta'zi:] *f* imagination; **p~los** *adj* unimaginative; **p~ren** *vi* to fantasize; **p~voll** *adj* imaginative

phantastisch [fan'tastıʃ] *adj* fantastic

Pharmazeut(in) [farma'tsɔʏt(ın)] (-en, -en) *m(f)* pharmacist

Phase ['fa:zə] *f* phase

Philippinen [fılı'pi:nən] *pl* Philippines

Philologe [filo'lo:gə] (-n, -n) *m* philologist

Philologie [filolo'gi:] *f* philology

Philosoph [filo'zo:f] (-en, -en) *m* philosopher; **~ie** [-'fi:] *f* philosophy; **p~isch** *adj* philosophical

Phlegma ['flɛgma] (-s) *nt* lethargy; **p~tisch** [flɛ'gma:tıʃ] *adj* lethargic

Phonetik [fo'ne:tık] *f* phonetics *sg*

phonetisch *adj* phonetic

Phosphor ['fɔsfɔr] (-s) *m* phosphorus

Photo *etc* ['fo:to] (-s, -s) *nt* = **Foto** *etc*

Phrase ['fra:zə] *f* phrase; (*pej*) hollow phrase

Physik [fy'zi:k] *f* physics *sg*; **p~alisch** [-'ka:lıʃ] *adj* of physics; **~er(in)** ['fy:zikər(ın)] (-s, -) *m(f)* physicist

Physiologe [fyzio'lo:gə] (-n, -n) *m* physiologist

Physiologie [fyziolo'gi:] *f* physiology

physisch ['fy:zıʃ] *adj* physical

Pianist(in) [pia'nıst(ın)] *m(f)* pianist

Pickel ['pıkəl] (-s, -) *m* pimple; (*Werkzeug*) pickaxe; (*Berg~*) ice-axe; **p~ig** *adj* pimply

picken ['pıkən] *vi* to pick, to peck

Picknick ['pıknık] (-s, -e *od* -s) *nt* picnic; **~ machen** to have a picnic

piepen ['pi:pən] *vi* to chirp

piepsen ['pi:psən] *vi* to chirp

Pietät [pie'tɛ:t] *f* piety, reverence; **p~los** *adj* impious, irreverent

Pigment [pı'gmɛnt] *nt* pigment

Pik [pi:k] (-s, -s) *nt* (*KARTEN*) spades

pikant [pi'kant] *adj* spicy, piquant; (*anzüglich*) suggestive

Pilger ['pılgər] (-s, -) *m* pilgrim; **~fahrt** *f* pilgrimage

Pille ['pılə] *f* pill

Pilot [pi'lo:t] (-en, -en) *m* pilot

Pils [pıls] (-, -) *nt* lager

Pilz [pılts] (-es, -e) *m* fungus; (*eßbar*) mushroom; (*giftig*) toadstool; **~krankheit** *f* fungal disease

pingelig ['pɪŋəlɪç] (*umg*) *adj* fussy
Pinguin ['pɪŋguiːn] (-s, -e) *m* penguin
Pinie ['piːniə] *f* pine
pinkeln ['pɪŋkəln] (*umg*) *vi* to pee
Pinsel ['pɪnzəl] (-s, -) *m* paintbrush
Pinzette [pɪn'tsɛtə] *f* tweezers *pl*
Pionier [pio'niːr] (-s, -e) *m* pioneer;
(*MIL*) sapper, engineer
Pirat [pi'raːt] (-en, -en) *m* pirate;
~**ensender** *m* pirate radio station
Piste ['pɪstə] *f* (*SKI*) run, piste; (*AVIAT*)
runway
Pistole [pɪs'toːlə] *f* pistol
Pizza ['pɪtsa] (-, -s) *f* pizza
Pkw [peːkaːveː] (-(s), -(s)) *m abk* =
Personenkraftwagen
plädieren [plɛ'diːrən] *vi* to plead
Plädoyer [plɛdoaˈjeː] (-s, -s) *nt* speech
for the defence; (*fig*) plea
Plage ['plaːgə] *f* plague; (*Mühe*)
nuisance; ~**geist** *m* pest, nuisance;
p~n *vt* to torment ♦ *vr* to toil, to slave
Plakat [pla'kaːt] (-(e)s, -e) *nt* placard;
poster
Plan [plaːn] (-(e)s, ⁻e) *m* plan; (*Karte*)
map
Plane *f* tarpaulin
planen *vt* to plan; (*Mord etc*) to plot
Planer (-s, -) *m* planner
Planet [pla'neːt] (-en -en) *m* planet
plangemäß *adv* according to schedule
od plan; (*EISENB*) on time
planieren [pla'niːrən] *vt* to plane, to
level
Planke ['plaŋkə] *f* plank
planlos *adj* (*Vorgehen*) unsystematic;
(*Umherlaufen*) aimless
planmäßig *adj* according to plan;
systematic; (*EISENB*) scheduled
Planschbecken *nt* paddling pool
planschen ['planʃən] *vi* to splash
Plansoll (-s) *nt* output target
Planstelle *f* post
Plantage [plan'taːʒə] *f* plantation
Planung *f* planning
Planwirtschaft *f* planned economy
plappern ['plapərn] *vi* to chatter
plärren ['plɛrən] *vi* (*Mensch*) to cry, to
whine; (*Radio*) to blare
Plasma ['plasma] (-s, **Plasmen**) *nt*

plasma
Plastik¹ ['plastɪk] *f* sculpture
Plastik² (-s) *nt* (*Kunststoff*) plastic;
~**folie** *f* plastic film
plastisch ['plastɪʃ] *adj* plastic; **stell dir
das ~ vor!** just picture it!
Platane [pla'taːnə] *f* plane (tree)
Platin ['plaːtiːn] (-s) *nt* platinum
Platitüde [platiˈtyːdə] *f* platitude
platonisch [pla'toːnɪʃ] *adj* platonic
platsch [platʃ] *excl* splash; ~**en** *vi* to
splash
plätschern ['plɛtʃərn] *vi* to babble
platschnaß *adj* drenched
platt [plat] *adj* flat; (*umg: überrascht*)
flabbergasted; (*fig: geistlos*) flat, boring; ~**deutsch** *adj* low German; **P~e** *f*
(*Speisen~,* PHOT. TECH) plate;
(*Steinplatte*) flag; (*Kachel*) tile;
(*Schalplatte*) record; **P~enspieler** *m*
record player; **P~enteller** *m* turntable;
P~fuß *m* flat foot
Platz [plats] (-es, ⁻e) *m* place; (*Sitz~*)
seat; (*Raum*) space, room; (*in Stadt*)
square; (*Sport~*) playing field; ~
nehmen to take a seat; **jdm ~ machen**
to make room for sb; ~**angst** *f* (*MED*)
agoraphobia; (*umg*) claustrophobia;
~**anweiser(in)** (-s, -) *m(f)* usher(ette)
Plätzchen ['plɛtsçən] *nt* spot; (*Gebäck*)
biscuit
Platz- *zW:* **p~en** *vi* to burst; (*Bombe*)
to explode; **vor Wut p~en** (*umg*) to be
bursting with anger; ~**karte** *f* seat reservation; ~**mangel** *m* lack of space;
~**patrone** *f* blank cartridge; ~**regen** *m*
downpour; ~**wunde** *f* cut
Plauderei [plaudə'rai] *f* chat, conversation; (*RADIO*) talk
plaudern ['plaudərn] *vi* to chat, to talk
plausibel [plau'ziːbəl] *adj* plausible
plazieren [pla'tsiːrən] *vt* to place ♦ *vr*
(*SPORT*) to be placed; (*TENNIS*) to be
seeded
Pleite ['plaitə] *f* bankruptcy; (*umg:
Reinfall*) flop; ~ **machen** to go bust;
p~ (*umg*) *adj* broke
Plenum ['pleːnʊm] (-s) *nt* plenum
Plombe ['plɔmbə] *f* lead seal; (*Zahn~*)
filling

plombieren [plɔm'biːrən] *vt* to seal; (*Zahn*) to fill

plötzlich ['plœtslɪç] *adj* sudden ♦ *adv* suddenly

plump [plʊmp] *adj* clumsy; (*Hände*) coarse; (*Körper*) shapeless; **~sen** (*umg*) *vi* to plump down, to fall

Plunder ['plʊndər] (-s) *m* rubbish

plündern ['plʏndərn] *vt* to plunder; (*Stadt*) to sack ♦ *vi* to plunder

Plünderung ['plʏndəruŋ] *f* plundering, sack, pillage

Plural ['pluːraːl] (-s, -e) *m* plural; **p~istisch** [plura'lɪstɪʃ] *adj* pluralistic

Plus [plʊs] (-, -) *nt* plus; (*FIN*) profit; (*Vorteil*) advantage; **p~** *adv* plus

Plüsch [plyːʃ] (-(e)s, -e) *m* plush

Pluspol *m* (*ELEK*) positive pole

Pluspunkt *m* point; (*fig*) point in sb's favour

PLZ *abk* = **Postleitzahl**

Po [poː] (-s, -s; *umg*) *m* bottom, bum

Pöbel ['pøːbəl] (-s) *m* mob, rabble; **~ei** [-'laı] *f* vulgarity; **p~haft** *adj* low, vulgar

pochen ['pɔxən] *vi* to knock; (*Herz*) to pound; **auf etw** *akk* **~** (*fig*) to insist on sth

Pocken ['pɔkən] *pl* smallpox *sg*

Podium ['poːdiʊm] *nt* podium; **~sdiskussion** *f* panel discussion

Poesie [poe'ziː] *f* poetry

Poet [po'eːt] (-en, -en) *m* poet; **p~isch** *adj* poetic

Pointe [po'ɛ̃ːtə] *f* point

Pokal [po'kaːl] (-s, -e) *m* goblet; (*SPORT*) cup; **~spiel** *nt* cup-tie

Pökelfleisch *nt* salt meat

pökeln ['pøːkəln] *vt* to pickle, to salt

Pol [poːl] (-s, -e) *m* pole; **p~ar** [po'laːr] *adj* polar; **~arkreis** *m* Arctic circle

Pole (-n, -n) *m* Pole

polemisch [po'leːmɪʃ] *adj* polemical

Polen (-s) *nt* Poland

Police [po'liːs(ə)] *f* insurance policy

Polier [po'liːr] (-s, -e) *m* foreman

polieren *vt* to polish

Poliklinik ['poːlikliːnɪk] *f* outpatients (department) *sg*

Polin *f* Pole

Politik [poli'tiːk] *f* politics *sg*; (*eine bestimmte*) policy; **~er(in)** [po'liːtikər(ın)] (-s, -) *m(f)* politician

politisch [po'liːtɪʃ] *adj* political

Politur [poli'tuːr] *f* polish

Polizei [poli'tsaı] *f* police; **~beamte(r)** *m* police officer; **p~lich** *adj* police; **sich p~lich melden** to register with the police; **~revier** *nt* police station; **~staat** *m* police state; **~streife** *f* police patrol; **~stunde** *f* closing time; **~wache** *f* police station

Polizist(in) [poli'tsɪst(ın)] (-en, -en) *m(f)* policeman (woman)

Pollen ['pɔlən] (-s, -) *m* pollen

polnisch ['pɔlnɪʃ] *adj* Polish

Polster ['pɔlstər] (-s, -) *nt* cushion; (*~ung*) upholstery; (*in Kleidung*) padding; (*fig: Geld*) reserves *pl*; **~er** (-s, -) *m* upholsterer; **~möbel** *pl* upholstered furniture *sg*; **p~n** *vt* to upholster; to pad; **~ung** *f* upholstery

Polterabend *m* party on eve of wedding

poltern ['pɔltərn] *vi* (*Krach machen*) to crash; (*schimpfen*) to rant

Polyp [po'lyːp] (-en, -en) *m* polyp; (*umg*) cop; **~en** *pl* (*MED*) adenoids

Pomade [po'maːdə] *f* pomade

Pommes frites [pɔm'frıt] *pl* chips, French fried potatoes

Pomp [pɔmp] (-(e)s) *m* pomp

Pony ['pɔni] (-s, -s) *nt* (*Pferd*) pony ♦ *m* (*Frisur*) fringe

Popmusik ['pɔpmuziːk] *f* pop music

Popo [po'poː] (-s, -s; *umg*) *m* bottom, bum

populär [popu'lɛːr] *adj* popular

Popularität [populari'tɛːt] *f* popularity

Pore ['poːrə] *f* pore

Pornographie [pɔrnogra'fiː] *f* pornography

porös [po'røːs] *adj* porous

Porree ['pɔre] (-s, -s) *m* leek

Portal [pɔr'taːl] (-s, -e) *nt* portal

Portefeuille [pɔrt'føːj] *nt* (*POL, FIN*) portfolio

Portemonnaie [pɔrtmɔ'nɛː] (-s, -s) *nt* purse

Portier [pɔrti'eː] (-s, -s) *m* porter

Portion [pɔrtsi'oːn] f portion, helping; (*umg*: *Anteil*) amount

Porto ['pɔrto] (-s, -s) nt postage; **p~frei** adj post-free, (postage) prepaid

Porträt [pɔr'trɛː] (-s, -s) nt portrait; **p~ieren** [pɔrtrɛ'tiːrən] vt to paint, to portray

Portugal ['pɔrtugal] (-s) nt Portugal

Portugiese [pɔrtu'giːzə] (-n, -n) m Portuguese

Portu'giesin f Portuguese

portu'giesisch adj Portuguese

Porzellan [pɔrtsɛ'laːn] (-s, -e) nt china, porcelain; (*Geschirr*) china

Posaune [po'zaunə] f trombone

Pose ['poːzə] f pose

posieren [po'ziːrən] vi to pose

Position [pozitsi'oːn] f position

positiv ['poːzitiːf] adj positive; **P~** (-s, -e) nt (*PHOT*) positive

possessiv ['pɔsesiːf] adj possessive; **P~pronomen** (-s, -e) nt possessive pronoun

possierlich [pɔ'siːrlɪç] adj funny

Post [pɔst] (-, -en) f post (office); (*Briefe*) mail; **~amt** nt post office; **~anweisung** f postal order, money order; **~bote** m postman; **~en** (-s, -) m post, position; (*COMM*) item; (*auf Liste*) entry; (*MIL*) sentry; (*Streik~*) picket; **~er** (-s, -(s)) nt poster; **~fach** nt post-office box; **~karte** f postcard; **p~lagernd** adv poste restante (*BRIT*), general delivery (*US*); **~leitzahl** f postal code; **~scheckkonto** nt postal giro account; **~sparkasse** f post office savings bank; **~stempel** m postmark; **~wertzeichen** nt postage stamp

potent [po'tɛnt] adj potent

Potential [potɛntsi'aːl] (-s, -e) nt potential

potentiell [potɛntsi'ɛl] adj potential

Potenz [po'tɛnts] f power; (*eines Mannes*) potency

Pracht [praxt] (-) f splendour, magnificence

prächtig ['prɛçtɪç] adj splendid

Prachtstück nt showpiece

prachtvoll adj splendid, magnificent

Prädikat [prɛdi'kaːt] (-(e)s, -e) nt title; (*GRAM*) predicate; (*Zensur*) distinction

Prag [praːk] (-s) nt Prague

prägen ['prɛːgən] vt to stamp; (*Münze*) to mint; (*Ausdruck*) to coin; (*Charakter*) to form

prägnant [prɛ'gnant] adj precise, terse

Prägung ['prɛːguŋ] f minting; forming; (*Eigenart*) character, stamp

prahlen ['praːlən] vi to boast, to brag

Prahlerei [praːlə'rai] f boasting

Praktik ['praktɪk] f practice; **p~abel** [-'kaːbəl] adj practicable; **~ant(in)** [-'kant(ɪn)] m(f) trainee; **~um** (-s, **Praktika** od **Praktiken**) nt practical training

praktisch ['praktɪʃ] adj practical, handy; **~er Arzt** general practitioner

praktizieren [prakti'tsiːrən] vt, vi to practise

Praline [pra'liːnə] f chocolate

prall [pral] adj firmly rounded; (*Segel*) taut; (*Arme*) plump; (*Sonne*) blazing; **~en** vi to bounce, to rebound; (*Sonne*) to blaze

Prämie ['prɛːmiə] f premium; (*Belohnung*) award, prize; **p~ren** [prɛ'miːrən] vt to give an award to

Pranger ['praŋər] (-s, -) m (*HIST*) pillory; **jdn an den ~ stellen** (*fig*) to pillory sb

Präparat [prɛpa'raːt] (-(e)s, -e) nt (*BIOL*) preparation; (*MED*) medicine

Präposition [prɛpozitsi'oːn] f preposition

Präsens ['prɛːzɛns] (-) nt present tense

präsentieren [prɛzɛn'tiːrən] vt to present

Präservativ [prɛzɛrva'tiːf] (-s, -e) nt contraceptive

Präsident(in) [prɛzi'dɛnt(ɪn)] m(f) president; **~schaft** f presidency

Präsidium [prɛ'ziːdium] nt presidency, chair(manship); (*Polizei~*) police headquarters pl

prasseln ['prasəln] vi (*Feuer*) to crackle; (*Hagel*) to drum; (*Wörter*) to rain down

Praxis ['praksɪs] (-, **Praxen**) f practice; (*Behandlungsraum*) surgery; (*von Anwalt*) office

präzis [prɛ'tsiːs] adj precise; **P~ion**

[prɛtsiˈtsi̯oːn] f precision
predigen [ˈpreːdɪgən] vt, vi to preach
Prediger (-s, -) m preacher
Predigt [ˈpreːdɪçt] (-, -en) f sermon
Preis [praɪs] (-es, -e) m price; (*Sieges~*) prize; **um keinen ~** not at any price
Preiselbeere f cranberry
preis- zW: **~en** [ˈpraɪzən] (*unreg*) vi to praise; **~geben** (*unreg*) vt to abandon; (*opfern*) to sacrifice; (*zeigen*) to expose; **~gekrönt** adj prize-winning; **P~gericht** nt jury; **~günstig** adj inexpensive; **P~lage** f price range; **P~träger(in)** m(f) prizewinner; **~wert** adj inexpensive
prekär [preˈkɛːr] adj precarious
Prell- [prɛl] zW: **~bock** m buffers pl; **p~en** vt to bump; (*fig*) to cheat, to swindle; **~ung** f bruise
Premiere [prəmiˈɛːrə] f premiere
Premierminister [prəmɪˈɛːmɪnɪstər] m prime minister, premier
Presse [ˈprɛsə] f press; **~freiheit** f freedom of the press; **p~n** vt to press; **~verlautbarung** f press release
pressieren [prɛˈsiːrən] vi to (be in a) hurry
Preßluft [ˈprɛsluft] f compressed air; **~bohrer** m pneumatic drill
Prestige [prɛsˈtiːʒə] (-s) nt prestige
Preuß- [ˈprɔʏs] zW: **~e** (-n, -n) m Prussian; **~en** (-s) nt Prussia; **~in** f Prussian; **p~isch** adj Prussian
prickeln [ˈprɪkəln] vt, vi to tingle; to tickle
Priester [ˈpriːstər] (-s, -) m priest
Prima [ˈpriːma] (-, **Primen**) f sixth form, top class
prima adj inv first-class, excellent
primär [priˈmɛːr] adj primary
Primel [ˈpriːməl] (-, -n) f primrose
primitiv [primiˈtiːf] adj primitive
Prinz [prɪnts] (-en, -en) m prince; **Prinzessin** [prɪnˈtsɛsɪn] f princess
Prinzip [prɪnˈtsiːp] (-s, -ien) nt principle; **p~iell** [-i̯ˈɛl] adj, adv on principle; **p~ienlos** adj unprincipled
Priorität [prioriˈtɛːt] f priority
Prise [ˈpriːzə] f pinch
Prisma [ˈprɪsma] (-s, **Prismen**) nt prism

privat [priˈvaːt] adj private
Pro (-) nt pro
pro [proː] präp +akk per
Probe [ˈproːbə] f test; (*Teststück*) sample; (*THEAT*) rehearsal; **jdn auf die ~ stellen** to put sb to the test; **~exemplar** nt specimen copy; **~fahrt** f test drive; **p~n** vt to try; (*THEAT*) to rehearse; **p~weise** adv on approval; **~zeit** f probation period
probieren [proˈbiːrən] vt to try; (*Wein, Speise*) to taste, to sample ♦ vi to try; to taste
Problem [proˈbleːm] (-s, -e) nt problem; **~atik** [-ˈmaːtɪk] f problem; **p~atisch** [-ˈmaːtɪʃ] adj problematic; **p~los** adj problem-free
Produkt [proˈdʊkt] (-(e)s, -e) nt product; (*AGR*) produce no pl; **~ion** [prodʊkˈtsi̯oːn] f production; output; **p~iv** [-ˈtiːf] adj productive; **~ivi'tät** f productivity
Produzent [produˈtsɛnt] m manufacturer; (*Film*) producer
produzieren [produˈtsiːrən] vt to produce
Professor [proˈfɛsor] m professor
Profi [ˈproːfi] (-s, -s) m (*umg, SPORT*) pro
Profil [proˈfiːl] (-s, -e) nt profile; (*fig*) image; **p~ieren** [profiˈliːrən] vr to create an image for o.s.
Profit [proˈfiːt] (-(e)s, -e) m profit; **p~ieren** [profiˈtiːrən] vi: **p~ieren (von)** to profit (from)
Prognose [proˈgnoːzə] f prediction, prognosis
Programm [proˈgram] (-s, -e) nt programme; (*COMPUT*) program; **p~ieren** [-ˈmiːrən] vt to programme; (*COMPUT*) to program; **~ierer(in)** (-s, -) m(f) programmer
progressiv [progrɛˈsiːf] adj progressive
Projekt [proˈjɛkt] (-(e)s, -e) nt project; **~or** [proˈjɛktor] m projector
proklamieren [proklaˈmiːrən] vt to proclaim
Prolet [proˈleːt] (-en, -en) m prole, pleb; **~ariat** [-ariˈaːt] (-(e)s, -e) nt proletariat; **~arier** [-ˈtaːriər] (-s, -) m proletarian
Prolog [proˈloːk] (-(e)s, -e) m prologue

Promenade [promə'na:də] f promenade
Promille [pro'mɪlə] (-(s), -) nt alcohol level
prominent [promi'nɛnt] adj prominent
Prominenz [promi'nɛnts] f VIPs pl
Promotion [promotsi'o:n] f doctorate, Ph.D.
promovieren [promo'vi:rən] vi to do a doctorate od Ph.D.
prompt [prɔmpt] adj prompt
Pronomen [pro'no:mɛn] (-s, -) nt pronoun
Propaganda [propa'ganda] (-) f propaganda
Propeller [pro'pɛlər] (-s, -) m propeller
Prophet [pro'fe:t] (-en, -en) m prophet
prophezeien [profe'tsaɪən] vt to prophesy
Prophezeiung f prophecy
Proportion [proportsi'o:n] f proportion; **p~al** [-'na:l] adj proportional
Prosa ['pro:za] (-) f prose; **p~isch** [pro'za:ɪʃ] adj prosaic
prosit ['pro:zɪt] excl cheers
Prospekt [pro'spɛkt] (-(e)s, -e) m leaflet, brochure
prost [pro:st] excl cheers
Prostituierte [prostitu'i:rtə] f prostitute
Prostitution [prostitutsi'o:n] f prostitution
Protest [pro'tɛst] (-(e)s, -e) m protest; **~ant(in)** [protɛs'tant] m(f) Protestant; **p~antisch** [protɛs'tantɪʃ] adj Protestant; **p~ieren** [protɛs'ti:rən] vi to protest
Prothese [pro'te:zə] f artificial limb; (Zahn~) dentures pl
Protokoll [proto'kɔl] (-s, -e) nt register; (von Sitzung) minutes pl; (diplomatisch) protocol; (Polizei~) statement; **p~ieren** [-'li:rən] vt to take down in the minutes
protzen ['prɔtsən] vi to show off
protzig adj ostentatious
Proviant [provi'ant] (-s, -e) m provisions pl, supplies pl
Provinz [pro'vɪnts] (-, -en) f province; **p~i'ell** adj provincial
Provision [provizi'o:n] f (COMM) commission
provisorisch [provi'zo:rɪʃ] adj provi-

sional
Provokation [provokatsi'o:n] f provocation
provozieren [provo'tsi:rən] vt to provoke
Prozedur [protse'du:r] f procedure; (pej) carry-on
Prozent [pro'tsɛnt] (-(e)s, -e) nt per cent, percentage; **~satz** m percentage; **p~ual** [-u'a:l] adj percentage cpd; as a percentage
Prozeß [pro'tsɛs] (-sses, -sse) m trial, case
Prozession [protsɛsi'o:n] f procession
prüde ['pry:də] adj prudish; **P~rie** [-'ri:] f prudery
Prüf- ['pry:f] zW: **p~en** vt to examine, to test; (nach~) to check; **~er** (-s, -) m examiner; **~ling** m examinee; **~ung** f examination; checking; **~ungsausschuß** m examining board
Prügel ['pry:gəl] (-s, -) m cudgel ♦ pl (Schläge) beating; **~ei** [-'laɪ] f fight; **~knabe** m scapegoat; **p~n** vt to beat ♦ vr to fight; **~strafe** f corporal punishment
Prunk [prʊŋk] (-(e)s) m pomp, show; **p~voll** adj splendid, magnificent
PS [pe:'ɛs] abk (= Pferdestärke) H.P.
Psalm [psalm] (-s, -en) m psalm
pseudo- ['psɔydo] in zW pseudo
pst [pst] excl psst!
Psych- ['psyç] zW: **~iater** [-i'a:tər] (-s, -) m psychiatrist; **p~isch** adj psychological; **~oanalyse** [-o'ana'ly:zə] f psychoanalysis; **~ologe** [-o'lo:gə] (-n, -n) m psychologist; **~olo'gie** f psychology; **p~ologisch** adj psychological
Pubertät [puber'tɛ:t] f puberty
Publikum ['pu:blikʊm] (-s) nt audience; (SPORT) crowd
publizieren [publi'tsi:rən] vt to publish, to publicize
Pudding ['pʊdɪŋ] (-s, -e od -s) m blancmange
Pudel ['pu:dəl] (-s) m poodle
Puder ['pu:dər] (-s, -) m powder; **~dose** f powder compact; **p~n** vt to powder; **~zucker** m icing sugar
Puff₁ [pʊf] (-s, -e) m (Wäsche~) linen basket; (Sitz~) pouf

Puff² (-s, -̈e; *umg*) *m* (*Stoß*) push

Puff³ (-s, -; *umg*) *m od nt* (*Bordell*) brothel

Puffer (-s, -) *m* buffer; ~**speicher** *m* (*COMPUT*) buffer

Pullover [pʊ'loːvər] (-s, -) *m* pullover, jumper

Puls [pʊls] (-es, -e) *m* pulse; ~**ader** *f* artery; **p~ieren** [pʊl'ziːrən] *vi* to throb, to pulsate

Pult [pʊlt] (-(e)s, -e) *nt* desk

Pulver ['pʊlfər] (-s, -) *nt* powder; **p~ig** *adj* powdery; ~**schnee** *m* powdery snow

pummelig ['pʊməlɪç] *adj* chubby

Pumpe ['pʊmpə] *f* pump; **p~n** *vt* to pump; (*umg*) to lend; to borrow

Punkt [pʊŋkt] (-(e)s, -e) *m* point; (*bei Muster*) dot; (*Satzzeichen*) full stop; **p~ieren** [-'tiːrən] *vt* to dot; (*MED*) to aspirate

pünktlich ['pʏŋktlɪç] *adj* punctual; **P~keit** *f* punctuality

Punktsieg *m* victory on points

Punktzahl *f* score

Punsch [pʊnʃ] (-(e)s, -e) *m* punch

Pupille [pu'pɪlə] *f* pupil

Puppe ['pʊpə] *f* doll; (*Marionette*) puppet; (*Insekten~*) pupa, chrysalis; **Puppenspieler** *m* puppeteer

pur [puːr] *adj* pure; (*völlig*) sheer; (*Whisky*) neat

Püree [py'reː] (-s, -s) *nt* mashed potatoes *pl*

Purzelbaum *m* somersault

purzeln ['pʊrtsəln] *vi* to tumble

Puste ['puːstə] (-; *umg*) *f* puff; (*fig*) steam; **p~n** *vi* to puff, to blow

Pute ['puːtə] *f* turkey-hen; ~**r** (-s, -) *m* turkey-cock

Putsch [pʊtʃ] (-(e)s, -e) *m* revolt, putsch

Putz [pʊts] (-es) *m* (*Mörtel*) plaster, roughcast

putzen *vt* to clean; (*Nase*) to wipe, to blow ♦ *vr* to clean o.s.; to dress o.s. up

Putz- *zW*: ~**frau** *f* charwoman; **p~ig** *adj* quaint, funny; ~**lappen** *m* cloth

Puzzle ['pasəl] (-s, -s) *nt* jigsaw

Pyjama [py'dʒaːma] (-s, -s) *m* pyjamas

pl

Pyramide [pyra'miːdə] *f* pyramid

Pyrenäen [pyre'nɛːən] *pl* Pyrenees

Q

Quacksalber ['kvakzalbər] (-s, -) *m* quack (doctor)

Quader ['kvaːdər] (-s, -) *m* square stone; (*MATH*) cuboid

Quadrat [kva'draːt] (-(e)s, -e) *nt* square; **q~isch** *adj* square; ~**meter** *m* square metre

quaken ['kvaːkən] *vi* to croak; (*Ente*) to quack

quäken ['kvɛːkən] *vi* to screech

Qual [kvaːl] (-, -en) *f* pain, agony; (*seelisch*) anguish

Quäl- ['kvɛːl] *zW*: **q~en** *vt* to torment ♦ *vr* to struggle; (*geistig*) to torment o.s.; ~**erei** [-ə'rai] *f* torture, torment; ~**geist** *m* pest

qualifizieren [kvalifi'tsiːrən] *vt* to qualify; (*einstufen*) to label ♦ *vr* to qualify

Qualität [kvali'tɛːt] *f* quality; **Qualitätsware** *f* article of high quality

Qualle ['kvalə] *f* jellyfish

Qualm [kvalm] (-(e)s, -e) *m* thick smoke; **q~en** *vt, vi* to smoke

qualvoll ['kvaːlfɔl] *adj* excruciating, painful, agonizing

Quant- ['kvant] *zW*: ~**entheorie** *f* quantum theory; ~**ität** [-i'tɛːt] *f* quantity; **q~itativ** [-ita'tiːf] *adj* quantitative; ~**um** (-s, **Quanten**) *nt* quantity, amount

Quarantäne [karan'tɛːnə] *f* quarantine

Quark [kvark] (-s) *m* curd cheese; (*umg*) rubbish

Quarta ['kvarta] (-, **Quarten**) *f* third year of secondary school

Quartal [kvar'taːl] (-s, -e) *nt* quarter (year)

Quartier [kvar'tiːr] (-s, -e) *nt* accommodation; (*MIL*) quarters *pl*; (*Stadt~*) district

Quarz [kvaːrts] (-es, -e) *m* quartz

quasseln ['kvasəln] (*umg*) *vi* to natter

Quatsch [kvatʃ] (-es) m rubbish; **q~en** vi to chat, to natter

Quecksilber ['kvɛkzɪlbər] nt mercury

Quelle ['kvɛlə] f spring; (eines Flusses) source; **q~n** (unreg) vi (hervor~) to pour od gush forth; (schwellen) to swell

quer [kveːr] adv crossways, diagonally; (rechtwinklig) at right angles; ~ **auf dem Bett** across the bed; **Q~balken** m crossbeam; ~**feldein** adv across country; **Q~flöte** f flute; **Q~schnitt** m cross-section; ~**schnittgelähmt** adj paralysed below the waist; **Q~straße** f intersecting road

quetschen ['kvɛtʃən] vt to squash, to crush; (MED) to bruise

Quetschung f bruise, contusion

quieken ['kviːkən] vi to squeak

quietschen ['kviːtʃən] vi to squeak

Quint- ['kvɪnt] zW: ~**a** (-, **Quinten**) f second year of secondary school; ~**essenz** [-ɛsɛnts] f quintessence; ~**ett** [-'tɛt] (-(e)s, -e) nt quintet

Quirl [kvɪrl] (-(e)s, -e) m whisk

quitt [kvɪt] adj quits, even

Quitte f quince

quittieren [kvɪ'tiːrən] vt to give a receipt for; (Dienst) to leave

Quittung f receipt

Quiz [kvɪs] (-, -) nt quiz

quoll etc [kvɔl] vb siehe **quellen**

Quote ['kvoːtə] f number, rate

R

Rabatt [ra'bat] (-(e)s, -e) m discount

Rabatte f flowerbed, border

Rabattmarke f trading stamp

Rabe ['raːbə] (-n, -n) m raven

rabiat [rabi'aːt] adj furious

Rache ['raxə] (-) f revenge, vengeance

Rachen (-s, -) m throat

rächen ['rɛçən] vt to avenge, to revenge ♦ vr to take (one's) revenge; **das wird sich** ~ you'll pay for this

Rachitis [ra'xiːtɪs] (-) f rickets sg

Rad [raːt] (-(e)s, ⁼er) nt wheel; (Fahr~) bike

Radar ['raːdaːr] (-s) m od nt radar;

~**falle** f speed trap; ~**kontrolle** f radar-controlled speed trap

Radau [ra'dau] (-s; umg) m row

Raddampfer m paddle steamer

radebrechen vi insep: **deutsch** etc ~ to speak broken German etc

radfahr- zW: ~**en** (unreg) vi to cycle; **R~er(in)** m(f) cyclist, **R~weg** m cycle track od path

Radier- [ra'diːr] zW: **r~en** vt to rub out, to erase; (ART) to etch; ~**gummi** m rubber, eraser; ~**ung** f etching

Radieschen [ra'diːsçən] nt radish

radikal [radi'kaːl] adj radical; **R~e(r)** mf radical

Radio ['raːdio] (-s, -s) nt radio, wireless; **r~ak'tiv** adj radioactive; ~**aktivi'tät** f radioactivity; ~**apparat** m radio, wireless set

Radius ['raːdios] (-, **Radien**) m radius

Rad- zW: ~**kappe** f (AUT) hub cap; ~**rennen** nt cycle race; cycle racing; ~**sport** m cycling

raffen [rafən] vt to snatch, to pick up; (Stoff) to gather (up); (Geld) to pile up, to rake in

Raffinade [rafi'naːdə] f refined sugar

raffi'niert adj crafty, cunning

ragen ['raːgən] vi to tower, to rise

Rahm [raːm] (-s) m cream

Rahmen (-s, -) m frame(work); **im** ~ **des Möglichen** within the bounds of possibility; **r~** vt to frame; ~**plan** m outline plan

rahmig adj creamy

Rakete [ra'keːtə] f rocket; **Raketenstützpunkt** m missile base

rammen ['ramən] vt to ram

Rampe ['rampə] f ramp; **Rampenlicht** nt (THEAT) footlights pl

ramponieren [rampo'niːrən] (umg) vt to damage

Ramsch [ramʃ] (-(e)s, -e) m junk

ran [ran] (umg) adv = **heran**

Rand [rant] (-(e)s, ⁼er) m edge; (von Brille, Tasse etc) rim; (Hut~) brim; (auf Papier) margin; (Schmutz~, unter Augen) ring; (fig) verge, brink; **außer** ~ **und Band** wild; **am** ~**e bemerkt** mentioned in passing

randalieren [randa'li:rən] *vi* to (go on the) rampage

Rang [raŋ] (-(e)s, ⁻e) *m* rank; (*Stand*) standing; (*Wert*) quality; (*THEAT*) circle

Rangier- [rãʒiːr] *zW:* ~**bahnhof** *m* marshalling yard; **r~en** *vt* (*EISENB*) to shunt, to switch (*US*) ♦ *vi* to rank, to be classed; ~**gleis** *nt* siding

Ranke ['raŋkə] *f* tendril, shoot

rannte *etc* ['rantə] *vb siehe* **rennen**

ranzig ['rantsɪç] *adj* rancid

Rappe ['rapə] (-n, -n) *m* black horse

Rappen ['rapən] *m* (*FIN*) rappen, centime

rar [raːr] *adj* rare; **sich ~ machen** (*umg*) to keep o.s. to o.s.; **R~i'tät** *f* rarity; (*Sammelobjekt*) curio

rasant [ra'zant] *adj* quick, rapid

rasch [raʃ] *adj* quick

rascheln *vi* to rustle

Rasen ['raːzən] (-s, -) *m* lawn; grass

rasen *vi* to rave; (*schnell*) to race; ~**d** *adj* furious; ~**de Kopfschmerzen** a splitting headache

Rasenmäher (-s, -) *m* lawnmower

Rasenplatz *m* lawn

Rasier- [ra'ziːr] *zW:* ~**apparat** *m* shaver; ~**creme** *f* shaving cream; **r~en** *vt, vr* to shave; ~**klinge** *f* razor blade; ~**messer** *nt* razor; ~**pinsel** *m* shaving brush; ~**seife** *f* shaving soap *od* stick; ~**wasser** *nt* shaving lotion

Rasse ['rasə] *f* race; (*Tier~*) breed; ~**hund** *m* thoroughbred dog; **Rassenhaß** *m* race *od* racial hatred; **Rassentrennung** *f* racial segregation

Rassismus [ra'sɪsmʊs] *m* racism

Rast [rast] (-, -en) *f* rest; **r~en** *vi* to rest; ~**haus** *nt* (*AUT*) service station; ~**hof** *m* (*AUT*) service station; **r~los** *adj* tireless; (*unruhig*) restless; ~**platz** *m* (*AUT*) layby; ~**stätte** *f* (*AUT*) service station

Rasur [ra'zuːr] *f* shaving

Rat [raːt] (-(e)s, **-schläge**) *m* advice *no pl*; **ein ~** a piece of advice; **jdn zu ~e ziehen** to consult sb; **keinen ~ wissen** not to know what to do

Rate *f* instalment

raten (*unreg*) *vt, vi* to guess; (*empfehlen*): **jdm ~** to advise sb

Ratenzahlung *f* hire purchase

Ratgeber (-s, -) *m* adviser

Rathaus *nt* town hall

ratifizieren [ratifi'tsiːrən] *vt* to ratify

Ration [ratsi'oːn] *f* ration; **r~al** [-'naːl] *adj* rational; **r~ali'sieren** *vt* to rationalize; **r~ell** [-'nɛl] *adj* efficient; **r~ieren** [-'niːrən] *vt* to ration

Rat- *zW:* **r~los** *adj* at a loss, helpless; **r~sam** *adj* advisable; ~**schlag** *m* (piece of) advice

Rätsel ['rɛːtsəl] (-s, -) *nt* puzzle; (*Wort~*) riddle; **r~haft** *adj* mysterious; **es ist mir r~haft** it's a mystery to me

Ratte ['ratə] *f* rat; **Rattenfänger** (-s, -) *m* ratcatcher

rattern ['ratərn] *vi* to rattle, to clatter

Raub [raʊp] (-(e)s) *m* robbery; (*Beute*) loot, booty; ~**bau** *m* ruthless exploitation; **r~en** ['raʊbən] *vt* to rob; (*Mensch*) to kidnap, to abduct

Räuber ['rɔʏbər] (-s, -) *m* robber

Raub- *zW:* ~**mord** *m* robbery with murder; ~**tier** *nt* predator; ~**überfall** *m* robbery with violence; ~**vogel** *m* bird of prey

Rauch [raʊx] (-(e)s) *m* smoke; **r~en** *vt, vi* to smoke; ~**er(in)** (-s, -) *m(f)* smoker; ~**erabteil** *nt* (*EISENB*) smoker

räuchern ['rɔʏçərn] *vt* to smoke, to cure

Rauchfleisch *nt* smoked meat

rauchig *adj* smoky

rauf [raʊf] (*umg*) *adv* = **herauf**; **hinauf**

raufen *vt* (*Haare*) to pull out ♦ *vi, vr* to fight; **Raufe'rei** *f* brawl, fight

rauh [raʊ] *adj* rough, coarse; (*Wetter*) harsh; ~**reif** *m* hoarfrost

Raum [raʊm] (-(e)s, **Räume**) *m* space; (*Zimmer, Platz*) room; (*Gebiet*) area

räumen ['rɔʏmən] *vt* to clear; (*Wohnung, Platz*) to vacate; (*wegbringen*) to shift, to move; (*in Schrank etc*) to put away

Raum- *zW:* ~**fähre** *f* space shuttle; ~**fahrt** *f* space travel; ~**inhalt** *m* cubic capacity, volume

räumlich ['rɔʏmlɪç] *adj* spatial; **R~keiten** *pl* premises

Raum- *zW*: ~**mangel** *m* lack of space; ~**pflegerin** *f* cleaner; ~**schiff** *nt* spaceship; ~**schiffahrt** *f* space travel

Räumung ['rɔʏmʊŋ] *f* vacating, evacuation; clearing (away); **Räumungsverkauf** *m* clearance sale; (*bei Geschäftsaufgabe*) closing down sale

Raupe ['raʊpə] *f* caterpillar; (~*nkette*) (caterpillar) track; **Raupenschlepper** *m* caterpillar tractor

raus [raʊs] (*umg*) *adv* = **heraus; hinaus**

Rausch [raʊʃ] (-(e)s, **Räusche**) *m* intoxication

rauschen *vi* (*Wasser*) to rush; (*Baum*) to rustle; (*Radio etc*) to hiss; (*Mensch*) to sweep, to sail; ~**d** *adj* (*Beifall*) thunderous; (*Fest*) sumptuous

Rauschgift *nt* drug; ~**handel** *m* drug traffic; ~**süchtige(r)** *mf* drug addict

räuspern ['rɔʏspərn] *vr* to clear one's throat

Razzia ['ratsia] (-, **Razzien**) *f* raid

Reagenzglas [rea'gɛntsglaːs] *nt* test tube

reagieren [rea'giːrən] *vi*: ~ (**auf** +*akk*) to react (to)

Reakt- *zW*: ~**ion** [reaktsi'oːn] *f* reaction; **r~io'när** *adj* reactionary; ~**or** [re'aktɔr] *m* reactor

real [re'aːl] *adj* real, material; **R~ismus** [-'lɪsmʊs] *m* realism; ~**istisch** *adj* realistic; **R~schule** *f* secondary school

Rebe ['reːbə] *f* vine

Rebell [re'bɛl] (-en, -en) *m* rebel; ~**i'on** *f* rebellion; **r~isch** *adj* rebellious

Rechen ['rɛçən] (-s, -) *m* rake; **r~** *vt, vi* to rake

Rechen- *zW*: ~**fehler** *m* miscalculation; ~**maschine** *f* calculating machine; ~**schaft** *f* account; **für etw** ~**schaft ablegen** to account for sth; ~**schieber** *m* slide rule

Rech- ['rɛç] *zW*: **r~nen** *vt, vi* to calculate; **jdm/etw r~nen zu** to count sb/sth among; **r~nen mit** to reckon with; **r~nen auf** +*akk* to count on; ~**nen** *nt* arithmetic; ~**ner** (-s, -) *m* calculator; (*COMPUT*) computer; ~**nung** *f* calculation(s); (*COMM*) bill, check (*US*); **jdm/etw ~nung tragen** to take sb/ sth into account; ~**nungsjahr** *nt*

financial year; ~**nungsprüfer** *m* auditor

Recht [rɛçt] (-(e)s, -e) *nt* right; (*JUR*) law; **mit** ~ rightly, justly; **von** ~**s wegen** by rights

recht *adj* right ♦ *adv* (*vor Adjektiv*) really, quite; **das ist mir** ~ that suits me; **jetzt erst** ~ now more than ever; ~ **haben** to be right; **jdm** ~ **geben** to agree with sb

Rechte *f* right (hand); (*POL*) Right; **r~(r, s)** *adj* right; (*POL*) right-wing; **ein** ~**r** a right-winger; ~**(s)** *nt* right thing; **etwas/nichts** ~**s** something/nothing proper

recht- *zW*: **R~eck** (-s, -e) *nt* rectangle; ~**eckig** *adj* rectangular; ~**fertigen** *vt insep* to justify ♦ *vr insep* to justify o.s.; **R~fertigung** *f* justification; ~**mäßig** *adj* legal, lawful

rechts [rɛçts] *adv* on/to the right; **R~anwalt** *m* lawyer, barrister; **R~anwältin** *f* lawyer, barrister; **R~'außen** (-, -) *m* (*SPORT*) outside right

rechtschaffen *adj* upright

Rechtschreibung *f* spelling

Rechts- *zW*: ~**fall** *m* (law) case; ~**händer** (-s, -) *m* right-handed person; **r~kräftig** *adj* valid, legal; ~**kurve** *f* right-hand bend; ~**streit** *m* lawsuit; **r~verbindlich** *adj* legally binding; ~**verkehr** *m* driving on the right; **r~widrig** *adj* illegal; ~**wissenschaft** *f* jurisprudence

rechtwinklig *adj* right-angled

rechtzeitig *adj* timely ♦ *adv* in time

Reck [rɛk] (-(e)s, -e) *nt* horizontal bar; **r~en** *vt, vr* to stretch

Redakteur [redak'tøːr] *m* editor

Redaktion [redaktsi'oːn] *f* editing; (*Leute*) editorial staff; (*Büro*) editorial office(s)

Rede ['reːdə] *f* speech; (*Gespräch*) talk; **jdn zur** ~ **stellen** to take sb to task; ~**freiheit** *f* freedom of speech; **r~gewandt** *adj* eloquent; **r~n** *vi* to talk, to speak ♦ *vt* to say; (*Unsinn etc*) to talk; **Redensart** *f* set phrase; ~**wendung** *f* expression, idiom

redlich *adj* honest

Redner (-s, -) *m* speaker, orator
redselig *adj* talkative, loquacious
reduzieren [redu'tsiːrən] *vt* to reduce
Reede ['reːdə] *f* protected anchorage; ~**r** (-s, -) *m* shipowner; ~'**rei** *f* shipping line *od* firm
reell [re'ɛl] *adj* fair, honest; (*MATH*) real
Refer- *zW:* ~**at** [refe'raːt] (-(e)s, -e) *nt* report; (*Vortrag*) paper; (*Gebiet*) section; ~**ent** [refe'rɛnt] *m* speaker; (*Berichterstatter*) reporter; (*Sachbearbeiter*) expert; ~**enz** [refe'rɛnts] *f* reference; **r~ieren** [refe'riːrən] *vi:* **r~ieren über** +*akk* to speak *od* talk on
Reflex [re'flɛks] (-es, -e) *m* reflex; ~**bewegung** *f* reflex action; **r~iv** [-'ksiːf] *adj* (*GRAM*) reflexive
Reform [re'fɔrm] (-, -en) *f* reform; ~**ati'on** *f* reformation; ~**haus** *nt* health food shop; **r~ieren** [-'miːrən] *vt* to reform
Regal [re'gaːl] (-s, -e) *nt* (book)shelves *pl*, bookcase; stand, rack
Regel ['reːgəl] (-, -n) *f* rule; (*MED*) period; **r~mäßig** *adj* regular; ~**mäßigkeit** *f* regularity; **r~n** *vt* to regulate, to control; (*Angelegenheit*) to settle ♦ *vr:* **sich von selbst r~n** to take care of itself; **r~recht** *adj* regular, proper, thorough; ~**ung** *f* regulation; settlement; **r~widrig** *adj* irregular, against the rules
Regen ['reːgən] (-s, -) *m* rain; ~**bogen** *m* rainbow; ~**bogenpresse** *f* tabloids *pl*; ~**mantel** *m* raincoat, mac(kintosh); ~**schauer** *m* shower (of rain); ~**schirm** *m* umbrella; ~**wurm** *m* earthworm
Regie [re'ʒiː] *f* (*Film etc*) direction; (*THEAT*) production
Regier- [re'giːr] *zW:* **r~en** *vt, vi* to govern, to rule; ~**ung** *f* government; (*Monarchie*) reign; ~**ungswechsel** *m* change of government; ~**ungszeit** *f* period in government; (*von König*) reign
Regiment [regi'mɛnt] (-s, -er) *nt* regiment
Region [regi'oːn] *f* region
Regisseur [reʒɪ'søːr] *m* director; (*THEAT*) (stage) producer

Register [re'gɪstər] (-s, -) *nt* register; (*in Buch*) table of contents, index
registrieren [regɪs'triːrən] *vt* to register
Regler ['reːglər] (-s, -) *m* regulator, governor
reglos ['reːkloːs] *adj* motionless
regnen *vi unpers* to rain
regnerisch *adj* rainy
regulär [regu'lɛːr] *adj* regular
regulieren [regu'liːrən] *vt* to regulate; (*COMM*) to settle
Regung ['reːguŋ] *f* motion; (*Gefühl*) feeling, impulse; **regungslos** *adj* motionless
Reh [reː] (-(e)s, -e) *nt* deer, roe; ~**bock** *m* roebuck; ~**kalb** *nt* fawn; ~**kitz** *nt* fawn
Reib- ['raib] *zW:* ~**e** *f* grater; ~**eisen** *nt* grater; **r~en** (*unreg*) *vt* to rub; (*KOCH*) to grate; ~**e'rei** *f* friction *no pl*; ~**fläche** *f* rough surface; ~**ung** *f* friction; **r~ungslos** *adj* smooth
Reich [raiç] (-(e)s, -e) *nt* empire, kingdom; (*fig*) realm; **das Dritte ~** the Third Reich
reich *adj* rich
reichen *vi* to reach; (*genügen*) to be enough *od* sufficient ♦ *vt* to hold out; (*geben*) to pass, to hand; (*anbieten*) to offer; **jdm ~** to be enough *od* sufficient for sb
reich- *zW:* ~**haltig** *adj* ample, rich; ~**lich** *adj* ample, plenty of; **R~tum** (-s, -tümer) *m* wealth; **R~weite** *f* range
reif [raif] *adj* ripe; (*Mensch, Urteil*) mature
Reif[1] (-(e)s) *m* hoarfrost
Reif[2] (-(e)s, -e) *m* (*Ring*) ring, hoop
Reife (-) *f* ripeness; maturity; **r~n** *vi* to mature; to ripen
Reifen (-s, -) *m* ring, hoop; (*Fahrzeug~*) tyre; ~**druck** *m* tyre pressure; ~**panne** *f* puncture
Reihe ['raiə] *f* row; (*von Tagen etc, umg: Anzahl*) series *sg*; **der ~ nach** in turn; **er ist an der ~** it's his turn; **an die ~ kommen** to have one's turn; **Reihenfolge** *f* sequence; **alphabetische Reihenfolge** alphabetical order; **Reihenhaus** *nt* terraced house

Reim [raɪm] (-(e)s, -e) m rhyme; **r~en** vt to rhyme

rein¹ [raɪn] (umg) adv = **herein; hinein**

rein² adj pure; (sauber) clean ♦ adv purely; **etw ins ~e schreiben** to make a fair copy of sth; **etw ins ~e bringen** to clear sth up; **R~fall** (umg) m let-down; **R~gewinn** m net profit; **R~heit** f purity; cleanness; **~igen** vt to clean; (Wasser) to purify; **R~igung** f cleaning; purification; (Geschäft) cleaners; **chemische R~igung** dry cleaning; dry cleaners; **~lich** adj clean; **~rassig** adj pedigree; **R~schrift** f fair copy

Reis [raɪs] (-es, -e) m rice

Reise ['raɪzə] f journey; (Schiffs~) voyage; **~n** pl (Herum~) travels; **gute ~!** have a good journey; **~andenken** nt souvenir; **~büro** nt travel agency; **r~fertig** adj ready to start; **~führer** m guide(book); (Mensch) travel guide; **~gepäck** nt luggage; **~gesellschaft** f party of travellers; **~kosten** pl travelling expenses; **~leiter** m courier; **~lektüre** f reading matter for the journey; **r~n** vi to travel; **r~n nach** to go to; **Reisende(r)** mf traveller; **~paß** m passport; **~proviant** m food and drink for the journey; **~scheck** m traveller's cheque; **~ziel** nt destination

Reiß- ['raɪs] zW: **r~en** (unreg) vt to tear; (ziehen) to pull, to drag; (Witz) to crack ♦ vi to tear; to pull, to drag; **etw an sich r~en** to snatch sth up; (fig) to take over sth; **sich um etw r~en** to scramble for sth; **~nagel** m drawing pin (BRIT), thumbtack (US); **~verschluß** m zip(per), zip fastener; **~wolf** m shredder; **~zwecke** f = **~nagel**

Reit- ['raɪt] zW: **r~en** (unreg) vt, vi to ride; **~er** (-s, -) m rider; (MIL) cavalryman, trooper; **~erin** f rider; **~hose** f riding breeches pl; **~pferd** nt saddle horse; **~stiefel** m riding boot; **~zeug** nt riding outfit

Reiz [raɪts] (-es, -e) m stimulus; (angenehm) charm; (Verlockung) attraction; **r~bar** adj irritable; **~barkeit** f irritability; **r~en** vt to stimulate; (unangenehm) to irritate; (verlocken)

to appeal to, to attract; **r~end** adj charming; **r~voll** adj attractive

rekeln ['reːkəln] vr to stretch out; (lümmeln) to lounge od loll about

Reklamation [reklamatsi'oːn] f complaint

Reklame [re'klaːmə] f advertising; advertisement; **~ machen für etw** to advertise sth

rekonstruieren [rekɔnstru'iːrən] vt to reconstruct

Rekord [re'kɔrt] (-(e)s, -e) m record; **~leistung** f record performance

Rektor ['rɛktɔr] m (UNIV) rector, vice-chancellor; (SCH) headteacher (BRIT), principal (US); **~at** [-'rat] (-(e)s, -e) nt rectorate, vice-chancellorship; headship; (Zimmer) rector's etc office

Relais [rə'lɛː] (-, -) nt relay

relativ [rela'tiːf] adj relative; **R~ität** [relativi'tɛːt] f relativity

relevant [rele'vant] adj relevant

Relief [reli'ɛf] (-s, -s) nt relief

Religion [religi'oːn] f religion

religiös [religi'øːs] adj religious

Reling ['reːlɪŋ] (-, -s) f (NAUT) rail

Remoulade [remu'laːdə] f remoulade

Rendezvous [rãde'vuː] (-, -) nt rendezvous

Renn- ['rɛn] zW: **~bahn** f racecourse; (AUT) circuit, race track; **r~en** (unreg) vt, vi to run, to race; **~en** (-s, -) nt running; (Wettbewerb) race; **~fahrer** m racing driver; **~pferd** nt racehorse; **~wagen** m racing car

renovieren [reno'viːrən] vt to renovate

Renovierung f renovation

rentabel [rɛn'taːbəl] adj profitable, lucrative

Rentabilität [rɛntabili'tɛːt] f profitability

Rente ['rɛntə] f pension; **rentendynamisch** adj index-linked; **Rentenversicherung** f pension scheme

Rentier ['rɛntiːr] nt reindeer

rentieren [rɛn'tiːrən] vr to pay, to be profitable

Rentner(in) ['rɛntnər(ɪn)] (-s, -) m(f) pensioner

Reparatur [repara'tuːr] f repairing; repair; **~werkstatt** f repair shop; (AUT) garage

reparieren [repa'ri:rən] *vt* to repair

Reportage [repɔr'ta:ʒə] *f* (on-the-spot) report; *(TV, RADIO)* live commentary *od* coverage

Roportor [rɛ'pɔrtər] (ɑ,) *m* rɛportɛr, commentator

Repressalien [reprɛ'sa:liən] *pl* reprisals

Reprivatisierung [reprivati'zi:ruŋ] *f* denationalisation

Reproduktion [reprodʊktsi'o:n] *f* reproduction

reproduzieren [reprodu'tsi:rən] *vt* to reproduce

Reptil [rɛp'ti:l] (-s, -ien) *nt* reptile

Republik [repu'bli:k] *f* republic; **r~anisch** [-'ka:nɪʃ] *adj* republican

Reservat [rezɛr'va:t] (-(e)s, -e) *nt* reservation

Reserve [re'zɛrvə] *f* reserve; **~rad** *nt* *(AUT)* spare wheel; **~spieler** *m* reserve; **~tank** *m* reserve tank

reservieren [rezɛr'vi:rən] *vt* to reserve

Reservoir [rezɛrvo'a:r] (-s, -e) *nt* reservoir

Residenz [rezi'dɛnts] *f* residence, seat

resignieren [rezɪ'gni:rən] *vi* to resign

resolut [rezo'lu:t] *adj* resolute

Resonanz [rezo'nants] *f* resonance; *(fig)* response

Resopal [rezo'pa:l] (®; -s) *nt* Formica (®)

Resozialisierung [rezotsiali'zi:ruŋ] *f* rehabilitation

Respekt [rɛ'spɛkt] (-(e)s) *m* respect; **r~ieren** [-'ti:rən] *vt* to respect; **r~los** *adj* disrespectful; **r~voll** *adj* respectful

Ressort [rɛ'so:r] (-s, -s) *nt* department

Rest [rɛst] (-(e)s, -e) *m* remainder, rest; *(Über~)* remains *pl*

Restaurant [rɛsto'rã:] (-s, -s) *nt* restaurant

restaurieren [rɛstau'ri:rən] *vt* to restore

Rest- *zW:* **~betrag** *m* remainder, outstanding sum; **r~lich** *adj* remaining; **r~los** *adj* complete

Resultat [rezʊl'ta:t] (-(e)s, -e) *nt* result

Retorte [re'tɔrtə] *f* retort

Retouren [re'tu:rən] *pl* *(COMM)* returns

retten ['rɛtən] *vt* to save, to rescue

Rettich ['rɛtɪç] (-s, -e) *m* radish

Rettung *f* rescue; *(Hilfe)* help; **seine letzte ~** his last hope

Rettungs- *zW:* **~boot** *nt* lifeboat; **r~los** *adj* hopeless; **~ring** *m* lifebelt, life prɛsɛrvɛr *(US)*

retuschieren [retu'ʃi:rən] *vt* *(PHOT)* to retouch

Reue ['rɔyə] (-) *f* remorse; *(Bedauern)* regret; **r~n** *vt*: **es reut ihn** he regrets (it) *od* is sorry (about it)

reuig ['rɔyɪç] *adj* penitent

Revanche [re'vã:ʃə] *f* revenge; *(SPORT)* return match

revanchieren [revã'ʃi:rən] *vr* *(sich rächen)* to get one's own back, to have one's revenge; *(erwidern)* to reciprocate, to return the compliment

Revier [re'vi:r] (-s, -e) *nt* district; *(Jagd~)* preserve; *(Polizei~)* police station; beat

Revolte [re'vɔltə] *f* revolt

Revolution [revolutsi'o:n] *f* revolution; **~är** [-'nɛ:r] (-s, -e) *m* revolutionary; **r~ieren** [-'ni:rən] *vt* to revolutionize

Rezept [re'tsɛpt] (-(e)s, -e) *nt* recipe; *(MED)* prescription; **~ion** [retsɛptsi'o:n] *f* reception; **r~pflichtig** *adj* available only on prescription

rezitieren [retsi'ti:rən] *vt* to recite

R-Gespräch ['ɛrgəʃprɛ:ç] *nt* reverse charge call *(BRIT)*, collect call *(US)*

Rhabarber [ra'barbər] (-s) *m* rhubarb

Rhein [raɪn] (-s) *m* Rhine; **r~isch** *adj* Rhenish

Rhesusfaktor ['re:zusfaktɔr] *m* rhesus factor

rhetorisch [re'to:rɪʃ] *adj* rhetorical

Rheuma ['rɔyma] (-s) *nt* rheumatism; **~tismus** [rɔyma'tɪsmus] *m* rheumatism

Rhinozeros [ri'no:tserɔs] (- *od* -ses, -se) *nt* rhinoceros

rhythmisch ['rʏtmɪʃ] *adj* rhythmical

Rhythmus ['rʏtmus] *m* rhythm

richt- ['rɪçt] *zW:* **~en** *vt* to direct; *(Waffe)* to aim; *(einstellen)* to adjust; *(instandsetzen)* to repair; *(zurechtmachen)* to prepare; *(bestrafen)* to pass judgement on ♦ *vr:* **sich ~en nach** to go by; **~en an** +*akk* to direct at;

(fig) to direct to; ~en auf +*akk* to aim at; R~er(in) (-s, -) *m(f)* judge; ~erlich *adj* judicial

richtig *adj* right, correct; *(echt)* proper ♦ *adv (umg: sehr)* really; bin ich hier ~? am I in the right place?; der/die R~e the right one/person; das R~e the right thing, R~keit *f* correctness; R~stellung *f* correction, rectification

Richtpreis *m* recommended price

Richtung *f* direction; tendency, orientation

rieb *etc* [riːp] *vb siehe* **reiben**

riechen ['riːçən] *(unreg) vt, vi* to smell; an etw *dat* ~ to smell sth; nach etw ~ to smell of sth; ich kann das/ihn nicht ~ *(umg)* I can't stand it/him

rief *etc* [riːf] *vb siehe* **rufen**

Riegel ['riːgəl] (-s, -) *m* bolt; *(Schokolade usw)* bar

Riemen ['riːmən] (-s, -) *m* strap; *(Gürtel, TECH)* belt; *(NAUT)* oar

Riese ['riːzə] (-n, -n) *m* giant

rieseln *vi* to trickle; *(Schnee)* to fall gently

Riesenerfolg *m* enormous success

riesengroß *adj* colossal, gigantic, huge

riesig ['riːzɪç] *adj* enormous, huge, vast

riet *etc* [riːt] *vb siehe* **raten**

Riff [rɪf] (-(e)s, -e) *nt* reef

Rille ['rɪlə] *f* groove

Rind [rɪnt] (-(e)s, -er) *nt* ox; cow; cattle *pl*; *(KOCH)* beef

Rinde ['rɪndə] *f* rind; *(Baum~)* bark; *(Brot~)* crust

Rindfleisch *nt* beef

Rindvieh *nt* cattle *pl*; *(umg)* blockhead, stupid oaf

Ring [rɪŋ] (-(e)s, -e) *m* ring; ~buch *nt* ring binder; **Ringelnatter** *f* grass snake; r~en *(unreg) vi* to wrestle; ~en (-s) *nt* wrestling; ~finger *m* ring finger; ~kampf *m* wrestling bout; ~richter *m* referee; rings *adv:* rings um round; ringsherum *adv* round about; ~straße *f* ring road; ringsum(her) *adv (rundherum)* round about; *(überall)* all round

Rinn- ['rɪn] *zW:* ~e *f* gutter, drain; r~en *(unreg) vi* to run, to trickle;

~stein *m* gutter

Rippchen ['rɪpçən] *nt* small rib; cutlet

Rippe ['rɪpə] *f* rib; **Rippenfellentzündung** *f* pleurisy

Risiko ['riːziko] (-s, -s *od* Risiken) *nt* risk

riskant [rɪsˈkant] *adj* risky, hazardous

riskieren [rɪsˈkiːrən] *vt* to risk

Riß [rɪs] (-sses, -sse) *m* tear; *(in Mauer, Tasse etc)* crack; *(in Haut)* scratch; *(TECH)* design

rissig ['rɪsɪç] *adj* torn; cracked; scratched

Ritt [rɪt] (-(e)s, -e) *m* ride

ritt *etc vb siehe* **reiten**

Ritter (-s, -) *m* knight; r~lich *adj* chivalrous

Ritze ['rɪtsə] *f* crack, chink

Rivale [riˈvaːlə] (-n, -n) *m* rival

Rivalität [rivaliˈtɛːt] *f* rivalry

Rizinusöl ['riːtsinusøːl] *nt* castor oil

Robbe ['rɔbə] *f* seal

Roboter ['rɔbɔtər] (-s, -) *m* robot

roch *etc* [rɔx] *vb siehe* **riechen**

Rock [rɔk] (-(e)s, -e) *m* skirt; *(Jackett)* jacket; *(Uniform~)* tunic

Rodel ['roːdəl] (-s, -) *m* toboggan; ~bahn *f* toboggan run; r~n *vi* to toboggan

roden ['roːdən] *vt, vi* to clear

Rogen ['roːgən] (-s, -) *m* roe, spawn

Roggen ['rɔgən] (-s, -) *m* rye

roh [roː] *adj* raw; *(Mensch)* coarse, crude; R~bau *m* shell of a building; R~material *nt* raw material; R~öl *nt* crude oil

Rohr [roːr] (-(e)s, -e) *nt* pipe, tube; *(BOT)* cane; *(Schilf)* reed; *(Gewehr~)* barrel; ~bruch *m* burst pipe

Röhre ['røːrə] *f* tube, pipe; *(RADIO etc)* valve; *(Back~)* oven

Rohr- *zW:* ~leitung *f* pipeline; ~post *f* pneumatic postal system; ~zucker *m* cane sugar

Rohstoff *m* raw material

Rokoko ['rɔkoko] (-s) *nt* rococo

Roll- ['rɔl] *zW:* ~(l)aden *m* shutter; ~bahn *f (AVIAT)* runway; ~feld *nt (AVIAT)* runway

Rolle ['rɔlə] *f* roll; *(THEAT, soziologisch)*

role; (*Garn~ etc*) reel, spool; (*Walze*) roller; (*Wäsche~*) mangle; **keine ~ spielen** not to matter; **eine (wichtige) ~ spielen bei** to play a (major) part *od* role in; **r~n** *vt, vi* to roll; (*AVIAT*) to taxi; **~r** (-s, -) *m* scooter; (*Welle*) roller

Roll- *zW:* **~mops** *m* pickled herring; **~schuh** *m* roller skate; **~stuhl** *m* wheelchair; **~treppe** *f* escalator

Rom [roːm] (-s) *nt* Rome

Roman [roˈmaːn] (-s, -e) *m* novel; **~tik** [roˈmantɪk] *f* romanticism; **~tiker** [roˈmantikər] (-s, -) *m* romanticist; **r~tisch** [roˈmantɪʃ] *adj* romantic; **Romanze** [roˈmantsə] *f* romance

Römer [ˈrøːmər] (-s, -) *m* wineglass; (*Mensch*) Roman

römisch *adj* Roman

röntgen [ˈrœntɡən] *vt* to X-ray; **R~aufnahme** *f* X-ray; **R~bild** *nt* X-ray; **R~strahlen** *pl* X-rays

rosa [ˈroːza] *adj inv* pink, rose(-coloured)

Rose [ˈroːzə] *f* rose; **Rosenkohl** *m* Brussels sprouts *pl*; **Rosenkranz** *m* rosary

rosig [ˈroːzɪç] *adj* rosy

Rosine [roˈziːnə] *f* raisin, currant

Roß [rɔs] (-sses, -sse) *nt* horse, steed; **~kastanie** *f* horse chestnut

Rost [rɔst] (-(e)s, -e) *m* rust; (*Gitter*) grill, gridiron; (*Bett~*) springs *pl*; **~braten** *m* roast(ed) meat, joint; **r~en** *vi* to rust

rösten [ˈrøːstən] *vt* to roast; to toast; to grill

Rost- *zW:* **r~frei** *adj* rust-free; rust-proof; stainless; **r~ig** *adj* rusty; **~schutz** *m* rust-proofing

rot [roːt] *adj* red; **in den ~en Zahlen** in the red; **das R~e Meer** the Red Sea

Röte [ˈrøːtə] (-) *f* redness; **Röteln** *pl* German measles *sg*; **r~n** *vt, vr* to redden

rothaarig *adj* red-haired

rotieren [roˈtiːrən] *vi* to rotate

Rot- *zW:* **~kehlchen** *nt* robin; **~stift** *m* red pencil; **~wein** *m* red wine

Rouge [ruːʒ] *nt* blusher

Roulade [ruˈlaːdə] *f* (*KOCH*) beef olive

Route [ˈruːtə] *f* route

Routine [ruˈtiːnə] *f* experience; routine

Rübe [ˈryːbə] *f* turnip; **gelbe ~** carrot; **rote ~** beetroot (*BRIT*), beet (*US*)

rüber [ˈryːbər] (*umg*) *adv* = **herüber**; **hinüber**

Rubin [ruˈbiːn] (-s, -e) *m* ruby

Rubrik [ruˈbriːk] *f* heading; (*Spalte*) column

Ruck [rʊk] (-(e)s, -e) *m* jerk, jolt

Rück- [ˈrʏk] *zW:* **~antwort** *f* reply, answer; **r~bezüglich** *adj* reflexive; **r~blickend** *adj* retrospective

Rücken [ˈrʏkən] (-s, -) *m* back; (*Berg~*) ridge

rücken *vt, vi* to move

Rücken- *zW:* **~mark** *nt* spinal cord; **~schwimmen** *nt* backstroke; **~wind** *m* following wind

Rück- *zW:* **~erstattung** *f* return, restitution; **~fahrkarte** *f* return (ticket); **~fahrt** *f* return journey; **~fall** *m* relapse; **r~fällig** *adj* relapsing; **r~fällig werden** to relapse; **~flug** *m* return flight; **~frage** *f* question; **~gabe** *f* return; **~gang** *m* decline, fall; **r~gängig** *adj*: **etw r~gängig machen** to cancel sth; **~grat** (-(e)s, -e) *nt* spine, backbone; **~kehr** (-, -en) *f* return; **~licht** *nt* back light; **r~lings** *adv* from behind; backwards; **~nahme** *f* taking back; **~porto** *nt* return postage; **~reise** *f* return journey; (*NAUT*) home voyage; **~ruf** *m* recall

Rucksack [ˈrʊkzak] *m* rucksack

Rück- *zW:* **~schau** *f* reflection; **~schluß** *m* conclusion; **~schritt** *m* retrogression; **r~schrittlich** *adj* reactionary; retrograde; **~seite** *f* back; (*von Münze etc*) reverse; **~sicht** *f* consideration; **~sicht nehmen auf** +*akk* to show consideration for; **r~sichtslos** *adj* inconsiderate; (*Fahren*) reckless; (*unbarmherzig*) ruthless; **r~sichtsvoll** *adj* considerate; **~sitz** *m* back seat; **~spiegel** *m* (*AUT*) rear-view mirror; **~spiel** *nt* return match; **~sprache** *f* further discussion *od* talk; **~stand** *m* arrears *pl*; **r~ständig** *adj* backward, out-of-date; (*Zahlungen*) in arrears; **~stoß** *m* recoil; **~strahler** (-s, -) *m* rear reflector; **~tritt** *m* resignation; **~trittbremse** *f* pedal brake; **~vergütung** *f* repayment; (*COMM*) refund; **~versicherung** *f* reinsurance; **r~wärtig** *adj* rear; **r~wärts** *adv* backward(s), back; **~wärtsgang** *m* (*AUT*) reverse gear; **~weg** *m* return journey, way back; **r~wirkend** *adj* retroactive; **~wirkung** *f* reaction; retrospective effect; **~zahlung** *f* repayment; **~zug** *m* retreat

Rudel ['ruːdəl] (-s, -) *nt* pack; herd
Ruder ['ruːdər] (-s, -) *nt* oar; (*Steuer*) rudder; **~boot** *nt* rowing boat; **r~n** *vt, vi* to row
Ruf [ruːf] (-(e)s, -e) *m* call, cry; (*Ansehen*) reputation; **r~en** (*unreg*) *vt, vi* to call; to cry; **~name** *m* usual (first) name; **~nummer** *f* (tele)phone number; **~zeichen** *nt* (*RADIO*) call sign; (*TEL*) ringing tone
Rüge ['ryːgə] *f* reprimand, rebuke
Ruhe ['ruːə] (-) *f* rest; (*Ungestörtheit*) peace, quiet; (*Gelassenheit, Stille*) calm; (*Schweigen*) silence; **jdn in ~ lassen** to leave sb alone; **sich zur ~ setzen** to retire; **~!** be quiet!, silence!; **r~n** *vi* to rest; **~pause** *f* break; **~platz** *m* resting place; **~stand** *m* retirement; **~stätte** *f*: **letzte ~stätte** final resting place; **~störung** *f* breach of the peace; **~tag** *m* (*von Geschäft*) closing day
ruhig ['ruːɪç] *adj* quiet; (*bewegungslos*) still; (*Hand*) steady; (*gelassen, friedlich*) calm; (*Gewissen*) clear; **kommen Sie ~ herein** just come on in; **tu das ~** feel free to do that
Ruhm [ruːm] (-(e)s) *m* fame, glory
rühmen ['ryːmən] *vt* to praise ♦ *vr* to boast
Ruhr [ruːr] (-) *f* dysentery
Rühr- ['ryːr] *zW*: **~ei** *nt* scrambled egg; **r~en** *vt, vr* (*auch fig*) to move, to stir ♦ *vi*: **r~en von** to come *od* stem from; **r~en an** +*akk* to touch; (*fig*) to touch on; **r~end** *adj* touching, moving; **r~ig** *adj* active, lively; **r~selig** *adj* senti-

mental, emotional; **~ung** *f* emotion
Ruin [ruˈiːn] (-s, -e) *m* ruin; **~e** *f* ruin; **r~ieren** [ruiˈniːrən] *vt* to ruin
rülpsen ['rʏlpsən] *vi* to burp, to belch
Rum [rʊm] (-s, -s) *m* rum
rum (*umg*) *adv* = **herum**
Rumän- [ruˈmɛːn] *zW*: **~e** (-n, -n) *m* Ro(u)manian; **~ien** (-s) *nt* Ro(u)mania; **~in** *f* Ro(u)manian; **r~isch** *adj* Ro(u)manian
Rummel ['rʊməl] (-s; *umg*) *m* hubbub; (*Jahrmarkt*) fair; **~platz** *m* fairground, fair
Rumpf [rʊmpf] (-(e)s, ⸚e) *m* trunk, torso; (*AVIAT*) fuselage; (*NAUT*) hull
rümpfen ['rʏmpfən] *vt* (*Nase*) to turn up
rund [rʊnt] *adj* round ♦ *adv* (*etwa*) around; **~ um etw** round sth; **R~brief** *m* circular; **R~e** ['rʊndə] *f* round; (*in Rennen*) lap; (*Gesellschaft*) circle; **R~fahrt** *f* (round) trip
Rundfunk ['rʊntfʊŋk] (-(e)s) *m* broadcasting; **im ~** on the radio; **~gerät** *nt* wireless set; **~sendung** *f* broadcast, radio programme
Rund- *zW*: **r~heraus** *adv* straight out, bluntly; **r~herum** *adv* round about; all round; **r~lich** *adj* plump, rounded; **~reise** *f* round trip; **~schreiben** *nt* (*COMM*) circular
runter ['rʊntər] (*umg*) *adv* = **herunter**; **hinunter**
Runzel ['rʊntsəl] (-, -n) *f* wrinkle; **r~ig** *adj* wrinkled; **r~n** *vt* to wrinkle; **die Stirn r~n** to frown
Rupfen ['rʊpfən] (-s, -) *m* sackcloth
rupfen *vt* to pluck
ruppig ['rʊpɪç] *adj* rough, gruff
Rüsche ['ryːʃə] *f* frill
Ruß [ruːs] (-es) *m* soot
Russe ['rʊsə] (-n, -n) *m* Russian
Rüssel ['rʏsəl] (-s, -) *m* snout; (*Elefanten~*) trunk
rußig ['ruːsɪç] *adj* sooty
Russin ['rʊsɪn] *f* Russian
russisch *adj* Russian
Rußland ['rʊslant] (-s) *nt* Russia
rüsten ['rʏstən] *vt* to prepare ♦ *vi* to prepare; (*MIL*) to arm ♦ *vr* to prepare (o.s.); to arm o.s.

rüstig ['rʏstɪç] *adj* sprightly, vigorous
Rüstung ['rʏstʊŋ] *f* preparation; arming; (*Ritter~*) armour; (*Waffen etc*) armaments *pl*; **Rüstungskontrolle** *f* arms control
Rute ['ruːtə] *f* rod
Rutsch [rʊtʃ] (-(e)s, -e) *m* slide; (*Erd~*) landslide; ~**bahn** *f* slide; **r~en** *vi* to slide; (*ausrutschen*) to slip; **r~ig** *adj* slippery
rütteln ['rʏtəln] *vt, vi* to shake, to jolt

S

S. *abk* (= *Seite*) p.; = **Schilling**
s. *abk* (= *siehe*) see
Saal [zaːl] (-(e)s, **Säle**) *m* hall; room
Saarland ['zaːrlant] *nt*: **das ~** the Saar(land)
Saat [zaːt] (-, -en) *f* seed; (*Pflanzen*) crop; (*Säen*) sowing
Säbel ['zɛːbəl] (-s, -) *m* sabre, sword
Sabotage [zabo'taːʒə] *f* sabotage
sabotieren [zabo'tiːrən] *vt* to sabotage
Sach- [zax] *zW*: ~**bearbeiter** *m* specialist; **s~dienlich** *adj* relevant, helpful; ~**e** *f* thing; (*Angelegenheit*) affair, business; (*Frage*) matter; (*Pflicht*) task; **zur ~e** to the point; **s~kundig** *adj* expert; **s~lich** *adj* matter-of-fact; objective; (*Irrtum, Angabe*) factual
sächlich ['zɛxlɪç] *adj* neuter
Sachschaden *m* material damage
Sachsen ['zaksən] (-s) *nt* Saxony
sächsisch ['zɛksɪʃ] *adj* Saxon
sacht(e) ['zaxt(ə)] *adv* softly, gently
Sachverständige(r) *mf* expert
Sack [zak] (-(e)s, ẹ) *m* sack; ~**gasse** *f* cul-de-sac, dead-end street (*US*)
Sadismus [za'dɪsmʊs] *m* sadism
Sadist [za'dɪst] *m* sadist; **s~isch** *adj* sadistic
säen ['zɛːən] *vt, vi* to sow
Saft [zaft] (-(e)s, ẹ) *m* juice; (*BOT*) sap; **s~ig** *adj* juicy; **s~los** *adj* dry
Sage ['zaːgə] *f* saga
Säge ['zɛːgə] *f* saw; ~**mehl** *nt* sawdust
sagen ['zaːgən] *vt, vi* to say; (*mitteilen*): **jdm ~** to tell sb; **~ Sie**

ihm, daß ... tell him ...
sägen *vt, vi* to saw
sagenhaft *adj* legendary; (*umg*) great, smashing
sah *etc* [zaː] *vb siehe* **sehen**
Sahne ['zaːnə] (-) *f* cream
Saison [zɛ'zõː] (-, -s) *f* season; ~**arbeiter** *m* seasonal worker
Saite ['zaɪtə] *f* string; **Saiteninstrument** *nt* string instrument
Sakko ['zako] (-s, -s) *m od nt* jacket
Sakrament [zakra'mɛnt] *nt* sacrament
Sakristei [zakrɪs'taɪ] *f* sacristy
Salat [za'laːt] (-(e)s, -e) *m* salad; (*Kopf~*) lettuce; ~**soße** *f* salad dressing
Salbe ['zalbə] *f* ointment
Salbei [zal'baɪ] (-s *od* -) *m od f* sage
salben *vt* to anoint
Saldo ['zaldo] (-s, **Salden**) *m* balance
Salmiak [zalmi'ak] (-s) *m* sal ammoniac; ~**geist** *m* liquid ammonia
salopp [za'lɔp] *adj* casual
Salpeter [zal'peːtər] (-s) *m* saltpetre; ~**säure** *f* nitric acid
Salve ['zalvə] *f* salvo
Salz [zalts] (-es, -e) *nt* salt; **s~en** (*unreg*) *vt* to salt; **s~ig** *adj* salty; ~**kartoffeln** *pl* boiled potatoes; ~**säure** *f* hydrochloric acid
Samen ['zaːmən] (-s, -) *m* seed; (*ANAT*) sperm
Sammelband *m* anthology
sammeln ['zaməln] *vt* to collect ♦ *vr* to assemble, to gather; (*konzentrieren*) to concentrate
Sammlung ['zamlʊŋ] *f* collection; assembly, gathering; concentration
Samstag ['zamstaːk] *m* Saturday; **s~s** *adv* (on) Saturdays
Samt [zamt] (-(e)s, -e) *m* velvet
samt *präp* +*dat* (along) with, together with; ~ **und sonders** each and every one (of them)
sämtlich ['zɛmtlɪç] *adj* all (the), entire
Sand [zant] (-(e)s, -e) *nt* sand
Sandale [zan'daːlə] *f* sandal
Sand- *zW*: ~**bank** *f* sandbank; **s~ig** ['zandɪç] *adj* sandy; ~**kasten** *m* sandpit; ~**kuchen** *m* Madeira cake; ~**papier** *nt*

sandpaper; ~**stein** *m* sandstone;
s~**strahlen** *vt insep* to sandblast ♦ *vi*
insep to sandblast
sandte *etc* ['zantə] *vb siehe* **senden**
Sanduhr *f* hourglass
sanft [zanft] *adj* soft, gentle; ~**mütig**
adj gentle, meek
sang *etc* [zaŋ] *vb siehe* **singen**
Sänger(in) ['zɛŋər(ɪn)] (-s, -) *m(f)*
singer
Sani- *zW*: s~**eren** [za'niːrən] *vt* to re-
develop; (*Betrieb*) to make financially
sound ♦ *vr* to line one's pockets; to
become financially sound; s~**tär**
[zani'tɛːr] *adj* sanitary; s~**täre Anlagen**
sanitation *sg*; ~**täter** [zani'tɛːtər] (-s, -)
m first-aid attendant; (*MIL*) (medical)
orderly
sanktionieren [zaŋktsio'niːrən] *vt* to
sanction
Saphir ['zaːfiːr] (-s, -e) *m* sapphire
Sardelle [zar'dɛlə] *f* anchovy
Sardine [zar'diːnə] *f* sardine
Sardinien [zar'diːniən] (-s) *nt* Sardinia
Sarg [zark] (-(e)s, ⁻e) *m* coffin
Sarkasmus [zar'kasmʊs] *m* sarcasm
sarkastisch [zar'kastɪʃ] *adj* sarcastic
saß *etc* [zaːs] *vb siehe* **sitzen**
Satan ['zaːtan] (-s, -e) *m* Satan; devil
Satellit [zatɛ'liːt] (-en, -en) *m* satellite;
~**enfoto** *nt* satellite picture
Satire [za'tiːrə] *f* satire
satirisch [za'tiːrɪʃ] *adj* satirical
satt [zat] *adj* full; (*Farbe*) rich, deep;
jdn/etw ~ sein *od* **haben** to be fed up
with sb/sth; **sich ~ hören/sehen an** +*dat*
to hear/see enough of; **sich ~ essen** to
eat one's fill; ~ **machen** to be filling
Sattel ['zatəl] (-s, ⁻) *m* saddle; (*Berg*)
ridge; s~n *vt* to saddle; ~**schlepper** *m*
articulated lorry
sättigen ['zɛtɪgən] *vt* to satisfy; (*CHEM*)
to saturate
Satz [zats] (-es, ⁻e) *m* (*GRAM*) sentence;
(*Neben~, Adverbial~*) clause; (*Theorem*) theorem; (*MUS*) movement;
(*TENNIS, Briefmarken etc*) set; (*Kaffee*)
grounds *pl*; (*COMM*) rate; (*Sprung*)
jump; ~**teil** *m* part of a sentence;
~**zeichen** *nt* punctuation mark

Sau [zau] (-, **Säue**) *f* sow; (*umg*) dirty
pig
sauber ['zaubər] *adj* clean; (*ironisch*)
fine; ~**halten** (*unreg*) *vt* to keep clean;
S~**keit** *f* cleanness; (*einer Person*)
cleanliness
säuberlich ['zɔybərlɪç] *adv* neatly
saubermachen *vt, vi* to clean
säubern *vt* to clean; (*POL etc*) to purge
Säuberung *f* cleaning; purge
Sauce ['zoːsə] *f* sauce, gravy
sauer ['zauər] *adj* sour; (*CHEM*) acid;
(*umg*) cross; **Saurer Regen** acid rain
Sauerei [zauə'rai] (*umg*) *f* rotten state
of affairs, scandal; (*Schmutz etc*)
mess; (*Unanständigkeit*) obscenity
Sauer- *zW*: ~**milch** *f* sour milk; ~**stoff**
m oxygen; ~**teig** *m* leaven
saufen ['zaufən] (*unreg; umg*) *vt, vi* to
drink, to booze
Säufer ['zɔyfər] (-s, -; *umg*) *m* boozer
saugen ['zaugən] (*unreg*) *vt, vi* to suck
Sauger ['zaugər] (-s, -) *m* dummy,
comforter (*US*); (*auf Flasche*) teat;
(*Staub~*) vacuum cleaner, hoover (®)
Säugetier ['zɔygə-] *nt* mammal
Säugling *m* infant, baby
Säule ['zɔylə] *f* column, pillar
Saum [zaum] (-(e)s, **Säume**) *m* hem;
(*Naht*) seam
säumen ['zɔymən] *vt* to hem; to seam ♦
vi to delay, to hesitate
Sauna ['zauna] (-, -s) *f* sauna
Säure ['zɔyrə] *f* acid; (*Geschmack*)
sourness, acidity
sausen ['zauzən] *vi* to blow; (*umg:
eilen*) to rush; (*Ohren*) to buzz; **etw ~
lassen** (*umg*) not to bother with sth
Saustall ['zauʃtal] (*umg*) *m* pigsty
Saxophon [zakso'foːn] (-s, -e) *nt* saxo-
phone
SB *abk* = **Selbstbedienung**
S-Bahn *f abk* (= *Schnellbahn*) high
speed railway; (= *Stadtbahn*) suburban
railway
schaben ['ʃaːbən] *vt* to scrape
schäbig ['ʃɛːbɪç] *adj* shabby
Schablone [ʃa'bloːnə] *f* stencil;
(*Muster*) pattern; (*fig*) convention
Schach [ʃax] (-s, -s) *nt* chess;

(*Stellung*) check; ~**brett** *nt* chessboard; ~**figur** *f* chessman; **'s~'matt** *adj* checkmate; ~**spiel** *nt* game of chess

Schacht [ʃaxt] (-(e)s, ̈e) *m* shaft

Schachtel (-, -n) *f* box; (*pej*: *Frau*) bag, cow

schade [ˈʃaːdə] *adj* a pity *od* shame ♦ *excl*: (**wie**) ~! (what a) pity *od* shame; **sich** *dat* **zu ~ sein für etw** to consider o.s. too good for sth

Schädel [ˈʃɛːdəl] (-s, -) *m* skull; ~**bruch** *m* fractured skull

Schaden [ˈʃaːdən] (-s, ̈) *m* damage; (*Verletzung*) injury; (*Nachteil*) disadvantage; **s~** *vi* +*dat* to hurt; **einer Sache s~** to damage sth; ~**ersatz** *m* compensation, damages *pl*; ~**freude** *f* malicious glee

schadhaft [ˈʃaːthaft] *adj* faulty, damaged

schäd- [ˈʃɛːt] *zW*: ~**igen** [ˈʃɛdɪgən] *vt* to damage; (*Person*) to do harm to, to harm; ~**lich** *adj*: ~**lich (für)** harmful (to); **S~lichkeit** *f* harmfulness; **S~ling** *m* pest

Schadstoff [ˈʃaːtʃtɔf] *m* harmful substance

Schaf [ʃaːf] (-(e)s, ̈e) *nt* sheep; ~**bock** *m* ram

Schäfer [ˈʃɛːfər] (-s, -e) *m* shepherd; ~**hund** *m* Alsatian (dog) (*BRIT*), German shepherd (dog) (*US*)

Schaffen [ˈʃafən] (-s) *nt* (creative) activity

schaffen¹ (*unreg*) *vt* to create; (*Platz*) to make

schaffen² *vt* (*erreichen*) to manage, to do; (*erledigen*) to finish; (*Prüfung*) to pass; (*transportieren*) to take ♦ *vi* (*umg*: *arbeiten*) to work; **sich** *dat* **etw ~** to get o.s. sth; **sich an etw** *dat* **zu ~ machen** to busy o.s. with sth

Schaffner(in) [ˈʃafnər(ɪn)] (-s, -) *m(f)* (*Bus~*) conductor(tress); (*EISENB*) guard

Schaft [ʃaft] (-(e)s, ̈e) *m* shaft; (*von Gewehr*) stock; (*von Stiefel*) leg; (*BOT*) stalk; tree trunk; ~**stiefel** *m* high boot

Schakal [ʃaˈkaːl] (-s, -e) *m* jackal

Schal [ʃaːl] (-s, -e *od* -s) *m* scarf

schal *adj* flat; (*fig*) insipid

Schälchen [ˈʃɛːlçən] *nt* cup, bowl

Schale [ˈʃaːlə] *f* skin; (*abgeschält*) peel; (*Nuß~*, *Muschel~*, *Ei~*) shell; (*Geschirr*) dish, bowl

schälen [ˈʃɛːlən] *vt* to peel; to shell ♦ *vr* to peel

Schall [ʃal] (-(e)s, -e) *m* sound; ~**dämpfer** (-s, -) *m* (*AUT*) silencer; **s~dicht** *adj* soundproof; **s~en** *vi* to (re)sound; **s~end** *adj* resounding, loud; ~**mauer** *f* sound barrier; ~**platte** *f* (gramophone) record

Schalt- [ʃalt] *zW*: ~**bild** *nt* circuit diagram; ~**brett** *nt* switchboard; **s~en** *vt* to switch, to turn ♦ *vi* (*AUT*) to change (gear); (*umg*: *begreifen*) to catch on; ~**er** (-s, -) *m* counter; (*an Gerät*) switch; ~**erbeamte(r)** *m* counter clerk; ~**hebel** *m* switch; (*AUT*) gear-lever; ~**jahr** *nt* leap year; ~**ung** *f* switching; (*ELEK*) circuit; (*AUT*) gear change

Scham [ʃaːm] (-) *f* shame; (~*gefühl*) modesty; (*Organe*) private parts *pl*

schämen [ˈʃɛːmən] *vr* to be ashamed

schamlos *adj* shameless

Schande [ˈʃandə] (-) *f* disgrace

schändlich [ˈʃɛntlɪç] *adj* disgraceful, shameful

Schändung [ˈʃɛndʊŋ] *f* violation, defilement

Schankerlaubnis [ˈʃaŋk-] *f* (publican's) licence

Schanktisch *m* bar

Schanze [ˈʃantsə] *f* (*Sprung~*) skijump

Schar [ʃaːr] (-, -en) *f* band, company; (*Vögel*) flock; (*Menge*) crowd; **in ~en** in droves; **s~en** *vr* to assemble, to rally

scharf [ʃarf] *adj* sharp; (*Essen*) hot, spicy; (*Munition*) live; ~ **nachdenken** to think hard; **auf etw** *akk* ~ **sein** (*umg*) to be keen on sth

Schärfe [ˈʃɛrfə] *f* sharpness; (*Strenge*) rigour; **s~n** *vt* to sharpen

Scharf- *zW*: **s~machen** (*umg*) *vt* to stir up; ~**richter** *m* executioner; ~**schütze** *m* marksman, sharpshooter; ~**sinn** *m* penetration, astuteness;

s~**sinnig** adj astute, shrewd

Scharnier [ʃarˈniːr] (-s, -e) nt hinge

Schärpe [ˈʃɛrpə] f sash

scharren [ˈʃarən] vt, vi to scrape, to scratch

Schaschlik [ˈʃaʃlɪk] (-s, -s) m od nt (shish) kebab

Schatten [ˈʃatən] (-s, -) m shadow; ~**bild** nt silhouette; ~**riß** m silhouette; ~**seite** f shady side, dark side, ~**wirtschaft** f black economy

schattieren [ʃaˈtiːrən] vt, vi to shade

schattig [ˈʃatɪç] adj shady

Schatulle [ʃaˈtʊlə] f casket; (Geld~) coffer

Schatz [ʃats] (-es, ⁻e) m treasure; (Person) darling

schätz- [ˈʃɛts] zW: ~**bar** adj assessable; S~**chen** nt darling, love; ~**en** vt (abschätzen) to estimate; (Gegenstand) to value; (würdigen) to value, to esteem; (vermuten) to reckon; S~**ung** f estimate; estimation; valuation; **nach meiner S~ung** ... I reckon that ...; ~**ungsweise** adv approximately; it is thought

Schau [ʃau] (-) f show; (Ausstellung) display, exhibition; **etw zur ~ stellen** to make a show of sth, to show sth off; ~**bild** nt diagram

Schauder [ˈʃaudər] (-s, -s) m shudder; (wegen Kälte) shiver; s~**haft** adj horrible; s~**n** vi to shudder; to shiver

schauen [ˈʃauən] vi to look

Schauer [ˈʃauər] (-s, -) m (Regen~) shower; (Schreck) shudder; ~**geschichte** f horror story; s~**lich** adj horrific, spine-chilling

Schaufel [ˈʃaufəl] (-, -n) f shovel; (NAUT) paddle; (TECH) scoop; s~**n** vt to shovel, to scoop

Schau- zW: ~**fenster** nt shop window; ~**fensterbummel** m window shopping (expedition); ~**kasten** m showcase

Schaukel [ˈʃaukəl] (-, -n) f swing; s~**n** vi to swing, to rock; ~**pferd** nt rocking horse; ~**stuhl** m rocking chair

Schaum [ʃaum] (-(e)s, Schäume) m foam; (Seifen~) lather

schäumen [ˈʃɔymən] vi to foam

Schaum- zW: ~**gummi** m foam (rubber); s~**ig** adj frothy, foamy; ~**wein** m sparkling wine

Schauplatz m scene

schaurig adj horrific, dreadful

Schau- zW: ~**spiel** nt spectacle; (THEAT) play; ~**spieler(in)** m(f) actor(actress); s~**spielern** vi insep to act; ~**spielhaus** nt theatre

Scheck [ʃɛk] (-s, -s) m cheque; ~**heft** m cheque book; ~**karte** f cheque card

scheffeln [ˈʃɛfəln] vt to amass

Scheibe [ˈʃaibə] f disc; (Brot etc) slice; (Glas~) pane; (MIL) target

Scheiben- zW: ~**bremse** f (AUT) disc brake; ~**waschanlage** f (AUT) windscreen washers pl; ~**wischer** m (AUT) windscreen wiper

Scheich [ʃaiç] (-s, -e od -s) m sheik(h)

Scheide [ˈʃaidə] f sheath; (Grenze) boundary; (ANAT) vagina; s~**n** (unreg) vt to separate; (Ehe) to dissolve ♦ vi to depart; to part; **sich s~n lassen** to get a divorce

Scheidung f (Ehe~) divorce

Schein [ʃain] (-(e)s, -e) m light; (An~) appearance; (Geld) (bank)note; (Bescheinigung) certificate; **zum ~** in pretence; s~**bar** adj apparent; s~**en** (unreg) vi to shine; (Anschein haben) to seem; s~**heilig** adj hypocritical; ~**werfer** (-s, -) m floodlight; spotlight; (Suchwerfer) searchlight; (AUT) headlamp

Scheiß- [ʃais] (umg) in zW bloody

Scheiße (-; umg) f shit

Scheit [ʃait] (-(e)s, -e od -er) nt log

Scheitel [ˈʃaitəl] (-s, -) m top; (Haar~) parting; s~**n** vt to part

scheitern [ˈʃaitərn] vi to fail

Schelle [ˈʃɛlə] f small bell; s~**n** vi to ring

Schellfisch [ˈʃɛlfɪʃ] m haddock

Schelm [ʃɛlm] (-(e)s, -e) m rogue; s~**isch** adj mischievous, roguish

Schelte [ˈʃɛltə] f scolding; s~**n** (unreg) vt to scold

Schema [ˈʃeːma] (-s, -s od -ta) nt scheme, plan; (Darstellung) schema; **nach ~** quite mechanically; s~**tisch**

[ʃe'maːtɪʃ] adj schematic; (pej) mechanical

Schemel ['ʃeːməl] (-s, -) m (foot)stool

Schenkel ['ʃɛŋkəl] (-s, -) m thigh

schenken ['ʃɛŋkən] vt (auch fig) to give; (Getränk) to pour; **sich** dat **etw ~** (umg) to skip sth; **das ist geschenkt!** (billig) that's a giveaway!; (nichts wert) that's worthless!

Scherbe ['ʃɛrbə] f broken piece, fragment; (archäologisch) potsherd

Schere ['ʃeːrə] f scissors pl; (groß) shears pl; **s~n** (unreg) vt to cut; (Schaf) to shear; (kümmern) to bother ♦ vr to care; **scher dich zum Teufel!** get lost!; **~'rei** (umg) f bother, trouble

Scherz [ʃɛrts] (-es, -e) m joke; fun; **~frage** f conundrum; **s~haft** adj joking, jocular

Scheu [ʃɔʏ] (-) f shyness; (Angst) fear; (Ehrfurcht) awe; **s~** adj shy; **s~en** vr: **sich s~en vor** +dat to be afraid of, to shrink from ♦ vt to shun ♦ vi (Pferd) to shy

scheuern ['ʃɔʏərn] vt to scour, to scrub

Scheuklappe f blinker

Scheune ['ʃɔʏnə] f barn

Scheusal ['ʃɔʏzaːl] (-s, -e) nt monster

scheußlich ['ʃɔʏslɪç] adj dreadful, frightful; **S~keit** f dreadfulness

Schi [ʃiː] m = Ski

Schicht [ʃɪçt] (-, -en) f layer; (Klasse) class, level; (in Fabrik etc) shift; **~arbeit** f shift work; **s~en** vt to layer, to stack

schick [ʃɪk] adj stylish, chic

schicken vt to send ♦ vr: **sich ~** (in +akk) to resign o.s. (to) ♦ vb unpers (anständig sein) to be fitting

schicklich adj proper, fitting

Schicksal (-s, -e) nt fate; **Schicksalsschlag** m great misfortune, blow

Schieb- ['ʃiːb] zW: **~edach** nt (AUT) sun roof; **s~en** (unreg) vt (auch Drogen) to push; (Schuld) to put ♦ vi to push; **~etür** f sliding door; **~ung** f fiddle

Schieds- ['ʃiːts] zW: **~gericht** nt court of arbitration; **~richter** m referee; umpire; (Schlichter) arbitrator; **~ver-**

fahren nt arbitration

schief [ʃiːf] adj crooked; (Ebene) sloping; (Turm) leaning; (Winkel) oblique; (Blick) funny; (Vergleich) distorted ♦ adv crooked(ly); (ansehen) askance; **etw ~ stellen** to slope sth

Schiefer ['ʃiːfər] (-s, -) m slate; **~dach** nt slate roof; **~tafel** f (child's) slate

schiefgehen (unreg; umg) vi to go wrong

schielen ['ʃiːlən] vi to squint; **nach etw ~** (fig) to eye sth

schien etc [ʃiːn] vb siehe scheinen

Schienbein nt shinbone

Schiene ['ʃiːnə] f rail; (MED) splint; **s~n** vt to put in splints

schier [ʃiːr] adj (fig) sheer ♦ adv nearly, almost

Schieß- ['ʃiːs] zW: **~bude** f shooting gallery; **s~en** (unreg) vt to shoot; (Ball) to kick; (Geschoß) to fire ♦ vi to shoot; (Salat etc) to run to seed; **s~en auf** +akk to shoot at; **~e'rei** f shooting incident, shoot-up; **~pulver** nt gunpowder; **~scharte** f embrasure

Schiff [ʃɪf] (-(e)s, -e) nt ship, vessel; (Kirchen~) nave; **~bau** m shipbuilding; **~bruch** m shipwreck; **s~brüchig** adj shipwrecked; **~chen** nt small boat; (Weben) shuttle; (Mütze) forage cap; **~er** (-s, -) m bargeman, boatman; **~(f)ahrt** f shipping; (Reise) voyage; **~(fahrts)linie** f shipping route

Schikane [ʃiˈkaːnə] f harassment; dirty trick; **mit allen ~n** with all the trimmings

schikanieren [ʃikaˈniːrən] vt to harass, to torment

Schild¹ [ʃɪlt] (-(e)s, -e) m shield; **etw im ~e führen** to be up to sth

Schild² (-(e)s, -er) nt sign; nameplate; (Etikett) label

Schilddrüse f thyroid gland

schildern ['ʃɪldərn] vt to depict, to portray

Schilderung f description, portrayal

Schildkröte f tortoise; (Wasser~) turtle

Schilf [ʃɪlf] (-(e)s, -e) nt (Pflanze) reed; (Material) reeds pl, rushes pl; **~rohr** nt

(Pflanze) reed
schillern ['ʃɪlərn] *vi* to shimmer; **~d** *adj* iridescent
Schilling ['ʃɪlɪŋ] *m* schilling
Schimmel ['ʃɪməl] (**-s**, **-**) *m* mould; *(Pferd)* white horse; **s~ig** *adj* mouldy; **s~n** *vi* to get mouldy
schimmern ['ʃɪmərn] *vi* to glimmer, to shimmer
Schimpanse [ʃɪm'panzə] (**-n**, **-n**) *m* chimpanzee
schimpfen ['ʃɪmpfən] *vt* to scold ♦ *vi* to curse, to complain; to scold
Schimpfwort *nt* term of abuse
schinden ['ʃɪndən] *(unreg) vt* to maltreat, to drive too hard ♦ *vr:* **sich ~** **(mit)** to sweat and strain (at), to toil away (at); **Eindruck ~** *(umg)* to create an impression
Schinde'rei *f* grind, drudgery
Schinken ['ʃɪŋkən] (**-s**, **-**) *m* ham
Schippe ['ʃɪpə] *f* shovel; **s~n** *vt* to shovel
Schirm [ʃɪrm] (**-(e)s**, **-e**) *m* *(Regen~)* umbrella; *(Sonnen~)* parasol, sunshade; *(Wand~, Bild~)* screen; *(Lampen~)* (lamp)shade; *(Mützen~)* peak; *(Pilz~)* cap; **~mütze** *f* peaked cap; **~ständer** *m* umbrella stand
schizophren [ʃitso'freːn] *adj* schizophrenic
Schlacht [ʃlaxt] (**-**, **-en**) *f* battle; **s~en** *vt* to slaughter, to kill; **~enbummler** *m* visiting *od* away football supporter; **~er** (**-s**, **-**) *m* butcher; **~feld** *nt* battlefield; **~haus** *nt* slaughterhouse, abattoir; **~hof** *m* slaughterhouse, abattoir; **~schiff** *nt* battleship; **~vieh** *nt* animals kept for meat; beef cattle
Schlacke ['ʃlakə] *f* slag
Schlaf [ʃlaːf] (**-(e)s**) *m* sleep; **~anzug** *m* pyjamas *pl*
Schläfe ['ʃlɛːfə] *f (ANAT)* temple
schlafen ['ʃlaːfən] *(unreg) vi* to sleep; **~ gehen** to go to bed; **S~gehen** (**-s**) *nt* going to bed; **Schlafenszeit** *f* bedtime
schlaff [ʃlaf] *adj* slack; *(energielos)* limp; *(erschöpft)* exhausted
Schlaf- *zW:* **~gelegenheit** *f* sleeping accommodation; **~lied** *nt* lullaby;

s~los *adj* sleepless; **~losigkeit** *f* sleeplessness, insomnia; **~mittel** *nt* sleeping pill
schläfrig ['ʃlɛːfrɪç] *adj* sleepy
Schlaf- *zW:* **~saal** *m* dormitory; **~sack** *m* sleeping bag; **~tablette** *f* sleeping pill; **~wagen** *m* sleeping car, sleeper; **s~wandeln** *vi insep* to sleepwalk; **~zimmer** *nt* bedroom
Schlag [ʃlaːk] (**(e)s**, **⁻e**) *m (auch fig)* blow; *(auch MED)* stroke; *(Puls~, Herz~)* beat; *(ELEK)* shock; *(Blitz~)* bolt, stroke; *(Autotür)* car door; *(umg: Portion)* helping; *(Art)* kind, type; **Schläge** *pl (Tracht Prügel)* beating *sg*; **mit einem ~** all at once; **~ auf ~** in rapid succession; **~ auf ~** in **~fall** *m* stroke; **s~artig** *adj* sudden, without warning; **~baum** *m* barrier; **s~en** ['ʃlaːgən] *(unreg) vt, vi* to strike, to hit; *(wiederholt schlagen, besiegen)* to beat; *(Glocke)* to ring; *(Stunde)* to strike; *(Sahne)* to whip; *(Schlacht)* to fight ♦ *vr* to fight; **nach jdm s~en** *(fig)* to take after sb; **sich gut s~en** *(fig)* to do well; **~er** ['ʃlaːgər] (**-s**, **-**) *m (auch fig)* hit
Schläger ['ʃlɛːgər] *m* brawler; *(SPORT)* bat; *(TENNIS etc)* racket; *(GOLF)* club; hockey stick; *(Waffe)* rapier; **Schläge'rei** *f* fight, punch-up
Schlagersänger(in) *m(f)* pop singer
Schlag- *zW:* **s~fertig** *adj* quick-witted; **~fertigkeit** *f* ready wit, quickness of repartee; **~loch** *nt* pothole; **~sahne** *f* (whipped) cream; **~seite** *f (NAUT)* list; **~wort** *nt* slogan, catch phrase; **~zeile** *f* headline; **~zeug** *nt* percussion; drums *pl*; **~zeuger** (**-s**, **-**) *m* drummer
Schlamassel [ʃla'masəl] (**-s**, **-**; *umg) m* mess
Schlamm [ʃlam] (**-(e)s**, **-e**) *m* mud; **s~ig** *adj* muddy
Schlamp- *zW:* **~e** *(umg) f* slut; **s~en** *(umg) vi* to be sloppy; **~e'rei** *(umg) f* disorder, untidiness; sloppy work
Schlange ['ʃlaŋə] *f* snake; *(Menschen~)* queue *(BRIT)*, line-up *(US)*; **~ stehen** to (form a) queue, to line up; **Schlangenbiß** *m* snake bite;

Schlangengift *nt* snake venom;
Schlangenlinie *f* wavy line
schlank [ʃlaŋk] *adj* slim, slender;
S~heit *f* slimness, slenderness;
S~heitskur *f* diet
schlapp [ʃlap] *adj* limp; (*locker*) slack;
S~e (*umg*) *f* setback
Schlaraffenland [ʃla'rafənlant] *nt* land
of milk and honey
schlau [ʃlau] *adj* crafty, cunning
Schlauch [ʃlaux] (-(e)s, **Schläuche**) *m*
hose; (*in Reifen*) inner tube; (*umg*:
Anstrengung) grind; **~boot** *nt* rubber
dinghy; **s~en** (*umg*) *vt* to tell on, to
exhaust; **s~los** *adj* (*Reifen*) tubeless
Schlauheit *f* cunning
Schläue [ʃlɔyə] (-) *f* cunning
Schlaukopf *m* clever dick
schlecht [ʃlɛçt] *adj* bad ♦ *adv* badly; ~
gelaunt in a bad mood; ~ **und recht**
after a fashion; **jdm ist** ~ sb feels sick
od bad; **~gehen** (*unreg*) *vi unpers*:
jdm geht es ~ sb is in a bad way;
S~igkeit *f* badness; bad deed; **~ma-
chen** *vt* to run down
schlecken [ʃlɛkən] *vt, vi* to lick
Schlegel [ʃle:gəl] (-s, -) *m* (drum)stick;
(*Hammer*) mallet, hammer; (*KOCH*)
leg
schleichen [ʃlaɪçən] (*unreg*) *vi* to
creep, to crawl; **~d** *adj* gradual; creep-
ing
Schleier [ʃlaɪər] (-s, -) *m* veil; **s~haft**
(*umg*) *adj*: **jdm s~haft sein** to be a
mystery to sb
Schleif- [ʃlaɪf] *zW*: **~e** *f* loop; (*Band*)
bow; **s~en** *vt, vi* to drag ♦ *vt* (*unreg*)
to grind; (*Edelstein*) to cut; (*MIL*:
Soldaten) to drill; **~stein** *m* grindstone
Schleim [ʃlaɪm] (-(e)s, -e) *m* slime;
(*MED*) mucus; (*KOCH*) gruel; **s~ig** *adj*
slimy
Schlemm- [ʃlɛm] *zW*: **s~en** *vi* to
feast; **~er** (-s, -) *m* gourmet; **~e'rei** *f*
gluttony, feasting
schlendern [ʃlɛndərn] *vi* to stroll
schlenkern [ʃlɛŋkərn] *vt, vi* to swing, to
dangle
Schlepp- [ʃlɛp] *zW*: **~e** *f* train; **s~en**
vt to drag; (*Auto, Schiff*) to tow; (*tra-*

gen) to lug; **s~end** *adj* dragging, slow;
~er (-s, -) *m* tractor; (*Schiff*) tug
Schleuder [ʃlɔydər] (-, -n) *f* catapult;
(*Wäsche~*) spin-drier; (*Butter~ etc*)
centrifuge; **s~n** *vt* to hurl; (*Wäsche*) to
spin-dry ♦ *vi* (*AUT*) to skid; **~preis** *m*
give-away price; **~sitz** *m* (*AVIAT*)
ejector seat; (*fig*) hot seat; **~ware** *f*
cheap *od* cut-price goods *pl*
schleunigst [ʃlɔynıçst] *adv* straight
away
Schleuse [ʃlɔyzə] *f* lock; (*~ntor*) sluice
schlicht [ʃlıçt] *adj* simple, plain; **~en** *vt*
(*glätten*) to smooth, to dress; (*Streit*)
to settle; **S~er** (-s, -) *m* mediator, arbitrator; **S~ung** *f* settlement; arbitration
Schlick [ʃlık] (-(e)s, -e) *m* mud; (*Öl~*)
slick
schlief *etc* [ʃli:f] *vb siehe* **schlafen**
Schließ- [ʃli:s] *zW*: **~e** *f* fastener;
s~en (*unreg*) *vt* to close, to shut;
(*beenden*) to close; (*Freundschaft,
Bündnis, Ehe*) to enter into; (*folgern*):
s~en (aus) to infer (from) ♦ *vi, vr* to
close, to shut; **etw in sich s~en** to include sth; **~fach** *nt* locker; **s~lich** *adv*
finally; **s~lich doch** after all
Schliff [ʃlıf] (-(e)s, -e) *m* cut(ting);
(*fig*) polish
schlimm [ʃlım] *adj* bad; **~er** *adj*
worse; **~ste(r, s)** *adj* worst; **~stenfalls**
adv at (the) worst
Schlinge [ʃlıŋə] *f* loop; (*bes Henker~*)
noose; (*Falle*) snare; (*MED*) sling; **~l**
(-s, -) *m* rascal; **s~n** (*unreg*) *vt* to
wind; (*essen*) to bolt, to gobble ♦ *vi*
(*essen*) to bolt one's food, to gobble;
s~rn *vi* to roll
Schlips [ʃlıps] (-es, -e) *m* tie
Schlitten [ʃlıtən] (-s, -) *m* sledge,
sleigh; **~bahn** *f* toboggan run; **~fahren**
(-s) *nt* tobogganing
schlittern [ʃlıtərn] *vi* to slide
Schlittschuh [ʃlıtʃu:] *m* skate; ~
laufen to skate; **~bahn** *f* skating rink;
~läufer(in) *m(f)* skater
Schlitz [ʃlıts] (-es, -e) *m* slit; (*für
Münze*) slot; (*Hosen~*) flies *pl*;
s~äugig *adj* slant-eyed; **s~en** *vt* to slit
Schloß [ʃlɔs] (-sses, ⁼sser) *nt* lock; (*an*

Schmuck etc) clasp; (*Bau*) castle; chateau

schloß *etc vb siehe* **schließen**

Schlosser ['ʃlɔsər] (-s, -) *m* (*Auto~*) fitter; (*für Schlüssel etc*) locksmith; **~ei** [-'raɪ] *f* metal (working) shop

Schlot [ʃloːt] (-(e)s, -e) *m* chimney; (*NAUT*) funnel

schlottern ['ʃlɔtərn] *vi* to shake, to tremble; (*Kleidung*) to be baggy

Schlucht [ʃluxt] (-, -en) *f* gorge, ravine

schluchzen ['ʃluxtsən] *vi* to sob

Schluck [ʃlʊk] (-(e)s, -e) *m* swallow; (*Menge*) drop; **~auf** (-s, -s) *m* hiccups *pl*; **s~en** *vt, vi* to swallow

schludern ['ʃluːdərn] *vi* to skimp, to do sloppy work

schlug *etc* [ʃluːk] *vb siehe* **schlagen**

Schlummer ['ʃlʊmər] (-s) *m* slumber; **s~n** *vi* to slumber

Schlund [ʃlʊnt] (-(e)s, ⁼e) *m* gullet; (*fig*) jaw

schlüpfen ['ʃlʏpfən] *vi* to slip; (*Vogel etc*) to hatch (out)

Schlüpfer ['ʃlʏpfər] (-s, -) *m* panties *pl*, knickers *pl*

schlüpfrig ['ʃlʏpfrɪç] *adj* slippery; (*fig*) lewd; **S~keit** *f* slipperiness; (*fig*) lewdness

schlurfen ['ʃlʊrfən] *vi* to shuffle

schlürfen ['ʃlʏrfən] *vt, vi* to slurp

Schluß [ʃlʊs] (-sses, ⁼sse) *m* end; (*~folgerung*) conclusion; **am ~** at the end; **~ machen mit** to finish with

Schlüssel ['ʃlʏsəl] (-s, -) *m* (*auch fig*) key; (*Schraub~*) spanner, wrench; (*MUS*) clef; **~bein** *nt* collarbone; **~blume** *f* cowslip, primrose; **~bund** *m* bunch of keys; **~loch** *nt* keyhole; **~position** *f* key position; **~wort** *nt* keyword

schlüssig ['ʃlʏsɪç] *adj* conclusive

Schluß- *zW*: **~licht** *nt* taillight; (*fig*) tailender; **~strich** *m* (*fig*) final stroke; **~verkauf** *m* clearance sale

schmächtig ['ʃmɛçtɪç] *adj* slight

schmackhaft ['ʃmakhaft] *adj* tasty

schmal [ʃmaːl] *adj* narrow; (*Person, Buch etc*) slender, slim; (*karg*) meagre

schmälern ['ʃmɛːlərn] *vt* to diminish;

(*fig*) to belittle

Schmalfilm *m* cine film

Schmalz [ʃmalts] (-es, -e) *nt* dripping, lard; (*fig*) sentiment, schmaltz; **s~ig** *adj* (*fig*) schmaltzy

schmarotzen [ʃma'rɔtsən] *vi* to sponge; (*BOT*) to be parasitic

Schmarotzer (-s, -) *m* parasite; sponger

Schmarren ['ʃmarən] (-s, -) *m* (*ÖSTERREICHISCH*) small piece of pancake; (*fig*) rubbish, tripe

schmatzen ['ʃmatsən] *vi* to smack one's lips; to eat noisily

schmecken ['ʃmɛkən] *vt, vi* to taste; **es schmeckt ihm** he likes it

Schmeichel- ['ʃmaɪçəl] *zW*: **~ei** [-'laɪ] *f* flattery; **s~haft** *adj* flattering; **s~n** *vi* to flatter

schmeißen ['ʃmaɪsən] (*unreg; umg*) *vt* to throw, to chuck

Schmeißfliege *f* bluebottle

Schmelz [ʃmɛlts] (-es, -e) *m* enamel; (*Glasur*) glaze; (*von Stimme*) melodiousness; **s~bar** *adj* fusible; **s~en** (*unreg*) *vt* to melt; (*Erz*) to smelt ♦ *vi* to melt; **~punkt** *m* melting point; **~wasser** *nt* melted snow

Schmerz [ʃmɛrts] (-es, -en) *m* pain; (*Trauer*) grief; **s~empfindlich** *adj* sensitive to pain; **s~en** *vt, vi* to hurt; **~ensgeld** *nt* compensation; **s~haft** *adj* painful; **s~lich** *adj* painful; **s~los** *adj* painless; **s~stillend** *adj* soothing; **~tablette** *f* painkiller

Schmetterling ['ʃmɛtərlɪŋ] *m* butterfly

Schmied [ʃmiːt] (-(e)s, -e) *m* blacksmith; **~e** ['ʃmiːdə] *f* smithy, forge; **~eeisen** *nt* wrought iron; **s~en** *vt* to forge; (*Pläne*) to devise, to concoct

schmiegen ['ʃmiːgən] *vt* to press, to nestle ♦ *vr*: **sich ~ (an +akk)** to cuddle up (to), to nestle (up to)

Schmier- ['ʃmiːr] *zW*: **~e** *f* grease; (*THEAT*) greasepaint, make-up; **s~en** *vt* to smear; (*ölen*) to lubricate, to grease; (*bestechen*) to bribe; (*schreiben*) to scrawl ♦ *vi* to scrawl; **~fett** *nt* grease; **~fink** *m* messy person; **~geld** *nt* bribe; **s~ig** *adj* greasy; ~**seife** f soft soap

Schminke ['ʃmɪŋkə] f make-up; s~**n** vt, vr to make up

schmirgeln ['ʃmɪrgəln] vt to sand (down)

Schmirgelpapier nt emery paper

schmollen ['ʃmɔlən] vi to sulk, to pout

Schmorbraten m stewed od braised meat

schmoren ['ʃmoːrən] vt to stew, to braise

Schmuck [ʃmʊk] (-(e)s, -e) m jewellery; (Verzierung) decoration

schmücken ['ʃmʏkən] vt to decorate

Schmuck- zW: s~**los** adj unadorned, plain; ~**losigkeit** f simplicity; ~**sachen** pl jewels, jewellery sg

Schmuggel ['ʃmʊgəl] (-s) m smuggling; s~**n** vt, vi to smuggle

Schmuggler (-s, -) m smuggler

schmunzeln ['ʃmʊntsəln] vi to smile benignly

Schmutz [ʃmʊts] (-es) m dirt, filth; ~**fink** m filthy creature; ~**fleck** m stain; s~**ig** adj dirty

Schnabel ['ʃnaːbəl] (-s, ⁻) m beak, bill; (Ausguß) spout

Schnake ['ʃnaːkə] f cranefly; (Stechmücke) gnat

Schnalle ['ʃnalə] f buckle, clasp; s~**n** vt to buckle

Schnapp- ['ʃnap] zW: s~**en** vt to grab, to catch ♦ vi to snap; ~**schloß** nt spring lock; ~**schuß** m (PHOT) snapshot

Schnaps [ʃnaps] (-es, ⁻e) m spirits pl; schnapps

schnarchen ['ʃnarçən] vi to snore

schnauben ['ʃnaubən] vi to snort ♦ vr to blow one's nose

schnaufen ['ʃnaufən] vi to puff, to pant

Schnauzbart m moustache

Schnauze ['ʃnautsə] f snout, muzzle; (Ausguß) spout; (umg) gob

Schnecke ['ʃnɛkə] f snail; **Schneckenhaus** nt snail's shell

Schnee [ʃneː] (-s) m snow; (Ei~) beaten egg white; ~**ball** m snowball; ~**flocke** f snowflake; ~**gestöber** nt snowstorm; ~**glöckchen** nt snowdrop;

~**kette** f (AUT) snow chain; ~**pflug** m snowplough; ~**schmelze** f thaw; ~**wehe** f snowdrift

Schneid [ʃnait] (-(e)s; umg) m pluck

Schneide ['ʃnaidə] f edge; (Klinge) blade; s~**n** (unreg) vt to cut; (kreuzen) to cross, to intersect with ♦ vr to cut o.s.; to cross, to intersect; **schneidend** adj cutting; ~**r** (-s, -) m tailor; ~**rin** f dressmaker; **schneidern** vt to make ♦ vi to be a tailor; ~**zahn** m incisor

schneien ['ʃnaiən] vi unpers to snow

Schneise ['ʃnaizə] f clearing

schnell [ʃnɛl] adj quick, fast ♦ adv quick, quickly, fast; **S~hefter** (-s, -) m loose-leaf binder; **S~igkeit** f speed; **S~imbiß** m (Lokal) snack bar; **S~kochtopf** m (Dampfkochtopf) pressure cooker; **S~reinigung** f dry cleaner's; ~**stens** adv as quickly as possible; **S~straße** f expressway; **S~zug** m fast od express train

schneuzen ['ʃnɔytsən] vr to blow one's nose

schnippisch ['ʃnɪpɪʃ] adj sharp-tongued

Schnitt [ʃnɪt] (-(e)s, -e) m cut(ting); (~punkt) intersection; (Quer~) (cross) section; (Durch~) average; (~muster) pattern; (an Buch) edge; (umg: Gewinn) profit

schnitt etc vb siehe **schneiden**

Schnitt- zW: ~**blumen** pl cut flowers; ~**e** f slice; (belegt) sandwich; ~**fläche** f section; ~**lauch** m chive; ~**muster** nt pattern; ~**punkt** m (point of) intersection; ~**stelle** f (COMPUT) interface; ~**wunde** f cut

Schnitz- ['ʃnɪts] zW: ~**arbeit** f wood carving; ~**el** (-s, -) nt chip; (KOCH) escalope; s~**en** vt to carve; ~**er** (-s, -) m carver; (umg) blunder; ~**e'rei** f carving; carved woodwork

schnodderig ['ʃnɔdərɪç] (umg) adj snotty

Schnorchel ['ʃnɔrçəl] (-s, -) m snorkel

Schnörkel ['ʃnœrkəl] (-s, -) m flourish; (ARCHIT) scroll

schnorren ['ʃnɔrən] vt, vi to cadge

schnüffeln ['ʃnʏfəln] vi to sniff; **S~**

(umg) nt (von Klebstoff etc) glue-sniffing etc
Schnüffler (-s, -) m snooper
Schnuller ['ʃnʊlər] (-s, -) m dummy, comforter (US)
Schnupfen ['ʃnʊpfən] (-s, -) m cold
schnuppern ['ʃnʊpərn] vi to sniff
Schnur [ʃnuːr] (-, ⁼e) f string, cord; (ELEK) flex
schnüren ['ʃnyːrən] vt to tie
schnurgerade adj straight (as a die)
Schnurrbart m moustache
schnurren ['ʃnʊrən] vi to purr; (Kreisel) to hum
Schnürschuh m lace-up (shoe)
Schnürsenkel m shoelace
schnurstracks adv straight (away)
Schock [ʃɔk] (-(e)s, -e) m shock; **s~ieren** [ʃɔˈkiːrən] vt to shock, to outrage
Schöffe ['ʃœfə] (-n, -n) m lay magistrate
Schokolade [ʃokoˈlaːdə] f chocolate
Scholle ['ʃɔlə] f clod; (Eis~) ice floe; (Fisch) plaice

SCHLÜSSELWORT

schon [ʃoːn] adv 1 (bereits) already; **er ist schon da** he's there already, he's already there; **ist er schon da?** is he there yet?; **warst du schon einmal da?** have you ever been there?; **ich war schon einmal da** I've been there before; **das war schon immer so** that has always been the case; **schon oft** often; **hast du schon gehört?** have you heard?
2 (bestimmt) all right; **du wirst schon sehen** you'll see (all right); **das wird schon noch gut** that'll be OK
3 (bloß) just; **allein schon das Gefühl ...** just the very feeling ...; **schon der Gedanke** the very thought; **wenn ich das schon höre** I only have to hear that
4 (einschränkend): **ja schon, aber ...** yes (well), but ...
5: **schon möglich** possible; **schon gut!** OK!; **du weißt schon** you know; **komm schon!** come on!

---

schön [ʃøːn] adj beautiful; (nett) nice;

~e Grüße best wishes; ~e Ferien have a nice holiday; ~en Dank (many) thanks
schonen ['ʃoːnən] vt to look after ♦ vr to take it easy; ~d adj careful, gentle
Schön- zW: ~heit f beauty; ~heitsfehler m blemish, flaw; ~heitsoperation f cosmetic surgery; **s~machen** vr to make o.s. look nice
Schon- zW: ~ung f good care; (Nachsicht) consideration; (Forst) plantation of young trees; **s~ungslos** adj unsparing, harsh; ~zeit f close season
Schöpf- ['ʃœpf] zW: **s~en** vt to scoop, to ladle; (Mut) to summon up; (Luft) to breathe in; ~er (-s, -) m creator; **s~erisch** adj creative; ~kelle f ladle; ~löffel m skimmer, scoop; ~ung f creation
Schorf ['ʃɔrf] (-(e)s, -e) m scab
Schornstein ['ʃɔrnʃtain] m chimney; (NAUT) funnel; ~feger (-s, -) m chimney sweep
Schoß [ʃoːs] (-es, ⁼e) m lap; (Rock~) coat tail
schoß etc vb siehe **schießen**
Schoßhund m pet dog, lapdog
Schote ['ʃoːtə] f pod
Schotte ['ʃɔtə] m Scot, Scotsman
Schotter ['ʃɔtər] (-s) m broken stone, road metal; (EISENB) ballast
Schott- [ʃɔt] zW: ~in f Scot, Scotswoman; **s~isch** adj Scottish, Scots; ~land nt Scotland
schraffieren [ʃraˈfiːrən] vt to hatch
schräg [ʃrɛːk] adj slanting, not straight; **etw ~ stellen** to put sth at an angle; ~ **gegenüber** diagonally opposite; **S~e** f slant; **S~strich** m oblique stroke
Schramme ['ʃramə] f scratch; **s~n** vt to scratch
Schrank [ʃraŋk] (-(e)s, ⁼e) m cupboard; (Kleider~) wardrobe; ~e f barrier; ~enwärter m (EISENB) level crossing attendant; ~koffer m trunk
Schraube ['ʃraubə] f screw; **s~n** vt to screw; **Schraubenschlüssel** m spanner; **Schraubenzieher** (-s, -) m screwdriver
Schraubstock ['ʃraupʃtɔk] m (TECH)

vice

Schreck [ʃrɛk] (-(e)s, -e) *m* terror;
fright; ~en (-s, -) *m* terror; fright;
s~en *vt* to frighten, to scare;
~gespenst *nt* spectre, nightmare;
s~haft *adj* jumpy, easily frightened;
s~lich *adj* terrible, dreadful
Schrei [ʃraɪ] (-(e)s, -e) *m* scream;
(*Ruf*) shout
Schreib- [ˈʃraɪb] *zW:* ~block *m* writing
pad; ~dichte *f:* einfache/doppelte
~dichte (*Diskette*) single/double
density; s~en (*unreg*) *vt, vi* to write;
(*buchstabieren*) to spell; ~en (-s, -) *nt*
letter, communication; s~faul *adj* bad
about writing letters; ~fehler *m* spelling mistake; ~maschine *f* typewriter;
~papier *nt* notepaper; ~tisch *m* desk;
~ung *f* spelling; ~waren *pl* stationery
sg; ~warenhandlung *f* stationer's;
~weise *f* spelling; way of writing;
~zentrale *f* typing pool; ~zeug *nt* writing materials *pl*
schreien [ˈʃraɪən] (*unreg*) *vt, vi* to
scream; (*rufen*) to shout; ~d *adj* (*fig*)
glaring; (*Farbe*) loud
Schreiner [ˈʃraɪnər] (-s, -) *m* joiner;
(*Zimmermann*) carpenter; (*Möbel~*)
cabinetmaker; ~ei [-ˈraɪ] *f* joiner's
workshop
schreiten [ˈʃraɪtən] (*unreg*) *vi* to stride
schrieb *etc* [ʃriːp] *vb siehe* **schreiben**
Schrift [ʃrɪft] (-, -en) *f* writing; handwriting; (~*art*) script; (*Gedrucktes*)
pamphlet, work; ~deutsch *nt* written
German; ~führer *m* secretary; s~lich
adj written ♦ *adv* in writing; ~setzer
m compositor; ~sprache *f* written
language; ~steller(in) (-s, -) *m(f)*
writer; ~stück *nt* document
schrill [ʃrɪl] *adj* shrill
Schritt [ʃrɪt] (-(e)s, -e) *m* step; (*Gang-
art*) walk; (*Tempo*) pace; (*von Hose*)
crutch; ~ fahren to drive at walking
pace; ~macher (-s, -) *m* pacemaker;
~(t)empo *nt:* im ~(t)empo at a walking pace
schroff [ʃrɔf] *adj* steep; (*zackig*)
jagged; (*fig*) brusque; (*ungeduldig*)
abrupt

schröpfen [ˈʃrœpfən] *vt* (*fig*) to fleece
Schrot [ʃroːt] (-(e)s, -e) *m od nt* (*Blei*)
(small) shot; (*Getreide*) coarsely
ground grain, groats *pl;* ~flinte *f* shotgun
Schrott [ʃrɔt] (-(e)s, -e) *m* scrap metal;
~haufen *m* scrap heap; s~reif *adj*
ready for the scrap heap
schrubben [ˈʃrʊbən] *vt* to scrub
Schrubber (-s, -) *m* scrubbing brush
schrumpfen [ˈʃrʊmpfən] *vi* to shrink;
(*Apfel*) to shrivel
Schub- [ˈʃuːb] *zW:* ~fach *nt* drawer;
~karren *m* wheelbarrow; ~lade *f*
drawer
schüchtern [ˈʃʏçtərn] *adj* shy; S~heit *f*
shyness
Schuft [ʃʊft] (-(e)s, -e) *m* scoundrel
schuften (*umg*) *vi* to graft, to slave
away
Schuh [ʃuː] (-(e)s, -e) *m* shoe; ~band
nt shoelace; ~creme *f* shoe polish;
~löffel *m* shoehorn; ~macher (-s, -) *m*
shoemaker
Schul- *zW:* ~aufgaben *pl* homework
sg; ~besuch *m* school attendance;
~buch *nt* school book
Schuld [ʃʊlt] (-, -en) *f* guilt; (*FIN*) debt;
(*Verschulden*) fault; s~ *adj:* s~ sein od
haben (an +*dat*) to be to blame (for);
er ist *od* hat s~ it's his fault; jdm s~
geben to blame sb; s~en [ˈʃʊldən] *vt* to
owe; s~enfrei *adj* free from debt;
~gefühl *nt* feeling of guilt; s~ig *adj*
guilty; (*gebührend*) due; s~ig an etw
dat sein to be guilty of sth; jdm etw
s~ig sein to owe sb sth; jdm etw s~ig
bleiben not to provide sb with sth;
s~los *adj* innocent, without guilt; ~ner
(-s, -) *m* debtor; ~schein *m* promissory
note, IOU; ~spruch *m* verdict of guilty
Schule [ˈʃuːlə] *f* school; s~n *vt* to train,
to school
Schüler(in) [ˈʃyːlər(ɪn)] (-s, -) *m(f)*
pupil; ~lotse *m* pupil acting as road
crossing warden
Schul- *zW:* ~ferien *pl* school holidays;
s~frei *adj:* s~freier Tag holiday;
s~frei sein to be a holiday; ~hof *m*
playground; ~jahr *nt* school year;

~**junge** *m* schoolboy; ~**mädchen** *nt* schoolgirl; **s~pflichtig** *adj* of school age; ~**schiff** *nt* (*NAUT*) training ship; ~**stunde** *f* period, lesson; ~**tasche** *f* school bag

Schulter ['ʃʊltər] (-, -n) *f* shoulder; ~**blatt** *nt* shoulder blade; **s~n** *vt* to shoulder

Schulung *f* education, schooling

Schulzeugnis *nt* school report

Schund [ʃʊnt] (-(e)s) *m* trash, garbage; ~**roman** *m* trashy novel

Schuppe ['ʃʊpə] *f* scale; ~**n** *pl* (*Haarschuppen*) dandruff *sg*

Schuppen (-s, -) *m* shed

schuppen *vt* to scale ♦ *vr* to peel

schuppig ['ʃʊpıç] *adj* scaly

Schur [ʃuːr] (-, -en) *f* shearing

schüren ['ʃyːrən] *vt* to rake; (*fig*) to stir up

schürfen ['ʃʏrfən] *vt, vi* to scrape, to scratch; (*MIN*) to prospect

Schurke ['ʃʊrkə] (-n, -n) *m* rogue

Schürze ['ʃʏrtsə] *f* apron

Schuß [ʃʊs] (-sses, -sse) *m* shot; (*WEBEN*) woof; ~**bereich** *m* effective range

Schüssel ['ʃʏsəl] (-, -n) *f* bowl

Schuß- *zW:* ~**linie** *f* line of fire; ~**verletzung** *f* bullet wound; ~**waffe** *f* firearm; ~**weite** *f* range (of fire)

Schuster ['ʃuːstər] (-s, -) *m* cobbler, shoemaker

Schutt [ʃʊt] (-(e)s) *m* rubbish; (*Bau~*) rubble; ~**abladeplatz** *m* refuse dump

Schüttelfrost *m* shivering

schütteln ['ʃʏtəln] *vt, vr* to shake

schütten ['ʃʏtən] *vt* to pour; (*Zucker, Kies etc*) to tip; (*ver~*) to spill ♦ *vi unpers* to pour (down)

Schutthalde *f* dump

Schutthaufen *m* heap of rubble

Schutz [ʃʊts] (-es) *m* protection; (*Unterschlupf*) shelter; **jdn in ~ nehmen** to stand up for sb; ~**anzug** *m* overalls *pl*; ~**blech** *nt* mudguard; ~**brille** *f* goggles *pl*

Schütze ['ʃʏtsə] (-n, -n) *m* gunman; (*Gewehr~*) rifleman; (*Scharf~, Sport~*) marksman; (*ASTROL*) Sagitta-

rius

schützen *vt* to protect; ~ **vor** +*dat od* **gegen** to protect from

Schützenfest *nt* fair featuring shooting matches

Schutz- *zW:* ~**engel** *m* guardian angel; ~**gebiet** *nt* protectorate; (*Naturschutzgebiet*) reserve; ~**impfung** *f* immunisation; **s~los** *adj* defenceless; ~**mann** (*pl* -**leute** *od* -**männer**) *m* policeman; ~**patron** *m* patron saint

Schwaben ['ʃvaːbən] *nt* Swabia

schwäbisch ['ʃvɛːbıʃ] *adj* Swabian

schwach [ʃvax] *adj* weak, feeble

Schwäche ['ʃvɛçə] *f* weakness; **s~n** *vt* to weaken

Schwachheit *f* weakness

schwächlich *adj* weakly, delicate

Schwächling *m* weakling

Schwach- *zW:* ~**sinn** *m* imbecility; **s~sinnig** *adj* mentally deficient; (*Idee*) idiotic; ~**strom** *m* weak current

Schwächung ['ʃvɛçʊŋ] *f* weakening

schwafeln ['ʃvaːfəln] *vi* to drivel

Schwager ['ʃvaːgər] (-s, -) *m* brother-in-law

Schwägerin ['ʃvɛːgərın] *f* sister-in-law

Schwalbe ['ʃvalbə] *f* swallow

Schwall [ʃval] (-(e)s, -e) *m* surge; (*Worte*) flood, torrent

Schwamm [ʃvam] (-(e)s, -e) *m* sponge; (*Pilz*) fungus

schwamm *etc vb siehe* **schwimmen**

schwammig *adj* spongy; (*Gesicht*) puffy

Schwan [ʃvaːn] (-(e)s, -e) *m* swan

schwanen *vi unpers:* **jdm schwant etw** sb has a foreboding of sth

schwanger ['ʃvaŋər] *adj* pregnant

schwängern ['ʃvɛŋərn] *vt* to make pregnant

Schwangerschaft *f* pregnancy

Schwank [ʃvaŋk] (-(e)s, -e) *m* funny story

schwanken *vi* to sway; (*taumeln*) to stagger, to reel; (*Preise, Zahlen*) to fluctuate; (*zögern*) to hesitate, to vacillate

Schwankung *f* fluctuation

Schwanz [ʃvants] (-es, -e) *m* tail

schwänzen ['ʃvɛntsən] (*umg*) *vt* to skip, to cut ♦ *vi* to play truant

Schwarm [ʃvarm] (-(e)s, ⁼e) *m* swarm; (*umg*) heart-throb, idol

schwärm- ['ʃvɛrm] *zW*: ~**en** *vi* to swarm; ~**en für** to be mad *od* wild about; **S~erei** [-ə'raɪ] *f* enthusiasm; ~**erisch** *adj* impassioned, effusive

Schwarte ['ʃvartə] *f* hard skin; (*Speck~*) rind

schwarz [ʃvarts] *adj* black; ~**es Brett** notice board; **ins S~e treffen** (*auch fig*) to hit the bull's eye; **in den ~en Zahlen** in the black; **S~arbeit** *f* illicit work, moonlighting; **S~brot** *nt* black bread

Schwärze ['ʃvɛrtsə] *f* blackness; (*Farbe*) blacking; (*Drucker~*) printer's ink; ~**n** *vt* to blacken

Schwarz- *zW*: **s~fahren** (*unreg*) *vi* to travel without paying; to drive without a licence; ~**handel** *m* black-market (trade); **s~hören** *vi* to listen to the radio without a licence; ~**markt** *m* black market; **s~sehen** (*unreg*; *umg*) *vi* to see the gloomy side of things; (*TV*) to watch TV without a licence; ~**seher** *m* pessimist; (*TV*) viewer without a licence; ~**wald** *m* Black Forest; **s~weiß** *adj* black and white

schwatzen ['ʃvatsən] *vi* to chatter

schwätzen ['ʃvɛtsən] *vi* to chatter

Schwätzer ['ʃvɛtsər] (-s, -) *m* gasbag; ~**in** *f* chatterbox, gossip

schwatzhaft *adj* talkative, gossipy

Schwebe ['ʃveːbə] *f*: **in der ~** (*fig*) in abeyance; ~**bahn** *f* overhead railway; ~**balken** *m* (*SPORT*) beam; **s~n** *vi* to drift, to float; (*hoch*) to soar

Schwed- ['ʃveːd] *zW*: ~**e** *m* Swede; ~**en** *nt* Sweden; ~**in** *f* Swede; **s~isch** *adj* Swedish

Schwefel ['ʃveːfəl] (-s) *m* sulphur; **s~ig** *adj* sulphurous; ~**säure** *f* sulphuric acid

Schweig- ['ʃvaɪg] *zW*: ~**egeld** *nt* hush money; ~**en** (-s) *nt* silence; **s~en** (*unreg*) *vi* to be silent; to stop talking; **s~sam** ['ʃvaɪkzaːm] *adj* silent, taciturn; ~**samkeit** *f* taciturnity, quietness

Schwein [ʃvaɪn] (-(e)s, -e) *nt* pig; (*umg*) (good) luck

Schweine- *zW*: ~**fleisch** *nt* pork; ~**rei** *f* mess; (*Gemeinheit*) dirty trick; ~**stall** *m* pigsty

schweinisch *adj* filthy

Schweinsleder *nt* pigskin

Schweiß [ʃvaɪs] (-es) *m* sweat, perspiration; **s~en** *vt*, *vi* to weld; ~**er** (-s, -) *m* welder; ~**füße** *pl* sweaty feet; ~**naht** *f* weld

Schweiz [ʃvaɪts] *f* Switzerland; ~**er(in)** *m(f)* Swiss; **s~erisch** *adj* Swiss

schwelgen ['ʃvɛlgən] *vi* to indulge

Schwelle ['ʃvɛlə] *f* (*auch fig*) threshold; doorstep; (*EISENB*) sleeper (*BRIT*), tie (*US*)

schwellen (*unreg*) *vi* to swell

Schwellung *f* swelling

Schwenk- ['ʃvɛŋk] *zW*: **s~bar** *adj* swivel-mounted; **s~en** *vt* to swing; (*Fahne*) to wave; (*abspülen*) to rinse ♦ *vi* to turn, to swivel; (*MIL*) to wheel; ~**ung** *f* turn; wheel

schwer [ʃveːr] *adj* heavy; (*schwierig*) difficult, hard; (*schlimm*) serious, bad ♦ *adv* (*sehr*) very (much); (*verletzt etc*) seriously, badly; **S~arbeiter** *m* manual worker, labourer; **S~e** *f* weight, heaviness; (*PHYS*) gravity; ~**elos** *adj* weightless; (*Kammer*) zero-G; ~**erziehbar** *adj* difficult (to bring up); ~**fallen** (*unreg*) *vi*: **jdm ~fallen** to be difficult for sb; ~**fällig** *adj* ponderous; **S~gewicht** *nt* heavyweight; (*fig*) emphasis; ~**hörig** *adj* hard of hearing; **S~industrie** *f* heavy industry; **S~kraft** *f* gravity; **S~kranke(r)** *mf* person who is seriously ill; ~**lich** *adv* hardly; ~**machen** *vt*: **jdm/sich etw ~machen** to make sth difficult for sb/o.s.; ~**mütig** *adj* melancholy; ~**nehmen** (*unreg*) *vt* to take to heart; **S~punkt** *m* centre of gravity; (*fig*) emphasis, crucial point

Schwert [ʃveːrt] (-(e)s, -er) *nt* sword; ~**lilie** *f* iris

schwer- *zW*: ~**tun** (*unreg*) *vi*: **sich** *dat od akk* ~**tun** to have difficulties; **S~verbrecher(in)** *m(f)* criminal, serious offender; ~**verdaulich** *adj* indigestible, heavy; ~**verletzt** *adj* badly injured; ~**wiegend** *adj* weighty, important

Schwester ['ʃvɛstər] (-, -n) f sister; (*MED*) nurse; s~**lich** adj sisterly

Schwieger- ['ʃviːgər] zW: ~**eltern** pl parents-in-law; ~**mutter** f mother-in-law; ~**sohn** m son-in-law; ~**tochter** f daughter-in-law; ~**vater** m father-in-law

Schwiele ['ʃviːlə] f callus

schwierig ['ʃviːrɪç] adj difficult, hard; S~**keit** f difficulty

Schwimm- ['ʃvɪm] zW: ~**bad** nt swimming baths pl; ~**becken** nt swimming pool; s~**en** (*unreg*) vi to swim; (*treiben, nicht sinken*) to float; (*fig: unsicher sein*) to be all at sea; ~**er** (-s, -) m swimmer; (*Angeln*) float; ~**lehrer** m swimming instructor; ~**weste** f life jacket

Schwindel ['ʃvɪndəl] (-s) m giddiness; dizzy spell; (*Betrug*) swindle, fraud; (*Zeug*) stuff; s~**frei** adj: s~**frei sein** to have a good head for heights; s~**n** (*umg*) vi (*lügen*) to fib; **jdm schwindelt es** sb feels dizzy

schwinden ['ʃvɪndən] (*unreg*) vi to disappear; (*sich verringern*) to decrease; (*Kräfte*) to decline

Schwindler ['ʃvɪndlər] m swindler; (*Lügner*) liar

schwindlig adj dizzy; **mir ist ~** I feel dizzy

Schwing- ['ʃvɪŋ] zW: s~**en** (*unreg*) vt to swing; (*Waffe etc*) to brandish ♦ vi to swing; (*vibrieren*) to vibrate; (*klingen*) to sound; ~**tür** f swing door(s); ~**ung** f vibration; (*PHYS*) oscillation

Schwips [ʃvɪps] (-es, -e) m: **einen ~ haben** to be tipsy

schwirren ['ʃvɪrən] vi to buzz

schwitzen ['ʃvɪtsən] vi to sweat, to perspire

schwören ['ʃvøːrən] (*unreg*) vt, vi to swear

schwul [ʃvuːl] (*umg*) adj gay, queer

schwül [ʃvyːl] adj sultry, close; S~**e** (-) f sultriness, closeness

schwülstig ['ʃvʏlstɪç] adj pompous

Schwung [ʃvʊŋ] (-(e)s, ⁻e) m swing; (*Triebkraft*) momentum; (*fig: Energie*) verve, energy; (*umg: Menge*) batch; s~**haft** adj brisk, lively; s~**voll** adj vigorous

Schwur [ʃvuːr] (-(e)s, ⁻e) m oath; ~**gericht** nt court with a jury

sechs [zɛks] num six; ~**hundert** num six hundred; ~**te(r, s)** adj sixth; S~**tel** (-s, -) nt sixth

sechzehn ['zɛçtseːn] num sixteen

sechzig ['zɛçtsɪç] num sixty

See¹ [zeː] (-, -n) f sea

See² (-s, -n) m lake

See- zW: ~**bad** nt seaside resort; ~**fahrt** f seafaring; (*Reise*) voyage; ~**gang** m (motion of the) sea; ~**hund** m seal; ~**igel** ['zeːʔiːgəl] m sea urchin; s~**krank** adj seasick; ~**krankheit** f seasickness; ~**lachs** m rock salmon

Seele ['zeːlə] f soul; **seelenruhig** adv calmly

Seeleute ['zeːlɔʏtə] pl seamen

Seel- zW: s~**isch** adj mental; ~**sorge** f pastoral duties pl; ~**sorger** (-s, -) m clergyman

See- zW: ~**macht** f naval power; ~**mann** (pl -**leute**) m seaman, sailor; ~**meile** f nautical mile; ~**not** f distress; ~**pferd(chen)** nt sea horse; ~**räuber** m pirate; ~**rose** f water lily; ~**stern** m starfish; s~**tüchtig** adj seaworthy; ~**weg** m sea route; **auf dem ~weg** by sea; ~**zunge** f sole

Segel ['zeːgəl] (-s, -) nt sail; ~**boot** nt yacht; ~**fliegen** (-s) nt gliding; ~**flieger** m glider pilot; ~**flugzeug** nt glider; s~**n** vt, vi to sail; ~**schiff** nt sailing vessel; ~**sport** m sailing; ~**tuch** nt canvas

Segen ['zeːgən] (-s, -) m blessing; **segensreich** adj beneficial

Segler ['zeːglər] (-s, -) m sailor, yachtsman

segnen ['zeːgnən] vt to bless

Seh- [zeː] zW: s~**en** (*unreg*) vt, vi to see; (*in bestimmte Richtung*) to look; **mal s~en**(, **ob ...**) let's see (if ...); **siehe Seite 5** see page 5; s~**enswert** adj worth seeing; ~**enswürdigkeiten** pl sights (of a town); ~**er** (-s, -) m seer; ~**fehler** m sight defect

Sehne ['ze:nə] f sinew; (an Bogen) string
sehnen vr: sich ~ nach to long od yearn for
sehnig adj sinewy
Sehn- zW: s~lich adj ardent; ~sucht f longing; s~süchtig adj longing
sehr [ze:r] adv very; (mit Verben) a lot, (very) much; zu ~ too much; ~ geehrte(r) ... dear ...
seicht [zaɪçt] adj (auch fig) shallow
Seide ['zaɪdə] f silk; s~n adj silk; **Seidenpapier** nt tissue paper
seidig ['zaɪdɪç] adj silky
Seife ['zaɪfə] f soap
Seifen- zW: ~lauge f soapsuds pl; ~schale f soap dish; ~schaum m lather
seihen ['zaɪən] vt to strain, to filter
Seil [zaɪl] (-(e)s, -e) nt rope; cable; ~bahn f cable railway; ~hüpfen (-s) nt skipping; ~springen (-s) nt skipping; ~tänzer(in) m(f) tightrope walker

---

sein [zaɪn] (pt war, pp gewesen) vi **1** to be; **ich bin** I am; **du bist** you are; **er/sie/es ist** he/she/it is; **wir sind/ihr seid/sie sind** we/you/they are; **wir waren** we were; **wir sind gewesen** we have been

2: seien Sie nicht böse don't be angry; **sei so gut und ...** be so kind as to ...; **das wäre gut** that would od that'd be a good thing; **wenn ich Sie wäre** if I were od was you; **das wär's** that's all, that's it; **morgen bin ich in Rom** tomorrow I'll od I will od I shall be in Rome; **waren Sie mal in Rom?** have you ever been to Rome?

3: wie ist das zu verstehen? how is that to be understood?; **er ist nicht zu ersetzen** he cannot be replaced; **mit ihr ist nicht zu reden** you can't talk to her

4: mir ist kalt I'm cold; **was ist?** what's the matter?, what is it?; **ist was?** is something the matter?; **es sei denn, daß ...** unless ...; **wie dem auch sei** be that as it may; **wie wäre es mit**

...? how od what about ...?; **laß das sein!** stop that!

---

sein(e) ['zaɪn(ə)] adj his; its; ~e(r, s) pron his; its; ~er (gen von er) pron of him; ~erseits adv for his part; ~erzeit adv in those days, formerly; ~esgleichen pron people like him; ~etwegen adv (für ihn) for his sake; (wegen ihm) on his account; (von ihm aus) as far as he is concerned; ~etwillen adv: um ~etwillen = ~etwegen; ~ige pron: der/die/das ~ige his
Seismograph [zaɪsmo'graːf] (-en, -en) m seismograph
seit [zaɪt] präp +dat since ♦ konj since; **er ist ~ einer Woche hier** he has been here for a week; ~ **langem** for a long time; ~**dem** [zaɪt'de:m] adv, konj since
Seite ['zaɪtə] f side; (Buch~) page; (MIL) flank
Seiten- zW: ~ansicht f side view; ~hieb m (fig) passing shot, dig; s~s präp +gen on the part of; ~schiff nt aisle; ~sprung m extramarital escapade; ~stechen nt (a) stitch; ~straße f side road
seither [zaɪt'he:r] adv, konj since (then)
seitlich adj on one od the side; side cpd
seitwärts adv sidewards
Sekretär [zekre'tɛːr] m secretary; (Möbel) bureau; ~in f secretary
Sekretariat [zekretari'aːt] (-(e)s, -e) nt secretary's office, secretariat
Sekt [zɛkt] (-(e)s, -e) m champagne
Sekte ['zɛktə] f sect
Sekunde [ze'kʊndə] f second
selber ['zɛlbər] = selbst
Selbst [zɛlpst] (-) nt self

---

selbst pron **1: ich/er/wir selbst** I myself/he himself/we ourselves; **sie ist die Tugend selbst** she's virtue itself; **er braut sein Bier selbst** he brews his own beer; **wie geht's? - gut, und selbst?** how are things? - fine, and yourself?

2 (ohne Hilfe) alone, on my/his/one's etc own; **von selbst** by itself; **er kam von selbst** he came of his own accord

♦ *adv* even; **selbst wenn** even if; **selbst Gott** even God (himself)

Selbstachtung *f* self-respect
selbständig ['zɛlpʃtɛndɪç] *adj* independent; **S~keit** *f* independence
Selbst- *zW:* **~auslöser** *m* (PHOT) delayed-action shutter release; **~bedienung** *f* self-service; **~befriedigung** *f* masturbation; **~beherrschung** *f* self-control; **s~bewußt** *adj* (self-)confident; **~bewußtsein** *nt* self-confidence; **~erhaltung** *f* self-preservation; **~erkenntnis** *f* self-knowledge; **s~gefällig** *adj* smug, self-satisfied; **s~gemacht** *adj* home-made; **~gespräch** *nt* conversation with o.s.; **~kostenpreis** *m* cost price; **s~los** *adj* unselfish, selfless; **~mord** *m* suicide; **~mörder(in)** *m(f)* suicide; **s~mörderisch** *adj* suicidal; **s~sicher** *adj* self-assured; **s~tätig** *adj* automatic; **s~verständlich** *adj* obvious ♦ *adv* naturally; **ich halte das für s~verständlich** I take that for granted; **~vertrauen** *nt* self-confidence; **~verwaltung** *f* autonomy, self-government
selig ['ze:lɪç] *adj* happy, blissful; (REL) blessed; (tot) late; **S~keit** *f* bliss
Sellerie ['zɛləri:] (-s, -(s) *od* -, -) *m od f* celery
selten ['zɛltən] *adj* rare ♦ *adv* seldom, rarely; **S~heit** *f* rarity
Selterswasser ['zɛltərsvasər] *nt* soda water
seltsam ['zɛltza:m] *adj* strange, curious; **~erweise** *adv* curiously, strangely; **S~keit** *f* strangeness
Semester [ze'mɛstər] (-s, -) *nt* semester
Semi- [zemi] *in* zW semi-; **~kolon** [-'ko:lɔn] (-s, -s) *nt* semicolon
Seminar [-'na:r] (-s, -e) *nt* seminary; (Kurs) seminar; (UNIV: Ort) department building
Semmel ['zɛməl] (-, -n) *f* roll
sen. *abk* (= senior) sen.
Senat [ze'na:t] (-(e)s, -e) *m* senate, council
Sende- ['zɛndə] *zW:* **~bereich** *m* transmission range; **~folge** *f* (Serie)

series; **s~n** (unreg) *vt* to send; (RADIO, TV) to transmit, to broadcast ♦ *vi* to transmit, to broadcast; **~r** (-s, -) *m* station; (Anlage) transmitter; **~reihe** *f* series (of broadcasts)
Sendung ['zɛndʊŋ] *f* consignment; (Aufgabe) mission; (RADIO, TV) transmission; (Programm) programme
Senf [zɛnf] (-(e)s, -e) *m* mustard
Senk- ['zɛŋk] *zW:* **~blei** *nt* plumb; **~e** *f* depression; **s~en** *vt* to lower ♦ *vr* to sink, to drop gradually; **s~recht** *adj* vertical, perpendicular; **~rechte** *f* perpendicular; **~rechtstarter** *m* (AVIAT) vertical take-off plane; (fig) high-flyer
Sensation [zɛnzatsi'o:n] *f* sensation; **s~ell** [-'nɛl] *adj* sensational
Sense ['zɛnzə] *f* scythe
sensibel [zɛn'zi:bəl] *adj* sensitive
sentimental [zɛntimɛn'ta:l] *adj* sentimental; **S~i'tät** *f* sentimentality
separat [zepa'ra:t] *adj* separate
September [zɛp'tɛmbər] (-(s), -) *m* September
Serie ['ze:riə] *f* series; **serienweise** *adv* in series
seriös [zeri'ø:s] *adj* serious, bona fide
Serum ['ze:rʊm] (-s, Seren) *nt* serum
Service¹ [zɛr'vi:s] (-(s), -) *nt* (Geschirr) set, service
Service² (-, -s) *m* service
servieren [zɛr'vi:rən] *vt, vi* to serve
Serviette [zɛrvi'ɛtə] *f* napkin, serviette
Sessel ['zɛsəl] (-s, -) *m* armchair; **~lift** *m* chairlift
seßhaft ['zɛshaft] *adj* settled; (ansässig) resident
setzen ['zɛtsən] *vt* to put, to set; (Baum etc) to plant; (Segel, TYP) to set ♦ *vr* to settle; (Person) to sit down ♦ *vi* (springen) to leap; (wetten) to bet
Setz- ['zɛts] *zW:* **~er** (-s, -) *m* (TYP) compositor; **~e'rei** *f* caseroom; **~ling** *m* young plant
Seuche ['zɔʏçə] *f* epidemic; **Seuchengebiet** *nt* infected area
seufzen ['zɔʏftsən] *vt, vi* to sigh
Seufzer ['zɔʏftsər] (-s, -) *m* sigh
Sex [zɛks] (-(es)) *m* sex; **~ualität** [-uali'tɛt] *f* sex, sexuality; **s~uell** [-u'ɛl]

adj sexual
sezieren [zeˈtsiːrən] *vt* to dissect
Shampoo [ʃamˈpuː] (-s, -s) *nt* shampoo
Sibirien [ziˈbiːriən] *nt* Siberia
sibirisch [ziˈbiːrɪʃ] *adj* Siberian

| *SCHLÜSSELWORT* |

sich [zɪç] *pron* 1 (*akk*): **er/sie/es ... sich** he/she/it ... himself/herself/itself; **sie** *pl*/**man ... sich** they/one ... themselves/oneself; **Sie ... sich** you ... yourself/yourselves *pl*; **sich wiederholen** to repeat oneself/itself
2 (*dat*): **er/sie/es ... sich** he/she/it ... to himself/herself/itself; **sie** *pl*/**man ... sich** they/one ... to themselves/oneself; **Sie ... sich** you ... to yourself/yourselves *pl*; **sie hat sich einen Pullover gekauft** she bought herself a jumper; **sich die Haare waschen** to wash one's hair
3 (*mit Präposition*): **haben Sie Ihren Ausweis bei sich?** do you have your pass on you?; **er hat nichts bei sich** he's got nothing on him; **sie bleiben gern unter sich** they keep themselves to themselves
4 (*einander*) each other, one another; **sie bekämpfen sich** they fight each other *od* one another
5: **dieses Auto fährt sich gut** this car drives well; **hier sitzt es sich gut** it's good to sit here

---

Sichel [ˈzɪçəl] (-, -n) *f* sickle; (*Mond~*) crescent
sicher [ˈzɪçər] *adj* safe; (*gewiß*) certain; (*zuverlässig*) secure, reliable; (*selbst~*) confident; **vor jdm/etw ~ sein** to be safe from sb/sth; **ich bin nicht ~** I'm not sure *od* certain; **~ nicht** surely not; **aber ~!** of course!; **~gehen** (*unreg*) *vi* to make sure
Sicherheit [ˈzɪçərhaɪt] *f* safety; (*auch FIN*) security; (*Gewißheit*) certainty; (*Selbst~*) confidence
Sicherheits- *zW*: **~abstand** *m* safe distance; **~glas** *nt* safety glass; **~gurt** *m* safety belt; **s~halber** *adv* for safety; to be on the safe side; **~nadel** *f* safety pin; **~vorkehrung** *f* safety precaution

sicher- *zW*: **~lich** *adv* certainly, surely; **~n** *vt* to secure; (*schützen*) to protect; (*Waffe*) to put the safety catch on; **jdm etw ~n** to secure sth for sb; **sich** *dat* **etw ~n** to secure sth (for o.s.); **~stellen** *vt* to impound; (*COMPUT*) to save; **S~ung** *f* (*Sichern*) securing; (*Vorrichtung*) safety device; (*an Waffen*) safety catch; (*ELEK*) fuse; **S~ungskopie** *f* back-up copy
Sicht [zɪçt] (-) *f* sight; (*Aus~*) view; **auf** *od* **nach ~** (*FIN*) at sight; **auf lange ~** on a long-term basis; **s~bar** *adj* visible; **s~en** *vt* to sight; (*auswählen*) to sort out; **s~lich** *adj* evident, obvious; **~verhältnisse** *pl* visibility *sg*; **~vermerk** *m* visa
sickern [ˈzɪkərn] *vi* to trickle, to seep
Sie [ziː] (*nom, akk*) *pron* you
sie [ziː] *pron* (*sg: nom*) she; it; (: *akk*) her; it; (*pl: nom*) they; (: *akk*) them
Sieb [ziːp] (-(e)s, -e) *nt* sieve; (*KOCH*) strainer; **s~en**[1] [ˈziːbən] *vt* to sift; (*Flüssigkeit*) to strain
sieben[2] [ˈziːbən] *num* seven; **~hundert** *num* seven hundred; **S~sachen** *pl* belongings
siebte(r, s) [ˈziːptə(r, s)] *adj* seventh; **Siebtel** (-s, -) *nt* seventh
siebzehn [ˈziːptseːn] *num* seventeen
siebzig [ˈziːptsɪç] *num* seventy
sieden [ˈziːdən] *vt, vi* to boil, to simmer
Siedepunkt *m* boiling point
Siedlung *f* settlement; (*Häuser~*) housing estate
Sieg [ziːk] (-(e)s, -e) *m* victory
Siegel [ˈziːgəl] (-s, -) *nt* seal; **~lack** *m* sealing wax; **~ring** *m* signet ring
Sieg- *zW*: **s~en** *vi* to be victorious; (*SPORT*) to win; **~er** (-s, -) *m* victor; (*SPORT etc*) winner; **siegessicher** *adj* sure of victory; **s~reich** *adj* victorious
siehe *etc* [ˈziːə] *vb siehe* **sehen**
siehst *etc* [ziːst] *vb siehe* **sehen**
siezen [ˈziːtsən] *vt* to address as "Sie"
Signal [zɪˈgnaːl] (-s, -e) *nt* signal
Silbe [ˈzɪlbə] *f* syllable
Silber [ˈzɪlbər] (-s) *nt* silver; **s~n** *adj* silver; **~papier** *nt* silver paper
Silhouette [ziluˈɛtə] *f* silhouette

Silo ['zi:lo] (-s, -s) nt od m silo

Silvester [zɪl'vɛstər] (-s, -) nt New Year's Eve, Hogmanay (SCOTTISH); **~abend** m = **Silvester**

simpel ['zɪmpəl] adj simple

Sims [zɪms] (-es, -e) nt od m (Kamin~) mantelpiece; (Fenster~) (window)sill

simulieren [zɪmu'li:rən] vt to simulate, (vortäuschen) to feign ♦ vi to feign illness

simultan [zimʊl'ta:n] adj simultaneous

Sinfonie [zɪnfo'ni:] f symphony

singen ['zɪŋən] (unreg) vt, vi to sing

Singular ['zɪŋgula:r] m singular

Singvogel ['zɪŋfo:gəl] m songbird

sinken ['zɪŋkən] (unreg) vi to sink; (Preise etc) to fall, to go down

Sinn [zɪn] (-(e)s, -e) m mind; (Wahrnehmungs~) sense; (Bedeutung) sense, meaning; ~ **für etw** sense of sth; **von ~en sein** to be out of one's mind; **es hat keinen ~** there's no point; **~bild** nt symbol; **s~en** (unreg) vi to ponder; **auf etw** akk **s~en** to contemplate sth; **~estäuschung** f illusion; **s~gemäß** adj faithful; (Wiedergabe) in one's own words; **s~ig** adj clever; **s~lich** adj sensual, sensuous; (Wahrnehmung) sensory; **~lichkeit** f sensuality; **s~los** adj senseless; meaningless; **~losigkeit** f senselessness; meaninglessness; **s~voll** adj meaningful; (vernünftig) sensible

Sintflut ['zɪntflu:t] f Flood

Siphon [zi'fõ:] (-s, -s) m siphon

Sippe ['zɪpə] f clan, kin

Sippschaft ['zɪpʃaft] (pej) f relations pl, tribe; (Bande) gang

Sirene [zi're:nə] f siren

Sirup ['zi:rʊp] (-s, -e) m syrup

Sitt- ['zɪt] zW: **~e** f custom; **~en** pl (Sittlichkeit) morals; **~enpolizei** f vice squad; **s~lich** adj moral; **~lichkeit** f morality; **~lichkeitsverbrechen** nt sex offence; **s~sam** adj modest, demure

Situation [zituatsi'o:n] f situation

Sitz [zɪts] (-es, -e) m seat; **der Anzug hat einen guten ~** the suit is a good fit; **s~en** (unreg) vi to sit; (Bemerkung, Schlag) to strike home, to tell; (Gelerntes) to have sunk in; **s~en bleiben** to remain seated; **s~enbleiben** (unreg) vi (SCH) to have to repeat a year; **auf etw** dat **s~enbleiben** to be lumbered with sth; **s~end** adj (Tätigkeit) sedentary; **s~enlassen** (unreg) vt (SCH) to make (sb) repeat a year, (Mädchen) to jilt; (Wartenden) to stand up; **etw auf sich** dat **s~enlassen** to take sth lying down; **~gelegenheit** f place to sit down; **~platz** m seat; **~streik** m sit-down strike; **~ung** f meeting

Sizilien [zi'tsi:liən] nt Sicily

Skala ['ska:la] (-, Skalen) f scale

Skalpell [skal'pɛl] (-s, -e) nt scalpel

Skandal [skan'da:l] (-s, -e) m scandal; **s~ös** [skanda'lø:s] adj scandalous

Skandinav- [skandi'na:v] zW: **~ien** [-iən] nt Scandinavia; **~ier(in)** m(f) Scandinavian; **s~isch** adj Scandinavian

Skelett [ske'lɛt] (-(e)s, -e) nt skeleton

Skepsis ['skɛpsɪs] (-) f scepticism

skeptisch ['skɛptɪʃ] adj sceptical

Ski [ʃi:] (-s, -er) m ski; **~ laufen** od **fahren** to ski; **~fahrer** m skier; **~läufer** m skier; **~lehrer** m ski instructor; **~lift** m ski-lift; **~springen** nt ski-jumping; **~stock** m ski-pole

Skizze ['skɪtsə] f sketch

skizzieren [skɪ'tsi:rən] vt, vi to sketch

Sklave ['skla:və] (-n, -n) m slave; **~'rei** f slavery; **Sklavin** f slave

Skonto ['skɔnto] (-s, -s) m od nt discount

Skorpion [skɔrpi'o:n] (-s, -e) m scorpion; (ASTROL) Scorpio

Skrupel ['skru:pəl] (-s, -) m scruple; **s~los** adj unscrupulous

Slalom ['sla:lɔm] (-s, -s) m slalom

Slip (-s, -s) m (under)pants

Smaragd [sma'rakt] (-(e)s, -e) m emerald

Smoking ['smo:kɪŋ] (-s, -s) m dinner jacket

SCHLÜSSELWORT

---

so [zo:] adv **1** (sosehr) so; **so groß/schön** etc so big/nice etc; **so groß/schön wie** ... as big/nice as ...; **das hat ihn so**

geärgert, daß ... that annoyed him so much that ...; **so einer wie ich** somebody like me; **na so was!** well, well! **2** (*auf diese Weise*) like this; **mach es nicht so** don't do it like that; **so oder so** in one way or the other; **und so weiter** and so on; ... **oder so was** ... or something like that; **das ist gut so** that's fine **3** (*umg: umsonst*): **ich habe es so bekommen** I got it for nothing ♦ konj: **so daß** so that; **so wie es jetzt ist** as things are at the moment ♦ excl: **so?** really?; **so, das wär's** so, that's it then

s.o. *abk* = **siehe oben**
sobald [zo'balt] *konj* as soon as
Socke ['zɔkə] *f* sock
Sockel ['zɔkəl] (**-s, -**) *m* pedestal, base
Sodawasser ['zoːdavasər] *nt* soda water
Sodbrennen ['zoːtbrɛnən] (**-s, -**) *nt* heartburn
soeben [zoˈeːbən] *adv* just (now)
Sofa ['zoːfa] (**-s, -s**) *nt* sofa
sofern [zoˈfɛrn] *konj* if, provided (that)
sofort [zoˈfɔrt] *adv* immediately, at once; **~ig** *adj* immediate
Software ['sɔftwɛər] *f* software
so- *zW*: **~gar** [zoˈgaːr] *adv* even; **~genannt** [ˈzoːgənant] *adj* so-called; **~gleich** [zoˈglaɪç] *adv* straight away, at once
Sohle ['zoːlə] *f* sole; (*Tal~ etc*) bottom; (*MIN*) level
Sohn [zoːn] (**-(e)s, ̈e**) *m* son
solang(e) [zoˈlaŋ(ə)] *konj* as *od* so long as
solch [zɔlç] *pron* such; **ein ~e(r, s)** ... such a ...
Sold [zɔlt] (**-(e)s, -e**) *m* pay
Soldat [zɔlˈdaːt] (**-en, -en**) *m* soldier
Söldner ['zœldnər] (**-s, -**) *m* mercenary
solidarisch [zoliˈdaːrɪʃ] *adj* in *od* with solidarity; **sich ~ erklären** to declare one's solidarity
solid(e) [zoˈliːd(ə)] *adj* solid; (*Leben, Person*) respectable
Solist(in) [zoˈlɪst(ɪn)] *m(f)* soloist
Soll [zɔl] (**-(s), -(s)**) *nt* (*FIN*) debit (side); (*Arbeitsmenge*) quota, target

sollen ['zɔlən] (*pt* **sollte**, *pp* **gesollt** *od* (*als Hilfsverb*) **sollen**) *Hilfsverb* **1** (*Pflicht, Befehl*) to be supposed to; **du hättest nicht gehen sollen** you shouldn't have gone, you oughtn't to have gone; **soll ich?** shall I?; **soll ich dir helfen?** shall I help you?; **sag ihm, er soll warten** tell him he's to wait; **was soll ich machen?** what should I do?
2 (*Vermutung*): **sie soll verheiratet sein** she's said to be married; **was soll das heißen?** what's that supposed to mean?; **man sollte glauben, daß** ... you would think that ...; **sollte das passieren, ...** if that should happen ...
♦ vt, vi: **was soll das?** what's all this?; **das sollst du nicht** you shouldn't do that; **was soll's?** what the hell!

Solo ['zoːlo] (**-s, -s** *od* **Soli**) *nt* solo
somit [zoˈmɪt] *konj* and so, therefore
Sommer ['zɔmər] (**-s, -**) *m* summer; **s~lich** *adj* summery; summer; **~schlußverkauf** *m* summer sale; **~sprossen** *pl* freckles
Sonate [zoˈnaːtə] *f* sonata
Sonde ['zɔndə] *f* probe
Sonder- ['zɔndər] *in zW* special; **~angebot** *nt* special offer; **s~bar** *adj* strange, odd; **~fahrt** *f* special trip; **~fall** *m* special case; **s~gleichen** *adj inv* without parallel, unparalleled; **s~lich** *adj* particular; (*außergewöhnlich*) remarkable; (*eigenartig*) peculiar; **s~n** *konj* but ♦ vt to separate; **nicht nur ..., s~n auch** not only ..., but also; **~preis** *m* special price; **~zug** *m* special train
Sonett [zoˈnɛt] (**-(e)s, -e**) *nt* sonnet
Sonnabend ['zɔnˈaːbənt] *m* Saturday
Sonne ['zɔnə] *f* sun; **s~n** *vr* to sun o.s.
Sonnen- *zW*: **~aufgang** *m* sunrise; **s~baden** *vi* to sunbathe; **~brand** *m* sunburn; **~brille** *f* sunglasses *pl*; **~creme** *f* suntan lotion; **~energie** *f* solar energy; **~finsternis** *f* solar eclipse; **~schein** *m* sunshine; **~schirm** *m* parasol, sunshade; **~stich** *m* sun-

stroke; ~**uhr** f sundial; ~**untergang** m
sunset; ~**wende** f solstice
sonnig ['zɔnɪç] adj sunny
Sonntag ['zɔntaːk] m Sunday; **s~s** adv
(on) Sundays
sonst [zɔnst] adv otherwise; (mit pron,
in Fragen) else; (zu anderer Zeit) at
other times, normally ♦ konj otherwise;
~ **noch etwas?** anything else?; ~ **nichts**
nothing else; ~**ig** adj other; ~**jemand**
pron anybody (at all); ~**wo** adv somewhere else; ~**woher** adv from somewhere else; ~**wohin** adv somewhere
else
sooft [zo''ɔft] konj whenever
Sopran [zo'praːn] (-s, -e) m soprano
Sorge ['zɔrgə] f care, worry
sorgen vi: **für jdn** ~ to look after sb ♦
vr: **sich** ~ **(um)** to worry (about); **für**
etw ~ to take care of or see to sth;
~**frei** adj carefree; **S~kind** nt problem
child; ~**voll** adj troubled, worried
Sorgerecht nt custody (of a child)
Sorg- [zɔrk] zW: ~**falt** (-) f
care(fulness); **s~fältig** adj careful;
s~los adj careless; (ohne Sorgen) carefree; **s~sam** adj careful
Sorte ['zɔrtə] f sort; (Waren~) brand;
~**n** pl (FIN) foreign currency sg
sortieren [zɔr'tiːrən] vt to sort (out)
Sortiment [zɔrti'mɛnt] nt assortment
sosehr [zo'zeːr] konj as much as
Soße ['zoːsə] f sauce; (Braten~) gravy
Souffleur [zu'fløːr] m prompter
Souffleuse [zu'fløːzə] f prompter
soufflieren [zu'fliːrən] vt, vi to prompt
souverän [zuvə'rɛːn] adj sovereign;
(überlegen) superior
so- zW: ~**viel** [zo'fiːl] konj: ~**viel ich**
weiß as far as I know ♦ pron: ~**viel**
(wie) as much as; **rede nicht** ~**viel**
don't talk so much; ~**weit** [zo'vaɪt] konj
as far as ♦ adj: ~**weit sein** to be ready;
~**weit wie** od **als möglich** as far as
possible; **ich bin** ~**weit zufrieden** by
and large I'm quite satisfied; ~**wenig**
[zo've:nɪç] konj little as ♦ pron: ~**wenig**
(wie) as little (as); ~**wie** [zo'viː] konj
(sobald) as soon as; (ebenso) as well
as; ~**wieso** [zovi'zoː] adv anyway

sowjetisch [zɔ'vjɛtɪʃ] adj Soviet
Sowjetunion f Soviet Union
sowohl [zo'voːl] konj: ~ ... **als** od **wie**
auch both ... and
sozial [zotsi'aːl] adj social; **S~abgaben**
pl national insurance contributions;
S~demokrat m social democrat;
~**demokratisch** adj social democratic;
~**i'sieren** vt to socialize; **S~ismus**
[-'lɪsmʊs] m socialism; **S~ist** [-'lɪst] m
socialist; ~**istisch** adj socialist;
S~politik f social welfare policy;
S~produkt nt (net) national product;
S~staat m welfare state
Sozio- [zotsio] zW: ~**loge** [-'loːgə] (-n,
-n) m sociologist; ~**logie** [-lo'giː] f sociology; **s~logisch** [-'loːgɪʃ] adj sociological
sozusagen [zotsu'zaːgən] adv so to
speak
Spachtel ['ʃpaxtəl] (-s, -) m spatula
spähen ['ʃpɛːən] vi to peep, to peek
Spalier [ʃpa'liːr] (-s, -e) nt (Gerüst)
trellis; (Leute) guard of honour
Spalt [ʃpalt] (-(e)s, -e) m crack; (Tür~)
chink; (fig: Kluft) split; ~**e** f crack,
fissure; (Gletscherspalte) crevasse; (in
Text) column; **s~en** vt, vr (auch fig) to
split; ~**ung** f splitting
Span [ʃpaːn] (-(e)s, ²e) m shaving
Spanferkel nt sucking-pig
Spange ['ʃpaŋə] f clasp; (Haar~) hair
slide; (Schnalle) buckle; (Armreif)
bangle
Spanien ['ʃpaːniən] nt Spain
Spanier(in) m(f) Spaniard
spanisch adj Spanish
Spann- ['ʃpan] zW: ~**beton** m pre-
stressed concrete; ~**e** f (Zeitspanne)
space; (Differenz) gap; **s~en** vt
(straffen) to tighten, to tauten; (befestigen) to brace ♦ vi to be tight; **s~end**
adj exciting, gripping; ~**ung** f tension;
(ELEK) voltage; (fig) suspense; (unangenehm) tension
Spar- ['ʃpaːr] zW: ~**buch** nt savings
book; ~**büchse** f moneybox; **s~en** vt,
vi to save; **sich** dat **etw s~en** to save
o.s. sth; (Bemerkung) to keep sth to
o.s.; **mit etw s~en** to be sparing with
sth; **an etw** dat **s~en** to economize on

sth; ~**er** (-s, -) *m* saver

Spargel ['ʃpargəl] (-s, -) *m* asparagus

Sparkasse *f* savings bank

Sparkonto *nt* savings account

spärlich ['ʃpɛːrlɪç] *adj* meagre; (*Bekleidung*) scanty

Spar- *zW:* ~**maßnahme** *f* economy measure, cut; s~**sam** *adj* economical, thrifty; ~**samkeit** *f* thrift, economizing; ~**schwein** *nt* piggy bank

Sparte ['ʃpartə] *f* field; line of business; (*PRESSE*) column

Spaß [ʃpaːs] (-es, ⁻e) *m* joke; (*Freude*) fun; **jdm** ~ **machen** to be fun (for sb); **viel** ~! have fun!; s~**en** *vi* to joke; **mit ihm ist nicht zu** s~**en** you can't take liberties with him; s~**haft** *adj* funny, droll; s~**ig** *adj* funny, droll; ~**verderber** (-s, -) *m* spoilsport

spät [ʃpɛːt] *adj, adv* late; **wie** ~ **ist es?** what's the time?

Spaten ['ʃpaːtən] (-s, -) *m* spade

später *adj, adv* later

spätestens *adv* at the latest

Spatz [ʃpats] (-en, -en) *m* sparrow

spazier- [ʃpa'tsiːr] *zW:* ~**en** *vi* to stroll, to walk; ~**enfahren** (*unreg*) *vi* to go for a drive; ~**engehen** (*unreg*) *vi* to go for a walk; **S**~**gang** *m* walk; **S**~**stock** *m* walking stick; **S**~**weg** *m* path, walk

SPD [ʃpeː'deː] (-) *f abk* (= *Sozialdemokratische Partei Deutschlands*) Social Democratic Party

Specht [ʃpɛçt] (-(e)s, -e) *m* woodpecker

Speck [ʃpɛk] (-(e)s, -e) *m* bacon

Spediteur [ʃpedi'tøːr] *m* carrier; (*Möbel~*) furniture remover

Spedition [ʃpeditsi'oːn] *f* carriage; (*Speditionsfirma*) road haulage contractor; removal firm

Speer [ʃpeːr] (-(e)s, -e) *m* spear; (*SPORT*) javelin

Speiche ['ʃpaɪçə] *f* spoke

Speichel ['ʃpaɪçəl] (-s) *m* saliva, spit(tle)

Speicher ['ʃpaɪçər] (-s, -) *m* storehouse; (*Dach~*) attic, loft; (*Korn~*) granary; (*Wasser~*) tank; (*TECH*) store; (*COMPUT*) memory; s~**n** *vt* to store; (*COMPUT*) to save

speien ['ʃpaɪən] (*unreg*) *vt, vi* to spit; (*erbrechen*) to vomit; (*Vulkan*) to spew

Speise ['ʃpaɪzə] *f* food; ~**eis** [-'aɪs] *nt* ice-cream; ~**kammer** *f* larder, pantry; ~**karte** *f* menu; s~**n** *vt* to feed; to eat ♦ *vi* to dine; ~**röhre** *f* gullet, oesophagus; ~**saal** *m* dining room; ~**wagen** *m* dining car

Speku- [ʃpeku] *zW:* ~**lant** [-'lant] *m* speculator; ~**lation** [-latsi'oːn] *f* speculation; s~**lieren** [-'liːrən] *vi* (*fig*) to speculate; **auf etw** *akk* s~**lieren** to have hopes of sth

Spelunke [ʃpe'lʊŋkə] *f* dive

Spende ['ʃpɛndə] *f* donation; s~**n** *vt* to donate, to give; ~**r** (-s, -) *m* donor, donator

spendieren [ʃpɛn'diːrən] *vt* to pay for, to buy; **jdm etw** ~ to treat sb to sth, to stand sb sth

Sperling ['ʃpɛrlɪŋ] *m* sparrow

Sperma ['ʃpɛrma] (-s, **Spermen**) *nt* sperm

Sperr- ['ʃpɛr] *zW:* ~**e** *f* barrier; (*Verbot*) ban; s~**en** *vt* to block; (*SPORT*) to suspend, to bar; (*vom Ball*) to obstruct; (*einschließen*) to lock; (*verbieten*) to ban ♦ *vr* to baulk, to jib(e); ~**gebiet** *nt* prohibited area; ~**holz** *nt* plywood; s~**ig** *adj* bulky; ~**sitz** *m* (*THEAT*) stalls *pl*; ~**stunde** *f* closing time

Spesen ['ʃpeːzən] *pl* expenses; ~**abrechnung** *f* expense account

Spezial- [ʃpetsi'aːl] *in zW* special; s~**angefertigt** *adj* custom-built; (*Kleidung*) tailor-made; s~**i'sieren** *vr* to specialize; ~**i'sierung** *f* specialization; ~**ist** [-'lɪst] *m* specialist; ~**i'tät** *f* speciality

speziell [ʃpetsi'ɛl] *adj* special

spezifisch [ʃpe'tsiːfɪʃ] *adj* specific

Sphäre ['sfɛːrə] *f* sphere

Spiegel ['ʃpiːgəl] (-s, -) *m* mirror; (*Wasser~*) level; (*MIL*) tab; ~**bild** *nt* reflection; s~**bildlich** *adj* reversed; ~**ei** ['aɪ] *nt* fried egg; s~**n** *vt* to mirror, to reflect ♦ *vr* to be reflected ♦ *vi* to gleam; (*widerspiegeln*) to be reflective; ~**schrift** *f* mirror-writing; ~**ung** *f* re-

flection
Spiel [ʃpiːl] (-(e)s, -e) nt game;
(*Schau~*) play; (*Tätigkeit*) play(ing);
(*KARTEN*) deck; (*TECH*) (free) play;
s~en vt, vi to play; (*um Geld*) to
gamble; (*THEAT*) to perform, to act;
s~end adv easily; **~er** (-s, -) m player; (*um Geld*) gambler; **~e'rei** f trifling
pastime; **~feld** nt pitch, field; **~film** m
feature film; **~plan** m (*THEAT*) programme; **~platz** m playground;
~raum m room to manoeuvre, scope;
~regel f rule; **~sachen** pl toys; **~ver-
derber** (-s, -) m spoilsport; **~waren** pl
toys; **~zeug** nt toy(s)
Spieß [ʃpiːs] (-es, -e) m spear; (*Brat~*)
spit; **~bürger** m bourgeois; **~er** (-s, -;
umg) m bourgeois; **~rutenlaufen** nt
running the gauntlet
Spikes [spaɪks] pl spikes; (*AUT*) studs
Spinat [ʃpiˈnaːt] (-(e)s, -e) m spinach
Spind [ʃpɪnt] (-(e)s, -e) m od nt locker
Spinn- [ˈʃpɪn] zW: **~e** f spider; **s~en**
(*unreg*) vt, vi to spin; (*umg*) to talk
rubbish; (*verrückt sein*) to be crazy od
mad; **~e'rei** f spinning mill; **~rad** nt
spinning-wheel; **~webe** f cobweb
Spion [ʃpiˈoːn] (-s, -e) m spy; (*in Tür*)
spyhole; **~age** [ʃpioˈnaːʒə] f espionage;
s~ieren [ʃpioˈniːrən] vi to spy
Spirale [ʃpiˈraːlə] f spiral
Spirituosen [ʃpirituˈoːzən] pl spirits
Spiritus [ˈʃpiːritus] (-, -se) m
(methylated) spirit
Spital [ʃpiˈtaːl] (-s, ⸚er) nt hospital
spitz [ʃpɪts] adj pointed; (*Winkel*)
acute; (*fig: Zunge*) sharp; (: *Bemerkung*) caustic; **S~bogen** m pointed
arch; **S~bube** m rogue
Spitze f point, tip; (*Berg~*) peak;
(*Bemerkung*) taunt, dig; (*erster Platz*)
lead, top; (*meist pl: Gewebe*) lace
Spitzel (-s, -) m police informer
spitzen vt to sharpen
Spitzen- zW: **~leistung** f top
performance; **~lohn** m top wages pl;
~marke f brand leader; **~sportler** m
top-class sportsman
spitzfindig adj (over)subtle
Spitzname m nickname

Splitter [ˈʃplɪtər] (-s, -) m splinter;
s~nackt adj stark naked
sponsern [ˈspɔnzərn, ˈʃpɔnzərn] vt to
sponsor
spontan [ʃpɔnˈtaːn] adj spontaneous
Sport [ʃpɔrt] (-(e)s, -e) m sport; (*fig*)
hobby; **~lehrer(in)** m(f) games od P.E.
teacher; **~ler(in)** (-s, -) m(f)
sportsman(woman); **s~lich** adj sporting; (*Mensch*) sporty; **~platz** m playing od sports field; **~verein** m sports
club; **~wagen** m sports car
Spott [ʃpɔt] (-(e)s) m mockery,
ridicule; **s~billig** adj dirt-cheap; **s~en**
vi to mock; **s~en** (*über +akk*) to mock
(at), to ridicule
spöttisch [ˈʃpœtɪʃ] adj mocking
sprach etc [ʃpraːx] vb siehe **sprechen**
Sprach- zW: **s~begabt** adj good at
languages; **~e** f language; **~fehler** m
speech defect; **~führer** m phrasebook;
~gefühl nt feeling for language;
~labor nt language laboratory; **s~lich**
adj linguistic; **s~los** adj speechless
sprang etc [ʃpraŋ] vb siehe **springen**
Spray [spreː] (-s, -s) m od nt spray
Sprech- [ˈʃprɛç] zW: **~anlage** f intercom; **s~en** (*unreg*) vi to speak, to talk
♦ vt to say; (*Sprache*) to speak;
(*Person*) to speak to; **mit jdm s~en** to
speak to sb; **das spricht für ihn** that's a
point in his favour; **~er(in)** (-s, -) m(f)
speaker; (*für Gruppe*) spokes-
man(woman); (*RADIO, TV*) announcer;
~stunde f consultation (hour); (*doctor's*) surgery; **~stundenhilfe** f
(doctor's) receptionist; **~zimmer** nt
consulting room, surgery, office (*US*)
Spreng- [ˈʃprɛŋ] zW: **~arbeiten** pl
blasting operations; **s~en** vt to
sprinkle; (*mit Sprengstoff*) to blow up;
(*Gestein*) to blast; (*Versammlung*) to
break up; **~kopf** m warhead; **~ladung**
f explosive charge; **~stoff** m
explosive(s)
Spreu [ʃprɔy] (-) f chaff
sprichst etc [ʃprɪçst] vb siehe **sprechen**
Sprichwort nt proverb
sprichwörtlich adj proverbial
Spring- [ˈʃprɪŋ] zW: **~brunnen** m

fountain; **s~en** (*unreg*) *vi* to jump; (*Glas*) to crack; (*mit Kopfsprung*) to dive; **~er** (-s, -) *m* jumper; (*Schach*) knight

Spritz- ['ʃprɪts] *zW:* **~e** *f* syringe; injection; (*an Schlauch*) nozzle; **s~en** *vt* to spray; (*MED*) to inject ♦ *vi* to splash; (*heraus~*) to spurt; (*MED*) to give injections; **~pistole** *f* spray gun

spröde ['ʃprø:də] *adj* brittle; (*Person*) reserved, coy

Sprosse ['ʃprɔsə] *f* rung

Spruch [ʃprʊx] (-(e)s, ⸗e) *m* saying, maxim; (*JUR*) judgement

Sprudel ['ʃpru:dəl] (-s, -) *m* mineral water; lemonade; **s~n** *vi* to bubble

Sprüh- ['ʃpry:] *zW:* **~dose** *f* aerosol (can); · **s~en** *vi* to spray; (*fig*) to sparkle ♦ *vt* to spray; **~regen** *m* drizzle

Sprung [ʃprʊŋ] (-(e)s, ⸗e) *m* jump; (*Riß*) crack; **~brett** *nt* springboard; **s~haft** *adj* erratic; (*Aufstieg*) rapid; **~schanze** *f* skijump

Spucke ['ʃpʊkə] (-) *f* spit; **s~n** *vt*, *vi* to spit

Spuk [ʃpu:k] (-(e)s, -e) *m* haunting; (*fig*) nightmare; **s~en** *vi* (*Geist*) to walk; **hier spukt es** this place is haunted

Spule ['ʃpu:lə] *f* spool; (*ELEK*) coil

Spül- ['ʃpy:l] *zW:* **~e** *f* (kitchen) sink; **s~en** *vt*, *vi* to rinse; (*Geschirr*) to wash up; (*Toilette*) to flush; **~maschine** *f* dishwasher; **~mittel** *nt* washing-up liquid; **~stein** *m* sink; **~ung** *f* rinsing; flush; (*MED*) irrigation

Spur [ʃpu:r] (-, -en) *f* trace; (*Fuß~, Rad~, Tonband~*) track; (*Fährte*) trail; (*Fahr~*) lane

spürbar *adj* noticeable, perceptible

spüren ['ʃpy:rən] *vt* to feel

spurlos *adv* without (a) trace

Spurt [ʃpʊrt] (-(e)s, -s *od* -e) *m* spurt

sputen ['ʃpu:tən] *vr* to make haste

St. *abk* = **Stück**; (= *Sankt*) St.

Staat [ʃta:t] (-(e)s, -en) *m* state; (*Prunk*) show; (*Kleidung*) finery; **mit etw ~ machen** to show off *od* parade sth; **s~enlos** *adj* stateless; **s~lich** *adj*

state(-); state-run

Staats- *zW:* **~angehörigkeit** *f* nationality; **~anwalt** *m* public prosecutor; **~bürger** *m* citizen; **~dienst** *m* civil service; **s~feindlich** *adj* subversive; **~mann** (*pl* -männer) *m* statesman; **~sekretär** *m* secretary of state

Stab [ʃta:p] (-(e)s, ⸗e) *m* rod; (*Gitter~*) bar; (*Menschen*) staff; **~hochsprung** *m* pole vault

stabil [ʃta'bi:l] *adj* stable; (*Möbel*) sturdy; **~isieren** *vt* to stabilize

Stachel ['ʃtaxəl] (-s, -n) *m* spike; (*von Tier*) spine; (*von Insekten*) sting; **~beere** *f* gooseberry; **~draht** *m* barbed wire; **s~ig** *adj* prickly; **~schwein** *nt* porcupine

Stadion ['ʃta:diɔn] (-s, Stadien) *nt* stadium

Stadium ['ʃta:diʊm] *nt* stage, phase

Stadt [ʃtat] (-, ⸗e) *f* town

Städt- ['ʃtɛ:t] *zW:* **~chen** *nt* small town; **~ebau** *m* town planning; **~er(in)** (-s, -) *m(f)* town dweller; **s~isch** *adj* municipal; (*nicht ländlich*) urban

Stadt- *zW:* **~mauer** *f* city wall(s); **~mitte** *f* town centre; **~plan** *m* street map; **~rand** *m* outskirts *pl*; **~rundfahrt** *f* tour of a/the city; **~teil** *m* district, part of town; **~zentrum** *nt* town centre

Staffel ['ʃtafəl] (-, -n) *f* rung; (*SPORT*) relay (team); (*AVIAT*) squadron; **s~n** *vt* to graduate

Stahl [ʃta:l] (-(e)s, ⸗e) *m* steel

stahl *etc vb siehe* **stehlen**

stak *etc* [ʃta:k] *vb siehe* **stecken**

Stall [ʃtal] (-(e)s, ⸗e) *m* stable; (*Kaninchen~*) hutch; (*Schweine~*) sty; (*Hühner~*) henhouse

Stamm [ʃtam] (-(e)s, ⸗e) *m* (*Baum~*) trunk; (*Menschen~*) tribe; (*GRAM*) stem; **~baum** *m* family tree; (*von Tier*) pedigree; **s~eln** *vt*, *vi* to stammer; **s~en** *vi:* **s~en von** *od* **aus** to come from; **~gast** *m* regular (customer)

stämmig ['ʃtɛmɪç] *adj* sturdy; (*Mensch*) stocky

Stammtisch ['ʃtamtɪʃ] m table for the regulars

stampfen ['ʃtampfən] vt, vi to stamp; (stapfen) to tramp; (mit Werkzeug) to pound

Stand [ʃtant] (-(e)s, ⁼e) m position; (Wasser~, Benzin~ etc) level; (Stehen) standing position; (Zu~) state; (Spiel~) score; (Messe~ etc) stand; (Klasse) class; (Beruf) profession

stand etc vb siehe **stehen**

Standard ['ʃtandart] (-s, -s) m standard

Ständer ['ʃtɛndər] (-s, -) m stand

Standes- ['ʃtandəs] zW: **~amt** nt registry office; **~beamte(r)** m registrar; **s~gemäß** adj, adv according to one's social position; **~unterschied** m social difference

Stand- zW: **s~haft** adj steadfast; **~haftigkeit** f steadfastness; **s~halten** (unreg) vi: (jdm/etw) s~halten to stand firm (against sb/sth), to resist (sb/sth)

ständig ['ʃtɛndɪç] adj permanent; (ununterbrochen) constant, continual

Stand- zW: **~licht** nt sidelights pl, parking lights pl (US); **~ort** m location; (MIL) garrison; **~punkt** m standpoint

Stange ['ʃtaŋə] f stick; (Stab) pole, bar; rod; (Zigaretten) carton; **von der ~** (COMM) off the peg; **eine ~ Geld** (umg) quite a packet

Stanniol [ʃtani'o:l] (-s, -e) nt tinfoil

Stapel ['ʃta:pəl] (-s, -) m pile; (NAUT) stocks pl; **~lauf** m launch; **s~n** vt to pile (up)

Star¹ [ʃtaːr] (-(e)s, -e) m starling; (MED) cataract

Star² (-s, -s) m (Film~ etc) star

starb etc [ʃtarp] vb siehe **sterben**

stark [ʃtark] adj strong; (heftig, groß) heavy; (Maßangabe) thick

Stärke ['ʃtɛrkə] f strength; heaviness; thickness; (KOCH, Wäsche~) starch; **s~n** vt to strengthen; (Wäsche) to starch

Starkstrom m heavy current

Stärkung ['ʃtɛrkʊŋ] f strengthening; (Essen) refreshment

starr [ʃtar] adj stiff; (unnachgiebig) rigid; (Blick) staring; **~en** vi to stare;

~en vor od **von** to be covered in; (Waffen) to be bristling with; **S~heit** f rigidity; **~köpfig** adj stubborn; **S~sinn** m obstinacy

Start [ʃtart] (-(e)s, -e) m start; (AVIAT) takeoff; **~automatik** f (AUT) automatic choke; **~bahn** f runway; **s~en** vt to start ♦ vi to start; to take off; **~er** (-s, -) m starter; **~erlaubnis** f takeoff clearance

Station [ʃtatsi'oːn] f station; hospital ward; **s~ieren** [-'niːrən] vt to station

Statist [ʃta'tɪst] m extra, supernumerary

Statistik f statistics sg; **~er** (-s, -) m statistician

statistisch adj statistical

Stativ [ʃta'tiːf] (-s, -e) nt tripod

statt [ʃtat] konj instead of ♦ präp (+gen od dat) instead of

Stätte ['ʃtɛtə] f place

statt- zW: **~finden** (unreg) vi to take place; **~haft** adj admissible; **~lich** adj imposing, handsome

Statue ['ʃtaːtuə] f statue

Status ['ʃtaːtʊs] (-, -) m status; **~symbol** nt status symbol

Statuten [ʃta'tuːtən] pl rules

Stau [ʃtaʊ] (-(e)s, -e) m blockage; (Verkehrs~) (traffic) jam

Staub [ʃtaʊp] (-(e)s, -e) m dust; **s~en** ['ʃtaʊbən] vi to be dusty; **s~ig** adj dusty; **~sauger** m vacuum cleaner; **~tuch** nt duster

Staudamm m dam

Staude ['ʃtaʊdə] f shrub

stauen ['ʃtaʊən] vt (Wasser) to dam up; (Blut) to stop the flow of ♦ vr (Wasser) to become dammed up; (MED, Verkehr) to become congested; (Menschen) to collect; (Gefühle) to build up

staunen ['ʃtaʊnən] vi to be astonished; **S~** (-s) nt amazement

Stauung ['ʃtaʊʊŋ] f (von Wasser) damming-up; (von Blut, Verkehr) congestion

Std. abk (= Stunde) hr.

Steak [steːk] nt steak

Stech- ['ʃtɛç] zW: **s~en** (unreg) vt (mit Nadel etc) to prick; (mit Messer) to stab; (mit Finger) to poke; (Biene etc) to sting; (Mücke) to bite; (Sonne) to burn; (KARTEN) to take; (ART) to engrave; (Torf, Spargel) to cut; **in See s~en** to put to sea; **~en** (-s, -) nt (SPORT) play-off; jump-off; **s~end** adj piercing, stabbing; (Geruch) pungent; **~palme** f holly; **~uhr** f time clock

Steck- ['ʃtɛk] zW: **~brief** m "wanted" poster; **~dose** f (wall) socket; **s~en** vt to put, to insert; (Nadel) to stick; (Pflanzen) to plant; (beim Nähen) to pin ♦ vi (auch unreg) to be; (festsitzen) to be stuck; (Nadeln) to stick; **s~enbleiben** (unreg) vi to get stuck; **s~enlassen** (unreg) vt to leave in; **~enpferd** nt hobby-horse; **~er** (-s, -) m plug; **~nadel** f pin; **~rübe** f turnip

Steg [ʃteːk] (-(e)s, -e) m small bridge; (Anlege~) landing stage; **~reif** m: **aus dem ~reif** just like that

stehen ['ʃteːən] (unreg) vi to stand; (sich befinden) to be; (in Zeitung) to say; (still~) to have stopped ♦ vi unpers: **es steht schlecht um jdn/etw** things are bad for sb/sth; **zu jdm/etw ~** to stand by sb/sth; **jdm ~** to suit sb; **wie steht's?** how are things?; (SPORT) what's the score?; **~ bleiben** to remain standing; **~bleiben** (unreg) vi (Uhr) to stop; (Fehler) to stay as it is; **~lassen** (unreg) vt to leave; (Bart) to grow

Stehlampe ['ʃteːlampə] f standard lamp

stehlen ['ʃteːlən] (unreg) vt to steal

Stehplatz ['ʃteːplats] m standing place

steif [ʃtaɪf] adj stiff; **S~heit** f stiffness

Steig- ['ʃtaɪk] zW: **~bügel** m stirrup; **~eisen** nt crampon; **s~en** (unreg) vi to rise; (klettern) to climb; **s~en in** +akk/**auf** +akk to get in/on; **s~ern** vt to raise; (GRAM) to compare ♦ vi (Auktion) to bid ♦ vr to increase; **~erung** f raising; (GRAM) comparison; **~ung** f incline, gradient, rise

steil [ʃtaɪl] adj steep

Stein [ʃtaɪn] (-(e)s, -e) m stone; (in Uhr) jewel; **~bock** m (ASTROL) Capricorn; **~bruch** m quarry; **~butt** (-s, -e) m turbot; **s~ern** adj (made of) stone; (fig) stony; **~gut** nt stoneware;

s~hart adj hard as stone; **s~ig** adj stony; **s~igen** vt to stone; **~kohle** f mineral coal

Stelle ['ʃtɛlə] f place; (Arbeit) post, job; (Amt) office; **an Ihrer/meiner ~** in your/my place

stellen vt to put; (Uhr etc) to set, (zur Verfügung ~) to supply; (fassen: Dieb) to apprehend ♦ vr (sich aufstellen) to stand; (sich einfinden) to present o.s.; (bei Polizei) to give o.s. up; (vorgeben) to pretend (to be); **sich zu etw ~** to have an opinion of sth

Stellen- zW: **~angebot** nt offer of a post; (in Zeitung) "vacancies"; **~gesuch** nt application for a post; **~vermittlung** f employment agency

Stell- zW: **~ung** f position; (MIL) line; **~ung nehmen zu** to comment on; **~ungnahme** f comment; **s~vertretend** adj deputy, acting; **s~vertreter** m deputy; **~werk** nt (EISENB) signal box

Stelze ['ʃtɛltsə] f stilt

Stemmbogen m (SKI) stem turn

stemmen ['ʃtɛmən] vt to lift (up); (drücken) to press; **sich ~ gegen** (fig) to resist, to oppose

Stempel ['ʃtɛmpəl] (-s, -) m stamp; (BOT) pistil; **~kissen** nt inkpad; **s~n** vt to stamp; (Briefmarke) to cancel; **s~n gehen** (umg) to be od go on the dole

Stengel ['ʃtɛŋəl] (-s, -) m stalk

Steno- [ʃteno] zW: **~gramm** [-'gram] nt shorthand report; **~graphie** [-gra'fiː] f shorthand; **s~graphieren** [-gra'fiːrən] vt, vi to write (in) shorthand; **~typist(in)** [-ty'pɪst(ɪn)] m(f) shorthand typist

Stepp- ['ʃtɛp] zW: **~decke** f quilt; **~e** f prairie; steppe; **s~en** vt to stitch ♦ vi to tap-dance

Sterb- ['ʃtɛrb] zW: **Sterbefall** m death; **s~en** (unreg) vi to die; **s~lich** ['ʃtɛrplɪç] adj mortal; **~lichkeit** f mortality; **~lichkeitsziffer** f death rate

stereo- ['steːreo] in zW stereo(-); **S~anlage** f stereo (system); **~typ** [ʃteːreo'tyːp] adj stereotype

steril [ʃteˈriːl] adj sterile; **~i'sieren** vt to sterilize; **S~i'sierung** f sterilization

Stern [ʃtɛrn] (-(e)s, -e) m star; **~bild** nt

constellation; ~**schnuppe** f meteor, falling star; ~**stunde** f historic moment

stet [ʃteːt] adj steady; ~**ig** adj constant, continual; ~**s** adv continually, always

Steuer[1] [ˈʃtɔyər] (-s, -) nt (NAUT) helm; (~ruder) rudder; (AUT) steering wheel

Steuer[2] (-, -n) f tax

Stouor zW. erklärung f tax return; ~**freibetrag** m tax allowance; ~**klasse** f tax group; ~**knuppel** m control column; (AVIAT, COMPUT) joystick; ~**mann** (pl -**männer** od -**leute**) m helmsman; s~**n** vt, vi to steer; (Flugzeug) to pilot; (Entwicklung, Tonstärke) to control; ~**paradies** nt tax haven; ~**rad** nt steering wheel; ~**ung** f (auch AUT) steering; piloting; control; (Vorrichtung) controls pl; ~**vergünstigung** f tax relief; ~**zahler** (-s, -) m taxpayer

Steward [ˈstjuːart] (-s, -s) m steward; **Stewardeß** [ˈstjuːərdɛs] (-, -**essen**) f stewardess; air hostess

Stich [ʃtɪç] (-(e)s, -e) m (Insekten~) sting; (Messer~) stab; (beim Nähen) stitch; (Färbung) tinge; (KARTEN) trick; (ART) engraving; **jdn im ~ lassen** to leave sb in the lurch; s~**eln** vi (fig) to jibe; s~**haltig** adj sound, tenable; ~**probe** f spot check; ~**wahl** f final ballot; ~**wort** nt cue; (in Wörterbuch) headword; (für Vortrag) note

sticken [ˈʃtɪkən] vt, vi to embroider

Sticke'rei f embroidery

stickig adj stuffy, close

Stickstoff m nitrogen

Stief- [ˈʃtiːf] in zW step

Stiefel [ˈʃtiːfəl] (-s, -) m boot

Stief- zW: ~**kind** nt stepchild; (fig) Cinderella; ~**mutter** f stepmother; ~**mütterchen** nt pansy

Stiege [ˈʃtiːgə] f staircase

stiehlst etc [ʃtiːlst] vb siehe **stehlen**

Stiel [ʃtiːl] (-(e)s, -e) m handle; (BOT) stalk

Stier (-(e)s, -e) m bull; (ASTROL) Taurus

stier [ʃtiːr] adj staring, fixed; ~**en** vi to stare

Stift [ʃtɪft] (-(e)s, -e) m peg; (Nagel) tack; (Farb~) crayon; (Blei~) pencil ♦ nt (charitable) foundation; (ECCL) religious institution; s~**en** vt to found; (Unruhe) to cause; (spenden) to contribute; ~**er(in)** (-s, -) m(f) founder; ~**ung** f donation; (Organisation) foundation; ~**zahn** m post crown

Stil [ʃtiːl] (-(e)s, -e) m style

still [ʃtɪl] adj quiet; (unbewegt) still; (heimlich) secret; **S~er Ozean** Pacific; **S~e** f stillness, quietness; **in aller S~e** quietly; ~**en** vt to stop; (befriedigen) to satisfy; (Säugling) to breast-feed; ~**halten** (unreg) vi to keep still; ~**(l)egen** vt to close down; **S~(l)egung** f shut-down; ~**schweigen** (unreg) vi to be silent; **S~schweigen** nt silence; ~**schweigend** adj silent; (Einverständnis) tacit ♦ adv silently; tacitly; **S~stand** m standstill; ~**stehen** (unreg) vi to stand still

Stimm- [ˈʃtɪm] zW: ~**bänder** pl vocal chords; s~**berechtigt** adj entitled to vote; ~**e** f voice; (Wahlstimme) vote; s~**en** vt (MUS) to tune ♦ vi to be right; **das s~te ihn traurig** that made him feel sad; s~**en für/gegen** to vote for/against; s~**t so!** that's right; ~**enmehrheit** f majority (of votes); ~**enthaltung** f abstention; ~**gabel** f tuning fork; ~**recht** nt right to vote; ~**ung** f mood; atmosphere; s~**ungsvoll** adj enjoyable; full of atmosphere; ~**zettel** m ballot paper

stinken [ˈʃtɪŋkən] (unreg) vi to stink

Stipendium [ʃtiˈpɛndiʊm] nt grant

stirbst etc [ʃtɪrpst] vb siehe **sterben**

Stirn [ʃtɪrn] (-, -en) f forehead, brow; (Frechheit) impudence; ~**höhle** f sinus; ~**runzeln** (-s) nt frown(ing)

stöbern [ˈʃtøːbərn] vi to rummage

stochern [ˈʃtɔxərn] vi to poke (about)

Stock[1] [ʃtɔk] (-(e)s, ⁻e) m stick; (BOT) stock

Stock[2] (-(e)s, - od ~**werke**) m storey

stocken vi to stop, to pause; ~**d** adj halting

Stockung f stoppage

Stockwerk nt storey, floor

Stoff [ʃtɔf] (-(e)s, -e) m (Gewebe) material, cloth; (Materie) matter; (von

Buch etc) subject (matter); **s~lich** *adj* material; **~wechsel** *m* metabolism
stöhnen ['ʃtøːnən] *vi* to groan
stoisch ['ʃtoːɪʃ] *adj* stoical
Stollen ['ʃtɔlən] (-s, -) *m* (*MIN*) gallery; (*KOCH*) cake eaten at Christmas; (*von Schuhen*) stud
stolpern ['ʃtɔlpərn] *vi* to stumble, to trip
Stolz [ʃtɔlts] (-es) *m* pride; **s~** *adj* proud; **s~ieren** [ʃtɔl'tsiːrən] *vi* to strut
stopfen ['ʃtɔpfən] *vt* (*hinein~*) to stuff; (*voll~*) to fill (up); (*nähen*) to darn ♦ *vi* (*MED*) to cause constipation
Stopfgarn *nt* darning thread
Stoppel ['ʃtɔpəl] (-, -n) *f* stubble
Stopp- ['ʃtɔp] *zW*: **s~en** *vt* to stop; (*mit Uhr*) to time ♦ *vi* to stop; **~schild** *nt* stop sign; **~uhr** *f* stopwatch
Stöpsel ['ʃtœpsəl] (-s, -) *m* plug; (*für Flaschen*) stopper
Storch [ʃtɔrç] (-(e)s, ̈e) *m* stork
Stör- ['ʃtøːr] *zW*: **s~en** *vt* to disturb; (*behindern, RADIO*) to interfere with ♦ *vr*: **sich an etw** *dat* **s~en** to let sth bother one; **s~end** *adj* disturbing, annoying; **~enfried** (-(e)s, -e) *m* troublemaker
störrisch ['ʃtœrɪʃ] *adj* stubborn, perverse
Störsender *m* jammer
Störung *f* disturbance; interference
Stoß [ʃtoːs] (-es, ̈e) *m* (*Schub*) push; (*Schlag*) blow; knock; (*mit Schwert*) thrust; (*mit Fuß*) kick; (*Erd~*) shock; (*Haufen*) pile; **~dämpfer** (-s, -) *m* shock absorber; **s~en** (*unreg*) *vt* (*mit Druck*) to shove, to push; (*mit Schlag*) to knock, to bump; (*mit Fuß*) to kick; (*Schwert etc*) to thrust; (*anstoßen: Kopf etc*) to get a knock ♦ *vr* to get a knock ♦ *vi*: **s~en an** *od* **auf** +*akk* to bump into; (*finden*) to come across; (*angrenzen*) to be next to; **sich s~en an** +*dat* (*fig*) to take exception to; **~stange** *f* (*AUT*) bumper
stottern ['ʃtɔtərn] *vt, vi* to stutter
Str. *abk* (= *Straße*) St.
Straf- ['ʃtraːf] *zW*: **~anstalt** *f* penal institution; **~arbeit** *f* (*SCH*) punishment; lines *pl*; **s~bar** *adj* punishable; **~bar-**

keit *f* criminal nature; **~e** *f* punishment; (*JUR*) penalty; (*Gefängnisstrafe*) sentence; (*Geldstrafe*) fine; **s~en** *vt* to punish
straff [ʃtraf] *adj* tight; (*streng*) strict; (*Stil etc*) concise; (*Haltung*) erect; **~en** *vt* to tighten, to tauten
Strafgefangene(r) *mf* prisoner, convict
Strafgesetzbuch *nt* penal code
sträflich ['ʃtrɛːflɪç] *adj* criminal
Sträfling *m* convict
Straf- *zW*: **~porto** *nt* excess postage (charge); **~predigt** *f* telling-off; **~raum** *m* (*SPORT*) penalty area; **~recht** *nt* criminal law; **~stoß** *m* (*SPORT*) penalty (kick); **~tat** *f* punishable act; **~zettel** *m* ticket
Strahl [ʃtraːl] (-s, -en) *m* ray, beam; (*Wasser~*) jet; **s~en** *vi* to radiate; (*fig*) to beam; **~entherapie** *f* radiotherapy; **~ung** *f* radiation
Strähne ['ʃtrɛːnə] *f* strand
stramm [ʃtram] *adj* tight; (*Haltung*) erect; (*Mensch*) robust
strampeln ['ʃtrampəln] *vi* to kick (about), to fidget
Strand [ʃtrant] (-(e)s, ̈e) *m* shore; (*mit Sand*) beach; **~bad** *nt* open-air swimming pool, lido; **s~en** ['ʃtrandən] *vi* to run aground; (*fig: Mensch*) to fail; **~gut** *nt* flotsam; **~korb** *m* beach chair
Strang [ʃtran] (-(e)s, ̈e) *m* cord, rope; (*Bündel*) skein
Strapaz- *zW*: **~e** [ʃtra'paːtsə] *f* strain, exertion; **s~ieren** [ʃtrapa'tsiːrən] *vt* (*Material*) to treat roughly, to punish; (*Mensch, Kräfte*) to wear out, to exhaust; **s~ierfähig** *adj* hard-wearing; **s~iös** [ʃtrapatsi'øːs] *adj* exhausting, tough
Straße ['ʃtraːsə] *f* street, road
Straßen- *zW*: **~bahn** *f* tram, streetcar (*US*); **~beleuchtung** *f* street lighting; **~feger** (-s, -) *m* roadsweeper; **~kehrer** (-s, -) *m* roadsweeper; **~sperre** *f* roadblock; **~verkehrsordnung** *f* highway code
Strateg- [ʃtra'teːg] *zW*: **~e** (-n, -n) *m* strategist; **~ie** [ʃtrate'giː] *f* strategy;

s~isch adj strategic

sträuben ['ʃtrɔʏbən] vt to ruffle ♦ vr to bristle; (Mensch): **sich (gegen etw)** ~ to resist (sth)

Strauch [ʃtraʊx] (-(e)s, **Sträucher**) m bush, shrub

Strauß¹ [ʃtraʊs] (-es, **Sträuße**) m bunch; bouquet

Strauß² (-es, -e) m ostrich

Streb- ['ʃtreːb] zW: **s~en** vi to strive, to endeavour; **s~en nach** to strive for; ~**er** (-s, -; pej) m pusher, climber; (SCH) swot (BRIT); **s~sam** adj industrious

Strecke ['ʃtrɛkə] f stretch; (Entfernung) distance; (EISENB, MATH) line; **s~n** vt to stretch; (Waffen) to lay down; (KOCH) to eke out ♦ vr to stretch (o.s.)

Streich [ʃtraɪç] (-(e)s, -e) m trick, prank; (Hieb) blow; **s~eln** vt to stroke; **s~en** (unreg) vt (berühren) to stroke; (auftragen) to spread; (anmalen) to paint; (durchstreichen) to delete; (nicht genehmigen) to cancel ♦ vi (berühren) to brush; (schleichen) to prowl; ~**holz** nt match; ~**instrument** nt string instrument

Streif- ['ʃtraɪf] zW: ~**e** f patrol; **s~en** vt (leicht berühren) to brush against, to graze; (Blick) to skim over; (Thema, Problem) to touch on; (abstreifen) to take off ♦ vi (gehen) to roam; ~**en** (-s, -) m (Linie) stripe; (Stück) strip; (Film) film; ~**endienst** m patrol duty; ~**enwagen** m patrol car; ~**schuß** m graze, grazing shot; ~**zug** m scouting trip

Streik [ʃtraɪk] (-(e)s, -s) m strike; ~**brecher** (-s, -) m blackleg, strikebreaker; **s~en** vi to strike; ~**kasse** f strike fund; ~**posten** m (strike) picket

Streit [ʃtraɪt] (-(e)s, -e) m argument; dispute; **s~en** (unreg) vi, vr to argue; to dispute; ~**frage** f point at issue; **s~ig** adj: **jdm etw s~ig machen** to dispute sb's right to sth; ~**igkeiten** pl quarrel sg, dispute sg; ~**kräfte** pl (MIL) armed forces

streng [ʃtrɛŋ] adj severe; (Lehrer, Maßnahme) strict; (Geruch etc) sharp;

S~e (-) f severity; strictness; sharpness; ~**genommen** adv strictly speaking; ~**gläubig** adj orthodox, strict; ~**stens** adv strictly

Streu [ʃtrɔʏ] (-, -en) f litter, bed of straw; **s~en** vt to strew, to scatter, to spread; ~**ung** f dispersion

Strich [ʃtrɪç] (-(e)s, -e) m (Linie) line; (Feder~, Pinsel~) stroke; (von Geweben) nap; (von Fell) pile; **auf den** ~ **gehen** (umg) to walk the streets; **jdm gegen den** ~ **gehen** to rub sb up the wrong way; **einen** ~ **machen durch** to cross out; (fig) to foil; ~**mädchen** nt streetwalker; ~**punkt** m semicolon; **s~weise** adv here and there

Strick [ʃtrɪk] (-(e)s, -e) m rope; **s~en** vt, vi to knit; ~**jacke** f cardigan; ~**leiter** f rope ladder; ~**nadel** f knitting needle; ~**waren** pl knitwear sg

strikt ['ʃtrɪkt] adj strict

strittig ['ʃtrɪtɪç] adj disputed, in dispute

Stroh [ʃtroː] (-(e)s, -e) nt straw; ~**blume** f everlasting flower; ~**dach** nt thatched roof; ~**halm** m (drinking) straw

Strom [ʃtroːm] (-(e)s, ⁓e) m river; (fig) stream; (ELEK) current; **s~abwärts** [-ʼapvɛrts] adv downstream; **s~aufwärts** [-ʼaʊfvɛrts] adv upstream

strömen ['ʃtrøːmən] vi to stream, to pour

Strom- zW: ~**kreis** m circuit; **s~linienförmig** adj streamlined; ~**rechnung** f electricity bill; ~**sperre** f power cut

Strömung ['ʃtrøːmʊŋ] f current

Strophe ['ʃtroːfə] f verse

strotzen ['ʃtrɔtsən] vi: ~ **vor** od **von** to abound in, to be full of

Strudel ['ʃtruːdəl] (-s, -) m whirlpool, vortex; (KOCH) strudel

Struktur [ʃtrʊkˈtuːr] f structure

Strumpf [ʃtrʊmpf] (-(e)s, ⁓e) m stocking; ~**band** nt garter; ~**hose** f (pair of) tights

Stube ['ʃtuːbə] f room

Stuben- zW: ~**arrest** m confinement to one's room; (MIL) confinement to quarters; ~**hocker** (umg) m stay-at-home; **s~rein** adj house-trained

Stuck [ʃtʊk] (-(e)s) m stucco
Stück [ʃtʏk] (-(e)s, -e) nt piece; (etwas)
bit; (THEAT) play; ~**chen** nt little
piece; ~**lohn** m piecework wages pl;
s~weise adv bit by bit, piecemeal;
(COMM) individually; ~**werk** nt bits and
pieces pl
Student(in) [ʃtuˈdɛnt(ɪn)] m(f) student;
s~isch adj student, academic
Studie [ˈʃtuːdiə] f study
studieren [ʃtuˈdiːrən] vt, vi to study
Studio [ˈʃtuːdio] (-s, -s) nt studio
Studium [ˈʃtuːdiʊm] nt studies pl
Stufe [ˈʃtuːfə] f step; (Entwicklungs~)
stage; **stufenweise** adv gradually
Stuhl [ʃtuːl] (-(e)s, :e) m chair; ~**gang**
m bowel movement
stülpen [ˈʃtʏlpən] vt (umdrehen) to turn
upside down; (bedecken) to put
stumm [ʃtʊm] adj silent; (MED) dumb
Stummel [ˈʃtʊməl] (-s, -) m stump; (Zi-
garetten~) stub
Stummfilm m silent film
Stummheit f silence; dumbness
Stümper [ˈʃtʏmpər] (-s, -) m incompetent, duffer; **s~haft** adj bungling,
incompetent; **s~n** vi to bungle
Stumpf [ʃtʊmpf] (-(e)s, :e) m stump;
s~ adj blunt; (teilnahmslos, glanzlos)
dull; (Winkel) obtuse; ~**sinn** m tedious-
ness; **s~sinnig** adj dull
Stunde [ˈʃtʊndə] f hour; (SCH) lesson
stunden vt: **jdm etw ~** to give sb time
to pay sth; **S~geschwindigkeit** f average speed per hour; **S~kilometer** pl
kilometres per hour; ~**lang** adj for
hours; **S~lohn** m hourly wage; **S~plan**
m timetable; ~**weise** adj by the hour;
every hour
stündlich [ˈʃtʏntlɪç] adj hourly
Stups [ʃtʊps] (-es, -e; umg) m push;
~**nase** f snub nose
stur [ʃtuːr] adj obstinate, pigheaded
Sturm [ʃtʊrm] (-(e)s, :e) m storm, gale;
(MIL etc) attack, assault
stürm- [ˈʃtʏrm] zW: ~**en** vi (Wind) to
blow hard, to rage; (rennen) to storm ♦
vt (MIL, fig) to storm ♦ vb unpers: es
~**t** there's a gale blowing; **S~er** (-s, -)
m (SPORT) forward, striker; ~**isch** adj
stormy

Sturmwarnung f gale warning
Sturz [ʃtʊrts] (-es, :e) m fall; (POL)
overthrow
stürzen [ˈʃtʏrtsən] vt (werfen) to hurl;
(POL) to overthrow; (umkehren) to
overturn ♦ vr to rush; (hinein~) to
plunge ♦ vi to fall; (AVIAT) to dive;
(rennen) to dash
Sturzflug m nose-dive
Sturzhelm m crash helmet
Stute [ˈʃtuːtə] f mare
Stützbalken m brace, joist
Stütze [ˈʃtʏtsə] f support; help
stutzen [ˈʃtʊtsən] vt to trim; (Ohr,
Schwanz) to dock; (Flügel) to clip ♦ vi
to hesitate; to become suspicious
stützen vt (auch fig) to support;
(Ellbogen etc) to prop up
stutzig adj perplexed, puzzled;
(mißtrauisch) suspicious
Stützpunkt m point of support; (von
Hebel) fulcrum; (MIL, fig) base
Styropor [ʃtyroˈpoːr] (®; -s) nt polystyrene
s.u. abk = **siehe unten**
Subjekt [zʊpˈjɛkt] (-(e)s, -e) nt subject;
s~iv [-ˈtiːf] adj subjective; ~**ivi'tät** f
subjectivity
Substantiv [ˈzʊpstantiːf] (-s, -e) nt noun
Substanz [zʊpˈstants] f substance
subtil [zʊpˈtiːl] adj subtle
subtrahieren [zʊptraˈhiːrən] vt to subtract
Subvention [zʊpvɛntsiˈoːn] f subsidy;
s~ieren [-ˈniːrən] vt to subsidize
Such- [ˈzuːx] zW: ~**aktion** f search; ~**e**
f search; **s~en** vt to look (for), to
seek; (versuchen) to try ♦ vi to seek, to
search; ~**er** (-s, -) m seeker, searcher;
(PHOT) viewfinder
Sucht [zʊxt] (-, :e) f mania; (MED)
addiction, craving
süchtig [ˈzʏçtɪç] adj addicted; **S~e(r)**
mf addict
Süd- [ˈzyːt] zW: ~**en** [ˈzyːdən] (-s) m
south; ~**früchte** pl Mediterranean fruit
sg; **s~lich** adj southern; **s~lich von** (to
the) south of; ~**pol** m South Pole;
s~wärts adv southwards

süffig ['zʏfɪç] *adj (Wein)* pleasant to the taste
süffisant [zʏfi'zant] *adj* smug
suggerieren [zʊge'riːrən] *vt* to suggest
Sühne ['zyːnə] *f* atonement, expiation; s~n *vt* to atone for, to expiate
Sultan ['zʊltan] (-s, -e) *m* sultan; ~ine [zʊlta'niːnə] *f* sultana
Sülze ['zʏltsə] *f* brawn
Summe ['zʊmə] *f* sum, total
summen *vt, vi* to buzz; *(Lied)* to hum
Sumpf [zʊmpf] (-(e)s, -e) *m* swamp, marsh; s~ig *adj* marshy
Sünde ['zʏndə] *f* sin; **Sündenbock** *(umg) m* scapegoat; **Sündenfall** *m* Fall (of man); ~r(in) (-s, -) *m(f)* sinner
Super ['zuːpər] (-s) *nt (Benzin)* four star (petrol) *(BRIT)*, premium *(US)*; ~lativ [-latiːf] (-s, -e) *m* superlative; ~markt *m* supermarket
Suppe ['zʊpə] *f* soup
süß [zyːs] *adj* sweet; S~e (-) *f* sweetness; ~en *vt* to sweeten; S~igkeit *f* sweetness; *(Bonbon etc)* sweet *(BRIT)*, candy *(US)*; ~lich *adj* sweetish; *(fig)* sugary; S~speise *f* pudding, sweet; S~stoff *m* sweetener; S~wasser *nt* fresh water
Sylvester [zʏl'vɛstər] (-s, -) *nt* = Silvester
Symbol [zʏm'boːl] (-s, -e) *nt* symbol; s~isch *adj* symbolic(al)
Symmetrie [zʏme'triː] *f* symmetry
symmetrisch [zʏ'meːtrɪʃ] *adj* symmetrical
Sympathie [zʏmpa'tiː] *f* liking, sympathy; **sympathisch** [zʏm'paːtɪʃ] *adj* likeable; **er ist mir sympathisch** I like him; **sympathi'sieren** *vi* to sympathize
Symptom [zʏmp'toːm] (-s, -e) *nt* symptom; s~atisch [zʏmpto'maːtɪʃ] *adj* symptomatic
Synagoge [zʏna'goːgə] *f* synagogue
synchron [zʏn'kroːn] *adj* synchronous; S~getriebe *nt* synchromesh (gears *pl*); ~i'sieren *vt* to synchronize; *(Film)* to dub
Synonym [zyno'nyːm] (-s, -e) *nt* synonym; s~ *adj* synonymous
Synthese [zʏn'teːzə] *f* synthesis

synthetisch [zʏn'teːtɪʃ] *adj* synthetic
Syphilis ['zyːfilɪs] (-) *f* syphilis
Syr- ['zyːr] *zW:* ~er(in) *m(f)* Syrian; ~ien *nt* Syria; s~isch *adj* Syrian
System [zʏs'teːm] (-s, -e) *nt* system; s~atisch [zʏste'maːtɪʃ] *adj* systematic; s~ati'sieren *vt* to systematize; ~platte *f* system disk
Szene ['stseːnə] *f* scene; ~rie [stsenə'riː] *f* scenery

T

t *abk* (= *Tonne*) t
Tabak ['taːbak] (-s, -e) *m* tobacco
Tabell- [ta'bɛl] *zW:* t~arisch [tabɛ'laːrɪʃ] *adj* tabular; ~e *f* table; ~enführer *m* top of the table, league leader
Tablett [ta'blɛt] *nt* tray; ~e *f* tablet, pill
Tabu [ta'buː] *nt* taboo; t~ *adj* taboo
Tachometer [taxo'meːtər] (-s, -) *m* *(AUT)* speedometer
Tadel ['taːdəl] (-s, -) *m* censure; scolding; *(Fehler)* fault, blemish; t~los *adj* faultless, irreproachable; t~n *vt* to scold; **tadelnswert** *adj* blameworthy
Tafel ['taːfəl] (-, -n) *f (auch MATH)* table; *(Anschlag~)* board; *(Wand~)* blackboard; *(Schiefer~)* slate; *(Gedenk~)* plaque; *(Illustration)* plate; *(Schalt~)* panel; *(Schokolade etc)* bar
Taft [taft] (-(e)s, -e) *m* taffeta
Tag [taːk] (-(e)s, -e) *m* day; daylight; **unter/über** ~e *(MIN)* underground/on the surface; **an den** ~ **kommen** to come to light; **guten** ~! good morning/afternoon!; t~aus *adv:* t~aus, t~ein day in, day out; ~dienst *m* day duty
Tage- ['taːgə] *zW:* ~buch ['taːgəbuːx] *nt* diary, journal; ~geld *nt* daily allowance; t~lang *adv* for days; t~n *vi* to sit, to meet ♦ *vb unpers:* es tagt dawn is breaking
Tages- *zW:* ~ablauf *m* course of the day; ~anbruch *m* dawn; ~karte *f* menu of the day; *(Fahrkarte)* day ticket; ~licht *nt* daylight; ~ordnung *f* agenda; ~zeit *f* time of day; ~zeitung *f* daily (paper)

täglich ['tɛ:klɪç] *adj, adv* daily
tagsüber ['ta:ks'y:bər] *adv* during the day
Tagung *f* conference
Taille ['taljə] *f* waist
Takt [takt] (-(e)s, -e) *m* tact; (*MUS*) time; **~gefühl** *nt* tact
Taktik *f* tactics *pl*
taktisch *adj* tactical
Takt- *zW:* **t~los** *adj* tactless; **~losigkeit** *f* tactlessness; **~stock** *m* (conductor's) baton; **t~voll** *adj* tactful
Tal [ta:l] (-(e)s, -er) *nt* valley
Talent [ta'lɛnt] (-(e)s, -e) *nt* talent; **t~iert** [talɛn'ti:rt] *adj* talented, gifted
Talisman ['ta:lɪsman] (-s, -e) *m* talisman
Talsohle *f* bottom of a valley
Talsperre *f* dam
Tamburin [tambu'ri:n] (-s, -e) *nt* tambourine
Tampon ['tampɔn] (-s, -s) *m* tampon
Tang [taŋ] (-(e)s, -e) *m* seaweed
Tangente [taŋ'gɛntə] *f* tangent
tangieren [taŋ'gi:rən] *vt* to touch; to affect
Tank [taŋk] (-s, -s) *m* tank; **t~en** *vi* to fill up with petrol (*BRIT*) *od* gas (*US*); (*AVIAT*) to (re)fuel; **~er** (-s, -) *m* tanker; **~schiff** *nt* tanker; **~stelle** *f* petrol (*BRIT*) *od* gas (*US*) station; **~wart** *m* petrol pump (*BRIT*) *od* gas station (*US*) attendant
Tanne ['tanə] *f* fir; **Tannenbaum** *m* fir tree; **Tannenzapfen** *m* fir cone
Tante ['tantə] *f* aunt
Tanz [tants] (-es, -e) *m* dance; **t~en** *vt, vi* to dance
Tänzer(in) ['tɛntsər(ɪn)] (-s, -) *m(f)* dancer
Tanzfläche *f* (dance) floor
Tanzschule *f* dancing school
Tapete [ta'pe:tə] *f* wallpaper; **Tapetenwechsel** *m* (*fig*) change of scenery
tapezieren [tape'tsi:rən] *vt* to (wall)paper
Tapezierer [tape'tsi:rər] (-s, -) *m* (interior) decorator
tapfer ['tapfər] *adj* brave; **T~keit** *f* courage, bravery
Tarif [ta'ri:f] (-s, -e) *m* tariff, (scale of) fares *od* charges; **~lohn** *m* standard wage rate; **~verhandlungen** *pl* wage negotiations
Tarn- ['tarn] *zW:* **t~en** *vt* to camouflage; (*Person, Absicht*) to disguise; **~farbe** *f* camouflage paint; **~ung** *f* camouflaging; disguising
Tasche ['taʃə] *f* pocket; handbag
Taschen- *in zW* pocket; **~buch** *nt* paperback; **~dieb** *m* pickpocket; **~geld** *nt* pocket money; **~lampe** *f* (electric) torch, flashlight (*US*); **~messer** *nt* penknife; **~tuch** *nt* handkerchief
Tasse ['tasə] *f* cup
Tastatur [tasta'tu:r] *f* keyboard
Taste ['tastə] *f* push-button control; (*an Schreibmaschine*) key; **t~n** *vt* to feel, to touch ♦ *vi* to feel, to grope ♦ *vr* to feel one's way
Tat [ta:t] (-, -en) *f* act, deed, action; **in der ~** indeed, as a matter of fact; **t~** *etc vb siehe* **tun**; **~bestand** *m* facts *pl* of the case; **t~enlos** *adj* inactive
Tät- ['tɛ:t] *zW:* **~er(in)** (-s, -) *m(f)* perpetrator, culprit; **t~ig** *adj* active; **in einer Firma t~ig sein** to work for a firm; **~igkeit** *f* activity; (*Beruf*) occupation; **t~lich** *adj* violent; **~lichkeit** *f* violence; **~lichkeiten** *pl* (*Schläge*) blows
tätowieren [tɛto'vi:rən] *vt* to tattoo
Tatsache *f* fact
tatsächlich *adj* actual ♦ *adv* really
Tau¹ [tau] (-(e)s, -e) *nt* rope
Tau² (-(e)s) *m* dew
taub [taup] *adj* deaf; (*Nuß*) hollow; **T~heit** *f* deafness; **~stumm** *adj* deaf-and-dumb
Taube ['taubə] *f* dove; pigeon; **Taubenschlag** *m* dovecote; **hier geht es zu wie in einem Taubenschlag** it's a hive of activity here
Tauch- ['taux] *zW:* **t~en** *vt* to dip ♦ *vi* to dive; (*NAUT*) to submerge; **~er** (-s, -) *m* diver; **~eranzug** *m* diving suit; **~sieder** (-s, -) *m* immersion coil (*for boiling water*)
tauen ['tauən] *vt, vi* to thaw ♦ *vb unpers:* **es taut** it's thawing

Tauf- ['tauf] *zW:* ~**becken** *nt* font; ~**e** *f* baptism; **t~en** *vt* to christen, to baptize; ~**name** *m* Christian name; ~**pate** *m* godfather; ~**patin** *f* godmother; ~**schein** *m* certificate of baptism

taug- ['taug] *zW:* ~**en** *vi* to be of use; ~**en für** to do for, to be good for; **nicht** ~**en** to be no good *od* useless; **Taugenichts** (-es, -e) *m* good-for-nothing; ~**lich** ['tauklıç] *adj* suitable; (*MIL*) fit (for service)

Taumel ['tauməl] (-s) *m* dizziness; (*fig*) frenzy; **t~n** *vi* to reel, to stagger

Tausch [tauʃ] (-(e)s, -e) *m* exchange; **t~en** *vt* to exchange, to swap

täuschen ['tɔyʃən] *vt* to deceive ♦ *vi* to be deceptive ♦ *vr* to be wrong; ~**d** *adj* deceptive

Tauschhandel *m* barter

Täuschung *f* deception; (*optisch*) illusion

tausend ['tauzənt] *num* (a) thousand; **T~füßler** (-s, -) *m* centipede; millipede

Tauwetter *nt* thaw

Taxi ['taksi] (-(s), -(s)) *nt* taxi; ~**fahrer** *m* taxi driver; ~**stand** *m* taxi rank

Tech- ['teç] *zW:* ~**nik** *f* technology; (*Methode, Kunstfertigkeit*) technique; ~**niker** (-s, -) *m* technician; **t~nisch** *adj* technical; ~**nolo'gie** *f* technology; **t~no'logisch** *adj* technological

TEE [teːʔeːˈʔeː] (-, -(s)) *m abk* (= *Trans-Europ-Express*) Trans-European Express

Tee [teː] (-s, -s) *m* tea; ~**kanne** *f* teapot; ~**löffel** *m* teaspoon

Teer [teːr] (-(e)s, -e) *m* tar; **t~en** *vt* to tar

Teesieb *nt* tea strainer

Teich [taıç] (-(e)s, -e) *m* pond

Teig [taık] (-(e)s, -e) *m* dough; **t~ig** ['taıgıç] *adj* doughy; ~**waren** *pl* pasta *sg*

Teil [taıl] (-(e)s, -e) *m od nt* part; (*An~*) share; (*Bestand~*) component; **zum** ~ partly; **t~bar** *adj* divisible; ~**betrag** *m* instalment; ~**chen** *nt* (atomic) particle; **t~en** *vt, vr* to divide; (*mit jdm*) to share; **t~haben** (*unreg*) *vi:* **t~haben an** +*dat* to share

in; ~**haber** (-s, -) *m* partner; ~**kaskoversicherung** *f* third party, fire and theft insurance; ~**nahme** *f* participation; (*Mitleid*) sympathy; **t~nahmslos** *adj* disinterested, apathetic; **t~nehmen** (*unreg*) *vi:* **t~nehmen an** +*dat* to take part in; ~**nehmer** (-s,) *m* participant; **t~s** *adv* partly, ~**ung** *f* division; **t~weise** *adv* partially, in part; ~**zahlung** *f* payment by instalments

Teint [tɛ̃ː] (-s, -s) *m* complexion

Telefax ['telefaks] *nt* fax

Telefon [tele'foːn] (-s, -e) *nt* telephone; ~**amt** *nt* telephone exchange; ~**anruf** *m* (tele)phone call; ~**at** [telefo'naːt] (-(e)s, -e) *nt* (tele)phone call; ~**buch** *nt* telephone directory; **t~ieren** [telefo'niːrən] *vi* to telephone; **t~isch** [-ıʃ] *adj* telephone; (*Benachrichtigung*) by telephone; ~**ist(in)** [telefo'nıst(ın)] *m(f)* telephonist; ~**nummer** *f* (tele)phone number; ~**verbindung** *f* telephone connection; ~**zelle** *f* telephone kiosk, callbox; ~**zentrale** *f* telephone exchange

Telegraf [tele'graːf] (-en, -en) *m* telegraph; ~**enleitung** *f* telegraph line; ~**enmast** *m* telegraph pole; ~**ie** [-'fiː] *f* telegraphy; **t~ieren** [-'fiːrən] *vt, vi* to telegraph, to wire; **t~isch** *adj* telegraphic

Telegramm [tele'gram] (-s, -e) *nt* telegram, cable; ~**adresse** *f* telegraphic address

Tele- *zW:* ~**objektiv** ['teːleʔɔpjɛktiːf] *nt* telephoto lens; ~**pathie** [telepa'tiː] *f* telepathy; **t~pathisch** [tele'paːtıʃ] *adj* telepathic; ~**skop** [tele'skoːp] (-s, -e) *nt* telescope

Telex ['teːlɛks] (-es, -e) *nt* telex

Teller ['tɛlər] (-s, -) *m* plate

Tempel ['tɛmpəl] (-s, -) *m* temple

Temperament [tɛmpera'mɛnt] *nt* temperament; (*Schwung*) vivacity, liveliness; **t~los** *adj* spiritless; **t~voll** *adj* high-spirited, lively

Temperatur [tɛmpera'tuːr] *f* temperature

Tempo¹ ['tɛmpo] (-s, -s) *nt* speed, pace; ~! get a move on!

Tempo² (-s, **Tempi**) nt (MUS) tempo
Tendenz [tɛn'dɛnts] f tendency; (Absicht) intention; **t~iös** [-i'øːs] adj biased, tendentious
tendieren [tɛn'diːrən] vi: ~ **zu** to show a tendency to, to incline towards
Tennis ['tɛnɪs] (-) nt tennis; **~platz** m tennis court; **~schläger** m tennis racket; **~spieler(in)** m(f) tennis player
Tenor [te'noːr] (-s, -e) m tenor
Teppich ['tɛpɪç] (-s, -e) m carpet; **~boden** m wall-to-wall carpeting
Termin [tɛr'miːn] (-s, -e) m (Zeitpunkt) date; (Frist) time limit, deadline; (Arzt~ etc) appointment; **~kalender** m diary, appointments book
Termite [tɛr'miːtə] f termite
Terpentin [tɛrpɛn'tiːn] (-s, -e) nt turpentine, turps sg
Terrasse [tɛ'rasə] f terrace
Terrine [tɛ'riːnə] f tureen
territorial [tɛritori'aːl] adj territorial
Territorium [tɛri'toːriʊm] nt territory
Terror ['tɛrɔr] (-s) m terror; reign of terror; **t~isieren** [tɛrori'ziːrən] vt to terrorize; **~ismus** [-'rɪsmʊs] m terrorism; **~ist** [-'rɪst] m terrorist
Terz [tɛrts] (-, -en) f (MUS) third; **~ett** [tɛr'tsɛt] (-(e)s, -e) nt trio
Tesafilm ['teːzafɪlm] ® m Sellotape ® (BRIT), Scotch tape ® (US)
Test [tɛst] (-s, -s) m test
Testament [tɛsta'mɛnt] nt will, testament; (REL) Testament; **t~arisch** [-'taːrɪʃ] adj testamentary; **Testamentsvollstrecker** m executor (of a will)
Testbild nt (TV) test card
testen vt to test
Tetanus ['teːtanʊs] (-) m tetanus; **~impfung** f (anti-)tetanus injection
teuer ['tɔyər] adj dear, expensive; **T~ung** f increase in prices; **T~ungszulage** f cost of living bonus
Teufel ['tɔyfəl] (-s, -) m devil
teuflisch ['tɔyflɪʃ] adj fiendish, diabolical
Text [tɛkst] (-(e)s, -e) m text; (Lieder~) words pl; **t~en** vi to write the words
textil [tɛks'tiːl] adj textile; **T~ien** pl textiles; **T~industrie** f textile industry; **T~waren** pl textiles

Theater [te'aːtər] (-s, -) nt theatre; (umg) fuss; ~ **spielen** (auch fig) to playact; **~besucher** m playgoer; **~kasse** f box office; **~stück** nt (stage-)play
Theke ['teːkə] f (Schanktisch) bar; (Ladentisch) counter
Thema ['teːma] (-s, **Themen** od -ta) nt theme, topic, subject
Themse ['tɛmzə] f Thames
Theo- [teo] zW: **~loge** [-'loːgə] (-n, -n) m theologian; **~logie** [-lo'giː] f theology; **t~logisch** [-'loːgɪʃ] adj theological; **~retiker** [-'reːtikər] (-s, -) m theorist; **t~retisch** [-'reːtɪʃ] adj theoretical; **~rie** [-'riː] f theory
Thera- [tera] zW: **~peut** [-'pɔyt] (-en, -en) m therapist; **t~peutisch** [-'pɔytɪʃ] adj therapeutic; **~pie** [-'piː] f therapy
Therm- zW: **~albad** [tɛr'maːlbaːt] nt thermal bath; thermal spa; **~odrucker** ['tɛrmo-] m thermal printer; **~ometer** [tɛrmo'meːtər] (-s, -) nt thermometer; **~osflasche** ['tɛrmɔsflaʃə] f Thermos ® flask; **~ostat** [tɛrmo'staːt] (-(e)s od -en, -e(n)) m thermostat
These ['teːzə] f thesis
Thrombose [trɔm'boːzə] f thrombosis
Thron [troːn] (-(e)s, -e) m throne; **~folge** f succession (to the throne)
Thunfisch ['tuːnfɪʃ] m tuna
Thymian ['tyːmiaːn] (-s, -e) m thyme
Tick [tɪk] (-(e)s, -s) m tic; (Eigenart) quirk; (Fimmel) craze
ticken vi to tick
tief [tiːf] adj deep; (~sinnig) profound; (Ausschnitt, Preis, Ton) low; **T~** (-s, -s) nt (MET) depression; **T~druck** m low pressure; **T~e** f depth; **T~ebene** f plain; **T~enpsychologie** f depth psychology; **T~enschärfe** f (PHOT) depth of focus; **T~garage** f underground garage; **~gekühlt** adj frozen; **~greifend** adj far-reaching; **T~kühlfach** nt deep-freeze compartment; **T~kühltruhe** f deep-freeze, freezer; **T~land** nt lowlands pl; **T~punkt** m low point; (fig) low ebb; **T~schlag** m (BOXEN, fig) blow below the belt; **~schürfend** adj profound; **T~see** f

deep sea; ~**sinnig** *adj* profound;
melancholy; **T~stand** *m* low level;
Tiefstwert *m* minimum *od* lowest value
Tier [tiːr] (-(e)s, -e) *nt* animal; ~**arzt** *m*
vet(erinary surgeon); ~**garten** *m*
zoo(logical gardens *pl*); **t~isch** *adj*
animal; (*auch fig*) brutish; (*fig: Ernst
etc*) deadly; ~**kreis** *m* zodiac; ~**kunde**
f zoology; **t~liebend** *adj* fond of
animals; ~**quälerei** [-kvɛːlə'raɪ] *f* cruelty
to animals; ~**schutzverein** *m* society
for the prevention of cruelty to animals
Tiger(in) ['tiːgər(ɪn)] (-s, -) *m*
tiger(gress)
tilgen ['tɪlgən] *vt* to erase; (*Sünden*) to
expiate; (*Schulden*) to pay off
Tinte ['tɪntə] *f* ink; **Tintenfisch** *m*
cuttlefish; **Tintenstift** *m* copying *od* indelible pencil
Tip [tɪp] *m* tip; **tippen** *vt, vi* to tap, to
touch; (*umg: schreiben*) to type; (*im
Lotto etc*) to bet (on); **auf jdn tippen**
(*umg: raten*) to tip sb, to put one's
money on sb (*fig*)
Tipp- ['tɪp] *zW:* ~**fehler** (*umg*) *m* typing
error; **t~topp** (*umg*) *adj* tip-top;
~**zettel** *m* (pools) coupon
Tirol [ti'roːl] *nt* the Tyrol; ~**er(in)** *m(f)*
Tyrolean; **t~isch** *adj* Tyrolean
Tisch [tɪʃ] (-(e)s, -e) *m* table; **bei** ~ at
table; **vor/nach** ~ before/after eating;
unter den ~ **fallen** (*fig*) to be dropped;
~**decke** *f* tablecloth; ~**ler** (-s, -) *m*
carpenter, joiner; ~**le'rei** *f* joiner's
workshop; (*Arbeit*) carpentry, joinery;
t~lern *vi* to do carpentry *etc*; ~**rede** *f*
after-dinner speech; ~**tennis** *nt* table
tennis
Titel ['tiːtəl] (-s, -) *m* title; ~**anwärter**
m (*SPORT*) challenger; ~**bild** *nt* cover
(picture); (*von Buch*) frontispiece;
~**geschichte** *f* main story; ~**rolle** *f* title
role; ~**seite** *f* cover; (*Buch~*) title
page; ~**verteidiger** *m* defending
champion, title holder
Toast [toːst] (-(e)s, -s *od* -e) *m* toast;
~**er** (-s, -) *m* toaster
tob- ['toːb] *zW:* ~**en** *vi* to rage;
(*Kinder*) to romp about; **T~sucht** *f*
raving madness; ~**süchtig** *adj*

maniacal
Tochter ['tɔxtər] (-, ⸚) *f* daughter;
~**gesellschaft** *f* subsidiary (company)
Tod [toːt] (-(e)s, -e) *m* death; **t~ernst**
adj deadly serious ♦ *adv* in dead earnest
Todes- ['toːdəs] *zW:* ~**angst** [-aŋst] *f*
mortal fear; ~**anzeige** *f* obituary
(notice); ~**fall** *m* death; ~**strafe** *f*
death penalty; ~**ursache** *f* cause of
death; ~**urteil** *nt* death sentence; ~**verachtung** *f* utter disgust
todkrank *adj* dangerously ill
tödlich ['tøːtlɪç] *adj* deadly, fatal
tod- *zW:* ~**müde** *adj* dead tired;
~**schick** (*umg*) *adj* smart, classy; ~**sicher** (*umg*) *adj* absolutely *od* dead
certain; **T~sünde** *f* deadly sin
Toilette [toa'lɛtə] *f* toilet, lavatory;
(*Frisiertisch*) dressing table; (*Kleidung*) outfit
Toiletten- *zW:* ~**artikel** *pl* toiletries,
toilet articles; ~**papier** *nt* toilet paper;
~**tisch** *m* dressing table
toi, toi, toi ['tɔy 'tɔy 'tɔy] *excl* touch
wood
tolerant [tole'rant] *adj* tolerant
Toleranz [tole'rants] *f* tolerance
tolerieren [tole'riːrən] *vt* to tolerate
toll [tɔl] *adj* mad; (*Treiben*) wild;
(*umg*) terrific; ~**en** *vi* to romp;
T~kirsche *f* deadly nightshade; ~**kühn**
adj daring; **T~wut** *f* rabies
Tomate [to'maːtə] *f* tomato;
Tomatenmark *nt* tomato puree
Ton[1] [toːn] (-(e)s, -e) *m* (*Erde*) clay
Ton[2] (-(e)s, ⸚e) *m* (*Laut*) sound; (*MUS*)
note; (*Redeweise*) tone; (*Farb~,
Nuance*) shade; (*Betonung*) stress;
~**abnehmer** *m* pick-up; **t~angebend**
adj leading; ~**art** *f* (musical) key;
~**band** *nt* tape; ~**bandgerät** *nt* tape recorder
tönen ['tøːnən] *vi* to sound ♦ *vt* to
shade; (*Haare*) to tint
tönern ['tøːnərn] *adj* clay
Ton- *zW:* ~**fall** *m* intonation; ~**film** *m*
sound film; ~**leiter** *f* (*MUS*) scale; **t~los**
adj soundless
Tonne ['tɔnə] *f* barrel; (*Maß*) ton

Tonspur f soundtrack
Tontaube f clay pigeon
Tonwaren pl pottery sg, earthenware sg
Topf [tɔpf] (-(e)s, ⸚e) m pot; ~**blume** f pot plant
Töpfer ['tœpfər] (-s, -) m potter; ~**ei** [-'raɪ] f piece of pottery; potter's workshop; ~**scheibe** f potter's wheel
topographisch [topo'gra:fɪʃ] adj topographic
Tor¹ [to:r] (-en, -en) m fool
Tor² (-(e)s, -e) nt gate; (SPORT) goal; ~**bogen** m archway
Torf [tɔrf] (-(e)s) m peat
Torheit f foolishness; foolish deed
Torhüter (-s, -) m goalkeeper
töricht ['tø:rɪçt] adj foolish
torkeln ['tɔrkəln] vi to stagger, to reel
Torpedo [tɔr'pe:do] (-s, -s) m torpedo
Torte ['tɔrtə] f cake; (Obst~) flan, tart
Tortur [tɔr'tu:r] f ordeal
Torwart (-(e)s, -e) m goalkeeper
tosen ['to:zən] vi to roar
tot [to:t] adj dead
total [to'ta:l] adj total; ~**itär** [totali'tɛ:r] adj totalitarian; **T~schaden** m (AUT) complete write-off
Tote(r) mf dead person
töten ['tø:tən] vt, vi to kill
Toten- ['to:tən] zW: ~**bett** nt deathbed; **t~blaß** adj deathly pale, white as a sheet; ~**kopf** m skull; ~**schein** m death certificate; ~**stille** f deathly silence
tot- zW: ~**fahren** (unreg) vt to run over; ~**geboren** adj stillborn; ~**lachen** (umg) vr to laugh one's head off
Toto ['to:to] (-s, -s) m od nt pools pl; ~**schein** m pools coupon
tot- zW: ~**sagen** vt: jdn ~**sagen** to say that sb is dead; **T~schlag** m manslaughter; ~**schlagen** (unreg) vt (auch fig) to kill; ~**schweigen** (unreg) vt to hush up; ~**stellen** vr to pretend to be dead
Tötung ['tø:tʊŋ] f killing
Toupet [tu'pe:] (-s, -s) nt toupee
toupieren [tu'pi:rən] vt to back-comb
Tour [tu:r] (-, -en) f tour, trip;

(Umdrehung) revolution; (Verhaltensart) way; **in einer** ~ incessantly; ~**enzähler** m rev counter; ~**ismus** [tu'rɪsmʊs] m tourism; ~**ist** [tu'rɪst] m tourist; ~**istenklasse** f tourist class; **Tournee** [tʊr'ne:] (-, -n) f (THEAT etc) tour; **auf Tournee gehen** to go on tour
Trab [tra:p] (-(e)s) m trot
Trabant [tra'bant] m satellite; ~**enstadt** f satellite town
traben vi to trot
Tracht [traxt] (-, -en) f (Kleidung) costume, dress; **eine ~ Prügel** a sound thrashing; **t~en** vi: **t~en (nach)** to strive (for); **jdm nach dem Leben t~en** to seek to kill sb; **danach t~en, etw zu tun** to strive od endeavour to do sth
trächtig ['trɛçtɪç] adj (Tier) pregnant
Tradition [traditsi'o:n] f tradition; **t~ell** [-'nɛl] adj traditional
traf etc [tra:f] vb siehe **treffen**
Tragbahre f stretcher
tragbar adj (Gerät) portable; (Kleidung) wearable; (erträglich) bearable
träge ['trɛ:gə] adj sluggish, slow; (PHYS) inert
tragen ['tra:gən] (unreg) vt to carry; (Kleidung, Brille) to wear; (Namen, Früchte) to bear; (erdulden) to endure ♦ vi (schwanger sein) to be pregnant; (Eis) to hold; **sich mit einem Gedanken** ~ to have an idea in mind; **zum T~ kommen** to have an effect
Träger ['trɛ:gər] (-s, -) m carrier; wearer; bearer; (Ordens~) holder; (an Kleidung) (shoulder) strap; (Körperschaft etc) sponsor; ~**rakete** f launch vehicle; ~**rock** m skirt with shoulder straps
Tragfläche f (AVIAT) wing
Tragflügelboot nt hydrofoil
Trägheit ['trɛ:khaɪt] f laziness; (PHYS) inertia
Tragik ['tra:gɪk] f tragedy
tragisch ['tra:gɪʃ] adj tragic
Tragödie [tra'gø:diə] f tragedy
Tragweite f range; (fig) scope
Train- ['trɛ:n] zW: ~**er** (-s, -) m (SPORT) trainer, coach; (Fußball) manager; **t~ieren** [trɛ'ni:rən] vt, vi to train;

(*Mensch*) to train, to coach; (*Übung*) to practise; ~**ing** (-s, -s) *nt* training; ~**ingsanzug** *m* track suit
Traktor ['traktɔr] *m* tractor; (*von Drucker*) tractor feed
trällern ['trɛlərn] *vt, vi* to trill, to sing
trampeln ['trampəln] *vt, vi* to trample, to stamp
trampen ['trɛmpən] *vi* to hitch-hike
Tran [tra:n] (-(e)s, -e) *m* train oil, blubber
Tranchierbesteck [trã'ʃiːrbəʃtɛk] *nt* (pair of) carvers *pl*
tranchieren [trã'ʃiːrən] *vt* to carve
Träne ['trɛːnə] *f* tear; **t~n** *vi* to water; **Tränengas** *nt* teargas
trank *etc* [traŋk] *vb siehe* **trinken**
tränken ['trɛŋkən] *vt* (*Tiere*) to water
Trans- *zW:* ~**formator** [transfɔr'maːtɔr] *m* transformer; ~**istor** [tran'zistɔr] *m* transistor; **t~itiv** ['tranzitiːf] *adj* transitive; ~**itverkehr** *m* transit traffic; ~**itvisum** *nt* transit visa; **t~parent** [transpa'rɛnt] *adj* transparent; ~**parent** (-(e)s, -e) *nt* (*Bild*) transparency; (*Spruchband*) banner; **t~pirieren** [tran-spiˈriːrən] *vi* to perspire; ~**plantation** [transplantatsi'oːn] *f* transplantation; (*Hauttransplantation*) graft(ing)
Transport [trans'pɔrt] (-(e)s, -e) *m* transport; **t~ieren** [transpɔr'tiːrən] *vt* to transport; ~**kosten** *pl* transport charges, carriage *sg*; ~**mittel** *nt* means *sg* of transportation; ~**unternehmen** *nt* carrier
Trapez [tra'peːts] (-es, -e) *nt* trapeze; (*MATH*) trapezium
Traube ['traubə] *f* grape; bunch (of grapes); **Traubenzucker** *m* glucose
trauen ['trauən] *vi:* jdm/etw ~ to trust sb/sth ♦ *vr* to dare ♦ *vt* to marry
Trauer ['trauər] (-) *f* sorrow; (*für Verstorbenen*) mourning; ~**fall** *m* death, bereavement; ~**kleidung** *f* mourning; **t~n** *vi* to mourn; um jdn t~n to mourn (for) sb; ~**rand** *m* black border; ~**spiel** *nt* tragedy
traulich ['trauliç] *adj* cosy, intimate
Traum [traum] (-(e)s, **Träume**) *m* dream

Trauma (-s, -men) *nt* trauma
träum- ['trɔym] *zW:* ~**en** *vt, vi* to dream; **T~er** (-s, -) *m* dreamer; **T~e'rei** *f* dreaming; ~**erisch** *adj* dreamy
traumhaft *adj* dreamlike; (*fig*) wonderful
traurig ['trauriç] *adj* sad; **T~keit** *f* sadness
Trau- ['trau] *zW:* ~**ring** *m* wedding ring; ~**schein** *m* marriage certificate; ~**ung** *f* wedding ceremony; ~**zeuge** *m* witness (to a marriage)
treffen ['trɛfən] (*unreg*) *vt* to strike, to hit; (*Bemerkung*) to hurt; (*begegnen*) to meet; (*Entscheidung etc*) to make; (*Maßnahmen*) to take ♦ *vi* to hit ♦ *vr* to meet; er hat es gut getroffen he did well; ~ auf +*akk* to come across, to meet with; es traf sich, daß ... it so happened that ...; es trifft sich gut it's convenient; wie es so trifft as these things happen; **T~** (-s, -) *nt* meeting; ~**d** *adj* pertinent, apposite
Treffer (-s, -) *m* hit; (*Tor*) goal; (*Los*) winner
Treffpunkt *m* meeting place
Treib- ['traib] *zW:* ~**eis** *nt* drift ice; **t~en** (*unreg*) *vt* to drive; (*Studien etc*) to pursue; (*Sport*) to do, to go in for ♦ *vi* (*Schiff etc*) to drift; (*Pflanzen*) to sprout; (*KOCH: aufgehen*) to rise; (*Tee, Kaffee*) to be diuretic; Unsinn t~en to fool around; ~**haus** *nt* greenhouse; ~**stoff** *m* fuel
Trend [trɛnt] (-s, -s) *m* trend; ~**wende** *f* trend away (from sth)
trenn- ['trɛn] *zW:* ~**bar** *adj* separable; ~**en** *vt* to separate; (*teilen*) to divide ♦ *vr* to separate; sich ~**en** von to part with; **T~schärfe** *f* (*RADIO*) selectivity; **T~ung** *f* separation; **T~wand** *f* partition (wall)
Trepp- ['trɛp] *zW:* **t~ab** *adv* downstairs; **t~auf** *adv* upstairs; ~**e** *f* stair(case); ~**engeländer** *nt* banister; ~**enhaus** *nt* staircase
Tresor [tre'zoːr] (-s, -e) *m* safe
treten ['treːtən] (*unreg*) *vi* to step; (*Tränen, Schweiß*) to appear ♦ *vt* (mit

Fußtritt) to kick; (*nieder~*) to tread, to trample; ~ **nach** to kick at; ~ **in** +*akk* to step in(to); **in Verbindung** ~ to get in contact; **in Erscheinung** ~ to appear

treu [trɔy] *adj* faithful, true; **T~e** (-) *f* loyalty, faithfulness; **T~händer** (-s, -) *m* trustee; **T~handgesellschaft** *f* trust company; ~**herzig** *adj* innocent; ~**los** *adj* faithless

Tribüne [tri'byːnə] *f* grandstand; (*Redner~*) platform

Trichter ['trɪçtər] (-s, -) *m* funnel; (*in Boden*) crater

Trick [trɪk] (-s, -e *od* -s) *m* trick; ~**film** *m* cartoon

Trieb [triːp] (-(e)s, -e) *m* urge, drive; (*Neigung*) inclination; (*an Baum etc*) shoot; **t~** *etc vb siehe* **treiben**; ~**feder** *f* (*fig*) motivating force; ~**kraft** *f* (*fig*) drive; ~**täter** *m* sex offender; ~**werk** *nt* engine

triefen ['triːfən] *vi* to drip

triffst *etc* [trɪfst] *vb siehe* **treffen**

triftig ['trɪftɪç] *adj* good, convincing

Trikot [tri'koː] (-s, -s) *nt* vest; (*SPORT*) shirt

Trimester [tri'mɛstər] (-s, -) *nt* term

trimmen ['trɪmən] *vr* to do keep fit exercises

trink- ['trɪŋk] *zW:* ~**bar** *adj* drinkable; ~**en** (*unreg*) *vt, vi* to drink; **T~er** (-s, -) *m* drinker; **T~geld** *nt* tip; **T~spruch** *m* toast; **T~wasser** *nt* drinking water

Tripper ['trɪpər] (-s, -) *m* gonorrhoea

Tritt [trɪt] (-(e)s, -e) *m* step; (*Fuß~*) kick; ~**brett** *nt* (*EISENB*) step; (*AUT*) running-board

Triumph [tri'ʊmf] (-(e)s, -e) *m* triumph; ~**bogen** *m* triumphal arch; **t~ieren** [-'fiːrən] *vi* to triumph; (*jubeln*) to exult

trocken ['trɔkən] *adj* dry; **T~element** *nt* dry cell; **T~haube** *f* hair-dryer; **T~heit** *f* dryness; ~**legen** *vt* (*Sumpf*) to drain; (*Kind*) to put a clean nappy on; **T~milch** *f* dried milk

trocknen ['trɔknən] *vt, vi* to dry

Trödel ['trøːdəl] (-s; *umg*) *m* junk; ~**markt** *m* flea market; **t~n** (*umg*) *vi* to dawdle

Trog [troːk] (-(e)s, ²e) *m* trough

Trommel ['trɔməl] (-, -n) *f* drum; ~**fell** *nt* eardrum; **t~n** *vt, vi* to drum

Trommler ['trɔmlər] (-s, -) *m* drummer

Trompete [trɔm'peːtə] *f* trumpet; ~**r** (-s, -) *m* trumpeter

Tropen ['troːpən] *pl* tropics; ~**helm** *m* sun helmet

tröpfeln ['trœpfəln] *vi* to drop, to trickle

Tropfen ['trɔpfən] (-s, -) *m* drop; **t~** *vt, vi* to drip ♦ *vb unpers:* **es tropft** a few raindrops are falling; **t~weise** *adv* in drops

Tropfsteinhöhle *f* stalactite cave

tropisch ['troːpɪʃ] *adj* tropical

Trost [troːst] (-es) *m* consolation, comfort; **t~bedürftig** *adj* in need of consolation

tröst- ['trøːst] *zW:* ~**en** *vt* to console, to comfort; **T~er(in)** (-s, -) *m(f)* comfort(er); ~**lich** *adj* comforting

trost- *zW:* ~**los** *adj* bleak; (*Verhältnisse*) wretched; **T~preis** *m* consolation prize; ~**reich** *adj* comforting

Trott [trɔt] (-(e)s, -e) *m* trot; (*Routine*) routine; ~**el** (-s, -; *umg*) *m* fool, dope; **t~en** *vi* to trot; **Trottoir** [trɔto'aːr] (-s, -s *od* -e) *nt* pavement, sidewalk (*US*)

Trotz [trɔts] (-es) *m* pigheadedness; **etw aus** ~ **tun** to do sth just to show them; **jdm zum** ~ in defiance of sb; **t~** *präp* (+*gen od dat*) in spite of; **t~dem** *adv* nevertheless, all the same ♦ *konj* although; **t~ig** *adj* defiant, pig-headed; ~**kopf** *m* obstinate child; ~**reaktion** *f* fit of pique

trüb [tryːp] *adj* dull; (*Flüssigkeit, Glas*) cloudy; (*fig*) gloomy

Trubel ['truːbəl] (-s) *m* hurly-burly

trüb- ['tryːb] *zW:* ~**en** ['tryːbən] *vt* to cloud ♦ *vr* to become clouded; **T~heit** *f* dullness; cloudiness; gloom; **T~sal** (-, -e) *f* distress; ~**selig** *adj* sad, melancholy; **T~sinn** *m* depression; ~**sinnig** *adj* depressed, gloomy

Trüffel ['trʏfəl] (-, -n) *f* truffle

trug *etc* [truːk] *vb siehe* **tragen**

trügen ['tryːgən] (*unreg*) *vt* to deceive ♦ *vi* to be deceptive

trügerisch *adj* deceptive

Trugschluß ['tru:gʃlʊs] *m* false conclusion

Truhe ['tru:ə] *f* chest

Trümmer ['trʏmər] *pl* wreckage *sg*; (*Bau~*) ruins; **~haufen** *m* heap of rubble

Trumpf [trʊmpf] (-(e)s, ⁼e) *m* (*auch fig*) trump; **t~en** *vt, vi* to trump

Trunk [trʊŋk] (-(e)s, ⁼e) *m* drink; **t~en** *adj* intoxicated; **~enheit** *f* intoxication; **~enheit am Steuer** drunken driving; **~sucht** *f* alcoholism

Trupp [trʊp] (-s, -s) *m* troop; **~e** *f* troop; (*Waffengattung*) force; (*Schauspiel~*) troupe; **~en** *pl* (MIL) troops; **~enübungsplatz** *m* training area

Truthahn ['tru:tha:n] *m* turkey

Tschech- ['tʃɛç] *zW:* **~e** *m* Czech, Czechoslovak(ian); **~in** *f* Czech, Czechoslovak(ian); **t~isch** *adj* Czech, Czechoslovak(ian); **~oslowake** [-oslo'va:kə] *m* Czech, Czechoslovak(ian); **~oslowakei** [-oslova'kaɪ] *f*: **die ~oslowakei** Czechoslovakia; **~oslowakin** *f* Czech, Czechoslovak(ian); **t~oslowakisch** [-oslo'va:kɪʃ] *adj* Czech, Czechoslovak(ian)

tschüs [tʃʏs] *excl* cheerio

T-Shirt ['ti:ʃœrt] *nt* T-shirt

Tube ['tu:bə] *f* tube

Tuberkulose [tuberku'lo:zə] *f* tuberculosis

Tuch [tu:x] (-(e)s, ⁼er) *nt* cloth; (*Hals~*) scarf; (*Kopf~*) headscarf; (*Hand~*) towel

tüchtig ['tʏçtɪç] *adj* efficient, (cap)able; (*umg: kräftig*) good, sound; **T~keit** *f* efficiency, ability

Tücke ['tʏkə] *f* (*Arglist*) malice; (*Trick*) trick; (*Schwierigkeit*) difficulty, problem; **seine ~n haben** to be temperamental

tückisch ['tʏkɪʃ] *adj* treacherous; (*böswillig*) malicious

Tugend ['tu:gənt] (-, -en) *f* virtue; **t~haft** *adj* virtuous

Tüll [tʏl] (-s, -e) *m* tulle

Tülle *f* spout

Tulpe ['tʊlpə] *f* tulip

Tumor ['tu:mɔr] (-s, -e) *m* tumour

Tümpel ['tʏmpəl] (-s, -) *m* pool, pond

Tumult [tu'mʊlt] (-(e)s, -e) *m* tumult

tun [tu:n] (*unreg*) *vt* (*machen*) to do; (*legen*) to put ♦ *vi* to act ♦ *vr:* **es tut sich etwas/viel** something/a lot is happening; **jdm etw ~** (*antun*) to do sth to sb; **etw tut es auch** sth will do; **das tut nichts** that doesn't matter; **das tut nichts zur Sache** that's neither here nor there; **so ~, als ob** to act as if

tünchen ['tʏnçən] *vt* to whitewash

Tunesien [tu'ne:ziən] *nt* Tunisia

Tunke ['tʊŋkə] *f* sauce; **t~n** *vt* to dip, to dunk

tunlichst ['tu:nlɪçst] *adv* if at all possible; **~ bald** as soon as possible

Tunnel ['tʊnəl] (-s, -s *od* -) *m* tunnel

Tupfen ['tʊpfən] (-s, -) *m* dot, spot; **t~** *vt, vi* to dab; (*mit Farbe*) to dot

Tür [ty:r] (-, -en) *f* door

Turban ['tʊrba:n] (-s, -e) *m* turban

Turbine [tʊr'bi:nə] *f* turbine

Türk- [tʏrk] *zW:* **~e** *m* Turk; **~ei** [tʏr'kaɪ] *f*: **die ~ei** Turkey; **~in** *f* Turk

Türkis [tʏr'ki:s] (-es, -e) *m* turquoise; **t~** *adj* turquoise

türkisch ['tʏrkɪʃ] *adj* Turkish

Turm [tʊrm] (-(e)s, ⁼e) *m* tower; (*Kirch~*) steeple; (*Sprung~*) diving platform; (*SCHACH*) castle, rook

türmen ['tʏrmən] *vr* to tower up ♦ *vt* to heap up ♦ *vi* (*umg*) to scarper, to bolt

Turn- ['tʊrn] *zW:* **t~en** *vt* to do gymnastic exercises ♦ *vt* to perform; **~en** (-s) *nt* gymnastics; (*SCH*) physical education, P.E.; **~er(in)** (-s, -) *m(f)* gymnast; **~halle** *f* gym(nasium); **~hose** *f* gym shorts *pl*

Turnier [tʊr'ni:r] (-s, -e) *nt* tournament

Turn- *zW:* **~schuh** *m* gym shoe; **~verein** *m* gymnastics club; **~zeug** *nt* gym things *pl*

Tusche ['tʊʃə] *f* Indian ink

tuscheln ['tʊʃəln] *vt, vi* to whisper

Tuschkasten *m* paintbox

Tüte ['ty:tə] *f* bag

tuten ['tu:tən] *vi* (AUT) to hoot (BRIT), to honk (US)

TÜV [tʏf] (-s, -s) *m abk* (= *Technischer Überwachungsverein*) MOT

Typ [ty:p] (-s, -en) *m* type; ~**e** *f* (*TYP*) type; ~**enraddrucker** *m* daisy-wheel printer

Typhus ['ty:fʊs] (-) *m* typhoid (fever)

typisch ['ty:pɪʃ] *adj*: ~ (**für**) typical (of)

Tyrann [ty'ran] (-en, -en) *m* tyrant; ~**ei** [-'naɪ] *f* tyranny; **t~isch** *adj* tyrannical; **t~i'sieren** *vt* to tyrannize

U

u. *abk* = **und**

u.a. *abk* = **unter anderem**

U-Bahn ['u:ba:n] *f* underground, tube

übel ['y:bəl] *adj* bad; (*moralisch*) bad, wicked; **jdm ist** ~ sb feels sick; **Ü~** (-s, -) *nt* evil; (*Krankheit*) disease; ~**gelaunt** *adj* bad-tempered; **Ü~keit** *f* nausea; ~**nehmen** (*unreg*) *vt*: **jdm eine Bemerkung** *etc* ~**nehmen** to be offended at sb's remark *etc*

üben ['y:bən] *vt, vi* to exercise, to practise

SCHLÜSSELWORT

über ['y:bər] *präp* +*dat* **1** (*räumlich*) over, above; **zwei Grad über Null** two degrees above zero
2 (*zeitlich*) over; **über der Arbeit einschlafen** to fall asleep over one's work
♦ *präp* +*akk* **1** (*räumlich*) over; (*hoch über auch*) above; (*quer über auch*) across
2 (*zeitlich*) over; **über Weihnachten** over Christmas; **über kurz oder lang** sooner or later
3 (*mit Zahlen*): **Kinder über 12 Jahren** children over *od* above 12 years of age; **ein Scheck über 200 Mark** a cheque for 200 marks
4 (*auf dem Wege*) via; **nach Köln über Aachen** to Cologne via Aachen; **ich habe es über die Auskunft erfahren** I found out from information
5 (*betreffend*) about; **ein Buch über ...** a book about *od* on ...; **über jdn/etw lachen** to laugh about *od* at sb/sth
6: **Macht über jdn haben** to have power

over sb; **sie liebt ihn über alles** she loves him more than everything
♦ *adv* over; **über und über** over and over; **den ganzen Tag über** all day long; **jdm in etw** *dat* **über sein** to be superior to sb in sth

überall [y:bər'al] *adv* everywhere; ~**'hin** *adv* everywhere

überanstrengen [y:bər'anʃtrɛŋən] *vt insep* to overexert ♦ *vr insep* to overexert o.s.

überarbeiten [y:bər'arbaɪtən] *vt insep* to revise, to rework ♦ *vr insep* to overwork (o.s.)

überaus ['y:bər'aus] *adv* exceedingly

überbelichten ['y:bərbəlɪçtən] *vt* (*PHOT*) to overexpose

über'bieten (*unreg*) *vt insep* to outbid; (*übertreffen*) to surpass; (*Rekord*) to break

Überbleibsel ['y:bərblaɪpsəl] (-s, -) *nt* residue, remainder

Überblick ['y:bərblɪk] *m* view; (*fig: Darstellung*) survey, overview; (*Fähigkeit*): ~ (**über** +*akk*) grasp (of), overall view (of); **ü~en** [-'blɪkən] *vt insep* to survey

überbring- [y:bər'brɪŋ] *zW*: ~**en** (*unreg*) *vt insep* to deliver, to hand over; **Ü~er** (-s, -) *m* bearer; **Ü~ung** *f* delivery

überbrücken [y:bər'brʏkən] *vt insep* to bridge (over)

über'dauern *vt insep* to outlast

über'denken (*unreg*) *vt insep* to think over

überdies [y:bər'di:s] *adv* besides

überdimensional ['y:bərdimɛnziona:l] *adj* oversize

Überdruß ['y:bərdrʊs] (-sses) *m* weariness; **bis zum** ~ ad nauseam

überdrüssig ['y:bərdrʏsɪç] *adj* (+*gen*) tired (of), sick (of)

übereifrig ['y:bər'aɪfrɪç] *adj* overkeen

übereilt [y:bər''aɪlt] *adj* (over)hasty, premature

überein- [y:bər''aɪn] *zW*: ~**ander** [y:bər'aɪ'nandər] *adv* one upon the other; (*sprechen*) about each other;

~kommen (*unreg*) *vi* to agree; **Ü~kunft** (-, **-künfte**) *f* agreement; **~stimmen** *vi* to agree; **Ü~stimmung** *f* agreement

überempfindlich ['y:bər'ɛmpfɪntlɪç] *adj* hypersensitive

überfahren [y:bər'fa:rən] (*unreg*) *vt insep* (*AUT*) to run over; (*fig*) to walk all over

Überfahrt ['y:bərfa:rt] *f* crossing

Überfall ['y:bərfal] *m* (*Bank~*, *MIL*) raid; (*auf jdn*) assault; **ü~en** [-'falən] (*unreg*) *vt insep* to attack; (*Bank*) to raid; (*besuchen*) to drop in on, to descend on

überfällig ['y:bərfɛlɪç] *adj* overdue

über'fliegen (*unreg*) *vt insep* to fly over, to overfly; (*Buch*) to skim through

Überfluß ['y:bərflʊs] *m*: ~ (**an** +*dat*) (super)abundance (of), excess (of)

überflüssig ['y:bərflʏsɪç] *adj* superfluous

über'fordern *vt insep* to demand too much of; (*Kräfte etc*) to overtax

über'führen *vt insep* (*Leiche etc*) to transport; (*Täter*) to have convicted

Überführung *f* transport; conviction; (*Brücke*) bridge, overpass

Übergabe ['y:bərga:bə] *f* handing over; (*MIL*) surrender

Übergang ['y:bərgaŋ] *m* crossing; (*Wandel*, *Überleitung*) transition

Übergangs- *zW*: **~erscheinung** *f* transitory phenomenon; **~lösung** *f* provisional solution, stopgap; **~stadium** *nt* transitional stage; **~zeit** *f* transitional period

über'geben (*unreg*) *vt insep* to hand over; (*MIL*) to surrender ♦ *vr insep* to be sick; **dem Verkehr ~** to open to traffic

übergehen ['y:bərge:ən] (*unreg*) *vi* (*Besitz*) to pass; (*zum Feind etc*) to go over, to defect; ~ **in** +*akk* to turn into; **über'gehen** (*unreg*) *vt insep* to pass over, to omit

Übergewicht ['y:bərgəvɪçt] *nt* excess weight; (*fig*) preponderance

überglücklich ['y:bərglʏklɪç] *adj* overjoyed

übergroß ['y:bərgro:s] *adj* outsize, huge

überhandnehmen [y:bər'hantne:mən] (*unreg*) *vi* to gain the ascendancy

überhaupt [y:bər'haupt] *adv* at all; (*im allgemeinen*) in general; (*besonders*) especially; ~ **nicht/keine** not/none at all

überheblich [y:bər'he:plɪç] *adj* arrogant; **Ü~keit** *f* arrogance

über'holen *vt insep* to overtake; (*TECH*) to overhaul

überholt *adj* out-of-date, obsolete

über'hören *vt insep* not to hear; (*absichtlich*) to ignore

überirdisch ['y:bər'ɪrdɪʃ] *adj* supernatural, unearthly

über'laden (*unreg*) *vt insep* to overload ♦ *adj* (*fig*) cluttered

über'lassen (*unreg*) *vt insep*: **jdm etw** ~ to leave sth to sb ♦ *vr insep*: **sich einer Sache** *dat* ~ to give o.s. over to sth

über'lasten *vt insep* to overload; (*Mensch*) to overtax

überlaufen ['y:bərlaufən] (*unreg*) *vi* (*Flüssigkeit*) to flow over; (*zum Feind etc*) to go over, to defect; ~ **sein** to be inundated *od* besieged; **über'laufen** (*unreg*) *vt insep* (*Schauer etc*) to come over

Überläufer ['y:bərlɔyfər] (-s, -) *m* deserter

über'leben *vt insep* to survive; **Ü~de(r)** *mf* survivor

über'legen *vt insep* to consider ♦ *adj* superior; **ich muß es mir** ~ I'll have to think about it; **Ü~heit** *f* superiority

Überlegung *f* consideration, deliberation

über'liefern *vt insep* to hand down, to transmit

Überlieferung *f* tradition

überlisten [y:bər'lɪstən] *vt insep* to outwit

überm ['y:bərm] = **über dem**

Übermacht ['y:bərmaxt] *f* superior force, superiority

übermächtig ['y:bərmɛçtɪç] *adj* superior (in strength); (*Gefühl etc*) overwhelming

übermannen [y:bər'manən] *vt insep* to

overcome

Übermaß ['y:bərmaːs] *nt*: ~ **(an** +*dat)* excess (of)

übermäßig ['y:bərmɛːsɪç] *adj* excessive

Übermensch ['y:bərmɛnʃ] *m* superman; **ü~lich** *adj* superhuman

übermitteln [y:bər'mɪtəln] *vt insep* to convey

übermorgen ['y:bərmɔrgən] *adv* the day after tomorrow

Übermüdung [y:bər'my:dʊŋ] *f* fatigue, overtiredness

Übermut ['y:bərmuːt] *m* exuberance

übermütig ['y:bərmyːtɪç] *adj* exuberant, high-spirited; ~ **werden** to get over-confident

übernachten [y:bər'naxtən] *vi insep*: **(bei jdm)** ~ to spend the night (at sb's place)

Übernachtung [y:bər'naxtʊŋ] *f* over-night stay

Übernahme ['y:bərna:mə] *f* taking over *od* on, acceptance

über'nehmen (*unreg*) *vt insep* to take on, to accept; (*Amt, Geschäft*) to take over ♦ *vr insep* to take on too much

über'prüfen *vt insep* to examine, to check

Überprüfung *f* examination

überqueren [y:bər'kveːrən] *vt insep* to cross

überragen [y:bər'raːgən] *vt insep* to tower above; (*fig*) to surpass

überraschen [y:bər'raʃən] *vt insep* to surprise

Überraschung *f* surprise

überreden [y:bər'reːdən] *vt insep* to persuade

überreichen [y:bər'raɪçən] *vt insep* to present, to hand over

Überreste ['y:bərrɛstə] *pl* remains, remnants

überrumpeln [y:bər'rʊmpəln] *vt insep* to take by surprise

überrunden [y:bər'rʊndən] *vt insep* to lap

übers ['y:bərs] = **über das**

Überschallflugzeug ['y:bərʃal-] *nt* supersonic jet

Überschallgeschwindigkeit *f* super-sonic speed

über'schätzen *vt insep* to overesti-mate

Überschlag ['y:bərʃlaːk] *m* (*FIN*) esti-mate; (*SPORT*) somersault; **ü~en** [-'ʃlaːgən] (*unreg*) *vt insep* (*berechnen*) to estimate; (*auslassen: Seite*) to omit ♦ *vr insep* to somersault; (*Stimme*) to crack; (*AVIAT*) to loop the loop; **'überschlagen** (*unreg*) *vt* (*Beine*) to cross ♦ *vi* (*Wellen*) to break; (*Funken*) to flash

überschnappen ['y:bərʃnapən] *vi* (*Stimme*) to crack; (*umg: Mensch*) to flip one's lid

über'schneiden (*unreg*) *vr insep* (*auch fig*) to overlap; (*Linien*) to inter-sect

über'schreiben (*unreg*) *vt insep* to provide with a heading; **jdm etw** ~ to transfer *od* make over sth to sb

über'schreiten (*unreg*) *vt insep* to cross over; (*fig*) to exceed; (*verletzen*) to transgress

Überschrift ['y:bərʃrɪft] *f* heading, title

Überschuß ['y:bərʃʊs] *m*: ~ **(an** +*dat)* surplus (of)

überschüssig ['y:bərʃʏsɪç] *adj* surplus, excess

über'schütten *vt insep*: **jdn/etw etw** ~ to pour sth over sb/sth; **jdn mit etw** ~ (*fig*) to shower sb with sth

überschwemmen [y:bər'ʃvɛmən] *vt in-sep* to flood

Überschwemmung *f* flood

überschwenglich ['y:bərʃvɛŋlɪç] *adj* effusive

Übersee ['y:bərzeː] *f*: **nach/in** ~ over-seas; **ü~isch** *adj* overseas

über'sehen (*unreg*) *vt insep* to look (out) over; (*fig: Folgen*) to see, to get an overall view of; (: *nicht beachten*) to overlook

über'senden (*unreg*) *vt insep* to send, to forward

übersetz- *zW*: **~en** [y:bər'zɛtsən] *vt in-sep* to translate; **'übersetzen** *vi* to cross; **Ü~er(in)** [-'zɛtsər(ɪn)] (**-s, -**) *m(f)* translator; **Ü~ung** [-zɛtsʊŋ] *f* transla-tion; (*TECH*) gear ratio

Übersicht ['y:bərzıçt] *f* overall view; (*Darstellung*) survey; **ü~lich** *adj* clear; (*Gelände*) open; **~lichkeit** *f* clarity, lucidity

übersiedeln ['y:bərzi:dəln] *vi sep* to move; **über'siedeln** *vi* to move

über'spannen *vt insep* (*zu sehr spannen*) to overstretch; (*überdecken*) to cover

über'spannt *adj* eccentric; (*Idee*) wild, crazy; **Ü~heit** *f* eccentricity

überspitzt [y:bər'ʃpıtst] *adj* exaggerated

über'springen (*unreg*) *vt insep* to jump over; (*fig*) to skip

überstehen [y:bər'ʃte:ən] (*unreg*) *vt insep* to overcome, to get over; (*Winter etc*) to survive, to get through; **'überstehen** (*unreg*) *vi* to project

über'steigen (*unreg*) *vt insep* to climb over; (*fig*) to exceed

über'stimmen *vt insep* to outvote

Überstunden ['y:bərʃtundən] *pl* overtime *sg*

über'stürzen *vt insep* to rush ♦ *vr insep* to follow (one another) in rapid succession

überstürzt *adj* (over)hasty

über'tönen *vt insep* to drown (out)

Übertrag ['y:bərtra:k] (-(e)s, -träge) *m* (*COMM*) amount brought forward; **ü~bar** [-'tra:kba:r] *adj* transferable; (*MED*) infectious; **ü~en** [-'tra:gən] (*unreg*) *vt insep* to transfer; (*RADIO*) to broadcast; (*übersetzen*) to render; (*Krankheit*) to transmit ♦ *vr insep* to spread ♦ *adj* figurative; **ü~en auf** +*akk* to transfer to; **jdm etw ü~en** to assign sth to sb; **sich ü~en auf** + *akk* to spread to; **~ung** [-'tra:gʊŋ] *f* transfer(ence); (*RADIO*) broadcast; rendering; transmission

über'treffen (*unreg*) *vt insep* to surpass

über'treiben (*unreg*) *vt insep* to exaggerate

Übertreibung *f* exaggeration

übertreten [y:bər'tre:tən] (*unreg*) *vt insep* to cross; (*Gebot etc*) to break; **'übertreten** (*unreg*) *vi* (*über Linie, Gebiet*) to step (over); (*SPORT*) to over-

step; (*zu anderem Glauben*) to be converted; **'~ (in** +*akk*) (*POL*) to go over ..(to)

Über'tretung *f* violation, transgression

übertrieben [y:bər'tri:bən] *adj* exaggerated, excessive

übervölkert [y:bər'fœlkərt] *adj* overpopulated

übervoll ['y:bərfɔl] *adj* overfull

übervorteilen [y:bər'fɔrtailən] *vt insep* to dupe, to cheat

über'wachen *vt insep* to supervise; (*Verdächtigen*) to keep under surveillance

Überwachung *f* supervision; surveillance

überwältigen [y:bər'vɛltıgən] *vt insep* to overpower; **~d** *adj* overwhelming

überweisen [y:bər'vaızən] (*unreg*) *vt insep* to transfer

Überweisung *f* transfer

über'wiegen (*unreg*) *vi insep* to predominate; **~d** *adj* predominant

über'winden (*unreg*) *vt insep* to overcome ♦ *vr insep* to make an effort, to bring o.s. (to do sth)

Überwindung *f* effort, strength of mind

Überzahl ['y:bərtsa:l] *f* superiority, superior numbers *pl*; **in der ~ sein** to be numerically superior

überzählig ['y:bərtsɛ:lıç] *adj* surplus

über'zeugen *vt insep* to convince; **~d** adj convincing

Überzeugung *f* conviction; **Überzeugungskraft** *f* power of persuasion

überziehen ['y:bərtsi:ən] (*unreg*) *vt* to put on; **über'ziehen** (*unreg*) *vt insep* to cover; (*Konto*) to overdraw

Überzug ['y:bərtsu:k] *m* cover; (*Belag*) coating

üblich ['y:plıç] *adj* usual

U-Boot ['u:bo:t] *nt* submarine

übrig ['y:brıç] *adj* remaining; **für jdn etwas ~ haben** (*umg*) to be fond of sb; **die ~en the others; das ~e the rest; im ~en besides; ~bleiben** (*unreg*) *vi* to remain, to be left (over); **übrigens** ['y:brıgəns] *adv* besides; (*nebenbei*

bemerkt) by the way; **~lassen** (*unreg*)
vt to leave (over)
Übung ['y:bʊŋ] *f* practice; (*Turn~*,
Aufgabe etc) exercise; **~ macht den
Meister** practice makes perfect
UdSSR [u:de:'ɛs'ɛs''ɛr] (-) *f* *abk* (=
*Union der Sozialistischen Sowjet-
republiken*) USSR
Ufer ['u:fər] (-s, -) *nt* bank; (*Meeres~*)
shore
Uhr [u:r] (-, -en) *f* clock; (*Armband~*)
watch; **wieviel ~ ist es?** what time is
it?; **1 ~** 1 o'clock; **20 ~** 8 o'clock, 20.00
(twenty hundred) hours; **~band** *nt*
watch strap; **~kette** *f* watch chain;
~macher (-s, -) *m* watchmaker; **~werk**
nt clockwork; works of a watch;
~zeiger *m* hand; **~zeigersinn** *m*: **im
~zeigersinn** clockwise; **entgegen dem
~zeigersinn** anticlockwise; **~zeit** *f* time
(of day)
Uhu ['u:hu] (-s, -s) *m* eagle owl
UKW [u:ka:'ve:] *abk* (= *Ultrakurzwelle*)
VHF
Ulk [ʊlk] (-s, -e) *m* lark; **u~ig** *adj* funny
Ulme ['ʊlmə] *f* elm
Ultimatum [ʊlti'ma:tʊm] (-s, Ultimaten)
nt ultimatum
ultraviolett ['ʊltravio'lɛt] *adj* ultraviolet

┌─────────────────┐
│ *SCHLÜSSELWORT* │
└─────────────────┘

um [ʊm] *präp* +*akk* **1** (*um herum*)
(a)round; **um Weihnachten** around
Christmas; **er schlug um sich** he hit
about him
2 (*mit Zeitangabe*) at; **um acht (Uhr)**
at eight (o'clock)
3 (*mit Größenangabe*) by; **etw um 4
cm kürzen** to shorten sth by 4 cm; **um
10% teurer** 10% more expensive; **um
vieles besser** better by far; **um nichts
besser** not in the least bit better; **um so
besser** so much the better
4: **der Kampf um den Titel** the battle
for the title; **um Geld spielen** to play
for money; **Stunde um Stunde** hour
after hour; **Auge um Auge** an eye for
an eye

♦ *präp* +*gen*: **um ... willen** for the sake
of ...; **um Gottes willen** for goodness *od*

(*stärker*) God's sake
♦ *konj*: **um ... zu** (in order) to ...; **zu
klug, um zu ...** too clever to ...; **um so
besser/schlimmer** so much the better/
worse
♦ *adv* **1** (*ungefähr*) about; **um (die) 30
Leute** about *od* around 30 people
2 (*vorbei*): **die 2 Stunden sind um** the
two hours are up

umändern ['ʊm'ɛndərn] *vt* to alter
Umänderung *f* alteration
umarbeiten ['ʊm'arbaɪtən] *vt* to re-
model; (*Buch etc*) to revise, to rework
umarmen [ʊm''armən] *vt insep* to embrace
Umbau ['ʊmbaʊ] (-(e)s, -e *od* -ten) *m*
reconstruction, alteration(s); **u~en** *vt*
to rebuild, to reconstruct
umbenennen ['ʊmbənɛnən] (*unreg*) *vt*
to rename
umbilden ['ʊmbɪldən] *vt* to reorganize;
(*POL: Kabinett*) to reshuffle
umbinden ['ʊmbɪndən] (*unreg*) *vt*
(*Krawatte etc*) to put on
umblättern ['ʊmblɛtərn] *vt* to turn over
umblicken ['ʊmblɪkən] *vr* to look around
umbringen ['ʊmbrɪŋən] (*unreg*) *vt* to
kill
Umbruch ['ʊmbrʊx] *m* radical change;
(*TYP*) make-up
umbuchen ['ʊmbu:xən] *vi* to change
one's reservation/flight *etc* ♦ *vt* to
change
umdenken ['ʊmdɛŋkən] (*unreg*) *vi* to
adjust one's views
umdrehen ['ʊmdre:ən] *vt* to turn
(round); (*Hals*) to wring ♦ *vr* to turn
(round)
Um'drehung *f* revolution; rotation
umeinander [ʊm'aɪ'nandər] *adv* round
one another; (*füreinander*) for one
another
umfahren ['ʊmfa:rən] (*unreg*) *vt* to run
over; **um'fahren** (*unreg*) *vt insep* to
drive round; to sail round
umfallen ['ʊmfalən] (*unreg*) *vi* to fall
down *od* over
Umfang ['ʊmfaŋ] *m* extent; (*von Buch*)
size; (*Reichweite*) range; (*Fläche*)

area; (*MATH*) circumference; **u~reich**
adj extensive; (*Buch etc*) voluminous
um'fassen *vt insep* to embrace;
(*umgeben*) to surround; (*enthalten*) to
include; **~d** *adj* comprehensive,
extensive
umformen ['ʊmfɔrmən] *vi* to transform
Umformer (-s, -) *m* (*ELEK*)
transformer, converter
Umfrage ['ʊmfraːgə] *f* poll
umfüllen ['ʊmfʏlən] *vt* to transfer;
(*Wein*) to decant
umfunktionieren ['ʊmfʊŋktsioniːrən] *vt*
to convert, to transform
Umgang ['ʊmgaŋ] *m* company; (*mit
jdm*) dealings *pl*; (*Behandlung*) way of
behaving
umgänglich ['ʊmgɛŋlɪç] *adj* sociable
Umgangsformen *pl* manners
Umgangssprache *f* colloquial
language
umgeben [ʊm'geːbən] (*unreg*) *vt insep*
to surround
Umgebung *f* surroundings *pl*; (*Milieu*)
environment; (*Personen*) people in
one's circle
umgehen [ʊm'geːən] (*unreg*) *vi* to go
(a)round; **im Schlosse ~** to haunt the
castle; **mit jdm grob** *etc* **~** to treat sb
roughly *etc*; **mit Geld sparsam ~** to be
careful with one's money; **um'gehen**
(*unreg*) *vt insep* to bypass; (*MIL*) to
outflank; (*Gesetz etc*) to circumvent;
(*vermeiden*) to avoid; **'umgehend** *adj*
immediate
Um'gehung *f* bypassing; outflanking;
circumvention; avoidance; **Umgehungsstraße** *f* bypass
umgekehrt ['ʊmgəkeːrt] *adj* reverse(d);
(*gegenteilig*) opposite ♦ *adv* the other
way around; **und ~** and vice versa
umgraben ['ʊmgraːbən] (*unreg*) *vt* to
dig up
Umhang ['ʊmhaŋ] *m* wrap, cape
umhauen ['ʊmhaʊən] *vt* to fell; (*fig*) to
bowl over
umher [ʊm'heːr] *adv* about, around;
~gehen (*unreg*) *vi* to walk about;
~ziehen (*unreg*) *vi* to wander from
place to place

umhinkönnen [ʊm'hɪnkœnən] (*unreg*)
vi: **ich kann nicht umhin, das zu tun I**
can't help doing it
umhören ['ʊmhøːrən] *vr* to ask around
Umkehr ['ʊmkeːr] (-) *f* turning back;
(*Änderung*) change; **u~en** *vi* to turn
back ♦ *vt* to turn round, to reverse;
(*Tasche etc*) to turn inside out; (*Gefäß
etc*) to turn upside down
umkippen ['ʊmkɪpən] *vt* to tip over ♦ *vi*
to overturn; (*umg: Mensch*) to keel
over; (*fig: Meinung ändern*) to change
one's mind
Umkleideraum ['ʊmklaɪdəraʊm] *m*
changing *od* dressing room
umkommen ['ʊmkɔmən] (*unreg*) *vi* to
die, to perish; (*Lebensmittel*) to go bad
Umkreis ['ʊmkraɪs] *m* neighbourhood;
im ~ von within a radius of
Umlage ['ʊmlaːgə] *f* share of the costs
Umlauf ['ʊmlaʊf] *m* (*Geld~*) circulation; (*von Gestirn*) revolution; **~bahn** *f*
orbit
Umlaut ['ʊmlaʊt] *m* umlaut
umlegen ['ʊmleːgən] *vt* to put on;
(*verlegen*) to move, to shift; (*Kosten*)
to share out; (*umkippen*) to tip over;
(*umg: töten*) to bump off
umleiten ['ʊmlaɪtən] *vt* to divert
Umleitung *f* diversion
umliegend ['ʊmliːgənt] *adj* surrounding
um'rahmen *vt insep* to frame
um'randen *vt insep* to border, to edge
umrechnen ['ʊmrɛçnən] *vt* to convert
Umrechnung *f* conversion; **Umrechnungskurs** *m* rate of exchange
um'reißen (*unreg*) *vt insep* to outline,
to sketch
um'ringen *vt insep* to surround
Umriß ['ʊmrɪs] *m* outline
umrühren ['ʊmryːrən] *vt, vi* to stir
ums [ʊms] = **um das**
Umsatz ['ʊmzats] *m* turnover
umschalten ['ʊmʃaltən] *vt* to switch
Umschau ['ʊmʃaʊ] *f* look(ing) round; **~
halten nach** to look around for; **u~en**
vr to look round
Umschlag ['ʊmʃlaːk] *m* cover; (*Buch~
auch*) jacket; (*MED*) compress;
(*Brief~*) envelope; (*Wechsel*) change;

(*von Hose*) turn-up; **u~en** ['ʊmʃlaːgən] (*unreg*) *vi* to change; (*NAUT*) to capsize ♦ *vt* to knock over; (*Ärmel*) to turn up; (*Seite*) to turn over; (*Waren*) to transfer; **~platz** *m* (*COMM*) distribution centre

umschreiben ['ʊmʃraɪbən] (*unreg*) *vt* (*neu~*) to rewrite; (*übertragen*) to transfer; **~ auf** +*akk* to transfer to; **um'schreiben** (*unreg*) *vt insep* to paraphrase; (*abgrenzen*) to define

umschulen ['ʊmʃuːlən] *vt* to retrain; (*Kind*) to send to another school

Umschweife ['ʊmʃvaɪfə] *pl*: **ohne ~** without beating about the bush, straight out

Umschwung ['ʊmʃvʊŋ] *m* change (around), revolution

umsehen ['ʊmzeːən] (*unreg*) *vr* to look around *od* about; (*suchen*): **sich ~ (nach)** to look out (for)

umseitig ['ʊmzaɪtɪç] *adv* overleaf

Umsicht ['ʊmzɪçt] *f* prudence, caution; **u~ig** *adj* cautious, prudent

umsonst [ʊm'zɔnst] *adv* in vain; (*gratis*) for nothing

umspringen ['ʊmʃprɪŋən] (*unreg*) *vi* to change; (*Wind auch*) to veer; **mit jdm ~** to treat sb badly

Umstand ['ʊmʃtant] *m* circumstance; **Umstände** *pl* (*fig: Schwierigkeiten*) fuss; **in anderen Umständen sein** to be pregnant; **Umstände machen** to go to a lot of trouble; **unter Umständen** possibly

umständlich ['ʊmʃtɛntlɪç] *adj* (*Methode*) cumbersome, complicated; (*Ausdrucksweise, Erklärung*) longwinded; (*Mensch*) ponderous

Umstandskleid *nt* maternity dress

Umstehende(n) ['ʊmʃteːəndə(n)] *pl* bystanders

umsteigen ['ʊmʃtaɪgən] (*unreg*) *vi* (*EISENB*) to change

umstellen ['ʊmʃtɛlən] *vt* (*an anderen Ort*) to change round, to rearrange; (*TECH*) to convert ♦ *vr* to adapt (o.s.); **sich auf etw** *akk* **~** to adapt to sth; **um'stellen** *vt insep* to surround

Umstellung ['ʊmʃtɛlʊŋ] *f* change;

(*Umgewöhnung*) adjustment; (*TECH*) conversion

umstimmen ['ʊmʃtɪmən] *vt* (*MUS*) to retune; **jdn ~** to make sb change his mind

umstoßen ['ʊmʃtoːsən] (*unreg*) *vt* to overturn; (*Plan etc*) to change, to upset

umstritten [ʊm'ʃtrɪtən] *adj* disputed

Umsturz ['ʊmʃtʊrts] *m* overthrow

umstürzen ['ʊmʃtʏrtsən] *vt* (*umwerfen*) to overturn ♦ *vi* to collapse, to fall down; (*Wagen*) to overturn

Umtausch ['ʊmtaʊʃ] *m* exchange; **u~en** *vt* to exchange

umwandeln ['ʊmvandəln] *vt* to change, to convert; (*ELEK*) to transform

umwechseln ['ʊmvɛksəln] *vt* to change

Umweg ['ʊmveːk] *m* detour, roundabout way

Umwelt ['ʊmvɛlt] *f* environment; **u~feindlich** *adj* ecologically harmful; **u~freundlich** *adj* not harmful to the environment; **~schutz** *m* conservation; **~schützer** *m* environmentalist; **~verschmutzung** *f* environmental pollution

umwenden ['ʊmvɛndən] (*unreg*) *vt, vr* to turn (round)

umwerben [ʊm'vɛrbən] (*unreg*) *vt insep* to court, to woo

umwerfen ['ʊmvɛrfən] (*unreg*) *vt* to upset, to overturn; (*Mantel*) to throw on; (*fig: erschüttern*) to upset, to throw

umziehen ['ʊmtsiːən] (*unreg*) *vt, vr* to change ♦ *vi* to move

umzingeln [ʊm'tsɪŋəln] *vt insep* to surround, to encircle

Umzug ['ʊmtsuːk] *m* procession; (*Wohnungs~*) move, removal

unab- ['ʊn'ap] *zW*: **~änderlich** *adj* irreversible, unalterable; **~hängig** *adj* independent; **U~hängigkeit** *f* independence; **~kömmlich** *adj* indispensable; **zur Zeit ~kömmlich** not free at the moment; **~lässig** *adj* incessant, constant; **~sehbar** *adj* immeasurable; (*Folgen*) unforeseeable; (*Kosten*) incalculable; **~sichtlich** *adj* unintentional; **~'wendbar** *adj* inevitable

unachtsam ['ʊn'axtzaːm] *adj* careless; **U~keit** *f* carelessness

unan- ['ʊn'an] zW: ~'**fechtbar** adj indisputable; ~**gebracht** adj uncalled-for; ~**gemessen** adj inadequate; ~**genehm** adj unpleasant; ~**gepaßt** adj nonconformist; **U~nehmlichkeit** f inconvenience; **U~nehmlichkeiten** pl (Ärger) trouble sg; ~**sehnlich** adj unsightly; ~**ständig** adj indecent, improper

unappetitlich ['ʊn'apetɪtlɪç] adj unsavoury

Unart ['ʊn'a:rt] f bad manners pl; (Angewohnheit) bad habit; **u~ig** adj naughty, badly behaved

unauf- ['ʊn'aʊf] zW: ~**fällig** adj unobtrusive; (Kleidung) inconspicuous; ~'**findbar** adj not to be found; ~**gefordert** adj unasked ♦ adv spontaneously; ~**haltsam** adj irresistible; ~'**hörlich** adj incessant, continuous; ~**merksam** adj inattentive; ~**richtig** adj insincere

unaus- ['ʊn'aʊs] zW: ~'**bleiblich** adj inevitable, unavoidable; ~**geglichen** adj unbalanced; ~'**sprechlich** adj inexpressible; ~'**stehlich** adj intolerable

unbarmherzig ['ʊnbarmhɛrtsɪç] adj pitiless, merciless

unbeabsichtigt ['ʊnbə'apzɪçtɪçt] adj unintentional

unbeachtet ['ʊnbə'axtət] adj unnoticed, ignored

unbedenklich ['ʊnbədɛŋklɪç] adj (Plan) unobjectionable ♦ adv without hesitation

unbedeutend ['ʊnbədɔʏtənt] adj insignificant, unimportant; (Fehler) slight

unbedingt ['ʊnbədɪŋt] adj unconditional ♦ adv absolutely; **mußt du ~ gehen?** do you really have to go?

unbefangen ['ʊnbəfaŋən] adj impartial, unprejudiced; (ohne Hemmungen) uninhibited; **U~heit** f impartiality; uninhibitedness

unbefriedigend ['ʊnbəfri:dɪgənt] adj unsatisfactory

unbefriedigt [-dɪçt] adj unsatisfied, dissatisfied

unbefugt ['ʊnbəfu:kt] adj unauthorized

unbegreiflich [ʊnbə'graɪflɪç] adj inconceivable

unbegrenzt ['ʊnbəgrɛntst] adj unlimited

unbegründet ['ʊnbəgryndət] adj unfounded

Unbehagen ['ʊnbəha:gən] nt discomfort

unbehaglich [-klɪç] adj uncomfortable; (Gefühl) uneasy

unbeholfen ['ʊnbəhɔlfən] adj awkward, clumsy; **U~heit** f awkwardness, clumsiness

unbeirrt ['ʊnbə'ɪrt] adj imperturbable

unbekannt ['ʊnbəkant] adj unknown

unbekümmert ['ʊnbəkʏmərt] adj unconcerned

unbeliebt ['ʊnbəli:pt] adj unpopular

unbequem ['ʊnbəkve:m] adj (Stuhl) uncomfortable; (Mensch) bothersome; (Regelung) inconvenient

unberechenbar [ʊnbə'rɛçənba:r] adj incalculable; (Mensch, Verhalten) unpredictable

unberechtigt ['ʊnbərɛçtɪçt] adj unjustified; (nicht erlaubt) unauthorized

unberührt ['ʊnbəry:rt] adj untouched, intact; **sie ist noch ~** she is still a virgin

unbescheiden ['ʊnbəʃaɪdən] adj presumptuous

unbeschreiblich [ʊnbə'ʃraɪplɪç] adj indescribable

unbesonnen ['ʊnbəzɔnən] adj unwise, rash, imprudent

unbeständig ['ʊnbəʃtɛndɪç] adj (Mensch) inconstant; (Wetter) unsettled; (Lage) unstable

unbestechlich [ʊnbə'ʃtɛçlɪç] adj incorruptible

unbestimmt ['ʊnbəʃtɪmt] adj indefinite; (Zukunft auch) uncertain

unbeteiligt ['ʊnbətaɪlɪçt] adj unconcerned, indifferent

unbewacht ['ʊnbəvaxt] adj unguarded, unwatched

unbeweglich ['ʊnbəve:klɪç] adj immovable

unbewußt ['ʊnbəvʊst] adj unconscious

unbrauchbar ['ʊnbraʊxba:r] adj (Arbeit) useless; (Gerät auch) unusable

und [ʊnt] konj and; ~ **so weiter** and so on

Undank ['ʊndaŋk] m ingratitude; **u~bar** adj ungrateful; ~**barkeit** f ingratitude

undefinierbar [ʊndefiˈniːrbaːr] *adj* indefinable

undenkbar [ʊnˈdɛŋkbaːr] *adj* inconceivable

undeutlich [ˈʊndɔʏtlɪç] *adj* indistinct

undicht [ˈʊndɪçt] *adj* leaky

Unding [ˈʊndɪŋ] *nt* absurdity

undurch- [ˈʊndʊrç] *zW*: **~führbar** [-ˈfyːrbaːr] *adj* impracticable; **~lässig** [-lɛsɪç] *adj* waterproof, impermeable; **~sichtig** [-zɪçtɪç] *adj* opaque; (*fig*) obscure

uneben [ˈʊnˈeːbən] *adj* uneven

unehelich [ˈʊnˈeːəlɪç] *adj* illegitimate

uneigennützig [ˈʊnˈaɪɡənnʏtsɪç] *adj* unselfish

uneinig [ˈʊnˈaɪnɪç] *adj* divided; **~ sein** to disagree; **U~keit** *f* discord, dissension

uneins [ˈʊnˈaɪns] *adj* at variance, at odds

unempfindlich [ˈʊnˈɛmpfɪntlɪç] *adj* insensitive; (*Stoff*) practical

unendlich [ʊnˈɛntlɪç] *adj* infinite; **U~keit** *f* infinity

unent- [ˈʊnˈɛnt] *zW*: **~behrlich** [-ˈbeːrlɪç] *adj* indispensable; **~geltlich** [-gɛltlɪç] *adj* free (of charge); **~schieden** [-ʃiːdən] *adj* undecided; **~schieden enden** (*SPORT*) to end in a draw; **~schlossen** [-ʃlɔsən] *adj* undecided; irresolute; **~wegt** [-ˈveːkt] *adj* unswerving; (*unaufhörlich*) incessant

uner- [ˈʊnˈɛr] *zW*: **~bittlich** [-ˈbɪtlɪç] *adj* unyielding, inexorable; **~fahren** [-faːrən] *adj* inexperienced; **~freulich** [-frɔʏlɪç] *adj* unpleasant; **~gründlich** [-ˈɡrʏntlɪç] *adj* unfathomable; **~heblich** [-heːplɪç] *adj* unimportant; **~hört** [-høːrt] *adj* unheard-of; (*Bitte*) outrageous; **~läßlich** [-ˈlɛslɪç] *adj* indispensable; **~laubt** [-laʊpt] *adj* unauthorized; **~meßlich** [-ˈmɛslɪç] *adj* immeasurable, immense; **~müdlich** [-ˈmyːtlɪç] *adj* indefatigable; **~sättlich** [-ˈzɛtlɪç] *adj* insatiable; **~schöpflich** [-ˈʃœpflɪç] *adj* inexhaustible; **~schütterlich** [-ˈʃʏtərlɪç] *adj* unshakeable; **~schwinglich** [-ˈʃvɪŋlɪç] *adj* (*Preis*) exorbitant; too expensive; **~träglich** [-ˈtrɛːklɪç] *adj* unbearable; (*Frechheit*) insufferable;

~wartet [-vartət] *adj* unexpected; **~wünscht** [-vʏnʃt] *adj* undesirable, unwelcome

unfähig [ˈʊnfɛːɪç] *adj* incapable; incompetent; **zu etw ~ sein** to be incapable of sth; **U~keit** *f* incapacity; incompetence

unfair [ˈʊnfɛːr] *adj* unfair

Unfall [ˈʊnfal] *m* accident; **~flucht** *f* hit-and-run (driving); **~stelle** *f* scene of the accident; **~versicherung** *f* accident insurance

unfaßbar [ʊnˈfasbaːr] *adj* inconceivable

unfehlbar [ʊnˈfeːlbaːr] *adj* infallible ♦ *adv* inevitably; **U~keit** *f* infallibility

unfit [ˈʊnfɪt] *adj* unfit

unfrei [ˈʊnfraɪ] *adj* not free, unfree; (*Paket*) unfranked; **~willig** *adj* involuntary, against one's will

unfreundlich [ˈʊnfrɔʏntlɪç] *adj* unfriendly; **U~keit** *f* unfriendliness

Unfriede(n) [ˈʊnfriːdə(n)] *m* dissension, strife

unfruchtbar [ˈʊnfrʊxtbaːr] *adj* infertile; (*Gespräche*) unfruitful; **U~keit** *f* infertility; unfruitfulness

Unfug [ˈʊnfuːk] (**-s**) *m* (*Benehmen*) mischief; (*Unsinn*) nonsense; **grober ~** (*JUR*) gross misconduct; malicious damage

Ungar(in) [ˈʊŋɡar(ɪn)] *m(f)* Hungarian; **u~isch** *adj* Hungarian; **~n** *nt* Hungary

ungeachtet [ˈʊnɡəˈaxtət] *präp* +*gen* notwithstanding

ungeahnt [ˈʊnɡəˈaːnt] *adj* unsuspected, undreamt-of

ungebeten [ˈʊnɡəbeːtən] *adj* uninvited

ungebildet [ˈʊnɡəbɪldət] *adj* uneducated; uncultured

ungedeckt [ˈʊnɡədɛkt] *adj* (*Scheck*) uncovered

Ungeduld [ˈʊnɡədʊlt] *f* impatience; **u~ig** [-dɪç] *adj* impatient

ungeeignet [ˈʊnɡəˈaɪɡnət] *adj* unsuitable

ungefähr [ˈʊnɡəfɛːr] *adj* rough, approximate; **das kommt nicht von ~** that's hardly surprising

ungefährlich *adj* not dangerous, harmless

ungehalten [ˈʊnɡəhaltən] *adj* indignant

ungeheuer [ˈʊngəhɔyər] *adj* huge ♦ *adv* (*umg*) enormously; **U~** (**-s, -**) *nt* monster; **~lich** [-ˈhɔyərlɪç] *adj* monstrous

ungehobelt [ˈʊngəhoːbəlt] *adj* (*fig*) uncouth

ungehörig [ˈʊngəhøːrɪç] *adj* impertinent, improper; **U~keit** *f* impertinence

ungehorsam [ˈʊngəhoːrzaːm] *adj* disobedient; **U~** *m* disobedience

ungeklärt [ˈʊngəklɛːrt] *adj* not cleared up; (*Rätsel*) unsolved

ungeladen [ˈʊngəlaːdən] *adj* not loaded; (*Gast*) uninvited

ungelegen [ˈʊngəleːgən] *adj* inconvenient

ungelernt [ˈʊngəlɛrnt] *adj* unskilled

ungelogen [ˈʊngəloːgən] *adv* really, honestly

ungemein [ˈʊngəmaɪn] *adj* uncommon

ungemütlich [ˈʊngəmyːtlɪç] *adj* uncomfortable; (*Person*) disagreeable

ungenau [ˈʊngənaʊ] *adj* inaccurate; **U~igkeit** *f* inaccuracy

ungeniert [ˈʊnʒeniːrt] *adj* free and easy, unceremonious ♦ *adv* without embarrassment, freely

ungenießbar [ˈʊngəniːsbaːr] *adj* inedible; undrinkable; (*umg*) unbearable

ungenügend [ˈʊngənyːgənt] *adj* insufficient, inadequate

ungepflegt [ˈʊngəpfleːkt] *adj* (*Garten etc*) untended; (*Person*) unkempt; (*Hände*) neglected

ungerade [ˈʊngəraːdə] *adj* uneven, odd

ungerecht [ˈʊngərɛçt] *adj* unjust; **~fertigt** *adj* unjustified; **U~igkeit** *f* injustice, unfairness

ungern [ˈʊngɛrn] *adv* unwillingly, reluctantly

ungeschehen [ˈʊngəʃeːən] *adj*: **~ machen** to undo

Ungeschicklichkeit [ˈʊngəʃɪklɪçkaɪt] *f* clumsiness

ungeschickt *adj* awkward, clumsy

ungeschminkt [ˈʊngəʃmɪŋkt] *adj* without make-up; (*fig*) unvarnished

ungesetzlich [ˈʊngəzɛtslɪç] *adj* illegal

ungestört [ˈʊngəʃtøːrt] *adj* undisturbed

ungestraft [ˈʊngəʃtraːft] *adv* with impunity

ungestüm [ˈʊngəʃtyːm] *adj* impetuous; tempestuous; **U~** (**-(e)s**) *nt* impetuosity; passion

ungesund [ˈʊngəzʊnt] *adj* unhealthy

ungetrübt [ˈʊngətryːpt] *adj* clear; (*fig*) untroubled; (*Freude*) unalloyed

Ungetüm [ˈʊngətyːm] (**-(e)s, -e**) *nt* monster

ungewiß [ˈʊngəvɪs] *adj* uncertain; **U~heit** *f* uncertainty

ungewöhnlich [ˈʊngəvøːnlɪç] *adj* unusual

ungewohnt [ˈʊngəvoːnt] *adj* unaccustomed

Ungeziefer [ˈʊngətsiːfər] (**-s**) *nt* vermin

ungezogen [ˈʊngətsoːgən] *adj* rude, impertinent; **U~heit** *f* rudeness, impertinence

ungezwungen [ˈʊngətsvʊŋən] *adj* natural, unconstrained

ungläubig [ˈʊnglɔybɪç] *adj* unbelieving; **die U~en** the infidel(s)

unglaublich [ʊnˈglaʊplɪç] *adj* incredible

ungleich [ˈʊnglaɪç] *adj* dissimilar; unequal ♦ *adv* incomparably; **~artig** *adj* different; **U~heit** *f* dissimilarity; inequality

Unglück [ˈʊnglyk] (**-(e)s, -e**) *nt* misfortune; (*Pech*) bad luck; (**~sfall**) calamity, disaster; (*Verkehrs~*) accident; **u~lich** *adj* unhappy; (*erfolglos*) unlucky; (*unerfreulich*) unfortunate; **u~licherweise** [-ˈvaɪzə] *adv* unfortunately; **u~selig** *adj* calamitous; (*Person*) unfortunate; **Unglücksfall** *m* accident, calamity

ungültig [ˈʊngyltɪç] *adj* invalid; **U~keit** *f* invalidity

ungünstig [ˈʊngynstɪç] *adj* unfavourable

ungut [ˈʊnguːt] *adj* (*Gefühl*) uneasy; **nichts für ~** no offence

unhaltbar [ˈʊnhaltbaːr] *adj* untenable

Unheil [ˈʊnhaɪl] *nt* evil; (*Unglück*) misfortune; **~ anrichten** to cause mischief; **u~bar** *adj* incurable; **u~bringend** *adj* fatal, fateful; **u~voll** *adj* disastrous

unheimlich [ˈʊnhaɪmlɪç] *adj* weird, uncanny ♦ *adv* (*umg*) tremendously

unhöflich [ˈʊnhøːflɪç] *adj* impolite; **U~keit** *f* impoliteness

unhygienisch ['ʊnhygɪ'eːnɪʃ] adj un-
hygienic
Uni ['ʊni] (-, -s; umg) f university
uni [y'niː] adj self-coloured
Uniform [uni'fɔrm] f uniform; **u~iert**
[-'miːrt] adj uniformed
uninteressant ['ʊnʔɪntɛrɛsant] adj
uninteresting
Universität [univɛrzi'tɛːt] f university
unkenntlich ['ʊnkɛntlɪç] adj unrecogniz-
able
Unkenntnis ['ʊnkɛntnɪs] f ignorance
unklar ['ʊnklaːr] adj unclear; **im ~en
sein über** +akk to be in the dark about;
U~heit f unclarity; (Unentschieden-
heit) uncertainty
unklug ['ʊnkluːk] adj unwise
Unkosten ['ʊnkɔstən] pl expense(s)
Unkraut ['ʊnkraʊt] nt weed; weeds pl
unlängst ['ʊnlɛŋst] adv not long ago
unlauter ['ʊnlaʊtər] adj unfair
unleserlich ['ʊnleːzərlɪç] adj illegible
unlogisch ['ʊnloːgɪʃ] adj illogical
unlösbar [ʊn'løːsbar] adj insoluble
unlöslich [ʊn'løːslɪç] adj insoluble
Unlust ['ʊnlʊst] f lack of enthusiasm;
u~ig adj unenthusiastic
unmäßig ['ʊnmɛːsɪç] adj immoderate
Unmenge ['ʊnmɛŋə] f tremendous
number, hundreds pl
Unmensch ['ʊnmɛnʃ] m ogre, brute;
u~lich adj inhuman, brutal; (ungeheuer) awful
unmerklich [ʊn'mɛrklɪç] adj imperceptible
unmißverständlich ['ʊnmɪsfɛrʃtɛntlɪç]
adj unmistakable
unmittelbar ['ʊnmɪtəlbaːr] adj immediate
unmöbliert ['ʊnmøbliːrt] adj un-
furnished
unmöglich ['ʊnmøːklɪç] adj impossible;
U~keit f impossibility
unmoralisch ['ʊnmoraːlɪʃ] adj immoral
Unmut ['ʊnmuːt] m ill humour
unnachgiebig ['ʊnnaːxgiːbɪç] adj unyielding
unnahbar [ʊn'naːbaːr] adj unapproach-
able
unnötig ['ʊnnøːtɪç] adj unnecessary

unnütz ['ʊnnʏts] adj useless
unordentlich ['ʊnʔɔrdəntlɪç] adj untidy
Unordnung ['ʊnʔɔrdnʊŋ] f disorder
unparteiisch ['ʊnpartaɪʃ] adj impartial;
U~e(r) m umpire; (FUSSBALL) referee
unpassend ['ʊnpasənt] adj inappropriate; (Zeit) inopportune
unpäßlich ['ʊnpɛslɪç] adj unwell
unpersönlich ['ʊnpɛrzøːnlɪç] adj
impersonal
unpolitisch ['ʊnpoliːtɪʃ] adj apolitical
unpraktisch ['ʊnpraktɪʃ] adj unpractical
unpünktlich ['ʊnpʏnktlɪç] adj un-
punctual
unrationell ['ʊnratsionɛl] adj inefficient
unrecht ['ʊnrɛçt] adj wrong; **U~** nt
wrong; **zu U~** wrongly; **U~ haben** to be
wrong; **~mäßig** adj unlawful, illegal
unregelmäßig ['ʊnreːgəlmɛsɪç] adj
irregular; **U~keit** f irregularity
unreif ['ʊnraɪf] adj (Obst) unripe; (fig)
immature
unrentabel ['ʊnrɛnta:bəl] adj unprofit-
able
unrichtig ['ʊnrɪçtɪç] adj incorrect, wrong
Unruhe ['ʊnruːə] f unrest; **~stifter** m
troublemaker
unruhig ['ʊnruːɪç] adj restless
uns [ʊns] (akk, dat von **wir**) pron us;
ourselves
unsachlich ['ʊnzaxlɪç] adj not to the
point, irrelevant
unsagbar [ʊn'zaːkbaːr] adj indescribable
unsanft ['ʊnzanft] adj rough
unsauber ['ʊnzaʊbər] adj unclean, dirty;
(fig) crooked; (MUS) fuzzy
unschädlich ['ʊnʃɛːtlɪç] adj harmless;
jdn/etw ~ machen to render sb/sth
harmless
unscharf ['ʊnʃarf] adj indistinct; (Bild
etc) out of focus, blurred
unscheinbar ['ʊnʃaɪnbaːr] adj insignificant; (Aussehen, Haus etc) un-
prepossessing
unschlagbar [ʊn'ʃlaːkbaːr] adj invincible
unschlüssig ['ʊnʃlʏsɪç] adj undecided
Unschuld ['ʊnʃʊlt] f innocence; **u~ig**
[-dɪç] adj innocent
unselbständig ['ʊnzɛlpʃtɛndɪç] adj
dependent, over-reliant on others

unser(e) ['ʊnzər(ə)] *adj* our; ~**e(r, s)** *pron* ours; ~**einer** *pron* people like us; ~**eins** *pron* = ~**einer**; ~**erseits** *adv* on our part; **unsertwegen** *adv* (*für uns*) for our sake; (*wegen uns*) on our account; **unsertwillen** *adv*: **um unsertwillen** = **unsertwegen**

unsicher ['ʊnzɪçər] *adj* uncertain; (*Mensch*) insecure; **U~heit** *f* uncertainty; insecurity

unsichtbar ['ʊnzɪçtbaːr] *adj* invisible

Unsinn ['ʊnzɪn] *m* nonsense; **u~ig** *adj* nonsensical

Unsitte ['ʊnzɪtə] *f* deplorable habit

unsittlich ['ʊnzɪtlɪç] *adj* indecent

unsportlich ['ʊnʃpɔrtlɪç] *adj* not sporty; unfit; (*Verhalten*) unsporting

unsre ['ʊnzrə] = **unsere**

unsterblich ['ʊnʃtɛrplɪç] *adj* immortal; **U~keit** *f* immortality

Unstimmigkeit ['ʊnʃtɪmɪçkaɪt] *f* inconsistency; (*Streit*) disagreement

unsympathisch ['ʊnzʏmpaːtɪʃ] *adj* unpleasant; **er ist mir** ~ I don't like him

untätig ['ʊntɛːtɪç] *adj* idle

untauglich ['ʊntaʊklɪç] *adj* unsuitable; (*MIL*) unfit

unteilbar ['ʊntaɪlbaːr] *adj* indivisible

unten ['ʊntən] *adv* below; (*im Haus*) downstairs; (*an der Treppe etc*) at the bottom; **nach** ~ down; ~ **am Berg** *etc* at the bottom of the mountain *etc*; **ich bin bei ihm** ~ **durch** (*umg*) he's through with me

---

SCHLÜSSELWORT

unter ['ʊntər] *präp* +*dat* **1** (*räumlich, mit Zahlen*) under; (*drunter*) underneath, below; **unter 18 Jahren** under 18 years

2 (*zwischen*) among(st); **sie waren unter sich** they were by themselves; **einer unter ihnen** one of them; **unter anderem** among other things

♦ *präp* +*akk* under, below

Unterarm ['ʊntərʔarm] *m* forearm

unter- *zW*: ~**belichten** *vt* (*PHOT*) to underexpose; **U~bewußtsein** *nt* subconscious; ~**bezahlt** *adj* underpaid

unterbieten [ʊntər'biːtən] (*unreg*) *vt insep* (*COMM*) to undercut; (*Rekord*) to lower

unterbinden [ʊntər'bɪndən] (*unreg*) *vt insep* to stop, to call a halt to

unterbrechen [ʊntər'brɛçən] (*unreg*) *vt insep* to interrupt

Unterbrechung *f* interruption

unterbringen ['ʊntərbrɪŋən] (*unreg*) *vt* (*in Koffer*) to stow; (*in Zeitung*) to place; (*Person: in Hotel etc*) to accommodate, to put up; (: *beruflich*): **jdn in einer Stellung** *od* **auf einem Posten** ~ to fix sb up with a job

unterdessen [ʊntər'dɛsən] *adv* meanwhile

Unterdruck ['ʊntərdrʊk] *m* low pressure

unterdrücken [ʊntər'drʏkən] *vt insep* to suppress; (*Leute*) to oppress

untere(r, s) ['ʊntərə(r, s)] *adj* lower

untereinander [ʊntər'aɪ'nandər] *adv* with each other; among themselves *etc*

unterentwickelt [ʊntər'ʔɛntvɪkəlt] *adj* underdeveloped

unterernährt [ʊntər'ʔɛrnɛːrt] *adj* undernourished, underfed

Unterernährung *f* malnutrition

Unter'führung *f* subway, underpass

Untergang ['ʊntərgaŋ] *m* (down)fall, decline; (*NAUT*) sinking; (*von Gestirn*) setting

unter'geben *adj* subordinate

untergehen ['ʊntərgeːən] (*unreg*) *vi* to go down; (*Sonne auch*) to set; (*Staat*) to fall; (*Volk*) to perish; (*Welt*) to come to an end; (*im Lärm*) to be drowned

Untergeschoß ['ʊntərgəʃɔs] *nt* basement

unter'gliedern *vt insep* to subdivide

Untergrund ['ʊntərgrʊnt] *m* foundation; (*POL*) underground; ~**bahn** *f* underground, tube, subway (*US*); ~**bewegung** *f* underground (movement)

unterhalb ['ʊntərhalp] *präp* +*gen* below ♦ *adv* below; ~ **von** below

Unterhalt ['ʊntərhalt] *m* maintenance; **u~en** [ʊntər'haltən] (*unreg*) *vt insep* to maintain; (*belustigen*) to entertain ♦ *vr insep* to talk; (*sich belustigen*) to enjoy o.s.; ~**ung** f maintenance; (*Belustigung*) entertainment, amusement; (*Gespräch*) talk

Unterhemd ['ʊntərhɛmt] nt vest, undershirt (*US*)

Unterhose ['ʊntərhoːzə] f underpants pl

unterirdisch ['ʊntər'ɪrdɪʃ] adj underground

Unterkiefer ['ʊntərkiːfər] m lower jaw

unterkommen ['ʊntərkɔmən] (*unreg*) vi to find shelter; to find work; **das ist mir noch nie untergekommen** I've never met with that

Unterkunft ['ʊntərkʊnft] (-, -künfte) f accommodation

Unterlage ['ʊntərlaːgə] f foundation; (*Beleg*) document; (*Schreib*~ etc) pad

unter'lassen (*unreg*) vt insep (*versäumen*) to fail to do; (*sich enthalten*) to refrain from

unterlaufen [ʊntər'laʊfən] (*unreg*) vi insep to happen ♦ adj: **mit Blut** ~ suffused with blood; (*Augen*) bloodshot

unterlegen ['ʊntərleːgən] vt to lay od put under; **unter'legen** adj inferior; (*besiegt*) defeated

Unterleib ['ʊntərlaɪp] m abdomen

unter'liegen (*unreg*) vi insep (+dat) to be defeated od overcome (by); (*unterworfen sein*) to be subject (to)

Untermiete ['ʊntərmiːtə] f: **zur** ~ **wohnen** to be a subtenant od lodger; ~**r(in)** m(f) subtenant, lodger

unter'nehmen (*unreg*) vt insep to undertake; **U**~ (-s, -) nt undertaking, enterprise (*auch COMM*)

Unternehmer [ʊntər'neːmər] (-s, -) m entrepreneur, businessman

Unterredung [ʊntər'reːdʊŋ] f discussion, talk

Unterricht ['ʊntərrɪçt] (-(e)s, -e) m instruction, lessons pl; **u**~**en** [ʊntər'rɪçtən] vt insep to instruct; (*SCH*) to teach ♦ vr insep: **sich u**~**en** (**über** +akk) to inform o.s. (about), to obtain information (about)

Unterrock ['ʊntərrɔk] m petticoat, slip

unter'sagen vt insep to forbid; **jdm etw untersagen** to forbid sb to do sth

unter'schätzen vt insep to underestimate

unter'scheiden (*unreg*) vt insep to distinguish ♦ vr insep to differ

Unter'scheidung f (*Unterschied*) distinction; (*Unterscheiden*) differentiation

Unterschied ['ʊntərʃiːt] (-(e)s, -e) m difference, distinction; **im** ~ **zu** as distinct from; **u**~**lich** adj varying, differing; (*diskriminierend*) discriminatory; **unterschiedslos** adv indiscriminately

unter'schlagen (*unreg*) vt insep to embezzle; (*verheimlichen*) to suppress

Unter'schlagung f embezzlement

Unterschlupf ['ʊntərʃlʊpf] (-(e)s, -schlüpfe) m refuge

unter'schreiben (*unreg*) vt insep to sign

Unterschrift ['ʊntərʃrɪft] f signature

Unterseeboot ['ʊntərzeːboːt] nt submarine

Untersetzer ['ʊntərzɛtsər] m tablemat; (*für Gläser*) coaster

untersetzt [ʊntər'zɛtst] adj stocky

unterste(r, s) ['ʊntərstə(r, s)] adj lowest, bottom

unterstehen [ʊntər'ʃteːən] (*unreg*) vi insep (+dat) to be under ♦ vr insep to dare; '**unterstehen** (*unreg*) vi to shelter

unterstellen [ʊntər'ʃtɛlən] vt insep to subordinate; (*fig*) to impute ♦ vt (*Auto*) to garage, to park ♦ vr to take shelter

unter'streichen (*unreg*) vt insep (*auch fig*) to underline

Unterstufe ['ʊntərʃtuːfə] f lower grade

unter'stützen vt insep to support

Unter'stützung f support, assistance

unter'suchen vt insep (*MED*) to examine; (*Polizei*) to investigate

Unter'suchung f examination; investigation, inquiry; **Untersuchungsausschuß** m committee of inquiry; **Untersuchungshaft** f imprisonment on remand

Untertan ['ʊntərtaːn] (-s, -en) m subject

untertänig ['ʊntərtɛːnɪç] adj submissive, humble

Untertasse ['ʊntərtasə] f saucer

untertauchen ['ʊntərtaʊxən] vi to dive; (*fig*) to disappear, to go underground

Unterteil ['ʊntərtaɪl] nt od m lower part, bottom; **u~en** [ʊntər'taɪlən] vt insep to divide up

Unterwäsche ['ʊntərvɛʃə] f underwear

unterwegs [ʊntər've:ks] adv on the way

unter'weisen (unreg) vt insep to instruct

unter'werfen (unreg) vt insep to subject; (Volk) to subjugate ♦ vr insep (+dat) to submit (to)

unterwürfig ['ʊntərvyrfɪç] adj obsequious, servile

unter'zeichnen vt insep to sign

unter'ziehen (unreg) vt insep to subject ♦ vr insep (+dat) to undergo; (einer Prüfung) to take

untreu ['ʊntrɔy] adj unfaithful; **U~e** f unfaithfulness

untröstlich [ʊn'trø:stlɪç] adj inconsolable

unüberlegt ['ʊn'y:bərle:kt] adj illconsidered ♦ adv without thinking

unübersehbar [ʊn'y:bər'ze:ba:r] adj incalculable

unumgänglich [ʊn'ʊm'gɛŋlɪç] adj indispensable, vital; absolutely necessary

unumwunden [ʊn'ʊm'vʊndən] adj candid ♦ adv straight out

ununterbrochen ['ʊn'ʊntərbrɔxən] adj uninterrupted

unver- [ʊnfɛr] zW: **~änderlich** [-'ʔɛndərlɪç] adj unchangeable; **~antwortlich** [-'ʔantvɔrtlɪç] adj irresponsible; (unentschuldbar) inexcusable; **~besserlich** [-'bɛsərlɪç] adj incorrigible; **~bindlich** [-'bɪntlɪç] adj not binding; (Antwort) curt ♦ adv (COMM) without obligation; **~blümt** [-'bly:mt] adj plain, blunt ♦ adv plainly, bluntly; **~daulich** [-'daʊlɪç] adj indigestible; **~dorben** [-'dɔrbən] adj unspoilt; **~einbar** [-'aɪnba:r] adj incompatible; **~fänglich** [-'fɛŋlɪç] adj harmless; **~froren** [-'fro:rən] adj impudent; **~hofft** [-'hɔft] adj unexpected; **~kennbar** [-'kɛnba:r] adj unmistakable; **~meidlich** [-'maɪtlɪç] adj unavoidable; **~mutet** [-'mu:tət] adj unexpected; **~nünftig** [-'nynftɪç] adj foolish; **~schämt** [-'ʃɛ:mt] adj impudent; **U~schämtheit** f impudence, insolence; **~sehens** [-'ze:əns] adv all of a sudden;

~sehrt [-'ze:rt] adj uninjured; **~söhnlich** [-'zø:nlɪç] adj irreconcilable; **~ständlich** [-'ʃtɛntlɪç] adj unintelligible; **~träglich** [-'trɛ:klɪç] adj quarrelsome; (Meinungen, MED) incompatible; **~wüstlich** [-'vy:stlɪç] adj indestructible; (Mensch) irrepressible; **~zeihlich** [-'tsaɪlɪç] adj unpardonable; **~züglich** [-'tsy:klɪç] adj immediate

unvollkommen ['ʊnfɔlkɔmən] adj imperfect

unvollständig adj incomplete

unvor- ['ʊnfo:r] zW: **~bereitet** adj unprepared; **~eingenommen** adj unbiased; **~hergesehen** [-he:rgəze:ən] adj unforeseen; **~sichtig** [-zɪçtɪç] adj careless, imprudent; **~stellbar** [-'ʃtɛlba:r] adj inconceivable; **~teilhaft** [-taɪlhaft] adj disadvantageous

unwahr ['ʊnva:r] adj untrue; **~scheinlich** adj improbable, unlikely ♦ adv (umg) incredibly

unweigerlich [ʊn'vaɪgərlɪç] adj unquestioning ♦ adv without fail

Unwesen ['ʊnve:zən] nt nuisance; (Unfug) mischief; **sein ~ treiben** to wreak havoc; **unwesentlich** adj inessential, unimportant; **unwesentlich besser** marginally better

Unwetter ['ʊnvɛtər] nt thunderstorm

unwichtig ['ʊnvɪçtɪç] adj unimportant

unwider- [ʊnvi:dər] zW: **~legbar** [-'le:kba:r] adj irrefutable; **~ruflich** [-'ru:flɪç] adj irrevocable; **~stehlich** [-'ʃte:lɪç] adj irresistible

unwill- ['ʊnvɪl] zW: **U~e(n)** m indignation; **~ig** adj indignant; (widerwillig) reluctant; **~kürlich** [-ky:rlɪç] adj involuntary ♦ adv instinctively; (lachen) involuntarily

unwirklich ['ʊnvɪrklɪç] adj unreal

unwirsch ['ʊnvɪrʃ] adj cross, surly

unwirtschaftlich ['ʊnvɪrtʃaftlɪç] adj uneconomical

unwissen- ['ʊnvɪsən] zW: **~d** adj ignorant; **U~heit** f ignorance; **~schaftlich** adj unscientific

unwohl ['ʊnvo:l] adj unwell, ill; **U~sein** (-s) nt indisposition

unwürdig ['ʊnvyrdɪç] adj unworthy

unzählig [ʊn'tsɛ:lıç] *adj* innumerable, countless

unzer- [ʊntsɛr] *zW:* ~**brechlich** [-'brɛçlıç] *adj* unbreakable; ~**störbar** [-'ʃtø:rba:r] *adj* indestructible; ~**trennlich** [-'trɛnlıç] *adj* inseparable

Unzucht ['ʊntsʊxt] *f* sexual offence

unzüchtig ['ʊntsʏçtıç] *adj* immoral; lewd

unzu- ['ʊntsu] *zW:* ~**frieden** *adj* dissatisfied; **U~friedenheit** *f* discontent; ~**länglich** ['ʊntsu:lɛŋlıç] *adj* inadequate; ~**lässig** ['ʊntsu:lɛsıç] *adj* inadmissible; ~**rechnungsfähig** ['ʊntsu:rɛçnʊŋsfɛ:ıç] *adj* irresponsible; ~**treffend** ['ʊntsu:-] *adj* incorrect; ~**verlässig** ['ʊntsu:-] *adj* unreliable

unzweideutig ['ʊntsvaɪdɔʏtıç] *adj* unambiguous

üppig ['ʏpıç] *adj* (*Frau*) curvaceous; (*Busen*) full, ample; (*Essen*) sumptuous; (*Vegetation*) luxuriant, lush

Ur- ['u:r] *in zW* original

uralt ['u:r'alt] *adj* ancient, very old

Uran ['u'ra:n] (-s) *nt* uranium

Ur- *zW:* ~**aufführung** *f* first performance; ~**einwohner** *m* original inhabitant; ~**eltern** *pl* ancestors; ~**enkel(in)** *m(f)* great-grandchild, great-grandson(daughter); ~**großmutter** *f* great-grandmother; ~**großvater** *m* great-grandfather; ~**heber** (-s, -) *m* originator; (*Autor*) author

Urin [u'ri:n] (-s, -e) *m* urine

Urkunde ['u:rkʊndə] *f* document, deed

Urlaub ['u:rlaʊp] (-(e)s, -e) *m* holiday(s *pl*) (*BRIT*), vacation (*US*); (*MIL etc*) leave; ~**er** [-laʊbər] (-s, -) *m* holidaymaker (*BRIT*), vacationer (*US*)

Urne ['ʊrnə] *f* urn

Ursache ['u:rzaxə] *f* cause; **keine ~** that's all right

Ursprung ['u:rʃprʊŋ] *m* origin, source; (*von Fluß*) source

ursprünglich [u:r'ʃprʏŋlıç] *adj* original ♦ *adv* originally

Urteil ['ʊrtaıl] (-s, -e) *nt* opinion; (*JUR*) sentence, judgement; **u~en** *vi* to judge; **Urteilsspruch** *m* sentence, verdict

Urwald *m* jungle

Urzeit *f* prehistoric times *pl*

USA [u:'ɛs''a:] *pl abk* (= *Vereinigte Staaten von Amerika*) USA

usw. *abk* (= *und so weiter*) etc

Utensilien [ʊtɛn'zi:lıən] *pl* utensils

Utopie [uto'pi:] *f* pipedream

utopisch [u'to:pıʃ] *adj* utopian

u.U. *abk* = **unter Umständen**

V

vag(e) [va:k, va:gə] *adj* vague

Vagina [va'gi:na] (-, **Vaginen**) *f* vagina

Vakuum ['va:kuʊm] (-s, **Vakua** *od* **Vakuen**) *nt* vacuum

Vanille [va'nıljə] (-) *f* vanilla

Variation [variatsi'o:n] *f* variation

variieren [vari'i:rən] *vt, vi* to vary

Vase ['va:zə] *f* vase

Vater ['fa:tər] (-s, -) *m* father; ~**land** *nt* native country; Fatherland

väterlich ['fɛ:tərlıç] *adj* fatherly; **väterlicherseits** *adv* on the father's side

Vaterschaft *f* paternity

Vaterunser (-s, -) *nt* Lord's prayer

Vati ['fa:ti] *m* daddy

v.Chr. *abk* (= *vor Christus*) B.C.

Vegetarier(in) [vege'ta:rıər(ın)] (-s, -) *m(f)* vegetarian

Veilchen ['faılçən] *nt* violet

Vene ['ve:nə] *f* vein

Venedig [ve'ne:dıç] *nt* Venice

Ventil [vɛn'ti:l] (-s, -e) *nt* valve

Ventilator [vɛnti'la:tɔr] *m* ventilator

verab- [fɛr''ap] *zW:* ~**reden** *vt* to agree, to arrange ♦ *vr:* **sich mit jdm** ~**reden** to arrange to meet sb; **mit jdm** ~**redet sein** to have arranged to meet sb; **V~redung** *f* arrangement; (*Treffen*) appointment; ~**scheuen** *vt* to detest, to abhor; ~**schieden** *vt* (*Gäste*) to say goodbye to; (*entlassen*) to discharge; (*Gesetz*) to pass ♦ *vr* to take one's leave; **V~schiedung** *f* leave-taking; discharge; passing

ver- [fɛr] *zW:* ~**achten** [-''axtən] *vt* to despise; ~**ächtlich** [-''ɛçtlıç] *adj* contemptuous; (*verachtenswert*) contemptible; **jdn** ~**ächtlich machen** to run sb

down; **V~achtung** f contempt
verallgemeinern [fɛr'algə'maɪnərn] vt to generalize
Verallgemeinerung f generalization
veralten [fɛr"altən] vi to become obsolete od out-of-date
Veranda [ve'randa] (-, **Veranden**) f veranda
veränder- [fɛr'ɛndər] zW: **~lich** adj changeable; **~n** vt, vr to change, to alter; **V~ung** f change, alteration
veran- [fɛr"an] zW: **~lagt** adj with a ... nature; **V~lagung** f disposition; **~lassen** vt to cause; **Maßnahmen ~lassen** to take measures; **sich ~laßt sehen** to feel prompted; **~schaulichen** vt to illustrate; **~schlagen** vt to estimate; **~stalten** vt to organize, to arrange; **V~stalter** (-s, -) m organizer; **V~staltung** f (Veranstalten) organizing; (Konzert etc) event, function
verantwort- [fɛr"antvɔrt] zW: **~en** vt to answer for ♦ vr to justify o.s.; **~lich** adj responsible; **V~ung** f responsibility; **~ungsbewußt** adj responsible; **~ungslos** adj irresponsible
verarbeiten [fɛr"arbaɪtən] vt to process; (geistig) to assimilate; **etw zu etw ~** to make sth into sth
Verarbeitung f processing; assimilation
verärgern [fɛr"ɛrgərn] vt to annoy
verausgaben [fɛr"ausgaːbən] vr to run out of money; (fig) to exhaust o.s.
veräußern [fɛr"ɔʏsərn] vt to dispose of, to sell
Verb [vɛrp] (-s, -en) nt verb
Verband [fɛr'bant] (-(e)s, ⁻e) m (MED) bandage, dressing; (Bund) association, society; (MIL) unit; **~kasten** m medicine chest, first-aid box; **~zeug** nt bandage
verbannen [fɛr'banən] vt to banish
Verbannung f exile
verbergen [fɛr'bɛrgən] (unreg) vt, vr: (sich) ~ (vor +dat) to hide (from)
verbessern [fɛr'bɛsərn] vt, vr to improve; (berichtigen) to correct (o.s.)
Verbesserung f improvement; correction

verbeugen [fɛr'bɔʏgən] vr to bow
Verbeugung f bow
ver'biegen (unreg) vi to bend
ver'bieten (unreg) vt to forbid; **jdm etw verbieten** to forbid sb to do sth
verbilligt [fɛr'bɪlɪçt] adj reduced
ver'binden (unreg) vt to connect; (kombinieren) to combine; (MED) to bandage ♦ vr (auch CHEM) to combine, to join; **jdm die Augen ~** to blindfold sb
verbindlich [fɛr'bɪntlɪç] adj binding; (freundlich) friendly; **V~keit** f obligation; (Höflichkeit) civility
Ver'bindung f connection; (Zusammensetzung) combination; (CHEM) compound; (UNIV) club
ver'bitten (unreg) vt: **sich dat etw ~** not to tolerate sth, not to stand for sth
verblassen [fɛr'blasən] vi to fade
Verbleib [fɛ'blaɪp] (-(e)s) m whereabouts; **v~en** [fɛr'blaɪbən] (unreg) vi to remain
verblüffen [fɛr'blʏfən] vt to stagger, to amaze
Verblüffung f stupefaction
ver'blühen vi to wither, to fade
ver'bluten vi to bleed to death
verborgen [fɛr'bɔrgən] adj hidden
Verbot [fɛr'boːt] (-(e)s, -e) nt prohibition, ban; **v~en** adj forbidden; **Rauchen v~en!** no smoking; **Verbotsschild** nt prohibitory sign
Verbrauch [fɛr'braux] (-(e)s) m consumption; **v~en** vt to use up; **~er** (-s, -) m consumer; **v~t** adj used up, finished; (Luft) stale; (Mensch) worn-out
Verbrechen [fɛr'brɛçən] (-s, -) nt crime; **v~** (unreg) vt to perpetrate
Verbrecher [fɛr'brɛçər] (-s, -) m criminal; **v~isch** adj criminal
ver'breiten vt, vr to spread; **sich über etw** akk **~** to expound on sth
verbreitern [fɛr'braɪtərn] vt to broaden
Verbreitung f spread(ing), propagation
verbrenn- [fɛr'brɛn] zW: **~bar** adj combustible; **~en** (unreg) vt to burn; (Leiche) to cremate; **V~ung** f burning; (in Motor) combustion; (von Leiche)

cremation; **V~ungsmotor** *m* internal combustion engine
ver'bringen (*unreg*) *vt* to spend
verbrühen [fɛr'bryːən] *vt* to scald
verbuchen [fɛr'buːxən] *vt* (*FIN*) to register, (*Erfolg*) to enjoy; (*Mißerfolg*) to suffer
verbunden [fɛr'bʊndən] *adj* connected; **jdm ~ sein** to be obliged *od* indebted to sb; „**falsch ~**" (*TEL*) "wrong number"
verbünden [fɛr'bʏndən] *vr* to ally o.s.
Verbundenheit *f* bond, relationship
Verbündete(r) [fɛr'bʏndətə(r)] *mf* ally
ver'bürgen *vr*: **sich ~ für** to vouch for
ver'büßen *vt*: **eine Strafe ~** to serve a sentence
Verdacht [fɛr'daxt] (**-(e)s**) *m* suspicion
verdächtig [fɛr'dɛçtɪç] *adj* suspicious, suspect; **~en** [fɛr'dɛçtɪgən] *vt* to suspect
verdammen [fɛr'damən] *vt* to damn, to condemn; **verdammt!** damn!
ver'dampfen *vi* to vaporize, to evaporate
ver'danken *vt*: **jdm etw ~** to owe sb sth
verdauen [fɛr'dauən] *vt* (*auch fig*) to digest
verdaulich [fɛr'daulɪç] *adj* digestible; **das ist schwer ~** that is hard to digest
Verdauung *f* digestion
Verdeck [fɛr'dɛk] (**-(e)s, -e**) *nt* (*AUT*) hood; (*NAUT*) deck; **v~en** *vt* to cover (up); (*verbergen*) to hide
ver'denken (*unreg*) *vt*: **jdm etw ~** to blame sb for sth, to hold sth against sb
Verderb- [fɛr'dɛrp] *zW*: **~en** [fɛr'dɛrbən] (**-s**) *nt* ruin; **v~en** (*unreg*) *vt* to spoil; (*schädigen*) to ruin; (*moralisch*) to corrupt ♦ *vi* (*Essen*) to spoil, to rot; (*Mensch*) to go to the bad; **es mit jdm v~en** to get into sb's bad books; **v~lich** *adj* (*Einfluß*) pernicious; (*Lebensmittel*) perishable
verdeutlichen [fɛr'dɔytlɪçən] *vt* to make clear
ver'dichten *vt, vr* to condense
ver'dienen *vt* to earn; (*moralisch*) to deserve
Ver'dienst (**-(e)s, -e**) *m* earnings *pl* ♦ *nt* merit; (*Leistung*): **~ (um)** service

(to)
verdient [fɛr'diːnt] *adj* well-earned; (*Person*) deserving of esteem; **sich um etw ~ machen** to do a lot for sth
verdoppeln [fɛr'dɔpəln] *vt* to double
verdorben [fɛr'dɔrbən] *adj* spoilt; (*geschädigt*) ruined; (*moralisch*) corrupt
verdrängen [fɛr'drɛŋən] *vt* to oust, to displace (*auch PHYS*); (*PSYCH*) to repress
ver'drehen *vt* (*auch fig*) to twist; (*Augen*) to roll; **jdm den Kopf ~** (*fig*) to turn sb's head
verdreifachen [fɛr'draifaxən] *vt* to treble
verdrießlich [fɛr'driːslɪç] *adj* peevish, annoyed
Verdruß [fɛr'drʊs] (**-sses, -sse**) *m* annoyance, worry
verdummen [fɛr'dʊmən] *vt* to make stupid ♦ *vi* to grow stupid
verdunkeln [fɛr'dʊŋkəln] *vt* to darken; (*fig*) to obscure ♦ *vr* to darken
Verdunk(e)lung *f* blackout; (*fig*) obscuring
verdünnen [fɛr'dʏnən] *vt* to dilute
verdunsten [fɛr'dʊnstən] *vi* to evaporate
verdursten [fɛr'dʊrstən] *vi* to die of thirst
verdutzt [fɛr'dʊtst] *adj* nonplussed, taken aback
verehr- [fɛr''eːr] *zW*: **~en** *vt* to venerate, to worship (*auch REL*); **jdm etw ~en** to present sb with sth; **V~er(in)** (**-s, -**) *m(f)* admirer, worshipper (*auch REL*); **~t** *adj* esteemed; **V~ung** *f* respect; (*REL*) worship
Verein [fɛr''ain] (**-(e)s, -e**) *m* club, association; **v~bar** *adj* compatible; **v~baren** [-baːrən] *vt* to agree upon; **~barung** *f* agreement; **v~fachen** [-faxən] *vt* to simplify; **v~igen** [-ɪgən] *vt*, *vr* to unite; **~igte Staaten** *pl* United States; **~igung** *f* union; (*Verein*) association; **v~t** *adj* united; **vereinzelt** *adj* isolated
vereiteln [fɛr''aitəln] *vt* to frustrate
ver'eitern *vi* to suppurate, to fester
verengen [fɛr''ɛŋən] *vr* to narrow
vererb- [fɛr''ɛrb] *zW*: **~en** *vt* to

bequeath; *(BIOL)* to transmit ♦ *vr* to be hereditary; **~lich** [fɛr'ʔɛrplɪç] *adj* hereditary; **V~ung** *f* bequeathing; *(BIOL)* transmission; *(Lehre)* heredity

verewigen [fɛr'ʔeːvɪgən] *vt* to immortalize ♦ *vr (umg)* to immortalize o.s.

ver'fahren *(unreg) vi* to act ♦ *vr* to get lost ♦ *adj* tangled; **~ mit** to deal with; **V~** (-s, -) *nt* procedure; *(TECH)* process; *(JUR)* proceedings *pl*

Verfall [fɛr'fal] (-(e)s) *m* decline; *(von Haus)* dilapidation; *(FIN)* expiry; **v~en** *(unreg) vi* to decline; *(Haus)* to be falling down; *(FIN)* to lapse; **v~en in** +*akk* to lapse into; **v~en auf** +*akk* to hit upon; **einem Laster v~en sein** to be addicted to a vice

ver'färben *vr* to change colour

Verfasser(in) [fɛr'fasər(ɪn)] (-s, -) *m(f)* author, writer

Verfassung *f (auch POL)* constitution

Verfassungs- *zW:* **~gericht** *nt* constitutional court; **v~mäßig** *adj* constitutional; **v~widrig** *adj* unconstitutional

ver'faulen *vi* to rot

ver'fehlen *vt* to miss; **etw für verfehlt halten** to regard sth as mistaken

verfeinern [fɛr'faɪnərn] *vt* to refine

ver'filmen *vt* to film

ver'fluchen *vt* to curse

verfolg- [fɛr'fɔlg] *zW:* **~en** *vt* to pursue; *(gerichtlich)* to prosecute; *(grausam, bes POL)* to persecute; **V~er** (-s, -) *m* pursuer; **V~ung** *f* pursuit; prosecution; persecution

verfremden [fɛr'frɛmdən] *vt* to make unfamiliar

verfrüht [fɛr'fryːt] *adj* premature

verfüg- [fɛr'fyːg] *zW:* **~bar** *adj* available; **~en** *vt* to direct, to order ♦ *vr* to proceed ♦ *vi:* **~en über** +*akk* to have at one's disposal; **V~ung** *f* direction, order; **zur V~ung** at one's disposal; **jdm zur V~ung stehen** to be available to sb

verführ- [fɛr'fyːr] *zW:* **~en** *vt* to tempt; *(sexuell)* to seduce; **V~er** *m* tempter; seducer; **~erisch** *adj* seductive; **V~ung** *f* seduction; *(Versuchung)* temptation

ver'gammeln *(umg) vi* to go to seed; *(Nahrung)* to go off

vergangen [fɛr'gaŋən] *adj* past; **V~heit** *f* past

vergänglich [fɛr'gɛŋlɪç] *adj* transitory; **V~keit** *f* transitoriness, impermanence

vergasen [fɛr'gaːzən] *vt (töten)* to gas

Vergaser (-s, -) *m (AUT)* carburettor

vergaß etc [fɛr'gaːs] *vb siehe* **vergessen**

vergeb- [fɛr'geːb] *zW:* **~en** *(unreg) vt (verzeihen)* to forgive; *(weggeben)* to give away; **jdm etw ~en** to forgive sb (for) sth; **~ens** *adv* in vain; **~lich** [fɛr'geːplɪç] *adv* in vain ♦ *adj* vain, futile; **V~ung** *f* forgiveness

ver'gehen *(unreg) vi* to pass by *od* away ♦ *vr* to commit an offence; **jdm vergeht etw** sb loses sth; **sich an jdm ~** to (sexually) assault sb; **V~** (-s, -) *nt* offence

ver'gelten *(unreg) vt:* **jdm etw vergelten** to pay sb back for sth, to repay sb for sth

Ver'geltung *f* retaliation, reprisal; **Vergeltungsschlag** *m (MIL)* reprisal

vergessen [fɛr'gɛsən] *(unreg) vt* to forget; **V~heit** *f* oblivion

vergeßlich [fɛr'gɛslɪç] *adj* forgetful; **V~keit** *f* forgetfulness

vergeuden [fɛr'gɔydən] *vt* to squander, to waste

vergewaltigen [fɛrgə'valtɪgən] *vt* to rape; *(fig)* to violate

Vergewaltigung *f* rape

vergewissern [fɛrgə'vɪsərn] *vr* to make sure

ver'gießen *(unreg) vt* to shed

vergiften [fɛr'gɪftən] *vt* to poison

Vergiftung *f* poisoning

Vergißmeinnicht [fɛr'gɪsmaɪnnɪçt] (-(e)s, -e) *nt* forget-me-not

vergißt etc [fɛr'gɪst] *vb siehe* **vergessen**

Vergleich [fɛr'glaɪç] (-(e)s, -e) *m* comparison; *(JUR)* settlement; **im ~ mit** *od* **zu** compared with *od* to; **v~bar** *adj* comparable; **v~en** *(unreg) vt* to compare ♦ *vr* to reach a settlement

vergnügen [fɛr'gnyːgən] *vr* to enjoy *od* amuse o.s.; **V~** (-s, -) *nt* pleasure; **viel V~!** enjoy yourself!

vergnügt [fɛrˈɡnyːkt] *adj* cheerful
Vergnügung *f* pleasure, amusement; **Vergnügungspark** *m* amusement park; **vergnügungssüchtig** *adj* pleasure-loving
vergolden [fɛrˈɡɔldən] *vt* to gild
vergöttern [fɛrˈɡœtərn] *vt* to idolize
ver'graben *vt* to bury
ver'greifen (*unreg*) *vr*: **sich an jdm ~** to lay hands on sb; **sich an etw ~** to misappropriate sth; **sich im Ton ~** to say the wrong thing
vergriffen [fɛrˈɡrɪfən] *adj* (*Buch*) out of print; (*Ware*) out of stock
vergrößern [fɛrˈɡrøːsərn] *vt* to enlarge; (*mengenmäßig*) to increase; (*Lupe*) to magnify
Vergrößerung *f* enlargement; increase; magnification; **Vergrößerungsglas** *nt* magnifying glass
Vergünstigung [fɛrˈɡʏnstɪɡʊŋ] *f* concession, privilege
vergüten [fɛrˈɡyːtən] *vt*: **jdm etw ~** to compensate sb for sth
Vergütung *f* compensation
verhaften [fɛrˈhaftən] *vt* to arrest
Verhaftung *f* arrest
ver'hallen *vi* to die away
ver'halten (*unreg*) *vr* to be, to stand; (*sich benehmen*) to behave ♦ *vt* to hold *od* keep back; (*Schritt*) to check; **sich ~ (zu)** (*MATH*) to be in proportion (to); **V~** (**-s**) *nt* behaviour
Verhältnis [fɛrˈhɛltnɪs] (**-ses, -se**) *nt* relationship; (*MATH*) proportion, ratio; **~se** *pl* (*Umstände*) conditions; **über seine ~se leben** to live beyond one's means; **v~mäßig** *adj* relative, comparative ♦ *adv* relatively, comparatively
verhandeln [fɛrˈhandəln] *vi* to negotiate; (*JUR*) to hold proceedings ♦ *vt* to discuss; (*JUR*) to hear; **über etw** *akk* **~** to negotiate sth *od* about sth
Verhandlung *f* negotiation; (*JUR*) proceedings *pl*; **Verhandlungspaket** *nt* package (of proposals)
ver'hängen *vt* (*fig*) to impose, to inflict
Verhängnis [fɛrˈhɛŋnɪs] (**-ses, -se**) *nt* fate, doom; **jdm zum ~ werden** to be

sb's undoing; **v~voll** *adj* fatal, disastrous
verharmlosen [fɛrˈharmloːzən] *vt* to make light of, to play down
verhärten [fɛrˈhɛrtən] *vr* to harden
verhaßt [fɛrˈhast] *adj* odious, hateful
verheerend [fɛrˈheːrənt] *adj* disastrous, devastating
verheimlichen [fɛrˈhaɪmlɪçən] *vt*: **jdm etw ~** to keep sth secret from sb
verheiratet [fɛrˈhaɪraːtət] *adj* married
ver'helfen (*unreg*) *vi*: **jdm ~ zu** to help sb to get
verherrlichen [fɛrˈhɛrlɪçən] *vt* to glorify
ver'hexen *vt* to bewitch; **es ist wie verhext** it's jinxed
ver'hindern *vt* to prevent; **verhindert sein** to be unable to make it
verhöhnen [fɛrˈhøːnən] *vt* to mock, to sneer at
Verhör [fɛrˈhøːr] (**-(e)s, -e**) *nt* interrogation; (*gerichtlich*) (cross-)examination; **v~en** *vt* to interrogate; to (cross-)examine ♦ *vr* to misunderstand, to mishear
ver'hungern *vi* to starve, to die of hunger
ver'hüten *vt* to prevent, to avert
Ver'hütung *f* prevention; **Verhütungsmittel** *nt* contraceptive
verirren [fɛrˈɪrən] *vr* to go astray
ver'jagen *vt* to drive away *od* out
verkalken [fɛrˈkalkən] *vi* to calcify; (*umg*) to become senile
verkannt [fɛrˈkant] *adj* unappreciated
Verkauf [fɛrˈkaʊf] *m* sale; **v~en** *vt* to sell
Verkäufer(in) [fɛrˈkɔʏfər(ɪn)] (**-s, -**) *m(f)* seller; salesman(woman); (*in Laden*) shop assistant
verkäuflich [fɛrˈkɔʏflɪç] *adj* saleable
Verkaufsbedingungen *pl* terms and conditions of sale
Verkehr [fɛrˈkeːr] (**-s, -e**) *m* traffic; (*Umgang, bes sexuell*) intercourse; (*Umlauf*) circulation; **v~en** *vi* (*Fahrzeug*) to ply, to run ♦ *vt, vr* to turn, to transform; **v~en mit** to associate with; **bei jdm v~en** (*besuchen*) to visit sb regularly

Verkehrs- *zW*: ~**ampel** *f* traffic lights *pl*; ~**amt** *nt* tourist office; ~**delikt** *nt* traffic offence; ~**stauung** *f* traffic jam, stoppage; ~**stockung** *f* traffic jam, stoppage; ~**teilnehmer** *m* road-user; ~**unfall** *m* traffic accident; ~**zeichen** *nt* traffic sign

verkehrt *adj* wrong; (*umgekehrt*) the wrong way round

ver'kennen (*unreg*) *vt* to misjudge, not to appreciate

ver'klagen *vt* to take to court

verkleiden [fɛr'klaɪdən] *vt, vr* to disguise (o.s.), to dress up

Verkleidung *f* disguise; (*ARCHIT*) wainscoting

verkleinern [fɛr'klaɪnərn] *vt* to make smaller, to reduce in size

verklemmt [fɛr'klɛmt] *adj* (*fig*) inhibited

ver'klingen (*unreg*) *vi* to die away

ver'kneifen (*umg*) *vt*: **sich** *dat* **etw ~** (*Lachen*) to stifle sth; (*Schmerz*) to hide sth; (*sich versagen*) to do without sth

verknüpfen [fɛr'knʏpfən] *vt* to tie (up), to knot; (*fig*) to connect

ver'kommen (*unreg*) *vi* to deteriorate, to decay; (*Mensch*) to go downhill, to come down in the world ♦ *adj* (*moralisch*) dissolute, depraved

verkörpern [fɛr'kœrpərn] *vt* to embody, to personify

verkraften [fɛr'kraftən] *vt* to cope with

ver'kriechen (*unreg*) *vr* to creep away, to creep into a corner

Verkrümmung *f* bend, warp; (*ANAT*) curvature

verkrüppelt [fɛr'krʏpəlt] *adj* crippled

verkrustet [fɛr'krʊstət] *adj* encrusted

ver'kühlen *vr* to get a chill

ver'kümmern *vi* to waste away

ver'künden [fɛr'kʏndən] *vt* to proclaim; (*Urteil*) to pronounce

ver'kürzen [fɛr'kʏrtsən] *vt* to shorten; (*Wort*) to abbreviate; **sich** *dat* **die Zeit ~** to while away the time

Verkürzung *f* shortening; abbreviation

Verlag [fɛr'laːk] (**-(e)s, -e**) *m* publishing firm

verlangen [fɛr'laŋən] *vt* to demand; to desire ♦ *vi*: **~ nach** to ask for, to desire; **~ Sie Herrn X** ask for Mr X; **V~** (**-s, -**) *nt*: **V~** (**nach**) desire (for); **auf jds V~** at sb's request

verlängern [fɛr'lɛŋərn] *vt* to extend; (*länger machen*) to lengthen

Verlängerung *f* extension; (*SPORT*) extra time; **Verlängerungsschnur** *f* extension cable

verlangsamen [fɛr'laŋzaːmən] *vt, vr* to decelerate, to slow down

Verlaß [fɛr'las] *m*: **auf ihn/das ist kein ~** he/it cannot be relied upon

ver'lassen (*unreg*) *vt* to leave ♦ *vr*: **sich ~ auf** +*akk* to depend on ♦ *adj* desolate; (*Mensch*) abandoned; **V~heit** *f* loneliness

verläßlich [fɛr'lɛslɪç] *adj* reliable

Verlauf [fɛr'laʊf] *m* course; **v~en** (*unreg*) *vi* (*zeitlich*) to pass; (*Farben*) to run ♦ *vr* to get lost; (*Menschenmenge*) to disperse

ver'lauten *vi*: **etw ~ lassen** to disclose sth; **wie verlautet** as reported

ver'legen *vt* to move; (*verlieren*) to mislay; (*Buch*) to publish ♦ *vr*: **sich auf etw** *akk* **~** to take up *od* to sth ♦ *adj* embarrassed; **nicht ~ um** never at a loss for; **V~heit** *f* embarrassment; (*Situation*) difficulty, scrape

Verleger [fɛr'leːgər] (**-s, -**) *m* publisher

Verleih [fɛr'laɪ] (**-(e)s, -e**) *m* hire service; **v~en** (*unreg*) *vt* to lend; (*Kraft, Anschein*) to confer, to bestow; (*Preis, Medaille*) to award; ~**ung** *f* lending; bestowal; award

ver'leiten *vt* to lead astray; **~ zu** to talk into, to tempt into

ver'lernen *vt* to forget, to unlearn

ver'lesen (*unreg*) *vt* to read out; (*aussondern*) to sort out ♦ *vr* to make a mistake in reading

verletz- [fɛr'lɛts] *zW*: ~**en** *vt* (*auch fig*) to injure, to hurt; (*Gesetz etc*) to violate; ~**end** *adj* (*fig: Worte*) hurtful; ~**lich** *adj* vulnerable, sensitive; **V~te(r)** *mf* injured person; **V~ung** *f* injury; (*Verstoß*) violation, infringement

verleumden [fɛr'lɔymdən] *vt* to slander

Verleumdung *f* slander, libel

ver'lieben *vr:* **sich ~ (in** +*akk*) to fall in love (with)
verliebt [fɛr'liːpt] *adj* in love; **V~heit** *f* being in love
verlieren [fɛr'liːrən] (*unreg*) *vt, vi* to lose ♦ *vr* to get lost
verlob- [fɛr'loːb] *zW:* **~en** *vr:* **sich ~en (mit)** to get engaged (to); **V~te(r)** [fɛr'loːptə(r)] *mf* fiancé(e); **V~ung** *f* engagement
ver'locken *vt* to entice, to lure
Ver'lockung *f* temptation, attraction
verlogen [fɛr'loːgən] *adj* untruthful; **V~heit** *f* untruthfulness
verlor *etc vb siehe* **verlieren**
verloren [fɛr'loːrən] *adj* lost; (*Eier*) poached ♦ *vb siehe* **verlieren; etw ~ geben** to give sth up for lost; **~gehen** (*unreg*) *vi* to get lost
verlosen [fɛr'loːzən] *vt* to raffle, to draw lots for
Verlosung *f* raffle, lottery
verlottern [fɛr'lɔtərn] (*umg*) *vi* to go to the dogs
verludern [fɛr'luːdərn] (*umg*) *vi* to go to the dogs
Verlust [fɛr'lʊst] (-(e)s, -e) *m* loss; (*MIL*) casualty
ver'machen *vt* to bequeath, to leave
Vermächtnis [fɛr'mɛçtnɪs] (-ses, -se) *nt* legacy
Vermählung [fɛr'mɛːlʊŋ] *f* wedding, marriage
vermehren [fɛr'meːrən] *vt, vr* to multiply; (*Menge*) to increase
Vermehrung *f* multiplying; increase
ver'meiden (*unreg*) *vt* to avoid
vermeintlich [fɛr'maɪntlɪç] *adj* supposed
Vermerk [fɛr'mɛrk] (-(e)s, -e) *m* note; (*in Ausweis*) endorsement; **v~en** *vt* to note
ver'messen (*unreg*) *vt* to survey ♦ *adj* presumptuous, bold; **V~heit** *f* presumptuousness; recklessness
Ver'messung *f* survey(ing)
ver'mieten *vt* to let, to rent (out); (*Auto*) to hire out, to rent
Ver'mieter(in) (-s, -) *m(f)* landlord(lady)
Ver'mietung *f* letting, renting (out);

(*von Autos*) hiring (out)
vermindern [fɛr'mɪndərn] *vt, vr* to lessen, to decrease; (*Preise*) to reduce
Verminderung *f* reduction
ver'mischen *vt, vr* to mix, to blend
vermissen [fɛr'mɪsən] *vt* to miss
vermißt [fɛr'mɪst] *adj* missing
vermitteln [fɛr'mɪtəln] *vi* to mediate ♦ *vt* (*Gespräch*) to connect; **jdm etw ~ to** help sb to obtain sth
Vermittler [fɛr'mɪtlər] (-s, -) *m* (*Schlichter*) agent, mediator
Vermittlung *f* procurement; (*Stellen~*) agency; (*TEL*) exchange; (*Schlichtung*) mediation
ver'mögen (*unreg*) *vt* to be capable of; **~ zu** to be able to; **V~** (-s, -) *nt* wealth; (*Fähigkeit*) ability; **ein V~ kosten** to cost a fortune; **~d** *adj* wealthy
vermuten [fɛr'muːtən] *vt* to suppose, to guess; (*argwöhnen*) to suspect
vermutlich *adj* supposed, presumed ♦ *adv* probably
Vermutung *f* supposition; suspicion
vernachlässigen [fɛr'naːxlɛsɪgən] *vt* to neglect
ver'nehmen (*unreg*) *vt* to perceive, to hear; (*erfahren*) to learn; (*JUR*) to (cross-)examine; **dem V~ nach** from what I/we *etc* hear
vernehmlich [fɛr'neːmlɪç] *adj* audible
Vernehmung *f* (cross-)examination
verneigen [fɛr'naɪgən] *vr* to bow
verneinen [fɛr'naɪnən] *vt* (*Frage*) to answer in the negative; (*ablehnen*) to deny; (*GRAM*) to negate; **~d** *adj* negative
Verneinung *f* negation
vernichten [fɛr'nɪçtən] *vt* to annihilate, to destroy; **~d** *adj* (*fig*) crushing; (*Blick*) withering; (*Kritik*) scathing
Vernichtung *f* destruction, annihilation
verniedlichen [fɛr'niːtlɪçən] *vt* to play down
Vernunft [fɛr'nʊnft] (-) *f* reason, understanding
vernünftig [fɛr'nʏnftɪç] *adj* sensible, reasonable
veröffentlichen [fɛr'œfəntlɪçən] *vt* to publish

Veröffentlichung f publication
verordnen [fɛr''ɔrdnən] vt (MED) to prescribe
Verordnung f order, decree; (MED) prescription
ver'pachten vt to lease (out)
ver'packen vt to pack
Ver'packung f packing, wrapping; **Verpackungsmaterial** nt packing, wrapping
ver'passen vt to miss; **jdm eine Ohrfeige ~** (umg) to give sb a clip round the ear
ver'pflanzen vt to transplant
Ver'pflanzung f transplant(ing)
ver'pflegen vt to feed, to cater for
Ver'pflegung f feeding, catering; (Kost) food; (in Hotel) board
verpflichten [fɛr'pflɪçtən] vt to oblige, to bind; (anstellen) to engage ♦ vr to undertake; (MIL) to sign on ♦ vi to carry obligations; **jdm zu Dank verpflichtet sein** to be obliged to sb
Verpflichtung f obligation, duty
verpönt [fɛr'pø:nt] adj disapproved (of), taboo
ver'prügeln (umg) vt to beat up, to do over
Verputz [fɛr'pʊts] m plaster, roughcast; **v~en** vt to plaster; (umg: Essen) to put away
Verrat [fɛr'ra:t] (-(e)s) m treachery; (POL) treason; **v~en** (unreg) vt to betray; (Geheimnis) to divulge ♦ vr to give o.s. away
Verräter(in) [fɛr'rɛ:tər(ɪn)] (-s, -) m(f) traitor(tress); **v~isch** adj treacherous
ver'rechnen vt: **~ mit** to set off against ♦ vr to miscalculate
Verrechnungsscheck [fɛr'rɛçnʊŋsʃɛk] m crossed cheque
verregnet [fɛr're:gnət] adj spoilt by rain, rainy
ver'reisen vi to go away (on a journey)
verrenken [fɛr'rɛŋkən] vt to contort; (MED) to dislocate; **sich dat den Knöchel ~** to sprain one's ankle
ver'richten vt to do, to perform
verriegeln [fɛr'ri:gəln] vt to bolt up, to lock

verringern [fɛr'rɪŋərn] vt to reduce ♦ vr to diminish
Verringerung f reduction; lessening
ver'rinnen (unreg) vi to run out od away; (Zeit) to elapse
ver'rosten vi to rust
verrotten [fɛr'rɔtən] vi to rot
ver'rücken vt to move, to shift
verrückt [fɛr'rʏkt] adj crazy, mad; **V~e(r)** mf lunatic; **V~heit** f madness, lunacy
Verruf [fɛr'ru:f] m: **in ~ geraten/bringen** to fall/bring into disrepute; **v~en** adj notorious, disreputable
Vers [fɛrs] (-es, -e) m verse
ver'sagen vt: **jdm/sich etw ~** to deny sb/o.s. sth ♦ vi to fail; **V~** (-s) nt failure
Versager [fɛr'za:gər] (-s, -) m failure
ver'salzen (unreg) vt to put too much salt in; (fig) to spoil
ver'sammeln vt, vr to assemble, to gather
Ver'sammlung f meeting, gathering
Versand [fɛr'zant] (-(e)s) m forwarding; dispatch; (~abteilung) dispatch department; **~haus** nt mail-order firm
versäumen [fɛr'zɔymən] vt to miss; (unterlassen) to neglect, to fail
ver'schaffen vt: **jdm/sich etw ~** to get od procure sth for sb/o.s.
verschämt [fɛr'ʃɛ:mt] adj bashful
verschandeln [fɛr'ʃandəln] (umg) vt to spoil
verschärfen [fɛr'ʃɛrfən] vt to intensify; (Lage) to aggravate ♦ vr to intensify; to become aggravated
ver'schätzen vr to be out in one's reckoning
ver'schenken vt to give away
ver'schicken vt to send off
ver'schieben (unreg) vt to shift; (EISENB) to shunt; (Termin) to postpone
verschieden [fɛr'ʃi:dən] adj different; (pl: mehrere) various; **sie sind ~ groß** they are of different sizes; **~e** pron pl various people/things; **~es** pron various things pl; **etwas V~es** something different; **V~heit** f difference; **verschiedentlich** adv several times

verschlafen [fɛrˈʃlaːfən] (*unreg*) *vt* to sleep through; (*fig: versäumen*) to miss ♦ *vi*, *vr* to oversleep ♦ *adj* sleepy

Verschlag [fɛrˈʃlaːk] *m* shed; **v~en** [fɛrˈʃlaːgən] (*unreg*) *vt* to board up ♦ *adj* cunning; **jdm den Atem v~en** to take sb's breath away; **an einen Ort v~en werden** to wind up in a place

verschlechtern [fɛrˈʃlɛçtərn] *vt* to make worse ♦ *vr* to deteriorate, to get worse

Verschlechterung *f* deterioration

Verschleiß [fɛrˈʃlaɪs] (**-es, -e**) *m* wear and tear; **v~en** (*unreg*) *vt* to wear out

ver'schleppen *vt* to carry off, to abduct; (*Krankheit*) to protract; (*zeitlich*) to drag out

ver'schleudern *vt* to squander; (*COMM*) to sell dirt-cheap

verschließbar *adj* lockable

verschließen [fɛrˈʃliːsən] (*unreg*) *vt* to close, to lock ♦ *vr*: **sich einer Sache** *dat* ~ to close one's mind to sth

verschlimmern [fɛrˈʃlɪmərn] *vt* to make worse, to aggravate ♦ *vr* to get worse, to deteriorate

verschlingen [fɛrˈʃlɪŋən] (*unreg*) *vt* to devour, to swallow up; (*Fäden*) to twist

verschlossen [fɛrˈʃlɔsən] *adj* locked; (*fig*) reserved; **V~heit** *f* reserve

ver'schlucken *vt* to swallow ♦ *vr* to choke

Verschluß [fɛrˈʃlʊs] *m* lock; (*von Kleid etc*) fastener; (*PHOT*) shutter; (*Stöpsel*) plug; **unter ~ halten** to keep under lock and key

verschlüsseln [fɛrˈʃlʏsəln] *vt* to encode

verschmähen [fɛrˈʃmɛːən] *vt* to disdain, to scorn

verschmerzen [fɛrˈʃmɛrtsən] *vt* to get over

verschmutzen [fɛrˈʃmʊtsən] *vt* to soil; (*Umwelt*) to pollute

verschneit [fɛrˈʃnaɪt] *adj* snowed up, covered in snow

verschollen [fɛrˈʃɔlən] *adj* lost, missing

ver'schonen *vt*: **jdn mit etw ~** to spare sb sth

verschönern [fɛrˈʃøːnərn] *vt* to decorate; (*verbessern*) to improve

ver'schreiben (*unreg*) *vt* (*MED*) to pre-scribe ♦ *vr* to make a mistake (in writing); **sich einer Sache** *dat* ~ to devote o.s. to sth

verschroben [fɛrˈʃroːbən] *adj* eccentric, odd

verschrotten [fɛrˈʃrɔtən] *vt* to scrap

verschuld- [fɛrˈʃʊld] *zW*: **~en** *vt* to be guilty of; **V~en** (**-s**) *nt* fault, guilt; **~et** *adj* in debt; **V~ung** *f* fault; (*Geld*) debts *pl*

ver'schütten *vt* to spill; (*zuschütten*) to fill; (*unter Trümmer*) to bury

ver'schweigen (*unreg*) *vt* to keep secret; **jdm etw ~** to keep sth from sb

verschwend- [fɛrˈʃvɛnd] *zW*: **~en** *vt* to squander; **V~er** (**-s, -**) *m* spendthrift; **~erisch** *adj* wasteful, extravagant; **V~ung** *f* waste; extravagance

verschwiegen [fɛrˈʃviːgən] *adj* discreet; (*Ort*) secluded; **V~heit** *f* discretion; seclusion

ver'schwimmen (*unreg*) *vi* to grow hazy, to become blurred

ver'schwinden (*unreg*) *vi* to dis-appear, to vanish; **V~** (**-s**) *nt* dis-appearance

verschwommen [fɛrˈʃvɔmən] *adj* hazy, vague

verschwör- [fɛrˈʃvøːr] *zW*: **~en** (*unreg*) *vr* to plot, to conspire; **V~er** (**-s, -**) *m* conspirator; **V~ung** *f* conspiracy, plot

ver'sehen (*unreg*) *vt* to supply, to provide; (*Pflicht*) to carry out; (*Amt*) to fill; (*Haushalt*) to keep ♦ *vr* (*fig*) to make a mistake; **ehe er (es) sich ~ hatte ...** before he knew it ...; **V~** (**-s, -**) *nt* oversight; **aus V~** by mistake; **ver-sehentlich** *adv* by mistake

Versehrte(r) [fɛrˈzeːrtə(r)] *mf* disabled person

ver'senden (*unreg*) *vt* to forward, to dispatch

ver'senken *vt* to sink ♦ *vr*: **sich ~ in** *+akk* to become engrossed in

versessen [fɛrˈzɛsən] *adj*: ~ **auf** *+akk* mad about

ver'setzen *vt* to transfer; (*verpfänden*) to pawn; (*umg*) to stand up ♦ *vr*: **sich in jdn** *od* **in jds Lage ~** to put o.s. in sb's place; **jdm einen Tritt/Schlag ~** to

kick/hit sb; **etw mit etw ~** to mix sth with sth; **jdn in gute Laune ~** to put sb in a good mood
Ver'setzung f transfer
verseuchen [fɛr'zɔyçən] vt to contaminate
versichern [fɛr'zɪçərn] vt to assure; (mit Geld) to insure
Versicherung f assurance; insurance; **Versicherungsgesellschaft** f insurance company; **Versicherungspolice** f insurance policy
ver'siegen vi to dry up
ver'sinken (unreg) vi to sink
versöhnen [fɛr'zø:nən] vt to reconcile ♦ vr to become reconciled
Versöhnung f reconciliation
ver'sorgen vt to provide, to supply; (Familie etc) to look after
Ver'sorgung f provision; (Unterhalt) maintenance; (Alters~ etc) benefit, assistance
verspäten [fɛr'ʃpɛːtən] vr to be late
Verspätung f delay; **~ haben** to be late
ver'sperren vt to bar, to obstruct
ver'spotten vt to ridicule, to scoff at
ver'sprechen (unreg) vt to promise; **sich** dat **etw von etw ~** to expect sth from sth; **V~ (-s, -)** nt promise
verstaatlichen [fɛr'ʃtaːtlɪçən] vt to nationalize
Verstand [fɛr'ʃtant] m intelligence; mind; **den ~ verlieren** to go out of one's mind; **über jds ~ gehen** to go beyond sb
verständig [fɛr'ʃtɛndɪç] adj sensible; **~en** [fɛr'ʃtɛndɪgən] vt to inform ♦ vr to communicate; (sich einigen) to come to an understanding; **V~ung** [fɛr'ʃtɛndɪgʊŋ] f communication; (Benachrichtigung) informing; (Einigung) agreement
verständ- [fɛr'ʃtɛnt] zW: **~lich** adj understandable, comprehensible; **V~lichkeit** f clarity, intelligibility; **V~nis (-ses, -se)** nt understanding; **~nislos** adj uncomprehending; **~nisvoll** adj understanding, sympathetic
verstärk- [fɛr'ʃtɛrk] zW: **~en** vt to strengthen; (Ton) to amplify; (erhöhen) to intensify ♦ vr to intensify;

V~er (-s, -) m amplifier; **V~ung** f strengthening; (Hilfe) reinforcements pl; (von Ton) amplification
verstauchen [fɛr'ʃtauxən] vt to sprain
verstauen [fɛr'ʃtauən] vt to stow away
Versteck [fɛr'ʃtɛk] (-(e)s, -e) nt hiding (place); **v~en** vt, vr to hide; **v~t** adj hidden
ver'stehen (unreg) vt to understand ♦ vr to get on; **das versteht sich (von selbst)** that goes without saying
versteigern [fɛr'ʃtaɪgərn] vt to auction
Versteigerung f auction
verstell- [fɛr'ʃtɛl] zW: **~bar** adj adjustable, variable; **~en** vt to move, to shift; (Uhr) to adjust; (versperren) to block; (fig) to disguise ♦ vr to pretend, to put on an act; **V~ung** f pretence
verstiegen [fɛr'ʃtiːgən] adj exaggerated
verstimmt [fɛr'ʃtɪmt] adj out of tune; (fig) cross, put out; (Magen) upset
verstohlen [fɛr'ʃtoːlən] adj stealthy
ver'stopfen vt to block, to stop up; (MED) to constipate
Ver'stopfung f obstruction; (MED) constipation
verstorben [fɛr'ʃtɔrbən] adj deceased, late
verstört [fɛr'ʃtøːrt] adj (Mensch) distraught
Verstoß [fɛr'ʃtoːs] m: **~ (gegen)** infringement (of), violation (of); **v~en** (unreg) vt to disown, to reject ♦ vi: **v~en gegen** to offend against
ver'streichen (unreg) vt to spread ♦ vi to elapse
ver'streuen vt to scatter (about)
verstümmeln [fɛr'ʃtʏməln] vt to maim, to mutilate (auch fig)
verstummen [fɛr'ʃtʊmən] vi to go silent; (Lärm) to die away
Versuch [fɛr'zuːx] (-(e)s, -e) m attempt; (SCI) experiment; **v~en** vt to try; (verlocken) to tempt ♦ vr: **sich an etw** dat **v~en** to try one's hand at sth; **Versuchskaninchen** nt (fig) guinea-pig; **versuchsweise** adv tentatively; **~ung** f temptation
versumpfen [fɛr'zʊmpfən] (umg) vi (fig) to get into a booze-up

versunken [fɛr'zʊŋkən] *adj* sunken; ~ **sein in** +*akk* to be absorbed *od* engrossed in

vertagen [fɛr'taːgən] *vt*, *vi* to adjourn

ver'tauschen *vt* to exchange; (*versehentlich*) to mix up

verteidig- [fɛr'taɪdɪg] *zW*: ~**en** *vt* to defend; **V~er** (-s, -) *m* defender; (*JUR*) defence counsel; **V~ung** *f* defence

ver'teilen *vt* to distribute; (*Rollen*) to assign; (*Salbe*) to spread

Verteilung *f* distribution, allotment

vertiefen [fɛr'tiːfən] *vt* to deepen ♦ *vr*: **sich in etw akk** ~ to become engrossed *od* absorbed in sth

Vertiefung *f* depression

vertikal [vɛrti'kaːl] *adj* vertical

vertilgen [fɛr'tɪlgən] *vt* to exterminate; (*umg*) to eat up, to consume

vertonen [fɛr'toːnən] *vt* to set to music

Vertrag [fɛr'traːk] (-(e)s, ⁻e) *m* contract, agreement; (*POL*) treaty; **v~en** [fɛr'traːgən] (*unreg*) *vt* to tolerate, to stand ♦ *vr* to get along; (*sich aussöhnen*) to become reconciled; **v~lich** *adj* contractual

verträglich [fɛr'trɛːklɪç] *adj* good-natured, sociable; (*Speisen*) easily digested; (*MED*) easily tolerated; **V~keit** *f* sociability; good nature; digestibility

Vertrags- *zW*: ~**bruch** *m* breach of contract; ~**partner** *m* party to a contract; **v~widrig** *adj* contrary to contract

vertrauen [fɛr'traʊən] *vi*: **jdm** ~ to trust sb; ~ **auf** +*akk* to rely on; **V~** (-s) *nt* confidence; ~**erweckend** *adj* inspiring trust; **vertrauensvoll** *adj* trustful; **vertrauenswürdig** *adj* trustworthy

vertraulich [fɛr'traʊlɪç] *adj* familiar; (*geheim*) confidential

vertraut [fɛr'traʊt] *adj* familiar; **V~heit** *f* familiarity

ver'treiben (*unreg*) *vt* to drive away; (*aus Land*) to expel; (*COMM*) to sell; (*Zeit*) to pass

vertret- [fɛr'treːt] *zW*: ~**en** (*unreg*) *vt* to represent; (*Ansicht*) to hold, to advocate; **sich** *dat* **die Beine** ~**en** to

stretch one's legs; **V~er** (-s, -) *m* representative; (*Verfechter*) advocate; **V~ung** *f* representation; advocacy

Vertrieb [fɛr'triːp] (-(e)s, -e) *m* marketing (department)

ver'trocknen *vi* to dry up

ver'trösten *vt* to put off

vertun [fɛr'tuːn] (*unreg*) *vt* to waste ♦ *vr* (*umg*) to make a mistake

vertuschen [fɛr'tʊʃən] *vt* to hush *od* cover up

verübeln [fɛr'yːbəln] *vt*: **jdm etw** ~ to be cross *od* offended with sb on account of sth

verüben [fɛr'yːbən] *vt* to commit

verun- [fɛr'ʊn] *zW*: ~**glimpfen** [-glɪmpfən] *vt* to disparage; ~**glücken** [-glʏkən] *vi* to have an accident; **tödlich** ~**glücken** to be killed in an accident; ~**reinigen** *vt* to soil; (*Umwelt*) to pollute; ~**sichern** *vt* to rattle; ~**treuen** [-trɔʏən] *vt* to embezzle

verur- [fɛr'uːr] *zW*: ~**sachen** [-zaxən] *vt* to cause; ~**teilen** [-taɪlən] *vt* to condemn; **V~teilung** *f* condemnation; (*JUR*) sentence

verviel- [fɛr'fiːl] *zW*: ~**fachen** [-faxən] *vt* to multiply; ~**fältigen** [-fɛltɪgən] *vt* to duplicate, to copy; **V~fältigung** *f* duplication, copying

vervollkommnen [fɛr'fɔlkɔmnən] *vt* to perfect

vervollständigen *vt* to complete

ver'wackeln *vt* (*Foto*) to blur

ver'wählen *vr* (*TEL*) to dial the wrong number

verwahr- [fɛr'vaːr] *zW*: ~**en** *vt* to keep, to lock away ♦ *vr* to protest; ~**losen** [-loːzən] *vi* to become neglected; (*moralisch*) to go to the bad; ~**lost** [-loːst] *adj* neglected; wayward

verwalt- [fɛr'valt] *zW*: ~**en** *vt* to manage; to administer; **V~er** (-s, -) *m* manager; (*Vermögensverwalter*) trustee; **V~ung** *f* administration; management; **V~ungsbezirk** *m* administrative district

ver'wandeln *vt* to change, to transform ♦ *vr* to change; to be transformed

Ver'wandlung *f* change, transformation

verwandt [fɛr'vant] *adj*: ~ (mit) related (to); V~e(r) *mf* relative, relation; V~schaft *f* relationship; (*Menschen*) relations *pl*

ver'warnen *vt* to caution

Ver'warnung *f* caution

ver'wechseln *vt*: verwechseln mit to confuse with; to mistake for; zum V~ ähnlich like as two peas

Ver'wechslung *f* confusion, mixing up

verwegen [fɛr've:gən] *adj* daring, bold

Verwehung [fɛr've:uŋ] *f* snowdrift; sanddrift

verweichlicht [fɛr'vaɪçlɪçt] *adj* effeminate, soft

ver'weigern *vt*: jdm etw ~ to refuse sb sth; den Gehorsam/die Aussage ~ to refuse to obey/testify

Ver'weigerung *f* refusal

Verweis [fɛr'vaɪs] (-es, -e) *m* reprimand, rebuke; (*Hinweis*) reference; v~en [fɛr'vaɪzən] (*unreg*) *vt* to refer; jdn von der Schule v~en to expel sb (from school); jdn des Landes v~en to deport *od* expel sb

ver'welken *vi* to fade

ver'wenden (*unreg*) *vt* to use; (*Mühe, Zeit, Arbeit*) to spend ♦ *vr* to intercede

Ver'wendung *f* use

ver'werfen (*unreg*) *vt* to reject

verwerflich [fɛr'vɛrflɪç] *adj* reprehensible

ver'werten *vt* to utilize

Ver'wertung *f* utilization

verwesen [fɛr'veɪzən] *vi* to decay

ver'wickeln *vt* to tangle (up); (*fig*) to involve ♦ *vr* to get tangled (up); jdn in etw *akk* ~ to involve sb in sth; sich in etw *akk* ~ to get involved in sth

verwildern [fɛr'vɪldərn] *vi* to run wild

ver'winden (*unreg*) *vt* to get over

verwirklichen [fɛr'vɪrklɪçən] *vt* to realize, to put into effect

Verwirklichung *f* realization

verwirren [fɛr'vɪrən] *vt* to tangle (up); (*fig*) to confuse

Verwirrung *f* confusion

verwittern [fɛr'vɪtərn] *vi* to weather

verwitwet [fɛr'vɪtvət] *adj* widowed

verwöhnen [fɛr'vø:nən] *vt* to spoil

verworfen [fɛr'vɔrfən] *adj* depraved

verworren [fɛr'vɔrən] *adj* confused

verwundbar [fɛr'vʊntba:r] *adj* vulnerable

verwunden [fɛr'vʊndən] *vt* to wound

verwunderlich [fɛr'vʊndərlɪç] *adj* surprising

Verwunderung [fɛr'vʊndərʊŋ] *f* astonishment

Verwundete(r) *mf* injured person

Verwundung *f* wound, injury

ver'wünschen *vt* to curse

verwüsten [fɛr'vy:stən] *vt* to devastate

verzagen [fɛr'tsa:gən] *vi* to despair

ver'zählen *vr* to miscount

verzehren [fɛr'tse:rən] *vt* to consume

ver'zeichnen *vt* to list; (*Niederlage, Verlust*) to register

Verzeichnis [fɛr'tsaɪçnɪs] (-ses, -se) *nt* list, catalogue; (*in Buch*) index

verzeih- [fɛr'tsaɪ] *zW*: ~en (*unreg*) *vt, vi* to forgive; jdm etw ~en to forgive sb for sth; ~lich *adj* pardonable; V~ung *f* forgiveness, pardon; V~ung! sorry!, excuse me!

Verzicht [fɛr'tsɪçt] (-(e)s, -e) *m*: ~ (auf +*akk*) renunciation (of); v~en *vi*: v~en auf +*akk* to forgo, to give up

ver'ziehen (*unreg*) *vi* to move ♦ *vt* to put out of shape; (*Kind*) to spoil; (*Pflanzen*) to thin out ♦ *vr* to go out of shape; (*Gesicht*) to contort; (*verschwinden*) to disappear; das Gesicht ~ to pull a face

verzieren [fɛr'tsi:rən] *vt* to decorate, to ornament

verzinsen [fɛr'tsɪnzən] *vt* to pay interest on

ver'zögern *vt* to delay

Ver'zögerung *f* delay, time-lag; Verzögerungstaktik *f* delaying tactics *pl*

verzollen [fɛr'tsɔlən] *vt* to pay duty on

verzückt [fɛr'tsʏkt] *adj* enraptured

Verzückung *f* ecstasy

verzweif- [fɛr'tsvaɪf] *zW*: ~eln *vi* to despair; ~elt *adj* desperate; V~lung *f* despair

verzwickt [fɛr'tsvɪkt] (*umg*) *adj*

awkward, complicated

Vesuv [ve'zu:f] (-(s)) *m* Vesuvius

Veto ['ve:to] (-s, -s) *nt* veto

Vetter ['fɛtər] (-s, -n) *m* cousin

vgl. *abk* (= *vergleiche*) cf.

v.H. *abk* (= *vom Hundert*) p.c.

vibrieren [vi'bri:rən] *vi* to vibrate

Video ['vi:deo] *nt* video; ~**gerät** *nt* video recorder; ~**recorder** *m* video recorder

Vieh [fi:] (-(e)s) *nt* cattle *pl*; **v**~**isch** *adj* bestial

viel [fi:l] *adj* a lot of, much ♦ *adv* a lot, much; ~**e** *pron pl* a lot of, many; ~ **zuwenig** much too little; ~**erlei** *adj* a great variety of; ~**es** *pron* a lot; ~**fach** *adj, adv* many times; **auf** ~**fachen Wunsch** at the request of many people; **V**~**falt** (-) *f* variety; ~**fältig** *adj* varied, many-sided

vielleicht [fi'laɪçt] *adv* perhaps

viel- *zW*: ~**mal(s)** *adv* many times; **danke** ~**mals** many thanks; ~**mehr** *adv* rather, on the contrary; ~**sagend** *adj* significant; ~**seitig** *adj* many-sided; ~**versprechend** *adj* promising

vier [fi:r] *num* four; **V**~**eck** (-(e)s, -e) *nt* four-sided figure; (*gleichseitig*) square; ~**eckig** *adj* four-sided; square; **V**~**taktmotor** *m* four-stroke engine; ~**te(r, s)** ['fi:rtə(r, s)] *adj* fourth; **V**~**tel** ['fɪrtəl] (-s, -) *nt* quarter; ~**teljährlich** *adj* quarterly; **V**~**telnote** *f* crotchet; **V**~**telstunde** [fɪrtəl'ʃtʊndə] *f* quarter of an hour; ~**zehn** ['fɪrtse:n] *num* fourteen; **in** ~**zehn Tagen** in a fortnight; ~**zehntägig** *adj* fortnightly; ~**zig** ['fɪrtsɪç] *num* forty

Villa ['vɪla] (-, **Villen**) *f* villa

violett [vio'lɛt] *adj* violet

Violin- [vio'li:n] *zW*: ~**e** *f* violin; ~**konzert** *nt* violin concerto; ~**schlüssel** *m* treble clef

Virus ['vi:rʊs] (-, **Viren**) *m od nt* virus

Visa ['vi:za] *pl von* **Visum**

vis-à-vis [viza'vi:] *adv* opposite

Visen ['vi:zən] *pl von* **Visum**

Visier [vi'zi:r] (-s, -e) *nt* gunsight; (*am Helm*) visor

Visite [vi'zi:tə] *f* (*MED*) visit;

Visitenkarte *f* visiting card

Visum ['vi:zʊm] (-s, **Visa** *od* **Visen**) *nt* visa

vital [vi'ta:l] *adj* lively, full of life, vital

Vitamin [vita'mi:n] (-s, -e) *nt* vitamin

Vogel ['fo:gəl] (-s, ⁼) *m* bird; **einen** ~ **haben** (*umg*) to have bats in the belfry; **jdm den** ~ **zeigen** (*umg*) to tap one's forehead (*meaning that one thinks sb stupid*); ~**bauer** *nt* birdcage; ~**scheuche** *f* scarecrow

Vogesen [vo'ge:zən] *pl* Vosges

Vokabel [vo'ka:bəl] (-, -n) *f* word

Vokabular [vokabu'la:r] (-s, -e) *nt* vocabulary

Vokal [vo'ka:l] (-s, -e) *m* vowel

Volk [fɔlk] (-(e)s, ⁼er) *nt* people; nation

Völker- ['fœlkər] *zW*: ~**recht** *nt* international law; **v**~**rechtlich** *adj* according to international law; ~**verständigung** *f* international understanding

Volks- *zW*: ~**abstimmung** *f* referendum; **v**~**eigen** *adj* state-owned; ~**fest** *nt* fair; ~**hochschule** *f* adult education classes *pl*; ~**lied** *nt* folksong; ~**republik** *f* people's republic; **die** ~**republik China** the People's Republic of China; ~**schule** *f* elementary school; ~**tanz** *m* folk dance; **v**~**tümlich** ['fɔlksty:mlɪç] *adj* popular; ~**wirtschaft** *f* economics *sg*; ~**zählung** *f* (national) census

voll [fɔl] *adj* full; **etw** ~ **machen** to fill sth up; ~ **und ganz** completely; **jdn für** ~ **nehmen** (*umg*) to take sb seriously; ~**auf** [fɔl'|aʊf] *adv* amply; **V**~**bart** *m* full beard; ~'**bringen** (*unreg*) *vt insep* to accomplish; ~'**enden** *vt insep* to finish, to complete; ~**ends** ['fɔlɛnts] *adv* completely; **V**~'**endung** *f* completion; ~**er** *adj* fuller; ~**er einer Sache** *gen* full of sth

Volleyball ['vɔlibal] *m* volleyball

Vollgas *nt*: **mit** ~ at full throttle; ~ **geben** to step on it

völlig ['fœlɪç] *adj* complete ♦ *adv* completely

voll- *zW*: ~**jährig** *adj* of age; **V**~**kaskoversicherung** *f* fully comprehensive insurance; ~'**kommen** *adj*

perfect; **V~'kommenheit** f perfection;
V~kornbrot nt wholemeal bread;
V~macht (-, **-en**) f authority, full
powers pl; **V~mond** m full moon;
V~pension f full board; **~schlank** adj:
Kleidung für V~schlanke clothes for the
fuller figure; **~ständig** adj complete;
~'strecken vt insep to execute;
~tanken vt, vi to fill up; **~zählig** adj
complete; in full number; **~'ziehen**
(unreg) vt insep to carry out ♦ vr insep
to happen; **V~'zug** m execution

Volt [vɔlt] (- od -(e)s, -) nt volt
Volumen [voˈluːmən] (-s, - od **Volumina**)
nt volume
vom [fɔm] = **von dem**

von [fɔn] präp +dat **1** (Ausgangspunkt)
from; **von ... bis** from ... to; **von
morgens bis abends** from morning till
night; **von ... nach ...** from ... to ...; **von
... an** from ...; **von ... aus** from ...; **von
dort aus** from there; **etw von sich aus
tun** to do sth of one's own accord; **von
mir aus** (umg) if you like, I don't
mind; **von wo/wann ...?** where/when ...
from?
2 (Ursache, im Passiv) by; **ein Gedicht
von Schiller** a poem by Schiller; **von
etw müde** tired from sth
3 (als Genitiv) of; **ein Freund von mir**
a friend of mine; **nett von dir** nice of
you; **jeweils zwei von zehn** two out of
every ten
4 (über) about; **er erzählte vom Urlaub**
he talked about his holiday
5: **von wegen!** (umg) no way!

voneinander [fɔnaɪˈnandər] adv from
each other
vonstatten [fɔnˈʃtatən] adv: **~ gehen** to
proceed, to go

vor [foːr] präp +dat **1** (räumlich) in
front of; **vor der Kirche links abbiegen**
turn left before the church
2 (zeitlich) before; **ich war vor ihm da**
I was there before him; **vor 2 Tagen** 2

days ago; **5** (**Minuten**) **vor 4** 5
(minutes) to 4; **vor kurzem** a little
while ago
3 (Ursache) with; **vor Wut/Liebe** with
rage/love; **vor Hunger sterben** to die of
hunger; **vor lauter Arbeit** because of
work
4: **vor allem, vor allen Dingen** most of
all
♦ prap +akk (räumlich) in front of
♦ adv: **vor und zurück** backwards and
forwards

Vorabend [ˈfoːrˈʔaːbənt] m evening
before, eve
voran [foˈran] adv before, ahead; **mach
~!** get on with it!; **~gehen** (unreg) vi
to go ahead; **einer Sache dat ~gehen** to
precede sth; **~gehend** adj previous;
~kommen (unreg) vi to come along, to
make progress
Voranschlag m estimate
Vorarbeiter m foreman
voraus [foˈraus] adv ahead; (zeitlich) in
advance; **jdm ~ sein** to be ahead of sb;
im ~ in advance; **~gehen** (unreg) vi to
go (on) ahead; (fig) to precede;
~haben (unreg) vt: **jdm etw ~haben** to
have the edge on sb in sth; **V~sage** f
prediction; **~sagen** vt to predict;
~sehen (unreg) vt to foresee; **~setzen**
vt to assume; **~gesetzt, daß ...** provided
that ...; **V~setzung** f requirement, prerequisite; **V~sicht** f foresight; **aller
V~sicht nach** in all probability; **~sicht-
lich** adv probably
Vorbehalt [ˈfoːrbəhalt] (-(e)s, -e) m
reservation, proviso; **v~en** (unreg) vt:
sich/jdm etw v~en to reserve sth (for
o.s.)/for sb; **v~los** adj unconditional ♦
adv unconditionally
vorbei [foːrˈbaɪ] adv by, past; **das ist ~**
that's over; **~gehen** (unreg) vi to pass
by, to go past
vor- zW: **~belastet** [ˈfoːrbəlastət] adj
(fig) handicapped; **~bereiten** [ˈfoːrbəraɪ-
tən] vt to prepare; **V~bereitung** f
preparation; **~bestraft** [ˈfoːrbəʃtraːft] adj
previously convicted, with a record
vorbeugen [ˈfoːrbɔygən] vt, vr to lean

forward ♦ *vi* +*dat* to prevent; ~**d** *adj* preventive

Vorbeugung *f* prevention; **zur ~ gegen** for the prevention of

Vorbild ['fo:rbɪlt] *nt* model; **sich** *dat* **jdn zum · nehmen** to model o.s. on sb; **v~lich** *adj* model, ideal

vorbringen ['fo:rbrɪŋən] (*unreg*) *vt* to advance, to state

Vorder- ['fɔrdər] *zW*: ~**achse** *f* front axle; ~**asien** *nt* the Near East; **v~e(r, s)** *adj* front; ~**grund** *m* foreground; **v~hand** *adv* for the present; ~**mann** (*pl* -**männer**) *m* man in front; **jdn auf ~mann bringen** (*umg*) to get sb in shape up; ~**seite** *f* front (side); **v~ste(r, s)** *adj* front

vordrängen ['fo:rdrɛŋən] *vr* to push to the front

voreilig ['fo:r'aɪlɪç] *adj* hasty, rash

voreingenommen ['fo:r'aɪngənɔmən] *adj* biased; **V~heit** *f* bias

vorenthalten ['fo:r'ɛnthaltən] (*unreg*) *vt*: **jdm etw ~** to withhold sth from sb

vorerst ['fo:r'e:rst] *adv* for the moment *od* present

Vorfahr ['fo:rfa:r] (-**en**, -**en**) *m* ancestor

vorfahren (*unreg*) *vi* to drive (on) ahead; (*vors Haus etc*) to drive up

Vorfahrt *f* (*AUT*) right of way; ~ **achten!** give way!

Vorfahrts- *zW*: ~**regel** *f* right of way; ~**schild** *nt* give way sign; ~**straße** *f* major road

Vorfall ['fo:rfal] *m* incident; **v~en** (*unreg*) *vi* to occur

vorfinden ['fo:rfɪndən] (*unreg*) *vt* to find

vorführen ['fo:rfy:rən] *vt* to show, to display; **dem Gericht ~** to bring before the court

Vorgabe ['fo:rga:bə] *f* (*SPORT*) start, handicap ♦ *in zW* (*COMPUT*) default

Vorgang ['fo:rgaŋ] *m* course of events; (*bes SCI*) process

Vorgänger(in) ['fo:rgɛŋər(ɪn)] (-**s**, -) *m(f)* predecessor

vorgeben ['fo:rge:bən] (*unreg*) *vt* to pretend, to use as a pretext; (*SPORT*) to give an advantage *od* a start of

vorgefaßt ['fo:rgəfast] *adj* preconceived

vorgefertigt ['fo:rgəfɛrtɪçt] *adj* prefabricated

vorgehen ['fo:rge:ən] (*unreg*) *vi* (*voraus*) to go (on) ahead; (*nach vorn*) to go up front; (*handeln*) to act, to proceed; (*Uhr*) to be fast; (*Vorrang haben*) to take precedence; (*passieren*) to go on; **V~** (-**s**) *nt* action

Vorgeschmack ['fo:rgəʃmak] *m* foretaste

Vorgesetzte(r) ['fo:rgəzɛtstə(r)] *mf* superior

vorgestern ['fo:rgɛstərn] *adv* the day before yesterday

vorhaben ['fo:rha:bən] (*unreg*) *vt* to intend; **hast du schon was vor?** have you got anything on?; **V~** (-**s**, -) *nt* intention

vorhalten ['fo:rhaltən] (*unreg*) *vt* to hold *od* put up ♦ *vi* to last; **jdm etw ~** (*fig*) to reproach sb for sth

Vorhaltung *f* reproach

vorhanden [fo:r'handən] *adj* existing; (*erhältlich*) available

Vorhang ['fo:rhaŋ] *m* curtain

Vorhängeschloß ['fo:rhɛŋəʃlɔs] *nt* padlock

vorher [fo:r'he:r] *adv* before(hand); ~**bestimmen** *vt* (*Schicksal*) to preordain; ~**gehen** (*unreg*) *vi* to precede; ~**ig** [fo:r'he:rɪç] *adj* previous

Vorherrschaft ['fo:rhɛrʃaft] *f* predominance, supremacy

vorherrschen ['fo:rhɛrʃən] *vi* to predominate

vorher- [fo:r'he:r] *zW*: **V~sage** *f* forecast; ~**sagen** *vt* to forecast, to predict; ~**sehbar** *adj* predictable; ~**sehen** (*unreg*) *vt* to foresee

vorhin [fo:r'hɪn] *adv* not long ago, just now; ~**ein** ['fo:rhɪnaɪn] *adv*: **im ~ein** beforehand

vorig ['fo:rɪç] *adj* previous, last

Vorkaufsrecht ['fo:rkaufsrɛçt] *nt* option to buy

Vorkehrung ['fo:rke:rʊŋ] *f* precaution

vorkommen ['fo:rkɔmən] (*unreg*) *vi* to come forward; (*geschehen, sich finden*) to occur; (*scheinen*) to seem (to be); **sich** *dat* **dumm** *etc* **~** to feel stupid *etc*;

V~ (-s, -) *nt* occurrence
Vorkriegs- ['fo:rkri:ks] *in zW* prewar
Vorladung ['fo:rla:duŋ] *f* summons *sg*
Vorlage ['fo:rla:gə] *f* model, pattern; (*Gesetzes~*) bill; (*SPORT*) pass
vorlassen ['fo:rlasən] (*unreg*) *vt* to admit; (*vorgehen lassen*) to allow to go in front
vorläufig ['fo:rləyfıç] *adj* temporary, provisional
vorlaut ['fo:rlaut] *adj* impertinent, cheeky
vorlesen ['fo:rle:zən] (*unreg*) *vt* to read (out)
Vorlesung *f* (*UNIV*) lecture
vorletzte(r, s) ['fo:rletstə(r, s)] *adj* last but one
Vorliebe ['fo:rli:bə] *f* preference, partiality
vorliebnehmen [fo:r'li:pne:mən] (*unreg*) *vi*: ~ **mit** to make do with
vorliegen ['fo:rli:gən] (*unreg*) *vi* to be (here); **etw liegt jdm vor** sb has sth; ~**d** *adj* present, at issue
vormachen ['fo:rmaxən] *vt*: **jdm etw** ~ to show sb how to do sth; (*fig*) to fool sb; to have sb on
Vormachtstellung ['fo:rmaxtʃtɛluŋ] *f* supremacy, hegemony
Vormarsch ['fo:rmarʃ] *m* advance
vormerken ['fo:rmɛrkən] *vt* to book
Vormittag ['fo:rmıta:k] *m* morning; **v~s** *adv* in the morning, before noon
Vormund ['fo:rmunt] (-(e)s, -e *od* -münder) *m* guardian
vorn ['fɔrn] *adv* in front; **von** ~ **anfangen** to start at the beginning; **nach** ~ **to the front**
Vorname ['fo:rna:mə] *m* first name, Christian name
vorne *adv* = **vorn**
vornehm ['fo:rne:m] *adj* distinguished; refined; elegant
vornehmen (*unreg*) *vt* (*fig*) to carry out; **sich** *dat* **etw** ~ to start on sth; (*beschließen*) to decide to do sth; **sich** *dat* **jdn** ~ to tell sb off
vornehmlich *adv* chiefly, specially
vornherein ['fɔrnhɛraın] *adv*: **von** ~ from the start

Vorort [fo:r'ɔrt] *m* suburb
Vorrang ['fo:rraŋ] *m* precedence, priority; **v~ig** *adj* of prime importance, primary
Vorrat ['fo:rra:t] *m* stock, supply
vorrätig ['fo:rre:tıç] *adj* in stock
Vorratskammer *f* pantry
Vorrecht ['fo:rreçt] *nt* privilege
Vorrichtung ['fo:rrıçtuŋ] *f* device, contrivance
vorrücken ['fo:rrʏkən] *vi* to advance ♦ *vt* to move forward
Vorsatz ['fo:rzats] *m* intention; (*JUR*) intent; **einen** ~ **fassen** to make a resolution
vorsätzlich ['fo:rzetslıç] *adj* intentional; (*JUR*) premeditated ♦ *adv* intentionally
Vorschau ['fo:rʃau] *f* (*RADIO, TV*) (programme) preview; (*Film*) trailer
Vorschlag ['fo:rʃla:k] *m* suggestion, proposal; **v~en** (*unreg*) *vt* to suggest, to propose
vorschnell ['fo:rʃnɛl] *adv* hastily, too quickly
vorschreiben ['fo:rʃraıbən] (*unreg*) *vt* to prescribe, to specify
Vorschrift ['fo:rʃrıft] *f* regulation(s); rule(s); (*Anweisungen*) instruction(s); **Dienst nach** ~ work-to-rule; **vorschriftsmäßig** *adj* as per regulations/instructions
Vorschuß ['fo:rʃus] *m* advance
vorsehen ['fo:rze:ən] (*unreg*) *vt* to provide for, to plan ♦ *vr* to take care, to be careful ♦ *vi* to be visible
Vorsehung *f* providence
vorsetzen ['fo:rzetsən] *vt* to move forward; (*anbieten*) to offer; ~ **vor** +*akk* to put in front of
Vorsicht ['fo:rzıçt] *f* caution, care; ~! look out!, take care!; (*auf Schildern*) caution!, danger!; ~, **Stufe!** mind the step!; **v~ig** *adj* cautious, careful; **vorsichtshalber** *adv* just in case
Vorsilbe ['fo:rzılbə] *f* prefix
Vorsitz ['fo:rzıts] *m* chair(manship); ~**ende(r)** *mf* chairman(woman)
Vorsorge ['fo:rzɔrgə] *f* precaution(s), provision(s); **v~n** *vi*: **v~n für** to make provision(s) for; ~**untersuchung** *f*

check-up

vorsorglich [ˈfoːrzɔrklıç] *adv* as a precaution

Vorspeise [ˈfoːrʃpaızə] *f* hors d'oeuvre, appetizer

Vorspiel [ˈfoːrʃpiːl] *nt* prelude

vorsprechen [ˈfoːrʃprɛçən] (*unreg*) *vt* to say out loud, to recite ♦ *vi:* **bei jdm ~** to call on sb

Vorsprung [ˈfoːrʃprʊŋ] *m* projection, ledge; (*fig*) advantage, start

Vorstadt [ˈfoːrʃtat] *f* suburbs *pl*

Vorstand [ˈfoːrʃtant] *m* executive committee; (*COMM*) board (of directors); (*Person*) director, head

vorstehen [ˈfoːrʃteːən] (*unreg*) *vi* to project; **etw** *dat* **~** (*fig*) to be the head of sth

vorstell- [ˈfoːrʃtɛl] *zW:* **~bar** *adj* conceivable; **~en** *vt* to put forward (*bekannt machen*) to introduce; (*darstellen*) to represent; **~en vor** +*akk* to put in front of; **sich** *dat* **etw ~en** to imagine sth; **V~ung** *f* (*Bekanntmachen*) introduction; (*THEAT etc*) performance; (*Gedanke*) idea, thought

Vorstrafe [ˈfoːrʃtraːfə] *f* previous conviction

Vortag [ˈfoːrtaːk] *m:* **am ~ einer Sache** *gen* on the day before sth

vortäuschen [ˈfoːrtɔʏʃən] *vt* to feign, to pretend

Vorteil [ˈfɔrtaıl] (**-s, -e**) *m:* **~ (gegenüber)** advantage (over); **im ~ sein** to have the advantage; **v~haft** *adj* advantageous

Vortrag [ˈfoːrtraːk] (**-(e)s, Vorträge**) *m* talk, lecture; **v~en** (*unreg*) *vt* to carry forward; (*fig*) to recite; (*Rede*) to deliver; (*Lied*) to perform; (*Meinung etc*) to express

vortrefflich [ˈfoːrtrɛflıç] *adj* excellent

vortreten [ˈfoːrtreːtən] (*unreg*) *vi* to step forward; (*Augen etc*) to protrude

vorüber [foˈryːbər] *adv* past, over; **~gehen** (*unreg*) *vi* to pass (by); **~gehen an** +*dat* (*fig*) to pass over; **~gehend** *adj* temporary, passing

Vorurteil [ˈfoːrʔʊrtaıl] *nt* prejudice

Vorverkauf [ˈfoːrfɛrkaʊf] *m* advance booking

Vorwahl [ˈfoːrvaːl] *f* preliminary election; (*TEL*) dialling code

Vorwand [ˈfoːrvant] (**-(e)s, Vorwände**) *m* pretext

vorwärts [ˈfoːrvɛrts] *adv* forward; **V~gang** *m* (*AUT etc*) forward gear; **~gehen** (*unreg*) *vi* to progress; **~kommen** (*unreg*) *vi* to get on, to make progress

vorweg [foːrˈvɛk] *adv* in advance; **V~nahme** *f* anticipation; **~nehmen** (*unreg*) *vt* to anticipate

vorweisen [ˈfoːrvaızən] (*unreg*) *vt* to show, to produce

vorwerfen [ˈfoːrvɛrfən] (*unreg*) *vt:* **jdm etw ~** to reproach sb for sth, to accuse sb of sth; **sich** *dat* **nichts vorzuwerfen haben** to have nothing to reproach o.s. with

vorwiegend [ˈfoːrviːgənt] *adj* predominant ♦ *adv* predominantly

Vorwort [ˈfoːrvɔrt] (**-(e)s, -e**) *nt* preface

Vorwurf [ˈfoːrvʊrf] *m* reproach; **jdm/ sich Vorwürfe machen** to reproach sb/ o.s.; **vorwurfsvoll** *adj* reproachful

vorzeigen [ˈfoːrtsaıgən] *vt* to show, to produce

vorzeitig [ˈfoːrtsaıtıç] *adj* premature

vorziehen [ˈfoːrtsiːən] (*unreg*) *vt* to pull forward; (*Gardinen*) to draw; (*lieber haben*) to prefer

Vorzug [ˈfoːrtsuːk] *m* preference; (*gute Eigenschaft*) merit, good quality; (*Vorteil*) advantage

vorzüglich [foːrˈtsyːklıç] *adj* excellent

vulgär [vʊlˈgɛːr] *adj* vulgar

Vulkan [vʊlˈkaːn] (**-s, -e**) *m* volcano

W

Waage [ˈvaːgə] *f* scales *pl*; (*ASTROL*) Libra; **w~recht** *adj* horizontal

Wabe [ˈvaːbə] *f* honeycomb

wach [vax] *adj* awake; (*fig*) alert; **W~e** *f* guard, watch; **W~e halten** to keep watch; **W~e stehen** to stand guard; **~en** *vi* to be awake; (*Wache halten*) to guard

Wacholder [va'xɔldər] (-s, -) m juniper

Wachs [vaks] (-es, -e) nt wax

wachsam ['vaxza:m] adj watchful, vigilant, alert; **W~keit** f vigilance

wachsen¹ (unreg) vi to grow

wachsen² vt (Skier) to wax

Wachstuch nt oilcloth

Wachstum (-s) nt growth

Wächter ['vɛçtər] (-s, -) m guard, warden, keeper; (Parkplatz~) attendant

wackel- ['vakəl] zW: **~ig** adj shaky, wobbly; **W~kontakt** m loose connection; **~n** vi to shake; (fig: Position) to be shaky

wacker ['vakər] adj valiant, stout ♦ adv well, bravely

Wade ['va:də] f (ANAT) calf

Waffe ['vafə] f weapon

Waffel ['vafəl] f waffle; wafer

Waffen- zW: **~schein** m gun licence; **~schieber** m gun-runner; **~stillstand** m armistice, truce

Wagemut ['va:gəmu:t] m daring

wagen ['va:gən] vt to venture, to dare

Wagen ['va:gən] (-s, -) m vehicle; (Auto) car; (EISENB) carriage; (Pferde~) cart; **~heber** (-s, -) m jack

Waggon [va'gõ:] (-s, -s) m carriage; (Güter~) goods van, freight truck (US)

waghalsig ['va:khalzıç] adj foolhardy

Wagnis ['va:knıs] (-ses, -se) nt risk

Wahl [va:l] (-, -en) f choice; (POL) election; **zweite ~** (COMM) seconds pl

wähl- ['vɛ:l] zW: **~bar** adj eligible; **~en** vt, vi to choose; (POL) to elect, to vote (for); (TEL) to dial; **W~er(in)** (-s, -) m(f) voter; **~erisch** adj fastidious, particular

Wahl- zW: **~fach** nt optional subject; **~gang** m ballot; **~kabine** f polling booth; **~kampf** m election campaign; **~kreis** m constituency; **~lokal** nt polling station; **w~los** adv at random; **~recht** nt franchise; **~spruch** m motto; **~urne** f ballot box

Wahn [va:n] (-(e)s) m delusion; folly; **~sinn** m madness; **w~sinnig** adj insane, mad ♦ adv (umg) incredibly

wahr [va:r] adj true

wahren vt to maintain, to keep

während ['vɛ:rənt] präp +gen during ♦ konj while; **~dessen** [vɛ:rənt'dɛsən] adv meanwhile

wahr- zW: **~haben** (unreg) vt: **etw nicht ~haben wollen** to refuse to admit sth; **~haft** adv (tatsächlich) truly; **~haftig** [va:r'haftıç] adj true, real ♦ adv really; **W~heit** f truth; **~nehmen** (unreg) vt to perceive, to observe; **W~nehmung** f perception; **~sagen** vi to prophesy, to tell fortunes; **W~sager(in)** (-s, -) m(f) fortune teller; **~scheinlich** [va:r'faınlıç] adj probable ♦ adv probably; **W~'scheinlichkeit** f probability; **aller W~scheinlichkeit nach** in all probability

Währung ['vɛ:rʊŋ] f currency

Wahrzeichen nt emblem

Waise ['vaızə] f orphan; **Waisenhaus** nt orphanage

Wald [valt] (-(e)s, -er) m wood(s); (groß) forest; **~sterben** nt dying of trees due to pollution

Wal(fisch) ['va:l(fıʃ)] (-(e)s, -e) m whale

Wall [val] (-(e)s, -e) m embankment; (Bollwerk) rampart

Wallfahr- zW: **w~en** (unreg) vi insep to go on a pilgrimage; **~er(in)** m(f) pilgrim; **~t** f pilgrimage

Walnuß ['valnʊs] f walnut

Walroß ['valrɔs] nt walrus

Walze ['valtsə] f (Gerät) cylinder; (Fahrzeug) roller; **w~n** vt to roll (out)

wälzen ['vɛltsən] vt to roll (over); (Bücher) to hunt through; (Probleme) to deliberate on ♦ vr to wallow; (vor Schmerzen) to roll about; (im Bett) to toss and turn

Walzer ['valtsər] (-s, -) m waltz

Wand [vant] (-, -e) f wall; (Trenn~) partition; (Berg~) precipice

Wandel ['vandəl] (-s) m change; **w~bar** adj changeable, variable; **w~n** vt, vr to change ♦ vi (gehen) to walk

Wander- ['vandər] zW: **~er** (-s, -) m hiker, rambler; **w~n** vi to hike; (Blick) to wander; (Gedanken) to stray; **~schaft** f travelling; **~ung** f walk, hike

Wandlung f change, transformation
Wange ['vaŋə] f cheek
wankelmütig [vaŋkəlmy:tıç] adj vacillating, inconstant
wanken ['vankən] vi to stagger; (fig) to waver
wann [van] adv when
Wanne ['vanə] f tub
Wanze ['vantsə] f bug
Wappen ['vapən] (-s, -) nt coat of arms, crest; ~kunde f heraldry
war etc [va:r] vb siehe **sein**
Ware ['va:rə] f ware
Waren- zW: ~haus nt department store; ~lager nt stock, store; ~probe f sample; ~zeichen nt: (**eingetragenes**) ~**zeichen** (registered) trademark
warf etc [va:rf] vb siehe **werfen**
warm [varm] adj warm; (Essen) hot
Wärm- ['verm] zW: ~e f warmth; w~en vt, vr to warm (up), to heat (up); ~flasche f hot-water bottle
warnen ['varnən] vt to warn
Warnung f warning
Warschau ['varʃau] nt Warsaw; ~er **Pakt** Warsaw Pact
warten ['vartən] vi: ~ (**auf** +akk) to wait (for); **auf sich** ~ **lassen** to take a long time
Wärter(in) ['vertər(ın)] (-s, -) m(f) attendant
Warte- ['vartə] zW: ~raum m (EISENB) waiting room; ~saal m (EISENB) waiting room; ~zimmer nt waiting room
Wartung f servicing; service; ~ **und Instandhaltung** maintenance
warum [va'rʊm] adv why
Warze [vartsə] f wart
was [vas] pron what; (umg: etwas) something; ~ **für (ein)** ... what sort of ...
waschbar adj washable
Waschbecken nt washbasin
Wäsche ['vɛʃə] f wash(ing); (Bett~) linen; (Unter~) underclothing
waschecht adj colourfast; (fig) genuine
Wäscheklammer f clothes peg (BRIT), clothspin (US)
Wäscheleine f washing line (BRIT)

waschen ['vaʃən] (unreg) vt, vi to wash
♦ vr to (have a) wash; **sich** dat **die Hände** ~ to wash one's hands
Wäsche'rei f laundry
Wasch- zW: ~küche f laundry room; ~lappen m face flannel, washcloth (US); (umg) sissy; ~maschine f washing machine; ~mittel nt detergent, washing powder; ~pulver nt detergent, washing powder; ~raum m washroom
Wasser ['vasər] (-s, -) nt water; ~ball m water polo; w~dicht adj waterproof; ~fall m waterfall; ~farbe f watercolour; w~gekühlt adj (AUT) water-cooled; ~hahn m tap, faucet (US); ~kraftwerk nt hydroelectric power station; ~leitung f water pipe; ~mann n (ASTROL) Aquarius
wässern ['vesərn] vt, vi to water
Wasser- zW: w~scheu adj afraid of (the) water; ~ski nt water-skiing; ~stoff m hydrogen; ~stoffbombe f hydrogen bomb; ~waage f spirit level; ~zeichen nt watermark
wäßrig ['vesrıç] adj watery
waten ['va:tən] vi to wade
watscheln ['va:tʃəln] vi to waddle
Watt¹ [vat] (-(e)s, -en) nt mud flats pl
Watt² (-s, -) nt (ELEK) watt
Watte f cotton wool, absorbent cotton (US)
WC ['ve:'tse:] (-s, -s) nt abk (= water closet) W.C.
Web- ['ve:b] zW: w~en (unreg) vt to weave; ~er (-s, -) m weaver; ~e'rei f (Betrieb) weaving mill; ~stuhl m loom
Wechsel ['vɛksəl] (-s, -) m change; (COMM) bill of exchange; ~beziehung f correlation; ~geld nt change; w~haft adj (Wetter) variable; ~jahre pl change of life sg; ~kurs m rate of exchange; w~n vt to change; (Blicke) to exchange ♦ vi to change; to vary; (Geldwechseln) to have change; ~sprechanlage f two-way intercom; ~strom m alternating current; ~stube f bureau de change; ~wirkung f interaction
wecken ['vɛkən] vt to wake (up); to call
Wecker ['vɛkər] (-s, -) m alarm clock

wedeln ['ve:dəln] *vi* (*mit Schwanz*) to wag; (*mit Fächer etc*) to wave

weder ['ve:dər] *konj* neither; ~ ... **noch** ... neither ... nor ...

Weg [ve:k] (-(e)s, -e) *m* way; (*Pfad*) path; (*Route*) route; **sich auf den ~ machen** to be on one's way; **jdm aus dem ~ gehen** to keep out of sb's way

weg [vɛk] *adv* away, off; **über etw** *akk* ~ **sein** to be over sth; **er war schon ~** he had already left; **Finger ~!** hands off!

Wegbereiter (-s, -) *m* pioneer

wegbleiben (*unreg*) *vi* to stay away

wegen ['ve:gən] *präp* +*gen* (*umg:* +*dat*) because of

weg- ['vɛk] *zW:* ~**fahren** (*unreg*) *vi* to drive away; to leave; ~**fallen** (*unreg*) *vi* to be left out; (*Ferien, Bezahlung*) to be cancelled; (*aufhören*) to cease; ~**gehen** (*unreg*) *vi* to go away; to leave; ~**lassen** (*unreg*) *vt* to leave out; ~**laufen** (*unreg*) *vi* to run away *od* off; ~**legen** *vt* to put aside; ~**machen** (*umg*) *vt* to get rid of; ~**müssen** (*unreg; umg*) *vi* to have to go; ~**nehmen** (*unreg*) *vt* to take away; ~**tun** (*unreg*) *vt* to put away; **W~weiser** ['ve:gvaɪzər] (-s, -) *m* road sign, signpost; ~**werfen** (*unreg*) *vt* to throw away; ~**werfend** *adj* disparaging; **W~werfgesellschaft** *f* throw-away society

weh [ve:] *adj* sore; ~ **tun** to hurt, to be sore; **jdm/sich** ~ **tun** to hurt sb/o.s.; ~**(e)** *excl:* ~**(e)**, **wenn du ...** woe betide you if ...; **o** ~! oh dear!; ~**e**! just you dare!; **W~en** *pl* (*MED*) labour pains

wehen *vt, vi* to blow; (*Fahnen*) to flutter

weh- *zW:* ~**leidig** *adj* whiny, whining; **W~mut** (-) *f* melancholy; ~**mütig** *adj* melancholy

Wehr[1] [ve:r] (-(e)s, -e) *nt* weir

Wehr[2] (-, -en) *f:* **sich zur** ~ **setzen** to defend o.s.; ~**dienst** *m* military service; **w~en** *vr* to defend o.s.; **w~los** *adj* defenceless; ~**pflicht** *f* compulsory military service; **w~pflichtig** *adj* liable for military service

Weib [vaɪp] (-(e)s, -er) *nt* woman, female; wife; ~**chen** *nt* female; **w~lich** *adj* feminine

weich [vaɪç] *adj* soft; **W~e** *f* (*EISENB*) points *pl*; ~**en** (*unreg*) *vi* to yield, to give way; **W~heit** *f* softness; ~**lich** *adj* soft, namby-pamby; **W~ling** *m* weakling

Weide ['vaɪdə] *f* (*Baum*) willow; (*Gras*) pasture; **w~n** *vi* to graze ♦ *vr:* **sich an etw** *dat* **w~n** to delight in sth

weidlich ['vaɪtlɪç] *adv* thoroughly

weigern ['vaɪgərn] *vr* to refuse

Weigerung ['vaɪgərʊŋ] *f* refusal

Weihe ['vaɪə] *f* consecration; (*Priester~*) ordination; **w~n** *vt* to consecrate; to ordain

Weiher (-s, -) *m* pond

Weihnacht- *zW:* ~**en** (-) *nt* Christmas; **w~lich** *adj* Christmas *cpd*; **Weihnachtsabend** *m* Christmas Eve; **Weihnachtslied** *nt* Christmas carol; **Weihnachtsmann** *m* Father Christmas, Santa Claus; **Weihnachtstag** *m* Christmas Day; **zweiter Weihnachtstag** Boxing Day

Weihrauch *m* incense

Weihwasser *nt* holy water

weil [vaɪl] *konj* because

Weile ['vaɪlə] (-) *f* while, short time

Wein [vaɪn] (-(e)s, -e) *m* wine; (*Pflanze*) vine; ~**bau** *m* cultivation of vines; ~**beere** *f* grape; ~**berg** *m* vineyard; ~**bergschnecke** *f* snail; ~**brand** *m* brandy

weinen *vt, vi* to cry; **das ist zum W~** it's enough to make you cry *od* weep

Wein- *zW:* ~**karte** *f* wine list; ~**lese** *f* vintage; ~**rebe** *f* vine; ~**stock** *m* vine; ~**traube** *f* grape

weise ['vaɪzə] *adj* wise; **W~(r)** *mf* wise old man(woman), sage

Weise ['vaɪzə] *f* manner, way; (*Lied*) tune; **auf diese** ~ in this way

weisen (*unreg*) *vt* to show

Weisheit ['vaɪshaɪt] *f* wisdom; **Weisheitszahn** *m* wisdom tooth

weiß [vaɪs] *adj* white ♦ *vb siehe* **wissen**; **W~brot** *nt* white bread; ~**en** *vt* to whitewash; **W~glut** *f* (*TECH*) incandescence; **jdn bis zur W~glut bringen** (*fig*) to make sb see red; **W~kohl** *m* (white) cabbage; **W~wein** *m* white wine

weit [vaɪt] *adj* wide; (*Begriff*) broad; (*Reise, Wurf*) long ♦ *adv* far; **wie ~ ist es ...?** how far is it ...?; **in ~er Ferne** in the far distance; **das geht zu ~** that's going too far; **~aus** *adv* by far; **~blickend** *adj* far-seeing; **W~e** *f* width; (*Raum*) space; (*von Entfernung*) distance; **~en** *vt, vr* to widen

weiter ['vaɪtər] *adj* wider; broader; farther (away); (*zusätzlich*) further ♦ *adv* further; **ohne ~es** without further ado; just like that; **~ nichts/niemand** nothing/nobody else; **~arbeiten** *vi* to go on working; **~empfehlen** (*unreg*) *vt* to recommend (to others); **W~fahrt** *f* continuation of the journey; **~gehen** (*unreg*) *vi* to go on; **~hin** *adv*: **etw ~hin tun** to go on doing sth; **~leiten** *vt* to pass on; **~machen** *vt, vi* to continue

weit- *zW*: **~gehend** *adj* considerable ♦ *adv* largely; **~läufig** *adj* (*Gebäude*) spacious; (*Erklärung*) lengthy; (*Verwandter*) distant; **~schweifig** *adj* long-winded; **~sichtig** *adj* (*MED*) long-sighted; (*fig*) far-sighted; **W~sprung** *m* long jump; **~verbreitet** *adj* widespread; **W~winkelobjektiv** *nt* (*PHOT*) wide-angle lens

Weizen ['vaɪtsən] (-s, -) *m* wheat

welche(r, s) ['vɛlçə(r, s)] *interrogativ pron* which; **welcher von beiden?** which (one) of the two?; **welchen hast du genommen?** which (one) did you take?; **welche eine ...!** what a ...!; **welche Freude!** what joy!
♦ *unbestimmt pron* some; (*in Fragen*) any; **ich habe welche** I have some; **haben Sie welche?** do you have any?
♦ *relativ pron* (*bei Menschen*) who; (*bei Sachen*) which, that; **welche(r, s) auch immer** whoever/whichever/ whatever

welk [vɛlk] *adj* withered; **~en** *vi* to wither

Wellblech *nt* corrugated iron

Welle ['vɛlə] *f* wave; (*TECH*) shaft; **Wellenbereich** *m* waveband; **Wellenlänge** *f* (*auch fig*) wavelength; **Wellensittich** *m* budgerigar

Welt [vɛlt] (-, -en) *f* world; **~all** *nt* universe; **~anschauung** *f* philosophy of life; **w~berühmt** *adj* world-famous; **w~fremd** *adj* unworldly; **~krieg** *m* world war; **w~lich** *adj* worldly; (*nicht kirchlich*) secular; **~macht** *f* world power; **~meister** *m* world champion; **~meisterschaft** *f* world championship(s *pl*); **~raum** *m* space; **~reise** *f* trip round the world; **~stadt** *f* metropolis; **w~weit** *adj* world-wide

wem [veːm] (*dat von* **wer**) *pron* to whom

wen [veːn] (*akk von* **wer**) *pron* whom

Wende ['vɛndə] *f* turn; (*Veränderung*) change; **~kreis** *m* (*GEOG*) tropic; (*AUT*) turning circle; **Wendeltreppe** *f* spiral staircase; **w~n** (*unreg*) *vt, vi, vr* to turn; **sich an jdn w~n** to go/come to sb; **~punkt** *m* turning point

Wendung *f* turn; (*Rede~*) idiom

wenig ['veːnɪç] *adj, adv* little; **~e** ['veːnɪgə] *pron pl* few *pl*; **~er** *adj* less; (*mit pl*) fewer ♦ *adv* less; **~ste(r, s)** *adj* least; **am ~sten** least; **~stens** *adv* at least

wenn [vɛn] *konj* **1** (*falls, bei Wünschen*) if; **wenn auch ..., selbst wenn ...** even if ...; **wenn ich doch ...** if only I ...
2 (*zeitlich*) when; **immer wenn** whenever

wennschon ['vɛnʃoːn] *adv*: **na ~** so what?; **~, dennschon!** in for a penny, in for a pound

wer [veːr] *pron* who

Werbe- ['vɛrbə] *zW*: **~fernsehen** *nt* commercial television; **w~n** (*unreg*) *vt* to win; (*Mitglied*) to recruit ♦ *vi* to advertise; **um jdn/etw w~n** to try to win sb/sth; **für jdn/etw w~n** to promote sb/sth; **~spot** *m* TV ad(vertisement)

Werbung *f* advertising; (*von Mitgliedern*) recruitment; **~ um jdn/etw** promotion of sb/sth

─────────────
│ *SCHLÜSSELWORT* │
─────────────

werden ['veːrdən] (*pt* **wurde**, *pp* **geworden** *od* (*bei Passiv*) **worden**) *vi* to become; **was ist aus ihm/aus der Sache geworden?** what became of him/it?; **es ist nichts/gut geworden** it came to nothing/turned out well; **es wird Nacht/Tag** it's getting dark/light; **mir wird kalt** I'm getting cold; **mir wird schlecht** I fell ill; **Erster werden** to come *od* be first; **das muß anders werden** that'll have to change; **rot/zu Eis werden** to turn red/to ice; **was willst du (mal) werden?** what do you want to be?; **die Fotos sind gut geworden** the photos have come out nicely

♦ *als Hilfsverb* **1** (*bei Futur*): **ich wird es tun** he will *od* he'll do it; **er wird das nicht tun** he will not *od* he won't do it; **es wird gleich regnen** it's going to rain
2 (*bei Konjunktiv*): **ich würde** ... I would ...; **er würde gern** ... he would *od* he'd like to ...; **ich würde lieber** ... I would *od* I'd rather ...
3 (*bei Vermutung*): **sie wird in der Küche sein** she will be in the kitchen
4 (*bei Passiv*): **gebraucht werden** to be used; **er ist erschossen worden** he has *od* he's been shot; **mir wurde gesagt, daß** ... I was told that ...

werfen ['vɛrfən] (*unreg*) *vt* to throw
Werft [vɛrft] (-, **-en**) *f* shipyard, dockyard
Werk [vɛrk] (-(**e**)**s**, **-e**) *nt* work; (*Tätigkeit*) job; (*Fabrik, Mechanismus*) works *pl*; **ans ~ gehen** to set to work; **~statt** (-, **-stätten**) *f* workshop; (*AUT*) garage; **~tag** *m* working day; **w~tags** *adv* on working days; **w~tätig** *adj* working; **~zeug** *nt* tool
Wermut ['veːrmuːt] (-(**e**)**s**) *m* wormwood; (*Wein*) vermouth
Wert [veːrt] (-(**e**)**s**, **-e**) *m* worth; (*FIN*) value; **~ legen auf** +*akk* to attach importance to; **es hat doch keinen ~** it's useless; **w~** *adj* worth; (*geschätzt*) dear; worthy; **das ist nichts/viel w~** it's not worth anything/it's worth a lot; **das ist es/er mir w~** it's/he's worth that to me; **w~en** *vt* to rate; **w~los** *adj* worthless; **~papier** *nt* security; **w~voll** *adj* valuable
Wesen ['veːzən] (-s, -) *nt* (*Geschöpf*) being; (*Natur, Character*) nature; **wesentlich** *adj* significant; (*beträchtlich*) considerable
weshalb [vɛs'halp] *adv* why
Wespe ['vɛspə] *f* wasp
wessen ['vɛsən] (*gen von* **wer**) *pron* whose
Weste ['vɛstə] *f* waistcoat, vest (*US*); (*Woll~*) cardigan
West- *zW*: **~deutschland** *nt* West Germany; **~en** (-s) *m* west; **~europa** *nt* Western Europe; **~falen** *nt* Westphalia; **~indien** *nt* the West Indies; **w~lich** *adj* western ♦ *adv* to the west
weswegen [vɛs'veːgən] *adv* why
wett [vɛt] *adj* even; **W~bewerb** *m* competition; **W~e** *f* bet, wager; **~en** *vt, vi* to bet
Wetter ['vɛtər] (-s, -) *nt* weather; **~bericht** *m* weather report; **~dienst** *m* meteorological service; **~lage** *f* (weather) situation; **~vorhersage** *f* weather forecast; **~warte** *f* weather station
Wett- *zW*: **~kampf** *m* contest; **~lauf** *m* race; **w~machen** *vt* to make good; **~streit** *m* contest
wichtig ['vɪçtɪç] *adj* important; **W~keit** *f* importance
wickeln ['vɪkəln] *vt* to wind; (*Haare*) to set; (*Kind*) to change; **jdn/etw in etw** *akk* **~** to wrap sb/sth in sth
Widder ['vɪdər] (-s, -) *m* ram; (*ASTROL*) Aries
wider ['viːdər] *präp* +*akk* against; **~'fahren** (*unreg*) *vi* to happen; **~'legen** *vt* to refute
widerlich ['viːdərlɪç] *adj* disgusting, repulsive
wider- ['viːdər] *zW*: **~rechtlich** *adj* unlawful; **W~rede** *f* contradiction; **W~ruf**

m retraction; countermanding; ~'**rufen**
(*unreg*) *vt insep* to retract;
(*Anordnung*) to revoke; (*Befehl*) to
countermand; ~'**setzen** *vr insep*: **sich
jdm/etw ~setzen** to oppose sb/sth
widerspenstig ['vi:dərʃpɛnstiç] *adj* wilful
wider'sprechen (*unreg*) *vi insep*: **jdm
~** to contradict sb
Widerspruch ['vi:dərʃprʊx] *m* contradiction; **widerspruchslos** *adv* without
arguing
Widerstand ['vi:dərʃtant] *m* resistance
Widerstands- *zW*: ~**bewegung** *f* resistance (movement); **w~fähig** *adj* resistant, tough; **w~los** *adj* unresisting
wider'stehen (*unreg*) *vi insep*: **jdm/
etw ~** to withstand sb/sth
wider- ['vi:dər] *zW*: ~**wärtig** *adj* nasty,
horrid; **W~wille** *m*: **W~wille (gegen)**
aversion (to); ~**willig** *adj* unwilling, reluctant
widmen ['vɪtmən] *vt* to dedicate; to
devote ♦ *vr* to devote o.s.
widrig ['vi:drɪç] *adj* (*Umstände*) adverse

| SCHLÜSSELWORT |

wie [vi:] *adv* how; **wie groß/schnell?**
how big/fast?; **wie wär's?** how about
it?; **wie ist er?** what's he like?; **wie gut
du das kannst!** you're very good at it;
wie bitte? pardon?; (*entrüstet*) I beg
your pardon!; **und wie!** and how!
♦ *konj* **1** (*bei Vergleichen*): **so schön
wie ...** as beautiful as ...; **wie ich schon
sagte** as I said; **wie du** like you; **singen
wie ein ...** to sing like a ...; **wie (zum
Beispiel)** such as (for example)
2 (*zeitlich*): **wie er das hörte, ging er**
when he heard that he left; **er hörte,
wie der Regen fiel** he heard the rain
falling

wieder ['vi:dər] *adv* again; ~ **da sein** to
be back (again); **gehst du schon ~?** are
you off again?; ~ **ein(e) ...** another ...;
W~aufbau [-''aufbau] *m* rebuilding;
~**aufnehmen** (*unreg*) *vt* to resume;
~**bekommen** (*unreg*) *vt* to get back;
~**bringen** (*unreg*) *vt* to bring back;

~**erkennen** (*unreg*) *vt* to recognize;
W~gabe *f* reproduction; ~**geben** (*unreg*) *vt* (*zurückgeben*) to return;
(*Erzählung etc*) to repeat; (*Gefühle
etc*) to convey; ~**gutmachen** *vt* to
make up for; (*Fehler*) to put right;
W~gutmachung *f* reparation; ~'**herstellen** *vt* to restore; ~'**holen** *vt insep*
to repeat; **W~'holung** *f* repetition;
W~hören *nt*: **auf W~hören** (*TEL*) goodbye; **W~kehr** (-) *f* return; (*von Vorfall*) repetition, recurrence; ~**sehen**
(*unreg*) *vt* to see again; **auf W~sehen**
goodbye; ~**um** *adv* again; (*andererseits*) on the other hand; **W~wahl** *f*
re-election
Wiege ['vi:gə] *f* cradle; **w~n[1]** *vt*
(*schaukeln*) to rock
wiegen[2] (*unreg*) *vt, vi* (*Gewicht*) to
weigh
wiehern ['vi:ərn] *vi* to neigh, to whinny
Wien [vi:n] *nt* Vienna; ~**er** *adj*
Viennese; ~**er(in)** *m(f)* Viennese; ~**er
Schnitzel** Wiener schnitzel
Wiese ['vi:zə] *f* meadow
Wiesel ['vi:zəl] (-s, -) *nt* weasel
wieso [vi:'zo:] *adv* why
wieviel [vi:'fi:l] *adj* how much; ~ **Menschen** how many people; ~**mal** *adv* how
often; ~**te(r, s)** *adj*: **zum ~ten Mal?**
how many times?; **den W~ten haben
wir?** what's the date?; **an ~ter Stelle?**
in what place?; **der ~te Besucher war
er?** how many visitors were there
before him?
wieweit [vi:'vait] *adv* to what extent
wild [vɪlt] *adj* wild; **W~** (-(e)s) *nt*
game; ~**ern** ['vɪldərn] *vi* to poach;
~'**fremd** (*umg*) *adj* quite strange *od* unknown; **W~heit** *f* wildness; **W~leder** *nt*
suede; **W~nis** (-, -se) *f* wilderness;
W~schwein *nt* (wild) boar
will *etc* [vɪl] *vb siehe* **wollen**
Wille ['vɪlə] (-ns, -n) *m* will; **w~n** *präp*
+*gen*: **um ... w~n** for the sake of ...;
willensstark *adj* strong-willed
will- *zW*: ~**ig** *adj* willing; **W~kommen**
(-s, -) *nt* welcome; ~**kommen**
[vɪl'kɔmən] *adj* welcome; **jdn ~kommen
heißen** to welcome sb; ~**kürlich** *adj*

arbitrary; (*Bewegung*) voluntary

wimmeln ['vɪməln] *vi*: ~ **(von)** to swarm (with)

wimmern ['vɪmərn] *vi* to whimper

Wimper ['vɪmpər] (-, -n) *f* eyelash

Wind [vɪnt] (-(e)s, -e) *m* wind; ~**beutel** *m* cream puff; (*fig*) rake; ~**e** ['vɪndə] *f* (*TECH*) winch, windlass; (*BOT*) bindweed; ~**el** ['vɪndəl] (-, -n) *f* nappy, diaper (*US*); **w~en** ['vɪndən] *vi unpers* to be windy ♦ *vt* (*unreg*) to wind; (*Kranz*) to weave; (*entwinden*) to twist ♦ *vr* (*unreg*) to wind; (*Person*) to writhe; ~**hund** *m* greyhound; (*Mensch*) fly-by-night; **w~ig** ['vɪndɪç] *adj* windy; (*fig*) dubious; ~**mühle** *f* windmill; ~**pocken** *pl* chickenpox *sg*; ~**schutzscheibe** *f* (*AUT*) windscreen, windshield (*US*); ~**stille** *f* calm; ~**stoß** *m* gust of wind

Wink [vɪŋk] (-(e)s, -e) *m* (*mit Hand*) wave; (*mit Kopf*) nod; (*Hinweis*) hint

Winkel ['vɪŋkəl] (-s, -) *m* (*MATH*) angle; (*Gerät*) set square; (*in Raum*) corner

winken ['vɪŋkən] *vt, vi* to wave

winseln ['vɪnzəln] *vi* to whine

Winter ['vɪntər] (-s, -) *m* winter; **w~lich** *adj* wintry; ~**sport** *m* winter sports *pl*

Winzer ['vɪntsər] (-s, -) *m* vine grower

winzig ['vɪntsɪç] *adj* tiny

Wipfel ['vɪpfəl] (-s, -) *m* treetop

wir [viːr] *pron* we; ~ **alle** all of us, we all

Wirbel ['vɪrbəl] (-s, -) *m* whirl, swirl; (*Trubel*) hurly-burly; (*Aufsehen*) fuss; (*ANAT*) vertebra; **w~n** *vi* to whirl, to swirl; ~**säule** *f* spine

wird [vɪrt] *vb siehe* **werden**

wirfst *etc* [vɪrfst] *vb siehe* **werfen**

wirken ['vɪrkən] *vi* to have an effect; (*erfolgreich sein*) to work; (*scheinen*) to seem ♦ *vt* (*Wunder*) to work

wirklich ['vɪrklɪç] *adj* real ♦ *adv* really; **W~keit** *f* reality

wirksam ['vɪrkzaːm] *adj* effective; **W~keit** *f* effectiveness, efficacy

Wirkung ['vɪrkʊŋ] *f* effect; **wirkungslos** *adj* ineffective; **wirkung bleiben** to have no effect; **wirkungsvoll** *adj* effective

wirr [vɪr] *adj* confused; wild; **W~warr**

['vɪrvar] (-s) *m* disorder, chaos

Wirsing ['vɪrzɪŋ] (-s) *m* savoy cabbage

wirst [vɪrst] *vb siehe* **werden**

Wirt(in) ['vɪrt(ɪn)] (-(e)s, -e) *m(f)* landlord(lady); ~**schaft** *f* (*Gaststätte*) pub; (*Haushalt*) housekeeping; (*eines Landes*) economy; (*umg: Durcheinander*) mess; **w~schaftlich** *adj* economical; (*POL*) economic

Wirtschafts- *zW*: ~**krise** *f* economic crisis; ~**prüfer** *m* chartered accountant; ~**wunder** *nt* economic miracle

Wirtshaus *nt* inn

Wisch [vɪʃ] (-(e)s, -e) *m* scrap of paper; **w~en** *vt* to wipe; ~**er** (-s, -) *m* (*AUT*) wiper

wispern ['vɪspərn] *vt, vi* to whisper

Wißbegier(de) ['vɪsbəgiːr(də)] *f* thirst for knowledge; **wißbegierig** *adj* inquisitive, eager for knowledge

wissen ['vɪsən] (*unreg*) *vt* to know; **was weiß ich!** I don't know!; **W~** (-s) *nt* knowledge; **W~schaft** *f* science; **W~schaftler(in)** (-s, -) *m(f)* scientist; ~**schaftlich** *adj* scientific; **wissenswert** *adj* worth knowing; **wissentlich** *adj* knowing

wittern ['vɪtərn] *vt* to scent; (*fig*) to suspect

Witterung *f* weather; (*Geruch*) scent

Witwe ['vɪtvə] *f* widow; ~**r** (-s, -) *m* widower

Witz [vɪts] (-es, -e) *m* joke; ~**blatt** *nt* comic (paper); ~**bold** (-(e)s, -e) *m* joker, wit; **w~ig** *adj* funny

wo [voː] *adv* where; (*umg: irgendwo*) somewhere; **im Augenblick, ~ ...** the moment (that) ...; **die Zeit, ~ ...** the time when ...; ~**anders** [voː''andərs] *adv* elsewhere; ~**andershin** *adv* somewhere else; ~**bei** [voː'baɪ] *adv* (*relativ*) by/with which; (*interrogativ*) what ... in/by/with

Woche ['vɔxə] *f* week

Wochen- *zW*: ~**ende** *nt* weekend; **w~lang** *adj, adv* for weeks; ~**schau** *f* newsreel

wöchentlich ['vœçəntlɪç] *adj, adv* weekly

wodurch [voː'dʊrç] *adv* (*relativ*)

through which; (interrogativ) what ...
through

wofür [vo:'fy:r] adv (relativ) for which;
(interrogativ) what ... for

wog etc [vo:k] vb siehe **wiegen**

Woge ['vo:gə] f wave

wo- zW: **~gegen** [vo:'ge:gən] adv (relativ) against which; (interrogativ)
what ... against; **~her** [vo:'he:r] adv
where ... from; **~hin** [vo:'hɪn] adv
where ... to

SCHLÜSSELWORT

wohl [vo:l] adv 1: **sich wohl fühlen** (zufrieden) to feel happy; (gesundheitlich)
to feel well; **wohl oder übel** whether one
likes it or not

2 (wahrscheinlich) probably; (gewiß)
certainly; (vielleicht) perhaps; **sie ist
wohl zu Hause** she's probably at home;
das ist doch wohl nicht dein Ernst!
surely you're not serious!; **das mag
wohl sein** that may well be; **ob das
wohl stimmt?** I wonder if that's true;
er weiß das sehr wohl he knows that
perfectly well

Wohl [vo:l] (-(e)s) nt welfare; **zum ~!**
cheers!; **w~auf** [vo:l''aʊf] adv well;
~behagen nt comfort; **~fahrt** f welfare; **~fahrtsstaat** m welfare state;
w~habend adj wealthy; **w~ig** adj con-
tented, comfortable; **w~schmeckend**
adj delicious; **~stand** m prosperity;
~standsgesellschaft f affluent society;
~tat f relief; act of charity; **~täter(in**
m(f) benefactor; **w~tätig** adj charitable; **w~tun** (unreg) vi: **jdm w~tun** to
do sb good; **w~verdient** adj well-
earned, well-deserved; **w~weislich** adv
prudently; **~wollen** (-s) nt good will;
w~wollend adj benevolent

wohn- ['vo:n] zW: **~en** vi to live;
W~gemeinschaft f (Menschen) people
sharing a flat; **~haft** adj resident;
~lich adj comfortable; **W~ort** m
domicile; **W~sitz** m place of residence;
W~ung f house; (Etagenwohnung) flat,
apartment (US); **W~wagen** m caravan; **W~zimmer** nt living room

wölben ['vœlbən] vt, vr to curve

Wölbung f curve

Wolf [vɔlf] (-(e)s, ⸚e) m wolf

Wolke ['vɔlkə] f cloud; **Wolkenkratzer**
m skyscraper

wolkig ['vɔlkɪç] adj cloudy

Wolle ['vɔlə] f wool; **w~n¹** adj woollen

SCHLÜSSELWORT

wollen² ['vɔlən] (pt **wollte**, pp **gewollt**
od (als Hilfsverb) **wollen**) vt, vi to
want; **ich will nach Hause** I want to go
home; **er will nicht** he doesn't want to;
er wollte das nicht he didn't want it;
wenn du willst if you like; **ich will, daß
du mir zuhörst** I want you to listen to
me

♦ Hilfsverb: **er will ein Haus kaufen** he
wants to buy a house; **ich wollte, ich
wäre ...** I wish I were ...; **etw gerade
tun wollen** to be going to do sth

wollüstig ['vɔlystɪç] adj lusty, sensual

wo- zW: **~mit** [vo:'mɪt] adv (relativ)
with which; (interrogativ) what ...
with; **~möglich** [vo:'mø:klɪç] adv probably, I suppose; **~nach** [vo:'na:x] adv
(relativ) after/for which; (interrogativ)
what ... for/after; **~ran** [vo:'ran] adv
(relativ) on/at which; (interrogativ)
what ... on/at; **~rauf** [vo:'raʊf] adv (relativ) on which; (interrogativ) what ...
on; **~raus** [vo:'raʊs] adv (relativ) from/
out of which; (interrogativ) what ...
from/out of; **~rin** [vo:'rɪn] adv (relativ)
in which; (interrogativ) what ... in

Wort [vɔrt] (-(e)s, ⸚er od -e) nt word;
jdn beim ~ nehmen to take sb at his
word; **mit anderen ~en** in other words;
w~brüchig adj not true to one's word

Wörterbuch ['vœrtərbu:x] nt dictionary

Wort- zW: **~führer** m spokesman;
w~karg adj taciturn; **~laut** m wording

wörtlich ['vœrtlɪç] adj literal

Wort- zW: **w~los** adj mute; **w~reich**
adj wordy, verbose; **~schatz** m
vocabulary; **~spiel** nt play on words,
pun

wo- zW: **~rüber** [vo:'ry:bər] adv (relativ) over/about which; (interrogativ)

what ... over/about; ~**rum** [voː'rʊm] *adv* (*relativ*) about/round which; (*interrogativ*) what ... about/round; ~**runter** [voː'rʊntər] *adv* (*relativ*) under which; (*interrogativ*) what ... under; ~**von** [voː'fɔn] *adv* (*relativ*) from which; (*interrogativ*) what ... from; ~**vor** [voː'foːr] *adv* (*relativ*) in front of/before which; (*interrogativ*) in front of/before what; of what; ~**zu** [voː'tsuː] *adv* (*relativ*) to/for which; (*interrogativ*) what ... for/to; (*warum*) why

Wrack [vrak] (-(e)s, -s) *nt* wreck

wringen ['vrɪŋən] (*unreg*) *vt* to wring

Wucher ['vuːxər] (-s) *m* profiteering; ~**er** (-s, -) *m* profiteer; **w**~**isch** *adj* profiteering; **w**~**n** *vi* (*Pflanzen*) to grow wild; ~**ung** *f* (*MED*) growth, tumour

Wuchs [vuːks] (-es) *m* (*Wachstum*) growth; (*Statur*) build

Wucht [vʊxt] (-) *f* force

wühlen ['vyːlən] *vi* to scrabble; (*Tier*) to root; (*Maulwurf*) to burrow; (*umg: arbeiten*) to slave away ♦ *vt* to dig

Wulst [vʊlst] (-es, ⁼e) *m* bulge; (*an Wunde*) swelling

wund [vʊnt] *adj* sore, raw; **W**~**e** ['vʊndə] *f* wound

Wunder ['vʊndər] (-s, -) *nt* miracle; **es ist kein** ~ it's no wonder; **w**~**bar** *adj* wonderful, marvellous; ~**kind** *nt* infant prodigy; **w**~**lich** *adj* odd, peculiar; **w**~**n** *vr* to be surprised ♦ *vt* to surprise; **sich w**~**n über** +*akk* to be surprised at; **w**~**schön** *adj* beautiful; **w**~**voll** *adj* wonderful

Wundstarrkrampf ['vʊntʃtarkrampf] *m* tetanus, lockjaw

Wunsch [vʊnʃ] (-(e)s, ⁼e) *m* wish

wünschen ['vʏnʃən] *vt* to wish; **sich** *dat* **etw** ~ to want sth, to wish for sth; **wünschenswert** *adj* desirable

wurde *etc* ['vʊrdə] *vb siehe* **werden**

Würde ['vʏrdə] *f* dignity; (*Stellung*) honour; **w**~**voll** *adj* dignified

würdig ['vʏrdɪç] *adj* worthy; (*würdevoll*) dignified; ~**en** ['vʏrdɪɡən] *vt* to appreciate; **jdn keines Blickes** ~**en** not to so much as look at sb

Wurf [vʊrf] (-s, ⁼e) *m* throw; (*Junge*) litter

Würfel ['vʏrfəl] (-s, -) *m* dice; (*MATH*) cube; ~**becher** *m* (dice) cup; **w**~**n** *vi* to play dice ♦ *vt* to dice; ~**zucker** *m* lump sugar

würgen ['vʏrɡən] *vt*, *vi* to choke

Wurm [vʊrm] (-(e)s, ⁼er) *m* worm

wurmen (*umg*) *vt* to rile, to nettle

wurmstichig *adj* worm-ridden

Wurst [vʊrst] (-, ⁼e) *f* sausage; **das ist mir** ~ (*umg*) I don't care, I don't give a damn

Würstchen ['vʏrstçən] *nt* sausage

Würze ['vʏrtsə] *f* seasoning, spice

Wurzel ['vʊrtsəl] (-, -n) *f* root

würzen ['vʏrtsən] *vt* to season, to spice

würzig *adj* spicy

wusch *etc* [vʊʃ] *vb siehe* **waschen**

wußte *etc* ['vʊstə] *vb siehe* **wissen**

wüst [vyːst] *adj* untidy, messy; (*ausschweifend*) wild; (*öde*) waste; (*umg: heftig*) terrible; **W**~**e** *f* desert

Wut [vuːt] (-) *f* rage, fury; ~**anfall** *m* fit of rage

wüten ['vyːtən] *vi* to rage; ~**d** *adj* furious, mad

X

X-Beine ['ɪksbaɪnə] *pl* knock-knees

x-beliebig [ɪksbə'liːbiç] *adj* any (whatever)

xerokopieren [kseroko'piːrən] *vt* to xerox, to photocopy

x-mal ['ɪksmaːl] *adv* any number of times, n times

Xylophon [ksylo'foːn] (-s, -e) *nt* xylophone

Y

Ypsilon ['ʏpsilɔn] (-(s), -s) *nt* the letter Y

Z

Zacke ['tsakə] f point; (Berg~) jagged peak; (Gabel~) prong; (Kamm~) tooth
zackig ['tsakɪç] adj jagged; (umg) smart; (Tempo) brisk
zaghaft ['tsa:khaft] adj timid
zäh [tsɛ:] adj tough; (Mensch) tenacious; (Flüssigkeit) thick; (schleppend) sluggish; **Z~igkeit** f toughness; tenacity
Zahl [tsa:l] (-, -en) f number; **z~bar** adj payable; **z~en** vt, vi to pay; **z~en bitte!** the bill please!
zählen ['tsɛ:lən] vt, vi to count; ~ **auf** +akk to count on; ~ **zu** to be numbered among
Zähler ['tsɛ:lər] (-s, -) m (TECH) meter; (MATH) numerator
Zahl- zW: **z~los** adj countless; **z~reich** adj numerous; **~tag** m payday; **~ung** f payment; **z~ungsfähig** adj solvent; **~ungsrückstände** pl arrears; **~wort** nt numeral
zahm [tsa:m] adj tame
zähmen ['tsɛ:mən] vt to tame; (fig) to curb
Zahn [tsa:n] (-(e)s, ⁼e) m tooth; **~arzt** m dentist; **~bürste** f toothbrush; **~creme** f toothpaste; **~fleisch** nt gums pl; **~pasta** f toothpaste; **~rad** nt cog(wheel); **~schmerzen** pl toothache sg; **~stein** m tartar; **~stocher** (-s, -) m toothpick
Zange [tsaŋə] f pliers pl; (Zucker~ etc) tongs pl; (Beiß~, ZOOL) pincers pl; (MED) forceps pl
zanken ['tsaŋkən] vi, vr to quarrel
zänkisch ['tsɛŋkɪʃ] adj quarrelsome
Zäpfchen ['tsɛpfçən] nt (ANAT) uvula; (MED) suppository
Zapfen ['tsapfən] (-s, -) m plug; (BOT) cone; (Eis~) icicle
zapfen vt to tap; **Z~streich** m (MIL) tattoo
zappeln ['tsapəln] vi to wriggle; to fidget
zart [tsart] adj (weich, leise) soft;

(Fleisch) tender; (fein, schwächlich) delicate; **Z~gefühl** nt tact; **Z~heit** f softness; tenderness; delicacy
zärtlich ['tsɛːrtlɪç] adj tender, affectionate; **Z~keiten** pl caresses
Zauber ['tsaubər] (-s, -) m magic; (~bann) spell; **~ei** [-'raɪ] f magic; **~er** (-s, -) m magician; conjuror; **z~haft** adj magical, enchanting; **~künstler** m conjuror; **z~n** vi to conjure, to practise magic
zaudern ['tsaudərn] vi to hesitate
Zaum [tsaum] (-(e)s, Zäume) m bridle; **etw im ~ halten** to keep sth in check
Zaun [tsaun] (-(e)s, Zäune) m fence; **~könig** m wren
z.B. abk (= zum Beispiel) e.g.
Zebra ['tse:bra] nt zebra; **~streifen** m zebra crossing
Zeche ['tsɛçə] f (Rechnung) bill; (Bergbau) mine
Zehe [tse:ə] f toe; (Knoblauch~) clove
zehn [tse:n] num ten; **~te(r, s)** adj tenth; **Z~tel** (-s, -) nt tenth (part)
Zeich- ['tsaɪç] zW: **~en** (-s, -) nt sign; **z~nen** vt to draw; (kennzeichnen) to mark; (unterzeichnen) to sign ♦ vi to draw; to sign; **~ner** (-s, -) m artist; **technischer ~ner** draughtsman; **~nung** f drawing; (Markierung) markings pl
Zeige- ['tsaɪgə] zW: **~finger** m index finger; **z~n** vt to show ♦ vi to point ♦ vr to show o.s.; **z~n auf** +akk to point to; to point at; **es wird sich z~n** time will tell; **es zeigte sich, daß ...** it turned out that ...; **~r** (-s, -) m pointer; (Uhrzeiger) hand
Zeile ['tsaɪlə] f line; (Häuser~) row
Zeit [tsaɪt] (-, -en) f time; (GRAM) tense; **zur ~** at the moment; **sich dat ~ lassen** to take one's time; **von ~ zu** from time to time; **~alter** nt age; **z~gemäß** adj in keeping with the times; **~genosse** m contemporary; **z~ig** adj early; **z~lich** adj temporal; **~lupe** f slow motion; **z~raubend** adj time-consuming; **~raum** m period; **~rechnung** f time, era; **nach/vor unserer ~rechnung** A.D./B.C.; **~schrift** f periodical; **~ung** f newspaper; **~ver-**

schwendung f waste of time; ~ver-treib m pastime, diversion; z~weilig adj temporary; z~weise adv for a time; ~wort nt verb; ~zünder m time fuse

Zelle ['tsɛlə] f cell; (Telefon~) callbox

Zellstoff m cellulose

Zelt [tsɛlt] (-(e)s, -e) nt tent; z~en vi to camp

Zement [tse'mɛnt] (-(e)s, -e) m cement; z~ieren [-'tiːrən] vt to cement

zensieren [tsɛn'ziːrən] vt to censor; (SCH) to mark

Zensur [tsɛn'zuːr] f censorship; (SCH) mark

Zentimeter [tsɛnti'meːtər] m od nt centimetre

Zentner ['tsɛntnər] (-s, -) m hundred-weight

zentral [tsɛn'traːl] adj central; Z~e f central office; (TEL) exchange; Z~einheit f central processing unit, CPU; Z~heizung f central heating

Zentrum ['tsɛntrʊm] (-s, Zentren) nt centre

zerbrechen [tsɛr'brɛçən] (unreg) vt, vi to break

zerbrechlich adj fragile

zer'drücken vt to squash, to crush; (Kartoffeln) to mash

Zeremonie [tseremo'niː] f ceremony

Zerfall [tsɛr'fal] m decay; z~en (unreg) vi to disintegrate, to decay; (sich gliedern): z~en (in +akk) to fall (into)

zer'gehen (unreg) vi to melt, to dissolve

zerkleinern [tsɛr'klaɪnərn] vt to reduce to small pieces

zerlegbar adj able to be dismantled

zerlegen [tsɛr'leːgən] vt to take to pieces; (Fleisch) to carve; (Satz) to analyse

zermürben [tsɛr'mʏrbən] vt to wear down

zerquetschen [tsɛr'kvɛtʃən] vt to squash

Zerrbild ['tsɛrbɪlt] nt caricature, distorted picture

zer'reißen (unreg) vt to tear to pieces ♦ vi to tear, to rip

zerren ['tsɛrən] vt to drag ♦ vi: ~ (an +dat) to tug (at)

zer'rinnen (unreg) vi to melt away

zerrissen [tsɛr'rɪsən] adj torn, tattered; Z~heit f tattered state; (POL) disunion, discord; (innere Zerrissenheit) disintegration

zerrütten [tsɛr'rʏtən] vt to wreck, to destroy

zerrüttet adj wrecked, shattered

zer'schlagen (unreg) vt to shatter, to smash ♦ vr to fall through

zer'schneiden (unreg) vt to cut up

zer'setzen vt, vr to decompose, to dissolve

zer'springen (unreg) vi to shatter, to burst

Zerstäuber [tsɛr'ʃtɔybər] (-s, -) m atomizer

zerstören [tsɛr'ʃtøːrən] vt to destroy

Zerstörung f destruction

zerstreu- [tsɛr'ʃtrɔy] zW: ~en vt to disperse, to scatter; (unterhalten) to divert; (Zweifel etc) to dispel ♦ vr to disperse, to scatter; to be dispelled; ~t adj scattered; (Mensch) absent-minded; **Zerstreutheit** f absent-mindedness; Z~ung f dispersion; (Ablenkung) diversion

zerstückeln [tsɛr'ʃtʏkəln] vt to cut into pieces

zer'teilen vt to divide into parts

Zertifikat [tsɛrtifi'kaːt] (-(e)s, -e) nt certificate

zer'treten (unreg) vt to crush underfoot

zertrümmern [tsɛr'trʏmərn] vt to shatter; (Gebäude etc) to demolish

zerzausen [tsɛr'tsaʊzən] vt (Haare) to ruffle up, to tousle

zetern ['tseːtərn] vi to shout, to shriek

Zettel ['tsɛtəl] (-s, -) m piece of paper, slip; (Notiz~) note; (Formular) form

Zeug [tsɔyk] (-(e)s, -e; umg) nt stuff; (Ausrüstung) gear; dummes ~ (stupid) nonsense; das ~ haben zu to have the makings of; sich ins ~ legen to put one's shoulder to the wheel

Zeuge ['tsɔygə] (-n, -n) m witness; z~n vi to bear witness, to testify ♦ vt (Kind) to father; es zeugt von ... it testifies to

...; **Zeugenaussage** f evidence; **Zeugin** ['tsɔʏgɪn] f witness

Zeugnis ['tsɔʏgnɪs] (-ses, -se) nt certificate; (*SCH*) report; (*Referenz*) reference; (*Aussage*) evidence, testimony; ~ **geben von** to be evidence of, to testify to

z.H(d). abk (= *zu Händen*) attn.

Zickzack ['tsɪktsak] (-(e)s, -e) m zigzag

Ziege ['tsi:gə] f goat; **Ziegenleder** nt kid (leather)

Ziegel ['tsi:gəl] (-s, -) m brick; (*Dach~*) tile

ziehen ['tsi:ən] (*unreg*) vt to draw; (*zerren*) to pull; (*SCHACH etc*) to move; (*züchten*) to rear ♦ vi to draw; (*um~, wandern*) to move; (*Rauch, Wolke etc*) to drift; (*reißen*) to pull ♦ vb unpers: **es zieht** there is a draught, it's draughty ♦ vr (*Gummi*) to stretch; (*Grenze etc*) to run; (*Gespräche etc*) to be drawn out; **etw nach sich** ~ to lead to sth, to entail sth

Ziehharmonika ['tsi:harmo:nika] f concertina; accordion

Ziehung ['tsi:ʊŋ] f (*Los~*) drawing

Ziel [tsi:l] (-(e)s, -e) nt (*einer Reise*) destination; (*SPORT*) finish; (*MIL*) target; (*Absicht*) goal; **z~en** vi: **z~en (auf +akk)** to aim (at); **z~los** adj aimless; ~**scheibe** f target; **z~strebig** adj purposeful

ziemlich ['tsi:mlɪç] adj quite a; fair ♦ adv rather; quite a bit

Zierde ['tsi:rdə] f ornament

zieren ['tsi:rən] vr to act coy

zierlich ['tsi:rlɪç] adj dainty; **Z~keit** f daintiness

Ziffer ['tsɪfər] (-, -n) f figure, digit; ~**blatt** nt dial, clock-face

zig [tsɪç] (*umg*) adj umpteen

Zigarette [tsiga'rɛtə] f cigarette

Zigaretten- zW: ~**automat** m cigarette machine; ~**schachtel** f cigarette packet; ~**spitze** f cigarette holder

Zigarillo [tsiga'rɪlo] (-s, -s) nt od m cigarillo

Zigarre [tsi'garə] f cigar

Zigeuner(in) [tsi'gɔʏnər(ɪn)] (-s, -) m(f) gipsy

Zimmer ['tsɪmər] (-s, -) nt room; ~**lautstärke** f reasonable volume; ~**mädchen** nt chambermaid; ~**mann** m carpenter; **z~n** vt to make (from wood); ~**nachweis** m accommodation office; ~**pflanze** f indoor plant

zimperlich ['tsɪmpərlɪç] adj squeamish; (*pingelig*) fussy, finicky

Zimt [tsɪmt] (-(e)s, -e) m cinnamon

Zink [tsɪŋk] (-(e)s) nt zinc

Zinn [tsɪn] (-(e)s) nt (*Element*) tin; (*in ~waren*) pewter; ~**soldat** m tin soldier

Zins [tsɪns] (-es, -en) m interest; **Zinseszins** m compound interest; ~**fuß** m rate of interest; **z~los** adj interest-free; ~**satz** m rate of interest

Zipfel ['tsɪpfəl] (-s, -) m corner; (*spitz*) tip; (*Hemd~*) tail; (*Wurst~*) end; ~**mütze** f stocking cap; nightcap

zirka ['tsɪrka] adv (round) about

Zirkel ['tsɪrkəl] (-s, -) m circle; (*MATH*) pair of compasses

Zirkus ['tsɪrkʊs] (-, -se) m circus

zischen ['tsɪʃən] vi to hiss

Zitat [tsi'ta:t] (-(e)s, -e) nt quotation, quote

zitieren [tsi'ti:rən] vt to quote

Zitronat [tsitro'na:t] (-(e)s, -e) nt candied lemon peel

Zitrone [tsi'tro:nə] f lemon; **Zitronenlimonade** f lemonade; **Zitronensaft** m lemon juice

zittern ['tsɪtərn] vi to tremble

zivil [tsi'vi:l] adj civil; (*Preis*) moderate; **Z~** (-s) nt plain clothes pl; (*MIL*) civilian clothing; **Z~bevölkerung** f civilian population; **Z~courage** f courage of one's convictions; **Z~dienstleistende(r)** mf *conscientious objector doing service (in the community)*; **Z~isation** [tsivilizatsi'o:n] f civilization; **Z~isationskrankheit** f disease peculiar to civilization; ~**isieren** vt to civilize; **Z~ist** [tsivi'lɪst] m civilian

zog etc [tso:k] vb siehe **ziehen**

zögern ['tsø:gərn] vi to hesitate

Zoll [tsɔl] (-(e)s, ⁼e) m customs pl; (*Abgabe*) duty; ~**abfertigung** f customs clearance; ~**amt** nt customs office; ~**beamte(r)** m customs official;

~**erklärung** f customs declaration; **z~frei** adj duty-free; ~**kontrolle** f customs check; **z~pflichtig** adj liable to duty, dutiable

Zone ['tso:nə] f zone

Zoo [tso:] (-s, -s) m zoo; ~**loge** [tsoo'lo:gə] (-n, -n) m zoologist; ~**lo'gie** f zoology, z **logisch** adj zoological

Zopf [tsɔpf] (-(e)s, ̈-e) m plait; pigtail; **alter ~** antiquated custom

Zorn [tsɔrn] (-(e)s) m anger; **z~ig** adj angry

zottig ['tsɔtɪç] adj shaggy

z.T. abk = **zum Teil**

│ SCHLÜSSELWORT │

zu [tsu:] präp +dat **1** (örtlich) to; **zum Bahnhof/Arzt gehen** to go to the station/ doctor; **zur Schule/Kirche gehen** to go to school/church; **sollen wir zu euch gehen?** shall we go to your place?; **sie sah zu ihm hin** she looked towards him; **zum Fenster herein** through the window; **zu meiner Linken** to od on my left

2 (zeitlich) at; **zu Ostern** at Easter; **bis zum 1. Mai** until May 1st; (nicht später als) by May 1st; **zu meiner Zeit** in my time

3 (Zusatz) with; **Wein zum Essen trinken** to drink wine with one's meal; **sich zu jdm setzen** to sit down beside sb; **setz dich doch zu uns** (come and) sit with us; **Anmerkungen zu etw** notes on sth

4 (Zweck) for; **Wasser zum Waschen** water for washing; **Papier zum Schreiben** paper to write on; **etw zum Geburtstag bekommen** to get sth for one's birthday

5 (Veränderung) into; **zu etw werden** to turn into sth; **jdn zu etw machen** to make sb (into) sth; **zu Asche verbrennen** to burn to ashes

6 (mit Zahlen): **3 zu 2** (SPORT) 3-2; **das Stück zu 2 Mark** at 2 marks each; **zum ersten Mal** for the first time

7: **zu meiner Freude** etc to my joy etc; **zum Glück** luckily; **zu Fuß** on foot; **es ist zum Weinen** it's enough to make you cry

♦ konj to; **etw zu essen** sth to eat; **um besser sehen zu können** in order to see better; **ohne es zu wissen** without knowing it; **noch zu bezahlende Rechnungen** bills that are still to be paid

♦ adv **1** (allzu) too; **zu sehr** too much

2 (örtlich) toward(s), **er kam auf mich zu** he came up to me

3 (geschlossen) shut!; closed; **die Geschäfte haben zu** the shops are closed; **„auf/zu"** (Wasserhahn etc) "on/off"

4 (umg: los): **nur zu!** just keep on!; **mach zu!** hurry up!

---

zuallererst [tsu"alər"e:rst] adv first of all

zuallerletzt [tsu"alər'lɛtst] adv last of all

Zubehör ['tsu:bəhø:r] (-(e)s, -e) nt accessories pl

zubereiten ['tsu:bəraɪtən] vt to prepare

zubilligen ['tsu:bɪlɪgən] vt to grant

zubinden ['tsu:bɪndən] (unreg) vt to tie up

zubringen ['tsu:brɪŋən] (unreg) vt (Zeit) to spend

Zubringer (-s, -) m (Straße) approach od slip road

Zucht [tsʊxt] (-, -en) f (von Tieren) breeding; (von Pflanzen) cultivation; (Rasse) breed; (Erziehung) raising; (Disziplin) discipline

züchten ['tsʏçtən] vt (Tiere) to breed; (Pflanzen) to cultivate, to grow

Züchter (-s, -) m breeder; grower

Zuchthaus nt prison, penitentiary (US)

züchtigen ['tsʏçtɪgən] vt to chastise

zucken ['tsʊkən] vi to jerk, to twitch; (Strahl etc) to flicker ♦ vt (Schultern) to shrug

Zucker ['tsʊkər] (-s, -) m sugar; (MED) diabetes; ~**dose** f sugar bowl; ~**guß** m icing; **z~krank** adj diabetic; **z~n** vt to sugar; ~**rohr** nt sugar cane; ~**rübe** f sugar beet

Zuckung ['tsʊkʊŋ] f convulsion, spasm; (leicht) twitch

zudecken ['tsu:dɛkən] vt to cover (up)

zudem [tsu'de:m] adv in addition (to this)

zudringlich ['tsu:drɪŋlɪç] *adj* forward, pushing, obtrusive

zudrücken ['tsu:drʏkən] *vt* to close; **ein Auge ~** to turn a blind eye

zueinander [tsu'aɪ'nandər] *adv* to one another; (*in Verbindung*) together

zuerkennen ['tsu:'ɛrkɛnən] (*unreg*) *vt* to award; **jdm etw ~** to award sth to sb, to award sb sth

zuerst [tsu'ɛːrst] *adv* first; (*zu Anfang*) at first; **~ einmal** first of all

Zufahrt ['tsu:faːrt] *f* approach; **Zufahrtsstraße** *f* approach road; (*von Autobahn etc*) slip road

Zufall ['tsu:fal] *m* chance; (*Ereignis*) coincidence; **durch ~** by accident; **so ein ~** what a coincidence; **z~en** (*unreg*) *vi* to close, to shut; (*Anteil, Aufgabe*) to fall

zufällig ['tsu:fɛlɪç] *adj* chance ♦ *adv* by chance; (*in Frage*) by any chance

Zuflucht ['tsu:fluxt] *f* recourse; (*Ort*) refuge

zufolge [tsu'fɔlgə] *präp* (+*dat od gen*) judging by; (*laut*) according to

zufrieden [tsu'friːdən] *adj* content(ed), satisfied; **Z~heit** *f* satisfaction, contentedness; **~stellen** *vt* to satisfy

zufrieren ['tsu:friːrən] (*unreg*) *vi* to freeze up od over

zufügen ['tsu:fyːgən] *vt* to add; (*Leid etc*): **(jdm) etw ~** to cause (sb) sth

Zufuhr ['tsu:fuːr] (-, -en) *f* (*Herbeibringen*) supplying; (*MET*) influx

Zug [tsu:k] (-(e)s, ⁼e) *m* (*EISENB*) train; (*Luft~*) draught; (*Ziehen*) pull(ing); (*Gesichts~*) feature; (*SCHACH etc*) move; (*Klingel~*) pull; (*Schrift~*) stroke; (*Atem~*) breath; (*Charakter~*) trait; (*an Zigarette*) puff, pull, drag; (*Schluck*) gulp; (*Menschengruppe*) procession; (*von Vögeln*) flight; (*MIL*) platoon; **etw in vollen Zügen genießen** to enjoy sth to the full

Zu- ['tsu:] *zW*: **~gabe** *f* extra; (*in Konzert etc*) encore; **~gang** *m* access, approach; **z~gänglich** *adj* accessible; (*Mensch*) approachable

zugeben ['tsu:geːbən] (*unreg*) *vt* (*beifügen*) to add, to throw in;

(*zugestehen*) to admit; (*erlauben*) to permit

zugehen ['tsu:geːən] (*unreg*) *vi* (*schließen*) to shut; **es geht dort seltsam zu** there are strange goings-on there; **auf jdn/etw ~** to walk towards sb/sth; **dem Ende ~** to be finishing

Zugehörigkeit ['tsu:gəhøːrɪçkaɪt] *f*: **~ (zu)** membership (of), belonging (to)

Zügel ['tsyːgəl] (-s, -) *m* rein(s); (*fig*) curb; **z~n** *vt* to curb; (*Pferd*) to rein in

zuge- ['tsu:gə] *zW*: **Z~ständnis** (-ses, -se) *nt* concession; **~stehen** (*unreg*) *vt* to admit; (*Rechte*) to concede; **~stiegen** *adj*: **noch jemand ~stiegen?** tickets please

zugig ['tsu:gɪç] *adj* draughty

zügig ['tsyːgɪç] *adj* speedy, swift

zugreifen ['tsu:graɪfən] (*unreg*) *vi* to seize *od* grab at; (*helfen*) to help; (*beim Essen*) to help o.s.

Zugriff ['tsu:grɪf] *m* (*COMPUT*) access

zugrunde [tsu'grundə] *adv*: **~ gehen** to collapse; (*Mensch*) to perish; **einer Sache** *dat* **etw ~ legen** to base sth on sth; **einer Sache** *dat* **~ liegen** to be based on sth; **~ richten** to ruin, to destroy

zugunsten [tsu'gunstən] *präp* (+*gen od dat*) in favour of

zugute [tsu'guːtə] *adv*: **jdm etw ~ halten** to concede sth to sb; **jdm ~ kommen** to be of assistance to sb

Zugvogel *m* migratory bird

Zuhälter ['tsu:hɛltər] (-s, -) *m* pimp

Zuhause [tsu'hauzə] (-) *nt* home

zuhören ['tsu:høːrən] *vi* to listen

Zuhörer (-s, -) *m* listener; **~schaft** *f* audience

zukleben ['tsu:kleːbən] *vt* to paste up

zukommen ['tsu:kɔmən] (*unreg*) *vi* to come up; **auf jdn ~** to come up to sb; **jdm etw ~ lassen** to give sb sth; **etw auf sich ~ lassen** to wait and see; **~ (sich gehören)** to be fitting for sb

Zukunft ['tsu:kunft] (-, **Zukünfte**) *f* future

zukünftig ['tsu:kʏnftɪç] *adj* future ♦ *adv* in future; **mein ~er Mann** my husband to be

Zulage ['tsu:laːgə] *f* bonus

zulassen ['tsu:lasən] (*unreg*) *vt* (*hereinlassen*) to admit; (*erlauben*) to permit; (*Auto*) to license; (*umg: nicht öffnen*) to (keep) shut

zulässig ['tsu:lɛsɪç] *adj* permissible, permitted

zuleide [tsu'laɪdə] *adv*: jdm etw ~ tun to hurt *od* harm sb

zuletzt [tsu'lɛtst] *adv* finally, at last

zuliebe [tsu'li:bə] *adv*: jdm ~ to please sb

zum [tsum] = zu dem; ~ dritten Mal for the third time; ~ Scherz as a joke; ~ Trinken for drinking

zumachen ['tsu:maxən] *vt* to shut; (*Kleidung*) to do up, to fasten ♦ *vi* to shut; (*umg*) to hurry up

zumal [tsu'ma:l] *konj* especially (as)

zumeist [tsu'maɪst] *adv* mostly

zumindest [tsu'mɪndəst] *adv* at least

zumut- *zW*: ~**bar** ['tsu:mu:tba:r] *adj* reasonable; ~**e** *adv*: wie ist ihm ~e? how does he feel?; ~**en** ['tsu:mu:tən] *vt*: (jdm) etw ~en to expect *od* ask sth (of sb); **Z~ung** ['tsu:mu:tʊŋ] *f* unreasonable expectation *od* demand, impertinence

zunächst [tsu'nɛ:çst] *adv* first of all; ~ einmal to start with

Zunahme ['tsu:na:mə] *f* increase

Zuname ['tsu:na:mə] *m* surname

Zünd- [tsʏnd] *zW*: **z~en** *vi* (*Feuer*) to light, to ignite; (*Motor*) to fire; (*begeistern*): bei jdm **z~en** to fire sb (with enthusiasm); **z~end** *adj* fiery; ~**er** (-s, -) *m* fuse; (*MIL*) detonator; ~**holz** [tsʏnt-] *nt* match; ~**kerze** *f* (*AUT*) spark(ing) plug; ~**schlüssel** *m* ignition key; ~**schnur** *f* fuse wire; ~**ung** *f* ignition

zunehmen ['tsu:ne:mən] (*unreg*) *vi* to increase, to grow; (*Mensch*) to put on weight

Zuneigung *f* affection

Zunft [tsʊnft] (-, ⁻e) *f* guild

zünftig ['tsʏnftɪç] *adj* proper, real; (*Handwerk*) decent

Zunge ['tsʊŋə] *f* tongue

zunichte [tsu'nɪçtə] *adv*: ~ machen to ruin, to destroy; ~ werden to come to nothing

zunutze [tsu'nʊtsə] *adv*: sich *dat* etw ~ machen to make use of sth

zuoberst [tsu'ʔo:bərst] *adv* at the top

zupfen ['tsʊpfən] *vt* to pull, to pick, to pluck; (*Gitarre*) to pluck

zur [tsu:r] = zu der

zurechnungsfähig ['tsu:rɛçnʊŋsfɛ:ɪç] *adj* responsible, accountable; **Z~keit** *f* responsibility, accountability

zurecht- [tsu'rɛçt] *zW*: ~**finden** (*unreg*) *vr* to find one's way (about); ~**kommen** (*unreg*) *vi* to (be able to) cope, to manage; ~**legen** *vt* to get ready; (*Ausrede etc*) to have ready; ~**machen** *vt* to prepare ♦ *vr* to get ready; ~**weisen** (*unreg*) *vt* to reprimand; **Z~weisung** *f* reprimand, rebuff

zureden ['tsu:re:dən] *vi*: jdm ~ to persuade *od* urge sb

zurück [tsu'rʏk] *adv* back; ~**behalten** (*unreg*) *vt* to keep back; ~**bekommen** (*unreg*) *vt* to get back; ~**bleiben** (*unreg*) *vi* (*Mensch*) to remain behind; (*nicht nachkommen*) to fall behind, to lag; (*Schaden*) to remain; ~**bringen** (*unreg*) *vt* to bring back; ~**fahren** (*unreg*) *vi* to travel back; (*vor Schreck*) to recoil, to start ♦ *vt* to drive back; ~**finden** (*unreg*) *vi* to find one's way back; ~**fordern** *vt* to demand back; ~**führen** *vt* to lead back; etw auf etw *akk* ~**führen** to trace sth back to sth; ~**geben** (*unreg*) *vt* to give back; (*antworten*) to retort with; ~**geblieben** *adj* retarded; ~**gehen** (*unreg*) *vi* to go back; (*fallen*) to go down, to fall; (*zeitlich*): ~**gehen** (auf +*akk*) to date back (to); ~**gezogen** *adj* retired, withdrawn; ~**halten** (*unreg*) *vt* to hold back; (*Mensch*) to restrain; (*hindern*) to prevent ♦ *vr* (*reserviert sein*) to be reserved; (*im Essen*) to hold back; ~**haltend** *adj* reserved; **Z~haltung** *f* reserve; ~**kehren** *vi* to return; ~**kommen** (*unreg*) *vi* to come back; auf etw *akk* ~**kommen** to return to sth; ~**lassen** (*unreg*) *vt* to leave behind; ~**legen** *vt* to put back; (*Geld*) to put by; (*reservieren*) to keep back;

(*Strecke*) to cover; ~**nehmen** (*unreg*) *vt* to take back; ~**schrecken** *vi*: ~**schrecken** (**vor** +*dat*) to shrink (from); ~**stellen** *vt* to put back, to replace; (*aufschieben*) to put off, to postpone; (*MIL*) to turn down; (*Interessen*) to defer; (*Ware*) to keep; ~**treten** (*unreg*) *vi* to step back; (*vom Amt*) to retire; **gegenüber etw** *od* **hinter etw** *dat* ~**treten** to diminish in importance in view of sth; ~**weisen** (*unreg*) *vt* to turn down; (*Mensch*) to reject; ~**zahlen** *vt* to repay, to pay back; ~**ziehen** (*unreg*) *vt* to pull back; (*Angebot*) to withdraw ♦ *vr* to retire

Zuruf ['tsuːruːf] *m* shout, cry

Zusage ['tsuːzaːgə] *f* promise; (*Annahme*) consent; **z~n** *vt* to promise ♦ *vi* to accept; **jdm z~n** (*gefallen*) to agree with *od* please sb

zusammen [tsuˈzamən] *adv* together; **Z~arbeit** *f* cooperation; ~**arbeiten** *vi* to cooperate; ~**beißen** (*unreg*) *vt* (*Zähne*) to clench; ~**bleiben** (*unreg*) *vi* to stay together; ~**brechen** (*unreg*) *vi* to collapse; (*Mensch auch*) to break down; ~**bringen** (*unreg*) *vt* to bring *od* get together; (*Geld*) to get; (*Sätze*) to put together; **Z~bruch** *m* collapse; ~**fassen** *vt* to summarize; (*vereinigen*) to unite; **Z~fassung** *f* summary, résumé; ~**fügen** *vt* to join (together), to unite; ~**halten** (*unreg*) *vi* to stick together; **Z~hang** *m* connection; **im/ aus dem Z~hang** in/out of context; ~**hängen** (*unreg*) *vi* to be connected *od* linked; ~**kommen** (*unreg*) *vi* to meet, to assemble; (*sich ereignen*) to occur at once *od* together; ~**legen** *vt* to put together; (*stapeln*) to pile up; (*falten*) to fold; (*verbinden*) to combine, to unite; (*Termine, Fest*) to amalgamate; (*Geld*) to collect; ~**nehmen** (*unreg*) *vt* to summon up ♦ *vr* to pull o.s. together; **alles ~genommen** all in all; ~**passen** *vi* to go well together, to match; ~**schließen** (*unreg*) *vt*, *vr* to join (together); **Z~schluß** *m* amalgamation; ~**schreiben** (*unreg*) *vt* to write as one word; (*Bericht*) to put together;

Z~sein (-s) *nt* get-together; ~**setzen** *vt* to put together ♦ *vr* (*Stoff*) to be composed of; (*Menschen*) to get together; **Z~setzung** *f* composition; ~**stellen** *vt* to put together; to compile; **Z~stoß** *m* collision; ~**stoßen** (*unreg*) *vi* to collide; **Z~treffen** *nt* meeting; coincidence; ~**treffen** (*unreg*) *vi* to coincide; (*Menschen*) to meet; ~**zählen** *vt* to add up; ~**ziehen** (*unreg*) *vt* (*verengern*) to draw together; (*vereinigen*) to bring together; (*addieren*) to add up ♦ *vr* to shrink; (*sich bilden*) to form, to develop

zusätzlich ['tsuːzɛtslɪç] *adj* additional ♦ *adv* in addition

zuschauen ['tsuːʃauən] *vi* to watch, to look on

Zuschauer(in) (-s, -) *m(f)* spectator ♦ *pl* (*THEAT*) audience *sg*

zuschicken ['tsuːʃɪkən] *vt*: (**jdm etw**) ~ to send *od* forward (sth to sb)

Zuschlag ['tsuːʃlaːk] *m* extra charge, surcharge; **z~en** ['tsuːʃlaːgən] (*unreg*) *vt* (*Tür*) to slam; (*Ball*) to hit; (*bei Auktion*) to knock down; (*Steine etc*) to knock into shape ♦ *vi* (*Fenster, Tür*) to shut; (*Mensch*) to hit, to punch; ~**karte** *f* (*EISENB*) surcharge ticket; **z~pflichtig** *adj* subject to surcharge

zuschneiden ['tsuːʃnaɪdən] (*unreg*) *vt* to cut out; to cut to size

zuschrauben ['tsuːʃraubən] *vt* to screw down *od* up

zuschreiben ['tsuːʃraɪbən] (*unreg*) *vt* (*fig*) to ascribe, to attribute; (*COMM*) to credit

Zuschrift ['tsuːʃrɪft] *f* letter, reply

zuschulden [tsuˈʃuldən] *adv*: **sich** *dat* **etw ~ kommen lassen** to make o.s. guilty of sth

Zuschuß ['tsuːʃus] *m* subsidy, allowance

zusehen ['tsuːzeːən] (*unreg*) *vi* to watch; (*dafür sorgen*) to take care; **jdm/etw ~** to watch sb/sth; ~**ds** *adv* visibly

zusenden ['tsuːzɛndən] (*unreg*) *vt* to forward, to send on

zusichern ['tsuːzɪçərn] *vt*: **jdm etw ~** to assure sb of sth

zuspielen ['tsuːʃpiːlən] *vt, vi* to pass
zuspitzen ['tsuːʃpɪtsən] *vt* to sharpen ♦ *vr* (*Lage*) to become critical
zusprechen ['tsuːʃprɛçən] (*unreg*) *vt* (*zuerkennen*) to award ♦ *vi* to speak; **jdm etw ~** to award sb sth *od* sth to sb; **jdm Trost ~** to comfort sb; **dem Essen/ Alkohol ~** to eat/drink a lot
Zustand ['tsuːʃtant] *m* state, condition; **z~e** [tsuːʃtɛndə] *adv:* **z~e bringen** to bring about; **z~e kommen** to come about
zuständig ['tsuːʃtɛndɪç] *adj* responsible; **Z~keit** *f* competence, responsibility
zustehen ['tsuːʃteːən] (*unreg*) *vi:* **jdm ~** to be sb's right
zustellen ['tsuːʃtɛlən] *vt* (*verstellen*) to block; (*Post etc*) to send
zustimmen ['tsuːʃtɪmən] *vi* to agree
Zustimmung *f* agreement, consent
zustoßen ['tsuːʃtoːsən] (*unreg*) *vi* (*fig*) to happen
zutage [tsuːtaːgə] *adv:* **~ bringen** to bring to light; **~ treten** to come to light
Zutaten ['tsuːtaːtən] *pl* ingredients
zutiefst [tsuːtiːfst] *adv* deeply
zutragen ['tsuːtraːgən] (*unreg*) *vt* to bring; (*Klatsch*) to tell ♦ *vr* to happen
zutrau- ['tsuːtrau] *zW:* **Z~en** (-s) *nt:* **Z~en (zu) traut** (in); **~en** *vt:* **jdm etw ~en** to credit sb with sth; **~lich** *adj* trusting, friendly; **Z~lichkeit** *f* trust
zutreffen ['tsuːtrɛfən] (*unreg*) *vi* to be correct; to apply; **Z~des bitte unterstreichen** please underline where applicable
Zutritt ['tsuːtrɪt] *m* access, admittance
Zutun ['tsuːtuːn] (-s) *nt* assistance
zuverlässig ['tsuːfɛrlɛsɪç] *adj* reliable; **Z~keit** *f* reliability
Zuversicht ['tsuːfɛrzɪçt] (-) *f* confidence; **z~lich** *adj* confident
zuviel [tsuːfiːl] *adv* too much
zuvor [tsuːfoːr] *adv* before, previously; **~kommen** (*unreg*) *vi* +*dat* to anticipate; **jdm ~kommen** to beat sb to it; **~kommend** *adj* obliging, courteous
Zuwachs ['tsuːvaks] (-es) *m* increase, growth; (*umg*) addition; **z~en** (*unreg*) *vi* to become overgrown; (*Wunde*) to

heal (up)
zuwege [tsuːveːgə] *adv:* **etw ~ bringen** to accomplish sth
zuweilen [tsuːvaɪlən] *adv* at times, now and then
zuweisen ['tsuːvaɪzən] (*unreg*) *vt* to assign, to allocate
zuwenden ['tsuːvɛndən] (*unreg*) *vt* (+*dat*) to turn (towards) ♦ *vr:* **sich jdm/etw ~** to devote o.s. to sb/sth; to turn to sb/sth; **jdm seine Aufmerksamkeit ~** to give sb one's attention
zuwenig [tsuːveːnɪç] *adv* too little
zuwider [tsuːviːdər] *adv:* **etw ist jdm ~** sb loathes sth, sb finds sth repugnant ♦ *präp* +*dat:* (**einer Sache**) **~** contrary to (sth); **~handeln** *vi:* **einer Sache** *dat* **~handeln** to act contrary to sth; **einem Gesetz ~handeln** to contravene a law
zuziehen ['tsuːtsiːən] (*unreg*) *vt* (*schließen: Vorhang*) to draw, to close; (*herbeirufen: Experten*) to call in ♦ *vi* to move in, to come; **sich** *dat* **etw ~** (*Krankheit*) to catch sth; (*Zorn*) to incur sth
zuzüglich ['tsuːtsyːklɪç] *präp* +*gen* plus, with the addition of
Zwang [tsvaŋ] (-(e)s, ⸗e) *m* compulsion, coercion
zwängen ['tsvɛŋən] *vt, vr* to squeeze
zwanglos *adj* informal
Zwangs- *zW:* **~arbeit** *f* forced labour; (*Strafe*) hard labour; **~jacke** *f* straitjacket; **~lage** *f* predicament, tight corner; **z~läufig** *adj* necessary, inevitable
zwanzig ['tsvantsɪç] *num* twenty
zwar [tsvaːr] *adv* to be sure, indeed; **das ist ~ ..., aber ...** that may be ... but ...; **und ~ am Sonntag** on Sunday to be precise; **und ~ so schnell, daß ...** in fact so quickly that ...
Zweck [tsvɛk] (-(e)s, -e) *m* purpose, aim; **es hat keinen ~** there's no point; **z~dienlich** *adj* practical; expedient
Zwecke *f* hobnail; (*Heft~*) drawing pin, thumbtack (*US*)
Zweck- *zW:* **z~los** *adj* pointless; **z~mäßig** *adj* suitable, appropriate; **z~s** *präp* +*gen* for the purpose of

zwei [tsvaɪ] *num* two; ~**deutig** *adj* ambiguous; (*unanständig*) suggestive; ~**erlei** *adj*: ~**erlei Stoff** two different kinds of material; ~**erlei Meinung** of differing opinions; ~**fach** *adj* double

Zweifel ['tsvaɪfəl] (-s, -) *m* doubt; z~**haft** *adj* doubtful, dubious; z~**los** *adj* doubtless; z~**n** *vi*: (**an etw** *dat*) z~**n** to doubt (sth)

Zweig [tsvaɪk] (-(e)s, -e) *m* branch; ~**stelle** *f* branch (office)

zwei- *zW*: ~**hundert** *num* two hundred; **Z~kampf** *m* duel; ~**mal** *adv* twice; ~**sprachig** *adj* bilingual; ~**spurig** *adj* (*AUT*) two-lane; ~**stimmig** *adj* for two voices; **Z~taktmotor** *m* two-stroke engine

zweit [tsvaɪt] *adv*: **zu ~** together; (*bei mehreren Paaren*) in twos; ~**beste(r, s)** *adj* second best; ~**e(r, s)** *adj* second; ~**ens** *adv* secondly; ~**größte(r, s)** *adj* second largest; ~**klassig** *adj* second-class; ~**letzte(r, s)** *adj* last but one, penultimate; ~**rangig** *adj* second-rate

Zwerchfell ['tsvɛrçfɛl] *nt* diaphragm

Zwerg [tsvɛrk] (-(e)s, -e) *m* dwarf

Zwetsch(g)e ['tsvɛtʃ(g)ə] *f* plum

Zwieback ['tsvi:bak] (-(e)s, -e) *m* rusk

Zwiebel ['tsvi:bəl] (-, -n) *f* onion; (*Blumen~*) bulb

Zwie- ['tsvi:] *zW*: z~**lichtig** *adj* shady, dubious; z~**spältig** *adj* (*Gefühle*) conflicting; (*Charakter*) contradictory; ~**tracht** *f* discord, dissension

Zwilling ['tsvɪlɪŋ] (-s, -e) *m* twin; ~**e** *pl* (*ASTROL*) Gemini

zwingen ['tsvɪŋən] (*unreg*) *vt* to force; ~**d** *adj* (*Grund etc*) compelling

zwinkern ['tsvɪŋkərn] *vi* to blink; (*absichtlich*) to wink

Zwirn [tsvɪrn] (-(e)s, -e) *m* thread

zwischen ['tsvɪʃən] *präp* (+*akk od dat*) between; **Z~bemerkung** *f* (incidental) remark; **Z~ding** *nt* cross; ~**durch** [-'dʊrç] *adv* in between; (*räumlich*) here and there; **Z~ergebnis** *nt* intermediate result; **Z~fall** *m* incident; **Z~frage** *f* question; **Z~handel** *m* middlemen *pl*; middleman's trade; **Z~landung** *f* (*AVIAT*) stopover; ~**menschlich** *adj* interpersonal; **Z~raum** *m* space; **Z~ruf** *m* interjection; **Z~station** *f* intermediate station; **Z~zeit** *f* interval; **in der Z~zeit** in the interim, meanwhile

Zwist [tsvɪst] (-es, -e) *m* dispute, feud

zwitschern ['tsvɪtʃərn] *vt*, *vi* to twitter, to chirp

zwo [tsvo:] *num* two

zwölf [tsvœlf] *num* twelve

Zyklus ['tsy:klʊs] (-, **Zyklen**) *m* cycle

Zylinder [tsi'lɪndər] (-s, -) *m* cylinder; (*Hut*) top hat; z~**förmig** *adj* cylindrical

Zyniker ['tsy:nikər] (-s, -) *m* cynic

zynisch ['tsy:nɪʃ] *adj* cynical

Zynismus [tsy'nɪsmʊs] *m* cynicism

Zypern ['tsy:pərn] *nt* Cyprus

Zyste ['tsʏstə] *f* cyst

z.Z(t). *abk* = **zur Zeit**

ENGLISH - GERMAN
ENGLISCH - DEUTSCH

A

A [eɪ] *n* (*MUS*) A *nt*; ~ **road** Hauptverkehrsstraße *f*

a [eɪ, ə] (*before vowel or silent h: an*) *indef art* **1** ein; eine; **a woman** eine Frau; **a book** ein Buch; **an eagle** ein Adler; **she's a doctor** sie ist Ärztin
2 (*instead of the number "one"*) ein; eine; **a year ago** vor einem Jahr; **a hundred/thousand** *etc* **pounds** (ein) hundert/(ein) tausend *etc* Pfund
3 (*in expressing ratios, prices etc*) pro; **3 a day/week** 3 pro Tag/Woche, 3 am Tag/in der Woche; **10 km an hour** 10 km pro Stunde/in der Stunde

A.A. *n abbr* = **Alcoholics Anonymous**; (*BRIT*) = **Automobile Association**
A.A.A. (*US*) *n abbr* = **American Automobile Association**
aback [ə'bæk] *adv*: **to be taken** ~ verblüfft sein
abandon [ə'bændən] *vt* (*give up*) aufgeben; (*desert*) verlassen ♦ *n* Hingabe *f*
abashed [ə'bæʃt] *adj* verlegen
abate [ə'beɪt] *vi* nachlassen, sich legen
abattoir ['æbətwɑ:*] (*BRIT*) *n* Schlachthaus *nt*
abbey ['æbɪ] *n* Abtei *f*
abbot ['æbət] *n* Abt *m*
abbreviate [ə'bri:vɪeɪt] *vt* abkürzen
abbreviation [əbri:vɪ'eɪʃən] *n* Abkürzung *f*
abdicate ['æbdɪkeɪt] *vt* aufgeben ♦ *vi* abdanken
abdomen ['æbdəmən] *n* Unterleib *m*
abduct [æb'dʌkt] *vt* entführen
aberration [æbə'reɪʃən] *n* (geistige) Verwirrung *f*
abet [ə'bet] *vt see* **aid**
abeyance [ə'beɪəns] *n*: **in** ~ in der

Schwebe; (*disuse*) außer Kraft
abhor [əb'hɔ:*] *vt* verabscheuen
abide [ə'baɪd] *vt* vertragen; leiden; ~ **by** *vt* sich halten an +*acc*
ability [ə'bɪlɪtɪ] *n* (*power*) Fähigkeit *f*; (*skill*) Geschicklichkeit *f*
abject ['æbdʒekt] *adj* (*liar*) übel; (*poverty*) größte(r, s); (*apology*) zerknirscht
ablaze [ə'bleɪz] *adj* in Flammen
able ['eɪbl] *adj* geschickt, fähig; **to be** ~ **to do sth** etw tun können; ~**-bodied** *adj* kräftig; (*seaman*) Voll-
ably ['eɪblɪ] *adv* geschickt
abnormal [æb'nɔ:məl] *adj* regelwidrig, abnorm
aboard [ə'bɔ:d] *adv, prep* an Bord +*gen*
abode [ə'bəud] *n*: **of no fixed** ~ ohne festen Wohnsitz
abolish [ə'bɒlɪʃ] *vt* abschaffen
abolition [æbə'lɪʃən] *n* Abschaffung *f*
abominable [ə'bɒmɪnəbl] *adj* scheußlich
aborigine [æbə'rɪdʒɪni:] *n* Ureinwohner *m*
abort [ə'bɔ:t] *vt* abtreiben; fehlgebären; ~**ion** [ə'bɔ:ʃən] *n* Abtreibung *f*; (*miscarriage*) Fehlgeburt *f*; ~**ive** *adj* mißlungen
abound [ə'baund] *vi* im Überfluß vorhanden sein; **to** ~ **in** Überfluß haben an +*dat*

about [ə'baut] *adv* **1** (*approximately*) etwa, ungefähr; **about a hundred/thousand** *etc* etwa hundert/tausend *etc*; **at about 2 o'clock** etwa um 2 Uhr; **I've just about finished** ich bin gerade fertig
2 (*referring to place*) herum, umher; **to leave things lying about** Sachen herumliegen lassen; **to run/walk** *etc* **about** herumrennen/gehen *etc*

3 : to be about to do sth im Begriff sein, etw zu tun; **he was about to go to bed** er wollte gerade ins Bett gehen
♦ *prep* **1** *(relating to)* über +*acc*; **a book about London** ein Buch über London; **what is it about?** worum geht es?; *(book etc)* wovon handelt es?; **we talked about it** wir haben darüber geredet; **what** *or* **how about doing this?** wollen wir das machen?
2 *(referring to place)* um (... herum); **to walk about the town** in der Stadt herumgehen; **her clothes were scattered about the room** ihre Kleider waren über das ganze Zimmer verstreut

about-face [ə'baut'feɪs] *n* Kehrtwendung *f*

about-turn [ə'baut'tɜ:n] *n* Kehrtwendung *f*

above [ə'bʌv] *adv* oben ♦ *prep* über; ~ **all** vor allem; ~ **board** *adj* offen, ehrlich

abrasive [ə'breɪzɪv] *adj* Abschleif-; *(personality)* zermürbend, aufreibend

abreast [ə'brest] *adv* nebeneinander; **to keep** ~ **of** Schritt halten mit

abridge [ə'brɪdʒ] *vt* (ab)kürzen

abroad [ə'brɔ:d] *adv* *(be)* im Ausland; *(go)* ins Ausland

abrupt [ə'brʌpt] *adj* *(sudden)* abrupt, jäh; *(curt)* schroff

abscess ['æbses] *n* Geschwür *nt*

abscond [əb'skɒnd] *vi* flüchten, sich davonmachen

abseil ['æbsaɪl] *vi* *(also:* ~ *down)* sich abseilen

absence ['æbsəns] *n* Abwesenheit *f*

absent ['æbsənt] *adj* abwesend, nicht da; *(lost in thought)* geistesabwesend; ~**ee** [æbsən'ti:] *n* Abwesende(r) *m*; ~**eeism** [æbsən'ti:ɪzəm] *n* Fehlen *nt* (am Arbeitsplatz/in der Schule); ~-**minded** *adj* zerstreut

absolute ['æbsəlu:t] *adj* absolut; *(power)* unumschränkt; *(rubbish)* vollkommen, rein; ~**ly** [æbsə'lu:tlɪ] *adv* absolut, vollkommen; ~**ly!** ganz bestimmt!

absolve [əb'zɒlv] *vt* entbinden; freispre-

chen

absorb [əb'zɔ:b] *vt* aufsaugen, absorbieren; *(fig)* ganz in Anspruch nehmen, fesseln; **to be** ~**ed in a book** in ein Buch vertieft sein; ~**ent** *adj* absorbierend; ~**ent cotton** *(US)* *n* Verbandwatte *f*; ~**ing** *adj* aufsaugend; *(fig)* packend

absorption [əb'zɔ:pʃən] *n* Aufsaugung *f*, Absorption *f*; *(fig)* Versunkenheit *f*

abstain [əb'steɪn] *vi* *(in vote)* sich enthalten; **to** ~ **from** *(keep from)* sich enthalten +*gen*

abstemious [əb'sti:mɪəs] *adj* enthaltsam

abstention [əb'stenʃən] *n* *(in vote)* (Stimm)enthaltung *f*

abstinence ['æbstɪnəns] *n* Enthaltsamkeit *f*

abstract ['æbstrækt] *adj* abstrakt

absurd [əb'sɜ:d] *adj* absurd

abundance [ə'bʌndəns] *n*: ~ *(of)* Überfluß *m* (an +*dat*)

abundant [ə'bʌndənt] *adj* reichlich

abuse [*n* ə'bju:s, *vb* ə'bju:z] *n* *(rude language)* Beschimpfung *f*; *(ill usage)* Mißbrauch *m*; *(bad practice)* (Amts)mißbrauch *m* ♦ *vt* *(misuse)* mißbrauchen

abusive [ə'bju:sɪv] *adj* beleidigend, Schimpf-

abysmal [ə'bɪzməl] *adj* scheußlich; *(ignorance)* bodenlos

abyss [ə'bɪs] *n* Abgrund *m*

AC *abbr* (= *alternating current*) Wechselstrom *m*

academic [ækə'demɪk] *adj* akademisch; *(theoretical)* theoretisch ♦ *n* Akademiker(in) *m(f)*

academy [ə'kædəmɪ] *n* *(school)* Hochschule *f*; *(society)* Akademie *f*

accelerate [æk'seləreɪt] *vi* schneller werden; *(AUT)* Gas geben ♦ *vt* beschleunigen

acceleration [ækselə'reɪʃən] *n* Beschleunigung *f*

accelerator [ək'seləreɪtə*] *n* Gas(pedal) *nt*

accent ['æksent] *n* Akzent *m*, Tonfall *m*; *(mark)* Akzent *m*; *(stress)* Betonung *f*

accept [ək'sept] *vt* *(take)* annehmen;

(*agree to*) akzeptieren; ~**able** *adj* annehmbar; ~**ance** *n* Annahme *f*

access ['ækses] *n* Zugang *m*; ~**ible** [æk'sesɪbl] *adj* (*easy to approach*) zugänglich; (*within reach*) (leicht) erreichbar

accessory [æk'sesərɪ] *n* Zubehörteil *nt*; **toilet accessories** Toilettenartikel *pl*

accident ['æksɪdənt] *n* Unfall *m*; (*coincidence*) Zufall *m*; **by** ~ zufällig; ~**al** [æksɪ'dentl] *adj* unbeabsichtigt; ~**ally** [æksɪ'dentəlɪ] *adv* zufällig; ~-**prone** *adj*: **to be** ~-**prone** zu Unfällen neigen

acclaim [ə'kleɪm] *vt* zujubeln +*dat* ♦ *n* Beifall *m*

acclimate [ə'klaɪmət] (*US*) *vt* = **acclimatize**

acclimatize [ə'klaɪmətaɪz] *vt*: **to become** ~**d** (**to**) sich gewöhnen (an +*acc*), sich akklimatisieren (in +*dat*)

accolade ['ækəlcɪd] *n* Auszeichnung *f*

accommodate [ə'kɒmədeɪt] *vt* unterbringen; (*hold*) Platz haben für; (*oblige*) (aus)helfen +*dat*

accommodating [ə'kɒmədeɪtɪŋ] *adj* entgegenkommend

accommodation [əkɒmə'deɪʃən] (*US* ~**s**) *n* Unterkunft *f*

accompaniment [ə'kʌmpənɪmənt] *n* Begleitung *f*

accompany [ə'kʌmpənɪ] *vt* begleiten

accomplice [ə'kʌmplɪs] *n* Helfershelfer *m*, Komplize *m*

accomplish [ə'kʌmplɪʃ] *vt* (*fulfil*) durchführen; (*finish*) vollenden; (*aim*) erreichen; ~**ed** *adj* vollendet, ausgezeichnet; ~**ment** *n* (*skill*) Fähigkeit *f*; (*completion*) Vollendung *f*; (*feat*) Leistung *f*

accord [ə'kɔːd] *n* Übereinstimmung *f* ♦ *vt* gewähren; **of one's own** ~ freiwillig; ~**ing to** *prep* nach, laut +*gen*; ~**ance** *n*: **in** ~**ance with** in Übereinstimmung mit; ~**ingly** *adv* danach, dementsprechend

accordion [ə'kɔːdɪən] *n* Akkordeon *nt*

accost [ə'kɒst] *vt* ansprechen

account [ə'kaʊnt] *n* (*bill*) Rechnung *f*; (*narrative*) Bericht *m*; (*report*) Rechenschaftsbericht *m*; (*in bank*) Konto *nt*; (*importance*) Geltung *f*; ~**s** *npl* (*FIN*) Bücher *pl*; **on** ~ auf Rechnung; **of no** ~ ohne Bedeutung; **on no** ~ keinesfalls; **on** ~ **of** wegen; **to take into** ~ berücksichtigen; ~ **for** *vt fus* (*expenditure*) Rechenschaft ablegen für; **how do you** ~ **for that?** wie erklären Sie (sich) das?; ~**able** *adj* verantwortlich; ~**ancy** [ə'kaʊntənsɪ] *n* Buchhaltung *f*; ~**ant** [ə'kaʊntənt] *n* Wirtschaftsprüfer(in) *m(f)*; ~ **number** *n* Kontonummer *f*

accredited [ə'kredɪtɪd] *adj* (offiziell) zugelassen

accrue [ə'kruː] *vi* sich ansammeln

accumulate [ə'kjuːmjʊleɪt] *vt* ansammeln ♦ *vi* sich ansammeln

accuracy ['ækjʊrəsɪ] *n* Genauigkeit *f*

accurate ['ækjʊrɪt] *adj* genau; ~**ly** *adv* genau, richtig

accusation [ækjuː'zeɪʃən] *n* Anklage *f*, Beschuldigung *f*

accuse [ə'kjuːz] *vt* anklagen, beschuldigen; ~**d** *n* Angeklagte(r) *mf*

accustom [ə'kʌstəm] *vt*: **to** ~ **sb** (**to sth**) jdn (an etw *acc*) gewöhnen; ~**ed** *adj* gewohnt

ace [eɪs] *n* As *nt*; (*inf*) As *nt*, Kanone *f*

ache [eɪk] *n* Schmerz *m* ♦ *vi* (*be sore*) schmerzen, weh tun

achieve [ə'tʃiːv] *vt* zustande bringen; (*aim*) erreichen; ~**ment** *n* Leistung *f*; (*act*) Erreichen *nt*

acid ['æsɪd] *n* Säure *f* ♦ *adj* sauer, scharf; ~ **rain** *n* Saure(r) Regen *m*

acknowledge [ək'nɒlɪdʒ] *vt* (*receipt*) bestätigen; (*admit*) zugeben; ~**ment** *n* Anerkennung *f*; (*letter*) Empfangsbestätigung *f*

acne ['æknɪ] *n* Akne *f*

acorn ['eɪkɔːn] *n* Eichel *f*

acoustic [ə'kuːstɪk] *adj* akustisch; ~**s** *npl* Akustik *f*

acquaint [ə'kweɪnt] *vt* vertraut machen; **to be** ~**ed with sb** mit jdm bekannt sein; ~**ance** *n* (*person*) Bekannte(r) *mf*; (*knowledge*) Kenntnis *f*

acquiesce [ækwɪ'es] *vi*: **to** ~ (**in**) sich abfinden (mit)

acquire [ə'kwaɪə*] *vt* erwerben

acquisition [ækwɪˈzɪʃən] n Errungenschaft f; (act) Erwerb m

acquisitive [əˈkwɪzɪtɪv] adj gewinnsüchtig

acquit [əˈkwɪt] vt (free) freisprechen; to ~ o.s. well sich bewähren; ~tal n Freispruch m

acre [ˈeɪkə*] n Morgen m

acrid [ˈækrɪd] adj (smell, taste) bitter; (smoke) beißend

acrimonious [ækrɪˈməʊnɪəs] adj bitter

acrobat [ˈækrəbæt] n Akrobat m

across [əˈkrɒs] prep über +acc ♦ adv hinüber, herüber; **he lives ~ the river** er wohnt auf der anderen Seite des Flusses; **ten metres ~** zehn Meter breit; **he lives ~ from us** er wohnt uns gegenüber

acrylic [əˈkrɪlɪk] adj Acryl-

act [ækt] n (deed) Tat f; (JUR) Gesetz nt; (THEAT) Akt m; (: turn) Nummer f ♦ vi (take action) handeln; (behave) sich verhalten; (pretend) vorgeben; (THEAT) spielen ♦ vt (in play) spielen; **to ~ as** fungieren als; ~ing adj stellvertretend ♦ n Schauspielkunst f; (performance) Aufführung f

action [ˈækʃən] n (deed) Tat f; Handlung f; (motion) Bewegung f; (way of working) Funktionieren nt; (battle) Einsatz m, Gefecht nt; (lawsuit) Klage f, Prozeß m; **out of ~** (person) nicht einsatzfähig; (thing) außer Betrieb; **to take ~** etwas unternehmen; ~ **replay** n (TV) Wiederholung f

activate [ˈæktɪveɪt] vt (mechanism) betätigen; (CHEM, PHYS) aktivieren

active [ˈæktɪv] adj (brisk) rege, tatkräftig; (working) aktiv; (GRAM) aktiv, Tätigkeits-; ~ly adv aktiv; (dislike) offen

activity [ækˈtɪvɪtɪ] n Aktivität f; (doings) Unternehmungen pl; (occupation) Tätigkeit f

actor [ˈæktə*] n Schauspieler m

actress [ˈæktrɪs] n Schauspielerin f

actual [ˈæktjʊəl] adj wirklich; ~ly adv tatsächlich; ~ly no eigentlich nicht

acumen [ˈækjʊmen] n Scharfsinn m

acute [əˈkjuːt] adj (severe) heftig, akut; (keen) scharfsinnig

ad [æd] n abbr = **advertisement**

A.D. adv abbr (= Anno Domini) n.Chr.

Adam [ˈædəm] n Adam m

adamant [ˈædəmənt] adj eisern; hartnäckig

adapt [əˈdæpt] vt anpassen ♦ vi: to ~ (to) sich anpassen (an +acc); ~able adj anpassungsfähig; ~ation [ædæpˈteɪʃən] n (THEAT etc) Bearbeitung f; (adjustment) Anpassung f; ~er n (ELEC) Zwischenstecker m; ~or n (ELEC) Zwischenstecker m

add [æd] vt (join) hinzufügen; (numbers: also: ~ up) addieren; ~ vi (make sense) stimmen; ~ **up to** vt fus ausmachen

adder [ˈædə*] n Kreuzotter f, Natter f

addict [ˈædɪkt] n Süchtige(r) mf; ~ed [əˈdɪktɪd] adj: ~ed to -süchtig; ~ion [əˈdɪkʃən] n Sucht f; ~ive adj: to be ~ive süchtig machen

addition [əˈdɪʃən] n Anhang m, Addition f; (MATH) Addition f, Zusammenzählen nt; **in ~** zusätzlich, außerdem; ~al adj zusätzlich, weiter

additive [ˈædɪtɪv] n Zusatz m

address [əˈdres] n Adresse f; (speech) Ansprache f ♦ vt (letter) adressieren; (speak to) ansprechen; (make speech to) eine Ansprache halten an +acc

adept [ˈædept] adj geschickt; **to be ~ at** gut sein in +dat

adequate [ˈædɪkwɪt] adj angemessen

adhere [ədˈhɪə*] vi: to ~ to haften an +dat; (fig) festhalten an +dat

adhesive [ədˈhiːzɪv] adj klebend; Kleb(e)- ♦ n Klebstoff m; ~ **tape** n (BRIT) Klebestreifen m; (US) Heftpflaster nt

ad hoc [ædˈhɒk] adj (decision, committee) Ad-hoc- ♦ adv (decide, appoint) ad hoc

adjacent [əˈdʒeɪsənt] adj benachbart; ~ **to** angrenzend an +acc

adjective [ˈædʒəktɪv] n Adjektiv nt, Eigenschaftswort nt

adjoining [əˈdʒɔɪnɪŋ] adj benachbart, Neben-

adjourn [əˈdʒɜːn] vt vertagen ♦ vi abbrechen

adjudicate [əˈdʒuːdɪkeɪt] *vi* entscheiden, ein Urteil fällen

adjust [əˈdʒʌst] *vt* (*alter*) anpassen; (*put right*) regulieren, richtig stellen ♦ *vi* sich anpassen; **~able** *adj* verstellbar

ad-lib [ædˈlɪb] *vt, vi* improvisieren ♦ *adv*: **ad lib** aus dem Stegreif

administer [ædˈmɪnɪstə*] *vt* (*manage*) verwalten; (*dispense*) ausüben; (*justice*) sprechen; (*medicine*) geben

administration [ədmɪnɪsˈtreɪʃən] *n* Verwaltung *f*; (*POL*) Regierung *f*

administrative [ədˈmɪnɪstrətɪv] *adj* Verwaltungs-

administrator [ədˈmɪnɪstreɪtə*] *n* Verwaltungsbeamte(r) *m*

admiral [ˈædmərəl] *n* Admiral *m*

Admiralty [ˈædmərəltɪ] (*BRIT*) *n* Admiralität *f*

admiration [ædmɪˈreɪʃən] *n* Bewunderung *f*

admire [ədˈmaɪə*] *vt* (*respect*) bewundern; (*love*) verehren; **~r** *n* Bewunderer *m*

admission [ədˈmɪʃən] *n* (*entrance*) Einlaß *m*; (*fee*) Eintritt(spreis *m*) *m*; (*confession*) Geständnis *nt*

admit [ədˈmɪt] *vt* (*let in*) einlassen; (*confess*) gestehen; (*accept*) anerkennen; **~tance** *n* Zulassung *f*; **~tedly** *adv* zugegebenermaßen

admonish [ədˈmɒnɪʃ] *vt* ermahnen

ad nauseam [ædˈnɔːsɪæm] *adv* (*repeat, talk*) endlos

ado [əˈduː] *n*: **without more ~** ohne weitere Umstände

adolescence [ædəˈlesns] *n* Jugendalter *nt*

adolescent [ædəˈlesnt] *adj* jugendlich ♦ *n* Jugendliche(r) *mf*

adopt [əˈdɒpt] *vt* (*child*) adoptieren; (*idea*) übernehmen; **~ion** [əˈdɒpʃən] *n* Adoption *f*; Übernahme *f*

adore [əˈdɔː*] *vt* anbeten; verehren

adorn [əˈdɔːn] *vt* schmücken

Adriatic [eɪdrɪˈætɪk] *n*: **the ~** (**Sea**) die Adria

adrift [əˈdrɪft] *adv* Wind und Wellen preisgegeben

adult [ˈædʌlt] *n* Erwachsene(r) *mf*

adultery [əˈdʌltərɪ] *n* Ehebruch *m*

advance [ədˈvɑːns] *n* (*progress*) Vorrücken *nt*; (*money*) Vorschuß *m* ♦ *vt* (*move forward*) vorrücken; (*money*) vorschießen; (*argument*) vorbringen ♦ *vi* vorwärtsgehen; **in ~** im voraus; **~d** *adj* (*ahead*) vorgerückt; (*modern*) fortgeschritten; (*study*) für Fortgeschrittene; **~ment** *n* Förderung *f*; (*promotion*) Beförderung *f*

advantage [ədˈvɑːntɪdʒ] *n* Vorteil *m*; **to have an ~ over sb** jdm gegenüber im Vorteil sein; **to take ~ of** (*misuse*) ausnutzen; (*profit from*) Nutzen ziehen aus; **~ous** [ædvənˈteɪdʒəs] *adj* vorteilhaft

advent [ˈædvent] *n* Ankunft *f*; **A~** Advent *m*

adventure [ədˈventʃə*] *n* Abenteuer *nt*

adventurous [ədˈventʃərəs] *adj* abenteuerlich, waghalsig

adverb [ˈædvɜːb] *n* Adverb *nt*, Umstandswort *nt*

adversary [ˈædvəsərɪ] *n* Gegner *m*

adverse [ˈædvɜːs] *adj* widrig

adversity [ədˈvɜːsɪtɪ] *n* Widrigkeit *f*, Mißgeschick *nt*

advert [ˈædvɜːt] *n* Anzeige *f*

advertise [ˈædvətaɪz] *vt* werben für ♦ *vi* annoncieren; **to ~ for sth** etw (per Anzeige) suchen

advertisement [ədˈvɜːtɪsmənt] *n* Anzeige *f*, Inserat *nt*

advertiser [ˈædvətaɪzə*] *n* (*in newspaper etc*) Inserent *m*

advertising [ˈædvətaɪzɪŋ] *n* Werbung *f*

advice [ədˈvaɪs] *n* Rat(schlag) *m*; (*notification*) Benachrichtigung *f*

advisable [ədˈvaɪzəbl] *adj* ratsam

advise [ədˈvaɪz] *vt*: **to ~ (sb)** (jdm) raten

advisedly [ədˈvaɪzədlɪ] *adv* (*deliberately*) bewußt

adviser *n* Berater *m*

advisory [ədˈvaɪzərɪ] *adj* beratend, Beratungs-

advocate [*vb* ˈædvəkeɪt, *n* ˈædvəkət] *vt* vertreten ♦ *n* Befürworter(in) *m(f)*

Aegean [iːˈdʒiːən] *n*: **the ~** (**Sea**) die Ägäis

aerial ['ɛərɪəl] n Antenne f ♦ adj Luft-
aerobics [ɛər'əʊbɪks] n Aerobic nt
aerodrome ['ɛərədrəʊm] (BRIT) n Flugplatz m
aerodynamic ['ɛərəʊdaɪ'næmɪk] adj
aerodynamisch
aeroplane ['ɛərəpleɪn] n Flugzeug nt
aerosol ['ɛərəsɒl] n Aerosol nt;
Sprühdose f
aesthetic [ɪs'θetɪk] adj ästhetisch
afar [ə'fɑː*] adv: from ~ aus der Ferne
affable ['æfəbl] adj umgänglich
affair [ə'fɛə*] n (concern) Angelegenheit
f; (event) Ereignis nt; (love ~) Verhältnis nt
affect [ə'fekt] vt (influence) (ein)wirken
auf +acc; (move deeply) bewegen; this
change doesn't ~ us diese Änderung betrifft uns nicht; ~ed adj affektiert,
gekünstelt
affection [ə'fekʃən] n Zuneigung f; ~ate
[ə'fekʃənɪt] adj liebevoll
affiliated [ə'fɪlɪeɪtɪd] adj angeschlossen
affinity [ə'fɪnɪtɪ] n (attraction) gegen-
seitige Anziehung f; (relationship) Verwandtschaft f
affirmation [æfə'meɪʃən] n Behauptung f
affirmative [ə'fɜːmətɪv] adj bestätigend
affix [ə'fɪks] vt aufkleben, anheften
afflict [ə'flɪkt] vt quälen, heimsuchen
affluence ['æfluəns] n (wealth) Wohlstand m
affluent ['æfluənt] adj wohlhabend,
Wohlstands-
afford [ə'fɔːd] vt sich dat leisten; (yield)
bieten, einbringen
affront [ə'frʌnt] n Beleidigung f
Afghanistan [æf'gænɪstɑːn] n Afghanistan nt
afield [ə'fiːld] adv: far ~ weit fort
afloat [ə'fləʊt] adj: to be ~ schwimmen
afoot [ə'fʊt] adv im Gang
afraid [ə'freɪd] adj ängstlich; to be ~ of
Angst haben vor +dat; to be ~ to do
sth sich scheuen, etw zu tun; I am ~ I
have ... ich habe leider ...; I'm ~ so/not
leider/leider nicht; I am ~ that ... ich
fürchte(, daß) ...
afresh [ə'freʃ] adv von neuem
Africa ['æfrɪkə] n Afrika nt; ~n adj

afrikanisch ♦ n Afrikaner(in) m(f)
aft [ɑːft] adv achtern
after ['ɑːftə*] prep nach; (following,
seeking) hinter ... dat ... her; (in
imitation) nach, im Stil von ♦ adv: soon
~ bald danach ♦ conj nachdem; what
are you ~? was wollen Sie?; ~ he left
nachdem er gegangen war; ~ you!
nach Ihnen!; ~ all letzten Endes; ~-
effects npl Nachwirkungen pl; ~life n
Leben nt nach dem Tode; ~math n
Auswirkungen pl; ~noon n Nachmittag
m; ~s (inf) n (dessert) Nachtisch m;
~-sales service (BRIT) n Kundendienst
m; ~-shave (lotion) n Rasierwasser nt;
~thought n nachträgliche(r) Einfall
m; ~wards adv danach, nachher
again [ə'gen] adv wieder, noch einmal;
(besides) außerdem, ferner; ~ and ~
immer wieder
against [ə'genst] prep gegen
age [eɪdʒ] n (of person) Alter nt; (in
history) Zeitalter nt ♦ vi altern, alt
werden ♦ vt älter machen; to come of
~ mündig werden; 20 years of ~ 20
Jahre alt; it's been ~s since ... es ist
ewig her, seit ...; ~d ['eɪdʒɪd] adj ...
Jahre alt, -jährig; (elderly) betagt ♦
npl: the ~d die Alten pl; ~ group n
Altersgruppe f; ~ limit n Altersgrenze f
agency ['eɪdʒənsɪ] n Agentur f; Vermittlung f; (CHEM) Wirkung f; through or
by the ~ of ... mit Hilfe von ...
agenda [ə'dʒendə] n Tagesordnung f
agent ['eɪdʒənt] n (COMM) Vertreter m;
(spy) Agent m
aggravate ['ægrəveɪt] vt (make worse)
verschlimmern; (irritate) reizen
aggregate ['ægrɪgɪt] n Summe f
aggression [ə'greʃən] n Aggression f
aggressive [ə'gresɪv] adj aggressiv
aggrieved [ə'griːvd] adj bedrückt, verletzt
aghast [ə'gɑːst] adj entsetzt
agile ['ædʒaɪl] adj flink; agil; (mind)
rege
agitate ['ædʒɪteɪt] vt rütteln; to ~ for
sich starkmachen für
ago [ə'gəʊ] adv: two days ~ vor zwei
Tagen; not long ~ vor kurzem; it's so

long ~ es ist schon so lange her
agog [ə'gɒg] *adj* gespannt
agonizing ['ægənaızıŋ] *adj* quälend
agony ['ægənı] *n* Qual *f*; **to be in ~** Qualen leiden
agree [ə'griː] *vt (date)* vereinbaren ♦ *vi (have same opinion, correspond)* übereinstimmen; *(consent)* zustimmen; *(be in harmony)* sich vertragen; **to ~ to sth** einer Sache *dat* zustimmen; **to ~ that ...** *(admit)* zugeben, daß ...; **to ~ to do sth** sich bereit erklären, etw zu tun; **garlic doesn't ~ with me** Knoblauch vertrage ich nicht; **I ~** einverstanden, ich stimme zu; **to ~ on sth** sich auf etw *acc* einigen; **~able** *adj (pleasing)* liebenswürdig; *(willing to consent)* einverstanden; **~d** *adj* vereinbart; **~ment** *n (agreeing)* Übereinstimmung *f*; *(contract)* Vereinbarung *f*, Vertrag *m*; **to be in ~ment** übereinstimmen
agricultural [ægrı'kʌltʃərəl] *adj* landwirtschaftlich, Landwirtschafts-
agriculture ['ægrıkʌltʃə*] *n* Landwirtschaft *f*
aground [ə'graund] *adv*: **to run ~** auf Grund laufen
ahead [ə'hed] *adv* vorwärts; **to be ~** voraus sein; **~ of time** der Zeit voraus; **go right** *or* **straight ~** gehen Sie geradeaus; **fahren Sie geradeaus**
aid [eıd] *n (assistance)* Hilfe *f*, Unterstützung *f*; *(person)* Hilfe *f*; *(thing)* Hilfsmittel *nt* ♦ *vt* unterstützen, helfen +*dat*; **in ~ of** zugunsten +*gen*; **to ~ and abet sb** jdm Beihilfe leisten
aide [eıd] *n (person)* Gehilfe *m*; *(MIL)* Adjutant *m*
AIDS [eıdz] *n abbr (= acquired immune deficiency syndrome)* Aids *nt*
ailing ['eılıŋ] *adj* kränkelnd
ailment ['eılmənt] *n* Leiden *nt*
aim [eım] *vt (gun, camera)* richten ♦ *vi (with gun: also: take ~)* zielen; *(intend)* beabsichtigen ♦ *n (intention)* Absicht *f*, Ziel *nt*; *(pointing)* Zielen *nt*, Richten *nt*; **to ~ at sth** auf etw *acc* richten; *(fig)* etw anstreben; **to ~ to do sth** vorhaben, etw zu tun; **~less** *adj* ziellos; **~lessly** *adv* ziellos

ain't [eınt] *(inf)* = am not; are not; is not; has not; have not
air [ɛə*] *n* Luft *f*; *(manner)* Miene *f*, Anschein *m*; *(MUS)* Melodie *f* ♦ *vt* lüften; *(fig)* an die Öffentlichkeit bringen ♦ *cpd* Luft-; **by ~** *(travel)* auf dem Luftweg; **to be on the ~** *(RADIO, TV: programme)* gesendet werden; **~ bed** *(BRIT)* *n* Luftmatratze *f*; **~-borne** *adj* in der Luft; **~-conditioned** *adj* mit Klimaanlage; **~-conditioning** *n* Klimaanlage *f*; **~craft** *n* Flugzeug *nt*, Maschine *f*; **~craft carrier** *n* Flugzeugträger *m*; **~field** *n* Flugplatz *m*; **~ force** *n* Luftwaffe *f*; **~ freshener** *n* Raumspray *nt*; **~gun** *n* Luftgewehr *nt*; **~ hostess** *(BRIT)* *n* Stewardeß *f*; **~ letter** *(BRIT)* *n* Luftpostbrief *m*; **~lift** *n* Luftbrücke *f*; **~line** *n* Luftverkehrsgesellschaft *f*; **~liner** *n* Verkehrsflugzeug *nt*; **~lock** *n* Luftblase *f*; **~mail** *n*: **by ~mail** mit Luftpost; **~plane** *(US)* *n* Flugzeug *nt*; **~port** *n* Flughafen *m*, Flugplatz *m*; **~ raid** *n* Luftangriff *m*; **~sick** *adj* luftkrank; **~strip** *n* Landestreifen *m*; **~ terminal** *n* Terminal *m*; **~tight** *adj* luftdicht; **~ traffic controller** *n* Fluglotse *m*; **~y** *adj* luftig; *(manner)* leichtfertig
aisle [aıl] *n* Gang *m*
ajar [ə'dʒɑː*] *adv* angelehnt; einen Spalt offen
akin [ə'kın] *adj*: **~ to** ähnlich +*dat*
alacrity [ə'lækrıtı] *n* Bereitwilligkeit *f*
alarm [ə'lɑːm] *n (warning)* Alarm *m*; *(bell etc)* Alarmanlage *f*; *(anxiety)* Sorge *f* ♦ *vt* erschrecken; **~ clock** *n* Wecker *m*
alas [ə'læs] *excl* ach
Albania [æl'beınıə] *n* Albanien *nt*
albeit [ɔːl'biːıt] *conj* obgleich
album [ælbəm] *n* Album *nt*
alcohol ['ælkəhɒl] *n* Alkohol *m*; **~ic** [ælkə'hɒlık] *adj (drink)* alkoholisch ♦ *n* Alkoholiker(in) *m(f)*; **~ism** *n* Alkoholismus *m*
alderman ['ɔːldəmən] *(irreg)* *n* Stadtrat *m*
ale [eıl] *n* Ale *nt*
alert [ə'lɜːt] *adj* wachsam ♦ *n* Alarm *m*

♦ *vt* alarmieren; **to be on the** ~ wachsam sein
algebra ['ældʒıbrə] *n* Algebra *f*
Algeria [æl'dʒıərıə] *n* Algerien *nt*
alias ['eılıəs] *adv* alias ♦ *n* Deckname *m*
alibi ['ælıbaı] *n* Alibi *nt*
alien ['eılıən] *n* Ausländer *m* ♦ *adj* (*foreign*) ausländisch; (*strange*) fremd; ~ **to** fremd +*dat*; ~**ate** *vt* entfremden
alight [ə'laıt] *adj* brennend; (*of building*) in Flammen ♦ *vi* (*descend*) aussteigen; (*bird*) sich setzen
align [ə'laın] *vt* ausrichten
alike [ə'laık] *adj* gleich, ähnlich ♦ *adv* gleich, ebenso; **to look** ~ sich *dat* ähnlich sehen
alimony ['ælımənı] *n* Unterhalt *m*, Alimente *pl*
alive [ə'laıv] *adj* (*living*) lebend; (*lively*) lebendig, aufgeweckt; ~ (**with**) (*full of*) voll (von), wimmelnd (von)

KEYWORD
---

all [ɔːl] *adj* alle(r, s); **all day/night** den ganzen Tag/die ganze Nacht; **all men are equal** alle Menschen sind gleich; **all five came** alle fünf kamen; **all the books/food** die ganzen Bücher/das ganze Essen; **all the time** die ganze Zeit (über); **all his life** sein ganzes Leben (lang)
♦ *pron* **1** alles; **I ate it all, I ate all of it** ich habe alles gegessen; **all of us/the boys went** wir gingen alle/alle Jungen gingen; **we all sat down** wir setzten uns alle
2 (*in phrases*): **above all** vor allem; **after all** schließlich; **at all: not at all** (*in answer to question*) überhaupt nicht; (*in answer to thanks*) gern geschehen; **I'm not at all tired** ich bin überhaupt nicht müde; **anything at all will do** es ist egal, welche(r, s); **all in all** alles in allem
♦ *adv* ganz; **all alone** ganz allein; **it's not as hard as all that** so schwer ist es nun auch wieder nicht; **all the more/the better** um so mehr/besser; **all but** fast; **the score is 2 all** es steht 2 zu 2

---

allay [ə'leı] *vt* (*fears*) beschwichtigen
all clear ['ɔːl'klıə*] *n* Entwarnung *f*
allegation [ælı'geıʃən] *n* Behauptung *f*
allege [ə'ledʒ] *vt* (*declare*) behaupten; (*falsely*) vorgeben; ~**dly** [ə'ledʒıdlı] *adv* angeblich
allegiance [ə'liːdʒəns] *n* Treue *f*
allergic [ə'lɜːdʒık] *adj*: ~ (**to**) allergisch (gegen)
allergy ['ælədʒı] *n* Allergie *f*
alleviate [ə'liːvıeıt] *vt* lindern
alley ['ælı] *n* Gasse *f*, Durchgang *m*
alliance [ə'laıəns] *n* Bund *m*, Allianz *f*
allied ['ælaıd] *adj* vereinigt; (*powers*) alliiert; ~ (**to**) verwandt (mit)
alligator ['ælıgeıtə*] *n* Alligator *m*
all-in ['ɔːlın] (*BRIT*) *adj*, *adv* (*charge*) alles inbegriffen, Gesamt-; ~ **wrestling** *n* Freistilringen *nt*
all-night ['ɔːl'naıt] *adj* (*café, cinema*) die ganze Nacht geöffnet, Nacht-
allocate ['æləkeıt] *vt* zuteilen
allot [ə'lɒt] *vt* zuteilen; ~**ment** *n* (*share*) Anteil *m*; (*plot*) Schrebergarten *m*
all-out ['ɔːl'aʊt] *adj* total; **all out** *adv* mit voller Kraft
allow [ə'laʊ] *vt* (*permit*) erlauben (*sb jdm*), gestatten; (*grant*) bewilligen; (*deduct*) abziehen; (*concede*): **to** ~ **that ...** annehmen, daß ...; **to** ~ **sb sth** jdm etw erlauben, jdm etw gestatten; **to** ~ **sb to do sth** jdm erlauben or gestatten, etw zu tun; ~ **for** *vt fus* berücksichtigen, einplanen; ~**ance** *n* Beihilfe *f*; **to make** ~**ances for** berücksichtigen
alloy ['ælɔı] *n* Metallegierung *f*
all right *adv* (*well*) gut; (*correct*) richtig; (*as answer*) okay
all-round ['ɔːl'raʊnd] *adj* (*sportsman*) allseitig, Allround-; (*view*) Rundum-
all-time ['ɔːl'taım] *adj* (*record, high*) ... aller Zeiten, Höchst-
allude [ə'luːd] *vi*: **to** ~ **to** hinweisen auf +*acc*, anspielen auf +*acc*
alluring [ə'ljʊərıŋ] *adj* verlockend
allusion [ə'luːʒən] *n* Anspielung *f*
ally [*n* 'ælaı, *vb* ə'laı] *n* Verbündete(r) *mf*; (*POL*) Alliierte(r) *m* ♦ *vr*: **to** ~

o.s. with sich verbünden mit
almighty [ɔːˈmaɪtɪ] *adj* allmächtig
almond [ˈɑːmənd] *n* Mandel *f*
almost [ˈɔːlməust] *adv* fast, beinahe
alms [ɑːmz] *npl* Almosen *nt*
aloft [əˈlɒft] *adv* (*be*) in der Luft;
(*throw*) in die Luft
alone [əˈləun] *adj, adv* allein; to **leave**
sth ~ etw sein lassen; let ~ ... geschweige denn ...
along [əˈlɒŋ] *prep* entlang, längs ♦ *adv*
(*onward*) vorwärts, weiter; ~ **with**
zusammen mit; he was **limping** ~ er
humpelte einher; **all** ~ (*all the time*)
die ganze Zeit; ~**side** *adv* (*walk*)
nebenher; (*come*) nebendran; (*be*)
daneben ♦ *prep* (*walk, compared with*)
neben +*dat*; (*come*) neben +*acc*; (*be*)
entlang, neben +*dat*; (*of ship*)
längsseits +*gen*
aloof [əˈluːf] *adj* zurückhaltend ♦ *adv*
fern; to **stand** ~ abseits stehen
aloud [əˈlaud] *adv* laut
alphabet [ˈælfəbet] *n* Alphabet *nt*; ~**ical**
[ælfəˈbetɪkl] *adj* alphabetisch
alpine [ˈælpaɪn] *adj* alpin, Alpen-
Alps [ælps] *npl*: the ~ die Alpen *pl*
already [ɔːlˈredɪ] *adv* schon, bereits
alright [ˈɔːlˈraɪt] (*BRIT*) *adv* = **all right**
Alsatian [ælˈseɪʃən] *n* (*dog*) Schäferhund
m
also [ˈɔːlsəu] *adv* auch, außerdem
altar [ˈɔːltə*] *n* Altar *m*
alter [ˈɔːltə*] *vt* ändern; (*dress*)
umändern; ~**ation** [ɒltəˈreɪʃən] *n*
Änderung *f*; Umänderung *f*; (*to
building*) Umbau *m*
alternate [*adj* ɒlˈtɜːnɪt, *vb* ˈɒltɜːneɪt] *adj*
abwechselnd ♦ *vi* abwechseln; on ~
days jeden zweiten Tag
alternating [ˈɒltəneɪtɪŋ] *adj*: ~ **current**
Wechselstrom *m*
alternative [ɒlˈtɜːnətɪv] *adj* andere(r, s)
♦ *n* Alternative *f*; ~**ly** *adv* im anderen
Falle; ~**ly one could** ... oder man
könnte ...
alternator [ˈɒltɜːneɪtə*] *n* (*AUT*)
Lichtmaschine *f*
although [ɔːlˈðəu] *conj* obwohl
altitude [ˈæltɪtjuːd] *n* Höhe *f*

alto [ˈæltəu] *n* Alt *m*
altogether [ɔːltəˈgeðə*] *adv* (*on the
whole*) im ganzen genommen; (*entirely*) ganz und gar
aluminium [æljuˈmɪnɪəm] (*BRIT*) *n*
Aluminium *nt*
aluminum [əˈluːmɪnəm] (*US*) *n*
Aluminium *nt*
always [ˈɔːlweɪz] *adv* immer
am [æm] *see* be
a.m. *adv abbr* (= *ante meridiem*) vor-
mittags
amalgamate [əˈmælgəmeɪt] *vi*
(*combine*) sich vereinigen ♦ *vt* (*mix*)
amalgamieren
amass [əˈmæs] *vt* anhäufen
amateur [ˈæmətɜ:*] *n* Amateur *m*; (*pej*)
Amateur *m*, Stümper *m*; ~**ish** (*pej*) *adj*
dilettantisch, stümperhaft
amaze [əˈmeɪz] *vt* erstaunen; to **be** ~**d**
(**at**) erstaunt sein (über); ~**ment** *n*
höchste(s) Erstaunen *nt*
amazing [əˈmeɪzɪŋ] *adj* höchst erstaunlich
Amazon [ˈæməzən] *n* (*GEOG*) Amazonas
m
ambassador [æmˈbæsədə*] *n* Bot-
schafter *m*
amber [ˈæmbə*] *n* Bernstein *m*; at ~
(*BRIT*: *AUT*) (auf) gelb
ambiguous [æmˈbɪgjuəs] *adj* zweideutig;
(*not clear*) unklar
ambition [æmˈbɪʃən] *n* Ehrgeiz *m*
ambitious [æmˈbɪʃəs] *adj* ehrgeizig
ambivalent [æmˈbɪvələnt] *n* (*attitude*)
zwiespältig
amble [ˈæmbl] *vi* (*usu*: ~ **along**)
schlendern
ambulance [ˈæmbjuləns] *n*
Krankenwagen *m*; ~**man** (*irreg*) *n*
Sanitäter *m*
ambush [ˈæmbuʃ] *n* Hinterhalt *m* ♦ *vt*
(aus dem Hinterhalt) überfallen
amenable [əˈmiːnəbl] *adj* gefügig; ~
(**to**) (*reason*) zugänglich (+*dat*);
(*flattery*) empfänglich (für); (*law*)
unterworfen (+*dat*)
amend [əˈmend] *vt* (*law etc*) abändern,
ergänzen; to **make** ~**s** etw wiedergutmachen; ~**ment** *n* Abänderung *f*

amenities [əˈmiːnɪtɪz] *npl* Einrichtungen *pl*

America [əˈmerɪkə] *n* Amerika *nt*; **~n** *adj* amerikanisch ♦ *n* Amerikaner(in) *m(f)*

amiable [ˈeɪmɪəbl] *adj* liebenswürdig

amicable [ˈæmɪkəbl] *adj* freundschaftlich; *(settlement)* gütlich

amid(st) [əˈmɪd(st)] *prep* mitten in *or* unter +*dat*

amiss [əˈmɪs] *adv*: **to take sth ~** etw übelnehmen; **there's something ~** da stimmt irgend etwas nicht

ammonia [əˈməʊnɪə] *n* Ammoniak *nt*

ammunition [æmjʊˈnɪʃən] *n* Munition *f*

amnesia [æmˈniːzɪə] *n* Gedächtnisverlust *m*

amnesty [ˈæmnɪstɪ] *n* Amnestie *f*

amok [əˈmɔk] *adv*: **to run ~** Amok laufen

among(st) [əˈmʌŋ(st)] *prep* unter

amoral [eɪˈmɔrəl] *adj* unmoralisch

amorous [ˈæmərəs] *adj* verliebt

amount [əˈmaʊnt] *n* *(of money)* Betrag *m*; *(of water, sand)* Menge *f* ♦ *vi*: **to ~ to** *(total)* sich belaufen auf +*acc*; **a great ~ of time/energy** ein großer Aufwand an Zeit/Energie *(dat)*; **this ~s to treachery** das kommt Verrat gleich; **it ~s to the same** es läuft aufs gleiche hinaus; **he won't ~ to much** aus ihm wird nie was

amp(ere) [ˈæmp(eə*)] *n* Ampere *nt*

amphibian [æmˈfɪbɪən] *n* Amphibie *f*

amphibious [æmˈfɪbɪəs] *adj* amphibisch, Amphibien-

ample [ˈæmpl] *adj* *(portion)* reichlich; *(dress)* weit, groß; **~ time** genügend Zeit

amplifier [ˈæmplɪfaɪə*] *n* Verstärker *m*

amuck [əˈmʌk] *adv* = **amok**

amuse [əˈmjuːz] *vt* *(entertain)* unterhalten; *(make smile)* belustigen; **~ment** *n* *(feeling)* Unterhaltung *f*; *(recreation)* Zeitvertreib *m*; **~ment arcade** *n* Spielhalle *f*

an [æn] *see* **a**

anaemia [əˈniːmɪə] *n* Anämie *f*

anaemic [əˈniːmɪk] *adj* blutarm

anaesthetic [ænɪsˈθetɪk] *n* Betäubungs-

mittel *nt*; **under ~** unter Narkose

anaesthetist [ænˈiːsθɪtɪst] *n* Anästhesist(in) *m(f)*

analgesic [ænælˈdʒiːsɪk] *n* schmerzlindernde(s) Mittel *nt*

analog(ue) [ˈænəlɒg] *adj* Analog-

analogy [əˈnælədʒɪ] *n* Analogie *f*

analyse [ˈænəlaɪz] *(BRIT)* *vt* analysieren

analyses [əˈnælɪsiːz] *(BRIT)* *npl of* **analysis**

analysis [əˈnælɪsɪs] *(pl* **analyses**) *n* Analyse *f*

analyst [ˈænəlɪst] *n* Analytiker(in) *m(f)*

analytic(al) [ænəˈlɪtɪk(əl)] *adj* analytisch

analyze [ˈænəlaɪz] *(US)* *vt* = **analyse**

anarchy [ˈænəkɪ] *n* Anarchie *f*

anathema [əˈnæθɪmə] *n* *(fig)* Greuel *nt*

anatomy [əˈnætəmɪ] *n* *(structure)* anatomische(r) Aufbau *m*; *(study)* Anatomie *f*

ancestor [ˈænsestə*] *n* Vorfahr *m*

anchor [ˈæŋkə*] *n* Anker *m* ♦ *vi* *(also:* **to drop ~**) ankern, vor Anker gehen ♦ *vt* verankern; **to weigh ~** den Anker lichten; **~age** *n* Ankerplatz *m*

anchovy [ˈæntʃəvɪ] *n* Sardelle *f*

ancient [ˈeɪnʃənt] *adj* alt; *(car etc)* uralt

ancillary [ænˈsɪlərɪ] *adj* Hilfs-

and [ænd] *conj* und; **~ so on** und so weiter; **try ~ come** versuche zu kommen; **better ~ better** immer besser

Andes [ˈændiːz] *npl*: **the ~** die Anden *pl*

anemia [əˈniːmɪə] *(US)* *n* = **anaemia**

anesthetic [ænɪsˈθetɪk] *(US)* *n* = **anaesthetic**

anew [əˈnjuː] *adv* von neuem

angel [ˈeɪndʒəl] *n* Engel *m*

anger [ˈæŋgə*] *n* Zorn *m* ♦ *vt* ärgern

angina [ænˈdʒaɪnə] *n* Angina *f*

angle [ˈæŋgl] *n* Winkel *m*; *(point of view)* Standpunkt *m*

angler *n* Angler *m*

Anglican [ˈæŋglɪkən] *adj* anglikanisch ♦ *n* Anglikaner(in) *m(f)*

angling [ˈæŋglɪŋ] *n* Angeln *nt*

Anglo- [ˈæŋgləʊ] *prefix* Anglo-

angrily [ˈæŋgrɪlɪ] *adv* ärgerlich, böse

angry [ˈæŋgrɪ] *adj* ärgerlich, ungehalten, böse; *(wound)* entzündet; **to be ~ with**

sb auf jdn böse sein; **to be ~ at sth** über etw *acc* verärgert sein
anguish ['æŋgwɪʃ] *n* Qual *f*
angular ['æŋgjʊlə*] *adj* eckig, winkelförmig; *(face)* kantig
animal ['ænɪməl] *n* Tier *nt*; *(living creature)* Lebewesen *nt* ♦ *adj* tierisch
animate [*vb* 'ænɪmeɪt, *adj* 'ænɪmət] *vt* beleben ♦ *adj* lebhaft; **~d** *adj* lebendig; *(film)* Zeichentrick-
animosity [ænɪ'mɒsɪtɪ] *n* Feindseligkeit *f*, Abneigung *f*
aniseed ['ænɪsiːd] *n* Anis *m*
ankle ['æŋkl] *n* (Fuß)knöchel *m*; **~ sock** *n* Söckchen *nt*
annex [*n* 'æneks, *vb* ə'neks] *n* *(also: BRIT: annexe)* Anbau *m* ♦ *vt* anfügen; *(POL)* annektieren, angliedern
annihilate [ə'naɪəleɪt] *vt* vernichten
anniversary [ænɪ'vɜːsərɪ] *n* Jahrestag *m*
annotate ['ænəteɪt] *vt* kommentieren
announce [ə'naʊns] *vt* ankündigen, anzeigen; **~ment** *n* Ankündigung *f*; *(official)* Bekanntmachung *f*; **~r** *n* Ansager(in) *m(f)*
annoy [ə'nɔɪ] *vt* ärgern; **don't get ~ed!** reg' dich nicht auf!; **~ance** *n* Ärgernis *nt*, Störung *f*; **~ing** *adj* ärgerlich; *(person)* lästig
annual ['ænjʊəl] *adj* jährlich; *(salary)* Jahres- ♦ *n* *(plant)* einjährige Pflanze *f*; *(book)* Jahrbuch *nt*; **~ly** *adv* jährlich
annul [ə'nʌl] *vt* aufheben, annullieren; **~ment** *n* Aufhebung *f*, Annullierung *f*
annum ['ænəm] *n see* **per**
anomaly [ə'nɒmədɪ] *n* Abweichung *f* von der Regel
anonymous [ə'nɒnɪməs] *adj* anonym
anorak ['ænəræk] *n* Anorak *m*, Windjacke *f*
anorexia [ænə'reksɪə] *n* *(MED)* Magersucht *f*
another [ə'nʌðə*] *adj, pron (different)* ein(e) andere(r, s); *(additional)* noch eine(r, s); *see also* **one**
answer ['ɑːnsə*] *n* Antwort *f* ♦ *vi* antworten; *(on phone)* sich melden ♦ *vt* *(person)* antworten *+dat*; *(letter, question)* beantworten; *(telephone)* gehen an *+acc*, abnehmen; *(door)*

öffnen; **in ~ to your letter** in Beantwortung Ihres Schreibens; **to ~ the phone** ans Telefon gehen; **to ~ the bell** *or* **the door** aufmachen; **~ back** *vi* frech sein; **~ for** *vt*: **to ~ for sth** für etw verantwortlich sein; **~able** *adj*: **to be ~able to sb for sth** jdm gegenüber für etw verantwortlich sein; **~ing machine** *n* Anrufbeantworter *m*
ant [ænt] *n* Ameise *f*
antagonism [æn'tægənɪzəm] *n* Antagonismus *m*
antagonize [æn'tægənaɪz] *vt* reizen
Antarctic [ænt'ɑːktɪk] *adj* antarktisch ♦ *n*: **the ~** die Antarktis
antelope ['æntɪləʊp] *n* Antilope *f*
antenatal [æntɪ'neɪtl] *adj* vor der Geburt; **~ clinic** *n* Sprechstunde *f* für werdende Mütter
antenna [æn'tenə] *n* *(BIOL)* Fühler *m*; *(RADIO)* Antenne *f*
antennae [æn'teniː] *npl of* **antenna**
anthem ['ænθəm] *n* Hymne *f*; **national ~** Nationalhymne *f*
anthology [æn'θɒlədʒɪ] *n* Gedichtsammlung *f*, Anthologie *f*
anti- ['æntɪ] *prefix* Gegen-, Anti-
anti-aircraft ['æntɪ'ɛəkrɑːft] *adj* Flugabwehr-
antibiotic ['æntɪbaɪ'ɒtɪk] *n* Antibiotikum *nt*
antibody ['æntɪbɒdɪ] *n* Antikörper *m*
anticipate [æn'tɪsɪpeɪt] *vt* *(expect: trouble, question)* erwarten, rechnen mit; *(look forward to)* sich freuen auf *+acc*; *(do first)* vorwegnehmen; *(foresee)* ahnen, vorhersehen
anticipation [æntɪsɪ'peɪʃən] *n* Erwartung *f*; *(foreshadowing)* Vorwegnahme *f*
anticlimax ['æntɪ'klaɪmæks] *n* Ernüchterung *f*
anticlockwise ['æntɪ'klɒkwaɪz] *adv* entgegen dem Uhrzeigersinn
antics ['æntɪks] *npl* Possen *pl*
anticyclone ['æntɪ'saɪkləʊn] *n* Hoch *nt*, Hochdruckgebiet *nt*
antidote ['æntɪdəʊt] *n* Gegenmittel *nt*
antifreeze ['æntɪfriːz] *n* Frostschutzmittel *nt*
antihistamine [æntɪ'hɪstəmiːn] *n* Anti-

histamin *nt*

antiquated ['æntɪkweɪtɪd] *adj* antiquiert

antique [æn'tiːk] *n* Antiquität *f* ♦ *adj* antik; (*old-fashioned*) altmodisch; ~ **shop** *n* Antiquitätenladen *m*

antiquity [æn'tɪkwɪtɪ] *n* Altertum *nt*

antiseptic [æntɪ'septɪk] *n* Antiseptikum *nt* ♦ *adj* antiseptisch

antisocial [æntɪ'səʊʃl] *adj* (*person*) ungesellig; (*law*) unsozial

antlers ['æntləz] *npl* Geweih *nt*

anus ['eɪnəs] *n* After *m*

anvil ['ænvɪl] *n* Amboß *m*

anxiety [æŋ'zaɪətɪ] *n* Angst *f*; (*worry*) Sorge *f*

anxious ['æŋkʃəs] *adj* ängstlich; (*worried*) besorgt; **to be** ~ **to do sth** etw unbedingt tun wollen

---
KEYWORD
---

any ['enɪ] *adj* **1** (*in questions etc*): **have you any butter?** haben Sie (etwas) Butter?; **have you any children?** haben Sie Kinder?; **if there are any tickets left** falls noch Karten da sind
2 (*with negative*): **I haven't any money/books** ich habe kein Geld/keine Bücher
3 (*no matter which*) jede(r, s) (beliebige); **any colour (at all)** jede beliebige Farbe; **choose any book you like** nehmen Sie ein beliebiges Buch
4 (*in phrases*): **in any case** in jedem Fall; **any day now** jeden Tag; **at any moment** jeden Moment; **at any rate** auf jeden Fall
♦ *pron* **1** (*in questions etc*): **have you got any?** haben Sie welche?; **can any of you sing?** kann (irgend)einer von euch singen?
2 (*with negative*): **I haven't any (of them)** ich habe keinen/keines (davon)
3 (*no matter which one(s)*): **take any of those books (you like)** nehmen Sie irgendeines dieser Bücher
♦ *adv* **1** (*in questions etc*): **do you want any more soup/sandwiches?** möchten Sie noch Suppe/Brote?; **are you feeling any better?** fühlen Sie sich etwas besser?

2 (*with negative*): **I can't hear him any more** ich kann ihn nicht mehr hören

anybody ['enɪbɒdɪ] *pron* (*no matter who*) jede(r); (*in questions etc*) (irgend) jemand, (irgend) eine(r); (*with negative*): **I can't see** ~ ich kann niemanden sehen

anyhow ['enɪhaʊ] *adv* (*at any rate*): **I shall go** ~ ich gehe sowieso; (*haphazardly*): **do it** ~ machen Sie es, wie Sie wollen

anyone ['enɪwʌn] *pron* = **anybody**

KEYWORD
---

anything ['enɪθɪŋ] *pron* **1** (*in questions etc*) (irgend) etwas; **can you see anything?** können Sie etwas sehen?
2 (*with negative*): **I can't see anything** ich kann nichts sehen
3 (*no matter what*): **you can say anything you like** Sie können sagen, was Sie wollen; **anything will do** irgend etwas (, wird genügen), irgendeine(r, s) (wird genügen); **he'll eat anything** er ißt alles

---

anyway ['enɪweɪ] *adv* (*at any rate*) auf jeden Fall; (*besides*): ~, **I couldn't come even if I wanted to** jedenfalls könnte ich nicht kommen, selbst wenn ich wollte; **why are you phoning,** ~? warum rufst du überhaupt an?

anywhere ['enɪwɛə*] *adv* (*in questions etc*) irgendwo; (: *with direction*) irgendwohin; (*no matter where*) überall; (: *with direction*) überallhin; (*with negative*): **I can't see him** ~ ich kann ihn nirgendwo *or* nirgends sehen; **can you see him** ~? siehst du ihn irgendwo?; **put the books down** ~ leg die Bücher irgendwohin

apart [ə'pɑːt] *adv* (*parted*) auseinander; (*away*) beiseite, abseits; **10 miles** ~ 10 Meilen auseinander; **to take** ~ auseinandernehmen; ~ **from** *prep* außer

apartheid [ə'pɑːteɪt] *n* Apartheid *f*

apartment [ə'pɑːtmənt] (*US*) *n* Wohnung *f*; ~ **building** (*US*) *n* Wohnhaus *nt*

apathy ['æpəθɪ] *n* Teilnahmslosigkeit *f*,

Apathie f

ape [eɪp] n (Menschen)affe m ♦ vt nachahmen

aperture ['æpətjʊə*] n Öffnung f; (PHOT) Blende f

apex ['eɪpeks] n Spitze f

apiece [ə'piːs] adv pro Stück; (per poreon) pro Kopf

apologetic [əpɒlə'dʒetɪk] adj entschuldigend; to be ~ sich sehr entschuldigen

apologize [ə'pɒlədʒaɪz] vi: to ~ (for sth to sb) sich (für etw bei jdm) entschuldigen

apology [ə'pɒlədʒɪ] n Entschuldigung f

apostle [ə'pɒsl] n Apostel m

apostrophe [ə'pɒstrəfɪ] n Apostroph m

appal [ə'pɔːl] vt erschrecken; ~ling [ə'pɔːlɪŋ] adj schrecklich

apparatus [æpə'reɪtəs] n Gerät nt

apparel [ə'pærəl] (US) n Kleidung f

apparent [ə'pærənt] adj offenbar; ~ly adv anscheinend

apparition [æpə'rɪʃən] n (ghost) Erscheinung f, Geist m; (appearance) Erscheinen nt

appeal [ə'piːl] vi dringend ersuchen; (JUR) Berufung einlegen ♦ n Aufruf m; (JUR) Berufung f; to ~ for dringend bitten um; to ~ to sich wenden an +acc; (to public) appellieren an +acc; it doesn't ~ to me es gefällt mir nicht; ~ing adj ansprechend

appear [ə'pɪə*] vi (come into sight) erscheinen; (be seen) auftauchen; (seem) scheinen; it would ~ that ... anscheinend ...; ~ance n (coming into sight) Erscheinen nt; (outward show) Äußere(s) nt

appease [ə'piːz] vt beschwichtigen

appendices [ə'pendɪsiːz] npl of appendix

appendicitis [əpendɪ'saɪtɪs] n Blinddarmentzündung f

appendix [ə'pendɪks] (pl appendices) n (in book) Anhang m; (MED) Blinddarm m

appetite ['æpɪtaɪt] n Appetit m; (fig) Lust f

appetizer ['æpətaɪzə*] n Appetitanreger m

appetizing ['æpɪtaɪzɪŋ] adj appetitanregend

applaud [ə'plɔːd] vi Beifall klatschen, applaudieren ♦ vt Beifall klatschen +dat

applause [ə'plɔːz] n Beifall m, Applaus m

apple ['æpl] n Apfel m; ~ tree n Apfelbaum m

appliance [ə'plaɪəns] n Gerät nt

applicable [ə'plɪkəbl] adj anwendbar; (in forms) zutreffend

applicant ['æplɪkənt] n Bewerber(in) m(f)

application [æplɪ'keɪʃən] n (request) Antrag m; (for job) Bewerbung f; (putting into practice) Anwendung f; (hard work) Fleiß m; ~ form n Bewerbungsformular nt

applied [ə'plaɪd] adj angewandt

apply [ə'plaɪ] vi (be suitable) zutreffen; (ask): to ~ (to) sich wenden (an +acc); (request): to ~ for sich melden für ♦ vt (place on) auflegen; (cream) anwenden; to ~ for sth sich um etw bewerben; to ~ the brakes die Bremsen betätigen; to ~ o.s. to sth sich bei etw anstrengen

appoint [ə'pɔɪnt] vt (to office) ernennen, berufen; (settle) festsetzen; ~ment n (meeting) Verabredung f; (at hairdresser etc) Bestellung f; (in business) Termin m; (choice for a position) Ernennung f; (UNIV) Berufung f

appraisal [ə'preɪzl] n Beurteilung f

appreciable [ə'priːʃəbl] adj (perceptible) merklich; (able to be estimated) abschätzbar

appreciate [ə'priːʃɪeɪt] vt (value) zu schätzen wissen; (understand) einsehen ♦ vi (increase in value) im Wert steigen

appreciation [əpriːʃɪ'eɪʃən] n Wertschätzung f; (COMM) Wertzuwachs m

appreciative [ə'priːʃɪətɪv] adj (showing thanks) dankbar; (showing liking) anerkennend

apprehend [æprɪ'hend] vt (arrest) festnehmen; (understand) erfassen

apprehension [æprɪ'henʃən] n Angst f

apprehensive [æprɪ'hensɪv] *adj* furchtsam

apprentice [ə'prentɪs] *n* Lehrling *m*; **~ship** *n* Lehrzeit *f*

approach [ə'prəʊtʃ] *vi* sich nähern ♦ *vt* herantreten an +*acc*; (*problem*) herangehen an +*acc* ♦ *n* Annäherung *f*; (*to problem*) Ansatz *m*; (*path*) Zugang *m*, Zufahrt *f*; **~able** *adj* zugänglich

appropriate [*adj* ə'prəʊprɪət, *vb* ə'prəʊprɪeɪt] *adj* angemessen; (*remark*) angebracht ♦ *vt* (*take for o.s.*) sich aneignen; (*set apart*) bereitstellen

approval [ə'pruːvəl] *n* (*show of satisfaction*) Beifall *m*; (*permission*) Billigung *f*; **on ~** (*COMM*) bei Gefallen

approve [ə'pruːv] *vt, vi* billigen; **I don't ~ of it/him** ich halte nichts davon/von ihm; **~d school** (*BRIT*) *n* Erziehungsheim *nt*

approximate [*adj* ə'prɒksɪmɪt, *vb* ə'prɒksɪmeɪt] *adj* annähernd, ungefähr ♦ *vt* nahekommen +*dat*; **~ly** *adv* rund, ungefähr

apricot ['eɪprɪkɒt] *n* Aprikose *f*

April ['eɪprəl] *n* April *m*; **~ Fools' Day** *n* der erste April

apron ['eɪprən] *n* Schürze *f*

apt [æpt] *adj* (*suitable*) passend; (*able*) begabt; (*likely*): **to be ~ to do sth** dazu neigen, etw zu tun

aptitude ['æptɪtjuːd] *n* Begabung *f*

aqualung ['ækwəlʌŋ] *n* Unterwasseratmungsgerät *nt*

aquarium [ə'kwɛərɪəm] *n* Aquarium *nt*

Aquarius [ə'kwɛərɪəs] *n* Wassermann *m*

aquatic [ə'kwætɪk] *adj* Wasser-

Arab ['ærəb] *n* Araber(in) *m(f)*

Arabia [ə'reɪbɪə] *n* Arabien *nt*

Arabian [ə'reɪbɪən] *adj* arabisch

Arabic ['ærəbɪk] *adj* arabisch ♦ *n* Arabisch *nt*; **~ numerals** arabische Ziffern

arable ['ærəbl] *adj* bebaubar, Kultur-

arbitrary ['ɑːbɪtrərɪ] *adj* willkürlich

arbitration [ɑːbɪ'treɪʃən] *n* Schlichtung *f*

arc [ɑːk] *n* Bogen *m*

arcade [ɑː'keɪd] *n* Säulengang *m*

arch [ɑːtʃ] *n* Bogen *m* ♦ *vt* überwölben; (*back*) krumm machen

archaeologist [ɑːkɪ'ɒlədʒɪst] *n* Archäologe *m*

archaeology [ɑːkɪ'ɒlədʒɪ] *n* Archäologie *f*

archaic [ɑː'keɪɪk] *adj* altertümlich

archbishop ['ɑːtʃ'bɪʃəp] *n* Erzbischof *m*

archenemy ['ɑːtʃ'enəmɪ] *n* Erzfeind *m*

archeology *etc* [ɑːkɪ'ɒlədʒɪ] (*US*) = **archaelogy** *etc*

archer ['ɑːtʃə*] *n* Bogenschütze *m*; **~y** *n* Bogenschießen *nt*

archipelago [ɑːkɪ'pelɪgəʊ] *n* Archipel *m*; (*sea*) Inselmeer *nt*

architect ['ɑːkɪtekt] *n* Architekt(in) *m(f)*; **~ural** [ɑːkɪ'tektʃərəl] *adj* architektonisch; **~ure** ['ɑːkɪtektʃə*] *n* Architektur *f*

archives ['ɑːkaɪvz] *npl* Archiv *nt*

archway ['ɑːtʃweɪ] *n* Bogen *m*

Arctic ['ɑːktɪk] *adj* arktisch ♦ *n*: **the ~** die Arktis

ardent ['ɑːdənt] *adj* glühend

arduous ['ɑːdjʊəs] *adj* mühsam

are [ɑː*] *see* **be**

area ['ɛərɪə] *n* Fläche *f*; (*of land*) Gebiet *nt*; (*part of sth*) Teil *m*, Abschnitt *m*

arena [ə'riːnə] *n* Arena *f*

aren't [ɑːnt] = **are not**

Argentina [ɑːdʒən'tiːnə] *n* Argentinien *nt*

Argentinian [ɑːdʒən'tɪnɪən] *adj* argentinisch ♦ *n* Argentinier(in) *m(f)*

arguably ['ɑːgjʊəblɪ] *adv* wohl

argue ['ɑːgjuː] *vi* diskutieren; (*angrily*) streiten

argument ['ɑːgjʊmənt] *n* (*theory*) Argument *nt*; (*reasoning*) Argumentation *f*; (*row*) Auseinandersetzung *f*, Streit *m*; **to have an ~** sich streiten; **~ative** [ɑːgjʊ'mɛntətɪv] *adj* streitlustig

aria ['ɑːrɪə] *n* Arie *f*

arid ['ærɪd] *adj* trocken

Aries ['ɛəriːz] *n* Widder *m*

arise [ə'raɪz] (*pt* **arose**, *pp* **arisen**) *vi* aufsteigen; (*get up*) aufstehen; (*difficulties etc*) entstehen; (*case*) vorkommen; **to ~ from sth** herrühren von etw; **arisen** [ə'rɪzn] *pp* of **arise**

aristocracy [ærɪs'tɒkrəsɪ] *n* Adel *m*, Aristokratie *f*

aristocrat ['ærɪstəkræt] *n* Adlige(r) *mf*,

Aristokrat(in) *m(f)*
arithmetic [ə'rıθmətık] *n* Rechnen *nt*,
Arithmetik *f*
ark [ɑːk] *n*: **Noah's A~** die Arche Noah
arm [ɑːm] *n* Arm *m*; (*branch of
military service*) Zweig *m* ♦ *vt*
bewaffnen; **~s** *npl* (*weapons*) Waffen *pl*
armaments [ˈɑːməmənts] *npl* Ausrüstung *f*
armchair *n* Lehnstuhl *m*
armed *adj* (*forces*) Streit-, bewaffnet;
(*robbery*) bewaffnet
armistice [ˈɑːmɪstɪs] *n* Waffenstillstand
m
armour [ˈɑːmə*] (*US* **armor**) *n* (*knight's*)
Rüstung *f*; (*MIL*) Panzerplatte *f*; **~ed
car** *n* Panzerwagen *m*; **~y** *n*
Waffenlager *nt*; (*factory*) Waffenfabrik
f
armpit [ˈɑːmpɪt] *n* Achselhöhle *f*
armrest [ˈɑːmrest] *n* Armlehne *f*
army [ˈɑːmɪ] *n* Armee *f*, Heer *nt*; (*host*)
Heer *nt*
aroma [əˈrəumə] *n* Duft *m*, Aroma *nt*;
~tic [ærəˈmætɪk] *adj* aromatisch, würzig
arose [əˈrəuz] *pt of* **arise**
around [əˈraund] *adv* ringsherum;
(*almost*) ungefähr ♦ *prep* um ... herum;
is he ~? ist er hier?
arouse [əˈrauz] *vt* wecken
arrange [əˈreɪndʒ] *vt* (*time, meeting*)
festsetzen; (*holidays*) festlegen;
(*flowers, hair, objects*) anordnen; **I ~d
to meet him** ich habe mit ihm ausgemacht, ihn zu treffen; **it's all ~d** es
ist alles arrangiert; **~ment** *n* (*order*)
Reihenfolge *f*; (*agreement*) Vereinbarung *f*; **~ments** *npl* (*plans*) Pläne *pl*
array [əˈreɪ] *n* (*collection*) Ansammlung
f
arrears [əˈrɪəz] *npl* (*of debts*) Rückstand
m; (*of work*) Unerledigte(s) *nt*; **in ~**
im Rückstand
arrest [əˈrest] *vt* (*person*) verhaften;
(*stop*) aufhalten ♦ *n* Verhaftung *f*;
under ~ in Haft
arrival [əˈraɪvəl] *n* Ankunft *f*
arrive [əˈraɪv] *vi* ankommen; **to ~ at** ankommen in +*dat*, ankommen bei
arrogance [ˈærəgəns] *n* Überheblichkeit

f, Arroganz *f*
arrogant [ˈærəgənt] *adj* überheblich,
arrogant
arrow [ˈærəu] *n* Pfeil *m*
arse [ɑːs] (*inf!*) *n* Arsch *m* (*!*)
arsenal [ˈɑːsɪnl] *n* Waffenlager *nt*,
Zeughaus *nt*
arsenic [ˈɑːsnɪk] *n* Arsen *nt*
arson [ˈɑːsn] *n* Brandstiftung *f*
art [ɑːt] *n* Kunst *f*; **A~s** *npl* (*UNIV*) Gei-
steswissenschaften *pl*
artery [ˈɑːtərɪ] *n* Schlagader *f*, Arterie *f*
artful [ˈɑːtful] *adj* verschlagen
art gallery *n* Kunstgalerie *f*
arthritis [ɑːˈθraɪtɪs] *n* Arthritis *f*
artichoke [ˈɑːtɪtʃəuk] *n* Artischocke *f*;
Jerusalem ~ Erdartischocke *f*
article [ˈɑːtɪkl] *n* (*PRESS, GRAM*) Artikel
m; (*thing*) Gegenstand *m*, Artikel *m*;
(*clause*) Abschnitt *m*, Paragraph *m*; **to
do one's ~s** (*JUR*) seine Referendarzeit
ableisten; **~ of clothing** Kleidungsstück
nt
articulate [*adj* ɑːˈtɪkjulɪt, *vb* ɑːˈtɪkjuleɪt]
adj (*able to express o.s.*) redegewandt;
(*speaking clearly*) deutlich, verständlich ♦ *vt* (*connect*) zusammen-
fügen, gliedern; **to be ~** sich gut ausdrücken können; **~d vehicle** *n* Sattelschlepper *m*
artificial [ɑːtɪˈfɪʃəl] *adj* künstlich,
Kunst-; **~ respiration** *n* künstliche Atmung *f*
artisan [ˈɑːtɪzæn] *n* gelernte(r)
Handwerker *m*
artist [ˈɑːtɪst] *n* Künstler(in) *m(f)*; **~ic**
[ɑːˈtɪstɪk] *adj* künstlerisch; **~ry** *n*
künstlerische(s) Können *nt*
artless [ˈɑːtlɪs] *adj* ungekünstelt;
(*character*) arglos
art school *n* Kunsthochschule *f*

KEYWORD

---

as [æz] *conj* **1** (*referring to time*) als; **as
the years went by** mit den Jahren; **he
came in as I was leaving** als er hereinkam, ging ich gerade; **as from
tomorrow** ab morgen
2 (*in comparisons*): **as big as** so groß
wie; **twice as big as** zweimal so groß

wie; **as much/many** soviel/so viele wie; **as soon as** sobald

3 (*since, because*) da; **he left early as he had to be home by 10** er ging früher, da er um 10 zu Hause sein mußte

4 (*referring to manner, way*) wie; **do as you wish** mach was du willst; **as she said** wie sie sagte

5 (*concerning*): **as for** *or* **to that** was das betrifft *or* angeht

6: **as if** *or* **though** als ob

♦ *prep* als; **he works as a driver** er arbeitet als Fahrer; **he gave it to me as a present** er hat es mir als Geschenk gegeben; *see also* **long**; **such**; **well**

a.s.a.p. *abbr* = **as soon as possible**

ascend [ə'send] *vi* aufsteigen ♦ *vt* besteigen; **~ancy** *n* Oberhand *f*

ascent [ə'sent] *n* Aufstieg *m*; Besteigung *f*

ascertain [æsə'teɪn] *vt* feststellen

ascribe [əs'kraɪb] *vt*: **to ~ sth to sth /sth to sb** etw einer Sache/jdm etw zuschreiben

ash [æʃ] *n* Asche *f*; (*tree*) Esche *f*

ashamed [ə'ʃeɪmd] *adj* beschämt; **to be ~ of sth** sich für etw schämen

ashen ['æʃən] *adj* (*pale*) aschfahl

ashore [ə'ʃɔː*] *adv* an Land

ashtray ['æʃtreɪ] *n* Aschenbecher *m*

Ash Wednesday *n* Aschermittwoch *m*

Asia ['eɪʃə] *n* Asien *nt*; **~n** *adj* asiatisch ♦ *n* Asiat(in) *m(f)*; **~tic** [eɪsɪ'ætɪk] *adj* asiatisch

aside [ə'saɪd] *adv* beiseite ♦ *n* beiseite gesprochene Worte *pl*

ask [ɑːsk] *vt* fragen; (*permission*) bitten um; **~ him his name** frage ihn nach seinem Namen; **he ~ed to see you** er wollte dich sehen; **to ~ sb to do sth** jdn bitten, etw zu tun; **to ~ sb about sth** jdn nach etw fragen; **to ~ (sb) a question** jdn etwas fragen; **to ~ sb out to dinner** jdn zum Essen einladen; **~ after** *vt fus* fragen nach; **~ for** *vt fus* bitten um

askance [əs'kɑːns] *adv*: **to look ~ at sb** jdn schief ansehen

askew [əs'kjuː] *adv* schief

asking price ['ɑːskɪŋ-] *n* Verkaufspreis *m*

asleep [ə'sliːp] *adj*: **to be ~** schlafen; **to fall ~** einschlafen

asparagus [əs'pærəgəs] *n* Spargel *m*

aspect ['æspekt] *n* Aspekt *m*

aspersions [əs'pɜːʃənz] *npl*: **to cast ~ on sb/sth** sich abfällig über jdn/etw äußern

asphyxiation [əsfɪksɪ'eɪʃən] *n* Erstickung *f*

aspirations [æspə'reɪʃənz] *npl*: **to have ~ towards sth** etw anstreben

aspire [əs'paɪə*] *vi*: **to ~ to** streben nach

aspirin ['æsprɪn] *n* Aspirin *nt*

ass [æs] *n* (*also fig*) Esel *m*; (*US*: *inf!*) Arsch *m* (*!*)

assailant [ə'seɪlənt] *n* Angreifer *m*

assassin [ə'sæsɪn] *n* Attentäter(in) *m(f)*; **~ate** [ə'sæsɪneɪt] *vt* ermorden

assassination [əsæsɪ'neɪʃən] *n* (geglückte(s)) Attentat *nt*

assault [ə'sɔːlt] *n* Angriff *m* ♦ *vt* überfallen; (*woman*) herfallen über +*acc*

assemble [ə'sembl] *vt* versammeln; (*parts*) zusammensetzen ♦ *vi* sich versammeln

assembly [ə'semblɪ] *n* (*meeting*) Versammlung *f*; (*construction*) Zusammensetzung *f*, Montage *f*; **~ line** *n* Fließband *nt*

assent [ə'sent] *n* Zustimmung *f*

assert [ə'sɜːt] *vt* erklären; **~ion** [ə'sɜːʃən] *n* Behauptung *f*

assess [ə'ses] *vt* schätzen; **~ment** *n* Bewertung *f*, Einschätzung *f*; **~or** *n* Steuerberater *m*

asset ['æset] *n* Vorteil *m*, Wert *m*; **~s** *npl* (*FIN*) Vermögen *nt*; (*estate*) Nachlaß *m*

assiduous [ə'sɪdjuəs] *adj* fleißig, aufmerksam

assign [ə'saɪn] *vt* zuweisen

assignment [ə'saɪnmənt] *n* Aufgabe *f*, Auftrag *m*

assimilate [ə'sɪmɪleɪt] *vt* sich aneignen, aufnehmen

assist [ə'sɪst] *vt* beistehen +*dat*; **~ance** *n* Unterstützung *f*, Hilfe *f*; **~ant** *n* Assistent(in) *m(f)*, Mitarbeiter(in) *m(f)*;

(*BRIT: also: shop* ~ant) Verkäufer(in) m(f)

assizes [ə'saızız] *npl* Landgericht *nt*

associate [*n* ə'səʊʃɪɪt, *vb* ə'səʊʃɪeɪt] *n* (*partner*) Kollege *m*, Teilhaber *m*; (*member*) außerordentliche(s) Mitglied *nt* ♦ *vt* verbinden ♦ *vi* (*keep company*) verkehren

association [əsəʊsɪ'eɪʃən] *n* Verband *m*, Verein *m*; (*PSYCH*) Assoziation *f*; (*link*) Verbindung *f*

assorted [ə'sɔːtɪd] *adj* gemischt

assortment [ə'sɔːtmənt] *n* Sammlung *f*; (*COMM*): ~ (**of**) Sortiment *nt* (von), Auswahl *f* (an +*dat*)

assume [ə'sjuːm] *vt* (*take for granted*) annehmen; (*put on*) annehmen, sich geben; ~**d name** *n* Deckname *m*

assumption [ə'sʌmpʃən] *n* Annahme *f*

assurance [ə'ʃʊərəns] *n* (*firm statement*) Versicherung *f*; (*confidence*) Selbstsicherheit *f*; (*insurance*) (Lebens)versicherung *f*

assure [ə'ʃʊə*] *vt* (*make sure*) sicherstellen; (*convince*) versichern +*dat*; (*life*) versichern

asterisk ['æstərɪsk] *n* Sternchen *nt*

astern [əs'tɜːn] *adv* achtern

asthma ['æsmə] *n* Asthma *nt*

astonish [əs'tɒnɪʃ] *vt* erstaunen; ~**ment** *n* Erstaunen *nt*

astound [əs'taʊnd] *vt* verblüffen

astray [əs'treɪ] *adv* in die Irre; auf Abwege; **to go** ~ (*go wrong*) sich vertun; **to lead** ~ irreführen

astride [əs'traɪd] *adv* rittlings ♦ *prep* rittlings auf

astrologer [əs'trɒlədʒə*] *n* Astrologe *m*, Astrologin *f*

astrology [əs'trɒlədʒɪ] *n* Astrologie *f*

astronaut ['æstrənɔːt] *n* Astronaut(in) m(f)

astronomer [əs'trɒnəmə*] *n* Astronom *m*

astronomical [æstrə'nɒmɪkəl] *adj* astronomisch; (*success*) riesig

astronomy [əs'trɒnəmɪ] *n* Astronomie *f*

astute [əs'tjuːt] *adj* scharfsinnig; schlau, gerissen

asylum [ə'saɪləm] *n* (*home*) Heim *nt*;

(*refuge*) Asyl *nt*

| KEYWORD |
---

at [æt] *prep* **1** (*referring to position, direction*) an +*dat*, bei +*dat*; (*with place*) in +*dat*; **at the top** an der Spitze; **at home/school** zu Hause/in der Schule; **at the baker's** beim Bäcker; **to look at sth** auf etw *acc* blicken; **to throw sth at sb** etw nach jdm werfen

2 (*referring to time*): **at 4 o'clock** um 4 Uhr; **at night** bei Nacht; **at Christmas** zu Weihnachten; **at times** manchmal

3 (*referring to rates, speed etc*): **at £1 a kilo** zu £1 pro Kilo; **two at a time** zwei auf einmal; **at 50 km/h** mit 50 km/h

4 (*referring to manner*): **at a stroke** mit einem Schlag; **at peace** in Frieden

5 (*referring to activity*): **to be at work** bei der Arbeit sein; **to play at cowboys** Cowboy spielen; **to be good at sth** gut in etw *dat* sein

6 (*referring to cause*): **shocked/ surprised/annoyed at sth** schockiert/ überrascht/verärgert über etw *acc*; **I went at his suggestion** ich ging auf seinen Vorschlag hin

---

ate [et, eɪt] *pt of* eat

atheist ['eɪθɪɪst] *n* Atheist(in) m(f)

Athens ['æθɪnz] *n* Athen *nt*

athlete ['æθliːt] *n* Athlet *m*, Sportler *m*

athletic [æθ'letɪk] *adj* sportlich, athletisch; ~**s** *n* Leichtathletik *f*

Atlantic [ət'læntɪk] *adj* atlantisch ♦ *n*: **the** ~ (**Ocean**) der Atlantik

atlas ['ætləs] *n* Atlas *m*

atmosphere ['ætməsfɪə*] *n* Atmosphäre *f*

atom ['ætəm] *n* Atom *nt*; (*fig*) bißchen *nt*; ~**ic** [ə'tɒmɪk] *adj* atomar, Atom-; ~(**ic**) **bomb** *n* Atombombe *f*; ~**izer** ['ætəmaɪzə*] *n* Zerstäuber *m*

atone [ə'təʊn] *vi* sühnen; **to** ~ **for sth** etw sühnen

atrocious [ə'trəʊʃəs] *adj* gräßlich

atrocity [ə'trɒsɪtɪ] *n* Scheußlichkeit *f*; (*deed*) Greueltat *f*

attach [ə'tætʃ] *vt* (*fasten*) befestigen; **to**

be ~ed to sb/sth an jdm/etw hängen; to ~ **importance** *etc* **to sth** Wichtigkeit *etc* auf etw *acc* legen, einer Sache *dat* Wichtigkeit *etc* beimessen

attaché case [əˈtæʃeɪ-] *n* Aktenkoffer *m*

attachment [əˈtætʃmənt] *n* (*tool*) Zubehörteil *nt*; (*love*): ~ (**to sb**) Zuneigung *f* (zu jdm)

attack [əˈtæk] *vt* angreifen ♦ *n* Angriff *m*; (MED) Anfall *m*; ~**er** *n* Angreifer(in) *m(f)*

attain [əˈteɪn] *vt* erreichen; ~**ments** *npl* Kenntnisse *pl*

attempt [əˈtempt] *n* Versuch *m* ♦ *vt* versuchen; ~**ed murder** Mordversuch *m*

attend [əˈtend] *vt* (*go to*) teilnehmen (an +*dat*); (*lectures*) besuchen; **to** ~ **to** (*needs*) nachkommen +*dat*; (*person*) sich kümmern um; ~**ance** *n* (*presence*) Anwesenheit *f*; (*people present*) Besucherzahl *f*; **good** ~**ance** gute Teilnahme; ~**ant** *n* (*companion*) Begleiter(in) *m(f)*; Gesellschafter(in) *m(f)*; (*in car park etc*) Wächter(in) *m(f)*; (*servant*) Bedienstete(r) *mf* ♦ *adj* begleitend; (*fig*) damit verbunden

attention [əˈtenʃən] *n* Aufmerksamkeit *f*; (*care*) Fürsorge *f*; (*for machine etc*) Pflege *f* ♦ *excl* (MIL) Achtung!; **for the** ~ **of** ... zu Händen (von) ...

attentive [əˈtentɪv] *adj* aufmerksam

attest [əˈtest] *vi*: **to** ~ **to** sich verbürgen für

attic [ˈætɪk] *n* Dachstube *f*, Mansarde *f*

attitude [ˈætɪtjuːd] *n* (*mental*) Einstellung *f*

attorney [əˈtɜːnɪ] *n* (*solicitor*) Rechtsanwalt *m*; **A~ General** *n* Justizminister *m*

attract [əˈtrækt] *vt* anziehen; (*attention*) erregen; ~**ion** [əˈtrækʃən] *n* Anziehungskraft *f*; (*thing*) Attraktion *f*; ~**ive** *adj* attraktiv

attribute [*n* ˈætrɪbjuːt, *vb* əˈtrɪbjuːt] *n* Eigenschaft *f*, Attribut *nt* ♦ *vt* zuschreiben

attrition [əˈtrɪʃən] *n*: **war of** ~ Zermürbungskrieg *m*

aubergine [ˈəʊbəʒiːn] *n* Aubergine *f*

auburn [ˈɔːbən] *adj* kastanienbraun

auction [ˈɔːkʃən] *n* (*also*: **sale by** ~) Versteigerung *f*, Auktion *f* ♦ *vt* versteigern; ~**eer** [ɔːkʃəˈnɪə*] *n* Versteigerer *m*

audacity [ɔːˈdæsɪtɪ] *n* (*boldness*) Wagemut *m*; (*impudence*) Unverfrorenheit *f*

audible [ˈɔːdɪbl] *adj* hörbar

audience [ˈɔːdɪəns] *n* Zuhörer *pl*, Zuschauer *pl*; (*with king etc*) Audienz *f*

audiotypist [ˈɔːdɪəʊˈtaɪpɪst] *n* Phonotypistin *f*

audiovisual [ˈɔːdɪəʊˈvɪzjʊəl] *adj* audiovisuell

audit [ˈɔːdɪt] *vt* prüfen

audition [ɔːˈdɪʃən] *n* Probe *f*

auditor [ˈɔːdɪtə*] *n* Rechnungsprüfer *m*, Buchprüfer *m*

auditorium [ɔːdɪˈtɔːrɪəm] *n* Zuschauerraum *m*

augment [ɔːgˈment] *vt* vermehren

augur [ˈɔːgə*] *vi* bedeuten, voraussagen; **this** ~**s well** das ist ein gutes Omen

August [ˈɔːgəst] *n* August *m*

aunt [ɑːnt] *n* Tante *f*; ~**ie** *n* Tantchen *nt*; ~**y** *n* = **auntie**

au pair [ˈəʊˈpɛə*] *n* (*also*: ~ **girl**) Aupair-Mädchen *nt*

aura [ˈɔːrə] *n* Nimbus *m*

auspices [ˈɔːspɪsɪz] *npl*: **under the** ~ **of** unter der Schirmherrschaft von

auspicious [ɔːsˈpɪʃəs] *adj* günstig; verheißungsvoll

austere [ɒsˈtɪə*] *adj* streng; (*room*) nüchtern

austerity [ɒsˈterɪtɪ] *n* Strenge *f*; (POL) wirtschaftliche Einschränkung *f*

Australia [ɒsˈtreɪlɪə] *n* Australien *nt*; ~**n** *adj* australisch ♦ *n* Australier(in) *m(f)*

Austria [ˈɒstrɪə] *n* Österreich *nt*; ~**n** *adj* österreichisch ♦ *n* Österreicher(in) *m(f)*

authentic [ɔːˈθentɪk] *adj* echt, authentisch

author [ˈɔːθə*] *n* Autor *m*, Schriftsteller *m*; (*beginner*) Urheber *m*, Schöpfer *m*

authoritarian [ɔːθɒrɪˈtɛərɪən] *adj* autoritär

authoritative [ɔːˈθɒrɪtətɪv] *adj* (*account*) maßgeblich; (*manner*) herrisch

authority [ɔː'θɒrɪtɪ] n (power) Autorität f; (expert) Autorität f, Fachmann m; **the authorities** npl (ruling body) die Behörden pl

authorize ['ɔːθəraɪz] vt bevollmächtigen; (permit) genehmigen

auto ['ɔːtəʊ] (US) n Auto nt, Wagen m

autobiography [ɔːtəʊbaɪ'ɒgrəfɪ] n Autobiographie f

autograph ['ɔːtəgrɑːf] n (of celebrity) Autogramm nt ♦ vt mit Autogramm versehen

automatic [ɔːtə'mætɪk] adj automatisch ♦ n (gun) Selbstladepistole f; (car) Automatik m; ~**ally** adv automatisch

automation [ɔːtə'meɪʃən] n Automatisierung f

automobile ['ɔːtəməbiːl] (US) n Auto(mobil) nt

autonomous [ɔː'tɒnəməs] adj autonom

autumn ['ɔːtəm] n Herbst m

auxiliary [ɔːg'zɪlɪərɪ] adj Hilfs-

Av. abbr = avenue

avail [ə'veɪl] vt: to ~ o.s. of sth sich einer Sache gen bedienen ♦ n: to no ~ nutzlos

availability [əveɪlə'bɪlɪtɪ] n Erhältlichkeit f, Vorhandensein nt

available [ə'veɪləbl] adj erhältlich; zur Verfügung stehend; (person) erreichbar, abkömmlich

avalanche ['ævəlɑːnʃ] n Lawine f

avarice ['ævərɪs] n Habsucht f, Geiz m

Ave. abbr = avenue

avenge [ə'vendʒ] vt rächen, sühnen

avenue ['ævənjuː] n Allee f

average ['ævərɪdʒ] n Durchschnitt m ♦ adj durchschnittlich, Durchschnitts- ♦ vt (figures) den Durchschnitt nehmen von; (perform) durchschnittlich leisten; (in car etc) im Schnitt fahren; on ~ durchschnittlich, im Durchschnitt; ~ **out** vi: to ~ out at im Durchschnitt betragen

averse [ə'vɜːs] adj: to be ~ to doing sth eine Abneigung dagegen haben, etw zu tun

avert [ə'vɜːt] vt (turn away) abkehren; (prevent) abwehren

aviary ['eɪvɪərɪ] n Vogelhaus nt

aviation [eɪvɪ'eɪʃən] n Luftfahrt f, Flugwesen nt

avid ['ævɪd] adj: ~ (for) gierig (auf +acc)

avocado [ævə'kɑːdəʊ] n (also: BRIT: ~ pear) Avocado(birne) f

avoid [ə'vɔɪd] vt vermeiden; ~**ance** n Vermeidung f

await [ə'weɪt] vt erwarten, entgegensehen +dat

awake [ə'weɪk] (pt awoke, pp awoken or awaked) adj wach ♦ vt (auf)wecken ♦ vi aufwachen; to be ~ wach sein; ~**ning** n Erwachen nt

award [ə'wɔːd] n (prize) Preis m ♦ vt: to ~ (sb sth) (jdm etw) zuerkennen

aware [ə'weə*] adj bewußt; to be ~ sich bewußt sein; ~**ness** n Bewußtsein nt

awash [ə'wɒʃ] adj überflutet

away [ə'weɪ] adv weg, fort; two hours ~ by car zwei Autostunden entfernt; the holiday was two weeks ~ es war noch zwei Wochen bis zum Urlaub; ~ **match** n (SPORT) Auswärtsspiel nt

awe [ɔː] n Ehrfurcht f; ~-**inspiring** adj ehrfurchtgebietend; ~**some** adj ehrfurchtgebietend

awful ['ɔːful] adj (very bad) furchtbar; ~**ly** adv furchtbar, sehr

awhile [ə'waɪl] adv eine Weile

awkward ['ɔːkwəd] adj (clumsy) ungeschickt, linkisch; (embarrassing) peinlich

awning ['ɔːnɪŋ] n Markise f

awoke [ə'wəʊk] pt of awake; **awoken** [ə'wəʊkən] pp awake

awry [ə'raɪ] adv schief; to go ~ (person) fehlgehen; (plans) schiefgehen

axe [æks] (US ax) n Axt f, Beil nt ♦ vt (end suddenly) streichen

axes[1] ['æksɪz] npl of axe

axes[2] ['æksiːz] npl of axis

axis ['æksɪs] (pl axes) n Achse f

axle ['æksl] n Achse f

ay(e) [aɪ] excl (yes) ja

azalea [ə'zeɪlɪə] n Azalee f

B

B [biː] n (MUS) H nt
B.A. n abbr = **Bachelor of Arts**
babble ['bæbl] vi schwätzen; (stream) murmeln
baby ['beɪbɪ] n Baby nt; ~ **carriage** (US) n Kinderwagen m; ~-**sit** vi Kinder hüten, babysitten; ~-**sitter** n Babysitter m
bachelor ['bætʃələ*] n Junggeselle m; B~ **of Arts** Bakkalaureus m der philosophischen Fakultät; B~ **of Science** Bakkalaureus m der Naturwissenschaften
back [bæk] n (of person, horse) Rücken m; (of house) Rückseite f; (of train) Ende nt; (FOOTBALL) Verteidiger m ♦ vt (support) unterstützen; (wager) wetten auf +acc; (car) rückwärts fahren ♦ vi (go backwards) rückwärts gehen or fahren ♦ adj hintere(r, s) ♦ adv zurück; (to the rear) nach hinten; ~ **down** vi zurückstecken; ~ **out** vi sich zurückziehen; (inf) kneifen; ~ **up** vt (support) unterstützen; (car) zurücksetzen; (COMPUT) eine Sicherungskopie machen von; ~**bencher** (BRIT) n Parlamentarier(in) m(f); ~**bone** n Rückgrat nt; (support) Rückhalt m; ~**cloth** n Hintergrund m; ~**date** vt rückdatieren; ~**drop** n (THEAT) = **backcloth**; (background) Hintergrund m; ~**fire** vi (plan) fehlschlagen; (TECH) fehlzünden; ~**ground** n Hintergrund m; (person's education) Vorbildung f; **family** ~**ground** Familienverhältnisse pl; ~**hand** n (TENNIS: also: ~hand stroke) Rückhand f; ~**handed** adj (shot) Rückhand-; (compliment) zweifelhaft; ~**hander** (BRIT) n (bribe) Schmiergeld nt; ~**ing** n (support) Unterstützung f; ~**lash** n (fig) Gegenschlag m; ~**log** n (of work) Rückstand m; ~ **number** n (PRESS) alte Nummer f; ~**pack** n Rucksack m; ~ **pay** n (Gehalts- or Lohn)nachzahlung f; ~ **payments** npl Zahlungsrückstände

pl; ~ **seat** n (AUT) Rücksitz m; ~**side** (inf) n Hintern m; ~**stage** adv hinter den Kulissen; ~**stroke** n Rückenschwimmen nt; **Zusatz-**; (plane) Sonder-; (COMPUT) Sicherungs- ♦ n (see adj) Zusatzzug m; Sondermaschine f; Sicherungskopie f; ~**ward** adj (less developed) zurückgeblieben; (primitive) rückständig; ~**wards** adv rückwärts; ~**water** n (fig) Kaff nt; ~**yard** n Hinterhof m
bacon ['beɪkən] n Schinkenspeck m
bacteria [bæk'tɪərɪə] npl Bakterien pl
bad [bæd] adj schlecht, schlimm; **to go** ~ schlecht werden
bade [bæd] pt of **bid**
badge [bædʒ] n Abzeichen nt
badger ['bædʒə*] n Dachs m
badly ['bædlɪ] adv schlecht, schlimm; ~ **wounded** schwerverwundet; **he needs it** ~ er braucht es dringend; **to be** ~ **off** **(for money)** dringend Geld nötig haben
badminton ['bædmɪntən] n Federball m, Badminton nt
bad-tempered ['bæd'tempəd] adj schlecht gelaunt
baffle ['bæfl] vt (puzzle) verblüffen
bag [bæg] n (sack) Beutel m; (paper) Tüte f; (hand~) Tasche f; (suitcase) Koffer m; (booty) Jagdbeute f; (inf: old woman) alte Schachtel f ♦ vt (put in sack) in einen Sack stecken; (hunting) erlegen; ~**s** of (inf: lots of) eine Menge +acc; ~**gage** ['bægɪdʒ] n Gepäck nt; ~**gy** ['bægɪ] adj bauschig, sackartig; ~**pipes** ['bægpaɪps] npl Dudelsack m
Bahamas [bə'hɑːməz] npl: **the** ~ die Bahamas pl
bail [beɪl] n (money) Kaution f ♦ vt (prisoner: usu: grant ~ to) gegen Kaution freilassen; (boat: also: ~ out) ausschöpfen; **on** ~ (prisoner) gegen Kaution freigelassen; **to** ~ **sb out** die Kaution für jdn stellen; see also **bale**
bailiff ['beɪlɪf] n Gerichtsvollzieher(in) m(f)
bait [beɪt] n Köder m ♦ vt mit einem Köder versehen; (fig) ködern
bake [beɪk] vt, vi backen; ~**d beans**

gebackene Bohnen *pl*; ~**r** *n* Bäcker *m*;
~**ry** *n* Bäckerei *f*
baking ['beɪkɪŋ] *n* Backen *nt*; ~ **powder**
n Backpulver *nt*
balance ['bæləns] *n* (*scales*) Waage *f*;
(*equilibrium*) Gleichgewicht *nt*; (*FIN*:
state of account) Saldo *m*; (*difference*)
Bilanz *f*, (*amount remaining*) Restbe-
trag *m* ♦ *vt* (*weigh*) wägen; (*make
equal*) ausgleichen; ~ **of trade/
payments** Handels-/Zahlungsbilanz *f*;
~**d** *adj* ausgeglichen; ~ **sheet** *n* Bilanz
f, Rechnungsabschluß *m*
balcony ['bælkənɪ] *n* Balkon *m*
bald [bɔːld] *adj* kahl; (*statement*) knapp
bale [beɪl] *n* Ballen *m*; ~ **out** *vi* (*from a
plane*) abspringen Ballen *m*
baleful ['beɪlful] *adj* (*sad*) unglückselig;
(*evil*) böse
ball [bɔːl] *n* Ball *m*; ~ **bearing** *n*
Kugellager *nt*
ballet ['bæleɪ] *n* Ballett *nt*; ~ **dancer** *n*
Ballettänzer(in) *m(f)*
balloon [bə'luːn] *n* (Luft)ballon *m*
ballot ['bælət] *n* (geheime) Abstimmung
f
ballpoint (pen) ['bɔːlpɔɪnt] *n*
Kugelschreiber *m*
ballroom ['bɔːlrum] *n* Tanzsaal *m*
balm [baːm] *n* Balsam *m*
Baltic ['bɔːltɪk] *n*: **the ~ (Sea)** die
Ostsee
balustrade [bæləs'treɪd] *n* Brüstung *f*
bamboo [bæm'buː] *n* Bambus *m*
ban [bæn] *n* Verbot *nt* ♦ *vt* verbieten
banana [bə'nɑːnə] *n* Banane *f*
band [bænd] *n* Band *nt*; (*group*) Gruppe
f; (*of criminals*) Bande *f*; (*MUS*)
Kapelle *f*, Band *f*; ~ **together** *vi* sich
zusammentun
bandage ['bændɪdʒ] *n* Verband *m*;
(*elastic*) Bandage *f* ♦ *vt* (*cut*) verbinden; (*broken limb*) bandagieren
bandaid ['bændeɪd] *n* (*US*) *n* Heftpflaster
nt
bandwagon ['bændwægən] *n*: **to jump
on the ~** (*fig*) auf den fahrenden Zug
aufspringen
bandy ['bændɪ] *vt* wechseln; ~**-legged**
['bændɪ'legɪd] *adj* o-beinig

bang [bæŋ] *n* (*explosion*) Knall *m*;
(*blow*) Hieb *m* ♦ *vt*, *vi* knallen
bangle ['bæŋgl] *n* Armspange *f*
bangs [bæŋz] (*US*) *npl* (*fringe*) Pony *m*
banish ['bænɪʃ] *vt* verbannen
banister(s) ['bænɪstə(z)] *n(pl)*
(Treppen)geländer *nt*
bank [bæŋk] *n* (*raised ground*) Erdwall
m; (*of lake etc*) Ufer *nt*; (*FIN*) Bank *f* ♦
vt (*tilt*: *AVIAT*) in die Kurve bringen;
(*money*) einzahlen; ~ **on** *vt fus*: **to ~
on sth** mit etw rechnen; ~ **account** *n*
Bankkonto *nt*; ~ **card** *n* Scheckkarte *f*;
~**er** *n* Bankier *m*; ~**er's card** (*BRIT*) *n*
= **bank card**; **B~ holiday** (*BRIT*) *n*
gesetzliche(r) Feiertag *m*; ~**ing** *n*
Bankwesen *nt*; ~**note** *n* Banknote *f*; ~
rate *n* Banksatz *m*
bankrupt ['bæŋkrʌpt] *adj*: **to be ~**
bankrott sein; **to go ~** Bankrott machen; ~**cy** *n* Bankrott *m*
bank statement *n* Kontoauszug *m*
banner ['bænə*] *n* Banner *nt*
banns [bænz] *npl* Aufgebot *nt*
baptism ['bæptɪzəm] *n* Taufe *f*
baptize [bæp'taɪz] *vt* taufen
bar [baː*] *n* (*rod*) Stange *f*; (*obstacle*)
Hindernis *nt*; (*of chocolate*) Tafel *f*; (*of
soap*) Stück *nt*; (*for food, drink*) Buffet
nt, Bar *f*; (*pub*) Wirtschaft *f*; (*MUS*)
Takt(strich) *m* ♦ *vt* (*fasten*) verriegeln;
(*hinder*) versperren; (*exclude*) ausschließen; **behind ~s** hinter Gittern; **the
B~**: **to be called to the B~** als Anwalt
zugelassen werden; ~ **none** ohne Ausnahme
barbaric [baː'bærɪk] *adj* primitiv,
unkultiviert
barbecue ['baːbɪkjuː] *n* Barbecue *nt*
barbed wire ['baːbd-] *n* Stacheldraht *m*
barber ['baːbə*] *n* Herrenfriseur *m*
bar code *n* (*on goods*) Registrierkode *f*
bare [beə*] *adj* nackt; (*trees, country*)
kahl; (*mere*) bloß ♦ *vt* entblößen;
~**back** *adv* ungesattelt; ~**faced** *adj*
unverfroren; ~**foot** *adj*, *adv* barfuß;
~**ly** *adv* kaum, knapp
bargain ['baːgɪn] *n* (*sth cheap*)
günstiger Kauf; (*agreement*: *written*)
Kaufvertrag *m*; (: *oral*) Geschäft *nt*;

into the ~ obendrein; ~ for vt: he got more than he ~ed for er erlebte sein blaues Wunder

barge [bɑːdʒ] n Lastkahn m; ~ in vi hereinplatzen; ~ into vt rennen gegen

bark [bɑːk] n (of tree) Rinde f; (of dog) Bellen nt ♦ vi (dog) bellen

barley ['bɑːlɪ] n Gerste f; ~ sugar n Malzbonbon nt

barmaid ['bɑːmeɪd] n Bardame f

barman ['bɑːmən] (irreg) n Barkellner m

barn [bɑːn] n Scheune f

barometer [bə'rɒmɪtə*] n Barometer nt

baron ['bærən] n Baron m; ~ess n Baronin f

barracks ['bærəks] npl Kaserne f

barrage ['bærɑːʒ] n (gunfire) Sperrfeuer nt; (dam) Staudamm m; Talsperre f

barrel ['bærəl] n Faß nt; (of gun) Lauf m

barren ['bærən] adj unfruchtbar

barricade [bærɪ'keɪd] n Barrikade f ♦ vt verbarrikadieren

barrier ['bærɪə*] n (obstruction) Hindernis nt; (fence) Schranke f

barring ['bɑːrɪŋ] prep abgesehen von

barrister ['bærɪstə*] (BRIT) n Rechtsanwalt m

barrow ['bærəʊ] n (cart) Schubkarren m

bartender ['bɑːtendə*] (US) n Barmann or -kellner m

barter ['bɑːtə*] vt handeln

base [beɪs] n (bottom) Boden m, Basis f; (MIL) Stützpunkt m ♦ vt gründen; (opinion, theory): to be ~d on basieren auf +dat ♦ adj (low) gemein; ~ball ['beɪsbɔːl] n Baseball m; ~ment ['beɪsmənt] n Kellergeschoß nt

bases¹ ['beɪsɪz] npl of base

bases² ['beɪsiːz] npl of basis

bash [bæʃ] (inf) vt (heftig) schlagen

bashful ['bæʃfʊl] adj schüchtern

basic ['beɪsɪk] adj grundlegend; ~ally adv im Grunde

basil ['bæzl] n Basilikum nt

basin ['beɪsn] n (dish) Schüssel f; (for washing, also valley) Becken nt; (dock) (Trocken)becken nt

basis ['beɪsɪs] (pl **bases**) n Basis f, Grundlage f

bask [bɑːsk] vi: to ~ in the sun sich sonnen

basket ['bɑːskɪt] n Korb m; ~ball n Basketball m

bass [beɪs] n (MUS, also instrument) Baß m; (voice) Baßstimme f

bassoon [bə'suːn] n Fagott nt

bastard ['bɑːstəd] n Bastard m; (inf!) Arschloch nt (!)

bastion ['bæstɪən] n (also fig) Bollwerk nt

bat [bæt] n (SPORT) Schlagholz nt; Schläger m; (ZOOL) Fledermaus f ♦ vt: he didn't ~ an eyelid er hat nicht mit der Wimper gezuckt

batch [bætʃ] n (of letters) Stoß m; (of samples) Satz m

bated ['beɪtɪd] adj: with ~ breath mit angehaltenem Atem

bath [bɑːθ, pl bɑːðz] n Bad nt; (~ tub) Badewanne f ♦ vt baden; to have a ~ baden; see also baths

bathe [beɪð] vt, vi baden; ~r n Badende(r) mf

bathing ['beɪðɪŋ] n Baden nt; ~ cap n Badekappe f; ~ costume n Badeanzug m; ~ suit (US) n Badeanzug m; ~ trunks (BRIT) npl Badehose f

bathrobe ['bɑːθrəʊb] n Bademantel m

bathroom ['bɑːθrʊm] n Bad(ezimmer nt) nt

baths [bɑːðz] npl (Schwimm)bad nt

bath towel n Badetuch nt

batman ['bætmən] (irreg) n (Offiziers)bursche m

baton ['bætən] n (of police) Gummiknüppel m; (MUS) Taktstock m

batter ['bætə*] vt verprügeln ♦ n Schlagteig m; (for cake) Biskuitteig m; ~ed adj (hat, pan) verbeult

battery ['bætərɪ] n (ELEC) Batterie f; (MIL) Geschützbatterie f

battle ['bætl] n Schlacht f; (small) Gefecht nt ♦ vi kämpfen; ~field n Schlachtfeld nt; ~ship n Schlachtschiff nt

bawdy ['bɔːdɪ] adj unflätig

bawl [bɔːl] vi brüllen

bay [beɪ] n (of sea) Bucht f ♦ vi bellen; **to keep at ~** unter Kontrolle halten
bay window n Erkerfenster nt
bazaar [bəˈzaː*] n Basar m
B. & B. abbr = **bed and breakfast**
BBC n abbr (= British Broadcasting Corporation) BBC f or m
B.C. adv abbr (= before Christ) v.Chr.

KEYWORD
---

be [biː] (pt **was, were**, pp **been**) aux vb **1** (with present participle: forming continuous tenses): **what are you doing?** was machst du (gerade)?; **it is raining** es regnet; **I've been waiting for you for hours** ich warte schon seit Stunden auf dich
2 (with pp: forming passives): **to be killed** getötet werden; **the thief was nowhere to be seen** der Dieb war nirgendwo zu sehen
3 (in tag questions): **it was fun, wasn't it?** es hat Spaß gemacht, nicht wahr?
4 (+to +infin): **the house is to be sold** das Haus soll verkauft werden; **he's not to open it** er darf es nicht öffnen
♦ vb +complement **1** (usu): **I'm tired** bin ich müde; **I'm hot/cold** mir ist heiß/kalt; **he's a doctor** er ist Arzt; **2 and 2 are 4** 2 und 2 ist or sind 4; **she's tall/pretty** sie ist groß/hübsch; **be careful/quiet** sei vorsichtig/ruhig
2 (of health): **how are you?** wie geht es dir?; **he's very ill** er ist sehr krank; **I'm fine now** jetzt geht es mir gut
3 (of age): **how old are you?** wie alt bist du?; **I'm sixteen (years) old** ich bin sechzehn (Jahre alt)
4 (cost): **how much was the meal?** was or wieviel hat das Essen gekostet?; **that'll be £5.75, please** das macht £5.75, bitte
♦ vi **1** (exist, occur etc) sein; **is there a God?** gibt es einen Gott?; **be that as it may** wie dem auch sei; **so be it** also gut
2 (referring to place) sein; **I won't be here tomorrow** iche werde morgen nicht hier sein
3 (referring to movement): **where have you been?** wo bist du gewesen?; **I've been in the garden** ich war im Garten
♦ impers vb **1** (referring to time, distance, weather) sein; **it's 5 o'clock** es ist 5 Uhr; **it's 10 km to the village** es sind 10 km bis zum Dorf; **it's too hot/cold** es ist zu heiß/kalt
2 (emphatic): **it's me** ich bin's; **it's the postman** es ist der Briefträger

---

beach [biːtʃ] n Strand m ♦ vt (ship) auf den Strand setzen
beacon [ˈbiːkən] n (signal) Leuchtfeuer nt; (traffic ~) Bake f
bead [biːd] n Perle f; (drop) Tropfen m
beak [biːk] n Schnabel m
beaker [ˈbiːkə*] n Becher m
beam [biːm] n (of wood) Balken m; (of light) Strahl m; (smile) strahlende(s) Lächeln nt ♦ vi strahlen
bean [biːn] n Bohne f; **~ sprouts** npl Sojasprossen pl
bear [bɛə*] (pt **bore**, pp **borne**) n Bär m ♦ vt (weight, crops) tragen; (tolerate) ertragen; (young) gebären ♦ vi: **to ~ right/left** sich rechts/links halten; **~ out** vt (suspicions etc) bestätigen; **~ up** vi sich halten
beard [bɪəd] n Bart m; **~ed** adj bärtig
bearer [ˈbɛərə*] n Träger m
bearing [ˈbɛərɪŋ] n (posture) Haltung f; (relevance) Relevanz f ♦ n; (relation) Bedeutung f; (TECH) Kugellager nt; **~s** npl (direction) Orientierung f; (also: **ball ~s**) (Kugel)lager nt
beast [biːst] n Tier nt, Vieh nt; (person) Biest nt; **~ly** adj viehisch; (inf) scheußlich
beat [biːt] (pt **beat**, pp **beaten**) n (stroke) Schlag m; (pulsation) (Herz)schlag m; (police round) Runde f; Revier nt; (MUS) Takt m; Beat m ♦ vt, vi schlagen; **to ~ it** abhauen; **off the ~en track** abgelegen; **~ off** vt abschlagen; **~ up** vt zusammenschlagen; **beaten** pp of **beat**; **~ing** n Prügel pl
beautiful [ˈbjuːtɪful] adj schön; **~ly** adv ausgezeichnet
beauty [ˈbjuːtɪ] n Schönheit f; **~ salon** n Schönheitssalon m; **~ spot** n Schönheitsfleck m; (BRIT: TOURISM)

(besonders) schöne(r) Ort m

beaver ['biːvə*] n Biber m

became [bɪ'keɪm] pt of become

because [bɪ'kɒz] conj weil ♦ prep: ~ of wegen +gen or (inf) dat

beck [bek] n: to be at the ~ and call of sb nach jds Pfeife tanzen

beckon ['bekən] vt, vi: to ~ to sb jdm ein Zeichen geben

become [bɪ'kʌm] (irreg: like come) vi werden ♦ vt werden; (clothes) stehen +dat

becoming [bɪ'kʌmɪŋ] adj (suitable) schicklich; (clothes) kleidsam

bed [bed] n Bett nt; (of river) Flußbett nt; (foundation) Schicht f; (in garden) Beet nt; **to go to ~** zu Bett gehen; **single/double ~** Einzel/Doppelbett nt; **~ and breakfast** n Übernachtung f mit Frühstück; **~clothes** npl Bettwäsche f; **~ding** n Bettzeug nt

bedlam ['bedləm] n (uproar) tolle(s) Durcheinander nt

bedraggled [bɪ'drægld] adj ramponiert

bed: ~ridden adj bettlägerig; **~room** n Schlafzimmer nt; **~side** n: at the ~side am Bett; **~sit(ter)** (BRIT) n Einzimmerwohnung f, möblierte(s) Zimmer nt; **~spread** n Tagesdecke f; **~time** n Schlafenszeit f

bee [biː] n Biene f

beech [biːtʃ] n Buche f

beef [biːf] n Rindfleisch nt; **roast ~** Roastbeef nt; **~burger** n Hamburger m

beehive ['biːhaɪv] n Bienenstock m

beeline ['biːlaɪn] n: to make a ~ for schnurstracks zugehen auf +acc

been [biːn] pp of be

beer [bɪə*] n Bier nt

beet [biːt] n (vegetable) Rübe f; (US: also: red ~) rote Bete f or Rübe f

beetle ['biːtl] n Käfer m

beetroot ['biːtruːt] (BRIT) n rote Bete f

before [bɪ'fɔː*] prep vor ♦ conj bevor ♦ adv (of time) zuvor; früher; **the week ~** die Woche zuvor or vorher; **I've done it ~** das hab' ich schon mal getan; **~hand** adv im voraus

beg [beg] vt, vi (implore) dringend bitten; (alms) betteln

began [bɪ'gæn] pt of begin

beggar ['begə*] n Bettler(in) m(f)

begin [bɪ'gɪn] (pt began, pp begun) vt, vi anfangen, beginnen; (found) gründen; **to ~ doing** or **to do sth** anfangen or beginnen, etw zu tun; **to ~ with** zunächst (einmal); **~ner** n Anfänger m; **~ning** n Anfang m

begun [bɪ'gʌn] pp of begin

behalf [bɪ'hɑːf] n: on ~ of im Namen +gen; on my ~ für mich

behave [bɪ'heɪv] vi sich benehmen

behaviour [bɪ'heɪvjə*] (US **behavior**) n Benehmen nt

behead [bɪ'hed] vt enthaupten

beheld [bɪ'held] pt, pp of behold

behind [bɪ'haɪnd] prep hinter ♦ adv (late) im Rückstand; (in the rear) hinten ♦ n (inf) Hinterteil nt; **~ the scenes** (fig) hinter den Kulissen

behold [bɪ'həʊld] (irreg: like hold) vt erblicken

beige [beɪʒ] adj beige

Beijing ['beɪ'dʒɪŋ] n Peking nt

being ['biːɪŋ] n (existence) (Da)sein nt; (person) Wesen nt; **to come into ~** entstehen

belated [bɪ'leɪtɪd] adj verspätet

belch [beltʃ] vi rülpsen ♦ vt (smoke) ausspeien

belfry ['belfrɪ] n Glockenturm m

Belgian ['beldʒən] adj belgisch ♦ n Belgier(in) m(f)

Belgium ['beldʒəm] n Belgien nt

belie [bɪ'laɪ] vt Lügen strafen +acc

belief [bɪ'liːf] n Glaube m; (conviction) Überzeugung f; **~ in sb/sth** Glaube an jdn/etw

believe [bɪ'liːv] vt glauben +dat; (think) glauben, meinen, denken ♦ vi (have faith) glauben; **to ~ in sth** an etw acc glauben; **~r** n Gläubige(r) mf

belittle [bɪ'lɪtl] vt herabsetzen

bell [bel] n Glocke f

belligerent [bɪ'lɪdʒərənt] adj (person) streitsüchtig; (country) kriegsführend

bellow ['beləʊ] vt, vi brüllen

bellows ['beləʊz] npl (TECH) Gebläse nt; (for fire) Blasebalg m

belly ['belɪ] n Bauch m

belong [bɪ'lɒŋ] *vi* gehören; **to ~ to sb** jdm gehören; **to ~ to a club** *etc* einem Club *etc* angehören; **it does not ~ here** es gehört nicht hierher; **~ings** *npl* Habe *f*
beloved [bɪ'lʌvɪd] *adj* innig geliebt ♦ *n* Geliebte(r) *mf*
below [bɪ'ləʊ] *prep* unter ♦ *adv* unten
belt [belt] *n* (*band*) Riemen *m*; (*round waist*) Gürtel *m* ♦ *vt* (*fasten*) mit Riemen befestigen; (*inf:* *beat*) schlagen; **~way** (*US*) *n* (*AUT: ring road*) Umgehungsstraße *f*
bemused [bɪ'mjuːzd] *adj* verwirrt
bench [bentʃ] *n* (*seat*) Bank *f*; (*workshop*) Werkbank *f*; (*judge's seat*) Richterbank *f*; (*judges*) Richter *pl*
bend [bend] (*pt, pp* **bent**) *vt* (*curve*) biegen; (*stoop*) beugen ♦ *vi* sich biegen; sich beugen ♦ *n* Biegung *f*; (*BRIT: in road*) Kurve *f*; **~ down** or **over** *vi* sich bücken
beneath [bɪ'niːθ] *prep* unter ♦ *adv* darunter
benefactor ['benɪfæktə*] *n* Wohltäter(in) *m(f)*
beneficial [benɪ'fɪʃl] *adj* vorteilhaft; (*to health*) heilsam
benefit ['benɪfɪt] *n* (*advantage*) Nutzen *m* ♦ *vt* fördern ♦ *vi*: **to ~ (from)** Nutzen ziehen (aus)
Benelux ['benɪlʌks] *n* Beneluxstaaten *pl*
benevolent [bɪ'nevələnt] *adj* wohlwollend
benign [bɪ'naɪn] *adj* (*person*) gütig; (*climate*) mild
bent [bent] *pt, pp of* **bend** ♦ *n* (*inclination*) Neigung *f* ♦ *adj* (*inf:* *dishonest*) unehrlich; **to be ~ on** versessen sein auf +*acc*
bequest [bɪ'kwest] *n* Vermächtnis *nt*
bereaved [bɪ'riːvd] *npl*: **the ~** die Hinterbliebenen *pl*
bereft [bɪ'reft] *adj*: **~ of** bar +*gen*
beret ['bereɪ] *n* Baskenmütze *f*
Berlin [bɜː'lɪn] *n* Berlin *nt*
berm [bɜːm] (*US*) *n* (*AUT*) Seitenstreifen *m*
Bermuda [bɜː'mjuːdə] *n* Bermuda *nt*
berry ['berɪ] *n* Beere *f*

berserk [bə'sɜːk] *adj*: **to go ~** wild werden
berth [bɜːθ] *n* (*for ship*) Ankerplatz *m*; (*in ship*) Koje *f*; (*in train*) Bett *nt* ♦ *vt* am Kai festmachen ♦ *vi* anlegen
beseech [bɪ'siːtʃ] (*pt, pp* **besought**) *vt* anflehen
beset [bɪ'set] (*pt, pp* **beset**) *vt* bedrängen
beside [bɪ'saɪd] *prep* neben, bei; (*except*) außer; **to be ~ o.s. (with)** außer sich sein (vor +*dat*); **that's ~ the point** das tut nichts zur Sache
besides [bɪ'saɪdz] *prep* außer, neben ♦ *adv* außerdem
besiege [bɪ'siːdʒ] *vt* (*MIL*) belagern; (*surround*) umlagern, bedrängen
besought [bɪ'sɔːt] *pt, pp of* **beseech**
best [best] *adj* beste(r, s) ♦ *adv* am besten; **the ~ part of** (*quantity*) das meiste +*gen*; **at ~** höchstens; **to make the ~ of it** das Beste daraus machen; **to do one's ~** sein Bestes tun; **to the ~ of my knowledge** meines Wissens; **to the ~ of my ability** so gut ich kann; **for the ~** zum Besten; **~ man** *n* Trauzeuge *m*
bestow [bɪ'stəʊ] *vt* verleihen
bet [bet] (*pt, pp* **bet** or **betted**) *n* Wette *f* ♦ *vt, vi* wetten
betray [bɪ'treɪ] *vt* verraten
better ['betə*] *adj, adv* besser ♦ *vt* verbessern; ♦ *n*: **to get the ~ of sb** jdn überwinden; **the ~ thought ~ of it** er hat sich eines Besseren besonnen; **you had ~ leave** Sie gehen jetzt wohl besser; **to get ~** (*MED*) gesund werden; **~ off** *adj* (*richer*) wohlhabender
betting ['betɪŋ] *n* Wetten *nt*; **~ shop** (*BRIT*) *n* Wettbüro *nt*
between [bɪ'twiːn] *prep* zwischen; (*among*) unter ♦ *adv* dazwischen
beverage ['bevərɪdʒ] *n* Getränk *nt*
bevy ['bevɪ] *n* Schar *f*
beware [bɪ'wɛə*] *vt, vi* sich hüten vor +*dat*; **"~ of the dog"** „Vorsicht, bissiger Hund!"
bewildered [bɪ'wɪldəd] *adj* verwirrt
bewitching [bɪ'wɪtʃɪŋ] *adj* bestrickend
beyond [bɪ'jɒnd] *prep* (*place*) jenseits +*gen*; (*time*) über ... hinaus; (*out of*

reach) außerhalb +*gen* ♦ *adv* darüber hinaus; ~ **doubt** ohne Zweifel; ~ **repair** nicht mehr zu reparieren

bias ['baɪəs] *n* (*slant*) Neigung *f*; (*prejudice*) Vorurteil *nt*; ~**(s)ed** *adj* voreingenommen

bib [bɪb] *n* Latz *m*

Bible ['baɪbl] *n* Bibel *f*

bicarbonate of soda [baɪ'kɑ:bənɪt-] *n* Natron *nt*

bicker ['bɪkə*] *vi* zanken

bicycle ['baɪsɪkl] *n* Fahrrad *nt*

bid [bɪd] (*pt* **bade** *or* **bid, pp bid(den)**) *n* (*offer*) Gebot *nt*; (*attempt*) Versuch *m* ♦ *vt, vi* (*offer*) bieten; **to ~ farewell** Lebewohl sagen; **bidden** ['bɪdn] *pp of* **bid;** ~**der** *n* (*person*) Steigerer *m*; **the highest ~der** der Meistbietende; ~**ding** *n* (*command*) Geheiß *nt*

bide [baɪd] *vt*: **to ~ one's time** abwarten

bifocals [baɪ'fəʊkəlz] *npl* Bifokalbrille *f*

big [bɪg] *adj* groß

big dipper [-'dɪpə*] *n* Achterbahn *f*

bigheaded ['bɪg'hedɪd] *adj* eingebildet

bigot ['bɪgət] *n* Frömmler *m*; ~**ed** *adj* bigott; ~**ry** *n* Bigotterie *f*

big top *n* Zirkuszelt *nt*

bike [baɪk] *n* Rad *nt*

bikini [bɪ'ki:nɪ] *n* Bikini *m*

bile [baɪl] *n* (*BIOL*) Galle *f*

bilingual [baɪ'lɪŋgwəl] *adj* zweisprachig

bill [bɪl] *n* (*account*) Rechnung *f*; (*POL*) Gesetzentwurf *m*; (*US: FIN*) Geldschein *m*; **to fit** *or* **fill the ~** (*fig*) der/die/das richtige sein; **"post no ~s"** „Plakate ankleben verboten"; ~**board** *n* Reklameschild *nt*

billet ['bɪlɪt] *n* Quartier *nt*

billfold ['bɪlfəʊld] (*US*) *n* Geldscheintasche *f*

billiards ['bɪljədz] *n* Billard *nt*

billion ['bɪljən] *n* (*BRIT*) Billion *f*; (*US*) Milliarde *f*

bin [bɪn] *n* Kasten *m*; (*dust*~) (Abfall)eimer *m*

bind [baɪnd] (*pt, pp* **bound**) *vt* (*tie*) binden; (*tie together*) zusammenbinden; (*oblige*) verpflichten; ~**ing** *n* (Buch)einband *m* ♦ *adj* verbindlich

binge [bɪndʒ] (*inf*) *n* Sauferei *f*

bingo ['bɪŋgəʊ] *n* Bingo *nt*

binoculars [bɪ'nɒkjʊləz] *npl* Fernglas *nt*

bio... [baɪəʊ] *prefix*: ~**chemistry** *n* Biochemie *f*; ~**graphy** [baɪ'ɒgrəfɪ] *n* Biographie *f*; ~**logical** [baɪə'lɒdʒɪkəl] *adj* biologisch; ~**logy** [baɪ'ɒlədʒɪ] *n* Biologie *f*

birch [bɜːtʃ] *n* Birke *f*

bird [bɜːd] *n* Vogel *m*; (*BRIT: inf: girl*) Mädchen *nt*; ~**'s-eye view** *n* Vogelschau *f*; ~ **watcher** *n* Vogelbeobachter(in) *m(f)*

Biro ['baɪrəʊ] (®) *n* Kugelschreiber *m*

birth [bɜːθ] *n* Geburt *f*; **to give ~ to** zur Welt bringen; ~ **certificate** *n* Geburtsurkunde *f*; ~ **control** *n* Geburtenkontrolle *f*; ~**day** *n* Geburtstag *m*; ~**place** *n* Geburtsort *m*; ~ **rate** *n* Geburtenrate *f*

biscuit ['bɪskɪt] *n* Keks *m*

bisect [baɪ'sekt] *vt* halbieren

bishop ['bɪʃəp] *n* Bischof *m*

bit [bɪt] *pt of* **bite** ♦ *n* bißchen, Stückchen *nt*; (*horse's*) Gebiß *nt*; (*COMPUT*) Bit *nt*; **a ~ tired** etwas müde

bitch [bɪtʃ] *n* (*dog*) Hündin *f*; (*unpleasant woman*) Weibsstück *nt*

bite [baɪt] (*pt* **bit**, *pp* **bitten**) *vt, vi* beißen ♦ *n* Biß *m*; (*mouthful*) Bissen *m*; **to ~ one's nails** Nägel kauen; **let's have a ~ to eat** laß uns etwas essen

biting ['baɪtɪŋ] *adj* beißend

bitten ['bɪtn] *pp of* **bite**

bitter ['bɪtə*] *adj* bitter; (*memory etc*) schmerzlich; (*person*) verbittert ♦ *n* (*BRIT: beer*) dunkle(s) Bier *nt*; ~**ness** *n* Bitterkeit *f*

blab [blæb] *vi* klatschen ♦ *vt* (*also*: ~ **out**) ausplaudern

black [blæk] *adj* schwarz; (*night*) finster ♦ *vt* schwärzen; (*shoes*) wichsen; (*eye*) blau schlagen; (*BRIT: INDUSTRY*) boykottieren; **to give sb a ~ eye** jdm ein blaues Auge schlagen; **in the ~** (*bank account*) in den schwarzen Zahlen; ~ **and blue** *adj* grün und blau; ~**berry** *n* Brombeere *f*; ~**bird** *n* Amsel *f*; ~**board** *n* (Wand)tafel *f*; ~**currant** *n* schwarze Johannisbeere *f*; ~**en** *vt* schwärzen; (*fig*) verunglimpfen; ~ **ice**

n Glatteis *nt*; ~**jack** (*US*) *n* Siebzehn und Vier; ~**leg** (*BRIT*) *n* Streikbrecher(in) *m(f)*; ~**list** *n* schwarze Liste *f*; ~**mail** *n* Erpressung *f* ♦ *vt* erpressen; ~ **market** *n* Schwarzmarkt *m*; ~**out** *n* Verdunklung *f*; (*MED*): **to have a ~out** bewußtlos werden; **B**~ **Sea** *n*: **the B**~ **Sea** das Schwarze Meer; ~**sheep** *n* schwarze(s) Schaf *nt*; ~**smith** *n* Schmied *m*; ~ **spot** *n* (*AUT*) Gefahrenstelle *f*; (*for unemployment etc*) schwer betroffene(s) Gebiet *nt*

bladder ['blædə*] *n* Blase *f*

blade [bleɪd] *n* (*of weapon*) Klinge *f*; (*of grass*) Halm *m*; (*of oar*) Ruderblatt *nt*

blame [bleɪm] *n* Tadel *m*, Schuld *f* ♦ *vt* Vorwürfe machen +*dat*; **to ~ sb for sth** jdm die Schuld an etw *dat* geben; **he is to ~** er ist daran schuld

bland [blænd] *adj* mild

blank [blæŋk] *adj* leer, unbeschrieben; (*look*) verdutzt; (*verse*) Blank- ♦ *n* (*space*) Lücke *f*; Zwischenraum *m*; (*cartridge*) Platzpatrone *f*; ~ **cheque** *n* Blankoscheck *m*; (*fig*) Freibrief *m*

blanket ['blæŋkɪt] *n* (Woll)decke *f*

blare [bleə*] *vi* (*radio*) plärren; (*horn*) tuten; (*MUS*) schmettern

blasé ['blɑːzeɪ] *adj* blasiert

blast [blɑːst] *n* Explosion *f*; (*of wind*) Windstoß *m* ♦ *vt* (*blow up*) sprengen; ~! (*inf*) verflixt!; ~**off** *n* (*SPACE*) (Raketen)abschuß *m*

blatant ['bleɪtənt] *adj* offenkundig

blaze [bleɪz] *n* (*fire*) lodernde(s) Feuer *nt* ♦ *vi* lodern ♦ *vt*: **to ~ a trail** Bahn brechen

blazer ['bleɪzə*] *n* Blazer *m*

bleach [bliːtʃ] *n* (*also:* **household ~**) Bleichmittel *nt* ♦ *vt* bleichen

bleachers ['bliːtʃəz] (*US*) *npl* (*SPORT*) unüberdachte Tribüne *f*

bleak [bliːk] *adj* kahl, rauh; (*future*) trostlos

bleary-eyed ['blɪərɪ'aɪd] *adj* triefäugig; (*on waking up*) mit verschlafenen Augen

bleat [bliːt] *vi* blöken; (*fig: complain*) meckern

bled [bled] *pt, pp* of **bleed**

bleed [bliːd] (*pt, pp* **bled**) *vi* bluten ♦ *vt* (*draw blood*) zur Ader lassen; **to ~ to death** verbluten

bleeper [bliːpə*] *n* (*of doctor etc*) Funkrufempfänger *m*

blemish ['blemɪʃ] *n* Makel *m* ♦ *vt* verunstalten

blend [blend] *n* Mischung *f* ♦ *vt* mischen ♦ *vi* sich mischen

bless [bles] (*pt, pp* **blessed** *or* **blest**) *vt* segnen; (*give thanks*) preisen; (*make happy*) glücklich machen; ~ **you!** Gesundheit!; ~**ing** *n* Segen *m*; (*at table*) Tischgebet *nt*; (*happiness*) Wohltat *f*; Segen *m*; (*good wish*) Glück *nt*

blest [blest] *pt, pp* of **bless**

blew [bluː] *pt* of **blow**

blight [blaɪt] *vt* zunichte machen

blimey ['blaɪmɪ] (*BRIT: inf*) *excl* verflucht

blind [blaɪnd] *adj* blind; (*corner*) unübersichtlich ♦ *n* (*for window*) Rouleau *nt* ♦ *vt* blenden; ~ **alley** *n* Sackgasse *f*; ~**fold** *n* Augenbinde *f* ♦ *adj, adv* mit verbundenen Augen ♦ *vt*: **to ~fold sb** jdm die Augen verbinden; ~**ly** *adv* blind; (*fig*) blindlings; ~**ness** *n* Blindheit *f*; ~ **spot** *n* (*AUT*) tote(r) Winkel *m*; (*fig*) schwache(r) Punkt *m*

blink [blɪŋk] *vi* blinzeln; ~**ers** *npl* Scheuklappen *pl*

bliss [blɪs] *n* (Glück)seligkeit *f*

blister ['blɪstə*] *n* Blase *f* ♦ *vi* Blasen werfen

blithe [blaɪð] *adj* munter

blitz [blɪts] *n* Luftkrieg *m*

blizzard ['blɪzəd] *n* Schneesturm *m*

bloated ['bləʊtɪd] *adj* aufgedunsen; (*inf: full*) nudelsatt

blob [blɒb] *n* Klümpchen *nt*

bloc [blɒk] *n* (*POL*) Block *m*

block [blɒk] *n* (*of wood*) Block *m*, Klotz *m*; (*of houses*) Häuserblock *m* ♦ *vt* hemmen; ~**ade** [blɒ'keɪd] *n* Blockade *f* ♦ *vt* blockieren; ~**age** *n* Verstopfung *f*; ~**buster** *n* Knüller *m*; ~ **of flats** (*BRIT*) *n* Häuserblock *m*; ~ **letters** *npl* Blockbuchstaben *pl*

bloke [bləʊk] (*BRIT: inf*) *n* Kerl *m*, Typ *m*

blond(e) [blɔnd] *adj* blond ♦ *n* Blondine *f*

blood [blʌd] *n* Blut *nt*; ~ **donor** *n* Blutspender *m*; ~ **group** *n* Blutgruppe *f*; ~ **pressure** *n* Blutdruck *m*; ~**shed** *n* Blutvergießen *nt*; ~**shot** *adj* blutunterlaufen; ~**stained** *adj* blutbefleckt; ~**stream** *n* Blut *nt*, Blutkreislauf *m*; ~ **test** *n* Blutprobe *f*; ~**thirsty** *adj* blutrünstig; ~**y** *adj* blutig; (*BRIT: inf*) verdammt; ~**y-minded** (*BRIT: inf*) *adj* stur

bloom [bluːm] *n* Blüte *f*; (*freshness*) Glanz *m* ♦ *vi* blühen

blossom ['blɔsəm] *n* Blüte *f* ♦ *vi* blühen

blot [blɔt] *n* Klecks *m* ♦ *vt* beklecksen; (*ink*) (ab)löschen; ~ **out** *vt* auslöschen

blotchy ['blɔtʃɪ] *adj* fleckig

blotting paper ['blɔtɪŋ-] *n* Löschpapier *nt*

blouse [blauz] *n* Bluse *f*

blow [bləu] (*pt* **blew**, *pp* **blown**) *n* Schlag *m* ♦ *vt* blasen ♦ *vi* (*wind*) wehen; **to** ~ **one's nose** sich *dat* die Nase putzen; ~ **away** *vt* wegblasen; ~ **down** *vt* unwehen; ~ **out** *vi* ausgehen; ~ **over** *vi* vorübergehen; ~ **up** *vi* explodieren ♦ *vt* sprengen; ~**dry** *n*: **to have a** ~**dry** sich fönen lassen ♦ *vt* fönen; ~**lamp** (*BRIT*) *n* Lötlampe *f*; **blown** [bləun] *pp of* **blow**; ~**out** *n* (*AUT*) geplatzte(r) Reifen *m*; ~**torch** *n* = **blowlamp**

blue [bluː] *adj* blau; (*inf: unhappy*) niedergeschlagen; (*obscene*) pornographisch; (*joke*) anzüglich; **out of the** ~ (*fig*) aus heiterem Himmel; **the** ~**s** traurig sein; ~**bell** *n* Glockenblume *f*; ~**bottle** *n* Schmeißfliege *f*; ~ **film** *n* Pornofilm *m*; ~**print** *n* (*fig*) Entwurf *m*

bluff [blʌf] *vi* bluffen, täuschen ♦ *n* (*deception*) Bluff *m*; **to call sb's** ~ es darauf ankommen lassen

blunder ['blʌndə*] *n* grobe(r) Fehler *m*, Schnitzer *m* ♦ *vi* einen groben Fehler machen

blunt [blʌnt] *adj* (*knife*) stumpf; (*talk*) unverblümt ♦ *vt* abstumpfen

blur [blɜː*] *n* Fleck *m* ♦ *vt* verschwommen machen

blurb [blɜːb] *n* Waschzettel *m*

blurt [blɜːt] *vt*: **to** ~ **out** herausplatzen mit

blush [blʌʃ] *vi* erröten ♦ *n* (Scham)röte *f*

blustery ['blʌstərɪ] *adj* stürmisch

boar [bɔː*] *n* Keiler *m*, Eber *m*

board [bɔːd] *n* (*of wood*) Brett *nt*; (*of card*) Pappe *f*; (*committee*) Ausschuß *m*; (*of firm*) Aufsichtsrat *m*; (*SCH*) Direktorium *nt* ♦ *vt* (*train*) einsteigen in +*acc*; (*ship*) an Bord gehen +*gen*; **on** ~ (*AVIAT, NAUT*) an Bord; ~ **and lodging** Unterkunft *f* und Verpflegung; **full/half** ~ Voll-/Halbpension *f*; **to go by the** ~ flachfallen, über Bord gehen; ~ **up** *vt* mit Brettern vernageln; ~**er** *n* Kostgänger *m*; (*SCH*) Internatsschüler(in) *m(f)*; ~**ing card** *n* (*AVIAT, NAUT*) Bordkarte *f*; ~**ing house** *n* Pension *f*; ~**ing school** *n* Internat *nt*; ~ **room** *n* Sitzungszimmer *nt*

boast [bəust] *vi* prahlen ♦ *vt* sich rühmen +*gen* ♦ *n* Großtuerei *f*; Prahlerei *f*; **to** ~ **about** *or* **of sth** mit etw prahlen

boat [bəut] *n* Boot *nt*; (*ship*) Schiff *nt*; ~**er** *n* (*hat*) Kreissäge *f*; ~**swain** *n* = **bosun**

bob [bɔb] *vi* sich auf und nieder bewegen ♦ *n* (*BRIT: inf*) = **shilling**; ~ **up** *vi* auftauchen

bobbin ['bɔbɪn] *n* Spule *f*

bobby ['bɔbɪ] (*BRIT: inf*) *n* Bobby *m*

bobsleigh ['bɔbsleɪ] *n* Bob *m*

bode [bəud] *vi*: **to** ~ **well/ill** ein gutes/ schlechtes Zeichen sein

bodily ['bɔdɪlɪ] *adj, adv* körperlich

body ['bɔdɪ] *n* Körper *m*; (*dead*) Leiche *f*; (*group*) Mannschaft *f*; (*AUT*) Karosserie *f*; (*trunk*) Rumpf *m*; ~**guard** *n* Leibwache *f*; ~**work** *n* Karosserie *f*

bog [bɔg] *n* Sumpf *m* ♦ *vt*: **to get** ~**ged down** sich festfahren

boggle ['bɔgl] *vi* stutzen; **the mind** ~**s** es ist kaum auszumalen

bogus ['bəugəs] *adj* unecht, Schein-

boil [bɔɪl] *vt, vi* kochen ♦ *n* (*MED*) Geschwür *nt*; **to come to the** (*BRIT*) *or* **a** (*US*) ~ zu kochen anfangen; **to** ~ **down**

to (fig) hinauslaufen auf +acc; ~ **over** vi überkochen; ~**ed potatoes** npl Salzkartoffeln pl; ~**er** n Boiler m; ~**er suit** (BRIT) n Arbeitsanzug m; ~**ing point** n Siedepunkt m
boisterous ['bɔɪstərəs] adj ungestüm
bold [bəʊld] adj (fearless) unerschrocken; (handwriting) fest und klar
bollard ['bɒləd] n (NAUT) Poller m; (BRIT: AUT) Pfosten m
bolster ['bəʊlstə*] n Polster nt; ~ **up** vt unterstützen
bolt [bəʊlt] n Bolzen m; (lock) Riegel m ♦ adv: ~ **upright** kerzengerade ♦ vt verriegeln; (swallow) verschlingen ♦ vi (horse) durchgehen
bomb [bɒm] n Bombe f ♦ vt bombardieren; ~**ard** [bɒm'ba:d] vt bombardieren; ~**ardment** [bɒm'ba:d-mənt] n Beschießung f; ~**shell** n (fig) Bombe f
bona fide ['bəʊnə'faɪdɪ] adj echt
bond [bɒnd] n (link) Band nt; (FIN) Schuldverschreibung f
bondage ['bɒndɪdʒ] n Sklaverei f
bone [bəʊn] n Knochen m; (of fish) Gräte f; (piece of ~) Knochensplitter m ♦ vt die Knochen herausnehmen +dat; (fish) entgräten; ~ **idle** adj stinkfaul
bonfire ['bɒnfaɪə*] n Feuer nt im Freien
bonnet ['bɒnɪt] n Haube f; (for baby) Häubchen nt; (BRIT: AUT) Motorhaube f
bonus ['bəʊnəs] n Bonus m; (annual ~) Prämie f
bony ['bəʊnɪ] adj knochig, knochendürr
boo [bu:] vt auspfeifen
booby trap ['bu:bɪ-] n Falle f
book [bʊk] n Buch nt ♦ vt (ticket etc) vorbestellen; (person) verwarnen; ~**s** npl (COMM) Bücher pl; ~**case** n Bücherregal nt, Bücherschrank m; ~**ing office** (BRIT) n (RAIL) Fahrkarten-schalter m; (THEAT) Vorverkaufsstelle f; ~**-keeping** n Buchhaltung f; ~**let** n Broschüre f; ~**maker** n Buchmacher m; ~**seller** n Buchhändler m; ~**shop** n Buchhandlung f; ~ **store** n Buchhand-lung f
boom [bu:m] n (noise) Dröhnen nt;

(busy period) Hochkonjunktur f ♦ vi dröhnen
boon [bu:n] n Wohltat f, Segen m
boost [bu:st] n Auftrieb m; (fig) Re-klame f ♦ vt Auftrieb geben; ~**er** n (MED) Wiederholungsimpfung f
boot [bu:t] n Stiefel m; (BRIT: AUT) Kofferraum m ♦ vt (kick) einen Fuß-tritt geben; (COMPUT) laden; **to** ~ (in addition) obendrein
booth [bu:ð] n (at fair) Bude f; (tele-phone ~) Zelle f; (voting ~) Kabine f
booty ['bu:tɪ] n Beute f
booze [bu:z] (inf) n Alkohol m, Schnaps m ♦ vi saufen
border ['bɔ:də*] n Grenze f; (edge) Kante f; (in garden) (Blumen)rabatte f ♦ adj Grenz-; **the B~s** Grenzregion f zwischen England und Schottland; ~ **on** vt grenzen an +acc; ~**line** n Grenze f
bore [bɔ:*] pt of bear ♦ vt bohren; (weary) langweilen ♦ n (person) Lang-weiler m; (thing) langweilige Sache f; (of gun) Kaliber nt; **I am** ~**d** ich lang-weile mich; ~**dom** n Langeweile f
boring ['bɔ:rɪŋ] adj langweilig
born [bɔ:n] adj: **to be** ~ geboren werden
borne [bɔ:n] pp of bear
borough ['bʌrə] n Stadt(gemeinde) f, Stadtbezirk m
borrow ['bɒrəʊ] vt borgen
bosom ['bʊzəm] n Busen m
boss [bɒs] n Chef m, Boß m ♦ vt: **to** ~ **around** herumkommandieren; ~**y** adj herrisch
bosun ['bəʊsn] n Bootsmann m
botany ['bɒtənɪ] n Botanik f
botch [bɒtʃ] vt (also: ~ up) verpfu-schen
both [bəʊθ] adj beide(s) ♦ pron beide(s) ♦ adv: ~ **X and Y** sowohl X wie or als auch Y; ~ **(of) the books** beide Bücher
bother ['bɒðə*] vt (pester) quälen ♦ vi (fuss) sich aufregen ♦ n Mühe f, Um-stand m; **to** ~ **doing sth** sich dat die Mühe machen, etw zu tun; **what a** ~! wie ärgerlich!
bottle ['bɒtl] n Flasche f ♦ vt (in Fla-schen) abfüllen; ~ **up** vt aufstauen;

~**neck** n (also fig) Engpaß m; ~-**opener** n Flaschenöffner m

bottom ['bɒtəm] n Boden m; (of person) Hintern m; (riverbed) Flußbett nt ♦ adj unterste(r, s)

bough [baʊ] n Zweig m, Ast m

bought [bɔːt] pt, pp of **buy**

boulder ['bəʊldə*] n Felsbrocken m

bounce [baʊns] vi (ball) hochspringen; (person) herumhüpfen; (cheque) platzen ♦ vt (auf)springen lassen ♦ n (rebound) Aufprall m; ~**r** n Rausschmeißer m

bound [baʊnd] pt, pp of **bind** ♦ n Grenze f; (leap) Sprung m ♦ vi (spring, leap) (auf)springen ♦ adj (obliged) gebunden, verpflichtet; **out of** ~**s** Zutritt verboten; **to be** ~ **to do sth** verpflichtet sein, etw zu tun; **it's** ~ **to happen** es muß so kommen; **to be** ~ **for ...** nach ... fahren

boundary ['baʊndərɪ] n Grenze f

bouquet [bʊ'keɪ] n Strauß m; (of wine) Blume f

bourgeois ['bʊəʒwɑː] adj kleinbürgerlich, bourgeois ♦ n Spießbürger(in) m(f)

bout [baʊt] n (of illness) Anfall m; (of contest) Kampf m

bow[1] [bəʊ] n (ribbon) Schleife f; (weapon, MUS) Bogen m

bow[2] [baʊ] n (with head, body) Verbeugung f; (of ship) Bug m ♦ vi sich verbeugen; (submit): **to** ~ **to** to sich beugen +dat

bowels ['baʊəlz] npl Darm m; (centre) Innere nt

bowl [bəʊl] n (basin) Schüssel f; (of pipe) (Pfeifen)kopf m; (wooden ball) (Holz)kugel f ♦ vt, vi (die Kugel) rollen; ~**s** n (game) Bowls-Spiel nt

bow-legged ['bəʊ'legɪd] adj o-beinig

bowler ['bəʊlə*] n Werfer m; (BRIT: also: ~ **hat**) Melone f

bowling ['bəʊlɪŋ] n Kegeln nt; ~ **alley** n Kegelbahn f; ~ **green** n Rasen m zum Bowling-Spiel

bow tie ['bəʊ-] n Fliege f

box [bɒks] n (also: cardboard ~) Schachtel f; (bigger) Kasten m; (THEAT) Loge f ♦ vt einpacken ♦ vi

boxen; ~**er** n Boxer m; ~**ing** n (SPORT) Boxen nt; **B**~**ing Day** (BRIT) n zweite(r) Weihnachtsfeiertag m; ~**ing gloves** npl Boxhandschuhe pl; ~**ing ring** n Boxring m; ~ **office** n (Theater)kasse f; ~**room** n Rumpelkammer f

boy [bɔɪ] n Junge m

boycott ['bɔɪkɒt] n Boykott m ♦ vt boykottieren

boyfriend ['bɔɪfrend] n Freund m

boyish ['bɔɪʃ] adj jungenhaft

B.R. n abbr = **British Rail**

bra [brɑː] n BH m

brace [breɪs] n (TECH) Stütze f; (MED) Klammer f ♦ vt stützen; ~**s** npl (BRIT) Hosenträger pl; **to** ~ **o.s. for sth** (fig) sich auf etw acc gefaßt machen

bracelet ['breɪslɪt] n Armband nt

bracing ['breɪsɪŋ] adj kräftigend

bracken ['brækən] n Farnkraut nt

bracket ['brækɪt] n Halter m, Klammer f; (in punctuation) Klammer f; (group) Gruppe f ♦ vt einklammern; (fig) in dieselbe Gruppe einordnen

brag [bræg] vi sich rühmen

braid [breɪd] n (hair) Flechte f; (trim) Borte f

Braille [breɪl] n Blindenschrift f

brain [breɪn] n (ANAT) Gehirn nt; (intellect) Intelligenz f, Verstand m; (person) kluge(r) Kopf m; ~**s** npl (intelligence) Verstand m; ~**child** n Erfindung f; ~**wash** vt eine Gehirnwäsche vornehmen bei; ~**wave** n Geistesblitz m; ~**y** adj gescheit

braise [breɪz] vt schmoren

brake [breɪk] n Bremse f ♦ vt, vi bremsen; ~ **fluid** n Bremsflüssigkeit f; ~ **light** n Bremslicht nt

bramble ['bræmbl] n Brombeere f

bran [bræn] n Kleie f; (food) Frühstückflocken pl

branch [brɑːntʃ] n Ast m; (division) Zweig m ♦ vi (also: ~ out: road) sich verzweigen

brand [brænd] n (COMM) Marke f, Sorte f; (on cattle) Brandmal nt ♦ vt brandmarken; (COMM) ein Warenzeichen geben +dat

brandish ['brændɪʃ] *vt* (drohend) schwingen

brand-new ['brænd'njuː] *adj* funkelnagelneu

brandy ['brændɪ] *n* Weinbrand *m*, Kognak *m*

brash [bræʃ] *adj* unverschämt

brass [brɑːs] *n* Messing *nt*; **the** (MUS) das Blech; ~ **band** *n* Blaskapelle *f*

brassière ['bræsɪə*] *n* Büstenhalter *m*

brat [bræt] *n* Gör *nt*

bravado [brə'vɑːdəʊ] *n* Tollkühnheit *f*

brave [breɪv] *adj* tapfer ♦ *n* indianische(r) Krieger *m* ♦ *vt* die Stirn bieten +*dat*

bravery ['breɪvərɪ] *n* Tapferkeit *f*

brawl [brɔːl] *n* Rauferei *f*

brawn [brɔːn] *n* (ANAT) Muskeln *pl*; (*strength*) Muskelkraft *f*

bray [breɪ] *vi* schreien

brazen ['breɪzn] *adj* (*shameless*) unverschämt ♦ *vt*: **to ~ it out** sich mit Lügen und Betrügen durchsetzen

brazier ['breɪzɪə*] *n* (*of workmen*) offene(r) Kohlenofen *m*

Brazil [brə'zɪl] *n* Brasilien *nt*; ~**ian** *adj* brasilianisch ♦ *n* Brasilianer(in) *m(f)*

breach [briːtʃ] *n* (*gap*) Lücke *f*; (MIL) Durchbruch *m*; (*of discipline*) Verstoß *m* (gegen die Disziplin); (*of faith*) Vertrauensbruch *m* ♦ *vt* durchbrechen; ~ **of contract** Vertragsbruch *m*; ~ **of the peace** öffentliche Ruhestörung *f*

bread [bred] *n* Brot *nt*; ~ **and butter** Butterbrot *nt*; ~**bin** *n* Brotkasten *m*; ~**box** (US) *n* Brotkasten *m*; ~**crumbs** *npl* Brotkrumen *pl*; (COOK) Paniermehl *nt*; ~**line** *n*: **to be on the ~line** sich gerade so durchschlagen

breadth [bretθ] *n* Breite *f*

breadwinner ['bredwɪnə*] *n* Ernährer *m*

break [breɪk] (*pt* **broke**, *pp* **broken**) *vt* (*destroy*) (ab- *or* zer)brechen; (*promise*) brechen, nicht einhalten ♦ *vi* (*fall apart*) auseinanderbrechen; (*collapse*) zusammenbrechen; (*dawn*) anbrechen ♦ *n* (*gap*) Lücke *f*; (*chance*) Chance *f*, Gelegenheit *f*; (*fracture*) Bruch *m*; (*rest*) Pause *f*; ~ **down** *vt*

(*figures, data*) aufschlüsseln; (*undermine*) überwinden ♦ *vi* (*car*) eine Panne haben; (*person*) zusammenbrechen; ~ **even** *vi* die Kosten decken; ~ **free** *vi* sich losreißen; ~ **in** *vt* (*animal*) abrichten; (*horse*) zureiten ♦ *vi* (*burglar*) einbrechen; ~ **into** *vt fus* (*house*) einbrechen in +*acc*; ~ **loose** *vi* sich losreißen; ~ **off** *vi* abbrechen; ~ **open** *vt* (*door etc*) aufbrechen; ~ **out** *vi* ausbrechen; **to ~ out in spots** Pickel bekommen; ~ **up** *vi* zerbrechen; (*fig*) sich zerstreuen; (BRIT: SCH) in die Ferien gehen ♦ *vt* brechen; ~**age** *n* Bruch *m*, Beschädigung *f*; ~**down** *n* (TECH) Panne *f*; (MED: *also:* **nervous ~down**) Zusammenbruch *m*; ~**down van** (BRIT) *n* Abschleppwagen *m*; ~**er** *n* Brecher *m*

breakfast ['brekfəst] *n* Frühstück *nt*

break: ~**-in** *n* Einbruch *m*; ~**ing** *n*: ~**ing and entering** (JUR) Einbruch *m*; ~**through** *n* Durchbruch *m*; ~**water** *n* Wellenbrecher *m*

breast [brest] *n* Brust *f*; ~**-feed** (*irreg: like* **feed**) *vt, vi* stillen; ~**-stroke** *n* Brustschwimmen *nt*

breath [breθ] *n* Atem *m*; **out of ~** außer Atem; **under one's ~** flüsternd

Breathalyzer ['breθəlaɪzə*] (®) *n* Röhrchen *nt*

breathe [briːð] *vt, vi* atmen; ~ **in** *vt, vi* einatmen; ~ **out** *vt, vi* ausatmen; ~**r** *n* Verschnaufpause *f*

breathing ['briːðɪŋ] *n* Atmung *f*

breathless ['breθlɪs] *adj* atemlos

breathtaking ['breθteɪkɪŋ] *adj* atemberaubend

bred [bred] *pt, pp of* **breed**

breed [briːd] (*pt, pp* **bred**) *vi* sich vermehren ♦ *vt* züchten ♦ *n* (*race*) Rasse *f*, Zucht *f*; ~**er** *n* (*person*) Züchter *m*; ~**ing** *n* Züchtung *f*; (*upbringing*) Erziehung *f*; (*education*) Bildung *f*

breeze [briːz] *n* Brise *f*

breezy ['briːzɪ] *adj* windig; (*manner*) munter

brevity ['brevɪtɪ] *n* Kürze *f*

brew [bruː] *vt* brauen; (*plot*) anzetteln ♦ *vi* (*storm*) sich zusammenziehen;

~ery n Brauerei f
bribe ['braɪb] n Bestechungsgeld nt/ Bestechungsgeschenk nt ♦ vt bestechen; **~ry** ['braɪbərɪ] n Bestechung f
bric-a-brac ['brɪkəbræk] n Nippes pl
brick [brɪk] n Backstein m; **~layer** n Maurer m; **~works** n Ziegelei f
bridal ['braɪdl] adj Braut-
bride [braɪd] n Braut f; **~groom** n Bräutigam m; **~smaid** n Brautjungfer f
bridge [brɪdʒ] n Brücke f; (NAUT) Kommandobrücke f; (CARDS) Bridge nt; (ANAT) Nasenrücken m ♦ vt eine Brücke schlagen über +acc; (fig) überbrücken
bridle ['braɪdl] n Zaum m ♦ vt (fig) zügeln; (horse) aufzäumen; **~ path** n Reitweg m
brief [briːf] adj kurz ♦ n (JUR) Akten pl ♦ vt instruieren; **~s** npl (underwear) Schlüpfer m, Slip m; **~case** n Aktentasche f; **~ing** n (genaue) Anweisung f; **~ly** adv kurz
brigadier [brɪgə'dɪə*] n Brigadegeneral m
bright [braɪt] adj hell; (cheerful) heiter; (idea) klug; **~en (up)** ['braɪtn-] vt aufhellen; (person) aufheitern ♦ vi sich aufheitern
brilliance ['brɪljəns] n Glanz m; (of person) Scharfsinn m
brilliant ['brɪljənt] adj glänzend
brim [brɪm] n Rand m
brine [braɪn] n Salzwasser nt
bring [brɪŋ] (pt, pp brought) vt bringen; **~ about** vt zustande bringen; **~ back** vt zurückbringen; **~ down** vt (price) senken; **~ forward** vt (meeting) vorverlegen; (COMM) übertragen; **~ in** vt hereinbringen; (harvest) einbringen; **~ off** vt davontragen; (success) erzielen; **~ out** vt (object) herausbringen; **~ round** or **to** vt wieder zu sich bringen; **~ up** vt aufziehen; (question) zur Sprache bringen
brink [brɪŋk] n Rand m
brisk [brɪsk] adj lebhaft
brisket ['brɪskɪt] n Bruststück nt
bristle ['brɪsl] n Borste f ♦ vi sich

sträuben; **bristling with** strotzend vor +dat
Britain ['brɪtən] n (also: Great ~) Großbritannien nt
British ['brɪtɪʃ] adj britisch ♦ npl: **the ~** die Briten pl; **the ~ Isles** npl die Britischen Inseln pl; **~ Rail** n die Britischen Eisenbahnen pl
Briton ['brɪtən] n Brite m, Britin f
brittle ['brɪtl] adj spröde
broach [brəʊtʃ] vt (subject) anschneiden
broad [brɔːd] adj breit; (hint) deutlich; (daylight) hellicht; (general) allgemein; (accent) stark; **in ~ daylight** am hellichten Tag; **~cast** (pt, pp broadcast) n Rundfunkübertragung f ♦ vt, vi übertragen, senden; **~en** vt erweitern ♦ vi sich erweitern; **~ly** adv allgemein gesagt; **~-minded** adj tolerant
broccoli ['brɒkəlɪ] n Brokkoli pl
brochure ['brəʊʃʊə*] n Broschüre f
broil [brɔɪl] vt (grill) grillen
broke [brəʊk] pt of break ♦ adj (inf) pleite
broken ['brəʊkən] pp of break ♦ adj: **~ leg** gebrochenes Bein; **in ~ English** in gebrochenem Englisch; **~-hearted** adj untröstlich
broker ['brəʊkə*] n Makler m
brolly ['brɒlɪ] (BRIT: inf) n Schirm m
bronchitis [brɒŋ'kaɪtɪs] n Bronchitis f
bronze [brɒnz] n Bronze f
brooch [brəʊtʃ] n Brosche f
brood [bruːd] n Brut f ♦ vi brüten
brook [brʊk] n Bach m
broom [bruːm] n Besen m; **~stick** n Besenstiel m
Bros. abbr = Brothers
broth [brɒθ] n Suppe f, Fleischbrühe f
brothel ['brɒθl] n Bordell nt
brother ['brʌðə*] n Bruder m; **~-in-law** n Schwager m
brought [brɔːt] pt, pp of bring
brow [braʊ] n (eyebrow) (Augen)braue f; (forehead) Stirn f; (of hill) Bergkuppe f
brown [braʊn] adj braun ♦ n Braun nt ♦ vt bräunen; **~ bread** n Mischbrot nt; **B~ie** n Wichtel m; **~ paper**

Packpapier *nt*; ~ **sugar** *n* braune(r) Zucker *m*

browse [brauz] *vi* (*in books*) blättern; (*in shop*) schmökern, herumschauen

bruise [bru:z] *n* Bluterguß *m*, blaue(r) Fleck *m* ♦ *vt* einen blauen Fleck geben ♦ *vi* einen blauen Fleck bekommen

brunt [brʌnt] *n* volle Wucht *f*

brush [brʌʃ] *n* Bürste *f*; (*for sweeping*) Handbesen *m*; (*for painting*) Pinsel *m*; (*fight*) kurze(r) Kampf *m*; (*MIL*) Scharmützel *nt*; (*fig*) Auseinandersetzung *f* ♦ *vt* (*clean*) bürsten; (*sweep*) fegen; (*usu*: ~ *past*, ~ *against*) streifen; ~ **aside** *vt* abtun; ~ **up** *vt* (*knowledge*) auffrischen; ~**wood** *n* Gestrüpp *nt*

brusque [bru:sk] *adj* schroff

Brussels ['brʌslz] *n* Brüssel *nt*; ~ **sprout** *n* Rosenkohl *m*

brutal ['bru:tl] *adj* brutal

brute [bru:t] *n* (*person*) Scheusal *nt* ♦ *adj*: **by** ~ **force** mit roher Kraft

B.Sc. *n abbr* = **Bachelor of Science**

bubble ['bʌbl] *n* (Luft)blase *f* ♦ *vi* sprudeln; (*with joy*) übersprudeln; ~ **bath** *n* Schaumbad *nt*; ~**gum** *n* Kaugummi *m or nt*

buck [bʌk] *n* Bock *m*; (*US*: *inf*) Dollar *m* ♦ *vi* bocken; **to pass the** ~ (**to sb**) die Verantwortung (auf jdn) abschieben; ~ **up** (*inf*) *vi* sich zusammenreißen

bucket ['bʌkɪt] *n* Eimer *m*

buckle ['bʌkl] *n* Schnalle *f* ♦ *vt* (an- or zusammen)schnallen ♦ *vi* (*bend*) sich verziehen

bud [bʌd] *n* Knospe *f* ♦ *vi* knospen, keimen

Buddhism ['budɪzəm] *n* Buddhismus *m*

budding ['bʌdɪŋ] *adj* angehend

buddy ['bʌdɪ] (*inf*) *n* Kumpel *m*

budge [bʌdʒ] *vt*, *vi* (sich) von der Stelle rühren

budgerigar ['bʌdʒərɪga:*] *n* Wellensittich *m*

budget ['bʌdʒɪt] *n* Budget *nt*; (*POL*) Haushalt *m* ♦ *vi*: **to** ~ **for sth** etw einplanen

budgie ['bʌdʒɪ] *n* = **budgerigar**

buff [bʌf] *adj* (*colour*) lederfarben ♦ *n* (*enthusiast*) Fan *m*

buffalo ['bʌfələu] (*pl* ~ *or* ~**es**) *n* (*BRIT*) Büffel *m*; (*US*: *bison*) Bison *m*

buffer ['bʌfə*] *n* Puffer *m*; (*COMPUT*) Pufferspeicher *m*

buffet¹ ['bʌfɪt] *n* (*blow*) Schlag *m* ♦ *vt* (herum)stoßen

buffet² ['bufeɪ] (*BRIT*) *n* (*bar*) Imbißraum *m*, Erfrischungsraum *m*; (*food*) (kaltes) Büffet *nt*; ~ **car** (*BRIT*) *n* Speisewagen *m*

bug [bʌg] *n* (*also fig*) Wanze *f* ♦ *vt* verwanzen

bugle ['bju:gl] *n* Jagdhorn *nt*; (*MIL*: *MUS*) Bügelhorn *nt*

build [bɪld] (*pt*, *pp* **built**) *vt* bauen ♦ *n* Körperbau *m*; ~ **up** *vt* aufbauen; ~**er** *n* Bauunternehmer *m*; ~**ing** *n* Gebäude *nt*; ~**ing society** (*BRIT*) *n* Bausparkasse *f*

built [bɪlt] *pt*, *pp of* **build**

built-in *adj* (*cupboard*) eingebaut

built-up area *n* Wohngebiet *nt*

bulb [bʌlb] *n* (*BOT*) (Blumen)zwiebel *f*; (*ELEC*) Glühlampe *f*, Birne *f*

Bulgaria [bʌl'geərɪə] *n* Bulgarien *nt*; ~**n** *adj* bulgarisch ♦ *n* Bulgare *m*, Bulgarin *f*; (*LING*) Bulgarisch *nt*

bulge [bʌldʒ] *n* (Aus)bauchung *f* ♦ *vi* sich (aus)bauchen

bulk [bʌlk] *n* Größe *f*, Masse *f*; (*greater part*) Großteil *m*; **in** ~ (*COMM*) en gros; **the** ~ **of** der größte Teil +*gen*; ~**head** *n* Schott *nt*; ~**y** *adj* (sehr) umfangreich; (*goods*) sperrig

bull [bul] *n* (*animal*) Bulle *m*; (*cattle*) Stier *m*; (*papal*) Bulle *f*; ~**dog** *n* Bulldogge *f*

bulldozer ['buldəuzə*] *n* Planierraupe *f*

bullet ['bulɪt] *n* Kugel *f*

bulletin ['bulɪtɪn] *n* Bulletin *nt*, Bekanntmachung *f*

bulletproof ['bulɪtpru:f] *adj* kugelsicher

bullfight ['bulfaɪt] *n* Stierkampf *m*; ~**er** *n* Stierkämpfer *m*; ~**ing** *n* Stierkampf *m*

bullion ['buliən] *n* Barren *m*

bullock ['bulək] *n* Ochse *m*

bullring ['bulrɪŋ] *n* Stierkampfarena *f*

bull's-eye ['bulzaɪ] n Zentrum nt
bully ['bulɪ] n Raufbold m ♦ vt einschüchtern
bum [bʌm] n (inf: backside) Hintern m; (tramp) Landstreicher m
bumblebee ['bʌmblbiː] n Hummel f
bump [bʌmp] n (blow) Stoß m; (swelling) Beule f ♦ vt, vi stoßen, prallen; ~ **into** vt fus stoßen gegen ♦ vt (person) treffen; ~ **cars** (US) npl (dodgems) Autoskooter pl; ~**er** n (AUT) Stoßstange f ♦ adj (edition) dick; (harvest) Rekord-
bumptious ['bʌmpʃəs] adj aufgeblasen
bumpy ['bʌmpɪ] adj holprig
bun [bʌn] n Korinthenbrötchen nt
bunch [bʌntʃ] n (of flowers) Strauß m; (of keys) Bund m; (of people) Haufen m
bundle ['bʌndl] n Bündel nt ♦ vt (also: ~ up) bündeln
bungalow ['bʌŋgələu] n einstöckige(s) Haus nt, Bungalow m
bungle ['bʌŋgl] vt verpfuschen
bunion ['bʌnjən] n entzündete(r) Fußballen m
bunk [bʌŋk] n Schlafkoje f; ~ **beds** npl Etagenbett nt
bunker ['bʌŋkə*] n (coal store) Kohlenbunker m; (GOLF) Sandloch nt
bunny ['bʌnɪ] n (also: ~ rabbit) Häschen nt
bunting ['bʌntɪŋ] n Fahnentuch nt
buoy [bɔɪ] n Boje f; (life~) Rettungsboje f; ~ **up** vt Auftrieb geben +dat; ~**ant** adj (floating) schwimmend; (fig) heiter
burden ['bɜːdn] n (weight) Ladung f, Last f; (fig) Bürde f ♦ vt belasten
bureau ['bjuərəu] n (pl ~x) n (BRIT: writing desk) Sekretär m; (US: chest of drawers) Kommode f; (for information etc) Büro nt
bureaucracy [bjuˈrɒkrəsɪ] n Bürokratie f
bureaucrat ['bjuərəkræt] n Bürokrat(in) m(f)
bureaux ['bjuərəuz] npl of **bureau**
burglar ['bɜːglə*] n Einbrecher m; ~ **alarm** n Einbruchssicherung f; ~**y** n Einbruch m

burial ['berɪəl] n Beerdigung f
burly ['bɜːlɪ] adj stämmig
Burma ['bɜːmə] n Birma nt
burn [bɜːn] (pt, pp burned or burnt) vt verbrennen ♦ vi brennen ♦ n Brandwunde f; ~ **down** vt, vi abbrennen; ~**er** n Brenner m, ~**ing** adj brennend; **burnt** [bɜːnt] pt, pp of **burn**
burrow ['bʌrəu] n (of fox) Bau m; (of rabbit) Höhle f ♦ vt eingraben
bursar ['bɜːsə*] n Kassenverwalter m, Quästor m; ~**y** n (BRIT) Stipendium nt
burst [bɜːst] (pt, pp burst) vt zerbrechen ♦ vi platzen ♦ n Explosion f; (outbreak) Ausbruch m; (in pipe) Bruch(stelle f) m; **to ~ into flames** in Flammen aufgehen; **to ~ into tears** in Tränen ausbrechen; **to ~ out laughing** in Gelächter ausbrechen; ~ **into** vt fus (room etc) platzen in +acc; ~ **open** vi aufbrechen
bury ['berɪ] vt vergraben; (in grave) beerdigen
bus [bʌs] n (Auto)bus m, Omnibus m
bush [buʃ] n Busch m; **to beat about the** ~ wie die Katze um den heißen Brei herumgehen
bushy ['buʃɪ] adj buschig
busily ['bɪzɪlɪ] adv geschäftig
business ['bɪznɪs] n Geschäft nt; (concern) Angelegenheit f; **it's none of your** ~ es geht dich nichts an; **to mean** ~ es ernst meinen; **to be away on** ~ geschäftlich verreist sein; **it's my** ~ **to ...** es ist meine Sache, zu ...; ~**like** adj geschäftsmäßig; ~**man** (irreg) n Geschäftsmann m; ~ **trip** n Geschäftsreise f; ~**woman** (irreg) n Geschäftsfrau f
busker ['bʌskə*] (BRIT) n Straßenmusikant m
bus stop n Bushaltestelle f
bust [bʌst] n Büste f ♦ adj (broken) kaputt(gegangen); (business) pleite; **to go** ~ pleite machen
bustle ['bʌsl] n Getriebe nt ♦ vi hasten
bustling ['bʌslɪŋ] adj geschäftig
busy ['bɪzɪ] adj beschäftigt; (road) belebt ♦ vt: **to ~ o.s.** sich beschäftigen; ~**body** n Übereifrige(r)

mf; ~ **signal** (*US*) *n* (*TEL*) Besetztzeichen *nt*

but [bʌt] *conj* 1 (*yet*) aber; **not X but Y** nicht X sondern Y

2 (*however*): **I'd love to come, but I'm busy** ich würde gern kommen, bin aber beschäftigt

3 (*showing disagreement, surprise etc*): **but that's fantastic!** (aber) das ist ja fantastisch!

♦ *prep* (*apart from, except*): **nothing but trouble** nichts als Ärger; **no-one but him can do it** niemand außer ihn kann es machen; **but for you/your help** ohne dich/deine Hilfe; **anything but that** alles, nur das nicht

♦ *adv* (*just, only*): **she's but a child** sie ist noch ein Kind; **had I but known** wenn ich es nur gewußt hätte; **I can but try** ich kann es immerhin versuchen; **all but finished** so gut wie fertig

butcher ['butʃə*] *n* Metzger *m*; (*murderer*) Schlächter *m* ♦ *vt* schlachten; (*kill*) abschlachten; ~**'s** (**shop**) *n* Metzgerei *f*

butler ['bʌtlə*] *n* Butler *m*

butt [bʌt] *n* (*cask*) große(s) Faß *nt*; (*BRIT*: *fig*: *target*) Zielscheibe *f*; (*thick end*) dicke(s) Ende *nt*; (*of gun*) Kolben *m*; (*of cigarette*) Stummel *m* ♦ *vt* (*mit dem Kopf*) stoßen; ~ **in** *vi* (*interrupt*) sich einmischen

butter ['bʌtə*] *n* Butter *f* ♦ *vt* buttern; ~ **bean** *n* Wachsbohne *f*; ~**cup** *n* Butterblume *f*

butterfly ['bʌtəflaɪ] *n* Schmetterling *m*; (*SWIMMING*: *also* ~ **stroke**) Butterflystil *m*

buttocks ['bʌtəks] *npl* Gesäß *nt*

button ['bʌtn] *n* Knopf *m* ♦ *vt*, *vi* (*also*: ~ **up**) zuknöpfen

buttress ['bʌtrɪs] *n* Strebepfeiler *m*; Stützbogen *m*

buxom ['bʌksəm] *adj* drall

buy [baɪ] (*pt, pp* **bought**) *vt* kaufen ♦ *n* Kauf *m*; **to** ~ **sb a drink** jdm einen Drink spendieren; ~**er** *n* Käufer(in)

m(f)

buzz [bʌz] *n* Summen *nt* ♦ *vi* summen

buzzer ['bʌzə*] *n* Summer *m*

buzz word *n* Modewort *nt*

by [baɪ] *prep* 1 (*referring to cause, agent*) von, durch; **killed by lightning** vom Blitz getötet; **a painting by Picasso** ein Gemälde von Picasso

2 (*referring to method, manner, means*): **by bus/car/train** mit dem Bus/ Auto/Zug; **to pay by cheque** per Scheck bezahlen; **by moonlight** bei Mondschein; **by saving hard, he** ... indem er eisern sparte, ... er ...

3 (*via, through*) über +*acc*; **he came in by the back door** er kam durch die Hintertür herein

4 (*close to, past*) bei, an +*dat*; **a holiday by the sea** ein Urlaub am Meer; **she rushed by me** sie eilte an mir vorbei

5 (*not later than*): **by 4 o'clock** bis 4 Uhr; **by this time tomorrow** morgen um diese Zeit; **by the time I got here it was too late** als ich hier ankam, war es zu spät

6 (*during*): **by day** bei Tag

7 (*amount*): **by the kilo/metre** kiloweise/meterweise; **paid by the hour** stundenweise bezahlt

8 (*MATH, measure*): **to divide by 3** durch 3 teilen; **to multiply by 3** mit 3 malnehmen; **a room 3 metres by 4** ein Zimmer 3 mal 4 Meter; **it's broader by a metre** es ist (um) einem Meter breiter

9 (*according to*) nach; **it's all right by me** von mir aus gern

10: (**all**) **by oneself** *etc* ganz allein

11: **by the way** übrigens ♦ *adv*

♦ *adv* 1 *see* **go**; **pass** *etc*

2: **by and by** irgendwann; (*with past tenses*) nach einiger Zeit; **by and large** (*on the whole*) im großen und ganzen

bye(-bye) ['baɪ('baɪ)] *excl* (auf) Wiedersehen

by(e)-law ['baɪlɔ:] *n* Verordnung *f*

by-election ['baɪɪ'lekʃən] (*BRIT*) *n* Nachwahl *f*

bygone ['baɪgɒn] *adj* vergangen ♦ *n*: let ~s be ~s laß(t) das Vergangene vergangen sein

bypass ['baɪpɑːs] *n* Umgehungsstraße *f* ♦ *vt* umgehen

by-product ['baɪprɒdʌkt] *n* Nebenprodukt *nt*

bystander ['baɪstændə*] *n* Zuschauer *m*

byte [baɪt] *n* (*COMPUT*) Byte *nt*

byword ['baɪwɜːd] *n* Inbegriff *m*

C

C [siː] *n* (*MUS*) C *nt*
C. *abbr* (= *centigrade*) C
C.A. *abbr* = **chartered accountant**
cab [kæb] *n* Taxi *nt*; (*of train*) Führerstand *m*; (*of truck*) Führersitz *m*

cabaret ['kæbəreɪ] *n* Kabarett *nt*

cabbage ['kæbɪdʒ] *n* Kohl(kopf) *m*

cabin ['kæbɪn] *n* Hütte *f*; (*NAUT*) Kajüte *f*; (*AVIAT*) Kabine *f*; ~ **cruiser** *n* Motorjacht *f*

cabinet ['kæbɪnɪt] *n* Schrank *m*; (*for china*) Vitrine *f*; (*POL*) Kabinett *nt*; ~-**maker** *n* Kunsttischler *m*

cable ['keɪbl] *n* Drahtseil *nt*, Tau *nt*; (*TEL*) (Leitungs)kabel *nt*; (*telegram*) Kabel *nt* ♦ *vt* kabeln, telegraphieren; ~-**car** *n* Seilbahn *f*; ~ **television** *n* Kabelfernsehen *nt*

cache [kæʃ] *n* geheime(s) (Waffen)lager *nt*; geheime(s) (Proviant)lager *nt*

cackle ['kækl] *vi* gackern

cacti ['kæktaɪ] *npl of* **cactus**

cactus ['kæktəs] (*pl* **cacti**) *n* Kaktus *m*, Kaktee *f*

caddie ['kædɪ] *n* (*GOLF*) Golfjunge *m*

caddy *n* = **caddie**

cadet [kə'det] *n* Kadett *m*

cadge [kædʒ] *vt* schmarotzen

Caesarean [siː'zeərɪən] *adj*: ~ (**section**) Kaiserschnitt *m*

café ['kæfɪ] *n* Café *nt*, Restaurant *nt*

cafeteria [kæfɪ'tɪərɪə] *n* Selbstbedienungsrestaurant *nt*

caffein(e) ['kæfiːn] *n* Koffein *nt*

cage [keɪdʒ] *n* Käfig *m* ♦ *vt* einsperren

cagey ['keɪdʒɪ] *adj* geheimnistuerisch, zurückhaltend

cagoule [kə'guːl] *n* Windhemd *nt*

Cairo ['kaɪərəʊ] *n* Kairo *nt*

cajole [kə'dʒəʊl] *vt* überreden

cake [keɪk] *n* Kuchen *m*; (*of soap*) Stück *nt*; ~**d** *adj* verkrustet

calamity [kə'læmɪtɪ] *n* Unglück *nt*, (Schicksals)schlag *m*

calcium ['kælsɪəm] *n* Kalzium *nt*

calculate ['kælkjʊleɪt] *vt* berechnen, kalkulieren; **calculating** *adj* berechnend; **calculation** [kælkjʊ'leɪʃən] *n* Berechnung *f*; **calculator** *n* Rechner *m*

calculus ['kælkjʊləs] *n* Infinitesimalrechnung *f*

calendar ['kælɪndə*] *n* Kalender *m*; ~ **month** *n* Kalendermonat *m*

calf [kɑːf] (*pl* **calves**) *n* Kalb *nt*; (*also*: ~*skin*) Kalbsleder *nt*; (*ANAT*) Wade *f*

calibre ['kælɪbə*] (*US* **caliber**) *n* Kaliber *nt*

call [kɔːl] *vt* rufen; (*name*) nennen; (*meeting*) einberufen; (*awaken*) wecken; (*TEL*) anrufen ♦ *vi* (*shout*) rufen; (*visit*: *also*: ~ **in**, ~ **round**) vorbeikommen ♦ *n* (*shout*) Ruf *m*; (*TEL*) Anruf *m*; **to be** ~**ed** heißen; **on** ~ in Bereitschaft; ~ **back** *vi* (*return*) wiederkommen; (*TEL*) zurückrufen; ~ **for** *vt fus* (*demand*) erfordern, verlangen; (*fetch*) abholen; ~ **off** *vt* (*cancel*) absagen; ~ **on** *vt fus* (*visit*) besuchen; (*turn to*) bitten; ~ **out** *vi* rufen; ~ **up** *vt* (*MIL*) einberufen; ~**box** (*BRIT*) *n* Telefonzelle *f*; ~**er** *n* Besucher(in) *m(f)*; (*TEL*) Anrufer *m*; ~ **girl** *n* Call-Girl *nt*; ~-**in** (*US*) *n* (*phone-in*) Phone-in *nt*; ~**ing** *n* (*vocation*) Berufung *f*; ~**ing card** (*US*) *n* Visitenkarte *f*

callous ['kæləs] *adj* herzlos

calm [kɑːm] *n* Ruhe *f*; (*NAUT*) Flaute *f* ♦ *vt* beruhigen ♦ *adj* ruhig; (*person*) gelassen; ~ **down** *vi* sich beruhigen ♦ *vt* beruhigen

Calor gas ['kælə-] (®) *n* Propangas *nt*

calorie ['kælərɪ] *n* Kalorie *f*

calve [kɑːv] *vi* kalben

calves [kɑːvz] *npl of* **calf**
camber ['kæmbə*] *n* Wölbung *f*
Cambodia [kæm'bəʊdjə] *n* Kambodscha *nt*
came [keɪm] *pt of* **come**
camel ['kæməl] *n* Kamel *nt*
cameo ['kæmɪəʊ] *n* Kamee *f*
camera ['kæmərə] *n* Fotoapparat *m*, (*CINE*, *TV*) Kamera *f*; **in ~** unter Ausschluß der Öffentlichkeit; **~man** (*irreg*) *n* Kameramann *m*
camouflage ['kæməflɑːʒ] *n* Tarnung *f* ♦ *vt* tarnen
camp [kæmp] *n* Lager *nt* ♦ *vi* zelten, campen ♦ *adj* affektiert
campaign [kæm'peɪn] *n* Kampagne *f*; (*MIL*) Feldzug *m* ♦ *vi* Krieg führen; (*fig*) werben, Propaganda machen; (*POL*) den Wahlkampf führen
campbed ['kæmp'bed] (*BRIT*) *n* Campingbett *nt*
camper ['kæmpə*] *n* Camper(in) *m(f)*; (*vehicle*) Camping-wagen *m*
camping ['kæmpɪŋ] *n*: **to go ~** zelten, Camping machen
campsite ['kæmpsaɪt] *n* Campingplatz *m*
campus ['kæmpəs] *n* Universitätsgelände *nt*, Campus *m*
can¹ [kæn] *n* Büchse *f*, Dose *f*; (*for water*) Kanne *f* ♦ *vt* konservieren, in Büchsen einmachen

---
KEYWORD
---

can² [kæn] (*negative* **cannot, can't**; *conditional* **could**) *aux vb* **1** (*be able to, know how to*) können; **I can see you tomorrow, if you like** ich könnte Sie morgen sehen, wenn Sie wollen; **I can swim** ich kann schwimmen; **can you speak German?** sprechen Sie Deutsch? **2** (*may*) können, dürfen; **could I have a word with you?** könnte ich Sie kurz sprechen?

Canada ['kænədə] *n* Kanada *nt*
Canadian [kə'neɪdɪən] *adj* kanadisch ♦ *n* Kanadier(in) *m(f)*
canal [kə'næl] *n* Kanal *m*
canary [kə'nɛərɪ] *n* Kanarienvogel *m*
cancel ['kænsəl] *vt* absagen; (*delete*)

durchstreichen; (*train*) streichen; **~lation** [kænsə'leɪʃən] *n* Absage *f*, Streichung *f*
cancer ['kænsə*] *n* (*also*: *ASTROL*: *C~*) Krebs *m*
candid ['kændɪd] *adj* offen, ehrlich
candidate ['kændɪdeɪt] *n* Kandidat(in) *m(f)*
candle ['kændl] *n* Kerze *f*; **~light** *n* Kerzenlicht *nt*; **~stick** *n* (*also*: ~ *holder*) Kerzenhalter *m*
candour ['kændə*] (*US* **candor**) *n* Offenheit *f*
candy ['kændɪ] *n* Kandis(zucker) *m*; (*US*) Bonbons *pl*; **~-floss** (*BRIT*) *n* Zuckerwatte *f*
cane [keɪn] *n* (*BOT*) Rohr *nt*; (*stick*) Stock *m* ♦ *vt* (*BRIT*: *SCH*) schlagen
canine ['kænaɪn] *adj* Hunde-
canister ['kænɪstə*] *n* Blechdose *f*
cannabis ['kænəbɪs] *n* Hanf *m*, Haschisch *nt*
canned [kænd] *adj* Büchsen-, eingemacht
cannibal ['kænɪbəl] *n* Menschenfresser *m*
cannon ['kænən] (*pl* ~ *or* ~s) *n* Kanone *f*
cannot ['kænɒt] = **can not**
canny ['kænɪ] *adj* schlau
canoe [kə'nuː] *n* Kanu *nt*
canon ['kænən] *n* (*clergyman*) Domherr *m*; (*standard*) Grundsatz *m*
canonize ['kænənaɪz] *vt* heiligsprechen
can-opener [-'əʊpnə*] *n* Büchsenöffner *m*
canopy ['kænəpɪ] *n* Baldachin *m*
can't [kɑːnt] – **can not**
cantankerous [kæn'tæŋkərəs] *adj* zänkisch, mürrisch
canteen [kæn'tiːn] *n* Kantine *f*; (*BRIT*: *of cutlery*) Besteckkasten *m*; (*bottle*) Feldflasche *f*
canter ['kæntə*] *n* Kanter *m* ♦ *vi* in kurzem Galopp reiten
canvas ['kænvəs] *n* Segeltuch *nt*; (*sail*) Segel *nt*; (*for painting*) Leinwand *f*; **under ~** (*camping*) in Zelten
canvass ['kænvəs] *vi* um Stimmen werben; **~ing** *n* Wahlwerbung *f*

canyon ['kænjən] *n* Felsenschlucht *f*

cap [kæp] *n* Mütze *f*; (*of pen*) Kappe *f*; (*of bottle*) Deckel *m* ♦ *vt* (*surpass*) übertreffen; (*SPORT*) aufstellen

capability [keɪpə'bɪlɪtɪ] *n* Fähigkeit *f*

capable ['keɪpəbl] *adj* fähig

capacity [kə'pæsɪtɪ] *n* Fassungsvermögen *nt*; (*ability*) Fähigkeit *f*; (*position*) Eigenschaft *f*

cape [keɪp] *n* (*garment*) Cape *nt*, Umhang *m*; (*GEOG*) Kap *nt*

caper ['keɪpə*] *n* (*COOK*: *usu*: ~s) Kaper *f*; (*prank*) Kapriole *f*

capital ['kæpɪtl] *n* (~ *city*) Hauptstadt *f*; (*FIN*) Kapital *nt*; (~ *letter*) Großbuchstabe *m*; ~ **gains tax** *n* Kapitalertragssteuer *f*; ~**ism** *n* Kapitalismus *m*; ~**ist** *adj* kapitalistisch ♦ *n* Kapitalist(in) *m(f)*; ~**ize** *vi*: **to** ~**ize on** Kapital schlagen aus; ~ **punishment** *n* Todesstrafe *f*

capitulate [kə'pɪtjuleɪt] *vi* kapitulieren

capricious [kə'prɪʃəs] *adj* launisch

Capricorn ['kæprɪkɔːn] *n* Steinbock *m*

capsize [kæp'saɪz] *vt, vi* kentern

capsule ['kæpsjuːl] *n* Kapsel *f*

captain ['kæptɪn] *n* Kapitän *m*; (*MIL*) Hauptmann *m* ♦ *vt* anführen

caption ['kæpʃən] *n* (*heading*) Überschrift *f*; (*to picture*) Unterschrift *f*

captivate ['kæptɪveɪt] *vt* fesseln

captive ['kæptɪv] *n* Gefangene(r) *mf* ♦ *adj* gefangen(gehalten)

captivity [kæp'tɪvɪtɪ] *n* Gefangenschaft *f*

capture ['kæptʃə*] *vt* gefangennehmen; (*place*) erobern; (*attention*) erregen ♦ *n* Gefangennahme *f*; (*data* ~) Erfassung *f*

car [kɑː*] *n* Auto *nt*, Wagen *m*; (*RAIL*) Wagen *m*

carafe [kə'ræf] *n* Karaffe *f*

caramel ['kærəməl] *n* Karamelle *f*

carat ['kærət] *n* Karat *nt*

caravan ['kærəvæn] *n* (*BRIT*) Wohnwagen *m*; (*in desert*) Karawane *f*; ~ **site** (*BRIT*) *n* Campingplatz *m* für Wohnwagen

carbohydrate [kɑːbəu'haɪdreɪt] *n* Kohlenhydrat *nt*

carbon ['kɑːbən] *n* Kohlenstoff *m*; ~ **copy** *n* Durchschlag *m*; ~ **paper** *n* Kohlepapier *nt*

carburettor ['kɑːbjuretə*] (*US* **carburetor**) *n* Vergaser *m*

carcass ['kɑːkəs] *n* Kadaver *m*

card [kɑːd] *n* Karte *f*; ~**board** *n* Pappe *f*; ~ **game** *n* Kartenspiel *nt*

cardiac ['kɑːdɪæk] *adj* Herz-

cardigan ['kɑːdɪgən] *n* Strickjacke *f*

cardinal ['kɑːdɪnl] *adj*: ~ **number** Kardinalzahl *f* ♦ *n* (*REL*) Kardinal *m*

card index *n* Kartei *f*; (*in library*) Katalog *m*

care [kɛə*] *n* (*of teeth, car etc*) Pflege *f*; (*of children*) Fürsorge *f*; (*carefulness*) Sorgfalt *f*; (*worry*) Sorge *f* ♦ *vi*: **to** ~ **about** sich kümmern um; ~ **of** bei; **in sb's** ~ in jds Obhut; **I don't** ~ das ist mir egal; **I couldn't** ~ **less** es ist mir doch völlig egal; **to take** ~ aufpassen; **to take** ~ **of** sorgen für; **to take** ~ **to do sth** sich bemühen, etw zu tun; ~ **for** *vt* sorgen für; (*like*) mögen

career [kə'rɪə*] *n* Karriere *f*, Laufbahn *f* ♦ *vi* (*also*: ~ **along**) rasen

carefree ['kɛəfriː] *adj* sorgenfrei

careful ['kɛəful] *adj* sorgfältig; (**be**) ~! paß auf!

careless ['kɛəlɪs] *adj* nachlässig; ~**ness** *n* Nachlässigkeit *f*

caress [kə'res] *n* Liebkosung *f* ♦ *vt* liebkosen

caretaker ['kɛəteɪkə*] *n* Hausmeister *m*

car-ferry ['kɑːferɪ] *n* Autofähre *f*

cargo ['kɑːgəu] (*pl* ~**es**) *n* Schiffsladung *f*

car hire *n* Autovermietung *f*

Caribbean [kærɪ'biːən] *n*: **the** ~ (**Sea**) die Karibik

caricature ['kærɪkətjuə*] *n* Karikatur *f*

caring ['kɛərɪŋ] *adj* (*society, organization*) sozial eingestellt; (*person*) liebevoll

carnage ['kɑːnɪdʒ] *n* Blutbad *nt*

carnal ['kɑːnl] *adj* fleischlich

carnation [kɑː'neɪʃən] *n* Nelke *f*

carnival ['kɑːnɪvl] *n* Karneval *m*, Fasching *m*; (*US*: *fun fair*) Kirmes *f*

carnivorous [kɑː'nɪvərəs] *adj* fleischfressend

carol ['kærəl] n: **(Christmas)** ~ (Weihnachts)lied nt

carp [kɑːp] n (fish) Karpfen m; ~ **at** vt herumnörgeln an +dat

car park (BRIT) n Parkplatz m; (covered) Parkhaus nt

carpenter ['kɑːpɪntə*] n Zimmermann m

carpentry ['kɑːpɪntrɪ] n Zimmerei f

carpet ['kɑːpɪt] n Teppich m ♦ vt mit einem Teppich auslegen; ~ **slippers** npl Pantoffeln pl; ~ **sweeper** n Teppichkehrer m

carriage ['kærɪdʒ] n Kutsche f; (RAIL, of typewriter) Wagen m; (of goods) Beförderung f; (bearing) Haltung f; ~ **return** n (on typewriter) Rücklauftaste f; ~**way** (BRIT) n (part of road) Fahrbahn f

carrier ['kærɪə*] n Träger(in) m(f); (COMM) Spediteur m; ~ **bag** (BRIT) n Tragetasche m

carrot ['kærət] n Möhre f, Karotte f

carry ['kærɪ] vt, vi tragen; **to get carried away** (fig) sich nicht mehr bremsen können; ~ **on** vi (continue) weitermachen; (inf: complain) Theater machen; ~ **out** vt (orders) ausführen; (investigation) durchführen; ~**cot** (BRIT) n Babytragetasche f; ~**on** (inf) n (fuss) Theater nt

cart [kɑːt] n Wagen m, Karren m ♦ vt schleppen

cartilage ['kɑːtɪlɪdʒ] n Knorpel m

carton ['kɑːtən] n Karton m; (of milk) Tüte f

cartoon [kɑː'tuːn] n (PRESS) Karikatur f; (comic strip) Comics pl; (CINE) (Zeichen)trickfilm m

cartridge ['kɑːtrɪdʒ] n Patrone f

carve [kɑːv] vt (wood) schnitzen; (stone) meißeln; (meat) (vor-) schneiden; ~ **up** vt aufschneiden

carving ['kɑːvɪŋ] n Schnitzerei f; ~ **knife** n Tranchiermesser nt

car wash n Autowäsche f

cascade [kæs'keɪd] n Wasserfall m ♦ vi kaskadenartig herabfallen

case [keɪs] n (box) Kasten m; (BRIT:

also: suit~) Koffer m; (JUR, matter) Fall m; **in** ~ falls, im Falle; **in any** ~ jedenfalls, auf jeden Fall

cash [kæʃ] n (Bar)geld nt ♦ vt einlösen; ~ **on delivery** per Nachnahme; ~ **book** n Kassenbuch nt; ~ **card** n Scheckkarte f; ~ **desk** (BRIT) n Kasse f; ~ **dispenser** n Geldautomat m

cashew [kæ'ʃuː] n (also: ~ nut) Cashewnuß f

cash flow n Cash-flow m

cashier [kæ'ʃɪə*] n Kassierer(in) m(f)

cashmere ['kæʃmɪə*] n Kaschmirwolle f

cash register n Registrierkasse f

casing ['keɪsɪŋ] n Gehäuse nt

casino [kə'siːnəʊ] n Kasino nt

cask [kɑːsk] n Faß nt

casket ['kɑːskɪt] n Kästchen nt; (US: coffin) Sarg m

casserole ['kæsərəʊl] n Kasserolle f; (food) Auflauf m

cassette [kæ'set] n Kassette f; ~ **player** n Kassettengerät nt

cast [kɑːst] (pt, pp cast) vt werfen; (horns) verlieren; (metal) gießen; (THEAT) besetzen; (vote) abgeben ♦ n (THEAT) Besetzung f; (also: plaster ~) Gipsverband m; ~ **off** vi (NAUT) losmachen

castaway ['kɑːstəweɪ] n Schiffbrüchige(r) mf

caste [kɑːst] n Kaste f

caster sugar ['kɑːstə-] (BRIT) n Streuzucker m

casting vote ['kɑːstɪŋ-] (BRIT) n entscheidende Stimme f

cast iron n Gußeisen nt

castle ['kɑːsl] n Burg f; Schloß nt; (CHESS) Turm m

castor ['kɑːstə*] n (wheel) Laufrolle f

castor oil n Rizinusöl nt

castrate [kæs'treɪt] vt kastrieren

casual ['kæʒjʊl] adj (attitude) nachlässig; (dress) leger; (meeting) zufällig; (work) Gelegenheits-; ~**ly** adv (dress) zwanglos, leger; (remark) beiläufig

casualty ['kæʒjʊltɪ] n Verletzte(r) mf; (dead) Tote(r) mf; (also: ~ department) Unfallstation f

cat [kæt] n Katze f
catalogue ['kætəlɔg] (US **catalog**) n Katalog m ♦ vt katalogisieren
catalyst ['kætəlɪst] n Katalysator m
catapult ['kætəpʌlt] n Schleuder f
cataract ['kætərækt] n (MED) graue(r) Star m
catarrh [kə'tɑ:*] n Katarrh m
catastrophe [kə'tæstrəfɪ] n Katastrophe f
catch [kætʃ] (pt, pp **caught**) vt fangen; (arrest) fassen; (train) erreichen; (person: by surprise) ertappen; (also: ~ up) einholen ♦ vi (fire) in Gang kommen; (in branches etc) hängenbleiben ♦ n (fish etc) Fang m; (trick) Haken m; (of lock) Sperrhaken m; **to ~ an illness** sich dat eine Krankheit holen; **to ~ fire** Feuer fangen; ~ **on** vi (understand) begreifen; (grow popular) ankommen; ~ **up** vi (fig) aufholen
catching ['kætʃɪŋ] adj ansteckend
catchment area ['kætʃmənt-] (BRIT) n Einzugsgebiet nt
catch phrase n Slogan m
catchy ['kætʃɪ] adj (tune) eingängig
catechism ['kætɪkɪzəm] n Katechismus m
categoric(al) [kætə'gɔrɪk(l)] adj kategorisch
category ['kætɪgərɪ] n Kategorie f
cater ['keɪtə*] vi versorgen; ~ **for** (BRIT) vt fus (party) ausrichten; (needs) eingestellt sein auf +acc; ~**er** n Lieferant(in) m(f) von Speisen und Getränken; ~**ing** n Gastronomie f
caterpillar ['kætəpɪlə*] n Raupe f; ~ **track** n Gleiskette f
cathedral [kə'θi:drəl] n Kathedrale f, Dom m
catholic ['kæθəlɪk] adj (tastes etc) vielseitig; **C~** adj (REL) katholisch ♦ n Katholik(in) m(f)
cat's-eye ['kætsaɪ] (BRIT) n (AUT) Katzenauge nt
cattle ['kætl] npl Vieh nt
catty ['kætɪ] adj gehässig
caucus ['kɔ:kəs] n (POL) Gremium nt; (US: meeting) Sitzung f

caught [kɔ:t] pt, pp of **catch**
cauliflower ['kɒlɪflauə*] n Blumenkohl m
cause [kɔ:z] n Ursache f; (purpose) Sache f ♦ vt verursachen
causeway ['kɔ:zweɪ] n Damm m
caustic ['kɔ:stɪk] adj ätzend; (fig) bissig
caution ['kɔ:ʃən] n Vorsicht f; (warning) Verwarnung f ♦ vt verwarnen
cautious ['kɔ:ʃəs] adj vorsichtig
cavalier [kævə'lɪə*] adj blasiert
cavalry ['kævəlrɪ] n Kavallerie f
cave [keɪv] n Höhle f; ~ **in** vi einstürzen; ~**man** (irreg) n Höhlenmensch m
cavern ['kævən] n Höhle f
caviar(e) ['kævɪɑ:*] n Kaviar m
cavity ['kævɪtɪ] n Loch nt
cavort [kə'vɔ:t] vi umherspringen
C.B. n abbr (= Citizens' Band (Radio)) CB
C.B.I. n abbr (= Confederation of British Industry) ≈ BDI m
cc n abbr = **carbon copy**; **cubic centimetres**
cease [si:s] vi aufhören ♦ vt beenden; ~**fire** n Feuereinstellung f; ~**less** adj unaufhörlich
cedar ['si:də*] n Zeder f
cede [si:d] vt abtreten
ceiling ['si:lɪŋ] n Decke f; (fig) Höchstgrenze f
celebrate ['selɪbreɪt] vt, vi feiern; ~**d** adj gefeiert
celebration [selɪ'breɪʃən] n Feier f
celebrity [sɪ'lebrɪtɪ] n gefeierte Persönlichkeit f
celery ['selərɪ] n Sellerie m or f
celestial [sɪ'lestɪəl] adj himmlisch
celibacy ['selɪbəsɪ] n Zölibat nt or m
cell [sel] n Zelle f; (ELEC) Element nt
cellar ['selə*] n Keller m
'cello ['tʃeləu] n Cello nt
cellophane ['seləfeɪn] (®) n Cellophan nt (®)
cellular ['seljulə*] adj zellular
cellulose ['seljuləus] n Zellulose f
Celt [kelt, selt] n Kelte m, Keltin f; ~**ic** ['keltɪk, 'seltɪk] adj keltisch
cement [sɪ'ment] n Zement m ♦ vt

zementieren; ~ **mixer** n Betonmisch-
maschine f
cemetery ['semɪtrɪ] n Friedhof m
cenotaph ['senətɑːf] n Ehrenmal nt
censor ['sensə*] n Zensor m ♦ vt
zensieren; ~**ship** n Zensur f
censure ['senʃə*] vt rügen
census ['sensəs] n Volkszählung f
cent [sent] n (US: coin) Cent m; see also
per cent
centenary [sen'tiːnərɪ] n Jahrhundert-
feier f
center ['sentə*] (US) n = **centre**
centigrade ['sentɪgreɪd] adj Celsius
centimetre ['sentɪmiːtə*] (US **centi-
meter**) n Zentimeter nt
centipede ['sentɪpiːd] n Tausendfüßler
m
central ['sentrəl] adj zentral; **C~ America** n Mittelamerika nt; ~ **heating** n
Zentralheizung f; ~**ize** vt zentralisieren
centre ['sentə*] (US **center**) n Zentrum
nt ♦ vt zentrieren; ~**-forward** n (SPORT)
Mittelstürmer m; ~**-half** n (SPORT)
Stopper m
century ['sentjʊrɪ] n Jahrhundert nt
ceramic [sɪ'ræmɪk] adj keramisch; ~**s**
npl Keramiken pl
cereal ['sɪərɪəl] n (grain) Getreide nt;
(at breakfast) Getreideflocken pl
cerebral ['serɪbrəl] adj zerebral;
(intellectual) geistig
ceremony ['serɪmənɪ] n Zeremonie f; **to
stand on** ~ förmlich sein
certain ['sɜːtən] adj sicher; (particular)
gewiß; **for** ~ ganz bestimmt; ~**ly** adv
sicher, bestimmt; ~**ty** n Gewißheit f
certificate [sə'tɪfɪkɪt] n Bescheinigung f;
(SCH etc) Zeugnis nt
certified mail ['sɜːtɪfaɪd-] (US) n Einschreiben nt
certified public accountant
['sɜːtɪfaɪd-] (US) n geprüfte(r) Buchhalter
m
certify ['sɜːtɪfaɪ] vt bescheinigen
cervical ['sɜːvɪkl] adj (smear, cancer)
Gebärmutterhals-
cervix ['sɜːvɪks] n Gebärmutterhals m
cessation [se'seɪʃən] n Einstellung f,
Ende nt

cesspit ['sespɪt] n Senkgrube f
cf. abbr (= compare) vgl.
ch. abbr (= chapter) Kap.
chafe [tʃeɪf] vt scheuern
chaffinch ['tʃæfɪntʃ] n Buchfink m
chagrin ['ʃægrɪn] n Verdruß m
chain [tʃeɪn] n Kette f ♦ vt (also: ~ up)
anketten; ~ **reaction** n Kettenreaktion
f; ~**-smoke** vi kettenrauchen; ~ **store**
n Kettenladen m
chair [tʃeə*] n Stuhl m; (arm~) Sessel
m; (UNIV) Lehrstuhl m ♦ vt (meeting)
den Vorsitz führen bei; ~**lift** n Sessellift
m; ~**man** (irreg) n Vorsitzende(r) m
chalet ['ʃæleɪ] n Chalet nt
chalice ['tʃælɪs] n Kelch m
chalk ['tʃɔːk] n Kreide f
challenge ['tʃælɪndʒ] n Herausforderung
f ♦ vt herausfordern; (contest) bestreiten
challenging ['tʃælɪndʒɪŋ] adj (tone) her-
ausfordernd; (work) anspruchsvoll
chamber ['tʃeɪmbə*] n Kammer f; ~ **of
commerce** Handelskammer f; ~**maid** n
Zimmermädchen nt; ~ **music** n
Kammermusik f
chamois ['ʃæmwɑː] n Gemse f
champagne [ʃæm'peɪn] n Champagner
m, Sekt m
champion ['tʃæmpɪən] n (SPORT) Mei-
ster(in) m(f); (of cause) Verfechter(in)
m(f); ~**ship** n Meisterschaft f
chance [tʃɑːns] n (luck) Zufall m;
(possibility) Möglichkeit f;
(opportunity) Gelegenheit f, Chance f;
(risk) Risiko nt ♦ adj zufällig ♦ vt: **to** ~
it es darauf ankommen lassen; **by** ~
zufällig; **to take a** ~ ein Risiko eingehen
chancellor ['tʃɑːnsələ*] n Kanzler m;
C~ of the Exchequer (BRIT) n
Schatzkanzler m
chandelier [ʃændɪ'lɪə*] n Kronleuchter
m
change [tʃeɪndʒ] vt ändern; (replace,
COMM: money) wechseln; (exchange)
umtauschen; (transform) verwandeln ♦
vi sich ändern; (~ trains) umsteigen;
(~ clothes) sich umziehen ♦ n Veränderung f; (money returned)

Wechselgeld *nt*; (*coins*) Kleingeld *nt*; **to ~ one's mind** es sich *dat* anders überlegen; **to ~ into sth** (*be transformed*) sich in etw *acc* verwandeln; **for a ~** zur Abwechslung; **~able** *adj* (*weather*) wechselhaft; **~ machine** *n* Geldwechselautomat *m*; **~over** *n* Umstellung *f*

changing ['tʃeɪndʒɪŋ] *adj* veränderlich; **~ room** (*BRIT*) *n* Umkleideraum *m*

channel ['tʃænl] *n* (*stream*) Bachbett *nt*; (*NAUT*) Straße *f*; (*TV*) Kanal *m*; (*fig*) Weg *m* ♦ *vt* (*efforts*) lenken; **the (English) C~** der Ärmelkanal; **C~ Islands** *npl*: **the C~ Islands** die Kanalinseln *pl*

chant [tʃɑːnt] *n* Gesang *m*; (*of football fans etc*) Sprechchor *m* ♦ *vt* intonieren

chaos ['keɪɒs] *n* Chaos *nt*

chap [tʃæp] (*inf*) *n* Kerl *m*

chapel ['tʃæpəl] *n* Kapelle *f*

chaperon ['ʃæpərəʊn] *n* Anstandsdame *f*

chaplain ['tʃæplɪn] *n* Kaplan *m*

chapped ['tʃæpt] *adj* (*skin, lips*) spröde

chapter ['tʃæptə*] *n* Kapitel *nt*

char [tʃɑː*] *vt* (*burn*) verkohlen ♦ *n* (*BRIT*) = **charlady**

character ['kærɪktə*] *n* Charakter *m*, Wesen *nt*; (*in novel, film*) Figur *f*; **~istic** [kærɪktə'rɪstɪk] *adj*: **~istic (of sb/ sth)** (für jdn/etw) charakteristisch ♦ *n* Kennzeichen *nt*; **~ize** *vt* charakterisieren, kennzeichnen

charade [ʃə'rɑːd] *n* Scharade *f*

charcoal ['tʃɑːkəʊl] *n* Holzkohle *f*

charge [tʃɑːdʒ] *n* (*cost*) Preis *m*; (*JUR*) Anklage *f*; (*explosive*) Ladung *f*; (*attack*) Angriff *m* ♦ *vt* (*gun, battery*) laden; (*price*) verlangen; (*JUR*) anklagen; (*MIL*) angreifen ♦ *vi* (*rush*) (an)stürmen; **bank ~s** Bankgebühren *pl*; **free of ~** kostenlos; **to reverse the ~s** (*TEL*) ein R-Gespräch führen; **to be in ~ of** verantwortlich sein für; **to take ~** (die Verantwortung) übernehmen; **to ~ sth (up) to sb's account** jdm etw in Rechnung stellen; **~ card** *n* Kundenkarte *f*

charitable ['tʃærɪtəbl] *adj* wohltätig; (*lenient*) nachsichtig

charity ['tʃærɪtɪ] *n* (*institution*) Hilfswerk *nt*; (*attitude*) Nächstenliebe *f*

charlady ['tʃɑːleɪdɪ] (*BRIT*) *n* Putzfrau *f*

charlatan ['ʃɑːlətən] *n* Scharlatan *m*

charm [tʃɑːm] *n* Charme *m*; (*spell*) Bann *m*; (*object*) Talisman *m* ♦ *vt* bezaubern; **~ing** *adj* reizend

chart [tʃɑːt] *n* Tabelle *f*; (*NAUT*) Seekarte *f* ♦ *vt* (*course*) abstecken

charter ['tʃɑːtə*] *vt* chartern ♦ *n* Schutzbrief *m*; **~ed accountant** *n* Wirtschaftsprüfer(in) *m(f)*; **~ flight** *n* Charterflug *m*

charwoman ['tʃɑːwʊmən] *n* = **charlady**

chase [tʃeɪs] *vt* jagen, verfolgen ♦ *n* Jagd *f*

chasm ['kæzəm] *n* Kluft *f*

chassis ['ʃæsɪ] *n* Fahrgestell *nt*

chastity ['tʃæstɪtɪ] *n* Keuschheit *f*

chat [tʃæt] *vi* (*also: have a ~*) plaudern ♦ *n* Plauderei *f*; **~ show** (*BRIT*) *n* Talkshow *f*

chatter ['tʃætə*] *vi* schwatzen; (*teeth*) klappern ♦ *n* Geschwätz *nt*; **~box** *n* Quasselstrippe *f*

chatty ['tʃætɪ] *adj* geschwätzig

chauffeur ['ʃəʊfə*] *n* Chauffeur *m*

chauvinist ['ʃəʊvɪnɪst] *n* (*male ~*) Chauvi *m* (*inf*); (*nationalist*) Chauvinist(in) *m(f)*

cheap [tʃiːp] *adj, adv* billig; **~ly** *adv* billig

cheat [tʃiːt] *vt, vi* betrügen; (*SCH*) mogeln ♦ *n* Betrüger(in) *m(f)*

check [tʃek] *vt* (*examine*) prüfen; (*make sure*) nachsehen; (*control*) kontrollieren; (*restrain*) zügeln; (*stop*) anhalten ♦ *n* (*examination, restraint*) Kontrolle *f*; (*bill*) Rechnung *f*; (*pattern*) Karo(muster) *nt*; (*US*) = **cheque** ♦ *adj* (*pattern, cloth*) kariert; **~ in** *vi* (*in hotel, airport*) einchecken ♦ *vt* (*luggage*) abfertigen lassen; **~ out** *vi* (*of hotel*) abreisen; **~ up** *vi* nachschauen; **~ up on** *vt* kontrollieren; **~ered** (*US*) *adj* = **chequered**; **~ers** (*US*) *n* (*draughts*) Damespiel *nt*; **~-in (desk)** *n* Abfertigung *f*; **~ing account** (*US*) *n* (*current account*) Girokonto *nt*; **~mate** *n* Schachmatt *nt*; **~out** *n* Kasse *f*;

~**point** n Kontrollpunkt m; ~ **room** (US) n (left-luggage office) Gepäckaufbewahrung f; ~**up** n (Nach)prüfung f; (MED) (ärztliche) Untersuchung f

cheek [tʃiːk] n Backe f; (fig) Frechheit f; ~**bone** n Backenknochen m; ~**y** adj frech

cheep [tʃiːp] vi piepsen

cheer [tʃɪə*] n (usu pl) Hurra- or Beifallsruf m ♦ vt zujubeln; (encourage) aufmuntern ♦ vi jauchzen; ~**s!** Prost!; ~ **up** vi bessere Laune bekommen ♦ vt aufmuntern; ~ **up!** nun lach doch mal!; ~**ful** adj fröhlich

cheerio ['tʃɪərɪˈəʊ] (BRIT) excl tschüs!

cheese [tʃiːz] n Käse m; ~**board** n (gemischte) Käseplatte f

cheetah ['tʃiːtə] n Gepard m

chef [ʃef] n Küchenchef m

chemical ['kemɪkəl] adj chemisch ♦ n Chemikalie f

chemist ['kemɪst] n (BRIT: pharmacist) Apotheker m, Drogist m; (scientist) Chemiker m; ~**ry** n Chemie f; ~**'s** (shop) (BRIT) n Apotheke f, Drogerie f

cheque [tʃek] (BRIT) n Scheck m; ~**book** n Scheckbuch nt; ~ **card** n Scheckkarte f

chequered ['tʃekəd] adj (fig) bewegt

cherish ['tʃerɪʃ] vt (person) lieben; (hope) hegen

cherry ['tʃerɪ] n Kirsche f

chess [tʃes] n Schach nt; ~**board** n Schachbrett nt; ~**man** (irreg) n Schachfigur f

chest [tʃest] n (ANAT) Brust f; (box) Kiste f; ~ **of drawers** n Kommode f

chestnut ['tʃesnʌt] n Kastanie f; ~ **tree** n Kastanienbaum m

chew [tʃuː] vt, vi kauen; ~**ing gum** n Kaugummi m

chic [ʃiːk] adj schick, elegant

chick [tʃɪk] n Küken nt; (US: inf: girl) Biene f

chicken ['tʃɪkɪn] n Huhn nt; (food) Hähnchen nt; ~ **out** (inf) vi kneifen (inf)

chickenpox ['tʃɪkɪnpɒks] n Windpocken pl

chicory ['tʃɪkərɪ] n (in coffee) Zichorie f; (plant) Chicorée f

chief [tʃiːf] n (of tribe) Häuptling m; (COMM) Chef m ♦ adj Haupt-; ~ **executive** n Geschäftsführer(in) m(f); ~**ly** adv hauptsächlich

chiffon ['ʃɪfɒn] n Chiffon m

chilblain ['tʃɪlbleɪn] n Frostbeule f

child [tʃaɪld] (pl **children**) n Kind nt, ~**birth** n Entbindung f; ~**hood** n Kindheit f; ~**ish** adj kindisch; ~**like** adj kindlich; ~ **minder** (BRIT) n Tagesmutter f

children ['tʃɪldrən] npl of **child**

Chile ['tʃɪlɪ] n Chile nt; ~**an** adj chilenisch

chill [tʃɪl] n Kühle f; (MED) Erkältung f ♦ vt (CULIN) kühlen

chilli ['tʃɪlɪ] n Peperoni pl; (meal, spice) Chili m

chilly ['tʃɪlɪ] adj kühl, frostig

chime [tʃaɪm] n Geläut nt ♦ vi ertönen

chimney ['tʃɪmnɪ] n Schornstein m; ~ **sweep** n Schornsteinfeger(in) m(f)

chimpanzee [tʃɪmpænˈziː] n Schimpanse m

chin [tʃɪn] n Kinn nt

China ['tʃaɪnə] n China nt

china ['tʃaɪnə] n Porzellan nt

Chinese [tʃaɪˈniːz] adj chinesisch ♦ n (inv) Chinese m, Chinesin f; (LING) Chinesisch

chink [tʃɪŋk] n (opening) Ritze f; (noise) Klirren nt

chip [tʃɪp] n (of wood etc) Splitter m (in poker etc; US: crisp) Chip m ♦ vt absplittern; ~**s** npl (BRIT: COOK) Pommes frites pl; ~ **in** vi Zwischenbemerkungen machen

chiropodist [kɪˈrɒpədɪst] (BRIT) n Fußpfleger(in) m(f)

chirp [tʃɜːp] vi zwitschern

chisel ['tʃɪzl] n Meißel m

chit [tʃɪt] n Notiz f

chitchat ['tʃɪttʃæt] n Plauderei f

chivalrous ['ʃɪvəlrəs] adj ritterlich

chivalry ['ʃɪvəlrɪ] n Ritterlichkeit f

chives [tʃaɪvz] npl Schnittlauch m

chlorine ['klɔːriːn] n Chlor nt

chock [tʃɒk] n Bremsklotz m; ~**-a-block** adj vollgepfropft; ~**-full** adj vollge-

pfropft
chocolate ['tʃɒklɪt] n Schokolade f
choice [tʃɔɪs] n Wahl f; (of goods) Auswahl f ♦ adj Qualitäts-
choir ['kwaɪə*] n Chor m; ~**boy** n Chorknabe m
choke [tʃəʊk] vi ersticken ♦ vt erdrosseln; (block) (ab)drosseln ♦ n (AUT) Starterklappe f
cholera ['kɒlərə] n Cholera f
cholesterol [kɒ'lestərəl] n Cholesterin nt
choose [tʃuːz] (pt chose, pp chosen) vt wählen
choosy ['tʃuːzɪ] adj wählerisch
chop [tʃɒp] vt (wood) spalten; (COOK: also: ~ up) (zer)hacken ♦ n Hieb m; (COOK) Kotelett nt; ~**s** npl (jaws) Lefzen pl
chopper ['tʃɒpə*] n (helicopter) Hubschrauber m
choppy ['tʃɒpɪ] adj (sea) bewegt
chopsticks ['tʃɒpstɪks] npl (Eß)stäbchen pl
choral ['kɔːrəl] adj Chor-
chord [kɔːd] n Akkord m
chore [tʃɔː*] n Pflicht f; ~**s** npl (housework) Hausarbeit f
choreographer [kɒrɪ'ɒgrəfə*] n Choreograph(in) m(f)
chorister ['kɒrɪstə*] n Chorsänger(in) m(f)
chortle ['tʃɔːtl] vi glucksen
chorus ['kɔːrəs] n Chor m; (in song) Refrain m
chose [tʃəʊz] pt of choose
chosen ['tʃəʊzn] pp of choose
Christ [kraɪst] n Christus m
christen ['krɪsn] vt taufen
Christian ['krɪstɪən] adj christlich ♦ n Christ(in) m(f); ~**ity** [krɪstɪ'ænɪtɪ] n Christentum nt; ~ **name** n Vorname m
Christmas ['krɪsməs] n Weihnachten pl; ~ **card** n Weihnachtskarte f; ~ **Day** n der erste Weihnachtstag; ~ **Eve** n Heiligabend m; ~ **tree** n Weihnachtsbaum m
chrome [krəʊm] n = chromium plating
chromium ['krəʊmɪəm] n Chrom nt; ~ **plating** n Verchromung f
chronic ['krɒnɪk] adj chronisch

chronicle ['krɒnɪkl] n Chronik f
chronological [krɒnə'lɒdʒɪkəl] adj chronologisch
chubby ['tʃʌbɪ] adj rundlich
chuck [tʃʌk] vt werfen; (BRIT: also: ~ up) hinwerfen; ~ **out** vt (person) rauswerfen; (old clothes etc) wegwerfen
chuckle ['tʃʌkl] vi in sich hineinlachen
chug [tʃʌg] vi tuckern
chum [tʃʌm] n Kumpel m
chunk [tʃʌŋk] n Klumpen m; (of food) Brocken m
church [tʃɜːtʃ] n Kirche f; ~**yard** n Kirchhof m
churlish ['tʃɜːlɪʃ] adj grob
churn [tʃɜːn] n (for butter) Butterfaß nt; (for milk) Milchkanne f; ~ **out** (inf) vt produzieren
chute [ʃuːt] n Rutsche f; (rubbish ~) Müllschlucker m
CIA (US) n abbr (= Central Intelligence Agency) CIA m
CID (BRIT) n abbr (= Criminal Investigation Department) ≈ Kripo f
cider ['saɪdə*] n Apfelwein m
cigar [sɪ'gɑː*] n Zigarre f
cigarette [sɪgə'ret] n Zigarette f; ~ **case** n Zigarettenetui nt; ~ **end** n Zigarettenstummel m; ~ **holder** n Zigarettenspitze f
Cinderella [sɪndə'relə] n Aschenbrödel nt
cinders ['sɪndəz] npl Asche f
cine-camera ['sɪnɪ'kæmərə] (BRIT) n Filmkamera f
cine-film ['sɪnɪfɪlm] (BRIT) n Schmalfilm m
cinema ['sɪnəmə] n Kino nt
cinnamon ['sɪnəmən] n Zimt m
cipher ['saɪfə*] n (code) Chiffre f
circle ['sɜːkl] n Kreis m; (in cinema etc) Rang m ♦ vi kreisen ♦ vt (surround) umgeben; (move round) kreisen um
circuit ['sɜːkɪt] n (track) Rennbahn f; (lap) Runde f; (ELEC) Stromkreis m; ~**ous** [sɜː'kjuːɪtəs] adj weitschweifig
circular ['sɜːkjʊlə*] adj rund ♦ n Rundschreiben nt
circulate ['sɜːkjʊleɪt] vi zirkulieren ♦ vt in Umlauf setzen; **circulation**

[sɜːkjʊ'leɪʃən] n (of blood) Kreislauf m; (of newspaper) Auflage f; (of money) Umlauf m

circumcise ['sɜːkəmsaɪz] vt beschneiden

circumference [sə'kʌmfərəns] n (Kreis)umfang m

circumspect ['sɜːkəmspekt] adj umsichtig

circumstances ['sɜːkəmstənsəz] npl Umstände pl; (financial condition) Verhältnisse pl

circumvent [sɜːkəm'vent] vt umgehen

circus ['sɜːkəs] n Zirkus m

cistern ['sɪstən] n Zisterne f; (of W.C.) Spülkasten m

cite [saɪt] vt zitieren, anführen

citizen ['sɪtɪzn] n Bürger(in) m(f); ~ship n Staatsbürgerschaft f

citrus fruit ['sɪtrəs-] Zitrusfrucht f

city ['sɪtɪ] n Großstadt f; the C~ die City, das Finanzzentrum Londons

civic ['sɪvɪk] adj (of town) städtisch; (of citizen) Bürger-; ~ centre n Stadtverwaltung f

civil ['sɪvɪl] adj bürgerlich; (not military) zivil; (polite) höflich; ~ engineer n Bauingenieur m; ~ian [sɪ'vɪlɪən] n Zivilperson f ♦ adj zivil, Zivil-

civilization [sɪvɪlaɪ'zeɪʃən] n Zivilisation f

civilized ['sɪvɪlaɪzd] adj zivilisiert

civil ~ law n Zivilrecht nt; ~ servant n Staatsbeamte(r) m; C~ Service n Staatsdienst m; ~ war n Bürgerkrieg m

clad [klæd] adj: ~ in gehüllt in +acc

claim [kleɪm] vt beanspruchen; (have opinion) behaupten ♦ vi (for insurance) Ansprüche geltend machen ♦ n (demand) Forderung f; (right) Anspruch m; (pretension) Behauptung f; ~ant n Antragsteller(in) m(f)

clairvoyant [kleə'vɔɪənt] n Hellseher(in) m(f)

clam [klæm] n Venusmuschel f

clamber ['klæmbə*] vi kraxeln

clammy ['klæmɪ] adj klamm

clamour ['klæmə*] vi: to ~ for sth nach etw verlangen

clamp [klæmp] n Schraubzwinge f ♦ vt einspannen; ~ down on vt fus Maßnahmen ergreifen gegen

clan [klæn] n Clan m

clandestine [klæn'destɪn] adj geheim

clang [klæŋ] vi scheppern

clap [klæp] vi klatschen ♦ vt Beifall klatschen +dat ♦ n (of hands) Klatschen nt; (of thunder) Donnerschlag m; ~ping n Klatschen nt

claret ['klærɪt] n rote(r) Bordeaux(wein) m

clarify ['klærɪfaɪ] vt klären, erklären

clarinet [klærɪ'net] n Klarinette f

clarity ['klærɪtɪ] n Klarheit f

clash [klæʃ] n (fig) Konflikt m ♦ vi zusammenprallen; (colours) sich beißen; (argue) sich streiten

clasp [klɑːsp] n Griff m; (on jewels, bag) Verschluß m ♦ vt umklammern

class [klɑːs] n Klasse f ♦ vt einordnen; ~-conscious adj klassenbewußt

classic ['klæsɪk] n Klassiker m ♦ adj klassisch; ~al adj klassisch

classified ['klæsɪfaɪd] adj (information) Geheim-; ~ advertisement n Kleinanzeige f

classify ['klæsɪfaɪ] vt klassifizieren

classmate ['klɑːsmeɪt] n Klassenkamerad(in) m(f)

classroom ['klɑːsrʊm] n Klassenzimmer nt

clatter ['klætə*] vi klappern; (feet) trappeln

clause [klɔːz] n (JUR) Klausel f; (GRAM) Satz m

claustrophobia [klɒstrə'fəʊbɪə] n Platzangst f

claw [klɔː] n Kralle f ♦ vt (zer)kratzen

clay [kleɪ] n Lehm m; (for pots) Ton m

clean [kliːn] adj sauber ♦ vt putzen; (clothes) reinigen; ~ out vt gründlich putzen; ~ up vt aufräumen; ~-cut adj (person) adrett; (clear) klar; ~er n (person) Putzfrau f; ~ing n Putzen nt; (clothes) Reinigung f; ~liness ['klenlɪnɪs] n Reinlichkeit f

cleanse [klenz] vt reinigen; ~r n (for face) Reinigungsmilch f

clean-shaven ['kliːn'ʃeɪvn] adj glattrasiert

cleansing department ['klenzɪŋ-] (*BRIT*) n Stadtreinigung f

clear ['klɪə*] adj klar; (*road*) frei ♦ vt (*road etc*) freimachen; (*obstacle*) beseitigen; (*JUR: suspect*) freisprechen ♦ vi klarwerden; (*fog*) sich lichten ♦ adv: ~ of von ... entfernt; ~ up vt aufräumen; (*solve*) aufklären; ~ance ['klɪərəns] n (*removal*) Räumung f; (*free space*) Lichtung f; (*permission*) Freigabe f; ~-cut adj (*case*) eindeutig; ~ing n Lichtung f; ~ing bank (*BRIT*) n Clearingbank f; ~ly adv klar; (*obviously*) eindeutig; ~way (*BRIT*) n (Straße f mit) Halteverbot nt

cleaver ['kli:və*] n Hackbeil f

clef [klef] n Notenschlüssel m

cleft [kleft] n (*in rock*) Spalte f

clemency ['klemənsɪ] n Milde f

clench [klentʃ] vt (*teeth*) zusammenbeißen; (*fist*) ballen

clergy ['klɜːdʒɪ] n Geistliche(n) pl; ~man (*irreg*) n Geistliche(r) m

clerical ['klerɪkəl] adj (*office*) Schreib-, Büro-; (*REL*) geistlich

clerk [klɑːk, (*US*) klɜːk] n (*in office*) Büroangestellte(r) mf; (*US: sales person*) Verkäufer(in) m(f)

clever ['klevə*] adj klug; (*crafty*) schlau

cliché ['kliːʃeɪ] n Klischee nt

click [klɪk] vt (*heels*) zusammenklappen; (*tongue*) schnalzen mit

client ['klaɪənt] n Klient m(f); ~ele [kliːɒnˈtel] n Kundschaft f

cliff [klɪf] n Klippe f

climate ['klaɪmɪt] n Klima nt

climax ['klaɪmæks] n Höhepunkt m

climb [klaɪm] vt besteigen ♦ vi steigen, klettern ♦ n Aufstieg m; ~-down n Abstieg m; ~er n Bergsteiger(in) m(f); ~ing n Bergsteigen nt

clinch [klɪntʃ] vt (*decide*) entscheiden; (*deal*) festmachen

cling [klɪŋ] (*pt, pp* clung) vi (*clothes*) eng anliegen; to ~ to sich festklammern an +dat

clinic ['klɪnɪk] n Klinik f; ~al adj klinisch

clink [klɪŋk] vi klimpern

clip [klɪp] n Spange f; (*also: paper* ~) Klammer f ♦ vt (*papers*) heften; (*hair, hedge*) stutzen; ~pers npl (*for hedge*) Heckenschere f; (*for hair*) Haarschneidemaschine f; ~ping n Ausschnitt m

cloak [kləʊk] n Umhang m ♦ vt hüllen; ~room n (*for coats*) Garderobe f; (*BRIT: W.C.*) Toilette f

clock [klɒk] n Uhr f; ~ in or on vi stempeln; ~ off or out vi stempeln; ~wise adv im Uhrzeigersinn; ~work n Uhrwerk nt ♦ adj zum Aufziehen

clog [klɒg] n Holzschuh m ♦ vt verstopfen

cloister ['klɔɪstə*] n Kreuzgang m

clone [kləʊn] n Klon m

close¹ [kləʊs] adj (*near*) in der Nähe; (*friend, connection, print*) eng; (*relative*) nahe; (*result*) knapp; (*examination*) eingehend; (*weather*) schwül; (*room*) stickig ♦ adv nahe, dicht; ~ by in der Nähe; ~ at hand in der Nähe; to have a ~ shave (*fig*) mit knapper Not davorkommen

close² [kləʊz] vt (*shut*) schließen; (*end*) beenden ♦ vi (*shop etc*) schließen; (*door etc*) sich schließen ♦ n Ende nt; ~ down vi schließen; ~d [kləʊzd] adj (*shop etc*) geschlossen; ~d shop n Gewerkschaftszwang m

close-knit [kləʊsˈnɪt] adj eng zusammengewachsen

closely ['kləʊslɪ] adv eng; (*carefully*) genau

closet ['klɒzɪt] n Schrank m

close-up ['kləʊsʌp] n Nahaufnahme f

closure ['kləʊʒə*] n Schließung f

clot [klɒt] n (*of blood*) Blutgerinnsel nt; (*fool*) Blödmann m ♦ vi gerinnen

cloth [klɒθ] n (*material*) Tuch nt; (*rag*) Lappen m

clothe [kləʊð] vt kleiden; ~s npl Kleider pl; ~s brush n Kleiderbürste f; ~s line n Wäscheleine f; ~s peg (*US* ~s pin) n Wäscheklammer f

clothing ['kləʊðɪŋ] n Kleidung f

cloud [klaʊd] n Wolke f; ~burst n Wolkenbruch m; ~y adj bewölkt; (*liquid*) trüb

clout [klaʊt] *vt* hauen
clove [kləʊv] *n* Gewürznelke *f*; ~ **of garlic** Knoblauchzehe *f*
clover ['kləʊvə*] *n* Klee *m*
clown [klaʊn] *n* Clown *m* ♦ *vi (also:* ~ *about,* ~ *around)* kaspern
cloying ['klɔɪɪŋ] *adj (taste, smell)* übersüß
club [klʌb] *n (weapon)* Knüppel *m*; *(society)* Klub *m; (also: golf* ~) Golfschläger *m* ♦ *vt* prügeln ♦ *vi:* **to** ~ **together** zusammenlegen; ~**s** *npl (CARDS)* Kreuz *nt*; ~ **car** *(US) n (RAIL)* Speisewagen *m*; ~**house** *n* Klubhaus *nt*
cluck [klʌk] *vi* glucken
clue [kluː] *n* Anhaltspunkt *m; (in crosswords)* Frage *f*; **I haven't a** ~ (ich hab') keine Ahnung
clump [klʌmp] *n* Gruppe *f*
clumsy ['klʌmzɪ] *adj (person)* unbeholfen; *(shape)* unförmig
clung [klʌŋ] *pt, pp of* **cling**
cluster ['klʌstə*] *n (of trees etc)* Gruppe *f* ♦ *vi* sich drängen, sich scharen
clutch [klʌtʃ] *n* Griff *m; (AUT)* Kupplung *f* ♦ *vt* sich festklammern an +*dat*
clutter ['klʌtə*] *vt* vollpropfen; *(desk)* übersäen
CND *n abbr* = **Campaign for Nuclear Disarmament**
Co. *abbr* = **county; company**
c/o *abbr* (= *care of)* c/o
coach [kəʊtʃ] *n (bus)* Reisebus *m; (horse-drawn)* Kutsche *f; (RAIL)* (Personen)wagen *m; (trainer)* Trainer *m* ♦ *vt (SCH)* Nachhilfeunterricht geben +*dat; (SPORT)* trainieren; ~ **trip** *n* Busfahrt *f*
coagulate [kəʊ'ægjʊleɪt] *vi* gerinnen
coal [kəʊl] *n* Kohle *f*; ~ **face** *n* Streb *m*; ~ **field** *n* Kohlengebiet *nt*
coalition [kəʊə'lɪʃən] *n* Koalition *f*
coalman ['kəʊlmən] *(irreg) n* Kohlenhändler *m*
coal merchant *n* = **coalman**
coal mine *n* Kohlenbergwerk *nt*
coarse [kɔːs] *adj* grob; *(fig)* ordinär
coast [kəʊst] *n* Küste *f* ♦ *vi* dahinrollen; *(AUT)* im Leerlauf fahren; ~**al** *adj* Küsten-; ~**guard** *n* Küstenwache *f*;

~**line** *n* Küste(nlinie) *f*
coat [kəʊt] *n* Mantel *m; (on animals)* Fell *nt; (of paint)* Schicht *f* ♦ *vt* überstreichen; ~ **of arms** *n* Wappen *nt*; ~**hanger** *n* Kleiderbügel *m*; ~**ing** *n* Überzug *m; (of paint)* Schicht *f*
coax [kəʊks] *vt* beschwatzen
cob [kɒb] *n see* **corn**
cobbler ['kɒblə*] *n* Schuster *m*
cobbles ['kɒblz] *npl* Pflastersteine *pl*
cobblestones ['kɒblstəʊnz] *npl* Pflastersteine *pl*
cobweb ['kɒbweb] *n* Spinnennetz *nt*
cocaine [kə'keɪn] *n* Kokain *nt*
cock [kɒk] *n* Hahn *m* ♦ *vt (gun)* entsichern; ~**erel** *n* junge(r) Hahn *m*; ~**-eyed** *adj (fig)* verrückt
cockle ['kɒkl] *n* Herzmuschel *f*
cockney ['kɒknɪ] *n* echte(r) Londoner *m*
cockpit ['kɒkpɪt] *n (AVIAT)* Pilotenkanzel *f*
cockroach ['kɒkrəʊtʃ] *n* Küchenschabe *f*
cocktail ['kɒkteɪl] *n* Cocktail *m*; ~ **cabinet** *n* Hausbar *f*; ~ **party** *n* Cocktailparty *f*
cocoa ['kəʊkəʊ] *n* Kakao *m*
coconut ['kəʊkənʌt] *n* Kokosnuß *f*
cocoon [kə'kuːn] *n* Kokon *m*
cod [kɒd] *n* Kabeljau *m*
C.O.D. *abbr* = **cash on delivery**
code [kəʊd] *n* Kode *m; (JUR)* Kodex *m*
cod-liver oil ['kɒdlɪvər-] *n* Lebertran *m*
coercion [kəʊ'ɜːʃən] *n* Zwang *m*
coffee ['kɒfɪ] *n* Kaffee *m*; ~ **bar** *(BRIT) n* Café *nt*; ~ **bean** *n* Kaffeebohne *f*; ~ **break** *n* Kaffeepause *f*; ~ **grounds** *npl* Kaffeesatz *m*; ~**pot** *n* Kaffeekanne *f*; ~ **table** *n* Couchtisch *m*
coffin ['kɒfɪn] *n* Sarg *m*
cog [kɒg] *n* (Rad)zahn *m*
cogent ['kəʊdʒənt] *adj* triftig, überzeugend, zwingend
cognac ['kɒnjæk] *n* Kognak *m*
coherent [kəʊ'hɪərənt] *adj* zusammenhängend; *(person)* verständlich
cohesion [kəʊ'hiːʒən] *n* Zusammenhang *m*
coil [kɔɪl] *n* Rolle *f; (ELEC)* Spule *f; (contraceptive)* Spirale *f* ♦ *vt* aufwickeln

coin [kɔɪn] n Münze f ♦ vt prägen; ~**age** n (word) Prägung f; ~**-box** (BRIT) n Münzfernsprecher m

coincide [kəʊɪn'saɪd] vi (happen together) zusammenfallen; (agree) übereinstimmen; ~**nce** [kəʊ'ɪnsɪdəns] n Zufall m

Coke [kəʊk] (®) n (drink) Coca-Cola f (®)

coke n Koks m

colander ['kʌləndə*] n Durchschlag m

cold [kəʊld] adj kalt ♦ n Kälte f; (MED) Erkältung f; **I'm ~** mir ist kalt; **to catch ~** sich erkälten; **in ~ blood** kaltblütig; **to give sb the ~ shoulder** jdm die kalte Schulter zeigen; ~**ly** adv kalt; ~**-shoulder** vt die kalte Schulter zeigen +dat; ~ **sore** n Erkältungsbläschen nt

coleslaw ['kəʊlslɔː] n Krautsalat m

colic ['kɒlɪk] n Kolik f

collaborate [kə'læbəreɪt] vi zusammenarbeiten

collaboration [kəlæbə'reɪʃən] n Zusammenarbeit f; (POL) Kollaboration f

collapse [kə'læps] vi (people) zusammenbrechen; (things) einstürzen ♦ n Zusammenbruch m; Einsturz m

collapsible [kə'læpsəbl] adj zusammenklappbar, Klapp-

collar ['kɒlə*] n Kragen m; ~**bone** n Schlüsselbein nt

collateral [kɒ'lætərəl] n (zusätzliche) Sicherheit f

colleague ['kɒliːg] n Kollege m, Kollegin f

collect [kə'lekt] vt sammeln; (BRIT: call and pick up) abholen ♦ vi sich sammeln ♦ adv: **to call ~** (US: TEL) ein R-Gespräch führen; ~**ion** [kə'lekʃən] n Sammlung f; (REL) Kollekte f; (of post) Leerung f

collective [kə'lektɪv] adj gemeinsam; (POL) kollektiv

collector [kə'lektə*] n Sammler m; (tax ~) (Steuer)einnehmer m

college ['kɒlɪdʒ] n (UNIV) College nt; (TECH) Fach-, Berufsschule f

collide [kə'laɪd] vi zusammenstoßen

colliery ['kɒlɪərɪ] (BRIT) n Zeche f

collision [kə'lɪʒən] n Zusammenstoß m

colloquial [kə'ləʊkwɪəl] adj umgangssprachlich

collusion [kə'luːʒən] n geheime(s) Einverständnis nt

colon ['kəʊlɒn] n Doppelpunkt m; (MED) Dickdarm m

colonel ['kɜːnl] n Oberst m

colonial [kə'ləʊnɪəl] adj Kolonial-

colonize ['kɒlənaɪz] vt kolonisieren

colony ['kɒlənɪ] n Kolonie f

colour ['kʌlə*] (US color) n Farbe f ♦ vt (also fig) färben ♦ vi sich verfärben; ~**s** npl (of club) Fahne f; ~ **bar** n Rassenschranke f; ~**-blind** adj farbenblind; ~**ed** adj farbig; ~**eds** npl (people) Farbige pl; ~ **film** n Farbfilm m; ~**ful** adj bunt; (personality) schillernd; ~**ing** n (complexion) Gesichtsfarbe f; (substance) Farbstoff m; ~ **scheme** n Farbgebung f; ~ **television** n Farbfernsehen nt

colt [kəʊlt] n Fohlen nt

column ['kɒləm] n Säule f; (MIL) Kolonne f; (of print) Spalte f; ~**ist** ['kɒləmnɪst] n Kolumnist m

coma ['kəʊmə] n Koma nt

comb [kəʊm] n Kamm m ♦ vt kämmen; (search) durchkämmen

combat ['kɒmbæt] n Kampf m ♦ vt bekämpfen

combination [kɒmbɪ'neɪʃən] n Kombination f

combine [vb kəm'baɪn, n 'kɒmbaɪn] vt verbinden ♦ vi sich vereinigen ♦ n (COMM) Konzern m; ~ (**harvester**) n Mähdrescher m

combustion [kəm'bʌstʃən] n Verbrennung f

come [kʌm] (pt **came**, pp **come**) vi kommen; **to ~ undone** aufgehen; ~ **about** vi geschehen; ~ **across** vt fus (find) stoßen auf +acc; ~ **away** vi (person) weggehen; (handle etc) abgehen; ~ **back** vi zurückkommen; ~ **by** vt fus (find): **to ~ by sth** zu etw kommen; ~ **down** vi (price) fallen; ~ **forward** vi (volunteer) sich melden; ~ **from** vt fus (result) kommen von; **where do you ~ from?** wo kommen Sie her?; **I ~ from London** ich komme aus London; **~ in** *vi* hereinkommen; *(train)* einfahren; **~ in for** *vt fus* abkriegen; **~ into** *vt fus (inherit)* erben; **~ off** *vi (handle)* abgehen; *(succeed)* klappen; **~ on** *vi (progress)* vorankommen; **~ on!** komm!; *(hurry)* beeil dich!; **~ out** *vi* herauskommen; **~ round** *vi (MED)* wieder zu sich kommen; **~ to** *vi (MED)* wieder zu sich kommen ♦ *vt fus (bill)* sich belaufen auf +*acc*; **~ up** *vi* hochkommen; *(sun)* aufgehen; *(problem)* auftauchen; **~ up against** *vt fus (resistance, difficulties)* stoßen auf +*acc*; **~ upon** *vt fus* stoßen auf +*acc*; **~ up with** *vt fus* sich einfallen lassen

comedian [kə'miːdɪən] *n* Komiker *m*

comedienne [kəmiːdɪ'en] *n* Komikerin *f*

comedown ['kʌmdaʊn] *n* Abstieg *m*

comedy ['kɒmədɪ] *n* Komödie *f*

comet ['kɒmɪt] *n* Komet *m*

comeuppance [kʌm'ʌpəns] *n*: **to get one's ~** seine Quittung bekommen

comfort ['kʌmfət] *n* Komfort *m*; *(consolation)* Trost *m* ♦ *vt* trösten; **~able** *adj* bequem; **~ably** *adv* (*sit etc*) bequem; (*live*) angenehm; **~ station** *(US)* *n* öffentliche Toilette *f*

comic ['kɒmɪk] *n* Comic(heft) *nt*; *(comedian)* Komiker *m* ♦ *adj* (*also*: **~al**) komisch

coming ['kʌmɪŋ] *n* Kommen *nt*; **~(s) and going(s)** *n(pl)* Kommen und Gehen *nt*

comma ['kɒmə] *n* Komma *nt*

command [kə'mɑːnd] *n* Befehl *m*; *(control)* Führung *f*; *(MIL)* Kommando *nt*; *(mastery)* Beherrschung *f* ♦ *vt* befehlen +*dat*; *(MIL)* kommandieren; *(be able to get)* verfügen über +*acc*; **~eer** [kɒmən'dɪə*] *vt* requirieren; **~er** *n* Kommandant *m*

commandment [kə'mɑːndmənt] *n* *(REL)* Gebot *nt*

commando [kə'mɑːndəʊ] *n* Kommandotruppe *nt*; *(person)* Mitglied *nt* einer Kommandotruppe

commemorate [kə'meməreɪt] *vt* gedenken +*gen*

commence [kə'mens] *vt*, *vi* beginnen

commend [kə'mend] *vt* *(recommend)* empfehlen; *(praise)* loben

commensurate [kə'mensjʊrɪt] *adj*: **~ with sth** einer Sache *dat* entsprechend

comment ['kɒment] *n* Bemerkung *f* ♦ *vi*: **to ~ (on)** sich äußern (zu); **~ary** ['kɒməntrɪ] *n* Kommentar *m*; **~ator** ['kɒmənteɪtə*] *n* Kommentator *m*; *(TV)* Reporter(in) *m(f)*

commerce ['kɒmɜːs] *n* Handel *m*

commercial [kə'mɜːʃəl] *adj* kommerziell, geschäftlich; *(training)* kaufmännisch ♦ *n* *(TV)* Fernsehwerbung *f*; **~ break** *n* Werbespot *m*; **~ize** *vt* kommerzialisieren

commiserate [kə'mɪzəreɪt] *vi*: **to ~ with** Mitleid haben mit

commission [kə'mɪʃən] *n* *(act)* Auftrag *m*; *(fee)* Provision *f*; *(body)* Kommission *f* ♦ *vt* beauftragen; *(MIL)* zum Offizier ernennen; *(work of art)* in Auftrag geben; **out of ~** außer Betrieb; **~aire** [kəmɪʃə'neə*] *(BRIT)* *n* Portier *m*; **~er** *n* *(POLICE)* Polizeipräsident *m*

commit [kə'mɪt] *vt* *(crime)* begehen; *(entrust)* anvertrauen; **to ~ o.s.** sich festlegen; **~ment** *n* Verpflichtung *f*

committee [kə'mɪtɪ] *n* Ausschuß *m*

commodity [kə'mɒdɪtɪ] *n* Ware *f*

common ['kɒmən] *adj* *(cause)* gemeinsam; *(pej)* gewöhnlich; *(widespread)* üblich, häufig ♦ *n* Gemeindeland *nt*; **C~s** *npl* *(BRIT)*: **the C~s** das Unterhaus; **~er** *n* Bürgerliche(r) *mf*; **~ law** *n* Gewohnheitsrecht *nt*; **~ly** *adv* gewöhnlich; **C~ Market** *n* Gemeinsame(r) Markt *m*; **~place** *adj* alltäglich; **~room** *n* Gemeinschaftsraum *m*; **~ sense** *n* gesunde(r) Menschenverstand *m*; **C~wealth** *n*: **the C~wealth** das Commonwealth

commotion [kə'məʊʃən] *n* Aufsehen *nt*

communal ['kɒmjuːnl] *adj* Gemeinde-; Gemeinschafts-

commune [*n* 'kɒmjuːn, *vb* kə'mjuːn] *n* Kommune *f* ♦ *vi*: **to ~ with** sich mitteilen +*dat*

communicate [kə'mjuːnɪkeɪt] *vt* *(transmit)* übertragen ♦ *vi* *(be in* *touch*) in Verbindung stehen; (*make self understood*) sich verständigen

communication [kəmjuːnɪ'keɪʃən] *n* (*message*) Mitteilung *f*; (*making understood*) Kommunikation *f*; ~s *npl* (*transport etc*) Verkehrswege *pl*; ~ **cord** (*BRIT*) *n* Notbremse *f*

communion [kə'mjuːnɪən] *n* (*also: Holy C~*) Abendmahl *nt*, Kommunion *f*

communism ['kɒmjʊnɪzəm] *n* Kommunismus *m*

communist ['kɒmjʊnɪst] *n* Kommunist(in) *m(f)* ♦ *adj* kommunistisch

community [kə'mjuːnɪtɪ] *n* Gemeinschaft *f*; ~ **centre** *n* Gemeinschaftszentrum *nt*; ~ **chest** (*US*) *n* Wohltätigkeitsfonds *m*

commutation ticket [kɒmjʊ'teɪʃən-] (*US*) *n* Zeitkarte *f*

commute [kə'mjuːt] *vi* pendeln ♦ *vt* umwandeln; ~**r** *n* Pendler *m*

compact [*adj* kəm'pækt, *n* 'kɒmpækt] *adj* kompakt ♦ *n* (*for make-up*) Puderdose *f*; ~ **disc** *n* Compact-disc *f*

companion [kəm'pænɪən] *n* Begleiter(in) *m(f)*; ~**ship** *n* Gesellschaft *f*

company ['kʌmpənɪ] *n* Gesellschaft *f*; (*COMM*) Firma *f*, Gesellschaft *f*; **to keep sb** ~ jdm Gesellschaft leisten; ~ **secretary** (*BRIT*) *n* ≈ Prokurist(in) *m(f)*

comparable ['kɒmpərəbl] *adj* vergleichbar

comparative [kəm'pærətɪv] *adj* (*relative*) relativ; ~**ly** *adv* verhältnismäßig

compare [kəm'pɛə*] *vt* vergleichen ♦ *vi* sich vergleichen lassen

comparison [kəm'pærɪsn] *n* Vergleich *m*; **in** ~ (**with**) im Vergleich (mit *or* zu)

compartment [kəm'pɑːtmənt] *n* (*RAIL*) Abteil *nt*; (*in drawer etc*) Fach *nt*

compass ['kʌmpəs] *n* Kompaß *m*; ~**es** *npl* (*MATH etc: also: pair of ~es*) Zirkel *m*

compassion [kəm'pæʃən] *n* Mitleid *nt*; ~**ate** *adj* mitfühlend

compatible [kəm'pætɪbl] *adj* vereinbar; (*COMPUT*) kompatibel

compel [kəm'pɛl] *vt* zwingen

compendium [kəm'pendɪəm] *n* Kompendium *nt*

compensate ['kɒmpenseɪt] *vt* entschädigen ♦ *vi*: **to** ~ **for** Ersatz leisten für

compensation [kɒmpen'seɪʃən] *n* Entschädigung *f*

compère ['kɒmpɛə*] *n* Conférencier *m*

compete [kəm'piːt] *vi* (*take part*) teilnehmen; (*vie with*) konkurrieren

competence ['kɒmpɪtəns] *n* Fähigkeit *f*

competent ['kɒmpɪtənt] *adj* kompetent

competition [kɒmpɪ'tɪʃən] *n* (*contest*) Wettbewerb *m*; (*COMM, rivalry*) Konkurrenz *f*

competitive [kəm'petɪtɪv] *adj* Konkurrenz-; (*COMM*) konkurrenzfähig

competitor [kəm'petɪtə*] *n* (*COMM*) Konkurrent(in) *m(f)*; (*participant*) Teilnehmer(in) *m(f)*

compile [kəm'paɪl] *vt* zusammenstellen

complacency [kəm'pleɪsnsɪ] *n* Selbstzufriedenheit *f*

complacent [kəm'pleɪsnt] *adj* selbstzufrieden

complain [kəm'pleɪn] *vi* sich beklagen; (*formally*) sich beschweren; ~**t** *n* Klage *f*; (*formal ~t*) Beschwerde *f*; (*MED*) Leiden *nt*

complement [*n* 'kɒmplɪmənt, *vb* 'kɒmplɪment] *n* Ergänzung *f*; (*ship's crew etc*) Bemannung *f* ♦ *vt* ergänzen; ~**ary** [kɒmplɪ'mentərɪ] *adj* (*sich*) ergänzend

complete [kəm'pliːt] *adj* (*full*) vollkommen, ganz; (*finished*) fertig ♦ *vt* vervollständigen; (*finish*) beenden; (*fill in: form*) ausfüllen; ~**ly** *adv* ganz

completion [kəm'pliːʃən] *n* Fertigstellung *f*; (*of contract etc*) Abschluß *m*

complex ['kɒmpleks] *adj* kompliziert

complexion [kəm'plekʃən] *n* Gesichtsfarbe *f*; (*fig*) Aspekt *m*

complexity [kəm'pleksɪtɪ] *n* Kompliziertheit *f*

compliance [kəm'plaɪəns] *n* Fügsamkeit *f*, Einwilligung *f*; **in** ~ **with sth** einer Sache *dat* gemäß

complicate ['kɒmplɪkeɪt] *vt* komplizieren; ~**d** *adj* kompliziert

complication [kɒmplɪ'keɪʃən] n Komplikation f

complicity [kən'plɪsɪtɪ] n: ~ (in) Mittäterschaft f (bei)

compliment [n 'kɒmplɪmənt, vb 'kɒmplɪment] n Kompliment nt ♦ vt ein Kompliment machen +dat; ~s npl (greetings) Grüße pl; **to pay sb a** ~ jdm ein Kompliment machen; ~ary [kɒmplɪ'mentərɪ] adj schmeichelhaft; (free) Frei-, Gratis-

comply [kəm'plaɪ] vi: **to** ~ **with** erfüllen +acc; entsprechen +dat

component [kəm'pəʊnənt] adj Teil- ♦ n Bestandteil m

compose [kəm'pəʊz] vt (music) komponieren; (poetry) verfassen; **to** ~ **o.s.** sich sammeln; ~**d** adj gefaßt; ~**r** n Komponist(in) m(f)

composite ['kɒmpəzɪt] adj zusammengesetzt

composition [kɒmpə'zɪʃən] n (MUS) Komposition f; (SCH) Aufsatz m; (structure) Zusammensetzung f, Aufbau m

compost ['kɒmpɒst] n Kompost m

composure [kəm'pəʊʒə*] n Fassung f

compound ['kɒmpaʊnd] n (CHEM) Verbindung f; (enclosure) Lager nt; (LING) Kompositum nt ♦ adj zusammengesetzt; (fracture) kompliziert; ~ **interest** n Zinseszins m

comprehend [kɒmprɪ'hend] vt begreifen

comprehension [kɒmprɪ'henʃən] n Verständnis nt

comprehensive [kɒmprɪ'hensɪv] adj umfassend ♦ n = **comprehensive school**; ~ **insurance** n Vollkasko nt; ~ **school** (BRIT) n Gesamtschule f

compress [vb kəm'pres, n 'kɒmpres] vt komprimieren ♦ n (MED) Kompresse f

comprise [kəm'praɪz] vt (also: **be** ~**d of**) umfassen, bestehen aus

compromise ['kɒmprəmaɪz] n Kompromiß m ♦ vt kompromittieren ♦ vi einen Kompromiß schließen

compulsion [kəm'pʌlʃən] n Zwang m

compulsive [kəm'pʌlsɪv] adj zwanghaft

compulsory [kəm'pʌlsərɪ] adj obligatorisch

computer [kəm'pjuːtə*] n Computer m, Rechner m; ~**ize** vt (information) computerisieren; (company, accounts) auf Computer umstellen; ~ **programmer** n Programmierer(in) m(f); ~ **programming** n Programmieren nt; ~ **science** n Informatik f

computing n (science) Informatik f; (work) Computerei f

comrade ['kɒmrɪd] n Kamerad m; (POL) Genosse m; ~**ship** n Kameradschaft f

con [kɒn] vt hereinlegen ♦ n Schwindel nt

concave [kɒn'keɪv] adj konkav

conceal [kən'siːl] vt (secret) verschweigen; (hide) verbergen

concede [kən'siːd] vt (grant) gewähren; (point) zugeben ♦ vi (admit defeat) nachgeben

conceit [kən'siːt] n Einbildung f; ~**ed** adj eingebildet

conceivable [kən'siːvəbl] adj vorstellbar

conceive [kən'siːv] vt (idea) ausdenken; (imagine) sich vorstellen; (baby) empfangen ♦ vi empfangen

concentrate ['kɒnsəntreɪt] vi sich konzentrieren ♦ vt konzentrieren; **to** ~ **on sth** sich auf etw acc konzentrieren

concentration [kɒnsən'treɪʃən] n Konzentration f; ~ **camp** n Konzentrationslager nt, KZ nt

concept ['kɒnsept] n Begriff m

conception [kən'sepʃən] n (idea) Vorstellung f; (BIOL) Empfängnis f

concern [kən'sɜːn] n (affair) Angelegenheit f; (COMM) Unternehmen nt; (worry) Sorge f ♦ vt (interest) angehen; (be about) handeln von; (have connection with) betreffen; **to be** ~**ed (about)** sich Sorgen machen (um); ~**ing** prep hinsichtlich +gen

concert ['kɒnsət] n Konzert nt

concerted [kən'sɜːtɪd] adj gemeinsam

concert hall n Konzerthalle f

concertina [kɒnsə'tiːnə] n Handharmonika f

concerto [kən'tʃɜːtəʊ] n Konzert nt

concession [kən'seʃən] n (yielding) Zugeständnis nt; **tax** ~ Steuer-Konzession

f

conciliation [kənsɪlɪ'eɪʃən] n Versöhnung f; (official) Schlichtung f

concise [kən'saɪs] adj präzis

conclude [kən'kluːd] vt (end) beenden; (treaty) (ab)schließen; (decide) schließen, folgern

conclusion [kən'kluːʒən] n (Ab)schluß m; (deduction) Schluß m

conclusive [kən'kluːsɪv] adj schlüssig

concoct [kən'kɒkt] vt zusammenbrauen; ~ion [kən'kɒkʃən] n Gebräu nt

concourse ['kɒŋkɔːs] n (Bahnhofs)halle f, Vorplatz m

concrete ['kɒŋkriːt] n Beton m ♦ adj konkret

concur [kən'kɜː*] vi übereinstimmen

concurrently [kən'kʌrəntlɪ] adv gleichzeitig

concussion [kɒn'kʌʃən] n (Gehirn-) erschütterung f

condemn [kən'dem] vt (JUR) verurteilen; (building) abbruchreif erklären

condensation [kɒnden'seɪʃən] n Kondensation f

condense [kən'dens] vi (CHEM) kondensieren ♦ vt (fig) zusammendrängen; ~d milk n Kondensmilch f

condescending [kɒndɪ'sendɪŋ] adj herablassend

condition [kən'dɪʃən] n (state) Zustand m; (presupposition) Bedingung f ♦ vt (hair etc) behandeln; (accustom) gewöhnen; ~s npl (circumstances) Verhältnisse pl; **on ~ that** ... unter der Bedingung, daß ...; ~al adj bedingt; (LING) Bedingungs-; ~er n (for hair) Spülung f; (for fabrics) Weichspüler m

condolences [kən'dəʊlənsɪz] npl Beileid nt

condom ['kɒndəm] n Kondom nt or m

condominium [kɒndə'mɪnɪəm] (US) n Eigentumswohnung f; (block) Eigentumsblock m

condone [kən'dəʊn] vt gutheißen

conducive [kən'djuːsɪv] adj: ~ **to** dienlich +dat

conduct [n 'kɒndʌkt, vb kən'dʌkt] n (behaviour) Verhalten nt; (manage-

ment) Führung f ♦ vt führen; (MUS) dirigieren; ~**ed tour** n Führung f; ~**or** [kən'dʌktə*] n (of orchestra) Dirigent m; (in bus, US: on train) Schaffner m; (ELEC) Leiter m; ~**ress** [kən'dʌktrɪs] n (in bus) Schaffnerin f

cone [kəʊn] n (MATH) Kegel m; (for ice cream) (Waffel)tüte f; (BOT) Tannenzapfen m

confectioner [kən'fekʃənə*] n Konditor m; ~'**s (shop)** n Konditorei f; ~**y** n Süßigkeiten pl

confederation [kənfedə'reɪʃən] n Bund m

confer [kən'fɜː*] vt (degree) verleihen ♦ vi (discuss) konferieren, verhandeln; ~**ence** ['kɒnfərəns] n Konferenz f

confess [kən'fes] vt, vi gestehen; (ECCL) beichten; ~**ion** [kən'feʃən] n Geständnis nt; (ECCL) Beichte f; ~**ional** [kən'feʃənl] n Beichtstuhl m

confetti [kən'fetɪ] n Konfetti nt

confide [kən'faɪd] vi: **to ~ in** (sich) anvertrauen +dat

confidence ['kɒnfɪdəns] n Vertrauen nt; (assurance) Selbstvertrauen nt; (secret) Geheimnis nt; **in ~** (speak, write) vertraulich; ~ **trick** n Schwindel m

confident ['kɒnfɪdənt] adj (sure) überzeugt; (self-assured) selbstsicher

confidential [kɒnfɪ'denʃəl] adj vertraulich

confine [kən'faɪn] vt (limit) beschränken; (lock up) einsperren; ~**d** adj (space) eng; ~**ment** n (in prison) Haft f; (MED) Wochenbett nt; ~**s** ['kɒnfaɪnz] npl Grenzen pl

confirm [kən'fɜːm] vt bestätigen; ~**ation** [kɒnfə'meɪʃən] n Bestätigung f; (REL) Konfirmation f; ~**ed** adj unverbesserlich; (bachelor) eingefleischt

confiscate ['kɒnfɪskeɪt] vt beschlagnahmen

conflict [n 'kɒnflɪkt, vb kən'flɪkt] n Konflikt m ♦ vi im Widerspruch stehen; ~**ing** [kən'flɪktɪŋ] adj widersprüchlich

conform [kən'fɔːm] vi: **to ~ (to)** (things) entsprechen +dat; (people) sich anpassen +*dat*; (*to rules*) sich richten (nach); ~**ist** *n* Konformist(in) *m(f)*

confound [kən'faʊnd] *vt* verblüffen; (*throw into confusion*) durcheinanderbringen

confront [kən'frʌnt] *vt* (*enemy*) entgegentreten +*dat*; (*problems*) sich stellen +*dat*; **to ~ sb with sth** jdn mit etw konfrontieren; ~**ation** [kɒnfrən-'teɪʃən] *n* Konfrontation *f*

confuse [kən'fju:z] *vt* verwirren; (*sth with sth*) verwechseln; ~**d** *adj* verwirrt; **confusing** *adj* verwirrend; **confusion** [kən'fju:ʒən] *n* (*perplexity*) Verwirrung *f*; (*mixing up*) Verwechslung *f*; (*tumult*) Aufruhr *m*

congeal [kən'dʒi:l] *vi* (*freeze*) gefrieren; (*clot*) gerinnen

congenial [kən'dʒi:nɪəl] *adj* angenehm

congenital [kən'dʒenɪtəl] *adj* angeboren

congested [kən'dʒestɪd] *adj* überfüllt

congestion [kən'dʒestʃən] *n* Stau *m*

conglomerate [kən'glɒmərət] *n* (*COMM, GEOL*) Konglomerat *nt*

conglomeration [kənglɒmə'reɪʃən] *n* Anhäufung *f*

congratulate [kən'grætjʊleɪt] *vt*: **to ~ sb (on sth)** jdn (zu etw) beglückwünschen

congratulations [kəngrætjʊ'leɪʃənz] *npl* Glückwünsche *pl*; ~! gratuliere!, herzlichen Glückwunsch!

congregate ['kɒŋgrɪgeɪt] *vi* sich versammeln

congregation [kɒŋgrɪ'geɪʃən] *n* Gemeinde *f*

congress ['kɒŋgres] *n* Kongreß *m*; ~**man** (*US: irreg*) *n* Mitglied *nt* des amerikanischen Repräsentantenhauses

conical ['kɒnɪkəl] *adj* kegelförmig

conifer ['kɒnɪfə*] *n* Nadelbaum *m*

conjecture [kən'dʒektʃə*] *n* Vermutung *f*

conjugal ['kɒndʒʊgəl] *adj* ehelich

conjugate ['kɒndʒʊgeɪt] *vt* konjugieren

conjunction [kən'dʒʌŋkʃən] *n* Verbindung *f*; (*GRAM*) Konjunktion *f*

conjunctivitis [kəndʒʌŋktɪ'vaɪtɪs] *n* Bindehautentzündung *f*

conjure ['kʌndʒə*] *vi* zaubern; ~ **up** *vt*

heraufbeschwören; ~**r** *n* Zauberkünstler(in) *m(f)*

conk out [kɒŋk-] (*inf*) *vi* den Geist aufgeben

conman ['kɒnmæn] (*irreg*) *n* Schwindler *m*

connect [kə'nekt] *vt* verbinden; (*ELEC*) anschließen; **to be ~ed with** ein Beziehung haben zu; (*be related to*) verwandt sein mit; ~**ion** [kə'nekʃən] *n* Verbindung *f*; (*relation*) Zusammenhang *m*; (*ELEC, TEL, RAIL*) Anschluß *m*

connive [kə'naɪv] *vi*: **to ~ at** stillschweigend dulden

connoisseur [kɒnɪ'sɜ:*] *n* Kenner *m*

conquer ['kɒŋkə*] *vt* (*feelings*) überwinden; (*enemy*) besiegen; (*country*) erobern; ~**or** *n* Eroberer *m*

conquest ['kɒŋkwest] *n* Eroberung *f*

cons [kɒnz] *npl see* **convenience; pro**

conscience ['kɒnʃəns] *n* Gewissen *nt*

conscientious [kɒnʃɪ'enʃəs] *adj* gewissenhaft

conscious ['kɒnʃəs] *adj* bewußt; (*MED*) bei Bewußtsein; ~**ness** *n* Bewußtsein *nt*

conscript ['kɒnskrɪpt] *n* Wehrpflichtige(r) *m*; ~**ion** [kən'skrɪpʃən] *n* Wehrpflicht *f*

consecrate ['kɒnsɪkreɪt] *vt* weihen

consecutive [kən'sekjʊtɪv] *adj* aufeinanderfolgend

consensus [kən'sensəs] *n* allgemeine Übereinstimmung *f*

consent [kən'sent] *n* Zustimmung *f* ♦ *vi* zustimmen

consequence ['kɒnsɪkwəns] *n* (*importance*) Bedeutung *f*; (*effect*) Folge *f*

consequently ['kɒnsɪkwəntlɪ] *adv* folglich

conservation [kɒnsə'veɪʃən] *n* Erhaltung *f*; (*nature ~*) Umweltschutz *m*

conservative [kən'sɜ:vətɪv] *adj* konservativ; **C~** (*BRIT*) *adj* konservativ ♦ *n* Konservative(r) *mf*

conservatory [kən'sɜ:vətrɪ] *n* (*room*) Wintergarten *m*

conserve [kən'sɜ:v] *vt* erhalten

consider [kən'sɪdə*] *vt* überlegen; (*take into account*) in Betracht ziehen;

(*regard as*) halten für; **to ~ doing sth** daran denken, etw zu tun

considerable [kən'sɪdərəbl] *adj* beträchtlich

considerably *adv* beträchtlich

considerate [kən'sɪdərɪt] *adj* rücksichtsvoll

consideration [kənsɪdə'reɪʃən] *n* Rücksicht(nahme) *f*; (*thought*) Erwägung *f*; (*reward*) Entgelt *nt*

considering [kən'sɪdərɪŋ] *prep* in Anbetracht +*gen*

consign [kən'saɪn] *vt* übergeben; **~ment** *n* Sendung *f*

consist [kən'sɪst] *vi*: **to ~ of** bestehen aus

consistency [kən'sɪstənsɪ] *n* (*of material*) Konsistenz *f*; (*of argument, person*) Konsequenz *f*

consistent [kən'sɪstənt] *adj* (*person*) konsequent; (*argument*) folgerichtig

consolation [kɒnsə'leɪʃən] *n* Trost *m*

console[1] [kən'səʊl] *vt* trösten

console[2] ['kɒnsəʊl] *n* Kontroll(pult) *nt*

consolidate [kən'sɒlɪdeɪt] *vt* festigen

consommé [kən'sɒmeɪ] *n* Fleischbrühe *f*

consonant ['kɒnsənənt] *n* Konsonant *m*

conspicuous [kən'spɪkjʊəs] *adj* (*prominent*) auffällig; (*visible*) deutlich sichtbar

conspiracy [kən'spɪrəsɪ] *n* Verschwörung *f*

conspire [kən'spaɪə*] *vi* sich verschwören

constable ['kʌnstəbl] (*BRIT*) *n* Polizist(in) *m(f)*; **chief ~** Polizeipräsident *m*

constabulary [kən'stæbjʊlərɪ] *n* Polizei *f*

constant ['kɒnstənt] *adj* (*continuous*) ständig; (*unchanging*) konstant; **~ly** *adv* ständig

constellation [kɒnstə'leɪʃən] *n* Sternbild *nt*

consternation [kɒnstə'neɪʃən] *n* Bestürzung *f*

constipated ['kɒnstɪpeɪtəd] *adj* verstopft

constipation [kɒnstɪ'peɪʃən] *n* Verstopfung *f*

constituency [kən'stɪtjʊənsɪ] *n* Wahlkreis *m*

constituent [kən'stɪtjʊənt] *n* (*person*) Wähler *m*; (*part*) Bestandteil *m*

constitute ['kɒnstɪtjuːt] *vt* (*make up*) bilden; (*amount to*) darstellen

constitution [kɒnstɪ'tjuːʃən] *n* Verfassung *f*; **~al** *adj* Verfassungs-

constraint [kən'streɪnt] *n* Zwang *m*; (*shyness*) Befangenheit *f*

construct [kən'strʌkt] *vt* bauen; **~ion** [kən'strʌkʃən] *n* Konstruktion *f*; (*building*) Bau *m*; **~ive** *adj* konstruktiv

construe [kən'struː] *vt* deuten

consul ['kɒnsl] *n* Konsul *m*; **~ate** ['kɒnsjʊlət] *n* Konsulat *nt*

consult [kən'sʌlt] *vt* um Rat fragen; (*doctor*) konsultieren; (*book*) nachschlagen in +*dat*; **~ant** *n* (*MED*) Facharzt *m*; (*other specialist*) Gutachter *m*; **~ation** [kɒnsəl'teɪʃən] *n* Beratung *f*; (*MED*) Konsultation *f*; **~ing room** *n* Sprechzimmer *nt*

consume [kən'sjuːm] *vt* verbrauchen; (*food*) konsumieren; **~r** *n* Verbraucher *m*; **~r goods** *npl* Konsumgüter *pl*; **~rism** *n* Konsum *m*; **~r society** *n* Konsumgesellschaft *f*

consummate ['kɒnsʌmeɪt] *vt* (*marriage*) vollziehen

consumption [kən'sʌmpʃən] *n* Verbrauch *m*; (*of food*) Konsum *m*

cont. *abbr* (= *continued*) Forts.

contact ['kɒntækt] *n* (*touch*) Berührung *f*; (*connection*) Verbindung *f*; (*person*) Kontakt *m* ♦ *vt* sich in Verbindung setzen mit; **~ lenses** *npl* Kontaktlinsen *pl*

contagious [kən'teɪdʒəs] *adj* ansteckend

contain [kən'teɪn] *vt* enthalten; **to ~ o.s.** sich zügeln; **~er** *n* Behälter *m*; (*transport*) Container *m*

contaminate [kən'tæmɪneɪt] *vt* verunreinigen

contamination [kəntæmɪ'neɪʃən] *n* Verunreinigung *f*

cont'd *abbr* (= *continued*) Forts.

contemplate ['kɒntəmpleɪt] *vt* (*look at*) (nachdenklich) betrachten; (*think about*) überdenken; (*plan*) vorhaben

contemporary [kən'tempərərɪ] *adj* zeitgenössisch ♦ *n* Zeitgenosse *m*

contempt [kən'tempt] *n* Verachtung *f*;
~ **of court** (*JUR*) Mißachtung *f* des
Gerichts; ~**ible** *adj* verachtenswert;
~**uous** *adj* verächtlich

contend [kən'tend] *vt* (*argue*)
behaupten ♦ *vi* kämpfen; ~**er** *n* (*for
post*) Bewerber(in) *m(f)*; (*SPORT*)
Wettkämpfer(in) *m(f)*

content [*adj, vb* kən'tent, *n* 'kɔntent] *adj*
zufrieden ♦ *vt* befriedigen ♦ *n* (*also:*
~**s**) Inhalt *m*; ~**ed** *adj* zufrieden

contention [kən'tenʃən] *n* (*dispute*)
Streit *m*; (*argument*) Behauptung *f*

contentment [kən'tentmənt] *n* Zu-
friedenheit *f*

contest [*n* 'kɔntest, *vb* kən'test] *n*
(Wett)kampf *m* ♦ *vt* (*dispute*) bestreiten; (*JUR*) anfechten; (*POL*)
kandidieren in +*dat*; ~**ant** [kən'testənt]
n Bewerber(in) *m(f)*

context ['kɔntekst] *n* Zusammenhang *m*

continent ['kɔntinənt] *n* Kontinent *m*;
the C~ (*BRIT*) das europäische Festland; ~**al** [kɔntɪ'nentl] *adj* kontinental;
~**al quilt** (*BRIT*) *n* Federbett *nt*

contingency [kən'tɪndʒənsɪ] *n*
Möglichkeit *f*

contingent [kən'tɪndʒənt] *n* Kontingent
nt

continual [kən'tɪnjuəl] *adj* (*endless*)
fortwährend; (*repeated*) immer wiederkehrend; ~**ly** *adv* immer wieder

continuation [kəntɪnju'eɪʃən] *n* Fortsetzung *f*

continue [kən'tɪnjuː] *vi* (*person*)
weitermachen; (*thing*) weitergehen ♦ *vt*
fortsetzen

continuity [kɔntɪ'njʊɪtɪ] *n* Kontinuität *f*

continuous [kən'tɪnjuəs] *adj* ununterbrochen; ~ **stationery** *n* Endlospapier *nt*

contort [kən'tɔːt] *vt* verdrehen; ~**ion**
[kən'tɔːʃən] *n* Verzerrung *f*

contour ['kɔntuə*] *n* Umriß *m*; (*also:* ~
line) Höhenlinie *f*

contraband ['kɔntrəbænd] *n* Schmuggel-
ware *f*

contraception [kɔntrə'sepʃən] *n*
Empfängnisverhütung *f*

contraceptive [kɔntrə'septɪv] *n*
empfängnisverhütende(s) Mittel *nt* ♦

adj empfängnisverhütend

contract [*n* 'kɔntrækt, *vb* kən'trækt] *n*
Vertrag *m* ♦ *vi* (*muscle, metal*) sich
zusammenziehen ♦ *vt* zusammenziehen;
to ~ to do sth (*COMM*) sich vertraglich
verpflichten, etw zu tun; ~**ion**
[kən'trækʃən] *n* (*shortening*) Verkürzung
f; ~**or** [kən'træktə*] *n* Unternehmer *m*

contradict [kɔntrə'dɪkt] *vt* widersprechen +*dat*; ~**ion** [kɔntrə'dɪkʃən] *n* Widerspruch *m*; ~**ory** *adj* widersprüchlich

contraption [kən'træpʃən] *n* (*inf*)
Apparat *m*

contrary[1] ['kɔntrərɪ] *adj* (*opposite*) entgegengesetzt ♦ *n* Gegenteil *nt*; **on the ~**
im Gegenteil

contrary[2] [kən'treərɪ] *adj* (*obstinate*)
widerspenstig

contrast [*n* 'kɔntrɑːst, *vb* kən'trɑːst] *n*
Kontrast *m* ♦ *vt* entgegensetzen; ~**ing**
[kən'trɑːstɪŋ] *adj* Kontrast-

contravene [kɔntrə'viːn] *vt* verstoßen
gegen

contribute [kən'trɪbjuːt] *vt, vi*: **to ~ to**
beitragen zu

contribution [kɔntrɪ'bjuːʃən] *n* Beitrag
m

contributor [kən'trɪbjʊtə*] *n* Bei-
tragende(r) *mf*

contrive [kən'traɪv] *vt* ersinnen ♦ *vi*: **to
~ to do sth** es schaffen, etw zu tun

control [kən'trəʊl] *vt* (*direct, test*) kontrollieren ♦ *n* Kontrolle *f*; ~**s** *npl* (*of
vehicle*) Steuerung *f*; (*of engine*)
Schalttafel *f*; **to be in ~ of** (*business,
office*) leiten; (*group of children*)
beaufsichtigen; **out of ~** außer Kontrolle; **under ~** unter Kontrolle; ~
panel *n* Schalttafel *f*; ~ **room** *n* Kon-
trollraum *m*; ~ **tower** *n* (*AVIAT*) Kon-
trollturm *m*

controversial [kɔntrə'vɜːʃəl] *adj* umstritten

controversy ['kɔntrəvɜːsɪ] *n* Kon-
troverse *f*

conurbation [kɔnɜː'beɪʃən] *n*
Ballungsgebiet *nt*

convalesce [kɔnvə'les] *vi* genesen;
~**nce** *n* Genesung *f*

convector [kən'vektə*] *n* Heizlüfter *m*

convene [kən'viːn] vt zusammenrufen ♦ vi sich versammeln

convenience [kən'viːnɪəns] n Annehmlichkeit f; **all modern ~s** mit allem Komfort; **all mod cons** (BRIT) mit allem Komfort; **at your ~** wann es Ihnen paßt

convenient [kən'viːnɪənt] adj günstig

convent ['kɒnvənt] n Kloster nt

convention [kən'venʃən] n Versammlung f; (custom) Konvention f; **~al** adj konventionell

converge [kən'vɜːdʒ] vi zusammenlaufen

conversant [kən'vɜːsənt] adj: **to be ~ with** bewandert sein in +dat

conversation [kɒnvə'seɪʃən] n Gespräch nt; **~al** adj Unterhaltungs-

converse [n 'kɒnvɜːs, vb kən'vɜːs] n Gegenteil nt ♦ vi sich unterhalten

conversion [kən'vɜːʃən] n Umwandlung f; (esp REL) Bekehrung f

convert [vb kən'vɜːt, n 'kɒnvɜːt] vt (change) umwandeln; (REL) bekehren ♦ n Bekehrte(r) mf; Konvertit(in) m(f); **~ible** n (AUT) Kabriolett nt ♦ adj umwandelbar; (FIN) konvertierbar

convex [kɒn'veks] adj konvex

convey [kən'veɪ] vt (carry) befördern; (feelings) vermitteln; **~or belt** n Fließband nt

convict [vb kən'vɪkt, n 'kɒnvɪkt] vt verurteilen ♦ n Häftling m; **~ion** [kən'vɪkʃən] n (verdict) Verurteilung f; (belief) Überzeugung f

convince [kən'vɪns] vt überzeugen; **~d** adj: **~d that** überzeugt davon, daß; **convincing** adj überzeugend

convoluted [kɒnvə'luːtɪd] adj verwickelt; (style) gewunden

convoy ['kɒnvɔɪ] n (of vehicles) Kolonne f; (protected) Konvoi m

convulse [kən'vʌls] vt zusammenzucken lassen; **to be ~d with laughter** sich vor Lachen krümmen

convulsion [kən'vʌlʃən] n (esp MED) Zuckung f, Krampf m

coo [kuː] vi gurren

cook [kʊk] vt, vi kochen ♦ n Koch m, Köchin f; **~ book** n Kochbuch nt; **~er** n Herd m; **~ery** n Kochkunst f; **~ery book** (BRIT) n = **cook book**; **~ie** (US) n Plätzchen nt; **~ing** n Kochen nt

cool [kuːl] adj kühl ♦ vt, vi (ab)kühlen; **~ down** vt, vi (fig) (sich) beruhigen; **~ness** n Kühle f; (of temperament) kühle(r) Kopf m

coop [kuːp] n Hühnerstall m ♦ vt: **~ up** (fig) einpferchen

cooperate [kəʊ'ɒpəreɪt] vi zusammenarbeiten; **cooperation** [kəʊɒpə'reɪʃən] n Zusammenarbeit f

cooperative [kəʊ'ɒpərətɪv] adj hilfsbereit; (COMM) genossenschaftlich ♦ n (of farmers) Genossenschaft f; (~ store) Konsumladen m

coordinate [vb kəʊ'ɔːdɪneɪt, n kəʊ'ɔːdɪnət] vt koordinieren ♦ n (MATH) Koordinate f; **~s** npl (clothes) Kombinationen pl

coordination [kəʊɔːdɪ'neɪʃən] n Koordination f

cop [kɒp] (inf) n Polyp m, Bulle m

cope [kəʊp] vi: **to ~ with** fertig werden mit

copious ['kəʊpɪəs] adj reichhaltig

copper ['kɒpə*] n (metal) Kupfer nt; (inf: policeman) Polyp m, Bulle m; **~s** npl (money) Kleingeld nt

coppice ['kɒpɪs] n Unterholz nt

copse [kɒps] n Unterholz nt

copulate ['kɒpjʊleɪt] vi sich paaren

copy ['kɒpɪ] n (imitation) Kopie f; (of book etc) Exemplar nt; (of newspaper) Nummer f ♦ vt kopieren, abschreiben; **~right** n Copyright nt

coral ['kɒrəl] n Koralle f; **~ reef** n Korallenriff nt

cord [kɔːd] n Schnur f; (ELEC) Kabel nt

cordial ['kɔːdɪəl] adj herzlich ♦ n Fruchtsaft m

cordon ['kɔːdn] n Absperrkette f; **~ off** vt abriegeln

corduroy ['kɔːdərɔɪ] n Kord(samt) m

core [kɔː*] n Kern m ♦ vt entkernen

cork [kɔːk] n (bark) Korkrinde f; (stopper) Korken m; **~screw** n Korkenzieher m

corn [kɔːn] n (BRIT: wheat) Getreide nt, Korn nt; (US: maize) Mais m; (on foot) Hühnerauge nt; **~ on the cob**

Maiskolben *m*

cornea ['kɔːnɪə] *n* Hornhaut *f*

corned beef ['kɔːnd-] *n* Corned Beef *nt*

corner ['kɔːnə*] *n* Ecke *f*; (*on road*) Kurve *f* ♦ *vt* in die Enge treiben; (*market*) monopolisieren ♦ *vi* (*AUT*) in die Kurve gehen; **~stone** *n* Eckstein *m*

cornet ['kɔːnɪt] *n* (*MUS*) Kornett *nt*; (*BRIT*: *of ice cream*) Eistüte *f*

cornflakes ['kɔːnfleɪks] *npl* Cornflakes *pl* (®)

cornflour ['kɔːnflauə*] (*BRIT*) *n* Maizena *nt* (®)

cornstarch ['kɔːnstɑːtʃ] (*US*) *n* Maizena *nt* (®)

Cornwall ['kɔːnwəl] *n* Cornwall *nt*

corny ['kɔːnɪ] *adj* (*joke*) blöd(e)

corollary [kə'rɒlərɪ] *n* Folgesatz *m*

coronary ['kɒrənərɪ] *n* (*also*: ~ *thrombosis*) Herzinfarkt *m*

coronation [kɒrə'neɪʃən] *n* Krönung *f*

coroner ['kɒrənə*] *n* Untersuchungsrichter *m*

coronet ['kɒrənɪt] *n* Adelskrone *f*

corporal ['kɔːpərəl] *n* Obergefreite(r) *m* ♦ *adj*: ~ **punishment** Prügelstrafe *f*

corporate ['kɔːpərɪt] *adj* gemeinschaftlich, korporativ

corporation [kɔːpə'reɪʃən] *n* (*of town*) Gemeinde *f*; (*COMM*) Körperschaft *f*, Aktiengesellschaft *f*

corps [kɔː*, *pl* kɔːz] (*pl* **corps**) *n* (Armee)korps *nt*

corpse [kɔːps] *n* Leiche *f*

corpuscle ['kɔːpʌsl] *n* Blutkörperchen *nt*

corral [kə'rɑːl] *n* Pferch *m*, Korral *m*

correct [kə'rekt] *adj* (*accurate*) richtig; (*proper*) korrekt ♦ *vt* korrigieren; **~ion** [kə'rekʃən] *n* Berichtigung *f*

correlation [kɒrɪ'leɪʃən] *n* Wechselbeziehung *f*

correspond [kɒrɪs'pɒnd] *vi* (*agree*) übereinstimmen; (*exchange letters*) korrespondieren; **~ence** *n* (*similarity*) Entsprechung *f*; (*letters*) Briefwechsel *m*, Korrespondenz *f*; **~ence course** *n* Fernkurs *m*; **~ent** *n* (*PRESS*) Berichterstatter *m*

corridor ['kɒrɪdɔː*] *n* Gang *m*

corroborate [kə'rɒbəreɪt] *vt* bestätigen

corrode [kə'rəud] *vt* zerfressen ♦ *vi* rosten

corrosion [kə'rəuʒən] *n* Korrosion *f*

corrugated ['kɒrəgeɪtɪd] *adj* gewellt; ~ **iron** *n* Wellblech *nt*

corrupt [kə'rʌpt] *adj* korrupt ♦ *vt* verderben; (*bribe*) bestechen; **~ion** [kə'rʌpʃən] *n* (*of society*) Verdorbenheit *f*; (*bribery*) Bestechung *f*

corset ['kɔːsɪt] *n* Korsett *nt*

Corsica ['kɔːsɪkə] *n* Korsika *nt*

cortège [kɔː'teɪʒ] *n* Zug *m*; (*of funeral*) Leichenzug *m*

cosh [kɒʃ] (*BRIT*) *n* Totschläger *m*

cosmetic [kɒz'metɪk] *n* Kosmetikum *nt*

cosmic ['kɒzmɪk] *adj* kosmisch

cosmonaut ['kɒzmənɔːt] *n* Kosmonaut(in) *m(f)*

cosmopolitan [kɒzmə'pɒlɪtən] *adj* international; (*city*) Welt-

cosmos ['kɒzmɒs] *n* Kosmos *m*

cosset ['kɒsɪt] *vt* verwöhnen

cost [kɒst] (*pt*, *pp* **cost**) *n* Kosten *pl*, Preis *m* ♦ *vt*, *vi* kosten; ~**s** *npl* (*JUR*) Kosten *pl*; **how much does it ~?** wieviel kostet das?; **at all ~s** um jeden Preis

co-star ['kəustɑː*] *n* zweite(r) *or* weitere(r) Hauptdarsteller(in) *m(f)*

cost-effective ['kɒstɪ'fektɪv] *adj* rentabel

costly ['kɒstlɪ] *adj* kostspielig

cost-of-living ['kɒstəv'lɪvɪŋ] *adj* (*allowance*, *index*) Lebenshaltungskosten-

cost price (*BRIT*) *n* Selbstkostenpreis *m*

costume ['kɒstjuːm] *n* Kostüm *nt*; (*fancy dress*) Maskenkostüm *nt*; (*BRIT*: *also*: *swimming* ~) Badeanzug *m*; ~ **jewellery** *n* Modeschmuck *m*

cosy ['kəuzɪ] (*BRIT*) *adj* behaglich; (*atmosphere*) gemütlich

cot [kɒt] *n* (*BRIT*: *child's*) Kinderbett(chen) *nt*; (*US*: *campbed*) Feldbett *nt*

cottage ['kɒtɪdʒ] *n* kleine(s) Haus *nt*; ~ **cheese** *n* Hüttenkäse *m*; ~ **industry** *n* Heimindustrie *f*; ~ **pie** *n* Auflauf *m* mit Hackfleisch und Kartoffelbrei *m*

cotton ['kɒtn] *n* Baumwolle *f*; (*thread*) Garn *nt*; ~ **on to** (*inf*) *vt* kapieren; ~ **candy** (*US*) *n* Zuckerwatte *f*; ~ **wool**

(BRIT) n Watte f
couch [kautʃ] n Couch f
couchette [ku:'ʃet] n *(on train, boat)* Liegewagenplatz m
cough [kɒf] vi husten ♦ n Husten m; ~ **drop** n Hustenbonbon nt
could [kud] pt of **can²**; ~**n't** = could not
council ['kaunsl] n *(of town)* Stadtrat m; ~ **estate** *(BRIT)* n Siedlung f des sozialen Wohnungsbaus; ~ **house** *(BRIT)* n Haus nt des sozialen Wohnungsbaus; ~**lor** ['kaunsɪlə*] n Stadtrat m/-rätin f
counsel ['kaunsl] n *(barrister)* Anwalt m; *(advice)* Rat(schlag) m ♦ vt beraten; ~**lor** n Berater m
count [kaunt] vt, vi zählen ♦ n *(reckoning)* Abrechnung f; *(nobleman)* Graf m; ~ **on** vt zählen auf +acc; ~**down** n Countdown m
countenance ['kauntɪnəns] n *(old)* Antlitz nt ♦ vt *(tolerate)* gutheißen
counter ['kauntə*] n *(in shop)* Ladentisch m; *(in café)* Theke f; *(in bank, post office)* Schalter m ♦ vt entgegnen; ~**act** [kauntə'rækt] vt entgegenwirken +dat; ~**-espionage** n Spionageabwehr f
counterfeit ['kauntəfi:t] n Fälschung f ♦ vt fälschen ♦ adj gefälscht
counterfoil ['kauntəfɔɪl] n *(Kontroll)abschnitt m
countermand ['kauntəmɑ:nd] vt rückgängig machen
counterpart ['kauntəpɑ:t] n *(object)* Gegenstück nt; *(person)* Gegenüber nt
counterproductive ['kauntəprə'dʌktɪv] adj destruktiv
countersign ['kauntəsaɪn] vt gegenzeichnen
countess ['kauntɪs] n Gräfin f
countless ['kauntlɪs] adj zahllos, unzählig
country ['kʌntrɪ] n Land nt; ~ **dancing** *(BRIT)* n Volkstanz m; ~ **house** n Landhaus nt; ~**man** *(irreg)* n *(national)* Landsmann m; *(rural)* Bauer m; ~**side** n Landschaft f
county ['kauntɪ] n Landkreis m; *(BRIT)* Grafschaft f

coup [ku:] *(pl ~s)* n Coup m; *(also:* ~ d'état)* Staatsstreich m, Putsch m
coupé n *(AUT)* Coupé nt
couple n Paar nt ♦ vt koppeln; **a** ~ **of** ein paar
coupon n Gutschein m
coups [ku:z] npl of **coup**
courage ['kʌrɪdʒ] n Mut m; ~**ous** [kə'reɪdʒəs] adj mutig
courgette [kuə'ʒet] *(BRIT)* n Zucchini f
courier ['kurɪə*] n *(for holiday)* Reiseleiter m; *(messenger)* Kurier m
course [kɔ:s] n *(race)* Bahn f; *(of stream)* Lauf m; *(golf ~)* Platz m; *(NAUT, SCH)* Kurs m; *(in meal)* Gang m; **of** ~ adv natürlich
court [kɔ:t] n *(royal)* Hof m; *(JUR)* Gericht nt ♦ vt *(woman)* gehen mit; *(danger)* herausfordern; **to take to** ~ vor Gericht bringen
courteous ['kɜ:tɪəs] adj höflich
courtesan [kɔ:tɪ'zæn] n Kurtisane f
courtesy ['kɜ:təsɪ] n Höflichkeit f
court-house ['kɔ:thaus] *(US)* n Gerichtsgebäude nt
courtier ['kɔ:tɪə*] n Höfling m
court-martial ['kɔ:t'mɑ:ʃəl] *(pl courts-martial)* n Kriegsgericht nt ♦ vt vor ein Kriegsgericht stellen
courtroom ['kɔ:trum] n Gerichtssaal m
courts-martial ['kɔ:ts'mɑ:ʃəl] npl of **court-martial**
courtyard ['kɔ:tjɑ:d] n Hof m
cousin ['kʌzn] n Cousin m, Vetter m; Kusine f
cove [kəuv] n kleine Bucht f
covenant ['kʌvənənt] n *(ECCL)* Bund m; *(JUR)* Verpflichtung f
cover ['kʌvə*] vt *(spread over)* bedecken; *(shield)* abschirmen; *(include)* sich erstrecken über +acc; *(protect)* decken; *(distance)* zurücklegen; *(report on)* berichten über +acc ♦ n *(lid)* Deckel m; *(for bed)* Decke f; *(MIL)* Bedeckung f; *(of book)* Einband m; *(of magazine)* Umschlag m; *(insurance)* Versicherung f; **to take** ~ *(from rain)* sich unterstellen; *(MIL)* in Deckung gehen; **under** ~ *(indoors)* drinnen; **under** ~ **of** im Schutze +gen;

under separate ~ (COMM) mit ge-
trennter Post; to ~ up for sb jdn
decken; ~age n (PRESS: reports)
Berichterstattung f; (distribution) Verbreitung f; ~ charge n Bedienungsgeld
nt; ~ing n Bedeckung f; ~ing letter
(US cover letter) n Begleitbrief m; ~
note n (INSURANCE) vorläufige(r) Ver-
sicherungsschein m

covert ['kʌvət] adj geheim
cover-up ['kʌvərʌp] n Vertuschung f
covet ['kʌvɪt] vt begehren
cow [kaʊ] n Kuh f ♦ vt einschüchtern
coward ['kaʊəd] n Feigling m; ~ice
['kaʊədɪs] n Feigheit f; ~ly adj feige
cowboy ['kaʊbɔɪ] n Cowboy m
cower ['kaʊə*] vi kauern
coxswain ['kɒksn] n (abbr: cox)
Steuermann m
coy [kɔɪ] adj schüchtern
coyote [kɔɪ'əʊtɪ] n Präriewolf m
cozy ['kəʊzɪ] (US) adj = cosy
CPA (US) n abbr = certified public
accountant
crab [kræb] n Krebs m; ~ apple n
Holzapfel m
crack [kræk] n Riß m, Sprung m;
(noise) Knall m ♦ vt (break) springen
lassen; (joke) reißen; (nut, safe)
knacken; (whip) knallen lassen ♦ vi
springen ♦ adj erstklassig; (troops)
Elite-; ~ downvi: to ~ down (on) hart
durchgreifen (bei); ~ up vi (fig)
zusammenbrechen; ~er n (firework)
Knallkörper m, Kracher m; (biscuit)
Keks m; (Christmas ~) Knallbonbon nt
crackle ['krækl] vi knistern; (fire)
prasseln
cradle ['kreɪdl] n Wiege f
craft [krɑːft] n (skill) (Hand- or
Kunst)fertigkeit f; (trade) Handwerk
nt; (NAUT) Schiff nt; ~sman (irreg) n
Handwerker m; ~smanship n (quality)
handwerkliche Ausführung f; (ability)
handwerkliche(s) Können nt; ~y adj
schlau
crag [kræg] n Klippe f
cram [kræm] vt vollstopfen ♦ vi (learn)
pauken; to ~ sth into sth etw in etw acc
stopfen

cramp [kræmp] n Krampf m ♦ vt (limit)
einengen; (hinder) hemmen; ~ed adj
(position) verkrampft; (space) eng
crampon ['kræmpən] n Steigeisen nt
cranberry ['krænbərɪ] n Preiselbeere f
crane [kreɪn] n (machine) Kran m;
(bird) Kranich m
crank [kræŋk] n (lever) Kurbel f;
(person) Spinner m; ~shaft n
Kurbelwelle f
cranny ['krænɪ] n see nook
crash [kræʃ] n (noise) Krachen nt; (with
cars) Zusammenstoß m; (with plane)
Absturz m; (COMM) Zusammenbruch m
♦ vt (plane) abstürzen mit ♦ vi (cars)
zusammenstoßen; (plane) abstürzen;
(economy) zusammenbrechen; (noise)
knallen; ~ course n Schnellkurs m; ~
helmet n Sturzhelm m; ~ landing n
Bruchlandung f
crass [kræs] adj kraß
crate [kreɪt] n (also fig) Kiste f
crater ['kreɪtə*] n Krater m
cravat(e) [krə'væt] n Halstuch nt
crave [kreɪv] vt verlangen nach
crawl [krɔːl] vi kriechen; (baby)
krabbeln ♦ n Kriechen nt; (swim)
Kraul nt
crayfish ['kreɪfɪʃ] n inv (freshwater)
Krebs m; (saltwater) Languste f
crayon ['kreɪən] n Buntstift m
craze [kreɪz] n Fimmel m
crazy ['kreɪzɪ] adj verrückt; ~ paving n
Mosaikpflaster nt
creak [kriːk] vi knarren
cream [kriːm] n (from milk) Rahm m,
Sahne f; (polish, cosmetic) Creme f;
(fig: people) Elite f ♦ adj cremfarbig;
~ cake n Sahnetorte f; ~ cheese n
Rahmquark m; ~y adj sahnig
crease [kriːs] n Falte f ♦ vt falten;
(untidy) zerknittern ♦ vi (wrinkle up)
knittern
create [krɪ'eɪt] vt erschaffen; (cause)
verursachen
creation [krɪ'eɪʃən] n Schöpfung f
creative [krɪ'eɪtɪv] adj kreativ
creator [krɪ'eɪtə*] n Schöpfer m
creature ['kriːtʃə*] n Geschöpf nt
creche [kreʃ] n Krippe f

credence ['kri:dəns] n: **to lend** or **give** ~ **to sth** etw dat Glauben schenken
credentials [krɪ'denʃəlz] npl Beglaubigungsschreiben nt
credibility [kredɪ'bɪlɪtɪ] n Glaubwürdigkeit f
credible ['kredɪbl] adj (person) glaubwürdig; (story) glaubhaft
credit ['kredɪt] n (also COMM) Kredit m ♦ vt Glauben schenken +dat; (COMM) gutschreiben; ~**s** npl (of film) Mitwirkenden pl; ~**able** adj rühmlich; ~ **card** n Kreditkarte f; ~**or** n Gläubiger m
creed [kri:d] n Glaubensbekenntnis nt
creek [kri:k] n (inlet) kleine Bucht f; (US: river) kleine(r) Wasserlauf m
creep [kri:p] (pt, pp **crept**) vi kriechen; ~**er** n Kletterpflanze f; ~**y** adj (frightening) gruselig
cremate [krɪ'meɪt] vt einäschern
cremation [krɪ'meɪʃən] n Einäscherung f
crêpe [kreɪp] n Krepp m; ~ **bandage** (BRIT) n Elastikbinde f
crept [krept] pt, pp of **creep**
crescent ['kresnt] n (of moon) Halbmond m
cress [kres] n Kresse f
crest [krest] n (of cock) Kamm m; (of wave) Wellenkamm m; (coat of arms) Wappen nt; ~**fallen** adj niedergeschlagen
Crete [kri:t] n Kreta nt
crevasse [krɪ'væs] n Gletscherspalte f
crevice ['krevɪs] n Riß m
crew [kru:] n Besatzung f, Mannschaft f; ~-**cut** n Bürstenschnitt m; ~-**neck** n runde(r) Ausschnitt m
crib [krɪb] n (bed) Krippe f ♦ vt (inf) spicken
crick [krɪk] n Muskelkrampf m
cricket ['krɪkɪt] n (insect) Grille f; (game) Kricket nt
crime [kraɪm] n Verbrechen nt
criminal ['krɪmɪnl] n Verbrecher m ♦ adj kriminell; (act) strafbar
crimson ['krɪmzn] adj leuchtend rot
cringe [krɪndʒ] vi sich ducken
crinkle ['krɪŋkl] vt zerknittern
cripple ['krɪpl] n Krüppel m ♦ vt

lahmlegen; (MED) verkrüppeln
crises ['kraɪsi:z] npl of **crisis**
crisis ['kraɪsɪs] (pl **crises**) n Krise f
crisp [krɪsp] adj knusprig; ~**s** (BRIT) npl Chips pl
crisscross ['krɪskrɒs] adj gekreuzt, Kreuz-
criteria [kraɪ'tɪərɪə] npl of **criterion**
criterion [kraɪ'tɪərɪən] (pl **criteria**) n Kriterium nt
critic ['krɪtɪk] n Kritiker(in) m(f); ~**al** adj kritisch; ~**ally** adv kritisch; (ill) gefährlich; ~**ism** ['krɪtɪsɪzəm] n Kritik f; ~**ize** ['krɪtɪsaɪz] vt kritisieren
croak [krəʊk] vi krächzen; (frog) quaken
crochet ['krəʊʃeɪ] n Häkelei f
crockery ['krɒkərɪ] n Geschirr nt
crocodile ['krɒkədaɪl] n Krokodil nt
crocus ['krəʊkəs] n Krokus m
croft [krɒft] (BRIT) n kleine(s) Pachtgut nt
crony ['krəʊnɪ] (inf) n Kumpel m
crook [krʊk] n (criminal) Gauner m; (stick) Hirtenstab m; ~**ed** ['krʊkɪd] adj krumm
crop [krɒp] n (harvest) Ernte f; (riding ~) Reitpeitsche f ♦ vt ernten; ~ **up** vi passieren
croquet ['krəʊkeɪ] n Krocket nt
croquette [krə'ket] n Krokette f
cross [krɒs] n Kreuz nt ♦ vt (road) überqueren; (legs) übereinander legen; kreuzen ♦ adj (annoyed) böse; ~ **out** vt streichen; ~ **over** vi hinübergehen; ~**bar** n Querstange f; ~**breed** n Kreuzung f; ~-**country** (**race**) n Geländelauf m; ~-**examine** vt ins Kreuzverhör nehmen; ~-**eyed** adj: **to be** ~-**eyed** schielen; ~**fire** n Kreuzfeuer nt; ~**ing** n (crossroads) (Straßen)kreuzung f; (of ship) Überfahrt f; (for pedestrians) Fußgängerüberweg m; ~**ing guard** (US) n Schülerlotse m; ~ **purposes** npl: **to be at** ~ **purposes** aneinander vorbeireden; ~-**reference** n Querverweis m; ~**roads** n Straßenkreuzung f; (fig) Scheideweg m; ~ **section** n Querschnitt m; ~**walk** (US) n Fußgängerüberweg m; ~**wind** n Seitenwind m; ~**word**

(puzzle) n Kreuzworträtsel nt
crotch [krɒtʃ] n Zwickel m; (ANAT) Unterleib nt
crotchet ['krɒtʃɪt] n Viertelnote f
crotchety ['krɒtʃɪtɪ] adj launenhaft
crouch [krautʃ] vi hocken
croupier ['kru:pɪeɪ] n Croupier m
crow [krəʊ] n (bird) Krähe f; (of cock) Krähen nt ♦ vi krähen
crowbar ['krəʊbɑ:ʳ] n Stemmeisen nt
crowd [kraud] n Menge f ♦ vt (fill) überfüllen ♦ vi drängen; ~ed adj überfüllt
crown [kraun] n Krone f; (of head, hat) Kopf m ♦ vt krönen; ~ jewels npl Kronjuwelen pl; ~ prince n Kronprinz m
crow's-feet ['krəʊzfi:t] npl Krähenfüße pl
crucial ['kru:ʃəl] adj entscheidend
crucifix ['kru:sɪfɪks] n Kruzifix nt; ~ion [kru:sɪ'fɪkʃən] n Kreuzigung f
crucify ['kru:sɪfaɪ] vt kreuzigen
crude [kru:d] adj (raw) roh; (humour, behaviour) grob; (basic) primitiv; ~ (oil) n Rohöl nt
cruel ['kruəl] adj grausam; ~ty n Grausamkeit f
cruet ['kru:ɪt] n Gewürzständer m
cruise [kru:z] n Kreuzfahrt f ♦ vi kreuzen; ~r n (MIL) Kreuzer m
crumb [krʌm] n Krume f
crumble ['krʌmbl] vt, vi zerbröckeln
crumbly ['krʌmblɪ] adj krümelig
crumpet ['krʌmpɪt] n Tee(pfann)kuchen m
crumple ['krʌmpl] vt zerknittern
crunch [krʌntʃ] n: the ~ (fig) der Knackpunkt ♦ vt knirschen; ~y adj knusprig
crusade [kru:'seɪd] n Kreuzzug m
crush [krʌʃ] n Gedränge nt ♦ vt zerdrücken; (rebellion) unterdrücken
crust [krʌst] n Kruste f
crutch [krʌtʃ] n Krücke f
crux [krʌks] n springende(r) Punkt m
cry [kraɪ] vi (shout) schreien; (weep) weinen ♦ n (call) Schrei m; ~ off vi (plötzlich) absagen
crypt [krɪpt] n Krypta f

cryptic ['krɪptɪk] adj hintergründig
crystal ['krɪstl] n Kristall m; (glass) Kristallglas nt; (mineral) Bergkristall m; ~-clear adj kristallklar
crystallize vt, vi kristallisieren; (fig) klären
cub [kʌb] n Junge(s) nt; (also: C~ Scout) Wölfling m
Cuba ['kju:bə] n Kuba nt; ~n adj kubanisch ♦ n Kubaner(in) m(f)
cubbyhole ['kʌbɪhəʊl] n Eckchen nt
cube [kju:b] n Würfel m ♦ vt (MATH) hoch drei nehmen; ~ root n Kubikwurzel f
cubic ['kju:bɪk] adj würfelförmig; (centimetre etc) Kubik-; ~ capacity n Fassungsvermögen nt
cubicle ['kju:bɪkl] n Kabine f
cuckoo ['kuku:] n Kuckuck m; ~ clock n Kuckucksuhr f
cucumber ['kju:kʌmbəʳ] n Gurke f
cuddle ['kʌdl] vt, vi herzen, drücken (inf)
cue [kju:] n (THEAT) Stichwort nt; (snooker ~) Billardstock m
cuff [kʌf] n (BRIT: of shirt, coat etc) Manschette f; Aufschlag m; (US) = turn-up; off the ~ aus dem Handgelenk; ~link n Manschettenknopf m
cuisine [kwɪ'zi:n] n Kochkunst f, Küche f
cul-de-sac ['kʌldəsæk] n Sackgasse f
culinary ['kʌlɪnərɪ] adj Koch-
cull [kʌl] vt (flowers) pflücken; (select) auswählen
culminate ['kʌlmɪneɪt] vi gipfeln
culmination [kʌlmɪ'neɪʃən] n Höhepunkt m
culottes [kju'lɒts] npl Hosenrock m
culpable ['kʌlpəbl] adj schuldig
culprit ['kʌlprɪt] n Täter m
cult [kʌlt] n Kult m
cultivate ['kʌltɪveɪt] vt (AGR) bebauen; (mind) bilden
cultivation [kʌltɪ'veɪʃən] n (AGR) Bebauung f; (of person) Bildung f
cultural ['kʌltʃərəl] adj kulturell, Kultur-
culture ['kʌltʃəʳ] n Kultur f; ~d adj gebildet
cumbersome ['kʌmbəsəm] adj (object)

sperrig
cummerbund [ˈkʌməbʌnd] n Kummerbund m
cumulative [ˈkjuːmjʊlətɪv] adj gehäuft
cunning [ˈkʌnɪŋ] n Verschlagenheit f ♦ adj schlau
cup [kʌp] n Tasse f; (prize) Pokal m
cupboard [ˈkʌbəd] n Schrank m
Cupid [ˈkjuːpɪd] n Amor m
cup tie (BRIT) n Pokalspiel nt
curate [ˈkjʊərɪt] n (Catholic) Kurat m; (Protestant) Vikar m
curator [kjʊˈreɪtə*] n Kustos m
curb [kɜːb] vt zügeln ♦ n (on spending etc) Einschränkung f; (US) Bordstein m
curdle [ˈkɜːdl] vi gerinnen
cure [kjʊə*] n Heilmittel nt; (process) Heilverfahren nt ♦ vt heilen
curfew [ˈkɜːfjuː] n Ausgangssperre f; Sperrstunde f
curio [ˈkjʊərɪəʊ] n Kuriosität f
curiosity [kjʊərɪˈɒsɪtɪ] n Neugier f
curious [ˈkjʊərɪəs] adj neugierig; (strange) seltsam
curl [kɜːl] n Locke f ♦ vt locken ♦ vi sich locken; ~ **up** vi sich zusammenrollen; (person) sich ankuscheln; ~**er** n Lockenwickler m; ~**y** [ˈkɜːlɪ] adj lockig
currant [ˈkʌrənt] n Korinthe f
currency [ˈkʌrənsɪ] n Währung f; **to gain** ~ **an** Popularität gewinnen
current [ˈkʌrənt] n Strömung f ♦ adj (expression) gängig, üblich; (issue) neueste; ~ **account** (BRIT) n Girokonto nt; ~ **affairs** npl Zeitgeschehen nt; ~**ly** adv zur Zeit
curricula [kəˈrɪkjʊlə] npl of curriculum
curriculum [kəˈrɪkjʊləm] (pl ~**s** or **curricula**) n Lehrplan m; ~ **vitae** n Lebenslauf m
curry [ˈkʌrɪ] n Currygericht nt ♦ vt: **to** ~ **favour with** sich einschmeicheln bei; ~ **powder** n Curry(pulver) nt
curse [kɜːs] vi (swear): **to** ~ **(at)** fluchen (auf or über) +acc ♦ vt (insult) verwünschen ♦ n Fluch m
cursor [ˈkɜːsə*] n (COMPUT) Cursor m
cursory [ˈkɜːsərɪ] adj flüchtig
curt [kɜːt] adj schroff
curtail [kɜːˈteɪl] vt abkürzen; (rights)
einschränken
curtain [ˈkɜːtn] n Vorhang m
curts(e)y n Knicks m ♦ vi knicksen
curve [kɜːv] n Kurve f; (of body, vase etc) Rundung f ♦ vi sich biegen; (hips, breasts) sich runden; (road) einen Bogen machen
cushion [ˈkʊʃən] n Kissen nt ♦ vt dämpfen
custard [ˈkʌstəd] n Vanillesoße f
custodian [kʌsˈtəʊdɪən] n Kustos m, Verwalter(in) m(f)
custody [ˈkʌstədɪ] n Aufsicht f; (police ~) Haft f; **to take into** ~ **verhaften**
custom [ˈkʌstəm] n (tradition) Brauch m; (COMM) Kundschaft f; ~**ary** adj üblich
customer [ˈkʌstəmə*] n Kunde m, Kundin f
customized [ˈkʌstəmaɪzd] adj (car etc) mit Spezialausrüstung
custom-made [ˈkʌstəmˈmeɪd] adj speziell angefertigt
customs [ˈkʌstəmz] npl Zoll m; ~ **officer** n Zollbeamte(r) m, Zollbeamtin f
cut [kʌt] (pt, pp **cut**) vt schneiden; (wages) kürzen; (prices) heruntersetzen ♦ vi schneiden; (intersect) sich schneiden ♦ n Schnitt m; (wound) Schnittwunde f; (in book, income etc) Kürzung f; (share) Anteil m; **to** ~ **a tooth** zahnen; ~ **down** vt (tree) fällen; (reduce) einschränken; ~ **off** vt (also fig) abschneiden; (allowance) sperren; ~ **out** vt (shape) ausschneiden; (delete) streichen; ~ **up** vt (meat) aufschneiden; ~**back** n Kürzung f; (CINE) Rückblende f
cute [kjuːt] adj niedlich
cuticle [ˈkjuːtɪkl] n Nagelhaut f
cutlery [ˈkʌtlərɪ] n Besteck nt
cutlet [ˈkʌtlɪt] n (pork) Kotelett nt; (veal) Schnitzel nt
cut: ~**out** n (cardboard ~out) Ausschneidemodell nt; ~**-price** (US ~**-rate**) adj verbilligt; ~**throat** n Verbrechertyp m ♦ adj mörderisch
cutting [ˈkʌtɪŋ] adj schneidend ♦ n (BRIT: PRESS) Ausschnitt m; (: RAIL) Durchstich m

CV *n abbr* = **curriculum vitae**

cwt *abbr* = **hundredweight(s)**

cyanide ['saɪənaɪd] *n* Zyankali *nt*

cycle ['saɪkl] *n* Fahrrad *nt*; *(series)* Reihe *f* ♦ *vi* radfahren; **cycling** ['saɪklɪŋ] *n* Radfahren *nt*; **cyclist** ['saɪklɪst] *n* Radfahrer(in) *m(f)*

cyclone ['saɪkləun] *n* Zyklon *m*

cygnet ['sɪgnɪt] *n* junge(r) Schwan *m*

cylinder ['sɪlɪndə*] *n* Zylinder *m*; *(TECH)* Walze *f*; ~**-head gasket** *n* Zylinderkopfdichtung *f*

cymbals ['sɪmbəlz] *npl* Becken *nt*

cynic ['sɪnɪk] *n* Zyniker(in) *m(f)*; ~**al** *adj* zynisch; ~**ism** ['sɪnɪsɪzəm] *n* Zynismus *m*

cypress ['saɪprəs] *n* Zypresse *f*

Cypriot ['sɪprɪət] *adj* zypriotisch ♦ *n* Zypriot(in) *m(f)*

Cyprus ['saɪprəs] *n* Zypern *nt*

cyst [sɪst] *n* Zyste *f*

cystitis [sɪs'taɪtɪs] *n* Blasenentzündung *f*

czar [zɑ:*] *n* Zar *m*

Czech [tʃek] *adj* tschechisch ♦ *n* Tscheche *m*, Tschechin *f*

Czechoslovakia [tʃekəslə'vækɪə] *n* die Tschechoslowakei; ~**n** *adj* tschechoslowakisch ♦ *n* Tschechoslowake *m*, Tchechoslowakin *f*

D

D [di:] *n (MUS)* D *nt*

dab [dæb] *vt (wound, paint)* betupfen ♦ *n (little bit)* bißchen *nt*; *(of paint)* Tupfer *m*

dabble ['dæbl] *vi*: **to** ~ **in sth** in etw *dat* machen

dad [dæd] *n* Papa *m*, Vati *m*; ~**dy** ['dædɪ] *n* Papa *m*, Vati *m*; ~**dy-long-legs** *n* Weberknecht *m*

daffodil ['dæfədɪl] *n* Osterglocke *f*

daft [dɑ:ft] *(inf) adj* blöd(e), doof

dagger ['dægə*] *n* Dolch *m*

daily ['deɪlɪ] *adj* täglich ♦ *n (PRESS)* Tageszeitung *f*; *(BRIT: cleaning woman)* Haushaltshilfe *f* ♦ *adv* täglich

dainty ['deɪntɪ] *adj* zierlich

dairy ['dɛərɪ] *n (shop)* Milchgeschäft *nt*; *(on farm)* Molkerei *f* ♦ *adj* Milch-; ~ **farm** *n* Hof *m* mit Milchwirtschaft; ~ **produce** *n* Molkereiprodukte *pl*; ~ **store** *(US) n* Milchgeschäft *nt*

dais ['deɪs] *n* Podium *nt*

daisy ['deɪzɪ] *n* Gänseblümchen *nt*; ~ **wheel** *n (on printer)* Typenrad *nt*

dale [deɪl] *n* Tal *nt*

dam [dæm] *n* (Stau)damm *m* ♦ *vt* stauen

damage ['dæmɪdʒ] *n* Schaden *m* ♦ *vt* beschädigen; ~**s** *npl (JUR)* Schaden(s)ersatz *m*

damn [dæm] *vt* verdammen ♦ *n (inf)*: **I don't give a** ~ das ist mir total egal ♦ *adj (: also:* ~**ed)** verdammt; ~ **it!** verflucht!; ~**ing** *adj* vernichtend

damp [dæmp] *adj* feucht ♦ *n* Feuchtigkeit *f* ♦ *vt (also:* ~**en)** befeuchten; *(discourage)* dämpfen

damson ['dæmzən] *n* Damaszenerpflaume *f*

dance [dɑ:ns] *n* Tanz *m* ♦ *vi* tanzen; ~ **hall** *n* Tanzlokal *nt*; ~**r** *n* Tänzer *m*

dancing ['dɑ:nsɪŋ] *n* Tanzen *nt*

dandelion ['dændɪlaɪən] *n* Löwenzahn *m*

dandruff ['dændrəf] *n* (Kopf)schuppen *pl*

Dane [deɪn] *n* Däne *m*, Dänin *f*

danger ['deɪndʒə*] *n* Gefahr *f*; ~! *(sign)* Achtung!; **to be in** ~ **of doing sth** Gefahr laufen, etw zu tun; ~**ous** *adj* gefährlich; ~**ously** *adv* gefährlich

dangle ['dæŋgl] *vi* baumeln ♦ *vt* herabhängen lassen

Danish ['deɪnɪʃ] *adj* dänisch ♦ *n* Dänisch *nt*

dapper ['dæpə*] *adj* elegant

dare [dɛə*] *vt* herausfordern ♦ *vi*: **to** ~ **(to) do sth** es wagen, etw zu tun; **I say** ich würde sagen; ~**-devil** *n* Draufgänger(in) *m(f)*

daring ['dɛərɪŋ] *adj (audacious)* verwegen; *(bold)* wagemutig; *(dress)* gewagt ♦ *n* Mut *m*

dark [dɑ:k] *adj* dunkel; *(fig)* düster, trübe; *(deep colour)* dunkel- ♦ *n* Dunkelheit *f*; **to be left in the** ~ **about** im dunkeln sein über *+acc*; **after** ~ nach Anbruch der Dunkelheit; ~**en** *vt*, *vi* verdunkeln; ~ **glasses** *npl* Sonnenbrille *f*; ~**ness** *n* Finsternis *nt*; ~**room** *n* Dunkelkammer *f*

darling ['dɑːlɪŋ] *n* Liebling *m* ♦ *adj* lieb

darn [dɑːn] *vt* stopfen

dart [dɑːt] *n* (*weapon*) Pfeil *m*; (*in sewing*) Abnäher *m* ♦ *vi* sausen; ~**s** *n* (*game*) Pfeilwerfen *nt*; ~**board** *n* Zielscheibe *f*

dash [dæʃ] *n* Sprung *m*; (*mark*) (Gedanken)strich *m*; (*small amount*) bißchen *nt* ♦ *vt* (*hopes*) zunichte machen ♦ *vi* stürzen; ~ **away** *vi* davonstürzen; ~ **off** *vi* davonstürzen

dashboard ['dæʃbɔːd] *n* Armaturenbrett *nt*

dashing ['dæʃɪŋ] *adj* schneidig

data ['deɪtə] *npl* Einzelheiten *pl*, Daten *pl*; ~ **base** *n* Datenbank *f*; ~ **processing** *n* Datenverarbeitung *f*

date [deɪt] *n* Datum *nt*; (*for meeting etc*) Termin *m*; (*with person*) Verabredung *f*; (*fruit*) Dattel *f* ♦ *vt* (*letter etc*) datieren; (*person*) gehen mit; ~ **of birth** Geburtsdatum *nt*; **to** ~ bis heute; **out of** ~ überholt; **up to** ~ (*clothes*) modisch; (*report*) up-to-date; (*with news*) auf dem laufenden; ~**d** *adj* altmodisch

daub [dɔːb] *vt* beschmieren; (*paint*) schmieren

daughter ['dɔːtə*] *n* Tochter *f*; ~**-in-law** *n* Schwiegertochter *f*

daunting ['dɔːntɪŋ] *adj* entmutigend

dawdle ['dɔːdl] *vi* trödeln

dawn [dɔːn] *n* Morgendämmerung *f* ♦ *vi* dämmern; (*fig*): **it ~ed on him that ...** es dämmerte ihm, daß ...

day [deɪ] *n* Tag *m*; **the** ~ **before/after** am Tag zuvor/danach; **the** ~ **after tomorrow** übermorgen; **the** ~ **before yesterday** vorgestern; **by** ~ am Tage; ~**break** *n* Tagesanbruch *m*; ~**dream** *vi* mit offenen Augen träumen; ~**light** *n* Tageslicht *nt*; ~ **return** (*BRIT*) *n* Tagesrückfahrkarte *f*; ~**time** *n* Tageszeit *f*; ~**-to-day** *adj* alltäglich

daze [deɪz] *vt* betäuben ♦ *n* Betäubung *f*; **in a** ~ benommen

dazzle ['dæzl] *vt* blenden

DC *abbr* (= *direct current*) Gleichstrom *m*

D-day ['diːdeɪ] *n* (*HIST*) *Tag der Invasion durch die Alliierten (6.6.44)*; (*fig*) der Tag X

deacon ['diːkən] *n* Diakon *m*

dead [ded] *adj* tot; (*without feeling*) gefühllos ♦ *adv* ganz; (*exactly*) genau ♦ *npl*: **the** ~ die Toten *pl*; **to shoot sb** ~ jdn erschießen; ~ **tired** todmüde; **to stop** ~ abrupt stehenbleiben; ~**en** *vt* (*pain*) abtöten; (*sound*) ersticken; ~ **end** *n* Sackgasse *f*; ~ **heat** *n* tote(s) Rennen *nt*; ~**line** *n* Stichtag *m*; ~**lock** *n* Stillstand *m*; ~**ly** *adj* tödlich; ~**pan** *adj* undurchdringlich; **D**~ **Sea** *n*: **the D**~ **Sea** das Tote Meer

deaf [def] *adj* taub; ~**en** *vt* taub machen; ~**-mute** *n* Taubstumme(r) *mf*; ~**ness** *n* Taubheit *f*

deal [diːl] (*pt, pp* **dealt**) *n* Geschäft *nt* ♦ *vt* austeilen; (*CARDS*) geben; **a great** ~ **of** sehr viel; ~ **in** *vt fus* handeln mit; ~ **with** *vt fus* (*person*) behandeln; (*subject*) sich befassen mit; (*problem*) in Angriff nehmen; ~**er** *n* (*COMM*) Händler *m*; (*CARDS*) Kartengeber *m*; ~**ings** *npl* (*FIN*) Geschäfte *pl*; (*relations*) Beziehungen *pl*; **dealt** [delt] *pt, pp of* **deal**

dean [diːn] *n* (*Protestant*) Superintendent *m*; (*Catholic*) Dechant *m*; (*UNIV*) Dekan *m*

dear [dɪə*] *adj* lieb; (*expensive*) teuer ♦ *n* Liebling *m* ♦ *excl*: ~ **me!** du liebe Zeit!; **D**~ **Sir** Sehr geehrter Herr!; **D**~ **John** Lieber John!; ~**ly** *adv* (*love*) herzlich; (*pay*) teuer

death [deθ] *n* Tod *m*; (*statistic*) Todesfall *m*; ~ **certificate** *n* Totenschein *m*; ~ **duties** (*BRIT*) *npl* Erbschaftssteuer *f*; ~**ly** *adj* totenähnlich, Toten-; ~ **penalty** *n* Todesstrafe *f*; ~ **rate** *n* Sterblichkeitsziffer *f*

debar [dɪ'bɑː*] *vt* ausschließen

debase [dɪ'beɪs] *vt* entwerten

debatable [dɪ'beɪtəbl] *adj* anfechtbar

debate [dɪ'beɪt] *n* Debatte *f* ♦ *vt* debattieren, diskutieren; (*consider*) überlegen

debauchery [dɪ'bɔːtʃərɪ] *n* Ausschweifungen *pl*

debilitating [dɪ'bɪlɪteɪtɪŋ] *adj* schwächend

debit ['debɪt] *n* Schuldposten *m* ♦ *vt* belasten

debris ['debriː] *n* Trümmer *pl*

debt [det] *n* Schuld *f*; **to be in** ~ verschuldet sein; ~**or** *n* Schuldner *m*

debunk [diː'bʌŋk] *vt* entlarven

decade ['dekeɪd] *n* Jahrzehnt *nt*

decadence ['dekədəns] *n* Dekadenz *f*

decaffeinated [diː'kæfɪneɪtɪd] *adj* koffeinfrei

decanter [dɪ'kæntə*] *n* Karaffe *f*

decay [dɪ'keɪ] *n* Verfall *m*; *(tooth ~)* Karies *m* ♦ *vi* verfallen; *(teeth, meat etc)* faulen; *(leaves etc)* verrotten

deceased [dɪ'siːst] *adj* verstorben

deceit [dɪ'siːt] *n* Betrug *m*; ~**ful** *adj* falsch

deceive [dɪ'siːv] *vt* täuschen

December [dɪ'sembə*] *n* Dezember *m*

decency ['diːsənsɪ] *n* Anstand *m*

decent [diːsənt] *adj* *(respectable)* anständig; *(pleasant)* annehmbar

deception [dɪ'sepʃən] *n* Betrug *m*

deceptive [dɪ'septɪv] *adj* irreführend

decibel ['desɪbel] *n* Dezibel *nt*

decide [dɪ'saɪd] *vt* entscheiden ♦ *vi* sich entscheiden; **to** ~ **on** **sth** etw beschließen; ~**d** *adj* entschieden; ~**dly** [dɪ'saɪdɪdlɪ] *adv* entschieden

deciduous [dɪ'sɪdjʊəs] *adj* Laub-

decimal ['desɪməl] *adj* dezimal ♦ *n* Dezimalzahl *f*; ~ **point** *n* Komma *nt*

decimate ['desɪmeɪt] *vt* dezimieren

decipher [dɪ'saɪfə*] *vt* entziffern

decision [dɪ'sɪʒən] *n* Entscheidung *f*, Entschluß *m*

decisive [dɪ'saɪsɪv] *adj* entscheidend; *(person)* entschlossen

deck [dek] *n* (*NAUT*) Deck *nt*; *(of cards)* Pack *m*; ~**chair** *n* Liegestuhl *m*

declaration [deklə'reɪʃən] *n* Erklärung *f*

declare [dɪ'kleə*] *vt* erklären; *(CUS-TOMS)* verzollen

decline [dɪ'klaɪn] *n* *(decay)* Verfall *m*; *(lessening)* Rückgang *m* ♦ *vt* *(invitation)* ablehnen ♦ *vi* *(of strength)* nachlassen; *(say no)* ablehnen

declutch ['diː'klʌtʃ] *vi* auskuppeln

decode ['diː'kəʊd] *vt* entschlüsseln

decompose [diːkəm'pəʊz] *vi* (sich) zersetzen

décor ['deɪkɔː*] *n* Ausstattung *f*

decorate ['dekəreɪt] *vt* *(room: paper)* tapezieren; *(: paint)* streichen; *(adorn)* (aus)schmücken; *(cake)* verzieren; *(honour)* auszeichnen

decoration [dekə'reɪʃən] *n* *(of house)* (Wand)dekoration *f*; *(medal)* Orden *m*

decorator ['dekəreɪtə*] *n* Maler *m*, Anstreicher *m*

decorum [dɪ'kɔːrəm] *n* Anstand *m*

decoy ['diːkɔɪ] *n* Lockvogel *m*

decrease [*n* 'diːkriːs, *vb* diː'kriːs] *n* Abnahme *f* ♦ *vt* vermindern ♦ *vi* abnehmen

decree [dɪ'kriː] *n* Erlaß *m*; ~ **nisi** *n* vorläufige(s) Scheidungsurteil *nt*

decrepit [dɪ'krepɪt] *adj* hinfällig

dedicate ['dedɪkeɪt] *vt* widmen

dedication [dedɪ'keɪʃən] *n* *(devotion)* Ergebenheit; *(in book)* Widmung *f*

deduce [dɪ'djuːs] *vt*: **to** ~ **sth** **(from sth)** etw (aus etw) ableiten, etw (aus etw) schließen

deduct [dɪ'dʌkt] *vt* abziehen; ~**ion** [dɪ'dʌkʃən] *n* *(of money)* Abzug *m*; *(conclusion)* (Schluß)folgerung *f*

deed *n* Tat *f*; *(document)* Urkunde *f*

deem [diːm] *vt*: **to** ~ **sb/sth** **(to be)** **sth** jdn/etw für etw halten

deep [diːp] *adj* tief ♦ *adv*: **the spectators stood 20** ~ die Zuschauer standen in 20 Reihen hintereinander; ~**en** *vt* vertiefen ♦ *vi* *(darkness)* tiefer werden; ~**-freeze** *n* Tiefkühlung *f*; ~**-fry** *vt* fritieren; ~**ly** *adv* tief; ~**-sea diving** *n* Tiefseetauchen *nt*; ~**-seated** *adj* tiefsitzend

deer [dɪə*] *n* Reh *nt*; ~**skin** *n* Hirsch-/Rehleder *nt*

deface [dɪ'feɪs] *vt* entstellen

defamation [defə'meɪʃən] *n* Verleumdung *f*

default [dɪ'fɔːlt] *n* Versäumnis *nt*; *(COMPUT)* Standardwert *m* ♦ *vi* versäumen; **by** ~ durch Nichterscheinen

defeat [dɪ'fiːt] *n* Niederlage *f* ♦ *vt*

schlagen; ~ist *adj* defätistisch ♦ *n*
Defätist *m*

defect [*n* di:fekt, *vb* dɪ'fekt] *n* Fehler *m* ♦
vi überlaufen; ~ive [dɪ'fektɪv] *adj*
fehlerhaft

defence [dɪ'fens] *n* Verteidigung *f*;
~less *adj* wehrlos

defend [dɪ'fend] *vt* verteidigen; ~ant *n*
Angeklagte(r) *m*; ~er *n* Verteidiger *m*

defense [dɪ'fens] (*US*) *n* = **defence**

defensive [dɪ'fensɪv] *adj* defensiv ♦ *n*:
on the ~ in der Defensive

defer [dɪ'fɜ:*] *vt* verschieben

deference ['defərəns] *n* Rücksichtnahme
f

defiance [dɪ'faɪəns] *n* Trotz *m*,
Unnachgiebigkeit *f*; in ~ of sth einer
Sache *dat* zum Trotz

defiant [dɪ'faɪənt] *adj* trotzig,
unnachgiebig

deficiency [dɪ'fɪʃənsɪ] *n* (*lack*) Mangel
m; (*weakness*) Schwäche *f*

deficient [dɪ'fɪʃənt] *adj* mangelhaft

deficit ['defɪsɪt] *n* Defizit *nt*

defile [*vb* dɪ'faɪl, *n* 'di:faɪl] *vt*
beschmutzen ♦ *n* Hohlweg *m*

define [dɪ'faɪn] *vt* bestimmen; (*explain*)
definieren

definite ['defɪnɪt] *adj* (*fixed*) definitiv;
(*clear*) eindeutig; ~ly *adv* bestimmt

definition [defɪ'nɪʃən] *n* Definition *f*;
(*PHOT*) Schärfe *f*

deflate [di:'fleɪt] *vt* die Luft ablassen
aus

deflect [dɪ'flekt] *vt* ablenken

deform [dɪ'fɔ:m] *vt* deformieren; ~ity *n*
Mißbildung *f*

defraud [dɪ'frɔ:d] *vt* betrügen

defray [dɪ'freɪ] *vt* (*costs*) übernehmen

defrost [dɪ'frɔst] *vt* (*fridge*) abtauen;
(*food*) auftauen; ~er (*US*) *n* (*demister*)
Gebläse *nt*

deft [deft] *adj* geschickt

defunct [dɪ'fʌŋkt] *adj* verstorben

defuse [di:'fju:z] *vt* entschärfen

defy [dɪ'faɪ] *vt* (*disobey*) sich
widersetzen +*dat*; (*orders, death*)
trotzen +*dat*; (*challenge*) herausfordern

degenerate [*vb* dɪ'dʒenəreɪt, *adj*
dɪ'dʒenərɪt] *vi* degenerieren ♦ *adj*

degeneriert

degrading [dɪ'greɪdɪŋ] *adj* erniedrigend

degree [dɪ'gri:] *n* Grad *m*; (*UNIV*)
Universitätsabschluß *m*; by ~s
allmählich; to some ~ zu einem
gewissen Grad

dehydrated [di:haɪ'dreɪtɪd] *adj* (*person*)
ausgetrocknet; (*food*) Trocken-

de-ice [di:'aɪs] *vt* enteisen

deign [deɪn] *vi* sich herablassen

deity ['di:ɪtɪ] *n* Gottheit *f*

dejected [dɪ'dʒektɪd] *adj* niedergeschlagen

delay [dɪ'leɪ] *vt* (*hold back*) aufschieben
♦ *vi* (*linger*) sich aufhalten ♦ *n* Aufschub *m*, Verzögerung *f*; (*of train etc*)
Verspätung *f*; to be ~ed (*train*) Verspätung haben; without ~ unverzüglich

delectable [dɪ'lektəbl] *adj* köstlich; (*fig*)
reizend

delegate [*n* 'delɪgɪt, *vb* 'delɪgeɪt] *n*
Delegierte(r) *mf* ♦ *vt* delegieren

delete [dɪ'li:t] *vt* (aus)streichen

deliberate [*adj* dɪ'lɪbərɪt, *vb* dɪ'lɪbəreɪt]
adj (*intentional*) absichtlich; (*slow*)
bedächtig ♦ *vi* (*consider*) überlegen;
(*debate*) sich beraten; ~ly *adv* absichtlich

delicacy ['delɪkəsɪ] *n* Zartheit *f*;
(*weakness*) Anfälligkeit *f*; (*food*)
Delikatesse *f*

delicate ['delɪkɪt] *adj* (*fine*) fein;
(*fragile*) zart; (*situation*) heikel; (*MED*)
empfindlich

delicatessen [delɪkə'tesn] *n* Feinkostge-
schäft *nt*

delicious [dɪ'lɪʃəs] *adj* lecker

delight [dɪ'laɪt] *n* Wonne *f* ♦ *vt* entzücken; to take ~ in sth Freude an etw
dat haben; ~ed *adj*: ~ed (at *or* with
sth) entzückt (über +*acc* etw); ~ed to
do sth etw sehr gern tun; ~ful *adj* entzückend, herrlich

delinquency [dɪ'lɪŋkwənsɪ] *n* Kriminalität *f*

delinquent [dɪ'lɪŋkwənt] *n* Straffäl-
lige(r) *mf* ♦ *adj* straffällig

delirious [dɪ'lɪrɪəs] *adj* im Fieberwahn

deliver [dɪ'lɪvə*] *vt* (*goods*) (ab)liefern;
(*letter*) zustellen; (*speech*) halten; ~y

n (Ab)lieferung *f*; (*of letter*) Zustellung *f*; (*of speech*) Vortragsweise *f*; (*MED*) Entbindung *f*; **to take ~y of** in Empfang nehmen

delude [dɪ'luːd] *vt* täuschen

deluge ['deljuːdʒ] *n* Überschwemmung *f*; (*fig*) Flut *f* ♦ *vt* überfluten

delusion [dɪ'luːʒən] *n* (Selbst)täuschung *f*

de luxe [dɪ'lʌks] *adj* Luxus-

delve [delv] *vi*: **to ~ into** sich vertiefen in +*acc*

demand [dɪ'mɑːnd] *vt* verlangen ♦ *n* (*request*) Verlangen *nt*; (*COMM*) Nachfrage *f*; **in ~** gefragt; **on ~** auf Verlangen; **~ing** *adj* anspruchsvoll

demarcation [diːmɑː'keɪʃən] *n* Abgrenzung *f*

demean [dɪ'miːn] *vt*: **to ~ o.s.** sich erniedrigen

demeanour [dɪ'miːnə*] (*US* **demeanor**) *n* Benehmen *nt*

demented [dɪ'mentɪd] *adj* wahnsinnig

demise [dɪ'maɪz] *n* Ableben *nt*

demister [diː'mɪstə*] *n* (*AUT*) Gebläse *nt*

demo ['deməʊ]. (*inf*) *n abbr* (= **demonstration**) Demo *f*

democracy [dɪ'mɒkrəsɪ] *n* Demokratie *f*

democrat ['deməkræt] *n* Demokrat *m*; **~ic** [demə'krætɪk] *adj* demokratisch

demolish [dɪ'mɒlɪʃ] *vt* abreißen; (*fig*) vernichten

demolition [demə'lɪʃən] *n* Abbruch *m*

demon ['diːmən] *n* Dämon *m*

demonstrate ['demənstreɪt] *vt*, *vi* demonstrieren

demonstration [demən'streɪʃən] *n* Demonstration *f*

demonstrator ['demənstreɪtə*] *n* (*POL*) Demonstrant(in) *m(f)*

demote [dɪ'məʊt] *vt* degradieren

demure [dɪ'mjʊə*] *adj* ernst

den [den] *n* (*of animal*) Höhle *f*; (*study*) Bude *f*

denatured alcohol [diː'neɪtʃəd-] (*US*) *n* ungenießbar gemachte(r) Alkohol *m*

denial [dɪ'naɪəl] *n* Leugnung *f*; **official ~** Dementi *nt*

denim ['denɪm] *adj* Denim-; **~s** *npl* Denim-Jeans *pl*

Denmark ['denmɑːk] *n* Dänemark *nt*

denomination [dɪnɒmɪ'neɪʃən] *n* (*ECCL*) Bekenntnis *nt*; (*type*) Klasse *f*; (*FIN*) Wert *m*

denominator [dɪ'nɒmɪneɪtə*] *n* Nenner *m*

denote [dɪ'nəʊt] *vt* bedeuten

denounce [dɪ'naʊns] *vt* brandmarken

dense [dens] *adj* dicht; (*stupid*) schwer von Begriff; **~ly** *adv* dicht

density ['densɪtɪ] *n* Dichte *f*; **single-/double-density disk** Diskette *f* mit einfacher/doppelter Dichte

dent [dent] *n* Delle *f* ♦ *vt* (*also*: **make a ~ in**) einbeulen

dental ['dentl] *adj* Zahn-; **~ surgeon** *n* = **dentist**

dentist ['dentɪst] *n* Zahnarzt(ärztin) *m(f)*; **~ry** *n* Zahnmedizin *f*

dentures ['dentʃəz] *npl* Gebiß *nt*

deny [dɪ'naɪ] *vt* leugnen; (*officially*) dementieren; (*help*) abschlagen

deodorant [diː'əʊdərənt] *n* Deodorant *nt*

depart [dɪ'pɑːt] *vi* abfahren; **to ~ from** (*fig: differ from*) abweichen von

department [dɪ'pɑːtmənt] *n* (*COMM*) Abteilung *f*; (*UNIV*) Seminar *nt*; (*POL*) Ministerium *nt*; **~ store** *n* Warenhaus *nt*

departure [dɪ'pɑːtʃə*] *n* (*of person*) Abreise *f*; (*of train*) Abfahrt *f*; (*of plane*) Abflug *m*; **new ~** Neuerung *f*; **~ lounge** *n* (*at airport*) Abflughalle *f*

depend [dɪ'pend] *vi*: **to ~ on** abhängen von; (*rely on*) angewiesen sein auf +*acc*; **it ~s** es kommt darauf an; **~ing on the result ...** abhängig vom Resultat ...; **~able** *adj* zuverlässig; **~ant** *n* Angehörige(r) *mf*; **~ence** *n* Abhängigkeit *f*; **~ent** *adj* abhängig ♦ *n* = **dependant**; **~ent on** abhängig von

depict [dɪ'pɪkt] *vt* schildern

depleted [dɪ'pliːtɪd] *adj* aufgebraucht

deplorable [dɪ'plɔːrəbl] *adj* bedauerlich

deplore [dɪ'plɔː*] *vt* mißbilligen

deploy [dɪ'plɔɪ] *vt* einsetzen

depopulation ['diːpɒpjʊ'leɪʃən] *n* Entvölkerung *f*

deport [dɪ'pɔːt] *vt* deportieren; **~ation** [diːpɔː'teɪʃən] *n* Abschiebung *f*

deportment [dɪ'pɔ:tmənt] n Betragen nt
depose [dɪ'pəʊz] vt absetzen
deposit [dɪ'pɒzɪt] n (in bank) Guthaben nt; (down payment) Anzahlung f; (security) Kaution f; (CHEM) Niederschlag m ♦ vt (in bank) deponieren; (put down) niederlegen; ~ **account** n Sparkonto nt
depot ['depəʊ] n Depot nt
depraved [dɪ'preɪvd] adj verkommen
depreciate [dɪ'pri:ʃɪeɪt] vi im Wert sinken; **depreciation** [dɪpri:ʃɪ'eɪʃən] n Wertminderung f
depress [dɪ'pres] vt (press down) niederdrücken; (in mood) deprimieren; ~**ed** adj deprimiert; ~**ing** adj deprimierend; ~**ion** [dɪ'preʃən] n (mood) Depression f; (in trade) Wirtschaftskrise f; (hollow) Vertiefung f; (MET) Tief(druckgebiet) nt
deprivation [deprɪ'veɪʃən] n Not f
deprive [dɪ'praɪv] vt: to ~ sb of sth jdn einer Sache gen berauben; ~**d** adj (child) sozial benachteiligt; (area) unterentwickelt
depth [depθ] n Tiefe f; in the ~s of despair in tiefster Verzweiflung
deputation [depjʊ'teɪʃən] n Abordnung f
deputize ['depjʊtaɪz] vi: to ~ (for sb) (jdn) vertreten
deputy ['depjʊtɪ] adj stellvertretend ♦ n (Stell)vertreter m
derail [dɪ'reɪl] vt: to be ~ed entgleisen; ~**ment** n Entgleisung f
deranged [dɪ'reɪndʒd] adj verrückt
derby ['dɑ:bɪ] (US) n (bowler hat) Melone f
derelict ['derɪlɪkt] adj verlassen
deride [dɪ'raɪd] vt auslachen
derisory [dɪ'raɪsərɪ] adj spöttisch
derivative [dɪ'rɪvətɪv] n Derivat nt ♦ adj abgeleitet
derive [dɪ'raɪv] vt (get) gewinnen; (deduce) ableiten ♦ vi (come from) abstammen
dermatitis [dɜ:mə'taɪtɪs] n Hautentzündung f
derogatory [dɪ'rɒgətərɪ] adj geringschätzig
derrick ['derɪk] n Drehkran m

derv [dɜ:v] (BRIT) n Dieselkraftstoff m
descend [dɪ'send] vt, vi hinuntersteigen; to ~ **from** abstammen von; ~**ant** n Nachkomme m
descent [dɪ'sent] n (coming down) Abstieg m; (origin) Abstammung f
describe [dɪs'kraɪb] vt beschreiben
description [dɪs'krɪpʃən] n Beschreibung f; (sort) Art f
descriptive [dɪs'krɪptɪv] adj beschreibend; (word) anschaulich
desecrate ['desɪkreɪt] vt schänden
desert [n 'dezət, vb dɪ'zɜ:t] n Wüste f ♦ vt verlassen; (temporarily) im Stich lassen ♦ vi (MIL) desertieren; ~**s** npl (what one deserves): to get one's just ~s seinen gerechten Lohn bekommen; ~**er** n Deserteur m; ~**ion** [dɪ'zɜ:ʃən] n (of wife) Verlassen nt; (MIL) Fahnenflucht f; ~ **island** n einsame Insel f
deserve [dɪ'zɜ:v] vt verdienen
deserving [dɪ'zɜ:vɪŋ] adj verdienstvoll
design [dɪ'zaɪn] n (plan) Entwurf m; (planning) Design nt ♦ vt entwerfen
designate [vb 'dezɪgneɪt, adj 'dezɪgnɪt] vt bestimmen ♦ adj designiert
designer [dɪ'zaɪnə*] n Designer(in) m(f); (TECH) Konstrukteur(in) m(f); (fashion ~) Modeschöpfer(in) m(f)
desirable [dɪ'zaɪərəbl] adj wünschenswert
desire [dɪ'zaɪə*] n Wunsch m, Verlangen nt ♦ vt (lust) begehren; (ask for) wollen
desk [desk] n Schreibtisch m; (BRIT: in shop, restaurant) Kasse f
desolate ['desəlɪt] adj öde; (sad) trostlos
desolation [desə'leɪʃən] n Trostlosigkeit f
despair [dɪs'peə*] n Verzweiflung f ♦ vi: to ~ (of) verzweifeln (an +dat)
despatch [dɪs'pætʃ] n, vt = dispatch
desperate ['despərɪt] adj verzweifelt; ~**ly** ['despərɪtlɪ] adv verzweifelt
desperation [despə'reɪʃən] n Verzweiflung f
despicable [dɪs'pɪkəbl] adj abscheulich
despise [dɪs'paɪz] vt verachten

despite [dɪs'paɪt] *prep* trotz +*gen*
despondent [dɪs'pɒndənt] *adj* mutlos
dessert [dɪ'zɜːt] *n* Nachtisch *m*;
~**spoon** *n* Dessertlöffel *m*
destination [destɪ'neɪʃən] *n* (*of person*)
(Reise)ziel *nt*; (*of goods*) Be-
stimmungsort *m*
destine ['destɪn] *vt* (*set apart*) bestimmen
destiny ['destɪnɪ] *n* Schicksal *nt*
destitute ['destɪtjuːt] *adj* notleidend
destroy [dɪs'trɔɪ] *vt* zerstören; ~**er** *n*
(*NAUT*) Zerstörer *m*
destruction [dɪs'trʌkʃən] *n* Zerstörung *f*
destructive [dɪs'trʌktɪv] *adj* zerstörend
detach [dɪ'tætʃ] *vt* loslösen; ~**able** *adj*
abtrennbar; ~**ed** *adj* (*attitude*) distanziert; (*house*) Einzel-; ~**ment** *n*
(*MIL*) Sonderkommando *nt*; (*fig*) Abstand *m*
detail ['diːteɪl] *n* Einzelheit *f*, Detail *nt* ♦
vt (*relate*) ausführlich berichten;
(*appoint*) abkommandieren; **in** ~ im
Detail; ~**ed** *adj* detailliert
detain [dɪ'teɪn] *vt* aufhalten; (*imprison*)
in Haft halten
detect [dɪ'tekt] *vt* entdecken; ~**ion**
[dɪ'tekʃən] *n* Aufdeckung *f*; ~**ive** *n*
Detektiv *m*; ~**ive story** *n* Kriminalge-
schichte *f*, Krimi *m*; ~**or** *n* Detektor *m*
détente [deɪtɑ̃ːnt] *n* Entspannung *f*
detention [dɪ'tenʃən] *n* Haft *f*; (*SCH*)
Nachsitzen *nt*
deter [dɪ'tɜː*] *vt* abschrecken
detergent [dɪ'tɜːdʒənt] *n* Waschmittel *nt*
deteriorate [dɪ'tɪərɪəreɪt] *vi* sich verschlechtern; **deterioration** [dɪtɪərɪə'reɪ-
ʃən] *n* Verschlechterung *f*
determination [dɪtɜːmɪ'neɪʃən] *n* Entschlossenheit *f*
determine [dɪ'tɜːmɪn] *vt* bestimmen;
~**d** *adj* entschlossen
deterrent [dɪ'terənt] *n* Abschreckungs-
mittel *nt*
detest [dɪ'test] *vt* verabscheuen
detonate ['detəneɪt] *vt* explodieren
lassen ♦ *vi* detonieren
detour ['diːtuə*] *n* Umweg *m*; (*US: AUT:
diversion*) Umleitung *f* ♦ *vt* (*US: traffic*)
umleiten

detract [dɪ'trækt] *vi*: **to** ~ **from**
schmälern
detriment ['detrɪmənt] *n*: **to the** ~ **of**
zum Schaden +*gen*; ~**al** [detrɪ'mentl] *adj*
schädlich
devaluation [dɪvæljʊ'eɪʃən] *n* Abwertung
f
devalue ['diː'væljuː] *vt* abwerten
devastate ['devəsteɪt] *vt* verwüsten
devastating ['devəsteɪtɪŋ] *adj* verheerend
develop [dɪ'veləp] *vt* entwickeln;
(*resources*) erschließen ♦ *vi* sich entwickeln; ~**ing country** *n* Entwick-
lungsland *nt*; ~**ment** *n* Entwicklung *f*
deviate ['diːvɪeɪt] *vi* abweichen; **devia-
tion** [diːvɪ'eɪʃən] *n* Abweichung *f*
device [dɪ'vaɪs] *n* Gerät *nt*
devil ['devl] *n* Teufel *m*; ~**ish** *adj*
teuflisch
devious ['diːvɪəs] *adj* (*means*) krumm;
(*person*) verschlagen
devise [dɪ'vaɪz] *vt* entwickeln
devoid [dɪ'vɔɪd] *adj*: ~ **of** ohne
devolution [diːvə'luːʃən] *n* (*POL*) Dezen-
tralisierung *f*
devote [dɪ'vəʊt] *vt*: **to** ~ **sth** (**to sth**)
etw (einer Sache *dat*) widmen; ~**d** *adj*
ergeben; ~**e** [devəʊ'tiː] *n* Anhänger(in)
m(f), Verehrer(in) *m(f)*
devotion [dɪ'vəʊʃən] *n* (*piety*) Andacht
f; (*loyalty*) Ergebenheit *f*, Hingabe *f*
devour [dɪ'vaʊə*] *vt* verschlingen
devout [dɪ'vaʊt] *adj* andächtig
dew [djuː] *n* Tau *m*
dexterity [deks'terɪtɪ] *n* Geschicklichkeit
f
DHSS (*BRIT*) *n abbr* = **Department of
Health and Social Security**
diabetes [daɪə'biːtiːz] *n* Zuckerkrankheit
f
diabetic [daɪə'betɪk] *adj* zuckerkrank;
(*food*) Diabetiker- ♦ *n* Diabetiker *m*
diabolical [daɪə'bɒlɪkl] (*inf*) *adj*
(*weather, behaviour*) saumäßig
diagnose ['daɪəgnəʊz] *vt* diagnostizieren
diagnoses [daɪəg'nəʊsiːz] *npl of* **diagnosis**
diagnosis [daɪəg'nəʊsɪs] *n* Diagnose *f*
diagonal [daɪ'ægənl] *adj* diagonal ♦ *n*

diagram 70 dinghy

Diagonale *f*
diagram ['daɪəgræm] *n* Diagramm *nt*, Schaubild *nt*
dial ['daɪəl] *n* (*TEL*) Wählscheibe *f*; (*of clock*) Zifferblatt *nt* ♦ *vt* wählen; ~ **code** (*US*) *n* = **dialling code**
dialect ['daɪəlekt] *n* Dialekt *m*
dialling code ['daɪəlɪŋ-] *n* Vorwahl *f*
dialling tone ['daɪəlɪŋ-] *n* Amtszeichen *nt*
dialogue ['daɪəlɒg] *n* Dialog *m*
dial tone (*US*) *n* = **dialling tone**
diameter [daɪˈæmɪtə*] *n* Durchmesser *m*
diamond ['daɪəmənd] *n* Diamant *m*; ~**s** *npl* (*CARDS*) Karo *nt*
diaper ['daɪəpə*] (*US*) *n* Windel *f*
diaphragm ['daɪəfræm] *n* Zwerchfell *nt*
diarrhoea [daɪəˈriːə] (*US* **diarrhea**) *n* Durchfall *m*
diary ['daɪərɪ] *n* Taschenkalender *m*; (*account*) Tagebuch *nt*
dice [daɪs] *n* Würfel *pl* ♦ *vt* in Würfel schneiden
dichotomy [dɪˈkɒtəmɪ] *n* Kluft *f*
dictate [dɪkˈteɪt] *vt* diktieren; ~**s** ['dɪkteɪts] *npl* Gebote *pl*
dictation [dɪkˈteɪʃən] *n* Diktat *nt*
dictator [dɪkˈteɪtə*] *n* Diktator *m*; ~**ship** [dɪkˈteɪtəʃɪp] *n* Diktatur *f*
diction ['dɪkʃən] *n* Ausdrucksweise *f*
dictionary ['dɪkʃənrɪ] *n* Wörterbuch *nt*
did [dɪd] *pt of* do
didn't ['dɪdənt] = **did not**
die [daɪ] *vi* sterben; **to be dying for sth** etw unbedingt haben wollen; **to be dying to do sth**, darauf brennen, etw zu tun; ~ **away** *vi* schwächer werden; ~ **down** *vi* nachlassen; ~ **out** *vi* aussterben
diehard *n* Dickkopf *m*; (*POL*) Reaktionär *m*
diesel ['diːzəl] *n* (*car*) Diesel *m*; ~ **engine** *n* Dieselmotor *m*; ~ **oil** *n* Dieselkraftstoff *m*
diet ['daɪət] *n* Nahrung *f*; (*special food*) Diät *f*; (*slimming*) Abmagerungskur *f* ♦ *vi* (*also*: *be on a* ~) eine Abmagerungskur machen
differ ['dɪfə*] *vi* sich unterscheiden; (*disagree*) anderer Meinung sein;

~**ence** *n* Unterschied *m*; ~**ent** *adj* anders; (*two things*) verschieden; ~**ential** [dɪfəˈrenʃəl] *n* (*in wages*) Lohnstufe *f*; ~**entiate** [dɪfəˈrenʃɪeɪt] *vt*, *vi* unterscheiden; ~**ently** *adv* anders; (*from one another*) unterschiedlich
difficult ['dɪfɪkəlt] *adj* schwierig; ~**y** *n* Schwierigkeit *f*
diffident ['dɪfɪdənt] *adj* schüchtern
diffuse [*adj* dɪˈfjuːs, *vb* dɪˈfjuːz] *adj* langatmig ♦ *vt* verbreiten
dig [dɪg] (*pt*, *pp* **dug**) *vt* graben ♦ *n* (*prod*) Stoß *m*; (*remark*) Spitze *f*; (*archaeological*) Ausgrabung *f*; ~ **in** *vi* (*MIL*) sich eingraben; ~ **into** *vt* (*sb's past*) wühlen in +*dat*; (*savings*) angreifen; ~ **up** *vt* ausgraben; (*fig*) aufgabeln
digest [*vb* daɪˈdʒest, *n* 'daɪdʒest] *vt* verdauen ♦ *n* Auslese *f*; ~**ion** [dɪˈdʒestʃən] *n* Verdauung *f*; ~**ive** *adj* (*juices*, *system*) Verdauungs-
digit ['dɪdʒɪt] *n* Ziffer *f*; (*ANAT*) Finger *m*; ~**al** *adj* digital, Digital-
dignified ['dɪgnɪfaɪd] *adj* würdevoll
dignity ['dɪgnɪtɪ] *n* Würde *f*
digress [daɪˈgres] *vi* abschweifen
digs [dɪgz] (*BRIT*: *inf*) *npl* Bude *f*
dilapidated [dɪˈlæpɪdeɪtɪd] *adj* baufällig
dilate [daɪˈleɪt] *vt* weiten ♦ *vi* sich weiten
dilemma [daɪˈlemə] *n* Dilemma *nt*
diligent ['dɪlɪdʒənt] *adj* fleißig
dilute [daɪˈluːt] *vt* verdünnen
dim [dɪm] *adj* trübe; (*stupid*) schwer von Begriff ♦ *vt* verdunkeln; **to** ~ **one's headlights** (*esp US*) abblenden
dime [daɪm] (*US*) *n* Zehncentstück *nt*
dimension [dɪˈmenʃən] *n* Dimension *f*
diminish [dɪˈmɪnɪʃ] *vt*, *vi* verringern
diminutive [dɪˈmɪnjʊtɪv] *adj* winzig ♦ *n* Verkleinerungsform *f*
dimmer ['dɪmə*] (*US*) *n* (*AUT*) Abblendschalter *m*; ~**s** *npl* Abblendlicht *nt*; (*sidelights*) Begrenzungsleuchten *pl*
dimple ['dɪmpl] *n* Grübchen *nt*
din [dɪn] *n* Getöse *nt*
dine [daɪn] *vi* speisen; ~**r** *n* Tischgast *m*; (*RAIL*) Speisewagen *m*
dinghy ['dɪŋgɪ] *n* Dinghy *nt*; **rubber** ~

Schlauchboot nt

dingy ['dɪndʒɪ] adj armselig

dining car ['daɪnɪŋ-] (BRIT) n Speisewagen m

dining room ['daɪnɪŋ-] n Eßzimmer nt; (in hotel) Speisezimmer nt

dinner ['dɪnə*] n (lunch) Mittagessen nt; (evening) Abendessen nt, (public) Festessen nt; ~ **jacket** n Smoking m; ~ **party** n Tischgesellschaft f; ~ **time** n Tischzeit f

dinosaur ['daɪnəsɔː*] n Dinosaurier m

dint [dɪnt] n: **by** ~ **of** durch

diocese ['daɪəsɪs] n Diözese f

dip [dɪp] n (hollow) Senkung f; (bathe) kurze(s) Baden nt ♦ vt eintauchen; (BRIT: AUT: lights) abblenden ♦ vi (slope) sich senken, abfallen

diploma [dɪ'pləʊmə] n Diplom nt

diplomacy [dɪ'pləʊməsɪ] n Diplomatie f

diplomat ['dɪpləmæt] n Diplomat(in) m(f); ~**ic** [dɪplə'mætɪk] adj diplomatisch

dip stick n Ölmeßstab m

dipswitch (BRIT) n (AUT) Abblendschalter m

dire [daɪə*] adj schrecklich

direct [daɪ'rekt] adj direkt ♦ vt leiten; (film) die Regie führen +gen; (aim) richten; (order) anweisen; **can you** ~ **me to ...?** können Sie mir sagen, wo ich zu ... komme?

direction [dɪ'rekʃən] n Richtung f; (CINE) Regie f; Leitung f; ~**s** npl (for use) Gebrauchsanleitung f; (orders) Anweisungen pl; **sense of** ~ Orientierungssinn m

directly [dɪ'rektlɪ] adv direkt; (at once) sofort

director [dɪ'rektə*] n Direktor m; (of film) Regisseur m

directory [dɪ'rektərɪ] n (TEL) Telefonbuch nt

dirt [dɜːt] n Schmutz m, Dreck m; ~-**cheap** adj spottbillig; ~**y** adj schmutzig ♦ vt beschmutzen; ~**y trick** n gemeine(r) Trick m

disability [dɪsə'bɪlɪtɪ] n Körperbehinderung f

disabled [dɪs'eɪbld] adj körperbehindert

disadvantage [dɪsəd'vaːntɪdʒ] n Nachteil m

disaffection [dɪsə'fekʃən] n Entfremdung f

disagree [dɪsə'griː] vi nicht übereinstimmen; (quarrel) (sich) streiten; (food): **to** ~ **with sb** jdm nicht bekommen; ~**able** adj unangenehm; ~**ment** n (between persons) Streit m; (between things) Widerspruch m

disallow [dɪsə'laʊ] vt nicht zulassen

disappear [dɪsə'pɪə*] vi verschwinden; ~**ance** n Verschwinden nt

disappoint [dɪsə'pɔɪnt] vt enttäuschen; ~**ed** adj enttäuscht; ~**ing** adj enttäuschend; ~**ment** n Enttäuschung f

disapproval [dɪsə'pruːvəl] n Mißbilligung f

disapprove [dɪsə'pruːv] vi: **to** ~ **of** mißbilligen

disarm [dɪs'aːm] vt entwaffnen; (POL) abrüsten; ~**ament** n Abrüstung f

disarray [dɪsə'reɪ] n: **to be in** ~ (army) in Auflösung (begriffen) sein; (clothes) in unordentlichem Zustand sein

disaster [dɪ'zaːstə*] n Katastrophe f

disastrous [dɪ'zaːstrəs] adj verhängnisvoll

disband [dɪs'bænd] vt auflösen ♦ vi auseinandergehen

disbelief ['dɪsbə'liːf] n Ungläubigkeit f

disc [dɪsk] n Scheibe f; (record) (Schall)platte f; (COMPUT) = **disk**

discard ['dɪskaːd] vt ablegen

discern [dɪ'sɜːn] vt erkennen; ~**ing** adj scharfsinnig

discharge [vb dɪs'tʃaːdʒ, n 'dɪstʃaːdʒ] vt (ship) entladen; (duties) nachkommen +dat; (dismiss) entlassen; (gun) abschießen; (JUR) freisprechen ♦ n (of ship, ELEC) Entladung f; (dismissal) Entlassung f; (MED) Ausfluß m

disciple [dɪ'saɪpl] n Jünger m

discipline ['dɪsɪplɪn] n Disziplin f ♦ vt (train) schulen; (punish) bestrafen

disc jockey n Diskjockey m

disclaim [dɪs'kleɪm] vt nicht anerkennen

disclose [dɪs'kləʊz] vt enthüllen

disclosure [dɪs'kləʊʒə*] n Enthüllung f

disco ['dɪskəʊ] n abbr = **discotheque**

discoloured [dɪs'kʌləd] (US **discolored**)

adj verfärbt

discomfort [dɪsˈkʌmfət] *n* Unbehagen *nt*

disconcert [dɪskənˈsɜːt] *vt* aus der Fassung bringen

disconnect [ˈdɪskəˈnekt] *vt* abtrennen

discontent [dɪskənˈtent] *n* Unzufriedenheit *f*; ~ed *adj* unzufrieden

discontinue [ˈdɪskənˈtɪnjuː] *vt* einstellen

discord [ˈdɪskɔːd] *n* Zwietracht *f*; (*noise*) Dissonanz *f*; ~ant [dɪsˈkɔːdənt] *adj* uneinig

discotheque [ˈdɪskəʊtek] *n* Diskothek *f*

discount [*n* ˈdɪskaʊnt, *vb* dɪsˈkaʊnt] *n* Rabatt *m* ♦ *vt* außer acht lassen

discourage [dɪsˈkʌrɪdʒ] *vt* entmutigen; (*prevent*) abraten

discouraging [dɪsˈkʌrɪdʒɪŋ] *adj* entmutigend

discourteous [dɪsˈkɜːtɪəs] *adj* unhöflich

discover [dɪsˈkʌvə*] *vt* entdecken; ~y *n* Entdeckung *f*

discredit [dɪsˈkredɪt] *vt* in Verruf bringen

discreet [dɪsˈkriːt] *adj* diskret

discrepancy [dɪsˈkrepənsɪ] *n* Diskrepanz *f*

discriminate [dɪsˈkrɪmɪneɪt] *vi* unterscheiden; **to ~ against** diskriminieren

discriminating [dɪsˈkrɪmɪneɪtɪŋ] *adj* anspruchsvoll

discrimination [dɪskrɪmɪˈneɪʃən] *n* Urteilsvermögen *nt*; (*pej*) Diskriminierung *f*

discuss [dɪsˈkʌs] *vt* diskutieren, besprechen; ~ion [dɪsˈkʌʃən] *n* Diskussion *f*, Besprechung *f*

disdain [dɪsˈdeɪn] *vt* verachten ♦ *n* Verachtung *f*

disease [dɪˈziːz] *n* Krankheit *f*

disembark [dɪsɪmˈbɑːk] *vt* aussteigen lassen ♦ *vi* von Bord gehen

disenchanted [ˈdɪsɪnˈtʃɑːntɪd] *adj* desillusioniert

disengage [dɪsɪnˈgeɪdʒ] *vt* (*AUT*) auskuppeln

disentangle [ˈdɪsɪnˈtæŋgl] *vt* entwirren

disfigure [dɪsˈfɪgə*] *vt* entstellen

disgrace [dɪsˈgreɪs] *n* Schande *f* ♦ *vt* Schande bringen über +*acc*; ~ful *adj* unerhört

disgruntled [dɪsˈgrʌntld] *adj* verärgert

disguise [dɪsˈgaɪz] *vt* verkleiden; (*feelings*) verhehlen ♦ *n* Verkleidung *f*; **in ~** verkleidet, maskiert

disgust [dɪsˈgʌst] *n* Abscheu *f* ♦ *vt* anwidern; ~ing *adj* widerlich

dish [dɪʃ] *n* Schüssel *f*; (*food*) Gericht *nt*; **to do** *or* **wash the ~es** abwaschen; ~ **up** *vt* auftischen; ~ **cloth** *n* Spüllappen *m*

dishearten [dɪsˈhɑːtn] *vt* entmutigen

dishevelled [dɪˈʃevəld] *adj* (*hair*) zerzaust; (*clothing*) ungepflegt

dishonest [dɪsˈɒnɪst] *adj* unehrlich; ~y *n* Unehrlichkeit *f*

dishonour [dɪsˈɒnə*] (*US* **dishonor**) *n* Unehre *f*; ~able *adj* unehrenhaft

dishtowel [ˈdɪʃtaʊəl] *n* Geschirrtuch *nt*

dishwasher [ˈdɪʃwɒʃə*] *n* Geschirrspülmaschine *f*

disillusion [dɪsɪˈluːʒən] *vt* enttäuschen, desillusionieren

disincentive [ˈdɪsɪnˈsentɪv] *n* Entmutigung *f*

disinfect [dɪsɪnˈfekt] *vt* desinfizieren; ~ant *n* Desinfektionsmittel *nt*

disintegrate [dɪsˈɪntɪgreɪt] *vi* sich auflösen

disinterested [dɪsˈɪntrɪstɪd] *adj* uneigennützig; (*inf*) uninteressiert

disjointed [dɪsˈdʒɔɪntɪd] *adj* unzusammenhängend

disk [dɪsk] *n* (*COMPUT*) Diskette *f*; **single-/double-sided ~** einseitige/ beidseitige Diskette; ~ **drive** *n* Diskettenlaufwerk *nt*; ~ette (*US*) *n* = **disk**

dislike [dɪsˈlaɪk] *n* Abneigung *f* ♦ *vt* nicht leiden können

dislocate [ˈdɪsləʊkeɪt] *vt* auskugeln

dislodge [dɪsˈlɒdʒ] *vt* verschieben; (*MIL*) aus der Stellung werfen

disloyal [dɪsˈlɔɪəl] *adj* treulos

dismal [ˈdɪzməl] *adj* trostlos, trübe

dismantle [dɪsˈmæntl] *vt* demontieren

dismay [dɪsˈmeɪ] *n* Bestürzung *f* ♦ *vt* bestürzen

dismiss [dɪsˈmɪs] *vt* (*employee*) entlassen; (*idea*) von sich weisen; (*send away*) wegschicken; (*JUR*) abweisen;

~al *n* Entlassung *f*
dismount [dɪs'maʊnt] *vi* absteigen
disobedience [dɪsə'biːdɪəns] *n* Ungehorsam *m*
disobedient [dɪsə'biːdɪənt] *adj* ungehorsam
disobey ['dɪsə'beɪ] *vt* nicht gehorchen +*dat*
disorder [dɪs'ɔːdə*] *n* (*confusion*) Verwirrung *f*; (*commotion*) Aufruhr *m*; (*MED*) Erkrankung *f*
disorderly [dɪs'ɔːdəlɪ] *adj* (*untidy*) unordentlich; (*unruly*) ordnungswidrig
disorganized [dɪs'ɔːgənaɪzd] *adj* unordentlich
disorientated [dɪs'ɔːrɪənteɪtɪd] *adj* verwirrt
disown [dɪs'əʊn] *vt* (*child*) verstoßen
disparaging [dɪs'pærɪdʒɪŋ] *adj* geringschätzig
disparity [dɪs'pærɪtɪ] *n* Verschiedenheit *f*
dispassionate [dɪs'pæʃnɪt] *adj* objektiv
dispatch [dɪs'pætʃ] *vt* (*goods*) abschicken, abfertigen ♦ *n* Absendung *f*; (*esp MIL*) Meldung *f*
dispel [dɪs'pel] *vt* zerstreuen
dispensary [dɪs'pensərɪ] *n* Apotheke *f*
dispense [dɪs'pens] *vt* verteilen, austeilen; ~ **with** *vt fus* verzichten auf +*acc* ~**r** *n* (*container*) Spender *m*
dispensing [dɪs'pensɪŋ] *adj*: ~ **chemist** (*BRIT*) Apotheker *m*
dispersal [dɪs'pɜːsəl] *n* Zerstreuung *f*
disperse [dɪs'pɜːs] *vt* zerstreuen ♦ *vi* sich verteilen
dispirited [dɪs'pɪrɪtɪd] *adj* niedergeschlagen
displace [dɪs'pleɪs] *vt* verschieben; ~**d person** *n* Verschleppte(r) *mf*
display [dɪs'pleɪ] *n* (*of goods*) Auslage *f*; (*of feeling*) Zurschaustellung *f* ♦ *vt* zeigen; (*ostentatiously*) vorführen; (*goods*) ausstellen
displease [dɪs'pliːz] *vt* mißfallen +*dat*
displeasure [dɪs'pleʒə*] *n* Mißfallen *nt*
disposable [dɪs'pəʊzəbl] *adj* Wegwerf-; ~ **nappy** *n* Papierwindel *f*
disposal [dɪs'pəʊzəl] *n* (*of property*) Verkauf *m*; (*throwing away*) Beseitigung *f*; **to be at one's** ~ einem zur Verfügung stehen

dispose [dɪs'pəʊz] *vi*: **to** ~ **of** loswerden
disposed [dɪs'pəʊzd] *adj* geneigt
disposition [dɪspə'zɪʃən] *n* Wesen *nt*
disproportionate [dɪsprə'pɔːʃnɪt] *adj* unverhältnismäßig
disprove [dɪs'pruːv] *vt* widerlegen
dispute [dɪs'pjuːt] *n* Streit *m*; (*also: industrial* ~) Arbeitskampf *m* ♦ *vt* bestreiten
disqualify [dɪs'kwɒlɪfaɪ] *vt* disqualifizieren
disquiet [dɪs'kwaɪət] *n* Unruhe *f*
disregard [dɪsrɪ'gɑːd] *vt* nicht (be)achten
disrepair ['dɪsrɪ'pɛə*] *n*: **to fall into** ~ verfallen
disreputable [dɪs'repjʊtəbl] *adj* verrufen
disrespectful [dɪsrɪs'pektfʊl] *adj* respektlos
disrupt [dɪs'rʌpt] *vt* stören; (*service*) unterbrechen; ~**ion** [dɪs'rʌpʃən] *n* Störung *f*; Unterbrechung *f*
dissatisfaction ['dɪssætɪs'fækʃən] *n* Unzufriedenheit *f*
dissatisfied ['dɪs'sætɪsfaɪd] *adj* unzufrieden
dissect [dɪ'sekt] *vt* zerlegen, sezieren
disseminate [dɪ'semɪneɪt] *vt* verbreiten
dissent [dɪ'sent] *n* abweichende Meinung *f*
dissertation [dɪsə'teɪʃən] *n* wissenschaftliche Arbeit *f*; (*Ph.D.*) Doktorarbeit *f*
disservice [dɪs'sɜːvɪs] *n*: **to do sb a** ~ jdm einen schlechten Dienst erweisen
dissident ['dɪsɪdənt] *adj* andersdenkend ♦ *n* Dissident *m*
dissimilar ['dɪ'sɪmɪlə*] *adj*: ~ (**to sb/sth**) (jdm/etw) unähnlich
dissipate ['dɪsɪpeɪt] *vt* (*waste*) verschwenden; (*scatter*) zerstreuen
dissociate [dɪ'səʊʃɪeɪt] *vt* trennen
dissolute ['dɪsəluːt] *adj* liederlich
dissolution [dɪsə'luːʃən] *n* Auflösung *f*
dissolve [dɪ'zɒlv] *vt* auflösen ♦ *vi* sich auflösen
dissuade [dɪ'sweɪd] *vt*: **to** ~ **sb from doing sth** jdn davon abbringen, etw zu tun

distance ['dɪstəns] n Entfernung f; **in the ~** in der Ferne

distant ['dɪstənt] adj entfernt, fern; (with time) fern; (formal) distanziert

distaste [dɪs'teɪst] n Abneigung f; **~ful** adj widerlich

distended [dɪs'tendɪd] adj (stomach) aufgebläht

distil [dɪs'tɪl] vt destillieren; **~lery** n Brennerei f

distinct [dɪs'tɪŋkt] adj (separate) getrennt; (clear) klar, deutlich; **as ~ from** im Unterschied zu; **~ion** [dɪs'tɪŋkʃən] n Unterscheidung f; (eminence) Auszeichnung f; **~ive** adj bezeichnend

distinguish [dɪs'tɪŋwɪʃ] vt unterscheiden; **~ed** adj (eminent) berühmt; **~ing** adj bezeichnend

distort [dɪs'tɔːt] vt verdrehen; (misrepresent) entstellen; **~ion** [dɪs'tɔːʃən] n Verzerrung f

distract [dɪs'trækt] vt ablenken; **~ing** adj verwirrend; **~ion** [dɪs'trækʃən] n (distress) Raserei f; (diversion) Zerstreuung f

distraught [dɪs'trɔːt] adj bestürzt

distress [dɪs'tres] n Not f; (suffering) Qual f ♦ vt quälen; **~ing** adj erschütternd; **~ signal** n Notsignal nt

distribute [dɪs'trɪbjuːt] vt verteilen

distribution [dɪstrɪ'bjuːʃən] n Verteilung f

distributor [dɪs'trɪbjʊtə*] n Verteiler m

district ['dɪstrɪkt] n (of country) Kreis m; (of town) Bezirk m; **~ attorney** (US) n Oberstaatsanwalt m; **~ nurse** n Kreiskrankenschwester f

distrust [dɪs'trʌst] n Mißtrauen nt ♦ vt mißtrauen +dat

disturb [dɪs'tɜːb] vt stören; (agitate) erregen; **~ance** n Störung f; **~ed** adj beunruhigt; **emotionally ~ed** emotional gestört; **~ing** adj beunruhigend

disuse ['dɪs'juːs] n: **to fall into ~** außer Gebrauch kommen

disused ['dɪs'juːzd] adj außer Gebrauch; (mine, railway line) stillgelegt

ditch [dɪtʃ] n Graben m ♦ vt (person) loswerden; (plan) fallenlassen

dither ['dɪðə*] vi verdattert sein

ditto ['dɪtəʊ] adv dito, ebenfalls

divan [dɪ'væn] n Liegesofa nt

dive [daɪv] n (into water) Kopfsprung m; (AVIAT) Sturzflug m ♦ vi tauchen; **~r** n Taucher m

diverge [daɪ'vɜːdʒ] vi auseinandergehen

diverse [daɪ'vɜːs] adj verschieden

diversion [daɪ'vɜːʃən] n Ablenkung f; (BRIT: AUT) Umleitung f

diversity [daɪ'vɜːsɪtɪ] n Vielfalt f

divert [daɪ'vɜːt] vt ablenken; (traffic) umleiten

divide [dɪ'vaɪd] vt teilen ♦ vi sich teilen; **~d highway** (US) n Schnellstraße f

dividend ['dɪvɪdend] n Dividende f

divine [dɪ'vaɪn] adj göttlich

diving ['daɪvɪŋ] n (SPORT) Turmspringen nt; (underwater ~) Tauchen nt; **~ board** n Sprungbrett nt

divinity [dɪ'vɪnɪtɪ] n Gottheit f; (subject) Religion f

division [dɪ'vɪʒən] n Teilung f; (MIL) Division f; (part) Abteilung f; (in opinion) Uneinigkeit f; (BRIT: POL) (Abstimmung f durch) Hammelsprung f

divorce [dɪ'vɔːs] n (Ehe)scheidung f ♦ vt scheiden; **~d** adj geschieden; **~e** [dɪvɔː'siː] n Geschiedene(r) mf

divulge [daɪ'vʌldʒ] vt preisgeben

D.I.Y. (BRIT) n abbr = **do-it-yourself**

dizzy ['dɪzɪ] adj schwindlig

DJ n abbr = **disc jockey**

KEYWORD

do [duː] (pt **did**, pp **done**) n (inf: party etc) Fete f
♦ aux vb **1** (in negative constructions and questions): **I don't understand** ich verstehe nicht; **didn't you know?** wußtest du das nicht?; **what do you think?** was meinen Sie?

2 (for emphasis, in polite expressions): **she does seem rather tired** sie scheint wirklich sehr müde zu sein; **do sit down/help yourself** setzen Sie sich doch hin/greifen Sie doch zu

3 (used to avoid repeating vb): **she swims better than I do** sie schwimmt besser als ich; **she lives in Glasgow - so**

do I sie wohnt in Glasgow - ich auch
4 (*in question tags*): **you like him, don't you?** du magst ihn doch, oder? ♦
vt
♦ *vt* **1** (*carry out, perform etc*) tun, machen; **what are you doing tonight?** was machst du heute abend?; **I've got nothing to do** ich habe nichts zu tun; **to do one's hair/nails** sich die Haare/Nägel machen
2 (*AUT etc*) fahren
♦ *vi* **1** (*act, behave*): **do as I do** mach es wie ich
2 (*get on, fare*): **he's doing well/badly at school** er ist gut/schlecht in der Schule; **how do you do?** guten Tag
3 (*be suitable*) gehen; (*be sufficient*) reichen; **to make do (with)** auskommen mit

do away with *vt* (*kill*) umbringen; (*abolish: law etc*) abschaffen
do up *vt* (*laces, dress, buttons*) zumachen; (*renovate: room, house*) renovieren
do with *vt* (*need*) brauchen; (*be connected*) zu tun haben mit
do without *vt, vi* auskommen ohne

docile ['dəʊsaɪl] *adj* gefügig
dock [dɒk] *n* Dock *nt*; (*JUR*) Anklagebank *f* ♦ *vi* ins Dock gehen; **~er** *n* Hafenarbeiter *m*; **~yard** *n* Werft *f*
doctor ['dɒktə*] *n* Arzt *m*, Ärztin *f*; (*UNIV*) Doktor *m* ♦ *vt* (*fig*) fälschen; (*drink etc*) etw beimischen +*dat*; **D~ of Philosophy** *n* Doktor *m* der Philosophie
doctrine ['dɒktrɪn] *n* Doktrin *f*
document ['dɒkjʊmənt] *n* Dokument *nt*; **~ary** [dɒkjʊ'mentərɪ] *n* Dokumentarbericht *m*; (*film*) Dokumentarfilm *m* ♦ *adj* dokumentarisch; **~ation** [dɒkjʊmen-'teɪʃən] *n* dokumentarische(r) Nachweis *m*
dodge [dɒdʒ] *n* Kniff *m* ♦ *vt* ausweichen +*dat*; **~ms** (*BRIT*) *npl* Autoskooter *m*
doe [dəʊ] *n* (*roe deer*) Ricke *f*; (*red deer*) Hirschkuh *f*; (*rabbit*) Weibchen *nt*
does [dʌz] *vb see* do; **~n't** = does not

dog [dɒg] *n* Hund *m*; **~ collar** *n* Hundehalsband *nt*; (*ECCL*) Kragen *m* des Geistlichen; **~-eared** *adj* mit Eselsohren
dogged ['dɒgɪd] *adj* hartnäckig
dogsbody ['dɒgzbɒdɪ] *n* Mädchen *nt* für alles
doings ['duːɪŋz] *npl* (*activities*) Treiben *nt*
do-it-yourself ['duːɪtjə'self] *n* Do it yourself *nt*
doldrums ['dɒldrəmz] *npl*: **to be in the ~** (*business*) Flaute haben; (*person*) deprimiert sein
dole [dəʊl] (*BRIT*) *n* Stempelgeld *nt*; **to be on the ~** stempeln gehen; **~ out** *vt* ausgeben, austeilen
doleful ['dəʊlful] *adj* traurig
doll [dɒl] *n* Puppe *f* ♦ *vt*: **to ~ o.s. up** sich aufdonnern
dollar ['dɒlə*] *n* Dollar *m*
dolphin ['dɒlfɪn] *n* Delphin *m*
domain [dəʊ'meɪn] *n* Domäne *f*
dome [dəʊm] *n* Kuppel *f*
domestic [də'mestɪk] *adj* häuslich; (*within country*) Innen-, Binnen-; (*animal*) Haus-; **~ated** *adj* (*person*) häuslich; (*animal*) zahm
dominant ['dɒmɪnənt] *adj* vorherrschend
dominate ['dɒmɪneɪt] *vt* beherrschen
domineering [dɒmɪ'nɪərɪŋ] *adj* herrisch
dominion [də'mɪnɪən] *n* (*rule*) Regierungsgewalt *f*; (*land*) Staatsgebiet *nt* mit Selbstverwaltung
domino ['dɒmɪnəʊ] (*pl* **~es**) *n* Dominostein *m*; **~es** *n* (*game*) Domino(spiel) *nt*
don [dɒn] (*BRIT*) *n* akademische(r) Lehrer *m*
donate [dəʊ'neɪt] *vt* (*blood, little money*) spenden; (*lot of money*) stiften
donation [dəʊ'neɪʃən] *n* Spende *f*
done [dʌn] *pp of* do
donkey ['dɒŋkɪ] *n* Esel *m*
donor ['dəʊnə*] *n* Spender *m*
don't [dəʊnt] = do not
doodle ['duːdl] *vi* kritzeln
doom [duːm] *n* böse(s) Geschick *nt*; (*downfall*) Verderben *nt* ♦ *vt*: **to be ~ed**

zum Untergang verurteilt sein; ~**sday** *n* der Jüngste Tag

door [dɔ:*] *n* Tür *f*; ~**bell** *n* Türklingel *f*; ~**handle** *n* Türklinke *f*; ~**man** (*irreg*) *n* Türsteher *m*; ~**mat** *n* Fußmatte *f*; ~**step** *n* Türstufe *f*; ~**way** *n* Türöffnung *f*

dope [dəʊp] *n* (*drug*) Aufputschmittel *nt* ♦ *vt* (*horse etc*) dopen

dopey ['dəʊpɪ] (*inf*) *adj* bekloppt

dormant ['dɔ:mənt] *adj* latent

dormice ['dɔ:maɪs] *npl of* **dormouse**

dormitory ['dɔ:mɪtrɪ] *n* Schlafsaal *m*

dormouse ['dɔ:maʊs] (*pl* -**mice**) *n* Haselmaus *f*

DOS [dɒs] *n abbr* (= *disk operating system*) DOS *nt*

dosage ['dəʊsɪdʒ] *n* Dosierung *f*

dose [dəʊs] *n* Dosis *f*

doss house ['dɒs-] (*BRIT*) *n* Bleibe *f*

dot [dɒt] *n* Punkt *m*; ~**ted with** übersät mit; **on the** ~ pünktlich

dote [dəʊt]: **to** ~ **on** *vt fus* vernarrt sein in +*acc*

dot matrix printer *n* Matrixdrucker *m*

double ['dʌbl] *adj, adv* doppelt ♦ *n* Doppelgänger *m* ♦ *vt* verdoppeln ♦ *vi* sich verdoppeln; ~**s** *npl* (*TENNIS*) Doppel *nt*; **on** *or* **at the** ~ im Laufschritt; ~ **bass** *n* Kontrabaß *m*; ~ **bed** *n* Doppelbett *nt*; ~ **bend** (*BRIT*) *n* S-Kurve *f*; ~**breasted** *adj* zweireihig; ~**cross** *vt* hintergehen; ~**decker** *n* Doppeldecker *m*; ~ **glazing** (*BRIT*) *n* Doppelverglasung *f*; ~ **room** *n* Doppelzimmer *nt*

doubly ['dʌblɪ] *adv* doppelt

doubt [daʊt] *n* Zweifel *m* ♦ *vt* bezweifeln; ~**ful** *adj* zweifelhaft; ~**less** *adv* ohne Zweifel

dough [dəʊ] *n* Teig *m*; ~**nut** *n* Berliner *m*

douse [daʊz] *vt* (*drench*) mit Wasser begießen, durchtränken; (*extinguish*) ausmachen

dove [dʌv] *n* Taube *f*; ~**tail** *vi* (*plans*) übereinstimmen

dowdy ['daʊdɪ] *adj* unmodern

down [daʊn] *n* (*fluff*) Flaum *m*; (*hill*) Hügel *m* ♦ *adv* unten; (*motion*) herunter; hinunter ♦ *prep*: **to go** ~ **the street** die Straße hinuntergehen ♦ *vt* niederschlagen; ~ **with X!** nieder mit X!; ~**and-out** *n* Tramp *m*; ~**at-heel** *adj* schäbig; ~**cast** *adj* niedergeschlagen; ~**fall** *n* Sturz *m*; ~**hearted** *adj* niedergeschlagen; ~**hill** *adv* bergab; ~ **payment** *n* Anzahlung *f*; ~**pour** *n* Platzregen *m*; ~**right** *adj* ausgesprochen; ~**stairs** *adv* unten; (*motion*) nach unten; ~**stream** *adv* flußabwärts; ~**to-earth** *adj* praktisch; ~**town** *adv* in der Innenstadt; (*motion*) in die Innenstadt; ~ **under** (*BRIT*: *inf*) *adv* in/nach Australien/Neuseeland; ~**ward** *adj* Abwärts-, nach unten ♦ *adv* abwärts, nach unten; ~**wards** *adv* abwärts, nach unten

dowry ['daʊrɪ] *n* Mitgift *f*

doz. *abbr* (= *dozen*) Dtzd.

doze [dəʊz] *vi* dösen; ~ **off** *vi* einnicken

dozen ['dʌzn] *n* Dutzend *nt*

Dr. *abbr* = **doctor; drive**

drab [dræb] *adj* düster, eintönig

draft [drɑ:ft] *n* Entwurf *m*; (*FIN*) Wechsel *m*; (*US*: *MIL*) Einberufung *f* ♦ *vt* skizzieren; *see also* **draught**

draftsman ['drɑ:ftsmən] (*US*: *irreg*) *n* = **draughtsman**

drag [dræg] *vt* schleppen; (*river*) mit einem Schleppnetz absuchen ♦ *vi* sich (dahin)schleppen ♦ *n* (*bore*) etwas Blödes; **in** ~ als Tunte; **a man in** ~ eine Tunte; ~ **on** *vi* sich in die Länge ziehen

dragon ['drægən] *n* Drache *m*; ~**fly** ['drægənflaɪ] *n* Libelle *f*

drain [dreɪn] *n* Abfluß *m*; (*fig*: *burden*) Belastung *f* ♦ *vt* ableiten; (*exhaust*) erschöpfen ♦ *vi* (*of water*) abfließen; ~**age** *n* Kanalisation *f*; ~**ing board** (*US* ~**board**) *n* Ablaufbrett *nt*; ~**pipe** *n* Abflußrohr *nt*

dram [dræm] *n* Schluck *m*

drama ['drɑ:mə] *n* Drama *nt*; ~**tic** [drə'mætɪk] *adj* dramatisch; ~**tist** ['dræmətɪst] *n* Dramatiker *m*; ~**tize** *vt* (*events*) dramatisieren; (*adapt*: *for TV, cinema*) bearbeiten

drank [dræŋk] *pt of* **drink**
drape [dreip] *vt* drapieren; **~r** (*BRIT*) *n* Tuchhändler *m*; **~s** (*US*) *npl* Vorhänge *pl*
drastic ['dræstik] *adj* drastisch
draught [drɑːft] (*US* **draft**) *n* Zug *m*; (*NAUT*) Tiefgang *m*; **~s** (*BRIT*) *n* Damespiel *nt*, **on ~** (*beer*) vom Faß, **~board** (*BRIT*) *n* Zeichenbrett *nt*
draughtsman ['drɑːftsmən] (*irreg*) *n* technische(r) Zeichner *m*
draw [drɔː] (*pt* **drew**, *pp* **drawn**) *vt* ziehen; (*crowd*) anlocken; (*picture*) zeichnen; (*money*) abheben; (*water*) schöpfen ♦ *vi* (*SPORT*) unentschieden spielen ♦ *n* Unentschieden *nt*; (*lottery*) Ziehung *f*; **~ near** *vi* näherrücken; **~ out** *vi* (*train*) ausfahren; (*lengthen*) sich hinziehen; **~ up** *vi* (*stop*) halten ♦ *vt* (*document*) aufsetzen; **~back** *n* Nachteil *m*; **~bridge** *n* Zugbrücke *f*
drawer [drɔː*] *n* Schublade *f*
drawing ['drɔːiŋ] *n* Zeichnung *f*; Zeichnen *nt*; **~ board** *n* Reißbrett *nt*; **~ pin** (*BRIT*) *n* Reißzwecke *f*; **~ room** *n* Salon *m*
drawl [drɔːl] *n* schleppende Sprechweise *f*
drawn [drɔːn] *pp of* **draw**
dread [dred] *n* Furcht *f* ♦ *vt* fürchten; **~ful** *adj* furchtbar
dream [driːm] (*pt, pp* **dreamed** *or* **dreamt**) *n* Traum *m* ♦ *vt* träumen ♦ *vi*: **to ~** (*about*) träumen (von); **~er** *n* Träumer *m*; **dreamt** [dremt] *pt, pp of* **dream**; **~y** *adj* verträumt
dreary ['driəri] *adj* trostlos, öde
dredge [dredʒ] *vt* ausbaggern
dregs [dregz] *npl* Bodensatz *m*; (*fig*) Abschaum *m*
drench [drentʃ] *vt* durchnässen
dress [dres] *n* Kleidung *f*; (*garment*) Kleid *nt* ♦ *vt* anziehen; (*MED*) verbinden; **to get ~ed** sich anziehen; **~ up** *vi* sich fein machen; **~ circle** (*BRIT*) *n* erste(r) Rang *m*; **~er** *n* (*furniture*) Anrichte *f*; **~ing** *n* (*MED*) Verband *m*; (*COOK*) Soße *f*; **~ing gown** (*BRIT*) *n* Morgenrock *m*; **~ing room** *n* (*THEAT*) Garderobe *f*; (*SPORT*) Umkleideraum

m; **~ing table** *n* Toilettentisch *m*; **~maker** *n* Schneiderin *f*; **~making** *n* Schneidern *nt*; **~ rehearsal** *n* Generalprobe *f*; **~ shirt** *n* Frackhemd *nt*; **~y** (*inf*) *adj* schick
drew [druː] *pt of* **draw**
dribble ['dribl] *vi* sabbern ♦ *vt* (*ball*) dribbeln
dried [draid] *adj* getrocknet; (*fruit*) Dörr-, gedörrte(r, s); **~ milk** *n* Milchpulver *nt*
drier ['draiə*] *n* = **dryer**
drift [drift] *n* Strömung *f*; (*snow~*) Schneewehe *f*; (*fig*) Richtung *f* ♦ *vi* sich treiben lassen; **~wood** *n* Treibholz *nt*
drill [dril] *n* Bohrer *m*; (*MIL*) Drill *m* ♦ *vt* bohren; (*MIL*) ausbilden ♦ *vi*: **to ~ (for)** bohren (nach)
drink [driŋk] (*pt* **drank**, *pp* **drunk**) *n* Getränk *nt*; (*spirits*) Drink *m* ♦ *vt, vi* trinken; **~er** *n* Trinker *m*; **~ing water** *n* Trinkwasser *nt*
drip [drip] *n* Tropfen *m* ♦ *vi* tropfen; **~-dry** *adj* bügelfrei; **~ping** *n* Bratenfett *nt*
drive [draiv] (*pt* **drove**, *pp* **driven**) *n* Fahrt *f*; (*road*) Einfahrt *f*; (*campaign*) Aktion *f*; (*energy*) Schwung *m*; (*SPORT*) Schlag *m*; (*also: disk ~*) Diskettenlaufwerk *nt* ♦ *vt* (*car*) fahren; (*animals, people, objects*) treiben; (*power*) antreiben ♦ *vi* fahren; **left-/right-hand ~** Links-/Rechtssteuerung *f*; **to ~ sb mad** jdn verrückt machen
drivel ['drivl] *n* Faselei *f*
driven ['drivn] *pp of* **drive**
driver ['draivə*] *n* Fahrer *m*; **~'s license** (*US*) *n* Führerschein *m*
driveway ['draivwei] *n* Auffahrt *f*; (*longer*) Zufahrtsstraße *f*
driving ['draiviŋ] *adj* (*rain*) stürmisch; **~ instructor** *n* Fahrlehrer *m*; **~ lesson** *n* Fahrstunde *f*; **~ licence** (*BRIT*) *n* Führerschein *m*; **~ mirror** *n* Rückspiegel *m*; **~ school** *n* Fahrschule *f*; **~ test** *n* Fahrprüfung *f*
drizzle ['drizl] *n* Nieselregen *m* ♦ *vi* nieseln
droll [drəul] *adj* drollig
drone [drəun] *n* (*sound*) Brummen *nt*;

(bee) Drohne *f*
drool [dru:l] *vi* sabbern
droop [dru:p] *vi* *(schlaff)* herabhängen
drop [drɒp] *n* *(of liquid)* Tropfen *m*; *(fall)* Fall *m* ♦ *vt* fallen lassen; *(lower)* senken; *(abandon)* fallenlassen ♦ *vi* *(fall)* herunterfallen; ~s *npl* *(MED)* Tropfen *pl*; ~ **off** *vi* *(sleep)* einschlafen ♦ *vt* *(passenger)* absetzen; ~ **out** *vi* *(withdraw)* ausscheiden; ~-**out** *n* Aussteiger *m*; ~**per** *n* Pipette *f*; ~**pings** *npl* Kot *m*
drought [draʊt] *n* Dürre *f*
drove [drəʊv] *pt of* **drive**
drown [draʊn] *vt* ertränken; *(sound)* übertönen ♦ *vi* ertrinken
drowsy ['draʊzɪ] *adj* schläfrig
drudgery ['drʌdʒərɪ] *n* Plackerei *f*
drug [drʌg] *n* *(MED)* Arznei *f*; *(narcotic)* Rauschgift *nt* ♦ *vt* betäuben; ~ **addict** *n* Rauschgiftsüchtige(r) *mf*; ~**gist** *(US)* *n* Drogist(in) *m(f)*; ~**store** *(US)* *n* Drogerie *f*
drum [drʌm] *n* Trommel *f* ♦ *vi* trommeln; ~**s** *npl* *(MUS)* Schlagzeug *nt*; ~**mer** *n* Trommler *m*
drunk [drʌŋk] *pp of* **drink** ♦ *adj* betrunken ♦ *n* *(also: ~ard)* Trinker(in) *m(f)*; ~**en** *adj* betrunken
dry [draɪ] *adj* trocken ♦ *vt* (ab)trocknen ♦ *vi* trocknen; ~ **up** *vi* austrocknen ♦ *vt* *(dishes)* abtrocknen; ~-**cleaning** *n* chemische Reinigung *f*; ~**er** *n* Trockner *m*; *(US: spin-dryer)* (Wäsche)schleuder *f*; ~ **goods store** *(US)* *n* Kurzwarengeschäft *nt*; ~**ness** *n* Trockenheit *f*; ~ **rot** *n* Hausschwamm *m*
dual ['djʊəl] *adj* doppelt; ~ **carriageway** *(BRIT)* *n* zweispurige Fahrbahn *f*; ~-**control** *adj* mit Doppelsteuerung; ~ **nationality** *n* doppelte Staatsangehörigkeit *f*; ~-**purpose** *adj* Mehrzweck-
dubbed [dʌbd] *adj* *(film)* synchronisiert
dubious ['dju:bɪəs] *adj* zweifelhaft
duchess ['dʌtʃɪs] *n* Herzogin *f*
duck [dʌk] *n* Ente *f* ♦ *vi* sich ducken; ~**ling** *n* Entchen *nt*
duct [dʌkt] *n* Röhre *f*
dud [dʌd] *n* Niete *f* ♦ *adj* *(cheque)* ungedeckt

due [dju:] *adj* fällig; *(fitting)* angemessen ♦ *n* Gebühr *f*; *(right)* Recht *nt* ♦ *adv* *(south etc)* genau; ~s *npl* *(for club, union)* Beitrag *m*; *(in harbour)* Gebühren *pl*; ~ **to** wegen +*gen*
duel ['djʊəl] *n* Duell *nt*
duet [dju:'et] *n* Duett *nt*
duffel ['dʌfl] *adj*: ~ **bag** Matchbeutel *m*, Matchsack *m*; ~ **coat** Dufflecoat *m*
dug [dʌg] *pt, pp of* **dig**
duke [dju:k] *n* Herzog *m*
dull [dʌl] *adj* *(colour, weather)* trübe; *(stupid)* schwer von Begriff; *(boring)* langweilig ♦ *vt* abstumpfen
duly ['dju:lɪ] *adv* ordnungsgemäß
dumb [dʌm] *adj* stumm; *(inf: stupid)* doof, blöde; ~**founded** [dʌm'faʊndɪd] *adj* verblüfft
dummy ['dʌmɪ] *n* Schneiderpuppe *f*; *(substitute)* Attrappe *f*; *(BRIT: for baby)* Schnuller *m* ♦ *adj* Schein-
dump [dʌmp] *n* Abfallhaufen *m*; *(MIL)* Stapelplatz *m*; *(inf: place)* Nest *nt* ♦ *vt* abladen, auskippen; ~**ing** *n* *(COMM)* Schleuderexport *m*; *(of rubbish)* Schuttabladen *nt*
dumpling ['dʌmplɪŋ] *n* Kloß *m*, Knödel *m*
dumpy ['dʌmpɪ] *adj* pummelig
dunce [dʌns] *n* Dummkopf *m*
dune [dju:n] *n* Düne *f*
dung [dʌŋ] *n* Dünger *m*
dungarees [dʌŋgə'ri:z] *npl* Latzhose *f*
dungeon ['dʌndʒən] *n* Kerker *m*
dupe [dju:p] *n* Gefoppte(r) *m* ♦ *vt* hintergehen, anführen
duplex ['dju:pleks] *(US)* *n* zweistöckige Wohnung *f*
duplicate [*n* 'dju:plɪkɪt, *vb* 'dju:plɪkeɪt] *n* Duplikat *nt* ♦ *vt* verdoppeln; *(make copies)* kopieren; **in** ~ in doppelter Ausführung
duplicity [dju:'plɪsɪtɪ] *n* Doppelspiel *nt*
durable ['djʊərəbl] *adj* haltbar
duration [djʊə'reɪʃən] *n* Dauer *f*
duress [djʊə'res] *n*: **under** ~ unter Zwang
during ['djʊərɪŋ] *prep* während +*gen*
dusk [dʌsk] *n* Abenddämmerung *f*
dust [dʌst] *n* Staub *m* ♦ *vt* abstauben;

(sprinkle) bestäuben; ~**bin** *(BRIT)* *n* Mülleimer *m*; ~**er** *n* Staubtuch *nt*; ~ **jacket** *n* Schutzumschlag *m*; ~**man** *(BRIT: irreg)* *n* Müllmann *m*; ~**y** *adj* staubig

Dutch [dʌtʃ] *adj* holländisch, niederländisch ♦ *n* *(LING)* Holländisch *nt*, Niederländisch *nt*; **the** ~ *npl* *(people)* die Holländer *pl*, die Niederländer *pl*; **to go** ~ getrennte Kasse machen; ~**man/woman** *(irreg)* *n* Holländer(in) *m(f)*, Niederländer(in) *m(f)*

dutiful ['djuːtɪful] *adj* pflichtbewußt

duty ['djuːtɪ] *n* Pflicht *f*; *(job)* Aufgabe *f*; *(tax)* Einfuhrzoll *m*; **on** ~ im Dienst; ~**-free** *adj* zollfrei

duvet ['duːveɪ] *(BRIT)* *n* Daunendecke *nt*

dwarf [dwɔːf] *(pl* **dwarves)** *n* Zwerg *m* ♦ *vt* überragen

dwarves [dwɔːvz] *npl of* **dwarf**

dwell [dwel] *(pt, pp* **dwelt)** *vi* wohnen; ~ **on** *vt fus* verweilen bei; ~**ing** *n* Wohnung *f*

dwelt [dwelt] *pt, pp of* **dwell**

dwindle ['dwɪndl] *vi* schwinden

dye [daɪ] *n* Farbstoff *m* ♦ *vt* färben

dying ['daɪɪŋ] *adj* *(person)* sterbend; *(moments)* letzt

dyke [daɪk] *(BRIT)* *n* *(channel)* Kanal *m*; *(barrier)* Deich *m*, Damm *m*

dynamic [daɪ'næmɪk] *adj* dynamisch

dynamite ['daɪnəmaɪt] *n* Dynamit *nt*

dynamo ['daɪnəməʊ] *n* Dynamo *m*

dyslexia [dɪs'leksɪə] *n* Legasthenie *f*

E

E [iː] *n* *(MUS)* E *nt*

each [iːtʃ] *adj* jeder/jede/jedes ♦ *pron* (ein) jeder/(eine) jede/(ein) jedes; ~ **other** einander, sich

eager ['iːgə*] *adj* eifrig

eagle ['iːgl] *n* Adler *m*

ear [ɪə*] *n* Ohr *nt*; *(of corn)* Ähre *f*; ~**ache** *n* Ohrenschmerzen *pl*; ~**drum** *n* Trommelfell *nt*

earl [ɜːl] *n* Graf *m*

early ['ɜːlɪ] *adj, adv* früh; ~ **retirement** *n* vorzeitige Pensionierung

earmark ['ɪəmɑːk] *vt* vorsehen

earn [ɜːn] *vt* verdienen

earnest ['ɜːnɪst] *adj* ernst; **in** ~ im Ernst

earnings ['ɜːnɪŋz] *npl* Verdienst *m*

earphones ['ɪəfəʊnz] *npl* Kopfhörer *pl*

earring ['ɪərɪŋ] *n* Ohrring *m*

earshot ['ɪəʃɒt] *n* Hörweite *f*

earth [ɜːθ] *n* Erde *f*; *(BRIT: ELEC)* Erdung *f* ♦ *vt* erden; ~**enware** *n* Steingut *nt*; ~**quake** *n* Erdbeben *nt*

earthy ['ɜːθɪ] *adj* roh; *(sensual)* sinnlich

earwig ['ɪəwɪg] *n* Ohrwurm *m*

ease [iːz] *n* *(simplicity)* Leichtigkeit *f*; *(social)* Ungezwungenheit *f* ♦ *vt* *(pain)* lindern; *(burden)* erleichtern; **at** ~ ungezwungen; *(MIL)* rührt euch!; ~ **off** *or* **up** *vi* nachlassen

easel ['iːzl] *n* Staffelei *f*

easily ['iːzɪlɪ] *adv* leicht

east [iːst] *n* Osten *m* ♦ *adj* östlich ♦ *adv* nach Osten

Easter ['iːstə*] *n* Ostern *nt*; ~ **egg** *n* Osterei *nt*

easterly ['iːstəlɪ] *adj* östlich, Ost-

eastern ['iːstən] *adj* östlich

East Germany *n* die DDR

eastward(s) ['iːstwəd(z)] *adv* ostwärts

easy ['iːzɪ] *adj* *(task)* einfach; *(life)* bequem; *(manner)* ungezwungen, natürlich ♦ *adv* leicht; ~ **chair** *n* Sessel *m*; ~**-going** *adj* gelassen; *(lax)* lässig

eat [iːt] *(pt* **ate,** *pp* **eaten)** *vt* essen; *(animals)* fressen; *(destroy)* (zer)fressen ♦ *vi* essen; fressen; ~ **away** *vt* zerfressen; ~ **into** *vt fus* zerfressen; **eaten** *pp of* **eat**

eau de Cologne [əʊdəkə'ləʊn] *n* Kölnisch Wasser *nt*

eaves [iːvz] *npl* Dachrand *m*

eavesdrop ['iːvzdrɒp] *vi* lauschen; **to** ~ **on sb** jdn belauschen

ebb [eb] *n* Ebbe *f* ♦ *vi* *(fig: also:* ~ **away)** (ab)ebben; ~ **tide** *n* Ebbe *f*

ebony ['ebənɪ] *n* Ebenholz *nt*

ebullient [ɪ'bʌlɪənt] *adj* sprudelnd, temperamentvoll

eccentric [ɪk'sentrɪk] *adj* exzentrisch ♦ *n* Exzentriker(in) *m(f)*

ecclesiastical [ɪkliːzɪ'æstɪkəl] *adj* kirchlich

echo ['ekəʊ] (*pl* ~es) *n* Echo *nt* ♦ *vt* zurückwerfen; (*fig*) nachbeten ♦ *vi* widerhallen

eclipse [ɪ'klɪps] *n* Finsternis *f* ♦ *vt* verfinstern

ecology [ɪ'kɒlədʒɪ] *n* Ökologie *f*

economic [iːkə'nɒmɪk] *adj* wirtschaftlich; ~**al** *adj* wirtschaftlich; (*person*) sparsam; ~**s** *n* Volkswirtschaft *f*

economist [ɪ'kɒnəmɪst] *n* Volkswirt(schaftler) *m*

economize [ɪ'kɒnəmaɪz] *vi* sparen

economy [ɪ'kɒnəmɪ] *n* (*thrift*) Sparsamkeit *f*; (*of country*) Wirtschaft *f*

ecstasy ['ekstəsɪ] *n* Ekstase *f*

ecstatic [eks'tætɪk] *adj* hingerissen

ecumenical [iːkjʊ'menɪkəl] *adj* ökumenisch

eczema ['eksɪmə] *n* Ekzem *nt*

edge [edʒ] *n* Rand *m*; (*of knife*) Schneide *f* ♦ *vt* (SEWING) einfassen; **on** ~ (*fig*) = **edgy**; **to** ~ **away from** langsam abrücken von; ~**ways** *adv*: **he couldn't get a word in** ~**ways** er kam überhaupt nicht zu Wort

edgy ['edʒɪ] *adj* nervös

edible ['edɪbl] *adj* eßbar

edict ['iːdɪkt] *n* Erlaß *m*

edifice ['edɪfɪs] *n* Gebäude *nt*

edit ['edɪt] *vt* redigieren; ~**ion** [ɪ'dɪʃən] *n* Ausgabe *f*; ~**or** *n* (*of newspaper*) Redakteur *m*; (*of book*) Lektor *m*; ~**orial** [edɪ'tɔːrɪəl] *adj* Redaktions- ♦ *n* Leitartikel *m*

educate ['edjʊkeɪt] *vt* erziehen, (aus)bilden

education [edjʊ'keɪʃən] *n* (*teaching*) Unterricht *m*; (*system*) Schulwesen *nt*; (*schooling*) Erziehung *f*; Bildung *f*; ~**al** *adj* pädagogisch

EEC *n abbr* (= *European Economic Community*) EG *f*

eel [iːl] *n* Aal *m*

eerie ['ɪərɪ] *adj* unheimlich

effect [ɪ'fekt] *n* Wirkung *f* ♦ *vt* bewirken; ~**s** *npl* (*sound, visual*) Effekte *pl*; **in** ~ in der Tat; **to take** ~ (*law*) in Kraft treten; (*drug*) wirken; ~**ive** *adj* wirksam, effektiv; ~**ively** *adv*

wirksam, effektiv

effeminate [ɪ'femɪnɪt] *adj* weibisch

effervescent [efə'vesnt] *adj* (*also fig*) sprudelnd

efficacy ['efɪkəsɪ] *n* Wirksamkeit *f*

efficiency [ɪ'fɪʃənsɪ] *n* Leistungsfähigkeit *f*

efficient [ɪ'fɪʃənt] *adj* tüchtig; (TECH) leistungsfähig; (*method*) wirksam

effigy ['efɪdʒɪ] *n* Abbild *nt*

effort ['efət] *n* Anstrengung *f*; ~**less** *adj* mühelos

effrontery [ɪ'frʌntərɪ] *n* Unverfrorenheit *f*

effusive [ɪ'fjuːsɪv] *adj* überschwenglich

e.g. *adv abbr* (= *exempli gratia*) z.B.

egalitarian [ɪgælɪ'tɛərɪən] *adj* Gleichheits-, egalitär

egg [eg] *n* Ei *nt*; ~ **on** *vt* anstacheln; ~**cup** *n* Eierbecher *m*; ~**plant** (*esp US*) *n* Aubergine *f*; ~**shell** *n* Eierschale *f*

ego ['iːgəʊ] *n* Ich *nt*, Selbst *nt*

egotism ['egəʊtɪzəm] *n* Ichbezogenheit *f*

egotist ['egəʊtɪst] *n* Egozentriker *m*

Egypt ['iːdʒɪpt] *n* Ägypten *nt*; ~**ian** [ɪ'dʒɪpʃən] *adj* ägyptisch ♦ *n* Ägypter(in) *m(f)*

eiderdown ['aɪdədaʊn] *n* Daunendecke *f*

eight [eɪt] *num* acht; ~**een** *num* achtzehn; ~**h** [eɪtθ] *adj* achte(r, s) ♦ *n* Achtel *nt*; ~**y** *num* achtzig

Eire ['ɛərə] *n* Irland *nt*

either ['aɪðə*] *conj*: ~ ... **or** entweder ... oder ♦ *pron*: ~ **of the two** eine(r, s) von beiden ♦ *adj*: **on** ~ **side** auf beiden Seiten ♦ *adv*: **I don't** ~ ich will nicht; **I don't want** ~ ich will keins von beiden

eject [ɪ'dʒekt] *vt* ausstoßen, vertreiben

eke [iːk] *vt*: **to** ~ **out** strecken

elaborate [*adj* ɪ'læbərɪt, *vb* ɪ'læbəreɪt] *adj* sorgfältig ausgearbeitet, ausführlich ♦ *vt* sorgfältig ausarbeiten ♦ *vi* ausführlich darstellen; ~**ly** *adv* genau, ausführlich

elapse [ɪ'læps] *vi* vergehen

elastic [ɪ'læstɪk] *n* Gummiband *nt* ♦ *adj* elastisch; ~ **band** (BRIT) *n* Gummiband *nt*

elated [ɪ'leɪtɪd] *adj* froh

elation [ɪˈleɪʃən] n gehobene Stimmung f

elbow [ˈelbəʊ] n Ellbogen m

elder [ˈeldə*] adj älter ♦ n Ältere(r) mf; ~**ly** adj ältere(r, s) ♦ npl: the ~**ly** die Älteren pl

eldest [ˈeldɪst] adj älteste(r, s) ♦ n Älteste(r) mf

elect [ɪˈlekt] vt wählen ♦ adj zukünftig; ~**ion** [ɪˈlekʃən] n Wahl f; ~**ioneering** [ɪlekʃəˈnɪərɪŋ] n Wahlpropaganda f; ~**or** n Wähler m; ~**oral** adj Wahl-; ~**orate** n Wähler pl, Wählerschaft f

electric [ɪˈlektrɪk] adj elektrisch, Elektro-; ~**al** adj elektrisch; ~ **blanket** n Heizdecke f; ~ **chair** n elektrische(r) Stuhl m; ~ **fire** n elektrische(r) Heizofen m

electrician [ɪlekˈtrɪʃən] n Elektriker m

electricity [ɪlekˈtrɪsɪtɪ] n Elektrizität f

electrify [ɪˈlektrɪfaɪ] vt elektrifizieren; (fig) elektrisieren

electrocute [ɪˈlektrəʊkjuːt] vt durch elektrischen Strom töten

electronic [ɪlekˈtrɒnɪk] adj elektronisch, Elektronen-; ~ **mail** n elektronische(r) Briefkasten m; ~**s** n Elektronik f

elegance [ˈelɪgəns] n Eleganz f

elegant [ˈelɪgənt] adj elegant

element [ˈelɪmənt] n Element nt; ~**ary** [elɪˈmentərɪ] adj einfach; (primary) Grund-

elephant [ˈelɪfənt] n Elefant m

elevate [ˈelɪveɪt] vt emporheben

elevation [elɪˈveɪʃən] n (height) Erhebung f; (ARCHIT) (Quer)schnitt m

elevator [ˈelɪveɪtə*] (US) n Fahrstuhl m, Aufzug m

eleven [ɪˈlevn] num elf; ~ **ses** (BRIT) npl ≈ zweite(s) Frühstück nt; ~**th** adj elfte(r, s)

elf [elf] (pl **elves**) n Elfe f

elicit [ɪˈlɪsɪt] vt herausbekommen

eligible [ˈelɪdʒəbl] adj wählbar; **to be** ~ **for a pension** pensionsberechtigt sein

eliminate [ɪˈlɪmɪneɪt] vt ausschalten

elimination [ɪlɪmɪˈneɪʃən] n Ausschaltung f

elite [eɪˈliːt] n Elite f

elm [elm] n Ulme f

elocution [eləˈkjuːʃən] n Sprecherziehung f

elongated [ˈiːlɒŋgeɪtɪd] adj verlängert

elope [ɪˈləʊp] vi entlaufen; ~**ment** n Entlaufen nt

eloquence [ˈeləkwəns] n Beredsamkeit f

eloquent [ˈeləkwənt] adj redegewandt

else [els] adv sonst; **who** ~? wer sonst?; **somebody** ~ jemand anders, or sonst; ~**where** adv anderswo, woanders

elucidate [ɪˈluːsɪdeɪt] vt erläutern

elude [ɪˈluːd] vt entgehen +dat

elusive [ɪˈluːsɪv] adj schwer faßbar

elves [elvz] npl of elf

emaciated [ɪˈmeɪsɪeɪtɪd] adj abgezehrt

emanate [ˈeməneɪt] vi: **to** ~ **from** ausströmen aus

emancipate [ɪˈmænsɪpeɪt] vt emanzipieren; (slave) freilassen

emancipation [ɪmænsɪˈpeɪʃən] n Emanzipation f; Freilassung f

embankment [ɪmˈbæŋkmənt] n (of river) Uferböschung f; (of road) Straßendamm m

embargo [ɪmˈbɑːgəʊ] (pl ~**es**) n Embargo nt

embark [ɪmˈbɑːk] vi sich einschiffen; ~ **on** vt fus unternehmen; ~**ation** [embɑːˈkeɪʃən] n Einschiffung f

embarrass [ɪmˈbærəs] vt in Verlegenheit bringen; ~**ed** adj verlegen; ~**ing** adj peinlich; ~**ment** n Verlegenheit f

embassy [ˈembəsɪ] n Botschaft f

embed [ɪmˈbed] vt einbetten

embellish [ɪmˈbelɪʃ] vt verschönern

embers [ˈembəz] npl Glut(asche) f

embezzle [ɪmˈbezl] vt unterschlagen; ~**ment** n Unterschlagung f

embitter [ɪmˈbɪtə*] vt verbittern

embody [ɪmˈbɒdɪ] vt (ideas) verkörpern; (new features) (in sich) vereinigen

embossed [ɪmˈbɒst] adj geprägt

embrace [ɪmˈbreɪs] vt umarmen (include) einschließen ♦ vi sich umarmen ♦ n Umarmung f

embroider [ɪmˈbrɔɪdə*] vt (be)sticken; (story) ausschmücken; ~**y** n Stickerei f

emerald [ˈemərəld] n Smaragd m

emerge [ɪˈmɜːdʒ] vi auftauchen; (truth)

herauskommen

emergence [ɪˈmɜːdʒəns] n Erscheinen nt

emergency [ɪˈmɜːdʒənsɪ] n Notfall m; ~ **cord** (US) n Notbremse f; ~ **exit** n Notausgang m; ~ **landing** n Notlandung f; ~ **services** npl Notdienste pl

emery board [ˈeməɪ-] n Papiernagelfeile f

emetic [ɪˈmetɪk] n Brechmittel nt

emigrant [ˈemɪgrənt] n Auswanderer m

emigrate [ˈemɪgreɪt] vi auswandern

emigration [emɪˈgreɪʃən] n Auswanderung f

eminence [ˈemɪnəns] n hohe(r) Rang m

eminent [ˈemɪnənt] adj bedeutend

emission [ɪˈmɪʃən] n Ausströmen nt

emit [ɪˈmɪt] vt von sich dat geben

emotion [ɪˈməʊʃən] n Emotion f, Gefühl nt; ~**al** adj (person) emotional; (scene) ergreifend

emotive [ɪˈməʊtɪv] adj gefühlsbetont

emperor [ˈempərə*] n Kaiser m

emphases [ˈemfəsiːz] npl of emphasis

emphasis [ˈemfəsɪs] n (LING) Betonung f; (fig) Nachdruck m

emphasize [ˈemfəsaɪz] vt betonen

emphatic [ɪmˈfætɪk] adj nachdrücklich; ~**ally** [ɪmˈfætɪkəlɪ] adv nachdrücklich

empire [ˈempaɪə*] n Reich nt

empirical [emˈpɪrɪkəl] adj empirisch

employ [ɪmˈplɔɪ] vt (hire) anstellen; (use) verwenden; ~**ee** [emplɔɪˈiː] n Angestellte(r) mf; ~**er** n Arbeitgeber(in) m(f); ~**ment** n Beschäftigung f; ~**ment agency** n Stellenvermittlung f

empower [ɪmˈpaʊə*] vt: to ~ sb to do sth jdm ermächtigen, etw zu tun

empress [ˈemprɪs] n Kaiserin f

emptiness [ˈemptɪnɪs] n Leere f

empty [ˈemptɪ] adj leer ♦ n (bottle) Leergut nt ♦ vt (contents) leeren; (container) ausleeren ♦ vi (water) abfließen; (river) münden; (house) sich leeren; ~**-handed** adj mit leeren Händen

emulate [ˈemjʊleɪt] vt nacheifern +dat

emulsion [ɪˈmʌlʃən] n Emulsion f

enable [ɪˈneɪbl] vt: to ~ sb to do sth es jdm ermöglichen, etw zu tun

enact [ɪnˈækt] vt (law) erlassen; (play)

aufführen; (role) spielen

enamel [ɪˈnæməl] n Email nt; (of teeth) (Zahn)schmelz m

encased [ɪnˈkeɪst] adj: ~ **in** (enclosed) eingeschlossen in +dat; (covered) verkleidet mit

enchant [ɪnˈtʃɑːnt] vt bezaubern; ~**ing** adj entzückend

encircle [ɪnˈsɜːkl] vt umringen

encl. abbr (= enclosed) Anl.

enclose [ɪnˈkləʊz] vt einschließen; to ~ **sth** (**in** or **with a letter**) etw (einem Brief) beilegen; ~**d** (in letter) beiliegend, anbei

enclosure [ɪnˈkləʊʒə*] n Einfriedung f; (in letter) Anlage f

encompass [ɪnˈkʌmpəs] vt (include) umfassen

encore [ˈɒŋkɔː*] n Zugabe f

encounter [ɪnˈkaʊntə*] n Begegnung f; (MIL) Zusammenstoß m ♦ vt treffen; (resistance) stoßen auf +acc

encourage [ɪnˈkʌrɪdʒ] vt ermutigen; ~**ment** n Ermutigung f, Förderung f

encouraging [ɪnˈkʌrɪdʒɪŋ] adj ermutigend, vielversprechend

encroach [ɪnˈkrəʊtʃ] vi: to ~ (**up**)**on** eindringen in +acc; (time) in Anspruch nehmen

encrusted [ɪnˈkrʌstəd] adj: ~ **with** besetzt mit

encumber [ɪnˈkʌmbə*] vt: to be ~**ed with** (parcels) beladen sein mit; (debts) belastet sein mit

encyclop(a)edia [ensaɪkləʊˈpiːdɪə] n Konversationslexikon nt

end [end] n Ende nt, Schluß m; (purpose) Zweck m ♦ vt (also: **bring to an** ~, **put an** ~ **to**) beenden ♦ vi zu Ende gehen; **in the** ~ zum Schluß; **on** ~ (object) hochkant; **to stand on** ~ (hair) zu Berge stehen; **for hours on** ~ stundenlang; ~ **up** vi landen

endanger [ɪnˈdeɪndʒə*] vt gefährden

endearing [ɪnˈdɪərɪŋ] adj gewinnend

endeavour [ɪnˈdevə*] (US **endeavor**) n Bestrebung f ♦ vi sich bemühen

ending [ˈendɪŋ] n Ende nt

endive [ˈendaɪv] n Endivie f

endless [ˈendlɪs] adj endlos

endorse [ɪn'dɔːs] vt unterzeichnen; (approve) unterstützen; ~ment n (on licence) Eintrag m
endow [ɪn'dau] vt: **to ~ sb with sth** jdm etw verleihen; (with money) jdm etw stiften
endurance [ɪn'djuərəns] n Ausdauer f
endure [ɪn'djuə*] vt ertragen ♦ vi (last) (fort)dauern
enemy ['enɪmɪ] n Feind m ♦ adj feindlich
energetic [enə'dʒetɪk] adj tatkräftig
energy ['enədʒɪ] n Energie f
enforce [ɪn'fɔːs] vt durchsetzen
engage [ɪn'geɪdʒ] vt (employ) einstellen; (in conversation) verwickeln; (TECH) einschalten ♦ vi ineinandergreifen; (clutch) fassen; **to ~ in** sich beteiligen an +dat; ~d adj verlobt; (BRIT: TEL, toilet) besetzt; (: busy) beschäftigt; **to get ~d** sich verloben; ~d **tone** (BRIT) n (TEL) Besetztzeichen nt; ~ment n (appointment) Verabredung f; (to marry) Verlobung f; (MIL) Gefecht nt; ~ment **ring** n Verlobungsring m
engaging [ɪn'geɪdʒɪŋ] adj gewinnend
engender [ɪn'dʒendə*] vt hervorrufen
engine ['endʒɪn] n (AUT) Motor m; (RAIL) Lokomotive f; ~ **driver** n Lok(omotiv)führer(in) m(f)
engineer [endʒɪ'nɪə*] n Ingenieur m; (US: RAIL) Lok(omotiv)führer(in) m(f); ~ing [endʒɪ'nɪərɪŋ] n Technik f
England ['ɪŋglənd] n England nt
English ['ɪŋglɪʃ] adj englisch ♦ n (LING) Englisch nt; **the ~** npl (people) die Engländer pl; **the ~ Channel** n der Ärmelkanal m; ~**man/woman** (irreg) n Engländer(in) m(f)
engraving [ɪn'greɪvɪŋ] n Stich m
engrossed [ɪn'grəust] adj vertieft
engulf [ɪn'gʌlf] vt verschlingen
enhance [ɪn'hɑːns] vt steigern, heben
enigma [ɪ'nɪgmə] n Rätsel nt; ~**tic** [enɪg'mætɪk] adj rätselhaft
enjoy [ɪn'dʒɔɪ] vt genießen; (privilege) besitzen; **to ~ o.s.** sich amüsieren; ~**able** adj erfreulich; ~**ment** n Genuß m, Freude f

enlarge [ɪn'lɑːdʒ] vt erweitern; (PHOT) vergrößern ♦ vi: **to ~ on sth** etw weiter ausführen; ~**ment** n Vergrößerung f
enlighten [ɪn'laɪtn] vt aufklären; ~**ment** n: **the E~ment** (HIST) die Aufklärung
enlist [ɪn'lɪst] vt gewinnen ♦ vi (MIL) sich melden
enmity ['enmɪtɪ] n Feindschaft f
enormity [ɪ'nɔːmɪtɪ] n Ungeheuerlichkeit f
enormous [ɪ'nɔːməs] adj ungeheuer
enough [ɪ'nʌf] adj, adv genug; **funnily ~** komischerweise
enquire [ɪn'kwaɪə*] vt, vi = inquire
enrage [ɪn'reɪdʒ] vt wütend machen
enrich [ɪn'rɪtʃ] vt bereichern
enrol [ɪn'rəul] vt einschreiben ♦ vi (register) sich anmelden; ~**ment** n (for course) Anmeldung f
en route [ãːn'ruːt] adv unterwegs
ensign ['ensaɪn, 'ensən] n (NAUT) Flagge f; (MIL) Fähnrich m
enslave [ɪn'sleɪv] vt versklaven
ensue [ɪn'sjuː] vi folgen, sich ergeben
ensure [ɪn'ʃuə*] vt garantieren
entail [ɪn'teɪl] vt mit sich bringen
entangle [ɪn'tæŋgl] vt verwirren, verstricken
enter ['entə*] vt eintreten in +dat, betreten; (club) beitreten +dat; (in book) eintragen ♦ vi hereinkommen, hineingehen; ~ **for** vt fus sich beteiligen an +dat; ~ **into** vt fus (agreement) eingehen; (plans) eine Rolle spielen bei; ~ **(up)on** vt fus beginnen
enteritis [entə'raɪtɪs] n Dünndarmentzündung f
enterprise ['entəpraɪz] n (in person) Initiative f; (COMM) Unternehmen nt
enterprising ['entəpraɪzɪŋ] adj unternehmungslustig
entertain [entə'teɪn] vt (guest) bewirten; (amuse) unterhalten; ~**er** n Unterhaltungskünstler(in) m(f); ~**ing** adj unterhaltsam; ~**ment** n Unterhaltung f
enthralled [ɪn'θrɔːld] adj gefesselt
enthusiasm [ɪn'θuːzɪæzəm] n Begeisterung f

enthusiast [ɪn'θuːzɪæst] n Enthusiast m; **~ic** [ɪnθuːzɪ'æstɪk] adj begeistert
entice [ɪn'taɪs] vt verleiten, locken
entire [ɪn'taɪə*] adj ganz; **~ly** adv ganz, völlig; **~ty** [ɪn'taɪərətɪ] n: **in its ~ty** in seiner Gesamtheit
entitle [ɪn'taɪtl] vt (allow) berechtigen; (name) betiteln; **~d** adj (book) mit dem Titel; **to be ~d to sth** das Recht auf etw acc haben; **to be ~d to do sth** das Recht haben, etw zu tun
entity ['entɪtɪ] n Ding nt, Wesen nt
entourage [ɒntu'rɑːʒ] n Gefolge nt
entrails ['entreɪlz] npl Eingeweide pl
entrance [n 'entrəns, vb ɪn'trɑːns] n Eingang m; (entering) Eintritt m; ♦ vt hinreißen; **~ examination** n Aufnahmeprüfung f; **~ fee** n Eintrittsgeld nt; **~ ramp** (US) n (AUT) Einfahrt f
entrant ['entrənt] n (for exam) Kandidat m; (in race) Teilnehmer m
entreat [ɪn'triːt] vt anflehen
entrenched [ɪn'trentʃt] adj (fig) verwurzelt
entrepreneur [ɒntrəprə'nɜː*] n Unternehmer(in) m(f)
entrust [ɪn'trʌst] vt: **to ~ sb with sth** or **sth to sb** jdm etw anvertrauen
entry ['entrɪ] n Eingang m; (THEAT) Auftritt m; (in account) Eintragung f; (in dictionary) Eintrag m; **"no ~"** "Eintritt verboten"; (for cars) "Einfahrt verboten"; **~ form** n Anmeldeformular nt; **~ phone** n Sprechanlage f
enumerate [ɪ'njuːməreɪt] vt aufzählen
enunciate [ɪ'nʌnsɪeɪt] vt aussprechen
envelop [ɪn'veləp] vt einhüllen
envelope ['envələup] n Umschlag m
enviable ['envɪəbl] adj beneidenswert
envious ['envɪəs] adj neidisch
environment [ɪn'vaɪərənmənt] n Umgebung f; (ECOLOGY) Umwelt f; **~al** [ɪnvaɪərən'mentl] adj Umwelt-
envisage [ɪn'vɪzɪdʒ] vt sich dat vorstellen
envoy ['envɔɪ] n Gesandte(r) mf
envy ['envɪ] n Neid m ♦ vt: **to ~ sb sth** jdn um etw beneiden
enzyme ['enzaɪm] n Enzym nt
ephemeral [ɪ'femərəl] adj flüchtig

epic ['epɪk] n Epos nt ♦ adj episch
epidemic [epɪ'demɪk] n Epidemie f
epilepsy ['epɪlepsɪ] n Epilepsie f
epileptic [epɪ'leptɪk] adj epileptisch ♦ n Epileptiker(in) m(f)
episode ['epɪsəud] n (incident) Vorfall m; (story) Episode f
epistle [ɪ'pɪsl] n Brief m
epitaph ['epɪtɑːf] n Grabinschrift f
epithet ['epɪθət] n Beiname m
epitome [ɪ'pɪtəmɪ] n Inbegriff m
epitomize [ɪ'pɪtəmaɪz] vt verkörpern
equable ['ekwəbl] adj ausgeglichen
equal ['iːkwl] adj gleich ♦ n Gleichgestellte(r) mf ♦ vt gleichkommen +dat; **~ to the task** der Aufgabe gewachsen; **~ity** [ɪ'kwɒlɪtɪ] n Gleichheit f; (~ rights) Gleichberechtigung f; **~ize** vt gleichmachen ♦ vi (SPORT) ausgleichen; **~izer** n (SPORT) Ausgleich(streffer) m; **~ly** adv gleich
equanimity [ekwə'nɪmɪtɪ] n Gleichmut m
equate [ɪ'kweɪt] vt gleichsetzen
equation [ɪ'kweɪʒən] n Gleichung f
equator [ɪ'kweɪtə*] n Äquator m
equestrian [ɪ'kwestrɪən] adj Reit-
equilibrium [iːkwɪ'lɪbrɪəm] n Gleichgewicht nt
equinox ['iːkwɪnɒks] n Tag- und Nachtgleiche f
equip [ɪ'kwɪp] vt ausrüsten; **~ment** n Ausrüstung f; (TECH) Gerät nt
equitable ['ekwɪtəbl] adj gerecht, billig
equities ['ekwɪtɪz] (BRIT) npl (FIN) Stammaktien pl
equivalent [ɪ'kwɪvələnt] adj gleichwertig, entsprechend ♦ n Äquivalent nt; (in money) Gegenwert m; **~ to** gleichwertig +dat, entsprechend +dat
equivocal [ɪ'kwɪvəkəl] adj zweideutig
era ['ɪərə] n Epoche f, Ära f
eradicate [ɪ'rædɪkeɪt] vt ausrotten
erase [ɪ'reɪz] vt ausradieren; (tape) löschen; **~r** n Radiergummi m
erect [ɪ'rekt] adj aufrecht ♦ vt errichten
erection [ɪ'rekʃən] n Errichtung f; (ANAT) Erektion f
ermine ['ɜːmɪn] n Hermelin(pelz) m
erode [ɪ'rəud] vt zerfressen; (land) aus-

waschen
erotic [ɪ'rɒtɪk] *adj* erotisch; ~**ism**
[ɪ'rɒtɪsɪzəm] *n* Erotik *f*
err [ɜː*] *vi* sich irren
errand ['erənd] *n* Besorgung *f*; ~ **boy** *n*
Laufbursche *m*
erratic [ɪ'rætɪk] *adj* unberechenbar
erroneous [ɪ'rəʊnɪəs] *adj* irrig
error ['erə*] *n* Fehler *m*
erudite ['erʊdaɪt] *adj* gelehrt
erupt [ɪ'rʌpt] *vi* ausbrechen; ~**ion**
[ɪ'rʌpʃən] *n* Ausbruch *m*
escalate ['eskəleɪt] *vi* sich steigern
escalator ['eskəleɪtə*] *n* Rolltreppe *f*
escape [ɪs'keɪp] *n* Flucht *f*; (*of gas*)
Entweichen *nt* ♦ *vi* entkommen;
(*prisoners*) fliehen; (*leak*) entweichen ♦
vt entkommen +*dat*
escapism [ɪs'keɪpɪzəm] *n* Flucht *f* (vor
der Wirklichkeit)
escort [*n* 'eskɔːt, *vb* ɪs'kɔːt] *n* (*person
accompanying*) Begleiter *m*; (*guard*)
Eskorte *f* ♦ *vt* (*lady*) begleiten; (*MIL*)
eskortieren
Eskimo ['eskɪməʊ] *n* Eskimo *m*
especially [ɪs'peʃəlɪ] *adv* besonders
espionage ['espɪənɑːʒ] *n* Spionage *f*
esplanade ['espləneɪd] *n* Promenade *f*
espouse [ɪ'spaʊz] *vt* Partei ergreifen für
Esquire [ɪs'kwaɪə*] *n*: **J. Brown** ~ Herrn
J. Brown
essay ['eseɪ] *n* Aufsatz *m*; (*LITER*)
Essay *m*
essence ['esəns] *n* (*quality*) Wesen *nt*;
(*extract*) Essenz *f*
essential [ɪ'senʃəl] *adj* (*necessary*)
unentbehrlich; (*basic*) wesentlich ♦ *n*
Allernötigste(s) *nt*; ~**ly** *adv* eigentlich
establish [ɪs'tæblɪʃ] *vt* (*set up*) gründen;
(*prove*) nachweisen; ~**ed** *adj* anerkannt; (*belief, laws etc*) herrschend;
~**ment** *n* (*setting up*) Einrichtung *f*;
the E~ment das Establishment
estate [ɪs'teɪt] *n* Gut *nt*; (*BRIT: housing*
~) Siedlung *f*; (*will*) Nachlaß *m*; ~
agent (*BRIT*) *n* Grundstücksmakler *m*;
~ **car** (*BRIT*) *n* Kombiwagen *m*
esteem [ɪs'tiːm] *n* Wertschätzung *f*
esthetic [ɪs'θetɪk] (*US*) *adj* = **aesthetic**
estimate [*n* 'estɪmət, *vb* 'estɪmeɪt] *n*

Schätzung *f*; (*of price*) (Kosten)voranschlag *m* ♦ *vt* schätzen
estimation [estɪ'meɪʃən] *n* Einschätzung
f; (*esteem*) Achtung *f*
estranged [ɪ'streɪndʒd] *adj* entfremdet
estuary ['estjʊərɪ] *n* Mündung *f*
etc *abbr* (= *et cetera*) usw
etching ['etʃɪŋ] *n* Kupferstich *m*
eternal [ɪ'tɜːnl] *adj* ewig
eternity [ɪ'tɜːnɪtɪ] *n* Ewigkeit *f*
ether ['iːθə*] *n* Äther *m*
ethical ['eθɪkəl] *adj* ethisch
ethics ['eθɪks] *n* Ethik *f* ♦ *npl* Moral *f*
Ethiopia [iːθɪ'əʊpɪə] *n* Äthiopien *nt*
ethnic ['eθnɪk] *adj* Volks-, ethnisch
ethos ['iːθɒs] *n* Gesinnung *f*
etiquette ['etɪket] *n* Etikette *f*
euphemism ['juːfɪmɪzəm] *n* Eu-
phemismus *m*
Eurocheque ['jʊərəʊ'tʃek] *n* Euroscheck
m
Europe ['jʊərəp] *n* Europa *nt*; ~**an**
[jʊərə'piːən] *adj* europäisch ♦ *n*
Europäer(in) *m(f)*
evacuate [ɪ'vækjʊeɪt] *vt* (*place*)
räumen; (*people*) evakuieren
evacuation [ɪvækjʊ'eɪʃən] *n* Räumung *f*;
Evakuierung *f*
evade [ɪ'veɪd] *vt* (*escape*) entkommen
+*dat*; (*avoid*) meiden; (*duty*) sich entziehen +*dat*
evaluate [ɪ'væljʊeɪt] *vt* bewerten;
(*information*) auswerten
evaporate [ɪ'væpəreɪt] *vi* verdampfen ♦
vt verdampfen lassen; ~**d milk** *n*
Kondensmilch *f*
evasion [ɪ'veɪʒən] *n* Umgehung *f*
evasive [ɪ'veɪzɪv] *adj* ausweichend
eve [iːv] *n*: **on the** ~ **of** am Vorabend
+*gen*
even ['iːvən] *adj* eben; gleichmäßig;
(*score etc*) unentschieden; (*number*)
gerade ♦ *adv*: ~ **you** sogar du; **to get** ~
with sb jdm heimzahlen; ~ **if** selbst
wenn; ~ **so** dennoch; ~ **out** *vi* sich ausgleichen
evening ['iːvnɪŋ] *n* Abend *m*; **in the** ~
abends, am Abend; ~ **class** *n* Abendschule *f*; ~ **dress** *n* (*man's*) Gesell-
schaftsanzug *m*; (*woman's*) Abendkleid

nt

event [ɪ'vent] n (happening) Ereignis nt; (SPORT) Disziplin f; **in the ~ of** im Falle +gen; **~ful** adj ereignisreich

eventual [ɪ'ventʃʋəl] adj (final) schließlich; **~ity** [ɪventʃʋ'ælɪtɪ] n Möglichkeit f; **~ly** adv (at last) am Ende; (given time) schließlich

ever ['evə*] adv (always) immer; (at any time) je(mals); **~ since** adv seitdem ♦ conj seit; **~green** n Immergrün nt; **~lasting** adj immerwährend

every ['evrɪ] adj jede(r, s); **~ other/ third day** jeden zweiten/dritten Tag; **~ one of them** alle; **I have ~ confidence in him** ich habe uneingeschränktes Vertrauen in ihn; **we wish you ~ success** wir wünschen Ihnen viel Erfolg; **he's ~ bit as clever as his brother** er ist genauso klug wie sein Bruder; **~ now and then** ab und zu; **~body** pron = everyone; **~day** adj (daily) täglich; (commonplace) alltäglich, Alltags-; **~one** pron jeder, alle pl; **~thing** pron alles; **~where** adv überall(hin); (wherever) wohin; **~where you go** wohin du auch gehst

evict [ɪ'vɪkt] vt ausweisen; **~ion** n Ausweisung f

evidence ['evɪdəns] n (sign) Spur f; (proof) Beweis m; (testimony) Aussage f

evident ['evɪdənt] adj augenscheinlich; **~ly** adv offensichtlich

evil ['iːvɪl] adj böse ♦ n Böse nt

evocative [ɪ'vɒkətɪv] adj: **to be ~ of sth** an etw acc erinnern

evoke [ɪ'vəʊk] vt hervorrufen

evolution [iːvə'luːʃən] n Entwicklung f; (of life) Evolution f

evolve [ɪ'vɒlv] vt entwickeln ♦ vi sich entwickeln

ewe [juː] n Mutterschaf nt

ex- [eks] prefix Ex-, Alt-, ehemalig

exacerbate [ek'sæsəbeɪt] vt verschlimmern

exact [ɪg'zækt] adj genau ♦ vt (demand) verlangen; **~ing** adj anspruchsvoll; **~itude** n Genauigkeit f

exaggerate [ɪg'zædʒəreɪt] vt, vi übertreiben

exaggeration [ɪgzædʒə'reɪʃən] n Übertreibung f

exalted [ɪg'zɔːltɪd] adj (position, style) hoch; (person) exaltiert

exam [ɪg'zæm] n abbr (SCH) = **examination**

examination [ɪgzæmɪ'neɪʃən] n Untersuchung f; (SCH) Prüfung f, Examen nt; (customs) Kontrolle f

examine [ɪg'zæmɪn] vt untersuchen; (SCH) prüfen; (consider) erwägen; **~r** n Prüfer m

example [ɪg'zɑːmpl] n Beispiel nt; **for ~** zum Beispiel

exasperate [ɪg'zɑːspəreɪt] vt zum Verzweifeln bringen

exasperating [ɪg'zɑːspəreɪtɪŋ] adj ärgerlich, zum Verzweifeln bringend

exasperation [ɪgzɑːspə'reɪʃən] n Verzweiflung f

excavate ['ekskəveɪt] vt ausgraben

excavation [ekskə'veɪʃən] n Ausgrabung f

exceed [ɪk'siːd] vt überschreiten; (hopes) übertreffen

excel [ɪk'sel] vi sich auszeichnen

excellence ['eksələns] n Vortrefflichkeit f

excellency ['eksələnsɪ] n: **His E~** Seine Exzellenz f

excellent ['eksələnt] adj ausgezeichnet

except [ɪk'sept] prep (also: **~ for, ~ing**) außer +dat ♦ vt ausnehmen; **~ion** [ɪk'sepʃən] n Ausnahme f; **to take ~ion to** Anstoß nehmen an +dat; **~ional** [ɪk'sepʃənl] adj außergewöhnlich

excerpt ['eksɜːpt] n Auszug m

excess [ek'ses] n Übermaß nt; **an ~ of** ein Übermaß an +dat; **~ baggage** n Mehrgepäck nt; **~ fare** n Nachlösegebühr f; **~ive** adj übermäßig

exchange [ɪks'tʃeɪndʒ] n Austausch m; (also: **telephone ~**) Zentrale f ♦ vt (goods) tauschen; (greetings) austauschen; (money, blows) wechseln; **~ rate** n Wechselkurs m

Exchequer [ɪks'tʃekə*] (BRIT) n: **the ~** das Schatzamt

excise [n 'eksaɪz, vb ek'saɪz] n Ver-

brauchssteuer *f* ♦ *vt* (*MED*) heraus-
schneiden
excite [ɪkˈsaɪt] *vt* erregen; **to get ~d**
sich aufregen; **~ment** *n* Aufregung *f*
exciting [ɪkˈsaɪtɪŋ] *adj* spannend
exclaim [ɪksˈkleɪm] *vi* ausrufen
exclamation [eksklǝˈmeɪʃǝn] *n* Ausruf
m; **~ mark** *n* Ausrufezeichen *nt*
exclude [ɪksˈkluːd] *vt* ausschließen
exclusion [ɪksˈkluːʒǝn] *n* Ausschluß *m*
exclusive [ɪksˈkluːsɪv] *adj* (*select*) exklusiv; (*sole*) ausschließlich, Allein-; **~
of** exklusive *+gen*; **~ly** *adv* nur, ausschließlich
excommunicate [ekskǝˈmjuːnɪkeɪt] *vt*
exkommunizieren
excrement [ˈekskrɪmǝnt] *n* Kot *m*
excruciating [ɪksˈkruːʃɪeɪtɪŋ] *adj*
qualvoll
excursion [ɪksˈkɜːʃǝn] *n* Ausflug *m*
excusable [ɪksˈkjuːzǝbl] *adj* entschuldbar
excuse [*n* ɪksˈkjuːs, *vb* ɪksˈkjuːz] *n* Entschuldigung *f* ♦ *vt* entschuldigen; **~
me!** entschuldigen Sie!
ex-directory [ˈeksdǝˈrektǝrɪ] (*BRIT*) *adj*:
to be ~ nicht im Telefonbuch stehen
execute [ˈeksɪkjuːt] *vt* (*carry out*) ausführen; (*kill*) hinrichten
execution [eksɪˈkjuːʃǝn] *n* Ausführung *f*;
(*killing*) Hinrichtung *f*; **~er** *n* Scharf-
richter *m*
executive [ɪgˈzekjʊtɪv] *n* (*COMM*) Ge-
schäftsführer *m*; (*POL*) Exekutive *f* ♦
adj Exekutiv-, ausführend
executor [ɪgˈzekjʊtǝ*] *n* Testamentsvollstrecker *m*
exemplary [ɪgˈzemplǝrɪ] *adj* musterhaft
exemplify [ɪgˈzemplɪfaɪ] *vt* veranschaulichen
exempt [ɪgˈzempt] *adj* befreit ♦ *vt* befreien; **~ion** [ɪgˈzempʃǝn] *n* Befreiung *f*
exercise [ˈeksǝsaɪz] *n* Übung *f* ♦ *vt*
(*power*) ausüben; (*muscle, patience*)
üben; (*dog*) ausführen ♦ *vi* Sport
treiben; **~ book** *n* (Schul)heft *nt*
exert [ɪgˈzɜːt] *vt* (*influence*) ausüben; **to
~ o.s.** sich anstrengen; **~ion** [ɪgˈzɜːʃǝn]
n Anstrengung *f*
exhale [eksˈheɪl] *vt, vi* ausatmen
exhaust [ɪgˈzɔːst] *n* (*fumes*) Abgase *pl*;

(*pipe*) Auspuffrohr *nt* ♦ *vt* erschöpfen;
~ed *adj* erschöpft; **~ion** [ɪgˈzɔːstʃǝn] *n*
Erschöpfung *f*; **~ive** *adj* erschöpfend
exhibit [ɪgˈzɪbɪt] *n* (*ART*) Ausstellungs-
stück *nt*; (*JUR*) Beweisstück *nt* ♦ *vt* ausstellen; **~ion** [eksɪˈbɪʃǝn] *n* (*ART*) Ausstellung *f*; (*of temper etc*) Zurschaustellung *f*; **~ionist** [eksɪˈbɪʃǝnɪst] *n*
Exhibitionist *m*
exhilarating [ɪgˈzɪlǝreɪtɪŋ] *adj* erhebend
exhort [ɪgˈzɔːt] *vt* ermahnen
exile [ˈeksaɪl] *n* Exil *nt*; (*person*) Ver-
bannte(r) *mf* ♦ *vt* verbannen
exist [ɪgˈzɪst] *vi* existieren; **~ence** *n* Existenz *f*; **~ing** *adj* bestehend
exit [ˈeksɪt] *n* Ausgang *m*; (*THEAT*)
Abgang *m* ♦ *vi* (*THEAT*) abtreten;
(*COMPUT*) aus einem Programm herausgehen; **~ ramp** (*US*) *n* (*AUT*) Ausfahrt *f*
exodus [ˈeksǝdǝs] *n* Auszug *m*
exonerate [ɪgˈzɒnǝreɪt] *vt* entlasten
exorbitant [ɪgˈzɔːbɪtǝnt] *adj* übermäßig;
(*price*) Phantasie-
exotic [ɪgˈzɒtɪk] *adj* exotisch
expand [ɪksˈpænd] *vt* ausdehnen ♦ *vi*
sich ausdehnen
expanse [ɪksˈpæns] *n* Fläche *f*
expansion [ɪksˈpænʃǝn] *n* Erweiterung *f*
expatriate [eksˈpætrɪt] *n* Ausländer(in)
m(f)
expect [ɪksˈpekt] *vt* erwarten; (*suppose*)
annehmen ♦ *vi*: **to be ~ing** ein Kind
erwarten; **~ancy** *n* Erwartung *f*; **~ant
mother** *n* werdende Mutter *f*; **~ation**
[ekspekˈteɪʃǝn] *n* Hoffnung *f*
expedience [ɪksˈpiːdɪǝns] *n* Zweckdien-
lichkeit *f*
expediency [ɪksˈpiːdɪǝnsɪ] *n* Zweckdien-
lichkeit *f*
expedient [ɪksˈpiːdɪǝnt] *adj* zweckdien-
lich ♦ *n* (Hilfs)mittel *nt*
expedition [eksprɪˈdɪʃǝn] *n* Expedition *f*
expel [ɪksˈpel] *vt* ausweisen; (*student*)
(ver)weisen
expend [ɪksˈpend] *vt* (*effort*) aufwenden; **~iture** [ɪkˈspendɪtʃǝ*] *n* Ausgaben *pl*
expense [ɪksˈpens] *n* Kosten *pl*; **~s** *npl*
(*COMM*) Spesen *pl*; **at the ~ of** auf Kosten von; **~ account** *n* Spesenkonto *nt*

expensive [ɪks'pensɪv] adj teuer
experience [ɪks'pɪərɪəns] n (incident) Erlebnis nt; (practice) Erfahrung f ♦ vt erleben; ~d adj erfahren
experiment [n ɪks'perɪmənt, vb ɪks'perɪment] n Versuch m, Experiment nt ♦ vi experimentieren; ~al [ɪksperɪ'mentl] adj experimentell
expert ['ekspəːt] n Fachmann m; (official) Sachverständige(r) m ♦ adj erfahren; ~ise [ekspəˈtiːz] n Sachkenntnis f
expire [ɪks'paɪə*] vi (end) ablaufen; (ticket) verfallen; (die) sterben
expiry [ɪks'paɪərɪ] n Ablauf m
explain [ɪks'pleɪn] vt erklären
explanation [eksplə'neɪʃən] n Erklärung f
explanatory [ɪks'plænətərɪ] adj erklärend
explicit [ɪks'plɪsɪt] adj ausdrücklich
explode [ɪks'pləud] vi explodieren ♦ vt (bomb) sprengen; (theory) platzen lassen
exploit [n 'eksplɔɪt, vb ɪks'plɔɪt] n (Helden)tat f ♦ vt ausbeuten; ~ation [eksplɔɪ'teɪʃən] n Ausbeutung f
exploration [eksplɔː'reɪʃən] n Erforschung f
exploratory [eks'plɔrətərɪ] adj Probe-
explore [ɪks'plɔː*] vt (travel) erforschen; (search) untersuchen; ~r n Erforscher(in) m(f)
explosion [ɪks'pləuʒən] n Explosion f; (fig) Ausbruch m
explosive [ɪks'pləuzɪv] adj explosiv, Spreng- ♦ n Sprengstoff m
exponent [eks'pəunənt] n Exponent m
export [vb eks'pɔːt, n 'ekspɔːt] vt exportieren ♦ n Export m ♦ cpd (trade) Export-; ~er n Exporteur m
expose [ɪks'pəuz] vt (to danger etc) aussetzen; (impostor) entlarven; to ~ sb to sth jdn einer Sache dat aussetzen; ~d [ɪks'pəuzd] adj (position) exponiert
exposure [ɪks'pəuʒə*] n (MED) Unterkühlung f; (PHOT) Belichtung f; ~ meter n Belichtungsmesser m
expound [ɪks'paund] vt entwickeln
express [ɪks'pres] adj ausdrücklich;

(speedy) Expreß-, Eil- ♦ n (RAIL) Schnellzug m ♦ adv (send) per Expreß ♦ vt ausdrücken; to ~ o.s. sich ausdrücken; ~ion [ɪks'preʃən] n Ausdruck m; ~ive adj ausdrucksvoll; ~ly adv ausdrücklich; ~way (US) n (urban motorway) Schnellstraße f
expulsion [ɪks'pʌlʃən] n Ausweisung f
expurgate ['ekspəːgeɪt] vt zensieren
exquisite [eks'kwɪzɪt] adj erlesen
extend [ɪks'tend] vt (visit etc) verlängern; (building) ausbauen; (hand) ausstrecken; (welcome) bieten ♦ vi (land) sich erstrecken
extension [ɪks'tenʃən] n Erweiterung f; (of building) Anbau m; (TEL) Apparat m
extensive [ɪks'tensɪv] adj (knowledge) umfassend; (use) weitgehend
extent [ɪks'tent] n Ausdehnung f; (fig) Ausmaß nt; to a certain ~ bis zu einem gewissen Grade; to such an ~ that ... dermaßen, daß ...; to what ~? inwieweit?
extenuating [eks'tenjueɪtɪŋ] adj mildernd
exterior [eks'tɪərɪə*] adj äußere(r, s), Außen- ♦ n Äußere(s) nt
exterminate [eks'tɜːmɪneɪt] vt ausrotten
extermination [ekstɜːmɪ'neɪʃən] n Ausrottung f
external [eks'tɜːnl] adj äußere(r, s), Außen-
extinct [ɪks'tɪŋkt] adj ausgestorben; ~ion [ɪks'tɪŋkʃən] n Aussterben nt
extinguish [ɪks'tɪŋgwɪʃ] vt (aus)löschen; ~er n Löschgerät nt
extort [ɪks'tɔːt] vt erpressen; ~ion [ɪks'tɔːʃən] n Erpressung f; ~ionate [ɪks'tɔːʃənɪt] adj überhöht, erpresserisch
extra ['ekstrə] adj zusätzlich ♦ adv besonders ♦ n (for car etc) Extra nt; (charge) Zuschlag m; (THEAT) Statist m ♦ prefix außer...
extract [vb ɪks'trækt, n 'ekstrækt] vt (heraus)ziehen ♦ n (from book etc) Auszug m; (COOK) Extrakt m
extracurricular ['ekstrəkə'rɪkjulə*] adj außerhalb des Stundenplans
extradite ['ekstrədaɪt] vt ausliefern

extramarital [ekstrə'mærɪtl] adj außerehelich
extramural [ekstrə'mjʊərl] adj (course) Volkshochschul-
extraordinary [ɪks'trɔːdnrɪ] adj außerordentlich; (amazing) erstaunlich
extravagance [ɪks'trævəgəns] n Verschwendung f; (lack of restraint) Zügellosigkeit f; (an ~) Extravaganz f
extravagant [ɪks'trævəgənt] adj extravagant
extreme [ɪks'triːm] adj (edge) äußerste(r, s), hinterste(r, s); (cold) äußerste(r, s); (behaviour) außergewöhnlich, übertrieben ♦ n Extrem nt; **~ly** adv äußerst, höchst
extremity [ɪks'tremɪtɪ] n (end) Spitze f, äußerste(s) Ende nt; (hardship) bitterste Not f; (ANAT) Hand f; Fuß m
extricate ['ekstrɪkeɪt] vt losmachen, befreien
extrovert ['ekstrəʊvɜːt] n extrovertierte(r) Mensch m
exuberant [ɪg'zuːbərənt] adj ausgelassen
exude [ɪg'zjuːd] vt absondern
exult [ɪg'zʌlt] vi frohlocken
eye [aɪ] n Auge nt; (of needle) Öhr nt ♦ vt betrachten; (up and down) mustern; **to keep an ~ on** aufpassen auf +acc; **~ball** n Augapfel m; **~bath** n Augenbad nt; **~brow** n Augenbraue f; **~brow pencil** n Augenbrauenstift m; **~drops** npl Augentropfen pl; **~lash** n Augenwimper f; **~lid** n Augenlid nt; **~liner** n Eyeliner nt; **~-opener** n: that was an **~-opener** das hat mir/ihm etc die Augen geöffnet; **~shadow** n Lidschatten m; **~sight** n Sehkraft f; **~sore** n Schandfleck m; **~ witness** n Augenzeuge m

F

F [ef] n (MUS) F nt
F. abbr (= Fahrenheit) F
fable ['feɪbl] n Fabel f
fabric ['fæbrɪk] n Stoff m; (fig) Gefüge nt
fabrication [fæbrɪ'keɪʃən] n Erfindung f

fabulous ['fæbjʊləs] adj sagenhaft
face [feɪs] n Gesicht nt; (surface) Oberfläche f; (of clock) Zifferblatt nt ♦ vt (point towards) liegen nach; (situation, difficulty) sich stellen +dat; **~ down** (person) mit dem Gesicht nach unten; (card) mit der Vorderseite nach unten; **to make** or **pull a ~** das Gesicht verziehen; **in the ~ of** angesichts +gen; **on the ~ of it** so, wie es aussieht; **~ to ~** Auge in Auge; **to ~ up to sth** einer Sache dat ins Auge sehen; **~ cloth** (BRIT) n Waschlappen m; **~ cream** n Gesichtscreme f; **~ lift** n Face-lifting nt; **~ powder** n (Gesichts)puder m
facet ['fæsɪt] n Aspekt m; (of gem) Facette f
facetious [fə'siːʃəs] adj witzig
face value n Nennwert m; **to take sth at (its) ~** (fig) etw für bare Münze nehmen
facial ['feɪʃəl] adj Gesichts-
facile ['fæsaɪl] adj oberflächlich; (US: easy) leicht
facilitate [fə'sɪlɪteɪt] vt erleichtern
facilities [fə'sɪlɪtɪz] npl Einrichtungen pl; **credit ~** Kreditmöglichkeiten pl
facing ['feɪsɪŋ] adj zugekehrt ♦ prep gegenüber
facsimile [fæk'sɪmɪlɪ] n Faksimile nt; (machine) Telekopierer m
fact [fækt] n Tatsache f; **in ~** in der Tat
faction ['fækʃən] n Splittergruppe f
factor ['fæktə*] n Faktor m
factory ['fæktərɪ] n Fabrik f
factual ['fæktjʊəl] adj sachlich
faculty ['fækəltɪ] n Fähigkeit f; (UNIV) Fakultät f; (US: teaching staff) Lehrpersonal nt
fad [fæd] n Tick m; (fashion) Masche f
fade [feɪd] vi (lose colour) verblassen; (grow dim) nachlassen; (sound, memory) schwächer werden; (wither) verwelken
fag [fæg] (inf) n (cigarette) Kippe f
fail [feɪl] vt (exam) nicht bestehen; (student) durchfallen lassen; (courage) verlassen; (memory) im Stich lassen ♦ vi (supplies) zu Ende gehen; (student) durchfallen; (eyesight) nachlassen;

(*light*) schwächer werden; (*crop*) fehlschlagen; (*remedy*) nicht wirken; **to ~ to do sth** (*neglect*) es unterlassen, etw zu tun; (*be unable*) es nicht schaffen, etw zu tun; **without ~** unbedingt; **~ing** *n* Schwäche *f* ♦ *prep* mangels +*gen*; **~ure** *n* (*person*) Versager *m*; (*act*) Versagen *nt*; (*TECH*) Defekt *m*

faint [feint] *adj* schwach ♦ *n* Ohnmacht *f* ♦ *vi* ohnmächtig werden

fair [fɛə*] *adj* (*just*) gerecht, fair; (*hair*) blond; (*skin*) hell; (*weather*) schön; (*not very good*) mittelmäßig; (*sizeable*) ansehnlich ♦ *adv* (*play*) fair ♦ *n* (*COMM*) Messe *f*; (*BRIT*: *fun~*) Jahrmarkt *m*; **~ly** *adv* (*honestly*) gerecht, fair; (*rather*) ziemlich; **~ness** *n* Fairneß *f*

fairy [ˈfɛərɪ] *n* Fee *f*; **~ tale** *n* Märchen *nt*

faith [feiθ] *n* Glaube *m*; (*trust*) Vertrauen *nt*; (*sect*) Bekenntnis *nt*; **~ful** *adj* treu; **~fully** *adv* treu; **yours ~fully** (*BRIT*) hochachtungsvoll

fake [feik] *n* (*thing*) Fälschung *f*; (*person*) Schwindler *m* ♦ *adj* vorgetäuscht ♦ *vt* fälschen

falcon [ˈfɔːlkən] *n* Falke *m*

fall [fɔːl] (*pt* **fell**, *pp* **fallen**) *n* Fall *m*, Sturz *m*; (*decrease*) Fallen *nt*; (*of snow*) (Schnee)fall *m*; (*US*: *autumn*) Herbst *m* ♦ *vi* (*also fig*) fallen; (*night*) hereinbrechen; **~s** *npl* (*waterfall*) Fälle *pl*; **to ~ flat** platt hinfallen; (*joke*) nicht ankommen; **~ back** *vi* zurückweichen; **~ back on** *vt fus* zurückgreifen auf +*acc*; **~ behind** *vi* zurückbleiben; **~ down** *vi* (*person*) hinfallen; (*building*) einstürzen; **~ for** *vt fus* (*trick*) hereinfallen auf +*acc*; (*person*) sich verknallen in +*acc*; **~ in** *vi* (*roof*) einstürzen; **~ off** *vi* herunterfallen; (*diminish*) sich vermindern; **~ out** *vi* sich streiten; (*MIL*) wegtreten; **~ through** *vi* (*plan*) ins Wasser fallen

fallacy [ˈfæləsɪ] *n* Trugschluß *m*

fallen [ˈfɔːlən] *pp* of **fall**

fallible [ˈfæləbl] *adj* fehlbar

fallout [ˈfɔːlaut] *n* radioaktive(r) Niederschlag *m*; **~ shelter** *n* Atombunker *m*

fallow [ˈfæləu] *adj* brach(liegend)

false [fɔːls] *adj* falsch; (*artificial*) künstlich; **under ~ pretences** unter Vorspiegelung falscher Tatsachen; **~ alarm** *n* Fehlalarm *m*; **~ teeth** (*BRIT*) *npl* Gebiß *nt*

falter [ˈfɔːltə*] *vi* schwanken, (*in speech*) stocken

fame [feim] *n* Ruhm *m*

familiar [fəˈmɪlɪə*] *adj* bekannt; (*intimate*) familiär; **to be ~ with** vertraut sein mit; **~ize** *vt* vertraut machen

family [ˈfæmɪlɪ] *n* Familie *f*; (*relations*) Verwandtschaft *f*; **~ business** *n* Familienunternehmen *nt*; **~ doctor** *n* Hausarzt *m*

famine [ˈfæmɪn] *n* Hungersnot *f*

famished [ˈfæmɪʃt] *adj* ausgehungert

famous [ˈfeiməs] *adj* berühmt; **~ly** *adv* (*get on*) prächtig

fan [fæn] *n* (*folding*) Fächer *m*; (*ELEC*) Ventilator *m*; (*admirer*) Fan *m* ♦ *vt* fächeln; **~ out** *vi* sich (fächerförmig) ausbreiten

fanatic [fəˈnætɪk] *n* Fanatiker(in) *m(f)*

fan belt *n* Keilriemen *m*

fanciful [ˈfænsɪful] *adj* (*odd*) seltsam; (*imaginative*) phantasievoll

fancy [ˈfænsɪ] *n* (*liking*) Neigung *f*; (*imagination*) Einbildung *f* ♦ *adj* schick ♦ *vt* (*like*) gern haben; wollen; (*imagine*) sich einbilden; **he fancies her** er mag sie; **~ dress** *n* Maskenkostüm *nt*; **~-dress ball** *n* Maskenball *m*

fang [fæŋ] *n* Fangzahn *m*; (*of snake*) Giftzahn *m*

fantastic [fænˈtæstɪk] *adj* phantastisch

fantasy [ˈfæntəzɪ] *n* Phantasie *f*

far [fɑː*] *adj* weit ♦ *adv* weit entfernt; (*very much*) weitaus; **by ~** bei weitem; **so ~** soweit; bis jetzt; **go as ~ as the farm** gehen Sie bis zum Bauernhof; **as ~ as I know** soweit *or* soviel ich weiß; **~away** *adj* weit entfernt

farce [fɑːs] *n* Farce *f*

farcical [ˈfɑːsɪkəl] *adj* lächerlich

fare [fɛə*] *n* Fahrpreis *m*; Fahrgeld *nt*; (*food*) Kost *f*

Far East *n*: **the ~** der Ferne Osten

farewell [feə'wel] n Abschied(sgruß) m
♦ excl lebe wohl!
farm [fɑːm] n Bauernhof m, Farm f ♦ vt
bewirtschaften; ~er n Bauer m,
Landwirt m; ~hand n Landarbeiter m;
~house n Bauernhaus nt; ~ing n
Landwirtschaft f; ~land n Ackerland
nt; • yard n Hof m
far-reaching ['fɑː'riːtʃɪŋ] adj weitrei-
chend
fart [fɑːt] (inf!) n Furz m ♦ vi furzen
farther ['fɑːðə*] adv weiter
farthest ['fɑːðɪst] adj fernste(r, s) ♦ adv
am weitesten
fascinate ['fæsɪneɪt] vt faszinieren
fascination [fæsɪ'neɪʃən] n Faszination f
fascism ['fæʃɪzəm] n Faschismus m
fashion ['fæʃən] n (of clothes) Mode f;
(manner) Art f (und Weise f) ♦ vt machen; in ~ in Mode; out of ~
unmodisch; ~able adj (clothes)
modisch; (place) elegant; ~ show n
Mode(n)schau f
fast [fɑːst] adj schnell; (firm) fest ♦ adv
schnell; fest ♦ n Fasten nt ♦ vi fasten;
to be ~ (clock) vorgehen
fasten ['fɑːsn] vt (attach) befestigen;
(with rope) zuschnüren; (seat belt)
festmachen; (coat) zumachen ♦ vi sich
schließen lassen; ~er n Verschluß m;
~ing n Verschluß m
fastidious [fæs'tɪdɪəs] adj wählerisch
fat [fæt] adj dick ♦ n Fett nt
fatal ['feɪtl] adj tödlich; (disastrous) verhängnisvoll; ~ity [fə'tælɪtɪ] n (road
death etc) Todesopfer nt; ~ly adv
tödlich
fate [feɪt] n Schicksal nt; ~ful adj (pro-
phetic) schicksalsschwer; (important)
schicksalhaft
father ['fɑːðə*] n Vater m; (REL) Pater
m; ~-in-law n Schwiegervater m; ~ly
adj väterlich
fathom ['fæðəm] n Klafter m ♦ vt ausloten; (fig) ergründen
fatigue [fə'tiːg] n Ermüdung f
fatten ['fætn] vt dick machen; (animals)
mästen ♦ vi dick werden
fatty ['fætɪ] adj fettig ♦ n (inf) Dicker-
chen nt

fatuous ['fætjʊəs] adj albern, affig
faucet ['fɔːsɪt] (US) n Wasserhahn m
fault [fɔːlt] n (defect) Defekt m; (ELEC)
Störung f; (blame) Schuld f; (GEOG)
Verwerfung f ♦ vt: to ~ sth etwas an
etw dat auszusetzen haben; it's your ~
du bist daran schuld; at ~ im Unrecht;
~less adj tadellos; ~y adj fehlerhaft,
defekt
favour ['feɪvə*] (US favor) n (approval)
Wohlwollen nt; (kindness) Gefallen m ♦
vt (prefer) vorziehen; in ~ of für;
zugunsten +gen; to find ~ with sb bei
jdm Anklang finden; ~able adj günstig;
~ite ['feɪvərɪt] adj Lieblings- ♦ n (child)
Liebling m; (SPORT) Favorit m
fawn [fɔːn] adj rehbraun ♦ n (colour)
Rehbraun nt; (animal) (Reh)kitz nt ♦
vi: to ~ (up)on (fig) katzbuckeln vor
+dat
fax [fæks] n (document) Fax nt; (machine) Telefax nt ♦ vt per Fax schicken
FBI ['efbiː'aɪ] (US) n abbr (= Federal
Bureau of Investigation) FBI nt
fear [fɪə*] n Furcht f ♦ vt fürchten; ~ful
adj (timid) furchtsam; (terrible)
fürchterlich; ~less adj furchtlos
feasible ['fiːzəbl] adj durchführbar
feast [fiːst] n Festmahl nt; (REL: also:
~ day) Feiertag m ♦ vi: to ~ (on) sich
gütlich tun (an +dat)
feat [fiːt] n Leistung f
feather ['feðə*] n Feder f
feature ['fiːtʃə*] n (Gesichts)zug m;
(important part) Grundzug m; (CINE,
PRESS) Feature nt ♦ vt darstellen;
(advertising etc) groß herausbringen ♦
vi vorkommen; featuring X mit X; ~
film n Spielfilm m
February ['februərɪ] n Februar m
fed [fed] pt, pp of feed
federal ['fedərəl] adj Bundes-
federation [fedə'reɪʃən] n (society) Verband m; (of states) Staatenbund m
fed up adj: to be ~ with sth etw satt
haben; I'm ~ ich habe die Nase voll
fee [fiː] n Gebühr f
feeble ['fiːbl] adj (person) schwach;
(excuse) lahm
feed [fiːd] (pt, pp fed) n (for baby)

Essen *nt*; (*for animals*) Futter *nt* ♦ *vt* füttern; (*support*) ernähren; (*data*) eingeben; **to ~ on** fressen; **~back** *n* (*information*) Feedback *nt*; **~ing bottle** (*BRIT*) *n* Flasche *f*

feel [fiːl] (*pt*, *pp* **felt**) *n*: **it has a soft ~** es fühlt sich weich an ♦ *vt* (*sense*) fühlen; (*touch*) anfassen; (*think*) meinen ♦ *vi* (*person*) sich fühlen; (*thing*) sich anfühlen; **to get the ~ of sth** sich an etw *acc* gewöhnen; **I ~ cold** mir ist kalt; **I ~ like a cup of tea** ich habe Lust auf eine Tasse Tee; **~ about** *or* **around** *vi* herumsuchen; **~er** *n* Fühler *m*; **~ing** *n* Gefühl *nt*; (*opinion*) Meinung *f*

feet [fiːt] *npl of* **foot**

feign [feɪn] *vt* vortäuschen

feline [ˈfiːlaɪn] *adj* katzenartig

fell [fel] *pt of* **fall** ♦ *vt* (*tree*) fällen

fellow [ˈfeləʊ] *n* (*man*) Kerl *m*; **~ citizen** *n* Mitbürger(in) *m(f)*; **~ countryman** (*irreg*) *n* Landsmann *m*; **~ men** *npl* Mitmenschen *pl*; **~ship** *n* (*group*) Körperschaft *f*; (*friendliness*) Kameradschaft *f*; (*scholarship*) Forschungsstipendium *nt*; **~ student** *n* Kommilitone *m*, Kommilitonin *f*

felony [ˈfelənɪ] *n* schwere(s) Verbrechen *nt*

felt [felt] *pt*, *pp of* **feel** ♦ *n* Filz *m*; **~-tip pen** *n* Filzstift *m*

female [ˈfiːmeɪl] *n* (*of animals*) Weibchen *nt* ♦ *adj* weiblich

feminine [ˈfemɪnɪn] *adj* (*LING*) weiblich; (*qualities*) fraulich

feminist [ˈfemɪnɪst] *n* Feminist(in) *m(f)*

fence [fens] *n* Zaun *m* ♦ *vt* (*also*: **~ in**) einzäunen ♦ *vi* fechten

fencing [ˈfensɪŋ] *n* Zaun *m*; (*SPORT*) Fechten *nt*

fend [fend] *vi*: **to ~ for o.s.** sich (allein) durchschlagen; **~ off** *vt* abwehren

fender [ˈfendə*] *n* Kaminvorsetzer *m*; (*US*: *AUT*) Kotflügel *m*

ferment [*vb* fəˈment, *n* ˈfɜːment] *vi* (*CHEM*) gären ♦ *n* (*excitement*) Unruhe *f*

fern [fɜːn] *n* Farn *m*

ferocious [fəˈrəʊʃəs] *adj* wild, grausam

ferret [ˈferɪt] *n* Frettchen *nt* ♦ *vt*: **to ~ out** aufspüren

ferry [ˈferɪ] *n* Fähre *f* ♦ *vt* übersetzen

fertile [ˈfɜːtaɪl] *adj* fruchtbar

fertilize [ˈfɜːtɪlaɪz] *vt* (*AGR*) düngen; (*BIOL*) befruchten; **~r** [ˈfɜːtɪlaɪzə*] *n* (Kunst)dünger *m*

fervent [ˈfɜːvənt] *adj* (*admirer*) glühend; (*hope*) innig

fervour [ˈfɜːvə*] (*US* **fervor**) *n* Leidenschaft *f*

fester [ˈfestə*] *vi* eitern

festival [ˈfestɪvəl] *n* (*REL etc*) Fest *nt*; (*ART*, *MUS*) Festspiele *pl*

festive [ˈfestɪv] *adj* festlich; **the ~ season** (*Christmas*) die Festzeit

festivities [fesˈtɪvɪtɪz] *npl* Feierlichkeiten *pl*

festoon [fesˈtuːn] *vt*: **to ~ with** schmücken mit

fetch [fetʃ] *vt* holen; (*in sale*) einbringen

fetching [ˈfetʃɪŋ] *adj* reizend

fête [feɪt] *n* Fest *nt*

fetus [ˈfiːtəs] (*US*) *n* = **foetus**

feud [fjuːd] *n* Fehde *f*

feudal [ˈfjuːdl] *adj* Feudal-

fever [ˈfiːvə*] *n* Fieber *nt*; **~ish** *adj* (*MED*) fiebrig; (*fig*) fieberhaft

few [fjuː] *adj* wenig; **a ~** einige; **~er** *adj* weniger; **~est** *adj* wenigste(r, s)

fiancé [fiˈɑːnseɪ] *n* Verlobte(r) *m*; **~e** *n* Verlobte *f*

fib [fɪb] *n* Flunkerei *f* ♦ *vi* flunkern

fibre [ˈfaɪbə*] (*US* **fiber**) *n* Faser *f*; **~glass** *n* Glaswolle *f*

fickle [ˈfɪkl] *adj* unbeständig

fiction [ˈfɪkʃən] *n* (*novels*) Romanliteratur *f*; (*story*) Erdichtung *f*; **~al** *adj* erfunden

fictitious [fɪkˈtɪʃəs] *adj* erfunden, fingiert

fiddle [ˈfɪdl] *n* Geige *f*; (*trick*) Schwindelei *f* ♦ *vt* (*BRIT*: *accounts*) frisieren; **~ with** *vt fus* herumfummeln an +*dat*

fidelity [fɪˈdelɪtɪ] *n* Treue *f*

fidget [ˈfɪdʒɪt] *vi* zappeln

field [fiːld] *n* Feld *nt*; (*range*) Gebiet *nt*;

~ **marshal** n Feldmarschall m; ~**work** n Feldforschung f

fiend [fi:nd] n Teufel m; ~**ish** adj teuflisch

fierce [fɪəs] adj wild

fiery ['faɪərɪ] adj (hot-tempered) hitzig

fifteen [fɪf'ti:n] num fünfzehn

fifth [fɪfθ] adj fünfte(r, s) ♦ n Fünftel nt

fifty ['fɪftɪ] num fünfzig; ~-**fifty** adj, adv halbe halbe, fifty fifty (inf)

fig [fɪg] n Feige f

fight [faɪt] (pt, pp fought) n Kampf m; (brawl) Schlägerei f; (argument) Streit m ♦ vt kämpfen gegen; sich schlagen mit; (fig) bekämpfen ♦ vi kämpfen; sich schlagen; streiten; ~**er** n Kämpfer(in) m(f); (plane) Jagdflugzeug nt; ~**ing** n Kämpfen nt; (war) Kampfhandlungen pl

figment ['fɪgmənt] n: ~ **of the imagination** reine Einbildung f

figurative ['fɪgərətɪv] adj bildlich

figure ['fɪgə*] n (of person) Figur f; (person) Gestalt f; (number) Ziffer f ♦ vt (US: imagine) glauben ♦ vi (appear) erscheinen; ~ **out** vt herausbekommen; ~**head** n (NAUT, fig) Galionsfigur f; ~ **of speech** n Redensart f

filament ['fɪləmənt] n Faden m; (ELEC) Glühfaden m

filch [fɪltʃ] (inf) vt filzen

file [faɪl] n (tool) Feile f; (dossier) Akte f; (folder) Aktenordner m; (COMPUT) Datei f; (row) Reihe f ♦ vt (metal, nails) feilen; (papers) abheften; (claim) einreichen ♦ vi: to ~ **in/out** hintereinander hereinkommen/hinausgehen; to ~ **past** vorbeimarschieren

filing ['faɪlɪŋ] n Ablage f; ~ **cabinet** n Aktenschrank m

fill [fɪl] vt füllen; (occupy) ausfüllen; (satisfy) sättigen ♦ n: to **eat one's** ~ sich richtig satt essen; ~ **in** vt (hole) (auf)füllen; (form) ausfüllen; ~ **up** vt (container) auffüllen; (form) ausfüllen ♦ vi (AUT) tanken

fillet ['fɪlɪt] n Filet nt; ~ **steak** n Filetsteak nt

filling ['fɪlɪŋ] n (COOK) Füllung f; (for

tooth) (Zahn)plombe f; ~ **station** n Tankstelle f

film [fɪlm] n Film m ♦ vt (scene) filmen; ~ **star** n Filmstar m; ~**strip** n Filmstreifen m

filter ['fɪltə*] n Filter m ♦ vt filtern; ~ **lane** (BRIT) n Abbiegespur f; ~-**tipped** adj Filter-

filth [fɪlθ] n Dreck m; ~**y** adj dreckig; (weather) scheußlich

fin [fɪn] n Flosse f

final ['faɪnl] adj letzte(r, s); End-; (conclusive) endgültig ♦ n (FOOTBALL etc) Endspiel nt; ~s npl (UNIV) Abschlußexamen nt; (SPORT) Schlußrunde f; ~**e** [fɪ'nɑ:lɪ] n (MUS) Finale nt; ~**ist** n (SPORT) Schlußrundenteilnehmer m; ~**ize** vt endgültige Form geben +dat; abschließen; ~**ly** adv (lastly) zuletzt; (eventually) endlich; (irrevocably) endgültig

finance [faɪ'næns] n Finanzwesen nt ♦ vt finanzieren; ~**s** npl (funds) Finanzen pl

financial [faɪ'nænʃəl] adj Finanz-; finanziell

find [faɪnd] (pt, pp found) vt finden ♦ n Fund m; to ~ **sb guilty** jdn für schuldig erklären; ~ **out** vt herausfinden; ~**ings** npl (JUR) Ermittlungsergebnis nt; (of report) Befund m

fine [faɪn] adj fein; (good) gut; (weather) schön ♦ adv (well) gut; (small) klein ♦ n (JUR) Geldstrafe f ♦ vt mit einer Geldstrafe belegen; ~ **arts** npl schöne(n) Künste pl

finery ['faɪnərɪ] n Putz m

finger ['fɪŋgə*] n Finger m ♦ vt befühlen; ~**nail** n Fingernagel m; ~**print** n Fingerabdruck m; ~**tip** n Fingerspitze f

finicky ['fɪnɪkɪ] adj pingelig

finish ['fɪnɪʃ] n Ende nt; (SPORT) Ziel nt; (of object) Verarbeitung f; (of paint) Oberflächenwirkung f ♦ vt beenden; (book) zu Ende lesen ♦ vi aufhören; (SPORT) ans Ziel kommen; to be ~**ed with sth** fertig sein mit etw; ~**ing line** n Ziellinie f; ~**ing school** n Mädchenpensionat nt

finite ['faɪnaɪt] adj endlich, begrenzt

Finland ['fɪnlənd] n Finnland nt
Finn [fɪn] n Finne m, Finnin f; **~ish** adj
finnisch ♦ n (LING) Finnisch nt
fir [fɜ:*] n Tanne f
fire [faɪə*] n Feuer nt; (in house etc)
Brand m ♦ vt (gun) abfeuern;
(imagination) entzünden; (dismiss) hinauswerfen ♦ vi (AUT) zünden; **to be on
~** brennen; **~ alarm** n Feueralarm m;
~arm n Schußwaffe f; **~ brigade**
(BRIT) n Feuerwehr f; **~ department**
(US) n Feuerwehr f; **~ engine** n
Feuerwehrauto nt; **~ escape** n
Feuerleiter f; **~ extinguisher** n
Löschgerät nt; **~man** (irreg) n
Feuerwehrmann m; **~place** n Kamin
m; **~side** n Kamin m; **~ station** n
Feuerwehrwache f; **~works** npl
Feuerwerk nt
firing ['faɪərɪŋ] n Schießen nt; **~ squad**
n Exekutionskommando nt
firm [fɜ:m] adj fest ♦ n Firma f
first [fɜ:st] adj erste(r, s) ♦ adv zuerst;
(arrive) als erste(r); (happen) zum er-
stenmal ♦ n (person: in race) Erste(r)
mf; (UNIV) Eins f; (AUT) erste(r) Gang
m; **at ~** zuerst; **~ of all** zu allererst; **~
aid** n Erste Hilfe f; **~-aid kit** n Ver-
bandskasten m; **~-class** adj erstklassig; (travel) erster Klasse; **~-hand**
adj aus erster Hand; **~ly** adv erstens;
~ name n Vorname m; **~-rate** adj
erstklassig
fiscal ['fɪskəl] adj Finanz-
fish [fɪʃ] n inv Fisch m ♦ vi fischen; angeln; **to go ~ing** angeln gehen; (in sea)
fischen gehen; **~erman** (irreg) n Fi-
scher m; **~ farm** n Fischzucht f; **~
fingers** (BRIT) npl Fischstäbchen pl;
~ing boat n Fischerboot nt; **~ing line**
n Angelschnur f; **~ing rod** n An-
gel(rute) f; **~monger's (shop)** n
Fischhändler m; **~ slice** n
Fischvorleger m; **~ sticks** (US) npl =
fish fingers; **~y** (inf) adj (suspicious)
faul
fission ['fɪʃən] n Spaltung f
fissure ['fɪʃə*] n Riß m
fist [fɪst] n Faust f
fit [fɪt] adj (MED) gesund; (SPORT) in

Form, fit; (suitable) geeignet ♦ vt
passen +dat; (insert, attach) einsetzen
♦ vi passen; (in space, gap) hineinpassen ♦ n (of clothes) Sitz m; (MED,
of anger) Anfall m; (of laughter)
Krampf m; **by ~s and starts** (move)
ruckweise; (work) unregelmäßig; **~ in**
vi hineinpassen; (fig: person) passen;
~ out vt (also: fit up) ausstatten; **~ful**
adj (sleep) unruhig; **~ment** n Ein-
richtungsgegenstand m; **~ness** n
(suitability) Eignung f; (MED) Gesundheit f; (SPORT) Fitneß f; **~ted carpet** n
Teppichboden m; **~ted kitchen** n Ein-
bauküche f; **~ter** n (TECH) Monteur m;
~ting adj passend ♦ n (of dress) Anprobe f; (piece of equipment)
(Ersatz)teil m; **~tings** npl (equipment)
Zubehör nt; **~ting room** n An-
proberaum m
five [faɪv] num fünf; **~r** (inf) n (BRIT)
Fünf-Pfund-Note f; (US) Fünf-Dollar-
Note f
fix [fɪks] vt befestigen; (settle) festsetzen; (repair) reparieren ♦ n: **in a ~**
in der Klemme; **~ up** vt (meeting)
arrangieren; **to ~ sb up with sth** jdm
etw acc verschaffen; **~ation** [fɪks'eɪʃən]
n Fixierung f; **~ed** [fɪkst] adj fest;
~ture ['fɪkstʃə*] n Installationsteil m;
(SPORT) Spiel nt
fizz [fɪz] vi sprudeln
fizzle ['fɪzl] vi: **to ~ out** verpuffen
fizzy ['fɪzɪ] adj Sprudel-, sprudelnd
flabbergasted ['flæbəgɑ:stɪd] (inf) adj
platt
flabby ['flæbɪ] adj wabbelig
flag [flæg] n Fahne f ♦ vi (strength)
nachlassen; (spirit) erlahmen; **~ down**
vt anhalten
flagpole ['flægpəʊl] n Fahnenstange f
flagrant ['fleɪgrənt] adj kraß
flair [flɛə*] n Talent nt
flak [flæk] n Flakfeuer nt
flake [fleɪk] n (of snow) Flocke f; (of
rust) Schuppe f ♦ vi (also: ~ off) abblättern
flamboyant [flæm'bɔɪənt] adj extravagant
flame [fleɪm] n Flamme f

flamingo [fləˈmɪŋgəʊ] n Flamingo m
flammable [ˈflæməbl] adj brennbar
flan [flæn] (BRIT) n Obsttorte f
flank [flæŋk] n Flanke f ♦ vt flankieren
flannel [ˈflænl] n Flanell m; (BRIT: also: face ~) Waschlappen m; (: inf) Geschwafel nt; ~s npl (trousers) Flanellhose f
flap [flæp] n Klappe f; (inf: crisis) (helle) Aufregung f ♦ vt (wings) schlagen mit ♦ vi flattern
flare [flɛə*] n (signal) Leuchtsignal nt; (in skirt etc) Weite f; ~ **up** vi aufflammen; (fig) aufbrausen; (revolt) (plötzlich) ausbrechen
flash [flæʃ] n Blitz m; (also: news ~) Kurzmeldung f; (PHOT) Blitzlicht nt ♦ vt aufleuchten lassen ♦ vi aufleuchten; **in a ~** im Nu; ~ **by** or **past** vi vorbeirasen; ~**back** n Rückblende f; ~**bulb** n Blitzlichtbirne f; ~ **cube** n Blitzwürfel m; ~**light** n Blitzlicht nt
flashy [ˈflæʃɪ] (pej) adj knallig
flask [flɑːsk] n (CHEM) Kolben m; (also: vacuum ~) Thermosflasche f (®)
flat [flæt] adj flach; (dull) matt; (MUS) erniedrigt; (beer) schal; (tyre) platt ♦ n (BRIT: rooms) Wohnung f; (MUS) b nt; (AUT) Platte(r) m; **to work ~ out** auf Hochtouren arbeiten; ~**ly** adv glatt; ~**ten** vt (also: ~ten out) ebnen
flatter [ˈflætə*] vt schmeicheln +dat; ~**ing** adj schmeichelhaft; ~**y** n Schmeichelei f
flatulence [ˈflætjʊləns] n Blähungen pl
flaunt [flɔːnt] vt prunken mit
flavour [ˈfleɪvə*] (US **flavor**) n Geschmack m ♦ vt würzen; ~**ed** adj: **strawberry-flavoured** mit Erdbeergeschmack; ~**ing** n Würze f
flaw [flɔː] n Fehler m; ~**less** adj einwandfrei
flax [flæks] n Flachs m; ~**en** adj flachsfarben
flea [fliː] n Floh m
fleck [flek] n (mark) Fleck m; (pattern) Tupfen m
fled [fled] pt, pp of **flee**
flee (pt, pp **fled**) vi fliehen ♦ vt fliehen vor +dat; (country) fliehen aus

fleece [fliːs] n Vlies nt ♦ vt (inf) schröpfen
fleet [fliːt] n Flotte f
fleeting [ˈfliːtɪŋ] adj flüchtig
Flemish [ˈflemɪʃ] adj flämisch
flesh [fleʃ] n Fleisch nt; ~ **wound** n Fleischwunde f
flew [fluː] pt of **fly**
flex [fleks] n Kabel nt ♦ vt beugen; ~**ibility** [fleksɪˈbɪlɪtɪ] n Biegsamkeit f; (fig) Flexibilität f; ~**ible** adj biegsam; (plans) flexibel
flick [flɪk] n leichte(r) Schlag m ♦ vt leicht schlagen; ~ **through** vt fus durchblättern
flicker [ˈflɪkə*] n Flackern nt ♦ vi flackern
flier [ˈflaɪə*] n Flieger m
flight [flaɪt] n Flug m; (fleeing) Flucht f; (also: ~ of steps) Treppe f; **to take** ~ **die** Flucht ergreifen; **to put to** ~ **in** die Flucht schlagen; ~ **attendant** (US) n Steward(eß) m(f); ~ **deck** n Flugdeck nt
flimsy [ˈflɪmzɪ] adj (thin) hauchdünn; (excuse) fadenscheinig
flinch [flɪntʃ] vi: **to** ~ (**away from**) zurückschrecken (vor +dat)
fling [flɪŋ] (pt, pp **flung**) vt schleudern
flint [flɪnt] n Feuerstein m
flip [flɪp] vt werfen
flippant [ˈflɪpənt] adj schnippisch
flipper [ˈflɪpə*] n Flosse f
flirt [flɜːt] vi flirten ♦ n: **he/she is a** ~ **er/sie** flirtet gern; ~**ation** [flɜːˈteɪʃən] n Flirt m
flit [flɪt] vi flitzen
float [fləʊt] n (FISHING) Schwimmer m; (esp in procession) Plattformwagen m ♦ vi schwimmen; (in air) schweben ♦ vt (COMM) gründen; (currency) floaten
flock [flɒk] n (of sheep, REL) Herde f; (of birds) Schwarm m; (of people) Schar f
flog [flɒg] vt prügeln; (inf: sell) verkaufen
flood [flʌd] n Überschwemmung f; (fig) Flut f ♦ vt überschwemmen; ~**ing** n Überschwemmung f; ~**light** n Flutlicht nt

floor [flɔ:*] n (Fuß)boden m; (storey)
Stock m ♦ vt (person) zu Boden
schlagen; **ground ~** (BRIT) Erdgeschoß
nt; **first ~** (BRIT) erste(r) Stock m; (US)
Erdgeschoß nt; **~board** n Diele f; **~
show** n Kabarettvorstellung f

flop [flɔp] n Plumps m; (failure)
Reinfall m ♦ vi (fail) durchfallen

floppy ['flɔpɪ] adj hängend; **~ (disk)** n
(COMPUT) Diskette f

flora ['flɔ:rə] n Flora f; **~l** adj Blumen-

florid ['flɔrɪd] adj (style) blumig

florist ['flɔrɪst] n Blumenhändler(in)
m(f); **~'s (shop)** n Blumengeschäft nt

flounce [flauns] n Volant m

flounder ['flaundə*] vi (fig) ins
Schleudern kommen ♦ n (ZOOL)
Flunder f

flour ['flauə*] n Mehl nt

flourish ['flʌrɪʃ] vi blühen; gedeihen ♦ n
(waving) Schwingen nt; (of trumpets)
Tusch m, Fanfare f; **~ing** adj blühend

flout [flaut] vt mißachten

flow [fləu] n Fließen nt; (of sea) Flut f
♦ vi fließen; **~ chart** n Flußdiagramm
nt

flower ['flauə*] n Blume f ♦ vi blühen;
~ bed n Blumenbeet nt; **~pot** n
Blumentopf m; **~y** adj (style)
blumenreich

flown [fləun] pp of **fly**

flu [flu:] n Grippe f

fluctuate ['flʌktjueɪt] vi schwanken

fluctuation [flʌktjʊ'eɪʃən] n Schwankung
f

fluency ['flu:ənsɪ] n Flüssigkeit f

fluent ['flu:ənt] adj fließend; **~ly** adv
fließend

fluff [flʌf] n Fussel f; **~y** adj flaumig

fluid ['flu:ɪd] n Flüssigkeit f ♦ adj
flüssig; (fig: plans) veränderbar

fluke [flu:k] (inf) n Dusel m

flung [flʌŋ] pt, pp of **fling**

fluoride ['fluəraɪd] n Fluorid nt

flurry ['flʌrɪ] n (of snow) Gestöber nt;
(of activity) Aufregung f

flush [flʌʃ] n Erröten nt; (of
excitement) Glühen nt ♦ vt (aus)spülen
♦ vi erröten ♦ adj glatt; **~ out** vt auf-
stöbern; **~ed** adj rot

flustered ['flʌstəd] adj verwirrt

flute [flu:t] n Querflöte f

flutter ['flʌtə*] n Flattern nt ♦ vi flattern

flux [flʌks] n: **in a state of ~** im Fluß

fly [flaɪ] (pt **flew**, pp **flown**) n (insect)
Fliege f; (on trousers: also: **flies**)
(Hosen)schlitz m ♦ vt fliegen ♦ vi
fliegen; (flee) fliehen; (flag) wehen; **~
away** or **off** vi (bird, insect)
wegfliegen; **~ing** n Fliegen nt ♦ adj:
with ~ing colours mit fliegenden
Fahnen; **~ing start** gute(r) Start m;
~ing visit Stippvisite f; **~ing saucer** n
fliegende Untertasse f; **~over** (BRIT) n
Überführung f; **~past** n Luftparade f;
~sheet n (for tent) Regendach nt

foal [fəul] n Fohlen nt

foam [fəum] n Schaum m ♦ vi
schäumen; **~ rubber** n Schaumgummi
m

fob [fɔb] vt: **to ~ sb off with sth** jdm
etw andrehen; (with promise) jdm etw
abspeisen

focal ['fəukəl] adj Brenn-

focus ['fəukəs] (pl **~es**) n Brennpunkt m
♦ vt (attention) konzentrieren;
(camera) scharf einstellen ♦ vi: **to ~
(on)** sich konzentrieren (auf +acc); **in
~** scharf eingestellt; **out of ~** unscharf

fodder ['fɔdə*] n Futter nt

foe [fəu] n Feind m

foetus ['fi:təs] (US **fetus**) n Fötus m

fog [fɔg] n Nebel m; **~gy** adj neblig; **~
lamp** n (AUT) Nebellampe f

foil [fɔɪl] vt vereiteln ♦ n (metal, also
fig) Folie f; (FENCING) Florett nt

fold [fəuld] n (bend, crease) Falte f;
(AGR) Pferch m ♦ vt falten; **~ up** vt
(map etc) zusammenfalten ♦ vi
(business) eingehen; **~er** n
Schnellhefter m; **~ing** adj (chair etc)
Klapp-

foliage ['fəulɪɪdʒ] n Laubwerk nt

folk [fəuk] npl Leute pl ♦ adj Volks-; **~s**
npl (family) Leute pl; **~lore** ['fəuklɔ:*] n
(study) Volkskunde f; (tradition) Folk-
lore f; **~ song** n Volkslied nt;
(modern) Folksong m

follow ['fɔləu] vt folgen +dat; (fashion)
mitmachen ♦ vi folgen; **~ up** vt ver-

folgen; ~**er** n Anhänger(in) m(f); ~**ing**
adj folgend ♦ n (people) Gefolgschaft f
folly ['fɒlɪ] n Torheit f
fond [fɒnd] adj: **to be ~ of** gern haben
fondle ['fɒndl] vt streicheln
font [fɒnt] n Taufbecken nt
food [fuːd] n Essen nt; Nahrung nt;
Futter nt; ~ **mixer** n Küchenmixer m;
~ **poisoning** n Lebensmittelvergiftung
f; ~ **processor** n Küchenmaschine f;
~**stuffs** npl Lebensmittel pl
fool [fuːl] n Narr m, Närrin f ♦ vt
(deceive) hereinlegen ♦ vi (also: ~
around) (herum)albern; ~**hardy** adj
tollkühn; ~**ish** adj albern; ~**proof** adj
idiotensicher
foot [fʊt] (pl **feet**) n Fuß m ♦ vt (bill)
bezahlen; **on ~** zu Fuß; ~**age** n (CINE)
Filmmaterial nt; ~**ball** n Fußball m;
(game: BRIT) Fußball m; (: US)
Football m; ~**ball player** n (BRIT: also:
~**baller**) Fußballspieler m, Fußballer
m; (US) Footballer m; ~**brake** n Fuß-
bremse f; ~**bridge** n Fußgängerbrücke
f; ~**hills** npl Ausläufer pl; ~**hold** n
Halt m; ~**ing** n Halt m; (fig) Verhältnis nt; ~**lights** npl Rampenlicht nt;
~**man** (irreg) n Bedienstete(r) m;
~**note** n Fußnote f; ~**path** n Fußweg
m; ~**print** n Fußabdruck m; ~**sore** adj
fußkrank; ~**step** n Schritt m; ~**wear** n
Schuhzeug nt

KEYWORD

for [fɔː*] prep **1** für; **is this for me?** ist
das für mich?; **the train for London** der
Zug nach London; **he went for the
paper** er ging die Zeitung holen; **give it
to me - what for?** gib es mir - warum?
2 (because of) wegen; **for this reason**
aus diesem Grunde
3 (referring to distance): **there are
roadworks for 5 km** die Baustelle ist 5
km lang; **we walked for miles** wir sind
meilenweit gegangen
4 (referring to time) seit; (: with
future sense) für; **he was away for 2
years** er war zwei Jahre lang weg
5 (with infin clauses): **it is not for me
to decide** das kann ich nicht ent-

scheiden; **for this to be possible ...**
damit dies möglich wird/wurde ...
6 (in spite of) trotz +gen (inf); **for all
his complaints** obwohl er sich ständig
beschwert
♦ conj denn

---

forage ['fɒrɪdʒ] n (Vieh)futter nt
foray ['fɒreɪ] n Raubzug m
forbad(e) [fə'bæd] pt of **forbid**
forbid [fə'bɪd] (pt **forbad(e)**, pp
forbidden) vt verbieten; ~**den** [fə'bɪdn]
pp of **forbid**; ~**ding** adj einschüchternd
force [fɔːs] n Kraft f; (compulsion)
Zwang m ♦ vt zwingen; (lock) aufbrechen; **the F~s** npl (BRIT) die Streitkräfte; **in ~** (rule) gültig; (group) in
großer Stärke; ~**d** [fɔːst] adj (smile)
gezwungen; (landing) Not-; ~**-feed** vt
zwangsernähren; ~**ful** adj (speech)
kraftvoll; (personality) resolut
forceps ['fɔːseps] npl Zange f
forcibly ['fɔːsəblɪ] adv zwangsweise
ford [fɔːd] n Furt f ♦ vt durchwaten
fore [fɔː*] n: **to the ~** in den Vordergrund
forearm ['fɔːrɑːm] n Unterarm m
foreboding [fɔː'bəʊdɪŋ] n Vorahnung f
forecast ['fɔːkɑːst] (irreg: like **cast**) n
Vorhersage f ♦ vt voraussagen
forecourt ['fɔːkɔːt] n (of garage) Vorplatz m
forefathers ['fɔːfɑːðəz] npl Vorfahren pl
forefinger ['fɔːfɪŋgə*] n Zeigefinger m
forefront ['fɔːfrʌnt] n Spitze f
forego [fɔː'gəʊ] (irreg: like **go**) vt verzichten auf +acc
foregone ['fɔːgɒn] adj: **it's a ~ conclusion** es steht von vornherein fest
foreground ['fɔːgraʊnd] n Vordergrund
m
forehead ['fɒrɪd] n Stirn f
foreign ['fɒrɪn] adj Auslands-; (accent)
ausländisch; (trade) Außen-; (body)
Fremd-; ~**er** n Ausländer(in) m(f); ~
exchange n Devisen pl; **F~ Office**
(BRIT) n Außenministerium nt; **F~
Secretary** (BRIT) n Außenminister m
foreleg ['fɔːleg] n Vorderbein nt
foreman ['fɔːmən] (irreg) n Vorarbeiter

m

foremost ['fɔːməʊst] *adj* erste(r, s) ♦ *adv*: **first and ~** vor allem

forensic [fəˈrensɪk] *adj* gerichtsmedizinisch

forerunner ['fɔːrʌnə*] *n* Vorläufer *m*

foresee [fɔːˈsiː] (*irreg: like* see) *vt* vorhersehen; **~able** *adj* absehbar

foreshadow [fɔːˈʃædəʊ] *vt* andeuten

foresight ['fɔːsaɪt] *n* Voraussicht *f*

forest ['fɒrɪst] *n* Wald *m*

forestall [fɔːˈstɔːl] *vt* zuvorkommen +*dat*

forestry ['fɒrɪstrɪ] *n* Forstwirtschaft *f*

foretaste ['fɔːteɪst] *n* Vorgeschmack *m*

foretell [fɔːˈtel] (*irreg: like* tell) *vt* vorhersagen

forever [fəˈrevə*] *adv* für immer

foreword ['fɔːwɜːd] *n* Vorwort *nt*

forfeit ['fɔːfɪt] *n* Einbuße *f* ♦ *vt* verwirken

forgave [fəˈgeɪv] *pt of* forgive

forge [fɔːdʒ] *n* Schmiede *f* ♦ *vt* fälschen; (*iron*) schmieden; **~ ahead** *vi* Fortschritte machen; **~r** *n* Fälscher *m*; **~ry** *n* Fälschung *f*

forget [fəˈget] (*pt* forgot, *pp* forgotten) *vt, vi* vergessen; **~ful** *adj* vergeßlich; **~-me-not** *n* Vergißmeinnicht *nt*

forgive [fəˈgɪv] (*pt* forgave, *pp* forgiven) *vt* verzeihen; **to ~ sb (for sth)** jdm (etw) verzeihen; **forgiven** *pp of* forgive; **~ness** *n* Verzeihung *f*

forgo [fɔːˈgəʊ] (*irreg: like* go) *vt* verzichten auf +*acc*

forgot [fəˈgɒt] *pt of* forget

forgotten [fəˈgɒtn] *pp of* forget

fork [fɔːk] *n* Gabel *f*; (*in road*) Gabelung *f* ♦ *vi* (*road*) sich gabeln; **~ out** (*inf*) *vt* (*pay*) blechen; **~-lift truck** *n* Gabelstapler *m*

forlorn [fəˈlɔːn] *adj* (*person*) verlassen; (*hope*) vergeblich

form [fɔːm] *n* Form *f*; (*type*) Art *f*; (*figure*) Gestalt *f*; (*SCH*) Klasse *f*; (*bench*) (Schul)bank *f*; (*document*) Formular *nt* ♦ *vt* formen; (*be part of*) bilden

formal ['fɔːməl] *adj* formell; (*occasion*) offiziell; **~ly** *adv* (*ceremoniously*) formell; (*officially*) offiziell

format ['fɔːmæt] *n* Format *nt* ♦ *vt* (*COMPUT*) formatieren

formation [fɔːˈmeɪʃən] *n* Bildung *f*; (*AVIAT*) Formation *f*

formative ['fɔːmətɪv] *adj* (*years*) formend

former ['fɔːmə*] *adj* früher; (*opposite of latter*) erstere(r, s); **~ly** *adv* früher

formidable ['fɔːmɪdəbl] *adj* furchtbar

formula (*pl* **~e** *or* **~s**) *n* Formel *f*; **formulae** ['fɔːmjuliː] *npl of* **formula**; **~te** ['fɔːmjuleɪt] *vt* formulieren

forsake [fəˈseɪk] (*pt* forsook, *pp* forsaken) *vt* verlassen; **forsaken** *pp of* forsake

forsook [fəˈsʊk] *pt* forsake

fort [fɔːt] *n* Feste *f*, Fort *nt*

forte ['fɔːtɪ] *n* Stärke *f*, starke Seite *f*

forth [fɔːθ] *adv*: **and so ~** und so weiter; **~coming** *adj* kommend; (*character*) entgegenkommend; **~right** *adj* offen; **~with** *adv* umgehend

fortification [fɔːtɪfɪˈkeɪʃən] *n* Befestigung *f*

fortify ['fɔːtɪfaɪ] *vt* (ver)stärken; (*protect*) befestigen

fortitude ['fɔːtɪtjuːd] *n* Seelenstärke *f*

fortnight ['fɔːtnaɪt] (*BRIT*) *n* vierzehn Tage *pl*; **~ly** (*BRIT*) *adj* zweiwöchentlich ♦ *adv* alle vierzehn Tage

fortress ['fɔːtrɪs] *n* Festung *f*

fortuitous [fɔːˈtjuːɪtəs] *adj* zufällig

fortunate ['fɔːtʃənɪt] *adj* glücklich; **~ly** *adv* glücklicherweise, zum Glück

fortune ['fɔːtʃən] *n* Glück *nt*; (*money*) Vermögen *nt*; **~-teller** *n* Wahrsager(in) *m(f)*

forty ['fɔːtɪ] *num* vierzig

forum ['fɔːrəm] *n* Forum *nt*

forward ['fɔːwəd] *adj* vordere(r, s); (*movement*) Vorwärts-; (*person*) vorlaut; (*planning*) Voraus- ♦ *adv* vorwärts ♦ *n* (*SPORT*) Stürmer *m* ♦ *vt* (*send*) schicken; (*help*) fördern; **~s** *adv* vorwärts

forwent [fɔːˈwent] *pt of* forgo

fossil ['fɒsl] *n* Fossil *nt*, Versteinerung *f*

foster ['fɒstə*] *vt* (*talent*) fördern; **~**

child n Pflegekind nt; ~ **mother** n Pflegemutter f

fought [fɔːt] pt, pp of **fight**

foul [faʊl] adj schmutzig; (language) gemein; (weather) schlecht ♦ n (SPORT) Foul nt ♦ vt (mechanism) blockieren; (SPORT) foulen; ~ **play** n (SPORT) Foulspiel nt; (LAW) Verbrechen nt

found [faʊnd] pt, pp of **find** ♦ vt gründen; ~**ation** [faʊnˈdeɪʃən] n (act) Gründung f; (fig) Fundament nt; (also: ~ **cream**) Grundierungscreme f; ~**ations** npl (of house) Fundament nt

founder [ˈfaʊndə*] n Gründer(in) m(f) ♦ vi sinken

foundry [ˈfaʊndrɪ] n Gießerei f

fount [faʊnt] n Quelle f; ~**ain** [ˈfaʊntɪn] n (Spring)brunnen m; ~**ain pen** n Füllfederhalter m

four [fɔː*] num vier; **on all** ~s auf allen vieren; ~**-poster** n Himmelbett nt; ~**some** n Quartett nt; ~**teen** num vierzehn; ~**teenth** adj vierzehnte(r, s); ~**th** adj vierte(r, s)

fowl [faʊl] n Huhn nt; (food) Geflügel nt

fox [fɒks] n Fuchs m ♦ vt täuschen; ~**trot** n Foxtrott m

foyer [ˈfɔɪeɪ] n Foyer nt, Vorhalle f

fraction [ˈfrækʃən] n (MATH) Bruch m; (part) Bruchteil m

fracture [ˈfræktʃə*] n (MED) Bruch m ♦ vt brechen

fragile [ˈfrædʒaɪl] adj zerbrechlich

fragment [ˈfrægmənt] n Bruchstück nt; (small part) Splitter m

fragrance [ˈfreɪgrəns] n Duft m

fragrant [ˈfreɪgrənt] adj duftend

frail [freɪl] adj schwach, gebrechlich

frame [freɪm] n Rahmen m; (of spectacles: also: ~s) Gestell nt; (body) Gestalt f ♦ vt einrahmen; **to** ~ **sb** (inf: incriminate) jdm etwas anhängen; ~ **of mind** Verfassung f; ~**work** n Rahmen m; (of society) Gefüge nt

France [frɑːns] n Frankreich nt

franchise [ˈfræntʃaɪz] n (POL) (aktives) Wahlrecht nt; (COMM) Lizenz f

frank [fræŋk] adj offen ♦ vt (letter) frankieren; ~**ly** adv offen gesagt; ~**ness** n Offenheit f

frantic [ˈfræntɪk] adj verzweifelt

fraternal [frəˈtɜːnl] adj brüderlich

fraternity [frəˈtɜːnɪtɪ] n (club) Vereinigung f; (spirit) Brüderlichkeit f; (US: SCH) Studentenverbindung f

fraternize [ˈfrætənaɪz] vi fraternisieren

fraud [frɔːd] n (trickery) Betrug m; (person) Schwindler(in) m(f)

fraudulent [ˈfrɔːdjʊlənt] adj betrügerisch

fraught [frɔːt] adj: ~ **with** voller +gen

fray [freɪ] n Rauferei f ♦ vt, vi ausfransen; **tempers were** ~**ed** die Gemüter waren erhitzt

freak [friːk] n Monstrosität f ♦ cpd (storm etc) anormal

freckle [ˈfrekl] n Sommersprosse f

free [friː] adj frei; (loose) lose; (liberal) freigebig ♦ vt (set free) befreien; (unblock) freimachen; ~ (**of charge**) gratis, umsonst; **for** ~ gratis, umsonst; ~**dom** [ˈfriːdəm] n Freiheit f; ~**-for-all** n (fight) allgemeine(s) Handgemenge nt; ~ **gift** n Geschenk nt; ~**hold property** n (freie(r)) Grundbesitz m; ~ **kick** n Freistoß m; ~**lance** adj frei; (artist) freischaffend; ~**ly** adv frei; (admit) offen; ~**mason** n Freimaurer m; ~**post** n ≈ Gebühr zahlt Empfänger; ~**-range** adj (hen) Farmhof-; (eggs) Land-; ~ **trade** n Freihandel m; ~**way** (US) n Autobahn f; ~**wheel** vi im Freilauf fahren; ~ **will** n: **of one's own** ~ **will** aus freien Stücken

freeze [friːz] (pt **froze**, pp **frozen**) vi gefrieren; (feel cold) frieren ♦ vt (also fig) einfrieren ♦ n (fig, FIN) Stopp m; ~**r** n Tiefkühltruhe f; (in fridge) Gefrierfach nt

freezing [ˈfriːzɪŋ] adj eisig; (~ cold) eiskalt; ~ **point** n Gefrierpunkt m

freight [freɪt] n Fracht f; ~ **train** n Güterzug m

French [frentʃ] adj französisch ♦ n (LING) Französisch nt; **the** ~ npl (people) die Franzosen pl; ~ **bean** n grüne Bohne f; ~ **fried potatoes** (BRIT) npl Pommes frites pl; ~ **fries** (US) npl Pommes frites pl; ~**man/woman** (irreg) n Franzose m/Französin f; ~ **window** n Verandatür f

frenzy ['frɛnzɪ] n Raserei f
frequency ['friːkwənsɪ] n Häufigkeit f;
(PHYS) Frequenz f
frequent [adj 'friːkwənt, vb friːˈkwɛnt] adj
häufig ♦ vt (regelmäßig) besuchen
fresco ['freskəu] n Fresko nt
fresh [frɛʃ] adj frisch; ~**en** vi (also:
~en up) (sich) auffrischen; (person)
sich frisch machen; ~**er** (BRIT: inf) n
(UNIV) Erstsemester nt; ~**ly** adv
gerade; ~**man** (US: irreg) n = fresher;
~**ness** n Frische f; ~**water** adj (fish)
Süßwasser-
fret [frɛt] vi sich dat Sorgen machen
friar ['fraɪə*] n Klosterbruder m
friction ['frɪkʃən] n (also fig) Reibung f
Friday ['fraɪdeɪ] n Freitag m
fridge [frɪdʒ] (BRIT) n Kühlschrank m
fried [fraɪd] adj gebraten
friend [frɛnd] n Freund(in) m(f);
~**liness** n Freundlichkeit f; ~**ly** adj
freundlich; (relations) freundschaftlich;
~**ship** n Freundschaft f
frieze [friːz] n Fries m
frigate ['frɪgɪt] n Fregatte f
fright [fraɪt] n Schrecken m; **to take** ~
es mit der Angst zu tun bekommen;
~**en** vt erschrecken; **to be** ~**ened** Angst
haben; ~**ening** adj schrecklich; ~**ful**
(inf) adj furchtbar; ~**fully** (inf) adv
furchtbar
frigid ['frɪdʒɪd] adj (woman) frigide
frill [frɪl] n Rüsche f
fringe [frɪndʒ] n Besatz m; (BRIT: of
hair) Pony m; (fig) Peripherie f; ~
benefits npl zusätzliche Leistungen pl
frisk [frɪsk] vt durchsuchen
frisky ['frɪskɪ] adj lebendig, ausgelassen
fritter ['frɪtə*] vt: **to** ~ **away** vergeuden
frivolous ['frɪvələs] adj frivol
frizzy ['frɪzɪ] adj kraus
fro [frəu] see **to**
frock [frɒk] n Kleid nt
frog [frɒg] n Frosch m; ~**man** (irreg) n
Froschmann m
frolic ['frɒlɪk] vi ausgelassen sein

+dat; **a letter/telephone call from my
sister** ein Brief/Anruf von meiner
Schwester; **where do you come from?**
woher kommen Sie?; **to drink from the
bottle** aus der Flasche trinken
2 (indicating time) von ... an; (: past)
seit; **from one o'clock to** or **until** or **till
two** von ein Uhr bis zwei; **from January
(on)** ab Januar
3 (indicating distance) von ... (entfernt)
4 (indicating price, number etc) ab
+dat; **from £10 ab £10; there were from
20 to 30 people there** es waren zwischen
20 und 30 Leute da
5 (indicating difference): **he can't tell
red from green** er kann nicht zwischen
rot und grün unterscheiden; **to be
different from sb/sth** anders sein als jd/
etw
6 (because of, on the basis of): **from
what he says** aus dem, was er sagt;
weak from hunger schwach vor Hunger

---

front [frʌnt] n Vorderseite f; (of house)
Fassade f; (promenade: also: sea ~)
Strandpromenade f; (MIL, POL, MET)
Front f; (fig: appearances) Fassade f
♦ adj (forward) vordere(r, s), Vorder-;
(first) vorderste(r, s); **in** ~ vorne; **in** ~
of vor; ~**age** n Vorderfront f; ~**al** adj
frontal, Vorder-; ~ **door** n Haustür f;
~**ier** ['frʌntɪə*] n Grenze f; ~ **page** n
Titelseite f; ~ **room** (BRIT) n
Wohnzimmer nt; ~-**wheel drive** n Vor-
derradantrieb m
frost [frɒst] n Frost m; ~**bite** n Erfrie-
rung f; ~**ed** adj (glass) Milch-; ~**y** adj
frostig
froth [frɒθ] n Schaum m
frown [fraun] n Stirnrunzeln nt ♦ vi die
Stirn runzeln
froze [frəuz] pt of **freeze**
frozen ['frəuzn] pp of **freeze**
frugal ['fruːgəl] adj sparsam, bescheiden
fruit [fruːt] n inv (as collective) Obst nt;
(particular) Frucht f; ~**erer** n Obst-
händler m; ~**erer's (shop)** n Obsthand-
lung f; ~**ful** adj fruchtbar; ~**ion**
[fruːˈɪʃən] n: **to come to** ~**ion** in

Erfüllung gehen; ~ **juice** n Fruchtsaft m; ~ **machine** (BRIT) n Spielautomat m; ~ **salad** n Obstsalat m

frustrate [frʌs'treɪt] vt vereiteln; ~**d** adj gehemmt; (PSYCH) frustriert

fry [fraɪ] (pt, pp **fried**) vt braten ♦ npl: **small** ~ kleine Fische pl; ~**ing pan** n Bratpfanne f

ft. abbr = **foot; feet**

fuddy-duddy ['fʌdɪdʌdɪ] n altmodische(r) Kauz m

fudge [fʌdʒ] n Fondant m

fuel [fjʊəl] n Treibstoff m; (for heating) Brennstoff m; (for lighter) Benzin nt; ~ **oil** n (diesel fuel) Heizöl nt; ~ **tank** n Tank m

fugitive ['fjuːdʒɪtɪv] n Flüchtling m

fulfil [fʊl'fɪl] vt (duty) erfüllen; (promise) einhalten; ~**ment** n Erfüllung f

full [fʊl] adj (box, bottle, price) voll; (person: satisfied) satt; (member, power, employment, moon) Voll-; (complete) vollständig, Voll-; (speed) höchste(r, s); (skirt) weit ♦ adv: **well** sehr wohl; **in** ~ vollständig; ~-**length** adj (lifesize) lebensgroß; **a** ~-**length photograph** eine Ganzaufnahme; ~ **moon** n Vollmond m; ~-**scale** adj (attack) General-; (drawing) in Originalgröße; ~ **stop** n Punkt m; ~-**time** adj (job) Ganztags- ♦ adv (work) ganztags ♦ n (SPORT) Spielschluß nt; ~**y** adv völlig; ~**y-fledged** adj (also fig) flügge

fulsome ['fʊlsəm] adj übertrieben

fumble ['fʌmbl] vi: **to** ~ (**with**) herumfummeln (an +dat)

fume [fjuːm] vi qualmen; (fig) kochen (inf); ~**s** npl (of fuel, car) Abgase pl

fumigate ['fjuːmɪgeɪt] vt ausräuchern

fun [fʌn] n Spaß m; **to make** ~ **of** sich lustig machen über +acc

function ['fʌŋkʃən] n Funktion f; (occasion) Veranstaltung f ♦ vi funktionieren; ~**al** adj funktionell

fund [fʌnd] n (money) Geldmittel pl, Fonds m; (store) Vorrat m; ~**s** npl (resources) Mittel pl

fundamental [fʌndə'mentl] adj fundamental, grundlegend

funeral ['fjuːnərəl] n Beerdigung f; ~ **parlour** n Leichenhalle f; ~ **service** n Trauergottesdienst m

funfair ['fʌnfɛə] (BRIT) n Jahrmarkt m

fungi ['fʌŋgaɪ] npl of **fungus**

fungus ['fʌŋgəs] n Pilz m

funnel ['fʌnl] n Trichter m; (NAUT) Schornstein m

funny ['fʌnɪ] adj komisch

fur [fɜː] n Pelz m; ~ **coat** n Pelzmantel m

furious ['fjʊərɪəs] adj wütend; (attempt) heftig

furlong ['fɜːlɒŋ] n = 201.17 m

furlough ['fɜːləʊ] n Urlaub m

furnace ['fɜːnɪs] n (Brenn)ofen m

furnish ['fɜːnɪʃ] vt einrichten; (supply) versehen; ~**ings** npl Einrichtung f

furniture ['fɜːnɪtʃə] n Möbel pl; **piece of** ~ Möbelstück nt

furrow ['fʌrəʊ] n Furche f

furry ['fɜːrɪ] adj (tongue) pelzig; (animal) Pelz-

further ['fɜːðə] adj weitere(r, s) ♦ adv weiter ♦ vt fördern; ~ **education** n Weiterbildung f; Erwachsenenbildung f; ~**more** adv ferner

furthest ['fɜːðɪst] superl of **far**

furtive ['fɜːtɪv] adj verstohlen

fury ['fjʊərɪ] n Wut f, Zorn m

fuse [fjuːz] n (ELEC) Sicherung f; (of bomb) Zünder m ♦ vt verschmelzen ♦ vi (BRIT: ELEC) durchbrennen; ~ **box** n Sicherungskasten m

fuselage ['fjuːzəlɑːʒ] n Flugzeugrumpf m

fusion ['fjuːʒən] n Verschmelzung f

fuss [fʌs] n Theater nt; ~**y** adj kleinlich

futile ['fjuːtaɪl] adj zwecklos, sinnlos

futility [fjuː'tɪlɪtɪ] n Zwecklosigkeit f

future ['fjuːtʃə] adj zukünftig ♦ n Zukunft f; **in (the)** ~ in Zukunft

fuze [fjuːz] (US) = **fuse**

fuzzy ['fʌzɪ] adj (indistinct) verschwommen; (hair) kraus

G

G [dʒiː] n (MUS) G nt
gabble ['gæbl] vi plappern
gable ['geɪbl] n Giebel m
gadget ['gædʒɪt] n Vorrichtung f
Gaelic ['geɪlɪk] adj gälisch ♦ n (LING) Gälisch nt
gaffe [gæf] n Fauxpas m
gag [gæg] n Knebel m; (THEAT) Gag m ♦ vt knebeln
gaiety ['geɪətɪ] n Fröhlichkeit f
gaily ['geɪlɪ] adv lustig, fröhlich
gain [geɪn] vt (obtain) erhalten; (win) gewinnen ♦ vi (clock) vorgehen ♦ n Gewinn m; **to ~ in** sth an etw dat gewinnen; **~ on** vt fus einholen
gait [geɪt] n Gang m
gal. abbr = **gallon**
gala ['gɑːlə] n Fest nt
galaxy ['gæləksɪ] n Sternsystem nt
gale [geɪl] n Sturm m
gallant ['gælənt] adj tapfer; (polite) galant; **~ry** n Tapferkeit f; Galanterie f
gallbladder ['gɔːl-] n Gallenblase f
gallery ['gælərɪ] n (also: art ~) Galerie f
galley ['gælɪ] n (ship's kitchen) Kombüse f; (ship) Galeere f
gallon ['gælən] n Gallone f
gallop ['gæləp] n Galopp m ♦ vi galoppieren
gallows ['gæləʊz] n Galgen m
gallstone ['gɔːlstəʊn] n Gallenstein m
galore [gə'lɔː*] adv in Hülle und Fülle
galvanize ['gælvənaɪz] vt (metal) galvanisieren; (fig) elektrisieren
gambit ['gæmbɪt] n (fig) (Schach)zug m
gamble ['gæmbl] vi (um Geld) spielen ♦ vt (risk) aufs Spiel setzen ♦ n Risiko nt; **~r** n Spieler(in) m(f)
gambling ['gæmblɪŋ] n Glücksspiel nt
game [geɪm] n Spiel nt; (hunting) Wild nt ♦ adj: **~ (for)** bereit (zu); **~keeper** n Wildhüter m
gammon ['gæmən] n geräucherte(r) Schinken m
gamut ['gæmət] n Tonskala f

gang [gæŋ] n (of criminals, youths) Bande f; (of workmen) Kolonne f ♦ vi: **to ~ up on** sb sich gegen jdn verschwören
gangrene ['gæŋgriːn] n Brand m
gangster ['gæŋstə*] n Gangster m
gangway ['gæŋweɪ] n (NAUT) Laufplanke f; (aisle) Gang m
gaol [dʒeɪl] (BRIT) n, vt = **jail**
gap [gæp] n Lücke f
gape [geɪp] vi glotzen
gaping ['geɪpɪŋ] adj (wound) klaffend; (hole) gähnend
garage ['gærɑːʒ] n Garage f; (for repair) (Auto)reparaturwerkstatt f; (for petrol) Tankstelle f
garbage ['gɑːbɪdʒ] n Abfall m; **~ can** (US) n Mülltonne f
garbled ['gɑːbld] adj (story) verdreht
garden ['gɑːdn] n Garten m; **~er** n Gärtner(in) m(f); **~ing** n Gärtnern nt
gargle ['gɑːgl] vi gurgeln
gargoyle ['gɑːgɔɪl] n Wasserspeier m
garish ['gɛərɪʃ] adj grell
garland ['gɑːlənd] n Girlande f
garlic ['gɑːlɪk] n Knoblauch m
garment ['gɑːmənt] n Kleidungsstück nt
garnish ['gɑːnɪʃ] vt (food) garnieren
garrison ['gærɪsən] n Garnison f
garrulous ['gærʊləs] adj geschwätzig
garter ['gɑːtə*] n Strumpfband nt; (US) Strumpfhalter m
gas [gæs] n Gas nt; (esp US: petrol) Benzin nt ♦ vt vergasen; **~ cooker** (BRIT) n Gasherd m; **~ cylinder** n Gasflasche f; **~ fire** n Gasofen m
gash [gæʃ] n klaffende Wunde f ♦ vt tief verwunden
gasket ['gæskɪt] n Dichtungsring m
gas mask n Gasmaske f
gas meter n Gaszähler m
gasoline ['gæsəliːn] (US) n Benzin nt
gasp [gɑːsp] vi keuchen; (in astonishment) tief Luft holen ♦ n Keuchen nt
gas ring n Gasring m
gassy ['gæsɪ] adj (drink) sprudelnd
gas tap n Gashahn m
gastric ['gæstrɪk] adj Magen-
gate [geɪt] n Tor nt; (barrier) Schranke

f; ~**crash** (*BRIT*) *vt* (*party*) platzen in +*acc*; ~**way** *n* Toreingang *m*
gather ['gæðə*] *vt* (*people*) versammeln; (*things*) sammeln; (*understand*) annehmen ♦ *vi* (*assemble*) sich versammeln; **to ~ speed** schneller werden; **to ~ (from)** schließen (aus); ~**ing** *n* Versammlung *f*
gauche [gəuʃ] *adj* linkisch
gaudy ['gɔːdɪ] *adj* schreiend
gauge [geɪdʒ] *n* (*instrument*) Meßgerät *nt*; (*RAIL*) Spurweite *f*; (*dial*) Anzeiger *m*; (*measure*) Maß *nt* ♦ *vt* (ab)messen; (*fig*) abschätzen
gaunt [gɔːnt] *adj* hager
gauntlet ['gɔːntlɪt] *n* (*knight's*) (Fehde)handschuh *m*
gauze [gɔːz] *n* Gaze *f*
gave [geɪv] *pt of* **give**
gay [geɪ] *adj* (*homosexual*) schwul; (*lively*) lustig
gaze [geɪz] *n* Blick *m* ♦ *vi* starren; **to ~ at sth** etw *dat* anstarren
gazelle [gə'zel] *n* Gazelle *f*
gazetteer [gæzɪ'tɪə*] *n* geographische(s) Lexikon *nt*
gazumping [gə'zʌmpɪŋ] (*BRIT*) *n* Verkauf eines Hauses an einen zweiten Bieter trotz Zusage an den ersten
GB *n abbr* = **Great Britain**
GCE (*BRIT*) *n abbr* = **General Certificate of Education**
GCSE (*BRIT*) *n abbr* = **General Certificate of Secondary Education**
gear [gɪə*] *n* Getriebe *nt*; (*equipment*) Ausrüstung *f*; (*AUT*) Gang *m* ♦ *vt* (*fig: adapt*): **to be ~ed to** ausgerichtet sein auf +*acc*; **top ~** höchste(r) Gang *m*; **high ~** (*US*) höchste(r) Gang *m*; **low ~** niedrige(r) Gang *m*; **in ~** eingekuppelt; ~ **box** *n* Getriebe(gehäuse) *nt*; ~ **lever** *n* Schalthebel *m*; ~ **shift** (*US*) *n* Schalthebel *m*
geese [giːs] *npl of* **goose**
gel [dʒel] *n* Gel *nt*
gelatin(e) ['dʒelətiːn] *n* Gelatine *f*
gelignite ['dʒelɪgnaɪt] *n* Plastiksprengstoff *m*
gem [dʒem] *n* Edelstein *m*; (*fig*) Juwel *nt*

Gemini ['dʒemɪniː] *n* Zwillinge *pl*
gender ['dʒendə*] *n* (*GRAM*) Geschlecht *nt*
gene [dʒiːn] *n* Gen *nt*
general ['dʒenərəl] *n* General *m* ♦ *adj* allgemein; ~ **delivery** (*US*) *n* Ausgabe(schalter *m*) *f* postlagernder Sendungen; ~ **election** *n* allgemeine Wahlen *pl*; ~**ization** ['dʒenərəlaɪ'zeɪʃən] *n* Verallgemeinerung *f*; ~**ize** *vi* verallgemeinern; ~**ly** *adv* allgemein, im allgemeinen; ~ **practitioner** *n* praktische(r) Arzt *m*, praktische Ärztin *f*
generate ['dʒenəreɪt] *vt* erzeugen
generation [dʒenə'reɪʃən] *n* Generation *f*; (*act*) Erzeugung *f*
generator ['dʒenəreɪtə*] *n* Generator *m*
generosity [dʒenə'rɒsɪtɪ] *n* Großzügigkeit *f*
generous ['dʒenərəs] *adj* großzügig
genetics [dʒɪ'netɪks] *n* Genetik *f*
Geneva [dʒɪ'niːvə] *n* Genf *nt*
genial ['dʒiːnɪəl] *adj* freundlich, jovial
genitals ['dʒenɪtlz] *npl* Genitalien *pl*
genius ['dʒiːnɪəs] *n* Genie *nt*
genocide ['dʒenəusaɪd] *n* Völkermord *m*
gent [dʒent] *n abbr* = **gentleman**
genteel [dʒen'tiːl] *adj* (*polite*) wohlanständig; (*affected*) affektiert
gentle ['dʒentl] *adj* sanft, zart
gentleman ['dʒentlmən] (*irreg*) *n* Herr *m*; (*polite*) Gentleman *m*
gentleness ['dʒentlnɪs] *n* Zartheit *f*, Milde *f*
gently ['dʒentlɪ] *adv* zart, sanft
gentry ['dʒentrɪ] *n* Landadel *m*
gents [dʒents] *n*: **G~** (*lavatory*) Herren *pl*
genuine ['dʒenjuɪn] *adj* echt
geographic(al) [dʒɪə'græfɪk(əl)] *adj* geographisch
geography [dʒɪ'ɒgrəfɪ] *n* Geographie *f*
geological [dʒɪəu'lɒdʒɪkəl] *adj* geologisch
geologist [dʒɪ'ɒlədʒɪst] *n* Geologe *m*, Geologin *f*
geology [dʒɪ'ɒlədʒɪ] *n* Geologie *f*
geometric(al) [dʒɪə'metrɪk(l)] *adj* geometrisch
geometry [dʒɪ'ɒmɪtrɪ] *n* Geometrie *f*

geranium [dʒɪ'reɪnɪəm] n Geranie f
geriatric [dʒerɪ'ætrɪk] adj Alten- ♦ n
Greis(in) m(f)
germ [dʒɜːm] n Keim m; (MED) Bazillus
m
German ['dʒɜːmən] adj deutsch ♦ n
Deutsche(r) mf; (LING) Deutsch nt; ~
measles n Röteln pl
Germany ['dʒɜːmənɪ] n Deutschland nt
germination [dʒɜːmɪ'neɪʃən] n Keimen
nt
gesticulate [dʒes'tɪkjʊleɪt] vi gesti-
kulieren
gesture ['dʒestʃə*] n Geste f

KEYWORD

get [get] (pt, pp **got**, pp **gotten** (US)) vi 1
(become, be) werden; **to get old/tired**
alt/müde werden; **to get married**
heiraten
2 (go) (an)kommen, gehen
3 (begin): **to get to know sb** jdn
kennenlernen; **let's get going** or **started**
fangen wir an!
4 (modal aux vb): **you've got to do it**
du mußt es tun
♦ vt **1**: **to get sth done** (do) etw machen; (have done) etw machen lassen;
to get sth going or **to go** etw in Gang
bringen or bekommen; **to get sb to do
sth** jdn dazu bringen, etw zu tun
2 (obtain: money, permission, results)
erhalten; (find: job, flat) finden; (fetch:
person, doctor, object) holen; **to get sth
for sb** jdm etw besorgen; **get me Mr
Jones, please** (TEL) verbinden Sie mich
bitte mit Mr Jones
3 (receive: present, letter) bekommen,
kriegen; (acquire: reputation etc)
erwerben
4 (catch) bekommen, kriegen; (hit:
target etc) treffen, erwischen; **get him!**
(to dog) faß!
5 (take, move) bringen; **to get sth to sb**
jdm etw bringen
6 (understand) verstehen; (hear) mitbekommen; **I've got it!** ich hab's!
7 (have, possess): **to have got sth** etw
haben
get about vi vi herumkommen;

(news) sich verbreiten
get along vi (people) (gut)
zurechtkommen; (depart) sich acc auf
den Weg machen
get at vt (facts) herausbekommen;
to get at sb (nag) an jdm herumnörgeln
get away vi (leave) sich acc davonmachen; (escape): **to get away from sth**
von etw dat entkommen; **to get away
with sth** mit etw davon kommen
get back vi (return) zurückkommen ♦
vt zurückbekommen
get by vi (pass) vorbeikommen;
(manage) zurechtkommen
get down vi (her)untergehen ♦ vt (depress) fertigmachen; **to get down to** in
Angriff nehmen; (find time to do)
kommen zu
get in vi (train) ankommen; (arrive
home) heimkommen
get into vt (enter) hinein-/
hereinkommen in +acc; (: car, train
etc) einsteigen in +acc; (clothes) anziehen
get off vi (from train etc) aussteigen;
(from horse) absteigen ♦ vt aussteigen
aus; absteigen von
get on vi (progress) vorankommen;
(be friends) auskommen; (age) alt
werden; (onto train etc) einsteigen;
(onto horse) aufsteigen ♦ vt einsteigen
in +acc; aufsteigen auf +acc
get out vi (of house) herauskommen;
(of vehicle) aussteigen ♦ vt (take out)
herausholen
get out of vt (duty etc) herumkommen um
get over vt (illness) sich acc erholen
von; (surprise) verkraften; (news)
fassen; (loss) sich abfinden mit
get round vt herumkommen; (fig:
person) herumkriegen
get through to vt (TEL) durchkommen zu
get together vi zusammenkommen
get up vi aufstehen ♦ vt hinaufbringen;
(go up) hinaufgehen; (organize) auf die
Beine stellen
get up to vt (reach) erreichen;

(*prank etc*) anstellen

getaway ['getəweɪ] n Flucht f

get-up ['getʌp] (*inf*) n Aufzug m

geyser ['giːzə*] n Geiser m; (*heater*) Durchlauferhitzer m

Ghana ['gɑːnə] n Ghana nt

ghastly ['gɑːstlɪ] adj (*horrible*) gräßlich

gherkin ['gɜːkɪn] n Gewürzgurke f

ghetto ['getəʊ] n G(h)etto nt

ghost [gəʊst] n Gespenst nt; ~ly adj gespenstisch

giant ['dʒaɪənt] n Riese m ♦ adj riesig, Riesen-

gibberish ['dʒɪbərɪʃ] n dumme(s) Geschwätz nt

gibe [dʒaɪb] n spöttische Bemerkung f

giblets ['dʒɪblɪts] npl Geflügelinnereien pl

Gibraltar [dʒɪ'brɔːltə*] n Gibraltar nt

giddiness ['gɪdɪnəs] n Schwindelgefühl nt

giddy ['gɪdɪ] adj schwindlig

gift [gɪft] n Geschenk nt; (*ability*) Begabung f; ~ed adj begabt; ~ token n Geschenkgutschein m; ~ voucher n Geschenkgutschein m

gigantic [dʒaɪ'gæntɪk] adj riesenhaft

giggle ['gɪgl] vi kichern ♦ n Gekicher nt

gild [gɪld] vt vergolden

gill [dʒɪl] n (*1/4 pint*) Viertelpinte f

gills [gɪlz] npl (*of fish*) Kiemen pl

gilt [gɪlt] n Vergoldung f ♦ adj vergoldet; ~-edged adj mündelsicher

gimmick ['gɪmɪk] n Gag m

gin [dʒɪn] n Gin m

ginger ['dʒɪndʒə*] n Ingwer m; ~ ale n Ingwerbier nt; ~ beer n Ingwerbier nt; ~bread n Pfefferkuchen m; ~-haired adj rothaarig

gingerly ['dʒɪndʒəlɪ] adv behutsam

gipsy ['dʒɪpsɪ] n Zigeuner(in) m(f)

giraffe [dʒɪ'rɑːf] n Giraffe f

girder ['gɜːdə*] n Eisenträger m

girdle ['gɜːdl] n Hüftgürtel m

girl [gɜːl] n Mädchen nt; ~friend n Freundin f; ~ish adj mädchenhaft

giro ['dʒaɪrəʊ] n (*bank* ~) Giro nt; (*post office* ~) Postscheckverkehr m

girth [gɜːθ] n (*measure*) Umfang m;

(*strap*) Sattelgurt m

gist [dʒɪst] n Wesentliche(s) nt

give [gɪv] (*pt* gave, *pp* given) vt geben ♦ vi (*break*) nachgeben; ~ away vt verschenken; (*betray*) verraten; ~ back vt zurückgeben; ~ in vi nachgeben ♦ vt (*hand in*) abgeben; ~ off vt abgeben; ~ out vt verteilen; (*announce*) bekanntgeben; ~ up vt, vi aufgeben; to ~ o.s. up sich stellen; (*after siege*) sich ergeben; ~ way vi (*BRIT: traffic*) Vorfahrt lassen; (*to feelings*): to ~ way to nachgeben +dat; **given** pp of **give**

glacier ['glæsɪə*] n Gletscher m

glad [glæd] adj froh

gladioli [glædɪ'əʊlaɪ] npl Gladiolen pl

gladly ['glædlɪ] adv gern(e)

glamorous ['glæmərəs] adj reizvoll

glamour ['glæmə*] n Glanz m

glance [glɑːns] n Blick m ♦ vi: to ~ (at) (hin)blicken (auf +acc); ~ off vt fus (*fly off*) abprallen von

glancing ['glɑːnsɪŋ] adj (*blow*) Streif-

gland [glænd] n Drüse f

glare [glɛə*] n (*light*) grelle(s) Licht nt; (*stare*) wilde(r) Blick m ♦ vi grell scheinen; (*angrily*): to ~ at böse ansehen

glaring ['glɛərɪŋ] adj (*injustice*) schreiend; (*mistake*) kraß

glass [glɑːs] n Glas nt; (*mirror: also: looking* ~) Spiegel m; ~es npl (*spectacles*). Brille f; ~house n Gewächshaus nt; ~ware n Glaswaren pl; ~y adj glasig

glaze [gleɪz] vt verglasen; (*finish with a* ~) glasieren ♦ n Glasur f; ~d adj (*eye*) glasig; (*pottery*) glasiert

glazier ['gleɪzɪə*] n Glaser m

gleam [gliːm] n Schimmer m ♦ vi schimmern; ~ing adj schimmernd

glean [gliːn] vt (*fig*) ausfindig machen

glee [gliː] n Frohsinn m

glen [glen] n Bergtal nt

glib [glɪb] adj oberflächlich

glide [glaɪd] vi gleiten; ~r n (*AVIAT*) Segelflugzeug nt

gliding ['glaɪdɪŋ] n Segelfliegen nt

glimmer ['glɪmə*] n Schimmer m

glimpse [glɪmps] n flüchtige(r) Blick m
♦ vt flüchtig erblicken
glint [glɪnt] n Glitzern nt ♦ vi glitzern
glisten ['glɪsn] vi glänzen
glitter ['glɪtə*] vi funkeln ♦ n Funkeln nt
gloat ['gləʊt] vi: to ~ over sich weiden
an +dat
global ['gləʊbl] adj global
globe [gləʊb] n Erdball m; (sphere)
Globus m
gloom [glu:m] n (darkness) Dunkel nt;
(depression) düstere Stimmung f; ~y
adj düster
glorify ['glɔːrɪfaɪ] vt verherrlichen
glorious ['glɔːrɪəs] adj glorreich
glory ['glɔːrɪ] n Ruhm m
gloss [glɒs] n (shine) Glanz m; ~ over
vt fus übertünchen
glossary ['glɒsərɪ] n Glossar nt
glossy ['glɒsɪ] adj (surface) glänzend
glove [glʌv] n Handschuh m; ~ compartment n (AUT) Handschuhfach nt
glow [gləʊ] vi glühen ♦ n Glühen nt
glower ['glaʊə*] vi: to ~ at finster an-
blicken
glucose ['glu:kəʊs] n Traubenzucker m
glue [glu:] n Klebstoff m ♦ vt kleben
glum [glʌm] adj bedrückt
glut [glʌt] n Überfluß m
glutton ['glʌtn] n Vielfraß m; a ~ for
work ein Arbeitstier nt; ~y n Völlerei f
glycerin(e) ['glɪsəriːn] n Glyzerin nt
gnarled [nɑːld] adj knorrig
gnat [næt] n Stechmücke f
gnaw [nɔː] vt nagen an +dat
gnome [nəʊm] n Gnom m
go [gəʊ] (pt went, pp gone; pl ~es) vi
gehen; (travel) reisen, fahren; (depart:
train) (ab)fahren; (be sold) verkauft
werden; (work) gehen, funktionieren;
(fit, suit) passen; (become) werden;
(break etc) nachgeben ♦ n (energy)
Schwung m; (attempt) Versuch m; he's
~ing to do it er wird es tun; to ~ for a
walk spazieren gehen; to ~ dancing
tanzen gehen; how did it ~? wie
war's?; to ~ with (be suitable) passen
zu; to have a ~ at sth etw versuchen;
to be on the ~ auf Trab sein; whose ~
is it? wer ist dran?; ~ about vi

(rumour) umgehen ♦ vt fus: how do I ~
about this? wie packe ich das an?; ~
ahead vi (proceed) weitergehen; ~
along vi dahingehen, dahinfahren ♦ vt
entlanggehen, entlangfahren; to ~
along with (agree to support) zustimmen +dat; ~ away vi (depart)
weggehen; ~ back vi (return)
zurückgehen; ~ back on vt fus
(promise) nicht halten; ~ by vi (years,
time) vergehen ♦ vt fus sich richten
nach; ~ down vi (sun) untergehen ♦ vt
fus hinuntergehen, hinunterfahren; ~
for vt fus (fetch) holen (gehen); (like)
mögen; (attack) sich stürzen auf +acc;
~ in vi hineingehen; ~ in for vt fus
(competition) teilnehmen an; ~ into vt
fus (enter) hineingehen in +acc;
(study) sich befassen mit; ~ off vi
(depart) weggehen; (lights) ausgehen;
(milk etc) sauer werden; (explode)
losgehen ♦ vt fus (dislike) nicht mehr
mögen; ~ on vi (continue)
weitergehen; (inf: complain) meckern;
(lights) angehen; to ~ on with sth mit
etw weitermachen; ~ out vi (fire,
light) ausgehen; (of house) hinaus-
gehen; ~ over vi (ship) kentern ♦ vt
fus (examine, check) durchgehen; ~
through vt fus (town etc) durchgehen,
durchfahren; ~ up vi (price) steigen;
~ without vt fus sich behelfen ohne;
(food) entbehren
goad [gəʊd] vt anstacheln
go-ahead ['gəʊəhed] adj zielstrebig;
(progressive) fortschrittlich ♦ n
grüne(s) Licht nt
goal [gəʊl] n Ziel nt; (SPORT) Tor nt;
~keeper n Torwart m; ~-post n
Torpfosten m
goat [gəʊt] n Ziege f
gobble ['gɒbl] vt (also: ~ down, ~ up)
hinunterschlingen
go-between ['gəʊbɪtwiːn] n Mittelsmann
m
goblet ['gɒblɪt] n Kelch(glas nt) m
god [gɒd] n Gott m; G~ n Gott m;
~child n Patenkind nt; ~daughter n
Patentochter f; ~dess n Göttin f;
~father n Pate m; ~-forsaken adj

gottverlassen; ~**mother** n Patin f;
~**send** n Geschenk nt des Himmels;
~**son** n Patensohn m
goggles ['gɒglz] npl Schutzbrille f
going ['gəʊɪŋ] n (HORSE-RACING) Bahn f
♦ adj (rate) gängig; (concern) gut-
gehend; **it's hard** ~ es ist schwierig
gold [gəʊld] n Gold nt ♦ adj golden;
~**en** adj golden, Gold-; ~**fish** n
Goldfisch m; ~ **mine** n Goldgrube f,
~-**plated** adj vergoldet; ~**smith** n
Goldschmied(in) m(f)
golf [gɒlf] n Golf nt; ~**ball** n Golfball m;
(on typewriter) Kugelkopf m; ~ **club** n
(society) Golfklub m; (stick) Golfschläger m; ~ **course** n Golfplatz m;
~**er** n Golfspieler(in) m(f)
gondola ['gɒndələ] n Gondel f
gone [gɒn] pp of **go**
gong [gɒŋ] n Gong m
good [gʊd] n (benefit) Wohl nt; (moral
excellence) Güte f ♦ adj gut; ~**s** npl
(merchandise etc) Waren pl, Güter pl;
a ~ deal (of) ziemlich viel; **a ~ many**
ziemlich viele; ~ **morning!** guten
Morgen!; ~ **afternoon!** guten Tag!; ~
evening! guten Abend!; ~ **night!** gute
Nacht!; ~**bye** excl auf Wiedersehen!;
G~ **Friday** n Karfreitag m; ~-**looking**
adj gutaussehend; ~-**natured** adj
gutmütig, (joke) harmlos; ~**ness** n
Güte f; (virtue) Tugend f; ~**s train**
(BRIT) n Güterzug m; ~**will** n (favour)
Wohlwollen nt; (COMM) Firmenansehen
nt
goose [guːs] (pl **geese**) n Gans f
gooseberry ['gʊzbərɪ] n Stachelbeere f
gooseflesh ['guːsfleʃ] n Gänsehaut f
goose pimples npl Gänsehaut f
gore [gɔː*] vt aufspießen ♦ n Blut nt
gorge [gɔːdʒ] n Schlucht f ♦ vt: **to ~
o.s.** (sich voll)fressen
gorgeous ['gɔːdʒəs] adj prächtig
gorilla [gə'rɪlə] n Gorilla m
gorse [gɔːs] n Stechginster m
gory ['gɔːrɪ] adj blutig
go-slow ['gəʊ'sləʊ] (BRIT) n Bummel-
streik m
gospel ['gɒspəl] n Evangelium nt
gossip ['gɒsɪp] n Klatsch m; (person)

Klatschbase f ♦ vi klatschen
got [gɒt] pt, pp of **get**
gotten ['gɒtən] (US) pp of **get**
gout [gaʊt] n Gicht f
govern ['gʌvən] vt regieren; verwalten
governess ['gʌvənɪs] n Gouvernante f
government ['gʌvnmənt] n Regierung f
governor ['gʌvənə*] n Gouverneur m
gown [gaʊn] n Gewand nt; (UNIV) Robe
f
G.P. n abbr = **general practitioner**
grab [græb] vt packen
grace [greɪs] n Anmut f; (blessing)
Gnade f; (prayer) Tischgebet nt ♦ vt
(adorn) zieren; (honour) auszeichnen; **5
days'** ~ 5 Tage Aufschub; ~**ful** adj an-
mutig
gracious ['greɪʃəs] adj gnädig; (kind)
freundlich
grade [greɪd] n Grad m; (slope) Gefälle
nt ♦ vt (classify) einstufen; ~ **crossing**
(US) n Bahnübergang m; ~ **school** (US)
n Grundschule f
gradient ['greɪdɪənt] n Steigung f;
Gefälle nt
gradual ['grædjʊəl] adj allmählich
graduate [n 'grædjʊɪt, vb 'grædjʊeɪt] n: **to
be a** ~ das Staatsexamen haben ♦ vi
das Staatsexamen machen
graduation [grædjʊ'eɪʃən] n Ab-
schlußfeier f
graffiti [grə'fiːtɪ] npl Graffiti pl
graft [grɑːft] n (hard work) Schufterei f;
(MED) Verpflanzung f ♦ vt propfen;
(fig) aufpropfen; (MED) verpflanzen
grain [greɪn] n Korn nt; (in wood) Mase-
rung f
gram [græm] n Gramm nt
grammar ['græmə*] n Grammatik f; ~
school (BRIT) n Gymnasium nt
grammatical [grə'mætɪkl] adj gram-
mat(ikal)isch
gramme [græm] n = **gram**
granary ['grænərɪ] n Kornspeicher m
grand [grænd] adj großartig; ~**children**
npl Enkel pl; ~**dad** n Opa m;
~**daughter** n Enkelin f; ~**eur** ['grændjə*]
n Erhabenheit f; ~**father** n Großvater
m; ~**iose** ['grændɪəʊs] adj (imposing)
großartig; (pompous) schwülstig; ~**ma**

n Oma *f*; **~mother** *n* Großmutter *f*;
~pa *n* = **~dad**; **~parents** *npl* Groß-
eltern *pl*; **~ piano** *n* Flügel *m*; **~son** *n*
Enkel *m*; **~stand** *n* Haupttribüne *f*
granite ['grænɪt] *n* Granit *m*
granny ['grænɪ] *n* Oma *f*
grant [grɑːnt] *vt* gewähren ♦ *n* Unterstützung *f*; (*UNIV*) Stipendium *nt*; **to
take sth for ~ed** etw als selbstverständlich (an)nehmen
granulated sugar ['grænjʊleɪtɪd-] *n*
Zuckerraffinade *f*
granule ['grænjuːl] *n* Körnchen *nt*
grape [greɪp] *n* (Wein)traube *f*
grapefruit ['greɪpfruːt] *n* Pampelmuse *f*,
Grapefruit *f*
graph [grɑːf] *n* Schaubild *nt*; **~ic**
['græfɪk] *adj* (*descriptive*) anschaulich;
(*drawing*) graphisch; **~ics** *npl* Grafik *f*
grapple ['græpl] *vi*: **to ~ with** kämpfen
mit
grasp [grɑːsp] *vt* ergreifen; (*understand*) begreifen ♦ *n* Griff *m*; (*of
subject*) Beherrschung *f*; **~ing** *adj*
habgierig
grass [grɑːs] *n* Gras *nt*; **~hopper** *n*
Heuschrecke *f*; **~land** *n* Weideland *nt*;
~-roots *adj* an der Basis; **~ snake** *n*
Ringelnatter *f*
grate [greɪt] *n* Kamin *m* ♦ *vi* (*sound*)
knirschen ♦ *vt* (*cheese etc*) reiben; **to ~
on the nerves** auf die Nerven gehen
grateful ['greɪtfʊl] *adj* dankbar
grater ['greɪtə*] *n* Reibe *f*
gratify ['grætɪfaɪ] *vt* befriedigen; **~ing**
['grætɪfaɪɪŋ] *adj* erfreulich
grating ['greɪtɪŋ] *n* (*iron bars*) Gitter *nt*
♦ *adj* (*noise*) knirschend
gratitude ['grætɪtjuːd] *n* Dankbarkeit *f*
gratuity [grə'tjuːɪtɪ] *n* Gratifikation *f*
grave [greɪv] *n* Grab *nt* ♦ *adj* (*serious*)
ernst
gravel ['grævəl] *n* Kies *m*
gravestone ['greɪvstəʊn] *n* Grabstein *m*
graveyard ['greɪvjɑːd] *n* Friedhof *m*
gravity ['grævɪtɪ] *n* Schwerkraft *f*;
(*seriousness*) Schwere *f*
gravy ['greɪvɪ] *n* (Braten)soße *f*
gray [greɪ] *adj* = **grey**
graze [greɪz] *vi* grasen ♦ *vt* (*touch*)

streifen; (*MED*) abschürfen ♦ *n* (*MED*)
Abschürfung *f*
grease [griːs] *n* (*fat*) Fett *nt*; (*lubricant*) Schmiere *f* ♦ *vt* (ab)schmieren;
~proof (*BRIT*) *adj* (*paper*) Butterbrot-
greasy ['griːsɪ] *adj* fettig
great [greɪt] *adj* groß; (*inf*: *good*)
prima; **~-grandfather** *n* Urgroßvater
m; **~-grandmother** *n* Urgroßmutter *f*;
~ly *adv* sehr; **~ness** *n* Größe *f*
Greece [griːs] *n* Griechenland *nt*
greed [griːd] *n* (*also*: **~iness**) Gier *f*;
(*meanness*) Geiz *m*; **~(iness) for** Gier
nach; **~y** *adj* gierig
Greek [griːk] *adj* griechisch ♦ *n* Grieche
m, Griechin *f*; (*LING*) Griechisch *nt*
green [griːn] *adj* grün ♦ *n* (*village* **~**)
Dorfwiese *f*; **~ belt** *n* Grüngürtel *m*; **~
card** *n* (*AUT*) grüne Versicherungskarte
f; **~ery** *n* Grün *nt*; **grüne(s) Laub** *nt*;
~gage *n* Reineclaude *f*; **~grocer** (*BRIT*)
n Obst- und Gemüsehändler *m*; **~house**
n Gewächshaus *nt*; **~ish** *adj* grünlich
Greenland ['griːnlənd] *n* Grönland *nt*
greet [griːt] *vt* grüßen; **~ing** *n* Gruß *m*;
~ing(s) card *n* Glückwunschkarte *f*
gregarious [grɪ'geərɪəs] *adj* gesellig
grenade [grɪ'neɪd] *n* Granate *f*
grew [gruː] *pt* of **grow**
grey [greɪ] *adj* grau; **~-haired** *adj*
grauhaarig; **~hound** *n* Windhund *m*;
~ish *adj* gräulich
grid [grɪd] *n* Gitter *nt*; (*ELEC*)
Leitungsnetz *nt*; (*on map*) Gitternetz *nt*
grief [griːf] *n* Gram *m*, Kummer *m*
grievance ['griːvəns] *n* Beschwerde *f*
grieve [griːv] *vi* sich grämen ♦ *vt* betrüben
grievous ['griːvəs] *adj*: **~ bodily harm**
(*JUR*) schwere Körperverletzung *f*
grill [grɪl] *n* Grill *m* ♦ *vt* (*BRIT*) grillen;
(*question*) in die Mangel nehmen
grille [grɪl] *n* (*on car etc*) (Kühler)gitter
nt
grim [grɪm] *adj* grimmig; (*situation*)
düster
grimace [grɪ'meɪs] *n* Grimasse *f* ♦ *vi*
Grimassen schneiden
grime [graɪm] *n* Schmutz *m*
grimy ['graɪmɪ] *adj* schmutzig

grin [grɪn] n Grinsen nt ♦ vi grinsen
grind [graɪnd] (pt, pp **ground**) vt mahlen; (US: meat) durch den Fleischwolf drehen; (sharpen) schleifen; (teeth) knirschen mit ♦ n (bore) Plackerei f
grip [grɪp] n Griff m; (suitcase) Handkoffer m ♦ vt packen; ~**ping** adj (exciting) spannend
grisly ['grɪzlɪ] adj gräßlich
gristle ['grɪsl] n Knorpel m
grit [grɪt] n Splitt m; (courage) Mut m ♦ vt (teeth) zusammenbeißen; (road) (mit Splitt be)streuen
groan [grəʊn] n Stöhnen nt ♦ vi stöhnen
grocer ['grəʊsə*] n Lebensmittelhändler m; ~**ies** npl Lebensmittel pl; ~'**s** (shop) n Lebensmittelgeschäft nt
groggy ['grɒgɪ] adj benommen
groin [grɔɪn] n Leistengegend f
groom [gruːm] n (also: bride~) Bräutigam m; (for horses) Pferdeknecht m ♦ vt (horse) striegeln; (well-)~**ed** gepflegt
groove [gruːv] n Rille f, Furche f
grope [grəʊp] vi tasten; ~ **for** vt fus suchen nach
gross [grəʊs] adj (coarse) dick, plump; (bad) grob, schwer; (COMM) brutto; ~**ly** adv höchst
grotesque [grəʊˈtesk] adj grotesk
grotto ['grɒtəʊ] n Grotte f
ground [graʊnd] pt, pp of **grind** ♦ n Boden m; (land) Grundbesitz m; (reason) Grund m; (US: also: ~ wire) Endleitung f ♦ vi (run ashore) stranden, auflaufen; ~**s** npl (dregs) Bodensatz m; (around house) (Garten)anlagen pl; **on the** ~ am Boden; **to the** ~ zu Boden; **to gain/lose** ~ Boden gewinnen/verlieren; ~ **cloth** (US) n = ~**sheet**; ~**ing** n (instruction) Anfangsunterricht m; ~**less** adj grundlos; ~**sheet** (BRIT) n Zeltboden m; ~ **staff** n Bodenpersonal nt; ~ **swell** n (of sea) Dünung f; (fig) Zunahme f; ~**work** n Grundlage f
group [gruːp] n Gruppe f ♦ vt (also: ~ together) gruppieren ♦ vi (also: ~ together) sich gruppieren

grouse [graʊs] n inv (bird) schottische(s) Moorhuhn nt ♦ vi (complain) meckern
grove [grəʊv] n Gehölz nt, Hain m
grovel ['grɒvl] vi (fig) kriechen
grow [grəʊ] (pt **grew**, pp **grown**) vi wachsen; (become) werden ♦ vt (raise) anbauen; ~ **up** vi aufwachsen; ~**er** n Züchter m; ~**ing** adj zunehmend
growl [graʊl] vi knurren
grown [grəʊn] pp of **grow**; ~-**up** n Erwachsene(r) mf
growth [grəʊθ] n Wachstum nt; (increase) Zunahme f; (of beard etc) Wuchs m
grub [grʌb] n Made f, Larve f; (inf: food) Futter nt; ~-**by** ['grʌbɪ] adj schmutzig
grudge [grʌdʒ] n Groll m ♦ vt: **to** ~ **sb sth** jdm etw misgönnen; **to bear sb a** ~ einen Groll gegen jdn hegen
gruelling ['grʊəlɪŋ] adj (climb, race) mörderisch
gruesome ['gruːsəm] adj grauenhaft
gruff [grʌf] adj barsch
grumble ['grʌmbl] vi murren
grumpy ['grʌmpɪ] adj verdrießlich
grunt [grʌnt] vi grunzen ♦ n Grunzen nt
G-string ['dʒiː-] n Minislip m
guarantee [gærənˈtiː] n Garantie f ♦ vt garantieren
guard [gɑːd] n (sentry) Wache f; (BRIT: RAIL) Zugbegleiter m ♦ vt bewachen; ~**ed** adj vorsichtig; ~**ian** n Vormund m; (keeper) Hüter m; ~'**s van** (BRIT) n (RAIL) Dienstwagen m
guerrilla [gəˈrɪlə] n Guerilla(kämpfer) m; ~ **warfare** n Guerillakrieg m
guess [ges] vt, vi (er)raten, schätzen ♦ n Vermutung f; ~**work** n Raterei f
guest [gest] n Gast m; ~-**house** n Pension f; ~ **room** n Gastzimmer nt
guffaw [gʌˈfɔː] vi schallend lachen
guidance ['gaɪdəns] n (control) Leitung f; (advice) Beratung f
guide [gaɪd] n Führer m; (also: girl ~) Pfadfinderin f ♦ vt führen; ~**book** n Reiseführer m; ~ **dog** n Blindenhund m; ~**lines** npl Richtlinien pl
guild [gɪld] n (HIST) Gilde f; ~**hall**

(BRIT) n Stadthalle f
guile [gaɪl] n Arglist f
guillotine [gɪlə'tiːn] n Guillotine f
guilt [gɪlt] n Schuld f; **~y** adj schuldig
guinea pig ['gɪnɪ-] n Meerschweinchen
nt; (fig) Versuchskaninchen nt
guise [gaɪz] n: **in the ~ of** in der Form
+gen
guitar [gɪ'tɑː*] n Gitarre f
gulf [gʌlf] n Golf m; (fig) Abgrund m
gull [gʌl] n Möwe f
gullet ['gʌlɪt] n Schlund m
gullible [gʌlɪbl] adj leichtgläubig
gully ['gʌlɪ] n (Wasser)rinne f
gulp [gʌlp] vt (also: ~ down) hinunter-
schlucken ♦ vi (gasp) schlucken
gum [gʌm] n (around teeth) Zahnfleisch
nt; (glue) Klebstoff m; (also: chewing-
~) Kaugummi m ♦ vt gummieren;
~boots (BRIT) npl Gummistiefel pl
gumption ['gʌmpʃən] (inf) n Mumm m
gun [gʌn] n Schußwaffe f; **~boat** n
Kanonenboot nt; **~fire** n Geschützfeuer
nt; **~man** (irreg) n bewaffnete(r) Verbrecher m; **~ner** n Kanonier m,
Artillerist m; **~point** n: **at ~point** mit
Waffengewalt; **~powder** n Schieß-
pulver nt; **~shot** n Schuß m; **~smith** n
Büchsenmacher(in) m(f)
gurgle ['gɜːgl] vi gluckern
guru ['guːruː] n Guru m
gush [gʌʃ] vi (rush out) hervorströmen;
(fig) schwärmen
gusset ['gʌsɪt] n Keil m, Zwickel m
gust [gʌst] n Windstoß m, Bö f
gusto ['gʌstəʊ] n Genuß m, Lust f
gut [gʌt] n (ANAT) Gedärme pl; (string)
Darm m; **~s** npl (fig) Schneid m
gutter ['gʌtə*] n Dachrinne f; (in street)
Gosse f
guttural ['gʌtərəl] adj guttural, Kehl-
guy [gaɪ] n (also: ~rope) Halteseil nt;
(man) Typ m, Kerl m
guzzle ['gʌzl] vt, vi (drink) saufen;
(eat) fressen
gym [dʒɪm] n (also: gymnasium)
Turnhalle f; (: gymnastics) Turnen nt;
~nast ['dʒɪmnæst] n Turner(in) m(f);
~nastics [dʒɪm'næstɪks] n Turnen nt,
Gymnastik f; **~ shoes** npl Turnschuhe

pl; **~ slip** (BRIT) n Schulträgerrock m
gynaecologist [gaɪnɪ'kɒlədʒɪst] (US
gynecologist) n Frauenarzt(ärztin) m(f)
gypsy ['dʒɪpsɪ] n = gipsy
gyrate [dʒaɪ'reɪt] vi kreisen

H

haberdashery [hæbə'dæʃərɪ] (BRIT) n
Kurzwaren pl
habit ['hæbɪt] n (An)gewohnheit f;
(monk's) Habit nt or m
habitable ['hæbɪtəbl] adj bewohnbar
habitat ['hæbɪtæt] n Lebensraum m
habitual [hə'bɪtjʊəl] adj gewohnheits-
mäßig; **~ly** adv gewöhnlich
hack [hæk] vt hacken ♦ n Hieb m;
(writer) Schreiberling m
hackneyed ['hæknɪd] adj abgedroschen
had [hæd] pt, pp of have
haddock ['hædək] (pl ~ or ~s) n
Schellfisch m
hadn't ['hædnt] = had not
haemorrhage ['hemərɪdʒ] (US hemorrhage) n Blutung f
haemorrhoids ['hemərɔɪdz] (US hemorrhoids) npl Hämorrhoiden pl
haggard ['hægəd] adj abgekämpft
haggle ['hægl] vi feilschen
Hague [heɪg] n: **The ~** Den Haag nt
hail [heɪl] n Hagel m ♦ vt umjubeln ♦ vi
hageln; **~stone** n Hagelkorn nt
hair [hɛə*] n Haar nt, Haare pl; (one ~)
Haar nt; **~brush** n Haarbürste f; **~cut**
n Haarschnitt m; **to get a ~cut** sich dat
die Haare schneiden lassen; **~do** n
Frisur f; **~dresser** n Friseur m,
Friseuse f; **~dresser's** n Friseursalon
m; **~ dryer** n Trockenhaube f; (hand-
held) Fön m; **~grip** n Klemme f; **~net**
n Haarnetz nt; **~pin** n Haarnadel f;
~pin bend (US **~pin curve**) n Haar-
nadelkurve f; **~raising** adj haarsträu-
bend; **~ remover** n Enthaarungsmittel
nt; **~ spray** n Haarspray nt; **~style** n
Frisur f; **~y** adj haarig
hake [heɪk] n Seehecht m
half [hɑːf] (pl **halves**) n Hälfte f ♦ adj
halb ♦ adv halb, zur Hälfte; **~-an-hour**

eine halbe Stunde; **two and a** ~ zweieinhalb; **to cut sth in** ~ etw halbieren; **~-back** n Läufer m; **~-breed** n Mischling m; **~-caste** n Mischling m; **~-hearted** adj lustlos; **~-hour** n halbe Stunde f; **~-penny** ['heɪpnɪ] (BRIT) n halbe(r) Penny m; **~-price:** (at) **~-price** zum halben Preis; **~-term** (BRIT) n (SCH) Ferien pl in der Mitte des Trimesters; **~-time** n Halbzeit f; **~-way** adv halbwegs, auf halbem Wege

halibut ['hælɪbət] n Heilbutt m

hall [hɔːl] n Saal m; (entrance ~) Hausflur m; (building) Halle f; ~ **of residence** (BRIT) n Studentenwohnheim nt

hallmark ['hɔːlmaːk] n Stempel m

hallo [hʌ'ləʊ] excl = hello

Hallowe'en ['hæləʊ'iːn] n Tag m vor Allerheiligen

hallucination [həluːsɪ'neɪʃən] n Halluzination f

hallway ['hɔːlweɪ] n Korridor m

halo ['heɪləʊ] n Heiligenschein m

halt [hɔːlt] n Halt m ♦ vt, vi anhalten

halve [haːv] vt halbieren

halves [haːvz] pl of **half**

ham [hæm] n Schinken m

hamburger ['hæmbɜːgə*] n Hamburger m

hamlet ['hæmlɪt] n Weiler m

hammer ['hæmə*] n Hammer m ♦ vt, vi hämmern

hammock ['hæmək] n Hängematte f

hamper ['hæmpə*] vt (be)hindern ♦ n Picknickkorb m

hamster ['hæmstə*] n Hamster m

hand [hænd] n Hand f; (of clock) (Uhr)zeiger m; (worker) Arbeiter m ♦ vt (pass) geben; **to give sb a** ~ jdm helfen; **at** ~ nahe; **to** ~ zur Hand; **in** ~ (under control) unter Kontrolle; (being done) im Gange; (extra) übrig; **on** ~ zur Verfügung; **on the one** ~ ..., **on the other** ~ ... einerseits ..., andererseits ...; ~ **in** vt abgeben; (forms) einreichen; ~ **out** vt austeilen; ~ **over** vt (deliver) übergeben; (surrender) abgeben; (: prisoner) ausliefern; **~bag** n Handtasche f; **~book** n Handbuch nt;

~brake n Handbremse f; **~cuffs** npl Handschellen pl; **~ful** n Handvoll f; (inf: person) Plage f

handicap ['hændɪkæp] n Handikap nt ♦ vt benachteiligen; **mentally/physically ~ped** geistig/körperlich behindert

handicraft ['hændɪkraːft] n Kunsthandwerk nt

handiwork ['hændɪwɜːk] n Arbeit f; (fig) Werk nt

handkerchief ['hæŋkətʃɪf] n Taschentuch nt

handle ['hændl] n (of door etc) Klinke f; (of cup etc) Henkel m; (for winding) Kurbel f ♦ vt (touch) anfassen; (deal with: things) sich befassen mit; (: people) umgehen mit; **~bar(s)** n(pl) Lenkstange f

hand: ~ **luggage** n Handgepäck nt; **~made** adj handgefertigt; **~out** n (distribution) Verteilung f; (charity) Geldzuwendung f; (leaflet) Flugblatt nt; **~rail** n Geländer nt; (on ship) Reling f; **~shake** n Händedruck f

handsome ['hænsəm] adj gutaussehend

handwriting ['hændraɪtɪŋ] n Handschrift f

handy ['hændɪ] adj praktisch; (shops) leicht erreichbar; **~man** ['hændɪmən] (irreg) n Bastler m

hang [hæŋ] (pt, pp hung) vt aufhängen; (criminal: pt, pp hanged) hängen ♦ vi hängen ♦ n: **to get the** ~ **of sth** (inf) den richtigen Dreh bei etw herauskriegen; ~ **about** vi sich herumtreiben; ~ **on** vi (wait) warten; ~ **up** vi (TEL) auflegen

hangar ['hæŋə*] n Hangar m

hanger ['hæŋə*] n Kleiderbügel m

hanger-on ['hæŋər'ɒn] n Anhänger(in) m(f)

hang-gliding ['hæŋglaɪdɪŋ] n Drachenfliegen nt

hangover ['hæŋəʊvə*] n Kater m

hang-up ['hæŋʌp] n Komplex m

hanker ['hæŋkə*] vi: **to** ~ **for** or **after** sich sehnen nach

hankie ['hæŋkɪ] n abbr = **handkerchief**

hanky ['hæŋkɪ] n abbr = **handkerchief**

haphazard ['hæp'hæzəd] adj zufällig

happen ['hæpən] *vi* sich ereignen, passieren; **as it ~s I'm going there today** zufällig(erweise) gehe ich heute (dort)hin; **~ing** *n* Ereignis *nt*

happily ['hæpɪlɪ] *adv* glücklich; (*fortunately*) glücklicherweise

happiness ['hæpɪnɪs] *n* Glück *nt*

happy ['hæpɪ] *adj* glücklich; **~ birthday!** alles Gute zum Geburtstag!; **~-go-lucky** *adj* sorglos

harass ['hærəs] *vt* plagen; **~ment** *n* Belästigung *f*

harbour ['hɑːbə*] (*US* **harbor**) *n* Hafen *m* ♦ *vt* (*hope etc*) hegen; (*criminal etc*) Unterschlupf gewähren

hard [hɑːd] *adj* (*firm*) hart; (*difficult*) schwer; (*harsh*) hart(herzig) ♦ *adv* (*work*) hart; (*try*) sehr; (*push, hit*) fest; **no ~ feelings!** ich nehme es dir nicht übel; **~ of hearing** schwerhörig; **to be ~ done by** übel dran sein: **~back** *n* kartonierte Ausgabe *f*; **~ cash** *n* Bargeld *nt*; **~ disk** *n* (*COMPUT*) Festplatte *f*; **~en** *vt* erhärten; (*fig*) verhärten ♦ *vi* hart werden; (*fig*) sich verhärten; **~-headed** *adj* nüchtern; **~ labour** *n* Zwangsarbeit *f*

hardly ['hɑːdlɪ] *adv* kaum

hard: **~ness** *n* Härte *f*; (*difficulty*) Schwierigkeit *f*; **~ship** *n* Not *f*; **~-up** *adj* knapp bei Kasse; **~ware** *n* Eisenwaren *pl*; (*COMPUT*) Hardware *f*; **~ware shop** *n* Eisenwarenhandlung *f*; **~-wearing** *adj* strapazierfähig; **~working** *adj* fleißig

hardy ['hɑːdɪ] *adj* widerstandsfähig

hare [heə*] *n* Hase *m*; **~-brained** *adj* schwachsinnig

harm [hɑːm] *n* Schaden *m* ♦ *vt* schaden +*dat*; **out of ~'s way** in Sicherheit; **~ful** *adj* schädlich; **~less** *adj* harmlos

harmonica [hɑːˈmɒnɪkə] *n* Mundharmonika *f*

harmonious [hɑːˈməʊnɪəs] *adj* harmonisch

harmonize ['hɑːmənaɪz] *vt* abstimmen ♦ *vi* harmonieren

harmony ['hɑːmənɪ] *n* Harmonie *f*

harness ['hɑːnɪs] *n* Geschirr *nt* ♦ *vt* (*horse*) anschirren; (*fig*) nutzbar ma-

chen

harp [hɑːp] *n* Harfe *f* ♦ *vi*: **to ~ on about sth** auf etw *dat* herumreiten

harpoon [hɑːˈpuːn] *n* Harpune *f*

harrowing ['hærəʊɪŋ] *adj* nervenaufreibend

harsh [hɑːʃ] *adj* (*rough*) rauh; (*severe*) streng; **~ness** *n* Härte *f*

harvest ['hɑːvɪst] *n* Ernte *f* ♦ *vt, vi* ernten; **~er** ['hɑːvɪstə*] *n* Mähbinder *m*

has [hæz] *vb see* **have**

hash [hæʃ] *vt* kleinhacken ♦ *n* (*mess*) Kuddelmuddel *m*; (*meat*) Haschee *nt*

hashish ['hæʃɪʃ] *n* Haschisch *nt*

hasn't ['hæznt] = **has not**

hassle ['hæsl] (*inf*) *n* Theater *nt*

haste [heɪst] *n* Eile *f*; **~n** ['heɪsn] *vt* beschleunigen ♦ *vi* eilen

hasty [heɪstɪ] *adj* hastig; (*rash*) vorschnell

hat [hæt] *n* Hut *m*

hatch [hætʃ] *n* (*NAUT: also:* **~way**) Luke *f*; (*in house*) Durchreiche *f* ♦ *vi* (*young*) ausschlüpfen ♦ *vt* (*brood*) ausbrüten; (*plot*) ausbrüten

hatchback ['hætʃbæk] *n* (*AUT*) (Auto *nt* mit) Heckklappe *f*

hatchet ['hætʃɪt] *n* Beil *nt*

hate [heɪt] *vt* hassen ♦ *n* Haß *m*; **~ful** *adj* verhaßt

hatred ['heɪtrɪd] *n* Haß *m*

haughty ['hɔːtɪ] *adj* hochnäsig, überheblich

haul [hɔːl] *vt* ziehen ♦ *n* (*catch*) Fang *m*; **~age** *n* Spedition *f*; **~ier** (*US* **~er**) *n* Spediteur *m*

haunch [hɔːntʃ] *n* Lende *f*

haunt [hɔːnt] *vt* (*ghost*) spuken in +*dat*; (*memory*) verfolgen; (*pub*) häufig besuchen ♦ *n* Lieblingsplatz *m*; **the castle is ~ed** in dem Schloß spukt es

---

KEYWORD

have [hæv] (*pt, pp* **had**) *aux vb* **1** haben; (*esp with vbs of motion*) sein; **to have arrived/slept** angekommen sein/geschlafen haben; **to have been** gewesen sein; **having eaten** *or* **when he had eaten, he left** nachdem er gegessen hatte, ging er

2 (*in tag questions*): **you've done it, haven't you?** du hast es doch gemacht, oder nicht?
3 (*in short answers and questions*): **you've made a mistake - so I have/no I haven't** du hast einen Fehler gemacht - ja, stimmt/nein; **we haven't paid - yes we have!** wir haben nicht bezahlt doch; **I've been there before, have you?** ich war schon einmal da, du auch?

♦ *modal aux vb* (*be obliged*): **to have (got) to do sth** etw tun müssen; **you haven't to tell her** du darfst es ihr nicht erzählen

♦ *vt* 1 (*possess*) haben; **he has (got) blue eyes** er hat blaue Augen; **I have (got) an idea** ich habe eine Idee
2 (*referring to meals etc*): **to have breakfast/a cigarette** frühstücken/eine Zigarette rauchen
3 (*receive, obtain etc*) haben; **may I have your address?** kann ich Ihre Adresse haben?; **to have a baby** ein Kind bekommen
4 (*maintain, allow*): **he will have it that he is right** er besteht darauf, daß er recht hat; **I won't have it** das lasse ich mir nicht bieten
5: **to have sth done** etw machen lassen; **to have sb do sth** jdn etw machen lassen; **he soon had them all laughing** er brachte sie alle zum Lachen
6 (*experience, suffer*): **she had her bag stolen** man hat ihr die Tasche gestohlen; **he had his arm broken** er hat sich den Arm gebrochen
7 (+*noun: take, hold etc*): **to have a walk/rest** spazierengehen/sich ausruhen; **to have a meeting/party** eine Besprechung/Party haben
have out *vt vt*: **to have it out with sb** (*settle a problem etc*) etw mit jdm bereden

haven ['heɪvn] *n* Zufluchtsort *m*
haven't ['hævnt] = **have not**
haversack ['hævəsæk] *n* Rucksack *m*
havoc ['hævək] *n* Verwüstung *f*
Hawaii [hə'waɪiː] *n* Hawaii *nt*
hawk [hɔːk] *n* Habicht *m*

hay [heɪ] *n* Heu *nt*; **~ fever** *n* Heuschnupfen *m*; **~stack** *n* Heuschober *m*
haywire ['heɪwaɪə*] (*inf*) *adj* durcheinander
hazard ['hæzəd] *n* Risiko *nt* ♦ *vt* aufs Spiel setzen; **~ous** *adj* gefährlich; **~ (warning) lights** *npl* (*AUT*) Warnblinklicht *nt*
haze [heɪz] *n* Dunst *m*
hazelnut ['heɪzlnʌt] *n* Haselnuß *f*
hazy ['heɪzɪ] *adj* (*misty*) dunstig; (*vague*) verschwommen
he [hiː] *pron* er
head [hed] *n* Kopf *m*; (*leader*) Leiter *m* ♦ *vt* (an)führen, leiten; (*ball*) köpfen; **~s (or tails)** Kopf (oder Zahl); **~ first** mit dem Kopf nach unten; **~ over heels** kopfüber; **~ for** *vt fus* zugehen auf +*acc*; **~ache** *n* Kopfschmerzen *pl*; **~dress** *n* Kopfschmuck *m*; **~ing** *n* Überschrift *f*; **~lamp** (*BRIT*) *n* Scheinwerfer *m*; **~land** *n* Landspitze *f*; **~light** *n* Scheinwerfer *m*; **~line** *n* Schlagzeile *f*; **~long** *adv* kopfüber; **~master** *n* (*of primary school*) Rektor *m*; (*of secondary school*) Direktor *m*; **~mistress** *n* Rektorin *f*; Direktorin *f*; **~ office** *n* Zentrale *f*; **~-on** *adj* Frontal-; **~phones** *npl* Kopfhörer *pl*; **~quarters** *npl* Zentrale *f*; (*MIL*) Hauptquartier *nt*; **~rest** *n* Kopfstütze *f*; **~room** *n* (*of bridges etc*) lichte Höhe *f*; **~scarf** *n* Kopftuch *nt*; **~strong** *adj* eigenwillig; **~ waiter** *n* Oberkellner *m*; **~way** *n* Fortschritte *pl*; **~wind** *n* Gegenwind *m*; **~y** *adj* berauschend
heal [hiːl] *vt* heilen ♦ *vi* verheilen
health [helθ] *n* Gesundheit *f*; **your ~!** prost!; **~ food** *n* Reformkost *f*; **the H~ Service** (*BRIT*) *n* das Gesundheitswesen; **~y** *adj* gesund
heap [hiːp] *n* Haufen *m* ♦ *vt* häufen
hear [hɪə*] (*pt, pp* **heard**) *vt* hören; (*listen to*) anhören ♦ *vi* hören; **heard** [hɜːd] *pt, pp of* **hear**; **~ing** *n* Gehör *nt*; (*JUR*) Verhandlung *f*; **~ing aid** *n* Hörapparat *m*; **~say** *n* Hörensagen *nt*
hearse [hɜːs] *n* Leichenwagen *m*
heart [hɑːt] *n* Herz *nt*; **~s** *npl* (*CARDS*) Herz *nt*; **by ~** auswendig; **~ attack** *n*

Herzanfall *m*; ~**beat** *n* Herzschlag *m*;
~**breaking** *adj* herzzerbrechend;
~**broken** *adj* untröstlich; ~**burn** *n* Sodbrennen *nt*; ~**failure** *n* Herzschlag *m*;
~**felt** *adj* aufrichtig
hearth [hɑ:θ] *n* Herd *m*
heartily ['hɑ:tɪlɪ] *adv* herzlich; (*eat*)
herzhaft
heartless ['hɑ:tlɪs] *adj* herzlos
hearty ['hɑ:tɪ] *adj* kräftig; (*friendly*)
freundlich
heat [hi:t] *n* Hitze *f*; (*of food, water etc*)
Wärme *f*; (*SPORT: also: qualifying* ~)
Ausscheidungsrunde *f* ♦ *vt* heizen;
(*substance*) heiß machen,
erhitzen; ~ **up** *vi* warm werden ♦ *vt*
aufwärmen; ~**ed** *adj* erhitzt; (*fig*)
hitzig; ~**er** *n* (Heiz)ofen *m*
heath [hi:θ] (*BRIT*) *n* Heide *f*
heathen ['hi:ðən] *n* Heide *m*/Heidin *f* ♦
adj heidnisch, Heiden-
heather ['heðə*] *n* Heidekraut *nt*
heating ['hi:tɪŋ] *n* Heizung *f*
heatstroke ['hi:tstrəʊk] *n* Hitzschlag *m*
heat wave *n* Hitzewelle *f*
heave [hi:v] *vt* hochheben; (*sigh*) ausstoßen ♦ *vi* wogen; (*breast*) sich heben
♦ *n* Heben *nt*
heaven ['hevn] *n* Himmel *m*; ~**ly** *adj*
himmlisch
heavily ['hevɪlɪ] *adv* schwer
heavy ['hevɪ] *adj* schwer; ~ **goods**
vehicle *n* Lastkraftwagen *m*; ~**weight**
n (*SPORT*) Schwergewicht *nt*
Hebrew ['hi:bru:] *adj* hebräisch ♦ *n*
(*LING*) Hebräisch *nt*
Hebrides ['hebrɪdi:z] *npl* Hebriden *pl*
heckle ['hekl] *vt* unterbrechen
hectic ['hektɪk] *adj* hektisch
he'd [hi:d] = **he had; he would**
hedge [hedʒ] *n* Hecke *f* ♦ *vt* einzäunen ♦
vi (*fig*) ausweichen; **to ~ one's bets**
sich absichern
hedgehog ['hedʒhɒg] *n* Igel *m*
heed [hi:d] *vt* (*also: take* ~ *of*)
beachten ♦ *n* Beachtung *f*; ~**less** *adj*
achtlos
heel [hi:l] *n* Ferse *f*; (*of shoe*) Absatz *m*
♦ *vt* (*shoes*) mit Absätzen versehen
hefty ['heftɪ] *adj* (*person*) stämmig;

(*portion*) reichlich
heifer ['hefə*] *n* Färse *f*
height [haɪt] *n* (*of person*) Größe *f*; (*of
object*) Höhe *f*; ~**en** *vt* erhöhen
heir [ɛə*] *n* Erbe *m*; ~**ess** ['ɛərɪs] *n*
Erbin *f*; ~**loom** *n* Erbstück *nt*
held [held] *pt, pp of* **hold**
helicopter ['helɪkɒptə*] *n* Hubschrauber
m
heliport ['helɪpɔ:t] *n* Hubschrauber-
landeplatz *m*
hell [hel] *n* Hölle *f* ♦ *excl* verdammt!
he'll [hi:l] = **he will; he shall**
hellish ['helɪʃ] *adj* höllisch, verteufelt
hello [hʌ'ləʊ] *excl* hallo
helm [helm] *n* Ruder *nt*, Steuer *nt*
helmet ['helmɪt] *n* Helm *m*
helmsman ['helmzmən] (*irreg*) *n*
Steuermann *m*
help [help] *n* Hilfe *f* ♦ *vt* helfen +*dat*; **I
can't ~ it** ich kann nichts dafür; ~
yourself bedienen Sie sich; ~**er** *n*
Helfer *m*; ~**ful** *adj* hilfreich; ~**ing** *n*
Portion *f*; ~**less** *adj* hilflos
hem [hem] *n* Saum *m* ♦ *vt* säumen; ~
in *vt* einengen
he-man ['hi:mæn] (*irreg; inf*) *n* Macho
m
hemorrhage ['hemərɪdʒ] (*US*) *n* =
haemorrhage
hemorrhoids ['hemərɔɪdz] (*US*) *npl* =
haemorrhoids
hen [hen] *n* Henne *f*
hence [hens] *adv* von jetzt an;
(*therefore*) daher; ~**forth** *adv* von nun
an; (*from then on*) von da an
henchman ['hentʃmən] (*irreg*) *n*
Gefolgsmann *m*
henpecked ['henpekt] *adj*: **to be ~**
unter dem Pantoffel stehen; ~ **husband**
Pantoffelheld *m*
her [hɜ:*] *pron* (*acc*) sie; (*dat*) ihr ♦ *adj*
ihr; *see also* **me; my**
herald ['herəld] *n* (Vor)bote *m* ♦ *vt* verkünden
heraldry ['herəldrɪ] *n* Wappenkunde *f*
herb [hɜ:b] *n* Kraut *nt*
herd [hɜ:d] *n* Herde *f*
here [hɪə*] *adv* hier; (*to this place*)
hierher; ~**after** *adv* hernach, künftig ♦

n Jenseits *nt*; ~**by** *adv* hiermit

hereditary [hɪ'redɪtərɪ] *adj* erblich

heredity [hɪ'redɪtɪ] *n* Vererbung *f*

heresy ['herəsɪ] *n* Ketzerei *f*

heretic ['herətɪk] *n* Ketzer *m*

heritage ['herɪtɪdʒ] *n* Erbe *nt*

hermetically [hɜ:'metɪkəlɪ] *adv*: ~ **sealed** hermetisch verschlossen

hermit ['hɜ:mɪt] *n* Einsiedler *m*

hernia ['hɜ:nɪə] *n* Bruch *m*

hero ['hɪərəʊ] (*pl* ~**es**) *n* Held *m*; ~**ic** [hɪ'rəʊɪk] *adj* heroisch

heroin ['herəʊɪn] *n* Heroin *nt*

heroine ['herəʊɪn] *n* Heldin *f*

heroism ['herəʊɪzəm] *n* Heldentum *nt*

heron ['herən] *n* Reiher *m*

herring ['herɪŋ] *n* Hering *m*

hers [hɜːz] *pron* ihre(r, s); *see also* **mine**

herself [hɜː'self] *pron* sich (selbst); (*emphatic*) selbst; *see also* **oneself**

he's [hiːz] = **he is**; **he has**

hesitant ['hezɪtənt] *adj* zögernd

hesitate ['hezɪteɪt] *vi* zögern

hesitation [hezɪ'teɪʃən] *n* Zögern *nt*

hew [hjuː] (*pt* **hewed**, *pp* **hewn**) *vt* hauen, hacken

hexagon ['heksəgən] *n* Sechseck *nt*; ~**al** [hek'sægənəl] *adj* sechseckig

heyday ['heɪdeɪ] *n* Blüte *f*, Höhepunkt *m*

HGV *n abbr* = **heavy goods vehicle**

hi [haɪ] *excl* he, hallo

hiatus [haɪ'eɪtəs] *n* (*gap*) Lücke *f*

hibernate ['haɪbəneɪt] *vi* Winterschlaf *m* halten

hibernation [haɪbə'neɪʃən] *n* Winterschlaf *m*

hiccough ['hɪkʌp] *vi* den Schluckauf haben; ~**s** *npl* Schluckauf *m*

hiccup ['hɪkʌp] = **hiccough**

hid [hɪd] *pt of* **hide**; **hidden** ['hɪdn] *pp of* **hide**

hide [haɪd] (*pt* **hid**, *pp* **hidden**) *n* (*skin*) Haut *f*, Fell *nt* ♦ *vt* verstecken ♦ *vi* sich verstecken; ~**-and-seek** *n* Versteckspiel *nt*; ~**away** *n* Versteck *nt*

hideous ['hɪdɪəs] *adj* abscheulich

hiding ['haɪdɪŋ] *n* (*beating*) Tracht *f* Prügel; **to be in** ~ (*concealed*) sich versteckt halten; ~ **place** *n* Versteck *nt*

hi-fi ['haɪfaɪ] *n* Hi-Fi *nt* ♦ *adj* Hi-Fi-

high [haɪ] *adj* hoch; (*wind*) stark ♦ *adv* hoch; ~**boy** (*US*) *n* (*tallboy*) hochbeinige Kommode *f*; ~**brow** *adj* (*betont*) intellektuell; ~**chair** *n* Hochstuhl *m*; ~**er education** *n* Hochschulbildung *f*; ~**-handed** *adj* eigenmächtig; ~**-heeled** *adj* hochhackig; ~**jack** *vt* = **hijack**; ~ **jump** *n* (*SPORT*) Hochsprung *m*; **the H~lands** *npl* das schottische Hochland; ~**light** *n* (*fig*) Höhepunkt *m* ♦ *vt* hervorheben; ~**ly** *adv* höchst; ~**ly strung** *adj* überempfindlich; ~**ness** *n* Höhe *f*; **Her H~ness** Ihre Hoheit *f*; ~**-pitched** *adj* hoch; ~**-rise block** *n* Hochhaus *nt*; ~ **school** (*US*) *n* Oberschule *f*; ~ **season** (*BRIT*) *n* Hochsaison *f*; ~ **street** (*BRIT*) *n* Hauptstraße *f*

highway ['haɪweɪ] *n* Landstraße *f*; **H~ Code** (*BRIT*) *n* Straßenverkehrsordnung *f*

hijack ['haɪdʒæk] *vt* entführen; ~**er** *n* Entführer(in) *m(f)*

hike [haɪk] *vi* wandern ♦ *n* Wanderung *f*; ~**r** *n* Wanderer *m*

hilarious [hɪ'lɛərɪəs] *adj* lustig

hill [hɪl] *n* Berg *m*; ~**side** *n* (Berg)hang *m*; ~**y** *adj* hügelig

hilt [hɪlt] *n* Heft *nt*; (**up**) **to the** ~ ganz und gar

him [hɪm] *pron* (*acc*) ihn; (*dat*) ihm; *see also* **me**

himself [hɪm'self] *pron* sich (selbst); (*emphatic*) selbst; *see also* **oneself**

hind [haɪnd] *adj* hinter, Hinter-

hinder ['hɪndə*] *vt* (*stop*) hindern; (*delay*) behindern

hindrance ['hɪndrəns] *n* (*delay*) Behinderung *f*; (*obstacle*) Hindernis *nt*

hindsight ['haɪndsaɪt] *n*: **with** ~ im nachhinein

Hindu ['hɪnduː] *n* Hindu *m*

hinge [hɪndʒ] *n* Scharnier *nt*; (*on door*) Türangel *f* ♦ *vi* (*fig*): **to** ~ **on** abhängen von

hint [hɪnt] *n* Tip *m*; (*trace*) Anflug *m* ♦ *vt*: **to** ~ **that** andeuten, daß ♦ *vi*: **to** ~ **at** andeuten

hip [hɪp] *n* Hüfte *f*

hippopotami [hɪpə'pɒtəmaɪ] *npl of* **hippopotamus**

hippopotamus [hɪpə'pɒtəməs] (*pl* ~es *or* **hippopotami**) *n* Nilpferd *nt*

hire ['haɪə*] *vt* (*worker*) anstellen; (*BRIT: car*) mieten ♦ *n* Miete *f*; **for ~** (*taxi*) frei; ~ **purchase** (*BRIT*) *n* Teilzahlungskauf *m*

his [hɪz] *adj* sein ♦ *pron* seine(r, s); *see also* **my**; **mine**

hiss [hɪs] *vi* zischen ♦ *n* Zischen *nt*

historian [hɪs'tɔːrɪən] *n* Historiker *m*

historic [hɪs'tɒrɪk] *adj* historisch

historical [hɪs'tɒrɪkəl] *adj* historisch, geschichtlich

history ['hɪstərɪ] *n* Geschichte *f*

hit [hɪt] (*pt, pp* **hit**) *vt* schlagen; (*injure*) treffen ♦ *n* (*blow*) Schlag *m*; (*success*) Erfolg *m*; (*MUS*) Hit *m*; **to ~ it off with sb** prima mit jdm auskommen; ~-**and-run driver** *n* jemand, der Fahrerflucht begeht

hitch [hɪtʃ] *vt* festbinden; (*also*: ~ *up*) hochziehen ♦ *n* (*difficulty*) Haken *m*; **to ~ a lift** trampen

hitchhike ['hɪtʃhaɪk] *vi* trampen; ~**r** *n* Tramper *m*

hitherto ['hɪðə'tuː] *adv* bislang

hive [haɪv] *n* Bienenkorb *m*; ~ **off** *vt* ausgliedern

HMS *abbr* = **His (Her) Majesty's Ship**

hoard [hɔːd] *n* Schatz *m* ♦ *vt* horten, hamstern

hoarding ['hɔːdɪŋ] *n* Bretterzaun *m*; (*BRIT: for advertising*) Reklamewand *f*

hoarfrost ['hɔː'frɒst] *n* (Rauh)reif *m*

hoarse [hɔːs] *adj* heiser, rauh

hoax [həʊks] *n* Streich *m*

hob [hɒb] *n* Kochmulde *f*

hobble ['hɒbl] *vi* humpeln

hobby ['hɒbɪ] *n* Hobby *nt*; ~-**horse** *n* (*fig*) Steckenpferd *nt*

hobo ['həʊbəʊ] (*US*) *n* Tippelbruder *m*

hock [hɒk] *n* (*wine*) weiße(r) Rheinwein *m*

hockey ['hɒkɪ] *n* Hockey *nt*

hoe [həʊ] *n* Hacke *f* ♦ *vt* hacken

hog [hɒg] *n* Schlachtschwein *nt* ♦ *vt* mit Beschlag belegen; **to go the whole ~** aufs Ganze gehen

hoist [hɔɪst] *n* Winde *f* ♦ *vt* hochziehen

hold [həʊld] (*pt, pp* **held**) *vt* halten; (*contain*) enthalten; (*be able to contain*) fassen; (*breath*) anhalten; (*meeting*) abhalten ♦ *vi* (*withstand pressure*) aushalten ♦ *n* (*grasp*) Halt *m*; (*NAUT*) Schiffsraum *m*; ~ **the line!** (*TEL*) bleiben Sie am Apparat!; **to ~ one's own** sich behaupten; ~ **back** *vt* zurückhalten; ~ **down** *vt* niederhalten; (*job*) behalten; ~ **off** *vt* (*enemy*) abwehren; ~ **on** *vi* sich festhalten; (*resist*) durchhalten; (*wait*) warten; ~ **on to** *vt fus* festhalten an +*dat*; (*keep*) behalten; ~ **out** *vt* hinhalten ♦ *vi* aushalten; ~ **up** *vt* (*delay*) aufhalten; (*rob*) überfallen; ~**all** (*BRIT*) *n* Reisetasche *f*; ~**er** *n* Behälter *m*; ~**ing** *n* (*share*) (Aktien)anteil *m*; ~**up** *n* (*BRIT: in traffic*) Stockung *f*; (*robbery*) Überfall *m*; (*delay*) Verzögerung *f*

hole [həʊl] *n* Loch *nt* ♦ *vt* durchlöchern

holiday ['hɒlədɪ] *n* (*day*) Feiertag *m*; **freie(r) Tag** *m*; (*vacation*) Urlaub *m*; (*SCH*) Ferien *pl*; ~ **camp** *n* Ferienlager *nt*; ~-**maker** (*BRIT*) *n* Urlauber(in) *m(f)*; ~ **resort** *n* Ferienort *m*

holiness ['həʊlɪnɪs] *n* Heiligkeit *f*

Holland ['hɒlənd] *n* Holland *nt*

hollow ['hɒləʊ] *adj* hohl; (*fig*) leer ♦ *n* Vertiefung *f*; ~ **out** *vt* aushöhlen

holly ['hɒlɪ] *n* Stechpalme *f*

holocaust ['hɒləkɔːst] *n* Inferno *nt*

holster ['həʊlstə*] *n* Pistolenhalfter *m*

holy ['həʊlɪ] *adj* heilig; **the H~ Ghost** *or* **Spirit** *n* der Heilige Geist

homage ['hɒmɪdʒ] *n* Huldigung *f*; **to pay ~ to** huldigen +*dat*

home [həʊm] *n* Zuhause *nt*; (*institution*) Heim *nt*, Anstalt *f* ♦ *adj* einheimisch; (*POL*) inner ♦ *adv* heim, nach Hause; **at ~** zu Hause; ~ **address** *n* Heimatadresse *f*; ~**coming** *n* Heimkehr *f*; ~ **computer** *n* Heimcomputer *m*; ~**land** Heimat(land *nt*) *f*; ~**less** *adj* obdachlos; ~**ly** *adj* häuslich; (*US: ugly*) unscheinbar; ~-**made** *adj* selbstgemacht; **H~ Office** (*BRIT*) *n* Innenministerium *nt*; ~ **rule** *n* Selbstverwaltung *f*; **H~ Secretary** (*BRIT*) *n*

Innenminister(in) *m(f)*; ~**sick** *adj*: **to
be** ~**sick** Heimweh haben; ~ **town** *n*
Heimatstadt *f*; ~**ward** *adj* (*journey*)
Heim-; ~**work** *n* Hausaufgaben *pl*
homicide ['hɒmɪsaɪd] (*US*) *n* Totschlag
m
homoeopathy [həʊmɪ'ɒpəθɪ] *n*
Homöopathie *f*
homogeneous [hɒmə'dʒiːnɪəs] *adj*
homogen
homosexual ['hɒməʊ'seksjʊəl] *adj*
homosexuell ♦ *n* Homosexuelle(r) *mf*
honest ['ɒnɪst] *adj* ehrlich; ~**ly** *adv* ehrlich; ~**y** *n* Ehrlichkeit *f*
honey ['hʌnɪ] *n* Honig *m*; ~**comb** *n*
Honigwabe *f*; ~**moon** *n* Flitterwochen
pl, Hochzeitsreise *f*; ~**suckle** *n* Geiß-
blatt *nt*
honk [hɒŋk] *vi* hupen
honor ['ɒnə*] (*US*) *vt*, *n* = **honour**
honorary ['ɒnərərɪ] *adj* Ehren-
honour ['ɒnə*] (*US* **honor**) *vt* ehren;
(*cheque*) einlösen ♦ *n* Ehre *f*; ~**able**
adj ehrenwert; (*intention*) ehrenhaft;
~**s degree** *n* (*UNIV*) akademischer Grad
mit Prüfung im Spezialfach
hood [hʊd] *n* Kapuze *f*; (*BRIT*: *AUT*)
Verdeck *nt*; (*US*) Kühlerhaube *f*
hoodlum ['huːdləm] *n* Rowdy *m*;
(*member of gang*) Gangster *m*
hoodwink ['hʊdwɪŋk] *vt* reinlegen
hoof [huːf] (*pl* **hooves**) *n* Huf *m*
hook [hʊk] *n* Haken *m* ♦ *vt* einhaken
hooligan ['huːlɪgən] *n* Rowdy *m*
hoop [huːp] *n* Reifen *m*
hoot [huːt] *vi* (*AUT*) hupen; ~**er** *n*
(*NAUT*) Dampfpfeife *f*; (*BRIT*: *AUT*)
(Auto)hupe *f*
hoover ['huːvə*] (®; *BRIT*) *n*
Staubsauger *m* ♦ *vt* staubsaugen
hooves [huːvz] *pl* of **hoof**
hop [hɒp] *vi* hüpfen, hopsen ♦ *n* (*jump*)
Hopser *m*
hope [həʊp] *vt*, *vi* hoffen ♦ *n* Hoffnung
f; **I** ~ **so/not** hoffentlich/hoffentlich
nicht; ~**ful** *adj* hoffnungsvoll; (*promising*) vielversprechend; ~**fully** *adv*
hoffentlich; ~**less** *adj* hoffnungslos
hops [hɒps] *npl* Hopfen *m*
horizon [hə'raɪzn] *n* Horizont *m*; ~**tal**

[hɒrɪ'zɒntl] *adj* horizontal
hormone ['hɔːməʊn] *n* Hormon *nt*
horn [hɔːn] *n* Horn *nt*; (*AUT*) Hupe *f*
hornet ['hɔːnɪt] *n* Hornisse *f*
horny ['hɔːnɪ] *adj* schwielig; (*US*: *inf*)
scharf
horoscope ['hɒrəskəʊp] *n* Horoskop *nt*
horrendous [hə'rendəs] *adj* abscheulich,
entsetzlich
horrible ['hɒrɪbl] *adj* fürchterlich
horrid ['hɒrɪd] *adj* scheußlich
horrify ['hɒrɪfaɪ] *vt* entsetzen
horror ['hɒrə*] *n* Schrecken *m*; ~ **film** *n*
Horrorfilm *m*
hors d'oeuvre [ɔː'dɜːvr] *n* Vorspeise *f*
horse [hɔːs] *n* Pferd *nt*; ~**back** *n*: **on**
~**back** beritten; ~ **chestnut** *n* Roßkas-
tanie *f*; ~**man/woman** (*irreg*) *n*
Reiter(in) *m(f)*; ~**power** *n* Pferdestärke *f*; ~**-racing** *n* Pferderennen *nt*;
~**radish** *n* Meerrettich *m*; ~**shoe** *n*
Hufeisen *nt*
horticulture ['hɔːtɪkʌltʃə*] *n* Gartenbau
m
hose [həʊz] *n* (*also*: ~**pipe**) Schlauch *m*
hosiery ['həʊzɪərɪ] *n* Strumpfwaren *pl*
hospitable [hɒs'pɪtəbl] *adj* gastfreund-
lich
hospital ['hɒspɪtl] *n* Krankenhaus *nt*
hospitality [hɒspɪ'tælɪtɪ] *n* Gastfreund-
schaft *f*
host [həʊst] *n* Gastgeber *m*; (*innkeeper*)
(Gast)wirt *m*; (*large number*) Heer-
schar *f*; (*ECCL*) Hostie *f*
hostage ['hɒstɪdʒ] *n* Geisel *f*
hostel ['hɒstəl] *n* Herberge *f*; (*also*:
youth ~) Jugendherberge *f*
hostess ['həʊstes] *n* Gastgeberin *f*
hostile ['hɒstaɪl] *adj* feindlich
hostility [hɒs'tɪlɪtɪ] *n* Feindschaft *f*;
hostilities *npl* (*fighting*) Feindselig-
keiten *pl*
hot [hɒt] *adj* heiß; (*drink, food, water*)
warm; (*spiced*) scharf; **I'm** ~ mir ist
heiß; ~**bed** *n* (*fig*) Nährboden *m*; ~
dog *n* heiße(s) Würstchen *nt*
hotel [həʊ'tel] *n* Hotel *nt*; ~**ier** *n*
Hotelier *m*
hot: ~**headed** *adj* hitzig; ~**house** *n*
Treibhaus *nt*; ~ **line** *n* (*POL*) heiße(r)

Draht *m*; ~**ly** *adv* (*argue*) hitzig; ~**plate** *n* Kochplatte *f*; ~**-water bottle** *n* Wärmflasche *f*
hound [haʊnd] *n* Jagdhund *m* ♦ *vt* hetzen
hour ['aʊə*] *n* Stunde *f*; (*time of day*) (Tages)zeit *f*; ~**ly** *adj, adv* stündlich
house [*n* haʊs, *pl* 'haʊzɪz, *vb* haʊz] *n* Haus *nt* ♦ *vt* unterbringen; **on the** ~ auf Kosten des Hauses; ~**boat** *n* Hausboot *nt*; ~**breaking** *n* Einbruch *m*; ~**-coat** *n* Morgenmantel *m*; ~**hold** *n* Haushalt *m*; ~**keeper** *n* Haushälterin *f*; ~**keeping** *n* Haushaltung *f*; ~**-warming party** *n* Einweihungsparty *f*; ~**wife** (*irreg*) *n* Hausfrau *f*; ~**work** *n* Hausarbeit *f*
housing ['haʊzɪŋ] *n* (*act*) Unterbringung *f*; (*houses*) Wohnungen *pl*; (*POL*) Wohnungsbau *m*; (*covering*) Gehäuse *nt*; ~ **estate** (*US* ~ **development**) *n* (Wohn)siedlung *f*
hovel ['hɒvəl] *n* elende Hütte *f*
hover ['hɒvə*] *vi* (*bird*) schweben; (*person*) herumstehen; ~**craft** *n* Luftkissenfahrzeug *nt*
how [haʊ] *adv* wie; ~ **are you?** wie geht es Ihnen?; ~ **much milk?** wieviel Milch?; ~ **many people?** wie viele Leute?
however [haʊ'evə*] *adv* (*but*) (je)doch, aber; ~ **you phrase it** wie Sie es auch ausdrücken
howl [haʊl] *n* Heulen *nt* ♦ *vi* heulen
H.P. *abbr* = **hire purchase**
h.p. *abbr* = **horsepower**
H.Q. *abbr* = **headquarters**
hub [hʌb] *n* Radnabe *f*
hubbub ['hʌbʌb] *n* Tumult *m*
hubcap ['hʌbkæp] *n* Radkappe *f*
huddle ['hʌdl] *vi:* **to** ~ **together** sich zusammendrängen
hue [hju:] *n* Färbung *f*; ~ **and cry** *n* Zetergeschrei *nt*
huff [hʌf] *n:* **to go into a** ~ einschnappen
hug [hʌg] *vt* umarmen ♦ *n* Umarmung *f*
huge [hju:dʒ] *adj* groß, riesig
hulk [hʌlk] *n* (*ship*) abgetakelte(s) Schiff *nt*; (*person*) Koloß *m*
hull [hʌl] *n* Schiffsrumpf *m*

hullo [hʌ'ləʊ] *excl* = **hello**
hum [hʌm] *vt, vi* summen
human ['hju:mən] *adj* menschlich ♦ *n* (*also:* ~ *being*) Mensch *m*
humane [hju:'meɪn] *adj* human
humanitarian [hju:mænɪ'tɛərɪən] *adj* humanitär
humanity [hju:'mænɪtɪ] *n* Menschheit *f*; (*kindliness*) Menschlichkeit *f*
humble ['hʌmbl] *adj* demütig; (*modest*) bescheiden ♦ *vt* demütigen
humbug ['hʌmbʌg] *n* Humbug *m*; (*BRIT: sweet*) Pfefferminzbonbon *nt*
humdrum ['hʌmdrʌm] *adj* stumpfsinnig
humid ['hju:mɪd] *adj* feucht; ~**ity** *n* Feuchtigkeit *f*
humiliate [hju:'mɪlɪeɪt] *vt* demütigen
humiliation [hju:mɪlɪ'eɪʃən] *n* Demütigung *f*
humility [hju:'mɪlɪtɪ] *n* Demut *f*
humor ['hju:mə*] (*US*) *n, vt* = **humour**
humorous ['hju:mərəs] *adj* humorvoll
humour ['hju:mə*] (*US* **humor**) *n* (*fun*) Humor *m*; (*mood*) Stimmung *f* ♦ *vt* bei Stimmung halten
hump [hʌmp] *n* Buckel *m*
hunch [hʌntʃ] *n* Buckel *m*; (*premonition*) (Vor)ahnung *f*; ~**back** *n* Bucklige(r) *mf*; ~**ed** *adj* gekrümmt
hundred ['hʌndrɪd] *num* hundert; ~**weight** *n* Zentner *m* (*BRIT:* = 50.8 kg; *US:* = 45.3 kg)
hung [hʌŋ] *pt, pp of* **hang**
Hungarian [hʌŋ'gɛərɪən] *adj* ungarisch ♦ *n* Ungar(in) *m(f)*; (*LING*) Ungarisch *nt*
Hungary ['hʌŋgərɪ] *n* Ungarn *nt*
hunger ['hʌŋgə*] *n* Hunger *m* ♦ *vi* hungern; ~ **strike** *n* Hungerstreik *m*
hungry ['hʌŋgrɪ] *adj* hungrig; **to be** ~ Hunger haben
hunk [hʌŋk] *n* (*of bread*) Stück *nt*
hunt [hʌnt] *vt, vi* jagen ♦ *n* Jagd *f*; **to** ~ **for** suchen; ~**er** *n* Jäger *m*; ~**ing** *n* Jagd *f*
hurdle ['hɜ:dl] *n* (*also fig*) Hürde *f*
hurl [hɜ:l] *vt* schleudern
hurrah [hʊ'rɑ:] *n* Hurra *nt*
hurray [hʊ'reɪ] *n* Hurra *nt*
hurricane ['hʌrɪkən] *n* Orkan *m*
hurried ['hʌrɪd] *adj* eilig; (*hasty*)

übereilt; ~**ly** *adv* übereilt, hastig
hurry ['hʌrɪ] *n* Eile *f* ♦ *vi* sich beeilen ♦ *vt* (an)treiben; *(job)* übereilen; **to be in a** ~ es eilig haben; ~ **up** *vi* sich beeilen ♦ *vt* *(person)* zur Eile antreiben; *(work)* vorantreiben
hurt [hɜːt] *(pt, pp* **hurt)** *vt* weh tun *+dat; (injure, fig)* verletzen ♦ *vi* weh tun; ~**ful** *adj* schädlich; *(remark)* verletzend
hurtle ['hɜːtl] *vi* sausen
husband ['hʌzbənd] *n* (Ehe)mann *m*
hush [hʌʃ] *n* Stille *f* ♦ *vt* zur Ruhe bringen ♦ *excl* pst, still
husk [hʌsk] *n* Spelze *f*
husky ['hʌskɪ] *adj (voice)* rauh ♦ *n* Eskimohund *m*
hustle ['hʌsl] *vt (push)* stoßen; *(hurry)* antreiben ♦ *n:* ~ **and bustle** Geschäftigkeit *f*
hut [hʌt] *n* Hütte *f*
hutch [hʌtʃ] *n* (Kaninchen)stall *m*
hyacinth ['haɪəsɪnθ] *n* Hyazinthe *f*
hybrid ['haɪbrɪd] *n* Kreuzung *f* ♦ *adj* Misch-
hydrant ['haɪdrənt] *n (also: fire* ~) Hydrant *m*
hydraulic [haɪ'drɒlɪk] *adj* hydraulisch
hydroelectric [haɪdrəʊɪ'lektrɪk] *adj* hydroelektrisch
hydrofoil ['haɪdrəʊfɔɪl] *n* Tragflügelboot *nt*
hydrogen ['haɪdrɪdʒən] *n* Wasserstoff *m*
hyena [haɪ'iːnə] *n* Hyäne *f*
hygiene ['haɪdʒiːn] *n* Hygiene *f*
hygienic [haɪ'dʒiːnɪk] *adj* hygienisch
hymn [hɪm] *n* Kirchenlied *nt*
hype [haɪp] *(inf)* Publicity *f*
hypermarket ['haɪpəˈmɑːkɪt] *(BRIT)* *n* Hypermarket *m*
hyphen ['haɪfən] *n* Bindestrich *m*
hypnosis [hɪp'nəʊsɪs] *n* Hypnose *f*
hypnotic [hɪp'nɒtɪk] *adj* hypnotisierend
hypnotize ['hɪpnətaɪz] *vt* hypnotisieren
hypocrisy [hɪ'pɒkrɪsɪ] *n* Heuchelei *f*
hypocrite ['hɪpəkrɪt] *n* Heuchler *m*
hypocritical [hɪpə'krɪtɪkəl] *adj* scheinheilig, heuchlerisch
hypothermia ['haɪpəʊ'θɜːmɪə] *n* Unterkühlung *f*

hypotheses [haɪ'pɒθɪsiːz] *npl of* **hypothesis**
hypothesis [haɪ'pɒθɪsɪs] *(pl* **hypotheses)** *n* Hypothese *f*
hypothetic(al) [haɪpəʊ'θetɪk(əl)] *adj* hypothetisch
hysterical [hɪs'terɪkəl] *adj* hysterisch
hysterics [hɪs'terɪks] *npl* hysterische(r) Anfall *m*

I

I [aɪ] *pron* ich
ice [aɪs] *n* Eis *nt* ♦ *vt (COOK)* mit Zuckerguß überziehen ♦ *vi (also:* ~ *up)* vereisen; ~ **axe** *n* Eispickel *m*; ~**berg** *n* Eisberg *m*; ~**box** *(US)* *n* Kühlschrank *m*; ~ **cream** *n* Eis *nt*; ~ **cube** *n* Eiswürfel *m*; ~ **hockey** *n* Eishockey *nt*
Iceland ['aɪslənd] *n* Island *nt*
ice: ~ **lolly** *(BRIT)* *n* Eis *nt* am Stiel; ~ **rink** *n* (Kunst)eisbahn *f*; ~ **skating** *n* Schlittschuhlaufen *nt*
icicle ['aɪsɪkl] *n* Eiszapfen *m*
icing ['aɪsɪŋ] *n (on cake)* Zuckerguß *m*; *(on window)* Vereisung *f*; ~ **sugar** *(BRIT)* *n* Puderzucker *m*
icon ['aɪkɒn] *n* Ikone *f*
icy ['aɪsɪ] *adj (slippery)* vereist; *(cold)* eisig
I'd [aɪd] = **I would; I had**
idea [aɪ'dɪə] *n* Idee *f*
ideal [aɪ'dɪəl] *n* Ideal *nt* ♦ *adj* ideal; ~**ist** *n* Idealist *m*
identical [aɪ'dentɪkəl] *adj* identisch; *(twins)* eineiig
identification [aɪdentɪfɪ'keɪʃən] *n* Identifizierung *f*; **means of** ~ Ausweispapiere *pl*
identify [aɪ'dentɪfaɪ] *vt* identifizieren; *(regard as the same)* gleichsetzen
Identikit picture [aɪ'dentɪkɪt-] *n* Phantombild *nt*
identity [aɪ'dentɪtɪ] *n* Identität *f*; ~ **card** *n* Personalausweis *m*
ideology [aɪdɪ'ɒlədʒɪ] *n* Ideologie *f*
idiom ['ɪdɪəm] *n (expression)* Redewendung *f*; *(dialect)* Idiom *nt*; ~**atic**

[ɪdɪə'mætɪk] *adj* idiomatisch
idiosyncrasy [ɪdɪə'sɪŋkrəsɪ] *n* Eigenart *f*
idiot ['ɪdɪət] *n* Idiot(in) *m(f)*; ~**ic**
[ɪdɪ'ɒtɪk] *adj* idiotisch
idle ['aɪdl] *adj* (*doing nothing*) untätig;
(*lazy*) faul; (*useless*) nutzlos; (*machine*) still(stehend); (*threat, talk*) leer
♦ *vi* (*machine*) leerlaufen ♦ *vt*: **to ~**
away the time die Zeit vertrödeln;
~**ness** *n* Müßiggang *m*; Faulheit *f*
idol ['aɪdl] *n* Idol *nt*; ~**ize** *vt* vergöttern
i.e. *abbr* (= *id est*) d.h.

KEYWORD

if [ɪf] *conj* **1** wenn; (*in case also*) falls;
if I were you wenn ich Sie wäre
2 (*although*): (**even**) **if** (selbst *or* auch)
wenn
3 (*whether*) ob
4: **if so/not** wenn ja/nicht; **if only ...**
wenn ... doch nur ...; **if only I could**
wenn ich doch nur könnte; *see also* **as**

---

ignite [ɪg'naɪt] *vt* (an)zünden ♦ *vi* sich
entzünden
ignition [ɪg'nɪʃən] *n* Zündung *f*; **to**
switch on/off the ~ den Motor anlassen/
abstellen; **~ key** *n* (*AUT*) Zündschlüssel
m
ignorance ['ɪgnərəns] *n* Unwissenheit *f*
ignorant ['ɪgnərənt] *adj* unwissend; **to**
be ~ of nicht wissen
ignore [ɪg'nɔ:*] *vt* ignorieren
I'll [aɪl] = **I will**; **I shall**
ill [ɪl] *adj* krank ♦ *n* Übel *nt* ♦ *adv*
schlecht; **to take** *or* **be taken ~** krank
werden; ~**-advised** *adj* unklug; ~**-at-**
ease *adj* unbehaglich
illegal [ɪ'li:gəl] *adj* illegal
illegible [ɪ'ledʒəbl] *adj* unleserlich
illegitimate [ɪlɪ'dʒɪtɪmət] *adj* unehelich
ill-fated [ɪl'feɪtɪd] *adj* unselig
ill feeling *n* Verstimmung *f*
illicit [ɪ'lɪsɪt] *adj* verboten
illiterate [ɪ'lɪtərət] *adj* ungebildet
ill-mannered ['ɪl'mænəd] *adj* ungehobelt
illness ['ɪlnəs] *n* Krankheit *f*
illogical [ɪ'lɒdʒɪkəl] *adj* unlogisch
ill-treat ['ɪl'tri:t] *vt* mißhandeln
illuminate [ɪ'lu:mɪneɪt] *vt* beleuchten

illumination [ɪlu:mɪ'neɪʃən] *n* Beleuchtung *f*; **~s** *pl* (*decorative lights*) festliche Beleuchtung *f*
illusion [ɪ'lu:ʒən] *n* Illusion *f*; **to be**
under the ~ that ... sich *dat* einbilden,
daß ...
illusory [ɪ'lu:sərɪ] *adj* trügerisch
illustrate ['ɪləstreɪt] *vt* (*book*) illustrieren; (*explain*) veranschaulichen
illustration [ɪləs'treɪʃən] *n* Illustration *f*;
(*explanation*) Veranschaulichung *f*
illustrious [ɪ'lʌstrɪəs] *adj* berühmt
ill will *n* Groll *m*
I'm [aɪm] = **I am**
image ['ɪmɪdʒ] *n* Bild *nt*; (*public ~*)
Image *nt*; ~**ry** *n* Symbolik *f*
imaginary [ɪ'mædʒɪnərɪ] *adj* eingebildet;
(*world*) Phantasie-
imagination [ɪmædʒɪ'neɪʃən] *n* Einbildung *f*; (*creative*) Phantasie *f*
imaginative [ɪ'mædʒɪnətɪv] *adj* phantasiereich, einfallsreich
imagine [ɪ'mædʒɪn] *vt* sich vorstellen;
(*wrongly*) sich einbilden
imbalance [ɪm'bæləns] *n* Unausgeglichenheit *f*
imbecile ['ɪmbəsi:l] *n* Schwachsinnige(r)
mf
imbue [ɪm'bju:] *vt*: **to ~ sth with** etw
erfüllen mit
imitate ['ɪmɪteɪt] *vt* imitieren
imitation [ɪmɪ'teɪʃən] *n* Imitation *f*
immaculate [ɪ'mækjʊlɪt] *adj* makellos;
(*dress*) tadellos; (*ECCL*) unbefleckt
immaterial [ɪmə'tɪərɪəl] *adj* unwesentlich; **it is ~ whether** ... es ist unwichtig,
ob ...
immature [ɪmə'tjʊə*] *adj* unreif
immediate [ɪ'mi:dɪət] *adj* (*instant*)
sofortig; (*near*) unmittelbar; (*relatives*) nächste(r, s); (*needs*) dringlich; ~**ly** *adv* sofort; ~**ly next to** direkt
neben
immense [ɪ'mens] *adj* unermeßlich
immerse [ɪ'mɜ:s] *vt* eintauchen; **to be**
~**d in** (*fig*) vertieft sein in +*acc*
immersion heater [ɪ'mɜ:ʃən-] (*BRIT*) *n*
Boiler *m*
immigrant ['ɪmɪgrənt] *n* Einwanderer *m*
immigrate ['ɪmɪgreɪt] *vi* einwandern

immigration [ɪmɪˈgreɪʃən] n Einwanderung f
imminent [ˈɪmɪnənt] adj bevorstehend
immobile [ɪˈməʊbaɪl] adj unbeweglich
immobilize [ɪˈməʊbɪlaɪz] vt lähmen
immoral [ɪˈmɒrəl] adj unmoralisch; ~ity [ɪməˈrælɪtɪ] n Unsittlichkeit f
immortal [ɪˈmɔːtl] adj unsterblich; ~ize vt unsterblich machen
immune [ɪˈmjuːn] adj (secure) sicher; (MED) immun; ~ from sicher vor +dat
immunity [ɪˈmjuːnɪtɪ] n (MED, JUR) Immunität f; (fig) Freiheit f
immunize [ˈɪmjʊnaɪz] vt immunisieren
imp [ɪmp] n Kobold m
impact [ˈɪmpækt] n Aufprall m; (fig) Wirkung f
impair [ɪmˈpɛə*] vt beeinträchtigen
impale [ɪmˈpeɪl] vt aufspießen
impart [ɪmˈpɑːt] vt mitteilen; (knowledge) vermitteln; (exude) abgeben
impartial [ɪmˈpɑːʃəl] adj unparteiisch
impassable [ɪmˈpɑːsəbl] adj unpassierbar
impasse [æmˈpɑːs] n Sackgasse f
impassive [ɪmˈpæsɪv] adj gelassen
impatience [ɪmˈpeɪʃəns] n Ungeduld f
impatient [ɪmˈpeɪʃənt] adj ungeduldig
impeccable [ɪmˈpekəbl] adj tadellos
impede [ɪmˈpiːd] vt (be)hindern
impediment [ɪmˈpedɪmənt] n Hindernis nt; (in speech) Sprachfehler m
impending [ɪmˈpendɪŋ] adj bevorstehend
impenetrable [ɪmˈpenɪtrəbl] adj (also fig) undurchdringlich
imperative [ɪmˈperətɪv] adj (necessary) unbedingt erforderlich ♦ n (GRAM) Imperativ m, Befehlsform f
imperceptible [ɪmpəˈseptəbl] adj nicht wahrnehmbar
imperfect [ɪmˈpɜːfɪkt] adj (faulty) fehlerhaft; ~ion [ɪmpɜːˈfekʃən] n Unvollkommenheit f; (fault) Fehler m
imperial [ɪmˈpɪərɪəl] adj kaiserlich; ~ism n Imperialismus m
impersonal [ɪmˈpɜːsnl] adj unpersönlich
impersonate [ɪmˈpɜːsəneɪt] vt sich ausgeben als; (for amusement) imitieren

impertinent [ɪmˈpɜːtɪnənt] adj unverschämt, frech
impervious [ɪmˈpɜːvɪəs] adj (fig): ~ (to) unempfänglich (für)
impetuous [ɪmˈpetjʊəs] adj ungestüm
impetus [ˈɪmpɪtəs] n Triebkraft f; (fig) Auftrieb m
impinge [ɪmˈpɪndʒ]: ~ on vt beeinträchtigen
implacable [ɪmˈplækəbl] adj unerbittlich
implement [n ˈɪmplɪmənt, vb ˈɪmplɪment] n Werkzeug nt ♦ vt ausführen
implicate [ˈɪmplɪkeɪt] vt verwickeln
implication [ɪmplɪˈkeɪʃən] n (effect) Auswirkung f; (in crime) Verwicklung f
implicit [ɪmˈplɪsɪt] adj (suggested) unausgesprochen; (utter) vorbehaltlos
implore [ɪmˈplɔː*] vt anflehen
imply [ɪmˈplaɪ] vt (hint) andeuten; (be evidence for) schließen lassen auf +acc
impolite [ɪmpəˈlaɪt] adj unhöflich
import [vb ɪmˈpɔːt, n ˈɪmpɔːt] vt einführen ♦ n Einfuhr f; (meaning) Bedeutung f
importance [ɪmˈpɔːtəns] n Bedeutung f
important [ɪmˈpɔːtənt] adj wichtig; it's not ~ es ist unwichtig
importer [ɪmˈpɔːtə*] n Importeur m
impose [ɪmˈpəʊz] vt, vi: to ~ (on) auferlegen (+dat); (penalty, sanctions) verhängen (gegen); to ~ (o.s.) on sb sich jdm aufdrängen
imposing [ɪmˈpəʊzɪŋ] adj eindrucksvoll
imposition [ɪmpəˈzɪʃən] n (of burden, fine) Auferlegung f; (SCH) Strafarbeit f; to be an ~ (on person) eine Zumutung sein
impossible [ɪmˈpɒsəbl] adj unmöglich
impostor [ɪmˈpɒstə*] n Hochstapler m
impotence [ˈɪmpətəns] n Impotenz f
impotent [ˈɪmpətənt] adj machtlos; (sexually) impotent
impound [ɪmˈpaʊnd] vt beschlagnahmen
impoverished [ɪmˈpɒvərɪʃt] adj verarmt
impracticable [ɪmˈpræktɪkəbl] adj undurchführbar
impractical [ɪmˈpræktɪkəl] adj unpraktisch
imprecise [ɪmprəˈsaɪs] adj ungenau
impregnable [ɪmˈpregnəbl] adj (castle)

uneinnehmbar

impregnate ['ɪmpregneɪt] *vt* (*saturate*) sättigen; (*fertilize*) befruchten

impress [ɪm'pres] *vt* (*influence*) beeindrucken; (*imprint*) (auf)drücken; **to ~ sth on sb** jdm etw einschärfen

impression [ɪm'preʃən] *n* Eindruck *m*; (*on wax, footprint*) Abdruck *m*; (*of book*) Auflage *f*; (*take-off*) Nachahmung *f*; **I was under the ~** ich hatte den Eindruck; **~able** *adj* leicht zu beeindrucken; **~ist** *n* Impressionist *m*

impressive [ɪm'presɪv] *adj* eindrucksvoll

imprint ['ɪmprɪnt] *n* Abdruck *m*

imprison [ɪm'prɪzn] *vt* ins Gefängnis schicken; **~ment** *n* Inhaftierung *f*

improbable [ɪm'prɒbəbl] *adj* unwahrscheinlich

impromptu [ɪm'prɒmptjuː] *adj, adv* aus dem Stegreif, improvisiert

improper [ɪm'prɒpə*] *adj* (*indecent*) unanständig; (*unsuitable*) unpassend

improve [ɪm'pruːv] *vt* verbessern ♦ *vi* besser werden; **~ment** *n* (Ver)besserung *f*

improvise ['ɪmprəvaɪz] *vt, vi* improvisieren

imprudent [ɪm'pruːdənt] *adj* unklug

impudent ['ɪmpjudənt] *adj* unverschämt

impulse ['ɪmpʌls] *n* Impuls *m*; **to act on ~** spontan handeln

impulsive [ɪm'pʌlsɪv] *adj* impulsiv

impunity [ɪm'pjuːnɪtɪ] *n* Straflosigkeit *f*

impure [ɪm'pjʊə*] *adj* (*dirty*) verunreinigt; (*bad*) unsauber

impurity [ɪm'pjʊərɪtɪ] *n* Unreinheit *f*; (*TECH*) Verunreinigung *f*

KEYWORD

in [ɪn] *prep* **1** (*indicating place, position*) in +*dat*; (*with motion*) in +*acc*; **here/there** hier/dort; **in London** in London; **in the United States** in den Vereinigten Staaten

2 (*indicating time: during*) in +*dat*; **in summer** im Sommer; **in 1988** im Jahre) 1988; **in the afternoon** nachmittags, am Nachmittag

3 (*indicating time: in the space of*) innerhalb von; **I'll see you in 2 weeks** *or* **in 2 weeks' time** ich sehe Sie in zwei Wochen

4 (*indicating manner, circumstances, state etc*) in +*dat*; **in the sun/rain** in der Sonne/im Regen; **in English/French** auf Englisch/Französisch; **in a loud/soft voice** mit lauter/leiser Stimme

5 (*with ratios, numbers*): **1 in 10** jeder zehnte; **20 pence in the pound** 20 Pence pro Pfund; **they lined up in twos** sie stellten sich in Zweierreihe auf

6 (*referring to people, works*): **the disease is common in children** die Krankheit ist bei Kindern häufig; **in Dickens** bei Dickens; **we have a loyal friend in him** er ist uns ein treurer Freund

7 (*indicating profession etc*): **to be in teaching/the army** Lehrer(in)/beim Militär sein; **to be in publishing** im Verlagswesen arbeiten

8 (*with present participle*): **in saying this, I ...** wenn ich das sage, ... ich; **in accepting this view, he ...** weil er diese Meinung akzeptierte, ... er

♦ *adv*: **to be in** (*person: at home, work*) dasein; (*train, ship, plane*) angekommen sein; (*in fashion*) in sein; **to ask sb in** jdn hereinbitten; **to run/limp etc in** hereingerannt/gehumpelt *etc* kommen

♦ *n*: **the ins and outs** (*of proposal, situation etc*) die Feinheiten

---

in. *abbr* = **inch**

inability [ɪnə'bɪlɪtɪ] *n* Unfähigkeit *f*

inaccessible [ɪnæk'sesəbl] *adj* unzugänglich

inaccurate [ɪn'ækjʊrɪt] *adj* ungenau; (*wrong*) unrichtig

inactivity [ɪnæk'tɪvɪtɪ] *n* Untätigkeit *f*

inadequate [ɪn'ædɪkwət] *adj* unzulänglich

inadvertently [ɪnəd'vɜːtəntlɪ] *adv* unabsichtlich

inadvisable [ɪnəd'vaɪzəbl] *adj* nicht ratsam

inane [ɪ'neɪn] *adj* dumm, albern

inanimate [ɪn'ænɪmət] *adj* leblos

inappropriate [ɪnə'prəʊprɪət] *adj* (*clothing*) ungeeignet; (*remark*) unange-

bracht
inarticulate [ɪnɑː'tɪkjʊlət] *adj* unklar
inasmuch as [ɪnəz'mʌtʃəz] *adv* da; *(in so far as)* soweit
inaudible [ɪn'ɔːdəbl] *adj* unhörbar
inaugural [ɪ'nɔːgjʊrəl] *adj* Eröffnungs-
inaugurate [ɪ'nɔːgjʊreɪt] *vt (open)* einweihen; *(admit to office)* (feierlich) einführen
inauguration [ɪnɔːgjʊ'reɪʃən] *n* Eröffnung *f*; *(feierliche)* Amtseinführung *f*
in-between [ɪnbɪ'twiːn] *adj* Zwischen-
inborn [ɪn'bɔːn] *adj* angeboren
inbred [ɪn'bred] *adj* angeboren
Inc. *abbr* = **incorporated**
incalculable [ɪn'kælkjʊləbl] *adj (consequences)* unabsehbar
incapable [ɪn'keɪpəbl] *adj*: ~ **(of doing sth)** unfähig(, etw zu tun)
incapacitate [ɪnkə'pæsɪteɪt] *vt* untauglich machen
incapacity [ɪnkə'pæsɪtɪ] *n* Unfähigkeit *f*
incarcerate [ɪn'kɑːsəreɪt] *vt* einkerkern
incarnation [ɪnkɑː'neɪʃən] *n (ECCL)* Menschwerdung *f*; *(fig)* Inbegriff *m*
incendiary [ɪn'sendɪərɪ] *adj* Brand-
incense [*n* 'ɪnsens, *vb* ɪn'sens] *n* Weihrauch *m* ♦ *vt* erzürnen
incentive [ɪn'sentɪv] *n* Anreiz *m*
incessant [ɪn'sesnt] *adj* unaufhörlich; **~ly** *adv* unaufhörlich
incest ['ɪnsest] *n* Inzest *m*
inch [ɪntʃ] *n* Zoll *m* ♦ *vi*: **to ~ forward** sich Stückchen für Stückchen vorwärts bewegen; **to be within an ~ of** kurz davor sein; **he didn't give an ~** er gab keinen Zentimeter nach
incidence ['ɪnsɪdəns] *n* Auftreten *nt*; *(of crime)* Quote *f*
incident ['ɪnsɪdənt] *n* Vorfall *m*; *(disturbance)* Zwischenfall *m*
incidental [ɪnsɪ'dentl] *adj (music)* Begleit-; *(unimportant)* nebensächlich; *(remark)* beiläufig; **~ly** *adv* übrigens
incinerator [ɪn'sɪnəreɪtə*] *n* Verbrennungsofen *m*
incipient [ɪn'sɪpɪənt] *adj* beginnend
incision [ɪn'sɪʒən] *n* Einschnitt *m*
incisive [ɪn'saɪsɪv] *adj (style)* treffend;

(person) scharfsinnig
incite [ɪn'saɪt] *vt* anstacheln
inclination [ɪnklɪ'neɪʃən] *n* Neigung *f*
incline [*n* 'ɪnklaɪn, *vb* ɪn'klaɪn] *n* Abhang *m* ♦ *vt* neigen; *(fig)* veranlassen ♦ *vi* sich neigen; **to be ~d to do sth** dazu neigen, etw zu tun
include [ɪn'kluːd] *vt* einschließen; *(on list, in group)* aufnehmen
including [ɪn'kluːdɪŋ] *prep*: ~ **X X** inbegriffen
inclusion [ɪn'kluːʒən] *n* Aufnahme *f*
inclusive [ɪn'kluːsɪv] *adj* einschließlich; *(COMM)* inklusive; ~ **of** einschließlich +*gen*
incoherent [ɪnkəʊ'hɪərənt] *adj* zusammenhanglos
income ['ɪnkʌm] *n* Einkommen *nt*; *(from business)* Einkünfte *pl*; ~ **tax** *n* Lohnsteuer *f*; *(of self-employed)* Einkommenssteuer *f*
incoming ['ɪnkʌmɪŋ] *adj*: ~ **flight** eintreffende Maschine *f*
incomparable [ɪn'kɒmpərəbl] *adj* unvergleichlich
incompatible [ɪnkəm'pætəbl] *adj* unvereinbar; *(people)* unverträglich
incompetence [ɪn'kɒmpɪtəns] *n* Unfähigkeit *f*
incompetent [ɪn'kɒmpɪtənt] *adj* unfähig
incomplete [ɪnkəm'pliːt] *adj* unvollständig
incomprehensible [ɪnkɒmprɪ'hensəbl] *adj* unverständlich
inconceivable [ɪnkən'siːvəbl] *adj* unvorstellbar
incongruous [ɪn'kɒŋgrʊəs] *adj* seltsam; *(remark)* unangebracht
inconsiderate [ɪnkən'sɪdərət] *adj* rücksichtslos
inconsistency [ɪnkən'sɪstənsɪ] *n* Widersprüchlichkeit *f*; *(state)* Unbeständigkeit *f*
inconsistent [ɪnkən'sɪstənt] *adj (action, speech)* widersprüchlich; *(person, work)* unbeständig; ~ **with** nicht übereinstimmend mit
inconspicuous [ɪnkən'spɪkjʊəs] *adj* unauffällig
incontinent [ɪn'kɒntɪnənt] *adj (MED)*

nicht fähig, Stuhl und Harn zurückzuhalten

inconvenience [ɪnkən'viːnɪəns] n Unbequemlichkeit f; (trouble to others) Unannehmlichkeiten pl

inconvenient [ɪnkən'viːnɪənt] adj ungelegen; (journey) unbequem

incorporate [ɪn'kɔːrpəreɪt] vt (include) aufnehmen; (contain) enthalten

incorporated [ɪn'kɔːpəreɪtɪd] adj: ~ **company** (US) eingetragene Aktiengesellschaft f

incorrect [ɪnkə'rekt] adj unrichtig

incorrigible [ɪn'kɒrɪdʒəbl] adj unverbesserlich

incorruptible [ɪnkə'rʌptəbl] adj unzerstörbar; (person) unbestechlich

increase [n 'ɪnkriːs, vb ɪn'kriːs] n Zunahme f; (pay ~) Gehaltserhöhung f; (in size) Vergrößerung f ♦ vt erhöhen; (wealth, rage) vermehren; (business) erweitern ♦ vi zunehmen; (prices) steigen; (in size) größer werden; (in number) sich vermehren

increasing [ɪn'kriːsɪŋ] adj (number) steigend

increasingly [ɪn'kriːsɪŋlɪ] adv zunehmend

incredible [ɪn'kredəbl] adj unglaublich

incredulous [ɪn'kredjʊləs] adj ungläubig

increment ['ɪnkrɪmənt] n Zulage f

incriminate [ɪn'krɪmɪneɪt] vt belasten

incubation [ɪnkjʊ'beɪʃən] n Ausbrüten nt

incubator ['ɪnkjʊbeɪtə*] n Brutkasten m

incumbent [ɪn'kʌmbənt] n Amtsinhaber(in) m(f) ♦ adj: **it is** ~ **on him to** ... es obliegt ihm, ...

incur [ɪn'kɜː*] vt sich zuziehen; (debts) machen

incurable [ɪn'kjʊərəbl] adj unheilbar; (fig) unverbesserlich

incursion [ɪn'kɜːʃən] n Einfall m

indebted [ɪn'detɪd] adj (obliged): ~ **(to sb)** (jdm) verpflichtet

indecent [ɪn'diːsnt] adj unanständig; ~ **assault** (BRIT) n Notzucht f; ~ **exposure** n Exhibitionismus m

indecisive [ɪndɪ'saɪsɪv] adj (battle) nicht entscheidend; (person) unentschlossen

indeed [ɪn'diːd] adv tatsächlich, in der

Tat; **yes** ~! Allerdings!

indefinite [ɪn'defɪnɪt] adj unbestimmt; ~**ly** adv auf unbestimmte Zeit; (wait) unbegrenzt lange

indelible [ɪn'deləbl] adj unauslöschlich

indemnify [ɪn'demnɪfaɪ] vt entschädigen; (safeguard) versichern

indemnity [ɪn'demnɪtɪ] n (insurance) Versicherung f; (compensation) Schadenersatz m

independence [ɪndɪ'pendəns] n Unabhängigkeit f

independent [ɪndɪ'pendənt] adj unabhängig

indestructible [ˌɪndɪs'trʌktəbl] adj unzerstörbar

indeterminate [ˌɪndɪ'tɜːmɪnɪt] adj unbestimmt

index ['ɪndeks] n Index m; ~ **card** n Karteikarte f; ~ **finger** n Zeigefinger m; ~**-linked** (US ~**ed**) adj (salaries) der Inflationsrate dat angeglichen; (pensions) dynamisch

India ['ɪndɪə] n Indien nt; ~**n** adj indisch ♦ n Inder(in) m(f); **Red** ~**n** Indianer(in) m(f); **the** ~**n Ocean** n der Indische Ozean

indicate ['ɪndɪkeɪt] vt anzeigen; (hint) andeuten

indication [ɪndɪ'keɪʃən] n Anzeichen nt; (information) Angabe f

indicative [ɪn'dɪkətɪv] adj: ~ **of** bezeichnend für ♦ n (GRAM) Indikativ m

indicator ['ɪndɪkeɪtə*] n (sign) (An)zeichen nt; (AUT) Richtungsanzeiger m

indices ['ɪndɪsiːz] npl of **index**

indict [ɪn'daɪt] vt anklagen; ~**ment** [ɪn'daɪtmənt] n Anklage f

indifference [ɪn'dɪfrəns] n Gleichgültigkeit f; Unwichtigkeit f

indifferent [ɪn'dɪfrənt] adj gleichgültig; (mediocre) mäßig

indigenous [ɪn'dɪdʒɪnəs] adj einheimisch

indigestion [ɪndɪ'dʒestʃən] n Verdauungsstörung f

indignant [ɪn'dɪgnənt] adj: **to be** ~ **about sth** über etw acc empört sein

indignation [ɪndɪg'neɪʃən] n Entrüstung

f

indignity [ɪn'dɪgnɪtɪ] *n* Demütigung *f*

indirect [ɪndɪ'rekt] *adj* indirekt; **~ly** *adv* indirekt

indiscreet [ɪndɪs'kriːt] *adj* (*insensitive*) taktlos; (*telling secrets*) indiskret

indiscretion [ɪndɪs'kreʃən] *n* Taktlosigkeit *f*; Indiskretion *f*

indiscriminate [ɪndɪs'krɪmɪnət] *adj* wahllos, kritiklos

indispensable [ɪndɪs'pensəbl] *adj* unentbehrlich

indisposed [ɪndɪs'pəʊzd] *adj* unpäßlich

indisputable [ɪndɪs'pjuːtəbl] *adj* unbestreitbar; (*evidence*) unanfechtbar

indistinct [ɪndɪs'tɪŋkt] *adj* undeutlich

individual [ɪndɪ'vɪdjʊəl] *n* Individuum *nt* ♦ *adj* individuell; (*case*) Einzel-; (*of, for one person*) eigen, individuell; (*characteristic*) eigentümlich; **~ly** *adv* einzeln, individuell

indivisible [ɪndɪ'vɪzəbl] *adj* unteilbar

indoctrinate [ɪn'dɒktrɪneɪt] *vt* indoktrinieren

indolent ['ɪndələnt] *adj* träge

Indonesia [ɪndəʊ'niːzɪə] *n* Indonesien *nt*

indoor ['ɪndɔː*] *adj* Haus-; Zimmer-; Innen-; (*SPORT*) Hallen-; **~s** [ɪn'dɔːz] *adv* drinnen, im Haus

induce [ɪn'djuːs] *vt* dazu bewegen; (*reaction*) herbeiführen; **~ment** *n* Veranlassung *f*; (*incentive*) Anreiz *m*

induction [ɪn'dʌkʃən] *n* (*MED: of birth*) Einleitung *f*; **~ course** (*BRIT*) *n* Einführungskurs *m*

indulge [ɪn'dʌldʒ] *vt* (*give way*) nachgeben +*dat*; (*gratify*) frönen +*dat* ♦ *vi*: **to ~ (in)** frönen (+*dat*); **~nce** *n* Nachsicht *f*; (*enjoyment*) Genuß *m*; **~nt** *adj* nachsichtig; (*pej*) nachgiebig

industrial [ɪn'dʌstrɪəl] *adj* Industrie-, industriell; (*dispute, injury*) Arbeits-; **~ action** *n* Arbeitskampfmaßnahmen *pl*; **~ estate** (*BRIT*) *n* Industriegebiet *nt*; **~ist** *n* Industrielle(r) *mf*; **~ize** *vt* industrialisieren; **~ park** (*US*) *n* Industriegebiet *nt*

industrious [ɪn'dʌstrɪəs] *adj* fleißig

industry ['ɪndəstrɪ] *n* Industrie *f*; (*diligence*) Fleiß *m*

inebriated [ɪ'niːbrɪeɪtɪd] *adj* betrunken

inedible [ɪn'edɪbl] *adj* ungenießbar

ineffective [ɪnɪ'fektɪv] *adj* unwirksam; (*person*) untauglich

ineffectual [ɪnɪ'fektjʊəl] *adj* = **ineffective**

inefficiency [ɪnɪ'fɪʃənsɪ] *n* Ineffizienz *f*

inefficient [ɪnɪ'fɪʃənt] *adj* ineffizient; (*ineffective*) unwirksam

inept [ɪ'nept] *adj* (*remark*) unpassend; (*person*) ungeeignet

inequality [ɪnɪ'kwɒlɪtɪ] *n* Ungleichheit *f*

inert [ɪ'nɜːt] *adj* träge; (*CHEM*) inaktiv; (*motionless*) unbeweglich

inertia [ɪ'nɜːʃə] *n* Trägheit *f*

inescapable [ɪnɪs'keɪpəbl] *adj* unvermeidbar

inevitable [ɪn'evɪtəbl] *adj* unvermeidlich

inexcusable [ɪnɪks'kjuːzəbl] *adj* unverzeihlich

inexhaustible [ɪnɪg'zɔːstəbl] *adj* unerschöpflich

inexorable [ɪn'eksərəbl] *adj* unerbittlich

inexpensive [ɪnɪks'pensɪv] *adj* preiswert

inexperience [ɪnɪks'pɪərɪəns] *n* Unerfahrenheit *f*; **~d** [ɪnɪks'pɪərɪənst] *adj* unerfahren

inexplicable [ɪnɪks'plɪkəbl] *adj* unerklärlich

inextricably [ɪnɪks'trɪkəblɪ] *adv* untrennbar

infallible [ɪn'fæləbl] *adj* unfehlbar

infamous ['ɪnfəməs] *adj* (*place*) verrufen; (*deed*) schändlich; (*person*) niederträchtig

infamy ['ɪnfəmɪ] *n* Verrufenheit *f*; Niedertracht *f*; (*disgrace*) Schande *f*

infancy ['ɪnfənsɪ] *n* frühe Kindheit *f*; (*fig*) Anfangsstadium *nt*

infant ['ɪnfənt] *n* kleine(s) Kind *nt*, Säugling *m*; **~ile** *adj* kindisch, infantil; **~ school** (*BRIT*) *n* Vorschule *f*

infatuated [ɪn'fætjʊeɪtɪd] *adj* vernarrt; **to become ~ with** sich vernarren in +*acc*

infatuation [ɪnfætjʊ'eɪʃən] *n*: **~ (with)** Vernarrtheit *f* (in +*acc*)

infect [ɪn'fekt] *vt* anstecken (*also fig*); **~ed with** (*illness*) infiziert mit; **~ion** [ɪn'fekʃən] *n* Infektion *f*; **~ious** [ɪn'fekʃəs]

adj ansteckend
infer [ɪnˈfɜː*] *vt* schließen; **~ence** [ˈɪnfərəns] *adj* Schlußfolgerung *f*
inferior [ɪnˈfɪərɪə*] *adj* (*rank*) untergeordnet; (*quality*) minderwertig ♦ *n* Untergebene(r) *m*; **~ity** [ɪnfɪrɪˈɒrɪtɪ] *n* Minderwertigkeit *f*; (*in rank*) untergeordnete Stellung *f*; **~ity complex** *n* Minderwertigkeitskomplex *m*
infernal [ɪnˈfɜːnl] *adj* höllisch
infertile [ɪnˈfɜːtaɪl] *adj* unfruchtbar
infertility [ɪnfɜːˈtɪlɪtɪ] *n* Unfruchtbarkeit *f*
infested [ɪnˈfestɪd] *adj*: **to be ~ with** wimmeln von
infidelity [ɪnfɪˈdelɪtɪ] *n* Untreue *f*
infighting [ˈɪnfaɪtɪŋ] *n* Nahkampf *m*
infiltrate [ˈɪnfɪltreɪt] *vt* infiltrieren; (*spies*) einschleusen ♦ *vi* (MIL, *liquid*) einsickern; (*POL*): **to ~ (into)** unterwandern (+*acc*)
infinite [ˈɪnfɪnɪt] *adj* unendlich
infinitive [ɪnˈfɪnɪtɪv] *n* Infinitiv *m*
infinity [ɪnˈfɪnɪtɪ] *n* Unendlichkeit *f*
infirm [ɪnˈfɜːm] *adj* gebrechlich
infirmary [ɪnˈfɜːmərɪ] *n* Krankenhaus *nt*
infirmity [ɪnˈfɜːmɪtɪ] *n* Schwäche *f*, Gebrechlichkeit *f*
inflamed [ɪnˈfleɪmd] *adj* entzündet
inflammable [ɪnˈflæməbl] (*BRIT*) *adj* feuergefährlich
inflammation [ɪnfləˈmeɪʃən] *n* Entzündung *f*
inflatable [ɪnˈfleɪtəbl] *adj* aufblasbar
inflate [ɪnˈfleɪt] *vt* aufblasen; (*tyre*) aufpumpen; (*prices*) hochtreiben
inflation [ɪnˈfleɪʃən] *n* Inflation *f*; **~ary** [ɪnˈfleɪʃnərɪ] *adj* (*increase*) inflationistisch; (*situation*) inflationär
inflexible [ɪnˈfleksəbl] *adj* (*person*) nicht flexibel; (*opinion*) starr; (*thing*) unbiegsam
inflict [ɪnˈflɪkt] *vt*: **to ~ sth on sb** jdm etw zufügen; (*wound*) jdm etw beibringen
influence [ˈɪnfluəns] *n* Einfluß *m* ♦ *vt* beeinflussen
influential [ɪnfluˈenʃəl] *adj* einflußreich
influenza [ɪnfluˈenzə] *n* Grippe *f*
influx [ˈɪnflʌks] *n* (*of people*) Zustrom

m; (*of ideas*) Eindringen *nt*
inform [ɪnˈfɔːm] *vt* informieren ♦ *vi*: **to ~ on sb** jdn denunzieren; **to keep sb ~ed** jdn auf dem laufenden halten
informal [ɪnˈfɔːml] *adj* zwanglos; **~ity** [ɪnfɔːˈmælɪtɪ] *n* Ungezwungenheit *f*
informant [ɪnˈfɔːmənt] *n* Informant(in) *m(f)*
information [ɪnfəˈmeɪʃən] *n* Auskunft *f*, Information *f*; **a piece of ~** eine Auskunft, eine Information; **~ office** *n* Informationsbüro *nt*
informative [ɪnˈfɔːmətɪv] *adj* informativ; (*person*) mitteilsam
informer [ɪnˈfɔːmə*] *n* Denunziant(in) *m(f)*
infra-red [ɪnfrəˈred] *adj* infrarot
infrequent [ɪnˈfriːkwənt] *adj* selten
infringe [ɪnˈfrɪndʒ] *vt* (*law*) verstoßen gegen; **~ upon** *vt* verletzen; **~ment** *n* Verstoß *m*, Verletzung *f*
infuriating [ɪnˈfjʊərɪeɪtɪŋ] *adj* ärgerlich
infusion [ɪnˈfjuːʒən] *n* (*tea etc*) Aufguß *m*
ingenious [ɪnˈdʒiːnɪəs] *adj* genial
ingenuity [ɪndʒɪˈnjuːɪtɪ] *n* Genialität *f*
ingenuous [ɪnˈdʒenjuəs] *adj* aufrichtig; (*naive*) naiv
ingot [ˈɪŋgət] *n* Barren *m*
ingrained [ɪnˈgreɪnd] *adj* tiefsitzend
ingratiate [ɪnˈgreɪʃɪeɪt] *vt*: **to ~ o.s. with sb** sich bei jdm einschmeicheln
ingratitude [ɪnˈgrætɪtjuːd] *n* Undankbarkeit *f*
ingredient [ɪnˈgriːdɪənt] *n* Bestandteil *m*; (*COOK*) Zutat *f*
inhabit [ɪnˈhæbɪt] *vt* bewohnen; **~ant** [ɪnˈhæbɪtənt] *n* Bewohner(in) *m(f)*; (*of island, town*) Einwohner(in) *m(f)*
inhale [ɪnˈheɪl] *vt* einatmen; (*MED, cigarettes*) inhalieren
inherent [ɪnˈhɪərənt] *adj*: **~ (in)** innewohnend (+*dat*)
inherit [ɪnˈherɪt] *vt* erben; **~ance** *n* Erbe *nt*, Erbschaft *f*
inhibit [ɪnˈhɪbɪt] *vt* hemmen; **to ~ sb from doing sth** jdn daran hindern, etw zu tun; **~ion** [ɪnhɪˈbɪʃən] *n* Hemmung *f*
inhospitable [ɪnhɒsˈpɪtəbl] *adj* (*person*) ungastlich; (*country*) unwirtlich

inhuman [ɪn'hjuːmən] *adj* unmenschlich
inimitable [ɪ'nɪmɪtəbl] *adj* unnachahmlich
iniquity [ɪ'nɪkwɪtɪ] *n* Ungerechtigkeit *f*
initial [ɪ'nɪʃəl] *adj* anfänglich, Anfangs- ♦ *n* Initiale *f* ♦ *vt* abzeichnen; (*POL*) paraphieren; ~**ly** *adv* anfangs
initiate [ɪ'nɪʃɪeɪt] *vt* einführen; (*negotiations*) einleiten; **to ~ sb into a secret** jdn in ein Geheimnis einweihen; **to ~ proceedings against sb** (*JUR*) gerichtliche Schritte gegen jdn einleiten
initiation [ɪnɪʃɪ'eɪʃən] *n* Einführung *f*; Einleitung *f*
initiative [ɪ'nɪʃətɪv] *n* Initiative *f*
inject [ɪn'dʒekt] *vt* einspritzen; (*fig*) einflößen; ~**ion** [ɪn'dʒekʃən] *n* Spritze *f*
injunction [ɪn'dʒʌŋkʃən] *n* Verfügung *f*
injure ['ɪndʒə*] *vt* verletzen; ~**d** *adj* (*person, arm*) verletzt
injury ['ɪndʒərɪ] *n* Verletzung *f*; **to play ~ time** (*SPORT*) nachspielen
injustice [ɪn'dʒʌstɪs] *n* Ungerechtigkeit *f*
ink [ɪŋk] *n* Tinte *f*
inkling ['ɪŋklɪŋ] *n* (dunkle) Ahnung *f*
inlaid ['ɪn'leɪd] *adj* eingelegt, Einlege-
inland [*adj* 'ɪnlənd, *adv* 'ɪnlænd] *adj* Binnen-; (*domestic*) Inlands- ♦ *adv* landeinwärts; ~ **revenue** (*BRIT*) *n* Fiskus *m*
in-laws ['ɪnlɔːz] *npl* (*parents-in-law*) Schwiegereltern *pl*; (*others*) angeheiratete Verwandte *pl*
inlet ['ɪnlet] *n* Einlaß *m*; (*bay*) kleine Bucht *f*
inmate ['ɪnmeɪt] *n* Insasse *m*
inn [ɪn] *n* Gasthaus *nt*, Wirtshaus *nt*
innate [ɪ'neɪt] *adj* angeboren
inner ['ɪnə*] *adj* inner, Innen-; (*fig*) verborgen; ~ **city** *n* Innenstadt *f*; ~ **tube** *n* (*of tyre*) Schlauch *m*
innings ['ɪnɪŋz] *n* (*CRICKET*) Innenrunde *f*
innocence ['ɪnəsns] *n* Unschuld *f*; (*ignorance*) Unkenntnis *f*
innocent ['ɪnəsnt] *adj* unschuldig
innocuous [ɪ'nɒkjuəs] *adj* harmlos
innovation [ɪnəʊ'veɪʃən] *n* Neuerung *f*
innuendo [ɪnjʊ'endəʊ] *n* (versteckte) Anspielung *f*

innumerable [ɪ'njuːmərəbl] *adj* unzählig
inoculation [ɪnɒkjʊ'leɪʃən] *n* Impfung *f*
inopportune [ɪn'ɒpətjuːn] *adj* (*remark*) unangebracht; (*visit*) ungelegen
inordinately [ɪ'nɔːdɪnɪtlɪ] *adv* unmäßig
inpatient ['ɪnpeɪʃənt] *n* stationäre(r) Patient *m*/stationäre Patientin *f*
input ['ɪnpʊt] *n* (*COMPUT*) Eingabe *f*, (*power ~*) Energiezufuhr *f*; (*of energy, work*) Aufwand *m*
inquest ['ɪnkwest] *n* gerichtliche Untersuchung *f*
inquire [ɪn'kwaɪə*] *vi* sich erkundigen ♦ *vt* (*price*) sich erkundigen nach; ~ **into** *vt* untersuchen
inquiry [ɪn'kwaɪərɪ] *n* (*question*) Erkundigung *f*; (*investigation*) Untersuchung *f*; ~ **office** (*BRIT*) *n* Auskunft(sbüro *nt*) *f*
inquisitive [ɪn'kwɪzɪtɪv] *adj* neugierig
inroad ['ɪnrəʊd] *n* (*MIL*) Einfall *m*; (*fig*) Eingriff *m*
ins. *abbr* = inches
insane [ɪn'seɪn] *adj* wahnsinnig; (*MED*) geisteskrank
insanity [ɪn'sænɪtɪ] *n* Wahnsinn *m*
insatiable [ɪn'seɪʃəbl] *adj* unersättlich
inscribe [ɪn'skraɪb] *vt* eingravieren; (*book etc*): **to ~ (to sb)** (jdm) widmen
inscription [ɪn'skrɪpʃən] *n* (*on stone*) Inschrift *f*; (*in book*) Widmung *f*
inscrutable [ɪn'skruːtəbl] *adj* unergründlich
insect ['ɪnsekt] *n* Insekt *nt*; ~**icide** [ɪn'sektɪsaɪd] *n* Insektenvertilgungsmittel *nt*
insecure [ɪnsɪ'kjʊə*] *adj* (*person*) unsicher; (*thing*) nicht fest *or* sicher
insecurity [ɪnsɪ'kjʊərɪtɪ] *n* Unsicherheit *f*
insemination [ɪnsemɪ'neɪʃən] *n*: **artificial ~** künstliche Befruchtung *f*
insensible [ɪn'sensɪbl] *adj* (*unconscious*) bewußtlos
insensitive [ɪn'sensɪtɪv] *adj* (*to pain*) unempfindlich; (*without feelings*) gefühllos
inseparable [ɪn'sepərəbl] *adj* (*people*) unzertrennlich; (*word*) untrennbar
insert [*vb* ɪn'sɜːt, *n* 'ɪnsɜːt] *vt* einfügen; (*coin*) einwerfen; (*stick into*) hinein-

stecken; (*advertisement*) aufgeben ♦ *n* (*in book*) Einlage *f*; (*in magazine*) Beilage *f*; ~**ion** [ɪn'sɜːʃən] *n* Einfügung *f*; (*PRESS*) Inserat *nt*

in-service ['ɪn'sɜːvɪs] *adj* (*training*) berufsbegleitend

inshore ['ɪn'ʃɔː*] *adj* Küsten- ♦ *adv* an der Küste

inside ['ɪn'saɪd] *n* Innenseite *f*, Innere(s) *nt* ♦ *adj* innere(r, s), Innen- ♦ *adv* (*place*) innen; (*direction*) nach innen, hinein ♦ *prep* (*place*) in +*dat*; (*direction*) in +*acc* ... hinein; (*time*) innerhalb +*gen*; ~**s** *npl* (*inf*) Eingeweide *nt*; ~ **10 minutes** unter 10 Minuten; ~ **forward** *n* (*SPORT*) Halbstürmer *m*; ~ **lane** *n* (*AUT: in Britain*) linke Spur; ~ **out** *adv* linksherum; (*know*) in- und auswendig

insidious [ɪn'sɪdɪəs] *adj* heimtückisch

insight ['ɪnsaɪt] *n* Einsicht *f*; ~ **into** Einblick *m* in +*acc*

insignificant [ɪnsɪg'nɪfɪkənt] *adj* unbedeutend

insincere [ɪnsɪn'sɪə*] *adj* unaufrichtig

insinuate [ɪn'sɪnjʊeɪt] *vt* (*hint*) andeuten

insipid [ɪn'sɪpɪd] *adj* fad(e)

insist [ɪn'sɪst] *vi*: **to** ~ (**on**) bestehen (auf +*acc*); ~**ence** *n* Bestehen *nt*; ~**ent** *adj* hartnäckig; (*urgent*) dringend

insole ['ɪnsəʊl] *n* Einlegesohle *f*

insolence ['ɪnsələns] *n* Frechheit *f*

insolent ['ɪnsələnt] *adj* frech

insoluble [ɪn'sɒljʊbl] *adj* unlösbar; (*CHEM*) unlöslich

insolvent [ɪn'sɒlvənt] *adj* zahlungsunfähig

insomnia [ɪn'sɒmnɪə] *n* Schlaflosigkeit *f*

inspect [ɪn'spekt] *vt* prüfen; (*officially*) inspizieren; ~**ion** [ɪn'spekʃən] *n* Inspektion *f*; ~**or** *n* (*official*) Inspektor *m*; (*police*) Polizeikommissar *m*; (*BRIT: on buses, trains*) Kontrolleur *m*

inspiration [ɪnspɪ'reɪʃən] *n* Inspiration *f*

inspire [ɪn'spaɪə*] *vt* (*person*) inspirieren; **to** ~ **sth in sb** (*respect*) jdm etw einflößen; (*hope*) etw in jdm wecken

instability [ɪnstə'bɪlɪtɪ] *n* Unbeständigkeit *f*, Labilität *f*

install [ɪn'stɔːl] *vt* (*put in*) installieren; (*telephone*) anschließen; (*establish*) einsetzen; ~**ation** [ɪnstə'leɪʃən] *n* (*of person*) (Amts)einsetzung *f*; (*of machinery*) Installierung *f*; (*machines etc*) Anlage *f*

instalment [ɪn'stɔːlmənt] (*US* **installment**) *n* Rate *f*; (*of story*) Fortsetzung *f*; **to pay in** ~**s** auf Raten zahlen

instance ['ɪnstəns] *n* Fall *m*; (*example*) Beispiel *nt*; **for** ~ zum Beispiel; **in the first** ~ zunächst

instant ['ɪnstənt] *n* Augenblick *m* ♦ *adj* augenblicklich, sofortig

instantaneous [ɪnstən'teɪnɪəs] *adj* unmittelbar

instant coffee *n* Pulverkaffee *m*

instantly ['ɪnstəntlɪ] *adv* sofort

instead [ɪn'sted] *adv* statt dessen; ~ **of** *prep* anstatt +*gen*

instep ['ɪnstep] *n* Spann *m*; (*of shoe*) Blatt *nt*

instigation [ɪnstɪ'geɪʃən] *n* Veranlassung *f*; (*of crime etc*) Anstiftung *f*

instil [ɪn'stɪl] *vt* (*fig*): **to** ~ **sth in sb** jdm etw beibringen

instinct ['ɪnstɪŋkt] *n* Instinkt *m*; ~**ive** [ɪn'stɪŋktɪv] *adj* instinktiv

institute ['ɪnstɪtjuːt] *n* Institut *nt* ♦ *vt* einführen; (*search*) einleiten

institution [ɪnstɪ'tjuːʃən] *n* Institution *f*; (*home*) Anstalt *f*

instruct [ɪn'strʌkt] *vt* anweisen; (*officially*) instruieren; ~**ion** [ɪn'strʌkʃən] *n* Unterricht *m*; ~**ions** *npl* (*orders*) Anweisungen *pl*; (*for use*) Gebrauchsanweisung *f*; ~**ive** *adj* lehrreich; ~**or** *n* Lehrer *m*; (*MIL*) Ausbilder *m*

instrument ['ɪnstrʊmənt] *n* Instrument *nt*; ~**al** [ɪnstrʊ'mentl] *adj* (*MUS*) Instrumental-; (*helpful*): ~**al** (**in**) behilflich (bei); ~ **panel** *n* Armaturenbrett *nt*

insubordinate [ɪnsə'bɔːdənət] *adj* aufsässig, widersetzlich

insubordination ['ɪnsəbɔːdɪ'neɪʃən] *n* Gehorsamsverweigerung *f*

insufferable [ɪn'sʌfərəbl] *adj* unerträglich

insufficient [ɪnsə'fɪʃənt] *adj* ungenügend
insular ['ɪnsjələ*] *adj* (*fig*) engstirnig
insulate ['ɪnsjʊleɪt] *vt* (*ELEC*) isolieren; (*fig*): **to ~ (from)** abschirmen (vor +*dat*)
insulating tape *n* Isolierband *nt*
insulation [ɪnsjʊ'leɪʃən] *n* Isolierung *f*
insulin ['ɪnsjʊlɪn] *n* Insulin *nt*
insult [*n* 'ɪnsʌlt, *vb* ɪn'sʌlt] *n* Beleidigung *f* ♦ *vt* beleidigen; **~ing** [ɪn'sʌltɪŋ] *adj* beleidigend
insuperable [ɪn'suːpərəbl] *adj* unüberwindlich
insurance [ɪn'ʃʊərəns] *n* Versicherung *f*; **fire/life ~** Feuer-/Lebensversicherung; **~ agent** *n* Versicherungsvertreter *m*; **~ policy** *n* Versicherungspolice *f*
insure [ɪn'ʃʊə*] *vt* versichern
insurrection [ɪnsə'rekʃən] *n* Aufstand *m*
intact [ɪn'tækt] *adj* unversehrt
intake ['ɪnteɪk] *n* (*place*) Einlaßöffnung *f*; (*act*) Aufnahme *f*; (*BRIT: SCH*): **an ~ of 200 a year** ein Neuzugang von 200 im Jahr
intangible [ɪn'tændʒəbl] *adj* nicht greifbar
integral ['ɪntɪgrəl] *adj* (*essential*) wesentlich; (*complete*) vollständig; (*MATH*) Integral-
integrate ['ɪntɪgreɪt] *vt* integrieren ♦ *vi* sich integrieren
integrity [ɪn'tegrɪtɪ] *n* (*honesty*) Redlichkeit *f*, Integrität *f*
intellect ['ɪntɪlekt] *n* Intellekt *m*; **~ual** [ɪntɪ'lektjʊəl] *adj* geistig, intellektuell ♦ *n* Intellektuelle(r) *mf*
intelligence [ɪn'telɪdʒəns] *n* (*understanding*) Intelligenz *f*; (*news*) Information *f*; (*MIL*) Geheimdienst *m*
intelligent [ɪn'telɪdʒənt] *adj* intelligent; **~ly** *adv* klug; (*write, speak*) verständlich
intelligentsia [ɪntelɪ'dʒentsɪə] *n* Intelligenz *f*
intelligible [ɪn'telɪdʒəbl] *adj* verständlich
intend [ɪn'tend] *vt* beabsichtigen; **that was ~ed for you** das war für dich gedacht
intense [ɪn'tens] *adj* stark, intensiv;

(*person*) ernsthaft; **~ly** *adv* äußerst; (*study*) intensiv
intensify [ɪn'tensɪfaɪ] *vt* verstärken, intensivieren
intensity [ɪn'tensɪtɪ] *n* Intensität *f*
intensive [ɪn'tensɪv] *adj* intensiv; **~ care unit** *n* Intensivstation *f*
intent [ɪn'tent] *n* Absicht *f* ♦ *adj*: **to be ~ on doing sth** fest entschlossen sein, etw zu tun; **to all ~s and purposes** praktisch
intention [ɪn'tenʃən] *n* Absicht *f*
intentional *adj* absichtlich; **~ly** *adv* absichtlich
intently [ɪn'tentlɪ] *adv* konzentriert
inter [ɪn'tɜ:*] *vt* beerdigen
interact [ɪntər'ækt] *vi* aufeinander einwirken; **~ion** *n* Wechselwirkung *f*
intercede [ɪntə'si:d] *vi* sich verwenden
intercept [ɪntə'sept] *vt* abfangen
interchange [*n* 'ɪntətʃeɪndʒ, *vb* ɪntə'tʃeɪndʒ] *n* (*exchange*) Austausch *m*; (*on roads*) Verkehrskreuz *nt* ♦ *vt* austauschen; **~able** [ɪntə'tʃeɪndʒəbl] *adj* austauschbar
intercom ['ɪntəkɒm] *n* (Gegen)sprechanlage *f*
intercourse ['ɪntəkɔ:s] *n* (*exchange*) Beziehungen *pl*; (*sexual*) Geschlechtsverkehr *m*
interface ['ɪntəfeɪs] *n* (*COMPUT*) Schnittstelle *f*, Interface *nt*
interfere [ɪntə'fɪə*] *vi*: **to ~ (with)** (*meddle*) sich einmischen (in +*acc*); (*disrupt*) stören (+*acc*)
interference [ɪntə'fɪərəns] *n* Einmischung *f*; (*TV*) Störung *f*
interim ['ɪntərɪm] *n*: **in the ~** inzwischen
interior [ɪn'tɪərɪə*] *n* Innere(s) *nt* ♦ *adj* innere(r, s), Innen-; **~ designer** *n* Innenarchitekt(in) *m(f)*
interjection [ɪntə'dʒekʃən] *n* Ausruf *m*
interlock [ɪntə'lɒk] *vi* ineinandergreifen

interloper ['ɪntələupə*] n Eindringling m
interlude ['ɪntəlu:d] n Pause f
intermarry [ɪntə'mærɪ] vi untereinander heiraten
intermediary [ɪntə'mi:dɪərɪ] n Vermittler m
intermediate [ɪntə'mi:dɪət] adj Zwischen-, Mittel-
interminable [ɪn'tɜ:mɪnəbl] adj endlos
intermission [ɪntə'mɪʃən] n Pause f
intermittent [ɪntə'mɪtənt] adj periodisch, stoßweise
intern [vb ɪn'tɜ:n, n 'ɪntɜ:n] vt internieren ♦ n (US) Assistenzarzt m/-ärztin f
internal [ɪn'tɜ:nl] adj (inside) innere(r, s); (domestic) Inlands-; **~ly** adv innen; (MED) innerlich; **"not to be taken ~ly"** „nur zur äußerlichen Anwendung"; **I~ Revenue Service** (US) n Finanzamt nt
international [ɪntə'næʃnəl] adj international ♦ n (SPORT) Nationalspieler(in) m(f); (: match) internationale(s) Spiel nt
interplay ['ɪntəpleɪ] n Wechselspiel nt
interpret [ɪn'tɜ:prɪt] vt (explain) auslegen, interpretieren; (translate) dolmetschen; **~ation** [ɪntɜ:prɪ'teɪʃən] n Interpretation f; **~er** n Dolmetscher(in) m(f)
interrelated [ɪntərɪ'leɪtɪd] adj untereinander zusammenhängend
interrogate [ɪn'terəgeɪt] vt verhören
interrogation [ɪntərə'geɪʃən] n Verhör nt
interrogative [ɪntə'rɒgətɪv] adj Frage-
interrupt [ɪntə'rʌpt] vt unterbrechen; **~ion** [ɪntə'rʌpʃən] n Unterbrechung f
intersect [ɪntə'sekt] vt (durch)schneiden ♦ vi sich schneiden; **~ion** [ɪntə'sekʃən] n (of roads) Kreuzung f; (of lines) Schnittpunkt m
intersperse [ɪntə'spɜ:s] vt: **to ~ sth with sth** etw mit etw durchsetzen
intertwine [ɪntə'twaɪn] vt verflechten ♦ vi sich verflechten
interval ['ɪntəvəl] n Abstand m; (BRIT: SCH, THEAT, SPORT) Pause f; **at ~s** in Abständen
intervene [ɪntə'vi:n] vi dazwischenliegen; (act): **to ~ (in)** einschreiten (gegen)

intervention [ɪntə'venʃən] n Eingreifen nt, Intervention f
interview ['ɪntəvju:] n (PRESS etc) Interview nt; (for job) Vorstellungsgespräch nt ♦ vt interviewen; **~er** n Interviewer m
intestine [ɪn'testɪn] n: **large/small ~** Dick-/Dünndarm m
intimacy ['ɪntɪməsɪ] n Intimität f
intimate [adj 'ɪntɪmət, vb 'ɪntɪmeɪt] adj (inmost) innerste(r, s); (knowledge) eingehend; (familiar) vertraut; (friends) eng ♦ vt andeuten
intimidate [ɪn'tɪmɪdeɪt] vt einschüchtern
intimidation [ɪntɪmɪ'deɪʃən] n Einschüchterung f
into ['ɪntu] prep (motion) in +acc ... hinein; **5 ~ 25** 25 durch 5
intolerable [ɪn'tɒlərəbl] adj unerträglich
intolerance [ɪn'tɒlərns] n Unduldsamkeit f
intolerant [ɪn'tɒlərənt] adj: **~ of** unduldsam gegen(über)
intoxicate [ɪn'tɒksɪkeɪt] vt berauschen; **~d** adj betrunken
intoxication [ɪntɒksɪ'keɪʃən] n Rausch m
intractable [ɪn'træktəbl] adj schwer zu handhaben; (problem) schwer lösbar
intransigent [ɪn'trænsɪdʒənt] adj unnachgiebig
intransitive [ɪn'trænsɪtɪv] adj intransitiv
intravenous [ɪntrə'vi:nəs] adj intravenös
in-tray ['ɪntreɪ] n Eingangskorb m
intrepid [ɪn'trepɪd] adj unerschrocken
intricate ['ɪntrɪkət] adj kompliziert
intrigue [ɪn'tri:g] n Intrige f ♦ vt faszinieren ♦ vi intrigieren
intriguing [ɪn'tri:gɪŋ] adj faszinierend
intrinsic [ɪn'trɪnsɪk] adj innere(r, s); (difference) wesentlich
introduce [ɪntrə'dju:s] vt (person) vorstellen; (sth new) einführen; (subject) anschneiden; **to ~ sb to sb** jdm jdn vorstellen; **to ~ sb to sth** jdn in etw acc einführen
introduction [ɪntrə'dʌkʃən] n Einführung f; (to book) Einleitung f
introductory [ɪntrə'dʌktərɪ] adj Einführungs-, Vor-
introspective [ɪntrəu'spektɪv] adj nach

innen gekehrt

introvert ['ɪntrəʊvɜːt] *n* Introvertierte(r) *mf* ♦ *adj* introvertiert

intrude [ɪn'truːd] *vi*: to ~ (on sb/sth) (jdn/etw) stören; ~r *n* Eindringling *m*

intrusion [ɪn'truːʒən] *n* Störung *f*

intrusive [ɪn'truːsɪv] *adj* aufdringlich

intuition [ɪntjuː'ɪʃən] *n* Intuition *f*

inundate ['ɪnʌndeɪt] *vt* (*also fig*) überschwemmen

invade [ɪn'veɪd] *vt* einfallen in +*acc*; ~r *n* Eindringling *m*

invalid [*n* 'ɪnvəlɪd, *adj* ɪn'vælɪd] *n* (*disabled*) Invalide *m* ♦ *adj* (*ill*) krank; (*disabled*) invalide; (*not valid*) ungültig

invaluable [ɪn'væljʊəbl] *adj* unschätzbar

invariable [ɪn'vɛərɪəbl] *adj* unveränderlich

invariably [ɪn'vɛərɪəblɪ] *adv* ausnahmslos

invasion [ɪn'veɪʒən] *n* Invasion *f*

invent [ɪn'vent] *vt* erfinden; ~ion [ɪn'venʃən] *n* Erfindung *f*; ~ive *adj* erfinderisch; ~or *n* Erfinder *m*

inventory ['ɪnvəntrɪ] *n* Inventar *nt*

inverse ['ɪn'vɜːs] *n* Umkehrung *f* ♦ *adj* umgekehrt

invert [ɪn'vɜːt] *vt* umdrehen; ~ed commas (*BRIT*) *npl* Anführungsstriche *pl*

invest [ɪn'vest] *vt* investieren

investigate [ɪn'vestɪgeɪt] *vt* untersuchen

investigation [ɪnvestɪ'geɪʃən] *n* Untersuchung *f*

investigator [ɪn'vestɪgeɪtə*] *n* Untersuchungsbeamte(r) *m*

investiture [ɪn'vestɪtʃə*] *n* Amtseinsetzung *f*

investment [ɪn'vestmənt] *n* Investition *f*

investor [ɪn'vestə*] *n* (Geld)anleger *m*

inveterate [ɪn'vetərət] *adj* unverbesserlich

invidious [ɪn'vɪdɪəs] *adj* unangenehm; (*distinctions, remark*) ungerecht

invigilate [ɪn'vɪdʒɪleɪt] *vi* (*in exam*) Aufsicht führen ♦ *vt* Aufsicht führen bei

invigorating [ɪn'vɪgəreɪtɪŋ] *adj* stärkend

invincible [ɪn'vɪnsəbl] *adj* unbesiegbar

inviolate [ɪn'vaɪələt] *adj* unverletzt

invisible [ɪn'vɪzəbl] *adj* unsichtbar; ~

ink *n* Geheimtinte *f*

invitation [ɪnvɪ'teɪʃən] *n* Einladung *f*

invite [ɪn'vaɪt] *vt* einladen

inviting [ɪn'vaɪtɪŋ] *adj* einladend

invoice ['ɪnvɔɪs] *n* Rechnung *f* ♦ *vt* (*goods*): to ~ sb for sth jdm etw *acc* in Rechnung stellen

invoke [ɪn'vəʊk] *vt* anrufen

involuntary [ɪn'vɒləntərɪ] *adj* unabsichtlich

involve [ɪn'vɒlv] *vt* (*entangle*) verwickeln; (*entail*) mit sich bringen; ~d *adj* verwickelt; ~ment *n* Verwicklung *f*

inward ['ɪnwəd] *adj* innere(r, s); (*curve*) Innen- ♦ *adv* nach innen; ~ly *adv* im Innern; ~s *adv* nach innen

I/O *abbr* (*COMPUT*: = *input/output*) I/O

iodine ['aɪədiːn] *n* Jod *nt*

iota [aɪ'əʊtə] *n* (*fig*) bißchen *nt*

IOU *n abbr* (= *I owe you*) Schuldschein *m*

IQ *n abbr* (= *intelligence quotient*) IQ *m*

IRA *n abbr* (= *Irish Republican Army*) IRA *f*

Iran [ɪ'rɑːn] *n* Iran *m*; ~ian *adj* iranisch ♦ *n* Iraner(in) *m(f)*; (*LING*) Iranisch *nt*

Iraq [ɪ'rɑːk] *n* Irak *m*; ~i *adj* irakisch ♦ *n* Iraker(in) *m(f)*; (*LING*) Irakisch *nt*

irascible [ɪ'ræsɪbl] *adj* reizbar

irate [aɪ'reɪt] *adj* zornig

Ireland ['aɪələnd] *n* Irland *nt*

iris ['aɪrɪs] (*pl* ~es) *n* Iris *f*

Irish ['aɪrɪʃ] *adj* irisch ♦ *npl*: the ~ die Iren *pl*; ~man (*irreg*) *n* Ire *m*, Irländer *m*; ~ Sea *n* Irische See *f*; ~woman (*irreg*) *n* Irin *f*, Irländerin *f*

irksome ['ɜːksəm] *adj* lästig

iron ['aɪən] *n* Eisen *nt*; (*for ironing*) Bügeleisen *nt* ♦ *adj* eisern ♦ *vt* bügeln; ~ out *vt* (*also fig*) ausbügeln; I~ Curtain *n* Eiserne(r) Vorhang *m*

ironic(al) [aɪ'rɒnɪk(əl)] *adj* ironisch; (*coincidence etc*) witzig

ironing ['aɪənɪŋ] *n* Bügeln *nt*; (*laundry*) Bügelwäsche *f*; ~ board *n* Bügelbrett *nt*

ironmonger ['aɪənmʌŋgə*] (*BRIT*) *n* Eisenwarenhändler *m*; ~'s (shop) *n* Eisenwarenhandlung *f*

iron ore ['aɪənɔː*] *n* Eisenerz *nt*

irony ['aɪərənɪ] n Ironie f
irrational [ɪ'ræʃənl] adj irrational
irreconcilable [ɪrekən'saɪləbl] adj unvereinbar
irrefutable [ɪrɪ'fjuːtəbl] adj unwiderlegbar
irregular [ɪ'regjʊlə*] adj unregelmäßig; (: shape) ungleich(mäßig); (fig) unüblich; (: behaviour) ungehörig; ~ity [ɪregjʊ'lærɪtɪ] n Unregelmäßigkeit f; Ungleichmäßigkeit f; (fig) Vergehen nt
irrelevant [ɪ'reləvənt] adj belanglos, irrelevant
irreparable [ɪ'repərəbl] adj nicht wiedergutzumachen
irreplaceable [ɪrɪ'pleɪsəbl] adj unersetzlich
irrepressible [ɪrɪ'presəbl] adj nicht zu unterdrücken; (joy) unbändig
irresistible [ɪrɪ'zɪstəbl] adj unwiderstehlich
irresolute [ɪ'rezəluːt] adj unentschlossen
irrespective [ɪrɪ'spektɪv]: ~ of prep ungeachtet +gen
irresponsible [ɪrɪ'spɒnsəbl] adj verantwortungslos
irreverent [ɪ'revərənt] adj respektlos
irrevocable [ɪ'revəkəbl] adj unwiderrufbar
irrigate ['ɪrɪgeɪt] vt bewässern
irrigation [ɪrɪ'geɪʃən] n Bewässerung f
irritable ['ɪrɪtəbl] adj reizbar
irritate ['ɪrɪteɪt] vt irritieren, reizen (also MED)
irritation [ɪrɪ'teɪʃən] n (anger) Ärger m; (MED) Reizung f
IRS n abbr = **Internal Revenue Service**
is [ɪz] vb see **be**
Islam ['ɪzlɑːm] n Islam m
island ['aɪlənd] n Insel f; ~er n Inselbewohner(in) m(f)
isle [aɪl] n (kleine) Insel f
isn't ['ɪznt] = **is not**
isolate ['aɪsəʊleɪt] vt isolieren; ~d adj isoliert; (case) Einzel-
isolation [aɪsəʊ'leɪʃən] n Isolierung f
Israel ['ɪzreɪəl] n Israel nt; ~i [ɪz'reɪlɪ] adj israelisch ♦ n Israeli mf
issue ['ɪʃuː] n (matter) Frage f; (outcome) Ausgang m; (of newspaper,

shares) Ausgabe f; (offspring) Nachkommenschaft f ♦ vt ausgeben; (warrant) erlassen; (documents) ausstellen; (orders) erteilen; (books) herausgeben; (verdict) aussprechen; **to be at ~** zur Debatte stehen; **to take ~ with sb over sth** jdm in etw dat widersprechen
isthmus ['ɪsməs] n Landenge f

KEYWORD
---

it [ɪt] pron **1** (specific: subject) er/sie/es; (: direct object) ihn/sie/es; (: indirect object) ihm/ihr/ihm; **about/from/in/of it** darüber/davon/darin/davon

2 (impers) es; **it's raining** es regnet; **it's Friday tomorrow** morgen ist Freitag; **who is it? - it's me** wer ist da? - ich (bin's)

Italian [ɪ'tæljən] adj italienisch ♦ n Italiener(in) m(f); (LING) Italienisch nt
italic [ɪ'tælɪk] adj kursiv; ~s npl Kursivschrift f
Italy ['ɪtəlɪ] n Italien nt
itch [ɪtʃ] n Juckreiz m; (fig) Lust f ♦ vi jucken; **to be ~ing to do sth** darauf brennen, etw zu tun; ~y adj juckend
it'd ['ɪtd] = **it would**; **it had**
item ['aɪtəm] n Gegenstand m; (on list) Posten m; (in programme) Nummer f; (in agenda) (Programm)punkt m; (in newspaper) (Zeitungs)notiz f; ~ize vt verzeichnen
itinerant [ɪ'tɪnərənt] adj (person) umherreisend
itinerary [aɪ'tɪnərərɪ] n Reiseroute f
it'll ['ɪtl] = **it will**; **it shall**
its [ɪts] adj (masculine, neuter) sein; (feminine) ihr
it's [ɪts] = **it is**; **it has**
itself [ɪt'self] pron sich (selbst); (emphatic) selbst
ITV (BRIT) n abbr = **Independent Television**
I.U.D. n abbr (= intra-uterine device) Pessar nt
I've [aɪv] = **I have**
ivory ['aɪvərɪ] n Elfenbein nt; ~ **tower** n (fig) Elfenbeinturm m

ivy ['aɪvɪ] n Efeu nt

J

jab [dʒæb] vt (hinein)stechen ♦ n Stich m, Stoß m; (inf) Spritze f
jabber ['dʒæbə*] vi plappern
jack [dʒæk] n (AUT) (Wagen)heber m; (CARDS) Bube m; ~ up vt aufbocken
jackal ['dʒækəl] n (ZOOL) Schakal m
jackdaw ['dʒækdɔ:] n Dohle f
jacket ['dʒækɪt] n Jacke f; (of book) Schutzumschlag m; (TECH) Ummantelung f
jackknife ['dʒæknaɪf] vi (truck) sich zusammenschieben
jack plug n (ELEC) Buchsenstecker m
jackpot ['dʒækpɒt] n Haupttreffer m
jade [dʒeɪd] n (stone) Jade m
jaded ['dʒeɪdɪd] adj ermattet
jagged ['dʒægɪd] adj zackig
jail [dʒeɪl] n Gefängnis nt ♦ vt einsperren; ~er n Gefängniswärter m
jam [dʒæm] n Marmelade f; (also: traffic ~) (Verkehrs)stau m; (inf: trouble) Klemme f ♦ vt (wedge) einklemmen; (cram) hineinzwängen; (obstruct) blockieren ♦ vi sich verklemmen; to ~ sth into sth etw in etw acc hineinstopfen
Jamaica [dʒə'meɪkə] n Jamaika nt
jangle ['dʒæŋgl] vt, vi klimpern
janitor ['dʒænɪtə*] n Hausmeister m
January ['dʒænjʊərɪ] n Januar m
Japan [dʒə'pæn] n Japan nt; ~ese [dʒæpə'ni:z] adj japanisch ♦ n inv Japaner(in) m(f); (LING) Japanisch nt
jar [dʒɑ:*] n Glas nt ♦ vi kreischen; (colours etc) nicht harmonieren
jargon ['dʒɑ:gən] n Fachsprache f, Jargon m
jaundice ['dʒɔ:ndɪs] n Gelbsucht f; ~d adj (fig) mißgünstig
jaunt [dʒɔ:nt] n Spritztour f; ~y adj (lively) munter; (brisk) flott
javelin ['dʒævlɪn] n Speer m
jaw [dʒɔ:] n Kiefer m
jay [dʒeɪ] n (ZOOL) Eichelhäher m
jaywalker ['dʒeɪwɔ:kə*] n unvorsichtige(r) Fußgänger m
jazz [dʒæz] n Jazz m; ~ up vt (MUS) verjazzen; (enliven) aufpolieren; ~y adj (colour) schreiend, auffallend
jealous ['dʒeləs] adj (envious) mißgünstig; (husband) eifersüchtig; ~y n Mißgunst f; Eifersucht f
jeans [dʒi:nz] npl Jeans pl
jeep [dʒi:p] n Jeep m
jeer [dʒɪə*] vi: to ~ (at sb) (über jdn) höhnisch lachen, (jdn) verspotten
jelly ['dʒelɪ] n Gelee nt; (dessert) Grütze f; ~fish n Qualle f
jeopardize ['dʒepədaɪz] vt gefährden
jeopardy ['dʒepədɪ] n: to be in ~ in Gefahr sein
jerk [dʒɜ:k] n Ruck m; (inf: idiot) Trottel m ♦ vt ruckartig bewegen ♦ vi sich ruckartig bewegen
jerkin ['dʒɜ:kɪn] n Wams nt
jerky ['dʒɜ:kɪ] adj (movement) ruckartig; (ride) rüttelnd
jersey ['dʒɜ:zɪ] n Pullover m
jest [dʒest] n Scherz m ♦ vi spaßen; in ~ im Spaß
Jesus ['dʒi:zəs] n Jesus m
jet [dʒet] n (stream: of water etc) Strahl m; (spout) Düse f; (AVIAT) Düsenflugzeug nt; ~-black adj rabenschwarz; ~ engine n Düsenmotor m; ~-lag n Jet-lag m
jettison ['dʒetɪsn] vt über Bord werfen
jetty ['dʒetɪ] n Landesteg m, Mole f
Jew [dʒu:] n Jude m
jewel ['dʒu:əl] n (also fig) Juwel nt; ~ler (US ~er) n Juwelier m; ~ler's (shop) n Juwelier m; ~lery (US ~ry) n Schmuck m
Jewess ['dʒu:ɪs] n Jüdin f
Jewish ['dʒu:ɪʃ] adj jüdisch
jib [dʒɪb] n (NAUT) Klüver m
jibe [dʒaɪb] n spöttische Bemerkung f
jiffy ['dʒɪfɪ] (inf) n: in a ~ sofort
jigsaw ['dʒɪgsɔ:] n (also: ~ puzzle) Puzzle(spiel) nt
jilt [dʒɪlt] vt den Laufpaß geben +dat
jingle ['dʒɪŋgl] n (advertisement) Werbesong m ♦ vi klimpern; (bells) bimmeln ♦ vt klimpern mit; bimmeln lassen

jinx [dʒɪŋks] *n*: there's a ~ on it es ist verhext

jitters ['dʒɪtəz] (*inf*) *npl*: to get the ~ einen Bammel kriegen

job [dʒɒb] *n* (*piece of work*) Arbeit *f*; (*position*) Stellung *f*; (*duty*) Aufgabe *f*; (*difficulty*) Mühe *f*; it's a good ~ he ... es ist ein Glück, daß er ...; just the ~ genau das Richtige; J~**centre** (*BRIT*) *n* Arbeitsamt *nt*; ~**less** *adj* arbeitslos

jockey ['dʒɒkɪ] *n* Jockei *m* ♦ *vi*: to ~ for **position** sich in eine gute Position drängeln

jocular ['dʒɒkjʊlə*] *adj* scherzhaft

jog [dʒɒɡ] *vt* (an)stoßen ♦ *vi* (*run*) joggen; to ~ **along** vor sich *acc* hinwursteln; (*work*) seinen Gang gehen; ~**ging** *n* Jogging *nt*

join [dʒɔɪn] *vt* (*club*) beitreten +*dat*; (*person*) sich anschließen +*dat*; (*put together*): to ~ (**sth to sth**) (etw mit etw) verbinden ♦ *vi* (*unite*) sich vereinigen ♦ *n* Verbindungsstelle *f*, Naht *f*; ~ **in** *vt, vi*: to ~ **in** (**sth**) (bei etw) mitmachen; ~ **up** *vi* (*MIL*) zur Armee gehen

joiner ['dʒɔɪnə*] *n* Schreiner *m*; ~**y** *n* Schreinerei *f*

joint [dʒɔɪnt] *n* (*TECH*) Fuge *f*; (*of bones*) Gelenk *nt*; (*of meat*) Braten *m*; (*inf: place*) Lokal *nt* ♦ *adj* gemeinsam; ~ **account** *n* (*with bank etc*) gemeinsame(s) Konto *nt*; ~**ly** *adv* gemeinsam

joist [dʒɔɪst] *n* Träger *m*

joke [dʒəʊk] *n* Witz *m* ♦ *vi* Witze machen; to play a ~ **on sb** jdm einen Streich spielen; ~**r** *n* Witzbold *m*; (*CARDS*) Joker *m*

jolly ['dʒɒlɪ] *adj* lustig ♦ *adv* (*inf*) ganz schön

jolt [dʒəʊlt] *n* (*shock*) Schock *m*; (*jerk*) Stoß *m* ♦ *vt* (*push*) stoßen; (*shake*) durchschütteln; (*fig*) aufrütteln ♦ *vi* holpern

Jordan ['dʒɔːdən] *n* Jordanien *nt*; (*river*) Jordan *m*

jostle ['dʒɒsl] *vt* anrempeln

jot [dʒɒt] *n*: not one ~ kein Jota *nt*; ~ **down** *vt* notieren; ~**ter** (*BRIT*) *n* Notiz-

block *m*

journal ['dʒɜːnl] *n* (*diary*) Tagebuch *nt*; (*magazine*) Zeitschrift *f*; ~**ese** *n* Zeitungsstil *m*; ~**ism** *n* Journalismus *m*; ~**ist** *n* Journalist(in) *m(f)*

journey ['dʒɜːnɪ] *n* Reise *f*

jovial ['dʒəʊvɪəl] *adj* jovial

joy [dʒɔɪ] *n* Freude *f*; ~**ful** *adj* freudig; ~**ous** *adj* freudig; ~ **ride** *n* Schwarzfahrt *f*; ~**stick** *n* Steuerknüppel *m*; (*COMPUT*) Joystick *m*

J.P. *n abbr* = **Justice of the Peace**

Jr *abbr* = **junior**

jubilant ['dʒuːbɪlənt] *adj* triumphierend

jubilee ['dʒuːbɪliː] *n* Jubiläum *nt*

judge [dʒʌdʒ] *n* Richter *m*; (*fig*) Kenner *m* ♦ *vt* (*JUR: person*) die Verhandlung führen über +*acc*; (*case*) verhandeln; (*assess*) beurteilen; (*estimate*) einschätzen; ~**ment** *n* (*JUR*) Urteil *nt*; (*ECCL*) Gericht *nt*; (*ability*) Urteilsvermögen *nt*

judicial [dʒuːˈdɪʃəl] *adj* gerichtlich, Justiz-

judiciary [dʒuːˈdɪʃɪərɪ] *n* Gerichtsbehörden *pl*; (*judges*) Richterstand *m*

judicious [dʒuːˈdɪʃəs] *adj* weise

judo ['dʒuːdəʊ] *n* Judo *nt*

jug [dʒʌɡ] *n* Krug *m*

juggernaut ['dʒʌɡənɔːt] (*BRIT*) *n* (*huge truck*) Schwertransporter *m*

juggle ['dʒʌɡl] *vt, vi* jonglieren; ~**r** *n* Jongleur *m*

Jugoslav *etc* ['juːɡəʊˈslɑːv] = **Yugoslav** *etc*

juice [dʒuːs] *n* Saft *m*

juicy ['dʒuːsɪ] *adj* (*also fig*) saftig

jukebox ['dʒuːkbɒks] *n* Musikautomat *m*

July [dʒuːˈlaɪ] *n* Juli *m*

jumble ['dʒʌmbl] *n* Durcheinander *nt* ♦ *vt* (*also*: ~ **up**) durcheinanderwerfen; (*facts*) durcheinanderbringen; ~ **sale** (*BRIT*) *n* Basar *m*, Flohmarkt *m*

jumbo (jet) *n* Jumbo(-Jet) *m*

jump [dʒʌmp] *vi* springen; (*nervously*) zusammenzucken ♦ *vt* überspringen ♦ *n* Sprung *m*; to ~ **the queue** (*BRIT*) sich vordrängeln

jumper ['dʒʌmpə*] *n* (*BRIT: pullover*) Pullover *m*; (*US: dress*) Trägerkleid *nt*;

~ **cables** (US) npl = jump leads

jump leads (BRIT) npl Überbrückungskabel nt

jumpy ['dʒʌmpɪ] adj nervös

Jun. abbr = junior

junction ['dʒʌŋkʃən] n (BRIT: of roads) (Straßen)kreuzung f; (RAIL) Knotenpunkt m

juncture ['dʒʌŋktʃə*] n: at this ~ in diesem Augenblick

June [dʒuːn] n Juni m

jungle ['dʒʌŋgl] n Dschungel m

junior ['dʒuːnɪə*] adj (younger) jünger; (after name) junior; (SPORT) Junioren-; (lower position) untergeordnet; (for young people) Junioren- ♦ n Jüngere(r) mf; ~ **school** (BRIT) n Grundschule f

junk [dʒʌŋk] n (rubbish) Plunder m; (ship) Dschunke f; ~ **food** n Plastikessen nt; ~**shop** n Ramschladen m

Junr abbr = junior

jurisdiction [dʒʊərɪs'dɪkʃən] n Gerichtsbarkeit f; (range of authority) Zuständigkeit(sbereich m) f

juror ['dʒʊərə*] n Geschworene(r) mf; (in competition) Preisrichter m

jury ['dʒʊərɪ] n (court) Geschworene pl; (in competition) Jury f

just [dʒʌst] adj gerecht ♦ adv (recently, now) gerade, eben; (barely) gerade noch; (exactly) genau, gerade; (only) nur, bloß; (a small distance) gleich; (absolutely) einfach; ~ **as I arrived** gerade als ich ankam; ~ **as nice** genauso nett; ~ **as well** um so besser; ~ **now** soeben, gerade; ~ **try** versuch es mal

justice ['dʒʌstɪs] n (fairness) Gerechtigkeit f; ~ **of the peace** n Friedensrichter m

justifiable ['dʒʌstɪfaɪəbl] adj berechtigt

justification [dʒʌstɪfɪ'keɪʃən] n Rechtfertigung f

justify ['dʒʌstɪfaɪ] vt rechtfertigen; (text) justieren

justly ['dʒʌstlɪ] adv (say) mit Recht; (condemn) gerecht

jut [dʒʌt] vi (also: ~ out) herausragen, vorstehen

juvenile ['dʒuːvənaɪl] adj (young) jugendlich; (for the young) Jugend- ♦ n Jugendliche(r) mf

juxtapose ['dʒʌkstəpəʊz] vt nebeneinanderstellen

K

K abbr (= one thousand) Tsd.; (= Kilobyte) K

kangaroo [kæŋgə'ruː] n Känguruh nt

karate [kə'rɑːtɪ] n Karate nt

kebab [kə'bæb] n Kebab m

keel [kiːl] n Kiel m; on an even ~ (fig) im Lot

keen [kiːn] adj begeistert; (intelligence, wind, blade) scharf; (sight, hearing) gut; **to be ~ to do** or **on doing sth** etw unbedingt tun wollen; **to be ~ on sth/sb** scharf auf etw/jdn sein

keep [kiːp] (pt, pp kept) vt (retain) behalten; (have) haben; (animals, one's word) halten; (support) versorgen; (maintain in state) halten; (preserve) aufbewahren; (restrain) abhalten ♦ vi (continue in direction) sich halten; (food) sich halten; (remain: quiet etc) bleiben ♦ n Unterhalt m; (tower) Burgfried m; (inf): **for** ~s für immer; **to ~ sth to o.s.** etw für sich behalten; **it ~s happening** es passiert immer wieder; ~ **back** vt fernhalten; (secret) verschweigen; ~ **on** vi: ~ **on doing sth** etw immer weiter tun; ~ **out** vt nicht hereinlassen; "~ **out**" „Eintritt verboten!"; ~ **up** vi Schritt halten ♦ vt aufrechterhalten; (continue) weitermachen; **to ~ up with** Schritt halten mit; ~**er** n Wärter(in) m(f); (goalkeeper) Torhüter(in) m(f); ~**-fit** n Keep-fit nt; ~**ing** n (care) Obhut f; **in** ~**ing with** in Übereinstimmung mit; ~**sake** n Andenken nt

keg [keg] n Faß nt

kennel ['kenl] n Hundehütte f; ~s npl (for boarding): **to put a dog in** ~s einen Hund in Pflege geben

Kenya ['kenjə] n Kenia nt; ~**n** adj kenianisch ♦ n Kenianer(in) m(f)

kept [kept] pt, pp of **keep**

kerb [kɜ:b] (BRIT) n Bordstein m
kernel [ˈkɜ:nl] n Kern m
kerosene [ˈkerəsi:n] n Kerosin nt
ketchup [ˈketʃəp] n Ketchup nt or m
kettle [ˈketl] n Kessel m; ~**drum** n Pauke f
key [ki:] n Schlüssel m; (of piano, typewriter) Taste f; (MUS) Tonart f ♦ vt (also: ~ in) eingeben; ~**board** n Tastatur f; ~**ed up** adj (person) überdreht; ~**hole** n Schlüsselloch nt; ~**note** n Grundton m; ~ **ring** n Schlüsselring m
khaki [ˈkɑ:kɪ] n K(h)aki nt ♦ adj k(h)aki(farben)
kibbutz [kɪˈbʊts] n Kibbutz m
kick [kɪk] vt einen Fußtritt geben +dat, treten ♦ vi treten; (baby) strampeln; (horse) ausschlagen ♦ n (Fuß)tritt m; (thrill) Spaß m; **he does it for** ~s er macht das aus Jux; ~ **off** vi (SPORT) anstoßen; ~**off** n (SPORT) Anstoß m
kid [kɪd] n (inf: child) Kind nt; (goat) Zicklein nt; (leather) Glacéleder nt ♦ vi (inf) Witze machen
kidnap [ˈkɪdnæp] vt entführen; ~**per** n Entführer m; ~**ping** n Entführung f
kidney [ˈkɪdnɪ] n Niere f
kill [kɪl] vt töten, umbringen ♦ vi töten ♦ n Tötung f; (hunting) (Jagd)beute f; ~**er** n Mörder(in) m(f); ~**ing** n Mord m; ~**joy** n Spaßverderber(in) m(f)
kiln [kɪln] n Brennofen m
kilo [ˈki:ləʊ] n Kilo nt; ~**byte** n (COMPUT) Kilobyte nt; ~**gram(me)** [ˈkɪləʊgræm] n Kilogramm nt; ~**metre** [ˈkɪləmi:tə*] (US **kilometer**) n Kilometer m; ~**watt** n Kilowatt nt
kilt [kɪlt] n Schottenrock m
kin [kɪn] n Verwandtschaft f
kind [kaɪnd] adj freundlich ♦ n Art f; a ~ **of** eine Art von; (**two**) **of a** ~ (zwei) von der gleichen Art; **in** ~ auf dieselbe Art; (in goods) in Naturalien
kindergarten [ˈkɪndəgɑ:tn] n Kindergarten m
kind-hearted [ˈkaɪndˈhɑ:tɪd] adj gutherzig
kindle [ˈkɪndl] vt (set on fire) anzünden; (rouse) reizen, (er)wecken

kindly [ˈkaɪndlɪ] adj freundlich ♦ adv liebenswürdig(erweise); **would you** ~ ...? wären Sie so freundlich und ...?
kindness [ˈkaɪndnəs] n Freundlichkeit f
kindred [ˈkɪndrɪd] n Verwandtschaft f ♦ adj: ~ **spirit** Gleichgesinnte(r) mf
king [kɪŋ] n König m; ~**dom** n Königreich nt; ~**fisher** n Eisvogel m; ~**-size** adj (cigarette) Kingsize
kinky [ˈkɪŋkɪ] (inf) adj (person, ideas) verrückt; (sexual) abartig
kiosk [ˈki:ɒsk] (BRIT) n (TEL) Telefonhäuschen nt
kipper [ˈkɪpə*] n Räucherhering m
kiss [kɪs] n Kuß m ♦ vt küssen ♦ vi: **they** ~**ed** sie küßten sich
kit [kɪt] n Ausrüstung f; (tools) Werkzeug nt
kitchen [ˈkɪtʃɪn] n Küche f; ~ **sink** n Spülbecken nt
kite [kaɪt] n Drachen m
kith [kɪθ] n: ~ **and kin** Blutsverwandte pl
kitten [ˈkɪtn] n Kätzchen nt
kitty [ˈkɪtɪ] n (money) Kasse f
km abbr (= kilometre) km
knack [næk] n Dreh m, Trick m
knapsack [ˈnæpsæk] n Rucksack m; (MIL) Tornister m
knead [ni:d] vt kneten
knee [ni:] n Knie nt; ~**cap** n Kniescheibe f
kneel [ni:l] (pt, pp **knelt**) vi (also: ~ **down**) knien
knell [nel] n Grabgeläute nt
knelt [nelt] pt, pp of **kneel**
knew [nju:] pt of **know**
knickers [ˈnɪkəz] (BRIT) npl Schlüpfer m
knife [naɪf] (pl **knives**) n Messer nt ♦ vt erstechen
knight [naɪt] n Ritter m; (chess) Springer m; ~**hood** n (title): **to get a** ~**hood** zum Ritter geschlagen werden
knit [nɪt] vt stricken ♦ vi stricken; (bones) zusammenwachsen; ~**ting** n (occupation) Stricken nt; (work) Strickzeug nt; ~**ting machine** n Strickmaschine f; ~**ting needle** n Stricknadel f; ~**wear** n Strickwaren pl
knives [naɪvz] pl of **knife**

knob [nɒb] n Knauf m; (on instrument) Knopf m; (BRIT: of butter etc) kleine(s) Stück nt

knock [nɒk] vt schlagen; (criticize) heruntermachen ♦ vi: to ~ at or on the door an die Tür klopfen ♦ n Schlag m; (on door) Klopfen nt; ~ down vt umwerfen; (with car) anfahren; ~ off vt (do quickly) hinhauen; (inf: steal) klauen ♦ vi (finish) Feierabend machen; ~ out vt ausschlagen; (BOXING) k.o. schlagen; ~ over vt (person, object) umwerfen; (with car) anfahren; ~er n (on door) Türklopfer m; ~-kneed adj x-beinig; ~out n K.o.-Schlag m; (fig) Sensation f

knot [nɒt] n Knoten m ♦ vt (ver)knoten

knotty ['nɒtɪ] adj (fig) kompliziert

know [nəʊ] (pt knew, pp known) vt, vi wissen; (be able to) können; (be acquainted with) kennen; (recognize) erkennen; to ~ how to do sth wissen, wie man etw macht, etw tun können; to ~ about or of sth/sb etw/jdn kennen; ~-all n Alleswisser m; ~-how n Kenntnis f, Know-how nt; ~ing adj (look, smile) wissend; ~ingly adv (intentionally) wissentlich

knowledge ['nɒlɪdʒ] n Wissen nt, Kenntnis f; ~able adj informiert

known [nəʊn] pp of know

knuckle ['nʌkl] n Fingerknöchel m

K.O. n abbr = knockout

Koran [kɔː'rɑːn] n Koran m

Korea [kə'rɪə] n Korea nt

kosher ['kəʊʃə*] adj koscher

L

l. abbr = litre

lab [læb] (inf) n Labor nt

label ['leɪbl] n Etikett nt ♦ vt etikettieren

labor etc (US) = **labour** etc

laboratory [lə'bɒrətərɪ] n Laboratorium nt

laborious [lə'bɔːrɪəs] adj mühsam

labour ['leɪbə*] (US labor) n Arbeit f; (workmen) Arbeitskräfte pl; (MED)

Wehen pl ♦ vi: to ~ (at) sich abmühen (mit) ♦ vt breittreten (inf); in ~ (MED) in den Wehen; L~ (BRIT: also the Labour party) die Labour Party; ~ed adj (movement) gequält; (style) schwerfällig; ~er n Arbeiter m; farm ~er (Land)arbeiter m

lace [leɪs] n (fabric) Spitze f; (of shoe) Schnürsenkel m; (braid) Litze f ♦ vt (also: ~ up) (zu)schnüren

lack [læk] n Mangel m ♦ vt nicht haben; sb ~s sth jdm fehlt etw nom; to be ~ing fehlen; sb is ~ing in sth es fehlt jdm an etw dat; through or for ~ of aus Mangel an +dat

lackadaisical [lækə'deɪzɪkəl] adj lasch

lacquer ['lækə*] n Lack m

lad [læd] n Junge m

ladder ['lædə*] n Leiter f; (BRIT: in tights) Laufmasche f ♦ vt (BRIT: tights) Laufmaschen bekommen in +dat

laden ['leɪdn] adj beladen, voll

ladle ['leɪdl] n Schöpfkelle f

lady ['leɪdɪ] n Dame f; (title) Lady f; young ~ junge Dame; the ladies' (room) die Damentoilette; ~bird (US ~bug) n Marienkäfer m; ~-in-waiting n Hofdame f; ~like adj damenhaft, vornehm; ~ship n: your ~ship Ihre Ladyschaft

lag [læg] vi (also: ~ behind) zurückbleiben ♦ vt (pipes) verkleiden

lager ['lɑːgə*] n helle(s) Bier nt

lagging ['lægɪŋ] n Isolierung f

lagoon [lə'guːn] n Lagune f

laid [leɪd] pt, pp of lay; ~ back (inf) adj cool

lain [leɪn] pp of lie

lair [leə*] n Lager nt

laity ['leɪtɪ] n Laien pl

lake [leɪk] n See m

lamb [læm] n Lamm nt; (meat) Lammfleisch nt; ~ chop n Lammkotelett nt; lambswool n Lammwolle f

lame [leɪm] adj lahm; (excuse) faul

lament [lə'ment] n Klage f ♦ vt beklagen

laminated ['læmɪneɪtɪd] adj beschichtet

lamp [læmp] n Lampe f; (in street) Straßenlaterne f

lampoon [læm'puːn] vt verspotten
lamppost ['læmppəʊst] n Laternenpfahl m
lampshade ['læmpʃeɪd] n Lampenschirm m
lance [lɑːns] n Lanze f ♦ vt (MED) aufschneiden; ~ **corporal** (BRIT) n Obergefreite(r) m
land [lænd] n Land nt ♦ vi (from ship) an Land gehen; (AVIAT, end up) landen ♦ vt (obtain) kriegen; (passengers) absetzen; (goods) abladen; (troops, space probe) landen; ~**ing** n Landung f; (on stairs) (Treppen)absatz m; ~**ing gear** n Fahrgestell nt; ~**ing stage** (BRIT) n Landesteg m; ~**ing strip** n Landebahn f; ~**lady** n (Haus)wirtin f; ~**locked** adj landumschlossen, Binnen-; ~**lord** n (of house) Hauswirt m, Besitzer m; (of pub) Gastwirt m; (of land) Grundbesitzer m; ~**mark** n Wahrzeichen nt; (fig) Meilenstein m; ~**owner** n Grundbesitzer m
landscape ['lændskeɪp] n Landschaft f
landslide ['lændslaɪd] n (GEOG) Erdrutsch m; (POL) überwältigende(r) Sieg m
lane [leɪn] n (in town) Gasse f; (in country) Weg m; (of motorway) Fahrbahn f, Spur f; (SPORT) Bahn f
language ['læŋgwɪdʒ] n Sprache f; bad ~ unanständige Ausdrücke pl; ~ **laboratory** n Sprachlabor nt
languid ['læŋgwɪd] adj schlaff, matt
languish ['læŋgwɪʃ] vi schmachten
lank [læŋk] adj dürr
lanky ['læŋkɪ] adj schlaksig
lantern ['læntən] n Laterne f
lap [læp] n Schoß m; (SPORT) Runde f ♦ vt (also: ~ up) auflecken ♦ vi (water) plätschern
lapel [lə'pel] n Revers nt or m
Lapland ['læplænd] n Lappland nt
lapse [læps] n (moral) Fehltritt m ♦ vi (decline) nachlassen; (expire) ablaufen; (claims) erlöschen; to ~ into bad habits sich schlechte Gewohnheiten angewöhnen
larceny ['lɑːsənɪ] n Diebstahl m
lard [lɑːd] n Schweineschmalz nt

larder ['lɑːdə*] n Speisekammer f
large [lɑːdʒ] adj groß; at ~ auf freiem Fuß; ~**ly** adv zum größten Teil; ~-**scale** adj groß angelegt, Groß-
largesse [lɑː'ʒes] n Freigebigkeit f
lark [lɑːk] n (bird) Lerche f; (joke) Jux m; ~ **about** (inf) vi herumalbern
laryngitis [lærɪn'dʒaɪtɪs] n Kehlkopfentzündung f
larynx ['lærɪŋks] n Kehlkopf m
lascivious [lə'sɪvɪəs] adj wollüstig
laser ['leɪzə*] n Laser m; ~ **printer** n Laserdrucker m
lash [læʃ] n Peitschenhieb m; (eye~) Wimper f ♦ vt (rain) schlagen gegen; (whip) peitschen; (bind) festbinden; ~ **out** vi (with fists) um sich schlagen; (spend money) sich in Unkosten stürzen ♦ vt (money etc) springen lassen
lass [læs] n Mädchen nt
lasso [læ'suː] n Lasso nt
last [lɑːst] adj letzte(r, s) ♦ adv zuletzt; (last time) das letztemal ♦ vi (continue) dauern; (remain good) sich halten; (money) ausreichen; at ~ endlich; ~ **night** gestern abend; ~ **week** letzte Woche; ~ **but one** vorletzte(r, s); ~-**ditch** adj (attempt) in letzter Minute; ~**ing** adj dauerhaft; (shame etc) andauernd; ~**ly** adv schließlich; ~-**minute** adj in letzter Minute
latch [lætʃ] n Riegel m
late [leɪt] adj spät; (dead) verstorben ♦ adv spät; (after proper time) zu spät; to be ~ zu spät kommen; of ~ in letzter Zeit; in ~ May Ende Mai; ~**comer** n Nachzügler(in) m(f); ~**ly** adv in letzter Zeit
lateness ['leɪtnəs] n (of person) Zuspätkommen nt; (of train) Verspätung f; ~ **of the hour** die vorgerückte Stunde
later ['leɪtə*] adj (date etc) später; (version etc) neuer ♦ adv später
lateral ['lætərəl] adj seitlich
latest ['leɪtɪst] adj (fashion) neueste(r, s) ♦ n (news) Neu(e)ste(s) nt; at the ~ spätestens
lathe [leɪð] n Drehbank f
lather ['lɑːðə*] n (Seifen)schaum m ♦ vt

einschäumen ♦ *vi* schäumen
Latin ['lætɪn] *n* Latein *nt* ♦ *adj* lateinisch; (*Roman*) römisch; ~ **America** *n* Lateinamerika *nt*; ~-**American** *adj* lateinamerikanisch
latitude ['lætɪtjuːd] *n* (*GEOG*) Breite *f*; (*freedom*) Spielraum *m*
latter ['lætə*] *adj* (*second of two*) letztere; (*coming at end*) letzte(r, s), später ♦ *n*: **the** ~ der/die/das letztere, die letzteren; ~**ly** *adv* in letzter Zeit
lattice ['lætɪs] *n* Gitter *nt*
laudable ['lɔːdəbl] *adj* löblich
laugh [lɑːf] *n* Lachen *nt* ♦ *vi* lachen; ~ **at** *vt* lachen über +*acc*; ~ **off** *vt* lachend abtun; ~**able** *adj* lachhaft; ~**ing stock** *n* Zielscheibe *f* des Spottes; ~**ter** *n* Gelächter *nt*
launch [lɔːntʃ] *n* (*of ship*) Stapellauf *m*; (*of rocket*) Abschuß *m*; (*boat*) Barkasse *f*; (*of product*) Einführung *f* ♦ *vt* (*set afloat*) vom Stapel lassen; (*rocket*) (ab)schießen; (*product*) auf den Markt bringen; ~**ing** *n* Stapellauf *m*; ~**(ing) pad** *n* Abschußrampe *f*
launder ['lɔːndə*] *vt* waschen
laundrette [lɔːn'drɛt] (*BRIT*) *n* Waschsalon *m*
Laundromat ['lɔːndrəmæt] (*US*) *n* Waschsalon *m*
laundry ['lɔːndrɪ] *n* (*place*) Wäscherei *f*; (*clothes*) Wäsche *f*; **to do the** ~ waschen
laureate ['lɔːrɪət] *adj see* **poet**
laurel ['lɔrəl] *n* Lorbeer *m*
lava ['lɑːvə] *n* Lava *f*
lavatory ['lævətrɪ] *n* Toilette *f*
lavender ['lævɪndə*] *n* Lavendel *m*
lavish ['lævɪʃ] *n* (*extravagant*) verschwenderisch; (*generous*) großzügig ♦ *vt* (*money*): **to** ~ **sth on sth** etw auf etw *acc* verschwenden; (*attention, gifts*): **to** ~ **sth on sb** jdn mit etw überschütten
law [lɔː] *n* Gesetz *nt*; (*system*) Recht *nt*; (*as studies*) Jura *no art*; ~-**abiding** *adj* gesetzestreu; ~ **and order** *n* Recht *nt* und Ordnung *f*; ~ **court** *n* Gerichtshof *m*; ~**ful** *adj* gesetzlich; ~**less** *adj* gesetzlos
lawn [lɔːn] *n* Rasen *m*; ~**mower** *n*

Rasenmäher *m*; ~ **tennis** *n* Rasentennis *m*
law school *n* Rechtsakademie *f*
lawsuit ['lɔːsuːt] *n* Prozeß *m*
lawyer ['lɔːjə*] *n* Rechtsanwalt *m*, Rechtsanwältin *f*
laxative ['læksətɪv] *n* Abführmittel *nt*
laxity ['læksɪtɪ] *n* Laxheit *f*
lay [leɪ] (*pt, pp* **laid**) *pt of* **lie** ♦ *adj* Laien- ♦ *vt* (*place*) legen; (*table*) decken; (*egg*) legen; (*trap*) stellen; (*money*) wetten; ~ **aside** *vt* zurücklegen; ~ **by** *vt* (*set aside*) beiseite legen; ~ **down** *vt* hinlegen; (*rules*) vorschreiben; (*arms*) strecken; **to** ~ **down the law** Vorschriften machen; ~ **off** *vt* (*workers*) (vorübergehend) entlassen; ~ **on** *vt* (*water, gas*) anschließen; (*concert etc*) veranstalten; ~ **out** *vt* (*her*)auslegen; (*money*) ausgeben; (*corpse*) aufbahren; ~ **up** *vt* (*subj: illness*) ans Bett fesseln; (*supplies*) anlegen; ~**about** *n* Faulenzer *m*; ~-**by** (*BRIT*) *n* Parkbucht *f*; (*bigger*) Rastplatz *m*
layer ['leɪə*] *n* Schicht *f*
layette [leɪ'et] *n* Babyausstattung *f*
layman ['leɪmən] *n* Laie *m*
layout ['leɪaʊt] *n* Anlage *f*; (*ART*) Layout *nt*
laze [leɪz] *vi* faulenzen
laziness ['leɪzɪnəs] *n* Faulheit *f*
lazy ['leɪzɪ] *adj* faul; (*slow-moving*) träge
lb. *abbr* = **pound** (*weight*)
lead¹ [led] *n* (*chemical*) Blei *nt*; (*of pencil*) (Bleistift)mine *f* ♦ *adj* bleiern, Blei-
lead² [liːd] (*pt, pp* **led**) *n* (*front position*) Führung *f*; (*distance, time ahead*) Vorsprung *f*; (*example*) Vorbild *nt*; (*clue*) Tip *m*; (*of police*) Spur *f*; (*THEAT*) Hauptrolle *f*; (*dog's*) Leine *f* ♦ *vt* (*guide*) führen; (*group etc*) leiten ♦ *vi* (*be first*) führen; **in the** ~ (*SPORT, fig*) in Führung; ~ **astray** *vt* irreführen; ~ **away** *vt* wegführen; (*prisoner*) abführen; ~ **back** *vi* zurückführen; ~ **on** *vt* anführen; ~ **on to** *vt* (*induce*) dazu bringen; ~ **to** *vt* (*street*)

(hin)führen nach; (result in) führen zu;
~ **up to** vt (drive) führen zu; (speaker
etc) hinführen auf +acc

leaden ['lɛdn] adj (sky, sea) bleiern;
(heavy: footsteps) bleischwer

leader ['liːdə*] n Führer m, Leiter m;
(of party) Vorsitzende(r) m; (PRESS)
Leitartikel m; ~**ship** n (office) Leitung
f; (quality) Führerschaft f

leading ['liːdɪŋ] adj führend; ~ **lady** n
(THEAT) Hauptdarstellerin f; ~ **light** n
(person) führende(r) Geist m

leaf [liːf] (pl **leaves**) n Blatt nt ♦ vi: to
~ **through** durchblättern; **to turn over a
new** ~ einen neuen Anfang machen

leaflet ['liːflɪt] n (advertisement)
Prospekt m; (pamphlet) Flugblatt nt;
(for information) Merkblatt nt

league [liːg] n (union) Bund m; (SPORT)
Liga f; **to be in** ~ **with** unter einer
Decke stecken mit

leak [liːk] n undichte Stelle f; (in ship)
Leck nt ♦ vt (liquid etc) durchlassen ♦
vi (pipe etc) undicht sein; (liquid etc)
auslaufen; **the information was** ~**ed to
the enemy** die Information wurde dem
Feind zugespielt; ~ **out** vi (liquid etc)
auslaufen; (information) durchsickern

leaky ['liːkɪ] adj undicht

lean [liːn] (pt, pp **leaned** or **leant**) adj
mager ♦ vi sich neigen ♦ vt (an)lehnen;
to ~ **against sth** an etw dat angelehnt
sein; sich an etw acc anlehnen; ~ **back**
vi sich zurücklehnen; ~ **forward** vi sich
vorbeugen; ~ **on** vt fus sich stützen auf
+ acc; ~ **out** vi sich hinauslehnen; ~
over vi sich hinüberbeugen; ~**ing**
Neigung f ♦ adj schief; **leant** [lɛnt] pt,
pp of **lean**; ~**-to** n Anbau m

leap [liːp] (pt, pp **leaped** or **leapt**) n
Sprung m ♦ vi springen; ~**frog** n Bock-
springen nt; **leapt** [lɛpt] pt, pp of **leap**;
~ **year** n Schaltjahr nt

learn [lɜːn] (pt, pp **learned** or **learnt**) vt,
vi lernen; (find out) erfahren; **to** ~ **how
to do sth** etw (er)lernen; ~**ed** ['lɜːnɪd]
adj gelehrt; ~**er** n Anfänger(in) m(f);
(AUT: BRIT: also ~ **driver**) Fahr-
schüler(in) m(f); ~**ing** n Gelehrsamkeit f; **learnt** [lɜːnt] pt, pp of **learn**

lease [liːs] n (of property) Mietvertrag
m ♦ vt pachten

leash [liːʃ] n Leine f

least [liːst] adj geringste(r, s) ♦ adv am
wenigsten ♦ n Mindeste(s) nt; **the** ~
possible effort möglichst geringer Aufwand; **at** ~ zumindest; **not in the** ~!
durchaus nicht!

leather ['lɛðə*] n Leder nt

leave [liːv] (pt, pp **left**) vt verlassen; (~
behind) zurücklassen; (forget) ver-
gessen; (allow to remain) lassen;
(after death) hinterlassen; (entrust): **to**
~ **sth to sb** jdm etw überlassen ♦ vi
weggehen, wegfahren; (for journey)
abreisen; (bus, train) abfahren ♦ n
Erlaubnis f; (MIL) Urlaub m; **to be left**
(remain) übrigbleiben; **there's some
milk left over** es ist noch etwas Milch
übrig; **on** ~ auf Urlaub; ~ **behind** vt
(person, object) dalassen; (: forget)
liegenlassen, stehenlassen; ~ **out** vt
auslassen; ~ **of absence** n Urlaub m

leaves [liːvz] pl of **leaf**

Lebanon ['lɛbənən] n Libanon m

lecherous ['lɛtʃərəs] adj lüstern

lecture ['lɛktʃə*] n Vortrag m; (UNIV)
Vorlesung f ♦ vi einen Vortrag halten;
(UNIV) lesen ♦ vt (scold) abkanzeln; **to
give a** ~ **on sth** einen Vortrag über
etwas halten; ~**r** ['lɛktʃərə*] n Vor-
tragende(r) mf; (BRIT: UNIV) Do-
zent(in) m(f)

led [lɛd] pt, pp of **lead**[2]

ledge [lɛdʒ] n Leiste f; (window ~)
Sims m or nt; (of mountain)
(Fels)vorsprung m

ledger ['lɛdʒə*] n Hauptbuch nt

lee [liː] n Windschatten m; (NAUT) Lee f

leech [liːtʃ] n Blutegel m

leek [liːk] n Lauch m

leer [lɪə*] vi: **to** ~ (**at sb**) (nach jdm)
schielen

leeway ['liːweɪ] n (fig): **to have some** ~
etwas Spielraum haben

left [lɛft] pt, pp of **leave** ♦ adj linke(r, s)
♦ n (side) linke Seite f ♦ adv links; **on
the** ~ links; **to the** ~ nach links; **the L**~
(POL) die Linke f; ~**-handed** adj
linkshändig; ~**-hand side** n linke Seite

f; ~**-luggage (office)** (*BRIT*) *n* Gepäckaufbewahrung *f*; ~**-overs** *npl* Reste *pl*; ~**-wing** *adj* linke(r, s)

leg [lɛg] *n* Bein *nt*; (*of meat*) Keule *f*; (*stage*) Etappe *f*; **1st/2nd** ~ (*SPORT*) 1./2. Etappe

legacy ['lɛgəsɪ] *n* Erbe *nt*, Erbschaft *f*

legal ['liːgəl] *adj* gesetzlich; (*allowed*) legal; ~ **holiday** (*US*) *n* gesetzliche(r) Feiertag *m*; ~**ize** *vt* legalisieren; ~**ly** *adv* gesetzlich; legal; ~ **tender** *n* gesetzliche(s) Zahlungsmittel *nt*

legend ['lɛdʒənd] *n* Legende *f*; ~**ary** *adj* legendär

legible ['lɛdʒəbl] *adj* leserlich

legislation [lɛdʒɪs'leɪʃən] *n* Gesetzgebung *f*

legislative ['lɛdʒɪslətɪv] *adj* gesetzgebend

legislature ['lɛdʒɪslətʃə*] *n* Legislative *f*

legitimate [lɪ'dʒɪtɪmət] *adj* rechtmäßig, legitim; (*child*) ehelich

legroom ['lɛgrʊm] *n* Platz *m* für die Beine

leisure ['lɛʒə*] *n* Freizeit *f*; **to be at** ~ Zeit haben; ~**ly** *adj* gemächlich

lemon ['lɛmən] *n* Zitrone *f*; (*colour*) Zitronengelb *nt*; ~**ade** [lɛmə'neɪd] *n* Limonade *f*

lend [lɛnd] (*pt, pp* **lent**) *vt* leihen; **to** ~ **sb sth** jdm etw leihen; ~**ing library** *n* Leihbibliothek *f*

length [lɛŋθ] *n* Länge *f*; (*section of road, pipe etc*) Strecke *f*; (*of material*) Stück *nt*; **at** ~ (*lengthily*) ausführlich; (*at last*) schließlich; ~**en** *vt* verlängern ♦ *vi* länger werden; ~**ways** *adv* längs; ~**y** *adj* sehr lang, langatmig

lenient ['liːnɪənt] *adj* nachsichtig

lens [lɛnz] *n* Linse *f*; (*PHOT*) Objektiv *nt*

Lent [lɛnt] *n* Fastenzeit *f*

lent *pt, pp of* **lend**

lentil ['lɛntl] *n* Linse *f*

Leo ['liːəʊ] *n* Löwe *m*

leotard ['liːətɑːd] *n* Trikot *nt*, Gymnastikanzug *m*

leper ['lɛpə*] *n* Leprakranke(r) *mf*

leprosy ['lɛprəsɪ] *n* Lepra *f*

lesbian ['lɛzbɪən] *adj* lesbisch ♦ *n* Lesbierin *f*

less [lɛs] *adj, adv, pron* weniger; ~ **than half** weniger als die Hälfte; ~ **than ever** weniger denn je; ~ **and** ~ immer weniger; **the** ~ **he works** je weniger er arbeitet

lessen ['lɛsn] *vi* abnehmen ♦ *vt* verringern, verkleinern

lesser ['lɛsə*] *adj* kleiner, geringer; **to a** ~ **extent** in geringerem Maße

lesson ['lɛsn] *n* (*SCH*) Stunde *f*; (*unit of study*) Lektion *f*; (*fig*) Lehre *f*; (*ECCL*) Lesung *f*; **a maths** ~ eine Mathestunde

lest [lɛst] *conj*: ~ **it happen** damit es nicht passiert

let [lɛt] (*pt, pp* **let**) *vt* lassen; (*BRIT: lease*) vermieten; **to** ~ **sb do sth** jdn etw tun lassen; **to** ~ **sb know sth** jdn etw wissen lassen; ~**'s go!** gehen wir!; ~ **him come** soll er doch kommen; ~ **down** *vt* hinunterlassen; (*disappoint*) enttäuschen; ~ **go** *vi* loslassen ♦ *vt* (*things*) loslassen; (*person*) gehen lassen; ~ **in** *vt* hereinlassen; (*water*) durchlassen; ~ **off** *vt* (*gun*) abfeuern; (*steam*) ablassen; (*forgive*) laufen lassen; ~ **on** *vi* durchblicken lassen; (*pretend*) vorgeben; ~ **out** *vt* herauslassen; (*scream*) fahren lassen; ~ **up** *vi* nachlassen; (*stop*) aufhören

lethal ['liːθəl] *adj* tödlich

letter ['lɛtə*] *n* (*of alphabet*) Buchstabe *m*; (*message*) Brief *m*; ~ **bomb** *n* Briefbombe *f*; ~**box** (*BRIT*) *n* Briefkasten *m*; ~**ing** *n* Beschriftung *f*; ~ **of credit** *n* Akkreditiv *m*

lettuce ['lɛtɪs] *n* (Kopf)salat *m*

let-up ['lɛtʌp] (*inf*) *n* Nachlassen *nt*

leukaemia [luːˈkiːmɪə] (*US* **leukemia**) *n* Leukämie *f*

level ['lɛvl] *adj* (*ground*) eben; (*at same height*) auf gleicher Höhe; (*equal*) gleich gut; (*head*) kühl ♦ *adv* auf gleicher Höhe ♦ *n* (*instrument*) Wasserwaage *f*; (*altitude*) Höhe *f*; (*flat place*) ebene Fläche *f*; (*position on scale*) Niveau *nt*; (*amount, degree*) Grad *m* ♦ *vt* (*ground*) einebnen; **to draw** ~ **with** gleichziehen mit; **to be** ~ **with** auf einer Höhe sein mit; **A** ~**s** (*BRIT*) ≈ Abitur *nt*; **O** ~**s** (*BRIT*) ≈ mittlere Reife f; **on the ~** (fig: honest) ehrlich; **to ~ sth at sb** (blow) jdm etw versetzen; (remark) etw gegen jdn richten; **~ off** or **out** vi flach or eben werden; (fig) sich ausgleichen; (plane) horizontal fliegen ♦ vt (ground) planieren; (differences) ausgleichen; **~crossing** (BRIT) n Bahnübergang m; **~-headed** adj vernünftig

lever ['li:və*] n Hebel m; (fig) Druckmittel nt ♦ vt (hoch)stemmen; **~age** n Hebelkraft f; (fig) Einfluß m

levity ['levɪtɪ] n Leichtfertigkeit f

levy ['levɪ] n (of taxes) Erhebung f; (tax) Abgaben pl; (MIL) Aushebung f ♦ vt erheben; (MIL) ausheben

lewd [lu:d] adj unzüchtig, unanständig

liability [laɪə'bɪlɪtɪ] n (burden) Belastung f; (duty) Pflicht f; (debt) Verpflichtung f; (proneness) Anfälligkeit f; (responsibility) Haftung f

liable ['laɪəbl] adj (responsible) haftbar; (prone) anfällig; **to be ~ for sth** etw dat unterliegen; **it's ~ to happen** es kann leicht vorkommen

liaise [li:'eɪz] vi: **to ~ (with sb)** (mit jdm) zusammenarbeiten

liaison [li:'eɪzɒn] n Verbindung f

liar ['laɪə*] n Lügner m

libel ['laɪbəl] n Verleumdung f ♦ vt verleumden

liberal ['lɪbərəl] adj (generous) großzügig; (open-minded) aufgeschlossen; (POL) liberal

liberate ['lɪbəreɪt] vt befreien

liberation [lɪbə'reɪʃən] n Befreiung f

liberty ['lɪbətɪ] n Freiheit f; (permission) Erlaubnis f; **to be at ~ to do sth** etw tun dürfen; **to take the ~ of doing sth** sich dat erlauben, etw zu tun

Libra ['li:brə] n Waage f

librarian [laɪ'breərɪən] n Bibliothekar(in) m(f)

library ['laɪbrərɪ] n Bibliothek f; (lending ~) Bücherei f

Libya ['lɪbɪə] n Libyen nt; **~n** adj libysch ♦ n Libyer(in) m(f)

lice [laɪs] npl of **louse**

licence ['laɪsəns] (US **license**) n (permit) Erlaubnis f; (also: driving ~, US

driver's license) Führerschein m; (excess) Zügellosigkeit f

license ['laɪsəns] n (US) = **licence** ♦ vt genehmigen, konzessionieren; **~d** adj (for alcohol) konzessioniert (für den Ausschank von Alkohol)

license plate (US) n (AUT) Nummernschild nt

licentious [laɪ'senʃəs] adj ausschweifend

lichen ['laɪkən] n Flechte f

lick [lɪk] vt lecken ♦ n Lecken nt; **a ~ of paint** ein bißchen Farbe

licorice ['lɪkərɪs] (US) n = **liquorice**

lid [lɪd] n Deckel m; (eye~) Lid nt

lido ['li:dəʊ] (BRIT) n Freibad nt

lie [laɪ] (pt **lay**, pp **lain**) vi (rest, be situated) liegen; (put o.s. in position) sich legen; (pt, pp **lied**: tell lies) lügen ♦ n Lüge f; **to ~ low** (fig) untertauchen; **~ about** vi (things) herumliegen; (people) faulenzen; **~-down** (BRIT) n: **to have a ~-down** ein Nickerchen machen; **~-in** (BRIT) n: **to have a ~-in** sich ausschlafen

lieu [lu:] n: **in ~ of** anstatt +gen

lieutenant [lef'tenənt, (US) lu'tenənt] n Leutnant m

life [laɪf] (pl **lives**) n Leben nt; **~ assurance** (BRIT) n = **~ insurance**; **~belt** (BRIT) n Rettungsring m; **~boat** n Rettungsboot nt; **~guard** n Rettungsschwimmer m; **~ insurance** n Lebensversicherung f; **~ jacket** n Schwimmweste f; **~less** adj (dead) leblos; (dull) langweilig; **~like** adj lebenswahr, naturgetreu; **~line** n Rettungsleine f; (fig) Rettungsanker m; **~long** adj lebenslang; **~ preserver** (US) n = **~belt**; **~-saver** n Lebensretter(in) m(f); **~ sentence** n lebenslängliche Freiheitsstrafe f; **~sized** adj in Lebensgröße; **~ span** n Lebensspanne f; **~style** n Lebensstil m; **~ support system** n (MED) Lebenserhaltungssystem nt; **~time** n: **in his ~time** während er lebte; **once in a ~time** einmal im Leben

lift [lɪft] vt hochheben ♦ vi sich heben ♦ n (BRIT: elevator) Aufzug m, Lift m; **to give sb a ~** jdn mitnehmen; **~-off** n

Abheben *nt* (vom Boden)
ligament ['lɪgəmənt] *n* Band *nt*
light [laɪt] (*pt, pp* **lighted** *or* **lit**) *n* Licht
nt; (*for cigarette etc*): **have you got a
~?** haben Sie Feuer? ♦ *vt* beleuchten;
(*lamp*) anmachen; (*fire, cigarette*) anzünden ♦ *adj* (*bright*) hell; (*pale*) hell-;
(*not heavy, easy*) leicht; (*punishment*)
milde; (*touch*) leicht; **~s** *npl* (*AUT*)
Beleuchtung *f*; **~ up** *vi* (*lamp*) angehen; (*face*) aufleuchten ♦ *vt*
(*illuminate*) beleuchten; (*lights*) anmachen; **~ bulb** *n* Glühbirne *f*; **~en** *vi*
(*brighten*) hell werden; (*lightning*)
blitzen ♦ *vt* (*give light to*) erhellen;
(*hair*) aufhellen; (*gloom*) aufheitern;
(*make less heavy*) leichter machen;
(*fig*) erleichtern; **~er** *n* Feuerzeug *nt*;
~-headed *adj* (*thoughtless*) leichtsinnig; (*giddy*) schwindlig; **~-hearted**
adj leichtherzig, fröhlich; **~house** *n*
Leuchtturm *m*; **~ing** *n* Beleuchtung *f*;
~ly *adv* leicht; (*irresponsibly*)
leichtfertig; **to get off ~ly** mit einem
blauen Auge davonkommen; **~ness** *n*
(*of weight*) Leichtigkeit *f*; (*of colour*)
Helle *f*
lightning ['laɪtnɪŋ] *n* Blitz *m*; **~ conductor** (*US* **~ rod**) *n* Blitzableiter *m*
light: **~ pen** *n* Lichtstift *m*; **~weight**
['laɪtweɪt] *adj* (*suit*) leicht; **~weight
boxer** *n* Leichtgewichtler *m*; **~ year** *n*
Lichtjahr *nt*
like [laɪk] *vt* mögen, gernhaben ♦ *prep*
wie ♦ *adj* (*similar*) ähnlich; (*equal*)
gleich ♦ *n*: **the ~** dergleichen; **I would
or I'd ~** ich möchte gern; **would you ~
a coffee?** möchten Sie einen Kaffee?; **to
be** *or* **look ~ sb/sth** jdm/etw ähneln;
that's just ~ him das ist typisch für
ihn; **do it ~ this** mach es so; **it is nothing ~ ...** es ist nicht zu vergleichen mit
...; **his ~s and dislikes** was er mag und
was er nicht mag; **~able** *adj* sympathisch
likelihood ['laɪklɪhʊd] *n* Wahrscheinlichkeit *f*
likely ['laɪklɪ] *adj* wahrscheinlich; **he's ~
to leave** er geht möglicherweise; **not ~!**
wohl kaum!

likeness ['laɪknɪs] *n* Ähnlichkeit *f*; (*portrait*) Bild *nt*
likewise ['laɪkwaɪz] *adv* ebenso
liking ['laɪkɪŋ] *n* Zuneigung *f*; (*taste*)
Vorliebe *f*
lilac ['laɪlək] *n* Flieder *m* ♦ *adj* (*colour*)
fliederfarben
lily ['lɪlɪ] *n* Lilie *f*; **~ of the valley** *n*
Maiglöckchen *nt*
limb [lɪm] *n* Glied *nt*
limber ['lɪmbə*]: **~ up** *vi* sich auflockern; (*fig*) sich vorbereiten
limbo ['lɪmbəʊ] *n*: **to be in ~** (*fig*) in der
Schwebe sein
lime [laɪm] *n* (*tree*) Linde *f*; (*fruit*)
Limone *f*; (*substance*) Kalk *m*
limelight ['laɪmlaɪt] *n*: **to be in the ~**
(*fig*) im Rampenlicht stehen
limestone ['laɪmstəʊn] *n* Kalkstein *m*
limit ['lɪmɪt] *n* Grenze *f*; (*inf*) Höhe *f* ♦
vt begrenzen, einschränken; **~ation** *n*
Einschränkung *f*; **~ed** *adj* beschränkt;
to be ~ed to sich beschränken auf
+*acc*; **~ed (liability) company** (*BRIT*) *n*
Gesellschaft *f* mit beschränkter Haftung
limp [lɪmp] *n* Hinken *nt* ♦ *vi* hinken ♦
adj schlaff
limpet ['lɪmpɪt] *n* (*fig*) Klette *f*
limpid ['lɪmpɪd] *adj* klar
line [laɪn] *n* Linie *f*; (*rope*) Leine *f*; (*on
face*) Falte *f*; (*row*) Reihe *f*; (*of hills*)
Kette *f*; (*US*: *queue*) Schlange *f*;
(*company*) Linie *f*, Gesellschaft *f*;
(*RAIL*) Strecke *f*; (*TEL*) Leitung *f*;
(*written*) Zeile *f*; (*direction*) Richtung
f; (*fig*: *business*) Branche *f*; (*range of
items*) Kollektion *f* ♦ *vt* (*coat*) füttern;
(*border*) säumen; **~s** *npl* (*RAIL*) Gleise
pl; **in ~ with** in Übereinstimmung mit;
~ up *vi* sich aufstellen ♦ *vt* aufstellen;
(*prepare*) sorgen für; (*support*)
mobilisieren; (*surprise*) planen
linear ['lɪnɪə*] *adj* gerade; (*measure*)
Längen-
lined [laɪnd] *adj* (*face*) faltig; (*paper*)
liniert
linen ['lɪnɪn] *n* Leinen *nt*; (*sheets etc*)
Wäsche *f*
liner ['laɪnə*] *n* Überseedampfer *m*
linesman ['laɪnzmən] (*irreg*) *n* (*SPORT*)

Linienrichter *m*
line-up ['laɪnʌp] *n* Aufstellung *f*
linger ['lɪŋgə*] *vi* (*remain long*) verweilen; (*taste*) (zurück)bleiben; (*delay*) zögern, verharren
lingerie ['lænʒəriː] *n* Damenunterwäsche *f*
lingering ['lɪŋgərɪŋ] *adj* (*doubt*) zurückbleibend; (*disease*) langwierig; (*taste*) nachhaltend; (*look*) lang
lingo ['lɪŋgəʊ] (*pl* ~es; *inf*) *n* Sprache *f*
linguist ['lɪŋgwɪst] *n* Sprachkundige(r) *mf*; (*UNIV*) Sprachwissenschaftler(in) *m(f)*
linguistic [lɪŋ'gwɪstɪk] *adj* sprachlich; sprachwissenschaftlich; ~s [lɪŋ'gwɪstɪks] *n* Sprachwissenschaft *f*, Linguistik *f*
lining ['laɪnɪŋ] *n* (*of clothes*) Futter *nt*
link [lɪŋk] *n* Glied *nt*; (*connection*) Verbindung *f* ♦ *vt* verbinden; ~s *npl* (*GOLF*) Golfplatz *m*; ~ up *vt* verbinden ♦ *vi* zusammenkommen; (*companies*) sich zusammenschließen; ~-up *n* (*TEL*) Verbindung *f*; (*of spaceships*) Kopplung *f*
lino ['laɪnəʊ] *n* = **linoleum**
linoleum [lɪ'nəʊlɪəm] *n* Linoleum *nt*
linseed oil ['lɪnsiːd-] *n* Leinöl *nt*
lion ['laɪən] *n* Löwe *m*; ~ess *n* Löwin *f*
lip [lɪp] *n* Lippe *f*; (*of jug*) Schnabel *m*; **to pay** ~ **service (to)** ein Lippenbekenntnis ablegen (zu); ~**read** (*irreg*) *vi* von den Lippen ablesen; ~ **salve** *n* Lippenbalsam *m*; ~**stick** *n* Lippenstift *m*
liqueur [lɪ'kjʊə*] *n* Likör *m*
liquid ['lɪkwɪd] *n* Flüßigkeit *f* ♦ *adj* flüssig
liquidate ['lɪkwɪdeɪt] *vt* liquidieren
liquidation [lɪkwɪ'deɪʃən] *n* Liquidation *f*
liquidize ['lɪkwɪdaɪz] *vt* (*CULIN*) (im Mixer) pürieren; ~**r** ['lɪkwɪdaɪzə*] *n* Mixgerät *nt*
liquor ['lɪkə*] *n* Alkohol *m*
liquorice ['lɪkərɪs] (*BRIT*) *n* Lakritze *f*
liquor store (*US*) *n* Spirituosengeschäft *nt*
Lisbon ['lɪzbən] *n* Lissabon *nt*
lisp [lɪsp] *n* Lispeln *nt* ♦ *vt*, *vi* lispeln
list [lɪst] *n* Liste *f*, Verzeichnis *nt*; (*of*

ship) Schlagseite *f* ♦ *vt* (*write down*) eine Liste machen von; (*verbally*) aufzählen ♦ *vi* (*ship*) Schlagseite haben
listen ['lɪsn] *vi* hören; ~ **to** *vt* zuhören +*dat*; ~**er** *n* (Zu)hörer(in) *m(f)*
listless ['lɪstləs] *adj* lustlos
lit [lɪt] *pt*, *pp* *of* **light**
liter ['liːtə*] (*US*) *n* = **litre**
literacy ['lɪtərəsɪ] *n* Fähigkeit *f* zu lesen und zu schreiben
literal ['lɪtərəl] *adj* buchstäblich; (*translation*) wortwörtlich; ~**ly** *adv* wörtlich; buchstäblich
literary ['lɪtərərɪ] *adj* literarisch
literate ['lɪtərət] *adj* des Lesens und Schreibens kundig
literature ['lɪtrətʃə*] *n* Literatur *f*
lithe [laɪð] *adj* geschmeidig
litigation [lɪtɪ'geɪʃən] *n* Prozeß *m*
litre ['liːtə*] (*US* **liter**) *n* Liter *m*
litter ['lɪtə*] *n* (*rubbish*) Abfall *m*; (*of animals*) Wurf *m* ♦ *vt* in Unordnung bringen; **to be** ~**ed with** übersät sein mit; ~ **bin** (*BRIT*) *n* Abfalleimer *m*
little ['lɪtl] *adj* klein ♦ *adv*, *n* wenig; **a** ~ ein bißchen; ~ **by** ~ nach und nach
live¹ [laɪv] *adj* lebendig; (*MIL*) scharf; (*ELEC*) geladen; (*broadcast*) live
live² [lɪv] *vi* leben; (*dwell*) wohnen ♦ *vt* (*life*) führen; ~ **down** *vt*: **I'll never** ~ **it down** das wird man mir nie vergessen; ~ **on** *vi* weiterleben ♦ *vt fus*: **to** ~ **on sth** von etw leben; ~ **together** *vi* zusammenleben; (*share a flat*) zusammenwohnen; ~ **up to** *vt* (*standards*) gerecht werden +*dat*; (*principles*) anstreben; (*hopes*) entsprechen +*dat*
livelihood ['laɪvlɪhʊd] *n* Lebensunterhalt *m*
lively ['laɪvlɪ] *adj* lebhaft, lebendig
liven up ['laɪvn-] *vt* beleben
liver ['lɪvə*] *n* (*ANAT*) Leber *f*
livery ['lɪvərɪ] *n* Livree *f*
lives [laɪvz] *pl of* **life**
livestock ['laɪvstɒk] *n* Vieh *nt*
livid ['lɪvɪd] *adj* bläulich; (*furious*) fuchsteufelswild
living ['lɪvɪŋ] *n* (Lebens)unterhalt *m* ♦ *adj* lebendig; (*language etc*) lebend; **to**

earn or make a ~ sich dat seinen
Lebensunterhalt verdienen; ~ **conditions** npl Wohnverhältnisse pl; ~ **room**
n Wohnzimmer nt; ~ **standards** npl
Lebensstandard m; ~ **wage** n ausrei-
chender Lohn m
lizard ['lɪzəd] n Eidechse f
load [ləʊd] n (burden) Last f; (amount)
Ladung f ♦ vt (also: ~ up) (be)laden;
(COMPUT) laden; (camera) Film einlegen in +acc; (gun) laden; **a ~ of, ~s
of** (fig) jede Menge; **~ed** adj beladen;
(dice) präpariert; (question) Fang-;
(inf: rich) steinreich; **~ing bay** n Lade-
platz m
loaf [ləʊf] (pl **loaves**) n Brot nt ♦ vi
(also: ~ about, ~ around) her-
umlungern, faulenzen
loan [ləʊn] n Leihgabe f; (FIN) Darlehen
nt ♦ vt leihen; **on ~** geliehen
loath [ləʊθ] adj: **to be ~ to do sth** etw
ungern tun
loathe [ləʊð] vt verabscheuen
loathing ['ləʊðɪŋ] n Abscheu f
loaves [ləʊvz] pl of **loaf**
lobby ['lɒbɪ] n Vorhalle f; (POL) Lobby f
♦ vt politisch beeinflussen (wollen)
lobe [ləʊb] n Ohrläppchen nt
lobster ['lɒbstə*] n Hummer m
local ['ləʊkəl] adj ortsansässig, Orts- ♦ n
(pub) Stammwirtschaft f; **the ~s** npl
(people) die Ortsansässigen pl; ~
anaesthetic n (MED) örtliche Betäubung
f; ~ **authority** n städtische Behörden
pl; ~ **call** n (TEL) Ortsgespräch nt; ~
government n Gemeinde-/Kreisverwal-
tung f; **~ity** [ləʊˈkælɪtɪ] n Ort m; **~ly**
adv örtlich, am Ort
locate [ləʊˈkeɪt] vt ausfindig machen;
(establish) errichten
location [ləʊˈkeɪʃən] n Platz m, Lage f;
on ~ (CINE) auf Außenaufnahme
loch [lɒx] (SCOTTISH) n See m
lock [lɒk] n Schloß nt; (NAUT) Schleuse
f; (of hair) Locke f ♦ vt (fasten)
(ver)schließen ♦ vi (door etc) sich
schließen (lassen); (wheels) blockieren
locker ['lɒkə*] n Spind m
locket ['lɒkɪt] n Medaillon nt
lock-out ['lɒkaʊt] n Aussperrung f

locksmith ['lɒksmɪθ] n Schlosser(in)
m(f)
lockup ['lɒkʌp] n (jail) Gefängnis nt;
(garage) Garage f
locomotive [ləʊkəˈməʊtɪv] n Lokomotive
f
locum ['ləʊkəm] n (MED) Vertreter(in)
m(f)
locust ['ləʊkəst] n Heuschrecke f
lodge [lɒdʒ] n (gatehouse) Pförtnerhaus
nt; (freemasons') Loge f ♦ vi (become
stuck) stecken(bleiben); (in Untermiete): **to ~ (with)** wohnen (bei) ♦ vt
(protest) einreichen; **~r** n (Unter-)
mieter m
lodgings ['lɒdʒɪŋz] n (Miet)wohnung f
loft [lɒft] n (Dach)boden m
lofty ['lɒftɪ] adj hoch(ragend); (proud)
hochmütig
log [lɒg] n Klotz m; (book) = **logbook**
logbook ['lɒgbʊk] n Bordbuch nt; (for
lorry) Fahrtenschreiber m; (AUT)
Kraftfahrzeugbrief m
loggerheads ['lɒgəhedz] npl: **to be at ~**
sich in den Haaren liegen
logic ['lɒdʒɪk] n Logik f; **~al** adj logisch
logistics [lɒˈdʒɪstɪks] npl Logistik f
logo ['ləʊgəʊ] n Firmenzeichen nt
loin [lɔɪn] n Lende f
loiter ['lɔɪtə*] vi herumstehen
loll [lɒl] vi (also: ~ about) sich rekeln
lollipop ['lɒlɪpɒp] n (Dauer)lutscher m;
~ **man/lady** (BRIT) n ≈ Schülerlotse m
London ['lʌndən] n London nt; **~er** n
Londoner(in) m(f)
lone [ləʊn] adj einsam
loneliness ['ləʊnlɪnəs] n Einsamkeit f
lonely ['ləʊnlɪ] adj einsam
loner ['ləʊnə*] n Einzelgänger(in) m(f)
long [lɒŋ] adj lang; (distance) weit ♦
adv lange ♦ vi: **to ~ for** sich sehnen
nach; **before ~** bald; **as ~ as** solange;
in the ~ run auf die Dauer; **don't be ~!**
beeil dich!; **how ~ is the street?** wie
lang ist die Straße?; **how ~ is the
lesson?** wie lange dauert die Stunde?; **6
metres ~** 6 Meter lang; **6 months ~** 6
Monate lang; **all night ~** die ganze
Nacht; **he no ~er comes** er kommt
nicht mehr; ~ **ago** vor langer Zeit; ~

before lange vorher; **at ~ last** endlich; **~-distance** *adj* Fern-

longevity [lɒnˈdʒɛvɪtɪ] *n* Langlebigkeit *f*

long: **~-haired** *adj* langhaarig; **~hand** *n* Langschrift *f*; **~ing** *n* Sehnsucht *f* ♦ *adj* sehnsüchtig

longitude [ˈlɒŋgɪtjuːd] *n* Längengrad *m*

long: **~ jump** *n* Weitsprung *m*; **~-lost** *adj* längst verloren geglaubt; **~-playing record** *n* Langspielplatte *f*; **~-range** *adj* Langstrecken-, Fern-; **~-sighted** *adj* weitsichtig; **~-standing** *adj* alt, seit langer Zeit bestehend; **~-suffering** *adj* schwer geprüft; **~-term** *adj* langfristig; **~ wave** *n* Langwelle *f*; **~-winded** *adj* langatmig

loo [luː] (*BRIT: inf*) *n* Klo *nt*

look [lʊk] *vi* schauen; (*seem*) aussehen; (*building etc*): **to ~ on to the sea** aufs Meer gehen ♦ *n* Blick *m*; **~s** *npl* (*appearance*) Aussehen *nt*; **~ after** *vt* (*care for*) sorgen für; (*watch*) aufpassen auf +*acc*; **~ at** *vt* ansehen; (*consider*) sich überlegen; **~ back** *vi* sich umsehen; (*fig*) zurückblicken; **~ down on** *vt* (*fig*) herabsehen auf +*acc*; **~ for** *vt* (*seek*) suchen; **~ forward to** *vt* sich freuen auf +*acc*; (*in letters*): **we ~ forward to hearing from you** wir hoffen, bald von Ihnen zu hören; **~ into** *vt* untersuchen; **~ on** *vi* zusehen; **~ out** *vi* hinaussehen; (*take care*) aufpassen; **~ out for** *vt* Ausschau halten nach; (*be careful*) achtgeben auf +*acc*; **~ round** *vi* sich umsehen; **~ to** *vt* (*take care of*) achtgeben auf +*acc*; (*rely on*) sich verlassen auf +*acc*; **~ up** *vi* aufblicken; (*improve*) sich bessern ♦ *vt* (*word*) nachschlagen; (*person*) besuchen; **~ up to** *vt* aufsehen zu; **~-out** *n* (*watch*) Ausschau *f*; (*person*) Wachposten *m*; (*place*) Ausguck *m*; (*prospect*) Aussichten *pl*; **to be on the ~-out for sth** nach etw Ausschau halten

loom [luːm] *n* Webstuhl *m* ♦ *vi* sich abzeichnen

loony [ˈluːnɪ] (*inf*) *n* Verrückte(r) *mf*

loop [luːp] *n* Schlaufe *f*; **~hole** *n* (*fig*) Hintertürchen *nt*

loose [luːs] *adj* lose, locker; (*free*) frei; (*inexact*) unpräzise ♦ *vt* lösen, losbinden; **~ change** *n* Kleingeld *nt*; **~ chippings** *npl* (*on road*) Rollsplit *m*; **~ end** *n*: **to be at a ~ end** (*BRIT*) *or* **at ~ ends** (*US*) nicht wissen, was man tun soll; **~ly** *adv* locker, lose; **~n** *vt* lockern, losmachen

loot [luːt] *n* Beute *f* ♦ *vt* plündern; **~ing** *n* Plünderung *f*

lop off *vt* abhacken

lopsided [ˈlɒpˈsaɪdɪd] *adj* schief

lord [lɔːd] *n* (*ruler*) Herr *m*; (*BRIT: title*) Lord *m*; **the L~** (*God*) der Herr; **the (House of) L~s** das Oberhaus; **~ship** *n*: **your L~ship** Eure Lordschaft

lore [lɔːᵊ] *n* Überlieferung *f*

lorry [ˈlɒrɪ] (*BRIT*) *n* Lastwagen *m*; **~ driver** (*BRIT*) *n* Lastwagenfahrer(in) *m(f)*

lose [luːz] (*pt, pp* **lost**) *vt* verlieren; (*chance*) verpassen ♦ *vi* verlieren; **to ~** (*time*) (*clock*) nachgehen; **~r** *n* Verlierer *m*

loss [lɒs] *n* Verlust *m*; **at a ~** (*COMM*) mit Verlust; (*unable*) außerstande

lost [lɒst] *pt, pp of* **lose** ♦ *adj* verloren; **~ property** (*US* **and found**) *n* Fundsachen *pl*

lot [lɒt] *n* (*quantity*) Menge *f*; (*fate, at auction*) Los *nt*; (*inf: people, things*) Haufen *m*; **the ~** alles; (*people*) alle; **a ~ of** (*with sg*) viel; (*with pl*) viele; **~s of** massenhaft, viel(e); **I read a ~** ich lese viel; **to draw ~s for sth** etw verlosen

lotion [ˈləʊʃən] *n* Lotion *f*

lottery [ˈlɒtərɪ] *n* Lotterie *f*

loud [laʊd] *adj* laut; (*showy*) schreiend ♦ *adv* laut; **~-hailer** (*BRIT*) *n* Megaphon *nt*; **~ly** *adv* laut; **~speaker** *n* Lautsprecher *m*

lounge [laʊndʒ] *n* (*in hotel*) Gesellschaftsraum *m*; (*in house*) Wohnzimmer *nt* ♦ *vi* sich herumlümmeln; **~ suit** (*BRIT*) *n* Straßenanzug *m*

louse [laʊs] (*pl* **lice**) *n* Laus *f*

lousy [ˈlaʊzɪ] *adj* (*fig*) miserabel

lout [laʊt] *n* Lümmel *m*

louvre [ˈluːvᵊ] (*US* **louver**) *adj* (*door,*

window) Jalousie-

lovable ['lʌvəbl] *adj* liebenswert

love [lʌv] *n* Liebe *f*; *(person)* Liebling *m*; *(SPORT)* null ♦ *vt (person)* lieben; *(activity)* gerne mögen; **to be in ~ with sb** in jdn verliebt sein; **to make ~** sich lieben; **for the ~ of** aus Liebe zu; **"15 ~"** *(TENNIS)* „15 null"; **to ~ to do sth** etw (sehr) gerne tun; **~ affair** *n (Liebes)verhältnis nt*; **~ letter** *n* Liebesbrief *m*; **~ life** *n* Liebesleben *nt*

lovely ['lʌvlɪ] *adj* schön

lover ['lʌvə*] *n* Liebhaber(in) *m(f)*

loving ['lʌvɪŋ] *adj* liebend, liebevoll

low [ləu] *adj* niedrig; *(rank)* niedere(r, s); *(level, note, neckline)* tief; *(intelligence, density)* gering; *(vulgar)* ordinär; *(not loud)* leise; *(depressed)* gedrückt ♦ *adv (not high)* niedrig; *(not loudly)* leise ♦ *n (low point)* Tiefstand *m*; *(MET)* Tief *nt*; **to feel ~** sich mies fühlen; **to turn (down) ~** leiser stellen; **~-cut** *adj (dress)* tiefausgeschnitten

lower ['ləuə*] *vt* herunterlassen; *(eyes, gun)* senken; *(reduce)* herabsetzen, senken ♦ *vr*: **to ~ o.s. to** *(fig)* sich herablassen zu

low: **~-fat** *adj* fettarm, Mager-; **~lands** *npl (GEOG)* Flachland *nt*; **~ly** *adj* bescheiden; **~-lying** *adj* tiefgelegen

loyal ['lɔɪəl] *adj* treu; **~ty** *n* Treue *f*

lozenge ['lɒzɪndʒ] *n* Pastille *f*

L.P. *n abbr* = **long-playing record**

L-plates ['elpleɪts] *(BRIT)* *npl* L-Schild *nt (für Fahrschüler)*

Ltd *abbr (= limited company)* GmbH.

lubricant ['lu:brɪkənt] *n* Schmiermittel *nt*

lubricate ['lu:brɪkeɪt] *vt* schmieren

lucid ['lu:sɪd] *adj* klar; *(sane)* bei klarem Verstand; *(moment)* licht

luck [lʌk] *n* Glück *nt*; **bad ~** Pech *nt*; **good ~!** viel Glück!; **~ily** *adv* glücklicherweise, zum Glück; **~y** *adj* Glücks-; **to be ~y** Glück haben

lucrative ['lu:krətɪv] *adj* einträglich

ludicrous ['lu:dɪkrəs] *adj* grotesk

lug [lʌg] *vt* schleppen

luggage ['lʌgɪdʒ] *n* Gepäck *nt*; **~ rack** *n* Gepäcknetz *nt*

lugubrious [lu:'gu:brɪəs] *adj* traurig

lukewarm ['lu:kwɔːm] *adj* lauwarm; *(indifferent)* lau

lull [lʌl] *n* Flaute *f* ♦ *vt* einlullen; *(calm)* beruhigen

lullaby ['lʌləbaɪ] *n* Schlaflied *nt*

lumbago [lʌm'beɪgəu] *n* Hexenschuß *m*

lumber ['lʌmbə*] *n* Plunder *m*; *(wood)* Holz *nt*; **~jack** *n* Holzfäller *m*

luminous ['lu:mɪnəs] *adj* Leucht-

lump [lʌmp] *n* Klumpen *m*; *(MED)* Schwellung *f*; *(in breast)* Knoten *m*; *(of sugar)* Stück *nt* ♦ *vt (also: ~ together)* zusammentun; *(judge together)* in einen Topf werfen; **~ sum** *n* Pauschalsumme *f*; **~y** *adj* klumpig

lunacy ['lu:nəsɪ] *n* Irrsinn *m*

lunar ['lu:nə*] *adj* Mond-

lunatic ['lu:nətɪk] *n* Wahnsinnige(r) *mf* ♦ *adj* wahnsinnig, irr; **~ asylum** *n* Irrenanstalt *f*

lunch [lʌntʃ] *n* Mittagessen *nt*

luncheon ['lʌntʃən] *n* Mittagessen *nt*; **~ meat** *n* Frühstücksfleisch *nt*; **~ voucher** *(BRIT)* *n* Essensmarke *f*

lunchtime *n* Mittagszeit *f*

lung [lʌŋ] *n* Lunge *f*

lunge [lʌndʒ] *vi (also: ~ forward)* (los)stürzen; **to ~ at** sich stürzen auf +acc

lurch [lɜːtʃ] *vi* taumeln; *(NAUT)* schlingern ♦ *n* Ruck *m*; *(NAUT)* Schlingern *nt*; **to leave sb in the ~** jdn im Stich lassen

lure [ljuə*] *n* Köder *m*; *(fig)* Lockung *f* ♦ *vt* (ver)locken

lurid ['ljuərɪd] *adj (shocking)* grausig, widerlich; *(colour)* grell

lurk [lɜːk] *vi* lauern

luscious ['lʌʃəs] *adj* köstlich

lush [lʌʃ] *adj* satt; *(vegetation)* üppig

lust [lʌst] *n (sensation)* Wollust *f*; *(greed)* Gier *f* ♦ *vi*: **to ~ after** gieren nach

lustre ['lʌstə*] *(US* **luster***)* *n* Glanz *m*

lusty ['lʌstɪ] *adj* gesund und munter

Luxembourg ['lʌksəmbɜːg] *n* Luxemburg *nt*

luxuriant [lʌg'zjuərɪənt] *adj* üppig

luxurious [lʌg'zjuərɪəs] *adj* luxuriös,

Luxus-
luxury ['lʌkʃərɪ] n Luxus m ♦ cpd Luxus-
lying ['laɪɪŋ] n Lügen nt ♦ adj verlogen
lynx [lɪŋks] n Luchs m
lyric ['lɪrɪk] n Lyrik f ♦ adj lyrisch; ~s
pl (words for song) (Lied)text m; ~al
adj lyrisch, gefühlvoll

M

m. abbr = metre; mile; million
M.A. n abbr = Master of Arts
mac [mæk] (BRIT: inf) n Regenmantel m
macaroni [mækə'rəʊnɪ] n Makkaroni pl
mace [meɪs] n Amtsstab m; (spice)
Muskat m
machine [mə'ʃiːn] n Maschine f ♦ vt
(dress etc) mit der Maschine nähen; ~
gun n Maschinengewehr nt; ~
language n (COMPUT) Maschinenspra-
che f; ~ry [mə'ʃiːnərɪ] n Maschinerie f
macho ['mætʃəʊ] adj macho
mackerel ['mækrəl] n Makrele f
mackintosh ['mækɪntɒʃ] (BRIT) n
Regenmantel m
mad [mæd] adj verrückt; (dog)
tollwütig; (angry) wütend; ~ about
(fond of) verrückt nach, versessen auf
+acc
madam ['mædəm] n gnädige Frau f
madden ['mædn] vt verrückt machen;
(make angry) ärgern
made [meɪd] pt, pp of make
Madeira [mə'dɪərə] n (GEOG) Madeira
nt; (wine) Madeira m
made-to-measure ['meɪdtə'meʒə*]
(BRIT) adj Maß-
madly ['mædlɪ] adv wahnsinnig
madman ['mædmən] (irreg) n Ver-
rückte(r) m, Irre(r) m
madness ['mædnəs] n Wahnsinn m
Madrid [mə'drɪd] n Madrid nt
Mafia ['mæfɪə] n Mafia f
magazine [mægə'ziːn] n Zeitschrift f;
(in gun) Magazin nt
maggot ['mægət] n Made f
magic ['mædʒɪk] n Zauberei f, Magie f;
(fig) Zauber m ♦ adj magisch, Zau-
ber-; ~al adj magisch; ~ian [mə'dʒɪʃən] n

Zauberer m
magistrate ['mædʒɪstreɪt] n (Frie-
dens)richter m
magnanimous [mæg'nænɪməs] adj
großmütig
magnesium [mæg'niːzɪəm] n Magnesium
nt
magnet ['mægnɪt] n Magnet m; ~ic
[mæg'netɪk] adj magnetisch; ~ic tape n
Magnetband nt; ~ism n Magnetismus
m; (fig) Ausstrahlungskraft f
magnificence [mæg'nɪfɪsəns] n Groß-
artigkeit f
magnificent [mæg'nɪfɪsənt] adj großartig
magnify ['mægnɪfaɪ] vt vergrößern;
~ing glass n Lupe f
magnitude ['mægnɪtjuːd] n (size) Größe
f; (importance) Ausmaß nt
magpie ['mægpaɪ] n Elster f
mahogany [mə'hɒgənɪ] n Mahagoni nt ♦
cpd Mahagoni-
maid [meɪd] n Dienstmädchen nt; old ~
alte Jungfer f
maiden ['meɪdn] n Maid f ♦ adj (flight,
speech) Jungfern-; ~ name n
Mädchenname m
mail [meɪl] n Post f ♦ vt aufgeben; ~
box n (US) Briefkasten m; ~ing list n
Anschreibeliste f; ~ order n Bestellung
f durch die Post; ~ order firm n Ver-
sandhaus nt
maim [meɪm] vt verstümmeln
main [meɪn] adj hauptsächlich, Haupt- ♦
n (pipe) Hauptleitung f; the ~s npl
(ELEC) das Stromnetz; in the ~ im
großen und ganzen; ~frame n
(COMPUT) Großrechner m; ~land n
Festland nt; ~ road n Hauptstraße f;
~stay n (fig) Hauptstütze f; ~stream n
Hauptrichtung f
maintain [meɪn'teɪn] vt (machine,
roads) instand halten; (support) unterhalten; (keep up) aufrechterhalten;
(claim) behaupten; (innocence)
beteuern
maintenance ['meɪntənəns] n (TECH)
Wartung f; (of family) Unterhalt m
maize [meɪz] n Mais m
majestic [mə'dʒestɪk] adj majestätisch
majesty ['mædʒɪstɪ] n Majestät f

major ['meɪdʒə*] n Major m ♦ adj (MUS)
Dur; (more important) Haupt-;
(bigger) größer
Majorca [mə'jɔːkə] n Mallorca nt
majority [mə'dʒɒrɪtɪ] n Mehrheit f; (JUR)
Volljährigkeit f
make [meɪk] (pt, pp made) vt machen;
(appoint) ernennen (zu); (cause to do
sth) veranlassen; (reach) erreichen;
(in time) schaffen; (earn) verdienen ♦
n Marke f; **to ~ sth happen** etw geschehen lassen; **to ~ it** es schaffen;
what time do you ~ it? wie spät hast du
es?; **to ~ do with** auskommen mit; **~
for** vi gehen/fahren nach; **~ out** vt
(write out) ausstellen; (understand)
verstehen; (write: cheque) ausstellen;
~ up vt machen; (face) schminken;
(quarrel) beilegen; (story etc) erfinden
♦ vi sich versöhnen; **~ up for** vt wiedergutmachen; (COMM) vergüten; **~-
believe** n Phantasie f; **~r** n (COMM)
Hersteller m; **~shift** adj behelfsmäßig,
Not-; **~up** n Schminke f, Make-up nt;
~-up remover n Make-up-Entferner m
making ['meɪkɪŋ] n: **in the ~** im Entstehen; **to have the ~s of** das Zeug
haben zu
malaise [mæ'leɪz] n Unbehagen nt
malaria [mə'leərɪə] n Malaria f
Malaya [mə'leɪə] n Malaya nt
Malaysia [mə'leɪzɪə] n Malaysia nt
male [meɪl] n Mann m; (animal)
Männchen nt ♦ adj männlich
malevolent [mə'levələnt] adj übelwol-
lend
malfunction [mæl'fʌŋkʃən] n (MED)
Funktionsstörung f; (of machine) Defekt m
malice ['mælɪs] n Bosheit f
malicious [mə'lɪʃəs] adj böswillig,
gehässig
malign [mə'laɪn] vt verleumden ♦ adj
böse
malignant [mə'lɪgnənt] adj bösartig
mall [mɔːl] n (also: shopping ~) Einkaufszentrum nt
malleable ['mælɪəbl] adj formbar
mallet ['mælɪt] n Holzhammer m
malnutrition ['mælnjuː'trɪʃən] n Unter-

ernährung f
malpractice [mæl'præktɪs] n Amtsver-
gehen nt
malt [mɔːlt] n Malz nt
Malta ['mɔːltə] n Malta nt; **Maltese**
['mɔːl'tiːz] adj inv maltesisch ♦ n inv
Malteser(in) m(f)
maltreat [mæl'triːt] vt mißhandeln
mammal ['mæməl] n Säugetier nt
mammoth ['mæməθ] n Mammut nt ♦
adj Mammut-
man [mæn] (pl men) n Mann m;
(human race) der Mensch, die Menschen pl ♦ vt bemannen
manage ['mænɪdʒ] vi zurechtkommen ♦
vt (control) führen, leiten; (cope with)
fertigwerden mit; **~able** adj (person,
animal) fügsam; (object) handlich;
~ment n (control) Führung f, Leitung
f; (directors) Management nt; **~r** n Ge-
schäftsführer m; **~ress** ['mænɪdʒə'res]
n Geschäftsführerin f; **~rial**
[mænə'dʒɪərɪəl] adj (post) leitend; (problem etc) Management-
managing ['mænɪdʒɪŋ] adj: **~ director**
Betriebsleiter m
mandarin ['mændərɪn] n (fruit)
Mandarine f
mandatory ['mændətərɪ] adj obligatorisch
mane [meɪn] n Mähne f
maneuver [mə'nuːvə*] (US) =
manoeuvre
manfully ['mænfʊlɪ] adv mannhaft
mangle ['mæŋgl] vt verstümmeln ♦ n
Mangel f
mango ['mæŋgəʊ] (pl ~es) n
Mango(pflaume) f
mangy ['meɪndʒɪ] adj (dog) räudig
manhandle ['mænhændl] vt grob
behandeln
manhole ['mænhəʊl] n (Straßen)schacht
m
manhood ['mænhʊd] n Mannesalter nt;
(manliness) Männlichkeit f
man-hour ['mæn'aʊə*] n Arbeitsstunde f
manhunt ['mænhʌnt] n Fahndung f
mania ['meɪnɪə] n Manie f; **~c** ['meɪnɪæk]
n Wahnsinnige(r) mf
manic ['mænɪk] adj (behaviour, activity)

hektisch; **~-depressive** *n* Manisch-Depressive(r) *mf*

manicure ['mænɪkjʊə*] *n* Maniküre *f*; **~ set** *n* Necessaire *nt*

manifest ['mænɪfest] *vt* offenbaren ♦ *adj* offenkundig; **~ation** *n* (*sign*) Anzeichen *nt*

manifesto [mænɪ'festəʊ] *n* Manifest *nt*

manipulate [mə'nɪpjʊleɪt] *vt* handhaben; (*fig*) manipulieren

mankind [mæn'kaɪnd] *n* Menschheit *f*

manly ['mænlɪ] *adj* männlich; mannhaft

man-made ['mæn'meɪd] *adj* (*fibre*) künstlich

manner ['mænə*] *n* Art *f*, Weise *f*; **~s** *npl* (*behaviour*) Manieren *pl*; **in a ~ of speaking** sozusagen; **~ism** *n* (*of person*) Angewohnheit *f*; (*of style*) Maniertheit *f*

manoeuvre [mə'nu:və*] (*US* **maneuver**) *vt, vi* manövrieren ♦ *n* (*MIL*) Feldzug *m*; (*general*) Manöver *nt*, Schachzug *m*

manor ['mænə*] *n* Landgut *nt*; **~ house** *n* Herrenhaus *nt*

manpower ['mænpaʊə*] *n* Arbeitskräfte *pl*

mansion ['mænʃən] *n* Villa *f*

manslaughter ['mænslɔ:tə*] *n* Totschlag *m*

mantelpiece ['mæntlpi:s] *n* Kaminsims *m*

mantle ['mæntl] *n* (*cloak*) lange(r) Umhang *m*

manual ['mænjʊəl] *adj* manuell, Hand- ♦ *n* Handbuch *nt*

manufacture [mænjʊ'fæktʃə*] *vt* herstellen ♦ *n* Herstellung *f*; **~r** *n* Hersteller *m*

manure [mə'njʊə*] *n* Dünger *m*

manuscript ['mænjʊskrɪpt] *n* Manuskript *nt*

Manx [mæŋks] *adj* der Insel Man

many ['menɪ] *adj, pron* viele; **a great ~** sehr viele; **~ a time** oft

map [mæp] *n* (Land)karte *f*; (*of town*) Stadtplan *m* ♦ *vt* eine Karte machen von; **~ out** *vt* (*fig*) ausarbeiten

maple ['meɪpl] *n* Ahorn *m*

mar [mɑ:*] *vt* verderben

marathon ['mærəθən] *n* (*SPORT*) Mara-

thonlauf *m*; (*fig*) Marathon *m*

marauder [mə'rɔ:də*] *n* Plünderer *m*

marble ['mɑ:bl] *n* Marmor *m*; (*for game*) Murmel *f*

March [mɑ:tʃ] *n* März *m*

march [mɑ:tʃ] *vi* marschieren ♦ *n* Marsch *m*; **~-past** *n* Vorbeimarsch *m*

mare [mɛə*] *n* Stute *f*

margarine [mɑ:dʒə'ri:n] *n* Margarine *f*

margin ['mɑ:dʒɪn] *n* Rand *m*; (*extra amount*) Spielraum *m*; (*COMM*) Spanne *f*; **~al** *adj* (*note*) Rand-; (*difference etc*) geringfügig; **~al (seat)** *n* (*POL*) Wahlkreis, der nur mit knapper Mehrheit gehalten wird

marigold ['mærɪgəʊld] *n* Ringelblume *f*

marijuana [mærɪ'wɑ:nə] *n* Marihuana *nt*

marina [mə'ri:nə] *n* Yachthafen *m*

marinate ['mærɪneɪt] *vt* marinieren

marine [mə'ri:n] *adj* Meeres-, See- ♦ *n* (*MIL*) Marineinfanterist *m*

marital ['mærɪtl] *adj* ehelich, Ehe-; **~ status** *n* Familienstand *m*

maritime ['mærɪtaɪm] *adj* See-

mark [mɑ:k] *n* (*coin*) Mark *f*; (*spot*) Fleck *m*; (*scar*) Kratzer *m*; (*sign*) Zeichen *nt*; (*target*) Ziel *nt*; (*SCH*) Note *f* ♦ *vt* (*make ~ on*) Flecken/Kratzer machen auf +*acc*; (*indicate*) markieren; (*exam*) korrigieren; **~ time** (*also fig*) auf der Stelle treten; **~ out** *vt* bestimmen; (*area*) abstecken; **~ed** *adj* deutlich; **~er** *n* (*in book*) (Lese)zeichen *nt*; (*on road*) Schild *nt*

market ['mɑ:kɪt] *n* Markt *m*; (*stock ~*) Börse *f* ♦ *vt* (*COMM: new product*) auf den Markt bringen; (*sell*) vertreiben; **~ garden** (*BRIT*) *n* Handelsgärtnerei *f*; **~ing** *n* Marketing *nt*; **~ research** *n* Marktforschung *f*; **~ value** *n* Marktwert *m*

marksman ['mɑ:ksmən] (*irreg*) *n* Scharfschütze *m*

marmalade ['mɑ:məleɪd] *n* Orangenmarmelade *f*

maroon [mə'ru:n] *vt* aussetzen ♦ *adj* (*colour*) kastanienbraun

marquee [mɑ:'ki:] *n* große(s) Zelt *nt*

marriage ['mærɪdʒ] *n* Ehe *f*; (*wedding*) Heirat *f*; **~ bureau** *n* Heiratsinstitut *nt*;

~ **certificate** n Heiratsurkunde f
married ['mærɪd] adj (person) verheiratet; (couple, life) Ehe-
marrow ['mærəu] n (Knochen)mark nt;
(vegetable) Kürbis m
marry ['mærɪ] vt (join) trauen; (take as
husband, wife) heiraten ♦ vi (also: get
married) heiraten
Mars [ma:z] n (planet) Mars m
marsh [ma:ʃ] n Sumpf m
marshal ['ma:ʃəl] n (US) Bezirkspolizei-
chef m ♦ vt (an)ordnen, arrangieren
marshy ['ma:ʃɪ] adj sumpfig
martial ['ma:ʃəl] adj kriegerisch; ~ **law**
n Kriegsrecht nt
martyr ['ma:tə*] n (also fig)
Märtyrer(in) m(f) ♦ vt zum Märtyrer
machen; ~**dom** n Martyrium nt
marvel ['ma:vəl] n Wunder nt ♦ vi: to ~
(at) sich wundern (über +acc); ~**lous**
(US ~**ous**) adj wunderbar
Marxist ['ma:ksɪst] n Marxist(in) m(f)
marzipan [ma:zɪ'pæn] n Marzipan nt
mascara [mæs'ka:rə] n Wimperntusche f
mascot ['mæskət] n Maskottchen nt
masculine ['mæskjulɪn] adj männlich
mash [mæʃ] n Brei m; ~**ed potatoes**
npl Kartoffelbrei m or -püree nt
mask [ma:sk] n (also fig) Maske f ♦ vt
maskieren, verdecken
mason ['meɪsn] n (stone~) Steinmetz
m; (free~) Freimaurer m; ~**ic**
[mə'sɒnɪk] adj Freimaurer-; ~**ry** n
Mauerwerk nt
masquerade [mæskə'reɪd] n Maskerade
f ♦ vi: to ~ as sich ausgeben als
mass [mæs] n Masse f; (greater part)
Mehrheit f; (REL) Messe f ♦ vi sich
sammeln; the ~**es** npl (people) die
Masse(n) f(pl)
massacre ['mæsəkə*] n Blutbad nt ♦ vt
niedermetzeln, massakrieren
massage ['mæsa:ʒ] n Massage f ♦ vt
massieren
massive ['mæsɪv] adj gewaltig, massiv
mass media npl Massenmedien pl
mass production n Massenproduktion
f
mast [ma:st] n Mast m
master ['ma:stə*] n Herr m; (NAUT)

Kapitän m; (teacher) Lehrer m;
(artist) Meister m ♦ vt meistern; (language etc) beherrschen; ~ **key** n
Hauptschlüssel m; ~**ly** adj meisterhaft;
~**mind** n Kapazität f ♦ vt geschickt
lenken; M~ **of Arts/Science** n Ma-
gister m der philosophischen/
naturwissenschaftlichen Fakultät;
~**piece** n Meisterwerk nt; ~ **plan** n
kluge(r) Plan m; ~**y** n Können nt
masturbate ['mæstəbeɪt] vi mastur-
bieren, onanieren
mat [mæt] n Matte f; (for table) Untersetzer m ♦ adj = **mat(t)**
match [mætʃ] n Streichholz nt; (sth
corresponding) Pendant nt; (SPORT)
Wettkampf m; (ball games) Spiel nt ♦
vt (be like, suit) passen zu; (equal)
gleichkommen +dat ♦ vi zusammen-
passen; it's a good ~ (for) es paßt gut
(zu); ~**box** n Streichholzschachtel f;
~**ing** adj passend
mate [meɪt] n (companion) Kamerad
m; (spouse) Lebensgefährte m; (of animal) Weibchen nt/Männchen nt;
(NAUT) Schiffsoffizier m ♦ vi (animals)
sich paaren ♦ vt (animals) paaren
material [mə'tɪərɪəl] n Material nt; (for
book, cloth) Stoff m ♦ adj (important)
wesentlich; (damage) Sach-; (comforts
etc) materiell; ~**s** npl (for building etc)
Materialien pl; ~**istic** adj materiali-
stisch; ~**ize** vi sich verwirklichen, zustande kommen
maternal [mə'tɜ:nl] adj mütterlich,
Mutter-
maternity [mə'tɜ:nɪtɪ] adj (dress)
Umstands-; (benefit) Wochen-; ~
hospital n Entbindungsheim nt
math [mæθ] (US) n = **maths**
mathematical [mæθə'mætɪkl] adj mathematisch
mathematics [mæθə'mætɪks] n Mathematik f
maths [mæθs] (US **math**) n Mathe f
matinée ['mætɪneɪ] n Matinee f
mating ['meɪtɪŋ] n Paarung f; ~ **call** n
Lockruf m
matrices ['meɪtrɪsiːz] npl of **matrix**
matriculation [mətrɪkjuˈleɪʃən] n Imma-

triculation *f*

matrimonial [mætrɪˈməʊnɪəl] *adj* ehelich, Ehe-

matrimony [ˈmætrɪmənɪ] *n* Ehestand *m*

matrix [ˈmeɪtrɪks] (*pl* **matrices**) *n* Matrize *f*; (*GEOL etc*) Matrix *f*

matron [ˈmeɪtrən] *n* (*MED*) Oberin *f*; (*SCH*) Hausmutter *f*; **~ly** *adj* matronenhaft

mat(t) [mæt] *adj* (*paint*) matt

matted [ˈmætɪd] *adj* verfilzt

matter [ˈmætə*] *n* (*substance*) Materie *f*; (*affair*) Angelegenheit *f* ♦ *vi* darauf ankommen; **no ~ how/what** egal wie/was; **what is the ~?** was ist los?; **as a ~ of course** selbstverständlich; **as a ~ of fact** eigentlich; **it doesn't ~** es macht nichts; **~-of-fact** *adj* sachlich, nüchtern

mattress [ˈmætrəs] *n* Matratze *f*

mature [məˈtjʊə*] *adj* reif ♦ *vi* reif werden

maturity [məˈtjʊərɪtɪ] *n* Reife *f*

maudlin [ˈmɔːdlɪn] *adj* gefühlsduselig

maul [mɔːl] *vt* übel zurichten

mauve [məʊv] *adj* mauve

maxima [ˈmæksɪmə] *npl of* **maximum**

maximum [ˈmæksɪməm] *adj* Höchst-, Maximal- ♦ *n* Maximum *nt*

May [meɪ] *n* Mai *m*

may [meɪ] (*conditional* **might**) *vi* (*be possible*) können; (*have permission*) dürfen; **he ~ come** er kommt vielleicht

maybe [ˈmeɪbiː] *adv* vielleicht

May Day *n* der 1. Mai

mayhem [ˈmeɪhem] *n* Chaos *nt*; (*US*) Körperverletzung *f*

mayonnaise [meɪəˈneɪz] *n* Mayonnaise *f*

mayor [mɛə*] *n* Bürgermeister *m*; **~ess** *n* (*wife*) (die) Frau *f* Bürgermeister; (*lady ~*) Bürgermeisterin *f*

maypole [ˈmeɪpəʊl] *n* Maibaum *m*

maze [meɪz] *n* Irrgarten *m*; (*fig*) Wirrwarr *nt*

M.D. *abbr* = **Doctor of Medicine**

KEYWORD

me [miː] *pron* **1** (*direct*) mich; **it's me** ich bin's

2 (*indirect*) mir; **give them to me** gib sie mir

3 (*after prep*: +*acc*) mich; (: +*dat*) mir; **with/without me** mit mir/ohne mich

meadow [ˈmedəʊ] *n* Wiese *f*

meagre [ˈmiːgə*] (*US* **meager**) *adj* dürftig, spärlich

meal [miːl] *n* Essen *nt*, Mahlzeit *f*; (*grain*) Schrotmehl *nt*; **to have a ~** essen (gehen); **~time** *n* Essenszeit *f*

mean [miːn] (*pt, pp* **meant**) *adj* (*stingy*) geizig; (*spiteful*) gemein; (*average*) durchschnittlich, Durchschnitts- ♦ *vt* (*signify*) bedeuten; (*intend*) vorhaben, beabsichtigen ♦ *n* (*average*) Durchschnitt *m*; **~s** *npl* (*wherewithal*) Mittel *pl*; (*wealth*) Vermögen *nt*; **do you ~ me?** meinst du mich?; **do you ~ it?** meinst du das ernst?; **what do you ~?** was willst du damit sagen?; **to be ~t for sb/sth** für jdn/etw bestimmt sein; **by ~s of** durch; **by all ~s** selbstverständlich; **by no ~s** keineswegs

meander [mɪˈændə*] *vi* sich schlängeln

meaning [ˈmiːnɪŋ] *n* Bedeutung *f*; (*of life*) Sinn *m*; **~ful** *adj* bedeutungsvoll; (*life*) sinnvoll; **~less** *adj* sinnlos

meanness [ˈmiːnnəs] *n* (*stinginess*) Geiz *m*; (*spitefulness*) Gemeinheit *f*

meant [ment] *pt, pp of* **mean**

meantime [ˈmiːntaɪm] *adv* inzwischen

meanwhile [ˈmiːnwaɪl] *adv* inzwischen

measles [ˈmiːzlz] *n* Masern *pl*

measly [ˈmiːzlɪ] (*inf*) *adj* poplig

measure [ˈmeʒə*] *vt, vi* messen ♦ *n* Maß *nt*; (*step*) Maßnahme *f*; **~d** *adj* (*slow*) gemessen; **~ments** *npl* Maße *pl*

meat [miːt] *n* Fleisch *nt*; **cold ~** Aufschnitt *m*; **~ ball** *n* Fleischkloß *m*; **~ pie** *n* Fleischpastete *f*; **~y** *adj* fleischig; (*fig*) gehaltvoll

Mecca [ˈmekə] *n* Mekka *nt* (*also fig*)

mechanic [mɪˈkænɪk] *n* Mechaniker *m*; **~al** *adj* mechanisch; **~s** *n* Mechanik *f* ♦ *npl* Technik *f*

mechanism [ˈmekənɪzəm] *n* Mechanismus *m*

mechanize [ˈmekənaɪz] *vt* mechanisieren

medal [ˈmedl] *n* Medaille *f*; (*decoration*)

Orden *m*; ~list (*US* ~ist) *n* Medaillengewinner(in) *m(f)*

meddle ['medl] *vi*: to ~ (in) sich einmischen (in +*acc*); to ~ with sth sich an etw *dat* zu schaffen machen

media ['mi:dɪə] *npl* Medien *pl*

mediaeval [medɪ'i:vəl] *adj* = **medieval**

median ['mi:dɪən] (*US*) *n* (*also*: ~ strip) Mittelstreifen *m*

mediate ['mi:dɪeɪt] *vi* vermitteln

mediation [mi:dɪ'eɪʃən] *n* Vermittlung *f*

mediator ['mi:dɪeɪtə*] *n* Vermittler *m*

Medicaid ['medɪkeɪd] (*US*) *n* medizinisches Versorgungsprogramm für Sozialschwache

medical ['medɪkəl] *adj* medizinisch; Medizin-; ärztlich ♦ *n* (ärztliche) Untersuchung *f*

Medicare ['medɪkeə*] (*US*) *n* staatliche Krankenversicherung besonders für Ältere

medicated ['medɪkeɪtɪd] *adj* medizinisch

medication [medɪ'keɪʃən] *n* (*drugs etc*) Medikamente *pl*

medicinal [me'dɪsɪnl] *adj* medizinisch, Heil-

medicine ['medsɪn] *n* Medizin *f*; (*drugs*) Arznei *f*

medieval [medɪ'i:vəl] *adj* mittelalterlich

mediocre [mi:dɪ'əʊkə*] *adj* mittelmäßig

mediocrity [mi:dɪ'ɒkrɪtɪ] *n* Mittelmäßigkeit *f*

meditate ['medɪteɪt] *vi* meditieren; to ~ (on sth) (über etw *acc*) nachdenken

meditation [medɪ'teɪʃən] *n* Nachsinnen *nt*; Meditation *f*

Mediterranean [medɪtə'reɪnɪən] *adj* Mittelmeer-; (*person*) südländisch; the ~ (Sea) das Mittelmeer

medium ['mi:dɪəm] *adj* mittlere(r, s), Mittel-, mittel- ♦ *n* Mitte *f*; (*means*) Mittel *nt*; (*person*) Medium *nt*; happy ~ goldener Mittelweg; ~ wave *n* Mittelwelle *f*

medley ['medlɪ] *n* Gemisch *nt*

meek [mi:k] *adj* sanft(mütig); (*pej*) duckmäuserisch

meet [mi:t] (*pt, pp* met) *vt* (*encounter*) treffen (*dat*), begegnen +*dat*; (*by arrangement*) sich treffen mit;

(*difficulties*) stoßen auf +*acc*; (*become acquainted with*) kennenlernen; (*fetch*) abholen; (*join*) zusammentreffen mit; (*satisfy*) entsprechen +*dat* ♦ *vi* sich treffen; (*become acquainted*) sich kennenlernen; ~ with *vt* (*problems*) stoßen auf +*acc*; (*US: people*) zusammentreffen mit; ~ing *n* Treffen *nt*; (*business meeting*) Besprechung *f*; (*of committee*) Sitzung *f*; (*assembly*) Versammlung *f*

megabyte ['megəbaɪt] *n* (*COMPUT*) Megabyte *nt*

megaphone ['megəfəʊn] *n* Megaphon *nt*

melancholy ['melənkəlɪ] *adj* (*person*) melancholisch; (*sight, event*) traurig

mellow ['meləʊ] *adj* mild, weich; (*fruit*) reif; (*fig*) gesetzt ♦ *vi* reif werden

melodious [mɪ'ləʊdɪəs] *adj* wohlklingend

melody ['melədɪ] *n* Melodie *f*

melon ['melən] *n* Melone *f*

melt [melt] *vi* schmelzen; (*anger*) verfliegen ♦ *vt* schmelzen; ~ away *vi* dahinschmelzen; ~ down *vt* einschmelzen; ~down *n* (*in nuclear reactor*) Kernschmelze *f*; ~ing point *n* Schmelzpunkt *m*; ~ing pot *n* (*fig*) Schmelztiegel *m*

member ['membə*] *n* Mitglied *nt*; (*of tribe, species*) Angehörige(r) *m*; (*ANAT*) Glied *nt*; M~ of Parliament (*BRIT*) *n* Parlamentsmitglied *nt*; M~ of the European Parliament (*BRIT*) *n* Mitglied *nt* des Europäischen Parlaments; ~ship *n* Mitgliedschaft *f*; to seek ~ship of einen Antrag auf Mitgliedschaft stellen; ~ship card *n* Mitgliedskarte *f*

memento [mə'mentəʊ] *n* Andenken *nt*

memo ['meməʊ] *n* Mitteilung *f*

memoirs ['memwɑːz] *npl* Memoiren *pl*

memorable ['memərəbl] *adj* denkwürdig

memoranda [memə'rændə] *npl of* **memorandum**

memorandum [memə'rændəm] (*pl* **memoranda**) *n* Mitteilung *f*

memorial [mɪ'mɔːrɪəl] *n* Denkmal *nt* ♦ *adj* Gedenk-

memorize ['meməraɪz] *vt* sich einprägen

memory ['memərɪ] *n* Gedächtnis *nt*; (*of computer*) Speicher *m*; (*sth recalled*)

Erinnerung f

men [men] pl of **man** ♦ npl (human race) die Menschen pl

menace ['menɪs] n Drohung f; Gefahr f ♦ vt bedrohen

menacing ['menɪsɪŋ] adj drohend

menagerie [mɪ'nædʒərɪ] n Tierschau f

mend [mend] vt reparieren, flicken ♦ vi (ver)heilen ♦ n ausgebesserte Stelle f; **on the ~** auf dem Wege der Besserung; **~ing** n (articles) Flickarbeit f

menial ['miːnɪəl] adj niedrig

meningitis [menɪn'dʒaɪtɪs] n Hirnhautentzündung f, Meningitis f

menopause ['menəupɔːz] n Wechseljahre pl, Menopause f

menstruation [menstrʊ'eɪʃən] n Menstruation f

mental ['mentl] adj geistig, Geistes-; (arithmetic) Kopf-; (hospital) Nerven-; (cruelty) seelisch; (inf: abnormal) verrückt; **~ity** [men'tælɪtɪ] n Mentalität f

menthol ['menθɒl] n Menthol nt

mention ['menʃən] n Erwähnung f ♦ vt erwähnen; **don't ~ it!** bitte (sehr), gern geschehen

mentor ['mentɔː*] n Mentor m

menu ['menjuː] n Speisekarte f

MEP n abbr = **Member of the European Parliament**

mercenary ['mɜːsɪnərɪ] adj (person) geldgierig; (MIL) Söldner- ♦ n Söldner m

merchandise ['mɜːtʃəndaɪz] n (Handels)ware f

merchant ['mɜːtʃənt] n Kaufmann m; **~ navy** (US **~ marine**) n Handelsmarine f

merciful ['mɜːsɪful] adj gnädig

merciless ['mɜːsɪləs] adj erbarmungslos

mercury ['mɜːkjurɪ] n Quecksilber nt

mercy ['mɜːsɪ] n Erbarmen nt; Gnade f; **at the ~ of** ausgeliefert +dat

mere [mɪə*] adj bloß

merely adv bloß

merge [mɜːdʒ] vt verbinden; (COMM) fusionieren ♦ vi verschmelzen; (roads) zusammenlaufen; (COMM) fusionieren; **~r** n (COMM) Fusion f

meringue [mə'ræŋ] n Baiser nt

merit ['merɪt] n Verdienst nt; (ad-

vantage) Vorzug m ♦ vt verdienen

mermaid ['mɜːmeɪd] n Wassernixe f

merry ['merɪ] adj fröhlich; **~-go-round** n Karussell nt

mesh [meʃ] n Masche f ♦ vi (gears) ineinandergreifen

mesmerize ['mezməraɪz] vt hypnotisieren; (fig) faszinieren

mess [mes] n Unordnung f; (dirt) Schmutz m; (trouble) Schwierigkeiten pl; (MIL) Messe f; **~ about** or **around** vi (play the fool) herumalbern; (do nothing in particular) herumgammeln; **~ about** or **around with** vt fus (tinker with) herummursken an +dat; **~ up** vt verpfuschen; (make untidy) in Unordnung bringen

message ['mesɪdʒ] n Mitteilung f; **to get the ~** kapieren

messenger ['mesɪndʒə*] n Bote m

Messrs ['mesəz] abbr (on letters) die Herren

messy ['mesɪ] adj schmutzig; (untidy) unordentlich

met [met] pt, pp of **meet**

metabolism [me'tæbəlɪzəm] n Stoffwechsel m

metal ['metl] n Metall nt

metaphor ['metəfɔː*] n Metapher f

mete [miːt]: **to ~ out** vt austeilen

meteorology [miːtɪə'rɒlədʒɪ] n Meteorologie f

meter ['miːtə*] n Zähler m; (US) = **metre**

method ['meθəd] n Methode f; **~ical** [mɪ'θɒdɪkəl] adj methodisch; **M~ist** ['meθədɪst] adj methodistisch ♦ n Methodist(in) m(f); **~ology** [meθə'dɒlədʒɪ] n Methodik f

meths [meθs] (BRIT) n = **methylated spirit(s)**

methylated spirit(s) ['meθɪleɪtɪd-] (BRIT) n (Brenn)spiritus m

meticulous [mɪ'tɪkjuləs] adj (über-)genau

metre ['miːtə*] (US **meter**) n Meter m or nt

metric ['metrɪk] adj (also: **~al**) metrisch

metropolitan [metrə'pɒlɪtən] adj der

Großstadt; **the M~ Police** (*BRIT*) *n* die Londoner Polizei

mettle ['metl] *n* Mut *m*

mew [mjuː] *vi* (*cat*) miauen

mews [mjuːz] *n*: ~ **cottage** (*BRIT*) ehemaliges Kutscherhäuschen

Mexican ['meksɪkən] *adj* mexikanisch ♦ *n* Mexikaner(in) *m(f)*

Mexico ['meksɪkəʊ] *n* Mexiko *nt*; ~ **City** *n* Mexiko City *f*

miaow [miːˈaʊ] *vi* miauen

mice [maɪs] *pl of* **mouse**

micro ['maɪkrəʊ] *n* (*also*: ~*computer*) Mikrocomputer *m*

microchip ['maɪkrəʊtʃɪp] *n* Mikrochip *m*

microcosm ['maɪkrəʊkɒzəm] *n* Mikrokosmos *m*

microfilm ['maɪkrəʊfɪlm] *n* Mikrofilm *m* ♦ *vt* auf Mikrofilm aufnehmen

microphone ['maɪkrəfəʊn] *n* Mikrophon *nt*

microprocessor ['maɪkrəʊ'prəʊsesə*] *n* Mikroprozessor *m*

microscope ['maɪkrəskəʊp] *n* Mikroskop *nt*

microwave ['maɪkrəʊweɪv] *n* (*also*: ~ *oven*) Mikrowelle(nherd *nt*) *f*

mid [mɪd] *adj*: **in ~ afternoon** am Nachmittag; **in ~ air** in der Luft; **in ~ May** Mitte Mai

midday ['mɪddeɪ] *n* Mittag *m*

middle ['mɪdl] *n* Mitte *f*; (*waist*) Taille *f* ♦ *adj* mittlere(r, s), Mittel-; **in the ~ of** mitten in +*dat*; **~-aged** *adj* mittleren Alters; **the M~ Ages** *npl* das Mittelalter; **~-class** *adj* Mittelstands-; **the M~ East** *n* der Nahe Osten; **~man** (*irreg*) *n* (*COMM*) Zwischenhändler *m*; **~ name** *n* zweiter Vorname *m*; **~ weight** *n* (*BOXING*) Mittelgewicht *nt*

middling ['mɪdlɪŋ] *adj* mittelmäßig

midge [mɪdʒ] *n* Mücke *f*

midget ['mɪdʒɪt] *n* Liliputaner(in) *m(f)*

Midlands ['mɪdləndz] *npl* Midlands *pl*

midnight ['mɪdnaɪt] *n* Mitternacht *f*

midriff ['mɪdrɪf] *n* Taille *f*

midst [mɪdst] *n*: **in the ~ of** (*persons*) mitten unter +*dat*; (*things*) mitten in +*dat*

midsummer ['mɪd'sʌmə*] *n* Hoch-

sommer *m*

midway ['mɪd'weɪ] *adv* auf halbem Wege ♦ *adj* Mittel-

midweek ['mɪd'wiːk] *adv* in der Mitte der Woche

midwife ['mɪdwaɪf] (*irreg*) *n* Hebamme *f*; **~ry** ['mɪdwɪfərɪ] *n* Geburtshilfe *f*

midwinter ['mɪd'wɪntə*] *n* tiefster(r) Winter *m*

might [maɪt] *vi see* **may** ♦ *n* Macht *f*, Kraft *f*; **~y** *adj*, *adv* mächtig

migraine ['miːgreɪn] *n* Migräne *f*

migrant ['maɪgrənt] *adj* Wander-; (*bird*) Zug-

migrate [maɪˈgreɪt] *vi* (ab)wandern; (*birds*) (fort)ziehen

migration [maɪˈgreɪʃən] *n* Wanderung *f*, Zug *m*

mike [maɪk] *n* = **microphone**

Milan [mɪˈlæn] *n* Mailand *nt*

mild [maɪld] *adj* mild; (*medicine, interest*) leicht; (*person*) sanft

mildew ['mɪldjuː] *n* (*on plants*) Mehltau *m*; (*on food*) Schimmel *m*

mildly ['maɪldlɪ] *adv* leicht; **to put it ~** gelinde gesagt

mile [maɪl] *n* Meile *f*; **~age** *n* Meilenzahl *f*; **~stone** *n* (*also fig*) Meilenstein *m*

militant ['mɪlɪtnt] *adj* militant

military ['mɪlɪtərɪ] *adj* militärisch, Militär-, Wehr-

militate ['mɪlɪteɪt] *vi*: **to ~ against** entgegenwirken +*dat*

militia [mɪˈlɪʃə] *n* Miliz *f*

milk [mɪlk] *n* Milch *f* ♦ *vt* (*also fig*) melken; **~ chocolate** *n* Milchschokolade *f*; **~man** (*irreg*) *n* Milchmann *m*; **~ shake** *n* Milchmixgetränk *nt*; **~y** *adj* milchig; **M~y Way** *n* Milchstraße *f*

mill [mɪl] *n* Mühle *f*; (*factory*) Fabrik *f* ♦ *vt* mahlen ♦ *vi* (*move around*) umherlaufen

millennia [mɪˈlenɪə] *npl of* **millennium**

millennium [mɪˈlenɪəm] (*pl* **~s** *or* **millennia**) *n* Jahrtausend *nt*

miller ['mɪlə*] *n* Müller *m*

millet ['mɪlɪt] *n* Hirse *f*

milligram(me) ['mɪlɪgræm] *n* Milli-

gramm *nt*
millimetre ['mɪlɪmiːtə*] (*US* **millimeter**) *n* Millimeter *m*
milliner ['mɪlɪnə*] *n* Hutmacher(in) *m(f)*; ~**y** ['mɪlɪnərɪ] *n* (*hats*) Hüte *pl*
million ['mɪljən] *n* Million *f*; **a ~ times** tausendmal; ~**aire** [mɪljə'nɛə*] *n* Millionär(in) *m(f)*
millstone ['mɪlstəʊn] *n* Mühlstein *m*
milometer [maɪ'lɒmɪtə*] *n* ≈ Kilometerzähler *m*
mime [maɪm] *n* Pantomime *f* ♦ *vt, vi* mimen
mimic ['mɪmɪk] *n* Mimiker *m* ♦ *vt, vi* nachahmen; ~**ry** ['mɪmɪkrɪ] *n* Nachahmung *f*; (*BIOL*) Mimikry *f*
min. *abbr* = **minutes; minimum**
minaret [mɪnə'rɛt] *n* Minarett *nt*
mince [mɪns] *vt* (zer)hacken ♦ *vi* (*walk*) trippeln ♦ *n* (*meat*) Hackfleisch *nt*; ~**meat** *n* süße Pastetenfüllung *f*; ~ **pie** *n* gefüllte (süße) Pastete *f*; ~**r** *n* Fleischwolf *m*
mind [maɪnd] *n* Verstand *m*, Geist *m*; (*opinion*) Meinung *f* ♦ *vt* aufpassen auf +*acc*; (*object to*) etwas haben gegen; **on my ~** auf den Herzen; **to my ~** meiner Meinung nach; **to be out of one's ~** wahnsinnig sein; **to bear** *or* **keep in ~** bedenken; **to change one's ~** es sich *dat* anders überlegen; **to make up one's ~** sich entschließen; **I don't ~** das macht mir nichts aus; ~ **you, ...** allerdings ...; **never ~!** macht nichts!; **"~ the step"** „Vorsicht Stufe"; ~ **your own business** kümmern Sie sich um Ihre eigenen Angelegenheiten; ~**er** *n* Aufpasser(in) *m(f)*; ~**ful** *adj*: ~**ful of** achtsam auf +*acc*; ~**less** *adj* sinnlos
mine¹ [maɪn] *n* (*coal*~) Bergwerk *nt*; (*MIL*) Mine *f* ♦ *vt* abbauen; (*MIL*) verminen
mine² [maɪn] *pron* meine(r, s); **that book is ~** das Buch gehört mir; **a friend of ~** ein Freund von mir
minefield ['maɪnfiːld] *n* Minenfeld *nt*
miner ['maɪnə*] *n* Bergarbeiter *m*
mineral ['mɪnərəl] *adj* mineralisch, Mineral- ♦ *n* Mineral *nt*; ~**s** *npl* (*BRIT: soft drinks*) alkoholfreie Getränke *pl*; ~

water *n* Mineralwasser *nt*
minesweeper ['maɪnswiːpə*] *n* Minensuchboot *nt*
mingle ['mɪŋgl] *vi*: **to ~** (**with**) sich mischen (unter +*acc*)
miniature ['mɪnɪtʃə*] *adj* Miniatur- ♦ *n* Miniatur *f*
minibus ['mɪnɪbʌs] *n* Kleinbus *m*
minim ['mɪnɪm] *n* halbe Note *f*
minima ['mɪnɪmə] *npl of* **minimum**
minimal ['mɪnɪməl] *adj* minimal
minimize ['mɪnɪmaɪz] *vt* auf das Mindestmaß beschränken
minimum ['mɪnɪməm] (*pl* **minima**) *n* Minimum *nt* ♦ *adj* Mindest-
mining ['maɪnɪŋ] *n* Bergbau *m* ♦ *adj* Bergbau-, Berg-
miniskirt ['mɪnɪskɜːt] *n* Minirock *m*
minister ['mɪnɪstə*] *n* (*BRIT: POL*) Minister *m*; (*ECCL*) Pfarrer *m* ♦ *vi*: **to ~ to sb** sich um jdn kümmern; ~**ial** [mɪnɪs'tɪərɪəl] *adj* ministeriell, Minister-
ministry ['mɪnɪstrɪ] *n* (*BRIT: POL*) Ministerium *nt*; (*ECCL: office*) geistliche(s) Amt *nt*
mink [mɪŋk] *n* Nerz *m*; ~ **coat** *n* Nerzmantel *m*
minnow ['mɪnəʊ] *n* Elritze *f*
minor ['maɪnə*] *adj* kleiner; (*operation*) leicht; (*problem, poet*) unbedeutend; (*MUS*) Moll ♦ *n* (*BRIT: under 18*) Minderjährige(r) *mf*
minority [maɪ'nɒrɪtɪ] *n* Minderheit *f*
mint [mɪnt] *n* Minze *f*; (*sweet*) Pfefferminzbonbon *nt* ♦ *vt* (*coins*) prägen; **the** (**Royal** (*BRIT*) *or* US (*US*)) **M~** die Münzanstalt; **in ~ condition** in tadellosem Zustand
minus ['maɪnəs] *n* Minuszeichen *nt*; (*amount*) Minusbetrag *m* ♦ *prep* minus, weniger
minuscule ['mɪnəskjuːl] *adj* winzig
minute¹ [maɪ'njuːt] *adj* winzig; (*detailed*) minuziös
minute² ['mɪnɪt] *n* Minute *f*; (*moment*) Augenblick *m*; ~**s** *npl* (*of meeting etc*) Protokoll *n*
miracle ['mɪrəkl] *n* Wunder *nt*
miraculous [mɪ'rækjʊləs] *adj* wunderbar
mirage ['mɪrɑːʒ] *n* Fata Morgana *f*

mire ['maɪə*] n Morast m
mirror ['mɪrə*] n Spiegel m ♦ vt (wider)spiegeln
mirth [mɜ:θ] n Heiterkeit f
misadventure [mɪsəd'ventʃə*] n Mißgeschick nt, Unfall m
misanthropist [mɪ'zænθrəpɪst] n Menschenfeind m
misapprehension ['mɪsæprɪ'henʃən] n Mißverständnis nt
misbehave ['mɪsbɪ'heɪv] vi sich schlecht benehmen
miscalculate ['mɪs'kælkjʊleɪt] vt falsch berechnen
miscarriage ['mɪskærɪdʒ] n (MED) Fehlgeburt f; ~ **of justice** Fehlurteil nt
miscellaneous [mɪsɪ'leɪnɪəs] adj verschieden
mischance [mɪs'tʃɑːns] n Mißgeschick nt
mischief ['mɪstʃɪf] n Unfug m
mischievous ['mɪstʃɪvəs] adj (person) durchtrieben; (glance) verschmitzt; (rumour) bösartig
misconception ['mɪskən'sepʃən] n fälschliche Annahme f
misconduct [mɪs'kɒndʌkt] n Vergehen nt; professional ~ Berufsvergehen nt
misconstrue [mɪskən'struː] vt mißverstehen
misdeed [mɪs'diːd] n Untat f
misdemeanour [mɪsdɪ'miːnə*] (US **misdemeanor**) n Vergehen nt
miser ['maɪzə*] n Geizhals m
miserable ['mɪzərəbl] adj (unhappy) unglücklich; (headache, weather) fürchterlich; (poor) elend; (contemptible) erbärmlich
miserly ['maɪzəlɪ] adj geizig
misery ['mɪzərɪ] n Elend nt, Qual f
misfire ['mɪs'faɪə*] vi (gun) versagen; (engine) fehlzünden; (plan) fehlgehen
misfit ['mɪsfɪt] n Außenseiter m
misfortune [mɪs'fɔːtʃən] n Unglück nt
misgiving(s) [mɪs'gɪvɪŋ(z)] n(pl) Bedenken pl
misguided ['mɪs'gaɪdɪd] adj fehlgeleitet; (opinions) irrig
mishandle ['mɪs'hændl] vt falsch handhaben
mishap ['mɪshæp] n Mißgeschick nt

misinform ['mɪsɪn'fɔːm] vt falsch unterrichten
misinterpret ['mɪsɪn'tɜːprɪt] vt falsch auffassen
misjudge ['mɪs'dʒʌdʒ] vt falsch beurteilen
mislay [mɪs'leɪ] (irreg: like **lay**) vt verlegen
mislead [mɪs'liːd] (irreg: like **lead**) vt (deceive) irreführen; ~**ing** adj irreführend
mismanage ['mɪs'mænɪdʒ] vt schlecht verwalten
misnomer ['mɪs'nəʊmə*] n falsche Bezeichnung f
misogynist [mɪ'sɒdʒɪnɪst] n Weiberfeind m
misplace ['mɪs'pleɪs] vt verlegen
misprint ['mɪsprɪnt] n Druckfehler m
Miss [mɪs] n Fräulein nt
miss [mɪs] vt (fail to hit, catch) verfehlen; (not notice) verpassen; (be too late) versäumen, verpassen; (omit) auslassen; (regret the absence of) vermissen ♦ vi fehlen ♦ n (shot) Fehlschuß m; (failure) Fehlschlag m; **I** ~ **you** du fehlst mir; ~ **out** vt auslassen
missal ['mɪsəl] n Meßbuch nt
misshapen ['mɪs'ʃeɪpən] adj mißgestaltet
missile ['mɪsaɪl] n Rakete f
missing ['mɪsɪŋ] adj (person) vermißt; (thing) fehlend; **to be** ~ fehlen
mission ['mɪʃən] n (work) Auftrag m; (people) Delegation f; (REL) Mission f; ~**ary** n Missionar(in) m(f)
misspell ['mɪs'spel] (irreg: like **spell**) vt falsch schreiben
misspent ['mɪs'spent] adj (youth) vergeudet
mist [mɪst] n Dunst m, Nebel m ♦ vi (also: ~ **over**, ~ **up**) sich trüben; (BRIT: windows) sich beschlagen
mistake [mɪs'teɪk] (irreg: like **take**) n Fehler m ♦ vt (misunderstand) mißverstehen; (mix up): **to** ~ (**sth for sth**) (etw mit etw) verwechseln; **to make a** ~ einen Fehler machen; **by** ~ aus Versehen; **to** ~ **A for B** A mit B verwechseln; **mistaken** pp of **mistake** ♦

adj (idea) falsch; **to be ~n** sich irren
mister ['mɪstə*] *n (inf)* Herr *m; see* **Mr**
mistletoe ['mɪsltəʊ] *n* Mistel *f*
mistook [mɪs'tʊk] *pt of* **mistake**
mistress ['mɪstrɪs] *n (teacher)* Lehrerin
f; (in house) Herrin *f; (lover)* Geliebte
f; see **Mrs**
mistrust ['mɪs'trʌst] *vt* mißtrauen +*dat*
misty ['mɪstɪ] *adj* neblig
misunderstand ['mɪsʌndə'stænd] *(irreg:
like* understand) *vt, vi* mißverstehen,
falsch verstehen; **~ing** *n* Mißverständnis *nt; (disagreement)* Meinungs-
verschiedenheit *f*
misuse [*n* 'mɪs'juːs, *vb* 'mɪs'juːz] *n* fal-
sche(r) Gebrauch *m* ♦ *vt* falsch gebrauchen
mitigate ['mɪtɪgeɪt] *vt* mildern
mitt(en) ['mɪt(n)] *n* Fausthandschuh *m*
mix [mɪks] *vt (blend)* (ver)mischen ♦ *vi
(liquids)* sich (ver)mischen lassen;
(people: get on) sich vertragen; *(:
associate)* Kontakt haben ♦ *n (mixture)*
Mischung *f;* **~ up** *vt* zusammenmi-
schen; *(confuse)* verwechseln; **~ed** *adj*
gemischt; **~ed-up** *adj* durcheinander;
~er *n (for food)* Mixer *m;* **~ture** *n*
Mischung *f;* **~-up** *n* Durcheinander *nt*
mm *abbr (= millimetre(s))* mm
moan [məʊn] *n* Stöhnen *nt; (complaint)*
Klage *f* ♦ *vi* stöhnen; *(complain)*
maulen
moat [məʊt] *n* (Burg)graben *m*
mob [mɒb] *n* Mob *m; (the masses)*
Pöbel *m* ♦ *vt (star)* herfallen über +*acc*
mobile ['məʊbaɪl] *adj* beweglich; *(library etc)* fahrbar ♦ *n (decoration)*
Mobile *nt;* **~ home** *n* Wohnwagen *m*
mobility [məʊ'bɪlɪtɪ] *n* Beweglichkeit *f*
mobilize ['məʊbɪlaɪz] *vt* mobilisieren
moccasin ['mɒkəsɪn] *n* Mokassin *m*
mock [mɒk] *vt* verspotten; *(defy)*
trotzen +*dat* ♦ *adj* Schein-; **~ery** *n*
Spott *m; (person)* Gespött *nt*
mod [mɒd] *adj see* **convenience**
mode [məʊd] *n* (Art *f* und) Weise *f*
model ['mɒdl] *n* Modell *nt; (example)*
Vorbild *nt; (in fashion)* Mannequin *nt* ♦
adj (railway) Modell-; *(perfect)*
Muster-; vorbildlich ♦ *vt (make)*

bilden; *(clothes)* vorführen ♦ *vi* als
Mannequin arbeiten
modem ['məʊdem] *n* Modem *nt*
moderate [*adj, n* 'mɒdərət, *vb* 'mɒdəreɪt]
adj gemäßigt ♦ *n (POL)* Gemäßigte(r)
mf ♦ *vi* sich mäßigen ♦ *vt* mäßigen
moderation [mɒdə'reɪʃən] *n* Mäßigung
f; **in ~** mit Maßen
modern ['mɒdən] *adj* modern; *(history,
languages)* neuere(r, s); *(Greek etc)*
Neu-; **~ize** *vt* modernisieren
modest ['mɒdɪst] *adj* bescheiden; **~y** *n*
Bescheidenheit *f*
modicum ['mɒdɪkəm] *n* bißchen *nt*
modification [mɒdɪfɪ'keɪʃən] *n* (Ab)än-
derung *f*
modify ['mɒdɪfaɪ] *vt* abändern
module ['mɒdjʊl] *n (component)*
(Bau)element *nt; (SPACE)* (Raum-)
kapsel *f*
mogul ['məʊgəl] *n (fig)* Mogul *m*
mohair ['məʊhɛə*] *n* Mohair *m*
moist [mɔɪst] *adj* feucht; **~en** ['mɔɪsn] *vt*
befeuchten; **~ure** ['mɔɪstʃə*] *n* Feuchtigkeit *f;* **~urizer** ['mɔɪstʃəraɪzə*] *n*
Feuchtigkeitscreme *f*
molar ['məʊlə*] *n* Backenzahn *m*
molasses [mə'læsɪz] *n* Melasse *f*
mold [məʊld] *(US)* = **mould**
mole [məʊl] *n (spot)* Leberfleck *m; (animal)* Maulwurf *m; (pier)* Mole *f*
molest [məʊ'lest] *vt* belästigen
mollycoddle ['mɒlɪkɒdl] *vt* verhätscheln
molt [məʊlt] *(US) vi* = **moult**
molten ['məʊltən] *adj* geschmolzen
mom [mɒm] *(US) n* = **mum**
moment ['məʊmənt] *n* Moment *m,*
Augenblick *m; (importance)* Tragweite
f; **at the ~** im Augenblick; **~ary** *adj*
kurz; **~ous** [məʊ'mentəs] *adj* folgen-
schwer
momentum [məʊ'mentəm] *n* Schwung
m; **to gather ~** in Fahrt kommen
mommy ['mɒmɪ] *(US) n* = **mummy**
Monaco ['mɒnəkəʊ] *n* Monaco *nt*
monarch ['mɒnək] *n* Herrscher(in)
m(f); **~y** *n* Monarchie *f*
monastery ['mɒnəstrɪ] *n* Kloster *nt*
monastic [mə'næstɪk] *adj* klösterlich,
Kloster-

Monday ['mʌndeɪ] n Montag m
monetary ['mʌnɪtərɪ] adj Geld-; (of currency) Währungs-
money ['mʌnɪ] n Geld nt; **to make ~** Geld verdienen; **~lender** n Geldverleiher m; **~ order** n Postanweisung f; **~-spinner** (inf) n Verkaufsschlager m (inf)
mongol ['mɒŋgəl] n (MED) mongoloide(s) Kind nt ♦ adj mongolisch; (MED) mongoloid
mongrel ['mʌŋgrəl] n Promenadenmischung f
monitor ['mɒnɪtə*] n (SCH) Klassenordner m; (television ~) Monitor m ♦ vt (broadcasts) abhören; (control) überwachen
monk [mʌŋk] n Mönch m
monkey ['mʌŋkɪ] n Affe m; **~ nut** (BRIT) n Erdnuß f; **~ wrench** n (TECH) Engländer m, Franzose m
monochrome ['mɒnəkrəum] adj schwarz-weiß
monopolize [mə'nɒpəlaɪz] vt beherrschen
monopoly [mə'nɒpəlɪ] n Monopol nt
monosyllable ['mɒnəsɪləbl] n einsilbige(s) Wort nt
monotone ['mɒnətəun] n gleichbleibende(r) Ton(fall) m; **to speak in a ~** monoton sprechen
monotonous [mə'nɒtənəs] adj eintönig
monotony [mə'nɒtənɪ] n Eintönigkeit f, Monotonie f
monsoon [mɒn'su:n] n Monsun m
monster ['mɒnstə*] n Ungeheuer nt; (person) Scheusal nt
monstrosity [mɒns'trɒsɪtɪ] n Ungeheuerlichkeit f; (thing) Monstrosität f
monstrous ['mɒnstrəs] adj (shocking) gräßlich, ungeheuerlich; (huge) riesig
month [mʌnθ] n Monat m; **~ly** adj monatlich, Monats- ♦ adv einmal im Monat ♦ n (magazine) Monatsschrift f
monument ['mɒnjumənt] n Denkmal nt; **~al** [mɒnju'mentl] adj (huge) gewaltig; (ignorance) ungeheuer
moo [mu:] vi muhen
mood [mu:d] n Stimmung f, Laune f; **to be in a good/bad ~** gute/schlechte

Laune haben; **~y** adj launisch
moon [mu:n] n Mond m; **~light** n Mondlicht nt; **~lighting** n Schwarzarbeit f; **~lit** adj mondhell
moor [muə*] n Heide f, Hochmoor nt ♦ vt (ship) festmachen, verankern ♦ vi anlegen; **~ings** npl Liegeplatz m
moorland ['muələnd] n Heidemoor nt
moose [mu:s] n Elch m
mop [mɒp] n Mop m ♦ vt (auf)wischen; **~ up** vt aufwischen
mope [məup] vi Trübsal blasen
moped ['məuped] n Moped nt
moral ['mɒrəl] adj moralisch; (values) sittlich; (virtuous) tugendhaft ♦ n Moral f; **~s** npl (ethics) Moral f; **~e** [mɒ'rɑ:l] n Moral f; **~ity** [mə'rælɪtɪ] n Sittlichkeit f
morass [mə'ræs] n Sumpf m
morbid ['mɔ:bɪd] adj krankhaft; (jokes) makaber

| KEYWORD |

more [mɔ:*] adj (greater in number etc) mehr; (additional) noch mehr; **do you want (some) more tea?** möchten Sie noch etwas Tee?; **I have no** or **I don't have any more money** ich habe kein Geld mehr
♦ pron (greater amount) mehr; (further or additional amount) noch mehr; **is there any more?** gibt es noch mehr?; (left over) ist noch etwas da?; **there's no more** es ist nichts mehr da
♦ adv mehr; **more dangerous/easily** etc (than) gefährlicher/einfacher etc (als); **more and more** immer mehr; **more and more excited** immer aufgeregter; **more or less** mehr oder weniger; **more than ever** mehr denn je; **more beautiful than ever** schöner denn je

moreover [mɔ:'rəuvə*] adv überdies
morgue [mɔ:g] n Leichenschauhaus nt
moribund ['mɒrɪbʌnd] adj aussterbend
Mormon ['mɔ:mən] n Mormone m, Mormonin f
morning ['mɔ:nɪŋ] n Morgen m; **in the ~** am Morgen; **7 o'clock in the ~** 7 Uhr morgens

Morocco [məˈrɒkəʊ] n Marokko nt
moron [ˈmɔːrɒn] n Schwachsinnige(r) mf
morose [məˈrəʊs] adj mürrisch
morphine [ˈmɔːfiːn] n Morphium nt
Morse [mɔːs] n (also: ~ code) Morsealphabet nt
morsel [ˈmɔːsl] n Bissen m
mortal [ˈmɔːtl] adj sterblich; (deadly) tödlich; (very great) Todes- ♦ n (human being) Sterbliche(r) mf; ~ity [mɔːˈtælɪtɪ] n Sterblichkeit f; (death rate) Sterblichkeitsziffer f
mortar [ˈmɔːtə*] n (for building) Mörtel m; (bowl) Mörser m; (MIL) Granatwerfer m
mortgage [ˈmɔːgɪdʒ] n Hypothek f ♦ vt hypothekarisch belasten; ~ company (US) n ≈ Bausparkasse f
mortify [ˈmɔːtɪfaɪ] vt beschämen
mortuary [ˈmɔːtjʊərɪ] n Leichenhalle f
mosaic [məʊˈzeɪɪk] n Mosaik nt
Moscow [ˈmɒskəʊ] n Moskau nt
Moslem [ˈmɒzləm] = **Muslim**
mosque [mɒsk] n Moschee f
mosquito [mɒsˈkiːtəʊ] (pl ~es) n Moskito m
moss [mɒs] n Moos nt
most [məʊst] adj meiste(r, s) ♦ adv am meisten; (very) höchst ♦ n das meiste, der größte Teil; (people) die meisten; ~ men die meisten Männer; at the (very) ~ allerhöchstens; to make the ~ of das Beste machen aus; a ~ interesting book ein höchst interessantes Buch; ~ly adv größtenteils
MOT (BRIT) n abbr (= Ministry of Transport): the ~ (test) ≈ der TÜV
motel [məʊˈtel] n Motel nt
moth [mɒθ] n Nachtfalter m; (wool-eating) Motte f; ~ball n Mottenkugel f
mother [ˈmʌðə*] n Mutter f ♦ vt bemuttern; ~hood n Mutterschaft f; ~-in-law n Schwiegermutter f; ~ly adj mütterlich; ~-to-be n werdende Mutter f; ~ tongue n Muttersprache f
motif [məʊˈtiːf] n Motiv nt
motion [ˈməʊʃən] n Bewegung f; (in meeting) Antrag m ♦ vt, vi: to ~ (to) sb jdm winken, jdm zu verstehen

geben; ~less adj regungslos; ~ picture n Film m
motivated [ˈməʊtɪveɪtɪd] adj motiviert
motivation [məʊtɪˈveɪʃən] n Motivierung f
motive [ˈməʊtɪv] n Motiv nt, Beweggrund m ♦ adj treibend
motley [ˈmɒtlɪ] adj bunt
motor [ˈməʊtə*] n Motor m; (BRIT: inf: vehicle) Auto nt ♦ adj Motor-; ~bike n Motorrad nt; ~boat n Motorboot nt; ~car (BRIT) n Auto nt; ~cycle n Motorrad nt; ~cycle racing n Motorradrennen nt; ~cyclist n Motorradfahrer(in) m(f); ~ing (BRIT) n Autofahren nt ♦ adj Auto-; ~ist [ˈməʊtərɪst] n Autofahrer(in) m(f); ~ racing (BRIT) n Autorennen nt; ~ scooter n Motorroller m; ~ vehicle n Kraftfahrzeug nt; ~way (BRIT) n Autobahn f
mottled [ˈmɒtld] adj gesprenkelt
motto [ˈmɒtəʊ] (pl ~es) n Motto nt
mould [məʊld] (US **mold**) n Form f; (mildew) Schimmel m ♦ vt (also fig) formen; ~er vi (decay) vermodern; ~y adj schimmelig
moult [məʊlt] (US **molt**) vi sich mausern
mound [maʊnd] n (Erd)hügel m
mount [maʊnt] n (liter: hill) Berg m; (horse) Pferd nt; (for jewel etc) Fassung f ♦ vt (horse) steigen auf +acc; (put in setting) fassen; (exhibition) veranstalten; (attack) unternehmen ♦ vi (also: ~ up) sich häufen; (on horse) aufsitzen
mountain [ˈmaʊntɪn] n Berg m ♦ cpd Berg-; ~eer [maʊntɪˈnɪə*] n Bergsteiger(in) m(f); ~eering n Bergsteigen nt; ~ous adj bergig; ~ rescue team n Bergwacht f; ~side n Berg(ab)hang m
mourn [mɔːn] vt betrauen, beklagen ♦ vi: to ~ (for sb) (um jdn) trauern; ~er n Trauernde(r) mf; ~ful adj traurig; ~ing n (grief) Trauer f ♦ cpd (dress) Trauer-; in ~ing (period etc) in Trauer; (dress) in Trauerkleidung f
mouse [maʊs] (pl mice) n Maus f; ~trap n Mausefalle f
mousse [muːs] n (CULIN) Creme f;

(*cosmetic*) Schaumfestiger *m*

moustache [məsˈtɑːʃ] *n* Schnurrbart *m*

mousy [ˈmaʊsɪ] *adj* (*colour*) mausgrau; (*person*) schüchtern

mouth [maʊθ, *pl* maʊðz] *n* Mund *m*; (*opening*) Öffnung *f*; (*of river*) Mündung *f*; (*of bottle*) Mundvoll *m*; ~ **organ** *n* Mundharmonika *f*; ~**piece** *n* Mundstück *nt*; (*fig*) Sprachrohr *nt*; ~**wash** *n* Mundwasser *nt*; ~**watering** *adj* lecker, appetitlich

movable [ˈmuːvəbl] *adj* beweglich

move [muːv] *n* (*movement*) Bewegung *f*; (*in game*) Zug *m*; (*step*) Schritt *m*; (*of house*) Umzug *m* ♦ *vt* bewegen; (*people*) transportieren; (*in job*) versetzen; (*emotionally*) bewegen ♦ *vi* sich bewegen; (*vehicle, ship*) fahren; (*go to another house*) umziehen; **to get a ~ on** sich beeilen; **to ~ sb to do sth** jdn veranlassen, etw zu tun; ~ **about** *or* **around** *vi* sich hin- und herbewegen; (*travel*) unterwegs sein; ~ **along** *vi* weitergehen; (*cars*) weiterfahren; ~ **away** *vi* weggehen; ~ **back** *vi* zurückgehen; (*to the rear*) zurückweichen; ~ **forward** *vi* vorwärtsgehen, sich vorwärtsbewegen ♦ *vt* vorschieben; (*time*) vorverlegen; ~ **in** *vi* (*to house*) einziehen; (*troops*) einrücken; ~ **on** *vi* weitergehen ♦ *vt* weitergehen lassen; ~ **out** *vi* (*of house*) ausziehen; (*troops*) abziehen; ~ **over** *vi* zur Seite rücken; ~ **up** *vi* aufsteigen; (*in job*) befördert werden ♦ *vt* nach oben bewegen; (*in job*) befördern; ~**ment** [ˈmuːvmənt] *n* Bewegung *f*

movie [ˈmuːvɪ] *n* Film *m*; **to go to the ~s** ins Kino gehen; ~ **camera** *n* Filmkamera *f*

moving [ˈmuːvɪŋ] *adj* beweglich; (*touching*) ergreifend

mow [məʊ] (*pt* **mowed**, *pp* **mowed** *or* **mown**) *vt* mähen; ~ **down** *vt* (*fig*) niedermähen; ~**er** *n* (*machine*) Mähmaschine *f*; (*lawn~*) Rasenmäher *m*; **mown** *pp of* **mow**

MP *n abbr* = **Member of Parliament**

m.p.h. *abbr* = **miles per hour**

Mr [ˈmɪstə*] (*US* **Mr.**) *n* Herr *m*

Mrs [ˈmɪsɪz] (*US* **Mrs.**) *n* Frau *f*

Ms [mɪz] (*US* **Ms.**) *n* (= **Miss** *or* **Mrs**) Frau *f*

M.Sc. *n abbr* = **Master of Science**

much [mʌtʃ] *adj* viel ♦ *adv* sehr; viel ♦ *n* viel, eine Menge; **how** ~ **is it?** wieviel kostet das?; **too** ~ zuviel; **it's not** ~ es ist nicht viel, **as** ~ **as** soeben, soviel; **however** ~ **he tries** sosehr er es auch versucht

muck [mʌk] *n* Mist *m*; (*fig*) Schmutz *m*; ~ **about** *or* **around** (*inf*): **to** ~ **about** *or* **around** (**with sth**) (an etw *dat*) herumalbern; ~ **up** *vt* (*inf*: *ruin*) vermasseln; (*dirty*) dreckig machen; ~**y** *adj* (*dirty*) dreckig

mucus [ˈmjuːkəs] *n* Schleim *m*

mud [mʌd] *n* Schlamm *m*

muddle [ˈmʌdl] *n* Durcheinander *nt* ♦ *vt* (*also*: ~ *up*) durcheinanderbringen; ~ **through** *vi* sich durchwursteln

muddy [ˈmʌdɪ] *adj* schlammig

mudguard [ˈmʌdgɑːd] *n* Schutzblech *nt*

mud-slinging [ˈmʌdslɪŋɪŋ] (*inf*) *n* Verleumdung *f*

muff [mʌf] *n* Muff *m* ♦ *vt* (*chance*) verpassen; (*lines*) verpatzen (*inf*)

muffin [ˈmʌfɪn] *n* süße(s) Teilchen *nt*

muffle [ˈmʌfl] *vt* (*sound*) dämpfen; (*wrap up*) einhüllen; ~**d** *adj* gedämpft

muffler [ˈmʌflə*] (*US*) *n* (*AUT*) Schalldämpfer *m*

mug [mʌg] *n* (*cup*) Becher *m*; (*inf*: *face*) Visage *f*; (: *fool*) Trottel *m* ♦ *vt* überfallen und ausrauben; ~**ging** *n* Überfall *m*

muggy [ˈmʌgɪ] *adj* (*weather*) schwül

mule [mjuːl] *n* Maulesel *m*

mull [mʌl]: ~ **over** *vt* nachdenken über +*acc*

mulled [mʌld] *adj* (*wine*) Glüh-

multi- [ˈmʌltɪ] *prefix* Multi-, multi-

multicoloured [ˈmʌltɪˈkʌləd] (*US* **multicolored**) *adj* mehrfarbig

multifarious [mʌltɪˈfɛərɪəs] *adj* mannigfaltig

multi-level [ˈmʌltɪlevl] (*US*) *adj* = **multistorey**

multiple [ˈmʌltɪpl] *n* Vielfache(s) *nt* ♦ *adj* mehrfach; (*many*) mehrere; ~

sclerosis n multiple Sklerose f
multiply ['mʌltɪplaɪ] vt: **to ~ (by)** multiplizieren (mit) ♦ vi (BIOL) sich vermehren
multistorey ['mʌltɪ'stɔːrɪ] (BRIT) adj (building, car park) mehrstöckig
multitude ['mʌltɪtjuːd] n Menge f
mum [mʌm] n (BRIT: inf) Mutti f ♦ adj: **to keep ~ (about)** den Mund halten (über +acc) ♦
mumble ['mʌmbl] vt, vi murmeln ♦ n Gemurmel nt
mummy ['mʌmɪ] n (dead body) Mumie f; (BRIT: inf) Mami f
mumps [mʌmps] n Mumps m
munch [mʌntʃ] vt, vi mampfen
mundane ['mʌn'deɪn] adj banal
municipal [mjuː'nɪsɪpəl] adj städtisch, Stadt-; **~ity** [mjuːnɪsɪ'pælɪtɪ] n Stadt f mit Selbstverwaltung
mural ['mjʊərəl] n Wandgemälde nt
murder ['mɜːdə*] n Mord m ♦ vt ermorden; **~er** n Mörder m; **~ous** adj Mord-; (fig) mörderisch
murky [mɜːkɪ] adj finster
murmur ['mɜːmə*] n Murmeln nt; (of water, wind) Rauschen nt ♦ vt, vi murmeln
muscle ['mʌsl] n Muskel m; **~ in** vi mitmischen
muscular ['mʌskjʊlə*] adj Muskel-; (strong) muskulös
muse [mjuːz] vi (nach)sinnen
museum [mjuː'zɪəm] n Museum nt
mushroom ['mʌʃruːm] n Champignon m; Pilz m ♦ vi (fig) emporschießen
music ['mjuːzɪk] n Musik f; (printed) Noten pl; **~al** adj (sound) melodisch; (person) musikalisch ♦ n (show) Musical nt; **~al instrument** n Musikinstrument nt; **~ hall** (BRIT) n Varieté nt; **~ian** [mjuː'zɪʃən] n Musiker(in) m(f)
musk [mʌsk] n Moschus m
Muslim ['mʌzlɪm] adj moslemisch ♦ n Moslem m
muslin ['mʌzlɪn] n Musselin m
mussel ['mʌsl] n Miesmuschel f
must [mʌst] vb aux müssen; (in negation) dürfen ♦ n Muß nt; **the film is a ~** den Film muß man einfach gesehen

haben
mustard ['mʌstəd] n Senf m
muster ['mʌstə*] vt (MIL) antreten lassen; (courage) zusammennehmen
mustn't ['mʌsnt] = must not
musty ['mʌstɪ] adj muffig
mute [mjuːt] adj stumm ♦ n (person) Stumme(r) mf; (MUS) Dämpfer m
muted ['mjuːtɪd] adj gedämpft
mutilate ['mjuːtɪleɪt] vt verstümmeln
mutilation [mjuːtɪ'leɪʃən] n Verstümmelung f
mutiny ['mjuːtɪnɪ] n Meuterei f ♦ vi meutern
mutter ['mʌtə*] vt, vi murmeln
mutton ['mʌtn] n Hammelfleisch nt
mutual ['mjuːtjʊəl] adj gegenseitig; beiderseitig; **~ly** adv gegenseitig; für beide Seiten
muzzle ['mʌzl] n (of animal) Schnauze f; (for animal) Maulkorb m; (of gun) Mündung f ♦ vt einen Maulkorb anlegen +dat
my [maɪ] adj mein; **this is ~ car** das ist mein Auto; **I've washed ~ hair** ich habe mir die Haare gewaschen
myopic [maɪ'ɒpɪk] adj kurzsichtig
myriad ['mɪrɪəd] n: **a ~ of** (people, things) unzählige
myself [maɪ'self] pron mich acc; mir dat; (emphatic) selbst; see also **oneself**
mysterious [mɪs'tɪərɪəs] adj geheimnisvoll
mystery ['mɪstərɪ] n (secret) Geheimnis nt; (sth difficult) Rätsel nt
mystify ['mɪstɪfaɪ] vt ein Rätsel sein +dat; verblüffen
mystique [mɪs'tiːk] n geheimnisvolle Natur f
myth [mɪθ] n Mythos m; (fig) Erfindung f; **~ology** [mɪ'θɒlədʒɪ] n Mythologie f

N

n/a abbr (= not applicable) nicht zutreffend
nab [næb] (inf) vt schnappen
nag [næg] n (horse) Gaul m; (person) Nörgler(in) m(f) ♦ vt, vi: **to ~ (at)** sb

an jdm herumnörgeln; **~ging** *adj*
(*doubt*) nagend ♦ *n* Nörgelei *f*
nail [neɪl] *n* Nagel *m* ♦ *vt* nageln; **to ~
sb down to doing sth** jdn darauf festnageln, etw zu tun; **~brush** *n*
Nagelbürste *f*; **~file** *n* Nagelfeile *f*; **~
polish** *n* Nagellack *m*; **~ polish remover** *n* Nagellackentferner *m*; **~
scissors** *npl* Nagelschere *f*; **~ varnish**
(*BRIT*) *n* = **~ polish**
naïve [naɪˈiːv] *adj* naiv
naked [ˈneɪkɪd] *adj* nackt
name [neɪm] *n* Name *m*; (*reputation*)
Ruf *m* ♦ *vt* nennen; (*sth new*)
benennen; (*appoint*) ernennen; **by ~**
mit Namen; **I know him only by ~** ich
kenne ihn nur dem Namen nach;
maiden ~ Mädchenname *m*; **what's
your ~?** wie heißen Sie?; **in the ~ of** im
Namen +*gen*; (*for the sake of*) um
+*gen* ...wıllen; **~less** *adj* namenlos;
~ly *adv* nämlich; **~sake** *n*
Namensvetter *m*
nanny [ˈnænɪ] *n* Kindermädchen *nt*
nap [næp] *n* (*sleep*) Nickerchen *nt*; (*on
cloth*) Strich *m* ♦ *vi*: **to be caught
~ping** (*fig*) überrumpelt werden
nape [neɪp] *n* Nacken *m*
napkin [ˈnæpkɪn] *n* (*at table*) Serviette
f; (*BRIT: for baby*) Windel *f*
nappy [ˈnæpɪ] (*BRIT*) *n* (*for baby*)
Windel *f*; **~ liner** *n* Windeleinlage *f*; **~
rash** *n* wunde Stellen *pl*
narcissi [nɑːˈsɪsaɪ] *npl of* **narcissus**
narcissus [nɑːˈsɪsəs] *n* (*BOT*) Narzisse *f*
narcotic [nɑːˈkɒtɪk] *adj* betäubend ♦ *n*
Betäubungsmittel *nt*
narrative [ˈnærətɪv] *n* Erzählung *f* ♦ *adj*
erzählend
narrator [nəˈreɪtə*] *n* Erzähler(in) *m(f)*
narrow [ˈnærəʊ] *adj* eng, schmal;
(*limited*) beschränkt ♦ *vi* sich verengen; **to have a ~ escape** mit knapper
Not davonkommen; **to ~ sth down to
sth** etw auf etw *acc* einschränken; **~ly**
adv (*miss*) knapp; (*escape*) mit
knapper Not; **~-minded** *adj* engstirnig
nasty [ˈnɑːstɪ] *adj* ekelhaft, fies;
(*business, wound*) schlimm
nation [ˈneɪʃən] *n* Nation *f*, Volk *nt*; **~al**

[ˈnæʃənl] *adj* national, National-, Landes-
♦ *n* Staatsangehörige(r) *mf*; **~al dress**
n Tracht *f*; **N~al Health Service** (*BRIT*)
n Staatliche(r) Gesundheitsdienst *m*;
N~al Insurance (*BRIT*) *n* Sozialversicherung *f*; **~alism** [ˈnæʃnəlɪzəm] *n* Na-
tionalismus *m*; **~alist** [ˈnæʃnəlɪst] *n*
Nationalist(in) *m(f)* ♦ *adj* nationali-
stisch; **~ality** [næʃəˈnælɪtɪ] *n* Staatsangehörigkeit *f*; **~alize** [ˈnæʃnəlaɪz] *vt*
verstaatlichen; **~ally** [ˈnæʃnəlɪ] *adv*
national, auf Staatsebene; **~-wide**
[ˈneɪʃənwaɪd] *adj, adv* allgemein,
landesweit
native [ˈneɪtɪv] *n* (*born in*) Einheimi-
sche(r) *mf*; (*original inhabitant*) Ein-
geborene(r) *mf* ♦ *adj* (*coming from a
certain place*) einheimisch; (*of the
original inhabitants*) Eingeborenen-;
(*belonging by birth*) heimatlich,
Heimat-; (*inborn*) angeboren, natürlich; **a ~ of Germany** ein gebürtiger
Deutscher; **a ~ speaker of French** ein
französischer Muttersprachler; **~
language** *n* Muttersprache *f*
Nativity [nəˈtɪvɪtɪ] *n*: **the ~** Christi
Geburt *no art*
NATO [ˈneɪtəʊ] *n abbr* (= *North Atlantic
Treaty Organization*) NATO *f*
natter [ˈnætə*] (*BRIT: inf*) *vi* quatschen
♦ *n* Gequatsche *nt*
natural [ˈnætʃrəl] *adj* natürlich; Natur-;
(*inborn*) (an)geboren; **~ gas** *n* Erdgas
nt; **~ist** *n* Naturkundler(in) *m(f)*; **~ize**
vt (*foreigner*) einbürgern; (*plant etc*)
einführen; **~ly** *adv* natürlich
nature [ˈneɪtʃə*] *n* Natur *f*; **by ~** von
Natur (aus)
naught [nɔːt] *n* = **nought**
naughty [ˈnɔːtɪ] *adj* (*child*) unartig, ungezogen; (*action*) ungehörig
nausea [ˈnɔːsɪə] *n* (*sickness*) Übelkeit *f*;
(*disgust*) Ekel *m*; **nauseate** [ˈnɔːsɪeɪt] *vt*
anekeln
nautical [ˈnɔːtɪkəl] *adj* nautisch; See-;
(*expression*) seemännisch
naval [ˈneɪvəl] *adj* Marine-, Flotten-; **~
officer** *n* Marineoffizier *m*
nave [neɪv] *n* Kirchen(haupt)schiff *nt*
navel [ˈneɪvəl] *n* Nabel *m*

navigate ['nævɪgeɪt] *vi* navigieren
navigation [nævɪ'geɪʃən] *n* Navigation *f*
navigator ['nævɪgeɪtə*] *n* Steuermann *m*; (*AVIAT*) Navigator *m*; (*AUT*) Beifahrer(in) *m(f)*
navvy ['nævɪ] (*BRIT*) *n* Straßenarbeiter *m*
navy ['neɪvɪ] *n* (Kriegs)marine *f* ♦ *adj* marineblau
Nazi ['nɑːtsɪ] *n* Nazi *m*
NB *abbr* (= *nota bene*) NB
near [nɪə*] *adj* nah ♦ *adv* in der Nähe ♦ *prep* (*also*: ~ *to*: *space*) in der Nähe +*gen*; (: *time*) um +*acc* ... herum ♦ *vt* sich nähern +*dat*; **a ~ miss** knapp daneben; **~by** *adj* nahe (gelegen) ♦ *adv* in der Nähe; **~ly** *adv* fast; **I ~ly fell** ich wäre fast gefallen; **~side** *n* (*AUT*) Beifahrerseite *f* ♦ *adj* auf der Beifahrerseite
neat ['niːt] *adj* (*tidy*) ordentlich; (*solution*) sauber; (*pure*) pur; **~ly** *adv* (*tidily*) ordentlich
nebulous ['nebjʊləs] *adj* nebulös
necessarily ['nesɪsərɪlɪ] *adv* unbedingt
necessary ['nesɪsərɪ] *adj* notwendig, nötig; **he did all that was ~** er erledigte alles, was nötig war
necessitate [nɪ'sesɪteɪt] *vt* erforderlich machen
necessity [nɪ'sesɪtɪ] *n* (*need*) Not *f*; (*compulsion*) Notwendigkeit *f*; **necessities** *npl* (*things needed*) das Notwendigste
neck [nek] *n* Hals *m* ♦ *vi* (*inf*) knutschen; **~ and ~** Kopf an Kopf
necklace ['neklɪs] *n* Halskette *f*
neckline ['neklaɪn] *n* Ausschnitt *m*
necktie ['nektaɪ] (*US*) *n* Krawatte *f*
née [neɪ] *adj* geborene
need [niːd] *n* Bedürfnis *nt*; (*lack*) Mangel *m*; (*necessity*) Notwendigkeit *f*; (*poverty*) Not *f* ♦ *vt* brauchen; **I ~ to do it** ich muß es tun; **you don't ~ to go** du brauchst nicht zu gehen
needle ['niːdl] *n* Nadel *f* ♦ *vt* (*fig*: *inf*) ärgern
needless ['niːdlɪs] *adj* unnötig; **~ to say** natürlich
needlework ['niːdlwɜːk] *n* Handarbeit *f*

needn't ['niːdnt] = **need not**
needy ['niːdɪ] *adj* bedürftig
negation [nɪ'geɪʃən] *n* Verneinung *f*
negative ['negətɪv] *n* (*PHOT*) Negativ *nt* ♦ *adj* negativ; (*answer*) abschlägig
neglect [nɪ'glekt] *vt* vernachlässigen ♦ *n* Vernachlässigung *f*
negligee ['neglɪʒeɪ] *n* Negligé *nt*
negligence ['neglɪdʒəns] *n* Nachlässigkeit *f*
negligible ['neglɪdʒəbl] *adj* unbedeutend, geringfügig
negotiable [nɪ'gəʊʃɪəbl] *adj* (*cheque*) übertragbar, einlösbar
negotiate [nɪ'gəʊʃɪeɪt] *vi* verhandeln ♦ *vt* (*treaty*) abschließen; (*difficulty*) überwinden; (*corner*) nehmen; **negotiation** [nɪgəʊʃɪ'eɪʃən] *n* Verhandlung *f*; **negotiator** *n* Unterhändler *m*
Negress ['niːgres] *n* Negerin *f*
Negro ['niːgrəʊ] *n* Neger *m* ♦ *adj* Neger-
neigh [neɪ] *vi* wiehern
neighbour ['neɪbə*] (*US* **neighbor**) *n* Nachbar(in) *m(f)*; **~hood** *n* Nachbarschaft *f*; Umgebung *f*; **~ing** *adj* benachbart, angrenzend
neither ['naɪðə*] *adj*, *pron* keine(r, s) (von beiden) ♦ *conj*: **he can't do it, and ~ can I** er kann es nicht und ich auch nicht ♦ *adv*: **~ good nor bad** weder gut noch schlecht
neon ['niːən] *n* Neon *nt*
nephew ['nefjuː] *n* Neffe *m*
nerve [nɜːv] *n* Nerv *m*; (*courage*) Mut *m*; (*impudence*) Frechheit *f*; **to have a fit of ~s** in Panik geraten; **~-racking** *adj* nervenaufreibend
nervous ['nɜːvəs] *adj* (*of the nerves*) Nerven-; (*timid*) nervös, ängstlich; **~ breakdown** *n* Nervenzusammenbruch *m*; **~ness** *n* Nervosität *f*
nest [nest] *n* Nest *nt* ♦ *vi* nisten; **~ egg** *n* (*fig*) Notgroschen *m*
nestle ['nesl] *vi* sich kuscheln
net [net] *n* Netz *nt* ♦ *adj* netto, Netto- ♦ *vt* netto einnehmen; **~ball** *n* Netzball *m*; **~ curtain** *n* Store *m*
Netherlands ['neðələndz] *npl*: **the ~** die Niederlande *pl*
nett [net] *adj* = **net**

netting ['netɪŋ] n Netz(werk) nt
nettle ['netl] n Nessel f
network ['netwɜːk] n Netz nt
neurotic [njʊə'rɒtɪk] adj neurotisch ♦ n Neurotiker(in) m(f)
neuter ['njuːtə*] adj (BIOL) geschlechtslos; (GRAM) sächlich ♦ vt kastrieren
neutral ['njuːtrəl] adj neutral ♦ n (AUT) Leerlauf m; ~ity n Neutralität f; ~ize vt (fig) ausgleichen
never ['nevə*] adv nie(mals); I ~ went ich bin gar nicht gegangen; ~ in my life nie im Leben; ~-ending adj endlos; ~theless [nevəðə'les] adv trotzdem, dennoch
new [njuː] adj neu; ~born adj neugeboren; ~comer ['njuːkʌmə*] n Neuankömmling m; ~-fangled (pej) adj neumodisch; ~-found adj neuentdeckt; ~ly adv frisch, neu; ~ly-weds npl Frischvermählte pl; ~ moon n Neumond m
news [njuːz] n Nachricht f; (RAD, TV) Nachrichten pl; a piece of ~ eine Nachricht; ~ agency n Nachrichtenagentur f; ~agent (BRIT) n Zeitungshändler m; ~caster n Nachrichtensprecher(in) m(f); ~ dealer (US) n = ~agent; ~ flash n Kurzmeldung f; ~letter n Rundschreiben nt; ~paper n Zeitung f; ~print n Zeitungspapier nt; ~reader n = ~caster; ~reel n Wochenschau f; ~stand n Zeitungsstand m
newt [njuːt] n Wassermolch m
New Year n Neujahr nt; ~'s Day n Neujahrstag m; ~'s Eve n Silvester(abend m) nt
New York [-'jɔːk] n New York nt
New Zealand [-'ziːlənd] n Neuseeland nt; ~er n Neuseeländer(in) m(f)
next [nekst] adj nächste(r, s) ♦ adv (after) dann, darauf; (~ time) das nächstemal; the ~ day am nächsten or folgenden Tag; ~ time das nächste Mal; ~ year nächstes Jahr; ~ door adv nebenan ♦ adj (neighbour, flat) von nebenan; ~ of kin n nächste(r) Verwandte(r) mf; ~ to prep neben; ~ to

nothing so gut wie nichts
NHS n abbr = National Health Service
nib [nɪb] n Spitze f
nibble ['nɪbl] vt knabbern an +dat
nice [naɪs] adj (person) nett; (thing) schön; (subtle) fein; ~-looking adj gutaussehend; ~ly adv gut, nett; niceties ['naɪsɪtɪz] npl Feinheiten pl
nick [nɪk] n Einkerbung f ♦ vt (inf: steal) klauen, in the ~ of time gerade rechtzeitig
nickel ['nɪkl] n Nickel nt; (US) Nickel m (5 cents)
nickname ['nɪkneɪm] n Spitzname m ♦ vt taufen
niece [niːs] n Nichte f
Nigeria [naɪ'dʒɪərɪə] n Nigeria nt
niggardly ['nɪgədlɪ] adj geizig
nigger ['nɪgə*] (inf) n (highly offensive) Nigger m
niggling ['nɪglɪŋ] adj pedantisch; (doubt, worry) quälend; (detail) kleinlich
night [naɪt] n Nacht f; (evening) Abend m; the ~ before last vorletzte Nacht; at or by ~ (after midnight) nachts; (before midnight) abends; ~cap n (drink) Schlummertrunk m; ~club n Nachtlokal nt; ~dress n Nachthemd nt; ~fall n Einbruch m der Nacht; ~ gown n = ~dress; ~ie ['naɪtɪ] (inf) n Nachthemd nt
nightingale ['naɪtɪŋgeɪl] n Nachtigall f
nightlife ['naɪtlaɪf] n Nachtleben nt
nightly ['naɪtlɪ] adj, adv jeden Abend; jede Nacht
nightmare ['naɪtmɛə*] n Alptraum m
night: ~ porter n Nachtportier m; ~ school n Abendschule f; ~ shift n Nachtschicht f; ~time n Nacht f
nil [nɪl] n Null f
Nile [naɪl] n: the ~ der Nil
nimble ['nɪmbl] adj beweglich
nine [naɪn] num neun; ~teen num neunzehn; ~ty num neunzig
ninth [naɪnθ] adj neunte(r, s)
nip [nɪp] vt kneifen ♦ n Kneifen nt
nipple ['nɪpl] n Brustwarze f
nippy ['nɪpɪ] (inf) adj (person) flink; (BRIT: car) flott; (: cold) frisch

nitrogen ['naɪtrədʒən] n Stickstoff m

KEYWORD

no [nəʊ] (pl ~es) adv (opposite of "yes") nein; **to answer no** (to question) mit Nein antworten; (to request) nein sagen; **no thank you** nein, danke ♦ adj (not any) kein(e); **I have no money/time** ich habe kein Geld/keine Zeit; **"no smoking"** „Rauchen verboten" ♦ n Nein nt; (no vote) Neinstimme f

nobility [nəʊ'bɪlɪtɪ] n Adel m
noble ['nəʊbl] adj (rank) adlig; (splendid) nobel, edel
nobody ['nəʊbədɪ] pron niemand, keiner
nocturnal [nɒk'tɜːnl] adj (tour, visit) nächtlich; (animal) Nacht-
nod [nɒd] vi nicken ♦ vt nicken mit ♦ n Nicken nt; ~ **off** vi einnicken
noise [nɔɪz] n (sound) Geräusch nt; (unpleasant, loud) Lärm m
noisy ['nɔɪzɪ] adj laut; (crowd) lärmend
nominal ['nɒmɪnl] adj nominell
nominate ['nɒmɪneɪt] vt (suggest) vorschlagen; (in election) aufstellen; (appoint) ernennen
nomination [nɒmɪ'neɪʃən] n (election) Nominierung f; (appointment) Ernennung f
nominee [nɒmɪ'niː] n Kandidat(in) m(f)
non- [nɒn] prefix Nicht-, un-; ~-**alcoholic** adj alkoholfrei; ~-**aligned** adj bündnisfrei
nonchalant ['nɒnʃələnt] adj lässig
non-committal ['nɒnkə'mɪtl] adj (reserved) zurückhaltend; (uncommitted) unverbindlich
nondescript ['nɒndɪskrɪpt] adj mittelmäßig
none [nʌn] adj, pron kein(e, er, es) ♦ adv: **he's ~ the worse for it** es hat ihm nicht geschadet; ~ **of you** keiner von euch; **I've ~ left** ich habe keinen mehr
nonentity [nɒ'nentɪtɪ] n Null f (inf)
nonetheless ['nʌnðə'les] adv nichtsdestoweniger
non-existent [nɒnɪg'zɪstənt] adj nicht vorhanden
non-fiction ['nɒn'fɪkʃən] n Sachbücher pl
nonplussed ['nɒn'plʌst] adj verdutzt
nonsense ['nɒnsəns] n Unsinn m
non: ~-**smoker** n Nichtraucher(in) m(f); ~-**stick** adj (pan, surface) Teflon-(®); ~-**stop** adj Nonstop-
noodles ['nuːdlz] npl Nudeln pl
nook [nʊk] n Winkel m; ~s **and crannies** Ecken und Winkel
noon [nuːn] n (12 Uhr) Mittag m
no one ['nəʊwʌn] pron = **nobody**
noose [nuːs] n Schlinge f
nor [nɔː*] conj = **neither** ♦ adv see **neither**
norm [nɔːm] n Norm f
normal ['nɔːməl] adj normal; ~**ly** adv normal; (usually) normalerweise
north [nɔːθ] n Norden m ♦ adj nördlich, Nord- ♦ adv nördlich, nach or im Norden; ~-**east** n Nordosten m; ~**erly** ['nɔːðəlɪ] adj nördlich; ~**ern** ['nɔːðən] adj nördlich, Nord-; **N~ern Ireland** n Nordirland nt; **N~ Pole** n Nordpol m; **N~ Sea** n Nordsee f; ~**ward(s)** ['nɔːθwəd(z)] adv nach Norden; ~-**west** n Nordwesten m
Norway ['nɔːweɪ] n Norwegen nt
Norwegian [nɔː'wiːdʒən] adj norwegisch ♦ n Norweger(in) m(f); (LING) Norwegisch nt
nose [nəʊz] n Nase f ♦ vi: **to ~ about** herumschnüffeln; ~**bleed** n Nasenbluten nt; ~-**dive** n Sturzflug m; ~**y** adj = **nosy**
nostalgia [nɒs'tældʒɪə] n Nostalgie f
nostril ['nɒstrɪl] n Nasenloch nt
nosy ['nəʊzɪ] (inf) adj neugierig
not [nɒt] adv nicht; **he is ~** or **isn't here** er ist nicht hier; **it's too late, isn't it?** es ist zu spät, oder or nicht wahr?; ~ **yet/now** noch nicht/nicht jetzt; see also **all**; **only**
notably ['nəʊtəblɪ] adv (especially) besonders; (noticeably) bemerkenswert
notary ['nəʊtərɪ] n Notar(in) m(f)
notch [nɒtʃ] n Kerbe f, Einschnitt m
note [nəʊt] n (MUS) Note f, Ton m; (short letter) Nachricht f; (POL) Note f; (comment, attention) Notiz f; (of lecture etc) Aufzeichnung f; (bank~)

Schein *m*; *(fame)* Ruf *m* ♦ *vt (observe)* bemerken; *(write down)* notieren; **~book** *n* Notizbuch *nt*; **~d** ['nəʊtɪd] *adj* bekannt; **~pad** *n* Notizblock *m*; **~paper** *n* Briefpapier *nt*

nothing ['nʌθɪŋ] *n* nichts; ~ **new/much** nichts Neues/nicht viel; **for** ~ umsonst

notice ['nəʊtɪs] *n (announcement)* Bekanntmachung *f*; *(warning)* Ankündigung *f*; *(dismissal)* Kündigung *f* ♦ *vt* bemerken; **to take** ~ **of** beachten; **at short** ~ kurzfristig; **until further** ~ bis auf weiteres; **to hand in one's** ~ kündigen; ~**able** *adj* merklich; ~**board** *n* Anschlagtafel *f*

notify ['nəʊtɪfaɪ] *vt* benachrichtigen

notion ['nəʊʃən] *n* Idee *f*

notorious [nəʊ'tɔːrɪəs] *adj* berüchtigt

notwithstanding [nɒtwɪθ'stændɪŋ] *adv* trotzdem; ~ **this** ungeachtet dessen

nought [nɔːt] *n* Null *f*

noun [naʊn] *n* Substantiv *nt*

nourish ['nʌrɪʃ] *vt* nähren; ~**ing** *adj* nahrhaft; ~**ment** *n* Nahrung *f*

novel ['nɒvəl] *n* Roman *m* ♦ *adj* neu(artig); ~**ist** *n* Schriftsteller(in) *m(f)*; ~**ty** *n* Neuheit *f*

November [nəʊ'vembə*] *n* November *m*

novice ['nɒvɪs] *n* Neuling *m*; *(ECCL)* Novize *m*

now [naʊ] *adv* jetzt; **right** ~ jetzt, gerade; **by** ~ inzwischen; **just** ~ gerade; ~ **and then,** ~ **and again** ab und zu, manchmal; **from** ~ **on** von jetzt an; ~**adays** ['naʊədeɪz] *adv* heutzutage

nowhere ['nəʊwɛə*] *adv* nirgends

nozzle ['nɒzl] *n* Düse *f*

nubile ['njuːbaɪl] *adj (woman)* gut entwickelt

nuclear ['njuːklɪə*] *adj (energy etc)* Atom-, Kern-

nuclei ['njuːklɪaɪ] *npl of* **nucleus**

nucleus ['njuːklɪəs] *n* Kern *m*

nude [njuːd] *adj* nackt ♦ *n (ART)* Akt *m*; **in the** ~ nackt

nudge [nʌdʒ] *vt* leicht anstoßen

nudist ['njuːdɪst] *n* Nudist(in) *m(f)*

nudity ['njuːdɪtɪ] *n* Nacktheit *f*

nuisance ['njuːsns] *n* Ärgernis *nt*; **what a** ~! wie ärgerlich!

nuke [njuːk] *(inf)* *n* Kernkraftwerk *nt* ♦ *vt* atomar vernichten

null [nʌl] *adj*: ~ **and void** null und nichtig

numb [nʌm] *adj* taub, gefühllos ♦ *vt* betäuben

number ['nʌmbə*] *n* Nummer *f*; *(numeral also)* Zahl *f*; *(quantity)* (An)zahl *f* ♦ *vt (give a* ~ *to)* numerieren; *(amount to)* sein; **to be** ~**ed among** gezählt werden zu; **a** ~ **of** *(several)* einige; **they were ten in** ~ sie waren zehn an der Zahl; ~ **plate** *(BRIT)* *n (AUT)* Nummernschild *nt*

numeral ['njuːmərəl] *n* Ziffer *f*

numerate ['njuːmərɪt] *adj* rechenkundig

numerical [njuː'merɪkəl] *adj (order)* zahlenmäßig

numerous ['njuːmərəs] *adj* zahlreich

nun [nʌn] *n* Nonne *f*

nurse [nɜːs] *n* Krankenschwester *f*; *(for children)* Kindermädchen *nt* ♦ *vt (patient)* pflegen; *(doubt etc)* hegen

nursery ['nɜːsərɪ] *n (for children)* Kinderzimmer *nt*; *(for plants)* Gärtnerei *f*; *(for trees)* Baumschule *f*; ~ **rhyme** *n* Kinderreim *m*; ~ **school** *n* Kindergarten *m*; ~ **slope** *(BRIT)* *n (SKI)* Idiotenhügel *m (inf)*, Anfängerhügel *m*

nursing ['nɜːsɪŋ] *n (profession)* Krankenpflege *f*; ~ **home** *n* Privatklinik *f*

nurture ['nɜːtʃə*] *vt* aufziehen

nut [nʌt] *n* Nuß *f*; *(screw)* Schraubenmutter *f*; *(inf)* Verrückte(r) *mf*; **he's** ~**s** *(inf)* er ist verrückt

nutcrackers ['nʌtkrækəz] *npl* Nußknacker *m*

nutmeg ['nʌtmeg] *n* Muskat(nuß *f*) *m*

nutrient ['njuːtrɪənt] *n* Nährstoff *m*

nutrition [njuː'trɪʃən] *n* Nahrung *f*

nutritious [njuː'trɪʃəs] *adj* nahrhaft

nutshell ['nʌtʃel] *n*: **in a** ~ in aller Kürze

nylon ['naɪlɒn] *n* Nylon *nt* ♦ *adj* Nylon-

O

oak [əʊk] n Eiche f ♦ adj Eichen(holz)-

O.A.P. abbr = **old-age pensioner**

oar [ɔː*] n Ruder nt

oases [əʊˈeɪsiːz] npl of **oasis**

oasis [əʊˈeɪsɪs] n Oase f

oath [əʊθ] n (statement) Eid m, Schwur m; (swearword) Fluch m

oatmeal [ˈəʊtmiːl] n Haferschrot m

oats [əʊts] npl Hafer m

obedience [əˈbiːdɪəns] n Gehorsam m

obedient [əˈbiːdɪənt] adj gehorsam

obesity [əʊˈbiːsɪtɪ] n Fettleibigkeit f

obey [əˈbeɪ] vt, vi: **to ~ (sb)** (jdm) gehorchen

obituary [əˈbɪtjʊərɪ] n Nachruf m

object [n ˈɒbdʒɪkt, vb əbˈdʒekt] n (thing) Gegenstand m, Objekt nt; (purpose) Ziel nt ♦ vi dagegen sein; **expense is no ~** Ausgaben spielen keine Rolle; **I ~!** ich protestiere!; **to ~ to sth** Einwände gegen etw haben; (morally) Anstoß an etw acc nehmen; **to ~ that** einwenden, daß; **~ion** [əbˈdʒekʃən] n (reason against) Einwand m, Einspruch m; (dislike) Abneigung f; **I have no ~ion to ...** ich habe nichts gegen ... einzuwenden; **~ionable** [əbˈdʒekʃnəbl] adj nicht einwandfrei; (language) anstößig; **~ive** [əbˈdʒektɪv] n Ziel nt ♦ adj objektiv

obligation [ɒblɪˈgeɪʃən] n Verpflichtung f; **without ~** unverbindlich

obligatory [ɒˈblɪgətərɪ] adj obligatorisch

oblige [əˈblaɪdʒ] vt (compel) zwingen; (do a favour) einen Gefallen tun +dat; **to be ~d to sb for sth** jdm für etw verbunden sein

obliging [əˈblaɪdʒɪŋ] adj entgegenkommend

oblique [əˈbliːk] adj schräg, schief ♦ n Schrägstrich m

obliterate [əˈblɪtəreɪt] vt auslöschen

oblivion [əˈblɪvɪən] n Vergessenheit f

oblivious [əˈblɪvɪəs] adj nicht bewußt

oblong [ˈɒblɒŋ] n Rechteck nt ♦ adj länglich

obnoxious [əbˈnɒkʃəs] adj widerlich

obscene [əbˈsiːn] adj obszön

obscenity [əbˈsenɪtɪ] n Obszönität f; **obscenities** npl (swearwords) Zoten pl

obscure [əbˈskjʊə*] adj unklar; (indistinct) undeutlich; (unknown) unbekannt, obskur; (dark) düster ♦ vt verdunkeln; (view) verbergen; (confuse) verwirren

obscurity [əbˈskjʊərɪtɪ] n Unklarheit f; (darkness) Dunkelheit f

obsequious [əbˈsiːkwɪəs] adj servil

observance [əbˈzɜːvəns] n Befolgung f

observant [əbˈzɜːvənt] adj aufmerksam

observation [ɒbzəˈveɪʃən] n (noticing) Beobachtung f; (surveillance) Überwachung f; (remark) Bemerkung f

observatory [əbˈzɜːvətrɪ] n Sternwarte f, Observatorium nt

observe [əbˈzɜːv] vt (notice) bemerken; (watch) beobachten; (customs) einhalten; **~r** n Beobachter(in) m(f)

obsess [əbˈses] vt verfolgen, quälen; **~ion** [əbˈseʃən] n Besessenheit f, Wahn m; **~ive** adj krankhaft

obsolescence [ɒbsəˈlesns] n Veralten nt

obsolete [ˈɒbsəliːt] adj überholt, veraltet

obstacle [ˈɒbstəkl] n Hindernis nt; **~ race** n Hindernisrennen nt

obstetrics [ɒbˈstetrɪks] n Geburtshilfe f

obstinate [ˈɒbstɪnət] adj hartnäckig, stur; **~ly** adv hartnäckig, stur

obstruct [əbˈstrʌkt] vt versperren; (pipe) verstopfen; (hinder) hemmen; **~ion** [əbˈstrʌkʃən] n Versperrung f; Verstopfung f; (obstacle) Hindernis nt

obtain [əbˈteɪn] vt erhalten, bekommen; (result) erzielen

obtrusive [əbˈtruːsɪv] adj aufdringlich

obvious [ˈɒbvɪəs] adj offenbar, offensichtlich; **~ly** adv offensichtlich

occasion [əˈkeɪʒən] n Gelegenheit f; (special event) Ereignis nt; (reason) Anlaß m ♦ vt veranlassen; **~al** adj gelegentlich; **~ally** adv gelegentlich

occupant [ˈɒkjʊpənt] n Inhaber(in) m(f); (of house etc) Bewohner(in) m(f)

occupation [ɒkjuˈpeɪʃən] n (employment) Tätigkeit f, Beruf m; (pastime) Beschäftigung f; (of country)

Besetzung *f*, Okkupation *f*; ~al hazard *n* Berufsrisiko *nt*

occupier ['ɒkjʊpaɪə*] *n* Bewohner(in) *m(f)*

occupy ['ɒkjʊpaɪ] *vt* (*take possession of*) besetzen; (*seat*) belegen; (*live in*) bewohnen; (*position, office*) bekleiden; (*position in sb's life*) einnehmen, (*time*) beanspruchen; to ~ o.s. with sth sich mit etw beschäftigen; to ~ o.s. by doing sth sich damit beschäftigen, etw zu tun

occur [ə'kɜː*] *vi* vorkommen; to ~ to sb jdm einfallen; ~rence *n* (*event*) Ereignis *nt*; (*appearing*) Auftreten *nt*

ocean ['əʊʃən] *n* Ozean *m*, Meer *nt*; ~-going *adj* Hochsee-

o'clock [ə'klɒk] *adv*: it is 5 ~ es ist 5 Uhr

OCR *n abbr* = **optical character reader**

octagonal [ɒk'tægənl] *adj* achteckig

October [ɒk'təʊbə*] *n* Oktober *m*

octopus ['ɒktəpəs] *n* Krake *f*; (*small*) Tintenfisch *m*

odd [ɒd] *adj* (*strange*) sonderbar; (*not even*) ungerade; (*the other part missing*) einzeln; (*surplus*) übrig; **60-~** so um die 60; **at ~ times** ab und zu; **to be the ~ one out** (*person*) das fünfte Rad am Wagen sein; (*thing*) nicht dazugehören; ~ity *n* (*strangeness*) Merkwürdigkeit *f*; (*queer person*) seltsame(r) Kauz *m*; (*thing*) Kuriosität *f*; ~-job man (*irreg*) *n* Mädchen *nt* für alles; ~ jobs *npl* gelegentlich anfallende Arbeiten; ~ly *adv* seltsam; ~ments *npl* Reste *pl*; ~s *npl* Chancen *pl*; (*betting*) Gewinnchancen *pl*; it makes no ~s es spielt keine Rolle; at ~s uneinig; ~s and ends *npl* Krimskrams *m*

odious ['əʊdɪəs] *adj* verhaßt; (*action*) abscheulich

odometer [əʊ'dɒmətə*] (*esp US*) *n* Tacho(meter) *m*

odour ['əʊdə*] (*US* **odor**) *n* Geruch *m*

KEYWORD
---

of [ɒv, əv] *prep* **1** von +*dat*, *use of gen*; the history of Germany die Geschichte

Deutschlands; **a friend of ours** ein Freund von uns; **a boy of 10** ein 10-jähriger Junge; **that was kind of you** das war sehr freundlich von Ihnen

2 (*expressing quantity, amount, dates etc*): **a kilo of flour** ein Kilo Mehl; **how much of this do you need?** wieviel brauchen Sie (davon)?; **there were 3 of them** (*people*) sie waren zu dritt; (*objects*) es gab 3 (davon); **a cup of tea/vase of flowers** eine Tasse Tee/Vase mit Blumen; **the 5th of July** der 5 Juli

3 (*from, out of*) aus; **a bridge made of wood** eine Holzbrücke, eine Brücke aus Holz

---

off [ɒf] *adj, adv* (*absent*) weg, fort; (*switch*) aus(geschaltet), ab(geschaltet); (*BRIT: food: bad*) schlecht; (*cancelled*) abgesagt ♦ *prep* von +*dat*; to be ~ (*to leave*) gehen; to be ~ sick krank sein; **a day** ~ ein freier Tag; to have an ~ day einen schlechten Tag haben; **he had his coat** ~ er hatte seinen Mantel aus; **10%** ~ (*COMM*) 10% Rabatt; **5 km** ~ (**the road**) 5 km (von der Straße) entfernt; ~ **the coast** vor der Küste; **I'm** ~ **meat** (*no longer eat it*) ich esse kein Fleisch mehr; (*no longer like it*) ich mag kein Fleisch mehr; **on the** ~ **chance** auf gut Glück

offal ['ɒfl] *n* Innereien *pl*

offbeat ['ɒfbiːt] *adj* unkonventionell

off-colour ['ɒf'kʌlə*] *adj* nicht wohl

offence [ə'fens] (*US* **offense**) *n* (*crime*) Vergehen *nt*, Straftat *f*; (*insult*) Beleidigung *f*; to take ~ at gekränkt sein wegen

offend [ə'fend] *vt* beleidigen; ~er *n* Gesetzesübertreter *m*

offense [ə'fens] (*US*) *n* = **offence**

offensive [ə'fensɪv] *adj* (*unpleasant*) übel, abstoßend; (*weapon*) Kampf-; (*remark*) verletzend ♦ *n* Angriff *m*

offer ['ɒfə*] *n* Angebot *f* ♦ *vt* anbieten; (*opinion*) äußern; (*resistance*) leisten; **on** ~ zum Verkauf angeboten; ~ing *n* Gabe *f*

offhand ['ɒf'hænd] *adj* lässig ♦ *adv* ohne weiteres

office ['ɒfɪs] n Büro nt; (position) Amt nt; **doctor's** ~ (US) Praxis f; **to take** ~ sein Amt antreten; (POL) die Regierung übernehmen; ~ **automation** n Büroautomatisierung f; ~ **block** (US = **building**) n Büro(hoch)haus nt; ~ **hours** npl Dienstzeit f; (US: MED) Sprechstunde f

officer ['ɒfɪsə*] n (MIL) Offizier m; (public ~) Beamte(r) m

official [ə'fɪʃəl] adj offiziell, amtlich ♦ n Beamte(r) m; ~**dom** n Beamtentum nt

officiate [ə'fɪʃɪeɪt] vi amtieren

officious [ə'fɪʃəs] adj aufdringlich

offing ['ɒfɪŋ] n: **in the** ~ in (Aus)sicht

off: ~**licence** (BRIT) n (shop) Wein- und Spirituosenhandlung f; ~**-peak** adj (charges) verbilligt; ~**-season** adj außer Saison

offset ['ɒfset] (irreg: like **set**) vt ausgleichen ♦ n (also: ~ **printing**) Offset(druck) m

offshoot ['ɒfʃuːt] n (fig: of organization) Zweig m; (: of discussion etc) Randergebnis nt

offshore ['ɒf'ʃɔː*] adv in einiger Entfernung von der Küste ♦ adj küstennah, Küsten-

offside ['ɒf'saɪd] adj (SPORT) im Abseits ♦ adv abseits ♦ n (AUT) Fahrerseite f

offspring ['ɒfsprɪŋ] n Nachkommenschaft f; (one) Sprößling m

off: ~**stage** adv hinter den Kulissen; ~**-the-cuff** adj unvorbereitet, aus dem Stegreif; ~**-the-peg** (US ~**-the-rack**) adv von der Stange; ~**-white** adj naturweiß

often ['ɒfən] adv oft

ogle ['əʊgl] vt liebäugeln mit

oh [əʊ] excl oh, ach

oil [ɔɪl] n Öl nt ♦ vt ölen; ~**can** n Ölkännchen nt; ~**field** n Ölfeld nt; ~**filter** n (AUT) Ölfilter m; ~**-fired** adj Öl-; ~ **painting** n Ölgemälde nt; ~**-rig** n Ölplattform f; ~**skins** npl Ölzeug nt; ~ **tanker** n (Öl)tanker m; ~ **well** n Ölquelle f; ~**y** adj ölig; (dirty) ölbeschmiert

ointment ['ɔɪntmənt] n Salbe f

O.K. ['əʊ'keɪ] excl in Ordnung, O.K. ♦ adj in Ordnung ♦ vt genehmigen

okay ['əʊ'keɪ] = **O.K.**

old [əʊld] adj alt; **how** ~ **are you?** wie alt bist du?; **he's 10 years** ~ er ist 10 Jahre alt; ~ **age** n Alter nt; ~**-age pensioner** (BRIT) n Rentner(in) m(f); ~**-fashioned** adj altmodisch

olive ['ɒlɪv] n (fruit) Olive f; (colour) Olive nt ♦ adj Oliven-; (coloured) olivenfarbig; ~ **oil** n Olivenöl nt

Olympic [əʊ'lɪmpɪk] adj olympisch; **the** ~ **Games, the** ~**s** die Olympischen Spiele

omelet(te) ['ɒmlət] n Omelett nt

omen ['əʊmən] n Omen nt

ominous ['ɒmɪnəs] adj bedrohlich

omission [əʊ'mɪʃən] n Auslassung f; (neglect) Versäumnis nt

omit [əʊ'mɪt] vt auslassen; (fail to do) versäumen

KEYWORD

on [ɒn] prep **1** (indicating position) auf +dat; (with vb of motion) auf +acc; (on vertical surface, part of body) an +dat/acc; **it's on the table** es ist auf dem Tisch; **she put the book on the table** sie legte das Buch auf den Tisch; **on the left** links

2 (indicating means, method, condition etc): **on foot** (go, be) zu Fuß; **on the train/plane** (go) mit dem Zug/Flugzeug; (be) im Zug/Flugzeug; **on the telephone/television** am Telefon/im Fernsehen; **to be on drugs** Drogen nehmen; **to be on holiday/business** im Urlaub/auf Geschäftsreise sein

3 (referring to time): **on Friday** (am) Freitag; **on Fridays** freitags; **on June 20th** am 20. Juni; **a week on Friday** Freitag in einer Woche; **on arrival he ... als er ankam, ... er ...**

4 (about, concerning) über +acc

♦ adv **1** (referring to dress) an; **she put her boots/hat on** sie zog ihre Stiefel an/setzte ihren Hut auf

2 (further, continuously) weiter; **to walk on** weitergehen

♦ adj **1** (functioning, in operation: machine, TV, light) an; (: tap) aufgedreht; (: brakes) angezogen; **is the**

meeting still on? findet die Versammlung noch statt?; there's a good film on es läuft ein guter Film
2: that's not on! (*inf: of behaviour*) das liegt nicht drin!

once [wʌns] *adv* einmal ♦ *conj* wenn ... einmal; ~ **he had left/it was done** nachdem er gegangen war/es fertig war; **at** ~ sofort; (*at the same time*) gleichzeitig; ~ **a week** einmal in der Woche; ~ **more** noch einmal; ~ **and for all** ein für allemal; ~ **upon a time** es war einmal
oncoming ['ɒnkʌmɪŋ] *adj* (*traffic*) Gegen-, entgegenkommend

KEYWORD

one [wʌn] *num* eins; (*with noun, referring back to noun*) ein/eine/ein; **it is one** (*o'clock*) es ist eins, es ist ein Uhr; **one hundred and fifty** einhundertfünfzig
♦ *adj* **1** (*sole*) einzige(r, s); **the one book which** das einzige Buch, welches
2 (*same*) derselbe/dieselbe/dasselbe; **they came in the one car** sie kamen alle in dem einen Auto
3 (*indef*): **one day I discovered ...** eines Tages bemerkte ich ...
♦ *pron* **1** eine(r, s); **do you have a red one?** haben Sie einen roten/eine rote/ein rotes?; **this one** diese(r, s); **that one** der/die/das; **which one?** welche(r, s)?; **one by one** einzeln
2: one another einander; **do you two ever see one another?** seht ihr beide euch manchmal?
3 (*impers*) man; **one never knows** man kann nie wissen; **to cut one's finger** sich in den Finger schneiden

one: ~**-armed bandit** *n* einarmiger Bandit *m*; ~**-day excursion** (*US*) *n* (*day return*) Tagesrückfahrkarte *f*; ~**-man** *adj* Einmann-; ~**-man band** *n* Einmannkapelle *f*; (*fig*) Einmannbetrieb *m*; ~**-off** (*BRIT: inf*) *n* Einzelfall *m*
oneself [wʌn'self] *pron* (*reflexive: after prep*) sich; (~ *personally*) sich selbst

or selber; (*emphatic*) (sich) selbst; **to hurt** ~ sich verletzen
one: ~**-sided** *adj* (*argument*) einseitig; ~**-to-one** *adj* (*relationship*) eins-zu-eins; ~**-upmanship** *n* die Kunst, anderen um eine Nasenlänge voraus zu sein; ~**-way** *adj* (*street*) Einbahn-
ongoing ['ɒngəʊɪŋ] *adj* momentan; (*progressing*) sich entwickelnd
onion ['ʌnjən] *n* Zwiebel *f*
on-line ['ɒn'laɪn] *adj* (*COMPUT*) rechnerabhängig; (: *switched on*) gekoppelt
onlooker ['ɒnlʊkə*] *n* Zuschauer(in) *m(f)*
only ['əʊnlɪ] *adv* nur, bloß ♦ *adj* einzige(r, s) ♦ *conj* nur, bloß; **an** ~ **child** ein Einzelkind; **not** ~ **... but also ...** nicht nur ... sondern auch ...
onset ['ɒnset] *n* (*beginning*) Beginn *m*
onshore ['ɒnʃɔː*] *adj* (*wind*) See-
onslaught ['ɒnslɔːt] *n* Angriff *m*
onto ['ɒntʊ] *prep* = **on to**
onus ['əʊnəs] *n* Last *f*, Pflicht *f*
onward(s) ['ɒnwəd(z)] *adv* (*place*) voran, vorwärts; **from that day onwards** von dem Tag an; **from today onwards** ab heute
ooze [uːz] *vi* sickern
opaque [əʊ'peɪk] *adj* undurchsichtig
OPEC ['əʊpek] *n abbr* (= *Organization of Petroleum-Exporting Countries*) OPEC *f*
open ['əʊpən] *adj* offen; (*public*) öffentlich; (*mind*) aufgeschlossen ♦ *vt* öffnen, aufmachen; (*trial, motorway, account*) eröffnen ♦ *vi* (*begin*) anfangen; (*shop*) aufmachen; (*door, flower*) aufgehen; (*play*) Premiere haben; **in the** ~ (**air**) im Freien; ~ **on to** *vt fus* sich öffnen auf +*acc*; ~ **up** *vt* (*route*) erschließen; (*shop, prospects*) eröffnen ♦ *vi* öffnen; ~**ing** *n* (*hole*) Öffnung *f*; (*beginning*) Anfang *m*; (*good chance*) Gelegenheit *f*; ~**ly** *adv* offen; (*publicly*) öffentlich; ~**-minded** *adj* aufgeschlossen; ~**-necked** *adj* offen; ~**-plan** *adj* (*office*) Großraum-; (*flat etc*) offen angelegt
opera ['ɒpərə] *n* Oper *f*; ~ **house** *n*

Opernhaus *nt*
operate ['ɒpəreɪt] *vt* (*machine*)
bedienen; (*brakes, light*) betätigen ♦ *vi*
(*machine*) laufen, in Betrieb sein;
(*person*) arbeiten; (*MED*): to ~ on
operieren
operatic [ɒpə'rætɪk] *adj* Opern-
operating ['ɒpəreɪtɪŋ] *adj*: ~ table/
theatre Operationstisch *m*/-saal *m*
operation [ɒpə'reɪʃən] *n* (*working*) Betrieb *m*; (*MED*) Operation *f*;
(*undertaking*) Unternehmen *nt*; (*MIL*)
Einsatz *m*; to be in ~ (*JUR*) in Kraft
sein; (*machine*) in Betrieb sein; to
have an ~ (*MED*) operiert werden; ~al
adj einsatzbereit
operative ['ɒpərətɪv] *adj* wirksam;
(*MED*) operativ
operator ['ɒpəreɪtə*] *n* (*of machine*)
Arbeiter *m*; (*TEL*) Telefonist(in) *m(f)*
ophthalmic [ɒf'θælmɪk] *adj* Augen-
opinion [ə'pɪnjən] *n* Meinung *f*; in my ~
meiner Meinung nach; ~ated *adj*
starrsinnig; ~ poll *n* Meinungsumfrage
f
opponent [ə'pəʊnənt] *n* Gegner *m*.
opportunity [ɒpə'tjuːnɪtɪ] *n* Gelegenheit
f, Möglichkeit *f*; to take the ~ of doing
sth die Gelegenheit ergreifen, etw zu
tun
oppose [ə'pəʊz] *vt* entgegentreten +*dat*;
(*argument, idea*) ablehnen; (*plan*)
bekämpfen; to be ~d to sth gegen etw
sein; as ~d to im Gegensatz zu
opposing [ə'pəʊzɪŋ] *adj* gegnerisch;
(*points of view*) entgegengesetzt
opposite ['ɒpəzɪt] *adj* (*house*) gegen-
überliegend; (*direction*) entgegengesetzt ♦ *adv* gegenüber ♦ *prep* gegenüber ♦ *n* Gegenteil *nt*
opposition [ɒpə'zɪʃən] *n* (*resistance*)
Widerstand *m*; (*POL*) Opposition *f*;
(*contrast*) Gegensatz *m*
oppress [ə'pres] *vt* unterdrücken; (*heat
etc*) bedrücken; ~ion [ə'preʃən] *n* Unterdrückung *f*; ~ive (*authority, law*)
repressiv; (*burden, thought*) be-
drückend; (*heat*) drückend
opt [ɒpt] *vi*: to ~ for sich entscheiden
für; to ~ to do sth sich entscheiden, etw

zu tun; to ~ out of sich drücken vor
+*dat*; (*of society*) ausflippen aus
optical ['ɒptɪkəl] *adj* optisch; ~ character reader *n* optische(s) Lesegerät *nt*
optician [ɒp'tɪʃən] *n* Optiker *m*
optimist ['ɒptɪmɪst] *n* Optimist *m*; ~ic
['ɒptɪ'mɪstɪk] *adj* optimistisch
optimum ['ɒptɪməm] *adj* optimal
option ['ɒpʃən] *n* Wahl *f*; (*COMM*)
Option *f*; to keep one's ~s open sich
alle Möglichkeiten offenhalten; ~al *adj*
freiwillig; (*subject*) wahlfrei; ~al
extras *npl* Extras auf Wunsch
opulent ['ɒpjʊlənt] *adj* sehr reich
or [ɔː*] *conj* oder; he could not read ~
write er konnte weder lesen noch
schreiben; ~ else sonst
oral ['ɔːrəl] *adj* mündlich ♦ *n* (*exam*)
mündliche Prüfung *f*
orange ['ɒrɪndʒ] *n* (*fruit*) Apfelsine *f*,
Orange *f*; (*colour*) Orange *nt* ♦ *adj*
orange
orator ['ɒrətə*] *n* Redner(in) *m(f)*
orbit ['ɔːbɪt] *n* Umlaufbahn *f*
orchard ['ɔːtʃəd] *n* Obstgarten *m*
orchestra ['ɔːkɪstrə] *n* Orchester *nt*;
(*US: seating*) Parkett *m*; ~l [ɔː'kestrəl]
adj Orchester-, orchestral
orchid ['ɔːkɪd] *n* Orchidee *f*
ordain [ɔː'deɪn] *vt* (*ECCL*) weihen;
(*decide*) verfügen
ordeal [ɔː'diːl] *n* Qual *f*
order ['ɔːdə*] *n* (*sequence*) Reihenfolge
f; (*good arrangement*) Ordnung *f*;
(*command*) Befehl *m*; (*JUR*) Anordnung
f; (*peace*) Ordnung *f*; (*condition*) Zustand *m*; (*rank*) Klasse *f*; (*COMM*) Bestellung *f*; (*ECCL, honour*) Orden *m* ♦ *vt*
(*also: put in ~*) ordnen; (*command*)
befehlen; (*COMM*) bestellen; in ~ in der
Reihenfolge; in (*working*) ~ in gutem
Zustand; in ~ to do sth um etw zu tun;
on ~ (*COMM*) auf Bestellung; to ~ sb to
do sth jdm befehlen, etw zu tun; to ~
sth (*command*) etw *acc* befehlen; to ~
form *n* Bestellschein *m*; ~ly *n* (*MIL*)
Sanitäter *m*; (*MED*) Pfleger *m* ♦ *adj*
(*tidy*) ordentlich; (*well-behaved*) ruhig
ordinary ['ɔːdnrɪ] *adj* gewöhnlich; out of
the ~ außergewöhnlich

ordnance ['ɔ:dnəns] n Artillerie f; O~ **Survey** (BRIT) n amtliche(r) Kartographiedienst m

ore [ɔ:*] n Erz nt

organ ['ɔ:gən] n (MUS) Orgel f; (BIOL, fig) Organ nt

organic [ɔ:'gænɪk] adj organisch

organization [ɔ:gənaɪ'zeɪʃən] n Organisation f; (make-up) Struktur f

organize ['ɔ:gənaɪz] vt organisieren; ~r n Organisator m, Veranstalter m

orgasm ['ɔ:gæzəm] n Orgasmus m

orgy ['ɔ:dʒɪ] n Orgie f

Orient ['ɔ:rɪənt] n Orient m

oriental [ɔ:rɪ'entəl] adj orientalisch

origin ['ɒrɪdʒɪn] n Ursprung m; (of the world) Anfang m, Entstehung f

original [ə'rɪdʒɪnl] adj (first) ursprünglich; (painting) original; (idea) originell ♦ n Original nt; ~ly adv ursprünglich; originell

originate [ə'rɪdʒɪneɪt] vi entstehen ♦ vt ins Leben rufen; to ~ from stammen aus

Orkneys ['ɔ:knɪz] npl (also: the Orkney Islands) die Orkneyinseln pl

ornament ['ɔ:nəmənt] n Schmuck m; (on mantelpiece) Nippesfigur f; ~al [ɔ:nə'mentl] adj Zier-

ornate [ɔ:'neɪt] adj reich verziert

orphan ['ɔ:fən] n Waise f, Waisenkind nt ♦ vt: to be ~ed Waise werden; ~age n Waisenhaus nt

orthodox ['ɔ:θədɒks] adj orthodox; ~y n Orthodoxie f; (fig) Konventionalität f

orthopaedic [ɔ:θəʊ'pi:dɪk] (US orthopedic) adj orthopädisch

ostensibly [ɒs'tensəblɪ] adv vorgeblich, angeblich

ostentatious [ɒsten'teɪʃəs] adj großtuerisch, protzig

ostracize ['ɒstrəsaɪz] vt ausstoßen

ostrich ['ɒstrɪtʃ] n Strauß m

other ['ʌðə*] adj andere(r, s) ♦ pron andere(r, s) ♦ adv: ~ than anders als; the ~ (one) der/die/das andere; the ~ day neulich; ~s (~ people) andere; ~wise adv (in a different way) anders; (or else) sonst

ouch [aʊtʃ] excl aua

ought [ɔ:t] vb aux sollen; I ~ to do it ich sollte es tun; this ~ to have been **corrected** das hätte korrigiert werden sollen

ounce [aʊns] n Unze f

our [aʊə*] adj unser; see also my; ~s pron unsere(r, s); see also mine; ~selves pron uns (selbst); (emphatic) (wir) selbst; see also oneself

oust [aʊst] vt verdrängen

out [aʊt] adv hinaus/heraus; (not indoors) draußen; (not alight) aus; (unconscious) bewußtlos; (results) bekanntgegeben; to eat/go ~ auswärts essen/ausgehen; ~ there da draußen; he is ~ (absent) er ist nicht da; he was ~ in his calculations seine Berechnungen waren nicht richtig; ~ **loud** laut; ~ of aus; (away from) außerhalb +gen; to be ~ of milk etc keine Milch etc mehr haben; ~ of order außer Betrieb; ~-and-out adj (liar, thief etc) ausgemacht

outback ['aʊtbæk] n Hinterland nt

outboard (motor) ['aʊtbɔ:d-] n Außenbordmotor m

outbreak ['aʊtbreɪk] n Ausbruch m

outburst ['aʊtbɜ:st] n Ausbruch m

outcast ['aʊtkɑ:st] n Ausgestoßene(r) mf

outcome ['aʊtkʌm] n Ergebnis nt

outcrop ['aʊtkrɒp] n (of rock) Felsnase f

outcry ['aʊtkraɪ] n Protest m

outdated [aʊt'deɪtɪd] adj überholt

outdo [aʊt'du:] (irreg: like do) vt übertrumpfen

outdoor ['aʊtdɔ:*] adj Außen-; (SPORT) im Freien; ~s adv im Freien

outer ['aʊtə*] adj äußere(r, s); ~ space n Weltraum m

outfit ['aʊtfɪt] n Kleidung f; ~ters (BRIT) n (for men's clothes) Herrenausstatter m

outgoing ['aʊtgəʊɪŋ] adj (character) aufgeschlossen; ~s (BRIT) npl Ausgaben pl

outgrow [aʊt'grəʊ] (irreg: like grow) vt (clothes) herauswachsen aus; (habit) ablegen

outhouse ['aʊthaʊs] n Nebengebäude nt

outing ['aʊtɪŋ] *n* Ausflug *m*
outlandish [aʊt'lændɪʃ] *adj* eigenartig
outlaw ['aʊtlɔ:] *n* Geächtete(r) *m* ♦ *vt* ächten; (*thing*) verbieten
outlay ['aʊtleɪ] *n* Auslage *f*
outlet ['aʊtlet] *n* Auslaß *m*, Abfluß *m*; (*also: retail ~*) Absatzmarkt *m*; (*US: ELEC*) Steckdose *f*; (*for emotions*) Ventil *nt*
outline ['aʊtlaɪn] *n* Umriß *m*
outlive [aʊt'lɪv] *vt* überleben
outlook ['aʊtlʊk] *n* (*also fig*) Aussicht *f*; (*attitude*) Einstellung *f*
outlying ['aʊtlaɪŋ] *adj* entlegen; (*district*) Außen-
outmoded [aʊt'məʊdɪd] *adj* veraltet
outnumber [aʊt'nʌmbə*] *vt* zahlenmäßig überlegen sein +*dat*
out-of-date [aʊtəv'deɪt] *adj* (*passport*) abgelaufen; (*clothes etc*) altmodisch; (*ideas etc*) überholt
out-of-the-way [aʊtəvðə'weɪ] *adj* abgelegen
outpatient ['aʊtpeɪʃənt] *n* ambulante(r) Patient *m*/ambulante Patientin *f*
outpost ['aʊtpəʊst] *n* (*MIL*, *fig*) Vorposten
output ['aʊtpʊt] *n* Leistung *f*, Produktion *f*; (*COMPUT*) Ausgabe *f*
outrage ['aʊtreɪdʒ] *n* (*cruel deed*) Ausschreitung *f*; (*indecency*) Skandal *m* ♦ *vt* (*morals*) verstoßen gegen; (*person*) empören; **~ous** [aʊt'reɪdʒəs] *adj* unerhört
outright [*adv* aʊt'raɪt, *adj* 'aʊtraɪt] *adv* (*at once*) sofort; (*openly*) ohne Umschweife ♦ *adj* (*denial*) völlig; (*sale*) Total-; (*winner*) unbestritten
outset ['aʊtset] *n* Beginn *m*
outside ['aʊt'saɪd] *n* Außenseite *f* ♦ *adj* äußere(r, s), Außen-; (*chance*) gering ♦ *adv* außen ♦ *prep* außerhalb +*gen*; **at the ~** (*fig*) maximal; **to go ~** nach draußen gehen; **~ lane** *n* (*AUT*) äußere Spur *f*; **~-left** *n* (*FOOTBALL*) Linksaußen *m*; **~ line** *n* (*TEL*) Amtsanschluß *m*; **~r** *n* Außenseiter(in) *m(f)*
outsize ['aʊtsaɪz] *adj* übergroß
outskirts ['aʊtskɜ:ts] *npl* Stadtrand *m*

outspoken [aʊt'spəʊkən] *adj* freimütig
outstanding [aʊt'stændɪŋ] *adj* hervorragend; (*debts etc*) ausstehend
outstay [aʊt'steɪ] *vt*: **to ~ one's welcome** länger bleiben als erwünscht
outstretched ['aʊtstretʃt] *adj* ausgestreckt
outstrip [aʊt'strɪp] *vt* übertreffen
out-tray ['aʊttreɪ] *n* Ausgangskorb *m*
outward ['aʊtwəd] *adj* äußere(r, s); (*journey*) Hin-; (*freight*) ausgehend ♦ *adv* nach außen; **~ly** *adv* äußerlich
outweigh [aʊt'weɪ] *vt* (*fig*) überwiegen
outwit [aʊt'wɪt] *vt* überlisten
oval ['əʊvəl] *adj* oval ♦ *n* Oval *nt*
ovary ['əʊvərɪ] *n* Eierstock *m*
ovation [əʊ'veɪʃən] *n* Beifallssturm *m*
oven ['ʌvn] *n* Backofen *m*; **~proof** *adj* feuerfest
over ['əʊvə*] *adv* (*across*) hinüber/herüber; (*finished*) vorbei; (*left*) übrig; (*again*) wieder, noch einmal ♦ *prep* über ♦ *prefix* (*excessively*) übermäßig; **~ here** hier(hin); **~ there** dort(hin); **all ~** (*everywhere*) überall; (*finished*) vorbei; **~ and ~** immer wieder; **~ and above** darüber hinaus; **to ask sb ~** jdn einladen; **to bend ~** sich bücken
overall [*adj*, *n* 'əʊvərɔ:l, *adv* əʊvər'ɔ:l] *adj* (*situation*) allgemein; (*length*) Gesamt- ♦ *n* (*BRIT*) Kittel *m* ♦ *adv* insgesamt; **~s** *npl* (*for man*) Overall *m*
overawe [əʊvər'ɔ:] *vt* (*frighten*) einschüchtern; (*make impression*) überwältigen
overbalance [əʊvə'bæləns] *vi* Übergewicht bekommen
overbearing [əʊvə'bɛərɪŋ] *adj* aufdringlich
overboard ['əʊvəbɔ:d] *adv* über Bord
overbook [əʊvə'bʊk] *vi* überbuchen
overcast ['əʊvəkɑ:st] *adj* bedeckt
overcharge ['əʊvə'tʃɑ:dʒ] *vt*: **to ~ sb** von jdm zuviel verlangen
overcoat ['əʊvəkəʊt] *n* Mantel *m*
overcome [əʊvə'kʌm] (*irreg: like* come) *vt* überwinden
overcrowded [əʊvə'kraʊdɪd] *adj* überfüllt
overcrowding [əʊvə'kraʊdɪŋ] *n* Über-

füllung *f*

overdo [əʊvə'duː] (*irreg: like* **do**) *vt*
(*cook too much*) verkochen;
(*exaggerate*) übertreiben

overdose ['əʊvədəʊs] *n* Überdosis *f*

overdraft ['əʊvədrɑːft] *n* (Konto)über-
ziehung *f*

overdrawn ['əʊvə'drɔːn] *adj* (*account*)
überzogen

overdue ['əʊvə'djuː] *adj* überfällig

overestimate ['əʊvər'estɪmeɪt] *vt* überschätzen

overexcited ['əʊvərɪk'saɪtɪd] *adj* überreizt; (*children*) aufgeregt

overflow [*vb* əʊvə'fləʊ, *n* 'əʊvəfləʊ] *vi*
überfließen ♦ *n* (*excess*) Überschuß *m*;
(*also: ~ pipe*) Überlaufrohr *nt*

overgrown ['əʊvə'grəʊn] *adj* (*garden*)
verwildert

overhaul [*vb* əʊvə'hɔːl, *n* 'əʊvəhɔːl] *vt*
(*car*) überholen; (*plans*) überprüfen ♦ *n*
Überholung *f*

overhead [*adv* əʊvə'hed, *adj, n* 'əʊvəhed]
adv oben ♦ *adj* Hoch-; (*wire*)
oberirdisch; (*lighting*) Decken- ♦ *n* (US)
= ~**s**; ~**s** *npl* (*costs*) allgemeine Unkosten *pl*

overhear [əʊvə'hɪə*] (*irreg: like* **hear**)
vt (mit an)hören

overheat [əʊvə'hiːt] *vi* (*engine*) heiß
laufen

overjoyed [əʊvə'dʒɔɪd] *adj* überglücklich

overkill ['əʊvəkɪl] *n* (*fig*) Rundumschlag
m

overland [*adj* 'əʊvəlænd, *adv* əʊvə'lænd]
adj Überland- ♦ *adv* (*travel*) über Land

overlap [*vb* əʊvə'læp, *n* 'əʊvəlæp] *vi* sich
überschneiden; (*objects*) sich teilweise
decken ♦ *n* Überschneidung *f*

overleaf [əʊvə'liːf] *adv* umseitig

overload ['əʊvə'ləʊd] *vt* überladen

overlook [əʊvə'lʊk] *vt* (*view from
above*) überblicken; (*not notice*)
übersehen; (*pardon*) hinwegsehen über
+*acc*

overnight [*adv* 'əʊvə'naɪt, *adj* 'əʊvənaɪt]
adv über Nacht ♦ *adj* (*journey*) Nacht-;
~ **stay** Übernachtung *f*

overpass ['əʊvəpɑːs] *n* Überführung *f*

overpower [əʊvə'paʊə*] *vt* überwältigen; ~**ing** *adj* überwältigend

overrate ['əʊvə'reɪt] *vt* überschätzen

override [əʊvə'raɪd] (*irreg: like* **ride**) *vt*
(*order, decision*) aufheben; (*objection*)
übergehen

overriding [əʊvə'raɪdɪŋ] *adj* vorherrschend

overrule [əʊvə'ruːl] *vt* verwerfen

overrun [əʊvə'rʌn] (*irreg: like* **run**) *vt*
(*country*) einfallen in; (*time limit*)
überziehen

overseas ['əʊvə'siːz] *adv* nach/in
Übersee ♦ *adj* überseeisch, Übersee-

overseer ['əʊvəsɪə*] *n* Aufseher *m*

overshadow [əʊvə'ʃædəʊ] *vt* über-
schatten

overshoot ['əʊvə'ʃuːt] (*irreg: like*
shoot) *vt* (*runway*) hinausschießen über
+*acc*

oversight ['əʊvəsaɪt] *n* (*mistake*) Versehen *nt*

oversleep ['əʊvə'sliːp] (*irreg: like* **sleep**)
vi verschlafen

overspill ['əʊvəspɪl] *n* (Bevölke-
rungs)überschuß *m*

overstate [əʊvə'steɪt] *vt* übertreiben

overstep [əʊvə'step] *vt*: **to ~ the mark**
zu weit gehen

overt [əʊ'vɜːt] *adj* offen(kundig)

overtake [əʊvə'teɪk] (*irreg: like* **take**)
vt, vi überholen

overthrow [əʊvə'θrəʊ] (*irreg: like*
throw) *vt* (*POL*) stürzen

overtime ['əʊvətaɪm] *n* Überstunden *pl*

overtone ['əʊvətəʊn] *n* (*fig*) Note *f*

overture ['əʊvətjʊə*] *n* Ouvertüre *f*

overturn [əʊvə'tɜːn] *vt, vi* umkippen

overweight ['əʊvə'weɪt] *adj* zu dick

overwhelm [əʊvə'welm] *vt* überwältigen; ~**ing** *adj* überwältigend

overwork ['əʊvə'wɜːk] *n* Überarbeitung
f ♦ *vt* überlasten ♦ *vi* sich überarbeiten

overwrought ['əʊvə'rɔːt] *adj* überreizt

owe [əʊ] *vt* schulden; **to ~ sth to sb**
(*money*) jdm etw schulden; (*favour
etc*) jdm etw verdanken

owing to ['əʊɪŋ-] *prep* wegen +*gen*

owl [aʊl] *n* Eule *f*

own [əʊn] *vt* besitzen ♦ *adj* eigen; **a**

room of my ~ mein eigenes Zimmer; **to get one's** ~ **back** sich rächen; **on one's** ~ **allein**; ~ **up** vi: **to** ~ **up** (**to sth**) (etw) zugeben; ~**er** n Besitzer(in) m(f); ~**ership** n Besitz m

ox [ɒks] (pl **oxen**) n Ochse m

oxen ['ɒksn] npl of ox

oxtail ['ɒksteɪl] n: ~ **soup** Ochsenschwanzsuppe f

oxygen ['ɒksɪdʒən] n Sauerstoff m; ~ **mask** n Sauerstoffmaske f; ~ **tent** n Sauerstoffzelt nt

oyster ['ɔɪstə*] n Auster f

oz. abbr = **ounce(s)**

P

p [piː] abbr = **penny**; **pence**

pa [pɑː] (inf) n Papa m

P.A. n abbr = **personal assistant**; **public address system**

p.a. abbr = **per annum**

pace [peɪs] n Schritt m; (speed) Tempo nt ♦ vi schreiten; **to keep** ~ **with** Schritt halten mit; ~-**maker** n Schrittmacher m

pacific [pə'sɪfɪk] adj pazifisch ♦ n: **the P~** (**Ocean**) der Pazifik

pacifist ['pæsɪfɪst] n Pazifist m

pacify ['pæsɪfaɪ] vt befrieden; (calm) beruhigen

pack [pæk] n (of goods) Packung f; (of hounds) Meute f; (of cards) Spiel nt; (gang) Bande f ♦ vt (case) packen; (clothes) einpacken ♦ vi packen; **to** ~ **sb off to** ... jdn nach ... schicken; ~ **it in!** laß es gut sein!

package ['pækɪdʒ] n Paket nt; ~ **tour** n Pauschalreise f

packed lunch ['pækt-] n Lunchpaket nt

packet ['pækɪt] n Päckchen nt

packing ['pækɪŋ] n (action) Packen nt; (material) Verpackung f; ~ **case** n (Pack)kiste f

pact [pækt] n Pakt m, Vertrag m

pad [pæd] n (of paper) (Schreib)block m; (stuffing) Polster nt ♦ vt polstern; ~**ding** n Polsterung f

paddle ['pædl] n Paddel nt; (US: for ta-

ble tennis) Schläger m ♦ vt (boat) paddeln ♦ vi (in sea) planschen; ~ **steamer** n Raddampfer m

paddling pool ['pædlɪŋ-] (BRIT) n Planschbecken nt

paddock ['pædək] n Koppel f

paddy field ['pædɪ-] n Reisfeld nt

padlock ['pædlɒk] n Vorhängeschloß nt ♦ vt verschließen

paediatrics [piːdɪ'ætrɪks] (US **pediatrics**) n Kinderheilkunde f

pagan ['peɪɡən] adj heidnisch ♦ n Heide m, Heidin f

page [peɪdʒ] n Seite f; (person) Page m ♦ vt (in hotel etc) ausrufen lassen

pageant ['pædʒənt] n Festzug m; ~**ry** n Gepränge nt

paid [peɪd] pt, pp of **pay** ♦ adj bezahlt; **to put** ~ **to** (BRIT) zunichte machen

pail [peɪl] n Eimer m

pain [peɪn] n Schmerz m; **to be in** ~ Schmerzen haben; **on** ~ **of death** bei Todesstrafe; **to take** ~**s to do sth** sich dat Mühe geben, etw zu tun; ~**ed** adj (expression) gequält; ~**ful** adj (physically) schmerzhaft; (embarrassing) peinlich; (difficult) mühsam; ~**fully** adv (fig: very) schrecklich; ~**killer** n Schmerzmittel nt; ~**less** adj schmerzlos; **painstaking** ['peɪnzteɪkɪŋ] adj gewissenhaft

paint [peɪnt] n Farbe f ♦ vt anstreichen; (picture) malen; **to** ~ **the door blue** die Tür blau streichen; ~**brush** n Pinsel m; ~**er** n Maler m; ~**ing** n Malerei f; (picture) Gemälde nt; ~**work** n Anstrich m; (of car) Lack m

pair [pɛə*] n Paar nt; ~ **of scissors** Schere f; ~ **of trousers** Hose f

pajamas [pə'dʒɑːməz] (US) npl Schlafanzug m

Pakistan [pɑːkɪ'stɑːn] n Pakistan nt; ~**i** adj pakistanisch ♦ n Pakistani mf

pal [pæl] (inf) n Kumpel m

palace ['pæləs] n Palast m, Schloß nt

palatable ['pælətəbl] adj schmackhaft

palate ['pælɪt] n Gaumen m

palatial [pə'leɪʃəl] adj palastartig

palaver [pə'lɑːvə*] (inf) n Theater nt

pale [peɪl] adj blaß, bleich ♦ n: **to be**

beyond the ~ die Grenzen überschreiten
Palestine ['pælɪstaɪn] n Palästina nt
Palestinian [pælɪs'tɪnɪən] adj palästinen-
sisch ♦ n Palästinenser(in) m(f)
palette ['pælɪt] n Palette f
paling ['peɪlɪŋ] n (stake) Zaunpfahl m;
(fence) Lattenzaun m
pall [pɔːl] n (of smoke) (Rauch)wolke f
♦ vi jeden Reiz verlieren, verblassen
pallet ['pælɪt] n (for goods) Palette f
pallid ['pælɪd] adj blaß, bleich
pallor ['pælə*] n Blässe f
palm [pɑːm] n (of hand) Handfläche f;
(also: ~ tree) Palme f ♦ vt: **to** ~ **sth
off on sb** jdm etw andrehen; **P**~ **Sunday** n Palmsonntag m
palpable ['pælpəbl] adj (also fig)
greifbar
palpitation [pælpɪ'teɪʃən] n Herzklopfen
nt
paltry ['pɔːltrɪ] adj armselig
pamper ['pæmpə*] vt verhätscheln
pamphlet ['pæmflət] n Broschüre f
pan [pæn] n Pfanne f ♦ vi (CINE)
schwenken
panacea [pænə'sɪə] n (fig) Allheilmittel
nt
panache [pə'næʃ] n Schwung m
pancake ['pænkeɪk] n Pfannkuchen m
pancreas ['pæŋkrɪəs] n Bauchspeichel-
drüse f
panda ['pændə] n Panda m; ~ **car**
(BRIT) n (Funk)streifenwagen m
pandemonium [pændɪ'məʊnɪəm] n Hölle
f; (noise) Höllenlärm m
pander ['pændə*] vi: **to** ~ **to** sich richten
nach
pane [peɪn] n (Fenster)scheibe f
panel ['pænl] n (of wood) Tafel f; (TV)
Diskussionsrunde f; ~**ling** (US **paneling**)
n Täfelung f
pang [pæŋ] n: ~**s of hunger** quälende(r)
Hunger m; ~**s of conscience**
Gewissensbisse pl
panic ['pænɪk] n Panik f ♦ vi in Panik
geraten; **don't** ~ (nur) keine Panik;
~**ky** adj (person) überängstlich; ~-
stricken adj von panischem Schrecken
erfaßt; (look) panisch
pansy ['pænzɪ] n (flower) Stiefmütter-

chen nt; (inf) Schwule(r) m
pant [pænt] vi keuchen; (dog) hecheln
panther ['pænθə*] n Panther m
panties ['pæntɪz] npl (Damen)slip m
pantihose ['pæntɪhəʊz] (US) n Strumpfhose f
pantomime ['pæntəmaɪm] (BRIT) n
Märchenkomödie f um Weihnachten
pantry ['pæntrɪ] n Vorratskammer f
pants [pænts] npl (BRIT: woman's)
Schlüpfer m; (: man's) Unterhose f;
(US: trousers) Hose f
papal ['peɪpəl] adj päpstlich
paper ['peɪpə*] n Papier nt; (news~)
Zeitung f; (essay) Referat nt ♦ adj
Papier-, aus Papier ♦ vt (wall)
tapezieren; ~**s** npl (identity ~s) Aus-
weis(papiere pl) nt; ~**back** n Taschenbuch nt; ~ **bag** n Tüte f; ~ **clip** n
Büroklammer f; ~ **hankie** n Tempota-
schentuch nt (®); ~**weight** n Briefbe-
schwerer m; ~**work** n Schreibarbeit f
par [pɑː*] n (COMM) Nennwert m;
(GOLF) Par nt; **on a** ~ **with** ebenbürtig
+dat
parable ['pærəbl] n (REL) Gleichnis nt
parachute ['pærəʃuːt] n Fallschirm m ♦
vi (mit dem Fallschirm) abspringen
parade [pə'reɪd] n Parade f ♦ vt auf-
marschieren lassen; (fig) zur Schau
stellen ♦ vi paradieren, vorbeimarschieren
paradise ['pærədaɪs] n Paradies nt
paradox ['pærədɒks] n Paradox nt;
~**ically** [pærə'dɒksɪkəlɪ] adv paradoxer-
weise
paraffin ['pærəfɪn] (BRIT) n Paraffin nt
paragon ['pærəgən] n Muster nt
paragraph ['pærəgrɑːf] n Absatz m
parallel ['pærəlel] adj parallel ♦ n
Parallele f
paralysis [pə'rælɪsɪs] n Lähmung f
paralyze ['pærəlaɪz] vt lähmen
parameter [pə'ræmɪtə*] n Parameter m;
~**s** npl (framework, limits) Rahmen m
paramount ['pærəmaʊnt] adj höchste(r,
s), oberste(r, s)
paranoid ['pærənɔɪd] adj paranoid
parapet ['pærəpɪt] n Brüstung f
paraphernalia ['pærəfə'neɪlɪə] n Zubehör

nt, Utensilien *pl*

paraphrase ['pærəfreɪz] *vt* umschreiben

paraplegic [pærə'pli:dʒɪk] *n* Querschnittsgelähmte(r) *mf*

parasite ['pærəsaɪt] *n* (*also fig*) Schmarotzer *m*, Parasit *m*

parasol ['pærəsɒl] *n* Sonnenschirm *m*

paratrooper ['pærətru:pə*] *n* Fallschirmjäger *m*

parcel ['pɑːsl] *n* Paket *nt* ♦ *vt* (*also*: ~ up) einpacken

parch [pɑːtʃ] *vt* (aus)dörren; ~ed *adj* ausgetrocknet; (*person*) am Verdursten

parchment ['pɑːtʃmənt] *n* Pergament *nt*

pardon ['pɑːdn] *n* Verzeihung *f* ♦ *vt* (*JUR*) begnadigen; ~ me!, I beg your ~! verzeihen Sie bitte!; ~ me? (*US*) wie bitte?; (I beg your) ~? wie bitte?

parent ['pɛərənt] *n* Elternteil *m*; ~s *npl* (*mother and father*) Eltern *pl*; ~al [pə'rentl] *adj* elterlich, Eltern-

parentheses [pə'renθɪsiːz] *npl of* **parenthesis**

parenthesis [pə'renθɪsɪs] *n* Klammer *f*; (*sentence*) Parenthese *f*

Paris ['pærɪs] *n* Paris *nt*

parish ['pærɪʃ] *n* Gemeinde *f*

parity ['pærɪtɪ] *n* (*FIN*) Umrechnungskurs *m*, Parität *f*

park [pɑːk] *n* Park *m* ♦ *vt, vi* parken

parking ['pɑːkɪŋ] *n* Parken *nt*; "no ~" „Parken verboten"; ~ lot (*US*) *n* Parkplatz *m*; ~ meter *n* Parkuhr *f*; ~ ticket *n* Strafzettel *m*

parlance ['pɑːləns] *n* Sprachgebrauch *m*

parliament ['pɑːləmənt] *n* Parlament *nt*; ~ary [pɑːlə'mentərɪ] *adj* parlamentarisch, Parlaments-

parlour ['pɑːlə*] (*US* parlor) *n* Salon *m*

parochial [pə'rəʊkɪəl] *adj* Gemeinde-; (*narrow-minded*) eng(stirnig)

parole [pə'rəʊl] *n*: on ~ (*prisoner*) auf Bewährung

paroxysm ['pærəksɪzəm] *n* Anfall *m*

parrot ['pærət] *n* Papagei *m*

parry ['pærɪ] *vt* parieren, abwehren

parsimonious [pɑːsɪ'məʊnɪəs] *adj* knauserig

parsley ['pɑːslɪ] *n* Petersilie *f*

parsnip ['pɑːsnɪp] *n* Pastinake *f*

parson ['pɑːsn] *n* Pfarrer *m*

part [pɑːt] *n* (*piece*) Teil *m*; (*THEAT*) Rolle *f*; (*of machine*) Teil *nt* ♦ *adv* = ~ly ♦ *vt* trennen; (*hair*) scheiteln ♦ *vi* (*people*) sich trennen; to take ~ in teilnehmen an +*dat*; to take sth in good ~ etw nicht übelnehmen; to take sb's ~ sich auf jds Seite *acc* stellen; for my ~ ich für meinen Teil; for the most ~ meistens, größtenteils; in ~ exchange (*BRIT*) in Zahlung; ~ with *vt fus* hergeben; (*renounce*) aufgeben; ~ial ['pɑːʃəl] *adj* (*incomplete*) teilweise; (*biased*) parteiisch; to be ~ial to eine (besondere) Vorliebe haben für

participant [pɑː'tɪsɪpənt] *n* Teilnehmer(in) *m(f)*

participate [pɑː'tɪsɪpeɪt] *vi*: to ~ (in) teilnehmen (an +*dat*)

participation [pɑːtɪsɪ'peɪʃən] *n* Teilnahme *f*; (*sharing*) Beteiligung *f*

participle ['pɑːtɪsɪpl] *n* Partizip *nt*

particle ['pɑːtɪkl] *n* Teilchen *nt*; (*GRAM*) Partikel *m*

particular [pə'tɪkjʊlə*] *adj* bestimmt; (*exact*) genau; (*fussy*) eigen; in ~ besonders; ~ly *adv* besonders; ~s *npl* (*details*) Einzelheiten *pl*; (*of person*) Personalien *pl*

parting ['pɑːtɪŋ] *n* (*separation*) Abschied *m*; (*BRIT*: *of hair*) Scheitel *m* ♦ *adj* Abschieds-

partition [pɑː'tɪʃən] *n* (*wall*) Trennwand *f*; (*division*) Teilung *f* ♦ *vt* aufteilen

partly ['pɑːtlɪ] *adv* zum Teil, teilweise

partner ['pɑːtnə*] *n* Partner *m* ♦ *vt* der Partner sein von; ~ship *n* Partnerschaft *f*; (*COMM*) Teilhaberschaft *f*

partridge ['pɑːtrɪdʒ] *n* Rebhuhn *nt*

part-time ['pɑːt'taɪm] *adj* Teilzeit- ♦ *adv* stundenweise

party ['pɑːtɪ] *n* (*POL, JUR*) Partei *f*; (*group*) Gesellschaft *f*; (*celebration*) Party *f* ♦ *adj* (*dress*) Party-; (*politics*) Partei-; ~ line *n* (*TEL*) Gemeinschaftsanschluß *m*

pass [pɑːs] *vt* (*on foot*) vorbeigehen an +*dat*; (*driving*) vorbeifahren an +*dat*; (*surpass*) übersteigen; (*hand on*) weitergeben; (*approve*) genehmigen;

(*time*) verbringen; (*exam*) bestehen ♦ *vi* (*go by*) vorbeigehen; vorbeifahren; (*years*) vergehen; (*be successful*) bestehen ♦ *n* (*in mountains, SPORT*) Paß *m*; (*permission*) Passierschein *m* (*in exam*): to get a ~ bestehen; to ~ sth through sth etw durch etw führen; to make a ~ at sb (*inf*) bei jdm Annäherungsversuche machen; ~ away *vi* (*euph*) verscheiden; ~ by *vi* vorbeigehen; vorbeifahren; (*years*) vergehen; ~ for *vt fus* gehalten werden für; ~ on *vt* weitergeben; ~ out *vi* (*faint*) ohnmächtig werden; ~ up *vt* vorbeigehen lassen; ~able *adj* (*road*) passierbar; (*fairly good*) passabel

passage ['pæsɪdʒ] *n* (*corridor*) Gang *m*; (*in book*) (Text)stelle *f*; (*voyage*) Überfahrt *f*; ~way *n* Durchgang *m*

passbook ['pɑːsbʊk] *n* Sparbuch *nt*

passenger ['pæsɪndʒə*] *n* Passagier *m*; (*on bus*) Fahrgast *m*

passer-by ['pɑːsə'baɪ] *n* Passant(in) *m(f)*

passing ['pɑːsɪŋ] *adj* (*car*) vorbeifahrend; (*thought, affair*) momentan ♦ *n*: in ~ en passant; ~ place *n* (*AUT*) Ausweichstelle *f*

passion ['pæʃən] *n* Leidenschaft *f*; ~ate *adj* leidenschaftlich

passive ['pæsɪv] *adj* passiv; (*LING*) passivisch

Passover ['pɑːsəʊvə*] *n* Passahfest *nt*

passport ['pɑːspɔːt] *n* (Reise)paß *m*; ~ control *n* Paßkontrolle *f*

password ['pɑːswɜːd] *n* Parole *f*, Kennwort *nt*, Losung *f*

past [pɑːst] *prep* (*motion*) an +*dat* ... vorbei; (*position*) hinter +*dat*; (*later than*) nach ♦ *adj* (*years*) vergangen; (*president etc*) ehemalig ♦ *n* Vergangenheit *f*; he's ~ forty er ist über vierzig; for the ~ few/3 days in den letzten paar/3 Tagen; to run ~ vorbeilaufen

pasta ['pæstə] *n* Teigwaren *pl*

paste [peɪst] *n* (*fish ~ etc*) Paste *f*; (*glue*) Kleister *m* ♦ *vt* kleben; (*put ~ on*) mit Kleister bestreichen

pasteurized ['pæstəraɪzd] *adj* pasteurisiert

pastime ['pɑːstaɪm] *n* Zeitvertreib *m*

pastor ['pɑːstə*] *n* Pfarrer *m*

pastry ['peɪstrɪ] *n* Blätterteig *m*; **pastries** *npl* (*tarts etc*) Stückchen *pl*

pasture ['pɑːstʃə*] *n* Weide *f*

pasty [*n* 'pæstɪ, *adj* peɪstɪ] *n* (Fleisch)pastete *f* ♦ *adj* bläßlich, käsig

pat [pæt] *n* leichte(r) Schlag *m*, Klaps *m* ♦ *vt* tätscheln

patch [pætʃ] *n* Fleck *m* ♦ *vt* flicken; (to go through) a bad ~ eine Pechsträhne (haben); ~ up *vt* flicken; (*quarrel*) beilegen; ~y *adj* (*irregular*) ungleichmäßig

pâté ['pæteɪ] *n* Pastete *f*

patent ['peɪtənt] *n* Patent *nt* ♦ *vt* patentieren lassen; (*by authorities*) patentieren ♦ *adj* offenkundig; ~ leather *n* Lackleder *nt*

paternal [pə'tɜːnl] *adj* väterlich

paternity [pə'tɜːnɪtɪ] *n* Vaterschaft *f*

path [pɑːθ] *n* Pfad *m*; Weg *m*; (*of the sun*) Bahn *f*

pathetic [pə'θetɪk] *adj* (*very bad*) kläglich

pathological [pæθə'lɒdʒɪkl] *adj* pathologisch

pathology [pə'θɒlədʒɪ] *n* Pathologie *f*

pathos ['peɪθɒs] *n* Rührseligkeit *f*

pathway ['pɑːθweɪ] *n* Weg *m*

patience ['peɪʃəns] *n* Geduld *f*; (*BRIT: CARDS*) Patience *f*

patient ['peɪʃənt] *n* Patient(in) *m(f)*, Kranke(r) *mf* ♦ *adj* geduldig

patio ['pætɪəʊ] *n* Terrasse *f*

patriotic [pætrɪ'ɒtɪk] *adj* patriotisch

patrol [pə'trəʊl] *n* Patrouille *f*; (*police*) Streife *f* ♦ *vt* patrouillieren in +*dat* ♦ *vi* (*police*) die Runde machen; (*MIL*) patrouillieren; ~ car *n* Streifenwagen *m*; ~man (*US: irreg*) *n* (Streifen)polizist *m*

patron ['peɪtrən] *n* (*in shop*) (Stamm)kunde *m*; (*in hotel*) (Stamm)gast *m*; (*supporter*) Förderer *m*; ~ of the arts Mäzen *m*; ~age ['pætrənɪdʒ] *n* Schirmherrschaft *f*; ~ize ['pætrənaɪz] *vt* (*support*) unterstützen; (*shop*) besuchen; (*treat condescendingly*) von oben herab behandeln; ~ saint *n* Schutzpatron(in) *m(f)*

patter ['pætə*] *n* (*sound: of feet*) Trappeln *nt*; (*: of rain*) Prasseln *nt*; (*sales talk*) Gerede *nt* ♦ *vi* (*feet*) trappeln; (*rain*) prasseln

pattern ['pætən] *n* Muster *nt*; (*SEWING*) Schnittmuster *nt*; (*KNITTING*) Strickanleitung *f*

paunch [pɔ:ntʃ] *n* Wanst *m*

pauper ['pɔ:pə*] *n* Arme(r) *mf*

pause [pɔ:z] *n* Pause *f* ♦ *vi* innehalten

pave [peɪv] *vt* pflastern; **to ~ the way for** den Weg bahnen für

pavement ['peɪvmənt] (*BRIT*) *n* Bürgersteig *m*

pavilion [pə'vɪlɪən] *n* Pavillon *m*; (*SPORT*) Klubhaus *nt*

paving ['peɪvɪŋ] *n* Straßenpflaster *nt*; **~ stone** *n* Pflasterstein *m*

paw [pɔ:] *n* Pfote *f*; (*of big cats*) Tatze *f*, Pranke *f* ♦ *vt* (*scrape*) scharren; (*handle*) betatschen

pawn [pɔ:n] *n* Pfand *nt*; (*chess*) Bauer *m* ♦ *vt* verpfänden; **~broker** *n* Pfandleiher *m*; **~shop** *n* Pfandhaus *nt*

pay [peɪ] (*pt, pp* **paid**) *n* Bezahlung *f*, Lohn *m* ♦ *vt* bezahlen ♦ *vi* zahlen; (*be profitable*) sich bezahlt machen; **to ~ attention (to)** achtgeben (auf +*acc*); **~ back** *vt* zurückzahlen; **~ for** *vt fus* bezahlen; **~ in** *vt* einzahlen; **~ off** *vt* abzahlen ♦ *vi* (*scheme, decision*) sich bezahlt machen; **~ up** *vi* bezahlen; **~able** *adj* zahlbar, fällig; **~ee** [per'i:] *n* Zahlungsempfänger *m*; **~ envelope** (*US*) *n* Lohntüte *f*; **~ment** *n* Bezahlung *f*; **advance ~ment** Vorauszahlung *f*; **monthly ~ment** monatliche Rate *f*; **~ packet** (*BRIT*) *n* Lohntüte *f*; **~ phone** *n* Münzfernsprecher *m*; **~roll** *n* Lohnliste *f*; **~ slip** *n* Lohn-/Gehaltsstreifen *m*

PC *n abbr* = **personal computer**

p.c. *abbr* = **per cent**

pea [pi:] *n* Erbse *f*

peace [pi:s] *n* Friede(n) *m*; **~able** *adj* friedlich; **~ful** *adj* friedlich, ruhig; **~keeping** *adj* Friedens-

peach [pi:tʃ] *n* Pfirsich *m*

peacock ['pi:kɒk] *n* Pfau *m*

peak [pi:k] *n* Spitze *f*; (*of mountain*)

Gipfel *m*; (*fig*) Höhepunkt *m*; **~ period** *n* Stoßzeit *f*, Hauptzeit *f*

peal [pi:l] *n* (Glocken)läuten *nt*; **~s of laughter** schallende(s) Gelächter *nt*

peanut ['pi:nʌt] *n* Erdnuß *f*; **~ butter** *n* Erdnußbutter *f*

pear [pɛə*] *n* Birne *f*

pearl [pɜ:l] *n* Perle *f*

peasant ['pezənt] *n* Bauer *m*

peat [pi:t] *n* Torf *m*

pebble ['pebl] *n* Kiesel *m*

peck [pek] *vt, vi* picken ♦ *n* (*with beak*) Schnabelhieb *m*; (*kiss*) flüchtige(r) Kuß *m*; **~ing order** *n* Hackordnung *f*; **~ish** (*BRIT: inf*) *adj* ein bißchen hungrig

peculiar [pɪ'kju:lɪə*] *adj* (*odd*) seltsam; **~ to** charakteristisch für; **~ity** [pɪkju:lɪ'ærɪtɪ] *n* (*singular quality*) Besonderheit *f*; (*strangeness*) Eigenartigkeit *f*

pedal ['pedl] *n* Pedal *nt* ♦ *vt, vi* (*cycle*) fahren, radfahren

pedantic [pɪ'dæntɪk] *adj* pedantisch

peddler ['pedlə*] *n* Hausierer(in) *m(f)*; (*of drugs*) Drogenhändler(in) *m(f)*

pedestal ['pedɪstl] *n* Sockel *m*

pedestrian [pɪ'destrɪən] *n* Fußgänger *m* ♦ *adj* Fußgänger-; (*humdrum*) langweilig; **~ crossing** (*BRIT*) *n* Fußgängerüberweg *m*

pediatrics [pi:dɪ'ætrɪks] (*US*) *n* = **paediatrics**

pedigree ['pedɪgri:] *n* Stammbaum *m* ♦ *cpd* (*animal*) reinrassig, Zucht-

pedlar ['pedlə*] *n* = **peddler**

pee [pi:] (*inf*) *vi* pissen, pinkeln

peek [pi:k] *vi* gucken

peel [pi:l] *n* Schale *f* ♦ *vt* schälen ♦ *vi* (*paint etc*) abblättern; (*skin*) sich schälen

peep [pi:p] *n* (*BRIT: look*) kurze(r) Blick *m*; (*sound*) Piepsen *nt* ♦ *vi* (*BRIT: look*) gucken; **~ out** *vi* herausgucken; **~hole** *n* Guckloch *nt*

peer [pɪə*] *vi* starren; (*peep*) gucken ♦ *n* (*nobleman*) Peer *m*; (*equal*) Ebenbürtige(r) *m*; **~age** *n* Peerswürde *f*

peeved [pi:vd] *adj* ärgerlich; (*person*) sauer

peevish ['pi:vɪʃ] *adj* verdrießlich

peg [peg] n (stake) Pflock m; (BRIT: also: clothes ~) Wäscheklammer f

Peking [pi:'kɪŋ] n Peking nt

pelican ['pelɪkən] n Pelikan m; ~ crossing (BRIT) n (AUT) Ampelüberweg m

pellet ['pelɪt] n Kügelchen nt

pelmet ['pelmɪt] n Blende f

pelt [pelt] vt bewerfen ♦ vi (rain) schütten ♦ n Pelz m, Fell nt

pelvis ['pelvɪs] n Becken nt

pen [pen] n (fountain ~) Federhalter m; (ball-point ~) Kuli m; (for sheep) Pferch m

penal ['pi:nl] adj Straf-; ~ize vt (punish) bestrafen; (disadvantage) benachteiligen; ~ty ['penəltɪ] n Strafe f; (FOOTBALL) Elfmeter m; ~ty (kick) n Elfmeter m

penance ['penəns] n Buße f

pence [pens] (BRIT) npl of penny

pencil ['pensl] n Bleistift m; ~ case n Federmäppchen nt; ~ sharpener n Bleistiftspitzer m

pendant ['pendənt] n Anhänger m

pending ['pendɪŋ] prep bis (zu) ♦ adj unentschieden, noch offen

pendulum ['pendjuləm] n Pendel nt

penetrate ['penɪtreɪt] vt durchdringen; (enter into) eindringen in +acc

penetration [penɪ'treɪʃən] n Durchdringen nt; Eindringen nt

penfriend ['penfrend] (BRIT) n Brieffreund(in) m(f)

penguin ['peŋgwɪn] n Pinguin m

penicillin [penɪ'sɪlɪn] n Penizillin nt

peninsula [pɪ'nɪnsjulə] n Halbinsel f

penis ['pi:nɪs] n Penis m

penitence ['penɪtəns] n Reue f

penitent ['penɪtənt] adj reuig

penitentiary [penɪ'tenʃərɪ] (US) n Zuchthaus nt

penknife ['pennaɪf] n Federmesser nt

pen name n Pseudonym nt

penniless ['penɪləs] adj mittellos

penny ['penɪ] (pl pennies or BRIT pence) n Penny m; (US) Centstück nt

penpal ['penpæl] n Brieffreund(in) m(f)

pension ['penʃən] n Rente f; ~er (BRIT) n Rentner(in) m(f); ~ fund n Rentenfonds m

pensive ['pensɪv] adj nachdenklich

Pentecost ['pentɪkɒst] n Pfingsten pl or nt

penthouse ['penthaus] n Dachterrassenwohnung f

pent-up ['pentʌp] adj (feelings) angestaut

penultimate [pɪ'nʌltɪmət] adj vorletzte(r, s)

people ['pi:pl] n (nation) Volk nt ♦ npl (persons) Leute pl; (inhabitants) Bevölkerung f ♦ vt besiedeln; several ~ came mehrere Leute kamen; ~ say that ... man sagt, daß ...

pep [pep] (inf) n Schwung m, Schmiß m; ~ up vt aufmöbeln

pepper ['pepə*] n Pfeffer m; (vegetable) Paprika m ♦ vt (pelt) bombardieren; ~mint n (plant) Pfefferminze f; (sweet) Pfefferminz nt

peptalk ['peptɔ:k] (inf) n Anstachelung f

per [pɜ:*] prep pro; ~ day/person pro Tag/Person; ~ annum adv pro Jahr; ~ capita adj (income) Pro-Kopf- ♦ adv pro Kopf

perceive [pə'si:v] vt (realize) wahrnehmen; (understand) verstehen

per cent [pə'sent] n Prozent nt

percentage [pə'sentɪdʒ] n Prozentsatz m

perception [pə'sepʃən] n Wahrnehmung f; (insight) Einsicht f

perceptive [pə'septɪv] adj (person) aufmerksam; (analysis) tiefgehend

perch [pɜ:tʃ] n Stange f; (fish) Flußbarsch m ♦ vi sitzen, hocken

percolator ['pɜ:kəleɪtə*] n Kaffeemaschine f

percussion [pɜ:'kʌʃən] n (MUS) Schlagzeug nt

peremptory [pə'remptərɪ] adj schroff

perennial [pə'renɪəl] adj wiederkehrend; (everlasting) unvergänglich

perfect [adj, n 'pɜ:fɪkt, vb pə'fekt] adj vollkommen; (crime, solution) perfekt ♦ n (GRAM) Perfekt nt ♦ vt vervollkommnen; ~ion [pə'fekʃən] n Vollkommenheit f; ~ionist [pə'fekʃənɪst] n Perfektionist m; ~ly adv vollkommen, perfekt; (quite) ganz, einfach

perforate ['pɜ:fəreɪt] vt durchlöchern

perforation [pə:fə'reɪʃən] n Perforieren nt; (line of holes) Perforation f
perform [pə'fɔ:m] vt (carry out) durchor ausführen; (task) verrichten; (THEAT) spielen, geben ♦ vi (THEAT) auftreten; ~**ance** n Durchführung f; (efficiency) Leistung f; (show) Vorstellung f; ~**er** n Künstler(in) m(f); ~**ing** adj (animal) dressiert
perfume [pə:fju:m] n Duft m; (lady's) Parfüm nt
perfunctory [pə'fʌŋktərɪ] adj oberflächlich, mechanisch
perhaps [pə'hæps] adv vielleicht
peril ['perɪl] n Gefahr f
perimeter [pə'rɪmɪtə*] n Peripherie f; (of circle etc) Umfang m
period ['pɪərɪəd] n Periode f; (GRAM) Punkt m; (MED) Periode f ♦ adj (costume) historisch; ~**ic** [pɪərɪ'ɒdɪk] adj periodisch; ~**ical** [pɪərɪ'ɒdɪkəl] n Zeitschrift f; ~**ically** [pɪərɪ'ɒdɪkəlɪ] adv periodisch
peripheral [pə'rɪfərəl] adj Rand-, peripher ♦ n (COMPUT) Peripheriegerät nt
perish ['perɪʃ] vi umkommen; (fruit) verderben; ~**able** adj leicht verderblich
perjury ['pə:dʒərɪ] n Meineid m
perk [pə:k] (inf) n (fringe benefit) Vergünstigung f; ~ **up** vi munter werden; ~**y** adj (cheerful) keck
perm [pə:m] n Dauerwelle f
permanent ['pə:mənənt] adj dauernd, ständig
permeate ['pə:mɪeɪt] vt, vi durchdringen
permissible [pə'mɪsəbl] adj zulässig
permission [pə'mɪʃən] n Erlaubnis f
permissive [pə'mɪsɪv] adj nachgiebig; **the** ~ **society** die permissive Gesellschaft
permit [n 'pə:mɪt, vb pə'mɪt] n Zulassung f ♦ vt erlauben, zulassen
pernicious [pə:'nɪʃəs] adj schädlich
perpendicular [pə:pən'dɪkjulə*] adj senkrecht
perpetrate ['pə:pɪtreɪt] vt begehen
perpetual [pə'petjuəl] adj dauernd, ständig
perpetuate [pə'petjueɪt] vt verewigen,

bewahren
perplex [pə'pleks] vt verblüffen
persecute ['pə:sɪkju:t] vt verfolgen
persecution [pə:sɪ'kju:ʃən] n Verfolgung f
perseverance [pə:sɪ'vɪərəns] n Ausdauer f
persevere [pə:sɪ'vɪə*] vi durchhalten
Persian ['pə:ʃən] adj persisch ♦ n Perser(in) m(f); **the** ~ **Gulf** der Persische Golf
persist [pə'sɪst] vi (in belief etc) bleiben; (rain, smell) andauern; (continue) nicht aufhören; **to** ~ **in** bleiben bei; ~**ence** n Beharrlichkeit f; ~**ent** adj beharrlich; (unending) ständig
person ['pə:sn] n Person f; **in** ~ persönlich; ~**able** adj gut aussehend; ~**al** adj persönlich; (private) privat; (of body) körperlich, Körper-; ~**al assistant** n Assistent(in) m(f); ~**al computer** n Personalcomputer m; ~**ality** [pə:sə'nælɪtɪ] n Persönlichkeit f; ~**ally** adv persönlich; ~**ify** [pə:'sɒnɪfaɪ] vt verkörpern
personnel [pə:sə'nel] n Personal nt
perspective [pə'spektɪv] n Perspektive f
Perspex ['pə:speks] (®) n Acrylglas nt
perspiration [pə:spə'reɪʃən] n Transpiration f
perspire [pəs'paɪə*] vi transpirieren
persuade [pə'sweɪd] vt überreden; (convince) überzeugen
persuasion [pə'sweɪʒən] n Überredung f; Überzeugung f
persuasive [pə'sweɪsɪv] adj überzeugend
pert [pə:t] adj keck
pertaining [pə:'teɪnɪŋ]: ~ **to** prep betreffend +acc
pertinent ['pə:tɪnənt] adj relevant
perturb [pə'tə:b] vt beunruhigen
peruse [pə'ru:z] vt lesen
pervade [pə:'veɪd] vt erfüllen
perverse [pə'və:s] adj pervers; (obstinate) eigensinnig
pervert [n 'pə:və:t, vb pə'və:t] n perverse(r) Mensch m ♦ vt verdrehen; (morally) verderben
pessimist ['pesɪmɪst] n Pessimist m;

~ic [pesɪ'mɪstɪk] adj pessimistisch
pest [pest] n (insect) Schädling m; (fig: person) Nervensäge f; (: thing) Plage f
pester ['pestə*] vt plagen
pesticide ['pestɪsaɪd] n Insektenvertilgungsmittel nt
pot [pɒt] n (animal) Haustier nt ♦ vt liebkosen, streicheln ♦ vi (inf) Petting machen
petal ['petl] n Blütenblatt nt
peter out ['piːtə-] vi allmählich zu Ende gehen
petite [pə'tiːt] adj zierlich
petition [pə'tɪʃən] n Bittschrift f
petrified ['petrɪfaɪd] adj versteinert; (person) starr (vor Schreck)
petrify ['petrɪfaɪ] vt versteinern; (person) erstarren lassen
petrol ['petrəl] (BRIT) n Benzin nt, Kraftstoff m; two-/four-star ~ ≈ Normal-/Superbenzin nt; ~ can n Benzinkanister m
petroleum [pɪ'trəʊlɪəm] n Petroleum nt
petrol: ~ pump (BRIT) n (in car) Benzinpumpe f; (at garage) Zapfsäule f; ~ station (BRIT) n Tankstelle f; ~ tank (BRIT) n Benzintank m
petticoat ['petɪkəʊt] n Unterrock m
petty ['petɪ] adj (unimportant) unbedeutend; (mean) kleinlich; ~ cash n Portokasse f; ~ officer n Maat m
petulant ['petjʊlənt] adj leicht reizbar
pew [pjuː] n Kirchenbank f
pewter ['pjuːtə*] n Zinn nt
pharmacist ['fɑːməsɪst] n Pharmazeut m; (druggist) Apotheker m
pharmacy ['fɑːməsɪ] n Pharmazie f; (shop) Apotheke f
phase [feɪz] n Phase f ♦ vt: to ~ sth in etw allmählich einführen; to ~ sth out etw auslaufen lassen
Ph.D. n abbr = Doctor of Philosophy
pheasant ['feznt] n Fasan m
phenomena [fɪ'nɒmɪnə] npl of phenomenon
phenomenon [fɪ'nɒmɪnən] n Phänomen nt
philanthropist [fɪ'lænθrəpɪst] n Philanthrop m, Menschenfreund m
Philippines ['fɪlɪpiːnz] npl: the ~ die Philippinen pl
philosopher [fɪ'lɒsəfə*] n Philosoph m
philosophical [fɪlə'sɒfɪkl] adj philosophisch
philosophy [fɪ'lɒsəfɪ] n Philosophie f
phlegm [flem] n (MED) Schleim m; (calmness) Gelassenheit f; ~atic [fleg'mætɪk] adj gelassen
phobia ['fəʊbjə] n Phobie f
phone [fəʊn] n Telefon nt ♦ vt, vi telefonieren, anrufen; to be on the ~ telephonieren; ~ back vt, vi zurückrufen; ~ up vt, vi anrufen; ~ book n Telefonbuch nt; ~ booth n Telefonzelle f; ~ box n Telefonzelle f; ~ call n Telefonanruf m; ~-in n (RADIO, TV) Phone-in nt
phonetics [fə'netɪks] n Phonetik f
phoney ['fəʊnɪ] (inf) adj unecht ♦ n (person) Schwindler m; (thing) Fälschung f; (banknote) Blüte f
phonograph ['fəʊnəgrɑːf] (US) n Grammophon nt
phony ['fəʊnɪ] adj, n = phoney
photo ['fəʊtəʊ] n Foto nt
photocopier ['fəʊtəʊkɒpɪə*] n Kopiergerät nt
photocopy ['fəʊtəʊkɒpɪ] n Fotokopie f ♦ vt fotokopieren
photogenic [fəʊtəʊ'dʒenɪk] adj fotogen
photograph ['fəʊtəgrɑːf] n Fotografie f, Aufnahme f ♦ vt fotografieren; ~er [fə'tɒgrəfə*] n Fotograf m; ~ic ['fəʊtə'græfɪk] adj fotografisch; ~y [fə'tɒgrəfɪ] n Fotografie f
phrase [freɪz] n Satz m; (expression) Ausdruck m ♦ vt ausdrücken, formulieren; ~ book n Sprachführer m
physical ['fɪzɪkəl] adj physikalisch; (bodily) körperlich, physisch; ~ education n Turnen nt; ~ly adv physikalisch
physician [fɪ'zɪʃən] n Arzt m
physicist ['fɪzɪsɪst] n Physiker(in) m(f)
physics ['fɪzɪks] n Physik f
physiotherapy [fɪzɪə'θerəpɪ] n Heilgymnastik f, Physiotherapie f
physique [fɪ'ziːk] n Körperbau m
pianist ['pɪənɪst] n Pianist(in) m(f)
piano [pɪ'ænəʊ] n Klavier nt
pick [pɪk] n (tool) Pickel m; (choice)

Auswahl f ♦ vt (fruit) pflücken; (choose) aussuchen; **take your** ~ such dir etwas aus; **to** ~ **sb's pocket** jdn bestehlen; ~ **off** vt (kill) abschießen; ~ **on** vt fus (person) herumhacken auf +dat; ~ **out** vt auswählen; ~ **up** vi (improve) sich erholen ♦ vt (lift up) aufheben; (learn) (schnell) mitbekommen; (collect) abholen; (girl) (sich dat) anlachen; (AUT: passenger) mitnehmen; (speed) gewinnen an +dat; **to** ~ **o.s. up** aufstehen

picket ['pɪkɪt] n (striker) Streikposten m ♦ vt (factory) Tonabnehmer m; (small truck) ~posten aufstellen vor +dat ♦ vi (Streik)posten stehen

pickle ['pɪkl] n (salty mixture) Pökel m; (inf) Klemme f ♦ vt (in Essig) einlegen; einpökeln

pickpocket ['pɪkpɒkɪt] n Taschendieb m

pick-up ['pɪkʌp] n (BRIT: on record player) Tonabnehmer m; (small truck) Lieferwagen m

picnic ['pɪknɪk] n Picknick nt ♦ vi picknicken

pictorial [pɪk'tɔːrɪəl] adj in Bildern

picture ['pɪktʃə*] n Bild nt ♦ vt (visualize) sich dat vorstellen; **the** ~**s** npl (BRIT) das Kino; **in the** ~ (fig) im Bild; ~ **book** n Bilderbuch nt

picturesque [pɪktʃə'resk] adj malerisch

pie [paɪ] n (meat) Pastete f; (fruit) Torte f

piece [piːs] n Stück nt ♦ vt: **to** ~ **together** zusammenstückeln; (fig) sich dat zusammenreimen; **to take to** ~**s** in Einzelteile zerlegen; ~**meal** adv stückweise, Stück für Stück; ~**work** n Akkordarbeit f

pie chart n Kreisdiagramm nt

pier [pɪə*] n Pier m, Mole f

pierce [pɪəs] vt durchstechen, durchbohren (also look); **piercing** ['pɪəsɪŋ] adj (cry) durchdringend

piety ['paɪətɪ] n Frömmigkeit f

pig [pɪg] n Schwein nt

pigeon ['pɪdʒən] n Taube f; ~**hole** n (compartment) Ablegefach nt

piggy bank ['pɪgɪ-] n Sparschwein nt

pigheaded ['pɪg'hedɪd] adj dickköpfig

piglet ['pɪglət] n Ferkel nt

pigskin ['pɪgskɪn] n Schweinsleder nt

pigsty ['pɪgstaɪ] n (also fig) Schweinestall m

pigtail ['pɪgteɪl] n Zopf m

pike [paɪk] n Pike f; (fish) Hecht m

pilchard ['pɪltʃəd] n Sardine f

pile [paɪl] n (of books, wood) Stapel m; (in ground) Pfahl m; (on carpet) Flausch m ♦ vt (also: ~ up) anhäufen ♦ vi (also: ~ up) sich anhäufen

piles [paɪlz] npl Hämorrhoiden pl

pile-up ['paɪlʌp] n (AUT) Massenzusammenstoß m

pilfering ['pɪlfərɪŋ] n Diebstahl m

pilgrim ['pɪlgrɪm] n Pilger(in) m(f); ~**age** n Wallfahrt f

pill [pɪl] n Tablette f, Pille f; **the** ~ die (Antibaby)pille

pillage ['pɪlɪdʒ] vt plündern

pillar ['pɪlə*] n Pfeiler m, Säule f (also fig); ~ **box** (BRIT) n Briefkasten m

pillion ['pɪljən] n Soziussitz m

pillory ['pɪlərɪ] vt (fig) anprangern

pillow ['pɪləʊ] n Kissen nt; ~**case** n Kissenbezug m

pilot ['paɪlət] n Pilot m; (NAUT) Lotse m ♦ adj (scheme etc) Versuchs- ♦ vt führen; (ship) lotsen; ~ **light** n Zündflamme f

pimp [pɪmp] n Zuhälter m

pimple ['pɪmpl] n Pickel m

pimply ['pɪmplɪ] adj pick(e)lig

pin [pɪn] n Nadel f; (for sewing) Stecknadel f; (TECH) Stift m, Bolzen m ♦ vt stecken; (keep in one position) pressen, drücken; **to** ~ **sth to sth** etw an etw acc heften; **to** ~ **sth on sb** (fig) jdm etw anhängen; ~**s and needles** Kribbeln nt; ~ **down** vt (fig: person): **to** ~ **sb down (to sth)** jdn (auf etw acc) festnageln

pinafore ['pɪnəfɔː*] n Schürze f; ~**dress** n Kleiderrock m

pinball ['pɪnbɔːl] n Flipper m

pincers ['pɪnsəz] npl Kneif- or Beißzange f; (MED) Pinzette f

pinch [pɪntʃ] n Zwicken nt, Kneifen nt; (of salt) Prise f ♦ vt zwicken, kneifen; (inf: steal) klauen; (: arrest)

schnappen ♦ vi (shoe) drücken; **at a ~**
notfalls, zur Not
pincushion ['pɪnkuʃən] n Nadelkissen nt
pine [paɪn] n (also: ~ **tree**) Kiefer f ♦
vi: **to ~ for** sich sehnen nach; **~ away**
vi sich zu Tode sehnen
pineapple ['paɪnæpl] n Ananas f
ping [pɪŋ] n Klingeln nt; **~-pong** ® n
Pingpong nt
pink [pɪŋk] adj rosa inv ♦ n Rosa nt;
(BOT) Nelke f
pinnacle ['pɪnəkl] n Spitze f
pinpoint ['pɪnpɔɪnt] vt festlegen
pinstripe ['pɪnstraɪp] n Nadelstreifen m
pint [paɪnt] n Pint nt; (BRIT: inf: of
beer) große(s) Bier nt
pioneer [paɪə'nɪə*] n Pionier m; (fig
also) Bahnbrecher m
pious ['paɪəs] adj fromm
pip [pɪp] n Kern m; **the ~s** npl (BRIT:
time signal on radio) das Zeitzeichen
pipe [paɪp] n (smoking) Pfeife f; (tube)
Rohr nt; (in house) (Rohr)leitung f ♦ vt
(durch Rohre) leiten; (MUS) blasen; **~s**
npl (also: bagpipes) Dudelsack m; **~
down** vi (be quiet) die Luft anhalten; **~
cleaner** n Pfeifenreiniger m; **~-
dream** n Luftschloß nt; **~line** n (for
oil) Pipeline f; **~r** n Pfeifer m;
(bagpipes) Dudelsackbläser m
piping ['paɪpɪŋ] adv: **~ hot** siedend heiß
piquant ['piːkənt] adj pikant
pique [piːk] n gekränkte(r) Stolz m
pirate ['paɪərɪt] n Pirat m, Seeräuber m;
~ radio (BRIT) n Piratensender m
Pisces ['paɪsiːz] n Fische pl
piss [pɪs] (inf) vi pissen; **~ed** (inf) adj
(drunk) voll
pistol ['pɪstl] n Pistole f
piston ['pɪstən] n Kolben m
pit [pɪt] n Grube f; (THEAT) Parterre nt;
(orchestra ~) Orchestergraben m ♦ vt
(mark with scars) zerfressen;
(compare): **to ~ sb against sb** jdn an
jdm messen; **the ~s** npl (MOTOR
RACING) die Boxen
pitch [pɪtʃ] n Wurf m; (of trader) Stand
m; (SPORT) (Spiel)feld nt; (MUS)
Tonlage f; (substance) Pech nt ♦ vt
werfen; (set up) aufschlagen ♦ vi

(NAUT) rollen; **to ~ a tent** ein Zelt aufbauen; **~-black** adj pechschwarz; **~ed
battle** n offene Schlacht f
pitcher ['pɪtʃə*] n Krug m
pitchfork ['pɪtʃfɔːk] n Heugabel f
piteous ['pɪtɪəs] adj kläglich,
erbärmlich
pitfall ['pɪtfɔːl] n (fig) Falle f
pith [pɪθ] n Mark nt
pithy ['pɪθɪ] adj prägnant
pitiful ['pɪtɪful] adj (deserving pity)
bedauernswert; (contemptible) jämmerlich
pitiless ['pɪtɪləs] adj erbarmungslos
pittance ['pɪtəns] n Hungerlohn m
pity ['pɪtɪ] n (sympathy) Mitleid nt ♦ vt
Mitleid haben mit; **what a ~!** wie
schade!
pivot ['pɪvət] n Drehpunkt m ♦ vi: **to ~
(on)** sich drehen (um)
pixie ['pɪksɪ] n Elf m, Elfe f
pizza ['piːtsə] n Pizza f
placard ['plækɑːd] n Plakat nt, Anschlag
m
placate [plə'keɪt] vt beschwichtigen
place [pleɪs] n Platz m; (spot) Stelle f;
(town etc) Ort m ♦ vt setzen, stellen,
legen; (order) aufgeben; (SPORT)
plazieren; (identify) unterbringen; **to
take ~** stattfinden; **out of ~** nicht am
rechten Platz; (fig: remark) unangebracht; **in the first ~** erstens; **to change
~s with sb** mit jdm den Platz tauschen;
to be ~d third (in race, exam) auf den
dritten Platz liegen
placid ['plæsɪd] adj gelassen, ruhig
plagiarism ['pleɪdʒɪərɪzəm] n Plagiat nt
plague [pleɪg] n Pest f; (fig) Plage f ♦
vt plagen
plaice [pleɪs] n Scholle f
plain [pleɪn] adj (clear) klar, deutlich;
(simple) einfach, schlicht; (not
beautiful) alltäglich ♦ n Ebene f; **in ~
clothes** (police) in Zivil(kleidung); **~
chocolate** n Bitterschokolade f
plaintiff ['pleɪntɪf] n Kläger m
plaintive ['pleɪntɪv] adj wehleidig
plait [plæt] n Zopf m ♦ vt flechten
plan [plæn] n Plan m ♦ vt, vi planen;
according to ~ planmäßig; **to ~ to do**

sth vorhaben, etw zu tun
plane [pleɪn] n Ebene f; (AVIAT)
Flugzeug nt; (tool) Hobel m; (tree)
Platane f
planet ['plænɪt] n Planet m
plank [plæŋk] n Brett nt
planning ['plænɪŋ] n Planung f; **family**
~ Familienplanung f; ~ **permission** n
Baugenehmigung f
plant [plɑːnt] n Pflanze f; (TECH) (Maschinen)anlage f; (factory) Fabrik f,
Werk nt ♦ vt pflanzen; (set firmly)
stellen
plantation [plæn'teɪʃən] n Plantage f
plaque [plæk] n Gedenktafel f; (on
teeth) (Zahn)belag m
plaster ['plɑːstə*] n Gips m; (in house)
Verputz m; (BRIT: also: sticking ~)
Pflaster nt; (for fracture: also: ~ of
Paris) Gipsverband m ♦ vt gipsen;
(hole) zugipsen; (ceiling) verputzen;
(fig: with pictures etc) bekleben, ver-
kleben; ~**ed** (inf) adj besoffen; ~**er** n
Gipser m
plastic ['plæstɪk] n Plastik nt or f ♦ adj
(made of ~) Plastik-; (ART) plastisch,
bildend; ~ **bag** n Plastiktüte f
plasticine ['plæstɪsiːn] (®) n Plastilin nt
plastic surgery n plastische Chirurgie
f
plate [pleɪt] n Teller m; (gold/silver ~)
vergoldete(s)/versilberte(s) Tafelge-
schirr nt; (flat sheet) Platte f; (in
book) (Bild)tafel f
plateau ['plætəʊ] (pl ~s or ~x) n
Plateau nt, Hochebene f
plateaux ['plætəʊz] npl of **plateau**
plate glass n Tafelglas nt
platform ['plætfɔːm] n (at meeting)
Plattform f, Podium nt; (RAIL) Bahnsteig m; (POL) Parteiprogramm nt; ~
ticket n Bahnsteigkarte f
platinum ['plætɪnəm] n Platin nt
platoon [plə'tuːn] n (MIL) Zug m
platter ['plætə*] n Platte f
plausible ['plɔːzɪbl] adj plausibel;
(person) überzeugend
play [pleɪ] n (also TECH) Spiel nt;
(THEAT) (Theater)stück nt ♦ vt spielen;
(another team) spielen gegen ♦ vi

spielen; **to ~ safe** auf Nummer sicher
gehen; ~ **down** vt herunterspielen; ~
up vi (cause trouble) frech werden;
(bad leg etc) weh tun ♦ vt (person)
plagen; **to ~ up to sb** jdm flattieren;
~-**acting** n Schauspielerei f; ~**boy** n
Playboy m; ~**er** n Spieler(in) m(f);
~**ful** adj spielerisch; ~**ground** n Spiel-
platz m; ~**group** n Kindergarten m;
~**ing card** n Spielkarte f; ~**ing field** n
Sportplatz m; ~**mate** n Spielkamerad
m; ~-**off** n (SPORT) Entscheidungsspiel
nt; ~**pen** n Laufstall m; ~**school** n =
~**group**; ~**thing** n Spielzeug nt;
~**wright** n Theaterschriftsteller m
plc abbr (= public limited company)
AG
plea [pliː] n Bitte f; (general appeal)
Appell m; (JUR) Plädoyer nt
plead [pliːd] vt (poverty) zur Entschuldigung anführen; (JUR: sb's case)
vertreten ♦ vi (beg) dringend bitten;
(JUR) plädieren; **to ~ with sb** jdn
dringend bitten
pleasant ['pleznt] adj angenehm; ~**ness**
n Angenehme(s) nt; (of person)
Freundlichkeit f; ~**ries** npl (polite
remarks) Nettigkeiten pl
please [pliːz] vt, vi (be agreeable to)
gefallen +dat; ~! bitte!; ~ **yourself!**
wie du willst!; ~**d** adj zufrieden;
(glad): ~**d** (about sth) erfreut (über
etw acc); ~**d to meet you** angenehm
pleasing ['pliːzɪŋ] adj erfreulich
pleasure ['pleʒə*] n Freude f; (old:
will) Wünsche pl ♦ cpd Vergnügungs-;
"**it's a ~**" „gern geschehen"
pleat [pliːt] n Falte f
plectrum ['plektrəm] n Plektron nt
pledge [pledʒ] n Pfand nt; (promise)
Versprechen nt ♦ vt verpfänden;
(promise) geloben, versprechen
plentiful ['plentɪfʊl] adj reichlich
plenty ['plentɪ] n Fülle f, Überfluß m; ~
of eine Menge, viel
pleurisy ['plʊərɪsɪ] n Rippenfellentzündung f
pliable ['plaɪəbl] adj biegsam; (person)
beeinflußbar
pliers ['plaɪəz] npl (Kneif)zange f

plight [plaɪt] n (Not)lage f
plimsolls ['plɪmsəlz] (BRIT) npl Turnschuhe pl
plinth [plɪnθ] n Sockel m
plod [plɒd] vi (work) sich abplagen; (walk) trotten; ~**der** n Arbeitstier nt
plonk [plɒŋk] n (BRIT: inf: wine) billige(r) Wein m ♦ vt: tö ~ sth down etw hinknallen
plot [plɒt] n Komplott nt; (story) Handlung f; (of land) Grundstück nt ♦ vt markieren; (curve) zeichnen; (movements) nachzeichnen ♦ vi (plan secretly) sich verschwören; ~**ter** n (instrument) Plotter m
plough [plaʊ] (US plow) n Pflug m ♦ vt pflügen; ~ **back** vt (COMM) wieder in das Geschäft stecken; ~ **through** vt fus (water) durchpflügen; (book) sich kämpfen durch
plow (US) = **plough**
ploy [plɔɪ] n Masche f
pluck [plʌk] vt (fruit) pflücken; (guitar) zupfen; (goose etc) rupfen ♦ n Mut m; **to** ~ **up courage** all seinen Mut zusammennehmen; ~**y** adj beherzt
plug [plʌg] n Stöpsel m; (ELEC) Stecker m; (inf: publicity) Schleichwerbung f; (AUT) Zündkerze f ♦ vt (zu)stopfen; (inf: advertise) Reklame machen für; ~ **in** vt (ELEC) anschließen
plum [plʌm] n Pflaume f, Zwetsch(g)e f ♦ adj (job etc) Bomben-
plumage ['pluːmɪdʒ] n Gefieder nt
plumb [plʌm] adj senkrecht ♦ n Lot nt ♦ adv (exactly) genau ♦ vt ausloten; (fig) sondieren
plumber ['plʌmə*] n Klempner m, Installateur m
plumbing ['plʌmɪŋ] n (craft) Installieren nt; (fittings) Leitungen pl
plume [pluːm] n Feder f; (of smoke etc) Fahne f
plummet ['plʌmɪt] vi (ab)stürzen
plump [plʌmp] adj rundlich, füllig ♦ vt plumpsen lassen; **to** ~ **for** (inf: choose) sich entscheiden für
plunder ['plʌndə*] n Plünderung f; (loot) Beute f ♦ vt plündern
plunge [plʌndʒ] n Sturz m ♦ vt stoßen ♦

vi (sich) stürzen; **to take the** ~ den Sprung wagen
plunging ['plʌndʒɪŋ] adj (neckline) offenherzig
pluperfect ['pluːpɜːfɪkt] n Plusquamperfekt nt
plural ['plʊərəl] n Plural m, Mehrzahl f
plus [plʌs] n (also: ~ **sign**) Plus(zeichen) nt ♦ prep plus, und; **ten/ twenty** ~ mehr als zehn/zwanzig
plush [plʌʃ] adj (also ~**y**: inf: luxurious) feudal
ply [plaɪ] vt (trade) (be)treiben; (with questions) zusetzen +dat; (ship, taxi) befahren ♦ vi (ship, taxi) verkehren ♦ n: **three-**~ (wool) Dreifach-; **to** ~ **sb with drink** jdn zum Trinken animieren; ~**wood** n Sperrholz nt
P.M. n abbr = **Prime Minister**
p.m. adv abbr (= post meridiem) nachmittags
pneumatic [njuː'mætɪk] adj pneumatisch; (TECH) Luft-; ~ **drill** n Preßlufthammer m
pneumonia [njuː'məʊnɪə] n Lungenentzündung f
poach [pəʊtʃ] vt (COOK) pochieren; (game) stehlen ♦ vi (steal) wildern; ~**ed** adj (egg) verloren; ~**er** n Wilddieb m; ~**ing** n Wildern nt
P.O. Box n abbr = **Post Office Box**
pocket ['pɒkɪt] n Tasche f; (of resistance) (Widerstands)nest nt ♦ vt einstecken; **to be out of** ~ (BRIT) draufzahlen; ~**book** n Taschenbuch nt; ~ **knife** n Taschenmesser nt; ~ **money** n Taschengeld nt
pod [pɒd] n Hülse f; (of peas also) Schote f
podgy ['pɒdʒɪ] adj pummelig
podiatrist [pɒ'diːətrɪst] (US) n Fußpfleger(in) m(f)
poem ['pəʊəm] n Gedicht nt
poet ['pəʊɪt] n Dichter m, Poet m; ~**ic** [pəʊ'etɪk] adj poetisch, dichterisch; ~ **laureate** n Hofdichter m; ~**ry** n Poesie f; (poems) Gedichte pl
poignant ['pɔɪnjənt] adj (touching) ergreifend
point [pɔɪnt] n (also in discussion,

scoring) Punkt *m*; (*spot*) Punkt *m*, Stelle *f*; (*sharpened tip*) Spitze *f*; (*moment*) (Zeit)punkt *m*; (*purpose*) Zweck *m*; (*idea*) Argument *nt*; (*decimal*) Dezimalstelle *f*; (*personal characteristic*) Seite *f* ♦ *vt* zeigen mit; (*gun*) richten ♦ *vi* zeigen; ~s *npl* (*RAIL*) Weichen *pl*; **to be on the ~ of doing sth** drauf und dran sein, etw zu tun; **to make a ~ of** Wert darauf legen; **to get the ~** verstehen, worum es geht; **to come to the ~** zur Sache kommen; **there's no ~ (in doing sth)** es hat keinen Sinn(, etw zu tun); ~ **out** *vt* hinweisen auf +*acc*; ~ **to** *vt fus* zeigen auf +*acc*; ~-**blank** *adv* (*at close range*) aus nächster Entfernung; (*bluntly*) unverblümt; ~**ed** *adj* (*also fig*) spitz, scharf; ~**edly** *adv* (*fig*) spitz; ~**er** *n* Zeigestock *m*; (*on dial*) Zeiger *m*; ~**less** *adj* sinnlos; ~ **of view** *n* Stand- *or* Gesichtspunkt *m*

poise [pɔɪz] *n* Haltung *f*; (*fig*) Gelassenheit *f*

poison [ˈpɔɪzn] *n* (*also fig*) Gift *nt* ♦ *vt* vergiften; ~**ing** *n* Vergiftung *f*; ~**ous** *adj* giftig, Gift-

poke [pəʊk] *vt* stoßen; (*put*) stecken; (*fire*) schüren; (*hole*) bohren; ~ **about** *vi* herumstochern; (*nose around*) herumwühlen

poker [ˈpəʊkə*] *n* Schürhaken *m*; (*CARDS*) Poker *nt*; ~-**faced** *adj* undurchdringlich

poky [ˈpəʊkɪ] *adj* eng

Poland [ˈpəʊlənd] *n* Polen *nt*

polar [ˈpəʊlə*] *adj* Polar-, polar; ~ **bear** *n* Eisbär *m*; ~**ize** *vt* polarisieren

Pole [pəʊl] *n* Pole *m*, Polin *f*

pole [pəʊl] *n* Stange *f*, Pfosten *m*; (*flag-~*, *telegraph* ~) Stange *f*, Mast *m*; (*ELEC*, *GEOG*) Pol *m*; (*SPORT*: *vaulting* ~) Stab *m*; (*ski* ~) Stock *m*; ~ **bean** (*US*) *n* (*runner bean*) Stangenbohne *f*; ~ **vault** *n* Stabhochsprung *m*

police [pəˈliːs] *n* Polizei *f* ♦ *vt* kontrollieren; ~ **car** *n* Polizeiwagen *m*; ~**man** (*irreg*) *n* Polizist *m*; ~ **state** *n* Polizeistaat *m*; ~ **station** *n*

(Polizei)revier *nt*, Wache *f*; ~**woman** (*irreg*) *n* Polizistin *f*

policy [ˈpɒlɪsɪ] *n* Politik *f*; (*insurance*) (Versicherungs)police *f*

polio [ˈpəʊlɪəʊ] *n* (spinale) Kinderlähmung *f*, Polio *f*

Polish [ˈpəʊlɪʃ] *adj* polnisch ♦ *n* (*LING*) Polnisch *nt*

polish [ˈpɒlɪʃ] *n* Politur *f*; (*for floor*) Wachs *nt*; (*for shoes*) Creme *f*; (*for nails*) Lack *m*; (*shine*) Glanz *m*; (*of furniture*) Politur *f*; (*fig*) Schliff *m* ♦ *vt* polieren; (*shoes*) putzen; (*fig*) den letzten Schliff geben +*dat*; ~ **off** *vt* (*inf*: *work*) erledigen; (: *food*) wegputzen; (: *drink*) hinunterschütten; ~**ed** *adj* (*also fig*) glänzend; (*manners*) verfeinert

polite [pəˈlaɪt] *adj* höflich; ~**ness** *n* Höflichkeit *f*

politic [ˈpɒlɪtɪk] *adj* (*prudent*) diplomatisch; ~**al** [pəˈlɪtɪkəl] *adj* politisch; ~**ally** *adv* politisch; ~**ian** [pɒlɪˈtɪʃən] *n* Politiker *m*; ~**s** *npl* Politik *f*

polka [ˈpɒlkə] *n* Polka *f*; ~ **dot** *n* Tupfen *m*

poll [pəʊl] *n* Abstimmung *f*; (*in election*) Wahl *f*; (*votes cast*) Wahlbeteiligung *f*; (*opinion* ~) Umfrage *f* ♦ *vt* (*votes*) erhalten

pollen [ˈpɒlən] *n* Blütenstaub *m*

pollination [pɒlɪˈneɪʃən] *n* Befruchtung *f*

polling [ˈpəʊlɪŋ] *n*: ~ **booth** (*BRIT*) *n* Wahlkabine *f*; ~ **day** (*BRIT*) *n* Wahltag *m*; ~ **station** (*BRIT*) *n* Wahllokal *nt*

pollute [pəˈluːt] *vt* verschmutzen, verunreinigen; **pollution** [pəˈluːʃən] *n* Verschmutzung *f*

polo [ˈpəʊləʊ] *n* Polo *nt*; ~-**neck** *n* Rollkragen *m*; Rollkragenpullover *m*

polystyrene [pɒlɪˈstaɪriːn] *n* Styropor *m*

polytechnic [pɒlɪˈteknɪk] *n* technische Hochschule *f*

polythene [ˈpɒlɪθiːn] *n* Plastik *nt*

pomegranate [ˈpɒməɡrænɪt] *n* Granatapfel *m*

pommel [ˈpʌml] *vt* mit den Fäusten bearbeiten ♦ *n* Sattelknopf *m*

pompom [ˈpɒmpɒm] *n* Troddel *f*, Pompon *m*

pompous ['pɒmpəs] adj aufgeblasen; (language) geschwollen

pond [pɒnd] n Teich m, Weiher m

ponder ['pɒndə*] vt nachdenken über +acc; ~ous adj schwerfällig

pong [pɒŋ] (BRIT: inf) n Mief m

pontiff ['pɒntɪf] n Pontifex m

pontificate [pɒn'tɪfɪkeɪt] vi (fig) geschwollen reden

pontoon [pɒn'tuːn] n Ponton m; (CARDS) 17-und-4 nt

pony ['pəʊnɪ] n Pony nt; ~tail n Pferdeschwanz m; ~ trekking (BRIT) n Ponyreiten nt

poodle ['puːdl] n Pudel m

pool [puːl] n (swimming ~) Schwimmbad nt; (: private) Swimmingpool m; (of spilt liquid, blood) Lache f; (fund) (gemeinsame) Kasse f; (billiards) Poolspiel nt ♦ vt (money etc) zusammenlegen; **typing** ~ Schreibzentrale f; (football) ~s Toto nt

poor [pʊə*] adj arm; (not good) schlecht ♦ npl: **the** ~ die Armen pl; ~**ly** adv schlecht; (dressed) ärmlich ♦ adj schlecht

pop [pɒp] n Knall m; (music) Popmusik f; (drink) Limo(nade) f; (US: inf) Pa m ♦ vt (put) stecken; (balloon) platzen lassen ♦ vi knallen; ~ **in** vi kurz vorbeigehen or vorbeikommen; ~ **out** vi (person) kurz rausgehen; (thing) herausspringen; ~ **up** vi auftauchen; ~**concert** n Popkonzert nt; ~**corn** n Puffmais m

pope [pəʊp] n Papst m

poplar ['pɒplə*] n Pappel f

poppy ['pɒpɪ] n Mohn m

Popsicle ['pɒpsɪkl] (®; US) n (ice lolly) Eis nt am Stiel

populace ['pɒpjʊləs] n Volk nt

popular ['pɒpjʊlə*] adj beliebt, populär; (of the people) volkstümlich; (widespread) allgemein; ~**ity** [pɒpjʊ'lærɪtɪ] n Beliebtheit f, Popularität f; ~**ize** vt popularisieren; ~**ly** adv allgemein, überall

population [pɒpjʊ'leɪʃən] n Bevölkerung f; (of town) Einwohner pl

populous ['pɒpjʊləs] adj dicht besiedelt

porcelain ['pɔːslɪn] n Porzellan nt

porch [pɔːtʃ] n Vorbau m, Veranda f

porcupine ['pɔːkjʊpaɪn] n Stachelschwein nt

pore [pɔː*] n Pore f ♦ vi: **to** ~ **over** brüten über +dat

pork [pɔːk] n Schweinefleisch nt

pornography [pɔː'nɒgrəfɪ] n Pornographie f

porous ['pɔːrəs] adj porös; (skin) porig

porpoise ['pɔːpəs] n Tümmler m

porridge ['pɒrɪdʒ] n Haferbrei m

port [pɔːt] n Hafen m; (town) Hafenstadt f; (NAUT: left side) Backbord nt; (wine) Portwein m; ~ **of call** Anlaufhafen m

portable ['pɔːtəbl] adj tragbar

portent ['pɔːtent] n schlimme(s) Vorzeichen nt

porter ['pɔːtə*] n Pförtner(in) m(f); (for luggage) (Gepäck)träger m

portfolio [pɔːt'fəʊlɪəʊ] n (case) Mappe f; (POL) Geschäftsbereich m; (FIN) Portefeuille nt; (of artist) Kollektion f

porthole ['pɔːthəʊl] n Bullauge nt

portion ['pɔːʃən] n Teil m, Stück nt; (of food) Portion f

portly ['pɔːtlɪ] adj korpulent, beleibt

portrait ['pɔːtrɪt] n Porträt nt

portray [pɔː'treɪ] vt darstellen; ~**al** n Darstellung f

Portugal ['pɔːtjʊgəl] n Portugal nt

Portuguese [pɔːtjʊ'giːz] adj portugiesisch ♦ n inv Portugiese m, Portugiesin f; (LING) Portugiesisch nt

pose [pəʊz] n Stellung f, Pose f; (affectation) Pose f ♦ vi posieren ♦ vt stellen

posh [pɒʃ] (inf) adj (piek)fein

position [pə'zɪʃən] n Stellung f; (place) Lage f; (job) Stelle f; (attitude) Standpunkt m ♦ vt aufstellen

positive ['pɒzɪtɪv] adj positiv; (convinced) sicher; (definite) eindeutig

posse ['pɒsɪ] (US) n Aufgebot nt

possess [pə'zes] vt besitzen; ~**ion** [pə'zeʃən] n Besitz m; ~**ive** adj besitzergreifend, eigensüchtig

possibility [pɒsə'bɪlɪtɪ] n Möglichkeit f

possible ['pɒsəbl] adj möglich; **as big**

as ~ so groß wie möglich, möglichst groß

possibly ['pɒsəblɪ] adv möglicherweise, vielleicht; **I cannot ~ come** ich kann unmöglich kommen

post [pəʊst] n (BRIT: letters, delivery) Post f; (pole) Pfosten m, Pfahl m; (place of duty) Posten m; (job) Stelle f ♦ vt (notice) anschlagen; (BRIT: letters) aufgeben; (: appoint) versetzen; (soldiers) aufstellen; ~**age** n Postgebühr f, Porto nt; ~**al** adj Post-; ~**al order** n Postanweisung f; ~**box** (BRIT) n Briefkasten m; ~**card** n Postkarte f; ~**code** (BRIT) n Postleitzahl f

postdate [pəʊst'deɪt] vt (cheque) nachdatieren

poster ['pəʊstə*] n Plakat nt, Poster nt

poste restante ['pəʊst'rɛstɑ̃:nt] n Aufbewahrungsstelle f für postlagernde Sendungen

posterior [pɒs'tɪərɪə*] (inf) n Hintern m

posterity [pɒs'tɛrɪtɪ] n Nachwelt f

postgraduate ['pəʊst'grædjʊət] n Weiterstudierende(r) mf

posthumous ['pɒstjʊməs] adj post(h)um

postman ['pəʊstmən] (irreg) n Briefträger m

postmark ['pəʊstmɑ:k] n Poststempel m

postmaster ['pəʊstmɑ:stə*] n Postmeister m

post-mortem ['pəʊst'mɔ:təm] n Autopsie f

post office n Postamt nt, Post f; (organization) Post f; **Post Office Box** n Postfach nt

postpone [pə'spəʊn] vt verschieben; ~**ment** n Verschiebung f

postscript ['pəʊsskrɪpt] n Postskript nt; (to affair) Nachspiel nt

postulate ['pɒstjʊleɪt] vt voraussetzen; (maintain) behaupten

posture ['pɒstʃə*] n Haltung f ♦ vi posieren

postwar ['pəʊst'wɔ:*] adj Nachkriegs-

posy ['pəʊzɪ] n Blumenstrauß m

pot [pɒt] n Topf m; (tea~) Kanne f; (inf: marijuana) Hasch m ♦ vt (plant) eintopfen; **to go to ~** (inf: work, performance) auf den Hund kommen

potato [pə'teɪtəʊ] (pl ~es) n Kartoffel f; ~ **peeler** n Kartoffelschäler m

potent ['pəʊtənt] adj stark; (argument) zwingend

potential [pə'tenʃəl] adj potentiell ♦ n Potential nt; ~**ly** adv potentiell

pothole ['pɒthəʊl] n (in road) Schlagloch nt; (BRIT: underground) Höhle f

potholing ['pɒthəʊlɪŋ] (BRIT) n: **to go ~** Höhlen erforschen

potion ['pəʊʃən] n Trank m

potluck ['pɒt'lʌk] n: **to take ~ with sth** etw auf gut Glück nehmen

potshot ['pɒtʃɒt] n: **to take a ~ at sth** auf etw acc ballern

potted ['pɒtɪd] adj (food) eingelegt, eingemacht; (plant) Topf-; (fig: book, version) konzentriert

potter ['pɒtə*] n Töpfer m ♦ vi herumhantieren; ~**y** n Töpferwaren pl; (place) Töpferei f

potty ['pɒtɪ] adj (inf: mad) verrückt ♦ n Töpfchen nt

pouch [paʊtʃ] n Beutel m

pouf(fe) [pu:f] n Sitzkissen nt

poultry ['pəʊltrɪ] n Geflügel nt

pounce [paʊns] vi sich stürzen ♦ n Sprung m, Satz m; **to ~ on** sich stürzen auf +acc

pound [paʊnd] n (FIN, weight) Pfund nt; (for cars, animals) Auslösestelle f ♦ vt (zer)stampfen ♦ vi klopfen, hämmern; ~ **sterling** n Pfund Sterling nt

pour [pɔ:*] vt gießen, schütten ♦ vi gießen; (crowds etc) strömen; ~ **away** vt abgießen; ~ **in** vi (people) hereinströmen; ~ **off** vt abgießen; ~ **out** vi (people) herausströmen ♦ vt (drink) einschenken; ~**ing** adj: ~**ing rain** strömende(r) Regen m

pout [paʊt] vi schmollen

poverty ['pɒvətɪ] n Armut f; ~-**stricken** adj verarmt, sehr arm

powder ['paʊdə*] n Pulver nt; (cosmetic) Puder m ♦ vt pulverisieren; **to ~ one's nose** sich dat die Nase pudern; ~ **compact** n Puderdose f; ~**ed milk** n Milchpulver nt; ~ **room** n Damentoilette f; ~**y** adj pulverig

power ['paʊə*] n (also POL) Macht f;

(*ability*) Fähigkeit *f*; (*strength*) Stärke *f*; (*MATH*) Potenz *f*; (*ELEC*) Strom *m* ♦ *vt* betreiben, antreiben; **to be in ~** (*POL etc*) an der Macht sein; **~ cut** *n* Stromausfall *m*; **~ed** *adj*: **~ed by** betrieben mit; **~ failure** (*US*) *n* Stromausfall *m*; **~ful** *adj* (*person*) mächtig; (*engine, government*) stark; **~less** *adj* machtlos; **~ point** (*BRIT*) *n* elektrische(r) Anschluß *m*; **~ station** *n* Elektrizitätswerk *m*

p.p. *abbr* (= *per procurationem*): **~ J. Smith** i.A. J. Smith

PR *n abbr* = **public relations**

practicable ['præktɪkəbl] *adj* durchführbar

practical ['præktɪkəl] *adj* praktisch; **~ity** [præktɪ'kælɪtɪ] *n* (*of person*) praktische Veranlagung *f*; (*of situation etc*) Durchführbarkeit *f*; **~ joke** *n* Streich *m*; **~ly** *adv* praktisch

practice ['præktɪs] *n* Übung *f*; (*reality, also of doctor, lawyer*) Praxis *f*; (*custom*) Brauch *m*; (*in business*) Usus *m* ♦ *vt, vi* (*US*) = **practise**; **in ~** (*in reality*) in der Praxis; **out of ~** außer Übung

practicing (*US*) *adj* = **practising**

practise ['præktɪs] (*US* **practice**) *vt* üben; (*profession*) ausüben ♦ *vi* (sich) üben; (*doctor, lawyer*) praktizieren

practising ['præktɪsɪŋ] (*US* **practicing**) *adj* praktizierend; (*Christian etc*) aktiv

practitioner [præk'tɪʃənə*] *n* praktische(r) Arzt *m*

pragmatic [præg'mætɪk] *adj* pragmatisch

prairie ['prɛərɪ] *n* Prärie *f*, Steppe *f*

praise [preɪz] *n* Lob *nt* ♦ *vt* loben; **~worthy** *adj* lobenswert

pram [præm] (*BRIT*) *n* Kinderwagen *m*

prance [prɑːns] *vi* (*horse*) tänzeln; (*person*) stolzieren; (: *gaily*) herumhüpfen

prank [præŋk] *n* Streich *m*

prattle ['prætl] *vi* schwatzen, plappern

prawn [prɔːn] *n* Garnele *f*; Krabbe *f*

pray [preɪ] *vi* beten; **~er** [prɛə*] *n* Gebet *nt*

preach [priːtʃ] *vi* predigen; **~er** *n* Prediger *m*

preamble [priː'æmbl] *n* Einleitung *f*

precarious [prɪ'kɛərɪəs] *adj* prekär, unsicher

precaution [prɪ'kɔːʃən] *n* (Vorsichts)maßnahme *f*

precede [prɪ'siːd] *vi* vorausgehen ♦ *vt* vorausgehen +*dat*; **~nce** ['presɪdəns] *n* Vorrang *m*; **~nt** ['presɪdənt] *n* Präzedenzfall *m*

preceding [prɪ'siːdɪŋ] *adj* vorhergehend

precept ['priːsept] *n* Gebot *nt*, Regel *f*

precinct ['priːsɪŋkt] *n* (*US*: *district*) Bezirk *m*; **~s** *npl* (*round building*) Gelände *nt*; (*area, environs*) Umgebung *f*; **pedestrian ~** Fußgängerzone *f*; **shopping ~** Geschäftsviertel *nt*

precious ['preʃəs] *adj* kostbar, wertvoll; (*affected*) preziös, geziert

precipice ['presɪpɪs] *n* Abgrund *m*

precipitate [*adj* prɪ'sɪpɪtɪt, *vb* prɪ'sɪpɪteɪt] *adj* überstürzt, übereilt ♦ *vt* hinunterstürzen; (*events*) heraufbeschwören

precise [prɪ'saɪs] *adj* genau, präzis; **~ly** *adv* genau, präzis

precision [prɪ'sɪʒən] *n* Präzision *f*

preclude [prɪ'kluːd] *vt* ausschließen

precocious [prɪ'kəʊʃəs] *adj* frühreif

preconceived ['priːkən'siːvd] *adj* (*idea*) vorgefaßt

precondition ['priːkən'dɪʃən] *n* Vorbedingung *f*, Voraussetzung *f*

precursor [priː'kɜːsə*] *n* Vorläufer *m*

predator ['predətə*] *n* Raubtier *nt*

predecessor ['priːdɪsesə*] *n* Vorgänger *m*

predestination [priːdestɪ'neɪʃən] *n* Vorherbestimmung *f*

predicament [prɪ'dɪkəmənt] *n* mißliche Lage *f*

predict [prɪ'dɪkt] *vt* voraussagen; **~able** *adj* vorhersagbar; **~ion** [prɪ'dɪkʃən] *n* Voraussage *f*

predominantly [prɪ'dɒmɪnəntlɪ] *adv* überwiegend, hauptsächlich

predominate [prɪ'dɒmɪneɪt] *vi* vorherrschen; (*fig*) vorherrschen, überwiegen

pre-eminent [priː'emɪnənt] *adj* hervorragend, herausragend

pre-empt [priː'empt] *vt* (*action, decision*) vorwegnehmen

preen [priːn] *vt* putzen; **to ~ o.s.** (*person*) sich brüsten

prefab ['priːfæb] *n* Fertighaus *nt*

prefabricated ['priːfæbrɪkeɪtɪd] *adj* vorgefertigt, Fertig-

preface ['prefɪs] *n* Vorwort *nt*

prefect ['priːfekt] *n* Präfekt *m*; (*SCH*) Aufsichtsschüler(in) *m(f)*

prefer [prɪ'fɜː*] *vt* vorziehen, lieber mögen; **to ~ to do sth** etw lieber tun; **~ably** *adv* vorzugsweise, am liebsten; **~ence** *n* Präferenz *f*, Vorzug *m*; **~ential** [prefə'renʃəl] *adj* bevorzugt, Vorzugs-

prefix ['priːfɪks] *n* Vorsilbe *f*, Präfix *nt*

pregnancy ['pregnənsɪ] *n* Schwangerschaft *f*

pregnant ['pregnənt] *adj* schwanger

prehistoric ['priːhɪs'tɒrɪk] *adj* prähistorisch, vorgeschichtlich

prejudice ['predʒʊdɪs] *n* (*opinion*) Vorurteil *nt*; (*bias*) Voreingenommenheit *f*; (*harm*) Schaden *m* ♦ *vt* beeinträchtigen; **~d** *adj* (*person*) voreingenommen

preliminary [prɪ'lɪmɪnərɪ] *adj* einleitend, Vor-

prelude ['preljuːd] *n* Vorspiel *nt*; (*fig*) Auftakt *m*

premarital ['priː'mærɪtl] *adj* vorehelich

premature ['premətʃʊə*] *adj* vorzeitig, verfrüht; (*birth*) Früh-

premeditated [priː'medɪteɪtɪd] *adj* geplant; (*murder*) vorsätzlich

premier ['premɪə*] *adj* erste(r, s) ♦ *n* Premier *m*

première [premɪ'ɛə*] *n* Premiere *f*; Uraufführung *f*

premise ['premɪs] *n* Voraussetzung *f*, Prämisse *f*; **~s** *npl* (*shop*) Räumlichkeiten *pl*; (*grounds*) Gelände *nt*; **on the ~s** im Hause

premium ['priːmɪəm] *n* Prämie *f*; **to be at a ~** über pari stehen; **~ bond** (*BRIT*) *n* Prämienanleihe *f*

premonition [premə'nɪʃən] *n* Vorahnung *f*

preoccupation [priːɒkjʊ'peɪʃən] *n* Sorge *f*

preoccupied [priː'ɒkjʊpaɪd] *adj* (*look*) geistesabwesend

prep [prep] *n* (*SCH*: *study*) Hausaufgabe *f*

prepaid ['priː'peɪd] *adj* vorausbezahlt; (*letter*) frankiert

preparation ['prepə'reɪʃən] *n* Vorbereitung *f*

preparatory [prɪ'pærətərɪ] *adj* Vor(bereitungs)-; **~ school** *n* *private* Vorbereitungsschule für die Public School (*BRIT*)/*die Hochschule* (*US*)

prepare [prɪ'pɛə*] *vt* vorbereiten ♦ *vi* sich vorbereiten; **to ~ for/~ sth for** sich/etw vorbereiten auf +*acc*; **to be ~d to ...** bereit sein zu ...

preponderance [prɪ'pɒndərəns] *n* Übergewicht *nt*

preposition [prepə'zɪʃən] *n* Präposition *f*, Verhältniswort *nt*

preposterous [prɪ'pɒstərəs] *adj* absurd

prep school *n* = preparatory school

prerequisite ['priː'rekwɪzɪt] *n* (unerläßliche) Voraussetzung *f*

prerogative [prɪ'rɒgətɪv] *n* Vorrecht *nt*

Presbyterian [prezbɪ'tɪərɪən] *adj* presbyterianisch ♦ *n* Presbyterier(in) *m(f)*

preschool ['priːskuːl] *adj* Vorschul-

prescribe [prɪs'kraɪb] *vt* vorschreiben; (*MED*) verschreiben

prescription [prɪs'krɪpʃən] *n* (*MED*) Rezept *nt*

presence ['prezns] *n* Gegenwart *f*; **~ of mind** Geistesgegenwart *f*

present [*adj, n* 'preznt, *vb* prɪ'zent] *adj* (*here*) anwesend; (*current*) gegenwärtig ♦ *n* Gegenwart *f*; (*gift*) Geschenk *nt* ♦ *vt* vorlegen; (*introduce*) vorstellen; (*show*) zeigen; (*give*): **to ~ sb with sth** jdm etw überreichen; **at ~** im Augenblick; **~able** [prɪ'zentəbl] *adj* präsentabel; **~ation** [prezən'teɪʃən] *n* Überreichung *f*; **~-day** *adj* heutig; **~er** [prɪ'zentə*] *n* (*RADIO, TV*) Moderator(in) *m(f)*; **~ly** *adv* bald; (*at present*) im Augenblick

preservation [prezə'veɪʃən] *n* Erhaltung *f*

preservative [prɪ'zɜːvətɪv] *n* Konservie-

rungsmittel *nt*
preserve [prɪ'zɜːv] *vt* erhalten; *(food)*
einmachen ♦ *n (jam)* Eingemachte(s)
nt; *(hunting)* Schutzgebiet *nt*
preside [prɪ'zaɪd] *vi* den Vorsitz haben
presidency ['prezɪdənsɪ] *n (POL)*
Präsidentschaft *f*
procident ['prezɪdənt] *n* Präsident *m*;
~**ial** [prezɪ'denʃəl] *adj* Präsidenten-;
(election) Präsidentschafts-; *(system)*
Präsidial-
press [pres] *n* Presse *f*; *(printing house)*
Druckerei *f* ♦ *vt* drücken; *(iron)*
bügeln; *(urge)* (be)drängen ♦ *vi (push)*
drücken; **to be** ~**ed for time** unter Zeit-
druck stehen; **to** ~ **for sth** drängen auf
etw *acc*; ~ **on** *vi* vorwärtsdrängen; ~
agency *n* Presseagentur *f*; ~ **conference** *n* Pressekonferenz *f*; ~**ing** *adj*
dringend; ~-**stud** *(BRIT)* *n* Druckknopf
m; ~-**up** *(BRIT)* *n* Liegestütz *m*
pressure [preʃə*] *n* Druck *m*; ~ **cooker**
n Schnellkochtopf *m*; ~ **gauge** *n*
Druckmesser *m*
pressurized ['preʃəraɪzd] *adj* Druck-
prestige [pres'tiːʒ] *n* Prestige *nt*
prestigious [pres'tɪdʒəs] *adj* Prestige-
presumably [prɪ'zjuːməblɪ] *adv* vermutlich
presume [prɪ'zjuːm] *vt, vi* annehmen; **to**
~ **to do sth** sich erlauben, etw zu tun
presumption [prɪ'zʌmpʃən] *n* Annahme
f
presumptuous [prɪ'zʌmptjuəs] *adj* an-
maßend
presuppose [priːsə'pəuz] *vt* voraussetzen
pretence [prɪ'tens] *(US* pretense) *n* Vorgabe *f*, Vortäuschung *f*; *(false claim)*
Vorwand *m*
pretend [prɪ'tend] *vt* vorgeben, so tun
als ob ... ♦ *vi* so tun; **to** ~ **to sth** Anspruch erheben auf etw *acc*
pretense [prɪ'tens] *(US)* *n* = **pretence**
pretension [prɪ'tenʃən] *n* Anspruch *m*;
(impudent claim) Anmaßung *f*
pretentious [prɪ'tenʃəs] *adj* angeberisch
pretext ['priːtekst] *n* Vorwand *m*
pretty ['prɪtɪ] *adj* hübsch ♦ *adv (inf)*
ganz schön
prevail [prɪ'veɪl] *vi* siegen; *(custom)*

vorherrschen; **to** ~ **against** *or* **over**
siegen über +*acc*; **to** ~ **(up)on sb to do**
sth jdn dazu bewegen, etw zu tun; ~**ing**
adj vorherrschend
prevalent ['prevələnt] *adj* vorherrschend
prevent [prɪ'vent] *vt (stop)* verhindern,
verhüten; **to** ~ **sb from doing sth** jdn
(daran) hindern, etw zu tun; ~**ative** *n*
Vorbeugungsmittel *nt*; ~**ion** [prɪ'venʃən]
n Verhütung *f*; ~**ive** *adj* vorbeugend,
Schutz-
preview ['priːvjuː] *n* private Vor-
aufführung *f*; *(trailer)* Vorschau *f*
previous ['priːvɪəs] *adj* früher, vorherig;
~**ly** *adv* früher
prewar ['priː'wɔː*] *adj* Vorkriegs-
prey [preɪ] *n* Beute *f*; ~ **on** *vt fus* Jagd
machen auf +*acc*; **it was** ~**ing on his**
mind es quälte sein Gewissen
price [praɪs] *n* Preis *m*; *(value)* Wert *m*
♦ *vt (label)* auszeichnen; ~**less** *adj*
(also fig) unbezahlbar; ~ **list** *n* Preisli-
ste *f*
prick [prɪk] *n* Stich *m* ♦ *vt, vi* stechen;
to ~ **up one's ears** die Ohren spitzen
prickle ['prɪkl] *n* Stachel *m*, Dorn *m*
prickly ['prɪklɪ] *adj* stachelig; *(fig:*
person) reizbar; ~ **heat** *n* Hitze-
bläschen *pl*
pride [praɪd] *n* Stolz *m*; *(arrogance)*
Hochmut *m* ♦ *vt*: **to** ~ **o.s. on sth** auf
etw *acc* stolz sein
priest [priːst] *n* Priester *m*; ~**ess** *n*
Priesterin *f*; ~**hood** *n* Priesteramt *nt*
prig [prɪg] *n* Selbstgefällige(r) *mf*
prim [prɪm] *adj* prüde
primarily ['praɪmərɪlɪ] *adv* vorwiegend
primary ['praɪmərɪ] *adj (main)* Haupt-;
(SCH) Grund-; ~ **school** *(BRIT)* *n*
Grundschule *f*
prime [praɪm] *adj* erste(r, s);
(excellent) erstklassig ♦ *vt* vorbereiten;
(gun) laden; **in the** ~ **of life** in der
Blüte der Jahre; **P~ Minister** *n*
Premierminister *m*, Ministerpräsident
m; ~**r** ['praɪmə*] *n* Fibel *f*
primeval [praɪ'miːvəl] *adj* vorzeitlich;
(forests) Ur-
primitive ['prɪmɪtɪv] *adj* primitiv
primrose ['prɪmrəuz] *n* (gelbe) Primel *f*

primus (stove) ['praıməs-] (®; *BRIT*) *n* Primuskocher *m*

prince [prɪns] *n* Prinz *m*; (*ruler*) Fürst *m*; **princess** [prɪn'ses] *n* Prinzessin *f*; Fürstin *f*

principal ['prɪnsɪpəl] *adj* Haupt- ♦ *n* (*SCH*) (Schul)direktor *m*, Rektor *m*; (*money*) (Grund)kapital *nt*; ~**ity** [prɪnsɪ'pælɪtɪ] *n* Fürstentum *nt*

principle ['prɪnsəpl] *n* Grundsatz *m*, Prinzip *nt*; **in** ~ im Prinzip; **on** ~ aus Prinzip, prinzipiell

print [prɪnt] *n* Druck *m*; (*made by feet, fingers*) Abdruck *m*; (*PHOT*) Abzug *m* ♦ *vt* drucken; (*name*) in Druckbuchstaben schreiben; (*PHOT*) abziehen; **out of** ~ vergriffen; ~**ed matter** *n* Drucksache *f*; ~**er** *n* Drucker *m*; ~**ing** *n* Drucken *nt*; (*of photos*) Abziehen *nt*; ~**out** *n* (*COMPUT*) Ausdruck *m*

prior ['praɪə*] *adj* früher ♦ *n* Prior *m*; ~ **to sth** vor etw *dat*; ~ **to going abroad, she had** ... bevor sie ins Ausland ging, hatte sie ...

priority [praɪ'ɒrɪtɪ] *n* Vorrang *m*; Priorität *f*

prise [praɪz] *vt*: **to** ~ **open** aufbrechen

prison ['prɪzn] *n* Gefängnis *nt* ♦ *adj* Gefängnis-; (*system etc*) Strafvollzugs-; ~**er** *n* Gefangene(r) *mf*

pristine ['prɪstiːn] *adj* makellos

privacy ['prɪvəsɪ] *n* Ungestörtheit *f*, Ruhe *f*; Privatleben *nt*

private ['praɪvɪt] *adj* privat, Privat-; (*secret*) vertraulich, geheim ♦ *n* einfache(r) Soldat *m*; "~" (*on envelope*) „persönlich"; **in** ~ privat, unter vier Augen; ~ **enterprise** *n* Privatunternehmen *nt*; ~ **eye** *n* Privatdetektiv *m*; ~**ly** *adv* privat; vertraulich, geheim; ~ **property** *n* Privatbesitz *m*; ~ **school** *n* Privatschule *f*; **privatize** *vt* privatisieren

privet ['prɪvɪt] *n* Liguster *m*

privilege ['prɪvɪlɪdʒ] *n* Privileg *nt*; ~**d** *adj* bevorzugt, privilegiert

privy ['prɪvɪ] *adj* geheim, privat; **P~ Council** *n* Geheime(r) Staatsrat *m*

prize [praɪz] *n* Preis *m* ♦ *adj* (*example*) erstklassig; (*idiot*) Voll- ♦ *vt*

(hoch)schätzen; ~**-giving** *n* Preisverteilung *f*; ~**winner** *n* Preisträger(in) *m(f)*

pro [prəʊ] *n* (*professional*) Profi *m*; **the** ~**s and cons** (*for and against*) das Für und Wider

probability [prɒbə'bɪlɪtɪ] *n* Wahrscheinlichkeit *f*

probable ['prɒbəbl] *adj* wahrscheinlich

probably *adv* wahrscheinlich

probation [prə'beɪʃən] *n* Probe(zeit) *f*; (*JUR*) Bewährung *f*; **on** ~ auf Probe; auf Bewährung

probe [prəʊb] *n* Sonde *f*; (*enquiry*) Untersuchung *f* ♦ *vt, vi* erforschen

problem ['prɒbləm] *n* Problem *nt*; ~**atic** [prɒblɪ'mætɪk] *adj* problematisch

procedure [prə'siːdʒə*] *n* Verfahren *nt*

proceed [prə'siːd] *vi* (*advance*) vorrücken; (*start*) anfangen; (*carry on*) fortfahren; (*set about*) vorgehen; ~**ings** *npl* Verfahren *nt*; ~**s** ['prəʊsiːdz] *npl* Erlös *m*

process ['prəʊses] *n* Prozeß *m*; (*method*) Verfahren *nt* ♦ *vt* bearbeiten; (*food*) verarbeiten; (*film*) entwickeln; ~**ing** *n* (*PHOT*) Entwickeln *nt*

procession [prə'seʃən] *n* Prozession *f*, Umzug *m*; **funeral** ~ Trauerprozession *f*

proclaim [prə'kleɪm] *vt* verkünden

proclamation [prɒklə'meɪʃən] *n* Verkündung *f*

procrastinate [prəʊ'kræstɪneɪt] *vi* zaudern

procreation [prəʊkrɪ'eɪʃən] *n* (Er)zeugung *f*

procure [prə'kjʊə*] *vt* beschaffen

prod [prɒd] *vt* stoßen ♦ *n* Stoß *m*

prodigal ['prɒdɪgəl] *adj*: ~ (**with** *or* **of**) verschwenderisch (mit)

prodigious [prə'dɪdʒəs] *adj* gewaltig; (*wonderful*) wunderbar

prodigy ['prɒdɪdʒɪ] *n* Wunder *nt*

produce [*n* 'prɒdjuːs, *vb* prə'djuːs] *n* (*AGR*) (Boden)produkte *pl*, (Natur)erzeugnis *nt* ♦ *vt* herstellen, produzieren; (*cause*) hervorrufen; (*farmer*) erzeugen; (*yield*) liefern, bringen; (*play*) inszenieren; ~**r** *n* Hersteller *m*, Produzent *m* (*also CINE*); Erzeuger *m*

product [ˈprɒdʌkt] n Produkt nt, Erzeugnis nt

production [prəˈdʌkʃən] n Produktion f, Herstellung f; (thing) Erzeugnis nt, Produkt nt; (THEAT) Inszenierung f; ~ **line** n Fließband nt

productive [prəˈdʌktɪv] adj produktiv; (fertile) ertragreich, fruchtbar

productivity [prɒdʌkˈtɪvɪtɪ] n Produktivität f

profane [prəˈfeɪn] adj (gottes)lästerlich; (lay) weltlich, profan

profess [prəˈfes] vt bekennen; (show) zeigen; (claim to be) vorgeben

profession [prəˈfeʃən] n Beruf m; (declaration) Bekenntnis nt; ~**al** n Fachmann m; (SPORT) Berufsspieler(in) m(f) ♦ adj Berufs-; (expert) fachlich; (player) professionell

professor [prəˈfesə*] n Professor m

proficiency [prəˈfɪʃənsɪ] n Können nt

proficient [prəˈfɪʃənt] adj fähig

profile [ˈprəʊfaɪl] n ·Profil nt; (fig: report) Kurzbiographie f

profit [ˈprɒfɪt] n Gewinn m ♦ vi: to ~ (by or from) profitieren (von); ~**ability** [prɒfɪtəˈbɪlɪtɪ] n Rentabilität f; ~**able** adj einträglich, rentabel

profiteering [prɒfɪˈtɪərɪŋ] n Profitmacherei f

profound [prəˈfaʊnd] adj tief

profuse [prəˈfjuːs] adj überreich; ~**ly** [prəˈfjuːslɪ] adv überschwenglich; (sweat) reichlich

profusion [prəˈfjuːʒən] n: ~ (of) Überfülle f (von), Überfluß m (an +dat)

progeny [ˈprɒdʒɪnɪ] n Nachkommenschaft f

programme [ˈprəʊgræm] (US **program**) n Programm nt ♦ vt planen; (computer) programmieren

programmer (US **programer**) n Programmierer(in) m(f)

programming [ˈprəʊgræmɪŋ] (US **programing**) n Programmieren nt

progress [n ˈprəʊgres, vb prəˈgres] n Fortschritt m ♦ vi fortschreiten, weitergehen; **in** ~ im Gang; ~**ion** [prəˈgreʃən] n Folge f; ~**ive** [prəˈgresɪv] adj fortschrittlich, progressiv

prohibit [prəˈhɪbɪt] vt verbieten; **to** ~ **sb from doing sth** jdm untersagen, etw zu tun; ~**ion** [prəʊɪˈbɪʃən] n Verbot nt; (US) Alkoholverbot nt, Prohibition f; ~**ive** adj (price etc) unerschwinglich

project [n ˈprɒdʒekt, vb prəˈdʒekt] n Projekt nt ♦ vt vorausplanen; (film etc) projizieren; (personality, voice) zum Tragen bringen ♦ vi (stick out) hervorragen, (her)vorstehen

projectile [prəˈdʒektaɪl] n Geschoß nt

projection [prəˈdʒekʃən] n Projektion f; (sth prominent) Vorsprung m

projector [prəˈdʒektə*] n Projektor m

proletariat [prəʊləˈtɛərɪət] n Proletariat nt

proliferate [prəˈlɪfəreɪt] vi sich vermehren

prolific [prəˈlɪfɪk] adj fruchtbar; (author etc) produktiv

prologue [ˈprəʊlɒg] n Prolog m; (event) Vorspiel nt

prolong [prəˈlɒŋ] vt verlängern

prom [prɒm] n abbr = **promenade**; **promenade concert** ♦ n (US: college ball) Studentenball m

promenade [prɒmɪˈnɑːd] n Promenade f; ~ **concert** n Promenadenkonzert nt

prominence [ˈprɒmɪnəns] n (große) Bedeutung f

prominent [ˈprɒmɪnənt] adj bedeutend; (politician) prominent; (easily seen) herausragend, auffallend

promiscuous [prəˈmɪskjʊəs] adj lose

promise [ˈprɒmɪs] n Versprechen nt; (hope: promise of sth) Aussicht f auf etw acc ♦ vt, vi versprechen

promising [ˈprɒmɪsɪŋ] adj vielversprechend

promontory [ˈprɒməntrɪ] n Vorsprung m

promote [prəˈməʊt] vt befördern; (help on) fördern, unterstützen; ~**r** n (in sport, entertainment) Veranstalter m; (for charity etc) Organisator m

promotion [prəˈməʊʃən] n (in rank) Beförderung f; (furtherance) Förderung f; (COMM): ~ (of) Werbung f (für)

prompt [prɒmpt] adj prompt, schnell ♦

adv (*punctually*) genau ♦ *n* (*COMPUT*) Meldung *f* ♦ *vt* veranlassen; (*THEAT*) soufflieren +*dat*; **to ~ sb to do sth** jdn dazu veranlassen, etw zu tun; **~ly** *adv* sofort

prone [prəʊn] *adj* hingestreckt; **to be ~ to sth** zu etw neigen

prong [prɒŋ] *n* Zinke *f*

pronoun ['prəʊnaʊn] *n* Fürwort *nt*

pronounce [prə'naʊns] *vt* aussprechen; (*JUR*) verkünden ♦ *vi* (*give an opinion*): **to ~ (on)** sich äußern (zu); **~d** *adj* ausgesprochen; **~ment** *n* Erklärung *f*

pronunciation [prənʌnsɪ'eɪʃən] *n* Aussprache *f*

proof [pruːf] *n* Beweis *m*; (*PRINT*) Korrekturfahne *f*; (*of alcohol*) Alkoholgehalt *m* ♦ *adj* sicher

prop [prɒp] *n* (*also fig*) Stütze *f*; (*THEAT*) Requisit *nt* ♦ *vt* (*also: ~ up*) (ab)stützen

propaganda [prɒpə'gændə] *n* Propaganda *f*

propagate ['prɒpəgeɪt] *vt* fortpflanzen; (*news*) propagieren, verbreiten

propel [prə'pel] *vt* (an)treiben; **~ler** *n* Propeller *m*; **~ling pencil** (*BRIT*) *n* Drehbleistift *m*

propensity [prə'pensɪtɪ] *n* Tendenz *f*

proper ['prɒpə*] *adj* richtig; (*seemly*) schicklich; **~ly** *adv* richtig; **~ noun** *n* Eigenname *m*

property ['prɒpətɪ] *n* Eigentum *nt*; (*quality*) Eigenschaft *f*; (*land*) Grundbesitz *m*; **~ owner** *n* Grundbesitzer *m*

prophecy ['prɒfɪsɪ] *n* Prophezeiung *f*

prophesy ['prɒfɪsaɪ] *vt* prophezeien

prophet ['prɒfɪt] *n* Prophet *m*

proportion [prə'pɔːʃən] *n* Verhältnis *nt*; (*share*) Teil *m* ♦ *vt*: **to ~ (to)** abstimmen (auf +*acc*); **~al** *adj* proportional; **~ate** *adj* verhältnismäßig

proposal [prə'pəʊzl] *n* Vorschlag *m*; (*of marriage*) Heiratsantrag *m*

propose [prə'pəʊz] *vt* vorschlagen; (*toast*) ausbringen ♦ *vi* (*offer marriage*) einen Heiratsantrag machen; **to ~ to do sth** beabsichtigen, etw zu tun

proposition [prɒpə'zɪʃən] *n* Angebot *nt*; (*statement*) Satz *m*

proprietor [prə'praɪətə*] *n* Besitzer *m*, Eigentümer *m*

propriety [prə'praɪətɪ] *n* Anstand *m*

pro rata [prəʊ'rɑːtə] *adv* anteilmäßig

prose [prəʊz] *n* Prosa *f*

prosecute ['prɒsɪkjuːt] *vt* (strafrechtlich) verfolgen

prosecution [prɒsɪ'kjuːʃən] *n* (*JUR*) strafrechtliche Verfolgung *f*; (*party*) Anklage *f*

prosecutor ['prɒsɪkjuːtə*] *n* Vertreter *m* der Anklage; **Public P~** Staatsanwalt *m*

prospect [*n* 'prɒspekt, *vb* prə'spekt] *n* Aussicht *f* ♦ *vt* auf Bodenschätze hin untersuchen ♦ *vi*: **to ~ (for)** suchen (nach); **~ing** [prə'spektɪŋ] *n* (*for minerals*) Suche *f*; **~ive** [prə'spektɪv] *adj* möglich; **~or** [prə'spektə*] *n* (Gold)sucher *m*; **~us** [prə'spektəs] *n* (Werbe)prospekt *m*

prosper ['prɒspə*] *vi* blühen, gedeihen; (*person*) erfolgreich sein; **~ity** [prɒ'sperɪtɪ] *n* Wohlstand *m*; **~ous** *adj* wohlhabend, reich

prostitute ['prɒstɪtjuːt] *n* Prostituierte *f*

prostrate ['prɒstreɪt] *adj* ausgestreckt (liegend); **~ with grief/exhaustion** von Schmerz/Erschöpfung übermannt

protagonist [prəʊ'tægənɪst] *n* Hauptperson *f*, Held *m*

protect [prə'tekt] *vt* (be)schützen; **~ion** *n* Schutz *m*; **~ive** *adj* Schutz-, (be)schützend

protégé ['prɒteʒeɪ] *n* Schützling *m*

protein ['prəʊtiːn] *n* Protein *nt*, Eiweiß *nt*

protest [*n* 'prəʊtest, *vb* prə'test] *n* Protest *m* ♦ *vi* protestieren ♦ *vt* (*affirm*) beteuern

Protestant ['prɒtɪstənt] *adj* protestantisch ♦ *n* Protestant(in) *m(f)*

protester [prə'testə*] *n* (*demonstrator*) Demonstrant(in) *m(f)*

protracted [prə'træktɪd] *adj* sich hinziehend

protrude [prə'truːd] *vi* (her)vorstehen

proud [praʊd] *adj*: **~ (of)** stolz (auf

+*acc*)

prove [pruːv] *vt* beweisen ♦ *vi*: **to ~ (to be) correct** sich als richtig erweisen; **to ~ o.s.** sich bewähren

proverb ['prɒvɜːb] *n* Sprichwort *nt*; **~ial** [prə'vɜːbɪəl] *adj* sprichwörtlich

provide [prə'vaɪd] *vt* versehen; (*supply*) besorgen; **to ~ sb with sth** jdn mit etw versorgen; **~ for** *vt fus* sorgen für; (*emergency*) Vorkehrungen treffen für; **~d (that)** *conj* vorausgesetzt (, daß); **P~nce** ['prɒvɪdəns] *n* die Vorsehung

providing [prə'vaɪdɪŋ] *conj* vorausgesetzt (, daß)

province ['prɒvɪns] *n* Provinz *f*; (*division of work*) Bereich *m*

provincial [prə'vɪnʃəl] *adj* provinziell, Provinz-

provision [prə'vɪʒən] *n* Vorkehrung *f*; (*condition*) Bestimmung *f*; **~s** *npl* (*food*) Vorräte *pl*, Proviant *m*; **~al** *adj* provisorisch

proviso [prə'vaɪzəʊ] *n* Bedingung *f*

provocative [prə'vɒkətɪv] *adj* provozierend

provoke [prə'vəʊk] *vt* provozieren; (*cause*) hervorrufen

prow [praʊ] *n* Bug *m*

prowess ['praʊes] *n* überragende(s) Können *nt*

prowl [praʊl] *vi* herumstreichen; (*animal*) schleichen ♦ *n*: **on the ~** umherstreifend; **~er** *n* Herumtreiber(in) *m(f)*

proximity [prɒk'sɪmɪtɪ] *n* Nähe *f*

proxy ['prɒksɪ] *n* (Stell)vertreter *m*; (*authority, document*) Vollmacht *f*; **by ~** durch einen Stellvertreter

prudence ['pruːdəns] *n* Umsicht *f*

prudent ['pruːdənt] *adj* klug, umsichtig

prudish ['pruːdɪʃ] *adj* prüde

prune [pruːn] *n* Backpflaume *f* ♦ *vt* ausputzen; (*fig*) zurechtstutzen

pry [praɪ] *vi*: **to ~ (into)** seine Nase stecken (in +*acc*)

PS *n abbr* (= *postscript*) PS

pseudo- ['sjuːdəʊ] *prefix* Pseudo-; **~nym** ['sjuːdənɪm] *n* Pseudonym *nt*, Deckname *m*

psychiatric [saɪkɪ'ætrɪk] *adj* psychiatrisch

psychiatrist [saɪ'kaɪətrɪst] *n* Psychiater *m*

psychic ['saɪkɪk] *adj* (*also:* **~al**) übersinnlich; (*person*) paranormal begabt

psychoanalyse [saɪkəʊ'ænəlaɪz] (*US* **psychoanalyze**) *vt* psychoanalytisch behandeln

psychoanalyst [saɪkəʊ'ænəlɪst] *n* Psychoanalytiker(in) *m(f)*

psychological [saɪkə'lɒdʒɪkəl] *adj* psychologisch

psychologist [saɪ'kɒlədʒɪst] *n* Psychologe *m*, Psychologin *f*

psychology [saɪ'kɒlədʒɪ] *n* Psychologie *f*

PTO *abbr* = **please turn over**

pub [pʌb] *n abbr* (= *public house*) Kneipe *f*

pubic ['pjuːbɪk] *adj* Scham-

public ['pʌblɪk] *adj* öffentlich ♦ *n* (*also:* **general ~**) Öffentlichkeit *f*; **in ~** in der Öffentlichkeit; **~ address system** *n* Lautsprecheranlage *f*

publican ['pʌblɪkən] *n* Wirt *m*

publication [pʌblɪ'keɪʃən] *n* Veröffentlichung *f*

public: **~ company** *n* Aktiengesellschaft *f*; **~ convenience** (*BRIT*) *n* öffentliche Toiletten *pl*; **~ holiday** *n* gesetzliche(r) Feiertag *m*; **~ house** (*BRIT*) *n* Lokal *nt*, Kneipe *f*

publicity [pʌb'lɪsɪtɪ] *n* Publicity *f*, Werbung *f*

publicize ['pʌblɪsaɪz] *vt* bekannt machen; (*advertise*) Publicity machen für

publicly ['pʌblɪklɪ] *adv* öffentlich

public: **~ opinion** *n* öffentliche Meinung *f*; **~ relations** *npl* Public Relations *pl*; **~ school** *n* (*BRIT*) Privatschule *f*; (*US*) staatliche Schule *f*; **~-spirited** *adj* mit Gemeinschaftssinn; **~ transport** *n* öffentliche Verkehrsmittel *pl*

publish ['pʌblɪʃ] *vt* veröffentlichen; (*event*) bekanntgeben; **~er** *n* Verleger *m*; **~ing** *n* (*business*) Verlagswesen *nt*

puce [pjuːs] *adj* violettbraun

pucker ['pʌkə*] *vt* (*face*) verziehen; (*lips*) kräuseln

pudding ['pʊdɪŋ] *n* (*BRIT*: *course*)

Nachtisch *m*; Pudding *m*; **black** ~ ≈ Blutwurst *f*

puddle ['pʌdl] *n* Pfütze *f*

puff [pʌf] *n* (*of wind etc*) Stoß *m*; (*cosmetic*) Puderquaste *f* ♦ *vt* blasen, pusten; (*pipe*) paffen ♦ *vi* keuchen, schnaufen; (*smoke*) paffen; **to** ~ **out smoke** Rauch ausstoßen; ~**ed** (*inf*) *adj* (*out of breath*) außer Puste; ~ **pastry** (*US* ~ **paste**) *n* Blätterteig *m*; ~**y** *adj* aufgedunsen

pull [pʊl] *n* Ruck *m*; (*influence*) Beziehung *f* ♦ *vt* ziehen; (*trigger*) abdrücken ♦ *vi* ziehen; **to** ~ **sb's leg** jdn auf den Arm nehmen; **to** ~ **to pieces** in Stücke reißen; (*fig*) verreißen; **to** ~ **one's punches** sich zurückhalten; **to** ~ **one's weight** sich in die Riemen legen; **to** ~ **o.s. together** sich zusammenreißen; ~ **apart** *vt* (*break*) zerreißen; (*dismantle*) auseinandernehmen; (*fighters*) trennen; ~ **down** *vt* (*house*) abreißen; ~ **in** *vi* hineinfahren; (*stop*) anhalten; (*RAIL*) einfahren; ~ **off** *vt* (*deal etc*) abschließen; ~ **out** *vi* (*car*) herausfahren; (*fig: partner*) aussteigen ♦ *vt* herausziehen; ~ **over** *vi* (*AUT*) an die Seite fahren; ~ **round** *vi* durchkommen; ~ **through** *vi* durchkommen; ~ **up** *vi* anhalten ♦ *vt* (*uproot*) herausreißen; (*stop*) anhalten

pulley ['pʊlɪ] *n* Rolle *f*, Flaschenzug *m*

pullover ['pʊləʊvə*] *n* Pullover *m*

pulp [pʌlp] *n* Brei *m*; (*of fruit*) Fruchtfleisch *nt*

pulpit ['pʊlpɪt] *n* Kanzel *f*

pulsate [pʌl'seɪt] *vi* pulsieren

pulse [pʌls] *n* Puls *m*

pummel ['pʌml] *vt* mit den Fäusten bearbeiten

pump [pʌmp] *n* Pumpe *f*; (*shoe*) leichter (Tanz)schuh *m* ♦ *vt* pumpen; ~ **up** *vt* (*tyre*) aufpumpen

pumpkin ['pʌmpkɪn] *n* Kürbis *m*

pun [pʌn] *n* Wortspiel *nt*

punch [pʌntʃ] *n* (*tool*) Locher *m*; (*blow*) (Faust)schlag *m*; (*drink*) Punsch *m*, Bowle *f* ♦ *vt* lochen; (*strike*) schlagen, boxen; ~**line** *n* Pointe *f*; ~-**up** (*BRIT: inf*) *n* Keilerei *f*

punctual ['pʌŋktjʊəl] *adj* pünktlich

punctuate ['pʌŋktjʊeɪt] *vt* mit Satzzeichen versehen; (*fig*) unterbrechen

punctuation [pʌŋktjʊ'eɪʃən] *n* Zeichensetzung *f*, Interpunktion *f*

puncture ['pʌŋktʃə*] *n* Loch *nt*; (*AUT*) Reifenpanne *f* ♦ *vt* durchbohren

pundit ['pʌndɪt] *n* Gelehrte(r) *m*

pungent ['pʌndʒənt] *adj* scharf

punish ['pʌnɪʃ] *vt* bestrafen; (*in boxing etc*) übel zurichten; ~**ment** *n* Strafe *f*; (*action*) Bestrafung *f*

punk [pʌŋk] *n* (*also*: ~ *rocker*) Punker(in) *m(f)*; (*also*: ~ *rock*) Punk *m*; (*US: inf: hoodlum*) Ganove *m*

punt [pʌnt] *n* Stechkahn *m*

punter ['pʌntə*] (*BRIT*) *n* (*better*) Wetter *m*

puny ['pjuːnɪ] *adj* kümmerlich

pup [pʌp] *n* = **puppy**

pupil ['pjuːpl] *n* Schüler(in) *m(f)*; (*in eye*) Pupille *f*

puppet ['pʌpɪt] *n* Puppe *f*; Marionette *f*

puppy ['pʌpɪ] *n* junge(r) Hund *m*

purchase ['pɜːtʃɪs] *n* Kauf *m*; (*grip*) Halt *m* ♦ *vt* kaufen, erwerben; ~**r** *n* Käufer(in) *m(f)*

pure [pjʊə*] *adj* (*also fig*) rein; ~**ly** ['pjʊəlɪ] *adv* rein

purgatory ['pɜːgətərɪ] *n* Fegefeuer *nt*

purge [pɜːdʒ] *n* (*also POL*) Säuberung *f*; (*medicine*) Abführmittel *nt* ♦ *vt* reinigen; (*body*) entschlacken

purify ['pjʊərɪfaɪ] *vt* reinigen

purity ['pjʊərɪtɪ] *n* Reinheit *f*

purl [pɜːl] *n* linke Masche *f*

purple ['pɜːpl] *adj* violett; (*face*) dunkelrot

purport [pɜː'pɔːt] *vi* vorgeben

purpose ['pɜːpəs] *n* Zweck *m*, Ziel *nt*; (*of person*) Absicht *f*; **on** ~ absichtlich; ~**ful** *adj* zielbewußt, entschlossen

purr [pɜː*] *n* Schnurren *nt* ♦ *vi* schnurren

purse [pɜːs] *n* Portemonnaie *nt*, Geldbeutel *m* ♦ *vt* (*lips*) zusammenpressen, schürzen

purser ['pɜːsə*] *n* Zahlmeister *m*

pursue [pə'sjuː] *vt* verfolgen; (*study*) nachgehen +*dat*; ~**r** *n* Verfolger *m*

pursuit [pə'sju:t] n Verfolgung f; (occupation) Beschäftigung f
purveyor [pɜ:'veɪə*] n Lieferant m
pus [pʌs] n Eiter m
push [pʊʃ] n Stoß m, Schub m; (MIL) Vorstoß m ♦ vt stoßen, schieben; (button) drücken; (idea) durchsetzen ♦ vi stoßen, schieben; ~ **aside** vt beiseiteschieben; ~ **off** (inf) vi abschieben; ~ **on** vi weitermachen; ~ **through** vt durchdrücken; (policy) durchsetzen; ~ **up** vt (total) erhöhen; (prices) hochtreiben; ~**chair** (BRIT) n (Kinder)sportwagen m; ~**over** (inf) n Kinderspiel nt; ~-**up** (US) n (press-up) Liegestütz m; ~**y** (inf) adj aufdringlich
puss [pʊs] n Mieze(katze) f; ~**y(-cat)** ['pʊsɪ(kæt)] n Mieze(katze) f
put [pʊt] (pt, pp **put**) vt setzen, stellen, legen; (express) ausdrücken, sagen; (write) schreiben; ~ **about** vi (turn back) wenden ♦ vt (spread) verbreiten; ~ **across** vt (explain) erklären; ~ **away** vt weglegen; (store) beiseitelegen; ~ **back** vt zurückstellen or -legen; ~ **by** vt zurücklegen, sparen; ~ **down** vt hinstellen or -legen; (rebellion) niederschlagen; (animal) einschläfern; (in writing) niederschreiben; ~ **forward** vt (idea) vorbringen; (clock) vorstellen; ~ **in** vt (application, complaint) einreichen; ~ **off** vt verschieben; (discourage): **to** ~ **sb off sth** jdn von etw abbringen; ~ **on** vt (clothes etc) anziehen; (light etc) anschalten, anmachen; (play etc) aufführen; (brake) anziehen; ~ **out** vt (hand etc) (her)ausstrecken; (news, rumour) verbreiten; (light etc) ausschalten, ausmachen; ~ **up** vt (tent) aufstellen; (building) errichten; (price) erhöhen; (person) unterbringen; ~ **up with** vt fus sich abfinden mit
putrid ['pju:trɪd] adj faul
putt [pʌt] vt (golf) putten ♦ n (golf) Putten nt; ~**ing green** n kleine(r) Golfplatz m nur zum Putten
putty ['pʌtɪ] n Kitt m; (fig) Wachs nt
put-up ['pʊtʌp] adj: ~ **job** abgekartete(s) Spiel nt

puzzle ['pʌzl] n Rätsel nt; (toy) Geduldspiel nt ♦ vt verwirren ♦ vi sich den Kopf zerbrechen
puzzling ['pʌzlɪŋ] adj rätselhaft, verwirrend
pyjamas [pɪ'dʒɑ:məz] (BRIT) npl Schlafanzug m, Pyjama m
pylon ['paɪlən] n Mast m
pyramid ['pɪrəmɪd] n Pyramide f

Q

quack [kwæk] n Quaken nt; (doctor) Quacksalber m ♦ vi quaken
quad [kwɒd] n abbr = **quadrangle**; **quadruplet**
quadrangle ['kwɒdræŋgl] n (court) Hof m; (MATH) Viereck nt
quadruple [kwɒ'dru:pl] adj vierfach ♦ vi sich vervierfachen ♦ vt vervierfachen
quadruplets [kwɒ'dru:pləts] npl Vierlinge pl
quagmire ['kwægmaɪə*] n Morast m
quail [kweɪl] n (bird) Wachtel f ♦ vi (vor Angst) zittern
quaint [kweɪnt] adj kurios; malerisch
quake [kweɪk] vi beben, zittern ♦ n abbr = **earthquake**
Quaker ['kweɪkə*] n Quäker(in) m(f)
qualification [kwɒlɪfɪ'keɪʃən] n Qualifikation f; (sth which limits) Einschränkung f
qualified ['kwɒlɪfaɪd] adj (competent) qualifiziert; (limited) bedingt
qualify ['kwɒlɪfaɪ] vt (prepare) befähigen; (limit) einschränken ♦ vi sich qualifizieren; **to** ~ **as a doctor/lawyer** sein juristisches/medizinisches Staatsexamen machen
quality ['kwɒlɪtɪ] n Qualität f; (characteristic) Eigenschaft f
qualm [kwɑ:m] n Bedenken nt
quandary ['kwɒndərɪ] n: **to be in a** ~ in Verlegenheit sein
quantity ['kwɒntɪtɪ] n Menge f; ~ **surveyor** n Baukostenkalkulator m
quarantine ['kwɒrənti:n] n Quarantäne f
quarrel ['kwɒrəl] n Streit m ♦ vi sich streiten; ~**some** adj streitsüchtig

quarry ['kwɒrɪ] n Steinbruch m; (animal) Wild nt; (fig) Opfer nt
quart [kwɔːt] n Quart nt
quarter ['kwɔːtə*] n Viertel nt; (of year) Quartal nt ♦ vt (divide) vierteln; (MIL) einquartieren; ~s npl (esp MIL) Quartier nt; ~ **final** n Viertelfinale nt; ~**ly** adj vierteljährlich; ~**master** n Quartiermeister m
quartet(te) [kwɔː'tet] n Quartett nt
quartz [kwɔːts] n Quarz m
quash [kwɒʃ] vt (verdict) aufheben
quasi- ['kwɑːzɪ] prefix Quasi-
quaver ['kweɪvə*] n (BRIT: MUS) Achtelnote f ♦ vi (tremble) zittern
quay [kiː] n Kai m
queasy ['kwiːzɪ] adj übel
queen [kwiːn] n Königin f; ~ **mother** n Königinmutter f
queer [kwɪə*] adj seltsam ♦ n (inf: homosexual) Schwule(r) m
quell [kwel] vt unterdrücken
quench [kwentʃ] vt (thirst) löschen
querulous ['kwerʊləs] adj nörglerisch
query ['kwɪərɪ] n (question) (An)frage f; (question mark) Fragezeichen nt ♦ vt in Zweifel ziehen, in Frage stellen
quest [kwest] n Suche f
question ['kwestʃən] n Frage f ♦ vt (ask) (be)fragen; (suspect) verhören; (doubt) in Frage stellen, bezweifeln; **beyond** ~ ohne Frage; **out of the** ~ ausgeschlossen; ~**able** adj zweifelhaft; ~**mark** n Fragezeichen nt
questionnaire [kwestʃə'nɛə*] n Fragebogen m
queue [kjuː] n (BRIT) Schlange f ♦ vi (also: ~ up) Schlange stehen
quibble ['kwɪbl] vi kleinlich sein
quick [kwɪk] adj schnell ♦ n (of nail) Nagelhaut f; **be** ~! mach schnell!; **cut to the** ~ (fig) tief getroffen; ~**en** vt (hasten) beschleunigen ♦ vi sich beschleunigen; ~**ly** adj schnell; ~**sand** n Treibsand m; ~**-witted** adj schlagfertig
quid [kwɪd] (BRIT: inf) n (£1) Pfund nt
quiet ['kwaɪət] adj (without noise) leise; (peaceful, calm) still, ruhig ♦ n Stille f, Ruhe f ♦ vt, vi (US) = ~**en**; **keep** ~! sei

still!; ~**en** vi (also: ~**en down**) ruhig werden ♦ vt (also: ~**en down**) beruhigen; ~**ly** adv leise, ruhig; ~**ness** n Ruhe f, Stille f
quilt [kwɪlt] n (continental ~) Steppdecke f
quin [kwɪn] n abbr = **quintuplet**
quinine [kwɪ'niːn] n Chinin nt
quintuplets [kwɪn'tjuːpləts] npl Fünflinge pl
quip [kwɪp] n witzige Bemerkung f
quirk [kwɜːk] n (oddity) Eigenart f
quit [kwɪt] (pt, pp **quit** or **quitted**) vt verlassen ♦ vi aufhören
quite [kwaɪt] adv (completely) ganz, völlig; (fairly) ziemlich; ~ **a few of them** ziemlich viele von ihnen; ~ (**so**)! richtig!
quits [kwɪts] adj quitt; **let's call it** ~ lassen wir's gut sein
quiver ['kwɪvə*] vi zittern ♦ n (for arrows) Köcher m
quiz [kwɪz] n (competition) Quiz nt ♦ vt prüfen; ~**zical** adj fragend
quorum ['kwɔːrəm] n beschlußfähige Anzahl f
quota ['kwəʊtə] n Anteil m; (COMM) Quote f
quotation [kwəʊ'teɪʃən] n Zitat nt; (price) Kostenvoranschlag m; ~ **marks** npl Anführungszeichen pl
quote [kwəʊt] n = **quotation** ♦ vi (from book) zitieren ♦ vt (from book) zitieren; (price) angeben

R

rabbi ['ræbaɪ] n Rabbiner m; (title) Rabbi m
rabbit ['ræbɪt] n Kaninchen nt; ~ **hole** n Kaninchenbau m; ~ **hutch** n Kaninchenstall m
rabble ['ræbl] n Pöbel m
rabies ['reɪbiːz] n Tollwut f
RAC (BRIT) n abbr = **Royal Automobile Club**
raccoon [rə'kuːn] n Waschbär m
race [reɪs] n (species) Rasse f; (competition) Rennen nt; (on foot)

Rennen *nt*, Wettlauf *m*; (*rush*) Hetze *f* ♦ *vt* um die Wette laufen mit; (*horses*) laufen lassen ♦ *vi* (*run*) rennen; (*in contest*) am Rennen teilnehmen; ~ **car** (*US*) *n* = **racing car**; ~ **car driver** (*US*) *n* = **racing driver**; ~**course** *n* (*for horses*) Rennbahn *f*; ~**horse** *n* Rennpferd *nt*; ~**track** *n* (*for cars etc*) Rennstrecke *f*

racial ['reɪʃəl] *adj* Rassen-; ~**ist** *adj* rassistisch ♦ *n* Rassist *m*

racing ['reɪsɪŋ] *n* Rennen *nt*; ~ **car** (*BRIT*) *n* Rennwagen *m*; ~ **driver** (*BRIT*) *n* Rennfahrer *m*

racism ['reɪsɪzəm] *n* Rassismus *m*

racist ['reɪsɪst] *n* Rassist *m* ♦ *adj* rassistisch

rack [ræk] *n* Ständer *m*, Gestell *nt* ♦ *vt* plagen; **to go to ~ and ruin** verfallen; **to ~ one's brains** sich *dat* den Kopf zerbrechen

racket ['rækɪt] *n* (*din*) Krach *m*; (*scheme*) (Schwindel)geschäft *nt*; (*TENNIS: also racquet*) (Tennis)schläger *m*

racoon [rə'ku:n] *n* = **raccoon**

racquet ['rækɪt] *n* (Tennis)schläger *m*

racy ['reɪsɪ] *adj* gewagt; (*style*) spritzig

radar ['reɪdɑ:*] *n* Radar *nt or* m

radial ['reɪdɪəl] *adj* (*also: US: ~-ply*) radial

radiance ['reɪdɪəns] *n* strahlende(r) Glanz *m*

radiant ['reɪdɪənt] *adj* strahlend; (*giving out rays*) Strahlungs-

radiate ['reɪdɪeɪt] *vi* ausstrahlen; (*roads, lines*) strahlenförmig wegführen ♦ *vt* ausstrahlen

radiation [reɪdɪ'eɪʃən] *n* (Aus)strahlung *f*

radiator ['reɪdɪeɪtə*] *n* (*for heating*) Heizkörper *m*; (*AUT*) Kühler *m*

radical ['rædɪkəl] *adj* radikal; ~**ly** *adv* radikal

radii ['reɪdɪaɪ] *npl of* **radius**

radio ['reɪdɪəʊ] *n* Rundfunk *m*, Radio *nt*; (*set*) Radio *nt*, Radioapparat *m*; **on the ~** im Radio; ~**active** [reɪdɪəʊ'æktɪv] *adj* radioaktiv; ~**logy** [reɪdɪ'ɒlədʒɪ] *n* Strahlenkunde *f*; ~ **station** *n* Rundfunk-

station *f*; ~**therapy** ['reɪdɪəʊ'θerəpɪ] *n* Röntgentherapie *f*

radish ['rædɪʃ] *n* (*big*) Rettich *m*; (*small*) Radieschen *nt*

radius ['reɪdɪəs] (*pl* **radii**) *n* Radius *m*; (*area*) Umkreis *m*

RAF *n abbr* = **Royal Air Force**

raffle ['ræfl] *n* Verlosung *f*, Tombola *f* ♦ *vt* verlosen

raft [rɑ:ft] *n* Floß *nt*

rafter ['rɑ:ftə*] *n* Dachsparren *m*

rag [ræg] *n* (*cloth*) Lumpen *m*, Lappen *m*; (*inf: newspaper*) Käseblatt *nt*; (*UNIV: for charity*) studentische Sammelaktion *f* ♦ *vt* (*BRIT*) auf den Arm nehmen; ~**s** *npl* (*cloth*) Lumpen *pl*; ~**-and-bone man** (*irreg; BRIT*) *n* = **ragman**; ~ **doll** *n* Flickenpuppe *f*

rage [reɪdʒ] *n* Wut *f*; (*fashion*) große Mode *f* ♦ *vi* wüten, toben

ragged ['rægɪd] *adj* (*edge*) gezackt; (*clothes*) zerlumpt

ragman ['rægmæn] (*irreg*) *n* Lumpensammler *m*

raid [reɪd] *n* Überfall *m*; (*MIL*) Angriff *m*; (*by police*) Razzia *f* ♦ *vt* überfallen; ~**er** *n* (*person*) (Bank)räuber *m*

rail [reɪl] *n* (*also: RAIL*) Schiene *f*; (*on stair*) Geländer *nt*; (*of ship*) Reling *f*; ~**s** *npl* (*RAIL*) Geleise *pl*; **by ~** per Bahn; ~**ing(s)** *n(pl)* Geländer *nt*; ~**road** (*US*) *n* Eisenbahn *f*; ~**way** (*BRIT*) *n* Eisenbahn *f*; ~**way line** (*BRIT*) *n* Eisenbahnlinie *f*; (*track*) Gleis *nt*; ~**wayman** (*irreg; BRIT*) *n* Eisenbahner *m*; ~**way station** (*BRIT*) *n* Bahnhof *m*

rain [reɪn] *n* Regen *m* ♦ *vt, vi* regnen; **in the ~** im Regen; **it's ~ing** es regnet; ~**bow** *n* Regenbogen *m*; ~**coat** *n* Regenmantel *m*; ~**drop** *n* Regentropfen *m*; ~**fall** *n* Niederschlag *m*; ~**y** *adj* (*region, season*) Regen-; (*day*) regnerisch, verregnet

raise [reɪz] *n* (*esp US: increase*) (Gehalts)erhöhung *f* ♦ *vt* (*lift*) (hoch)heben; (*increase*) erhöhen; (*question*) aufwerfen; (*doubts*) äußern; (*funds*) beschaffen; (*family*) großziehen; (*livestock*) züchten; **to ~ one's voice** die Stimme erheben

raisin ['reɪzən] n Rosine f
rake [reɪk] n Rechen m, Harke f; (person) Wüstling m ♦ vt rechen, harken; (with gun) (mit Feuer) bestreichen; (search) (durch)suchen
rakish ['reɪkɪʃ] adj verwegen
rally ['rælɪ] n (POL etc) Kundgebung f; (AUT) Rallye f ♦ vt (MIL) sammeln ♦ vi Kräfte sammeln; ~ round vt fus (sich) scharen um; (help) zu Hilfe kommen +dat ♦ vi zu Hilfe kommen
RAM [ræm] n abbr (= random access memory) RAM m
ram [ræm] n Widder m; (instrument) Ramme f ♦ vt (strike) rammen; (stuff) (hinein)stopfen
ramble ['ræmbl] n Wanderung f ♦ vi (talk) schwafeln; ~r n Wanderer m
rambling ['ræmblɪŋ] adj (speech) weitschweifig; (town) ausgedehnt
ramp [ræmp] n Rampe f; on/off ~ (US: AUT) Ein-/Ausfahrt f
rampage [ræm'peɪdʒ] n: to be on the ~ randalieren ♦ vi randalieren
rampant ['ræmpənt] adj wild wuchernd
rampart ['ræmpɑːt] n (Schutz)wall m
ramshackle ['ræmʃækl] adj baufällig
ran [ræn] pt of run
ranch [rɑːntʃ] n Ranch f
rancid ['rænsɪd] adj ranzig
rancour ['ræŋkə*] (US **rancor**) n Verbitterung f, Groll m
random ['rændəm] adj ziellos, wahllos ♦ n: at ~ aufs Geratewohl; ~ **access** n (COMPUT) wahlfreie(r) Zugriff m
randy ['rændɪ] (BRIT: inf) adj geil, scharf
rang [ræŋ] pt of ring
range [reɪndʒ] n Reihe f; (of mountains) Kette f; (COMM) Sortiment nt; (reach) (Reich)weite f; (of gun) Schußweite f; (for shooting practice) Schießplatz m; (stove) (großer) Herd m ♦ vt (set in row) anordnen, aufstellen; (roam) durchstreifen ♦ vi: to ~ over (wander) umherstreifen in +dat; (extend) sich erstrecken auf +acc; a ~ of (selection) eine (große) Auswahl an +dat; prices ranging from £5 to £10 Preise, die sich zwischen £5 und £10 bewegen; ~r

['reɪndʒə*] n Förster m
rank [ræŋk] n (row) Reihe f; (BRIT: also: taxi ~) (Taxi)stand m; (MIL) Rang m; (social position) Stand m ♦ vi (have ~): to ~ among gehören zu ♦ adj (strong-smelling) stinkend; (extreme) krass; the ~ and file (fig) die breite Masse
rankle ['ræŋkl] vi nagen
ransack ['rænsæk] vt (plunder) plündern; (search) durchwühlen
ransom ['rænsəm] n Lösegeld nt; to hold sb to ~ jdn gegen Lösegeld festhalten
rant [rænt] vi hochtrabend reden
rap [ræp] n Schlag m ♦ vt klopfen
rape [reɪp] n Vergewaltigung f; (BOT) Raps m ♦ vt vergewaltigen; ~(**seed**) **oil** n Rapsöl nt
rapid ['ræpɪd] adj rasch, schnell; ~**ity** [rə'pɪdɪtɪ] n Schnelligkeit f; ~**ly** adv schnell; ~**s** npl Stromschnellen pl
rapist ['reɪpɪst] n Vergewaltiger m
rapport [ræ'pɔː*] n gute(s) Verhältnis nt
rapture ['ræptʃə*] n Entzücken nt
rapturous ['ræptʃərəs] adj (applause) stürmisch; (expression) verzückt
rare [reə*] adj selten, rar; (underdone) nicht durchgebraten
rarely ['reəlɪ] adv selten
raring ['reərɪŋ] adj: to be ~ to go (inf) es kaum erwarten können, bis es losgeht
rarity ['reərɪtɪ] n Seltenheit f
rascal ['rɑːskəl] n Schuft m
rash [ræʃ] adj übereilt; (reckless) unbesonnen ♦ n (Haut)ausschlag m
rasher ['ræʃə*] n Speckscheibe f
raspberry ['rɑːzbərɪ] n Himbeere f
rasping ['rɑːspɪŋ] adj (noise) kratzend; (voice) krächzend
rat [ræt] n (animal) Ratte f; (person) Halunke m
rate [reɪt] n (proportion) Rate f; (price) Tarif m; (speed) Tempo nt ♦ vt (ein)schätzen; ~**s** npl (BRIT: tax) Grundsteuer f; to ~ as für etw halten; ~**able value** (BRIT) n Einheitswert m (als Bemessungsgrundlage); ~**payer** (BRIT) n Steuerzahler(in) m(f)
rather ['rɑːðə*] adv (in preference)

lieber, eher; (to some extent) ziemlich;
I would or **I'd ~ go** ich würde lieber
gehen
ratify ['rætɪfaɪ] vt bestätigen; (POL)
ratifizieren
rating ['reɪtɪŋ] n Klasse f; (BRIT: sailor)
Matrose m
ratio ['reɪʃɪəʊ] n Verhältnis nt; **in the ~
of 100 to 1** im Verhältnis 100 zu 1
ration ['ræʃən] n (usu pl) Ration f ♦ vt
rationieren
rational ['ræʃənl] adj rational; **~e**
[ræʃə'nɑːl] n Grundprinzip nt; **~ize**
['ræʃnəlaɪz] vt rationalisieren; **~ly** adv
rational
rat race n Konkurrenzkampf m
rattle ['rætl] n (sound) Rasseln nt; (toy)
Rassel f ♦ vi ratteln, klappern ♦ vt
rasseln mit; **~snake** n Klapperschlange
f
raucous ['rɔːkəs] adj heiser, rauh
ravage ['rævɪdʒ] vt verheeren; **~s** npl
verheerende Wirkungen pl
rave [reɪv] vi (talk wildly) phantasieren;
(rage) toben
raven ['reɪvn] n Rabe m
ravenous ['rævənəs] adj heißhungrig
ravine [rə'viːn] n Schlucht f
raving ['reɪvɪŋ] adj: **~ lunatic** völlig
Wahnsinnige(r) mf
ravishing ['rævɪʃɪŋ] adj atemberaubend
raw [rɔː] adj roh; (tender)
wund(gerieben); (inexperienced) unerfahren; **to get a ~ deal** (inf) schlecht
wegkommen; **~ material** n Roh-
material nt
ray [reɪ] n (of light) Strahl m; **~ of hope**
Hoffnungsschimmer m
raze [reɪz] vt (also: raze to the ground)
dem Erdboden gleichmachen
razor ['reɪzə*] n Rasierapparat m; **~
blade** n Rasierklinge f
Rd abbr = **road**
re [riː] prep (COMM) betreffs +gen
reach [riːtʃ] n Reichweite f; (of river)
Strecke f ♦ vt (arrive at) erreichen;
(give) reichen ♦ vi (stretch) sich erstrecken; **within ~** (shops etc) in
erreichbarer Weite or Entfernung; **out
of ~** außer Reichweite; **to ~ for** (try to

get) langen nach; **~ out** vi die Hand
ausstrecken; **to ~ out for sth** nach etw
greifen
react [riː'ækt] vi reagieren; **~ion**
[riː'ækʃən] n Reaktion f
reactor [riː'æktə*] n Reaktor m
read[1] [red] pt, pp of **read**[2]
read[2] [riːd] (pt, pp read) vt, vi lesen;
(aloud) vorlesen; **~ out** vt vorlesen;
~able adj leserlich; (worth reading)
lesenswert; **~er** n (person) Leser(in)
m(f); (book) Lesebuch nt; **~ership** n
Leserschaft f
readily ['redɪlɪ] adv (willingly)
bereitwillig; (easily) prompt
readiness ['redɪnəs] n (willingness)
Bereitwilligkeit f; (being ready) Bereitschaft f; **in ~** (prepared) bereit
reading ['riːdɪŋ] n Lesen nt
readjust ['riːə'dʒʌst] vt neu einstellen ♦
vi (person): **to ~ to** sich wieder anpassen an +acc
ready ['redɪ] adj (prepared, willing)
bereit ♦ adv: **~-cooked** vorgekocht ♦ n:
at the ~ bereit; **~-made** adj gebrauchsfertig, Fertig-; (clothes)
Konfektions-; **~ money** n Bargeld nt;
~ reckoner n Rechentabelle f; **~-to-
wear** adj Konfektions-
real [rɪəl] adj wirklich; (actual) eigentlich; (not fake) echt; **in ~ terms**
effektiv; **~ estate** n Grundbesitz m;
~istic [rɪə'lɪstɪk] adj realistisch;
~istically adv realistisch
reality [riː'ælɪtɪ] n Wirklichkeit f, Reali-
tät f; **in ~** in Wirklichkeit
realization [rɪəlaɪ'zeɪʃən] n (understanding) Erkenntnis f; (fulfilment)
Verwirklichung f
realize ['rɪəlaɪz] vt (understand) begreifen; (make real) verwirklichen;
(money) einbringen; **I didn't ~ ...** ich
wußte nicht...
really ['rɪəlɪ] adv wirklich
realm [relm] n Reich nt
realtor ['rɪəltɔː*] (US) n Grund-
stücksmakler(in) m(f)
reap [riːp] vt ernten
reappear ['riːə'pɪə*] vi wieder erscheinen

rear [rɪə*] *adj* hintere(r, s), Rück- ♦ *n* Rückseite *f*; (*last part*) Schluß *m* ♦ *vt* (*bring up*) aufziehen ♦ *vi* (*horse*) sich aufbäumen; ~**guard** *n* Nachhut *f*

rearmament ['riː'ɑːməmənt] *n* Wiederaufrüstung *f*

rearrange ['riːə'reɪndʒ] *vt* umordnen

rear-view mirror ['rɪəvjuː-] *n* Rückspiegel *m*

reason ['riːzn] *n* (*cause*) Grund *m*; (*ability to think*) Verstand *m*; (*sensible thoughts*) Vernunft *f* ♦ *vi* (*think*) denken; (*use arguments*) argumentieren; **it stands to ~ that** es ist logisch, daß; **to ~ with sb** mit jdm diskutieren; ~**able** *adj* vernünftig; ~**ably** *adv* vernünftig; (*fairly*) ziemlich; ~**ed** *adj* (*argument*) durchdacht; ~**ing** *n* Urteilen *nt*; (*argumentation*) Beweisführung *f*

reassurance ['riːə'ʃuərəns] *n* Beruhigung *f*; (*confirmation*) Bestätigung *f*

reassure ['riːə'ʃuə*] *vt* beruhigen; **to ~ sb of sth** jdm etw versichern

reassuring ['riːə'ʃuərɪŋ] *adj* beruhigend

rebate [n 'riːbeɪt] *n* Rückzahlung *f*

rebel [n 'rebl, vb rɪ'bel] *n* Rebell *m* ♦ *vi* rebellieren; ~**lion** [rɪ'beljən] *n* Rebellion *f*, Aufstand *m*

rebirth ['riː'bɜːθ] *n* Wiedergeburt *f*

rebound [vb rɪ'baʊnd, n 'riːbaʊnd] *vi* zurückprallen ♦ *n* Rückprall *m*

rebuff [rɪ'bʌf] *n* Abfuhr *f* ♦ *vt* abblitzen lassen

rebuild ['riː'bɪld] (*irreg*) *vt* wiederaufbauen; (*fig*) wiederherstellen

rebuke [rɪ'bjuːk] *n* Tadel *m* ♦ *vt* tadeln, rügen

rebut [rɪ'bʌt] *vt* widerlegen

recalcitrant [rɪ'kælsɪtrənt] *adj* widerspenstig

recall [rɪ'kɔːl] *vt* (*call back*) zurückrufen; (*remember*) sich erinnern an +*acc* ♦ *n* Rückruf *m*

recant [rɪ'kænt] *vi* widerrufen

recap ['riːkæp] *vt, vi* wiederholen

recapitulate [riːkə'pɪtjuleɪt] *vt, vi* = **recap**

rec'd *abbr* (= *received*) Eing.

recede [rɪ'siːd] *vi* zurückweichen

receding [rɪ'siːdɪŋ] *adj*: ~ **hairline** Stirnglatze *f*

receipt [rɪ'siːt] *n* (*document*) Quittung *f*; (*receiving*) Empfang *m*; ~**s** *npl* (ECON) Einnahmen *pl*

receive [rɪ'siːv] *vt* erhalten; (*visitors etc*) empfangen; ~**r** [rɪ'siːvə*] *n* (TEL) Hörer *m*

recent ['riːsnt] *adj* vor kurzem (geschehen), neuerlich; (*modern*) neu; ~**ly** *adv* kürzlich, neulich

receptacle [rɪ'septəkl] *n* Behälter *m*

reception [rɪ'sepʃən] *n* Empfang *m*; ~ **desk** *n* Empfang *m*; (*in hotel*) Rezeption *f*; ~**ist** *n* (*in hotel*) Empfangschef *m*, Empfangsdame *f*; (MED) Sprechstundenhilfe *f*

receptive [rɪ'septɪv] *adj* aufnahmebereit

recess [rɪ'ses] *n* (*break*) Ferien *pl*; (*hollow*) Nische *f*; ~**ion** [rɪ'seʃən] *n* Rezession *f*

recharge ['riː'tʃɑːdʒ] *vt* (*battery*) aufladen

recipe ['resɪpɪ] *n* Rezept *nt*

recipient [rɪ'sɪpɪənt] *n* Empfänger *m*

reciprocal [rɪ'sɪprəkəl] *adj* gegenseitig; (*mutual*) wechselseitig

recital [rɪ'saɪtl] *n* Vortrag *m*

recite [rɪ'saɪt] *vt* vortragen, aufsagen

reckless ['rekləs] *adj* leichtsinnig; (*driving*) fahrlässig

reckon ['rekən] *vt* (*count*) rechnen, berechnen, errechnen; (*estimate*) schätzen; (*think*): **I ~ that ...** ich nehme an, daß ...; ~ **on** *vt fus* rechnen mit; ~**ing** *n* (*calculation*) Rechnen *nt*

reclaim [rɪ'kleɪm] *vt* (*expenses*) zurückverlangen; (*land*): **to ~ (from sth)** (etw *dat*) gewinnen

reclamation [reklə'meɪʃən] *n* (*of land*) Gewinnung *f*

recline [rɪ'klaɪn] *vi* sich zurücklehnen

reclining [rɪ'klaɪnɪŋ] *adj* Liege-

recluse [rɪ'kluːs] *n* Einsiedler *m*

recognition [rekəg'nɪʃən] *n* (*recognizing*) Erkennen *nt*; (*acknowledgement*) Anerkennung *f*; **transformed beyond ~** völlig verändert

recognizable ['rekəgnaɪzəbl] *adj* erkennbar

recognize ['rekəgnaɪz] *vt* erkennen; (*POL, approve*) anerkennen; **to ~ as** anerkennen als; **to ~ by** erkennen an +*dat*

recoil [rɪ'kɔɪl] *vi* (*in horror*) zurückschrecken; (*rebound*) zurückprallen; (*person*); **to ~ from doing sth** davor zurückschrecken, etw zu tun

recollect [rekə'lekt] *vt* sich erinnern an +*acc*; **~ion** [rekə'lekʃən] *n* Erinnerung *f*

recommend [rekə'mend] *vt* empfehlen; **~ation** *n* Empfehlung *f*

recompense ['rekəmpens] *n* (*compensation*) Entschädigung *f*; (*reward*) Belohnung *f* ♦ *vt* entschädigen; belohnen

reconcile ['rekənsaɪl] *vt* (*facts*) vereinbaren; (*people*) versöhnen; **to ~ o.s. to sth** sich mit etw abfinden

reconciliation [rekənsɪlɪ'eɪʃən] *n* Versöhnung *f*

recondition ['riːkən'dɪʃən] *vt* (*machine*) generalüberholen

reconnaissance [rɪ'kɒnɪsəns] *n* Aufklärung *f*

reconnoitre [rekə'nɔɪtə*] (*US* **reconnoiter**) *vt* erkunden ♦ *vi* aufklären

reconsider ['riːkən'sɪdə*] *vt* von neuem erwägen, noch einmal überdenken ♦ *vi* es noch einmal überdenken

reconstruct ['riːkən'strʌkt] *vt* wiederaufbauen; (*crime*) rekonstruieren; **~ion** ['riːkən'strʌkʃən] *n* Rekonstruktion *f*

record [*n* 'rekɔːd, *vb* rɪ'kɔːd] *n* Aufzeichnung *f*; (*MUS*) Schallplatte *f*; (*best performance*) Rekord *m* ♦ *vt* aufzeichnen; (*music etc*) aufnehmen; **off the ~** *adj* vertraulich ♦ *adv* im Vertrauen; **in ~ time** in Rekordzeit; **~ card** *n* (*in file*) Karteikarte *f*; **~ed delivery** [rɪ'kɔːdɪd-] (*BRIT*) *n* (*POST*) Einschreiben *nt*; **~er** [rɪ'kɔːdə*] *n* (*TECH*) Registriergerät *nt*; (*MUS*) Blockflöte *f*; **~ holder** *n* (*SPORT*) Rekordinhaber *m*; **~ing** [rɪ'kɔːdɪŋ] *n* (*MUS*) Aufnahme *f*; **~ player** *n* Plattenspieler *m*

recount [rɪ'kaʊnt] *vt* (*tell*) berichten

re-count ['riːkaʊnt] *n* Nachzählung *f* ♦ *vt* nachzählen

recoup [rɪ'kuːp] *vt*: **to ~ one's losses** seinen Verlust wiedergutmachen

recourse [rɪ'kɔːs] *n*: **to have ~ to** Zuflucht nehmen zu *or* bei

recover [rɪ'kʌvə*] *vt* (*get back*) zurückerhalten ♦ *vi* sich erholen

re-cover [riː'kʌvə*] *vt* (*quilt etc*) neu überziehen

recovery [rɪ'kʌvərɪ] *n* Wiedererlangung *f*; (*of health*) Erholung *f*

recreate ['riːkrɪ'eɪt] *vt* wiederherstellen

recreation [rekrɪ'eɪʃən] *n* Erholung *f*; **~al** *adj* Erholungs-

recrimination [rɪkrɪmɪ'neɪʃən] *n* Gegenbeschuldigung *f*

recruit [rɪ'kruːt] *n* Rekrut *m* ♦ *vt* rekrutieren; **~ment** *n* Rekrutierung *f*

rectangle ['rektæŋgl] *n* Rechteck *nt*

rectangular [rek'tæŋgjələ*] *adj* rechteckig, rechtwinklig

rectify ['rektɪfaɪ] *vt* berichtigen

rector ['rektə*] *n* (*REL*) Pfarrer *m*; (*SCH*) Direktor(in) *m(f)*; **~y** ['rektərɪ] *n* Pfarrhaus *nt*

recuperate [rɪ'kuːpəreɪt] *vi* sich erholen

recur [rɪ'kɜː*] *vi* sich wiederholen; **~rence** *n* Wiederholung *f*; **~rent** *adj* wiederkehrend

red [red] *n* Rot *nt*; (*POL*) Rote(r) *m* ♦ *adj* rot; **in the ~** in den roten Zahlen; **~ carpet treatment** *n* Sonderbehandlung *f*, große(r) Bahnhof *m*; **R~ Cross** *n* Rote(s) Kreuz *nt*; **~currant** *n* rote Johannisbeere *f*; **~den** *vi* sich röten; (*blush*) erröten ♦ *vt* röten; **~dish** *adj* rötlich

redeem [rɪ'diːm] *vt* (*COMM*) einlösen; (*save*) retten

redeeming [rɪ'diːmɪŋ] *adj*: **~ feature** versöhnende(s) Moment *nt*

redeploy ['riːdɪ'plɔɪ] *vt* (*resources*) umverteilen

red-haired ['red'heəd] *adj* rothaarig

red-handed ['red'hændɪd] *adv*: **to be caught ~** auf frischer Tat ertappt werden

redhead ['redhed] *n* Rothaarige(r) *mf*

red herring *n* Ablenkungsmanöver *nt*

red-hot ['red'hɒt] *adj* rotglühend

redirect ['riːdaɪ'rekt] *vt* umleiten

red light *n*: **to go through a ~** (*AUT*)

bei Rot über die Ampel fahren; **red-light district** n Strichviertel nt

redo ['ri:'du:] (irreg: like do) vt nochmals machen

redolent ['redəʊlənt] adj: ~ of riechend nach; (fig) erinnernd an +acc

redouble [ri:'dʌbl] vt: to ~ one's efforts seine Anstrengungen verdoppeln

redress [rɪ'dres] n Entschädigung f ♦ vt wiedergutmachen

Red Sea n: the ~ das Rote Meer

redskin ['redskɪn] n Rothaut f

red tape n Bürokratismus m

reduce [rɪ'dju:s] vt (speed, temperature) vermindern; (photo) verkleinern; "~ speed now" (AUT) ≈ „langsam"; to ~ the price (to) den Preis herabsetzen (auf +acc); **at a ~d price** zum ermäßigten Preis

reduction [rɪ'dʌkʃən] n Verminderung f; Verkleinerung f; Herabsetzung f; (amount of money) Nachlaß m

redundancy [rɪ'dʌndənsɪ] n Überflüssigkeit f; (of workers) Entlassung f

redundant [rɪ'dʌndənt] adj überflüssig; (workers) ohne Arbeitsplatz; **to be made ~** arbeitslos werden

reed [ri:d] n Schilf nt; (MUS) Rohrblatt nt

reef [ri:f] n Riff nt

reek [ri:k] vi: to ~ (of) stinken (nach)

reel [ri:l] n Spule f, Rolle f ♦ vt (also: ~ in) wickeln, spulen ♦ vi (stagger) taumeln

ref [ref] (inf) n abbr (= referee) Schiri m

refectory [rɪ'fektərɪ] n (UNIV) Mensa f; (SCH) Speisesaal m; (ECCL) Refektorium nt

refer [rɪ'fɜ:*] vt: to ~ sb to sb/sth jdn an jdn/etw verweisen ♦ vi: to ~ to (to book) nachschlagen in +dat; (mention) sich beziehen auf +acc

referee [refə'ri:] n Schiedsrichter m; (BRIT: for job) Referenz f ♦ vt schiedsrichtern

reference ['refrəns] n (for job) Referenz f; (in book) Verweis m; (number, code) Aktenzeichen nt; (allusion): ~ (to) Anspielung (auf +acc); **with ~ to**

in bezug auf +acc; ~ **book** n Nachschlagewerk nt; ~ **number** n Aktenzeichen nt

referenda [refə'rendə] npl of **referendum**

referendum [refə'rendəm] (pl **-da**) n Volksabstimmung f

refill [vb 'ri:'fɪl, n 'ri:fɪl] vt nachfüllen ♦ n (for pen) Ersatzmine f

refine [rɪ'faɪn] vt (purify) raffinieren; ~**d** adj kultiviert; ~**ment** n Kultiviertheit f

reflect [rɪ'flekt] vt (light) reflektieren; (fig) (wider)spiegeln ♦ vi (meditate): to ~ (on) nachdenken (über +acc); it ~**s badly/well on him** das stellt ihn in ein schlechtes/gutes Licht; ~**ion** [rɪ'flekʃən] n Reflexion f; (image) Spiegelbild nt; (thought) Überlegung f; on ~**ion** wenn man sich dat das recht überlegt

reflex ['ri:fleks] adj Reflex- ♦ n Reflex m; ~**ive** [rɪ'fleksɪv] adj reflexiv

reform [rɪ'fɔ:m] n Reform f ♦ vt (person) bessern; **the R~ation** [refə'meɪʃən] n die Reformation; ~**atory** (US) n Besserungsanstalt f

refrain [rɪ'freɪn] vi: to ~ **from** unterlassen ♦ n Refrain m

refresh [rɪ'freʃ] vt erfrischen; ~**er course** (BRIT) n Wiederholungskurs m; ~**ing** adj erfrischend; ~**ments** npl Erfrischungen pl

refrigeration [rɪfrɪdʒə'reɪʃən] n Kühlung f

refrigerator [rɪ'frɪdʒəreɪtə*] n Kühlschrank m

refuel ['ri:'fjʊəl] vt, vi auftanken

refuge ['refju:dʒ] n Zuflucht f; **to take ~ in** sich flüchten in +acc

refugee [refjʊ'dʒi:] n Flüchtling m

refund [n 'ri:fʌnd, vb rɪ'fʌnd] n Rückvergütung f ♦ vt zurückerstatten

refurbish ['ri:'fɜ:bɪʃ] vt aufpolieren

refusal [rɪ'fju:zəl] n (Ver)weigerung f; **first ~** Vorkaufsrecht nt

refuse¹ [rɪ'fju:z] vt abschlagen ♦ vi sich weigern

refuse² ['refju:s] n Abfall m, Müll m; ~ **collection** n Müllabfuhr f

refute [rɪ'fju:t] vt widerlegen

regain [rɪ'geɪn] vt wiedergewinnen; (consciousness) wiedererlangen

regal ['ri:gəl] adj königlich

regalia [rɪ'geɪlɪə] npl Insignien pl

regard [rɪ'gɑ:d] n Achtung f ♦ vt ansehen; **to send one's ~s to sb** jdn grüßen lassen; **"with kindest ~s"** „mit freundlichen Grüßen"; ♦ vi (as ~s or with ~ to bezüglich +gen, in bezug auf +acc; **~less** adj; **~less of** ohne Rücksicht auf +acc ♦ adv trotzdem

regenerate [rɪ'dʒenəreɪt] vt erneuern

régime [reɪ'ʒi:m] n Regime nt

regiment [n 'redʒɪmənt, vb 'redʒɪment] n Regiment nt ♦ vt (fig) reglementieren; **~al** [redʒɪ'mentl] adj Regiments-

region ['ri:dʒən] n Region f; **in the ~ of** (fig) so um; **~al** adj örtlich, regional

register ['redʒɪstə*] n Register nt ♦ vt (list) registrieren; (emotion) zeigen; (write down) eintragen ♦ vi (at hotel) sich eintragen; (with police) sich melden; (make impression) wirken, ankommen; **to ~ with the police** sich bei der Polizei melden, sich polizeilich melden; **~ed** (BRIT) adj (letter) Einschreibe-, eingeschrieben; **~ed trademark** n eingetragene(s) Warenzeichen nt

registrar [redʒɪs'trɑ:*] n Standesbeamte(r) m

registration [redʒɪs'treɪʃən] n (act) Registrierung f; (AUT: also: ~ number) polizeiliche(s) Kennzeichen nt

registry ['redʒɪstrɪ] n Sekretariat nt; **~ office** (BRIT) n Standesamt nt; **to get married in a ~ office** standesamtlich heiraten

regret [rɪ'gret] n Bedauern nt ♦ vt bedauern; **~fully** adv mit Bedauern, ungern; **~table** adj bedauerlich

regroup ['ri:gru:p] vt umgruppieren ♦ vi sich umgruppieren

regular ['regjʊlə*] adj regelmäßig; (usual) üblich; (inf) regelrecht ♦ n (client etc) Stammkunde m; **~ity** [regjʊ'lærɪtɪ] n Regelmäßigkeit f; **~ly** adv regelmäßig

regulate ['regjʊleɪt] vt regeln, regulieren

regulation [regjʊ'leɪʃən] n (rule) Vor-

schrift f; (control) Regulierung f

rehabilitation ['ri:həbɪlɪ'teɪʃən] n (of criminal) Resozialisierung f

rehearsal [rɪ'hɜ:səl] n Probe f

rehearse [rɪ'hɜ:s] vt proben

reign [reɪn] n Herrschaft f ♦ vi herrschen

reimburse [ri:ɪm'bɜ:s] vt: **to ~ sb for sth** jdn für etw entschädigen, jdm etw zurückzahlen

rein [reɪn] n Zügel m

reincarnation ['ri:ɪnkɑ:'neɪʃən] n Wiedergeburt f

reindeer ['reɪndɪə*] n Ren nt

reinforce [ri:ɪn'fɔ:s] vt verstärken; **~d concrete** n Stahlbeton m; **~ment** n Verstärkung f; **~ments** npl (MIL) Verstärkungstruppen pl

reinstate ['ri:ɪn'steɪt] vt wiedereinsetzen

reissue ['ri:'ɪʃu:] vt neu herausgeben

reiterate [ri:'ɪtəreɪt] vt wiederholen

reject [n 'ri:dʒekt, vb rɪ'dʒekt] n (COMM) Ausschuß(artikel) m ♦ vt ablehnen; **~ion** ['ri:dʒekʃən] n Zurückweisung f

rejoice [rɪ'dʒɔɪs] vi: **to ~ at or over** sich freuen über +acc

rejuvenate [rɪ'dʒu:vɪneɪt] vt verjüngen

rekindle ['ri:'kɪndl] vt wieder anfachen

relapse [rɪ'læps] n Rückfall m

relate [rɪ'leɪt] vt (tell) erzählen; (connect) verbinden ♦ vi: **to ~ to** zusammenhängen mit; (form relationship) eine Beziehung aufbauen zu; **~d** adj: **~d (to)** verwandt (mit); **relating to** prep bezüglich +gen

relation [rɪ'leɪʃən] n Verwandte(r) mf; (connection) Beziehung f; **~ship** n Verhältnis nt, Beziehung f

relative ['relətɪv] n Verwandte(r) mf ♦ adj relativ; **~ly** adv verhältnismäßig

relax [rɪ'læks] vi (slacken) sich lockern; (muscles, person) sich entspannen ♦ vt (ease) lockern, entspannen; **~ation** [ri:læk'seɪʃən] n Entspannung f; **~ed** adj entspannt, locker; **~ing** adj entspannend

relay ['ri:leɪ] n (SPORT) Staffel f ♦ vt (message) weiterleiten; (RADIO, TV) übertragen

release [rɪ'li:s] n (freedom) Entlassung

f; *(TECH)* Auslöser *m* ♦ *vt* befreien;
(prisoner) entlassen; *(report, news)*
verlautbaren, bekanntgeben
relegate ['relǝgeɪt] *vt (SPORT)*: **to be ~d**
absteigen
relent [rɪ'lent] *vi* nachgeben; **~less** *adj*
unnachgiebig; **~lessly** *adv* unnachgiebig
relevant ['relǝvǝnt] *adj* wichtig,
relevant; **~ to** relevant für
reliability [rɪlaɪǝ'bɪlɪtɪ] *n* Zuverlässigkeit
f
reliable [rɪ'laɪǝbl] *adj* zuverlässig; **reli-
ably** *adv* zuverlässig; **to be ~ informed
that ...** aus zuverlässiger Quelle wissen,
daß ...
reliance [rɪ'laɪǝns] *n*: **~ (on)**
Abhängigkeit *f* (von)
relic ['relɪk] *n (from past)* Überbleibsel
nt; *(REL)* Reliquie *f*
relief [rɪ'liːf] *n* Erleichterung *f*; *(help)*
Hilfe *f*; *(person)* Ablösung *f*
relieve [rɪ'liːv] *vt (ease)* erleichtern;
(bring help) entlasten; *(person)*
ablösen; **to ~ sb of sth** jdm etw
abnehmen; **to ~ o.s.** *(euph)* sich
erleichtern *(euph)*
religion [rɪ'lɪdʒǝn] *n* Religion *f*
religious [rɪ'lɪdʒǝs] *adj* religiös; **~ly** *adv*
religiös; *(conscientiously)* gewissenhaft
relinquish [rɪ'lɪŋkwɪʃ] *vt* aufgeben
relish ['relɪʃ] *n* Würze *f* ♦ *vt* genießen;
to ~ doing gern tun
relocate ['riːlǝu'keɪt] *vt* verlegen ♦ *vi*
umziehen
reluctance [rɪ'lʌktǝns] *n* Widerstreben
nt, Abneigung *f*
reluctant [rɪ'lʌktǝnt] *adj* widerwillig;
~ly *adv* ungern
rely [rɪ'laɪ]: **to ~ on** *vt fus* sich verlassen
auf +*acc*
remain [rɪ'meɪn] *vi (be left)*
übrigbleiben; *(stay)* bleiben; **~der** *n*
Rest *m*; **~ing** *adj* übrig(geblieben); **~s**
npl Überreste *pl*
remand [rɪ'mɑːnd] *n*: **on ~ in** Untersuchungshaft ♦ *vt*: **to ~ in custody** in
Untersuchungshaft schicken; **~ home**
(BRIT) *n* Untersuchungsgefängnis *nt* für
Jugendliche

remark [rɪ'mɑːk] *n* Bemerkung *f* ♦ *vt*
bemerken; **~able** *adj* bemerkenswert;
~ably *adv* bemerkenswert
remarry ['riː'mærɪ] *vi* sich wieder ver-
heiraten
remedial [rɪ'miːdɪǝl] *adj* Heil-; *(teaching)* Hilfsschul-
remedy ['remǝdɪ] *n* Mittel *nt* ♦ *vt (pain)*
abhelfen +*dat*; *(trouble)* in Ordnung
bringen
remember [rɪ'membǝ*] *vt* sich erinnern
an +*acc*
remembrance [rɪ'membrǝns] *n* Erinnerung *f*; *(official)* Gedenken *nt*
remind [rɪ'maɪnd] *vt*: **to ~ sb to do sth**
jdn daran erinnern, etw zu tun; **to ~ sb
of sth** jdn an etw *acc* erinnern; **she ~s
me of her mother** sie erinnert mich an
ihre Mutter; **~er** *n* Mahnung *f*
reminisce [remɪ'nɪs] *vi* in Erinnerungen
schwelgen
reminiscent [remɪ'nɪsnt] *adj*: **to be ~ of
sth** an etw *acc* erinnern
remiss [rɪ'mɪs] *adj* nachlässig
remission [rɪ'mɪʃǝn] *n* Nachlaß *m*; *(of
debt, sentence)* Erlaß *m*
remit [rɪ'mɪt] *vt (money)*: **to ~ (to)**
überweisen (an +*acc*); **~tance** *n*
Geldanweisung *f*
remnant ['remnǝnt] *n* Rest *m*; **~s** *npl*
(COMM) Einzelstücke *pl*
remorse [rɪ'mɔːs] *n* Gewissensbisse *pl*;
~ful *adj* reumütig; **~less** *adj*
unbarmherzig; **~lessly** *adv* unbarmherzig
remote [rɪ'mǝut] *adj* abgelegen; *(slight)*
gering; **~ control** *n* Fernsteuerung *f*;
~ly *adv* entfernt
remould ['riːmǝuld] *(BRIT)* *n*
runderneuerte(r) Reifen *m*
removable [rɪ'muːvǝbl] *adj* entfernbar
removal [rɪ'muːvǝl] *n* Beseitigung *f*; *(of
furniture)* Umzug *m*; *(from office)* Entlassung *f*; **~ van** *(BRIT)* *n* Möbelwagen
m
remove [rɪ'muːv] *vt* beseitigen, entfernen; **~rs** *npl* Möbelspedition *f*
remuneration [rɪmjuːnǝ'reɪʃǝn] *n* Vergütung *f*, Honorar *nt*
render ['rendǝ*] *vt* machen; *(translate)*

übersetzen; ~**ing** *n* (*MUS*) Wiedergabe *f*
rendez-vous ['rɒndɪvuː] *n* Rendezvous
nt ♦ *vi* sich treffen
renew [rɪ'njuː] *vt* erneuern; (*contract,
licence*) verlängern; (*replace*) ersetzen; ~**al** *n* Erneuerung *f*; Verlängerung
f
renounce [rɪ'naʊns] *vt* (*give up*) verzichten auf +*acc*; (*disown*) verstoßen
renovate ['renəveɪt] *vt* renovieren;
(*building*) restaurieren
renown [rɪ'naʊn] *n* Ruf *m*; ~**ed** *adj*
namhaft
rent [rent] *n* Miete *f*; (*for land*) Pacht *f*
♦ *vt* (*hold as tenant*) mieten; pachten;
(*let*) vermieten; verpachten; (*car etc*)
mieten; (*firm*) vermieten; ~**al** *n* Miete
f
renunciation [rɪnʌnsɪ'eɪʃən] *n*: ~ (**of**)
Verzicht *m* (auf +*acc*)
reorganize [riː'ɔːgənaɪz] *vt* umgestalten,
reorganisieren
rep [rep] *n abbr* (*COMM*) = **representative**; (*THEAT*) = **repertory**
repair [rɪ'pɛə*] *n* Reparatur *f* ♦ *vt*
reparieren; (*damage*) wiedergutmachen; **in good/bad** ~ in gutem/
schlechtem Zustand; ~ **kit** *n*
Werkzeugkasten *m*
repartee [repɑː'tiː] *n* Witzeleien *pl*
repatriate [riː'pætrɪeɪt] *vt* in die Heimat
zurückschicken
repay [riː'peɪ] (*irreg*) *vt* zurückzahlen;
(*reward*) vergelten; ~**ment** *n*
Rückzahlung *f*; (*fig*) Vergeltung *f*
repeal [rɪ'piːl] *n* Aufhebung *f* ♦ *vt* aufheben
repeat [rɪ'piːt] *n* (*RADIO, TV*) Wieder-
holung(ssendung) *f* ♦ *vt* wiederholen;
~**edly** *adv* wiederholt
repel [rɪ'pel] *vt* (*drive back*)
zurückschlagen; (*disgust*) abstoßen;
~**lent** *adj* abstoßend ♦ *n*: **insect** ~**lent**
Insektenmittel *nt*
repent [rɪ'pent] *vt, vi*: **to** ~ (**of**)
bereuen; ~**ance** *n* Reue *f*
repercussion [riːpə'kʌʃən] *n* Auswirkung *f*; **to have** ~**s** ein Nachspiel haben
repertory ['repətərɪ] *n* Repertoire *nt*
repetition [repə'tɪʃən] *n* Wiederholung *f*

repetitive [rɪ'petɪtɪv] *adj* sich wieder-
holend
replace [rɪ'pleɪs] *vt* ersetzen; (*put back*)
zurückstellen; ~**ment** *n* Ersatz *m*
replay ['riːpleɪ] *n* (*of match*) Wieder-
holungsspiel *nt*; (*of tape, film*) Wiederholung *f*
replenish [rɪ'plenɪʃ] *vt* ergänzen
replete [rɪ'pliːt] *adj* (zum Platzen) voll
replica ['replɪkə] *n* Kopie *f*
reply [rɪ'plaɪ] *n* Antwort *f* ♦ *vi* antworten; ~ **coupon** *n* Antwortschein *m*
report [rɪ'pɔːt] *n* Bericht *m*; (*BRIT: SCH*)
Zeugnis *nt* ♦ *vt* (*tell*) berichten; (*give
information against*) melden; (*to
police*) anzeigen ♦ *vi* (*make report*)
Bericht erstatten; (*present o.s.*): **to** ~
(**to sb**) sich (bei jdm) melden; ~ **card**
(*US, SCOTTISH*) *n* Zeugnis *nt*; ~**edly** *adv*
wie verlautet; ~**er** *n* Reporter *m*
repose [rɪ'pəʊz] *n*: **in** ~ (*face, body*)
entspannt; (*mind*) gelassen
reprehensible [reprɪ'hensɪbl] *adj* tadelnswert
represent [reprɪ'zent] *vt* darstellen;
(*speak for*) vertreten; ~**ation**
[reprɪzen'teɪʃən] *n* Darstellung *f*; (*being
represented*) Vertretung *f*; ~**ations** *npl*
(*protest*) Vorhaltungen *pl*; ~**ative** *n*
(*person*) Vertreter *m*; (*US: POL*)
Abgeordnete(r) *mf* ♦ *adj* repräsentativ
repress [rɪ'pres] *vt* unterdrücken; ~**ion**
[rɪ'preʃən] *n* Unterdrückung *f*
reprieve [rɪ'priːv] *n* (*JUR*) Begnadigung
f; (*fig*) Gnadenfrist *f* ♦ *vt* (*JUR*) begnadigen
reprimand ['reprɪmɑːnd] *n* Verweis *m* ♦
vt einen Verweis erteilen +*dat*
reprint [*n* 'riːprɪnt, *vb* riː'prɪnt] *n* Neu-
druck *m* ♦ *vt* wieder abdrucken
reprisal [rɪ'praɪzəl] *n* Vergeltung *f*
reproach [rɪ'prəʊtʃ] *n* Vorwurf *m* ♦ *vt*
Vorwürfe machen +*dat*; **to** ~ **sb with
sth** jdm etw vorwerfen; ~**ful** *adj* vorwurfsvoll
reproduce [riːprə'djuːs] *vt* reproduzieren
♦ *vi* (*have offspring*) sich vermehren
reproduction [riːprə'dʌkʃən] *n* (*ART,
PHOT*) Reproduktion *f*; (*breeding*)
Fortpflanzung *f*

reproductive [riːprə'dʌktɪv] *adj* reproduktiv; (*breeding*) Fortpflanzungs-
reproof [rɪ'pruːf] *n* Tadel *m*
reprove [rɪ'pruːv] *vt* tadeln
reptile ['reptaɪl] *n* Reptil *nt*
republic [rɪ'pʌblɪk] *n* Republik *f*
repudiate [rɪ'pjuːdɪeɪt] *vt* zurückweisen
repugnant [rɪ'pʌgnənt] *adj* widerlich
repulse [rɪ'pʌls] *vt* (*drive back*) zurückschlagen; (*reject*) abweisen
repulsive [rɪ'pʌlsɪv] *adj* abstoßend
reputable ['repjʊtəbl] *adj* angesehen
reputation [repjʊ'teɪʃən] *n* Ruf *m*
repute [rɪ'pjuːt] *n* hohe(s) Ansehen *nt*; ~**d** *adj* angeblich; ~**dly** *adv* angeblich
request [rɪ'kwest] *n* Bitte *f* ♦ *vt* (*thing*) erbitten; **to ~ sth of** *or* **from sb** jdn um etw bitten; (*formally*) jdn um etw ersuchen; ~ **stop** (*BRIT*) *n* Bedarfshaltestelle *f*
require [rɪ'kwaɪə*] *vt* (*need*) brauchen; (*demand*) erfordern; ~**ment** *n* (*condition*) Anforderung *f*; (*need*) Bedarf *m*
requisite ['rekwɪzɪt] *n* Erfordernis *nt* ♦ *adj* erforderlich; **toilet ~s** (*BRIT*) Toilettenartikel *pl*
requisition [rekwɪ'zɪʃən] *n* Anforderung *f* ♦ *vt* beschlagnahmen
resale ['riːseɪl] *n* Weiterverkauf *m*
rescind [rɪ'sɪnd] *vt* aufheben
rescue ['reskjuː] *n* Rettung *f* ♦ *vt* retten; ~ **party** *n* Rettungsmannschaft *f*; ~**r** *n* Retter *m*
research [rɪ'sɜːtʃ] *n* Forschung *f* ♦ *vi* forschen ♦ *vt* erforschen; ~**er** *n* Forscher *m*
resemblance [rɪ'zembləns] *n* Ähnlichkeit *f*
resemble [rɪ'zembl] *vt* ähneln +*dat*
resent [rɪ'zent] *vt* übelnehmen; ~**ful** *adj* nachtragend, empfindlich; ~**ment** *n* Verstimmung *f*, Unwille *m*
reservation [rezə'veɪʃən] *n* (*booking*) Reservierung *f*; (*THEAT*) Vorbestellung *f*; (*doubt*) Vorbehalt *m*; (*land*) Reservat *nt*
reserve [rɪ'zɜːv] *n* (*store*) Vorrat *m*, Reserve *f*; (*manner*) Zurückhaltung *f*; (*game* ~) Naturschutzgebiet *nt*;

(*SPORT*) Ersatzspieler(in) *m(f)* ♦ *vt* reservieren; (*judgement*) sich *dat* vorbehalten; ~**s** *npl* (*MIL*) Reserve *f*; **in ~** in Reserve; ~**d** *adj* reserviert
reshape ['riː'ʃeɪp] *vt* umformen
reshuffle ['riː'ʃʌfl] *n* (*POL*): **cabinet ~** Kabinettsumbildung *f* ♦ *vt* (*POL*) umbilden
reside [rɪ'zaɪd] *vi* wohnen, ansässig sein
residence ['rezɪdəns] *n* (*house*) Wohnsitz *m*; (*living*) Aufenthalt *m*
resident ['rezɪdənt] *n* (*in house*) Bewohner *m*; (*in area*) Einwohner *m* ♦ *adj* wohnhaft, ansässig; ~**ial** [rezɪ'denʃəl] *adj* Wohn-
residue ['rezɪdjuː] *n* Rest *m*; (*CHEM*) Rückstand *m*; (*fig*) Bodensatz *m*
resign [rɪ'zaɪn] *vt* (*office*) aufgeben, zurücktreten von ♦ *vi* (*from office*) zurücktreten; (*employee*) kündigen; **to be ~ed to sth, to ~ o.s. to sth** sich mit etw abfinden; ~**ation** [rezɪg'neɪʃən] *n* (*from job*) Kündigung *f*; (*POL*) Rücktritt *m*; (*submission*) Resignation *f*; ~**ed** *adj* resigniert
resilience [rɪ'zɪlɪəns] *n* Spannkraft *f*; (*of person*) Unverwüstlichkeit *f*
resilient [rɪ'zɪlɪənt] *adj* unverwüstlich
resin ['rezɪn] *n* Harz *nt*
resist [rɪ'zɪst] *vt* widerstehen +*dat*; ~**ance** *n* Widerstand *m*
resolute ['rezəluːt] *adj* entschlossen, resolut; ~**ly** *adv* entschlossen, resolut
resolution [rezə'luːʃən] *n* (*firmness*) Entschlossenheit *f*; (*intention*) Vorsatz *m*; (*decision*) Beschluß *m*
resolve [rɪ'zɒlv] *n* Entschlossenheit *f* ♦ *vt* (*decide*) beschließen ♦ *vi* sich lösen; ~**d** *adj* (fest) entschlossen
resonant ['rezənənt] *adj* voll
resort [rɪ'zɔːt] *n* (*holiday place*) Erholungsort *m*; (*help*) Zuflucht *f* ♦ *vi*: **to ~ to** Zuflucht nehmen zu; **as a last ~** als letzter Ausweg
resound [rɪ'zaʊnd] *vi*: **to ~ (with)** widerhallen (von); ~**ing** [rɪ'zaʊndɪŋ] *adj* nachhallend; (*success*) groß
resource [rɪ'sɔːs] *n* Findigkeit *f*; ~**s** *npl* (*financial*) Geldmittel *pl*; (*natural*) Bodenschätze *pl*; ~**ful** *adj* findig

respect [rɪs'pekt] n Respekt m ♦ vt achten, respektieren; ~s npl (regards) Grüße pl; with ~ to in bezug auf +acc, hinsichtlich +gen; in this ~ in dieser Hinsicht; ~ability [rɪspektə'bɪlɪtɪ] n Anständigkeit f; ~able adj (decent) anständig; (fairly good) leidlich; ~ful adj höflich

respective [rɪs'pektɪv] adj jeweilig; ~ly adv beziehungsweise

respiration [respɪ'reɪʃən] n Atmung f

respite ['respaɪt] n Ruhepause f

resplendent [rɪs'plendənt] adj strahlend

respond [rɪs'pɒnd] vi antworten; (react): to ~ (to) reagieren (auf +acc)

response [rɪs'pɒns] n Antwort f; Reaktion f; (to advertisement etc) Resonanz f

responsibility [rɪspɒnsə'bɪlɪtɪ] n Verantwortung f

responsible [rɪs'pɒnsəbl] adj verantwortlich; (reliable) verantwortungsvoll

responsive [rɪs'pɒnsɪv] adj empfänglich

rest [rest] n Ruhe f; (break) Pause f; (remainder) Rest m ♦ vi sich ausruhen; (be supported) (auf)liegen ♦ vt (lean): to ~ sth on/against sth etw gegen etw acc lehnen; the ~ of them die übrigen; it ~s with him to ... es liegt bei ihm, zu ...

restaurant ['restərɒŋ] n Restaurant nt; ~ car (BRIT) n Speisewagen m

restful ['restfʊl] adj erholsam, ruhig

rest home n Erholungsheim nt

restitution [restɪ'tjuːʃən] n Rückgabe f; to make ~ to sb for sth jdn für etw entschädigen

restive ['restɪv] adj unruhig

restless ['restləs] adj unruhig

restoration [restə'reɪʃən] n Rückgabe f; (of building etc) Rückerstattung f

restore [rɪ'stɔː*] vt (order) wiederherstellen; (customs) wieder einführen; (person to position) wiedereinsetzen; (give back) zurückgeben; (paintings, buildings) restaurieren

restrain [rɪs'treɪn] vt zurückhalten; (curiosity etc) beherrschen; (person): to ~ sb from doing sth jdn davon abhalten, etw zu tun; ~ed adj (style

etc) gedämpft, verhalten; ~t n (self-control) Zurückhaltung f

restrict [rɪs'trɪkt] vt einschränken; ~ion [rɪs'trɪkʃən] n Einschränkung f; ~ive adj einschränkend

rest room (US) n Toilette f

restructure ['riː'strʌktʃə*] vt umstrukturieren

result [rɪ'zʌlt] n Resultat nt, Folge f; (of exam, game) Ergebnis nt ♦ vi; to ~ in sth etw zur Folge haben; as a ~ of als Folge +gen

resume [rɪ'zjuːm] vt fortsetzen; (occupy again) wieder einnehmen ♦ vi (work etc) wieder beginnen

résumé ['reɪzjuːmeɪ] n Zusammenfassung f

resumption [rɪ'zʌmpʃən] n Wiederaufnahme f

resurgence [rɪ'sɜːdʒəns] n Wiedererwachen n

resurrection [rezə'rekʃən] n Auferstehung f

resuscitate [rɪ'sʌsɪteɪt] vt wiederbeleben

resuscitation [rɪsʌsɪ'teɪʃən] n Wiederbelebung f

retail [n, adj 'riːteɪl, vb 'riːteɪl] n Einzelhandel m ♦ adj Einzelhandels- ♦ vt im kleinen verkaufen ♦ vi im Einzelhandel kosten; ~er ['riːteɪlə*] n Einzelhändler m, Kleinhändler m; ~ price n Ladenpreis m

retain [rɪ'teɪn] vt (keep) (zurück)behalten; ~er n (servant) Gefolgsmann m; (fee) (Honorar)vorschuß m

retaliate [rɪ'tælɪeɪt] vi zum Vergeltungsschlag ausholen

retaliation [rɪtælɪ'eɪʃən] n Vergeltung f

retarded [rɪ'tɑːdɪd] adj zurückgeblieben

retch [retʃ] vi würgen

retentive [rɪ'tentɪv] adj (memory) gut

reticent ['retɪsənt] adj schweigsam

retina ['retɪnə] n Netzhaut f

retinue ['retɪnjuː] n Gefolge nt

retire [rɪ'taɪə*] vi (from work) in den Ruhestand treten; (withdraw) sich zurückziehen; (go to bed) schlafen gehen; ~d adj (person) pensioniert, im Ruhestand; ~ment n Ruhestand m

retiring [rɪ'taɪərɪŋ] *adj* zurückhaltend

retort [rɪ'tɔːt] *n* (*reply*) Erwiderung *f*; (*SCI*) Retorte *f* ♦ *vi* (scharf) erwidern

retrace [rɪ'treɪs] *vt* zurückverfolgen; to ~ one's steps denselben Weg zurückgehen

retract [rɪ'trækt] *vt* (*statement*) zurücknehmen; (*claws*) einziehen ♦ *vi* einen Rückzieher machen; **~able** *adj* (*aerial*) ausziehbar

retrain [riː'treɪn] *vt* umschulen; **~ing** *n* Umschulung *f*

retread ['riːtred] *n* (*tyre*) Reifen *m* mit erneuerter Lauffläche

retreat [rɪ'triːt] *n* Rückzug *m*; (*place*) Zufluchtsort *m* ♦ *vi* sich zurückziehen

retribution [retrɪ'bjuːʃən] *n* Strafe *f*

retrieval [rɪ'triːvəl] *n* Wiedergewinnung *f*

retrieve [rɪ'triːv] *vt* wiederbekommen; (*rescue*) retten; **~r** *n* Apportierhund *m*

retrograde ['retrəʊɡreɪd] *adj* (*step*) Rück-; (*policy*) rückschrittlich

retrospect ['retrəʊspekt] *n*: **in ~** im Rückblick, rückblickend; **~ive** [retrəʊ'spektɪv] *adj* (*action*) rückwirkend; (*look*) rückblickend

return [rɪ'tɜːn] *n* Rückkehr *f*; (*profits*) Ertrag *m*; (*BRIT*: *rail ticket etc*) Rückfahrkarte *f*; (: *plane ticket*) Rückflugkarte *f* ♦ *adj* (*journey, match*) Rück- ♦ *vi* zurückkehren, zurückkommen ♦ *vt* zurückgeben, zurücksenden; (*pay back*) zurückzahlen; (*elect*) wählen; (*verdict*) aussprechen; **~s** *npl* (*COMM*) Gewinn *m*; (*receipts*) Einkünfte *pl*; **in ~** dafür; **by ~ of post** postwendend; **many happy ~s (of the day)!** herzlichen Glückwunsch zum Geburtstag!

reunion [riː'juːnjən] *n* Wiedervereinigung *f*; (*SCH etc*) Treffen *nt*

reunite ['riːjuː'naɪt] *vt* wiedervereinigen

rev [rev] *n abbr* (*AUT*: = *revolution*) Umdrehung *f* ♦ *vt* (*also*: ~ **up**: *engine*) auf Touren bringen ♦ *vi* (*also*: ~ **up**) den Motor auf Touren bringen

revamp ['riː'væmp] *vt* aufpolieren

reveal [rɪ'viːl] *vt* enthüllen; **~ing** *adj* aufschlußreich

reveille [rɪ'vælɪ] *n* Wecken *nt*

revel ['revl] *vi*: to ~ **in sth/in doing sth** seine Freude an etw *dat* haben/daran haben, etw zu tun

revelation [revə'leɪʃən] *n* Offenbarung *f*

revelry ['revlrɪ] *n* Rummel *m*

revenge [rɪ'vendʒ] *n* Rache *f*; to take ~ on sich rächen an +*dat*

revenue ['revənjuː] *n* Einnahmen *pl*

reverberate [rɪ'vɜːbəreɪt] *vi* widerhallen

revere [rɪ'vɪə*] *vt* (ver)ehren; **reverence** ['revərəns] *n* Ehrfurcht *f*

Reverend ['revərənd] *adj*: **the ~ Robert Martin** ≈ Pfarrer Robert Martin

reverent ['revərənt] *adj* ehrfurchtsvoll

reverie ['revərɪ] *n* Träumerei *f*

reversal [rɪ'vɜːsəl] *n* Umkehrung *f*

reverse [rɪ'vɜːs] *n* Rückseite *f*; (*AUT*: *gear*) Rückwärtsgang *m* ♦ *adj* (*order, direction*) entgegengesetzt ♦ *vt* umkehren ♦ *vi* (*BRIT*: *AUT*) rückwärts fahren; **~-charge call** (*BRIT*) *n* R-Gespräch *nt*; **reversing lights** *npl* (*AUT*) Rückfahrscheinwerfer *pl*

revert [rɪ'vɜːt] *vi*: to ~ **to** zurückkehren zu; (*to bad state*) zurückfallen in +*acc*

review [rɪ'vjuː] *n* (*MIL*) Truppenschau *f*; (*of book*) Rezension *f*; (*magazine*) Zeitschrift *f* ♦ *vt* Rückschau halten auf +*acc*; (*MIL*) mustern; (*book*) rezensieren; (*reexamine*) von neuem untersuchen; **~er** *n* (*critic*) Rezensent *m*

revile [rɪ'vaɪl] *vt* verunglimpfen

revise [rɪ'vaɪz] *vt* (*book*) überarbeiten; (*reconsider*) ändern, revidieren

revision [rɪ'vɪʒən] *n* Prüfung *f*; (*COMM*) Revision *f*; (*SCH*) Wiederholung *f*

revitalize ['riː'vaɪtəlaɪz] *vt* neu beleben

revival [rɪ'vaɪvəl] *n* Wiederbelebung *f*; (*REL*) Erweckung *f*; (*THEAT*) Wiederaufnahme *f*

revive [rɪ'vaɪv] *vt* wiederbeleben; (*fig*) wieder auffrischen ♦ *vi* wiedererwachen; (*fig*) wieder aufleben

revoke [rɪ'vəʊk] *vt* aufheben

revolt [rɪ'vəʊlt] *n* Aufstand *m*, Revolte *f* ♦ *vi* sich auflehnen ♦ *vt* entsetzen; **~ing** *adj* widerlich

revolution [revə'luːʃən] *n* (*turn*) Umdrehung *f*; (*POL*) Revolution *f*; **~ary** *adj* revolutionär ♦ *n* Revolutionär *m*;

~**ize** vt revolutionieren

revolve [rɪ'vɒlv] vi kreisen; (on own axis) sich drehen

revolver [rɪ'vɒlvə*] n Revolver m

revulsion [rɪ'vʌlʃən] n Ekel m

reward [rɪ'wɔ:d] n Belohnung f ♦ vt belohnen; ~**ing** adj lohnend

rewire [ri:'waɪə*] vt (house) neu verkabeln

reword [ri:'wɜ:d] vt anders formulieren

rewrite [ri:'raɪt] (irreg: like write) vt umarbeiten, neu schreiben

rheumatism ['ru:mətɪzəm] n Rheumatismus m, Rheuma nt

Rhine [raɪn] n: the ~ der Rhein

rhinoceros [raɪ'nɒsərəs] n Nashorn nt

Rhone [rəʊn] n: the ~ die Rhone

rhubarb ['ru:bɑ:b] n Rhabarber m

rhyme [raɪm] n Reim m

rhythm ['rɪðəm] n Rhythmus m

rib [rɪb] n Rippe f ♦ vt (mock) hänseln, aufziehen

ribald ['rɪbəld] adj saftig

ribbon ['rɪbən] n Band nt; **in** ~s (torn) in Fetzen

rice [raɪs] n Reis m; ~ **pudding** n Milchreis m

rich [rɪtʃ] adj reich; (food) reichhaltig ♦ npl: **the** ~ die Reichen pl; ~**es** npl Reichtum m; ~**ly** adv reich; (deserve) völlig; ~**ness** n Reichtum m; (of food) Reichhaltigkeit f

rickets ['rɪkɪts] n Rachitis f

rickety ['rɪkɪtɪ] adj wack(e)lig

rickshaw ['rɪkʃɔ:] n Rickscha f

ricochet ['rɪkəʃeɪ] n Abprallen nt; (shot) Querschläger m ♦ vi abprallen

rid [rɪd] (pt, pp rid) vt befreien; **to get** ~ **of** loswerden

ridden ['rɪdn] pp of ride

riddle ['rɪdl] n Rätsel nt ♦ vt: **to be** ~**d with** völlig durchlöchert sein von

ride [raɪd] (pt rode, pp ridden) n (in vehicle) Fahrt f; (on horse) Ritt m ♦ vt (horse) reiten; (bicycle) fahren ♦ vi fahren, reiten; **to take sb for a** ~ mit jdm eine Fahrt etc machen; (fig) jdn aufs Glatteis führen; **to** ~ **at anchor** (NAUT) vor Anker liegen; ~**r** n Reiter m; (addition) Zusatz m

ridge [rɪdʒ] n Kamm m; (of roof) First m

ridicule ['rɪdɪkju:l] n Spott m ♦ vt lächerlich machen

ridiculous [rɪ'dɪkjʊləs] adj lächerlich; ~**ly** adv lächerlich

riding ['raɪdɪŋ] n Reiten nt; ~ **school** n Reitschule f

rife [raɪf] adj weit verbreitet; **to be** grassieren; **to be** ~ **with** voll sein von

riffraff ['rɪfræf] n Pöbel m

rifle ['raɪfl] n Gewehr nt ♦ vt berauben; ~ **range** n Schießstand m

rift [rɪft] n Spalte f; (fig) Bruch m

rig [rɪg] n (outfit) Takelung f; (fig) Aufmachung f; (oil ~) Bohrinsel f ♦ vt (election etc) manipulieren; ~ **out** (BRIT) vt ausstatten; ~ **up** vt zusammenbasteln; ~**ging** n Takelage f

right [raɪt] adj (correct, just) richtig, recht; (~ side) rechte(r, s) ♦ n Recht nt; (not left, POL) Rechte f ♦ adv (on the ~) rechts; (to the ~) nach rechts; (look, work) richtig, recht; (directly) gerade; (exactly) genau ♦ vt in Ordnung bringen, korrigieren ♦ excl gut; **on the** ~ rechts; **to be in the** ~ im Recht sein; **by** ~**s** von Rechts wegen; **to be** ~ recht haben; ~ **away** sofort; ~ **now** in diesem Augenblick, eben; ~ **in the middle** genau in der Mitte; ~ **angle** n rechte(r) Winkel m; ~**eous** ['raɪtʃəs] adj rechtschaffen; ~**ful** adj rechtmäßig; ~-**handed** adj rechtshändig; ~-**hand man** (irreg) n rechte Hand f; ~-**hand side** n rechte Seite f; ~**ly** adv mit Recht; ~ **of way** n Vorfahrt f; ~-**wing** adj rechtsorientiert

rigid ['rɪdʒɪd] adj (stiff) starr, steif; (strict) streng; ~**ity** [rɪ'dʒɪdɪtɪ] n Starrheit f; Strenge f

rigmarole ['rɪgmərəʊl] n Gewäsch nt

rigor (US) n = rigour

rigorous ['rɪgərəs] adj streng

rigour ['rɪgə*] (US rigor) n Strenge f, Härte f

rile [raɪl] vt ärgern

rim [rɪm] n (edge) Rand m; (of wheel) Felge f

rind [raɪnd] n Rinde f

ring [rɪŋ] (pt **rang**, pp **rung**) n Ring m; (of people) Kreis m; (arena) Manege f; (of telephone) Klingeln nt ♦ vt, vi (bell) läuten; (BRIT) anrufen; ~ **back** (BRIT) vt, vi zurückrufen; ~ **off** (BRIT) vi aufhängen; ~ **up** (BRIT) vt anrufen; ~**ing** n Klingeln nt; (of large bell) Läuten nt; (in ears) Klingen nt; ~**ing tone** n (TEL) Rufzeichen nt

ringleader ['rɪŋliːdə*] n Anführer m, Rädelsführer m

ringlets ['rɪŋlɪts] npl Ringellocken pl

ring road (BRIT) n Umgehungsstraße f

rink [rɪŋk] n (ice ~) Eisbahn f

rinse [rɪns] n Spülen nt ♦ vt spülen

riot ['raɪət] n Aufruhr m ♦ vi randalieren; **to run** ~ (people) randalieren; (vegetation) wuchern; ~**er** n Aufrührer m; ~**ous** adj aufrührerisch; (noisy) lärmend; ~**ously** adv aufrührerisch

rip [rɪp] n Schlitz m, Riß m ♦ vt, vi (zer)reißen; ~**cord** ['rɪpkɔːd] n Reißleine f

ripe [raɪp] adj reif; ~**n** vi reifen ♦ vt reifen lassen

rip-off ['rɪpɒf] (inf) n: **it's a ~!** das ist Wucher!

ripple ['rɪpl] n kleine Welle f ♦ vt kräuseln ♦ vi sich kräuseln

rise [raɪz] (pt **rose**, pp **risen**) n (slope) Steigung f; (esp in wages: BRIT) Erhöhung f; (growth) Aufstieg m ♦ vi (sun) aufgehen; (smoke) aufsteigen; (mountain) sich erheben; (ground) ansteigen; (prices) steigen; (in revolt) sich erheben; **to give** ~ **to** Anlaß geben zu; **to** ~ **to the occasion** sich der Lage gewachsen zeigen; **risen** ['rɪzn] pp of **rise**

rising adj (increasing: tide, numbers, prices) steigend; (sun, moon) aufgehend ♦ n (uprising) Aufstand m

risk [rɪsk] n Gefahr f, Risiko nt ♦ vt (venture) wagen; (chance loss of) riskieren, aufs Spiel setzen; **to take** or **run the** ~ **of doing** das Risiko eingehen, zu tun; **at** ~ in Gefahr; **at one's own** ~ auf eigene Gefahr; ~**y** adj riskant

risqué ['riːskeɪ] adj gewagt

rissole ['rɪsəʊl] n Fleischklößchen nt

rite [raɪt] n Ritus m; **last** ~**s** Letzte Ölung f

ritual ['rɪtjʊəl] n Ritual nt ♦ adj ritual, Ritual-; (fig) rituell

rival ['raɪvəl] n Rivale m, Konkurrent m ♦ adj rivalisierend ♦ vt rivalisieren mit; (COMM) konkurrieren mit; ~**ry** n Rivalität f; Konkurrenz f

river ['rɪvə*] n Fluß m, Strom m ♦ cpd (port, traffic) Fluß-; **up/down** ~ flußaufwärts/-abwärts; ~**bank** n Flußufer nt; ~**bed** n Flußbett nt

rivet ['rɪvɪt] n Niete f ♦ vt (fasten) (ver)nieten

Riviera [rɪvɪ'ɛərə] n: **the** ~ die Riviera

road [rəʊd] n Straße f ♦ cpd Straßen-; **major/minor** ~ Haupt-/Nebenstraße f; ~**block** n Straßensperre f; ~**hog** n Verkehrsrowdy m; ~**map** n Straßenkarte f; ~ **safety** n Verkehrssicherheit f; ~**side** n Straßenrand m ♦ adj an der Landstraße (gelegen); ~ **sign** n Straßenschild nt; ~ **user** n Verkehrsteilnehmer m; ~**way** n Fahrbahn f; ~ **works** npl Straßenbauarbeiten pl; ~**worthy** adj verkehrssicher

roam [rəʊm] vi (umher)streifen ♦ vt durchstreifen

roar [rɔː*] n Brüllen nt, Gebrüll nt ♦ vi brüllen; **to** ~ **with laughter** vor Lachen brüllen; **to do a** ~**ing trade** ein Riesengeschäft machen

roast [rəʊst] n Braten m ♦ vt braten, schmoren; ~ **beef** n Roastbeef nt

rob [rɒb] vt bestehlen, berauben; (bank) ausrauben; **to** ~ **sb of sth** jdm etw rauben; ~**ber** n Räuber m; ~**bery** n Raub m

robe [rəʊb] n (dress) Gewand nt; (US) Hauskleid nt; (judge's) Robe f

robin ['rɒbɪn] n Rotkehlchen nt

robot ['rəʊbɒt] n Roboter m

rock [rɒk] n Felsen m; (BRIT: sweet) Zuckerstange f ♦ vt, vi wiegen, schaukeln; **on the** ~**s** (drink) mit Eis(würfeln); (marriage) gescheitert; (ship) aufgelaufen; ~ **and roll** n Rock and Roll m; ~-**bottom** n (fig) Tiefpunkt m; ~**ery** n Steingarten m

rocket ['rɒkɪt] n Rakete f
rocking chair ['rɒkɪŋ-] n Schaukelstuhl m
rocking horse ['rɒkɪŋ-] n Schaukelpferd nt
rocky ['rɒkɪ] adj felsig
rod [rɒd] n (bar) Stange f; (stick) Rute f
rode [rəud] pt of ride
rodent ['rəudənt] n Nagetier nt
roe [rəu] n (deer) Reh nt; (of fish: also: hard ~) Rogen m; soft ~ Milch f
rogue [rəug] n Schurke m
role [rəul] n Rolle f
roll [rəul] n Rolle f; (bread) Brötchen nt; (list) (Namens)liste f; (of drum) Wirbel m ♦ vt (turn) rollen, (herum)wälzen ♦ vi (swing) schlingern; (sound) rollen, grollen; ~ about or around vi herumkugeln; (ship) schlingern; (dog etc) sich wälzen; ~ by vi (time) verfließen; ~ in vi (mail) hereinkommen; ~ over vi sich (herum)drehen; ~ up vi (arrive) kommen, auftauchen ♦ vt (carpet) aufrollen; ~ call n Namensaufruf m; ~er n Rolle f, Walze f; (road roller) Straßenwalze f; ~er coaster n Achterbahn f; ~er skates npl Rollschuhe pl
rolling ['rəulɪŋ] adj (landscape) wellig; ~ pin n Nudel- or Wellholz nt; ~ stock n Wagenmaterial nt
ROM [rɒm] n abbr (= read only memory) ROM m
Roman ['rəumən] adj römisch ♦ n Römer(in) m(f); ~ Catholic adj römisch-katholisch ♦ n Katholik(in) m(f)
romance [rə'mæns] n Romanze f; (story) (Liebes)roman m
Romania [rəu'meɪnɪə] n = Rumania
Roman numeral n römische Ziffer
romantic [rəu'mæntɪk] adj romantisch; ~ism [rəu'mæntɪsɪzəm] n Romantik f
Rome [rəum] n Rom nt
romp [rɒmp] n Tollen nt ♦ vi (also: ~ about) herumtollen
rompers ['rɒmpəz] npl Spielanzug m
roof [ruːf] (pl roofs) n Dach nt; (of

mouth) Gaumen m ♦ vt überdachen, überdecken; ~ing n Deckmaterial nt; ~ rack n (AUT) Dachgepäckträger m
rook [ruk] n (bird) Saatkrähe f; (chess) Turm m
room [rum] n Zimmer nt, Raum m; (space) Platz m; (fig) Spielraum m; ~s npl (accommodation) Wohnung f; "~s to let (BRIT) or for rent (US)" „Zimmer zu vermieten"; single/double ~ Einzel-/Doppelzimmer nt; ~ing house (US) n Mietshaus nt (mit möblierten Wohnungen); ~-mate n Mitbewohner(in) m(f); ~ service n Zimmerbedienung f; ~y adj geräumig
roost [ruːst] n Hühnerstange f ♦ vi auf der Stange hocken
rooster ['ruːstə*] n Hahn m
root [ruːt] n (also fig) Wurzel f ♦ vi wurzeln; ~ about vi (fig) herumwühlen; ~ for vt fus Stimmung machen für; ~ out vt ausjäten; (fig) ausrotten
rope [rəup] n Seil nt ♦ vt (tie) festschnüren; to know the ~s sich auskennen; to ~ sb in jdn gewinnen; ~ off vt absperren; ~ ladder n Strickleiter f
rosary ['rəuzərɪ] n Rosenkranz m
rose [rəuz] pt of rise ♦ n Rose f ♦ adj Rosen-, rosenrot
rosé ['rəuzeɪ] n Rosé m
rosebud ['rəuzbʌd] n Rosenknospe f
rosebush ['rəuzbuʃ] n Rosenstock m
rosemary ['rəuzmərɪ] n Rosmarin m
rosette [rəu'zet] n Rosette f
roster ['rɒstə*] n Dienstplan m
rostrum ['rɒstrəm] n Rednerbühne f
rosy ['rəuzɪ] adj rosig
rot [rɒt] n Fäulnis f; (nonsense) Quatsch m ♦ vi verfaulen ♦ vt verfaulen lassen
rota ['rəutə] n Dienstliste f
rotary ['rəutərɪ] adj rotierend
rotate [rəu'teɪt] vt rotieren lassen; (two or more things in order) turnusmäßig wechseln ♦ vi rotieren
rotating [rəu'teɪtɪŋ] adj rotierend
rotation [rəu'teɪʃən] n Umdrehung f
rote [rəut] n: by ~ auswendig
rotten ['rɒtn] adj faul; (fig) schlecht, gemein; to feel ~ (ill) sich elend fühlen

rotund [rəʊ'tʌnd] adj rundlich
rouble ['ruːbl] (US **ruble**) n Rubel m
rough [rʌf] adj (not smooth) rauh; (path) uneben; (violent) roh, grob; (crossing) stürmisch; (without comforts) hart, unbequem; (unfinished, makeshift) grob; (approximate) ungefähr ♦ n (BRIT: person) Rowdy m, Rohling m; (GOLF): **in the ~** im Rauh ♦ vt: **to ~ it** primitiv leben; **to sleep ~** im Freien schlafen; **~age** n Ballaststoffe pl; **~-and-ready** adj provisorisch; (work) zusammengehauen; **~cast** n Rauhputz nt; **~ copy** n Entwurf m; **~ draft** n Entwurf m; **~en** vt aufrauhen; **~ly** adv grob; (about) ungefähr; **~ness** n Rauheit f; (of manner) Ungeschliffenheit f
roulette [ruː'let] n Roulett(e) nt
Roumania [ruː'meɪnɪə] n = **Rumania**
round [raʊnd] adj rund; (figures) aufgerundet ♦ adv (in a circle) rundherum ♦ prep um ... herum ♦ n Runde f; (of ammunition) Magazin nt ♦ vt (corner) biegen um; **all ~** überall; **the long way ~** der Umweg; **all the year ~** das ganze Jahr über; **it's just ~ the corner** (fig) es ist gerade um die Ecke; **~ the clock** rund um die Uhr; **to go ~ to sb's (house)** jdn besuchen; **to go ~ the back** hinterherum gehen; **to go ~ a house** um ein Haus herumgehen; **enough to go ~** genug für alle; **to go the ~s** (story) die Runde machen; **a ~ of applause** ein Beifall m; **a ~ of drinks** eine Runde Drinks; **a ~ or m of sandwiches** ein Sandwich nt or m, ein belegtes Brot; **~ off** vt abrunden; **~ up** vt (end) abschließen; (figures) aufrunden; (criminals) hochnehmen; **~about** n (BRIT: traffic) Kreisverkehr m; (: merry-go-round) Karussell nt ♦ adj auf Umwegen; **~ers** npl (game) ≈ Schlagball m; **~ly** adv (fig) gründlich; **~-shouldered** adj mit abfallenden Schultern; **~ trip** n Rundreise f; **~up** n Zusammentreiben nt, Sammeln nt
rouse [raʊz] vt (waken) (auf)wecken; (stir up) erregen
rousing ['raʊzɪŋ] adj (welcome)

stürmisch; (speech) zündend
route [ruːt] n Weg m, Route f; **~ map** (BRIT) n (for journey) Streckenkarte f
routine [ruː'tiːn] n Routine f ♦ adj Routine-
roving ['rəʊvɪŋ] adj (reporter) im Außendienst
row[1] [raʊ] n (noise) Lärm m; (dispute) Streit m ♦ vi sich streiten
row[2] [rəʊ] n (line) Reihe f ♦ vt, vi (boat) rudern; **in a ~** (fig) hintereinander
rowboat ['rəʊbəʊt] (US) n Ruderboot nt
rowdy ['raʊdɪ] adj rüpelhaft ♦ n (person) Rowdy m
rowing ['rəʊɪŋ] n Rudern nt; (SPORT) Rudersport m; **~ boat** (BRIT) n Ruderboot nt
royal ['rɔɪəl] adj königlich, Königs-; **R~ Air Force** n Königliche Luftwaffe f
royalty ['rɔɪəltɪ] n (family) königliche Familie f; (for book) Tantieme f
rpm abbr (= revs per minute) U/min
R.S.V.P. abbr (= répondez s'il vous plaît) u.A.w.g.
Rt. Hon. (BRIT) abbr (= Right Honourable) Abgeordnete(r) mf
rub [rʌb] n (with cloth) Polieren nt; (on person) Reiben nt ♦ vt reiben; **to ~ sb up** (BRIT) **or to ~ sb** (US) **the wrong way** jdn aufreizen; **~ off** vi (also fig); **to ~ off (on)** abfärben (auf +acc); **~ out** vt herausreiben; (with eraser) ausradieren
rubber ['rʌbə*] n Gummi m; (BRIT) Radiergummi m; **~ band** n Gummiband nt; **~ plant** n Gummibaum m; **~y** adj gummiartig
rubbish ['rʌbɪʃ] n (waste) Abfall m; (nonsense) Blödsinn m, Quatsch m; **~ bin** (BRIT) n Mülleimer m; **~ dump** n Müllabladeplatz m
rubble ['rʌbl] n (Stein)schutt m
ruby ['ruːbɪ] n Rubin m ♦ adj rubinrot
rucksack ['rʌksæk] n Rucksack m
ructions ['rʌkʃənz] npl Krach m
rudder ['rʌdə*] n Steuerruder nt
ruddy ['rʌdɪ] adj (colour) rötlich; (inf: bloody) verdammt
rude [ruːd] adj unverschämt; (shock)

hart; (*awakening*) unsanft; (*unrefined, rough*) grob; ~**ness** *n* Unverschämtheit *f*; Grobheit *f*

rudiment ['ruːdɪmənt] *n* Grundlage *f*

rueful ['ruːfʊl] *adj* reuevoll; (*situation*) beklagenswert

ruffian ['rʌfɪən] *n* Rohling *m*

ruffle ['rʌfl] *vt* kräuseln

rug [rʌg] *n* Brücke *f*; (*in bedroom*) Bettvorleger *m*; (*BRIT: for knees*) (Reise)decke *f*

rugby ['rʌgbɪ] *n* (*also:* ~ *football*) Rugby *nt*

rugged ['rʌgɪd] *adj* (*coastline*) zerklüftet; (*features*) markig

rugger ['rʌgə*] (*BRIT: inf*) *n* Rugby *nt*

ruin ['ruːɪn] *n* Ruine *f*; (*downfall*) Ruin *m* ♦ *vt* ruinieren; ~**s** *npl* (*fig*) Trümmer *pl*; ~**ous** *adj* ruinierend

rule [ruːl] *n* Regel *f*; (*government*) Regierung *f*; (*for measuring*) Lineal *nt* ♦ *vt* (*govern*) herrschen über +*acc*, regieren; (*decide*) anordnen, entscheiden; (*make lines on*) linieren ♦ *vi* herrschen, regieren; entscheiden; **as a** ~ in der Regel; ~ **out** *vt* ausschließen; ~**d** *adj* (*paper*) liniert; ~**r** *n* Lineal *nt*; Herrscher *m*

ruling ['ruːlɪŋ] *adj* (*party*) Regierungs-; (*class*) herrschend ♦ *n* (*JUR*) Entscheid *m*

rum [rʌm] *n* Rum *m*

Rumania [ruːˈmeɪnɪə] *n* Rumänien *nt*; ~**n** *adj* rumänisch ♦ *n* Rumäne *m*, Rumänin *f*; (*LING*) Rumänisch *nt*

rumble ['rʌmbl] *n* Rumpeln *nt*; (*of thunder*) Grollen *nt* ♦ *vi* rumpeln; grollen

rummage ['rʌmɪdʒ] *vi* durchstöbern

rumour ['ruːmə*] (*US* **rumor**) *n* Gerücht *nt* ♦ *vt*: **it is** ~**ed that** man sagt *or* man munkelt, daß

rump [rʌmp] *n* Hinterteil *nt*; ~ **steak** *n* Rumpsteak *nt*

rumpus ['rʌmpəs] *n* Spektakel *m*

run [rʌn] (*pt* **ran**, *pp* **run**) *n* Lauf *m*; (*in car*) (Spazier)fahrt *f*; (*series*) Serie *f*, Reihe *f*; (*ski* ~) (Ski)abfahrt *f*; (*in stocking*) Laufmasche *f* ♦ *vt* (*cause to* ~) laufen lassen; (*car, train, bus*)

fahren; (*race, distance*) laufen, rennen; (*manage*) leiten; (*COMPUT*) laufen lassen; (*pass: hand, eye*) gleiten lassen ♦ *vi* laufen; (*move quickly*) laufen, rennen; (*bus, train*) fahren; (*flow*) fließen, laufen; (*colours*) (ab)färben; **there was a** ~ **on** (*meat, tickets*) es gab einen Ansturm auf +*acc*; **on the** ~ auf der Flucht; **in the long** ~ auf die Dauer; **I'll** ~ **you to the station** ich fahre dich zum Bahnhof; **to** ~ **a risk** ein Risiko eingehen; ~ **about** *or* **around** *vi* (*children*) umherspringen; ~ **across** *vt fus* (*find*) stoßen auf +*acc*; ~ **away** *vi* weglaufen; ~ **down** *vi* (*clock*) ablaufen ♦ *vt* (*production, factory*) allmählich auflösen; (*with car*) überfahren; (*talk against*) heruntermachen; **to be** ~ **down** erschöpft *or* abgespannt sein; ~ **in** (*BRIT*) *vt* (*car*) einfahren; ~ **into** *vt fus* (*meet: person*) zufällig treffen; (: *trouble*) bekommen; (*collide with*) rennen gegen; fahren gegen; ~ **off** *vi* fortlaufen; ~ **out** *vi* (*person*) hinausrennen; (*liquid*) auslaufen; (*lease*) ablaufen; (*money*) ausgehen; **he ran out of money/petrol** ihm ging das Geld/ Benzin aus; ~ **over** *vt* (*in accident*) überfahren; ~ **through** *vt* (*instructions*) durchgehen; ~ **up** *vt* (*debt, bill*) machen; ~ **up against** *vt fus* (*difficulties*) stoßen auf +*acc*; ~**away** *adj* (*horse*) ausgebrochen; (*person*) flüchtig

rung [rʌŋ] *pp of* **ring** ♦ *n* Sprosse *f*

runner ['rʌnə*] *n* Läufer(in) *m(f)*; (*for sleigh*) Kufe *f*; ~ **bean** (*BRIT*) *n* Stangenbohne *f*; ~-**up** *n* Zweite(r) *mf*

running ['rʌnɪŋ] *n* (*of business*) Leitung *f*; (*of machine*) Betrieb *m* ♦ *adj* (*water*) fließend; (*commentary*) laufend; **to be in/out of the** ~ **for sth** im/aus dem Rennen für etw sein; **3 days** ~ 3 Tage lang *or* hintereinander

runny ['rʌnɪ] *adj* dünn; (*nose*) laufend

run-of-the-mill ['rʌnəvðəˈmɪl] *adj* gewöhnlich, alltäglich

run-up ['rʌnʌp] *n*: **the** ~ **to** (*election etc*) die Endphase vor +*dat*

runway ['rʌnweɪ] *n* Startbahn *f*

rupee [ruːˈpiː] *n* Rupie *f*

rupture [ˈrʌptʃə*] *n* (*MED*) Bruch *m* ♦ *vt*: **to ~ o.s.** sich *dat* einen Bruch zuziehen

rural [ˈruərəl] *adj* ländlich, Land-

ruse [ruːz] *n* Kniff *m*, List *f*

rush [rʌʃ] *n* Eile *f*, Hetze *f*; (*FIN*) starke Nachfrage *f* ♦ *vt* (*carry along*) auf dem schnellsten Wege schaffen *or* transportieren; (*attack*) losstürmen auf +*acc* ♦ *vi* (*hurry*) eilen, stürzen; **don't ~ me** dräng mich nicht; **~ hour** *n* Hauptverkehrszeit *f*

rusk [rʌsk] *n* Zwieback *m*

Russia [ˈrʌʃə] *n* Rußland *nt*; **~n** *adj* russisch ♦ *n* Russe *m*, Russin *f*; (*LING*) Russisch *nt*

rust [rʌst] *n* Rost *m* ♦ *vi* rosten

rustic [ˈrʌstɪk] *adj* bäuerlich, ländlich

rustle [ˈrʌsl] *vi* rauschen, rascheln ♦ *vt* rascheln lassen; (*cattle*) stehlen

rustproof [ˈrʌstpruːf] *adj* rostfrei

rusty [ˈrʌstɪ] *adj* rostig

rut [rʌt] *n* (*in track*) Radspur *f*; **to be in a ~** im Trott stecken

ruthless [ˈruːθləs] *adj* rücksichtslos

rye [raɪ] *n* Roggen *m*; **~ bread** *n* Roggenbrot *nt*

S

sabbath [ˈsæbəθ] *n* Sabbat *m*

sabotage [ˈsæbətɑːʒ] *n* Sabotage *f* ♦ *vt* sabotieren

saccharin [ˈsækərɪn] *n* Saccharin *nt*

sachet [ˈsæʃeɪ] *n* (*of shampoo etc*) Briefchen *nt*, Kissen *nt*

sack [sæk] *n* Sack *m* ♦ *vt* (*inf*) hinauswerfen; (*pillage*) plündern; **to get the ~** rausfliegen; **~ing** *n* (*material*) Sackleinen *nt*; (*inf*) Rausschmiß *m*

sacrament [ˈsækrəmənt] *n* Sakrament *nt*

sacred [ˈseɪkrɪd] *adj* heilig

sacrifice [ˈsækrɪfaɪs] *n* Opfer *nt* ♦ *vt* (*also fig*) opfern

sacrilege [ˈsækrɪlɪdʒ] *n* Schändung *f*

sad [sæd] *adj* traurig; **~den** *vt* traurig machen, betrüben

saddle [ˈsædl] *n* Sattel *m* ♦ *vt* (*burden*):

to ~ sb with sth jdm etw aufhalsen; **~bag** *n* Satteltasche *f*

sadistic [səˈdɪstɪk] *adj* sadistisch

sadly [ˈsædlɪ] *adv* traurig; (*unfortunately*) leider

sadness [ˈsædnəs] *n* Traurigkeit *f*

s.a.e. *abbr* (= *stamped addressed envelope*) frankierte(r) Rückumschlag *m*

safe [seɪf] *adj* (*free from danger*) sicher; (*careful*) vorsichtig ♦ *n* Safe *m*; **~ and sound** gesund und wohl; **(just) to be on the ~ side** um ganz sicher zu gehen; **~-conduct** *n* freie(s) Geleit *nt*; **~-deposit** *n* (*vault*) Tresorraum *m*; (*box*) Banksafe *m*; **~guard** *n* Sicherung *f* ♦ *vt* sichern, schützen; **~keeping** *n* sichere Verwahrung *f*; **~ly** *adv* sicher; (*arrive*) wohlbehalten

safety [ˈseɪftɪ] *n* Sicherheit *f*; **~ belt** *n* Sicherheitsgurt *m*; **~ pin** *n* Sicherheitsnadel *f*; **~ valve** *n* Sicherheitsventil *nt*

sag [sæg] *vi* (durch)sacken

sage [seɪdʒ] *n* (*herb*) Salbei *m*; (*person*) Weise(r) *mf*

Sagittarius [sædʒɪˈtɛərɪəs] *n* Schütze *m*

Sahara [səˈhɑːrə] *n*: **the ~ (Desert)** die (Wüste) Sahara

said [sed] *pt, pp of* **say**

sail [seɪl] *n* Segel *nt*; (*trip*) Fahrt *f* ♦ *vt* segeln ♦ *vi* segeln; (*begin voyage: person*) abfahren; (: *ship*) auslaufen; (*fig: cloud etc*) dahinsegeln; **to go for a ~** segeln gehen; **they ~ed into Copenhagen** sie liefen in Kopenhagen ein; **~ through** *vt fus, vi* (*fig*) (es) spielend schaffen; **~boat** (*US*) *n* Segelboot *nt*; **~ing** *n* Segeln *nt*; **~ing ship** *n* Segelschiff *nt*; **~or** *n* Matrose *m*, Seemann *m*

saint [seɪnt] *n* Heilige(r) *mf*; **~ly** *adj* heilig, fromm

sake [seɪk] *n*: **for the ~ of** um +*gen* willen

salad [ˈsæləd] *n* Salat *m*; **~ bowl** *n* Salatschüssel *f*; **~ cream** (*BRIT*) *n* gewürzte Mayonnaise *f*; **~ dressing** *n* Salatsoße *f*

salami [səˈlɑːmɪ] *n* Salami *f*

salary ['sælərɪ] n Gehalt nt
sale [seɪl] n Verkauf m; (reduced prices) Schlußverkauf m; **"for ~"** „zu verkaufen"; **on ~** zu verkaufen; **~room** n Verkaufsraum m; **~s assistant** n Verkäufer(in) m(f); **~s clerk** (US) n Verkäufer(in) m(f); **salesman** (irreg) n Verkäufer m; (representative) Vertreter m; **saleswoman** (irreg) n Verkäuferin f
salient ['seɪlɪənt] adj bemerkenswert
saliva [sə'laɪvə] n Speichel m
sallow ['sæləʊ] adj fahl; (face) bleich
salmon ['sæmən] n Lachs m
saloon [sə'luːn] n (BRIT: AUT) Limousine f; (ship's lounge) Salon m
salt [sɔːlt] n Salz nt ♦ vt (cure) einsalzen; (flavour) salzen; **~ away** (inf) vt (money) auf die hohe Kante legen; **~cellar** n Salzfaß nt; **~-water** adj Salzwasser-; **~y** adj salzig
salutary ['sæljʊtərɪ] adj nützlich
salute [sə'luːt] n (MIL) Gruß m; (with guns) Salutschüsse pl ♦ vt (MIL) salutieren
salvage ['sælvɪdʒ] n (from ship) Bergung f; (property) Rettung f ♦ vt bergen; retten
salvation [sæl'veɪʃən] n Rettung f; **S~ Army** n Heilsarmee f
same [seɪm] adj, pron (similar) gleiche(r, s); (identical) derselbe/dieselbe/dasselbe; **the ~ book as** das gleiche Buch wie; **at the ~ time** zur gleichen Zeit, gleichzeitig; (however) zugleich, andererseits; **all** or **just the ~** trotzdem; **the ~ to you!** gleichfalls!
sample ['sɑːmpl] n Probe f ♦ vt probieren
sanctify ['sæŋktɪfaɪ] vt weihen
sanctimonious [sæŋktɪ'məʊnɪəs] adj scheinheilig
sanction ['sæŋkʃən] n Sanktion f
sanctity ['sæŋktɪtɪ] n Heiligkeit f; (fig) Unverletzlichkeit f
sanctuary ['sæŋktjʊərɪ] n (for fugitive) Asyl nt; (refuge) Zufluchtsort m; (for animals) Schutzgebiet nt
sand [sænd] n Sand m ♦ vt (furniture) schmirgeln

sandal ['sændl] n Sandale f
sand: **~box** (US) n = sandpit; **~castle** n Sandburg f; **~ dune** n (Sand)düne f; **~paper** n Sandpapier nt; **~pit** n Sandkasten m; **~stone** n Sandstein m
sandwich ['sænwɪdʒ] n Sandwich m or nt ♦ vt (also: **~ in**) einklemmen; **cheese/ham** ~ Käse-/Schinkenbrot; **~ed between** eingeklemmt zwischen; **~ board** n Reklametafel f; **~ course** (BRIT) n theorie- und praxisabwechselnde(r) Ausbildungsgang
sandy ['sændɪ] adj sandig; (hair) rotblond
sane [seɪn] adj geistig gesund or normal; (sensible) vernünftig, gescheit
sang [sæŋ] pt of sing
sanitary ['sænɪtərɪ] adj hygienisch; **~ napkin** (US) n (Monats)binde f; **~ towel** n (Monats)binde f
sanitation [sænɪ'teɪʃən] n sanitäre Einrichtungen pl; **~ department** (US) n Stadtreinigung f
sanity ['sænɪtɪ] n geistige Gesundheit f; (good sense) Vernunft f
sank [sæŋk] pt of sink
Santa Claus [sæntə'klɔːz] n Nikolaus m, Weihnachtsmann m
sap [sæp] n (of plants) Saft m ♦ vt (strength) schwächen
sapling ['sæplɪŋ] n junge(r) Baum m
sapphire ['sæfaɪə*] n Saphir m
sarcasm ['sɑːkæzəm] n Sarkasmus m
sarcastic [sɑː'kæstɪk] adj sarkastisch
sardine [sɑː'diːn] n Sardine f
Sardinia [sɑː'dɪnɪə] n Sardinien nt
sardonic [sɑː'dɒnɪk] adj zynisch
sash [sæʃ] n Schärpe f
sat [sæt] pt, pp of sit
Satan ['seɪtn] n Satan m
satchel ['sætʃəl] n (for school) Schulmappe f
sated ['seɪtɪd] adj (appetite, person) gesättigt
satin ['sætɪn] n Satin m ♦ adj Satin-
satisfaction [sætɪs'fækʃən] n Befriedigung f, Genugtuung f
satisfactory [sætɪs'fæktərɪ] adj zufriedenstellend, befriedigend
satisfy ['sætɪsfaɪ] vt befriedigen, zu-

friedenstellen; (*convince*) überzeugen; (*conditions*) erfüllen; ~**ing** *adj* befriedigend; (*meal*) sättigend

saturate ['sætʃəreɪt] *vt* (durch)tränken

saturation [sætʃə'reɪʃən] *n* Durchtränkung *f*; (*CHEM, fig*) Sättigung *f*

Saturday ['sætədeɪ] *n* Samstag *m*, Sonnabend *m*

sauce [sɔːs] *n* Soße *f*, Sauce *f*; ~**pan** *n* Kasserolle *f*

saucer ['sɔːsə*] *n* Untertasse *f*

saucy ['sɔːsɪ] *adj* frech, keck

Saudi ['saudɪ]: ~ **Arabia** *n* Saudi-Arabien *nt*; ~ (**Arabian**) *adj* saudiarabisch ♦ *n* Saudiaraber(in) *m(f)*

sauna ['sɔːnə] *n* Sauna *f*

saunter ['sɔːntə*] *vi* schlendern

sausage ['sɒsɪdʒ] *n* Wurst *f*; ~ **roll** *n* Wurst *f* im Schlafrock, Wurstpastete *f*

sauté ['sauteɪ] *adj* Röst-

savage ['sævɪdʒ] *adj* wild ♦ *n* Wilde(r) *mf* ♦ *vt* (*animals*) zerfleischen; ~**ry** *n* Roheit *f*, Grausamkeit *f*

save [seɪv] *vt* retten; (*money, electricity etc*) sparen; (*strength etc*) aufsparen; (*COMPUT*) speichern ♦ *vi* (*also:* ~ **up**) sparen ♦ *n* (*SPORT*) (Ball)abwehr *f* ♦ *prep, conj* außer, ausgenommen

saving ['seɪvɪŋ] *adj*: **the** ~ **grace of** das Versöhnende an +*dat* ♦ *n* Sparen *nt*, Ersparnis *f*; ~**s** *npl* (*money*) Ersparnisse *pl*; ~**s account** *n* Sparkonto *nt*; ~**s bank** *n* Sparkasse *f*

saviour ['seɪvjə*] (*US* **savior**) *n* (*REL*) Erlöser *m*

savour ['seɪvə*] (*US* **savor**) *vt* (*taste*) schmecken; (*fig*) genießen; ~**y** *adj* pikant, würzig

saw [sɔː] (*pt* **sawed**, *pp* **sawed** *or* **sawn**) *pt of* **see** ♦ *n* (*tool*) Säge *f* ♦ *vt, vi* sägen; ~**dust** *n* Sägemehl *nt*; ~**mill** *n* Sägewerk *nt*; **sawn** [sɔːn] *pp of* **saw**; ~**n-off shotgun** *n* Gewehr *nt* mit abgesägtem Lauf

say [seɪ] (*pt, pp* **said**) *n*: **to have a/no** ~ **in sth** Mitspracherecht/kein Mitspracherecht bei etw haben ♦ *vt, vi* sagen; **let him have his** ~ laß ihn doch reden; **to** ~ **yes/no** ja/nein sagen; **that goes without** ~**ing** das versteht sich von

selbst; **that is to** ~ das heißt; ~**ing** *n* Sprichwort *nt*

scab [skæb] *n* Schorf *m*; (*pej*) Streikbrecher *m*

scaffold ['skæfəʊld] *n* (*for execution*) Schafott *nt*; ~**ing** *n* (Bau)gerüst *nt*

scald [skɔːld] *n* Verbrühung *f* ♦ *vt* (*burn*) verbrühen; (*clean*) (ab)brühen

scale [skeɪl] *n* (*of fish*) Schuppe *f*; (*MUS*) Tonleiter *f*; (*on map, size*) Maßstab *m*; (*gradation*) Skala *f* ♦ *vt* (*climb*) erklimmen; ~**s** *npl* (*balance*) Waage *f*; **on a large** ~ (*fig*) im großen, in großem Umfang; ~ **of charges** Gebührenordnung *f*; ~ **down** *vt* verkleinern; ~ **model** *n* maßstabgetreue(s) Modell *nt*

scallop ['skɒləp] *n* Kammuschel *f*

scalp [skælp] *n* Kopfhaut *f*

scamper ['skæmpə*] *vi*: **to** ~ **away** *or* **off** sich davonmachen

scampi ['skæmpɪ] *npl* Scampi *pl*

scan [skæn] *vt* (*examine*) genau prüfen; (*quickly*) überfliegen; (*horizon*) absuchen; (*poetry*) skandieren

scandal ['skændl] *n* Skandal *m*; (*piece of gossip*) Skandalgeschichte *f*

Scandinavia [skændɪ'neɪvɪə] *n* Skandinavien *nt*; ~**n** *adj* skandinavisch ♦ *n* Skandinavier(in) *m(f)*

scant [skænt] *adj* knapp; ~**ily** *adv* knapp, dürftig; ~**iness** *n* Knappheit *f*; ~**y** *adj* knapp, unzureichend

scapegoat ['skeɪpgəʊt] *n* Sündenbock *m*

scar [skɑː*] *n* Narbe *f* ♦ *vt* durch Narben entstellen

scarce [skɛəs] *adj* selten, rar; (*goods*) knapp; ~**ly** *adv* kaum

scarcity ['skɛəsɪtɪ] *n* Mangel *m*

scare ['skɛə*] *n* Schrecken *m* ♦ *vt* erschrecken; **bomb** ~ Bombendrohung *f*; **to** ~ **sb stiff** jdn zu Tode erschrecken; **to be** ~**d** Angst haben; ~**crow** *n* Vogelscheuche *f*

scarf [skɑːf] (*pl* **scarves**) *n* Schal *m*; (*head*~) Kopftuch *nt*

scarlet ['skɑːlət] *adj* scharlachrot ♦ *vt* Scharlachrot *nt*; ~ **fever** *n* Scharlach *m*

scarves [skɑːvz] *npl of* **scarf**

scary ['skɛərɪ] (*inf*) *adj* schaurig

scathing ['skeɪðɪŋ] *adj* scharf, ver-

nichtend
scatter ['skætə*] vt (sprinkle)
(ver)streuen; (disperse) zerstreuen ♦ vi
sich zerstreuen; ~**brained** adj
flatterhaft, schusselig
scavenger ['skævɪndʒə*] n (animal)
Aasfresser m
scenario [sɪ'nɑ:rɪəʊ] n (THEAT, CINE)
Szenarium nt; (fig) Szenario nt
scene [si:n] n (of happening) Ort m; (of
play, incident) Szene f; (view) Anblick
m; (argument) Szene f, Auftritt m; ~**ry**
['si:nərɪ] n (THEAT) Bühnenbild nt;
(landscape) Landschaft f
scenic ['si:nɪk] adj landschaftlich
scent [sent] n Parfüm nt; (smell) Duft
m ♦ vt parfümieren
sceptical ['skeptɪkəl] (US **skeptical**) adj
skeptisch
schedule ['ʃedju:l, (US) 'skedju:l] n (list)
Liste f; (plan) Programm nt; (of work)
Zeitplan m ♦ vt planen; on ~ pünktlich;
to be ahead of/behind ~ dem Zeitplan
voraus/im Rückstand sein; ~**d flight** n
(not charter) Linienflug m
scheme [ski:m] n Schema nt;
(dishonest) Intrige f; (plan of action)
Plan m ♦ vi intrigieren ♦ vt planen
scheming ['ski:mɪŋ] adj intrigierend
scholar ['skɒlə*] n Gelehrte(r) m;
(holding ~ship) Stipendiat m; ~**ly** adj
gelehrt; ~**ship** n Gelehrsamkeit f;
(grant) Stipendium nt
school [sku:l] n Schule f; (UNIV)
Fakultät f ♦ vt schulen; (dog)
trainieren; ~ **age** n schulpflichtige(s)
Alter nt; ~**book** n Schulbuch nt; ~**boy**
n Schüler m; ~**children** npl Schüler pl,
Schulkinder pl; ~**days** npl (alte)
Schulzeit f; ~**girl** n Schülerin f; ~**ing** n
Schulung f, Ausbildung f; ~**master** n
Lehrer m; ~**mistress** n Lehrerin f;
~**teacher** n Lehrer(in) m(f)
sciatica [saɪ'ætɪkə] n Ischias m or nt
science ['saɪəns] n Wissenschaft f;
(natural ~) Naturwissenschaft f
scientific [saɪən'tɪfɪk] adj wissenschaftlich; (natural sciences) naturwissen-
schaftlich
scientist ['saɪəntɪst] n Wissen-

schaftler(in) m(f)
scintillating ['sɪntɪleɪtɪŋ] adj sprühend
scissors ['sɪzəz] npl Schere f; a pair of
~ eine Schere
scoff [skɒf] vt (BRIT: inf: eat) fressen ♦
vi (mock): to ~ (at) spotten (über
+acc)
scold [skəʊld] vt schimpfen
scone [skɒn] n weiche(s) Teegebäck nt
scoop [sku:p] n Schaufel f; (news)
sensationelle Erstmeldung f; ~ **out** vt
herausschaufeln; (liquid) heraus-
schöpfen; ~ **up** vt aufschaufeln;
(liquid) aufschöpfen
scooter ['sku:tə*] n Motorroller m;
(child's) Roller m
scope [skəʊp] n Ausmaß nt;
(opportunity) (Spiel)raum m
scorch [skɔ:tʃ] n Brandstelle f ♦ vt versengen; ~**ing** adj brennend
score [skɔ:*] n (in game) Punktzahl f;
(final ~) (Spiel)ergebnis nt; (MUS)
Partitur f; (line) Kratzer m; (twenty)
zwanzig, zwanzig Stück ♦ vt (goal)
schießen; (points) machen; (mark) ein-
ritzen ♦ vi (keep record) Punkte
zählen; on that ~ in dieser Hinsicht;
what's the ~? wie steht's?; ~ **out** vt
ausstreichen; ~**board** n Anschreibetafel
f; ~**r** n Torschütze m; (recorder)
(Auf)schreiber m
scorn ['skɔ:n] n Verachtung f ♦ vt verhöhnen; ~**ful** adj verächtlich
Scorpio ['skɔ:pɪəʊ] n Skorpion m
Scot [skɒt] n Schotte m, Schottin f
Scotch [skɒtʃ] n Scotch m
scotch vt (end) unterbinden
scot-free ['skɒt'fri:] adv: to get off ~
(unpunished) ungeschoren davonkommen
Scotland ['skɒtlənd] n Schottland nt
Scots [skɒts] adj schottisch; ~**man/
woman** (irreg) n Schotte m/Schottin f
Scottish ['skɒtɪʃ] adj schottisch
scoundrel ['skaʊndrəl] n Schuft m
scour ['skaʊə*] vt (search) absuchen;
(clean) schrubben
scourge [skɜ:dʒ] n (whip) Geißel f;
(plague) Qual f
scout [skaʊt] n (MIL) Späher m; (also:

boy ~) Pfadfinder *m*; ~ **around** *vi*: to
~ **around (for)** sich umsehen (nach)
scowl [skaul] *n* finstere(r) Blick *m* ♦ *vi*
finster blicken
scrabble ['skræbl] *vi* (*also:* ~ *around*:
search) (herum)tasten; (*claw*): to ~
(at) kratzen (an +*dat*) ♦ *n*: S~ (®)
Scrabble *nt* (®)
scraggy ['skrægɪ] *adj* dürr, hager
scram [skræm] (*inf*) *vi* abhauen
scramble ['skræmbl] *n* (*climb*) Kletterei
f; (*struggle*) Kampf *m* ♦ *vi* klettern;
(*fight*) sich schlagen; to ~ **out/through**
krabbeln aus/durch; to ~ **for** sth sich
um etw raufen; ~**d eggs** *npl* Rührei *nt*
scrap [skræp] *n* (*bit*) Stückchen *nt*;
(*fight*) Keilerei *f*; (*also:* ~ *iron*) Schrott
m ♦ *vt* verwerfen ♦ *vi* (*fight*) streiten,
sich prügeln; ~**s** *npl* (*leftovers*) Reste
pl; (*waste*) Abfall *m*; ~**book** *n* Ein-
klebealbum *nt*; ~ **dealer** *n* Schrott-
händler(in) *m(f)*
scrape [skreɪp] *n* Kratzen *nt*; (*trouble*)
Klemme *f* ♦ *vt* kratzen; (*car*) zerkratzen; (*clean*) abkratzen ♦ *vi* (*make
harsh noise*) kratzen; to ~ **through**
gerade noch durchkommen; ~**r** *n*
Kratzer *m*
scrap: ~ **heap** *n* Schrotthaufen *m*; on
the ~ **heap** (*fig*) beim alten Eisen; ~
iron *n* Schrott *m*; ~ **merchant** (*BRIT*)
Altwarenhändler(in) *m(f)*
scrappy ['skræpɪ] *adj* zusammenge-
stoppelt
scratch [skrætʃ] *n* (*wound*) Kratzer *m*,
Schramme *f* ♦ *adj*: ~ **team**
zusammengewürfelte Mannschaft ♦ *vt*
kratzen; (*car*) zerkratzen ♦ *vi* (sich)
kratzen; to start from ~ ganz von vorne anfangen; to be up to ~ den Anforderungen entsprechen
scrawl [skrɔːl] *n* Gekritzel *nt* ♦ *vt*, *vi*
kritzeln
scrawny ['skrɔːnɪ] *adj* (*person, neck*)
dürr
scream [skriːm] *n* Schrei *m* ♦ *vi*
schreien
scree [skriː] *n* Geröll(halde *f*) *nt*
screech [skriːtʃ] *n* Schrei *m* ♦ *vi* kreischen

screen [skriːn] *n* (*protective*) Schutz-
schirm *m*; (*CINE*) Leinwand *f*; (*TV*)
Bildschirm *m* ♦ *vt* (*shelter*)
(be)schirmen; (*film*) zeigen, vorführen;
~**ing** *n* (*MED*) Untersuchung *f*; ~**play** *n*
Drehbuch *nt*
screw [skruː] *n* Schraube *f* ♦ *vt* (*fasten*)
schrauben; (*vulgar*) bumsen; ~ **up** *vt*
(*paper etc*) zerknüllen; (*inf: ruin*) vermasseln (*inf*); ~**driver** *n* Schraubenzieher *m*
scribble ['skrɪbl] *n* Gekritzel *nt* ♦ *vt*
kritzeln
script [skrɪpt] *n* (*handwriting*)
Handschrift *f*; (*for film*) Drehbuch *nt*;
(*THEAT*) Manuskript *nt*, Text *m*
Scripture ['skrɪptʃə*] *n* Heilige Schrift *f*
scroll [skrəul] *n* Schriftrolle *f*
scrounge [skraundʒ] (*inf*) *vt*: to ~ sth
off *or* from sb etw bei jdm abstauben ♦
n: on the ~ beim Schnorren
scrub [skrʌb] *n* (*clean*) Schrubben *nt*;
(*in countryside*) Gestrüpp *nt* ♦ *vt*
(*clean*) schrubben; (*reject*) fallenlassen
scruff [skrʌf] *n*: by the ~ of the neck am
Genick
scruffy ['skrʌfɪ] *adj* unordentlich, ver-
gammelt
scrum(mage) ['skrʌm(ɪdʒ)] *n* Getümmel
nt
scruple ['skruːpl] *n* Skrupel *m*,
Bedenken *nt*
scrupulous ['skruːpjuləs] *adj* peinlich
genau, gewissenhaft
scrutinize ['skruːtɪnaɪz] *vt* genau prüfen
scrutiny ['skruːtɪnɪ] *n* genaue Untersuchung *f*
scuff [skʌf] *vt* (*shoes*) abstoßen
scuffle ['skʌfl] *n* Handgemenge *nt*
scullery ['skʌlərɪ] *n* Spülküche *f*
sculptor ['skʌlptə*] *n* Bildhauer(in)
m(f)
sculpture ['skʌlptʃə*] *n* (*ART*)
Bildhauerei *f*; (*statue*) Skulptur *f*
scum [skʌm] *n* (*also fig*) Abschaum *m*
scupper ['skʌpə*] *vt* (*NAUT*) versenken;
(*fig*) zerstören
scurrilous ['skʌrɪləs] *adj* unflätig
scurry ['skʌrɪ] *vi* huschen
scuttle ['skʌtl] *n* (*also:* coal ~)

Kohleneimer *m* ♦ *vt* (*ship*) versenken ♦ *vi* (*scamper*): **to ~ away** *or* **off** sich davonmachen

scythe [saɪð] *n* Sense *f*

SDP (*BRIT*) *n abbr* = **Social Democratic Party**

sea [siː] *n* Meer *nt*, See *f*; (*fig*) Meer *nt* ♦ *adj* Meeres-, See-; **by ~** (*travel*) auf dem Seeweg; **on the ~** (*boat*) auf dem Meer; (*town*) am Meer; **out to ~** aufs Meer hinaus; **out at ~** aufs Meer; **to be all at ~** (*fig*) nicht durchblicken; **~board** *n* Küste *f*; **~ breeze** *n* Seewind *m*; **~food** *n* Meeresfrüchte *pl*; **~ front** *n* Strandpromenade *f*; **~going** *adj* seetüchtig, Hochsee-; **~gull** *n* Möwe *f*

seal [siːl] *n* (*animal*) Robbe *f*, Seehund *m*; (*stamp, impression*) Siegel *nt* ♦ *vt* versiegeln

sea level *n* Meeresspiegel *m*

sea lion *n* Seelöwe *m*

seam [siːm] *n* Saum *m*; (*edges joining*) Naht *f*; (*of coal*) Flöz *nt*

seaman ['siːmən] (*irreg*) *n* Seemann *m*

seamy ['siːmɪ] *adj* (*people, café*) zwielichtig; (*life*) anrüchig

seaplane ['siːpleɪn] *n* Wasserflugzeug *nt*

seaport ['siːpɔːt] *n* Seehafen *m*

search [sɜːtʃ] *n* (*for person, thing*) Suche *f*; (*of drawer, pockets, house*) Durchsuchung *f* ♦ *vi* suchen ♦ *vt* durchsuchen; **in ~ of** auf der Suche nach; **to ~ for** suchen nach; **~ through** *vt* durchsuchen; **~ing** *adj* (*look*) forschend; **~light** *n* Scheinwerfer *m*; **~ party** *n* Suchmannschaft *f*; **~ warrant** *n* Durchsuchungsbefehl *m*

seashore ['siːʃɔː*] *n* Meeresküste *f*

seasick ['siːsɪk] *adj* seekrank; **~ness** *n* Seekrankheit *f*

seaside ['siːsaɪd] *n* Küste *f*; **~ resort** *n* Badeort *m*

season ['siːzn] *n* Jahreszeit *f*; (*Christmas etc*) Zeit *f*, Saison *f* ♦ *vt* (*flavour*) würzen; **~al** *adj* Saison-; **~ed** *adj* (*fig*) erfahren; **~ing** *n* Gewürz *nt*, Würze *f*; **~ ticket** *n* (*RAIL*) Zeitkarte *f*; (*THEAT*) Abonnement *nt*

seat [siːt] *n* Sitz *m*, Platz *m*; (*in Parliament*) Sitz *m*; (*part of body*)

Gesäß *nt*; (*of trousers*) Hosenboden *m* ♦ *vt* (*place*) setzen; (*have space for*) Sitzplätze bieten für; **to be ~ed** sitzen; **~ belt** *n* Sicherheitsgurt *m*

sea water *n* Meerwasser *nt*

seaweed ['siːwiːd] *n* (See)tang *m*

seaworthy ['siːwɜːðɪ] *adj* seetüchtig

sec. *abbr* (= *second(s)*) Sek.

secluded [sɪ'kluːdɪd] *adj* abgelegen

seclusion [sɪ'kluːʒən] *n* Zurückgezogenheit *f*

second ['sekənd] *adj* zweite(r,s) ♦ *adv* (*in ~ position*) an zweiter Stelle ♦ *n* Sekunde *f*; (*person*) Zweite(r) *m*; (*COMM: imperfect*) zweite Wahl *f*; (*SPORT*) Sekundant *m*; (*AUT: also: ~ gear*) zweite(r) Gang *m*; (*BRIT: UNIV: degree*) mittlere Note bei Abschlußprüfungen ♦ *vt* (*support*) unterstützen; **~ary** *adj* zweitrangig; **~ary school** *n* höhere Schule *f*, Mittelschule *f*; **~class** *adj* zweiter Klasse; **~hand** *adj* aus zweiter Hand; (*car etc*) gebraucht; **~ hand** *n* (*on clock*) Sekundenzeiger *m*; **~ly** *adv* zweitens; **~ment** [sɪ'kɒndmənt] (*BRIT*) *n* Abordnung *f*; **~rate** *adj* mittelmäßig; **~ thoughts** *npl*: **to have ~ thoughts** sich etw *dat* anders überlegen; **on ~ thoughts** (*BRIT*) *or* **thought** (*US*) oder lieber nicht

secrecy ['siːkrəsɪ] *n* Geheimhaltung *f*

secret ['siːkrət] *n* Geheimnis *nt* ♦ *adj* geheim, Geheim-; **in ~** geheim

secretarial [sekrə'tɛərɪəl] *adj* Sekretärinnen-

secretary ['sekrətrɪ] *n* Sekretär(in) *m(f)*; (*government*) Minister *m*

secretion [sɪ'kriːʃən] *n* Absonderung *f*

secretive ['siːkrətɪv] *adj* geheimtuerisch

secretly *adv* geheim

sectarian [sek'tɛərɪən] *adj* konfessionsgebunden

section ['sekʃən] *n* Teil *m*; (*department*) Abteilung *f*; (*of document*) Abschnitt *m*

sector ['sektə*] *n* Sektor *m*

secular ['sekjʊlə*] *adj* weltlich, profan

secure [sɪ'kjʊə*] *adj* (*safe*) sicher; (*firmly fixed*) fest ♦ *vt* (*make firm*) befestigen, sichern; (*obtain*) sichern

security [sɪ'kjʊərɪtɪ] n Sicherheit f;
(pledge) Pfand nt; (document)
Wertpapier nt; (national ~) Staatssi-
cherheit f
sedan [sɪ'dæn] (US) n (AUT) Limousine f
sedate [sɪ'deɪt] adj gesetzt ♦ vt (MED)
ein Beruhigungsmittel geben +dat
sedation [sɪ'deɪʃən] n (MED) Einfluß m
von Beruhigungsmitteln
sedative ['sedətɪv] n Beruhigungsmittel
nt ♦ adj beruhigend, einschläfernd
sedentary ['sedntrɪ] adj (job) sitzend
sediment ['sedɪmənt] n (Boden)satz m
sedition [sə'dɪʃən] n Aufwiegelung f
seduce [sɪ'dju:s] vt verführen
seduction [sɪ'dʌkʃən] n Verführung f
seductive [sɪ'dʌktɪv] adj verführerisch
see [si:] (pt saw, pp seen) vt sehen;
(understand) (ein)sehen, erkennen;
(visit) besuchen ♦ vi (be aware) sehen;
(find out) nachsehen ♦ n (ECCL: R.C.)
Bistum nt; (: Protestant) Kirchenkreis
m; to ~ sb to the door jdn hinausbegleiten; to ~ that (ensure) dafür
sorgen, daß; ~ you soon! bis bald!; ~
about vt fus sich kümmern um; ~ off
vt: to ~ sb off jdn zum Zug etc begleiten; ~ through vt: to ~ sth through
etw durchfechten ♦ vt fus: to ~ through
sb/sth jdn/etw durchschauen; ~ to vt
fus: to ~ to it dafür sorgen
seed [si:d] n Samen m ♦ vt (TENNIS)
plazieren; to go to ~ (plant) schießen;
(fig) herunterkommen; ~ling n Setzling
m; ~y adj (café) übel; (person)
zweifelhaft
seeing ['si:ɪŋ] conj: ~ (that) da
seek [si:k] (pt, pp sought) vt suchen
seem [si:m] vi scheinen; it ~s that ... es
scheint, daß ...; ~ingly adv anscheinend
seen [si:n] pp of see
seep [si:p] vi sickern
seesaw ['si:sɔ:] n Wippe f
seethe [si:ð] vi: to ~ with anger vor
Wut kochen
see-through ['si:θru:] adj (dress etc)
durchsichtig
segment ['segmənt] n Teil m; (of
circle) Ausschnitt m

segregate ['segrɪgeɪt] vt trennen
seize [si:z] vt (grasp) (er)greifen,
packen; (power) ergreifen; (take
legally) beschlagnahmen; ~ (up)on vt
fus sich stürzen auf +acc; ~ up vi
(TECH) sich festfressen
seizure ['si:ʒə*] n (illness) Anfall m
seldom ['seldəm] adv selten
select [sɪ'lekt] adj ausgewählt ♦ vt auswählen; ~ion [sɪ'lekʃən] n Auswahl f;
~ive adj (person) wählerisch
self [self] (pl selves) pron selbst ♦ n
Selbst nt, Ich nt; the ~ das Ich; ~-
assured adj selbstbewußt; ~-catering
(BRIT) adj für Selbstversorger; ~-
centred (US self-centered) adj egozen-
trisch; ~-confidence n Selbstvertrauen
nt, Selbstbewußtsein nt; ~-conscious
adj gehemmt, befangen; ~-contained
adj (complete) (in sich) geschlossen;
(person) verschlossen; (BRIT: flat)
separat; ~-control n Selbstbeherrschung f; ~-defence (US self-defense) n
Selbstverteidigung f; (JUR) Notwehr f;
~-discipline n Selbstdisziplin f; ~-
employed adj frei(schaffend); ~-
evident adj offensichtlich; ~-governing
adj selbstverwaltet; ~-indulgent adj
zügellos; ~-interest n Eigennutz m;
~-ish adj egoistisch, selbstsüchtig;
~-ishness n Egoismus m, Selbstsucht f;
~-lessly adv selbstlos; ~-pity n
Selbstmitleid nt; ~-portrait n
Selbstbildnis nt; ~-possessed adj
selbstbeherrscht; ~-preservation n
Selbsterhaltung f; ~-reliant adj
unabhängig; ~-respect n Selbstachtung
f; ~-righteous adj selbstgerecht; ~-
sacrifice n Selbstaufopferung f; ~-
satisfied adj selbstzufrieden; ~-service
adj Selbstbedienungs-; ~-sufficient adj
selbstgenügsam; ~-taught adj selbst-
erlernt; ~-taught person Autodidakt m
sell [sel] (pt, pp sold) vt verkaufen ♦ vi
verkaufen; (goods) sich verkaufen; to
~ at or for £10 für £10 verkaufen; ~ off
vt verkaufen; ~ out vi alles verkaufen;
~-by date n Verfalldatum nt; ~er n
Verkäufer m; ~ing price n Verkaufspreis m

Sellotape ['seləuteɪp] (®; *BRIT*) *n* Tesafilm *m* (®)

sellout ['selaut] *n* (*of tickets*): **it was a ~** es war ausverkauft

selves [selvz] *npl of* **self**

semaphoro ['semɒfɔː*] *n* Winkzeichen *pl*

semblance ['semblɒns] *n* Anschein *m*

semen ['siːmən] *n* Sperma *nt*

semester [sɪ'mestə*] (*US*) *n* Semester *nt*

semi ['semɪ] *n* = **semidetached house**; **~circle** *n* Halbkreis *m*; **~colon** *n* Semikolon *nt*; **~conductor** *n* Halbleiter *m*; **~detached house** (*BRIT*) *n* halbe(s) Doppelhaus *nt*; **~final** *n* Halbfinale *nt*

seminary ['semɪnərɪ] *n* (*REL*) Priesterseminar *nt*

semiskilled ['semɪ'skɪld] *adj* angelernt

senate ['senɪt] *n* Senat *m*; **senator** *n* Senator *m*

send [send] (*pt*, *pp* **sent**) *vt* senden, schicken; (*inf*: *inspire*) hinreißen; **~ away** *vt* wegschicken; **~ away for** *vt fus* anfordern; **~ back** *vt* zurückschicken; **~ for** *vt fus* holen lassen; **~ off** *vt* (*goods*) abschicken; (*BRIT*: *SPORT*: *player*) vom Feld schicken; **~ out** *vt* (*invitation*) aussenden; **~ up** *vt* hinaufsenden; (*BRIT*: *parody*) verulken; **~er** *n* Absender *m*; **~-off** *n*: **to give sb a good ~-off** jdn (ganz) groß verabschieden

senior ['siːnɪə*] *adj* (*older*) älter; (*higher rank*) Ober- ♦ *n* (*older person*) Ältere(r) *m*; (*higher ranking*) Rangälteste(r) *m*; **~ citizen** *n* ältere(r) Mitbürger(in) *m(f)*; **~ity** [siːnɪ'ɒrɪtɪ] *n* (*of age*) höhere(s) Alter *nt*; (*in rank*) höhere(r) Dienstgrad *m*

sensation [sen'seɪʃən] *n* Gefühl *nt*; (*excitement*) Sensation *f*, Aufsehen *nt*

sense [sens] *n* Sinn *m*; (*understanding*) Verstand *m*, Vernunft *f*; (*feeling*) Gefühl *nt* ♦ *vt* fühlen, spüren; **~ of humour** Humor *m*; **to make ~** Sinn ergeben; **~less** *adj* sinnlos; (*unconscious*) besinnungslos

sensibility [sensɪ'bɪlɪtɪ] *n* Empfindsamkeit *f*; (*feeling hurt*) Empfindlichkeit *f*; **sensibilities** *npl* (*feelings*) Zartgefühl *nt*

sensible ['sensəbl] *adj* vernünftig

sensitive ['sensɪtɪv] *adj*: **~ (to)** empfindlich (gegen)

sensitivity [sensɪ'tɪvɪtɪ] *n* Empfindlichkeit *f*; (*artistic*) Feingefühl *nt*; (*tact*) Feinfühligkeit *f*

sensual ['sensjuəl] *adj* sinnlich

sensuous ['sensjuəs] *adj* sinnlich

sent [sent] *pt*, *pp of* **send**

sentence ['sentəns] *n* Satz *m*; (*JUR*) Strafe *f*; Urteil *nt* ♦ *vt*: **to ~ sb to death/to 5 years** jdn zum Tode/zu 5 Jahren verurteilen

sentiment ['sentɪmənt] *n* Gefühl *nt*; (*thought*) Gedanke *m*; **~al** [sentɪ'mentl] *adj* sentimental; (*of feelings rather than reason*) gefühlsmäßig

sentry ['sentrɪ] *n* (Schild)wache *f*

separate [*adj* 'seprət, *vb* 'sepəreɪt] *adj* getrennt, separat ♦ *vt* trennen ♦ *vi* sich trennen; **~ly** *adv* getrennt; **~s** *npl* (*clothes*) Röcke, Pullover *etc*

separation [sepə'reɪʃən] *n* Trennung *f*

September [sep'tembə*] *n* September *m*

septic ['septɪk] *adj* vereitert, septisch; **~ tank** *n* Klärbehälter *m*

sequel ['siːkwəl] *n* Folge *f*

sequence ['siːkwəns] *n* (Reihen)folge *f*

sequin ['siːkwɪn] *n* Paillette *f*

serene [sə'riːn] *adj* heiter

serenity [sɪ'renɪtɪ] *n* Heiterkeit *f*

sergeant ['saːdʒənt] *n* Feldwebel *m*; (*POLICE*) (Polizei)wachtmeister *m*

serial ['sɪərɪəl] *n* Fortsetzungsroman *m*; (*TV*) Fernsehserie *f* ♦ *adj* (*number*) (fort)laufend; **~ize** *vt* in Fortsetzungen veröffentlichen; in Fortsetzungen senden

series ['sɪərɪz] *n inv* Serie *f*, Reihe *f*

serious ['sɪərɪəs] *adj* ernst; (*injury*) schwer; **~ly** *adv* ernst(haft); (*hurt*) schwer; **~ness** *n* Ernst *m*, Ernsthaftigkeit *f*

sermon ['saːmən] *n* Predigt *f*

serrated [se'reɪtɪd] *adj* gezackt

servant ['saːvənt] *n* Diener(in) *m(f)*

serve [saːv] *vt* dienen +*dat*; (*guest, customer*) bedienen; (*food*) servieren ♦ *vi* dienen, nützen; (*at table*) servieren; (*TENNIS*) geben, aufschlagen; **it ~s him right** das geschieht ihm recht; **that'll ~**

as a table das geht als Tisch; **to ~ a summons (on sb)** (jdn) vor Gericht laden; **~ out** or **up** vt (*food*) auftragen, servieren
service ['sɜːvɪs] n (*help*) Dienst m; (*trains etc*) Verbindung f; (*hotel*) Service m, Bedienung f; (*set of dishes*) Service nt; (*REL*) Gottesdienst m; (*car*) Inspektion f; (*for TVs etc*) Kundendienst m; (*TENNIS*) Aufschlag m ♦ vt (*AUT, TECH*) warten, überholen; **the S~s** npl (*armed forces*) die Streitkräfte pl; **to be of ~ to sb** jdm einen großen Dienst erweisen; **~able** adj brauchbar; **~ area** n (*on motorway*) Raststätte f; **~ charge** (*BRIT*) n Bedienung f; **~man** (*irreg*) n (*soldier etc*) Soldat m; **~ station** n (*Groß*)tankstelle f
serviette [sɜːvɪ'et] n Serviette f
servile ['sɜːvaɪl] adj unterwürfig
session ['seʃən] n Sitzung f; (*POL*) Sitzungsperiode f; **to be in ~** tagen
set [set] (*pt, pp* set) n (*collection of things*) Satz m, Set nt; (*RADIO, TV*) Apparat m; (*TENNIS*) Satz m; (*group of people*) Kreis m; (*CINE*) Szene f; (*THEAT*) Bühnenbild nt ♦ adj festgelegt; (*ready*) bereit ♦ vt (*place*) setzen, stellen, legen; (*arrange*) (an)ordnen; (*table*) decken; (*time, price*) festsetzen; (*alarm, watch, task*) stellen; (*jewels*) (ein)fassen; (*exam*) ausarbeiten ♦ vi (*sun*) untergehen; (*become hard*) fest werden; (*bone*) zusammenwachsen; **to be ~ on doing sth** etw unbedingt tun wollen; **to ~ to music** vertonen; **to ~ on fire** anstecken; **to ~ free** freilassen; **to ~ sth going** etw in Gang bringen; **to ~ sail** losfahren; **~ about** vt fus (*task*) anpacken; **~ aside** vt beiseitelegen; **~ back** vt: **to ~ back (by)** zurückwerfen (um); **~ off** vi aufbrechen ♦ vt (*explode*) sprengen; (*alarm*) losgehen lassen; (*show up well*) hervorheben; **~ out** vi: **to ~ out to do sth** vorhaben, etw zu tun ♦ vt (*arrange*) anlegen, arrangieren; (*state*) darlegen; **~ up** vt (*organization*) aufziehen; (*record*) aufstellen; (*monument*) erstellen; **~back** n Rückschlag

m; **~ menu** n Tageskarte f
settee [se'tiː] n Sofa nt
setting ['setɪŋ] n Hintergrund m
settle ['setl] vt beruhigen; (*pay*) begleichen, bezahlen; (*agree*) regeln ♦ vi sich einleben; (*come to rest*) sich niederlassen; (*sink*) sich setzen; (*calm down*) sich beruhigen; **to ~ for sth** sich mit etw zufriedengeben; **to ~ on sth** sich für etw entscheiden; **to ~ up with** sb mit jdm abrechnen; **~ down** vi (*feel at home*) sich einleben; (*calm down*) sich beruhigen; **~ in** vi sich eingewöhnen; **~ment** n Regelung f; (*payment*) Begleichung f; (*colony*) Siedlung f; **~r** n Siedler m
setup ['setʌp] n (*situation*) Lage f
seven ['sevn] num sieben; **~teen** num siebzehn; **~th** adj siebte(r, s) ♦ n Siebtel nt; **~ty** num siebzig
sever ['sevə*] vt abtrennen
several ['sevrəl] adj mehrere, verschiedene ♦ pron mehrere; **~ of us** einige von uns
severance ['sevərəns] n: **~ pay** Abfindung f
severe [sɪ'vɪə*] adj (*strict*) streng; (*serious*) schwer; (*climate*) rauh
severity [sɪ'verɪtɪ] n Strenge f; Schwere f; Rauheit f
sew [səʊ] (*pt* sewed, *pp* sewn) vt, vi nähen; **~ up** vt zunähen
sewage ['sjuːɪdʒ] n Abwässer pl
sewer ['sjuə*] n (Abwasser)kanal m
sewing ['səʊɪŋ] n Näharbeit f; **~ machine** n Nähmaschine f
sewn [səʊn] pp of sew
sex [seks] n Sex m; (*gender*) Geschlecht nt; **to have ~ with** sb mit jdm Geschlechtsverkehr haben; **~ist** adj sexistisch ♦ n Sexist(in) m(f)
sexual ['seksjʊəl] adj sexuell, geschlechtlich, Geschlechts-
sexy ['seksɪ] adj sexy
shabby ['ʃæbɪ] adj (*also fig*) schäbig
shack [ʃæk] n Hütte f
shackles ['ʃæklz] npl (*also fig*) Fesseln pl, Ketten pl
shade [ʃeɪd] n Schatten m; (*for lamp*) Lampenschirm m; (*colour*) Farbton m

♦ *vt* abschirmen; **in the ~** im Schatten;
a ~ smaller ein bißchen kleiner
shadow ['ʃædəʊ] *n* Schatten *m* ♦ *vt*
(*follow*) beschatten ♦ *adj*: **~ cabinet**
(*BRIT: POL*) Schattenkabinett *nt*; **~y** *adj*
schattig
chady ['ʃɛɪdɪ] *adj* schattig; (*fig*)
zwielichtig
shaft [ʃɑːft] *n* (*of spear etc*) Schaft *m*;
(*in mine*) Schacht *m*; (*TECH*) Welle *f*;
(*of light*) Strahl *m*
shaggy ['ʃægɪ] *adj* struppig
shake [ʃeɪk] (*pt* **shook**, *pp* **shaken**) *vt*
schütteln, rütteln; (*shock*) erschüttern
♦ *vi* (*move*) schwanken; (*tremble*)
zittern, beben ♦ *n* (*jerk*) Schütteln *nt*,
Rütteln *nt*; **to ~ hands with** die Hand
geben +*dat*; **to ~ one's head** den Kopf
schütteln; **~ off** *vt* abschütteln; **~ up**
vt aufschütteln; (*fig*) aufrütteln;
shaken ['ʃeɪkn] *pp of* **shake**
shaky ['ʃeɪkɪ] *adj* zittrig; (*weak*) unsicher
shall [ʃæl] *vb aux*: **I ~ go** ich werde
gehen
shallow ['ʃæləʊ] *adj* seicht
sham [ʃæm] *n* Schein *m* ♦ *adj* unecht,
falsch
shambles ['ʃæmblz] *n* Durcheinander *nt*
shame [ʃeɪm] *n* Scham *f*; (*disgrace,
pity*) Schande *f* ♦ *vt* beschämen; **it is a
~ that** es ist schade, daß; **it is a ~ to
do** ... es ist eine Schande, ... zu tun;
what a ~! wie schade!; **~faced** *adj* beschämt; **~ful** *adj* schändlich; **~less** *adj*
schamlos
shampoo [ʃæm'puː] *n* Shampoo(n) *nt* ♦
vt (*hair*) waschen; **~ and set** *n* Waschen *nt* und Legen
shamrock ['ʃæmrɒk] *n* Kleeblatt *nt*
shandy ['ʃændɪ] *n* Bier *nt* mit Limonade
shan't [ʃɑːnt] = **shall not**
shanty town ['ʃæntɪ-] *n* Bidonville *f*
shape [ʃeɪp] *n* Form *f* ♦ *vt* formen, gestalten ♦ *vi* (*also*: **~ up**) sich entwickeln; **to take ~** Gestalt annehmen;
-shaped *suffix*: **heart-shaped** herz-
förmig; **~less** *adj* formlos; **~ly** *adj*
wohlproportioniert
share [ʃɛə*] *n* (An)teil *m*; (*FIN*) Aktie *f*

♦ *vt* teilen; **to ~ out (among/between)**
verteilen (unter/zwischen); **~holder** *n*
Aktionär(in) *m(f)*
shark [ʃɑːk] *n* Hai(fisch) *m*; (*swindler*)
Gauner *m*
sharp [ʃɑːp] *adj* scharf; (*pin*) spitz;
(*person*) clever; (*MUS*) erhöht ♦ *n*
(*MUS*) Kreuz *nt* ♦ *adv* (*MUS*) zu hoch;
nine o'clock ~ Punkt neun; **~en** *vt*
schärfen; (*pencil*) spitzen; **~ener** *n*
(*also*: *pencil ~ener*) Anspitzer *m*; **~-
eyed** *adj* scharfsichtig; **~ly** *adv* (*turn,
stop*) plötzlich; (*stand out, contrast*)
deutlich; (*criticize, retort*) scharf
shatter ['ʃætə*] *vt* zerschmettern; (*fig*)
zerstören ♦ *vi* zerspringen
shave [ʃeɪv] *n* Rasur *f* ♦ *vt* rasieren ♦ *vi*
sich rasieren; **to have a ~** sich rasieren
(lassen); **~r** *n* (*also*: *electric ~r*)
Rasierapparat *m*
shaving ['ʃeɪvɪŋ] *n* (*action*) Rasieren *nt*;
~s *npl* (*of wood etc*) Späne *pl*; **~ brush**
n Rasierpinsel *m*; **~ cream** *n* Rasier-
krem *f*
shawl [ʃɔːl] *n* Schal *m*, Umhang *m*
she [ʃiː] *pron* sie ♦ *adj* weiblich; **~-bear**
Bärenweibchen *nt*
sheaf [ʃiːf] (*pl* **sheaves**) *n* Garbe *f*
shear [ʃɪə*] (*pt* **~ed**, *pp* **~ed** *or* **shorn**)
vt scheren; **~ off** *vi* abbrechen; **~s** *npl*
Heckenschere *f*
sheath [ʃiːθ] *n* Scheide *f*; (*condom*)
Kondom *m* *or* *nt*
sheaves [ʃiːvz] *npl of* **sheaf**
shed [ʃed] (*pt, pp* **shed**) *n* Schuppen *m*;
(*for animals*) Stall *m* ♦ *vt* (*leaves etc*)
verlieren; (*tears*) vergießen
she'd [ʃiːd] = **she had; she would**
sheen [ʃiːn] *n* Glanz *m*
sheep [ʃiːp] *n inv* Schaf *nt*; **~dog** *n*
Schäferhund *m*; **~ish** *adj* verlegen;
~skin *n* Schaffell *nt*
sheer [ʃɪə*] *adj* bloß, rein; (*steep*) steil;
(*transparent*) (hauch)dünn ♦ *adv*
(*directly*) direkt
sheet [ʃiːt] *n* Bettuch *nt*, Bettlaken *nt*;
(*of paper*) Blatt *nt*; (*of metal etc*)
Platte *f*; (*of ice*) Fläche *f*
sheik(h) [ʃeɪk] *n* Scheich *m*
shelf [ʃelf] (*pl* **shelves**) *n* Bord *nt*, Regal

nt

shell [ʃel] n Schale f; (sea~) Muschel f; (explosive) Granate f ♦ vt (peas) schälen; (fire on) beschießen

she'll [ʃiːl] = she will; she shall

shellfish ['ʃelfɪʃ] n Schalentier nt; (as food) Meeresfrüchte pl

shelter ['ʃeltə*] n Schutz m; (air-raid ~) Bunker m ♦ vt schützen, bedecken; (refugees) aufnehmen ♦ vi sich unterstellen; ~ed adj (life) behütet; (spot) geschützt

shelve [ʃelv] vt aufschieben ♦ vi abfallen

shelves [ʃelvz] npl of shelf

shepherd ['ʃepəd] n Schäfer m ♦ vt treiben, führen; ~'s pie n Auflauf m aus Hackfleisch und Kartoffelbrei

sheriff ['ʃerɪf] n Sheriff m; (SCOTTISH) Friedensrichter m

sherry ['ʃerɪ] n Sherry m

she's [ʃiːz] = she is; she has

Shetland ['ʃetlənd] n (also: the ~s, the ~ Isles) die Shetlandinseln pl

shield [ʃiːld] n Schild m; (fig) Schirm m ♦ vt (be)schirmen; (TECH) abschirmen

shift [ʃɪft] n Verschiebung f; (work) Schicht f ♦ vt (ver)rücken, verschieben; (arm) wegnehmen ♦ vi sich verschieben; ~less adj (person) träge; ~ work n Schichtarbeit f; ~y adj verschlagen

shilly-shally ['ʃɪlɪʃælɪ] vi zögern

shin [ʃɪn] n Schienbein nt

shine [ʃaɪn] n (pt, pp shone) n Glanz m, Schein m ♦ vt polieren ♦ vi scheinen; (fig) glänzen; to ~ a torch on sb jdn (mit einer Lampe) anleuchten

shingle ['ʃɪŋgl] n Strandkies m; ~s npl (MED) Gürtelrose f

shiny ['ʃaɪnɪ] adj glänzend

ship [ʃɪp] n Schiff nt ♦ vt verschiffen; ~-building n Schiffbau m; ~ment n Schiffsladung f; ~per n Verschiffer m; ~ping n (act) Verschiffung f; (ships) Schiffahrt f; ~shape adj in Ordnung; ~wreck n Schiffbruch m; (destroyed ship) Wrack nt ♦ vt: to be ~wrecked Schiffbruch erleiden; ~yard n Werft f

shire ['ʃaɪə*] n (BRIT) Grafschaft f

shirk [ʃɜːk] vt ausweichen +dat

shirt [ʃɜːt] n (Ober)hemd nt; in ~ sleeves in Hemdsärmeln; ~y (inf) adj mürrisch

shit [ʃɪt] (inf!) excl Scheiße (!)

shiver ['ʃɪvə*] n Schauer m ♦ vi frösteln, zittern

shoal [ʃəul] n (Fisch)schwarm m

shock [ʃɒk] n Erschütterung f; (mental) Schock m; (ELEC) Schlag m ♦ vt erschüttern; (offend) schockieren; ~ absorber n Stoßdämpfer m; ~ing adj unerhört

shod [ʃɒd] pt, pp of shoe ♦ adj beschuht

shoddy ['ʃɒdɪ] adj schäbig

shoe [ʃuː] (pt, pp shod) n Schuh m; (of horse) Hufeisen nt ♦ vt (horse) beschlagen; ~brush n Schuhbürste f; ~horn n Schuhlöffel m; ~lace n Schnürsenkel m; ~ polish n Schuhcreme f; ~ shop n Schuhgeschäft nt; ~string n (fig): on a ~string mit sehr wenig Geld

shone [ʃɒn] pt, pp of shine

shoo [ʃuː] excl sch; (to dog etc) pfui

shook [ʃuk] pt of shake

shoot [ʃuːt] (pt, pp shot) n (branch) Schößling m ♦ vt (gun) abfeuern; (goal, arrow) schießen; (person) anschießen; (kill) erschießen; (film) drehen ♦ vi (gun, move quickly) schießen; to ~ (at) schießen (auf +acc); ~ down vt abschießen; ~ in vi hineinschießen; ~ out vi hinausschießen; ~ up vi (fig) aus dem Boden schießen; ~ing n Schießerei f; ~ing star n Sternschnuppe f

shop [ʃɒp] n (esp BRIT) Geschäft nt, Laden m; (work~) Werkstatt f ♦ vi (also: go ~ping) einkaufen gehen; ~ assistant (BRIT) n Verkäufer(in) m(f); ~ floor (BRIT) n Werkstatt f; ~keeper n Geschäftsinhaber m; ~lifting n Ladendiebstahl m; ~per n Käufer(in) m(f); ~ping n Einkaufen nt, Einkauf m; ~ping bag n Einkaufstasche f; ~ping centre (US ~ping center) n Einkaufszentrum nt; ~-soiled adj angeschmutzt; ~ steward (BRIT) n (INDUSTRY) Betriebsrat m; ~ window n

Schaufenster *nt*

shore [ʃɔː*] *n* Ufer *nt*; (*of sea*) Strand *m* ♦ *vt*: **to ~ up** abstützen

shorn [ʃɔːn] *pp of* **shear**

short [ʃɔːt] *adj* kurz; (*person*) klein; (*curt*) kurz angebunden; (*measure*) zu knapp ♦ *n* (*also*: **~ film**) Kurzfilm *m* ♦ *adv* (*suddenly*) plötzlich ♦ *vi* (ELEC) einen Kurzschluß haben; **~s** *npl* (*clothes*) Shorts *pl*; **to be ~ of sth** nicht genug von etw haben; **in ~** kurz gesagt; **~ of doing sth** ohne so weit zu gehen, etw zu tun; **everything ~ of ...** alles außer ...; **it is ~ for** das ist die Kurzform von; **to cut ~** abkürzen; **to fall ~ of sth** etw nicht erreichen; **to stop ~** plötzlich anhalten; **to stop ~ of** haltmachen vor; **~age** *n* Knappheit *f*, Mangel *m*; **~bread** *n* Mürbegebäck *nt*; **~-change** *vt*: **to ~-change sb** jdm zuwenig herausgeben; **~circuit** *n* Kurzschluß *m* ♦ *vi* einen Kurzschluß haben ♦ *vt* kurzschließen; **~coming** *n* Mangel *m*; **~(crust) pastry** (BRIT) *n* Mürbeteig *m*; **~ cut** *n* Abkürzung *f*; **~en** *vt* (ab)kürzen; (*clothes*) kürzer machen; **~fall** *n* Defizit *nt*; **~hand** (BRIT) *n* Stenographie *f*; **~hand typist** (BRIT) *n* Stenotypistin *f*; **~list** (BRIT) *n* (*for job*) engere Wahl *f*; **~-lived** *adj* kurzlebig; **~ly** *adv* bald; **~ness** *n* Kürze *f*; **~-sighted** (BRIT) *adj* (*also fig*) kurzsichtig; **~-staffed** *adj*: **to be ~-staffed** zu wenig Personal haben; **~ story** *n* Kurzgeschichte *f*; **~-tempered** *adj* leicht aufbrausend; **~-term** *adj* (*effect*) kurzfristig; **~ wave** *n* (RADIO) Kurzwelle *f*

shot [ʃɒt] *pt, pp of* **shoot** ♦ *n* (*from gun*) Schuß *m*; (*person*) Schütze *m*; (*try*) Versuch *m*; (*injection*) Spritze *f*; (PHOT) Aufnahme *f*; **like a ~** wie der Blitz; **~gun** *n* Schrotflinte *f*

should [ʃʊd] *vb aux*: **I ~ go now** ich sollte jetzt gehen; **he ~ be there now** er sollte eigentlich schon da sein; **I ~ go if I were you** ich würde gehen, wenn ich du wäre; **I ~ like to** ich möchte gerne

shoulder ['ʃəʊldə*] *n* Schulter *f*; (BRIT: *of road*): **hard ~** Seitenstreifen *m* ♦ *vt*

(*rifle*) schultern; (*fig*) auf sich nehmen; **~ bag** *n* Umhängetasche *f*; **~ blade** *n* Schulterblatt *nt*; **~ strap** *n* (MIL) Schulterklappe *f*; (*of dress etc*) Träger *m*

shouldn't ['ʃʊdnt] = **should not**

shout [ʃaʊt] *n* Schrei *m*; (*call*) Ruf *m* ♦ *vt* rufen ♦ *vi* schreien; **~ down** *vt* niederbrüllen; **~ing** *n* Geschrei *nt*

shove [ʃʌv] *n* Schubs *m*, Stoß *m* ♦ *vt* schieben, stoßen, schubsen; (*inf*: *put*): **to ~ sth in(to) sth** etw in etw *acc* hineinschieben; **~ off** *vi* (NAUT) abstoßen; (*fig*: *inf*) abhauen

shovel ['ʃʌvl] *n* Schaufel *f* ♦ *vt* schaufeln

show [ʃəʊ] (*pt* **showed**, *pp* **shown**) *n* (*display*) Schau *f*; (*exhibition*) Ausstellung *f*; (CINE, THEAT) Vorstellung *f*, Show *f* ♦ *vt* zeigen; (*kindness*) erweisen ♦ *vi* zu sehen sein; **to be on ~** (*exhibits etc*) ausgestellt sein; **to ~ sb in** jdn hereinführen; **to ~ sb out** jdn hinausbegleiten; **~ off** *vi* (*pej*) angeben ♦ *vt* (*display*) ausstellen; **~ up** *vi* (*stand out*) sich abheben; (*arrive*) erscheinen ♦ *vt* aufzeigen; (*unmask*) bloßstellen; **~ business** *n* Showbusineß *nt*; **~down** *n* Kraftprobe *f*

shower ['ʃaʊə*] *n* Schauer *m*; (*of stones*) (Stein)hagel *m*; (~ *bath*) Dusche *f* ♦ *vi* duschen ♦ *vt*: **to ~ sb with sth** jdn mit etw überschütten; **~proof** *adj* wasserabstoßend

showing ['ʃəʊɪŋ] *n* Vorführung *f*

show jumping *n* Turnierreiten *nt*

shown [ʃəʊn] *pp of* **show**

show: **~-off** ['ʃəʊɒf] *n* Angeber(in) *m(f)*; **~piece** ['ʃəʊpiːs] *n* Paradestück *nt*; **~room** ['ʃəʊrʊm] *n* Ausstellungsraum *m*

shrank [ʃræŋk] *pt of* **shrink**

shred [ʃred] *n* Fetzen *m* ♦ *vt* zerfetzen; (COOK) raspeln; **~der** *n* (*for vegetables*) Gemüseschneider *m*; (*for documents*) Reißwolf *m*

shrewd [ʃruːd] *adj* clever

shriek [ʃriːk] *n* Schrei *m* ♦ *vt, vi* kreischen, schreien

shrimp [ʃrɪmp] *n* Krabbe *f*, Garnele *f*

shrink [ʃrɪŋk] (*pt* **shrank**, *pp* **shrunk**) *vi* schrumpfen, eingehen ♦ *vt* einschrumpfen lassen; **to ~ from doing sth** davor zurückschrecken, etw zu tun; **~age** *n* Schrumpfung *f*; **~wrap** *vt* einschweißen

shrivel [ʃrɪvl] *vt*, *vi* (*also:* ~ *up*) schrumpfen, schrumpeln

shroud [ʃraʊd] *n* Leichentuch *nt* ♦ *vt*: **~ed in mystery** mit einem Geheimnis umgeben

Shrove Tuesday [ʃrəʊv-] *n* Fastnachtsdienstag *m*

shrub [ʃrʌb] *n* Busch *m*, Strauch *m*; **~bery** *n* Gebüsch *nt*

shrug [ʃrʌg] *n* Achselzucken *nt* ♦ *vt*, *vi*: **to ~ (one's shoulders)** die Achseln zucken; ~ **off** *vt* auf die leichte Schulter nehmen

shrunk [ʃrʌŋk] *pp of* **shrink**

shudder [ʃʌdə*] *n* Schauder *m* ♦ *vi* schaudern

shuffle [ʃʌfl] *n* (*CARDS*) (Karten)mischen *nt* ♦ *vt* (*cards*) mischen; **to ~ (one's feet)** schlurfen

shun [ʃʌn] *vt* scheuen, (ver)meiden

shunt [ʃʌnt] *vt* rangieren

shut [ʃʌt] (*pt*, *pp* **shut**) *vt* schließen, zumachen ♦ *vi* sich schließen (lassen); ~ **down** *vt*, *vi* schließen; ~ **off** *vt* (*supply*) abdrehen; ~ **up** *vi* (*keep quiet*) den Mund halten ♦ *vt* (*close*) zuschließen; **~ter** *n* Fensterladen *m*; (*PHOT*) Verschluß *m*

shuttle [ʃʌtl] *n* (*plane, train etc*) Pendelflugzeug *nt*/-zug *m etc*; (*space* ~) Raumtransporter *m*; (*also:* ~ *service*) Pendelverkehr *m*

shuttlecock [ʃʌtlkɒk] *n* Federball *m*

shy [ʃaɪ] *adj* schüchtern; **~ness** *n* Schüchternheit *f*

Siamese [saɪəˈmiːz] *adj*: ~ **cat** Siamkatze *f*

Siberia [saɪˈbɪərɪə] *n* Sibirien *nt*

sibling [ˈsɪblɪŋ] *n* Geschwister *nt*

Sicily [ˈsɪsɪlɪ] *n* Sizilien *nt*

sick [sɪk] *adj* krank; (*joke*) makaber; **I feel ~** mir ist schlecht; **I was ~** ich habe gebrochen; **to be ~ of sb/sth** jdn/ etw satt haben; ~ **bay** *n*

(Schiffs)lazarett *nt*; **~en** *vt* (*disgust*) krankmachen ♦ *vi* krank werden; **~ening** *adj* (*sight*) widerlich; (*annoying*) zum Weinen

sickle [ˈsɪkl] *n* Sichel *f*

sick: ~ **leave** *n*: **to be on ~ leave** krank geschrieben sein; **~ly** *adj* kränklich, blaß; (*causing nausea*) widerlich; **~ness** *n* Krankheit *f*; (*vomiting*) Übelkeit *f*, Erbrechen *nt*; ~ **pay** *n* Krankengeld *nt*

side [saɪd] *n* Seite *f* ♦ *adj* (*door, entrance*) Seiten-, Neben- ♦ *vi*: **to ~ with sb** jds Partei ergreifen; **by the ~ of** neben; ~ **by** ~ nebeneinander; **on all ~s** von allen Seiten; **to take ~s (with)** Partei nehmen (für); **~boards** (*BRIT*) *npl* Koteletten *pl*; **~burns** *npl* Koteletten *pl*; **~car** *n* Beiwagen *m*; ~ **drum** *n* (*MUS*) kleine Trommel; ~ **effect** *n* Nebenwirkung *f*; **~light** *n* (*AUT*) Parkleuchte *f*; **~line** *n* (*SPORT*) Seitenlinie *f*; (*fig: hobby*) Nebenbeschäftigung *f*; **~long** *adj* Seiten-; **~saddle** *adv* im Damensattel; ~ **show** *n* Nebenausstellung *f*; ~ **step** *vt* (*fig*) ausweichen; ~ **street** *n* Seitenstraße *f*; **~track** *vt* (*fig*) ablenken; **~walk** (*US*) *n* Bürgersteig *m*; **~ways** *adv* seitwärts

siding [ˈsaɪdɪŋ] *n* Nebengleis *nt*

sidle [ˈsaɪdl] *vi*: **to ~ up (to)** sich heranmachen (an *+acc*)

siege [siːdʒ] *n* Belagerung *f*

sieve [sɪv] *n* Sieb *nt* ♦ *vt* sieben

sift [sɪft] *vt* sieben; (*fig*) sichten

sigh [saɪ] *n* Seufzer *m* ♦ *vi* seufzen

sight [saɪt] *n* (*power of seeing*) Sehvermögen *nt*; (*look*) Blick *m*; (*fact of seeing*) Anblick *m*; (*of gun*) Visier *nt* ♦ *vt* sichten; **in ~** in Sicht; **out of ~** außer Sicht; **~seeing** *n* Besuch *m* von Sehenswürdigkeiten; **to go ~seeing** Sehenswürdigkeiten besichtigen

sign [saɪn] *n* Zeichen *nt*; (*notice, road etc*) Schild *nt* ♦ *vt* unterschreiben; **to ~ sth over to sb** jdm etw überschreiben; ~ **on** *vi* (*MIL*) sich verpflichten; (*as unemployed*) sich (arbeitslos) melden ♦ *vt* (*MIL*) verpflichten; (*employee*) anstellen; ~ **up**

vi (*MIL*) sich verpflichten ♦ *vt* verpflichten

signal ['sıgnl] *n* Signal *nt* ♦ *vt* ein Zeichen geben +*dat*; ~**man** (*irreg*) *n* (*RAIL*) Stellwerkswärter *m*

signature ['sıgnətʃə*] *n* Unterschrift *f*; ~ **tune** *n* Erkennungsmelodie *f*

signet ring ['sıgnət-] *n* Siegelring *m*

significance [sıg'nıfıkəns] *n* Bedeutung *f*

significant [sıg'nıfıkənt] *adj* (*meaning sth*) bedeutsam; (*important*) bedeutend

signify ['sıgnıfaı] *vt* bedeuten; (*show*) andeuten, zu verstehen geben

sign language *n* Zeichensprache *f*, Fingersprache *f*

signpost ['saınpəust] *n* Wegweiser *m*

silence ['saıləns] *n* Stille *f*; (*of person*) Schweigen *nt* ♦ *vt* zum Schweigen bringen; ~**r** *n* (*on gun*) Schalldämpfer *m*; (*BRIT: AUT*) Auspufftopf *m*

silent ['saılənt] *adj* still; (*person*) schweigsam; **to remain** ~ schweigen; ~ **partner** *n* (*COMM*) stille(r) Teilhaber *m*

silicon chip ['sılıkən-] *n* Siliciumchip *nt*

silk [sılk] *n* Seide *f* ♦ *adj* seiden, Seiden-; ~**y** *adj* seidig

silly ['sılı] *adj* dumm, albern

silt [sılt] *n* Schlamm *m*, Schlick *m*

silver ['sılvə*] *n* Silber *nt* ♦ *adj* silbern, Silber-; ~ **paper** (*BRIT*) *n* Silberpapier *nt*; ~**-plated** *adj* versilbert; ~**smith** *n* Silberschmied *m*; ~**ware** *n* Silber *nt*; ~**y** *adj* silbern

similar ['sımılə*] *adj*: ~ (**to**) ähnlich (+*dat*); ~**ity** [sımı'lærıtı] *n* Ähnlichkeit *f*; ~**ly** *adv* in ähnlicher Weise

simile ['sımılı] *n* Vergleich *m*

simmer ['sımə*] *vi* sieden ♦ *vt* sieden lassen

simpering ['sımpərıŋ] *adj* albern

simple ['sımpl] *adj* einfach; ~**(-minded)** *adj* einfältig; ~**ton** *n* Einfaltspinsel *m*

simplicity [sım'plısıtı] *n* Einfachheit *f*; (*of person*) Einfältigkeit *f*

simplify ['sımplıfaı] *vt* vereinfachen

simply ['sımplı] *adv* einfach

simulate ['sımjuleıt] *vt* simulieren

simultaneous [sıməl'teınıəs] *adj* gleichzeitig

sin [sın] *n* Sünde *f* ♦ *vi* sündigen

since [sıns] *adv* seither ♦ *prep* seit, seitdem ♦ *conj* (*time*) seit; (*because*) da, weil; ~ **then** seitdem

sincere [sın'sıə*] *adj* aufrichtig; ~**ly** *adv*: **yours** ~**ly** mit freundlichen Grüßen

sincerity [sın'serıtı] *n* Aufrichtigkeit *f*

sinew ['sınjuː] *n* Sehne *f*

sinful ['sınful] *adj* sündig, sündhaft

sing [sıŋ] (*pt* **sang**, *pp* **sung**) *vt, vi* singen

Singapore [sıŋgə'pɔː*] *n* Singapur *nt*

singe [sındʒ] *vt* versengen

singer ['sıŋə*] *n* Sänger(in) *m(f)*

single ['sıŋgl] *adj* (*one only*) einzig; (*bed, room*) Einzel-, einzeln; (*unmarried*) ledig; (*BRIT: ticket*) einfach; (*having one part only*) einzeln ♦ *n* (*BRIT: also:* ~ *ticket*) einfache Fahrkarte *f*; **in** ~ **file** hintereinander; ~ **out** *vt* aussuchen, auswählen; ~ **bed** *n* Einzelbett *nt*; ~**-breasted** *adj* einreihig; ~**-handed** *adj* allein; ~**-minded** *adj* zielstrebig; ~ **room** *n* Einzelzimmer *nt*; ~**s** *n* (*TENNIS*) Einzel *nt*

singlet ['sıŋglət] *n* Unterhemd *nt*

singly ['sıŋglı] *adv* einzeln, allein

singular ['sıŋgjulə*] *adj* (*GRAM*) Singular-; (*odd*) merkwürdig, seltsam ♦ *n* (*GRAM*) Einzahl *f*, Singular *m*

sinister ['sınıstə*] *adj* (*evil*) böse; (*ghostly*) unheimlich

sink [sıŋk] (*pt* **sank**, *pp* **sunk**) *n* Spülbecken *nt* ♦ *vt* (*ship*) versenken ♦ *vi* sinken; **to** ~ **sth into** (*teeth, claws*) etw schlagen in +*acc*; ~ **in** *vi* (*news etc*) eingehen

sinner ['sınə*] *n* Sünder(in) *m(f)*

sinus ['saınəs] *n* (*ANAT*) Sinus *m*

sip [sıp] *n* Schlückchen *nt* ♦ *vt* nippen an +*dat*

siphon ['saıfən] *n* Siphon(flasche *f*) *m*; ~ **off** *vt* absaugen; (*fig*) abschöpfen

sir [sɜː*] *n* (*respect*) Herr *m*; (*knight*) Sir *m*; **S~ John Smith** Sir John Smith; **yes** ~ ja(wohl, mein Herr)

siren ['saıərən] *n* Sirene *f*

sirloin ['sɜːlɔın] *n* Lendenstück *nt*

sissy ['sısı] (*inf*) *n* Waschlappen *m*

sister ['sɪstə*] n Schwester f; (BRIT: nurse) Oberschwester f; (nun) Ordensschwester f; ~-**in-law** n Schwägerin f

sit [sɪt] (pt, pp **sat**) vi sitzen; (hold session) tagen ♦ vt (exam) machen; ~ **down** vi sich hinsetzen; ~ **in on** vt fus dabeisein bei; ~ **up** vi (after lying) sich aufsetzen; (straight) sich gerade setzen; (at night) aufbleiben

sitcom ['sɪtkɒm] n abbr (= situation comedy) Situationskomödie f

site [saɪt] n Platz m; (also: building ~) Baustelle f ♦ vt legen

sitting ['sɪtɪŋ] n (meeting) Sitzung f; ~ **room** n Wohnzimmer nt

situated ['sɪtjʊeɪtɪd] adj: to be ~ liegen

situation [sɪtjʊ'eɪʃən] n Situation f, Lage f; (place) Lage f; (employment) Stelle f; "~s vacant" (BRIT) „Stellenangebote" pl

six [sɪks] num sechs; ~**teen** num sechzehn; ~**th** adj sechste(r, s) ♦ n Sechstel nt; ~**ty** num sechzig

size [saɪz] n Größe f; (of project) Umfang m; ~ **up** vt (assess) abschätzen, einschätzen; ~**able** adj ziemlich groß, ansehnlich

sizzle ['sɪzl] vi zischen; (COOK) brutzeln

skate [skeɪt] n Schlittschuh m; (fish: pl inv) Rochen m ♦ vi Schlittschuh laufen; ~**r** n Schlittschuhläufer(in) m(f)

skating ['skeɪtɪŋ] n Eislauf m; **to go** ~ Eislaufen gehen; ~ **rink** n Eisbahn f

skeleton ['skelɪtn] n Skelett nt; (fig) Gerüst nt; ~ **key** n Dietrich m; ~ **staff** n Notbesetzung f

skeptical ['skeptɪkl] (US) adj = **sceptical**

sketch [sketʃ] n Skizze f; (THEAT) Sketch m ♦ vt skizzieren; ~**book** n Skizzenbuch nt; ~**y** adj skizzenhaft

skewer ['skjʊə*] n Fleischspieß m

ski [ski:] n Ski m, Schi m ♦ vi Ski or Schi laufen; ~ **boot** n Skistiefel m

skid [skɪd] n (AUT) Schleudern nt ♦ vi rutschen; (AUT) schleudern

skier ['ski:ə*] n Skiläufer(in) m(f)

skiing ['ski:ɪŋ] n: **to go** ~ Skilaufen gehen

ski-jump n Sprungschanze f ♦ vi Ski

springen

skilful ['skɪlfʊl] adj geschickt

ski-lift n Skilift m

skill [skɪl] n Können nt; ~**ed** adj geschickt; (worker) Fach-, gelernt

skim [skɪm] vt (liquid) abschöpfen; (glide over) gleiten über +acc ♦ vi: ~ **through** (book) überfliegen; ~**med milk** n Magermilch f

skimp [skɪmp] vt (do carelessly) oberflächlich tun; ~**y** adj (work) schlecht gemacht; (dress) knapp

skin [skɪn] n Haut f; (peel) Schale f ♦ vt abhäuten; schälen; ~**-deep** adj oberflächlich; ~ **diving** n Schwimmtauchen nt; ~**ny** adj dünn; ~**tight** adj (dress etc) hauteng

skip [skɪp] n Sprung m ♦ vi hüpfen; (with rope) Seil springen ♦ vt (pass over) übergehen

ski pants npl Skihosen pl

ski pole n Skistock m

skipper ['skɪpə*] n Kapitän m ♦ vt führen

skipping rope ['skɪpɪŋ-] (BRIT) n Hüpfseil nt

skirmish ['skɜ:mɪʃ] n Scharmützel nt

skirt [skɜ:t] n Rock m ♦ vt herumgehen um; (fig) umgehen; ~**ing board** (BRIT) n Fußleiste f

ski suit n Skianzug m

skit [skɪt] n Parodie f

skittle ['skɪtl] n Kegel m; ~**s** n (game) Kegeln nt

skive [skaɪv] (BRIT: inf) vi schwänzen

skulk [skʌlk] vi sich herumdrücken

skull [skʌl] n Schädel m

skunk [skʌŋk] n Stinktier nt

sky [skaɪ] n Himmel m; ~**light** n Oberlicht nt; ~**scraper** n Wolkenkratzer m

slab [slæb] n (of stone) Platte f

slack [slæk] adj (loose) locker; (business) flau; (careless) nachlässig, lasch ♦ vi nachlässig sein ♦ n: **to take up the** ~ straffziehen; ~**s** npl (trousers) Hose(n pl) f; ~**en** vi (also: ~**en off**) locker werden; (: become slower) nachlassen, stocken ♦ vt (also: ~**en off**: loosen) lockern

slag [slæg] *n* Schlacke *f*; ~ **heap** *n* Halde *f*

slain [sleɪn] *pp of* **slay**

slam [slæm] *n* Knall *m* ♦ *vt* (*door*) zuschlagen; (*throw down*) knallen ♦ *vi* zuschlagen

slander ['slɑːndə*] *n* Verleumdung *f* ♦ *vt* verleumden

slant [slɑːnt] *n* Schräge *f*; (*fig*) Tendenz *f* ♦ *vt* schräg legen ♦ *vi* schräg liegen; ~**ed** *adj* schräg; ~**ing** *adj* schräg

slap [slæp] *n* Klaps *m* ♦ *vt* einen Klaps geben +*dat* ♦ *adv* (*directly*) geradewegs; ~**dash** *adj* salopp; ~**stick** *n* (*comedy*) Klamauk *m*; ~**-up** (*BRIT*) *adj* (*meal*) erstklassig, prima

slash [slæʃ] *n* Schnittwunde *f* ♦ *vt* (auf)schlitzen; (*expenditure*) radikal kürzen

slat [slæt] *n* (*of wood, plastic*) Leiste *f*

slate [sleɪt] *n* (*stone*) Schiefer *m*; (*roofing*) Dachziegel *m* ♦ *vt* (*criticize*) verreißen

slaughter ['slɔːtə*] *n* (*of animals*) Schlachten *nt*; (*of people*) Gemetzel *nt* ♦ *vt* schlachten; (*people*) niedermetzeln; ~**house** *n* Schlachthof *m*

Slav [slɑːv] *adj* slawisch

slave [sleɪv] *n* Sklave *m*, Sklavin *f* ♦ *vi* schuften, sich schinden; ~**ry** *n* Sklaverei *f*; (*work*) Schinderei *f*

slay [sleɪ] *n* (*pt* **slew**, *pp* **slain**) *vt* ermorden

sleazy ['sliːzɪ] *adj* (*place*) schmierig

sledge [sledʒ] *n* Schlitten *m*; ~**hammer** *n* Schmiedehammer *m*

sleek [sliːk] *adj* glatt; (*shape*) rassig

sleep [sliːp] (*pt*, *pp* **slept**) *n* Schlaf *m* ♦ *vi* schlafen; **to go to** ~ einschlafen; ~ **in** *vi* ausschlafen; (*oversleep*) verschlafen; ~**er** *n* (*person*) Schläfer *m*; (*BRIT*: *RAIL*) Schlafwagen *m*; (: *beam*) Schwelle *f*; ~**ing bag** *n* Schlafsack *m*; ~**ing car** *n* Schlafwagen *m*; ~**ing pill** *n* Schlaftablette *f*; ~**less** *adj* (*night*) schlaflos; ~**walker** *n* Schlafwandler(in) *m(f)*; ~**y** *adj* schläfrig

sleet [sliːt] *n* Schneeregen *m*

sleeve [sliːv] *n* Ärmel *m*; (*of record*) Umschlag *m*; ~**less** *adj* ärmellos

sleigh [sleɪ] *n* Pferdeschlitten *m*

sleight [slaɪt] *n*: ~ **of hand** Fingerfertigkeit *f*

slender ['slendə*] *adj* schlank; (*fig*) gering

slept [slept] *pt*, *pp of* **sleep**

slew [sluː] *vi* (*veer*) (herum)schwenken ♦ *pt of* **slay**

slice [slaɪs] *n* Scheibe *f* ♦ *vt* in Scheiben schneiden

slick [slɪk] *adj* (*clever*) raffiniert, aalglatt ♦ *n* Ölteppich *m*

slid [slɪd] *pt*, *pp of* **slide**

slide [slaɪd] (*pt*, *pp* **slid**) *n* Rutschbahn *f*; (*PHOT*) Dia(positiv) *nt*; (*BRIT*: *for hair*) (Haar)spange *f* ♦ *vt* schieben ♦ *vi* (*slip*) gleiten, rutschen; ~ **rule** *n* Rechenschieber *m*

sliding ['slaɪdɪŋ] *adj* (*door*) Schiebe-; ~ **scale** *n* gleitende Skala *f*

slight [slaɪt] *adj* zierlich; (*trivial*) geringfügig; (*small*) gering ♦ *n* Kränkung *f* ♦ *vt* (*offend*) kränken; **not in the** ~**est** nicht im geringsten; ~**ly** *adv* etwas, ein bißchen

slim [slɪm] *adj* schlank; (*book*) dünn; (*chance*) gering ♦ *vi* eine Schlankheitskur machen

slime [slaɪm] *n* Schleim *m*

slimming ['slɪmɪŋ] *n* Schlankheitskur *f*

slimy ['slaɪmɪ] *adj* glitschig; (*dirty*) schlammig; (*person*) schmierig

sling [slɪŋ] (*pt*, *pp* **slung**) *n* Schlinge *f*; (*weapon*) Schleuder *f* ♦ *vt* schleudern

slip [slɪp] *n* (*mistake*) Flüchtigkeitsfehler *m*; (*petticoat*) Unterrock *m*; (*of paper*) Zettel *m* ♦ *vt* (*put*) stecken, schieben ♦ *vi* (*lose balance*) ausrutschen; (*move*) gleiten, rutschen; (*decline*) nachlassen; (*move smoothly*): **to** ~ **in/out** (*person*) hinein-/hinausschlüpfen; **to give sb the** ~ jdm entwischen; ~ **of the tongue** Versprecher *m*; **it** ~**ped my mind** das ist mir entfallen; **to** ~ **sth on/off** etw über-/abstreifen; ~ **away** *vi* sich wegstehlen; ~ **by** *vi* (*time*) verstreichen; ~ **in** *vt* hineingleiten lassen ♦ *vi* (*errors*) sich einschleichen; ~**ped disc** *n* Bandscheibenschaden *m*

slipper ['slɪpə*] n Hausschuh m
slippery ['slɪpərɪ] adj glatt
slip: **~-road** (BRIT) n Auffahrt f/ Ausfahrt f; **~shod** ['slɪpʃɒd] adj schlampig; **~-up** ['slɪpʌp] n Panne f; **~way** ['slɪpweɪ] n Auslaufbahn f
slit [slɪt] (pt, pp slit) n Schlitz m ♦ vt aufschlitzen
slither ['slɪðə*] vi schlittern; (snake) sich schlängeln
sliver ['slɪvə*] n (of glass, wood) Splitter m; (of cheese etc) Scheibchen nt
slob [slɒb] (inf) n Klotz m
slog [slɒg] vi (work hard) schuften ♦ n: it was a ~ es war eine Plackerei
slogan ['sləugən] n Schlagwort nt; (COMM) Werbespruch m
slop [slɒp] vi (also: ~ over) überschwappen ♦ vt verschütten
slope [sləup] n Neigung f; (of mountains) (Ab)hang m ♦ vi: to ~ down sich senken; to ~ up ansteigen
sloping ['sləupɪŋ] adj schräg
sloppy ['slɒpɪ] adj schlampig
slot [slɒt] n Schlitz m ♦ vt: to ~ sth in etw einlegen
sloth [sləuθ] n (laziness) Faulheit f
slot machine n (BRIT: vending machine) Automat m; (for gambling) Spielautomat m
slouch [slautʃ] vi: to ~ about (laze) herumhängen (inf)
slovenly ['slʌvnlɪ] adj schlampig; (speech) salopp
slow [sləu] adj langsam ♦ adv langsam; to be ~ (clock) nachgehen; (stupid) begriffsstutzig sein; "~" (road sign) „Langsam"; in ~ motion in Zeitlupe; ~ **down** vi langsamer werden ♦ vt verlangsamen; ~ **up** vi sich verlangsamen, sich verzögern ♦ vt aufhalten, langsamer machen; **~ly** adv langsam
sludge [slʌdʒ] n Schlamm m
slug [slʌg] n Nacktschnecke f; (inf: bullet) Kugel f; **~gish** adj träge; (COMM) schleppend
sluice [slu:s] n Schleuse f
slumber ['slʌmbə*] n Schlummer m
slump [slʌmp] n Rückgang m ♦ vi fallen, stürzen

slung [slʌŋ] pt, pp of sling
slur [slɜ:*] n Undeutlichkeit f; (insult) Verleumdung f; **~red** [slɜ:d] adj (pronunciation) undeutlich
slush [slʌʃ] n (snow) Schneematsch m; ~ **fund** n Schmiergeldfonds m
slut [slʌt] n Schlampe f
sly [slaɪ] adj schlau
smack [smæk] n Klaps m ♦ vt einen Klaps geben +dat ♦ vi: to ~ of riechen nach; to ~ one's lips schmatzen, sich dat die Lippen lecken
small [smɔ:l] adj klein; in the ~ hours in den frühen Morgenstunden; ~ **ads** (BRIT) npl Kleinanzeigen pl; ~ **change** n Kleingeld nt; ~ **holder** (BRIT) n Kleinbauer m; **~pox** n Pocken pl; ~ **talk** n Geplauder nt
smart [smɑ:t] adj (fashionable) elegant, schick; (neat) adrett; (clever) clever; (quick) scharf ♦ vi brennen, schmerzen; **~en up** vi sich in Schale werfen ♦ vt herausputzen
smash [smæʃ] n Zusammenstoß m; (TENNIS) Schmetterball m ♦ vt (break) zerschmettern; (destroy) vernichten ♦ vi (break) zersplittern, zerspringen; **~ing** (inf) adj toll
smattering ['smætərɪŋ] n oberflächliche Kenntnis f
smear [smɪə*] n Fleck m ♦ vt beschmieren
smell [smel] (pt, pp smelt or smelled) n Geruch m; (sense) Geruchssinn m ♦ vt riechen ♦ vi: to ~ (of) riechen (nach); **~y** adj übelriechend
smelt [smelt] pt, pp of smell
smile [smaɪl] n Lächeln nt ♦ vi lächeln
smiling adj lächelnd
smirk [smɜ:k] n blöde(s) Grinsen nt
smith [smɪθ] n Schmied m; **~y** ['smɪðɪ] n Schmiede f
smock [smɒk] n Kittel m
smoke [sməuk] n Rauch m ♦ vt rauchen; (food) räuchern ♦ vi rauchen; **~d** adj (bacon) geräuchert; (glass) Rauch-; **~r** n Raucher(in) m(f); (RAIL) Raucherabteil nt; ~ **screen** n Rauchwand f
smoking ['sməukɪŋ] n: "no ~" „Rau-

chen verboten"

smoky ['sməʊkɪ] *adj* rauchig; (*room*) verraucht; (*taste*) geräuchert

smolder ['sməʊldə*] (*US*) *vi* = **smoulder**

smooth [smu:ð] *adj* glatt ♦ *vt* (*also:* ~ *out*) glätten, glattstreichen

smother ['smʌðə*] *vt* ersticken

smoulder ['sməʊldə*] (*US* **smolder**) *vi* schwelen

smudge [smʌdʒ] *n* Schmutzfleck *m* ♦ *vt* beschmieren

smug [smʌg] *adj* selbstgefällig

smuggle ['smʌgl] *vt* schmuggeln; ~**r** *n* Schmuggler *m*

smuggling ['smʌglɪŋ] *n* Schmuggel *m*

smutty ['smʌtɪ] *adj* schmutzig

snack [snæk] *n* Imbiß *m*; ~ **bar** *n* Imbißstube *f*

snag [snæg] *n* Haken *m*

snail [sneɪl] *n* Schnecke *f*

snake [sneɪk] *n* Schlange *f*

snap [snæp] *n* Schnappen *nt*; (*photograph*) Schnappschuß *m* ♦ *adj* (*decision*) schnell ♦ *vt* (*break*) zerbrechen; (*PHOT*) knipsen ♦ *vi* (*break*) brechen; (*speak*) anfauchen; **to** ~ **shut** zuschnappen; ~ **at** *vt fus* schnappen nach; ~ **off** *vt* (*break*) abbrechen; ~ **up** *vt* aufschnappen; ~**py** *adj* flott; ~**shot** *n* Schnappschuß *m*

snare [snɛə*] *n* Schlinge *f* ♦ *vt* mit einer Schlinge fangen

snarl [snɑ:l] *n* Zähnefletschen *nt* ♦ *vi* (*dog*) knurren

snatch [snætʃ] *n* (*small amount*) Bruchteil *m* ♦ *vt* schnappen, packen

sneak [sni:k] *vi* schleichen ♦ *n* (*inf*) Petze(r) *mf*

sneakers ['sni:kəz] (*US*) *npl* Freizeitschuhe *pl*

sneaky ['sni:kɪ] *adj* raffiniert

sneer [snɪə*] *n* Hohnlächeln *nt* ♦ *vi* spötteln

sneeze [sni:z] *n* Niesen *nt* ♦ *vi* niesen

sniff [snɪf] *n* Schnüffeln *nt* ♦ *vi* schnieben; (*smell*) schnüffeln ♦ *vt* schnuppern

snigger ['snɪgə*] *n* Kichern *nt* ♦ *vi* hämisch kichern

snip [snɪp] *n* Schnippel *m*, Schnipsel *m* ♦

vt schnippeln

sniper ['snaɪpə*] *n* Heckenschütze *m*

snippet ['snɪpɪt] *n* Schnipsel *m*; (*of conversation*) Fetzen *m*

snivelling ['snɪvlɪŋ] *adj* weinerlich

snooker ['snu:kə*] *n* Snooker *nt*

snoop [snu:p] *vi*: **to** ~ **about** herumschnüffeln

snooty ['snu:tɪ] (*inf*) *adj* hochnäsig

snooze [snu:z] *n* Nickerchen *nt* ♦ *vi* ein Nickerchen machen, dösen

snore [snɔ:*] *vi* schnarchen ♦ *n* Schnarchen *nt*

snorkel ['snɔ:kl] *n* Schnorchel *m*

snort [snɔ:t] *n* Schnauben *nt* ♦ *vi* schnauben

snout [snaʊt] *n* Schnauze *f*

snow [snəʊ] *n* Schnee *m* ♦ *vi* schneien; ~**ball** *n* Schneeball *m* ♦ *vi* eskalieren; ~**bound** *adj* eingeschneit; ~**drift** *n* Schneewehe *f*; ~**drop** *n* Schneeglöckchen *nt*; ~**fall** *n* Schneefall *m*; ~**flake** *n* Schneeflocke *f*; ~**man** (*irreg*) *n* Schneemann *m*; ~**plough** (*US* ~-**plow**) *n* Schneepflug *m*; ~ **shoe** *n* Schneeschuh *m*; ~ **storm** *n* Schneesturm *m*

snub [snʌb] *vt* schroff abfertigen ♦ *n* Verweis *m*; ~-**nosed** *adj* stupsnasig

snuff [snʌf] *n* Schnupftabak *m*

snug [snʌg] *adj* gemütlich, behaglich

snuggle ['snʌgl] *vi*: **to** ~ **up to sb** sich an jdn kuscheln

┌─────────────┐
│ *KEYWORD* │
└─────────────┘

so [səʊ] *adv* **1** (*thus*) so; (*likewise*) auch; **so saying he walked away** indem er das sagte, ging er; **if so** wenn ja; **I didn't do it - you did so!** ich hab das nicht gemacht - hast du wohl!; **so do I, so am I** *etc* ich tue auch; **so it is!** tatsächlich!; **I hope/think so** hoffentlich/ich glaube schon; **so far** bis jetzt

2 (*in comparisons etc: to such a degree*) so; **so quickly/big (that)** so schnell/groß, daß; **I'm so glad to see you** ich freue mich so, dich zu sehen

3: **so many** so viele; **so much work** so viel Arbeit; **I love you so much** ich liebe dich so sehr

4 (*phrases*): **10 or so** etwa 10; **so long!**
(*inf: goodbye*) tschüs!
♦ *conj* 1 (*expressing purpose*): **so as to**
um ... zu; **so** (*that*) damit
2 (*expressing result*) also; **so I was
right after all** ich hatte also doch recht;
so you see ... wie du siehst ...

soak [səuk] *vt* durchnässen; (*leave in
liquid*) einweichen ♦ *vi* (*ein*)weichen; ~
in *vi* einsickern; ~ **up** *vt* aufsaugen
so-and-so ['səuənsəu] *n* (*somebody*)
Soundso *m*
soap [səup] *n* Seife *f*; ~**flakes** *npl*
Seifenflocken *pl*; ~ **opera** *n*
Familienserie *f* (*im Fernsehen, Radio*);
~ **powder** *n* Waschpulver *nt*; ~**y** *adj*
seifig, Seifen-
soar [sɔː*] *vi* aufsteigen; (*prices*) in die
Höhe schnellen
sob [sɒb] *n* Schluchzen *nt* ♦ *vi*
schluchzen
sober ['səubə*] *adj* (*also fig*) nüchtern; ♦
~ **up** *vi* nüchtern werden
so-called ['səu'kɔːld] *adj* sogenannt
soccer ['sɒkə*] *n* Fußball *m*
sociable ['səuʃəbl] *adj* gesellig
social ['səuʃəl] *adj* sozial; (*friendly,
living with others*) gesellig ♦ *n*
gesellige(r) Abend *m*; ~ **club** *n* Verein
m (*für Freizeitgestaltung*); ~**ism** *n*
Sozialismus *m*; ~**ist** *n* Sozialist(in)
m(f) ♦ *adj* sozialistisch; ~**ize** *vi*: **to
~ize** (**with**) gesellschaftlich verkehren
(mit); ~**ly** *adv* gesellschaftlich, privat;
~ **security** *n* Sozialversicherung *f*; ~
work *n* Sozialarbeit *f*; ~ **worker** *n*
Sozialarbeiter(in) *m(f)*
society [sə'saɪətɪ] *n* Gesellschaft *f*;
(*fashionable world*) die große Welt
sociology [səusɪ'ɒlədʒɪ] *n* Soziologie *f*
sock [sɒk] *n* Socke *f*
socket ['sɒkɪt] *n* (*ELEC*) Steckdose *f*; (*of
eye*) Augenhöhle *f*; (*TECH*) Rohransatz
m
sod [sɒd] *n* Rasenstück *nt*; (*inf!*)
Saukerl *m* (*!*)
soda ['səudə] *n* Soda *f*; (*also:* ~ *water*)
Soda(wasser) *nt*; (*US: also:* ~ *pop*)
Limonade *f*

sodden ['sɒdn] *adj* durchweicht
sodium ['səudɪəm] *n* Natrium *nt*
sofa ['səufə] *n* Sofa *nt*
soft [sɒft] *adj* weich; (*not loud*) leise;
(*weak*) nachgiebig; ~ **drink** *n* alkohol-
freie(s) Getränk *nt*; ~**en** ['sɒfn] *vt*
weich machen; (*blow*) abschwächen,
mildern ♦ *vi* weich werden; ~**ly** *adv*
sanft; leise; ~**ness** *n* Weichheit *f*; (*fig*)
Sanftheit *f*
software ['sɒftweə*] *n* (*COMPUT*)
Software *f*
soggy ['sɒgɪ] *adj* (*ground*) sumpfig;
(*bread*) aufgeweicht
soil [sɔɪl] *n* Erde *f* ♦ *vt* beschmutzen;
~**ed** *adj* beschmutzt
solace ['sɒləs] *n* Trost *m*
solar ['səulə*] *adj* Sonnen-
sold [səuld] *pt, pp of* **sell**; ~ **out** (*COMM*)
ausverkauft
solder ['səuldə*] *vt* löten ♦ *n* Lötmetall
nt
soldier ['səuldʒə*] *n* Soldat *m*
sole [səul] *n* Sohle *f*; (*fish*) Seezunge *f* ♦
adj alleinig, Allein-; ~**ly** *adv* ausschließlich
solemn ['sɒləm] *adj* feierlich
sole trader *n* (*COMM*) Ein-
zelunternehmen *nt*
solicit [sə'lɪsɪt] *vt* (*request*) bitten um ♦
vi (*prostitute*) Kunden anwerben
solicitor [sə'lɪsɪtə*] *n* Rechtsanwalt *m*/
-anwältin *f*
solid ['sɒlɪd] *adj* (*hard*) fest; (*of same
material, not hollow*) massiv; (*without
break*) voll, ganz; (*reliable, sensible*)
solide ♦ *n* Festkörper *m*
solidarity [sɒlɪ'dærɪtɪ] *n* Solidarität *f*
solidify [sə'lɪdɪfaɪ] *vi* fest werden
solitary ['sɒlɪtərɪ] *adj* einsam, einzeln; ~
confinement *n* Einzelhaft *f*
solitude ['sɒlɪtjuːd] *n* Einsamkeit *f*
solo ['səuləu] *n* Solo *nt*
soloist ['səuləuɪst] *n* Solist(in) *m(f)*
soluble ['sɒljubl] *adj* (*substance*)
löslich; (*problem*) (auf)lösbar
solution [sə'luːʃən] *n* (*also fig*) Lösung
f; (*of mystery*) Erklärung *f*
solve [sɒlv] *vt* (auf)lösen
solvent ['sɒlvənt] *adj* (*FIN*)

zahlungsfähig ♦ *n* (*CHEM*)
Lösungsmittel *nt*
sombre ['sɒmbə*] (*US* **somber**) *adj*
düster

KEYWORD

some [sʌm] *adj* **1** (*a certain amount or
number of*) einige; (*a few*) ein paar,
(*with singular nouns*) etwas; **some tea/
biscuits** etwas Tee/ein paar Plätzchen;
I've got some money, but not much ich
habe ein bißchen Geld, aber nicht viel
2 (*certain: in contrasts*) manche(r, s);
some people say that ... manche Leute
sagen, daß ...
3 (*unspecified*) irgendein(e); **some
woman was asking for you** da hat eine
Frau nach Ihnen gefragt; **some day** eines Tages; **some day next week**
irgendwann nächste Woche
♦ *pron* **1** (*a certain number*) einige;
have you got some? haben Sie welche?
2 (*a certain amount*) etwas; **I've read
some of the book** ich habe das Buch
teilweise gelesen
♦ *adv*: **some 10 people** etwa 10 Leute

somebody ['sʌmbədɪ] *pron* = **someone**
somehow ['sʌmhau] *adv* irgendwie
someone ['sʌmwʌn] *pron* jemand;
(*direct obj*) jemand(en); (*indirect obj*)
jemandem
someplace ['sʌmpleɪs] (*US*) *adv* = **somewhere**
somersault ['sʌməsɔːlt] *n* Salto *m* ♦ *vi*
einen Salto machen
something ['sʌmθɪŋ] *pron* etwas
sometime ['sʌmtaɪm] *adv*
(*irgend*)einmal
sometimes ['sʌmtaɪmz] *adv* manchmal
somewhat ['sʌmwɒt] *adv* etwas
somewhere ['sʌmwɛə*] *adv* irgendwo;
(*to a place*) irgendwohin; ~ **else**
irgendwo anders
son [sʌn] *n* Sohn *m*
sonar ['səunɑː*] *n* Echolot *nt*
song [sɒŋ] *n* Lied *nt*
sonic ['sɒnɪk] *adj* Schall-; ~ **boom** *n*
Überschallknall *m*
son-in-law ['sʌnɪnlɔː] *n* Schwiegersohn

m
sonny ['sʌnɪ] (*inf*) *n* Kleine(r) *m*
soon [suːn] *adv* bald; ~ **afterwards** kurz
danach; ~**er** *adv* (*time*) früher; (*for
preference*) lieber; ~**er or later** früher
oder später
soot [sut] *n* Ruß *m*
soothe [suːð] *vt* (*person*) beruhigen;
(*pain*) lindern
sophisticated [sə'fɪstɪkeɪtɪd] *adj*
(*person*) kultiviert; (*machinery*) hoch-
entwickelt
sophomore ['sɒfəmɔː*] (*US*) *n* College-
Student *m* im 2. Jahr
soporific [sɒpə'rɪfɪk] *adj* einschläfernd
sopping ['sɒpɪŋ] *adj* patschnaß
soppy ['sɒpɪ] (*inf*) *adj* schmalzig
soprano [sə'prɑːnəu] *n* Sopran *m*
sorcerer ['sɔːsərə*] *n* Hexenmeister *m*
sordid ['sɔːdɪd] *adj* erbärmlich
sore [sɔː*] *adj* schmerzend; (*point*)
wund ♦ *n* Wunde *f*; ~**ly** *adv* (*tempted*)
stark, sehr
sorrow ['sɒrəu] *n* Kummer *m*, Leid *nt*;
~**ful** *adj* sorgenvoll
sorry ['sɒrɪ] *adj* traurig, erbärmlich; ~!
Entschuldigung!; **to feel** ~ **for sb** jdn
bemitleiden; **I feel** ~ **for him** er tut mir
leid
sort [sɔːt] *n* Art *f*, Sorte *f* ♦ *vt* (*also*: ~
out: *papers*) sortieren; (: *problems*)
sichten, in Ordnung bringen; ~**ing
office** *n* Sortierstelle *f*
SOS *n* SOS *nt*
so-so ['səu'səu] *adv* so(-so) la-la
sought [sɔːt] *pt, pp of* **seek**
soul [səul] *n* Seele *f*; (*music*) Soul *m*;
~-**destroying** *adj* trostlos; ~**ful** *adj*
seelenvoll
sound [saund] *adj* (*healthy*) gesund;
(*safe*) sicher; (*sensible*) vernünftig;
(*theory*) stichhaltig; (*thorough*) tüchtig,
gehörig ♦ *adv*: **to be** ~ **asleep** fest
schlafen ♦ *n* (*noise*) Geräusch *nt*, Laut
m; (*GEOG*) Sund *m* ♦ *vt* erschallen
lassen; (*alarm*) (Alarm) schlagen;
(*MED*) abhorchen ♦ *vi* (*make a* ~)
schallen, tönen; (*seem*) klingen; **to** ~
like sich anhören wie; ~ **out** *vt*
(*opinion*) erforschen; (*person*) auf den

Zahn fühlen +*dat*; ~ **barrier** *n* Schallmauer *f*; ~ **effects** *npl* Toneffekte *pl*; ~**ing** *n* (*NAUT etc*) Lotung *f*; ~**ly** *adv* (*sleep*) fest; (*beat*) tüchtig; ~**proof** *adj* (*room*) schalldicht; ~**-track** *n* Tonstreifen *m*; (*music*) Filmmusik *f*

soup [su:p] *n* Suppe *f*; **in the** ~ (*inf*) in der Tinte; ~ **plate** *n* Suppenteller *m*; ~**spoon** *n* Suppenlöffel *m*

sour ['savə*] *adj* (*also fig*) sauer; **it's** ~ **grapes** (*fig*) die Trauben hängen zu hoch

source [sɔ:s] *n* (*also fig*) Quelle *f*

south [sauθ] *n* Süden *m* ♦ *adj* Süd-, südlich ♦ *adv* nach Süden, südwärts; **S~ Africa** *n* Südafrika *nt*; **S~ African** *adj* südafrikanisch ♦ *n* Südafrikaner(in) *m(f)*; **S~ America** *n* Südamerika *nt*; **S~ American** *adj* südamerikanisch ♦ *n* Südamerikaner(in) *m(f)*; ~**-east** *n* Südosten *m*; ~**erly** ['sʌðəli] *adj* südlich; ~**ern** ['sʌðən] *adj* südlich, Süd-; **S~ Pole** *n* Südpol *m*; ~**ward(s)** *adv* südwärts, nach Süden; ~**west** *n* Südwesten *m*

souvenir [su:və'nıə*] *n* Souvenir *nt*

sovereign ['sɒvrın] *n* (*ruler*) Herrscher(in) *m(f)* ♦ *adj* (*independent*) souverän

soviet ['səuvıət] *adj* sowjetisch; **the S~ Union** die Sowjetunion

sow[1] [sau] *n* Sau *f*

sow[2] [səu] (*pt* **sowed**, *pp* **sown**) *vt* (*also fig*) säen

soy [sɔı] (*US*) *n* = **soya**

soya ['sɔıə] (*US* **soy**) *n*: ~ **bean** Sojabohne *f*; ~ **sauce** Sojasauce *f*

spa [spa:] *n* (*place*) Kurort *m*

space [speıs] *n* Platz *m*, Raum *m*; (*universe*) Weltraum *m*, All *nt*; (*length of time*) Abstand *m* ♦ *vt* (*also*: ~ *out*) verteilen; ~**craft** *n* Raumschiff *nt*; ~**man** (*irreg*) *n* Raumfahrer *m*; ~ **ship** *n* Raumschiff *nt*

spacing *n* Abstand *m*; (*also*: ~ *out*) Verteilung *f*

spacious ['speıʃəs] *adj* geräumig, weit

spade [speıd] *n* Spaten *m*; ~**s** *npl* (*CARDS*) Pik *nt*

Spain [speın] *n* Spanien *nt*

span [spæn] *n* Spanne *f*; (*of bridge etc*)

Spannweite *f* ♦ *vt* überspannen

Spaniard ['spænjəd] *n* Spanier(in) *m(f)*

Spanish ['spænıʃ] *adj* spanisch ♦ *n* (*LING*) Spanisch *nt*; **the** ~ *npl* (*people*) die Spanier *pl*

spank [spæŋk] *vt* verhauen, versohlen

spanner ['spænə*] (*BRIT*) *n* Schraubenschlüssel *m*

spar [spa:*] *n* (*NAUT*) Sparren *m* ♦ *vi* (*BOXING*) einen Sparring machen

spare [spɛə*] *adj* Ersatz- ♦ *n* = **spare part** ♦ *vt* (*lives, feelings*) verschonen; (*trouble*) ersparen; **to** ~ (*surplus*) übrig; ~ **part** *n* Ersatzteil *nt*; ~ **time** *n* Freizeit *f*; ~ **wheel** *n* (*AUT*) Reservereifen *m*

sparing ['spɛərıŋ] *adj*: **to be** ~ **with** geizen mit; ~**ly** *adv* sparsam; (*eat, spend etc*) in Maßen

spark [spa:k] *n* Funken *m*; ~**(ing) plug** *n* Zündkerze *f*

sparkle ['spa:kl] *n* Funkeln *nt*; (*gaiety*) Schwung *m* ♦ *vi* funkeln

sparkling ['spa:klıŋ] *adj* funkelnd; (*wine*) Schaum-; (*conversation*) spritzig, geistreich

sparrow ['spærəu] *n* Spatz *m*

sparse [spa:s] *adj* spärlich

spasm ['spæzəm] *n* (*MED*) Krampf *m*; (*fig*) Anfall *m*; ~**odic** [spæz'mɒdık] *adj* (*fig*) sprunghaft

spat [spæt] *pt, pp of* **spit**

spate [speıt] *n* (*fig*) Flut *f*, Schwall *m*; **in** ~ (*river*) angeschwollen

spatter ['spætə*] *vt* bespritzen, verspritzen

spatula ['spætjʊlə] *n* Spatel *m*

spawn [spɔ:n] *vi* laichen ♦ *n* Laich *m*

speak [spi:k] (*pt* **spoke**, *pp* **spoken**) *vt* sprechen, reden; (*truth*) sagen; (*language*) sprechen ♦ *vi*: **to** ~ (**to**) sprechen (mit *or* zu); **to** ~ **to sb** *of or* **about sth** mit jdm über etw *acc* sprechen; ~ **up!** sprich lauter!; ~**er** *n* Sprecher(in) *m(f)*, Redner(in) *m(f)*; (*loudspeaker*) Lautsprecher *m*; (*POL*): **the S~er** der Vorsitzende des Parlaments (*BRIT*) *or* des Kongresses (*US*)

spear [spıə*] *n* Speer *m* ♦ *vt* aufspießen; ~**head** *vt* (*attack etc*) anführen

spec [spek] (*inf*) *n*: on ~ auf gut Glück
special ['speʃəl] *adj* besondere(r, s);
~**ist** *n* (*TECH*) Fachmann *m*; (*MED*)
Facharzt *m*/Fachärztin *f*; ~**ity**
[speʃɪ'ælɪtɪ] *n* Spezialität *f*; (*study*)
Spezialgebiet *nt*; ~**ize** *vi*: to ~ize (**in**)
sich spezialisieren (auf +*acc*); ~**ly** *adv*
besonders; (*explicitly*) extra
species ['spi:ʃi:z] *n* Art *f*
specific [spə'sɪfɪk] *adj* spezifisch; ~**ally**
adv spezifisch
specification [spesɪfɪ'keɪʃən] *n* Angabe
f; (*stipulation*) Bedingung *f*; ~s *npl*
(*TECH*) technische Daten *pl*
specify ['spesɪfaɪ] *vt* genau angeben
specimen ['spesɪmɪn] *n* Probe *f*
speck [spek] *n* Fleckchen *nt*
speckled ['spekld] *adj* gesprenkelt
specs [speks] (*inf*) *npl* Brille *f*
spectacle ['spektəkl] *n* Schauspiel *nt*; ~s
npl (*glasses*) Brille *f*
spectacular [spek'tækjʊlə*] *adj*
sensationell; (*success etc*) spektakulär
spectator [spek'teɪtə*] *n* Zuschauer(in)
m(f)
spectre ['spektə*] (*US* **specter**) *n* Geist
m, Gespenst *nt*
speculate ['spekjʊleɪt] *vi* spekulieren
speech [spi:tʃ] *n* Sprache *f*; (*address*)
Rede *f*; (*manner of speaking*)
Sprechweise *f*; ~**less** *adj* sprachlos
speed [spi:d] *n* Geschwindigkeit *f*;
(*gear*) Gang *m* ♦ *vi* (*JUR*) (zu) schnell
fahren; **at full** *or* **top** ~ mit
Höchstgeschwindigkeit; ~ **up** *vt* beschleunigen ♦ *vi* schneller werden;
schneller fahren; ~**boat** *n* Schnellboot
nt; ~**ily** *adv* schleunigst; ~**ing** *n* Ge-
schwindigkeitsüberschreitung *f*; ~ **limit**
n Geschwindigkeitsbegrenzung *f*;
~**ometer** [spɪ'dɒmɪtə*] *n* Tachometer *m*;
~**way** *n* (*bike racing*) Motorradrenn-
strecke *f*; ~**y** *adj* schnell
spell [spel] (*pt, pp* **spelt** (*BRIT*) *or* ~**ed**)
n (*magic*) Bann *m*; (*period of time*)
Zeitlang *f* ♦ *vt* buchstabieren; (*imply*)
bedeuten; **to cast a** ~ **on sb** jdn ver-
zaubern; ~**bound** *adj* (wie) gebannt;
~**ing** *n* Rechtschreibung *f*
spelt [spelt] (*BRIT*) *pt, pp of* **spell**

spend [spend] (*pt, pp* **spent**) *vt* (*money*)
ausgeben; (*time*) verbringen; ~**thrift** *n*
Verschwender(in) *m(f)*
spent [spent] *pt, pp of* **spend**
sperm [spɜ:m] *n* (*BIOL*) Samenflüssigkeit
f
spew [spju:] *vt* (er)brechen
sphere [sfɪə*] *n* (*globe*) Kugel *f*; (*fig*)
Sphäre *f*, Gebiet *nt*
spherical ['sferɪkəl] *adj* kugelförmig
spice [spaɪs] *n* Gewürz *nt* ♦ *vt* würzen
spick-and-span ['spɪkən'spæn] *adj* blitz-
blank
spicy ['spaɪsɪ] *adj* würzig; (*fig*) pikant
spider ['spaɪdə*] *n* Spinne *f*
spike [spaɪk] *n* Dorn *m*, Spitze *f*
spill [spɪl] (*pt, pp* **spilt** *or* ~**ed**) *vt* verschütten ♦ *vi* sich ergießen; ~ **over** *vi*
überlaufen; (*fig*) sich ausbreiten
spilt [spɪlt] *pt, pp of* **spill**
spin [spɪn] (*pt, pp* **spun**) *n* (*trip in car*)
Spazierfahrt *f*; (*AVIAT*) (Ab)trudeln *nt*;
(*on ball*) Drall *m* ♦ *vt* (*thread*)
spinnen; (*like top*) (herum)wirbeln ♦ *vi*
sich drehen; ~ **out** *vt* in die Länge
ziehen
spinach ['spɪnɪtʃ] *n* Spinat *m*
spinal ['spaɪnl] *adj* Rückgrat-; ~ **cord** *n*
Rückenmark *nt*
spindly ['spɪndlɪ] *adj* spindeldürr
spin-dryer ['spɪn'draɪə*] (*BRIT*) *n*
Wäscheschleuder *f*
spine [spaɪn] *n* Rückgrat *nt*; (*thorn*)
Stachel *m*; ~**less** *adj* (*also fig*)
rückgratlos
spinning ['spɪnɪŋ] *n* Spinnen *nt*; ~ **top**
n Kreisel *m*; ~ **wheel** *n* Spinnrad *nt*
spin-off ['spɪnɒf] *n* Nebenprodukt *nt*
spinster ['spɪnstə*] *n* unverheiratete
Frau *f*; (*pej*) alte Jungfer *f*
spiral ['spaɪərl] *n* Spirale *f* ♦ *adj*
spiralförmig; (*movement etc*) in
Spiralen ♦ *vi* sich (hoch)winden; ~
staircase *n* Wendeltreppe *f*
spire ['spaɪə*] *n* Turm *m*
spirit ['spɪrɪt] *n* Geist *m*; (*humour,
mood*) Stimmung *f*; (*courage*) Mut *m*;
(*verve*) Elan *m*; (*alcohol*) Alkohol *m*;
~s *npl* (*drink*) Spirituosen *pl*; **in good**
~s gut aufgelegt; ~**ed** *adj* beherzt; ~

level n Wasserwaage f

spiritual ['spɪrɪtjʊəl] adj geistig,
seelisch; (REL) geistlich ♦ n Spiritual nt

spit [spɪt] (pt, pp spat) n (for roasting)
(Brat)spieß m; (saliva) Spucke f ♦ vi
spucken; (rain) sprühen; (make a
sound) zischen; (cat) fauchen

spite [spaɪt] n Gehässigkeit f ♦ vt
kränken; **in ~ of** trotz; **~ful** adj
gehässig

spittle ['spɪtl] n Speichel m, Spucke f

splash [splæʃ] n Spritzer m; (of colour)
(Farb)fleck m ♦ vt bespritzen ♦ vi
spritzen

spleen [spliːn] n (ANAT) Milz f

splendid ['splendɪd] adj glänzend

splendour ['splendə*] (US splendor) n
Pracht f

splint [splɪnt] n Schiene f

splinter ['splɪntə*] n Splitter m ♦ vi
(zer)splittern

split [splɪt] (pt, pp split) n Spalte f; (fig)
Spaltung f; (division) Trennung f ♦ vt
spalten ♦ vi (divide) reißen; ~ **up** vi
sich trennen

splutter ['splʌtə*] vi stottern

spoil [spɔɪl] (pt, pp spoilt or ~ed) vt
(ruin) verderben; (child) verwöhnen;
~s npl Beute f; **~sport** n
Spielverderber m; **spoilt** [spɔɪlt] pt, pp
of **spoil**

spoke [spəʊk] pt of **speak** ♦ n Speiche f

spoken ['spəʊkn] pp of **speak**

spokesman ['spəʊksmən] (irreg) n Spre-
cher m

spokeswoman ['spəʊkswʊmən] (irreg)
n Sprecherin f

sponge [spʌndʒ] n Schwamm m ♦ vt
abwaschen ♦ vi: **to ~ on** auf Kosten
leben +gen; ~ **bag** (BRIT) n
Kulturbeutel m; ~ **cake** n Rührkuchen
m

sponsor ['spɒnsə*] n Sponsor m ♦ vt
fördern; **~ship** n Finanzierung f; (public) Schirmherrschaft f

spontaneous [spɒn'teɪnɪəs] adj spontan

spooky ['spuːkɪ] (inf) adj gespenstisch

spool [spuːl] n Spule f, Rolle f

spoon [spuːn] n Löffel m; ~**-feed**
(irreg) vt mit dem Löffel füttern; (fig)

hochpäppeln; **~ful** n Löffel(voll) m

sport [spɔːt] n Sport m; (person)
feine(r) Kerl m; **~ing** adj (fair) sportlich, fair; **to give sb a ~ing chance** jdm
eine faire Chance geben; ~ **jacket** (US)
n = **sports jacket**; **~s car** n Sportwagen
m; **~s jacket** n Sportjackett nt; **~sman**
(irreg) n Sportler m; **~smanship** n
Sportlichkeit f; **~swear** n Sportkleidung
f; **~swoman** (irreg) n Sportlerin f; **~y**
adj sportlich

spot [spɒt] n Punkt m; (dirty)
Fleck(en) m; (place) Stelle f; (MED)
Pickel m ♦ vt erspähen; (mistake)
bemerken; **on the ~** an Ort und Stelle;
(at once) auf der Stelle; ~ **check** n
Stichprobe f; **~less** adj fleckenlos;
~light n Scheinwerferlicht nt; (lamp)
Scheinwerfer m; **~ted** adj gefleckt;
~ty adj (face) pickelig

spouse [spaʊz] n Gatte m/Gattin f

spout [spaʊt] n (of pot) Tülle f; (jet)
Wasserstrahl m ♦ vi speien

sprain [spreɪn] n Verrenkung f ♦ vt verrenken

sprang [spræŋ] pt of **spring**

sprawl [sprɔːl] vi sich strecken

spray [spreɪ] n Spray nt; (off sea)
Gischt f; (of flowers) Zweig m ♦ vt be-
sprühen, sprayen

spread [spred] (pt, pp spread) n
(extent) Verbreitung f; (inf: meal)
Schmaus m; (for bread) Aufstrich m ♦
vt ausbreiten; (scatter) verbreiten;
(butter) streichen ♦ vi sich ausbreiten;
~-eagled ['spredɪgld] adj: **to be ~-
eagled** alle viere von sich strecken

spree [spriː] n (shopping) Ein-
kaufsbummel m; **to go on a ~** einen
draufmachen

sprightly ['spraɪtlɪ] adj munter, lebhaft

spring [sprɪŋ] (pt sprang, pp sprung) n
(leap) Sprung m; (metal) Feder f;
(season) Frühling m; (water) Quelle f
♦ vi (leap) springen; ~ **up** vi (problem) auftauchen; **~board** n Sprungbrett nt; **~clean** n (also: ~-cleaning)
Frühjahrsputz m; **~time** n Frühling m;
~y adj federnd, elastisch

sprinkle ['sprɪŋkl] vt (salt) streuen;

(*liquid*) sprenkeln; to ~ water on, to ~ with water mit Wasser besprengen

sprinkler ['sprɪŋklə*] n (*for lawn*) Sprenger m; (*for fire fighting*) Sprinkler m

sprite [spraɪt] n Elfe f; Kobold m

sprout [spraʊt] vi sprießen; ~s npl (*also: Drussolo · o*) Rosenkohl m

spruce [spruːs] n Fichte f ♦ adj schmuck, adrett

sprung [sprʌŋ] pp of **spring**

spry [spraɪ] adj flink, rege

spun [spʌn] pt, pp of **spin**

spur [spɜː*] n Sporn m; (*fig*) Ansporn m ♦ vt (*also:* ~ on: *fig*) anspornen; on the ~ of the moment spontan

spurious ['spjʊərɪəs] adj falsch

spurn [spɜːn] vt verschmähen

spurt [spɜːt] n (*jet*) Strahl m; (*acceleration*) Spurt m ♦ vi (*liquid*) schießen

spy [spaɪ] n Spion(in) m(f) ♦ vi spionieren ♦ vt erspähen; ~ing n Spionage f

sq. abbr = **square**

squabble ['skwɒbl] n Zank m ♦ vi sich zanken

squad [skwɒd] n (*MIL*) Abteilung f; (*POLICE*) Kommando nt

squadron ['skwɒdrən] n (*cavalry*) Schwadron f; (*NAUT*) Geschwader nt; (*air force*) Staffel f

squalid ['skwɒlɪd] adj verkommen

squall [skwɔːl] n Bö f, Windstoß m

squalor ['skwɒlə*] n Verwahrlosung f

squander ['skwɒndə*] vt verschwenden

square [skwɛə*] n Quadrat nt; (*open space*) Platz m; (*instrument*) Winkel m; (*inf: person*) Spießer m ♦ adj viereckig; (*inf: ideas, tastes*) spießig ♦ vt (*arrange*) ausmachen; (*MATH*) ins Quadrat erheben ♦ vi (*agree*) übereinstimmen; all ~ quitt; a ~ meal eine ordentliche Mahlzeit; 2 metres ~ 2 Meter im Quadrat; 1 ~ metre 1 Quadratmeter; ~ly adv fest, gerade

squash [skwɒʃ] n (*BRIT: drink*) Saft m; (*game*) Squash nt ♦ vt zerquetschen

squat [skwɒt] adj untersetzt ♦ vi hocken; ~ter n Hausbesetzer m

squawk [skwɔːk] vi kreischen

squeak [skwiːk] vi quiek(s)en; (*spring, door etc*) quietschen

squeal [skwiːl] vi schrill schreien

squeamish ['skwiːmɪʃ] adj empfindlich

squeeze [skwiːz] n (*POL*) Geldknappheit f ♦ vt pressen, drücken; (*orange*) auspressen; ~ out vt ausquetschen

squelch [skwɛltʃ] vi platschen

squib [skwɪb] n Knallfrosch m

squid [skwɪd] n Tintenfisch m

squiggle ['skwɪgl] n Schnörkel m

squint [skwɪnt] vi schielen ♦ n: to have a ~ schielen; to ~ at sb/sth nach jdm/etw schielen

squire ['skwaɪə*] (*BRIT*) n Gutsherr m

squirm [skwɜːm] vi sich winden

squirrel ['skwɪrəl] n Eichhörnchen nt

squirt [skwɜːt] vt, vi spritzen

Sr abbr (= *senior*) sen.

St abbr (= *saint*) hl., St.; (= *street*) Str.

stab [stæb] n (*blow*) Stich m; (*inf: try*) Versuch m ♦ vt erstechen

stabilize ['steɪbəlaɪz] vt stabilisieren ♦ vi sich stabilisieren

stable ['steɪbl] adj stabil ♦ n Stall m

stack [stæk] n Stapel m ♦ vt stapeln

stadium ['steɪdɪəm] n Stadion nt

staff [stɑːf] n (*stick, MIL*) Stab m; (*personnel*) Personal nt; (*BRIT: SCH*) Lehrkräfte pl ♦ vt (*with people*) besetzen

stag [stæg] n Hirsch m

stage [steɪdʒ] n Bühne f; (*of journey*) Etappe f; (*degree*) Stufe f; (*point*) Stadium nt ♦ vt (*put on*) aufführen; (*simulate*) inszenieren; (*demonstration*) veranstalten; in ~s etappenweise; ~coach n Postkutsche f; ~ door n Bühneneingang m; ~ manager n Intendant m

stagger ['stægə*] vi wanken, taumeln ♦ vt (*amaze*) verblüffen; (*hours*) staffeln; ~ing adj unglaublich

stagnant ['stægnənt] adj stagnierend; (*water*) stehend

stagnate [stæg'neɪt] vi stagnieren

stag party n Männerabend m (vom Bräutigam vor der Hochzeit gegeben)

staid [steɪd] *adj* gesetzt

stain [steɪn] *n* Fleck *m* ♦ *vt* beflecken;
~ed glass window buntes Glasfenster
nt; ~less *adj* (*steel*) rostfrei; ~ remover *n* Fleckentferner *m*

stair [stɛə*] *n* (Treppen)stufe *f*; ~s *npl*
(*flight of steps*) Treppe *f*; ~case *n*
Treppenhaus *nt*, Treppe *f*; ~way *n*
Treppenaufgang *m*

stake [steɪk] *n* (*post*) Pfahl *m*; (*money*)
Einsatz *m* ♦ *vt* (*bet: money*) setzen; to
be at ~ auf dem Spiel stehen

stale [steɪl] *adj* alt; (*bread*) altbacken

stalemate [ˈsteɪlmeɪt] *n* (*CHESS*) Patt *nt*;
(*fig*) Stillstand *m*

stalk [stɔːk] *n* Stengel *m*, Stiel *m* ♦ *vt*
(*game*) jagen; ~ off *vi* abstolzieren

stall [stɔːl] *n* (*in stable*) Stand *m*, Box *f*;
(*in market*) (Verkaufs)stand *m* ♦ *vt*
(*AUT*) abwürgen ♦ *vi* (*AUT*) stehenbleiben; (*fig*) Ausflüchte machen; ~s
npl (*BRIT: THEAT*) Parkett *nt*

stallion [ˈstælɪən] *n* Zuchthengst *m*

stalwart [ˈstɔːlwət] *n* treue(r) Anhänger
m

stamina [ˈstæmɪnə] *n* Durchhaltevermögen *nt*, Zähigkeit *f*

stammer [ˈstæmə*] *n* Stottern *nt* ♦ *vt, vi*
stottern, stammeln

stamp [stæmp] *n* Briefmarke *f*; (*for
document*) Stempel *m* ♦ *vi* stampfen ♦
vt (*mark*) stempeln; (*mail*) frankieren;
(*foot*) stampfen mit; ~ album *n*
Briefmarkenalbum *nt*; ~ collecting *n*
Briefmarkensammeln *nt*

stampede [stæmˈpiːd] *n* panische Flucht
f

stance [stæns] *n* Haltung *f*

stand [stænd] (*pt, pp* stood) *n* (*for
objects*) Gestell *nt*; (*seats*) Tribüne *f* ♦
vi stehen; (*rise*) aufstehen; (*decision*)
feststehen ♦ *vt* setzen, stellen; (*endure*)
aushalten; (*person*) ausstehen;
(*nonsense*) dulden; to make a ~ Widerstand leisten; to ~ for parliament
(*BRIT*) für das Parlament kandidieren;
~ by (*be ready*) bereitstehen ♦ *vt
fus* (*opinion*) treu bleiben +*dat*; ~
down *vi* (*withdraw*) zurücktreten; ~
for *vt fus* (*signify*) stehen für; (*permit,*

tolerate) hinnehmen; ~ in for *vt fus*
einspringen für; ~ out *vi* (*be
prominent*) hervorstehen; ~ up *vi*
(*rise*) aufstehen; ~ up for *vt fus* sich
einsetzen für; ~ up to *vt fus*: to ~ up
to sth einer Sache *dat* gewachsen sein;
to ~ up to sb sich jdm gegenüber
behaupten

standard [ˈstændəd] *n* (*measure*) Norm
f; (*flag*) Fahne *f* ♦ *adj* (*size etc*)
Normal-; ~s *npl* (*morals*) Maßstäbe *pl*;
~ize *vt* vereinheitlichen; ~ lamp
(*BRIT*) *n* Stehlampe *f*; ~ of living *n*
Lebensstandard *m*

stand-by [ˈstændbaɪ] *n* Reserve *f*; to be
on ~ in Bereitschaft sein; ~ ticket *n*
(*AVIAT*) Standby-Ticket *nt*

stand-in [ˈstændɪn] *n* Ersatz *m*

standing [ˈstændɪŋ] *adj* (*erect*) stehend;
(*permanent*) ständig; (*invitation*) offen
♦ *n* (*duration*) Dauer *f*; (*reputation*)
Ansehen *nt*; of many years' ~ lang-
jährig; ~ order (*BRIT*) *n* (*at bank*)
Dauerauftrag *m*; ~ orders *npl* (*MIL*)
Vorschrift *f*; ~ room *n* Stehplatz *m*

stand-offish [ˈstændˈɒfɪʃ] *adj* zurückhaltend, sehr reserviert

standpoint [ˈstændpɔɪnt] *n* Standpunkt
m

standstill [ˈstændstɪl] *n*: to be at a ~
stillstehen; to come to a ~ zum Stillstand kommen

stank [stæŋk] *pt of* stink

staple [ˈsteɪpl] *n* (*in paper*) Heftklamme
f; (*article*) Haupterzeugnis *nt* ♦ *adj*
Grund-, Haupt- ♦ *vt* (*fest*)klammern;
~r *n* Heftmaschine *f*

star [stɑː*] *n* Stern *m*; (*person*) Star *m*
♦ *vi* die Hauptrolle spielen ♦ *vt*: ~ring
... in der Hauptrolle/den Hauptrollen ...

starboard [ˈstɑːbəd] *n* Steuerbord *nt*

starch [stɑːtʃ] *n* Stärke *f*

stardom [ˈstɑːdəm] *n* Berühmtheit *f*

stare [stɛə*] *n* starre(r) Blick *m* ♦ *vi*: to
~ at starren auf +*acc*, anstarren

starfish [ˈstɑːfɪʃ] *n* Seestern *m*

stark [stɑːk] *adj* öde ♦ *adv*: ~ naked
splitternackt

starling [ˈstɑːlɪŋ] *n* Star *m*

starry [ˈstɑːrɪ] *adj* Sternen-; ~-eyed *adj*

(innocent) blauäugig

start [stɑːt] *n* Anfang *m*; *(SPORT)* Start *m*; *(lead)* Vorsprung *m* ♦ *vt* in Gang setzen; *(car)* anlassen ♦ *vi* anfangen; *(car)* anspringen; *(on journey)* aufbrechen; *(SPORT)* starten; *(with fright)* zusammenfahren; **to ~ doing** *or* **to do sth** anfangen, etw zu tun; **~ off** *vi* anfangen; *(begin moving)* losgehen; losfahren; **~ up** *vi* anfangen; *(startled)* auffahren ♦ *vt* beginnen; *(car)* anlassen; *(engine)* starten; **~er** *n (AUT)* Anlasser *m*; *(for race)* Starter *m*; *(BRIT: COOK)* Vorspeise *f*; **~ing point** *n* Ausgangspunkt *m*

startle ['stɑːtl] *vt* erschrecken

startling ['stɑːtlɪŋ] *adj* erschreckend

starvation [stɑːˈveɪʃən] *n* Verhungern *nt*

starve [stɑːv] *vi* verhungern ♦ *vt* verhungern lassen; **I'm starving** ich sterbe vor Hunger

state [steɪt] *n (condition)* Zustand *m*; *(POL)* Staat *m* ♦ *vt* erklären; *(facts)* angeben; **the S~s** *(USA)* die Staaten; **to be in a ~** durchdrehen; **~ly** *adj* würdevoll; **~ment** *n* Aussage *f*; *(POL)* Erklärung *f*; **statesman** *(irreg) n* Staatsmann *m*

static ['stætɪk] *n (also:* **~ electricity)** Reibungselektrizität *f*

station ['steɪʃən] *n (RAIL etc)* Bahnhof *m*; *(police etc)* Wache *f*; *(in society)* Stand *m* ♦ *vt* stationieren

stationary ['steɪʃənərɪ] *adj* stillstehend; *(car)* parkend

stationer ['steɪʃənə*] *n* Schreibwarenhändler *m*; **~'s** *n (shop)* Schreibwarengeschäft *nt*; **~y** *n* Schreibwaren *pl*

station master *n* Bahnhofsvorsteher *m*

station wagon *n* Kombiwagen *m*

statistics [stəˈtɪstɪks] *n* Statistik *f*

statue ['stætjuː] *n* Statue *f*

stature ['stætʃə*] *n* Größe *f*

status ['steɪtəs] *n* Status *m*

statute ['stætjuːt] *n* Gesetz *nt*

statutory ['stætjʊtərɪ] *adj* gesetzlich

staunch [stɔːntʃ] *adj* standhaft

stave [steɪv] *n (MUS)* Notenlinien *pl* ♦ *vt:* **to ~ off** *(threat)* abwenden; *(attack)*

abwehren

stay [steɪ] *n* Aufenthalt *m* ♦ *vi* bleiben; *(reside)* wohnen; **to ~ put** an Ort und Stelle bleiben; **to ~ the night** übernachten; **~ behind** *vi* zurückbleiben; **~ in** *vi (at home)* zu Hause bleiben; **~ on** *vi (continue)* länger bleiben; **~ out** *vi (of house)* wegbleiben; **~ up** *vi (at night)* aufbleiben; **~ing power** *n* Durchhaltevermögen *nt*

stead [sted] *n:* **in sb's ~** an jds Stelle *dat*; **to stand sb in good ~** jdm zugute kommen

steadfast ['stedfəst] *adj* standhaft, treu

steadily ['stedɪlɪ] *adv* stetig, regelmäßig

steady ['stedɪ] *adj (firm)* fest, stabil; *(regular)* gleichmäßig; *(reliable)* beständig; *(hand)* ruhig; *(job, boyfriend)* fest ♦ *vt* festigen; **to ~ o.s. on/against sth** sich stützen auf/gegen etw *acc*

steak [steɪk] *n* Steak *nt*; *(fish)* Filet *nt*

steal [stiːl] *(pt* **stole**, *pp* **stolen)** *vt* stehlen ♦ *vi* stehlen; *(go stealthily)* sich stehlen

stealth [stelθ] *n* Heimlichkeit *f*; **~y** ['stelθɪ] *adj* verstohlen, heimlich

steam [stiːm] *n* Dampf *m* ♦ *vt (COOK)* im Dampfbad erhitzen ♦ *vi* dampfen; **~ engine** *n* Dampfmaschine *f*; **~er** *n* Dampfer *m*; **~roller** *n* Dampfwalze *f*; **~ship** *n* = **steamer**; **~y** *adj* dampfig

steel [stiːl] *n* Stahl *m* ♦ *adj* Stahl-; *(fig)* stählern; **~works** *n* Stahlwerke *pl*

steep [stiːp] *adj* steil; *(price)* gepfeffert ♦ *vt* einweichen

steeple ['stiːpl] *n* Kirchturm *m*; **~chase** *n* Hindernisrennen *nt*

steer [stɪə*] *vt, vi* steuern; *(car etc)* lenken; **~ing** *n (AUT)* Steuerung *f*; **~ing wheel** *n* Steuer- or Lenkrad *nt*

stellar ['stelə*] *adj* Stern(en)-

stem [stem] *n* Stiel *m* ♦ *vt* aufhalten; **~ from** *vt fus* abstammen von

stench [stentʃ] *n* Gestank *m*

stencil ['stensl] *n* Schablone *f* ♦ *vt* (auf)drucken

stenographer [steˈnɒɡrəfə*] *(US) n* Stenograph(in) *m(f)*

step [step] *n* Schritt *m*; *(stair)* Stufe *f* ♦

vi treten, schreiten; ~s *npl* (*BRIT*) = **stepladder**; **to take** ~s Schritte unternehmen; **in/out of** ~ **(with)** im/nicht im Gleichklang (mit); ~ **down** *vi* (*fig*) abtreten; ~ **off** *vt fus* aussteigen aus; ~ **up** *vt* steigern; ~**brother** *n* Stiefbruder *m*; ~**daughter** *n* Stieftochter *f*; ~**father** *n* Stiefvater *m*; ~**ladder** *n* Trittleiter *f*; ~**mother** *n* Stiefmutter *f*; ~**ping stone** *n* Stein *m*; (*fig*) Sprungbrett *nt*; ~**sister** *n* Stiefschwester *f*; ~**son** *n* Stiefsohn *m*

stereo ['steriəʊ] *n* Stereoanlage *f* ♦ *adj* (*also*: ~**phonic**) stereophonisch

stereotype ['stiəriətaip] *n* Prototyp *m*; (*fig*) Klischee *nt* ♦ *vt* stereotypieren; (*fig*) stereotyp machen

sterile ['sterail] *adj* steril; (*person*) unfruchtbar

sterling ['stɜːliŋ] *adj* (*FIN*) Sterling-; (*character*) gediegen ♦ *n* (*ECON*) das Pfund Sterling; **a pound** ~ ein Pfund Sterling

stern [stɜːn] *adj* streng ♦ *n* Heck *nt*, Achterschiff *nt*

stew [stjuː] *n* Eintopf *m* ♦ *vt, vi* schmoren

steward ['stjuːəd] *n* Steward *m*; ~**ess** *n* Stewardess *f*

stick [stik] (*pt, pp* **stuck**) *n* Stock *m*; (*of chalk etc*) Stück *nt* ♦ *vt* (*stab*) stechen; (*fix*) stecken; (*put*) stellen; (*gum*) (an)kleben; (*inf: tolerate*) vertragen ♦ *vi* (*stop*) steckenbleiben; (*get stuck*) klemmen; (*hold fast*) kleben, haften; ~ **out** *vi* (*project*) hervorstehen; ~ **up** *vi* (*project*) in die Höhe stehen; ~ **up for** *vt fus* (*defend*) eintreten für; ~**er** *n* Aufkleber *m*; ~**ing plaster** *n* Heftpflaster *nt*

stickler ['stiklə*] *n*: ~ (**for**) Pedant *m* (in +*acc*)

stick-up ['stikʌp] (*inf*) *n* (Raub)überfall *m*

sticky ['stiki] *adj* klebrig; (*atmosphere*) stickig

stiff [stif] *adj* steif; (*difficult*) hart; (*paste*) dick; (*drink*) stark; ~**en** *vt* versteifen, (ver)stärken ♦ *vi* sich versteifen; ~**ness** *n* Steifheit *f*

stifle ['staifl] *vt* unterdrücken

stifling ['staifliŋ] *adj* drückend

stigma ['stigmə] (*pl BOT, MED, REL* ~**ta**; *fig* ~**s**) *n* Stigma *nt*

stigmata ['stigmətə] *npl of* **stigma**

stile [stail] *n* Steige *f*

stiletto [sti'letəʊ] (*BRIT*) *n* (*also*: ~ **heel**) Pfennigabsatz *m*

still [stil] *adj* still ♦ *adv* (immer) noch; (*anyhow*) immerhin; ~**born** *adj* totgeboren; ~ **life** *n* Stilleben *nt*

stilt [stilt] *n* Stelze *f*

stilted ['stiltid] *adj* gestelzt

stimulate ['stimjuleit] *vt* anregen, stimulieren

stimuli ['stimjulai] *npl of* **stimulus**

stimulus ['stimjuləs] (*pl* -**li**) *n* Anregung *f*, Reiz *m*

sting [stiŋ] (*pt, pp* **stung**) *n* Stich *m*; (*organ*) Stachel *m* ♦ *vi* stechen; (*on skin*) brennen ♦ *vt* stechen

stingy ['stindʒi] *adj* geizig, knauserig

stink [stiŋk] (*pt* **stank**, *pp* **stunk**) *n* Gestank *m* ♦ *vi* stinken; ~**ing** *adj* (*fig*) widerlich

stint [stint] *n* Pensum *nt*; (*period*) Betätigung *f* ♦ *vi* knausern; **to do one's** ~ seine Arbeit tun; (*share*) seinen Teil beitragen

stipulate ['stipjuleit] *vt* festsetzen

stir [stɜː*] *n* Bewegung *f*; (*COOK*) Rühren *nt*; (*sensation*) Aufsehen *nt* ♦ *vt* (um)rühren ♦ *vi* sich rühren; ~ **up** *vt* (*mob*) aufhetzen; (*mixture*) umrühren; (*dust*) aufwirbeln

stirrup ['stirəp] *n* Steigbügel *m*

stitch [stitʃ] *n* (*with needle*) Stich *m*; (*MED*) Faden *m*; (*of knitting*) Masche *f*; (*pain*) Stich *m* ♦ *vt* nähen

stoat [stəʊt] *n* Wiesel *nt*

stock [stɔk] *n* Vorrat *m*; (*COMM*) (Waren)lager *nt*; (*live-*~) Vieh *nt*; (*COOK*) Brühe *f*; (*FIN*) Grundkapital *nt* ♦ *adj* stets vorrätig; (*standard*) Normal- ♦ *vt* (*in shop*) führen; ~**s** *npl* (*FIN*) Aktien *pl*; **in/out of** ~ vorrätig/nicht vorrätig; **to take** ~ **of** Inventur machen von; (*fig*) Bilanz ziehen aus; ~**s and shares** Effekten *pl*; ~ **up** *vi*: **to** ~ **up (with)** Reserven anlegen (von)

stockbroker ['stɔkbrəʊkə*] *n*

Börsenmakler m
stock cube n Brühwürfel m
stock exchange n Börse f
stocking ['stɒkɪŋ] n Strumpf m
stockist ['stɒkɪst] n Händler m
stock: ~ **market** n Börse f; ~ **phrase** n
Standardsatz m; ~**pile** ['stɒkpaɪl] n Vorrat m ♦ vt aufstapeln, **taking**
['stɒkteɪkɪŋ] (BRIT) n (COMM) Inventur f,
Bestandsaufnahme f
stocky ['stɒkɪ] adj untersetzt
stodgy ['stɒdʒɪ] adj pampig; (fig)
trocken
stoke [stəʊk] vt schüren
stole [stəʊl] pt of steal ♦ n Stola f
stolen ['stəʊlən] pp of steal
stolid ['stɒlɪd] adj stur
stomach ['stʌmək] n Bauch m, Magen
m ♦ vt vertragen; ~**ache** n Magen- or
Bauchschmerzen pl
stone [stəʊn] n Stein m; (BRIT: weight)
Gewichtseinheit f = 6.35 kg ♦ vt (olive)
entkernen; (kill) steinigen; ~**cold** adj
eiskalt; ~**deaf** adj stocktaub; ~**work** n
Mauerwerk nt
stony ['stəʊnɪ] adj steinig
stood [stʊd] pt, pp of stand
stool [stuːl] n Hocker m
stoop [stuːp] vi sich bücken
stop [stɒp] n Halt m; (bus ~) Haltestelle f; (punctuation) Punkt m ♦ vt anhalten; (bring to an end) aufhören
(mit), sein lassen ♦ vi aufhören;
(clock) stehenbleiben; (remain)
bleiben; to ~ **doing sth** aufhören, etw zu
tun; to ~ **dead** innehalten; ~ **off** vi
kurz haltmachen; ~ **up** vt (hole) zustopfen, verstopfen; ~**gap** n Notlösung
f; ~**lights** npl (AUT) Bremslichter pl;
~**over** n (on journey) Zwischenaufenthalt m
stoppage ['stɒpɪdʒ] n (An)halten nt;
(traffic) Verkehrsstockung f; (strike)
Arbeitseinstellung f
stopper ['stɒpə*] n Propfen m, Stöpsel
m
stop press n letzte Meldung f
stopwatch ['stɒpwɒtʃ] n Stoppuhr f
storage ['stɔːrɪdʒ] n Lagerung f; ~
heater n (Nachtstrom)speicherofen m

store [stɔː*] n Vorrat m; (place) Lager
nt, Warenhaus nt; (BRIT: large shop)
Kaufhaus nt; (US) Laden m ♦ vt
lagern; ~**s** npl (supplies) Vorräte pl; ~
up vt sich eindecken mit; ~**room** n
Lagerraum m, Vorratsraum m
storey ['stɔːrɪ] (US story) n Stock m
stork [stɔːk] n Storch m
storm [stɔːm] n (also fig) Sturm m ♦ vt,
vi stürmen; ~**y** adj stürmisch
story ['stɔːrɪ] n Geschichte f; (lie)
Märchen nt; (US) = storey; ~**book** n
Geschichtenbuch nt; ~**teller** n Geschichtenerzähler m
stout [staʊt] adj (bold) tapfer; (fat)
beleibt ♦ n Starkbier nt; (also: sweet
~) ≈ Malzbier nt
stove [stəʊv] n (Koch)herd m; (for
heating) Ofen m
stow [stəʊ] vt verstauen; ~**away** n
blinde(r) Passagier m
straddle ['strædl] vt (horse, fence)
rittlings sitzen auf +dat; (fig)
überbrücken
straggle ['strægl] vi (branches etc) wuchern; (people) nachhinken; ~**r** n
Nachzügler m; **straggling** adj (hair)
zottig; **straggly** adj (hair) zottig
straight [streɪt] adj gerade; (honest)
offen, ehrlich; (drink) pur ♦ adv
(direct) direkt, geradewegs; to **put** or
get sth ~ etw in Ordnung bringen;
~**away** sofort; ~ **off** sofort; ~**en** vt
(also: ~en out) gerade machen; (fig)
klarstellen; ~**faced** adv ohne die
Miene zu verziehen ♦ adj: to be ~**faced**
keine Miene verziehen; ~**forward** adj
einfach, unkompliziert
strain [streɪn] n Belastung f; (streak,
trace) Zug m; (of music) Fetzen m ♦
vt überanstrengen; (stretch) anspannen; (muscle) zerren; (filter)
(durch)seihen ♦ vi sich anstrengen;
~**ed** adj (laugh) gezwungen;
(relations) gespannt; ~**er** n Sieb nt
strait [streɪt] n Straße f, Meerenge f;
~**jacket** n Zwangsjacke f; ~**laced** adj
engherzig, streng
strand [strænd] n (of hair) Strähne f;
(also fig) Faden m; ~**ed** adj (also fig)

gestrandet

strange [streɪndʒ] *adj* fremd; (*unusual*) seltsam; **~r** *n* Fremde(r) *mf*

strangle ['stræŋgl] *vt* erwürgen; **~hold** *n* (*fig*) Umklammerung *f*

strap [stræp] *n* Riemen *m*; (*on clothes*) Träger *m* ♦ *vt* (*fasten*) festschnallen

strapping ['stræpɪŋ] *adj* stramm

strata ['strɑːtə] *npl of* **stratum**

stratagem ['strætɪdʒəm] *n* (Kriegs)list *f*

strategic [strə'tiːdʒɪk] *adj* strategisch

strategy ['strætədʒɪ] *n* (*fig*) Strategie *f*

stratum ['strɑːtəm] (*pl* **-ta**) *n* Schicht *f*

straw [strɔː] *n* Stroh *nt*; (*single stalk, drinking* ~) Strohhalm *m*; **that's the last** ~! das ist der Gipfel!

strawberry ['strɔːbərɪ] *n* Erdbeere *f*

stray [streɪ] *adj* (*animal*) verirrt; (*thought*) zufällig ♦ *vi* herumstreunen

streak ['striːk] *n* Streifen *m*; (*in character*) Einschlag *m*; (*in hair*) Strähne *f* ♦ *vt* streifen ♦ *vi* zucken; (*move quickly*) flitzen; **~ of bad luck** Pechsträhne *f*; **~y** *adj* gestreift; (*bacon*) durchwachsen

stream [striːm] *n* (*brook*) Bach *m*; (*fig*) Strom *m* ♦ *vt* (*SCH*) in (Leistungs)gruppen einteilen ♦ *vi* strömen; **to ~ in/out** (*people*) hinein-/hinausströmen

streamer ['striːmə*] *n* (*flag*) Wimpel *m*; (*of paper*) Luftschlange *f*

streamlined ['striːmlaɪnd] *adj* stromlinienförmig; (*effective*) rationell

street [striːt] *n* Straße *f* ♦ *adj* Straßen-; **~car** (*US*) *n* Straßenbahn *f*; ~ **lamp** *n* Straßenlaterne *f*; ~ **plan** *n* Stadtplan *m*; **~wise** (*inf*) *adj*: **to be ~wise** wissen, wo es lang geht

strength [streŋθ] *n* (*also fig*) Stärke *f*; Kraft *f*; **~en** *vt* (ver)stärken

strenuous ['strenjʊəs] *adj* anstrengend

stress [stres] *n* Druck *m*; (*mental*) Streß *m*; (*GRAM*) Betonung *f* ♦ *vt* betonen

stretch [stretʃ] *n* Strecke *f* ♦ *vt* ausdehnen, strecken ♦ *vi* sich erstrecken; (*person*) sich strecken; ~ **out** *vi* sich ausstrecken ♦ *vt* ausstrecken

stretcher ['stretʃə*] *n* Tragbahre *f*

strewn [struːn] *adj*: ~ **with** übersät mit

stricken ['strɪkən] *adj* (*person*) ergriffen; (*city, country*) heimgesucht; ~ **with** (*arthritis, disease*) leidend unter +*dat*

strict [strɪkt] *adj* (*exact*) genau; (*severe*) streng; **~ly** *adv* streng, genau

stridden ['strɪdn] *pp of* **stride**

stride [straɪd] (*pt* **strode**, *pp* **stridden**) *n* lange(r) Schritt *m* ♦ *vi* schreiten

strident ['straɪdənt] *adj* schneidend, durchdringend

strife [straɪf] *n* Streit *m*

strike [straɪk] (*pt, pp* **struck**) *n* Streik *m*; (*attack*) Schlag *m* ♦ *vt* (*hit*) schlagen; (*collide*) stoßen gegen; (*come to mind*) einfallen +*dat*; (*find*) finden ♦ *vi* (*stop work*) streiken; (*attack*) zuschlagen; (*clock*) schlagen; **on** ~ (*workers*) im Streik; **to** ~ **a match** ein Streichholz anzünden; ~ **down** *vt* (*lay low*) niederschlagen; ~ **out** *vt* (*cross out*) ausstreichen; ~ **up** *vt* (*music*) anstimmen; (*friendship*) schließen; **~r** *n* Streikende(r) *mf*

striking ['straɪkɪŋ] *adj* auffallend

string [strɪŋ] (*pt, pp* **strung**) *n* Schnur *f*; (*row*) Reihe *f*; (*MUS*) Saite *f* ♦ *vt*: **to** ~ **together** aneinanderreihen ♦ *vi*: **to** ~ **out** (sich) verteilen; **the ~s** *npl* (*MUS*) die Streichinstrumente *pl*; **to pull ~s** (*fig*) Fäden ziehen; ~ **bean** *n* grüne Bohne *f*; **~(ed) instrument** *n* (*MUS*) Saiteninstrument *nt*

stringent ['strɪndʒənt] *adj* streng

strip [strɪp] *n* Streifen *m* ♦ *vt* (*uncover*) abstreifen, abziehen; (*clothes*) ausziehen; (*TECH*) auseinandernehmen ♦ *vi* (*undress*) sich ausziehen; ~ **cartoon** *n* Bildserie *f*

stripe [straɪp] *n* Streifen *m*; **~d** *adj* gestreift

strip lighting *n* Neonlicht *nt*

stripper ['strɪpə*] *n* Stripteasetänzerin *f*

strive [straɪv] (*pt* **strove**, *pp* **striven**) *vi*: **to** ~ (**for**) streben (nach); **striven** ['strɪvn] *pp of* **strive**

strode [strəud] *pt of* **stride**

stroke [strəuk] *n* Schlag *m*; (*SWIMMING,*

ROWING) Stoß *m*; (*TECH*) Hub *m*; (*MED*) Schlaganfall *m*; (*caress*) Streicheln *nt* ♦ *vt* streicheln; **at a ~** mit einem Schlag

stroll [strəʊl] *n* Spaziergang *m* ♦ *vi* schlendern; **~er** (*US*) *n* (*pushchair*) Sportwagen *m*

strong [strɒŋ] *adj* stark; (*firm*) fest; **they are 50 ~** sie sind 50 Mann stark; **~box** *n* Kassette *f*; **~hold** *n* Hochburg *f*; **~ly** *adv* stark; **~room** *n* Tresor *m*

strove [strəʊv] *pt of* strive

struck [strʌk] *pt, pp of* strike

structure ['strʌktʃə*] *n* Struktur *f*, Aufbau *m*; (*building*) Bau *m*

struggle ['strʌgl] *n* Kampf *m* ♦ *vi* (*fight*) kämpfen

strum [strʌm] *vt* (*guitar*) klimpern auf +*dat*

strung [strʌŋ] *pt, pp of* string

strut [strʌt] *n* Strebe *f*, Stütze *f* ♦ *vi* stolzieren

stub [stʌb] *n* Stummel *m*; (*of cigarette*) Kippe *f* ♦ *vt*: **to ~ one's toe** sich *dat* den Zeh anstoßen; **~ out** *vt* ausdrücken

stubble ['stʌbl] *n* Stoppel *f*

stubborn ['stʌbən] *adj* hartnäckig

stucco ['stʌkəʊ] *n* Stuck *m*

stuck [stʌk] *pt, pp of* stick ♦ *adj* (*jammed*) klemmend; **~-up** *adj* hochnäsig

stud [stʌd] *n* (*button*) Kragenknopf *m*; (*place*) Gestüt *n* ♦ *vt* (*fig*): **~ded with** übersät mit

student ['stju:dənt] *n* Student(in) *m(f)*; (*US*) Student(in) *m(f)*, Schüler(in) *m(f)* ♦ *adj* Studenten-; **~ driver** (*US*) *n* Fahrschüler(in) *m(f)*

studio ['stju:dɪəʊ] *n* Studio *nt*; (*for artist*) Atelier *nt*; **~ apartment** (*US*) *n* Appartement *nt*; **~ flat** *n* Appartement *nt*

studious ['stju:dɪəs] *adj* lernbegierig

study ['stʌdɪ] *n* Studium *nt*; (*investigation*) Studium *nt*, Untersuchung *f*; (*room*) Arbeitszimmer *nt*; (*essay etc*) Studie *f* ♦ *vt* studieren; (*face*) erforschen; (*evidence*) prüfen ♦ *vi* studieren

stuff [stʌf] *n* Stoff *m*; (*inf*) Zeug *nt* ♦ *vt* stopfen, füllen; (*animal*) ausstopfen;

~ing *n* Füllung *f*; **~y** *adj* (*room*) schwül; (*person*) spießig

stumble ['stʌmbl] *vi* stolpern; **to ~ across** (*fig*) zufällig stoßen auf +*acc*

stumbling block ['stʌmblɪŋ-] *n* Hindernis *nt*

stump [stʌmp] *n* Stumpf *m* ♦ *vt* umwerfen

stun [stʌn] *vt* betäuben; (*shock*) niederschmettern

stung [stʌŋ] *pt, pp of* sting

stunk [stʌŋk] *pp of* stink

stunning ['stʌnɪŋ] *adj* betäubend; (*news*) überwältigend, umwerfend

stunt [stʌnt] *n* Kunststück *nt*, Trick *m*

stunted *adj* verkümmert

stuntman (*irreg*) *n* Stuntman *m*

stupefy ['stju:pɪfaɪ] *vt* betäuben; (*by news*) bestürzen

stupendous [stju'pendəs] *adj* erstaunlich, enorm

stupid ['stju:pɪd] *adj* dumm; **~ity** [stju:'pɪdɪtɪ] *n* Dummheit *f*

stupor ['stju:pə*] *n* Betäubung *f*

sturdy ['stɜ:dɪ] *adj* kräftig, robust

stutter ['stʌtə*] *n* Stottern *nt* ♦ *vi* stottern

sty [staɪ] *n* Schweinestall *m*

stye [staɪ] *n* Gerstenkorn *nt*

style [staɪl] *n* Stil *m*; (*fashion*) Mode *f*

stylish ['staɪlɪʃ] *adj* modisch

stylist ['staɪlɪst] *n* (*hair ~*) Friseur *m*, Friseuse *f*

stylus ['staɪləs] *n* (Grammophon)nadel *f*

suave [swɑ:v] *adj* zuvorkommend

sub... *prefix* Unter...; **~conscious** *adj* unterbewußt ♦ *n*: **the ~conscious** das Unterbewußte; **~contract** [sʌbkən'trækt] *vt* (vertraglich) untervermitteln; **~divide** *vt* unterteilen

subdue [səb'dju:] *vt* unterwerfen; **~d** *adj* (*lighting*) gedämpft; (*person*) still

subject [*n* 'sʌbdʒɪkt, *vb* səb'dʒekt] *n* (*of kingdom*) Untertan *m*; (*citizen*) Staatsangehörige(r) *mf*; (*topic*) Thema *nt*; (*SCH*) Fach *nt*; (*GRAM*) Subjekt *nt* ♦ *adj*: **to be ~ to** unterworfen sein +*dat*; (*exposed*) ausgesetzt sein +*dat* ♦ *vt* (*subdue*) unterwerfen; (*expose*) aussetzen; **~ive** [səb'dʒektɪv] *adj* subjektiv;

~ **matter** n Thema nt
subjugate ['sʌbdʒʊɡeɪt] vt unterjochen
subjunctive [səb'dʒʌŋktɪv] adj Konjunktiv- ♦ n Konjunktiv m
sublet ['sʌb'let] (irreg: like **let**) vt untervermieten
sublime [sə'blaɪm] adj erhaben
submachine gun ['sʌbmə'ʃiːn-] n Maschinenpistole f
submarine [sʌbmə'riːn] n Unterseeboot nt, U-Boot nt
submerge [səb'mɜːdʒ] vt untertauchen; (flood) überschwemmen ♦ vi untertauchen
submission [səb'mɪʃən] n (obedience) Gehorsam m; (claim) Behauptung f; (of plan) Unterbreitung f
submissive [səb'mɪsɪv] adj demütig, unterwürfig (pej)
submit [səb'mɪt] vt behaupten; (plan) unterbreiten ♦ vi (give in) sich ergeben
subnormal ['sʌb'nɔːməl] adj minderbegabt
subordinate [sə'bɔːdɪnət] adj untergeordnet ♦ n Untergebene(r) mf
subpoena [sə'piːnə] n Vorladung f ♦ vt vorladen
subscribe [səb'skraɪb] vi: **to ~ to** (view etc) unterstützen; (newspaper) abonnieren; ~r n (to periodical) Abonnent m; (TEL) Telefonteilnehmer m
subscription [səb'skrɪpʃən] n Abonnement nt; (money subscribed) (Mitglieds)beitrag m
subsequent ['sʌbsɪkwənt] adj folgend, später; ~**ly** adv später
subside [səb'saɪd] vi sich senken; ~**nce** [sʌb'saɪdəns] n Senkung f
subsidiary [səb'sɪdɪərɪ] adj Neben- ♦ n (company) Tochtergesellschaft f
subsidize ['sʌbsɪdaɪz] vt subventionieren
subsidy ['sʌbsɪdɪ] n Subvention f
subsistence [səb'sɪstəns] n Unterhalt m
substance ['sʌbstəns] n Substanz f
substantial [səb'stænʃəl] adj (strong) fest, kräftig; (important) wesentlich; ~**ly** adv erheblich
substantiate [səb'stænʃɪeɪt] vt begründen, belegen
substitute ['sʌbstɪtjuːt] n Ersatz m ♦ vt ersetzen
substitution [sʌbstɪ'tjuːʃən] n Ersetzung f
subterfuge ['sʌbtəfjuːdʒ] n Vorwand m; (trick) Trick m
subterranean [sʌbtə'reɪnɪən] adj unterirdisch
subtitle ['sʌbtaɪtl] n Untertitel m
subtle ['sʌtl] adj fein; ~**ty** n Feinheit f
subtotal [sʌb'təʊtl] n Zwischensumme f
subtract [səb'trækt] vt abziehen; ~**ion** [səb'trækʃən] n Abziehen nt, Subtraktion f
suburb ['sʌbɜːb] n Vorort m; **the ~s** die Außenbezirke pl; ~**an** [sə'bɜːbən] adj Vorort(s)-, Stadtrand-; ~**ia** [sə'bɜːbɪə] n Vorstadt f
subversive [səb'vɜːsɪv] adj subversiv
subway ['sʌbweɪ] n (US) U-Bahn f; (BRIT) Unterführung f
succeed [sək'siːd] vi (person) erfolgreich sein, Erfolg haben; (plan etc also) gelingen ♦ vt (nach)folgen +dat; **he ~ed in doing it** es gelang ihm, es zu tun; ~**ing** adj (nach)folgend
success [sək'ses] n Erfolg m; **to be ~ful (in doing sth)** Erfolg haben (bei etw); ~**ful** adj erfolgreich; ~**fully** adv erfolgreich
succession [sək'seʃən] n (Aufeinander)folge f; (to throne) Nachfolge f
successive [sək'sesɪv] adj aufeinanderfolgend
successor [sək'sesə*] n Nachfolger(in) m(f)
succinct [sək'sɪŋkt] adj knapp
succulent ['sʌkjʊlənt] adj saftig
succumb [sə'kʌm] vi: **to ~ (to)** erliegen (+dat); (yield) nachgeben (+dat)
such [sʌtʃ] adj solche(r, s); ~ **a book** so ein Buch; ~ **books** solche Bücher; ~ **courage** so ein Mut; ~ **a long trip** so eine lange Reise; ~ **a lot of** so viel(e); ~ **as** wie; **a noise** ~ **as** to ein derartiger Lärm, daß; **as** ~ an sich; ~**-and-~ a time/town** die und die Zeit/Stadt
suck [sʌk] vt saugen; (ice cream etc) lutschen; ~**er** (inf) n Idiot m
suction ['sʌkʃən] n Saugkraft f
sudden ['sʌdn] adj plötzlich; **all of a ~**

auf einmal; ~**ly** *adv* plötzlich

suds [sʌdz] *npl* Seifenlauge *f*; (*lather*) Seifenschaum *m*

sue [suː] *vt* verklagen

suede [sweɪd] *n* Wildleder *nt*

suet [suɪt] *n* Nierenfett *nt*

Suez ['suːɪz] *n*: the ~ Canal der Suezkanal

suffer ['sʌfə*] *vt* (cr)leiden ♦ *vi* leiden; ~**er** *n* Leidende(r) *mf*; ~**ing** *n* Leiden *nt*

suffice [sə'faɪs] *vi* genügen

sufficient [sə'fɪʃənt] *adj* ausreichend; ~**ly** *adv* ausreichend

suffix ['sʌfɪks] *n* Nachsilbe *f*

suffocate ['sʌfəkeɪt] *vt, vi* ersticken

suffocation [sʌfə'keɪʃən] *n* Ersticken *nt*

suffrage ['sʌfrɪdʒ] *n* Wahlrecht *nt*

suffused [sə'fjuːzd] *adj*: to be ~ with sth von etw erfüllt sein

sugar ['ʃugə*] *n* Zucker *m* ♦ *vt* zuckern; ~ **beet** *n* Zuckerrübe *f*; ~ **cane** *n* Zuckerrohr *nt*; ~**y** *adj* süß

suggest [sə'dʒest] *vt* vorschlagen; (*show*) schließen lassen auf +*acc*; ~**ion** [sə'dʒestʃən] *n* Vorschlag *m*; ~**ive** *adj* anregend; (*indecent*) zweideutig

suicide ['suɪsaɪd] *n* Selbstmord *m*; to commit ~ Selbstmord begehen

suit [suːt] *n* Anzug *m*; (*CARDS*) Farbe *f* ♦ *vt* passen +*dat*; (*clothes*) stehen +*dat*; **well** ~**ed** (*well matched: couple*) gut zusammenpassend; ~**able** *adj* geeignet, passend; ~**ably** *adv* passend, angemessen

suitcase ['suːtkeɪs] *n* (Hand)koffer *m*

suite [swiːt] *n* (*of rooms*) Zimmerflucht *f*; (*of furniture*) Einrichtung *f*; (*MUS*) Suite *f*

suitor ['suːtə*] *n* (*JUR*) Kläger(in) *m(f)*

sulfur ['sʌlfə*] (*US*) *n* = sulphur

sulk [sʌlk] *vi* schmollen; ~**y** *adj* schmollend

sullen ['sʌlən] *adj* mürrisch

sulphur ['sʌlfə*] (*US* sulfur) *n* Schwefel *m*

sultana [sʌl'tɑːnə] *n* (*fruit*) Sultanine *f*

sultry ['sʌltrɪ] *adj* schwül

sum [sʌm] *n* Summe *f*; (*money*) Betrag *m*, Summe *f*; (*arithmetic*) Rechen-

aufgabe *f*; ~ **up** *vt, vi* zusammenfassen

summarize ['sʌməraɪz] *vt* kurz zusammenfassen

summary ['sʌmərɪ] *n* Zusammenfassung *f* ♦ *adj* (*justice*) kurzerhand erteilt

summer ['sʌmə*] *n* Sommer *m* ♦ *adj* Sommer-; ~**house** *n* (*in garden*) Gartenhaus *nt*; ~**time** *n* Sommerzeit *f*

summit ['sʌmɪt] *n* Gipfel *m*; ~ (**conference**) *n* Gipfelkonferenz *f*

summon ['sʌmən] *vt* herbeirufen; (*JUR*) vorladen; (*gather up*) aufbringen; ~**s** (*JUR*) *n* Vorladung *f* ♦ *vt* vorladen

sump [sʌmp] (*BRIT*) *n* (*AUT*) Ölwanne *f*

sumptuous ['sʌmptjuəs] *adj* prächtig

sun [sʌn] *n* Sonne *f*; ~**bathe** *vi* sich sonnen; ~**burn** *n* Sonnenbrand *m*

Sunday ['sʌndeɪ] *n* Sonntag *m*; ~ **school** *n* Sonntagsschule *f*

sundial ['sʌndaɪəl] *n* Sonnenuhr *f*

sundown ['sʌndaʊn] *n* Sonnenuntergang *m*

sundry ['sʌndrɪ] *adj* verschieden; **all and ~** alle; **sundries** *npl* (*miscellaneous items*) Verschiedene(s) *nt*

sunflower ['sʌnflaʊə*] *n* Sonnenblume *f*

sung [sʌŋ] *pp of* sing

sunglasses ['sʌnglɑːsɪz] *npl* Sonnenbrille *f*

sunk [sʌŋk] *pp of* sink

sun: ~**light** ['sʌnlaɪt] *n* Sonnenlicht *nt*; ~**lit** ['sʌnlɪt] *adj* sonnenbeschienen; ~**ny** ['sʌnɪ] *adj* sonnig; ~**rise** ['sʌnraɪz] *n* Sonnenaufgang *m*; ~**set** ['sʌnset] *n* Sonnenuntergang *m*; ~**shade** ['sʌnʃeɪd] *n* Sonnenschirm *m*; ~**shine** ['sʌnʃaɪn] *n* Sonnenschein *m*; ~**stroke** ['sʌnstrəʊk] *n* Hitzschlag *m*; ~**tan** ['sʌntæn] *n* (Sonnen)bräune *f*; ~**tan oil** *n* Sonnenöl *nt*

super ['suːpə*] (*inf*) *adj* prima, klasse

superannuation ['suːpərænjʊ'eɪʃən] *n* Pension *f*

superb [suː'pɜːb] *adj* ausgezeichnet, hervorragend

supercilious [suːpə'sɪlɪəs] *adj* herablassend

superficial [suːpə'fɪʃəl] *adj* oberflächlich

superfluous [sʊ'pɜːfluəs] *adj* überflüssig

superhuman [suːpə'hjuːmən] *adj*

(effort) übermenschlich
superimpose ['suːpərɪm'pəuz] vt übereinanderlegen
superintendent [suːpərɪn'tendənt] n Polizeichef m
superior [suˈpɪərɪə*] adj überlegen; (better) besser ♦ n Vorgesetzte(r) mf; ~**ity** [suˈpɪərɪˈɒrɪtɪ] n Überlegenheit f
superlative [suːˈpɜːlətɪv] adj überragend
superman ['suːpəmæn] (irreg) n Übermensch m
supermarket ['suːpəmɑːkɪt] n Supermarkt m
supernatural [suːpəˈnætʃərəl] adj übernatürlich
superpower ['suːpəpauə*] n Weltmacht f
supersede [suːpəˈsiːd] vt ersetzen
supersonic ['suːpəˈsɒnɪk] adj Überschall-
superstition [suːpəˈstɪʃən] n Aberglaube m
superstitious [suːpəˈstɪʃəs] adj abergläubisch
supervise ['suːpəvaɪz] vt beaufsichtigen, kontrollieren
supervision [suːpəˈvɪʒən] n Aufsicht f
supervisor ['suːpəvaɪzə*] n Aufsichtsperson f; ~**y** adj Aufsichts-
supine ['suːpaɪn] adj auf dem Rücken liegend
supper ['sʌpə*] n Abendessen nt
supplant [səˈplɑːnt] vt (person, thing) ersetzen
supple ['sʌpl] adj geschmeidig
supplement [n 'sʌplɪmənt, vb sʌplɪˈment] n Ergänzung f; (in book) Nachtrag m ♦ vt ergänzen; ~**ary** [sʌplɪˈmentərɪ] adj ergänzend
supplier [səˈplaɪə*] n Lieferant m
supplies [səˈplaɪz] npl (food) Vorräte pl; (MIL) Nachschub m
supply [səˈplaɪ] vt liefern ♦ n Vorrat m; (supplying) Lieferung f ♦ adj (teacher etc) Aushilfs-; see also supplies
support [səˈpɔːt] n Unterstützung f; (TECH) Stütze f ♦ vt (hold up) stützen, tragen; (provide for) ernähren; (be in favour of) unterstützen; ~**er** n Anhänger(in) m(f)

suppose [səˈpəuz] vt, vi annehmen; to be ~**d** to do sth etw tun sollen; ~**dly** [səˈpəuzɪdlɪ] adv angeblich
supposing [səˈpəuzɪŋ] conj angenommen
supposition [sʌpəˈzɪʃən] n Voraussetzung f
suppress [səˈpres] vt unterdrücken; ~**ion** [səˈpreʃən] n Unterdrückung f
supremacy [suˈpremәsɪ] n Vorherrschaft f, Oberhoheit f
supreme [suˈpriːm] adj oberste(r, s), höchste(r, s)
surcharge ['sɜːtʃɑːdʒ] n Zuschlag m
sure [ʃuə*] adj sicher, gewiß; ~! (of course) klar!; to make ~ of sth/that sich einer Sache gen vergewissern/vergewissern, daß; ~ enough (with past) tatsächlich; (with future) ganz bestimmt; ~**-footed** adj sicher (auf den Füßen); ~**ly** adv (certainly) sicherlich, gewiß; ~**ly** it's wrong das ist doch wohl falsch
surety ['ʃuərətɪ] n Sicherheit f; (person) Bürge m
surf [sɜːf] n Brandung f
surface ['sɜːfɪs] n Oberfläche f ♦ vt (roadway) teeren ♦ vi auftauchen; ~ **mail** n gewöhnliche Post f
surfboard ['sɜːfbɔːd] n Wellenreiterbrett nt
surfeit ['sɜːfɪt] n Übermaß nt
surfing ['sɜːfɪŋ] n Wellenreiten nt
surge [sɜːdʒ] n Woge f ♦ vi wogen
surgeon ['sɜːdʒən] n Chirurg(in) m(f)
surgery ['sɜːdʒərɪ] n (BRIT: place) Praxis f; (: time) Sprechstunde f; (treatment) Operation f; to undergo ~ operiert werden; ~ **hours** (BRIT) npl Sprechstunden pl
surgical ['sɜːdʒɪkəl] adj chirurgisch; ~ **spirit** (BRIT) n Wundbenzin nt
surly ['sɜːlɪ] adj verdrießlich, grob
surmount [sɜːˈmaunt] vt überwinden
surname ['sɜːneɪm] n Zuname m
surpass [sɜːˈpɑːs] vt übertreffen
surplus ['sɜːpləs] n Überschuß m ♦ adj überschüssig, Über(schuß)-
surprise [səˈpraɪz] n Überraschung f ♦ vt überraschen

surprising [sə'praɪzɪŋ] *adj* überra-
schend; ~**ly** *adv* überraschend(erweise)
surrender [sə'rendə*] *n* Kapitulation *f* ♦
vi sich ergeben
surreptitious [sʌrəp'tɪʃəs] *adj* verstohlen
surrogate ['sʌrəgɪt] *n* Ersatz *m*; ~
mother *n* Leihmutter *f*
surround [sə'raʊnd] *vt* umgeben; ~**ing**
adj (*countryside*) umliegend; ~**ings** *npl*
Umgebung *f*; (*environment*) Umwelt *f*
surveillance [sɜː'veɪləns] *n*
Überwachung *f*
survey [*n* 'sɜːveɪ, *vb* sɜː'veɪ] *n* Übersicht *f*
♦ *vt* überblicken; (*land*) vermessen;
~**or** [sə'veɪə*] *n* Land(ver)messer(in)
m(f)
survival [sə'vaɪvəl] *n* Überleben *nt*
survive [sə'vaɪv] *vt, vi* überleben
survivor [sə'vaɪvə*] *n* Überlebende(r)
mf
susceptible [sə'septəbl] *adj*: ~ (**to**)
empfindlich (gegen); (*charms etc*)
empfänglich (für)
suspect [*n, adj* 'sʌspekt, *vb* səs'pekt] *n*
Verdächtige(r) *mf* ♦ *adj* verdächtig ♦
vt verdächtigen; (*think*) vermuten
suspend [səs'pend] *vt* verschieben;
(*from work*) suspendieren; (*hang up*)
aufhängen; (*SPORT*) sperren; ~**ed**
sentence *n* (*JUR*) zur Bewährung aus-
gesetzte Strafe; ~**er belt** *n*
Strumpf(halter)gürtel *m*; ~**ers** *npl*
(*BRIT*) Strumpfhalter *m*; (: *men's*)
Sockenhalter *m*; (*US*) Hosenträger *m*
suspense [səs'pens] *n* Spannung *f*
suspension [səs'penʃən] *n* (*from work*)
Suspendierung *f*; (*SPORT*) Sperrung *f*;
(*AUT*) Federung *f*; ~ **bridge** *n*
Hängebrücke *f*
suspicion [səs'pɪʃən] *n* Mißtrauen *nt*;
Verdacht *m*
suspicious [səs'pɪʃəs] *adj* mißtrauisch;
(*causing suspicion*) verdächtig
sustain [səs'teɪn] *vt* (*maintain*) aufrechterhalten; (*confirm*) bestätigen; (*JUR*)
anerkennen; (*injury*) davontragen; ~**ed**
adj (*effort*) anhaltend
sustenance ['sʌstɪnəns] *n* Nahrung *f*
swab [swɒb] *n* (*MED*) Tupfer *m*

swagger ['swægə*] *vi* stolzieren
swallow ['swɒləʊ] *n* (*bird*) Schwalbe *f*;
(*of food etc*) Schluck *m* ♦ *vt*
(ver)schlucken; ~ **up** *vt* verschlingen
swam [swæm] *pt of* swim
swamp [swɒmp] *n* Sumpf *m* ♦ *vt*
überschwemmen
swan [swɒn] *n* Schwan *m*
swap [swɒp] *n* Tausch *m* ♦ *vt*: to ~ sth
(**for** sth) etw (gegen etw) tauschen *or*
eintauschen
swarm [swɔːm] *n* Schwarm *m* ♦ *vi*: to ~
or be ~**ing with** wimmeln von
swarthy ['swɔːðɪ] *adj* dunkel, braun
swastika ['swɒstɪkə] *n* Hakenkreuz *nt*
swat [swɒt] *vt* totschlagen
sway [sweɪ] *vi* schwanken; (*branches*)
schaukeln, sich wiegen ♦ *vt* schwenken;
(*influence*) beeinflussen
swear [sweə*] (*pt* swore, *pp* sworn) *vi*
(*promise*) schwören; (*curse*) fluchen;
to ~ to sth schwören auf etw *acc*;
~**word** *n* Fluch *m*
sweat [swet] *n* Schweiß *m* ♦ *vi*
schwitzen
sweater ['swetə*] *n* Pullover *m*
sweatshirt ['swetʃɜːt] *n* Sweatshirt *nt*
sweaty ['swetɪ] *adj* verschwitzt
Swede [swiːd] *n* Schwede *m*, Schwedin *f*
swede [swiːd] (*BRIT*) *n* Steckrübe *f*
Sweden ['swiːdn] *n* Schweden *nt*
Swedish ['swiːdɪʃ] *adj* schwedisch ♦ *n*
(*LING*) Schwedisch *nt*
sweep [swiːp] (*pt, pp* swept) *n*
(*chimney* ~) Schornsteinfeger *m* ♦ *vt*
fegen, kehren ♦ *vi* (*go quickly*) rauschen; ~ **away** *vt* wegfegen; ~ **past** *vi*
vorbeisausen; ~ **up** *vt* zusammen-
kehren; ~**ing** *adj* (*gesture*)
schwungvoll; (*statement*) verallgemei-
nernd
sweet [swiːt] *n* (*course*) Nachtisch *m*;
(*candy*) Bonbon *nt* ♦ *adj* süß; ~**corn** *n*
Zuckermais *m*; ~**en** *vt* (*fig*)
versüßen; ~**heart** *n* Liebste(r) *mf*;
~**ness** *n* Süße *f*; ~ **pea** *n* Gartenwicke
f
swell [swel] (*pt* ~**ed**, *pp* swollen *or* ~**ed**)
n Seegang *m* ♦ *adj* (*inf*) todschick ♦ *vt*
(*numbers*) vermehren ♦ *vi* (*also*: ~ **up**)

(an)schwellen; ~**ing** n Schwellung f
sweltering ['sweltərɪŋ] adj drückend
swept [swept] pt, pp of sweep
swerve [swɜːv] vt, vi ausscheren
swift [swɪft] n Mauersegler m ♦ adj geschwind, schnell, rasch; ~**ly** adv geschwind, schnell, rasch
swig [swɪg] n Zug m
swill [swɪl] n (for pigs) Schweinefutter
nt ♦ vt spülen
swim [swɪm] (pt swam, pp swum) n: to
go for a ~ schwimmen gehen ♦ vi
schwimmen ♦ vt (cross)
(durch)schwimmen; ~**mer** n
Schwimmer(in) m(f); ~**ming** n
Schwimmen nt; ~**ming cap** n
Badehaube f, Badekappe f; ~**ming
costume** (BRIT) n Badeanzug m;
~**ming pool** n Schwimmbecken nt;
(private) Swimmingpool m; ~**suit** n
Badeanzug m
swindle ['swɪndl] n Schwindel m, Betrug
m ♦ vt betrügen
swine [swaɪn] n (also fig) Schwein nt
swing [swɪŋ] (pt, pp swung) n (child's)
Schaukel f; (movement) Schwung m;
(MUS) Swing m ♦ vt schwingen ♦ vi
schwingen, schaukeln; (turn quickly)
schwenken; **in full** ~ in vollem Gange;
~ **bridge** n Drehbrücke f; ~ **door**
(BRIT) n Schwingtür f
swingeing ['swɪndʒɪŋ] (BRIT) adj hart;
(taxation, cuts) extrem
swinging door (US) n Schwingtür f
swipe [swaɪp] n Hieb m ♦ vt (inf: hit)
hart schlagen; (: steal) klauen
swirl [swɜːl] vi wirbeln
swish [swɪʃ] adj (inf: smart) schick ♦
vi zischen; (grass, skirts) rascheln
Swiss [swɪs] adj Schweizer,
schweizerisch ♦ n Schweizer(in) m(f);
the ~ npl (people) die Schweizer pl
switch [swɪtʃ] n (ELEC) Schalter m;
(change) Wechsel m ♦ vt (ELEC)
schalten; (change) wechseln ♦ vi
wechseln; ~ **off** vt ab- or ausschalten;
~ **on** vt an- or einschalten; ~**board** n
Zentrale f; (board) Schaltbrett nt
Switzerland ['swɪtsələnd] n die Schweiz
swivel ['swɪvl] vt (also: ~ round)

drehen ♦ vi (also: ~ round) sich drehen
swollen ['swəʊlən] pp of swell
swoon [swuːn] vi (old) in Ohnmacht
fallen
swoop [swuːp] n Sturzflug m; (esp by
police) Razzia f ♦ vi (also: ~ down)
stürzen
swop [swɒp] = swap
sword [sɔːd] n Schwert nt; ~**fish** n
Schwertfisch m
swore [swɔː*] pt of swear
sworn [swɔːn] pp of swear
swot [swɒt] vt, vi pauken
swum [swʌm] pp of swim
swung [swʌŋ] pt, pp of swing
sycamore ['sɪkəmɔː*] n (US) Platane f;
(BRIT) Bergahorn m
syllable ['sɪləbl] n Silbe f
syllabus ['sɪləbəs] n Lehrplan m
symbol ['sɪmbəl] n Symbol nt; ~**ic(al)**
[sɪm'bɒlɪk(əl)] adj symbolisch
symmetry ['sɪmɪtrɪ] n Symmetrie f
sympathetic [sɪmpə'θetɪk] adj mitfühlend
sympathize ['sɪmpəθaɪz] vi mitfühlen;
~**r** n Mitfühlende(r) mf; (POL) Sympa-
thisant(in) m(f)
sympathy ['sɪmpəθɪ] n Mitleid nt, Mitgefühl nt; (condolence) Beileid nt; **with
our deepest** ~ mit tiefempfundenem
Beileid
symphony ['sɪmfənɪ] n Sinfonie f
symposium [sɪm'pəʊzɪəm] n Tagung f
symptom ['sɪmptəm] n Symptom nt;
~**atic** [sɪmptə'mætɪk] adj (fig): ~**atic of**
bezeichnend für
synagogue ['sɪnəgɒg] n Synagoge f
synchronize ['sɪŋkrənaɪz] vt synchroni-
sieren ♦ vi gleichzeitig sein or ablaufen
syncopated ['sɪŋkəpeɪtɪd] adj synkopiert
syndicate ['sɪndɪkət] n Konsortium nt
synonym ['sɪnənɪm] n Synonym nt
synonymous [sɪ'nɒnɪməs] adj gleichbedeutend
synopsis [sɪ'nɒpsɪs] n Zusammenfassung
f
syphon ['saɪfən] = siphon
Syria ['sɪrɪə] n Syrien nt
syringe [sɪ'rɪndʒ] n Spritze f
syrup ['sɪrəp] n Sirup m; (of sugar)

Melasse *f*

system ['sɪstəm] *n* System *nt*; ~**atic** [sɪstə'mætɪk] *adj* systematisch; ~ **disk** *n* (*COMPUT*) Systemdiskette *f*; ~**s analyst** *n* Systemanalytiker(in) *m(f)*

T

ta [tɑː] (*BRIT: inf*) *excl* danke
tab [tæb] *n* Aufhänger *m*; (*name* ~) Schild *nt*; **to keep** ~**s on** (*fig*) genau im Auge behalten
tabby ['tæbɪ] *n* (*also:* ~ **cat**) getigerte Katze *f*
table ['teɪbl] *n* Tisch *m*; (*list*) Tabelle *f* ♦ *vt* (*PARL: propose*) vorlegen, einbringen; **to lay** *or* **set the** ~ den Tisch decken; ~**cloth** ['teɪblklɒθ] *n* Tischtuch *nt*; ~ **of contents** *n* Inhaltsverzeichnis *nt*; ~ **d'hôte** ['tɑːbl'dəʊt] *n* Tagesmenü *nt*; ~ **lamp** *n* Tischlampe *f*; ~**mat** ['teɪblmæt] *n* Untersatz *m*; ~**spoon** ['teɪblspuːn] *n* Eßlöffel *m*; ~**spoonful** *n* Eßlöffel(voll) *m*
tablet ['tæblət] *n* (*MED*) Tablette *f*; (*for writing*) Täfelchen *nt*
table tennis ['teɪbltenɪs] *n* Tischtennis *nt*
table wine ['teɪblwaɪn] *n* Tafelwein *m*
tabloid ['tæblɔɪd] *n* Zeitung *f* in kleinem Format; (*pej*) Boulevardzeitung
tabulate ['tæbjʊleɪt] *vt* tabellarisch ordnen
tacit ['tæsɪt] *adj* stillschweigend; ~**ly** *adv* stillschweigend
taciturn ['tæsɪtɜːn] *adj* wortkarg
tack [tæk] *n* (*small nail*) Stift *m*; (*US: thumb*~) Reißzwecke *f*; (*stitch*) Heftstich *m*; (*NAUT*) Lavieren *nt*; (*course*) Kurs *m* ♦ *vt* (*nail*) nageln; (*stitch*) heften ♦ *vi* aufkreuzen
tackle ['tækl] *n* (*for lifting*) Flaschenzug *m*; (*NAUT*) Takelage *f*; (*SPORT*) Tackling *nt* ♦ *vt* (*deal with*) anpacken, in Angriff nehmen; (*person*) festhalten; (*player*) angehen
tacky ['tækɪ] *adj* klebrig
tact [tækt] *n* Takt *m*; ~**ful** *adj* taktvoll; ~**fully** *adv* taktvoll

tactical ['tæktɪkəl] *adj* taktisch
tactics ['tæktɪks] *npl* Taktik *f*
tactless ['tæktləs] *adj* taktlos; ~**ly** *adv* taktlos
tadpole ['tædpəʊl] *n* Kaulquappe *f*
taffy ['tæfɪ] (*US*) *n* Sahnebonbon *nt*
tag [tæg] *n* (*label*) Schild *nt*, Anhänger *m*; (*maker's name*) Etikett *nt*; (*phrase*) Floskel *f*; ~ **along** *vi* mitkommen
tail [teɪl] *n* Schwanz *m*; (*of list*) Schluß *m* ♦ *vt* folgen +*dat*; ~ **away** *or* **off** *vi* abfallen, schwinden; ~**back** (*BRIT*) *n* (*AUT*) (Rück)stau *m*; ~ **coat** *n* Frack *m*; ~ **end** *n* Schluß *m*, Ende *nt*; ~**gate** *n* (*AUT*) Heckklappe *f*
tailor ['teɪlə*] *n* Schneider *m*; ~**ing** *n* Schneidern *nt*; ~-**made** *adj* maßgeschneidert; (*fig*): ~-**made for sb** jdm wie auf den Leib geschnitten
tailwind ['teɪlwɪnd] *n* Rückenwind *m*
tainted ['teɪntɪd] *adj* verdorben
take [teɪk] (*pt* **took**, *pp* **taken**) *vt* nehmen; (*trip, exam, PHOT*) machen; (*capture: person*) fassen; (: *town; also COMM, FIN*) einnehmen; (*carry to a place*) bringen; (*get for o.s.*) sich *dat* nehmen; (*gain, obtain*) bekommen; (*put up with*) hinnehmen; (*respond to*) aufnehmen; (*interpret*) auffassen; (*assume*) annehmen; (*contain*) Platz haben für; (*GRAM*) stehen mit; **to** ~ **sth from sb** jdm etw wegnehmen; **to** ~ **sth from sth** (*MATH: subtract*) etw von etw abziehen; (*extract, quotation*) etw einer Sache *dat* entnehmen; ~ **after** *vt fus* ähnlich sein +*dat*; ~ **apart** *vt* auseinandernehmen; ~ **away** *vt* (*remove*) wegnehmen; (*carry off*) wegbringen; ~ **back** *vt* (*return*) zurückbringen; (*retract*) zurücknehmen; ~ **down** *vt* (*pull down*) abreißen; (*write down*) aufschreiben; ~ **in** *vt* (*deceive*) hereinlegen; (*understand*) begreifen; (*include*) einschließen; ~ **off** *vi* (*plane*) starten ♦ *vt* (*remove*) wegnehmen; (*clothing*) ausziehen; (*imitate*) nachmachen; ~ **on** *vt* (*undertake*) übernehmen; (*engage*) einstellen; (*opponent*) antreten gegen; ~ **out** *vt*

(girl, dog) ausführen; *(extract)* herausnehmen; *(insurance)* abschließen; *(licence)* sich *dat* geben lassen; *(book)* ausleihen; *(remove)* entfernen; **to ~ sth out of sth** *(drawer, pocket etc)* etw aus etw herausnehmen; **~ over** *vt* übernehmen ♦ *vi*: **to ~ over from sb** jdn ablösen; **~ to** *vt fus (like)* mögen; *(adopt as practice)* sich *dat* angewöhnen; **~ up** *vt (raise)* aufnehmen; *(dress etc)* kürzer machen; *(occupy)* in Anspruch nehmen; *(engage in)* sich befassen mit; **~away** *adj* zum Mitnehmen; **~-home pay** *n* Nettolohn *m*; **taken** ['teɪkn] *pp* of **take**; **~off** *n (AVIAT)* Start *m*; *(imitation)* Nachahmung *f*; **~out** *(US) adj* = **takeaway**; **~over** *n (COMM)* Übernahme *f*

takings ['teɪkɪŋz] *npl (COMM)* Einnahmen *pl*

talc [tælk] *n (also: talcum powder)* Talkumpuder *m*

tale [teɪl] *n* Geschichte *f*, Erzählung *f*; **to tell ~s** *(pej: lie)* Geschichten erfinden

talent ['tælənt] *n* Talent *nt*; **~ed** *adj* begabt

talk [tɔ:k] *n (conversation)* Gespräch *nt*; *(rumour)* Gerede *nt*; *(speech)* Vortrag *m* ♦ *vi* sprechen, reden; **~s** *pl (POL etc)* Gespräche *pl*; **to ~ about** sprechen von +*dat or* über +*acc*; **to ~ sb into doing sth** jdn überreden, etw zu tun; **to ~ sb out of doing sth** jdm ausreden, etw zu tun; **to ~ shop** fachsimpeln; **~ over** *vt* besprechen; **~ative** *adj* gesprächig

tall [tɔ:l] *adj* groß; *(building)* hoch; **to be 1 m 80 ~** 1,80 m groß sein; **~boy** *(BRIT) n* Kommode *f*; **~ story** *n* übertriebene Geschichte *f*

tally ['tælɪ] *n* Abrechnung *f* ♦ *vi* übereinstimmen

talon ['tælən] *n* Kralle *f*

tame [teɪm] *adj* zahm; *(fig)* fade

tamper ['tæmpə*] *vi*: **to ~ with** herumpfuschen an +*dat*

tampon ['tæmpən] *n* Tampon *m*

tan [tæn] *n (on skin)* (Sonnen)bräune *f*; *(colour)* Gelbbraun *nt* ♦ *adj* (gelb)braun ♦ *vt* bräunen; *(skins)* gerben ♦ *vi* braun werden

tang [tæŋ] *n* Schärfe *f*

tangent ['tændʒənt] *n* Tangente *f*; **to go off at a ~** *(fig)* vom Thema abkommen

tangerine [tændʒə'ri:n] *n* Mandarine *f*

tangible ['tændʒəbl] *adj* greifbar

tangle ['tæŋgl] *n* Durcheinander *nt*; *(trouble)* Schwierigkeiten *pl*; **to get in(to) a ~** sich verheddern

tank [tæŋk] *n (container)* Tank *m*, Behälter *m*; *(MIL)* Panzer *m*

tanker ['tæŋkə*] *n (ship)* Tanker *m*; *(vehicle)* Tankwagen *m*

tanned [tænd] *adj (skin)* gebräunt

tantalizing ['tæntəlaɪzɪŋ] *adj* verlockend; *(annoying)* quälend

tantamount ['tæntəmaʊnt] *adj*: **~ to** gleichbedeutend mit

tantrum ['tæntrəm] *n* Wutanfall *m*

tap [tæp] *n* Hahn *m*; *(gentle blow)* Klopfen *nt* ♦ *vt (strike)* klopfen; *(supply)* anzapfen; *(telephone)* abhören; **on ~** *(fig: resources)* zur Hand; **~-dancing** ['tæpdɑ:nsɪŋ] *n* Steppen *nt*

tape [teɪp] *n* Band *nt*; *(magnetic)* (Ton)band *nt*; *(adhesive)* Klebstreifen *m* ♦ *vt (record)* aufnehmen; **~ measure** *n* Maßband *nt*

tape recorder *n* Tonbandgerät *nt*

taper ['teɪpə*] *n* (dünne) Wachskerze *f* ♦ *vi* spitz zulaufen

tapestry ['tæpɪstrɪ] *n* Wandteppich *m*

tar [tɑ:*] *n* Teer *m*

target ['tɑ:gɪt] *n* Ziel *nt*; *(board)* Zielscheibe *f*; **~ practice** *n* Zielschießen *nt*

tariff ['tærɪf] *n (duty paid)* Zoll *m*; *(list)* Tarif *m*

tarmac ['tɑ:mæk] *n (AVIAT)* Rollfeld *nt*

tarnish ['tɑ:nɪʃ] *vt* matt machen; *(fig)* beflecken

tarpaulin [tɑ:'pɔ:lɪn] *n* Plane *f*

tarragon ['tærəgən] *n* Estragon *m*

tart [tɑ:t] *n* (Obst)torte *f*; *(inf)* Nutte *f* ♦ *adj* scharf; **~ up** *(inf) vt* aufmachen *(inf)*; *(person)* auftakeln *(inf)*

tartan ['tɑ:tən] *n* Schottenkaro *nt* ♦ *adj* mit Schottenkaro

tartar ['tɑ:tə*] *n* Zahnstein *m*; **~(e) sauce** *n* Remouladensoße *f*

task [tɑ:sk] *n* Aufgabe *f*; **to take sb to ~** sich *dat* jdn vornehmen; **~ force** *n*

Sondertrupp *m*

tassel ['tæsəl] *n* Quaste *f*

taste [teɪst] *n* Geschmack *m*; (*sense*) Geschmackssinn *m*; (*small quantity*) Kostprobe *f*; (*liking*) Vorliebe *f* ♦ *vt* schmecken; (*try*) probieren ♦ *vi* schmecken; **can I have a ~ of this wine?** kann ich diesen Wein probieren?; **to have a ~ for sth** etw mögen; **in good/bad ~** geschmackvoll/geschmacklos; **you can ~ the garlic (in it)** man kann den Knoblauch herausschmecken; **to ~ of sth** nach einer Sache schmecken; **~ful** *adj* geschmackvoll; **~fully** *adv* geschmackvoll; **~less** *adj* (*insipid*) fade; (*in bad ~*) geschmacklos; **~lessly** *adv* geschmacklos

tasty ['teɪstɪ] *adj* schmackhaft

tattered ['tætəd] *adj* = **in tatters**

tatters ['tætəz] *npl*: **in ~** in Fetzen

tattoo [tə'tu:] *n* (*MIL*) Zapfenstreich *m*; (*on skin*) Tätowierung *f* ♦ *vt* tätowieren

tatty ['tætɪ] (*BRIT: inf*) *adj* schäbig

taught [tɔːt] *pt, pp of* **teach**

taunt [tɔːnt] *n* höhnische Bemerkung *f* ♦ *vt* verhöhnen

Taurus ['tɔːrəs] *n* Stier *m*

taut [tɔːt] *adj* straff

tawdry ['tɔːdrɪ] *adj* (bunt und) billig

tawny ['tɔːnɪ] *adj* gelbbraun

tax [tæks] *n* Steuer *f* ♦ *vt* besteuern; (*strain*) strapazieren; (*strength*) angreifen; **~able** *adj* (*income*) steuerpflichtig; **~ation** [tæk'seɪʃən] *n* Besteuerung *f*; **~ avoidance** *n* Steuerumgehung *f*; **~ collector** *n* Steuereinnehmer *m*; **~ disc** (*BRIT*) *n* (*AUT*) Kraftfahrzeugsteuerplakette *f*; **~ evasion** *n* Steuerhinterziehung *f*; **~-free** *adj* steuerfrei

taxi ['tæksɪ] *n* Taxi *nt* ♦ *vi* (*plane*) rollen; **~ driver** *n* Taxifahrer *m*; **~ rank** (*BRIT*) *n* Taxistand *m*; **~ stand** *n* Taxistand *m*

tax: **~payer** ['tækspeɪə*] *n* Steuerzahler *m*; **~ relief** *n* Steuerermäßigung *f*; **~ return** *n* Steuererklärung *f*

TB *n abbr* (= *tuberculosis*) Tb *f*, Tbc *f*

tea [tiː] *n* Tee *m*; (*meal*) (frühes) Abendessen *nt*; **high ~** (*BRIT*)

Abendessen *nt*; **~ bag** *n* Teebeutel *m*; **~ break** (*BRIT*) *n* Teepause *f*

teach [tiːtʃ] (*pt, pp* **taught**) *vt* lehren; (*SCH*) lehren, unterrichten; (*show*): **to ~ sb sth** jdm etw beibringen ♦ *vi* lehren, unterrichten; **~er** *n* Lehrer(in) *m(f)*; **~ing** *n* (*~er's work*) Unterricht *m*; (*doctrine*) Lehre *f*

tea: **~ cosy** *n* Teewärmer *m*; **~cup** ['tiːkʌp] *n* Teetasse *f*; **~ leaves** *npl* Tee blätter *pl*

team [tiːm] *n* (*workers*) Team *nt*; (*SPORT*) Mannschaft *f*; (*animals*) Gespann *nt*

teapot ['tiːpɒt] *n* Teekanne *f*

tear[1] [tɛə*] (*pt* **tore**, *pp* **torn**) *n* Riß *m* ♦ *vt* zerreißen; (*muscle*) zerren ♦ *vi* (zer)reißen; (*rush*) rasen; **~ along** *vi* (*rush*) entlangrasen; **~ up** *vt* (*sheet of paper etc*) zerreißen

tear[2] [tɪə*] *n* Träne *f*

tearful ['tɪəfʊl] *adj* weinend; (*voice*) weinerlich

tear gas ['tɪəgæs] *n* Tränengas *nt*

tearoom ['tiːrʊm] *n* Teestube *f*

tease [tiːz] *n* Hänsler *m* ♦ *vt* necken

tea set *n* Teeservice *nt*

teaspoon ['tiːspuːn] *n* Teelöffel *m*

teat [tiːt] *n* (*of woman*) Brustwarze *f*; (*of animal*) Zitze *f*; (*of bottle*) Sauger *m*

tea time *n* (*in the afternoon*) Teestunde *f*; (*mealtime*) Abendessen *nt*

tea towel *n* Geschirrtuch *nt*

technical ['teknɪkəl] *adj* technisch; (*knowledge, terms*) Fach-; **~ity** [teknɪ'kælɪtɪ] *n* technische Einzelheit *f*; (*JUR*) Formsache *f*; **~ly** *adv* technisch; (*speak*) spezialisiert; (*fig*) genau genommen

technician [tek'nɪʃən] *n* Techniker *m*

technique [tek'niːk] *n* Technik *f*

technological [teknə'lɒdʒɪkəl] *adj* technologisch

technology [tek'nɒlədʒɪ] *n* Technologie *f*

teddy (bear) ['tedɪ(bɛə*)] *n* Teddybär *m*

tedious ['tiːdɪəs] *adj* langweilig, ermüdend; **~ly** *adv* langweilig, ermüdend

tee [tiː] *n* (*GOLF*) Abschlagstelle *f*;

(*object*) Tee *nt*
teem [tiːm] *vi* (*swarm*): to ~ (with) wimmeln (von); it is ~ing (with rain) es gießt in Strömen
teenage ['tiːneɪdʒ] *adj* (*fashions etc*) Teenager-, jugendlich; ~r *n* Teenager *m*, Jugendliche(r) *mf*
teens [tiːnz] *npl* Teenageralter *nt*; to be in one's ~ im Teenageralter sein
tee-shirt ['tiːʃɜːt] *n* T-Shirt *nt*
teeter ['tiːtə*] *vi* schwanken
teeth [tiːθ] *npl of* tooth
teethe [tiːð] *vi* zahnen
teething ring ['tiːðɪŋ-] *n* Beißring *m*
teething troubles ['tiːðɪŋ-] *npl* (*fig*) Kinderkrankheiten *pl*
teetotal ['tiː'təʊtl] *adj* abstinent
telecommunications ['telɪkəmjuːnɪ'keɪʃənz] *npl* Fernmeldewesen *nt*
telegram ['telɪgræm] *n* Telegramm *nt*
telegraph ['telɪgrɑːf] *n* Telegraph *m*
telephone ['telɪfəʊn] *n* Telefon *nt*, Fernsprecher *m* ♦ *vt* anrufen; (*message*) telefonisch mitteilen; ~ **booth** *n* Telefonzelle *f*; ~ **box** (*BRIT*) *n* Telefonzelle *f*; ~ **call** *n* Telefongespräch *nt*, Anruf *m*; ~ **directory** *n* Telefonbuch *nt*; ~ **number** *n* Telefonnummer *f*
telephonist [tə'lefənɪst] (*BRIT*) *n* Telefonist(in) *m(f)*
telephoto lens ['telɪfəʊtəʊ'lenz] *n* Teleobjektiv *nt*
telescope ['telɪskəʊp] *n* Teleskop *nt*, Fernrohr *nt* ♦ *vt* ineinanderschieben
televise ['telɪvaɪz] *vt* durch das Fernsehen übertragen
television ['telɪvɪʒən] *n* Fernsehen *nt*; ~ (**set**) *n* Fernsehapparat *m*, Fernseher *m*
telex ['teleks] *n* Telex *nt* ♦ *vt* per Telex schicken
tell [tel] (*pt, pp* told) *vt* (*story*) erzählen; (*secret*) ausplaudern; (*say, make known*) sagen; (*distinguish*) erkennen; (*be sure*) wissen ♦ *vi* (*talk*) sprechen; (*be sure*) wissen; (*divulge*) es verraten; (*have effect*) sich auswirken; to ~ sb to do sth jdm sagen, daß er etw tun soll; to ~ sb sth *or* sth to sb jdm etw sagen; to ~ sb by sth jdn an etw *dat* erkennen; to ~ sth from etw

unterscheiden von; to ~ of sth von etw sprechen; ~ off *vt*: to ~ sb off jdn ausschimpfen; ~er *n* Kassenbeamte(r) *mf*; ~ing *adj* verräterisch; (*blow*) hart; ~tale *adj* verräterisch
telly ['telɪ] (*BRIT*: *inf*) *n* *abbr* (= *television*) TV *nt*
temerity [tɪ'merɪtɪ] *n* (Toll)kühnheit *f*
temp [temp] *n abbr* (= *temporary*) Aushilfssekretärin *f* ♦ *vi* als Aushilfskraft arbeiten
temper ['tempə*] *n* (*disposition*) Temperament *nt*; (*anger*) Zorn *m* ♦ *vt* (*tone down*) mildern; (*metal*) härten; to be in a (bad) ~ wütend sein; to lose one's ~ die Beherrschung verlieren
temperament ['temprəmənt] *n* Temperament *nt*; ~al [temprə'mentl] *adj* (*moody*) launisch
temperance ['tempərəns] *n* Mäßigung *f*; (*abstinence*) Enthaltsamkeit *f*
temperate ['tempərət] *adj* gemäßigt
temperature ['temprɪtʃə*] *n* Temperatur *f*; (*MED*: *high* ~) Fieber *nt*; to have *or* run a ~ Fieber haben
tempest ['tempɪst] *n* (wilder) Sturm *m*
template ['templət] *n* Schablone *f*
temple ['templ] *n* Tempel *m*; (*ANAT*) Schläfe *f*
temporal ['tempərəl] *adj* (*of time*) zeitlich; (*worldly*) irdisch, weltlich
temporarily ['tempərərɪlɪ] *adv* zeitweilig, vorübergehend
temporary ['tempərərɪ] *adj* vorläufig; (*road, building*) provisorisch
tempt [tempt] *vt* (*persuade*) verleiten; (*attract*) reizen, (ver)locken; to ~ sb into doing sth jdn dazu verleiten, etw zu tun; ~ation [temp'teɪʃən] *n* Versuchung *f*; ~ing *adj* (*person*) verführerisch; (*object, situation*) verlockend
ten [ten] *num* zehn
tenable ['tenəbl] *adj* haltbar
tenacious [tə'neɪʃəs] *adj* zäh, hartnäckig; ~ly *adv* zäh, hartnäckig
tenacity [tə'næsɪtɪ] *n* Zähigkeit *f*, Hartnäckigkeit *f*
tenancy ['tenənsɪ] *n* Mietverhältnis *nt*
tenant ['tenənt] *n* Mieter *m*; (*of larger property*) Pächter *m*

tend [tend] vt (look after) sich kümmern um ♦ vi: **to ~ to do sth** etw gewöhnlich tun

tendency ['tendənsɪ] n Tendenz f; (of person) Tendenz f, Neigung f

tender ['tendə*] adj zart; (loving) zärtlich ♦ n (COMM: offer) Kostenanschlag m ♦ vt (an)bieten; (resignation) einreichen; ~**ness** n Zartheit f; (being loving) Zärtlichkeit f

tendon ['tendən] n Sehne f

tenement ['tenəmənt] n Mietshaus nt

tenet ['tenət] n Lehre f

tennis ['tenɪs] n Tennis nt; ~ **ball** n Tennisball m; ~ **court** n Tennisplatz m; ~ **player** n Tennisspieler(in) m(f); ~ **racket** n Tennisschläger m; ~ **shoes** npl Tennisschuhe pl

tenor ['tenə*] n Tenor m

tenpin bowling ['tenpɪn-] n Bowling nt

tense [tens] adj angespannt ♦ n Zeitform f

tension ['tenʃən] n Spannung f

tent [tent] n Zelt nt

tentacle ['tentəkl] n Fühler m; (of sea animals) Fangarm m

tentative ['tentətɪv] adj (movement) unsicher; (offer) Probe-; (arrangement) vorläufig; (suggestion) unverbindlich; ~**ly** adv versuchsweise; (try, move) vorsichtig

tenterhooks ['tentəhʊks] npl: **to be on ~** auf die Folter gespannt sein

tenth [tenθ] adj zehnte(r, s)

tent peg n Hering m

tent pole n Zeltstange f

tenuous ['tenjʊəs] adj schwach

tenure ['tenjʊə*] n (of land) Besitz m; (of office) Amtszeit f

tepid ['tepɪd] adj lauwarm

term [tɜːm] n (period of time) Zeit(raum m) f; (limit) Frist f; (SCH) Quartal nt; (UNIV) Trimester nt; (expression) Ausdruck m ♦ vt (be)nennen; ~**s** npl (conditions) Bedingungen pl; **in the short/long ~** auf kurze/lange Sicht; **to be on good ~s with sb** gut mit jdm auskommen; **to come to ~s with** (person) sich einigen mit; (problem) sich abfinden mit

terminal ['tɜːmɪnl] n (BRIT: also: coach ~) Endstation f; (AVIAT) Terminal m; (COMPUT) Terminal nt or m ♦ adj Schluß-; (MED) unheilbar

terminate ['tɜːmɪneɪt] vt beenden ♦ vi enden, aufhören

termini ['tɜːmɪnaɪ] npl of **terminus**

terminus ['tɜːmɪnəs] (pl **termini**) n Endstation f

terrace ['terəs] n (BRIT: row of houses) Häuserreihe f; (in garden etc) Terrasse f; **the ~s** npl (BRIT: SPORT) die Ränge; ~**d** adj (garden) terrassenförmig angelegt; (house) Reihen-

terrible ['terəbl] adj schrecklich, entsetzlich, fürchterlich

terribly ['terəblɪ] adv fürchterlich

terrific [təˈrɪfɪk] adj unwahrscheinlich; ~**!** klasse!

terrify ['terɪfaɪ] vt erschrecken

territorial [terɪˈtɔːrɪəl] adj Gebiets-, territorial

territory ['terɪtərɪ] n Gebiet nt

terror ['terə*] n Schrecken m; (POL) Terror m; ~**ist** n Terrorist(in) m(f); ~**ize** vt terrorisieren

terse [tɜːs] adj knapp, kurz, bündig

test [test] n Probe f; (examination) Prüfung f; (PSYCH, TECH) Test m ♦ vt prüfen; (PSYCH) testen

testicle ['testɪkl] n Hoden m

testify ['testɪfaɪ] vi aussagen; **to ~ to sth** etw bezeugen

testimony ['testɪmənɪ] n (JUR) Zeugenaussage f; (fig) Zeugnis nt

test match n (SPORT) Länderkampf m

test tube n Reagenzglas nt

testy ['testɪ] adj gereizt; reizbar

tetanus ['tetənəs] n Wundstarrkrampf m, Tetanus m

tetchy ['tetʃɪ] adj empfindlich

tether ['teðə*] vt anbinden ♦ n: **at the end of one's ~** völlig am Ende

text [tekst] n Text m; (of document) Wortlaut m; ~**book** n Lehrbuch nt

textiles ['tekstaɪlz] npl Textilien pl

texture ['tekstʃə*] n Beschaffenheit f

Thai [taɪ] adj thailändisch ♦ n Thailänder(in) m(f); (LING) Thailändisch nt; ~**land** n Thailand nt

Thames [temz] *n*: **the ~** die Themse
than [ðæn, ðən] *prep* (*in comparisons*)
als
thank [θæŋk] *vt* danken +*dat*; **you've
him to ~ for your success** Sie haben
Ihren Erfolg ihm zu verdanken; **~ you
(very much)** danke (vielmals), danke
schön; **~ful** *adj* dankbar; **~less** *adj*
undankbar; **~s** *npl* Dank *m* ♦ *excl*
danke!; **~s to** dank +*gen*; **T~sgiving
(Day)** (*US*) *n* Thanksgiving Day *m*

─────────────
⌐KEYWORD⌐
─────────────

that [ðæt] *adj* (*demonstrative*: *pl* those)
der/die/das; jene(r, s); **that one** das da
♦ *pron* **1** (*demonstrative*: *pl* those) das;
who's/what's that? wer ist da/was ist
das?; **is that you?** bist du das?; **that's
what he said** genau das hat er gesagt;
what happened after that? was
passierte danach?; **that is** das heißt
2 (*relative*: *sub*) der/die/das, die; (:
direct obj) den/die/das, die; (: *indirect
obj*) dem/der/dem, denen; **all (that) I
have** alles, was ich habe
3 (*relative*: *of time*): **the day (that)** an
dem Tag, als; **the winter (that)** he
came in dem Winter, in dem er kam
♦ *conj* daß; **he thought that I was ill** er
dachte, daß ich krank sei, er dachte,
ich sei krank
♦ *adv* (*demonstrative*) so; **I can't work
that much** ich kann nicht soviel
arbeiten

thatched [θætʃt] *adj* strohgedeckt;
(*cottage*) mit Strohdach
thaw [θɔ:] *n* Tauwetter *nt* ♦ *vi* tauen;
(*frozen foods, fig*: *people*) auftauen ♦ *vt*
(auf)tauen lassen

─────────────
⌐KEYWORD⌐
─────────────

the [ði:, ðə] *def art* **1** der/die/das; **to
play the piano/violin** Klavier/Geige
spielen; **I'm going to the butcher's/the
cinema** ich gehe zum Fleischer/ins
Kino; **Elizabeth the First** Elisabeth die
Erste
2 (+*adj to form noun*) das, die; **the
rich and the poor** die Reichen und die
Armen
3 (*in comparisons*): **the more he works
the more he earns** je mehr er arbeitet,
desto mehr verdient er

theatre ['θɪətə*] (*US* **theater**) *n* Theater
nt; (*for lectures etc*) Saal *m*; (*MED*)
Operationssaal *m*;   **~goer**   *n*
Theaterbesucher(in) *m(f)*
theatrical [θɪ'ætrɪkəl] *adj* Theater-;
(*career*) Schauspieler-; (*showy*) thea-
tralisch
theft [θeft] *n* Diebstahl *m*
their [ðɛə*] *adj* ihr; *see also* my; **~s**
pron ihre(r, s); *see also* mine
them [ðem, ðəm] *pron* (*acc*) sie; (*dat*)
ihnen; *see also* me
theme [θi:m] *n* Thema *nt*; (*MUS*) Motiv
nt; **~ song** *n* Titelmusik *f*
themselves [ðəm'selvz]   *pl*   *pron*
(*reflexive*) sich (selbst); (*emphatic*)
selbst; *see also* oneself
then [ðen] *adv* (*at that time*) damals;
(*next*) dann ♦ *conj* also, folglich; (*fur-
thermore*) ferner ♦ *adj* damalig; **from
~ on** von da an; **by ~** bis dahin; **the ~
president** der damalige Präsident
theology [θɪ'ɒlədʒɪ] *n* Theologie *f*
theoretical [θɪə'retɪkəl] *adj* theoretisch;
~ly *adv* theoretisch
theory ['θɪərɪ] *n* Theorie *f*
therapist ['θerəpɪst] *adj* Therapeut(in)
m(f)
therapy ['θerəpɪ] *n* Therapie *f*

─────────────
⌐KEYWORD⌐
─────────────

there [ðɛə*] *adv* **1**: **there is, there are**
es *or* da ist/sind; (*there exists/exist
also*) es gibt; **there are 3 of them** (*people, things*) es gibt 3 davon; **there has
been an accident** da war ein Unfall
2 (*referring to place*) da, dort; (*with
vb of movement*) dahin, dorthin; **put it
in/on there** leg es dahinein/dorthinauf
3: **there, there** (*esp to child*) na, na

thereabouts [ðɛərə'baʊts] *adv* (*place*)
dort irgendwo; (*amount*): **fifteen or ~**
so um fünfzehn (herum)
thereafter [ðɛər'ɑ:ftə*] *adv* danach

thereby [ðɛə'baɪ] *adv* dadurch, damit
therefore ['ðɛəfɔ:*] *adv* deshalb, daher
there's ['ðɛəz] = **there is; there has**
thermometer [θə'mɒmɪtə*] *n* Thermometer *nt*
Thermos ['θɜ:məs] (®) *n* Thermosflasche *f*
thesaurus [θɪ'sɔ:rəs] *n* Synonymwörterbuch *nt*
these [ðiːz] *pron, adj (pl)* diese
theses ['θiːsiːz] *npl of* thesis
thesis ['θiːsɪs] *(pl* theses) *n (for discussion)* These *f*; *(UNIV)* Dissertation *f*, Doktorarbeit *f*
they [ðeɪ] *pl pron* sie; *(people in general)* man; ~ **say that** ... *(it is said that)* es wird gesagt, daß ...; **~'d** = they had; they would; **~'ll** = they shall; = they will; **~'re** = they are; **~'ve** = they have
thick [θɪk] *adj* dick; *(forest)* dicht; *(liquid)* dickflüssig; *(slow, stupid)* dumm, schwer von Begriff ♦ *n*: **in the ~ of** mitten in +*dat*; **it's 20 cm ~** es ist 20 cm dick *or* stark; **~en** *vi (fog)* dichter werden ♦ *vt (sauce etc)* verdicken; **~ness** *n* Dicke *f*; Dichte *f*; Dickflüssigkeit *f*; **~set** *adj* untersetzt; **~skinned** *adj* dickhäutig
thief [θiːf] *(pl* thieves) *n* Dieb(in) *m(f)*
thieves [θiːvz] *npl of* thief
thieving ['θiːvɪŋ] *n* Stehlen *nt* ♦ *adj* diebisch
thigh [θaɪ] *n* Oberschenkel *m*
thimble ['θɪmbl] *n* Fingerhut *m*
thin [θɪn] *adj* dünn; *(person)* dünn, mager; *(excuse)* schwach ♦ *vt*: **to ~ (down)** *(sauce, paint)* verdünnen
thing [θɪŋ] *n* Ding *nt*; *(affair)* Sache *f*; **my ~s** meine Sachen *pl*; **the best ~ would be to ...** das beste wäre, ...; **how are ~s?** wie geht's?
think [θɪŋk] *(pt, pp* thought) *vt, vi* denken; **what did you ~ of them?** was halten Sie von ihnen?; **to ~ about sth/sb** nachdenken über etw/jdn; **I'll ~ about it** ich überlege es mir; **to ~ of doing sth** vorhaben *or* beabsichtigen, etw zu tun; **I ~ so/not** ich glaube (schon)/glaube nicht; **to ~ well of sb** viel von jdm

halten; **~ over** *vt* überdenken; **~ up** *vt* sich *dat* ausdenken; **~ tank** *n* Expertengruppe *f*
thinly ['θɪnlɪ] *adv* dünn; *(disguised)* kaum
third [θɜ:d] *adj* dritte(r, s) ♦ *n (person)* Dritte(r) *mf*; *(part)* Drittel *nt*; **~ly** *adv* drittens; **~ party insurance** *(BRIT)* n Haftpflichtversicherung *f*; **~-rate** *adj* minderwertig; **the T~ World** *n* die Dritte Welt *f*
thirst [θɜ:st] *n (also fig)* Durst *m*; **~y** *adj (person)* durstig; *(work)* durstig machend; **to be ~y** Durst haben
thirteen ['θɜ:'tiːn] *num* dreizehn
thirty ['θɜ:tɪ] *num* dreißig

this [ðɪs] *adj (demonstrative: pl these)* diese(r, s); **this evening** heute abend; **this one** diese(r, s) (da)
♦ *pron (demonstrative: pl these)* dies, das; **who/what is this?** wer/was ist das?; **this is where I** live hier wohne ich; **this is what he said** das hat er gesagt; **this is Mr Brown** *(in introductions/photo)* dies ist Mr Brown; *(on telephone)* hier ist Mr Brown
♦ *adv (demonstrative)*: **this high/long** *etc* so groß/lang *etc*

thistle ['θɪsl] *n* Distel *f*
thong [θɒŋ] *n* (Leder)riemen *m*
thorn [θɔ:n] *n* Dorn *m*; **~y** *adj* dornig; *(problem)* schwierig
thorough ['θʌrə] *adj* gründlich; **~bred** *n* Vollblut *nt* ♦ *adj* reinrassig, Vollblut-; **~fare** *n* Straße *f*; "no ~fare" „Durchfahrt verboten"; **~ly** *adv* gründlich; *(extremely)* äußerst
those [ðəʊz] *pl pron* die (da), jene ♦ *adj* die, jene
though [ðəʊ] *conj* obwohl ♦ *adv* trotzdem
thought [θɔ:t] *pt, pp of* think ♦ *n (idea)* Gedanke *m*; *(thinking)* Denken *nt*, Denkvermögen *nt*; **~ful** *adj (thinking)* gedankenvoll, nachdenklich; *(kind)* rücksichtsvoll, aufmerksam; **~less** *adj* gedankenlos, unbesonnen; *(unkind)*

rücksichtslos

thousand ['θaʊzənd] *num* tausend; **two ~** zweitausend; **~s of** Tausende (von); **~th** *adj* tausendste(r, s)

thrash [θræʃ] *vt* verdreschen; *(fig)* (vernichten) schlagen; **~ about** *vi* um sich schlagen; **~ out** *vt* ausdiskutieren

thread [θred] *n* Faden *m*, Garn *nt*; *(on screw)* Gewinde *nt*; *(in story)* Faden *m* ♦ *vt (needle)* einfädeln; **~bare** *adj (also fig)* fadenscheinig

threat [θret] *n* Drohung *f*; *(danger)* Gefahr *f*; **~en** *vt* bedrohen ♦ *vi* drohen; **to ~en sb with sth** jdm etw androhen

three [θriː] *num* drei; **~-dimensional** *adj* dreidimensional; **~-piece suit** *n* dreiteilige(r) Anzug *m*; **~-piece suite** *n* dreiteilige Polstergarnitur *f*; **~-ply** *adj (wool)* dreifach; *(wood)* dreischichtig; **~-wheeler** *n* Dreiradwagen *m*

thresh [θreʃ] *vt, vi* dreschen

threshold ['θreʃhəʊld] *n* Schwelle *f*

threw [θruː] *pt of* **throw**

thrift [θrɪft] *n* Sparsamkeit *f*; **~y** *adj* sparsam

thrill [θrɪl] *n* Reiz *m*, Erregung *f* ♦ *vt* begeistern, packen; **to be ~ed with** *(gift etc)* sich unheimlich freuen über +*acc*; **~er** *n* Krimi *m*; **~ing** *adj* spannend; *(news)* aufregend

thrive [θraɪv] *(pt* ~**d,** throve*, pp* ~**d,** thriven*) vi*: **to ~ (on)** gedeihen (bei); **thriven** ['θrɪvn] *pp of* **thrive**

thriving ['θraɪvɪŋ] *adj* blühend

throat [θrəʊt] *n* Hals *m*, Kehle *f*; **to have a sore ~** Halsschmerzen haben

throb [θrɒb] *n* Pochen *nt* ♦ *vi* klopfen, pochen

throes [θrəʊz] *npl*: **in the ~ of** mitten in +*dat*

throng [θrɒŋ] *n* (Menschen)schar *f* ♦ *vt* sich drängen in +*dat*

throttle ['θrɒtl] *n* Gashebel *m* ♦ *vt* erdrosseln

through [θruː] *prep* durch; *(time)* während +*gen*; *(because of)* aus, durch ♦ *adv* durch ♦ *adj (ticket, train)* durchgehend; *(finished)* fertig; **to put sb ~ (to)** jdn verbinden (mit); **to be ~** *(TEL)* eine Verbindung haben; *(have finished)* fertig sein; **no ~ way** *(BRIT)* Sackgasse *f*; **~out** [θruː'aʊt] *prep (place)* überall in +*dat*; *(time)* während +*gen* ♦ *adv* überall; die ganze Zeit

throve [θrəʊv] *pt of* **thrive**

throw [θrəʊ] *(pt* threw*, pp* thrown*) n* Wurf *m* ♦ *vt* werfen; **to ~ a party** eine Party geben; **~ away** *vt* wegwerfen; *(waste)* verschenken; *(money)* verschwenden; **~ off** *vt* abwerfen; *(pursuer)* abschütteln; **~ out** *vt* hinauswerfen; *(rubbish)* wegwerfen; *(plan)* verwerfen; **~ up** *vt, vi (vomit)* speien; **~away** *adj* Wegwerf-; **~-in** *n* Einwurf *m*; **thrown** [θrəʊn] *pp of* **throw**

thru [θruː] *(US)* = **through**

thrush [θrʌʃ] *n* Drossel *f*

thrust [θrʌst] *(pt, pp* thrust*) n (TECH)* Schubkraft *f* ♦ *vt, vi (push)* stoßen

thud [θʌd] *n* dumpfe(r) (Auf)schlag *m*

thug [θʌg] *n* Schlägertyp *m*

thumb [θʌm] *n* Daumen *m* ♦ *vt (book)* durchblättern; **to ~ a lift** per Anhalter fahren (wollen); **~tack** *(US)* *n* Reißzwecke *f*

thump [θʌmp] *n (blow)* Schlag *m*; *(noise)* Bums *m* ♦ *vi* hämmern, pochen ♦ *vt* schlagen auf +*acc*

thunder ['θʌndə*] *n* Donner *m* ♦ *vi* donnern; *(train etc)*: **to ~ past** vorbeidonnern ♦ *vt* brüllen; **~ bolt** *n* Blitz *nt*; **~clap** *n* Donnerschlag *m*; **~storm** *n* Gewitter *nt*, Unwetter *nt*; **~y** *adj* gewitterschwül

Thursday ['θɜːzdeɪ] *n* Donnerstag *m*

thus [ðʌs] *adv (in this way)* so; *(therefore)* somit, also, folglich

thwart [θwɔːt] *vt* vereiteln, durchkreuzen; *(person)* hindern

thyme [taɪm] *n* Thymian *m*

thyroid ['θaɪrɔɪd] *n* Schilddrüse *f*

tiara [tɪ'ɑːrə] *n* Diadem *nt*

tic [tɪk] *n* Tick *m*

tick [tɪk] *n (sound)* Ticken *nt*; *(mark)* Häkchen *nt* ♦ *vi* ticken ♦ *vt* abhaken; **in a ~** *(BRIT: inf)* sofort; **~ off** *vt* abhaken; *(person)* ausschimpfen; **~ over** *vi (engine)* im Leerlauf laufen; *(fig)* auf Sparflamme laufen

ticket ['tɪkɪt] *n (for travel)* Fahrkarte *f*;

(for entrance) (Eintritts)karte *f*; *(price ~)* Preisschild *nt*; *(luggage ~)* (Gepäck)schein *m*; *(raffle ~)* Los *nt*; *(parking ~)* Strafzettel *m*; *(in car park)* Parkschein *m*; *~* **collector** *n* Fahrkartenkontrolleur *m*; *~* **office** *n* (RAIL *etc*) Fahrkartenschalter *m*; (THEAT *etc*) Kasse *f*

tickle ['tɪkl] *n* Kitzeln *nt* ♦ *vt* kitzeln; *(amuse)* amüsieren

ticklish ['tɪklɪʃ] *adj (also fig)* kitzlig

tidal ['taɪdl] *adj* Flut-, Tide-; *~* **wave** *n* Flutwelle *f*

tidbit ['tɪdbɪt] (US) *n* Leckerbissen *m*

tiddlywinks ['tɪdlɪwɪŋks] *n* Floh(hüpf)spiel *nt*

tide [taɪd] *n* Gezeiten *pl*; **high/low** *~* Flut *f*/Ebbe *f*

tidy ['taɪdɪ] *adj* ordentlich ♦ *vt* aufräumen, in Ordnung bringen

tie [taɪ] *n* (BRIT: neck~) Kravatte *f*, Schlips *m*; *(sth connecting)* Band *nt*; (SPORT) Unentschieden *nt* ♦ *vt (fasten, restrict)* binden ♦ *vi* (SPORT) unentschieden spielen; *(in competition)* punktgleich sein; **to** *~* **in a bow** zur Schleife binden; **to** *~* **a knot in sth** einen Knoten in etw *acc* machen; *~* **down** *vt* festbinden; **to** *~* **sb down to** jdn binden an +*acc*; *~* **up** *vt (dog)* anbinden; *(parcel)* verschnüren; *(boat)* festmachen; *(person)* fesseln; **to be** *~***d up** *(busy)* beschäftigt sein

tier [tɪə*] *n* (on roof) Rang *m*; *(of cake)* Etage *f*

tiff [tɪf] *n* Krach *m*

tiger ['taɪgə*] *n* Tiger *m*

tight [taɪt] *adj (close)* eng, knapp; *(schedule)* gedrängt; *(firm)* fest; *(control)* streng; *(stretched)* stramm, (an)gespannt; *(inf: drunk)* blau, stramm ♦ *adv (squeeze)* fest; *~***en** *vt* anziehen, anspannen; *(restrictions)* verschärfen ♦ *vi* sich spannen; *~***-fisted** *adj* knauserig; *~***ly** *adv* eng; fest; *(stretched)* straff; *~***-rope** *n* Seil *nt*; *~***s** *npl (esp BRIT)* Strumpfhose *f*

tile [taɪl] *n* (on roof) Dachziegel *m*; *(on wall or floor)* Fliese *f*; *~***d** *adj (roof)* gedeckt, Ziegel-; *(floor, wall)* mit Fliesen belegt

till [tɪl] *n* Kasse *f* ♦ *vt* bestellen ♦ *prep, conj* = **until**

tiller ['tɪlə*] *n* Ruderpinne *f*

tilt [tɪlt] *vt* kippen, neigen ♦ *vi* sich neigen

timber ['tɪmbə*] *n* Holz *nt*; *(trees)* Baumbestand *m*

time [taɪm] *n* Zeit *f*; *(occasion)* Mal *nt*; *(rhythm)* Takt *m* ♦ *vt* zur rechten Zeit tun, zeitlich einrichten; *(SPORT)* stoppen; **in 2 weeks'** *~* in 2 Wochen; **a long** *~* lange; **for the** *~* **being** vorläufig; **4 at a** *~* zu jeweils 4; **from** *~* **to** *~* gelegentlich; **to have a good** *~* sich amüsieren; **in** *~* *(soon enough)* rechtzeitig; *(after some ~)* mit der Zeit; *(MUS)* im Takt; **in no** *~* im Handumdrehen; **any** *~* jederzeit; **on** *~* pünktlich, rechtzeitig; **five** *~***s** 5 fünfmal 5; **what** *~* **is it?** wieviel Uhr ist es?, wie spät ist es?; *~* **bomb** *n* Zeitbombe *f*; *~***-lag** *n (in travel)* Verzögerung *f*; *(difference)* Zeitunterschied *m*; *~***less** *adj (beauty)* zeitlos; *~* **limit** *n* Frist *f*; *~***ly** *adj* rechtzeitig; günstig; *~* **off** *n* freie Zeit *f*; *~***r** *n (~* switch: *in kitchen)* Schaltuhr *f*; *~* **scale** *n* Zeitspanne *f*; *~* **switch** *(BRIT)* Zeitschalter *m*; *~***table** *n* Fahrplan *m*; *(SCH)* Stundenplan *m*; *~* **zone** *n* Zeitzone *f*

timid ['tɪmɪd] *adj* ängstlich, schuchtern

timing ['taɪmɪŋ] *n* Wahl *f* des richtigen Zeitpunkts, Timing *nt*; *(AUT)* Einstellung *f*

timpani ['tɪmpənɪ] *npl* Kesselpauken *pl*

tin [tɪn] *n (metal)* Blech *nt*; *(BRIT: can)* Büchse *f*, Dose *f*; *~***foil** *n* Staniolpapier *nt*

tinge [tɪndʒ] *n (colour)* Färbung *f*; *(fig)* Anflug *m* ♦ *vt* färben; *~***d with** mit einer Spur von

tingle ['tɪŋgl] *n* Prickeln *nt* ♦ *vi* prickeln

tinker ['tɪŋkə*] *n* Kesselflicker *m*; *~* **with** *vt fus* herumpfuschen an +*dat*

tinkle ['tɪŋkl] *vi* klingeln

tinned [tɪnd] *(BRIT) adj (food)* Dosen-, Büchsen-

tin opener ['-əupnə*] *(BRIT) n* Dosen- *or* Büchsenöffner *m*

tinsel ['tɪnsəl] *n* Rauschgold *nt*

tint [tɪnt] *n* Farbton *m*; (*slight colour*) Anflug *m*; (*hair*) Tönung *f*; ~**ed** *adj* getönt

tiny ['taɪnɪ] *adj* winzig

tip [tɪp] *n* (*pointed end*) Spitze *f*; (*money*) Trinkgeld *nt*; (*hint*) Wink *m*, Tip *m* ♦ *vt* (*slant*) kippen; (*hat*) antippen; (~ *over*) umkippen; (*waiter*) ein Trinkgeld geben +*dat*; ~**-off** *n* Hinweis *m*, Tip *m*; ~**ped** (*BRIT*) *adj* (*cigarette*) Filter-

tipsy ['tɪpsɪ] *adj* beschwipst

tiptoe ['tɪptəʊ] *n*: on ~ auf Zehenspitzen

tiptop ['tɪp'tɒp] *adj*: in ~ **condition** tipptopp, erstklassig

tire ['taɪə*] *n* (*US*) = **tyre** ♦ *vt*, *vi* ermüden, müde machen/werden; ~**d** *adj* müde; **to be** ~**d of sth** etw satt haben; ~**less** *adj* unermüdlich; ~**lessly** *adv* unermüdlich; ~**some** *adj* lästig

tiring ['taɪərɪŋ] *adj* ermüdend

tissue ['tɪʃuː] *n* Gewebe *nt*; (*paper handkerchief*) Papiertaschentuch *nt*; ~ **paper** *n* Seidenpapier *nt*

tit [tɪt] *n* (*bird*) Meise *f*; ~ **for tat** wie du mir, so ich dir

titbit ['tɪtbɪt] (*US* **tidbit**) *n* Leckerbissen *m*

titillate ['tɪtɪleɪt] *vt* kitzeln

titivate ['tɪtɪveɪt] *vt* schniegeln

title ['taɪtl] *n* Titel *m*; ~ **deed** *n* Eigentumsurkunde *f*; ~ **role** *n* Hauptrolle *f*

titter ['tɪtə*] *vi* kichern

titular ['tɪtjʊlə*] *adj* (*in name only*) nominell

TM *abbr* (= *trademark*) Wz

to [tuː, tə] *prep* **1** (*direction*) zu, nach; **I go to France/school** ich gehe nach Frankreich/zur Schule; **to the left** nach links

2 (*as far as*) bis

3 (*with expressions of time*) vor; **a quarter to 5** Viertel vor 5

4 (*for, of*) für; **secretary to the director** Sekretärin zu des Direckators

5 (*expressing indirect object*): **to give sth to sb** jdm etw geben; **to talk to sb** mit jdm sprechen; **I sold it to a friend** ich habe es einem Freund verkauft

6 (*in relation to*) zu; **30 miles to the gallon** 30 Meilen pro Gallone

7 (*purpose, result*) zu; **to my surprise** zu meiner Überraschung

♦ *with vb* **1** (*infin*): **to go/eat** gehen/essen; **to want to do sth** etw tun wollen; **to try/start to do sth** versuchen/anfangen, etw zu tun; **he has a lot to lose** er hat viel zu verlieren

2 (*with vb omitted*): **I don't want to** ich will (es) nicht

3 (*purpose, result*) um; **I did it to help you** ich tat es, um dir zu helfen

4 (*after adj etc*): **ready to use** gebrauchsfertig; **too old/young to ...** zu alt/jung, um ... zu ...

♦ *adv*: **push/pull the door to** die Tür zuschieben/zuziehen

toad [təʊd] *n* Kröte *f*; ~**stool** *n* Giftpilz *m*

toast [təʊst] *n* (*bread*) Toast *m*; (*drinking*) Trinkspruch *m* ♦ *vt* trinken auf +*acc*; (*bread*) toasten; (*warm*) wärmen; ~**er** *n* Toaster *m*

tobacco [tə'bækəʊ] *n* Tabak *m*; ~**nist** [tə'bækənɪst] *n* Tabakhändler *m*; ~**nist's (shop)** *n* Tabakladen *m*

toboggan [tə'bɒgən] *n* (Rodel)schlitten *m*

today [tə'deɪ] *adv* heute; (*at the present time*) heutzutage

toddler ['tɒdlə*] *n* Kleinkind *nt*

toddy ['tɒdɪ] *n* (Whisky)grog *m*

to-do [tə'duː] *n* Theater *nt*

toe [təʊ] *n* Zehe *f*; (*of sock, shoe*) Spitze *f* ♦ *vt*: **to ~ the line** (*fig*) sich einfügen; ~**nail** *n* Zehennagel *m*

toffee ['tɒfɪ] *n* Sahnebonbon *nt*; ~ **apple** (*BRIT*) *n* kandierte(r) Apfel *m*

together [tə'geðə*] *adv* zusammen; (*at the same time*) gleichzeitig; ~ **with** zusammen mit; gleichzeitig mit; ~**ness** *n* (*company*) Beisammensein *nt*

toil [tɔɪl] *n* harte Arbeit *f*, Plackerei *f* ♦ *vi* sich abmühen, sich plagen

toilet ['tɔɪlət] *n* Toilette *f* ♦ *cpd* Toiletten-; ~ **bag** *n* Waschbeutel *m*; ~

paper *n* Toilettenpapier *nt*; **~ries** ['tɔɪlətrɪz] *npl* Toilettenartikel *pl*; **~ roll** *n* Rolle *f* Toilettenpapier; **~ water** *n* Toilettenwasser *nt*

token ['təʊkən] *n* Zeichen *nt*; (*gift* **~**) Gutschein *m*; **book/record ~** (*BRIT*) Bücher-/Plattengutschein *m*

Tokyo ['təʊkjəʊ] *n* Tokio *nt*

told [təʊld] *pt, pp of* **tell**

tolerable ['tɒlərəbl] *adj* (*bearable*) erträglich; (*fairly good*) leidlich

tolerant ['tɒlərnt] *adj*: **~ (of)** tolerant (gegenüber)

tolerate ['tɒləreɪt] *vt* dulden; (*noise*) ertragen

toll [təʊl] *n* Gebühr *f* ♦ *vi* (*bell*) läuten

tomato [tə'mɑːtəʊ] (*pl* **~es**) *n* Tomate *f*

tomb [tuːm] *n* Grab(mal) *nt*

tomboy ['tɒmbɔɪ] *n* Wildfang *m*

tombstone ['tuːmstəʊn] *n* Grabstein *m*

tomcat ['tɒmkæt] *n* Kater *m*

tomorrow [tə'mɒrəʊ] *n* Morgen *nt* ♦ *adv* morgen; **the day after ~** übermorgen; **~ morning** morgen früh; **a week ~** morgen in einer Woche

ton [tʌn] *n* Tonne *f* (*BRIT* = 1016*kg*; *US* = 907*kg*); (*NAUT: also: register ~*) Registertonne *f*; **~s of** (*inf*) eine Unmenge von

tone [təʊn] *n* Ton *m*; **~ down** *vt* (*criticism, demands*) mäßigen; (*colours*) abtonen; **~ up** *vt* in Form bringen; **~-deaf** *adj* ohne musikalisches Gehör

tongs [tɒŋz] *npl* Zange *f*; (*curling ~*) Lockenstab *m*

tongue [tʌŋ] *n* Zunge *f*; (*language*) Sprache *f*; **with ~ in cheek** scherzhaft; **~-tied** *adj* stumm, sprachlos; **~-twister** *n* Zungenbrecher *m*

tonic ['tɒnɪk] *n* (*MED*) Stärkungsmittel *nt*; (*drink*) Tonic *nt*

tonight [tə'naɪt] *adv* heute abend

tonsil ['tɒnsl] *n* Mandel *f*; **~litis** [tɒnsɪ'laɪtɪs] *n* Mandelentzündung *f*

too [tuː] *adv* zu; (*also*) auch; **~ bad!** Pech!

took [tʊk] *pt of* **take**

tool [tuːl] *n* (*also fig*) Werkzeug *nt*; **~box** *n* Werkzeugkasten *m*

toot [tuːt] *n* Hupen *nt* ♦ *vi* tuten; (*AUT*) hupen

tooth [tuːθ] (*pl* **teeth**) *n* Zahn *m*; **~ache** *n* Zahnschmerzen *pl*, Zahnweh *nt*; **~brush** *n* Zahnbürste *f*; **~paste** *n* Zahnpasta *f*; **~pick** *n* Zahnstocher *m*

top [tɒp] *n* Spitze *f*; (*of mountain*) Gipfel *m*; (*of tree*) Wipfel *m*; (*toy*) Kreisel *m*; (**~ gear**) vierte(r)/fünfte(r) Gang *m* ♦ *adj* oberste(r, s) ♦ *vt* (*list*) an erster Stelle stehen auf **+***dat*; **on ~ of** oben auf **+***dat*; **from ~ to bottom** von oben bis unten; **~ off** (*US*) *vt* auffüllen; **~ up** *vt* auffüllen; **~ floor** *n* oberste(s) Stockwerk *nt*; **~ hat** *n* Zylinder *m*; **~-heavy** *adj* kopflastig

topic ['tɒpɪk] *n* Thema *nt*, Gesprächsgegenstand *m*; **~al** *adj* aktuell

topless ['tɒpləs] *adj* (*bather etc*) oben ohne

top-level ['tɒp'levl] *adj* auf höchster Ebene

topmost ['tɒpməʊst] *adj* oberste(r, s)

topple ['tɒpl] *vt, vi* stürzen, kippen

top-secret ['tɒp'siːkrət] *adj* streng geheim

topsy-turvy ['tɒpsɪ'tɜːvɪ] *adv* durcheinander ♦ *adj* auf den Kopf gestellt

torch [tɔːtʃ] *n* (*BRIT: ELEC*) Taschenlampe *f*; (*with flame*) Fackel *f*

tore [tɔː*] *pt of* **tear**[1]

torment [*n* 'tɔːment, *vb* tɔː'ment] *n* Qual *f* ♦ *vt* (*distress*) quälen

torn [tɔːn] *pp of* **tear**[1] ♦ *adj* hin- und hergerissen

torrent ['tɒrənt] *n* Sturzbach *m*; **~ial** [tə'renʃəl] *adj* wolkenbruchartig

torrid ['tɒrɪd] *adj* heiß

tortoise ['tɔːtəs] *n* Schildkröte *f*; **~shell** ['tɔːtəʃel] *n* Schildpatt *m*

tortuous ['tɔːtjʊəs] *adj* gewunden

torture ['tɔːtʃə*] *n* Folter *f* ♦ *vt* foltern

Tory ['tɔːrɪ] (*BRIT*) *n* (*POL*) Tory *m* ♦ *adj* (*POL*) Tory-, konservativ

toss [tɒs] *vt* schleudern; **to ~ a coin** *or* **to ~ up for sth** etw mit einer Münze entscheiden; **to ~ and turn** (*in bed*) sich hin und her werfen

tot [tɒt] *n* (*small quantity*) bißchen *nt*; (*small child*) Knirps *m*

total ['təʊtl] n Gesamtheit f; (money)
Endsumme f ♦ adj Gesamt-, total ♦ vt
(add up) zusammenzählen; (amount to)
sich belaufen auf
totalitarian [təʊtælɪ'tɛərɪən] adj totalitär
totally ['təʊtəlɪ] adv total
totter [tɒtə*] vi wanken, schwanken
touch [tʌtʃ] n Berührung f; (sense of
feeling) Tastsinn m ♦ vt (feel)
berühren; (come against) leicht anstoßen; (emotionally) rühren; a ~ of
(fig) eine Spur von; to get in ~ with sb
sich mit jdm in Verbindung setzen; to
lose ~ (friends) Kontakt verlieren; ~
on vt fus (topic) berühren ♦ vt,
erwähnen; ~ up vt (paint) auffrischen;
~-and-go adj riskant, knapp; ~down
n Landen nt, Niedergehen nt; ~ing adj
rührend; ~line n Seitenlinie f; ~y adj
empfindlich, reizbar
tough [tʌf] adj zäh; (difficult) schwierig
♦ n Schläger(typ) m; ~en vt zäh machen; (make strong) abhärten
toupee ['tuːpeɪ] n Toupet nt
tour ['tʊə*] n Tour f ♦ vi umherreisen;
(THEAT) auf Tour sein; auf Tour gehen;
~ing n Umherreisen nt; (THEAT)
Tournee f
tourism ['tʊərɪzm] n Fremdenverkehr
m, Tourismus m
tourist ['tʊərɪst] n Tourist(in) m(f) ♦
cpd (class) Touristen-; ~ office n Ver-
kehrsamt nt
tournament ['tʊənəmənt] n Tournier nt
tousled ['taʊzld] adj zerzaust
tout [taʊt] vi: to ~ for auf Kundenfang
gehen für ♦ n: ticket ~ Kunden-
schlepper(in) m(f)
tow [təʊ] vt (ab)schleppen; on (BRIT) or
in (US) ~ (AUT) im Schlepp
toward(s) [tə'wɔːd(z)] prep (with time)
gegen; (in direction of) nach
towel ['taʊəl] n Handtuch nt; ~ling n
(fabric) Frottee nt or m; ~ rack (US) n
Handtuchstange f; ~ rail n Handtuchstange f
tower ['taʊə*] n Turm m; ~ block
(BRIT) n Hochhaus nt; ~ing adj
hochragend
town [taʊn] n Stadt f; to go to ~ (fig)

sich ins Zeug legen; ~ centre n
Stadtzentrum nt; ~ clerk n
Stadtdirektor m; ~ council n Stadtrat
m; ~ hall n Rathaus nt; ~ plan n
Stadtplan m; ~ planning n Stadtpla-
nung f
towrope ['təʊrəʊp] n Abschlepptau nt
tow truck (US) n (breakdown lorry)
Abschleppwagen m
toxic ['tɒksɪk] adj giftig, Gift-
toy [tɔɪ] n Spielzeug nt; ~ with vt fus
spielen mit; ~shop n Spielwarenge-
schäft nt
trace [treɪs] n Spur f ♦ vt (follow a
course) nachspüren +dat; (find out)
aufspüren; (copy) durchpausen; **tracing
paper** n Pauspapier nt
track [træk] n (mark) Spur f; (path)
Weg m; (race~) Rennbahn f; (RAIL)
Gleis nt ♦ vt verfolgen; to keep ~ of sb
jdn im Auge behalten; ~ down vt aufspüren; ~suit n Trainingsanzug m
tract [trækt] n (of land) Gebiet nt;
(booklet) Traktat nt
traction ['trækʃən] n (power) Zugkraft
f; (AUT: grip) Bodenhaftung f; (MED):
in ~ im Streckverband
trade [treɪd] n (commerce) Handel m;
(business) Geschäft nt, Gewerbe nt;
(people) Geschäftsleute pl; (skilled
manual work) Handwerk nt ♦ vi: to ~
(in) handeln (mit) ♦ vt tauschen; ~ in
vt in Zahlung geben; ~ fair n Messe nt;
~-in price n Preis m, zu dem etw in
Zahlung genommen wird; ~mark n
Warenzeichen nt; ~ name n
Handelsbezeichnung f; ~r n Händler
m; **tradesman** (irreg) n (shopkeeper)
Geschäftsmann m; (workman) Handwerker m; (delivery man) Lieferant m;
~ union n Gewerkschaft f; ~ unionist
n Gewerkschaftler(in) m(f)
trading ['treɪdɪŋ] n Handel m; ~ estate
(BRIT) n Industriegelände nt
tradition [trə'dɪʃən] n Tradition f; ~al
adj traditionell, herkömmlich
traffic ['træfɪk] n Verkehr m; (esp in
drugs): ~ (in) Handel m (mit) ♦ vi: to
~ in (esp drugs) handeln mit; ~ circle
(US) n Kreisverkehr m; ~ jam n Ver-

kehrsstauung f; ~ **lights** npl Verkehrsampel f; ~ **warden** n ≈ Verkehrspolizist m (ohne amtliche Befugnisse), Politesse f (ohne amtliche Befugnisse)

tragedy ['trædʒədɪ] n Tragödie f

tragic ['trædʒɪk] adj tragisch

trail [treɪl] n (track) Spur f; (of smoke) Rauchfahne f; (of dust) Staubwolke f; (road) Pfad m, Weg m ♦ vt (animal) verfolgen; (person) folgen +dat; (drag) schleppen ♦ vi (hang loosely) schleifen; (plants) sich ranken; (be behind) hinterherhinken; (SPORT) weit zurückliegen; (walk) zuckeln; ~ **behind** vi zurückbleiben; ~**er** n Anhänger m; (US: caravan) Wohnwagen m; (for film) Vorschau f; ~ **truck** (US) n Sattelschlepper m

train [treɪn] n Zug m; (of dress) Schleppe f; (series) Folge f ♦ vt (teach: person) ausbilden; (: animal) abrichten; (: mind) schulen; (SPORT) trainieren; (aim) richten ♦ vi (exercise) trainieren; (study) ausgebildet werden; ~ **of thought** Gedankengang m; **to** ~ **sth on** (aim) etw richten auf +acc; ~**ed** adj (eye) geschult; (person, voice) ausgebildet; ~**ee** [treɪ'niː] n Lehrling m; Praktikant(in) m(f); ~**er** n (SPORT) Trainer m; Ausbilder m; ~**ing** n (for occupation) Ausbildung f; (SPORT) Training nt; **in** ~**ing** im Training; ~**ing college** n Pädagogische Hochschule f, Lehrerseminar nt; ~**ing shoes** npl Turnschuhe pl

traipse [treɪps] vi latschen

trait [treɪ(t)] n Zug m, Merkmal nt

traitor ['treɪtə*] n Verräter m

trajectory [trə'dʒektərɪ] n Flugbahn f

tram ['træm] (BRIT) n (also: ~car) Straßenbahn f

tramp [træmp] n Landstreicher m ♦ vi (walk heavily) stampfen, stapfen; (travel on foot) wandern

trample ['træmpl] vt (nieder)trampeln ♦ vi (herum)trampeln; **to** ~ (underfoot) herumtrampeln auf +dat

tranquil ['træŋkwɪl] adj ruhig, friedlich;

~**lity** (US ~**ity**) n Ruhe f; ~**lizer** (US ~**izer**) n Beruhigungsmittel nt

transact [træn'zækt] vt abwickeln; ~**ion** [træn'zækʃən] n Abwicklung f; (piece of business) Geschäft nt, Transaktion f

transcend [træn'send] vt übersteigen

transcript ['trænskrɪpt] n Abschrift f, Kopie f; (JUR) Protokoll nt; ~**ion** [træn'skrɪpʃən] n Transkription f; (product) Abschrift f

transfer [n 'trænsfə*, vt træns'fɜː*] n (~ring) Übertragung f; (of business) Umzug m; (being ~red) Versetzung f; (design) Abziehbild nt; (SPORT) Transfer m ♦ vt (business) verlegen; (person) versetzen; (prisoner) überführen; (drawing) übertragen; (money) überweisen; **to** ~ **the charges** (BRIT: TEL) ein R-Gespräch führen

transform [træns'fɔːm] vt umwandeln; ~**ation** [trænsfə'meɪʃən] n Umwandlung f, Verwandlung f; ~**er** n (ELEC) Transformator m

transfusion [træns'fjuːʒən] n Blutübertragung f, Transfusion f

transient ['trænzɪənt] adj kurz(lebig)

transistor [træn'zɪstə*] n (ELEC) Transistor m; (radio) Transistorradio nt

transit ['trænzɪt] n: **in** ~ unterwegs

transition [træn'zɪʃən] n Übergang m; ~**al** adj Übergangs-

transitory ['trænzɪtərɪ] adj vorübergehend

translate [trænz'leɪt] vt, vi übersetzen

translation [trænz'leɪʃən] n Übersetzung f

translator [trænz'leɪtə*] n Übersetzer(in) m(f)

transmission [trænz'mɪʃən] n (of information) Übermittlung f; (ELEC, MED, TV) Übertragung f; (AUT) Getriebe nt

transmit [trænz'mɪt] vt (message) übermitteln; (ELEC, MED, TV) übertragen; ~**ter** n Sender m

transparency [træns'pɛərənsɪ] n Durchsichtigkeit f; (BRIT: PHOT) Dia(positiv) nt

transparent [træns'pærənt] adj durchsichtig; (fig) offenkundig

transpire [træns'paɪə*] vi (turn out) sich herausstellen; (happen) passieren

transplant [vb træns'plɑːnt, n 'trænsplɑːnt] vt umpflanzen; (MED, also fig: person) verpflanzen ♦ n (MED) Transplantation f; (organ) Transplantat nt

transport [n 'trænspɔːt, vb træns'pɔːt] n Transport m, Beförderung f ♦ vt befördern; transportieren; **means of** ~ Transportmittel nt; ~**ation** [trænspɔː'teɪʃən] n Transport m, Beförderung f; (means) Beförderungsmittel nt; (cost) Transportkosten pl; ~ **café** (BRIT) n Fernfahrerlokal nt

transverse ['trænzvɜːs] adj Quer-; (position) horizontal; (engine) querliegend

trap [træp] n Falle f; (carriage) zweirädrige(r) Einspänner m; (inf: mouth) Klappe f ♦ vt fangen; (person) in eine Falle locken; ~**door** n Falltür f

trappings ['træpɪŋz] npl Aufmachung f

trash [træʃ] n (rubbish) Plunder m; (nonsense) Mist m; ~ **can** (US) n Mülleimer m

travel ['trævl] n Reisen nt ♦ vi reisen ♦ vt (distance) zurücklegen; (country) bereisen; ~ **agency** n Reisebüro nt; ~ **agent** n Reisebürokaufmann(frau) m(f); ~**ler** (US ~**er**) n Reisende(r) mf; (salesman) Handlungsreisende(r) m; ~**ler's cheque** (US ~**er's check**) n Reisescheck m; ~**ling** (US ~**ing**) n Reisen nt; ~ **sickness** n Reisekrankheit f

tray [treɪ] n (tea ~) Tablett nt; (receptacle) Schale f; (for mail) Ablage f

treacherous ['tretʃərəs] adj verräterisch; (road) tückisch

treachery ['tretʃərɪ] n Verrat m

treacle ['triːkl] n Sirup m, Melasse f

tread [tred] (pt **trod**, pp **trodden**) n Schritt m, Tritt m; (of stair) Stufe f; (on tyre) Profil nt ♦ vi treten; ~ **on** vt fus treten auf +acc

treason ['triːzn] n Verrat m

treasure ['treʒə*] n Schatz m ♦ vt schätzen

treasurer ['treʒərə*] n Kassenverwalter

m, Schatzmeister m

treasury ['treʒərɪ] n (POL) Finanzministerium nt

treat [triːt] n besondere Freude f ♦ vt (deal with) behandeln; **to** ~ **sb to sth** jdm etw spendieren

treatise ['triːtɪz] n Abhandlung f

treatment ['triːtmənt] n Behandlung f

treaty ['triːtɪ] n Vertrag m

treble ['trebl] adj dreifach ♦ vt verdreifachen; ~ **clef** n Violinschlüssel m

tree [triː] n Baum m; ~ **trunk** n Baumstamm m

trek [trek] n Treck m, Zug m; (inf) anstrengende(r) Weg m ♦ vi trecken

trellis ['trelɪs] n Gitter nt; (for gardening) Spalier nt

tremble ['trembl] vi zittern; (ground) beben

trembling ['tremblɪŋ] n Zittern nt ♦ adj zitternd

tremendous [trə'mendəs] adj gewaltig, kolossal; (inf: very good) prima

tremor ['tremə*] n Zittern nt; (of earth) Beben nt

trench [trentʃ] n Graben m; (MIL) Schützengraben m

trend [trend] n Tendenz f; ~**y** (inf) adj modisch

trepidation [trepɪ'deɪʃən] n Beklommenheit f

trespass ['trespəs] vi: **to** ~ **on** widerrechtlich betreten; "no ~**ing**" „Betreten verboten"

tress [tres] n Locke f

trestle ['tresl] n Bock m; ~ **table** n Klapptisch m

trial ['traɪəl] n (JUR) Prozeß m; (test) Versuch m, Probe f; (hardship) Prüfung f; **by** ~ **and error** durch Ausprobieren

triangle ['traɪæŋgl] n Dreieck nt; (MUS) Triangel f

triangular [traɪ'æŋgjʊlə*] adj dreieckig

tribal ['traɪbəl] adj Stammes-

tribe [traɪb] n Stamm m; **tribesman** (irreg) n Stammesangehörige(r) m

tribulation [trɪbjʊ'leɪʃən] n Not f, Mühsal f

tribunal [traɪ'bjuːnl] n Gericht nt;

(inquiry) Untersuchungsausschuß *m*

tributary ['trɪbjʊtərɪ] *n* Nebenfluß *m*

tribute ['trɪbjuːt] *n (admiration)* Zeichen *nt* der Hochachtung; **to pay ~ to** sb/sth jdm/einer Sache Tribut zollen

trice [traɪs] *n*: **in a ~** im Nu

trick [trɪk] *n* Trick *m*; *(CARDS)* Stich *m* ♦ *vt* überlisten, beschwindeln; **to play a ~ on** sb jdm einen Streich spielen; **that should do the ~** daß müßte eigentlich klappen; **~ery** *n* Tricks *pl*

trickle ['trɪkl] *n* Tröpfeln *nt*; *(small river)* Rinnsal *nt* ♦ *vi* tröpfeln; *(seep)* sickern

tricky ['trɪkɪ] *adj (problem)* schwierig; *(situation)* kitzlig

tricycle ['traɪsɪkl] *n* Dreirad *nt*

trifle ['traɪfl] *n* Kleinigkeit *f*; *(COOK)* Trifle *m* ♦ *adv*: **a ~ ...** ein bißchen ...

trifling ['traɪflɪŋ] *adj* geringfügig

trigger ['trɪgə*] *n* Drücker *m*; **~ off** *vt* auslösen

trim [trɪm] *adj* gepflegt; *(figure)* schlank ♦ *n* (gute) Verfassung *f*; *(embellishment, on car)* Verzierung *f* ♦ *vt (clip)* schneiden; *(trees)* stutzen; *(decorate)* besetzen; *(sails)* trimmen; **~mings** *npl (decorations)* Verzierung *f*, Verzierungen *pl*; *(extras)* Zubehör *nt*

Trinity ['trɪnɪtɪ] *n*: **the ~** die Dreieinigkeit *f*

trinket ['trɪŋkɪt] *n* kleine(s) Schmuckstück *nt*

trip [trɪp] *n (kurze)* Reise *f*; *(outing)* Ausflug *m*; *(stumble)* Stolpern *nt* ♦ *vi (walk quickly)* trippeln; *(stumble)* stolpern; **on a ~** auf Reisen; **~ up** *vi* stolpern; *(fig)* stolpern, einen Fehler machen ♦ *vt* zu Fall bringen; *(fig)* hereinlegen

tripe [traɪp] *n (food)* Kutteln *pl*; *(rubbish)* Mist *m*

triple ['trɪpl] *adj* dreifach

triplets ['trɪplɪts] *npl* Drillinge *pl*

triplicate ['trɪplɪkət] *n*: **in ~** in dreifacher Ausfertigung

tripod ['traɪpɒd] *n (PHOT)* Stativ *nt*

trite [traɪt] *adj* banal

triumph ['traɪʌmf] *n* Triumph *m* ♦ *vi*: **to ~ (over)** triumphieren (über +*acc*);

~ant [traɪ'ʌmfənt] *adj* triumphierend

trivia ['trɪvɪə] *npl* Trivialitäten *pl*

trivial ['trɪvɪəl] *adj* gering(fügig), trivial

trod [trɒd] *pt of* **tread**; **~den** ['trɒdn] *pp of* **tread**

trolley ['trɒlɪ] *n* Handwagen *m*; *(in shop)* Einkaufswagen; *(for luggage)* Kofferkuli *m*; *(table)* Teewagen *m*; **~bus** *n* Oberleitungsbus *m*, Obus *m*

trombone [trɒm'bəʊn] *n* Posaune *f*

troop [truːp] *n* Schar *f*; *(MIL)* Trupp *m*; **~s** *npl* Truppen *pl*; **~ in/out** *vi* hinein-/hinausströmen; **~er** *n* Kavallerist *m*; **~ing the colour** *n (ceremony)* Fahnenparade *f*

trophy ['trəʊfɪ] *n* Trophäe *f*

tropic ['trɒpɪk] *n* Wendekreis *m*; **~al** *adj* tropisch

trot [trɒt] *n* Trott *m* ♦ *vi* trotten; **on the ~** *(BRIT: fig: inf)* in einer Tour

trouble ['trʌbl] *n (problems)* Ärger *m*; *(worry)* Sorge *f*; *(in country, industry)* Unruhen *pl*; *(effort)* Mühe *f*; *(MED)*: **stomach ~** Magenbeschwerden *pl* ♦ *vt (disturb)* stören; **~s** *npl (POL etc)* Unruhen *pl*; **to ~ to do** sth sich bemühen, etw zu tun; **to be in ~** Probleme or Ärger haben; **to go to the ~ of doing** sth sich die Mühe machen, etw zu tun; **what's the ~?** was ist los?; *(to sick person)* wo fehlt's?; **~d** *adj (person)* beunruhigt; *(country)* geplagt; **~-free** *adj* sorglos; **~maker** *n* Unruhestifter *m*; **~shooter** *n* Vermittler *m*; **~some** *adj* lästig, unangenehm; *(child)* schwierig

trough [trɒf] *n (vessel)* Trog *m*; *(channel)* Rinne *f*, Kanal *m*; *(MET)* Tief *nt*

trounce [traʊns] *vt (esp SPORT)* vernichtend schlagen

trousers ['traʊzəz] *npl* Hose *f*

trout [traʊt] *n* Forelle *f*

trowel ['traʊəl] *n* Kelle *f*

truant ['truːənt] *n*: **to play ~** *(BRIT)* (die Schule) schwänzen

truce [truːs] *n* Waffenstillstand *m*

truck [trʌk] *n* Lastwagen *m*; *(RAIL)* offene(r) Güterwagen *m*; **~ driver** *n* Lastwagenfahrer *m*; **~ farm** *(US)* *n*

Gemüsegärtnerei f

truculent ['trʌkjʊlənt] adj trotzig

trudge [trʌdʒ] vi sich (mühselig) dahin-schleppen

true [truː] adj (exact) wahr; (genuine) echt; (friend) treu

truffle ['trʌfl] n Trüffel f or m

truly ['truːlɪ] adv wirklich; **yours ~** Ihr sehr ergebener

trump [trʌmp] n (CARDS) Trumpf m; **~ed-up** adj erfunden

trumpet ['trʌmpɪt] n Trompete f

truncheon ['trʌntʃən] n Gummiknüppel m

trundle ['trʌndl] vt schieben ♦ vi: **to ~ along** entlangrollen

trunk [trʌŋk] n (of tree) (Baum)stamm m; (ANAT) Rumpf m; (box) Truhe f, Überseekoffer m; (of elephant) Rüssel m; (US: AUT) Kofferraum m; **~s** npl (also: swimming ~s) Badehose f

truss [trʌs] n (MED) Bruchband nt ♦ vt (also: ~ up) fesseln

trust [trʌst] n (confidence) Vertrauen nt; (for property etc) Treuhandvermögen nt ♦ vt (rely on) vertrauen +dat (acc), sich verlassen auf +acc; (hope) hoffen; (entrust): **to ~ sth to sb** jdm etw anver-trauen; **~ed** adj treu; **~ee** [trʌs'tiː] n Vermögensverwalter m; **~ful** adj ver-trauensvoll; **~ing** adj vertrauensvoll; **~worthy** adj vertrauenswürdig; (account) glaubwürdig; **~y** adj treu, zuverlässig

truth [truːθ, pl truːðz] n Wahrheit f; **~ful** adj ehrlich

try [traɪ] n Versuch m ♦ vt (attempt) versuchen; (test) (aus)probieren; (JUR: person) unter Anklage stellen; (: case) verhandeln ♦ vi (make effort) versu-chen, sich bemühen; **to have a ~** es versuchen; **to ~ to do sth** versuchen, etw zu tun; **~ on** vt (dress) an-probieren; (hat) aufprobieren; **~ out** vt ausprobieren; **~ing** adj schwierig

T-shirt ['tiːʃɜːt] n T-shirt nt

T-square ['tiːskweə*] n Reißschiene f

tub [tʌb] n Wanne f, Kübel m; (for margarine etc) Becher m

tubby ['tʌbɪ] adj rundlich

tube [tjuːb] n (pipe) Röhre f, Rohr nt; (for toothpaste etc) Tube f; (in London) U-Bahn f; (AUT: for tyre) Schlauch m; **~ station** n (in London) U-Bahnstation f

tubing ['tjuːbɪŋ] n Schlauch m; **a piece of ~** ein (Stück) Schlauch

tubular ['tjuːbjʊlə*] adj röhrenförmig

TUC (BRIT) n abbr = **Trades Union Con-gress**

tuck [tʌk] n (fold) Falte f, Einschlag m ♦ vt (put) stecken; (gather) fälteln, ein-schlagen; **~ away** vt wegstecken; **~ in** vt hineinstecken; (blanket etc) fest-stecken; (person) zudecken ♦ vi (eat) hineinhauen, zulangen; **~ up** vt (child) warm zudecken; **~ shop** n Süßwarenladen m

Tuesday ['tjuːzdeɪ] n Dienstag m

tuft [tʌft] n Büschel m

tug [tʌg] n (jerk) Zerren nt, Ruck m; (NAUT) Schleppdampfer m ♦ vt, vi zerren, ziehen; (boat) schleppen; **~-of-war** n Tauziehen nt

tuition [tjuː'ɪʃən] n (BRIT) Unterricht m; (: private ~) Privatunterricht m; (US: school fees) Schulgeld nt

tulip ['tjuːlɪp] n Tulpe f

tumble ['tʌmbl] n (fall) Sturz m ♦ vi fallen, stürzen; **~ to** vt fus kapieren; **~down** adj baufällig; **~ dryer** (BRIT) n Trockner m; **~r** ['tʌmblə*] n (glass) Trinkglas nt

tummy ['tʌmɪ] (inf) n Bauch m

tumour ['tjuːmə*] (US **tumor**) n Ge-schwulst f, Tumor m

tuna ['tjuːnə] n Thunfisch m

tune [tjuːn] n Melodie f ♦ vt (MUS) stimmen; (AUT) richtig einstellen; **to sing in ~/out of ~** richtig/falsch singen; **to be out of ~ with** nicht harmonieren mit; **~ in** vi einschalten; **~ up** vi (MUS) stimmen; **~ful** adj melodisch; **~r** n (person) (Instrumenten)stimmer m; (part of radio) Tuner m; **piano ~r** Klavierstimmer(in) m(f)

tunic ['tjuːnɪk] n Waffenrock m; (loose garment) lange Bluse f

tuning ['tjuːnɪŋ] n (RAD, AUT) Einstellen

nt; (*MUS*) Stimmen *nt*; ~ **fork** *n*
Stimmgabel *f*

Tunisia [tjuːˈnɪzɪə] *n* Tunesien *nt*

tunnel [ˈtʌnl] *n* Tunnel *m*, Unterführung
f ♦ *vi* einen Tunnel anlegen

turbulent [ˈtɜːbjʊlənt] *adj* stürmisch

tureen [tjʊˈriːn] *n* Terrine *f*

turf [tɜːf] *n* Rasen *m*; (*piece*) Sode *f* ♦
vt mit Grassoden belegen; ~ **out** (*inf*)
vt rauswerfen

turgid [ˈtɜːdʒɪd] *adj* geschwollen

Turk [tɜːk] *n* Türke *m*, Türkin *f*

Turkey [ˈtɜːkɪ] *n* Türkei *f*

turkey [ˈtɜːkɪ] *n* Puter *m*, Truthahn *m*

Turkish [ˈtɜːkɪʃ] *adj* türkisch ♦ *n* (*LING*)
Türkisch *nt*

turmoil [ˈtɜːmɔɪl] *n* Aufruhr *m*, Tumult
m

turn [tɜːn] *n* (*rotation*) (Um)drehung *f*;
(*performance*) (Programm)nummer *f*;
(*MED*) Schock *m* ♦ *vt* (*rotate*) umdrehen;
(*change position of*) umdrehen,
wenden; (*page*) umblättern; (*transform*): **to ~ sth into sth** etw in etw *acc*
verwandeln; (*direct*) zuwenden ♦ *vi*
(*rotate*) sich drehen; (*change direction:
in car*) abbiegen; (: *wind*) drehen; (~
round) umdrehen, wenden; (*become*)
werden; (*leaves*) sich verfärben;
(*milk*) sauer werden; (*weather*) umschlagen; **to do sb a good ~** jdm etwas
Gutes tun; **it's your ~** du bist dran *or*
an der Reihe; **in ~**, **by ~s**
abwechselnd; **to take ~s** sich
abwechseln; **it gave me quite a ~** das
hat mich schön erschreckt; "**no left ~**"
(*AUT*) „Linksabbiegen verboten"; ~
away *vi* sich abwenden; ~ **back** *vt* umdrehen; (*person*) zurückschicken;
(*clock*) zurückstellen ♦ *vi* umkehren; ~
down *vt* (*refuse*) ablehnen; (*fold
down*) umschlagen; ~ **in** *vi* (*go to bed*)
ins Bett gehen ♦ *vt* (*fold inwards*) ein-
wärts biegen; ~ **off** *vi* abbiegen ♦ *vt*
ausschalten; (*tap*) zudrehen; (*machine,
electricity*) abstellen; ~ **on** *vt* (*light*)
anschalten, einschalten; (*tap*) auf-
drehen; (*machine*) anstellen; ~ **out** *vi*
(*prove to be*) sich erweisen; (*people*)
sich entwickeln ♦ *vt* (*light*) aus-

schalten; (*gas*) abstellen; (*produce*)
produzieren; **how did the cake ~ out?**
wie ist der Kuchen geworden?; ~
round *vi* (*person, vehicle*) sich herumdrehen; (*rotate*) sich drehen; ~ **up** *vi*
auftauchen; (*happen*) passieren, sich
ereignen ♦ *vt* (*collar*) hochklappen,
hochstellen; (*nose*) rümpfen; (*increase:
radio*) lauter stellen; (: *heat*) höher
drehen; ~**ing** *n* (*in road*) Abzweigung
f; ~**ing point** *n* Wendepunkt *m*

turnip [ˈtɜːnɪp] *n* Steckrübe *f*

turnout [ˈtɜːnaʊt] *n* (Besucher)zahl *f*;
(*COMM*) Produktion *f*

turnover [ˈtɜːnəʊvə*] *n* Umsatz *m*; (*of
staff*) Wechsel *m*

turnpike [ˈtɜːnpaɪk] (*US*) *n*
gebührenpflichtige Straße *f*

turnstile [ˈtɜːnstaɪl] *n* Drehkreuz *nt*

turntable [ˈtɜːnteɪbl] *n* (*of record
player*) Plattenteller *m*; (*RAIL*) Dreh-
scheibe *f*

turn-up [ˈtɜːnʌp] (*BRIT*) *n* (*on trousers*)
Aufschlag *m*

turpentine [ˈtɜːpəntaɪn] *n* Terpentin *nt*

turquoise [ˈtɜːkwɔɪz] *n* (*gem*) Türkis *m*;
(*colour*) Türkis *nt* ♦ *adj* türkisfarben

turret [ˈtʌrɪt] *n* Turm *m*

turtle [ˈtɜːtl] *n* Schildkröte *f*; ~ **neck
(sweater)** *n* Pullover *m* mit Schild-
krötkragen *m*

tusk [tʌsk] *n* Stoßzahn *m*

tussle [ˈtʌsl] *n* Balgerei *f*

tutor [ˈtjuːtə*] *n* (*teacher*) Privatlehrer
m; (*college instructor*) Tutor *m*; ~**ial**
[tjuːˈtɔːrɪəl] *n* (*UNIV*) Kolloquium *nt*,
Seminarübung *f*

tuxedo [tʌkˈsiːdəʊ] (*US*) *n* Smoking *m*

TV [ˈtiːˈviː] *n abbr* (= *television*) TV *nt*

twang [twæŋ] *n* scharfe(r) Ton *m*; (*of
voice*) Näseln *nt*

tweezers [ˈtwiːzəz] *npl* Pinzette *f*

twelfth [twelfθ] *adj* zwölfte(r, s)

twelve [twelv] *num* zwölf; **at ~ o'clock**
(*midday*) um 12 Uhr; (*midnight*) um
Null Uhr

twentieth [ˈtwentɪɪθ] *adj* zwanzigste(r,
s)

twenty [ˈtwentɪ] *num* zwanzig

twice [twaɪs] *adv* zweimal; ~ **as much**

doppelt soviel

twiddle ['twidl] vt, vi: to ~ (with) sth an etw dat herumdrehen; to ~ one's thumbs (fig) Däumchen drehen

twig [twig] n dünne(r) Zweig m ♦ vt (inf) kapieren, merken

twilight ['twailait] n Zwielicht nt

twin [twin] n Zwilling m ♦ adj Zwillings-; (very similar) Doppel- ♦ vt (towns) zu Partnerstädten machen; ~-bedded room n Zimmer nt mit zwei Einzelbetten

twine [twain] n Bindfaden m ♦ vi (plants) sich ranken

twinge [twind3] n stechende(r) Schmerz m, Stechen nt

twinkle ['twiŋkl] n Funkeln nt, Blitzen nt ♦ vi funkeln

twirl [tw3:l] n Wirbel m ♦ vt, vi (herum)wirbeln

twist [twist] n (~ing) Drehung f; (bend) Kurve f ♦ vt (turn) drehen; (make crooked) verbiegen; (distort) verdrehen ♦ vi (wind) sich drehen; (curve) sich winden

twit [twit] (inf) n Idiot m

twitch [twitʃ] n Zucken nt ♦ vi zucken

two [tu:] num zwei; to put ~ and ~ together seine Schlüsse ziehen; ~-door adj zweitürig; ~-faced adj falsch; ~fold adj, adv zweifach, doppelt; to increase ~fold verdoppeln; ~-piece adj zweiteilig; ~-piece (suit) n Zweiteiler m; ~-piece (swimsuit) n zweiteilige(r) Badeanzug m; ~-seater n (plane, car) Zweisitzer m; ~some n Paar nt; ~-way adj (traffic) Gegen-

tycoon [tai'ku:n] n: (business) ~ (Industrie)magnat m

type [taip] n Typ m, Art f; (PRINT) Type f ♦ vt, vi maschineschreiben, tippen; ~-cast adj (THEAT, TV) auf eine Rolle festgelegt; ~face n Schrift f; ~script n maschinegeschriebene(r) Text m; ~writer n Schreibmaschine f; ~written adj maschinegeschrieben

typhoid ['taifɔid] n Typhus m

typical ['tipikəl] adj: ~ (of) typisch (für); ~ly adv typisch

typify ['tipifai] vt typisch sein für

typing ['taipiŋ] n Maschineschreiben nt

typist ['taipist] n Maschinenschreiber(in) m(f), Tippse f (inf)

tyrant ['taiərnt] n Tyrann m

tyre [taiə*] (US tire) n Reifen m; ~ pressure n Reifendruck m

U

U-bend ['ju:'bend] n (in pipe) U-Bogen m

ubiquitous [ju:'bikwitəs] adj überall zu findend; allgegenwärtig

udder ['ʌdə*] n Euter nt

UFO ['ju:fəu] n abbr (= unidentified flying object) UFO nt

ugh [3:h] excl hu

ugliness ['ʌglinəs] n Häßlichkeit f

ugly ['ʌgli] adj häßlich; (bad) böse, schlimm

UK n abbr = United Kingdom

ulcer ['ʌlsə*] n Geschwür nt

Ulster ['ʌlstə*] n Ulster nt

ulterior [ʌl'tiəriə*] adj: ~ motive Hintergedanke m

ultimate ['ʌltimət] adj äußerste(r, s), allerletzte(r, s); ~ly adv schließlich, letzten Endes

ultrasound ['ʌltrə'saund] n (MED) Ultraschall m

umbilical cord [ʌm'bilikl-] n Nabelschnur f

umbrella [ʌm'brelə] n Schirm m

umpire ['ʌmpaiə*] n Schiedsrichter m ♦ vt, vi schiedsrichtern

umpteen ['ʌmpti:n] (inf) num zig; for the ~th time zum X-ten Mal

UN n abbr = United Nations

unable [ʌn'eibl] adj: to be ~ to do sth etw nicht tun können

unaccompanied ['ʌnə'kʌmpənid] adj ohne Begleitung

unaccountably ['ʌnə'kauntəbli] adv unerklärlich

unaccustomed ['ʌnə'kʌstəmd] adj nicht gewöhnt; (unusual) ungewohnt; ~ to nicht gewöhnt an +acc

unanimous [ju:'næniməs] adj einmütig; (vote) einstimmig; ~ly adv einmütig;

einstimmig

unarmed [ʌn'ɑːmd] *adj* unbewaffnet

unashamed [ʌnə'ʃeɪmd] *adj* schamlos

unassuming [ʌnə'sjuːmɪŋ] *adj* bescheiden

unattached [ʌnə'tætʃt] *adj* ungebunden

unattended [ʌnə'tendɪd] *adj* (*person*) unbeaufsichtigt; (*thing*) unbewacht

unauthorized [ʌn'ɔːθəraɪzd] *adj* unbefugt

unavoidable [ʌnə'vɔɪdəbl] *adj* unvermeidlich

unaware [ʌnə'wɛə*] *adj*: **to be ~ of sth** sich *dat* einer Sache *gen* nicht bewußt sein; **~s** *adv* unversehens

unbalanced [ʌn'bælənst] *adj* unausgeglichen; (*mentally*) gestört

unbearable [ʌn'bɛərəbl] *adj* unerträglich

unbeatable [ʌn'biːtəbl] *adj* unschlagbar

unbeknown(st) [ʌnbɪ'nəʊn(st)] *adv*: **~ to me** ohne mein Wissen

unbelievable [ʌnbɪ'liːvəbl] *adj* unglaublich

unbend [ʌn'bend] (*irreg: like* bend) *vt* geradebiegen ♦ *vi* aus sich herausgehen

unbias(s)ed [ʌn'baɪəst] *adj* unparteiisch

unbreakable [ʌn'breɪkəbl] *adj* unzerbrechlich

unbridled [ʌn'braɪdld] *adj* ungezügelt

unbroken [ʌn'brəʊkən] *adj* (*period*) ununterbrochen; (*spirit*) ungebrochen; (*record*) unübertroffen

unburden [ʌn'bɜːdn] *vt*: **to ~ o.s.** (jdm) sein Herz ausschütten

unbutton [ʌn'bʌtn] *vt* aufknöpfen

uncalled-for [ʌn'kɔːldfɔː*] *adj* unnötig

uncanny [ʌn'kænɪ] *adj* unheimlich

unceasing [ʌn'siːsɪŋ] *adj* unaufhörlich

unceremonious [ʌnserɪ'məʊnɪəs] *adj* (*abrupt, rude*) brüsk; (*exit, departure*) überstürzt

uncertain [ʌn'sɜːtn] *adj* unsicher; (*doubtful*) ungewiß; (*unreliable*) unbeständig; (*vague*) undeutlich, vag(e); **~ty** *n* Ungewißheit *f*

unchanged [ʌn'tʃeɪndʒd] *adj* unverändert

unchecked [ʌn'tʃekt] *adj* ungeprüft; (*not stopped: advance*) ungehindert

uncivilized [ʌn'sɪvɪlaɪzd] *adj* unzivilisiert

uncle [ʌŋkl] *n* Onkel *m*

uncomfortable [ʌn'kʌmfətəbl] *adj* unbequem, ungemütlich

uncommon [ʌn'kɒmən] *adj* ungewöhnlich; (*outstanding*) außergewöhnlich

uncompromising [ʌn'kɒmprəmaɪzɪŋ] *adj* kompromißlos, unnachgiebig

unconcerned [ʌnkən'sɜːnd] *adj* unbekümmert; (*indifferent*) gleichgültig

unconditional [ʌnkən'dɪʃənl] *adj* bedingungslos

uncongenial [ʌnkən'dʒiːnɪəl] *adj* unangenehm

unconscious [ʌn'kɒnʃəs] *adj* (*MED*) bewußtlos; (*not meant*) unbeabsichtigt ♦ *n*: **the ~** das Unbewußte; **~ly** *adv* unbewußt

uncontrollable [ʌnkən'trəʊləbl] *adj* unkontrollierbar, unbändig

unconventional [ʌnkən'venʃənl] *adj* unkonventionell

uncouth [ʌn'kuːθ] *adj* grob

uncover [ʌn'kʌvə*] *vt* aufdecken

undecided [ʌndɪ'saɪdɪd] *adj* unschlüssig

undeniable [ʌndɪ'naɪəbl] *adj* unleugbar

under [ʌndə*] *prep* unter ♦ *adv* darunter; **~ there** da drunter; **~ repair** in Reparatur; **~age** [ʌndər'eɪdʒ] *adj* minderjährig

undercarriage [ʌndəkærɪdʒ] (*BRIT*) *n* (*AVIAT*) Fahrgestell *nt*

undercharge [ʌndə'tʃɑːdʒ] *vt*: **to ~ sb** jdm zu wenig berechnen

underclothes [ʌndəkləʊðz] *npl* Unterwäsche *f*

undercoat [ʌndəkəʊt] *n* (*paint*) Grundierung *f*

undercover [ʌndəkʌvə*] *adj* Geheim-

undercurrent [ʌndəkʌrənt] *n* Unterströmung *f*

undercut [ʌndəkʌt] (*irreg: like* cut) *vt* unterbieten

underdeveloped [ʌndədɪ'veləpt] *adj* Entwicklungs-, unterentwickelt

underdog [ʌndədɒg] *n* Unterlegene(r) *mf*

underdone [ʌndə'dʌn] *adj* (*COOK*) nicht

gar, nicht durchgebraten

underestimate [ˈʌndərˈestɪmeɪt] *vt* unterschätzen

underexposed [ˈʌndərɪksˈpəʊzd] *adj* unterbelichtet

underfed [ˈʌndəˈfed] *adj* unterernährt

underfoot [ˈʌndəˈfʊt] *adv* am Boden

undergo [ˈʌndəˈgəʊ] (*irreg: like* **go**) *vt* (*experience*) durchmachen; (*operation, test*) sich unterziehen +*dat*

undergraduate [ˈʌndəˈgrædjʊət] *n* Student(in) *m(f)*

underground [ˈʌndəgraʊnd] *n* U-Bahn *f* ♦ *adj* Untergrund-

undergrowth [ˈʌndəgrəʊθ] *n* Gestrüpp *nt*, Unterholz *nt*

underhand(ed) [ˈʌndəˈhænd(ɪd)] *adj* hinterhältig

underlie [ʌndəˈlaɪ] (*irreg: like* **lie**) *vt* (*form the basis of*) zugrundeliegen +*dat*

underline [ʌndəˈlaɪn] *vt* unterstreichen; (*emphasize*) betonen

underling [ˈʌndəlɪŋ] *n* Handlanger *m*

undermine [ʌndəˈmaɪn] *vt* untergraben

underneath [ʌndəˈniːθ] *adv* darunter ♦ *prep* unter

underpaid [ˈʌndəˈpeɪd] *adj* unterbezahlt

underpants [ˈʌndəpænts] *npl* Unterhose *f*

underpass [ˈʌndəpɑːs] (*BRIT*) *n* Unterführung *f*

underprivileged [ˈʌndəˈprɪvɪlɪdʒd] *adj* benachteiligt, unterprivilegiert

underrate [ʌndəˈreɪt] *vt* unterschätzen

undershirt [ˈʌndəʃɜːt] (*US*) *n* Unterhemd *nt*

undershorts [ˈʌndəʃɔːts] (*US*) *npl* Unterhose *f*

underside [ˈʌndəsaɪd] *n* Unterseite *f*

underskirt [ˈʌndəskɜːt] (*BRIT*) *n* Unterrock *m*

understand [ʌndəˈstænd] (*irreg: like* **stand**) *vt, vi* verstehen; **I ~ that ...** ich habe gehört, daß ...; **am I to ~ that ...?** soll das (etwa) heißen, daß ...; **what do you ~ by that?** was verstehen Sie darunter?; **it is understood that ...** es wurde vereinbart, daß ...; **to make o.s. understood** sich verständlich machen; **is that understood?** ist das klar?; **~able**

adj verständlich; **~ing** *n* Verständnis *nt* ♦ *adj* verständnisvoll

understatement [ˈʌndəsteɪtmənt] *n* Untertreibung *f*

understood [ʌndəˈstʊd] *pt, pp of* **understand** ♦ *adj* klar; (*implied*) angenommen

understudy [ˈʌndəstʌdɪ] *n* Ersatz(schau)spieler(in) *m(f)*

undertake [ʌndəˈteɪk] (*irreg: like* **take**) *vt* unternehmen ♦ *vi:* **to ~ to do sth** sich verpflichten, etw zu tun

undertaker [ˈʌndəteɪkə*] *n* Leichenbestatter *m*

undertaking [ʌndəˈteɪkɪŋ] *n* (*enterprise*) Unternehmen *nt*; (*promise*) Verpflichtung *f*

undertone [ˈʌndətəʊn] *n:* **in an ~** mit gedämpfter Stimme

underwater [ˈʌndəˈwɔːtə*] *adv* unter Wasser ♦ *adj* Unterwasser-

underwear [ˈʌndəwɛə*] *n* Unterwäsche *f*

underworld [ˈʌndəwɜːld] *n* (*of crime*) Unterwelt *f*

underwriter [ˈʌndəraɪtə*] *n* Assekurant *m*

undesirable [ʌndɪˈzaɪərəbl] *adj* unerwünscht

undies [ˈʌndɪz] (*inf*) *npl* (Damen)unterwäsche *f*

undisputed [ˈʌndɪsˈpjuːtɪd] *adj* unbestritten

undo [ʌnˈduː] (*irreg: like* **do**) *vt* (*unfasten*) öffnen, aufmachen; (*work*) zunichte machen; **~ing** *n* Verderben *nt*

undoubted [ʌnˈdaʊtɪd] *adj* unbezweifelt; **~ly** *adv* zweifellos, ohne Zweifel

undress [ʌnˈdres] *vt* ausziehen ♦ *vi* sich ausziehen

undue [ˈʌndjuː] *adj* übermäßig

undulating [ˈʌndjʊleɪtɪŋ] *adj* wellenförmig; (*country*) wellig

unduly [ʌnˈdjuːlɪ] *adv* übermäßig

unearth [ʌnˈɜːθ] *vt* (*dig up*) ausgraben; (*discover*) ans Licht bringen

unearthly [ʌnˈɜːθlɪ] *adj* (*hour*) nachtschlafen

uneasy [ʌnˈiːzɪ] *adj* (*worried*) unruhig; (*feeling*) ungut

uneconomic(al) [ˈʌniːkəˈnɒmɪk(əl)] *adj* unwirtschaftlich

uneducated [ˈʌnˈedjʊkeɪtɪd] *adj* ungebildet

unemployed [ˈʌnɪmˈplɔɪd] *adj* arbeitslos ♦ *npl*: the ~ die Arbeitslosen *pl*

unemployment [ˈʌnɪmˈplɔɪmənt] *n* Arbeitslosigkeit *f*

unending [ʌnˈendɪŋ] *adj* endlos

unerring [ˈʌnˈɜːrɪŋ] *adj* unfehlbar

uneven [ˈʌnˈiːvən] *adj* (surface) uneben; (quality) ungleichmäßig

unexpected [ʌnɪkˈspektɪd] *adj* unerwartet; ~**ly** *adv* unerwartet

unfailing [ʌnˈfeɪlɪŋ] *adj* nie versagend

unfair [ˈʌnˈfeə*] *adj* ungerecht, unfair

unfaithful [ˈʌnˈfeɪθfʊl] *adj* untreu

unfamiliar [ʌnfəˈmɪliə*] *adj* ungewohnt; (person, subject) unbekannt

unfashionable [ʌnˈfæʃnəbl] *adj* unmodern; (area, hotel etc) nicht in Mode

unfasten [ˈʌnˈfɑːsn] *vt* öffnen, aufmachen

unfavourable [ˈʌnˈfeɪvərəbl] (US **unfavorable**) *adj* ungünstig

unfeeling [ʌnˈfiːlɪŋ] *adj* gefühllos, kalt

unfinished [ˈʌnˈfɪnɪʃt] *adj* unvollendet

unfit [ˈʌnˈfɪt] *adj* ungeeignet; (in bad health) nicht fit; ~ **for sth** zu or für etw ungeeignet

unfold [ʌnˈfəʊld] *vt* entfalten; (paper) auseinanderfalten ♦ *vi* (develop) sich entfalten

unforeseen [ˈʌnfɔːˈsiːn] *adj* unvorhergesehen

unforgettable [ʌnfəˈgetəbl] *adj* unvergeßlich

unforgivable [ˈʌnfəˈgɪvəbl] *adj* unverzeihlich

unfortunate [ʌnˈfɔːtʃnət] *adj* unglücklich, bedauerlich; ~**ly** *adv* leider

unfounded [ˈʌnˈfaʊndɪd] *adj* unbegründet

unfriendly [ˈʌnˈfrendlɪ] *adj* unfreundlich

ungainly [ʌnˈgeɪnlɪ] *adj* linkisch

ungodly [ʌnˈgɒdlɪ] *adj* (hour) nachtschlafend; (row) heillos

ungrateful [ʌnˈgreɪtfʊl] *adj* undankbar

unhappiness [ʌnˈhæpɪnəs] *n* Unglück *nt*,

Unglückseligkeit *f*

unhappy [ʌnˈhæpɪ] *adj* unglücklich; ~ **with** (arrangements etc) unzufrieden mit

unharmed [ˈʌnˈhɑːmd] *adj* wohlbehalten, unversehrt

unhealthy [ʌnˈhelθɪ] *adj* ungesund

unheard-of [ʌnˈhɜːdɒv] *adj* unerhört

unhook [ʌnˈhʊk] *vt* (from wall) vom Haken nehmen; (dress) loshaken

unhurt [ˈʌnˈhɜːt] *adj* unverletzt

unidentified [ˈʌnaɪˈdentɪfaɪd] *adj* unbekannt, nicht identifiziert

uniform [ˈjuːnɪfɔːm] *n* Uniform *f* ♦ *adj* einheitlich; ~**ity** [juːnɪˈfɔːmɪtɪ] *n* Einheitlichkeit *f*

unify [ˈjuːnɪfaɪ] *vt* vereinigen

unilateral [ˈjuːnɪˈlætərəl] *adj* einseitig

uninhabited [ʌnɪnˈhæbɪtɪd] *adj* unbewohnt

unintentional [ˈʌnɪnˈtenʃənl] *adj* unabsichtlich

union [ˈjuːnjən] *n* (uniting) Vereinigung *f*; (alliance) Bund *m*, Union *f*; (trade ~) Gewerkschaft *f*; **U~ Jack** *n* Union Jack *m*

unique [juːˈniːk] *adj* einzig(artig)

unison [ˈjuːnɪzn] *n* Einstimmigkeit *f*; **in** ~ einstimmig

unit [ˈjuːnɪt] *n* Einheit *f*; **kitchen** ~ Küchenelement *nt*

unite [juːˈnaɪt] *vt* vereinigen ♦ *vi* sich vereinigen; ~**d** *adj* vereinigt; (together) vereint; **U~d Kingdom** *n* Vereinigte(s) Königreich *nt*; **U~d Nations (Organization)** *n* Vereinte Nationen *pl*; **U~d States (of America)** *n* Vereinigte Staaten *pl* (von Amerika)

unit trust (BRIT) *n* Treuhandgesellschaft *f*

unity [ˈjuːnɪtɪ] *n* Einheit *f*; (agreement) Einigkeit *f*

universal [juːnɪˈvɜːsəl] *adj* allgemein

universe [ˈjuːnɪvɜːs] *n* (Welt)all *nt*

university [juːnɪˈvɜːsɪtɪ] *n* Universität *f*

unjust [ˈʌnˈdʒʌst] *adj* ungerecht

unkempt [ˈʌnˈkempt] *adj* ungepflegt

unkind [ʌnˈkaɪnd] *adj* unfreundlich

unknown [ˈʌnˈnəʊn] *adj*: ~ **(to sb)** (jdm) unbekannt

unlawful [ʌnˈlɔːful] *adj* illegal
unleash [ˈʌnˈliːʃ] *vt* entfesseln
unless [ənˈles] *conj* wenn nicht, es sei denn; ~ **he comes** es sei denn, er kommt; ~ **otherwise stated** sofern nicht anders angegeben
unlike [ˈʌnˈlaɪk] *adj* unähnlich ♦ *prep* im Gegensatz zu
unlikely [ʌnˈlaɪklɪ] *adj* unwahrscheinlich
unlimited [ʌnˈlɪmɪtɪd] *adj* unbegrenzt
unlisted [ʌnˈlɪstɪd] (*US*) *adj* nicht im Telefonbuch stehend
unload [ˈʌnˈləud] *vt* entladen
unlock [ʌnˈlɒk] *vt* aufschließen
unlucky [ʌnˈlʌkɪ] *adj* unglücklich; (*person*) unglückselig; **to be** ~ Pech haben
unmarried [ˈʌnˈmærɪd] *adj* unverheiratet, ledig
unmask [ˈʌnˈmɑːsk] *vt* entlarven
unmistakable [ˈʌnmɪsˈteɪkəbl] *adj* unverkennbar
unmitigated [ʌnˈmɪtɪgeɪtɪd] *adj* ungemildert, ganz
unnatural [ʌnˈnætʃrəl] *adj* unnatürlich
unnecessary [ˈʌnˈnesəsərɪ] *adj* unnötig
unnoticed [ʌnˈnəutɪst] *adj*: **to go** ~ unbemerkt bleiben
UNO [ˈjuːnəu] *n abbr* = **United Nations Organization**
unobtainable [ˈʌnəbˈteɪnəbl] *adj*: **this number is** ~ kein Anschluß unter dieser Nummer
unobtrusive [ʌnəbˈtruːsɪv] *adj* unauffällig
unofficial [ʌnəˈfɪʃl] *adj* inoffiziell
unpack [ˈʌnˈpæk] *vt, vi* auspacken
unpalatable [ʌnˈpælətəbl] *adj* (*truth*) bitter
unparalleled [ʌnˈpærəleld] *adj* beispiellos
unpleasant [ʌnˈpleznt] *adj* unangenehm
unplug [ˈʌnˈplʌg] *vt* den Stecker herausziehen von
unpopular [ʌnˈpɒpjulə*] *adj* unbeliebt
unprecedented [ʌnˈpresɪdəntɪd] *adj* beispiellos
unpredictable [ʌnprɪˈdɪktəbl] *adj* unvorhersehbar; (*weather, person*) unberechenbar

unprofessional [ʌnprəˈfeʃənl] *adj* unprofessionell
unqualified [ˈʌnˈkwɒlɪfaɪd] *adj* (*success*) uneingeschränkt, voll; (*person*) unqualifiziert
unquestionably [ʌnˈkwestʃənəblɪ] *adv* fraglos
unravel [ʌnˈrævəl] *vt* (*disentangle*) ausfasern, entwirren; (*solve*) lösen
unreal [ˈʌnˈrɪəl] *adj* unwirklich
unrealistic [ʌnrɪəˈlɪstɪk] *adj* unrealistisch
unreasonable [ʌnˈriːznəbl] *adj* unvernünftig; (*demand*) übertrieben
unrelated [ʌnrɪˈleɪtɪd] *adj* ohne Beziehung; (*family*) nicht verwandt
unrelenting [ˈʌnrɪˈlentɪŋ] *adj* unerbittlich
unreliable [ʌnrɪˈlaɪəbl] *adj* unzuverlässig
unremitting [ʌnrɪˈmɪtɪŋ] *adj* (*efforts, attempts*) unermüdlich
unreservedly [ʌnrɪˈzɜːvɪdlɪ] *adv* offen; (*believe, trust*) uneingeschränkt; (*cry*) rückhaltlos
unrest [ʌnˈrest] *n* (*discontent*) Unruhe *f*; (*fighting*) Unruhen *pl*
unroll [ˈʌnˈrəul] *vt* aufrollen
unruly [ʌnˈruːlɪ] *adj* (*child*) undiszipliniert; schwer lenkbar
unsafe [ˈʌnˈseɪf] *adj* nicht sicher
unsaid [ʌnˈsed] *adj*: **to leave sth** ~ etw ungesagt lassen
unsatisfactory [ˈʌnsætɪsˈfæktərɪ] *adj* unbefriedigend; unzulänglich
unsavoury [ˈʌnˈseɪvərɪ] (*US* **unsavory**) *adj* (*fig*) widerwärtig
unscathed [ʌnˈskeɪðd] *adj* unversehrt
unscrew [ˈʌnˈskruː] *vt* aufschrauben
unscrupulous [ʌnˈskruːpjuləs] *adj* skrupellos
unsettled [ˈʌnˈsetld] *adj* (*person*) rastlos; (*weather*) wechselhaft
unshaven [ˈʌnˈʃeɪvn] *adj* unrasiert
unsightly [ʌnˈsaɪtlɪ] *adj* unansehnlich
unskilled [ˈʌnˈskɪld] *adj* ungelernt
unspeakable [ʌnˈspiːkəbl] *adj* (*joy*) unsagbar; (*crime*) scheußlich
unstable [ˈʌnˈsteɪbl] *adj* instabil; (*mentally*) labil
unsteady [ʌnˈstedɪ] *adj* unsicher; (*growth*) unregelmäßig

unstuck ['ʌn'stʌk] *adj*: to come ~ sich lösen; (*fig*) ins Wasser fallen

unsuccessful ['ʌnsək'sesful] *adj* erfolglos

unsuitable ['ʌn'suːtəbl] *adj* unpassend

unsure [ʌn'ʃuə*] *adj* unsicher; to be ~ of o.s. unsicher sein

unsuspecting ['ʌnsəs'pektɪŋ] *adj* nichtsahnend

unsympathetic ['ʌnsɪmpə'θetɪk] *adj* gefühllos; (*response*) abweisend; (*unlikeable*) unsympathisch

untapped ['ʌn'tæpt] *adj* (*resources*) ungenützt

unthinkable [ʌn'θɪŋkəbl] *adj* unvorstellbar

untidy [ʌn'taɪdɪ] *adj* unordentlich

untie [ʌn'taɪ] *vt* aufschnüren

until [ən'tɪl] *prep, conj* bis; ~ he comes bis er kommt; ~ then bis dann

untimely [ʌn'taɪmlɪ] *adj* (*death*) vorzeitig

untold ['ʌn'təʊld] *adj* unermeßlich

untoward [ʌntə'wɔːd] *adj* widrig

untranslatable [ʌntrænz'leɪtəbl] *adj* unübersetzbar

unused ['ʌn'juːzd] *adj* unbenutzt

unusual [ʌn'juːʒʊəl] *adj* ungewöhnlich

unveil [ʌn'veɪl] *vt* enthüllen

unwavering [ʌn'weɪvərɪŋ] *adj* standhaft, unerschütterlich

unwelcome [ʌn'welkəm] *adj* (*at a bad time*) unwillkommen; (*unpleasant*) unerfreulich

unwell ['ʌn'wel] *adj*: to feel *or* be ~ sich nicht wohl fühlen

unwieldy [ʌn'wiːldɪ] *adj* sperrig

unwilling ['ʌn'wɪlɪŋ] *adj*: to be ~ to do sth nicht bereit sein, etw zu tun; ~ly *adv* widerwillig

unwind ['ʌn'waɪnd] (*irreg: like* **wind²**) *vt* abwickeln ♦ *vi* (*relax*) sich entspannen

unwise [ʌn'waɪz] *adj* unklug

unwitting [ʌn'wɪtɪŋ] *adj* unwissentlich

unworkable [ʌn'wɜːkəbl] *adj* (*plan*) undurchführbar

unworthy [ʌn'wɜːðə] *adj* (*person*): ~ (of sth) (einer Sache *gen*) nicht wert

unwrap ['ʌn'ræp] *vt* auspacken

unwritten ['ʌn'rɪtn] *adj* ungeschrieben

KEYWORD

up [ʌp] *prep*: to be up sth oben auf etw *dat* sein; to go up sth (auf) etw *acc* hinauf gehen; go up that road gehen Sie die Straße hinauf
♦ *adv* **1** (*upwards, higher*) oben; put it up a bit higher stell es etwas weiter nach oben; up there da oben, dort oben; up above hoch oben
2: to be up (*out of bed*) auf sein; (*prices, level*) gestiegen sein; (*building, tent*) stehen
3: up to (*as far as*) bis; up to now bis jetzt
4: to be up to (*depending on*): it's up to you das hängt von dir ab; (*equal to*): he's not up to it (*job, task etc*) er ist dem nicht gewachsen; (*inf: be doing*): what is he up to? (*showing disapproval, suspicion*) was führt er im Schilde?; it's not up to me to decide die Entscheidung liegt nicht bei mir; his work is not up to the required standard seine Arbeit entspricht nicht dem geforderten Niveau
♦ *n*: ups and downs (*in life, career*) Höhen und Tiefen *pl*

---

up-and-coming [ʌpənd'kʌmɪŋ] *adj* aufstrebend

upbringing ['ʌpbrɪŋɪŋ] *n* Erziehung *f*

update [ʌp'deɪt] *vt* auf den neuesten Stand bringen

upgrade [ʌp'greɪd] *vt* höher einstufen

upheaval [ʌp'hiːvəl] *n* Umbruch *m*

uphill ['ʌp'hɪl] *adj* ansteigend; (*fig*) mühsam ♦ *adv*: to go ~ bergauf gehen/fahren

uphold [ʌp'həʊld] (*irreg: like* **hold**) *vt* unterstützen

upholstery [ʌp'həʊlstərɪ] *n* Polster *nt*; Polsterung *f*

upkeep ['ʌpkiːp] *n* Instandhaltung *f*

upon [ə'pɒn] *prep* auf

upper ['ʌpə*] *n* (*on shoe*) Oberleder *nt* ♦ *adj* obere(r, s), höhere(r, s); to have the ~ hand die Oberhand haben; ~ class *adj* vornehm; ~most *adj* oberste(r, s), höchste(r, s); **what was ~most in my mind** was mich in erster Linie beschäftigte

upright ['ʌpraɪt] *adj* aufrecht

uprising ['ʌpraɪzɪŋ] *n* Aufstand *m*

uproar ['ʌprɔ:*] *n* Aufruhr *m*

uproot [ʌp'ru:t] *vt* ausreißen

upset [*n* 'ʌpset, *vb, adj* ʌp'set] (*irreg: like* set) *n* Aufregung *f* ♦ *vt* (*overturn*) umwerfen; (*disturb*) aufregen, bestürzen; (*plans*) durcheinanderbringen ♦ *adj* (*person*) aufgeregt; (*stomach*) verdorben

upshot ['ʌpʃɒt] *n* (End)ergebnis *nt*

upside-down ['ʌpsaɪd'daʊn] *adv* verkehrt herum; (*fig*) drunter und drüber

upstairs ['ʌp'steəz] *adv* oben; (*go*) nach oben ♦ *adj* (*room*) obere(r, s), Ober- ♦ *n* obere(s) Stockwerk *nt*

upstart ['ʌpstɑ:t] *n* Emporkömmling *m*

upstream ['ʌp'stri:m] *adv* stromaufwärts

uptake ['ʌpteɪk] *n*: **to be quick on the ~** schnell begreifen; **to be slow on the ~** schwer von Begriff sein

uptight ['ʌp'taɪt] (*inf*) *adj* (*nervous*) nervös; (*inhibited*) verklemmt

up-to-date ['ʌptə'deɪt] *adj* (*clothes*) modisch, modern; (*information*) neueste(r, s)

upturn ['ʌptɜ:n] *n* Aufschwung *m*

upward ['ʌpwəd] *adj* nach oben gerichtet; **~(s)** *adv* aufwärts

uranium [jʊə'reɪnɪəm] *n* Uran *nt*

urban ['ɜ:bən] *adj* städtisch, Stadt-

urbane ['ɜ:'beɪn] *adj* höflich

urchin ['ɜ:tʃɪn] *n* (*boy*) Schlingel *m*; (*sea ~*) Seeigel *m*

urge [ɜ:dʒ] *n* Drang *m* ♦ *vt*: **to ~ sb to do sth** jdn (dazu) drängen, etw zu tun

urgency ['ɜ:dʒənsɪ] *n* Dringlichkeit *f*

urgent ['ɜ:dʒənt] *adj* dringend

urinal ['jʊərɪnl] *n* (*MED*) Urinflasche *f*; (*public*) Pissoir *nt*

urinate ['jʊərɪneɪt] *vi* urinieren

urine ['jʊərɪn] *n* Urin *m*, Harn *m*

urn [ɜ:n] *n* Urne *f*; (*tea ~*) Teemaschine *f*

us [ʌs] *pron* uns; *see also* me

US *n abbr* = United States

USA *n abbr* = United States of America

usage ['ju:zɪdʒ] *n* Gebrauch *m*; (*esp LING*) Sprachgebrauch *m*

use [*n* ju:s, *vb* ju:z] *n* (*employment*) Gebrauch *m*; (*point*) Zweck *m* ♦ *vt* gebrauchen; **in ~** in Gebrauch; **out of ~** außer Gebrauch; **to be of ~** nützlich sein; **it's no ~** es hat keinen Zweck; **what's the ~?** was soll's?; **~d to** (*accustomed to*) gewöhnt an +*acc*; **she ~d to live here** (*formerly*) sie hat früher mal hier gewohnt; **~ up** *vt* aufbrauchen, verbrauchen; **~d** *adj* (*car*) Gebrauchs-; **~ful** *adj* nützlich; **~fulness** *n* Nützlichkeit *f*; **~less** *adj* nutzlos, unnütz; **~r** *n* Benutzer *m*; **~r-friendly** *adj* (*computer*) benutzerfreundlich

usher ['ʌʃə*] *n* Platzanweiser *m*; **~ette** [ʌʃə'ret] *n* Platzanweiserin *f*

USSR *n*: **the ~** die UdSSR *f*

usual ['ju:ʒʊəl] *adj* gewöhnlich, üblich; **as ~** wie üblich; **~ly** *adv* gewöhnlich

usurp [ju:'zɜ:p] *vt* an sich reißen

utensil [ju:'tensl] *n* Gerät *nt*; **kitchen ~s** Küchengeräte *pl*

uterus ['ju:tərəs] *n* Gebärmutter *f*

utilitarian [ju:tɪlɪ'teərɪən] *adj* Nützlichkeits-

utility [ju:'tɪlɪtɪ] *n* (*usefulness*) Nützlichkeit *f*; (*also: public ~*) öffentliche(r) Versorgungsbetrieb *m*; **~ room** *n* Hauswirtschaftsraum *m*

utilize ['ju:tɪlaɪz] *vt* benützen

utmost ['ʌtməʊst] *adj* äußerste(r, s) ♦ *n*: **to do one's ~** sein möglichstes tun

utter ['ʌtə*] *adj* äußerste(r, s), höchste(r, s), völlig ♦ *vt* äußern, aussprechen; **~ance** *n* Äußerung *f*; **~ly** *adv* äußerst, absolut, völlig

U-turn ['ju:'tɜ:n] *n* (*AUT*) Kehrtwendung *f*

V

v *abbr* = verse; versus; volt; (= *vide*) siehe

vacancy ['veɪkənsɪ] *n* (*BRIT: job*) offene Stelle *f*; (*room*) freie(s) Zimmer *nt*

vacant ['veɪkənt] adj leer; (unoccupied) frei; (house) leerstehend, unbewohnt; (stupid) (gedanken)leer; ~ **lot** (US) n unbebaute(s) Grundstück nt

vacate [və'keɪt] vt (seat) frei machen; (room) räumen

vacation [və'keɪʃən] n Ferien pl, Urlaub m; ~**ist** (US) n Ferienreisende(r) mf

vaccinate ['væksɪneɪt] vt impfen

vaccine ['væksiːn] n Impfstoff m

vacuum ['vækjʊm] n Vakuum nt; ~ **bottle** (US) n Thermosflasche f; ~ **cleaner** n Staubsauger m; ~ **flask** (BRIT) n Thermosflasche f; ~-**packed** adj vakuumversiegelt

vagina [və'dʒaɪnə] n Scheide f

vagrant ['veɪɡrənt] n Landstreicher m

vague [veɪɡ] adj vag(e); (absent-minded) geistesabwesend; ~**ly** adv unbestimmt, vag(e)

vain [veɪn] adj eitel; (attempt) vergeblich; **in** ~ vergebens, umsonst

valentine ['væləntaɪn] n (also: ~ **card**) Valentinsgruß m

valet ['væleɪ] n Kammerdiener m

valiant ['væliənt] adj tapfer; ~**ly** adv tapfer

valid ['vælɪd] adj gültig; (argument) stichhaltig; (objection) berechtigt; ~**ity** [və'lɪdɪtɪ] n Gültigkeit f

valley ['vælɪ] n Tal nt

valour ['vælə*] (US **valor**) n Tapferkeit f

valuable ['væljʊəbl] adj wertvoll; (time) kostbar; ~**s** npl Wertsachen pl

valuation [væljʊ'eɪʃən] n (FIN) Schätzung f; Beurteilung f

value ['væljuː] n Wert m; (usefulness) Nutzen m ♦ vt (prize) (hoch)schätzen, werthalten; (estimate) schätzen; ~ **added tax** (BRIT) n Mehrwertsteuer f; ~**d** adj (hoch)geschätzt

valve [vælv] n Ventil nt; (BIOL) Klappe f; (RAD) Röhre f

van [væn] n Lieferwagen m; (BRIT: RAIL) Waggon m

vandal ['vændl] n Rowdy m

vandalize ['vændəlaɪz] vt mutwillig beschädigen

vanguard ['vænɡɑːd] n (fig) Spitze f

vanilla [və'nɪlə] n Vanille f

vanish ['vænɪʃ] vi verschwinden

vanity ['vænɪtɪ] n Eitelkeit f; ~ **case** n Schminkkoffer m

vantage ['vɑːntɪdʒ] n: ~ **point** gute(r) Aussichtspunkt m

vapour ['veɪpə*] (US **vapor**) n (mist) Dunst m; (gas) Dampf m

variable ['vɛərɪəbl] adj wechselhaft, veränderlich; (speed, height) regulierbar

variance ['vɛərɪəns] n: to be at ~ (with) nicht übereinstimmen (mit)

variation [vɛərɪ'eɪʃən] n Variation f; (of temperature, prices) Schwankung f

varicose ['værɪkəʊs] adj: ~ **veins** Krampfadern pl

varied ['vɛərɪd] adj unterschiedlich; (life) abwechslungsreich

variety [və'raɪətɪ] n (difference) Abwechslung f; (varied collection) Vielfalt f; (COMM) Auswahl f; (sort) Sorte f, Art f; ~ **show** n Varieté nt

various ['vɛərɪəs] adj verschieden; (several) mehrere

varnish ['vɑːnɪʃ] n Lack m; (on pottery) Glasur f ♦ vt lackieren

vary ['vɛərɪ] vt (alter) verändern; (give variety to) abwechslungsreicher gestalten ♦ vi sich (ver)ändern; (prices) schwanken; (weather) unterschiedlich sein

vase [vɑːz] n Vase f

Vaseline ['væsɪliːn] (®) n Vaseline f

vast [vɑːst] adj weit, groß, riesig

VAT [væt] n abbr (= value added tax) MwSt f

vat [væt] n große(s) Faß nt

vault [vɔːlt] n (of roof) Gewölbe nt; (tomb) Gruft f; (in bank) Tresorraum m; (leap) Sprung m ♦ vt (also: ~ **over**) überspringen

vaunted ['vɔːntɪd] adj: much-~ vielgerühmt

VCR n abbr = video cassette recorder

VD n abbr = venereal disease

VDU n abbr = visual display unit

veal [viːl] n Kalbfleisch nt

veer [vɪə*] vi sich drehen; (of car) ausscheren

vegetable ['vedʒətəbl] n Gemüse nt ♦ adj Gemüse-; ~**s** npl (CULIN) Gemüse *nt*

vegetarian [vedʒɪ'tɛərɪən] *n*
Vegetarier(in) *m(f)* ♦ *adj* vegetarisch

vegetate ['vedʒɪteɪt] *vi* (dahin)vege-
tieren

vehemence ['viːɪməns] *n* Heftigkeit *f*

vehement ['viːɪmənt] *adj* heftig

vehicle ['viːɪkl] *n* Fahrzeug *nt*; *(fig)* Mittel *nt*

veil [veɪl] *n (also fig)* Schleier *m* ♦ *vt*
verschleiern

vein [veɪn] *n* Ader *f*; *(mood)* Stimmung
f

velocity [vɪ'lɒsɪtɪ] *n* Geschwindigkeit *f*

velvet ['velvɪt] *n* Samt *m* ♦ *adj* Samt-

vendetta [ven'detə] *n* Fehde *f*; *(in
family)* Blutrache *f*

vending machine ['vendɪŋ-] *n* Automat
m

vendor ['vendɔː*] *n* Verkäufer *m*

veneer [və'nɪə*] *n* Furnier(holz) *nt*;
(fig) äußere(r) Anstrich *m*

venereal disease [vɪ'nɪərɪəl-] *n* Ge-
schlechtskrankheit *f*

Venetian blind [vɪ'niːʃən-] *n* Jalousie *f*

vengeance ['vendʒəns] *n* Rache *f*; **with
a ~** gewaltig

venison ['venɪsn] *n* Reh(fleisch) *nt*

venom ['venəm] *n* Gift *nt*

vent [vent] *n* Öffnung *f*; *(in coat)* Schlitz
m; *(fig)* Ventil *nt* ♦ *vt (emotion)*
abreagieren

ventilate ['ventɪleɪt] *vt* belüften

ventilator ['ventɪleɪtə*] *n* Ventilator *m*

ventriloquist [ven'trɪləkwɪst] *n*
Bauchredner *m*

venture ['ventʃə*] *n* Unternehmung *f*,
Projekt *nt* ♦ *vt* wagen; *(life)* aufs Spiel
setzen ♦ *vi* sich wagen

venue ['venjuː] *n* Schauplatz *m*

verb [vɜːb] *n* Zeitwort *nt*, Verb *nt*; **~al**
adj (spoken) mündlich; *(translation)*
wörtlich; **~ally** *adv* mündlich

verbatim [vɜː'beɪtɪm] *adv* Wort für Wort
♦ *adj* wortwörtlich

verbose [vɜː'bəus] *adj* wortreich

verdict ['vɜːdɪkt] *n* Urteil *nt*

verge [vɜːdʒ] *n (BRIT)* Rand *m* ♦ *vi:* to
~ on grenzen an +*acc*; **"soft ~s"** *(BRIT:
AUT)* „Seitenstreifen nicht befahrbar";

on the ~ of doing sth im Begriff, etw zu
tun

verify ['verɪfaɪ] *vt* (über)prüfen;
(confirm) bestätigen; *(theory)* beweisen

veritable ['verɪtəbl] *adj* wirklich, echt

vermin ['vɜːmɪn] *npl* Ungeziefer *nt*

vermouth ['vɜːməθ] *n* Wermut *m*

vernacular [və'nækjulə*] *n* Landesspra-
che *f*

versatile ['vɜːsətaɪl] *adj* vielseitig

versatility [vɜːsə'tɪlɪtɪ] *n* Vielseitigkeit *f*

verse [vɜːs] *n (poetry)* Poesie *f*;
(stanza) Strophe *f*; *(of Bible)* Vers *m*;
in ~ in Versform

versed [vɜːst] *adj:* **(well-)~ in**
bewandert in +*dat*, beschlagen in
+*dat*

version ['vɜːʃən] *n* Version *f*; *(of car)*
Modell *nt*

versus ['vɜːsəs] *prep* gegen

vertebrate ['vɜːtɪbrət] *adj (animal)*
Wirbel-

vertical ['vɜːtɪkəl] *adj* senkrecht

vertigo ['vɜːtɪgəu] *n* Schwindel *m*

verve [vɜːv] *n* Schwung *m*

very ['verɪ] *adv* sehr ♦ *adj (extreme)*
äußerste(r, s); **the ~ book which** genau
das Buch, welches; **the ~ last** der/die/
das allerletzte; **at the ~ least**
allerwenigstens; **~ much** sehr

vessel ['vesl] *n (ship)* Schiff *nt*;
(container) Gefäß *nt*

vest [vest] *n (BRIT)* Unterhemd *nt*; *(US:
waistcoat)* Weste *f*; **~ed interests** *npl*
finanzielle Beteiligung *f*; *(people)*
finanziell Beteiligte *pl*; *(fig)*
persönliche(s) Interesse *nt*

vestige ['vestɪdʒ] *n* Spur *f*

vestry ['vestrɪ] *n* Sakristei *f*

vet [vet] *n abbr (= veterinary surgeon)*
Tierarzt *m*/-ärztin *f* ♦ *vt* genau prüfen

veteran ['vetərn] *n* Veteran(in) *m(f)*

veterinarian [vetrə'neərɪən] *(US)* *n*
Tierarzt *m*/-ärztin *f*

veterinary ['vetrɪnərɪ] *adj* Veterinär-; **~
surgeon** *(BRIT)* *n* Tierarzt *m*/-ärztin *f*

veto ['viːtəu] *n (pl* **~es)** *n* Veto *nt* ♦ *vt*
sein Veto einlegen gegen

vex [veks] *vt* ärgern; **~ed** *adj* verärgert; **~ed question** umstrittene Frage

f

VHF *abbr* (= *very high frequency*) UKW *f*

via ['vaɪə] *prep* über +*acc*

viable ['vaɪəbl] *adj* (*plan*) durchführbar; (*company*) rentabel

vibrant ['vaɪbrənt] *adj* (*lively*) lebhaft; (*bright*) leuchtend; (*full of emotion*: *voice*) bebend

vibrate [vaɪ'breɪt] *vi* zittern, beben; (*machine*, *string*) vibrieren

vibration [vaɪ'breɪʃən] *n* Schwingung *f*; (*of machine*) Vibrieren *nt*

vicar ['vɪkə*] *n* Pfarrer *m*; ~**age** *n* Pfarrhaus *nt*

vicarious [vɪ'kɛərɪəs] *adj* nachempfunden

vice [vaɪs] *n* (*evil*) Laster *nt*; (*TECH*) Schraubstock *m*

vice-chairman *n* stellvertretende(r) Vorsitzende(r) *m*

vice-president *n* Vizepräsident *m*

vice squad *n* ≈ Sittenpolizei *f*

vice versa ['vaɪsɪ'vɜːsə] *adv* umgekehrt

vicinity [vɪ'sɪnɪtɪ] *n* Umgebung *f*; (*closeness*) Nähe *f*

vicious ['vɪʃəs] *adj* gemein, böse; ~ **circle** *n* Teufelskreis *m*

victim ['vɪktɪm] *n* Opfer *nt*; ~**ize** *vt* benachteiligen

victor ['vɪktə*] *n* Sieger *m*

Victorian [vɪk'tɔːrɪən] *adj* viktorianisch; (*fig*) (sitten)streng

victorious [vɪk'tɔːrɪəs] *adj* siegreich

victory ['vɪktərɪ] *n* Sieg *m*

video ['vɪdɪəʊ] *adj* Fernseh-, Bild- ♦ *n* (~ *film*) Video *nt*; (*also*: ~ *cassette*) Videokassette *f*; (: ~ *cassette recorder*) Videorekorder *m*; ~ **tape** *n* Videoband *nt*

vie [vaɪ] *vi* wetteifern

Vienna [vɪ'enə] *n* Wien *nt*

view [vjuː] *n* (*sight*) Sicht *f*, Blick *m*; (*scene*) Aussicht *f*; (*opinion*) Ansicht *f*; (*intention*) Absicht *f* ♦ *vt* (*situation*) betrachten; (*house*) besichtigen; **to have sth in** ~ etw beabsichtigen; **on** ~ ausgestellt; **in** ~ **of** wegen +*gen*, angesichts +*gen*; ~**er** *n* (~*finder*) Sucher *m*; (*PHOT*: *small projector*) Gucki *m*; (*TV*)

Fernsehzuschauer(in) *m(f)*; ~**finder** *n* Sucher *m*; ~**point** *n* Standpunkt *m*

vigil ['vɪdʒɪl] *n* (Nacht)wache *f*; ~**ance** *n* Wachsamkeit *f*; ~**ant** *adj* wachsam

vigorous ['vɪgərəs] *adj* kräftig; (*protest*) energisch, heftig; ~**ly** *adv* kräftig; energisch, heftig

vile [vaɪl] *adj* (*mean*) gemein; (*foul*) abscheulich

vilify ['vɪlɪfaɪ] *vt* verleumden

villa ['vɪlə] *n* Villa *f*

village ['vɪlɪdʒ] *n* Dorf *nt*; ~**r** *n* Dorfbewohner(in) *m(f)*

villain ['vɪlən] *n* Schurke *m*

vindicate ['vɪndɪkeɪt] *vt* rechtfertigen

vindictive [vɪn'dɪktɪv] *adj* nachtragend, rachsüchtig

vine [vaɪn] *n* Rebstock *m*, Rebe *f*

vinegar ['vɪnɪgə*] *n* Essig *m*

vineyard ['vɪnjəd] *n* Weinberg *m*

vintage ['vɪntɪdʒ] *n* (*of wine*) Jahrgang *m*; ~ **wine** *n* edle(r) Wein *m*

viola [vɪ'əʊlə] *n* Bratsche *f*

violate ['vaɪəleɪt] *vt* (*law*) übertreten; (*rights*, *rule*, *neutrality*) verletzen; (*sanctity*, *woman*) schänden

violation [vaɪə'leɪʃən] *n* Verletzung *f*; Übertretung *f*

violence ['vaɪələns] *n* (*force*) Heftigkeit *f*; (*brutality*) Gewalttätigkeit *f*

violent ['vaɪələnt] *adj* (*strong*) heftig; (*brutal*) gewalttätig, brutal; (*contrast*) kraß; (*death*) gewaltsam; ~**ly** *adv* heftig; gewalttätig, brutal; kraß; gewaltsam

violet ['vaɪələt] *n* Veilchen *nt* ♦ *adj* veilchenblau, violett

violin [vaɪə'lɪn] *n* Geige *f*, Violine *f*; ~**ist** *n* Geiger(in) *m(f)*

VIP *n abbr* (= *very important person*) VIP *m*

virgin ['vɜːdʒɪn] *n* Jungfrau *f* ♦ *adj* jungfräulich, unberührt; **the Blessed V~** die heilige Jungfrau Maria; ~**ity** [vɜː'dʒɪnɪtɪ] *n* Unschuld *f*

Virgo ['vɜːgəʊ] *n* Jungfrau *f*

virile ['vɪraɪl] *adj* männlich

virility [vɪ'rɪlɪtɪ] *n* Männlichkeit *f*

virtually ['vɜːtjʊəlɪ] *adv* praktisch, fast

virtue ['vɜːtjuː] *n* (*moral goodness*)

Tugend *f*; *(good quality)* Vorteil *m*, Vorzug *m*; **by ~ of** aufgrund +*gen*
virtuous ['vɜːtjʊəs] *adj* tugendhaft
virulent ['vɪrjʊlənt] *adj (poisonous)* bösartig; *(bitter)* scharf, geharnischt
virus ['vaɪərəs] *n* Virus *m*
visa ['viːzə] *n* Visum *nt*
vis-à-vis ['viːzəviː] *prep* gegenüber
viscous ['vɪskəs] *adj* zähflüssig
visibility [vɪzɪ'bɪlɪtɪ] *n (MET)* Sicht(weite) *f*
visible ['vɪzəbl] *adj* sichtbar
visibly ['vɪzəblɪ] *adv* sichtlich
vision ['vɪʒən] *n (ability)* Sehvermögen *nt*; *(foresight)* Weitblick *m*; *(in dream, image)* Vision *f*
visit ['vɪzɪt] *n* Besuch *m* ♦ *vt* besuchen; *(town, country)* fahren nach; **~ing** *adj (professor)* Gast-; **~ing card** *n* Visitenkarte *f*; **~ing hours** *npl (in hospital etc)* Besuchszeiten *pl*; **~or** *n (in house)* Besucher(in) *m(f)*; *(in hotel)* Gast *m*; **~ors' book** *n* Gästebuch *nt*
visor ['vaɪzə*] *n* Visier *nt*; *(on cap)* Schirm *m*; *(AUT)* Blende *f*
vista ['vɪstə] *n* Aussicht *f*
visual ['vɪzjʊəl] *adj* Seh-, visuell; **~ aid** *n* Anschauungsmaterial *nt*; **~ display unit** *n* Bildschirm(gerät *nt*) *m*; **~ize** ['vɪzjʊəlaɪz] *vt* sich +*dat* vorstellen
vital ['vaɪtl] *adj (important)* unerläßlich; *(necessary for life)* Lebens-, lebenswichtig; *(lively)* vital; **~ity** [vaɪ'tælɪtɪ] *n* Vitalität *f*; **~ly** *adv:* **~ly important** äußerst wichtig; **~ statistics** *npl (fig)* Maße *pl*
vitamin ['vɪtəmɪn] *n* Vitamin *nt*
vivacious [vɪ'veɪʃəs] *adj* lebhaft
vivid ['vɪvɪd] *adj (graphic)* lebendig; *(memory)* lebhaft; *(bright)* leuchtend; **~ly** *adv* lebendig; lebhaft; leuchtend
V-neck ['viː'nek] *n* V-Ausschnitt *m*
vocabulary [vəʊ'kæbjʊlərɪ] *n* Wortschatz *m*, Vokabular *nt*
vocal ['vəʊkəl] *adj* Vokal-, Gesang-; *(fig)* lautstark; **~ cords** *npl* Stimmbänder *pl*
vocation [vəʊ'keɪʃən] *n (calling)* Berufung *f*; **~al** *adj* Berufs-
vociferous [vəʊ'sɪfərəs] *adj* lautstark;

~ly *adv* lautstark
vodka ['vɒdkə] *n* Wodka *m*
vogue [vəʊg] *n* Mode *f*
voice [vɔɪs] *n* Stimme *f*; *(fig)* Mitspracherecht *nt* ♦ *vt* äußern
void [vɔɪd] *n* Leere *f* ♦ *adj (invalid)* nichtig, ungültig; *(empty):* **~ of** ohne, bar +*gen*; *see* **null**
volatile ['vɒlətaɪl] *adj (gas)* flüchtig; *(person)* impulsiv; *(situation)* brisant
volcano [vɒl'keɪnəʊ] *n* Vulkan *m*
volition [və'lɪʃən] *n* Wille *m*; **of one's own ~** aus freiem Willen
volley ['vɒlɪ] *n (of guns)* Salve *f*; *(of stones)* Hagel *m*; *(of words)* Schwall *m*; *(tennis)* Flugball *m*; **~ball** *n* Volleyball *m*
volt [vəʊlt] *n* Volt *nt*; **~age** *n* (Volt)spannung *f*
voluble ['vɒljʊbl] *adj* redselig
volume ['vɒljuːm] *n (book)* Band *m*; *(size)* Umfang *m*; *(space)* Rauminhalt *m*; *(of sound)* Lautstärke *f*
voluminous [və'luːmɪnəs] *adj* üppig; *(clothes)* wallend; *(correspondence, notes)* umfangreich
voluntarily ['vɒləntrəlɪ] *adv* freiwillig
voluntary ['vɒləntərɪ] *adj* freiwillig
volunteer [vɒlən'tɪə*] *n* Freiwillige(r) *mf* ♦ *vi* sich freiwillig melden; **to ~ to do sth** sich anbieten, etw zu tun
voluptuous [və'lʌptjʊəs] *adj* sinnlich
vomit ['vɒmɪt] *n* Erbrochene(s) *nt* ♦ *vt* spucken ♦ *vi* sich übergeben
vote [vəʊt] *n* Stimme *f*; *(ballot)* Abstimmung *f*; *(result)* Abstimmungsergebnis *nt*; *(franchise)* Wahlrecht *nt* ♦ *vt, vi* wählen; **~ of thanks** *n* Dankesworte *pl*; **~r** *n* Wähler(in) *m(f)*
voting ['vəʊtɪŋ] *n* Wahl *f*
voucher ['vaʊtʃə*] *n* Gutschein *m*
vouch for [vaʊtʃ-] *vt* bürgen für
vow [vaʊ] *n* Versprechen *nt*; *(REL)* Gelübde *nt* ♦ *vt* geloben
vowel ['vaʊəl] *n* Vokal *m*
voyage ['vɔɪɪdʒ] *n* Reise *f*
vulgar ['vʌlgə*] *adj (rude)* vulgär; *(of common people)* allgemein, Volks-; **~ity** [vʌl'gærɪtɪ] *n* Vulgarität *f*
vulnerable ['vʌlnərəbl] *adj (easily*

injured) verwundbar; (*sensitive*) verletzlich
vulture ['vʌltʃə*] n Geier m

W

wad [wɒd] n (*bundle*) Bündel nt; (*of paper*) Stoß m; (*of money*) Packen m
waddle ['wɒdl] vi watscheln
wade [weɪd] vi: **to ~ through** waten durch
wafer ['weɪfə*] n Waffel f; (*REL*) Hostie f; (*COMPUT*) Wafer f
waffle ['wɒfl] n Waffel f; (*inf: empty talk*) Geschwafel nt ♦ vi schwafeln
waft [wɑːft] vt, vi wehen
wag [wæg] vt (*tail*) wedeln mit ♦ vi wedeln
wage [weɪdʒ] n (*also: ~s*) (Arbeits)lohn m ♦ vt: **to ~ war** Krieg führen; **~ earner** n Lohnempfänger(in) m(f); **~ packet** n Lohntüte f
wager ['weɪdʒə*] n Wette f ♦ vt, vi wetten
waggle ['wægl] vt (*tail*) wedeln mit ♦ vi wedeln
wag(g)on ['wægən] n (*horse-drawn*) Fuhrwerk nt; (*US: AUT*) Wagen m; (*BRIT: RAIL*) Waggon m
wail [weɪl] n Wehgeschrei nt ♦ vi wehklagen, jammern
waist [weɪst] n Taille f; **~coat** (*BRIT*) n Weste f; **~line** n Taille f
wait [weɪt] n Wartezeit f ♦ vi warten; **to lie in ~ for sb** jdm auflauern; **I can't ~ to see him** ich kann's kaum erwarten, ihn zu sehen; **"no ~ing"** (*BRIT: AUT*) Halteverbot nt; **~ behind** vi zurückbleiben; **~ for** vt fus warten auf +acc; **~ on** vt fus bedienen; **~er** n Kellner m; **~ing list** n Warteliste f; **~ing room** n (*MED*) Wartezimmer nt; (*RAIL*) Wartesaal m; **~ress** n Kellnerin f
waive [weɪv] vt verzichten auf +acc
wake [weɪk] (*pt* woke, ~d, *pp* woken, ~d) vt wecken ♦ vi (*also: ~ up*) aufwachen ♦ n (*NAUT*) Kielwasser nt; (*for dead*) Totenwache f; **to ~ up to** (*fig*)

sich bewußt werden +gen
waken ['weɪkən] vt aufwecken
Wales [weɪlz] n Wales nt
walk [wɔːk] n Spaziergang m; (*gait*) Gang m; (*route*) Weg m ♦ vi gehen; (*stroll*) spazierengehen; (*longer*) wandern; **~s of life** Sphären pl; **a 10-minute ~** 10 Minuten zu Fuß; **to ~ out on sb** (*inf*) jdn sitzenlassen; **~er** n Spaziergänger m; (*hiker*) Wanderer m; **~ie-talkie** ['wɔːkɪ'tɔːkɪ] n tragbare(s) Sprechfunkgerät nt; **~ing** n Gehen nt; (*hiking*) Wandern nt ♦ adj Wander-; **~ing shoes** npl Wanderschuhe pl; **~ing stick** n Spazierstock m; **~out** n Streik m; **~over** (*inf*) n leichte(r) Sieg m; **~way** n Fußweg m
wall [wɔːl] n (*inside*) Wand f; (*outside*) Mauer f; **~ed** adj von Mauern umgeben
wallet ['wɒlɪt] n Brieftasche f
wallflower ['wɔːlflauə*] n Goldlack m; **to be a ~** (*fig*) ein Mauerblümchen sein
wallop ['wɒləp] (*inf*) vt schlagen, verprügeln
wallow ['wɒləu] vi sich wälzen
wallpaper ['wɔːlpeɪpə*] n Tapete f
wally ['wɒlɪ] (*inf*) n Idiot m
walnut ['wɔːlnʌt] n Walnuß f
walrus ['wɔːlrəs] n Walroß nt
waltz [wɔːlts] n Walzer m ♦ vi Walzer tanzen
wan [wɒn] adj bleich
wand [wɒnd] n (*also: magic ~*) Zauberstab m
wander ['wɒndə*] vi (*roam*) (herum)wandern; (*fig*) abschweifen
wane [weɪn] vi abnehmen; (*fig*) schwinden
wangle ['wæŋgl] (*BRIT: inf*) vt: **to ~ sth** etw richtig hindrehen
want [wɒnt] n (*lack*) Mangel m ♦ vt (*need*) brauchen; (*desire*) wollen; (*lack*) nicht haben; **~s** npl (*needs*) Bedürfnisse pl; **for ~ of** aus Mangel an +dat; **mangels** +gen; **to ~ to do sth** etw tun wollen; **to ~ sb to do sth** wollen, daß jd etw tut; **~ing** adj: **to be found ~ing** sich als unzulänglich erweisen

wanton ['wɒntən] *adj* mutwillig, zügellos

war [wɔː*] *n* Krieg *m*; **to make ~** Krieg führen

ward [wɔːd] *n* (*in hospital*) Station *f*; (*of city*) Bezirk *m*; (*child*) Mündel *nt*; **~ off** *vt* abwenden, abwehren

warden ['wɔːdən] *n* (*guard*) Wächter *m*, Aufseher *m*; (*BRIT: in youth hostel*) Herbergsvater *m*; (*UNIV*) Heimleiter *m*; (*BRIT: also: traffic ~*) ≈ Verkehrspolizist *m*, ≈ Politesse *f*

warder ['wɔːdə*] (*BRIT*) *n* Gefängniswärter *m*

wardrobe ['wɔːdrəub] *n* Kleiderschrank *m*; (*clothes*) Garderobe *f*

warehouse ['weəhaus] *n* Lagerhaus *nt*

wares [weəz] *npl* Ware *f*

warfare ['wɔːfeə*] *n* Krieg *m*; Kriegsführung *f*

warhead ['wɔːhed] *n* Sprengkopf *m*

warily ['weərɪlɪ] *adv* vorsichtig

warlike ['wɔːlaɪk] *adj* kriegerisch

warm [wɔːm] *adj* warm; (*welcome*) herzlich ♦ *vt*, *vi* wärmen; **I'm ~** mir ist warm; **~ up** *vt* aufwärmen ♦ *vi* warm werden; **~-hearted** *adj* warmherzig; **~ly** *adv* warm; herzlich; **warmth** *n* Wärme *f*; Herzlichkeit *f*

warn [wɔːn] *vt*: **to ~ (of** *or* **against)** warnen (vor +*dat*); **~ing** *n* Warnung *f*; **without ~ing** unerwartet; **~ing light** *n* Warnlicht *nt*; **~ing triangle** *n* (*AUT*) Warndreieck *nt*

warp [wɔːp] *vt* verziehen; **~ed** *adj* wellig; (*fig*) pervers

warrant ['wɒrənt] *n* (*for arrest*) Haftbefehl *m*

warranty ['wɒrəntɪ] *n* Garantie *f*

warren ['wɒrən] *n* Labyrinth *nt*

warrior ['wɒrɪə*] *n* Krieger *m*

Warsaw ['wɔːsɔː] *n* Warschau *nt*

warship ['wɔːʃɪp] *n* Kriegsschiff *nt*

wart [wɔːt] *n* Warze *f*

wartime ['wɔːtaɪm] *n* Krieg *m*

wary ['weərɪ] *adj* mißtrauisch

was [wɒz, wəz] *pt of* **be**

wash [wɒʃ] *n* Wäsche *f* ♦ *vt* waschen; (*dishes*) abwaschen ♦ *vi* sich waschen; (*do ~ing*) waschen; **to have a ~** sich waschen; **~ away** *vt* abwaschen, wegspülen; **~ off** *vt* abwaschen; **~ up** *vi* (*BRIT*) spülen; (*US*) sich waschen; **~able** *adj* waschbar; **~basin** *n* Waschbecken *nt*; **~ bowl** (*US*) *n* Waschbecken *nt*; **~ cloth** (*US*) *n* (*face cloth*) Waschlappen *m*; **~er** *n* (*TECH*) Dichtungsring *m*; (*machine*) Waschmaschine *f*; **~ing** *n* Wäsche *f*; **~ing machine** *n* Waschmaschine *f*; **~ing powder** (*BRIT*) *n* Waschpulver *nt*; **~ing-up** *n* Abwasch *m*; **~ing-up liquid** *n* Spülmittel *nt*; **~-out** (*inf*) *n* (*event*) Reinfall *m*; (*person*) Niete *f*; **~room** *n* Waschraum *m*

wasn't ['wɒznt] = **was not**

wasp [wɒsp] *n* Wespe *f*

wastage ['weɪstɪdʒ] *n* Verlust *m*; **natural ~** Verschleiß *m*

waste [weɪst] *n* (*wasting*) Verschwendung *f*; (*what is wasted*) Abfall *m* ♦ *adj* (*useless*) überschüssig, Abfall- ♦ *vt* (*object*) verschwenden; (*time, life*) vergeuden ♦ *vi*: **to ~ away** verfallen; **~s** *npl* (*land*) Einöde *f*; **to lay ~** verwüsten; **~ disposal unit** (*BRIT*) *n* Müllschlucker *m*; **~ful** *adj* verschwenderisch; (*process*) aufwendig; **~ ground** (*BRIT*) *n* unbebaute(s) Grundstück *nt*; **~land** *n* Ödland *nt*; **~paper basket** *n* Papierkorb *m*; **~ pipe** *n* Abflußrohr *nt*

watch [wɒtʃ] *n* Wache *f*; (*for time*) Uhr *f* ♦ *vt* ansehen; (*observe*) beobachten; (*be careful of*) aufpassen auf +*acc*; (*guard*) bewachen ♦ *vi* zusehen; **to be on the ~ (for sth)** (auf etw *acc*) aufpassen; **to ~ TV** fernsehen; **to ~ sb doing sth** jdm bei etw zuschauen; **~ out** *vi* Ausschau halten; (*be careful*) aufpassen; **~ out!** paß auf!; **~dog** *n* Wachthund *m*; (*fig*) Wächter *m*; **~ful** *adj* wachsam; **~maker** *n* Uhrmacher *m*; **~man** (*irreg*) *n* (*also: night ~man*) (Nacht)wächter *m*; **~ strap** *n* Uhrarmband *nt*

water ['wɔːtə*] *n* Wasser *nt* ♦ *vt* (be)gießen; (*river*) bewässern; (*horses*) tränken ♦ *vi* (*eye*) tränen; **~s** *npl* (*of sea, river etc*) Gewässer *nt*; **~**

verwässern; ~ **closet** (*BRIT*) *n* (Wasser)klosett *nt*; ~**colour** (*US* **watercolor**) *n* (*painting*) Aquarell *nt*; (*paint*) Wasserfarbe *f*; ~**cress** *n* (Brunnen)kresse *f*; ~**fall** *n* Wasserfall *m*; ~ **heater** *n* Heißwassergerät *nt*; ~**ing can** *n* Gießkanne *f*; ~ **level** *n* Wasserstand *m*; ~**lily** *n* Seerose *f*; ~**line** *n* Wasserlinie *f*; ~**logged** *adj* (*ground*) voll Wasser; (*wood*) mit Wasser vollgesogen; ~ **main** *n* Haupt(wasser)leitung *f*; ~**mark** *n* Wasserzeichen *nt*; (*on wall*) Wasserstandsmarke *f*; ~**melon** *n* Wassermelone *f*; ~ **polo** *n* Wasserball(spiel) *nt*; ~**proof** *adj* wasserdicht; ~**shed** *n* Wasserscheide *f*; ~-**skiing** *n* Wasserschilaufen *nt*; ~ **tank** *n* Wassertank *m*; ~**tight** *adj* wasserdicht; ~**way** *n* Wasserweg *m*; ~**works** *npl* Wasserwerk *nt*; ~**y** *adj* wäss(e)rig

watt [wɒt] *n* Watt *nt*

wave [weɪv] *n* Welle *f*; (*with hand*) Winken *nt* ♦ *vt* (*move to and fro*) schwenken; (*hand, flag*) winken mit; (*hair*) wellen ♦ *vi* (*person*) winken; (*flag*) wehen; ~**length** *n* (*also fig*) Wellenlänge *f*

waver ['weɪvə*] *vi* schwanken

wavy ['weɪvɪ] *adj* wellig

wax [wæks] *n* Wachs *nt*; (*sealing* ~) Siegellack *m*; (*in ear*) Ohrenschmalz *nt* ♦ *vt* (*floor*) (ein)wachsen ♦ *vi* (*moon*) zunehmen; ~**works** *npl* Wachsfigurenkabinett *nt*

way [weɪ] *n* Weg *m*; (*method*) Art und Weise *f*; (*direction*) Richtung *f*; (*habit*) Gewohnheit *f*; (*distance*) Entfernung *f*; (*condition*) Zustand *m*; **which** ~? - **this** ~ welche Richtung? - hier entlang; **on the** ~ (*en route*) unterwegs; **to be in the** ~ im Weg sein; **to go out of one's** ~ **to do sth** sich besonders anstrengen, um etw zu tun; **to lose one's** ~ sich verirren; "**give** ~" (*BRIT: AUT*) „Vorfahrt achten!"; **in a** ~ in gewisser Weise; **by the** ~ übrigens; **in some** ~s in gewisser Hinsicht; "~ **in**" (*BRIT*) „Eingang"; "~ **out**" „Ausgang"

waylay [weɪ'leɪ] (*irreg: like* **lay**) *vt* auflauern +*dat*

wayward ['weɪwəd] *adj* eigensinnig

W.C. (*BRIT*) *n* WC *nt*

we [wiː] *pl pron* wir

weak [wiːk] *adj* schwach; ~**en** *vt* schwächen ♦ *vi* schwächer werden; ~**ling** *n* Schwächling *m*; ~**ly** *adv* schwach; ~**ness** *n* Schwäche *f*

wealth [welθ] *n* Reichtum *m*; (*abundance*) Fülle *f*; ~**y** *adj* reich

wean [wiːn] *vt* entwöhnen

weapon ['wepən] *n* Waffe *f*

wear [weə*] (*pt* **wore**, *pp* **worn**) *n* (*clothing*): **sports/baby** ~ Sport-/Babykleidung *f*; (*use*) Verschleiß *m* ♦ *vt* (*have on*) tragen; (*smile etc*) haben; (*use*) abnutzen ♦ *vi* (*last*) halten; (*become old*) (sich) verschleißen; **evening** ~ Abendkleidung *f*; ~ **and tear** Verschleiß *m*; ~ **away** *vt* verbrauchen ♦ *vi* schwinden; ~ **down** *vt* (*people*) zermürben; ~ **off** *vi* sich verlieren; ~ **out** *vt* verschleißen; (*person*) erschöpfen

weary ['wɪərɪ] *adj* müde ♦ *vt* ermüden ♦ *vi* überdrüssig werden

weasel ['wiːzl] *n* Wiesel *nt*

weather ['weðə*] *n* Wetter *nt* ♦ *vt* verwittern lassen; (*resist*) überstehen; **under the** ~ (*fig: ill*) angeschlagen (*inf*); ~-**beaten** *adj* verwittert; ~**cock** *n* Wetterhahn *m*; ~ **forecast** *n* Wettervorhersage *f*; ~ **vane** *m* Wetterfahne *f*

weave [wiːv] (*pt* **wove**, *pp* **woven**) *vt* weben; ~**r** *n* Weber(in) *m(f)*; **weaving** *n* (*craft*) Webkunst *f*

web [web] *n* Netz *nt*; (*membrane*) Schwimmhaut *f*

wed [wed] (*pt, pp* **wedded**) *vt* heiraten ♦ *n*: **the newly-~s** *npl* die Frischvermählten *pl*

we'd [wiːd] = **we had; we would**

wedding ['wedɪŋ] *n* Hochzeit *f*; **silver/golden** ~ **anniversary** Silberhochzeit *f/* Goldene Hochzeit *f*; ~ **day** *n* Hochzeitstag *m*; ~ **dress** *n* Hochzeitskleid *nt*; ~ **present** *n* Hochzeitsgeschenk *nt*; ~ **ring** *n* Trauring *m*, Ehering *m*

wedge [wedʒ] n Keil m; (of cheese etc) Stück nt ♦ vt (fasten) festklemmen; (pack tightly) einkeilen

wedlock ['wedlɒk] n Ehe f

Wednesday ['wenzdeɪ] n Mittwoch m

wee [wiː] (SCOTTISH) adj klein, winzig

weed [wiːd] n Unkraut nt ♦ vt jäten; **~-killer** n Unkrautvertilgungsmittel nt; **~y** adj (person) schmächtig

week [wiːk] n Woche f; **a ~ today/on Friday** heute/Freitag in einer Woche; **~day** n Wochentag m; **~end** n Wochenende nt; **~ly** adj wöchentlich; (wages, magazine) Wochen- ♦ adv wöchentlich

weep [wiːp] (pt, pp **wept**) vi weinen; **~ing willow** n Trauerweide f

weigh [weɪ] vt, vi wiegen; **to ~ anchor** den Anker lichten; **~ down** vt niederdrücken; **~ up** vt abschätzen

weight [weɪt] n Gewicht nt; **to lose/put on ~** abnehmen/zunehmen; **~ing** n (allowance) Zulage f; **~-lifter** n Gewichtheber m; **~y** adj (heavy) gewichtig; (important) schwerwiegend

weir [wɪə*] n (Stau)wehr nt

weird [wɪəd] adj seltsam

welcome ['welkəm] n Willkommen nt, Empfang m ♦ vt begrüßen; **thank you - you're ~!** danke - nichts zu danken

weld [weld] n Schweißnaht f ♦ vt schweißen; **~ing** n Schweißen nt

welfare ['welfeə*] n Wohl nt; (social) Fürsorge f; **~ state** n Wohlfahrtsstaat m; **~ work** n Fürsorge f

well [wel] n Brunnen m; (oil ~) Quelle f ♦ adj (in good health) gesund ♦ adv gut ♦ excl nun!, na schön!; **I'm ~** es geht mir gut; **get ~ soon!** gute Besserung!; **as ~ auch; as ~ as** sowohl als auch; **~ done!** gut gemacht!; **to do ~** (person) gut zurechtkommen; (business) gut gehen; **~ up** vi emporsteigen; (fig) aufsteigen

we'll [wiːl] = we will; we shall

well: **~-behaved** ['welbɪ'heɪvd] adj wohlerzogen; **~-being** ['welbi:ɪŋ] n Wohl nt; **~-built** ['wel'bɪlt] adj kräftig gebaut; **~-deserved** ['weldɪ'zɜːvd] adj wohlverdient; **~-dressed** ['wel'drest] adj

gut gekleidet; **~-heeled** ['wel'hiːld] (inf) adj (wealthy) gut gepolstert

wellingtons ['welɪŋtənz] npl (also: wellington boots) Gummistiefel pl

well: **~-known** ['wel'nəʊn] adj bekannt; **~-mannered** ['wel'mænəd] adj wohlerzogen; **~-meaning** ['wel'miːnɪŋ] adj (person) wohlmeinend; (action) gutgemeint; **~-off** ['wel'ɒf] adj gut situiert; **~-read** ['wel'red] adj (sehr) belesen; **~-to-do** ['weltə'duː] adj wohlhabend; **~-wisher** ['welwɪʃə*] n Gönner m

Welsh [welʃ] adj walisisch ♦ n (LING) Walisisch nt; **the ~** npl (people) die Waliser pl; **~man/woman** (irreg) n Waliser(in) m(f); **~ rarebit** n überbackene Käseschnitte pl

went [went] pt of go

wept [wept] pt, pp of weep

were [wɜː*] pt pl of be

we're [wɪə*] = we are

weren't [wɜːnt] = were not

west [west] n Westen m ♦ adj West-, westlich ♦ adv westwärts, nach Westen; **the W~** der Westen; **the W~ Country** (BRIT) n der Südwesten Englands; **~erly** adj westlich; **~ern** adj westlich, West- ♦ n (CINE) Western m; **W~ Germany** n Westdeutschland nt, Bundesrepublik Deutschland f; **W~ Indian** adj westindisch ♦ n Westindier(in) m(f); **W~ Indies** npl Westindische Inseln pl; **~ward(s)** adv westwärts

wet [wet] adj naß; **to get ~** naß werden; **"~ paint"** „frisch gestrichen"; **~ blanket** n (fig) Triefel m; **~ suit** n Taucheranzug m

we've [wiːv] = we have

whack [wæk] n Schlag m ♦ vt schlagen

whale [weɪl] n Wal m

wharf [wɔːf] n Kai m

wharves [wɔːvz] npl of wharf

KEYWORD

---

what [wɒt] adj **1** (in direct/indirect questions) welche(r, s), was für ein(e); **what size is it?** welche Größe ist das?
2 (in exclamations) was für ein(e); **what a mess!** was für ein Durch-

einander!

♦ *pron* *(interrogative/relative)* was; **what are you doing?** was machst du gerade?; **what are you talking about?** wovon reden Sie?; **what is it called?** wie heißt das?; **what about ...?** wie wär's mit ...?; **I saw what you did** ich habe gesehen, was du gemacht hast

♦ *excl* *(disbelieving)* wie, was; **what, no coffee!** wie, kein Kaffee?; **I've crashed the car - what!** ich hatte einen Autounfall - was!

whatever [wɒt'evə*] *adj*: ~ **book** welches Buch (auch) ♦ *pron* was (auch) (immer); ~ **happens** was (immer) (auch) passiert; **nothing** ~ überhaupt gar nichts

wheat [wiːt] *n* Weizen *m*; ~ **germ** *n* Weizenkeim *m*

wheedle ['wiːdl] *vt*: **to** ~ **sb into doing sth** jdn dazu überreden, etw zu tun; **to** ~ **sth out of sb** jdm etw abluchsen

wheel [wiːl] *n* Rad *nt*; *(steering* ~*)* Lenkrad *nt*; *(disc)* Scheibe *f* ♦ *vt* schieben; ~**barrow** *n* Schubkarren *m*; ~**chair** *n* Rollstuhl *m*; ~ **clamp** *n* *(AUT)* Radblockierung *f* *(an falschparkenden Autos angebracht)*

wheeze [wiːz] *vi* keuchen

when [wen] *adv* wann

♦ *conj* **1** *(at, during, after the time that)* wenn; *(with past reference)* als; **she was reading when I came in** sie las, als ich hereinkam; **be careful when you cross the road** seien Sie vorsichtig, wenn Sie über die Straße gehen

2 *(on, at which)* als; **on the day when I met him** an dem Tag, an dem ich ihn traf

3 *(whereas)* wo ... doch

whenever [wen'evə*] *adv* wann (auch) immer ♦ *conj* jedesmal wenn

where [wɛə*] *adv* *(place)* wo; *(direction)* wohin; ~ **from** woher; ~**abouts** ['wɛərə'bauts] *adv* wo ♦ *n* Aufenthaltsort *m*; **nobody knows his**

~**abouts** niemand weiß, wo er ist; ~**as** [wɛər'æz] *conj* während, wo ... doch; ~**by** *pron* woran, wodurch, womit, wovon; ~**upon** *conj* worauf, wonach; *(at beginning of sentence)* daraufhin

wherever [wɛər'evə*] *adv* wo (immer)

wherewithal ['wɛəwiðɔːl] *n* nötige (Geld)mittel *pl*

whet [wet] *vt* *(appetite)* anregen

whether ['weðə*] *conj* ob; **I don't know** ~ **to accept or not** ich weiß nicht, ob ich es annehmen soll oder nicht; ~ **you go or not** ob du gehst oder nicht

which [witʃ] *adj* **1** *(interrogative: direct, indirect)* welche(r, s); **which one?** welche(r, s)?

2: **in which case** in diesem Fall; **by which time** zu dieser Zeit

♦ *pron* **1** *(interrogative)* welche(r, s); *(of people also)* wer

2 *(relative)* der/die/das; *(referring to people)* was; **the apple which you ate/ which is on the table** der Apfel, den du gegessen hast/der auf dem Tisch liegt; **he said he saw her, which is true** er sagte, er habe sie gesehen, was auch stimmt

whichever [witʃ'evə*] *adj* welche(r, s) auch immer; *(no matter which)* ganz gleich welche(r, s)

whiff [wif] *n* Hauch *m*

while [wail] *n* Weile *f* ♦ *conj* während; **for a** ~ eine Zeitlang; ~ **away** *vt* *(time)* sich *dat* vertreiben

whim [wim] *n* Laune *f*

whimper ['wimpə*] *n* Wimmern *nt* ♦ *vi* wimmern

whimsical ['wimzikəl] *adj* launisch

whine [wain] *n* Gewinsel *nt*, Gejammer *nt* ♦ *vi* heulen, winseln

whip [wip] *n* Peitsche *f*; *(POL)* Fraktionsführer *m* ♦ *vt* *(beat)* peitschen; *(snatch)* reißen; ~**ped cream** *n* Schlagsahne *f*; ~**-round** *(BRIT: inf)* *n* Geldsammlung *f*

whirl [wɜːl] *n* Wirbel *m* ♦ *vt, vi* (her-um)wirbeln; ~**pool** *n* Wirbel *m*; ~**wind**

n Wirbelwind *m*

whirr [wɜː*] *vi* schwirren, surren

whisk [wɪsk] *n* Schneebesen *m* ♦ *vt* (*cream etc*) schlagen; **to ~ sb away** *or* **off mit jdm davon sausen**

whisker ['wɪskə*] *n*: ~**s** (*of animal*) Barthaare *pl*; (*of man*) Backenbart *m*

whisky ['wɪskɪ] (*US, IRISH* **whiskey**) *n* Whisky *m*

whisper ['wɪspə*] *n* Flüstern *nt* ♦ *vt, vi* flüstern

whistle ['wɪsl] *n* Pfiff *m*; (*instrument*) Pfeife *f* ♦ *vt, vi* pfeifen

white [waɪt] *n* Weiß *nt*; (*of egg*) Eiweiß *nt* ♦ *adj* weiß; ~ **coffee** (*BRIT*) *n* Kaffee *m* mit Milch; ~-**collar worker** *n* Angestellte(r) *m*; ~ **elephant** *n* (*fig*) Fehlinvestition *f*; ~ **lie** *n* Notlüge *f*; ~**ness** *n* Weiß *nt*; ~ **paper** *n* (*POL*) Weißbuch *nt*; ~**wash** *n* (*paint*) Tünche *f*; (*fig*) Ehrenrettung *f* ♦ *vt* weißen, tünchen; (*fig*) reinwaschen

whiting ['waɪtɪŋ] *n* Weißfisch *m*

Whitsun ['wɪtsn] *n* Pfingsten *nt*

whittle ['wɪtl] *vt*: **to ~ away** *or* **down** stutzen, verringern

whizz [wɪz] *vi*: **to ~ past** *or* **by** vorbeizischen, vorbeischwirren; ~ **kid** (*inf*) *n* Kanone *f*

who [huː] *pron* **1** (*interrogative*) wer; (*acc*) wen; (*dat*) wem; **who is it?**, **who's there?** wer ist da?
2 (*relative*) der/die/das; **the man/ woman who spoke to me** der Mann/die Frau, der/die mit mir sprach

whodunit [huːˈdʌnɪt] (*inf*) *n* Krimi *m*

whoever [huːˈevə*] *pron* wer/wen/wem auch immer; (*no matter who*) ganz gleich wer/wen/wem

whole [həʊl] *adj* ganz ♦ *n* Ganze(s) *nt*; **the ~ of the town** die ganze Stadt; **on the ~** im großen und ganzen; **as a ~** im großen und ganzen; ~**hearted** *adj* rückhaltlos; ~**heartedly** *adv* von ganzem Herzen; ~**meal** *adj* (*bread, flour*) Vollkorn-; ~**sale** *n* Großhandel *m* ♦ *adj* (*trade*) Großhandels-; (*de-*

struction) Massen-; ~**saler** *n* Großhändler *m*; ~**some** *adj* bekömmlich, gesund; ~**wheat** *adj* = **wholemeal**

wholly ['həʊlɪ] *adv* ganz, völlig

whom [huːm] *pron* **1** (*interrogative*: *acc*) wen; (: *dat*) wem; **whom did you see?** wen haben Sie gesehen?; **to whom did you give it?** wem haben Sie es gegeben?
2 (*relative*: *acc*) den/die/das; (: *dat*) dem/der/dem; **the man whom I saw/to whom I spoke** der Mann, den ich sah/ mit dem ich sprach

whooping cough ['huːpɪŋ-] *n* Keuchhusten *m*

whore [hɔː*] *n* Hure *f*

whose [huːz] *adj* (*possessive*: *interrogative*) wessen; (: *relative*) dessen; (*after f and pl*) deren ♦ *pron* wessen; ~ **book is this?**, ~ **is this book?** wessen Buch ist dies?; ~ **is this?** wem gehört das?

why [waɪ] *adv* warum, weshalb
♦ *conj* warum, weshalb; **that's not why I'm here** ich bin nicht deswegen hier; **that's the reason why** deshalb
♦ *excl* (*expressing surprise, shock, annoyance*) na so was; (*explaining*) also dann; **why, it's you!** na so was, du bist es!

wick [wɪk] *n* Docht *m*

wicked ['wɪkɪd] *adj* böse

wicker ['wɪkə*] *n* (*also*: ~**work**) Korbgeflecht *nt*

wicket ['wɪkɪt] *n* Tor *nt*, Dreistab *m*

wide [waɪd] *adj* breit; (*plain*) weit; (*in firing*) daneben ♦ *adv*: **to open ~** weit öffnen; **to shoot ~** daneben schießen; ~-**angle lens** *n* Weitwinkelobjektiv *nt*; ~-**awake** *adj* hellwach; ~**ly** *adv* weit; (*known*) allgemein; ~**n** *vt* erweitern; ~ **open** *adj* weit geöffnet; ~**spread** *adj* weitverbreitet

widow ['wɪdəʊ] n Witwe f; ~**ed** adj verwitwet; ~**er** n Witwer m
width [wɪdθ] n Breite f, Weite f
wield [wiːld] vt schwingen, handhaben
wife [waɪf] (pl **wives**) n (Ehe)frau f, Gattin f
wig [wɪg] n Perücke f
wiggle ['wɪgl] n Wackeln nt ♦ vt wackeln mit ♦ vi wackeln
wild [waɪld] adj wild; (violent) heftig; (plan, idea) verrückt; ~**erness** ['wɪldənəs] n Wildnis f, Wüste f; ~-**goose chase** n (fig) fruchtlose(s) Unternehmen nt; ~**life** n Tierwelt f; ~**ly** adv wild, ungestüm; (exaggerated) irrsinnig; ~**s** npl: **the** ~**s** die Wildnis f
wilful ['wɪlfʊl] (US **willful**) adj (intended) vorsätzlich; (obstinate) eigensinnig

---

KEYWORD

will [wɪl] aux vb **1** (forming future tense) werden; **I will finish it tomorrow** ich mache es morgen zu Ende
2 (in conjectures, predictions): **he will** or **he'll be there by now** er dürfte jetzt da sein; **that will be the postman** das wird der Postbote sein
3 (in commands, requests, offers): **will you be quiet!** sei endlich still!; **will you help me?** hilfst du mir?; **will you have a cup of tea?** trinken Sie eine Tasse Tee?; **I won't put up with it!** das lasse ich mir nicht gefallen!
♦ vt wollen
♦ n Wille f; (JUR) Testament nt

---

willing ['wɪlɪŋ] adj gewillt, bereit; ~**ly** adv bereitwillig, gern; ~**ness** n (Bereit)willigkeit f
willow ['wɪləʊ] n Weide f
willpower ['wɪlpaʊə*] n Willenskraft f
willy-nilly ['wɪlɪ'nɪlɪ] adv einfach so
wilt [wɪlt] vi (ver)welken
wily ['waɪlɪ] adj gerissen
win [wɪn] (pt, pp **won**) n Sieg m ♦ vt, vi gewinnen; **to** ~ **sb over** or **round** jdn gewinnen, jdn dazu bringen
wince [wɪns] n Zusammenzucken nt ♦ vi zusammenzucken
winch [wɪntʃ] n Winde f

wind¹ [wɪnd] n Wind m; (MED) Blähungen pl
wind² [waɪnd] (pt, pp **wound**) vt (rope) winden; (bandage) wickeln ♦ vi (turn) sich winden; ~ **up** vt (clock) aufziehen; (debate) (ab)schließen
windfall ['wɪndfɔːl] n unverhoffte(r) Glücksfall m
winding ['waɪndɪŋ] adj (road) gewunden
wind instrument ['wɪndɪnstrʊmənt] n Blasinstrument nt
windmill ['wɪndmɪl] n Windmühle f
window ['wɪndəʊ] n Fenster nt; ~ **box** n Blumenkasten m; ~ **cleaner** n Fensterputzer m; ~ **envelope** n Fensterbriefumschlag m; ~ **ledge** n Fenstersims m; ~ **pane** n Fensterscheibe f; ~**sill** n Fensterbank f
windpipe ['wɪndpaɪp] n Luftröhre f
windscreen ['wɪndskriːn] (BRIT) n Windschutzscheibe f; ~ **washer** n Scheibenwaschanlage f; ~ **wiper** n Scheibenwischer m
windshield ['wɪndʃiːld] (US) n = windscreen
windswept ['wɪndswept] adj vom Wind gepeitscht; (person) zerzaust
windy ['wɪndɪ] adj windig
wine [waɪn] n Wein m; ~ **cellar** n Weinkeller m; ~**glass** n Weinglas nt; ~ **list** n Weinkarte f; ~ **merchant** n Weinhändler m; ~ **tasting** n Weinprobe f; ~ **waiter** n Weinkellner m
wing [wɪŋ] n Flügel m; (MIL) Gruppe f; ~**s** npl (THEAT) Seitenkulisse f; ~**er** n (SPORT) Flügelstürmer m
wink [wɪŋk] n Zwinkern nt ♦ vi zwinkern, blinzeln
winner ['wɪnə*] n Gewinner m; (SPORT) Sieger m
winning ['wɪnɪŋ] adj (team) siegreich, Sieger-; (goal) entscheidend; ~ **post** n Ziel nt; ~**s** npl Gewinn m
winter ['wɪntə*] n Winter m ♦ adj (clothes) Winter- ♦ vi überwintern; ~ **sports** npl Wintersport m
wintry ['wɪntrɪ] adj Winter-, winterlich
wipe [waɪp] n: **to give sth a** ~ etw (ab)wischen ♦ vt wischen; ~ **off** vt abwischen; ~ **out** vt (debt) löschen;

(destroy) auslöschen; ~ **up** *vt* aufwischen

wire ['waɪə*] *n* Draht *m*; *(telegram)* Telegramm *nt* ♦ *vt* telegrafieren; **to ~ sb** jdm telegrafieren

wireless ['waɪəlɪs] *(BRIT)* *n* Radio(apparat *m*) *nt*

wiring ['waɪərɪŋ] *n* elektrische Leitungen *pl*

wiry ['waɪərɪ] *adj* drahtig

wisdom ['wɪzdəm] *n* Weisheit *f*; *(of decision)* Klugheit *f*; ~ **tooth** *n* Weisheitszahn *m*

wise [waɪz] *adj* klug, weise ♦ *suffix*: timewise zeitlich gesehen

wish [wɪʃ] *n* Wunsch *m* ♦ *vt* wünschen; **best ~es** *(on birthday etc)* alles Gute; **with best ~es** herzliche Grüße; **to ~ sb goodbye** jdn verabschieden; **he ~ed me well** er wünschte mir Glück; **to ~ to do sth** etw tun wollen; ~ **for** *vt fus* sich *dat* wünschen; ~**ful thinking** *n* Wunschdenken *nt*

wishy-washy ['wɪʃɪ'wɒʃɪ] *(inf)* *adj (colour)* verwaschen; *(ideas, argument)* verschwommen

wisp [wɪsp] *n* (Haar)strähne *f*; *(of smoke)* Wölkchen *nt*

wistful ['wɪstfʊl] *adj* sehnsüchtig

wit [wɪt] *n (also:* ~s) Verstand *m no pl*; *(amusing ideas)* Witz *m*; *(person)* Witzbold *m*

witch [wɪtʃ] *n* Hexe *f*; ~**craft** *n* Hexerei *f*

KEYWORD

with [wɪð, wɪθ] *prep* **1** *(accompanying, in the company of)* mit; **we stayed with friends** wir übernachteten bei Freunden; **I'll be with you in a minute** einen Augenblick, ich bin sofort da; **I'm not with you** *(I don't understand)* das verstehe ich nicht; **to be with it** *(inf: up-to-date)* auf dem laufenden sein; *(: alert)* (voll) da sein *(inf)*

2 *(descriptive, indicating manner etc)* mit; **the man with the grey hat** der Mann mit dem grauen Hut; **red with anger** rot vor Wut

withdraw [wɪθ'drɔ:] *(irreg: like* **draw**) *vt* zurückziehen; *(money)* abheben; *(remark)* zurücknehmen ♦ *vi* sich zurückziehen; ~**al** *n* Zurückziehung *f*; Abheben *nt*; Zurücknahme *f*; *(person)* verschlossen

wither ['wɪðə*] *vi* (ver)welken

withhold [wɪθ'həʊld] *(irreg: like* **hold**) *vt*: **to ~ sth (from sb)** (jdm) etw vorenthalten

within [wɪð'ɪn] *prep* innerhalb +*gen* ♦ *adv* innen; ~ **sight of** in Sichtweite von; ~ **the week** innerhalb dieser Woche

without [wɪð'aʊt] *prep* ohne

withstand [wɪθ'stænd] *(irreg: like* **stand**) *vt* widerstehen +*dat*

witness ['wɪtnəs] *n* Zeuge *m*, Zeugin *f* ♦ *vt (see)* sehen, miterleben; *(document)* beglaubigen; ~ **box** *n* Zeugenstand *m*; ~ **stand** *(US)* *n* Zeugenstand *m*

witticism ['wɪtɪsɪzəm] *n* witzige Bemerkung *f*

witty ['wɪtɪ] *adj* witzig, geistreich

wives [waɪvz] *pl of* **wife**

wizard ['wɪzəd] *n* Zauberer *m*

wk *abbr* = **week**

wobble ['wɒbl] *vi* wackeln

woe [wəʊ] *n* Kummer *m*

woke [wəʊk] *pt of* **wake**

woken ['wəʊkən] *pp of* **wake**

woman ['wʊmən] *(pl* **women**) *n* Frau *f*; ~ **doctor** *n* Ärztin *f*; ~**ly** *adj* weiblich

womb [wu:m] *n* Gebärmutter *f*

women ['wɪmɪn] *npl of* **woman**; ~**'s lib** *(inf)* *n* Frauenrechtsbewegung *f*

won [wʌn] *pt, pp of* **win**

wonder ['wʌndə*] *n (marvel)* Wunder *nt*; *(surprise)* Staunen *nt*, Verwunderung *f* ♦ *vi* sich wundern ♦ *vt*: **I ~ whether ...** ich frage mich, ob ...; **it's no ~ that** es ist kein Wunder, daß; **to ~ at** sich wundern über +*acc*; **to ~ about** sich Gedanken machen über +*acc*; ~**ful** *adj* wunderbar, herrlich; ~**fully** *adv* wunderbar

won't [wəʊnt] = **will not**

wood [wʊd] *n* Holz *nt*; *(forest)* Wald *m*; ~ **carving** *n* Holzschnitzerei *f*; ~**ed** *adj* bewaldet; ~**en** *adj (also fig)* hölzern;

~**pecker** n Specht m; ~**wind** n Blasinstrumente pl; ~**work** n Holzwerk nt; (craft) Holzarbeiten pl; ~**worm** n Holzwurm m

wool [wʊl] n Wolle f; **to pull the ~ over sb's eyes** (fig) jdm Sand in die Augen streuen; ~**len** (US **woolen**) adj Woll-; ~**lens** npl Wollsachen pl; ~**ly** (US **wooly**) adj wollig; (fig) schwammig

word [wɜːd] n Wort nt; (news) Bescheid m ♦ vt formulieren; **in other ~s** anders gesagt; **to break/keep one's ~** sein Wort brechen/halten; ~**ing** n Wortlaut m; ~ **processing** n Textverarbeitung f; ~ **processor** n Textverarbeitungsgerät nt

wore [wɔː*] pt of **wear**

work [wɜːk] n Arbeit f; (ART, LITER) Werk nt ♦ vi arbeiten; (machine) funktionieren; (medicine) wirken; (succeed) klappen; ~**s** n sg (BRIT: factory) Fabrik f, Werk nt ♦ npl (of watch) Werk nt; **to be out of ~** arbeitslos sein; **in ~ing order** in betriebsfähigem Zustand; ~ **loose** vi sich lockern; ~ **on** vi weiterarbeiten ♦ vt fus (be engaged in) arbeiten an +dat; (influence) bearbeiten; ~ **out** vi (sum) aufgehen; (plan) klappen ♦ vt (problem) lösen; (plan) ausarbeiten; **it ~s out at £100** das gibt or macht £100; ~ **up** vt: **to get ~ed up** sich aufregen; ~**able** adj (soil) bearbeitbar; (plan) ausführbar; ~**aholic** [wɜːkəˈhɒlɪk] n Arbeitssüchtige(r) mf; ~**er** n Arbeiter(in) m(f); ~**force** n Arbeiterschaft f; ~**ing class** n Arbeiterklasse f; ~**ing-class** adj Arbeiter-; ~**man** (irreg) n Arbeiter m; ~**manship** n Arbeit f, Ausführung f; ~**sheet** n Arbeitsblatt nt; ~**shop** n Werkstatt f; ~ **station** n Arbeitsplatz m; ~**-to-rule** (BRIT) n Dienst m nach Vorschrift

world [wɜːld] n Welt f; **to think the ~ of sb** große Stücke auf jdn halten; ~**ly** adj weltlich, irdisch; ~**-wide** adj weltweit

worm [wɜːm] n Wurm m

worn [wɔːn] pp of **wear** ♦ adj (clothes) abgetragen; ~**-out** adj (object) abgenutzt; (person) völlig erschöpft

worried [ˈwʌrɪd] adj besorgt, beunruhigt

worry [ˈwʌrɪ] n Sorge f ♦ vt beunruhigen ♦ vi (feel uneasy) sich sorgen, sich dat Gedanken machen; ~**ing** adj beunruhigend

worse [wɜːs] adj schlechter, schlimmer ♦ adv schlimmer, ärger ♦ n Schlimmere(s) nt, Schlechtere(s) nt; **a change for the ~** eine Verschlechterung; ~**n** vt verschlimmern ♦ vi sich verschlechtern; ~ **off** adj (fig) schlechter dran

worship [ˈwɜːʃɪp] n Verehrung f ♦ vt anbeten; **Your W~** (BRIT: to mayor) Herr Bürgermeister, Frau Bürgermeister; (: to judge) Euer Ehren

worst [wɜːst] adj schlimmste(r, s), schlechteste(r, s) ♦ adv am schlimmsten, am ärgsten ♦ n Schlimmste(s) nt, Ärgste(s) nt; **at ~** schlimmstenfalls

worsted [ˈwʊstɪd] n Kammgarn m

worth [wɜːθ] n Wert m ♦ adj wert; **it's ~ it** es lohnt sich; **to be ~ one's while (to do sth)** die Mühe wert sein (, etw zu tun); ~**less** adj wertlos; (person) nichtsnutzig; ~**while** adj lohnend, der Mühe wert

worthy [ˈwɜːðɪ] adj wert, würdig

would [wʊd] aux vb **1** (conditional tense): **if you asked him he would do it** wenn du ihn fragtest, würde er es tun; **if you had asked him he would have done it** wenn du ihn gefragt hättest, hätte er es getan

2 (in offers, invitations, requests): **would you like a biscuit?** möchten Sie ein Plätzchen?; **would you ask him to come in?** würden Sie ihn bitte hineinbitten?

3 (in indirect speech): **I said I would do it** ich sagte, ich würde es tun

4 (emphatic): **it WOULD have to snow today!** es mußte ja ausgerechnet heute schneien!

5 (insistence): **she wouldn't behave** sie wollte sich partout nicht anständig benehmen

6 (conjecture): **it would have been midnight** es mag ungefähr Mitternacht gewesen sein; **it would seem so** es sieht wohl so aus

7 (indicating habit): **he would go there on Mondays** er ging jeden Montag dorthin

wouldn't ['wʊdnt] = **would not**

wound¹ [wuːnd] n (also fig) Wunde f ♦ vt verwunden, verletzen (also fig)

wound² [waʊnd] (pt, pp) of **wind**

wove [wəʊv] pt of **weave**; **~n** ['wəʊvən] pp of **weave**

wrangle ['ræŋgl] n Streit m ♦ vi sich zanken

wrap [ræp] n (stole) Schal m ♦ vt einwickeln; **~ up** vt einwickeln; (deal) abschließen; **~per** n Umschlag m, Schutzhülle f; **~ping paper** n Einwickelpapier nt

wrath [rɒθ] n Zorn m

wreak [riːk] vt (havoc) anrichten; (vengeance) üben

wreath [riːθ, pl riːðz] n Kranz m

wreck [rek] n (ship) Wrack nt; (sth ruined) Ruine f ♦ vt zerstören; **~age** n Trümmer pl

wren [ren] n Zaunkönig m

wrench [rentʃ] n (spanner) Schraubenschlüssel m; (twist) Ruck m ♦ vt reißen, zerren; **to ~ sth from sb** jdm etw entreißen or entwinden

wrestle ['resl] vi: **to ~ (with sb)** (mit jdm) ringen; **~r** n Ringer(in) m(f); **wrestling** n Ringen nt

wretched ['retʃɪd] adj (hovel) elend; (inf) verflixt; **I feel ~** mir ist elend

wriggle ['rɪgl] n Schlängeln nt ♦ vi sich winden

wring [rɪŋ] (pt, pp **wrung**) vt wringen

wrinkle ['rɪŋkl] n Falte f, Runzel f ♦ vt runzeln ♦ vi sich runzeln; (material) knittern

wrist [rɪst] n Handgelenk nt; **~watch** n Armbanduhr f

writ [rɪt] n gerichtliche(r) Befehl m

write [raɪt] (pt **wrote**, pp **written**) vt, vi schreiben; **~ down** vt aufschreiben; **~ off** vt (dismiss) abschreiben; **~ out** vt (essay) abschreiben; (cheque) ausstellen; **~ up** vt schreiben; **~-off** n: **it

is a ~-off** das kann man abschreiben; **~r** n Schriftsteller m

writhe [raɪð] vi sich winden

writing ['raɪtɪŋ] n (act) Schreiben nt; (hand~) (Hand)schrift f; **in ~** schriftlich; **~ paper** n Schreibpapier nt

written ['rɪtn] pp of **write**

wrong [rɒŋ] adj (incorrect) falsch; (morally) unrecht ♦ n Unrecht nt ♦ vt Unrecht tun +dat; **he was ~ in doing that** es war nicht recht von ihm, das zu tun; **you are ~ about that, you've got it ~** da hast du unrecht; **to be in the ~** im Unrecht sein; **what's ~ with your leg?** was ist mit deinem Bein los?; **to go ~** (plan) schiefgehen; (person) einen Fehler machen; **~ful** adj unrechtmäßig; **~ly** adv falsch; (accuse) zu Unrecht

wrote [rəʊt] pt of **write**

wrought [rɔːt] adj: **~ iron** Schmiedeeisen nt

wrung [rʌŋ] pt, pp of **wring**

wry [raɪ] adj ironisch

wt. abbr = **weight**

X

Xmas ['eksməs] n abbr = **Christmas**

X-ray ['eksreɪ] n Röntgenaufnahme f ♦ vt röntgen; **~s** npl Röntgenstrahlen pl

xylophone ['zaɪləfəʊn] n Xylophon nt

Y

yacht [jɒt] n Jacht f; **~ing** n (Sport)segeln nt; **~sman** n Sportsegler m

Yank [jæŋk] (inf) n Ami m

yap [jæp] vi (dog) kläffen

yard [jɑːd] n Hof m; (measure) (englische) Elle f, Yard nt (0,91 m); **~stick** n (fig) Maßstab m

yarn [jɑːn] n (thread) Garn nt; (story) (Seemanns)garn nt

yawn [jɔːn] n Gähnen nt ♦ vi gähnen; **~ing** adj (gap) gähnend

yd. abbr = **yard(s)**

yeah [jɛə] (inf) adv ja
year [jɪə*] n Jahr nt; **to be 8 ~s old** acht Jahre alt sein; **an eight-~-old child** ein achtjähriges Kind; **~ly** adj, adv jährlich
yearn [jɜːn] vi: **to ~ (for)** sich sehnen (nach); **~ing** n Verlangen nt, Sehnsucht f
yeast [jiːst] n Hefe f
yell [jel] n gellende(r) Schrei m ♦ vi laut schreien
yellow ['jeləʊ] adj gelb ♦ n Gelb nt
yelp [jelp] n Gekläff nt ♦ vi kläffen
yeoman ['jəʊmən] (irreg) n: **Y~ of the Guard** Leibgardist m
yes [jes] adv ja ♦ n Ja nt, Jawort nt; **to say ~** ja sagen; **to answer ~** mit Ja antworten
yesterday ['jestədeɪ] adv gestern ♦ n Gestern nt; **~ morning/evening** gestern morgen/abend; **all day ~** gestern den ganzen Tag; **the day before ~** vorgestern
yet [jet] adv noch; (in question) schon; (up to now) bis jetzt ♦ conj doch, dennoch; **it is not finished ~** es ist noch nicht fertig; **the best ~** das bisher beste; **as ~** bis jetzt; (in past) bis dahin
yew [juː] n Eibe f
yield [jiːld] n Ertrag m ♦ vt (result, crop) hervorbringen; (interest, profit) abwerfen; (concede) abtreten ♦ vi nachgeben; (MIL) sich ergeben; **"~"** (US: AUT) „Vorfahrt gewähren"
YMCA n abbr (= Young Men's Christian Association) CVJM m
yoga ['jəʊgə] n Joga m
yoghourt ['jɒgət] n Joghurt m
yog(h)urt ['jɒgət] n = **yoghourt**
yoke [jəʊk] n (also fig) Joch nt
yolk [jəʊk] n Eidotter m, Eigelb nt
yonder ['jɒndə*] adv dort drüben, da drüben ♦ adj jene(r, s) dort

KEYWORD

you [juː] pron **1** (subj, in comparisons: German familiar form: sg) du; (: pl) ihr; (in letters also) Du, Ihr; (: German polite form) Sie; **you Germans** ihr Deutschen; **she's younger than you**
sie ist jünger als du/Sie
2 (direct object, after prep +acc: German familiar form: sg) dich; (: pl) euch; (in letters also) Dich, Euch; (: German polite form) Sie; **I know you** ich kenne dich/euch/Sie
3 (indirect object, after prep +dat: German familiar form: sg) dir; (: pl) euch; (in letters also) Dir, Euch; (: German polite form) Ihnen; **I gave it to you** ich gab es dir/euch/Ihnen
4 (impers: one: subj) man; (: direct object) einen; (: indirect object) einem; **fresh air does you good** frische Luft tut gut

you'd [juːd] = **you had; you would**
you'll [juːl] = **you will; you shall**
young [jʌŋ] adj jung ♦ npl: **the ~** die Jungen pl; **~ish** adj ziemlich jung; **~ster** n Junge m, junge(r) Bursche m, junge(s) Mädchen nt
your ['jɔː*] adj (familiar: sg) dein; (: pl) euer, eure pl; (polite) Ihr; see also **my**
you're ['jʊə*] = **you are**
yours [jɔːz] pron (familiar: sg) deine(r, s); (: pl) eure(r, s); (polite) Ihre(r, s); **~ sincerely** mit freundlichen Grüßen; **~ faithfully** hochachtungsvoll; see also **mine**
yourself [jɔːˈself] pron (emphatic) selbst; (familiar: sg: acc) dich (selbst); (: dat) dir (selbst); (: pl) euch (selbst); (polite) sich (selbst); see also **oneself**
youth [juːθ, pl juːðz] n Jugend f; (young man) junge(r) Mann m; **~s** npl (young people) Jugendliche pl; **~ club** n Jugendzentrum nt; **~ful** adj jugendlich; **~ hostel** n Jugendherberge f
you've [juːv] = **you have**
YTS (BRIT) n abbr (= Youth Training Scheme) staatliches Förderprogramm für arbeitslose Jugendliche
Yugoslav ['juːgəʊˈslɑːv] adj jugoslawisch ♦ n Jugoslawe m, Jugoslawin f
Yugoslavia ['juːgəʊˈslɑːvɪə] n Jugoslawien nt
YWCA n abbr (= Young Women's

Christian Association) CVJF *m*

Z

zany ['zeɪnɪ] *adj* verrückt
zap [zæp] *vt* (*COMPUT*) löschen
zeal [ziːl] *n* Eifer *m*; **~ous** ['zeləs] *adj* eifrig
zebra ['ziːbrə] *n* Zebra *nt*; **~ crossing** (*BRIT*) *n* Zebrastreifen *m*
zero ['zɪərəʊ] *n* Null *f*; (*on scale*) Nullpunkt *m*
zest [zest] *n* Begeisterung *f*

zigzag ['zɪgzæg] *n* Zickzack *m*
zip [zɪp] *n* Reißverschluß *m* ♦ *vt* (*also*: **~ up**) den Reißverschluß zumachen +*gen*; **~ code** (*US*) *n* Postleitzahl *f*; **~ fastener** *n* Reißverschluß *m*; **~per** (*esp US*) *n* Reißverschluß *m*
zodiac ['zəʊdɪæk] *n* Tierkreis *m*
zombie ['zɒmbɪ] *n*: **like a ~** (*fig*) wie im Tran
zoo [zuː] *n* Zoo *m*
zoology [zəʊ'ɒlədʒɪ] *n* Zoologie *f*
zoom [zuːm] *vi*: **to ~ past** vorbeisausen; **~ lens** *n* Zoomobjektiv *nt*
zucchini [zuː'kiːnɪ] (*US*) *npl* Zucchini *pl*

USING YOUR COLLINS POCKET DICTIONARY

Introduction

We are delighted that you have decided to invest in this Collins Pocket Dictionary! Whether you intend to use it in school, at home, on holiday or at work, we are sure that you will find it very useful.

The purpose of this supplement is to help you become aware of the wealth of vocabulary and grammatical information your dictionary contains, to explain how this information is presented and also to point out some of the traps one can fall into when using a German-English English-German dictionary.

In the pages which follow you will find explanations and exercises (not too difficult!) designed to give you practice in exploring the dictionary's contents and in retrieving information for a variety of purposes. Answers are provided at the end. If you spend a little time on these pages you should be able to use your dictionary more efficiently and effectively. Have fun!

Contents

295

HOW INFORMATION IS PRESENTED IN YOUR DICTIONARY

A great deal of information is packed into your Collins Pocket Dictionary using colour, various typefaces, sizes of type, symbols, abbreviations and brackets. The purpose of this section is to acquaint you with the conventions used in presenting information.

Headwords

A headword is the word you look up in a dictionary. Headwords are listed in alphabetical order throughout the dictionary. They are printed in colour so that they stand out clearly from all the other words on the dictionary page.

Note that at the top of each page two headwords appear. These are guides to the alphabetical order of words on the page. They are there to help you scan through the dictionary more quickly to find the word you want.

The German alphabet consists of the same 26 letters as the English alphabet, plus the letter ß, which is used in some words instead of ss. Although certain letters in the German alphabet take umlaut (ä, ö, ü), this does not affect the order of words in the German-English section of the dictionary.

A Dictionary Entry

An entry is made up of a headword and all the information about that headword. Entries will be short or long depending on how frequently a word is used in either English or German and how many meanings it has. Inevitably, the fuller the dictionary entry the more care is needed in sifting through it to find the information you require.

Meanings

The translations of a headword are given in ordinary type. Where there is more than one meaning or usage, a semi-colon separates one from the other.

abladen['apla:dən] (*unreg*) *vt* to unload
Ablage ['apla:gə] *f* (*für Akten*) tray; (*für Kleider*) cloakroom
ablassen['aplasən] (*unreg*) *vt* (*Wasser, Dampf*) to let off; (*vom Preis*) to knock off ♦ *vi*: **von etw ~** to give sth up, to abandon sth

Betrag [bə'tra:k] (-(e)s, ⁼e) *m* amount; **b~en**[bə'tra:gən] (*unreg*) *vt* to amount

Ohnmacht ['o:nmaxt] *f* faint; (*fig*) impotence; **in ~ fallen** to faint
ohnmächtig['o:nmɛçtiç] *adj* in a faint, unconscious; (*fig*) weak, impotent; **sie ist ~** she has fainted
Ohr [o:r] (-(e)s, -en) *nt* ear; (*Gehör*) hearing
Öhr[ø:r] (-(e)s, -e) *nt* eye

quilt; (*Überwurf*) bedspread
Bettel- ['bɛtəl] *zW*: **b~arm** *adj* very

Gurt[gurt] (-(e)s, -e) *m* belt

klar [kla:r] *adj* clear; (*NAUT*) ready for sea; (*MIL*) ready for action; **sich** *dat* **im ~en sein über** +*akk* to be clear about; **ins ~e kommen** to get clear; (**na**) **~!** of course!

Zug [tsu:k] (-(e)s, ⁼e) *m* (*EISENB*) train; (*Luft~*) draught; (*Ziehen*) pull(ing); (*Gesichts~*) feature; (*SCHACH etc*) move; (*Klingel~*) pull; (*Schrift~*) stroke; (*Atem~*) breath; (*Charakter~*) trait; (*an Zigarette*) puff, pull, drag; (*Schluck*) gulp; (*Menschengruppe*) procession; (*von Vögeln*) flight; (*MIL*) platoon; **etw in vollen Zügen genießen** to enjoy sth to the full

In addition, you will often find other words appearing in *italics* in brackets before the translations. These either give some notion of the contexts in which the headword might appear (as with 'scharf' opposite — 'scharfes Essen', 'scharfe Munition', etc.) or else they provide synonyms (as with 'fremd' opposite — 'unvertraut', 'ausländisch', etc.).

Phonetic Spellings

In square brackets immediately after most headwords you will find the phonetic spelling of the word — i.e. its pronunciation. The phonetic transcription of German and English vowels and consonants is given on page x near the front of your dictionary.

Additional Information About Headwords

Information about the usage or form of certain headwords is given in brackets between the phonetics and the translation or translations. Have a look at the entries for 'KG', 'Filiale', 'löschen' and 'Bruch' opposite.

This information is usually given in abbreviated form. A helpful list of abbreviations is given on pages vi to viii at the front of your dictionary.

You should be particularly careful with colloquial words or phrases. Words labelled '(*umg*)' would not normally be used in formal speech, while those labelled '(*umg!*)' would be considered offensive.

Careful consideration of such style labels will provide indications as to the degree of formality and appropriateness of a word and could help you avoid many an embarrassing situation when using German!

Expressions in which the Headword Appears

An entry will often feature certain common expressions in which the headword appears. These expressions are in **bold** type but in black as opposed to colour. A swung dash (~) is used instead of repeating a headword in an entry. 'Schikane' and 'man' opposite illustrate this point.

Related Words

In the Pocket Dictionary words related to certain headwords are sometimes given at the end of an entry, as with 'Lohn' and 'accept' opposite. These are easily picked out as they are also in colour. To help you find these words, they are placed in alphabetical order after the headword to which they belong — see 'acceptable', 'acceptance' etc. opposite.

scharf [ʃarf] *adj* sharp; (*Essen*) hot, spicy; (*Munition*) live; **~ nachdenken** to think hard; **auf etw** *akk* **~ sein** (*umg*) to be keen on sth

fremd [fremt] *adj* (*unvertraut*) strange; (*ausländisch*) foreign; (*nicht eigen*) someone else's; **etw ist jdm ~** sth is foreign to sb; **~artig** *adj* strange;

gänzlich ['gɛntslɪç] *adj* complete, entire ♦ *adv* completely, entirely

Teufel ['tɔyfəl] (-s, -) *m* devil

KG [kaːˈgeː] (-, -s) *f abk* (= *Kommanditgesellschaft*) limited partnership

Filiale [filiˈaːlə] *f* (*COMM*) branch

löschen ['lœʃən] *vt* (*Feuer, Licht*) to put out, to extinguish; (*Durst*) to quench; (*COMM*) to cancel; (*COMPUT*) to delete; (*Tonband*) to erase; (*Fracht*) to unload ♦ *vi* (*Feuerwehr*) to put out a fire; (*Tinte*) to blot

Bruch [brʊx] (-(e)s, ⁼e) *m* breakage; (*zerbrochene Stelle*) break; (*fig*) split, breach; (*MED: Eingeweide~*) rupture, hernia; (*Bein~ etc*) fracture; (*MATH*) fraction

schenken ['ʃɛŋkən] *vt* (*auch fig*) to give; (*Getrank*) to pour; **sich** *dat* **etw ~** (*umg*) to skip sth; **das ist geschenkt!** (*billig*) that's a giveaway!; (*nichts wert*) that's worthless!

fuchsen (*umg*) *vt* to rile, to annoy

Arsch [arʃ] (-es, ⁼e; *umg!*) *m* arse (*BRIT!*), ass (*US!*)

Schikane [ʃiˈkaːnə] *f* harassment; dirty trick; **mit allen ~n** with all the trimmings

man [man] *pron* one, you; **~ sagt, ...** they *od* people say ...; **wie schreibt ~ das?** how do you write it?, how is it written?

Lohn [loːn] (-(e)s, ⁼e) *m* reward; (*Arbeits~*) pay, wages *pl*; **~büro** *nt* wages office; **~empfänger** *m* wage earner

accept [əkˈsɛpt] *vt* (*take*) annehmen; (*agree to*) akzeptieren; **~able** *adj* annehmbar; **~ance** *n* Annahme *f*

'Key' Words

Your Collins Pocket Dictionary gives special status to certain German and English words which can be looked on as 'key' words in each language. These are words which have many different usages. 'Werden', 'alle(r, s)' and 'sich' opposite are typical examples in German. You are likely to become familiar with them in your day-to-day language studies.

There will be occasions, however, when you want to check on a particular usage. Your dictionary can be very helpful here. Note how different parts of speech and different usages are clearly indicated by a combination of lozenges (♦) and numbers. In addition, further guides to usage are given in italics in brackets in the language of the user who needs them.

werden ['veːrdən] (*pt* **wurde**, *pp* **geworden** *od* (*bei Passiv*) **worden**) *vi* to become; **was ist aus ihm/aus der Sache geworden?** what became of him/it?; **es ist nichts/gut geworden** it came to nothing/turned out well; **es wird Nacht/Tag** it's getting dark/light; **mir wird kalt** I'm getting cold; **mir wird schlecht** I fell ill; **Erster werden** to come *od* be first; **das muß anders werden** that'll have to change; **rot/zu Eis werden** to turn red/to ice; **was willst du (mal) werden?** what do you want to be?; **die Fotos sind gut geworden** the photos have come out nicely

♦ *als Hilfsverb* **1** (*bei Futur*): **er wird es tun** he will *od* he'll do it; **er wird das nicht tun** he will not *od* he won't do it; **es wird gleich regnen** it's going to rain

2 (*bei Konjunktiv*): **ich würde ...** I would ...; **er würde gern ...** he would *od* he'd like to ...; **ich würde lieber ...** I would *od* I'd rather ...

3 (*bei Vermutung*): **sie wird in der Küche sein** she will be in the kitchen

4 (*bei Passiv*): **gebraucht werden** to be used; **er ist erschossen worden** he has *od* he's been shot; **mir wurde gesagt, daß ...** I was told that ...

alle(r, s) ['alə(r, s)] *adj* **1** (*sämtliche*) all; **wir alle** all of us; **alle Kinder waren da** all the children were there; **alle Kinder mögen ...** all children like ...; **alle beide** both of us/them; **sie kamen alle** they all came; **alles Gute** all the best; **alles in allem** all in all

2 (*mit Zeit- oder Maßangaben*) every; **alle vier Jahre** every four years; **alle fünf Meter** every five metres

♦ *pron* everything; **alles was er sagt** everything he says, all that he says

♦ *adv* (*zu Ende, aufgebraucht*) finished; **die Milch ist alle** the milk's all gone, there's no milk left; **etw alle machen** to finish sth up

sich [zɪç] *pron* **1** (*akk*): **er/sie/es ... sich** he/she/it ... himself/herself/itself; **sie** *pl*/**man ... sich** they/one ... themselves; **sie kamen alle** oneself; **Sie ... sich** you ... yourself/yourselves *pl*; **sich wiederholen** to repeat oneself/itself

2 (*dat*): **er/sie/es ... sich** he/she/it ... himself/herself/itself; **sie** *pl*/**man ... sich** they/one ... to themselves/oneself; **Sie ... sich** you ... to yourself/yourselves *pl*; **sie hat sich einen Pullover gekauft** she bought herself a jumper; **sich die Haare waschen** to wash one's hair

3 (*mit Präposition*): **haben Sie Ihren Ausweis bei sich?** do you have your pass on you?; **er hat nichts bei sich** he's got nothing on him; **sie bleiben gern unter sich** they keep themselves to themselves

4 (*einander*) each other, one another; **sie bekämpfen sich** they fight each other *od* one another

5: **dieses Auto fährt sich gut** this car drives well; **hier sitzt es sich gut** it's good to sit here

WORDGAME 1

HEADWORDS

Study the following sentences. In each sentence a wrong word spelt very
similarly to the correct word has deliberately been put in and the sentence
doesn't make sense. This word is shaded each time. Write out the correct
word, which you will find in your dictionary near the wrong word.

Example   Raufen verboten

['Raufen' (= 'to pull out') is the wrong word and
should be replaced by 'rauchen' (= 'to smoke')]

1. Hast du das Buch schon gekonnt?
2. Ich habe ein paar VW-Akten gekauft.
3. Wir waren gestern im Kilo.
4. Sollen wir die Theaterkarten schon kauen?
5. Unser Nachbar hat einen kleinen schwarzen
   Puder.
6. Ich zähle heute die Rechnung.
7. Der Student muß sich für den Kurs einschreiten.
8. Das neue Restaurant ist gar nicht über.
9. Gans viele Leute standen am Unfallort.
10. Ich habe meiner Tanne einen Brief geschrieben.

WORDGAME 2
DICTIONARY ENTRIES

Complete the crossword below by looking up the English words in the list and finding the correct German translations. There is a slight catch, however! All the English words can be translated several ways into German, but only one translation will fit correctly into each part of the crossword. So look carefully through the entries in the English-German section of your dictionary.

1. FAIR
2. CATCH
3. LEARN
4. FALL
5. HIT
6. HARD
7. CALF
8. PLACE
9. HOLD
10. PLACE
11. TRACK
12. HOME

303

WORDGAME 3

FINDING MEANINGS

In this list there are eight pairs of words that have some sort of connection with each other. For example, 'Diplom' (= 'diploma') and 'Student' (= 'student') are linked. Find the other pairs by looking up the words in your dictionary.

1. Morgenrock
2. Handtasche
3. Bett
4. Kirchturm
5. Fisch
6. Nest
7. Diplom
8. Lederwaren
9. Hausschuhe
10. Glockengeläut
11. Student
12. Decke
13. Elster
14. Buch
15. Schuppe
16. Regal

WORDGAME 4
SYNONYMS

Complete the crossword by supplying synonyms of the words below. You will sometimes find the words you are looking for in italics in brackets in the entries for the words in the list. Sometimes you will have to turn to the English-German section for help.

1. Art
2. sich bemühen
3. Feuer
4. sich ereignen
5. Arroganz

6. namhaft
7. Ladung
8. Plan
9. begegnen
10. Neigung

WORDGAME 5

SPELLING

You will often use your dictionary to check spellings. The person who has compiled this list of ten German words has made <u>three</u> spelling mistakes. Find the three words which have been misspelt and write them out correctly.

1. nachsehen
2. nacht
3. Nagetier
4. Name
5. Nature
6. neuriech
7. Nickerchen
8. Nimmersatt
9. nördlich
10. nötig

WORDGAME 6

ANTONYMS

Complete the crossword by supplying ANTONYMS (i.e. opposites) in German of the words below. Use your dictionary to help.

1. gestehen
2. enthüllen
3. unschuldig
4. kaufen
5. verbieten
6. Reichtum
7. ruhig
8. ankommen
9. ängstlich
10. schmutzig

WORDGAME 7

PHONETIC SPELLINGS

The phonetic transcriptions of ten German words are given below. If you study page x near the front of your dictionary you should be able to work out what the words are.

1. frika'dɛlə

2. ʃpuːr

3. faɪn

4. 'lyːgə

5. 'ʃtaxəl

6. 'naʊtɪʃ

7. gə'vœlbə

8. 'kɔʏçən

9. 'møːgən

10. 'glaʊbvʏrdɪç

WORDGAME 8

EXPRESSIONS IN WHICH THE HEADWORD APPEARS

If you look up the headword 'Satz' in the German-English section of your dictionary you will find that the word can have many meanings. Study the entry carefully and translate the following sentences into English.

1. Der Satz ist viel zu lang.

2. Unterstreicht jeden Satz, der mit einer Konjunktion beginnt.

3. Den Satz von Pythagoras kennt jeder.

4. Das Orchester hat den letzten Satz ganz ausgezeichnet gespielt.

5. Steffi Graf hat in der Meisterschaft keinen Satz verloren.

6. Der ganze Satz war in der Tasse.

7. Bei Lieferungen ins Ausland gilt ein anderer Satz.

8. Sie hat vor lauter Begeisterung einen großen Satz gemacht.

WORDGAME 9

RELATED WORDS

Fill in the blanks in the pairs of sentences below. The missing words are related to the headwords on the left. Choose the correct "relative" each time. You will find it in your dictionary near the headword provided.

HEADWORD	RELATED WORDS
Stellung	1. Ich habe die Uhr auf 1/2 6 _____. 2. Das Auto steht an der gleichen _____.
Hoffnung	3. _____ bleibt das Wetter so. 4. Sie _____, daß sie bald wieder gesund ist.
Betrug	5. Von ihm lassen wir uns nicht mehr _____. 6. Er ist als _____ bekannt.
sprechen	7. Hat er schon mit seiner Mutter _____? 8. Das Buch wurde in fünf _____ übersetzt.
Student	9. Er hat letztes Semester mit dem _____ begonnen. 10. Sie _____ Medizin.
kurz	11. Ich habe _____ noch mit ihm gesprochen. 12. Der Rock muß _____ werden.

310

WORDGAME 10
'KEY' WORDS

Study carefully the entry 'machen' in your dictionary and find translations for the following:

1. what are you doing (there)?

2. it's the cold that does that

3. that doesn't matter

4. I don't mind the cold

5. 3 and 5 are 8

6. to have the car done

7. how's the work going?

8   hurry up!

9. to set about sth

10. to turn the radio down

THE DICTIONARY AND GRAMMAR

While it is true that a dictionary can never be a substitute for a detailed grammar book, it nevertheless provides a great deal of grammatical information. If you know how to extract this information you will be able to use German more accurately both in speech and in writing.

The Collins Pocket Dictionary presents grammatical information as follows.

Parts of Speech

Parts of speech are given in italics immediately after the phonetic spellings of headwords. Abbreviated forms are used. Abbreviations can be checked on pages vi to viii.

Changes in parts of speech within an entry — for example, from adjective to pronoun to adverb, or from noun to intransitive verb to transitive verb — are indicated by means of lozenges (♦), as with the German 'alle(r, s)' and the English 'fast' opposite.

German Nouns

The gender of each noun in the German-English section of the dictionary is indicated in the following way:

m	=	Maskulinum
f	=	Femininum
nt	=	Neutrum

You will occasionally see *'m od nt'* or *'m od f'* beside an entry. This indicates that the noun can be either masculine or neuter (see 'Knäuel' opposite) or masculine or feminine (see 'Sellerie' opposite).

Feminine forms of nouns are shown, as with 'Lehrer(in)' opposite. This is marked *m(f)* to show that the feminine form has the ending '-in'. Nouns which have the ending '-(r)', like 'Angeklagte(r)' opposite, are formed from adjectives and are marked *mf* to show that they can be either masculine or feminine. Their spelling changes in the same way as adjectives, depending on their article and position in the sentence.

prosit ['proːzɪt] *excl* cheers

leiten ['laɪtən] *vt* to lead; (*Firma*) to manage; (*in eine Richtung*) to direct; (*ELEK*) to conduct

alle(r, s) ['alə(r, s)] *adj* **1** (*sämtliche*) all; **wir alle** all of us; **alle Kinder waren da** all the children were there; **alle Kinder mögen ...** all children like ...; **alle beide** both of us/them; **sie kamen alle** they all came; **alles Gute** all the best; **alles in allem** all in all

2 (*mit Zeit- oder Maßangaben*) every; **alle vier Jahre** every four years; **alle fünf Meter** every five metres

♦ *pron* everything; **alles was er sagt** everything he says, all that he says

♦ *adv* (*zu Ende, aufgebraucht*) finished; **die Milch ist alle** the milk's all gone, there's no milk left; **etw alle machen** to finish sth up

fast [faːst] *adj* schnell; (*firm*) fest ♦ *adv* schnell; fest ♦ *n* Fasten *nt* ♦ *vi* fasten; **to be ~** (*clock*) vorgehen

Knäuel ['knɔʏəl] (-s, -) *m od nt* (*Woll~*) ball; (*Menschen~*) knot

Sellerie ['zɛləriː] (-s, -(s) *od* -, -) *m od f* celery

Lehre ['leːrə] *f* teaching, doctrine; (*beruflich*) apprenticeship; (*moralisch*) lesson; (*TECH*) gauge; **l~n** *vt* to teach; **~r(in)** (-s, -) *m(f)* teacher;

Angeklagte(r) ['angəklaːktə(r)] *mf* accused

So many things depend on you knowing the correct gender of a German noun — whether you use 'er', 'sie' or 'es' to translate 'it'; whether you use 'er' or 'es' to translate 'he', 'sie' or 'es' to translate 'she'; the spelling of adjectives etc. If you are in any doubt as to the gender of a noun, it is always best to check it in your dictionary.

Genitive singular and nominative plural forms of many nouns are also given (see 'Bube' and 'Scheitel' opposite). A list of regular noun endings is given on page ix and nouns which have these forms will not show genitive singular and nominative plural at the headword (see 'Rasur' and 'Genesung' opposite). Nouns formed from two or more words do not have genitive singular and nominative plural shown if the last element appears in the dictionary as a headword. For example, if you want to know how to decline 'Tranchierbesteck', you will find the necessary information at 'Besteck'.

Adjectives

Adjectives are given in the form used when they come after a verb. If the adjective comes before a noun, the spelling changes, depending on the gender of the noun and on the article (if any) which comes before the adjective. Compare 'der Hund ist schwarz' with 'der schwarze Hund'. If you find an unfamiliar adjective in a text and want to look it up in the dictionary, you will have to decide what spelling changes have been made before you can know how it will appear in the dictionary.

Some adjectives are never used after a verb. In these cases, the dictionary shows all the possible nominative singular endings.

Adverbs

German adverbs come in three main types.

Some are just adjectives in their after-verb form, used as adverbs. Sometimes the meaning is similar to the meaning of the adjective (see 'laut'), sometimes it is rather different (see 'richtig').

Some adverbs are formed by adding '-weise', '-sweise' or 'erweise' to the adjective.

Other adverbs are not considered to be derived from particular adjectives.

In your dictionary, adjective-adverbs may be shown by a change of part of speech or by the mention 'adj, adv' at the beginning of the entry.

Fuß [fuːs] (-es, ⁻e) *m* foot; (*von Glas, Säule etc*) base; (*von Möbel*) leg; **zu ~**

Stube ['ʃtuːbə] *f* room

Mädchen ['mɛːtçən] *nt* girl; **m~haft** *adj* girlish; **~name** *m* maiden name

Rasur [ra'zuːr] *f* shaving

Genesung *f* recovery, convalescence

schwarz [ʃvarts] *adj* black; **~es Brett** notice board; **ins S~e treffen** (*auch fig*) to hit the bull's-eye; **in den ~en Zahlen** in the black; **S~arbeit** *f* illicit work, moonlighting; **S~brot** *nt* black bread

laut [laʊt] *adj* loud ♦ *adv* loudly; (*lesen*) aloud ♦ *prap* (+*gen od dat*) according to; **L~** (-(e)s, -e) *m* sound

richtig *adj* right, correct; (*echt*) proper ♦ *adv* (*umg: sehr*) really; **bin ich hier ~?** am I in the right place?; **der/die R~e** the right one/person; **das R~e** the right thing; **R~keit** *f* correctness; **R~stellung** *f* correction, rectification

leider ['laɪdər] *adv* unfortunately; **ja, ~** yes, I'm afraid so; **~ nicht** I'm afraid not

oben ['oːbən] *adv* above; (*in Haus*) upstairs;

Bube ['buːbə] (-n, -n) *m* (*Schurke*) rogue; (*KARTEN*) jack

Scheitel ['ʃaɪtəl] (-s, -) *m* top; (*Haar*) parting; **s~n** *vt* to part

Tranchierbesteck [trã'ʃiːrbəʃtɛk] *nt* (pair of) carvers *pl*

Besteck [bə'ʃtɛk] (-(e)s, -e) *nt* knife, fork and spoon, cutlery; (*MED*) set of instruments

besondere(r, s) [bə'zɔndərə(r, s)] *adj* special; (*eigen*) particular; (*gesondert*) separate; (*eigentümlich*) peculiar

letzte(r, s) ['lɛtstə(r, s)] *adj* last; (*neueste*) latest; **zum ~nmal** for the last time; **~ns** *adv* lately; **~re(r, s)** *adj* latter

beispielsweise *adv* for instance *od* example

Glück- *zW:* **g~lich** *adj* fortunate; (*froh*) happy; **g~licherweise** *adv* fortunately; **Glücksbringer** (-s, -) *m* lucky charm; **g~'selig** *adj* blissful

315

Adjective-plus-ending adverbs will usually appear as subentries.

Adverbs like 'oben' and 'leider' will usually appear as separate headwords.

Where a word in your text seems to be an adverb but does not appear in the dictionary, you should be able to work out a translation from the word it is related to, once you have found that in the dictionary.

Information about Verbs

A major problem facing language learners is that the form of a verb will change according to the subject and/or the tense being used. A typical German verb can take on many different forms — too many to list in a dictionary entry.

Yet, although verbs are listed in your dictionary in their infinitive forms only, this does not mean that the dictionary is of limited value when it comes to handling the verb system of the German language. On the contrary, it contains much valuable information.

First of all, your dictionary will help you with the meanings of unfamiliar verbs. If you came across the word 'füllt' in a text and looked it up in your dictionary you wouldn't find it. What you must do is assume that it is part of a verb and look for the infinitive form. Thus you will deduce that 'füllt' is a form of the verb 'füllen'. You now have the basic meaning of the word you are concerned with — something to do with the English verb 'fill' — and this should be enough to help you understand the text you are reading.

It is usually an easy task to make the connection between the form of a verb and the infinitive. For example, 'füllten', 'füllst', 'füllte' and 'gefüllt' are all recognizable as parts of the infinitive 'füllen'. However, sometimes it is less obvious — for example, 'hilft', 'halfen' and 'geholfen' are all parts of 'helfen'. The only real solution to this problem is to learn the various forms of the main German irregular verbs.

And this is the second source of help offered by your dictionary as far as verbs are concerned. The irregular verb lists on pages xi to xiv of the Collins Pocket Dictionary provide the main forms of the main tenses of the basic irregular verbs. (Verbs which consist of a basic verb with prefix usually follow the rules for the basic verb.) Consider the verb 'sehen' below where the following information is given:

infinitive	present indicative (2nd, 3rd sg.)	imperfect	past participle
sehen	siehst, sieht	sah	gesehen

In order to make maximum use of the information contained in these pages, a good working knowledge of the various rules affecting German verbs is required. You will acquire this in the course of your German studies and your Collins dictionary will serve as a useful 'aide-mémoire'. If you happen to forget how to form the second person singular form of the Past Tense of 'sehen' (i.e. how to translate 'You saw'), there will be no need to panic — your dictionary contains the information!

In addition, the main parts of the most common irregular verbs are listed in the body of the dictionary.

317

WORDGAME 11

PARTS OF SPEECH

In each sentence below a word has been shaded. Put a tick in the appropriate box to indicate the **part of speech** each time.

SENTENCE	Noun	Adj	Adv	Verb
1. Das Essen ist fertig.				
2. Er hat kein Recht dazu.				
3. Warum fahren wir nicht in die Stadt zum Essen?				
4. Ich gehe nicht mit essen.				
5. Rauchen ist strengstens verboten.				
6. Gehen Sie geradeaus und dann die erste Straße links.				
7. Das war aber ein interessanter Vortrag.				
8. Die Schauspielerin trug ein herrliches Kleid.				
9. Hast du schon von deiner Freundin gehört?				
10. Es ist immer noch recht sommerlich.				

WORDGAME 12
MEANING CHANGING WITH GENDER

Some German nouns change meaning according to their gender. Look at the pairs of sentences below and fill in the blanks with either 'ein, einen, eine' or 'der, den, die, das'.

1. Ist das _____ erste Band der Schillerausgabe?
   _____ Band ist nicht lang genug.

2. _____ Mark ist in letzter Zeit wieder gestiegen.
   Der Metzger löst _____ Mark aus den Knochen.

3. Was kostet _____ Bund Petersilie?
   _____ Bund an der Hose ist zu weit.

4. _____ Tau lag noch auf den Wiesen.
   Der Mann konnte _____ Tau nicht heben.

5. Wie steht mir _____ Hut?
   Wir müssen wirklich auf _____ Hut sein.

6. Vor vielen Jahren wurde hier _____ Wehr gebaut.
   _____ Wehr machte den Angriff unmöglich.

WORDGAME 13

ADJECTIVES

Try to work out how the adjectives in the following phrases will appear in the dictionary. Write your answer beside the phrase, then check in the dictionary.

1. ein englisches Buch

2. der rote Traktor

3. letzte Nacht

4. mein kleiner Bruder

5. eine lange Reise

6. guter Käse

7. das alte Trikot

8. schwarzes Brot

9. die große Kommode

10. ein heftiger Schlag

11. der siebte Sohn

12. die neuen Nachbarn

WORDGAME 14

VERB TENSES

Use your dictionary to help you fill in the blanks in the table below.
(Remember the important pages at the front of your dictionary.)

INFINITIVE	PRESENT TENSE	IMPERFECT	PERFECT TENSE
sehen		ich	
schlafen	du		
sein			ich
schlagen		ich	
anrufen			ich
abfahren	er		
studieren			ich
haben		ich	
anfangen	du		
waschen	er		
werden		ich	
nehmen			ich

WORDGAME 15
PAST PARTICIPLES

Use your dictionary to find the past participle of these verbs.

INFINITIVE	PAST PARTICIPLE
singen	
beißen	
bringen	
frieren	
reiben	
gewinnen	
helfen	
geschehen	
liegen	
lügen	
schneiden	
kennen	
mögen	
wissen	
können	

WORDGAME 16

IDENTIFYING INFINITIVES

In the sentences below you will see various German verbs shaded. Use your dictionary to help you find the INFINITIVE form of each verb.

1. Leider habe ich Ihren Namen vergessen.

2. Bitte ruf mich doch morgen früh mal an.

3. Er ist um 16 Uhr angekommen.

4. Sie hielt an ihrem Argument fest.

5. Wir waren im Sommer in Italien.

6. Ich würde gerne kommen, wenn ich nur könnte.

7. Die Maschine flog über den Nordpol.

8. Ich würde es ja machen, aber ich habe keine Zeit.

9. Wohin fährst du diesen Winter zum Skilaufen?

10. Wen habt ihr sonst noch eingeladen?

11. Er hat deinen Brief erst gestern bekommen.

12. Liest du das Buch nicht zu Ende?

13. Meine Mutter ist letztes Jahr gestorben.

14. Er hat den Zettel aus Versehen weggeworfen.

15. Ich nahm ihn jeden Tag mit nach Hause.

MORE ABOUT MEANING

In this section we will consider some of the problems associated with using a bilingual dictionary.

Overdependence on your dictionary

That the dictionary is an invaluable tool for the language learner is beyond dispute. Nevertheless, it is possible to become overdependent on your dictionary, turning to it in an almost automatic fashion every time you come up against a new German word or phrase. Tackling an unfamiliar text in this way will turn reading in German into an extremely tedious activity. If you stop to look up every new word you may actually be *hindering* your ability to read in German — you are so concerned with the individual words that you pay no attention to the text as a whole and to the context which gives them meaning. It is therefore important to develop appropriate reading skills — using clues such as titles, headlines, illustrations, etc., understanding relations within a sentence, etc. to predict or infer what a text is about.

A detailed study of the development of reading skills is not within the scope of this supplement; we are concerned with knowing how to use a dictionary, which is only one of several important skills involved in reading. Nevertheless, it may be instructive to look at one example. You see the following text in a German newspaper and are interested in working out what it is about.

Contextual clues here include the word in large type which you would probably recognize as a German name, something that looks like a date below, and the name and address at the bottom. Some 'form' words such as 'wir', 'sind', 'und' and 'Tochter' will be familiar to you from your general studies in German. Given that we are dealing with

> *Wir sind glücklich*
> *über die Geburt*
> *unserer Tochter*
>
> ## Julia
>
> am 5. November 1989
>
> *Christine und Artur Landgraf*
> *Vacher Straße 50 B, Köln*

a newspaper, you will probably have worked out by now that this could be an announcement placed in the 'Personal Column'.

So you have used a series of cultural, contextual and word-formation clues to get you to the point where you have understood that Christine and Artur Landgraf have placed this notice in the 'Personal Column' of the newspaper and that something happened to Julia on 5 November 1989. And you have reached this point *without* opening your dictionary once. Common sense and your knowledge of newspaper contents in this country might suggest that this must be an announcement of someone's birth or death. Thus 'glücklich' ('happy') and 'Geburt' ('birth') become the only words that you might have to look up in order to confirm that this is indeed a birth announcement.

When learning German we are helped by the fact that some German and English words look and sound alike and have exactly the same meaning. Such words are called 'COGNATES' i.e. words derived from the same root. Many words come from a common Latin root. Other words are the same or nearly the same in both languages because the German language has borrowed a word from English or vice versa. The dictionary should not be necessary where cognates are concerned — provided you know the English word that the German word resembles!

Words With More Than One Meaning

The need to examine with care *all* the information contained in a dictionary entry must be stressed. This is particularly important with the many German words which have more than one meaning. For example, the German 'Zeit' can mean 'grammatical tense' as well as 'time'. How you translated the word would depend on the context in which you found it.

Similarly, if you were trying to translate a phrase such as 'sich vor etwas drücken', you would have to look through the whole entry for 'drücken' to get the right translation. If you restricted your search to the first couple of lines of the entry and saw that the first meaning given is 'press', you might be tempted to assume that the idiom meant 'to press o.s. in front of sth'. But if you examined the entry closely you would see that 'sich vor etwas drücken' means 'to get out of (doing) sth', as in the sentence 'Sie drückt sich immer vor dem Abwasch'.

The same need for care applies when you are using the English-German section of your dictionary to translate a word from English into German. Watch out in particular for the lozenges indicating changes in parts of speech.

If you want to translate 'You can't fool me', the capital letters at 'Narr' and 'Närrin' will remind you that these words are nouns. But watch what you are doing with the verbs or you could end up with a mistranslation like 'Sie können mich nicht herumalbern'!

Phrasal Verbs

Another potential source of difficulty is English phrasal verbs. These consist of a common verb ('go', 'make', etc.) plus an adverb and/or a preposition to give English expressions such as 'to take after', 'to make out', etc. Entries for such verbs tend to be fairly full; therefore close examination of the contents is required. Note how these verbs appear in colour within the entry.

False Friends

fool [fuːl] *n* Narr *m*, Närrin *f* ♦ *vt* (*deceive*) hereinlegen ♦ *vi* (*also*: ~ *around*) (herum)albern; ~**hardy** *adj* tollkühn; ~**ish** *adj* albern; ~**proof** *adj* idiotensicher

make [meɪk] (*pt*, *pp* **made**) *vt* machen; (*appoint*) ernennen (zu); (*cause to do sth*) veranlassen; (*reach*) erreichen; (*in time*) schaffen; (*earn*) verdienen ♦ *n* Marke *f*; **to ~ sth happen** etw geschehen lassen; **to ~ it** es schaffen; **what time do you ~ it?** wie spät hast du es?; **to ~ do with** auskommen mit; ~ **for** *vi* gehen/fahren nach; ~ **out** *vt* (*write out*) ausstellen; (*understand*) verstehen; (*write*: *cheque*) ausstellen; ~ **up** *vt* machen; (*face*) schminken; (*quarrel*) beilegen; (*story etc*) erfinden ♦ *vi* sich versöhnen; ~ **up for** *vt* wiedergutmachen; (*COMM*) vergüten; ~**believe** *n* Phantasie *f*; ~**r** *n* (*COMM*) Hersteller *m*; ~**shift** *adj* behelfsmäßig, Not-; ~**-up** *n* Schminke *f*, Make-up *nt*; ~**-up remover** *n* Make-up-Entferner *m*

Some German and English words have similar forms *and* meanings. There are, however, German words which *look* like English words but have a completely *different* meaning. For example, 'blank' in German means 'bright'; 'Sense' means 'scythe'; 'bilden' means 'to educate'. This can easily lead to serious mistranslations.

Sometimes the meaning of the German word is close to the English. For example, 'die Chips' are 'potato crisps' rather than 'chips'; 'der Hund' means a dog of any sort, not just a 'hound'. But some German words have two meanings, one the same as the English, the other completely different! 'Golf' can mean 'gulf' as well as 'golf'; 'senden' can mean 'to send' but can also mean 'to transmit/broadcast'.

Such words are often referred to as 'false friends'. You will have to look at the context in which they appear in order to arrive at the correct meaning. If they seem to fit with the sense of the passage as a whole, it will probably not be necessary to look them up. If they don't make sense, however, you may be dealing with 'false friends'.

WORDGAME 17
WORDS IN CONTEXT

Study the sentences below. Translations of the underlined words are given at the bottom. Match the number of the sentence and the letter of the translation correctly each time.

1. Sprich bitte etwas lauter, ich kann dich nicht hören.

2. Er hört den ganzen Tag Radio.

3. Kannst du das Licht ausmachen, wenn du ins Bett gehst?

4. Können wir heute schon einen Termin ausmachen?

5. Seine Frau saß am Steuer, als der Unfall passierte.

6. Ich muß dieses Jahr viel Steuern nachzahlen.

7. Die Nachfrage nach japanischen Autos ist groß.

8. Aufgrund meiner Nachfrage konnte ich dann doch etwas erfahren.

9. Das Haus wird auf meinen Namen umgeschrieben.

10. Das Referat mußt du völlig umschreiben.

11. Sind die Äpfel schon reif?

12. Für ihr Alter wirkt sie schon ziemlich reif.

a. demand	e. ripe	i. steering wheel
b. transferred	f. inquiry	j. listens to
c. turn off	g. mature	k. agree
d. hear	h. rewrite	l. tax

WORDGAME 18

FALSE FRIENDS

Look at the advertisements below. The words which have been shaded resemble English words but have different meanings here. Find a correct translation for each word in the context.

Reformhaus
Neustr. 23
Sonderangebot:
Vollkornbrot 2,78 DM

1

2

Hotel Olympia
Alle Zimmer mit Dusche/WC
Gemütliche Atmosphäre
Bitte Prospekt anfordern

Heinrichstraße 51 —
7000 STUTTGART 25
Tel. 0711/21 56 93

3

KP-Chef Italiens fliegt
morgen nach New York

4

W. Meinzer   Lebensmittel
Heute Chips
im
Sonderangebot

5

**Der Mann
im
Smoking**

6

Reagan
will weiter
Präsident der
USA werden

7

**Nach der
Jahrtausendwende
erst mit 65 in
Rente**

8

Europaparlament

Fraktions-Flanke abdecken

9

**Reise sorgenfrei
mit diesen Drei**

**Reisescheck
Devisen
Sparkassenbuch**

BEZIRKSSPARKASSE HAUSACH
Hauptstr. 14

WORDGAME 19

WORDS WITH MORE THAN ONE MEANING

Look at the advertisements and headlines below. The words which have been shaded can have more than one meaning. Use your dictionary to help you work out the correct translation in the context.

1

Landespräsident tritt zurück

2

Vermögen:
Vom kleinen zum
großen Geld

3

Ich weiß, wie ich
Schmerzen schell los werde

Parazetamol
Von Apotheken

4

**Heinrich Wohnmobile
GmbH**
*Spezialisten bieten günstige
Preise*

Hotel Restaurant Seeberger

Alle Preise inklusive Bedienung

Marktplatz 12
Loßurg

Telefon (07165) 33 14

5

Müsli - Riegel

von Cadbury

— gibt Kraft und Energie!

6

Hotel - Pension Miramar

Behagliche Atmosphäre
Günstige Nachsaisonpreise

*Strandstr. 6,
2356 Eckernförde
Telefon (04269) 29 51*

7

Das Blatt
Finanz- und
Wirtschaftszeitung

8

HAVE FUN WITH YOUR DICTIONARY

Here are some word games for you to try. You will find your dictionary helpful as you attempt the activities.

WORDGAME 20
CODED WORDS

In the boxes below the letters of eight German words have been replaced by numbers. A number represents the same letter each time.

Try to crack the code and find the eight words. If you need help, use your dictionary.

Here is a clue: all the words you are looking for have something to do with TRANSPORT.

1 | W¹ | A² | G³ | ⁴ | ⁵ |

2 | ¹⁰ | ⁸ | ¹¹ | ¹¹ | ⁴ | ¹⁰ |

3 | ¹² | ² | ¹³ | ¹⁴ |

4 | ⁸ | ¹³ | ⁵ | ¹⁴ | ⁶ | ¹⁶ | ¹⁸ |

5 | ⁹ | ¹¹ | ¹⁶ | ³ | ¹⁵ | ⁴ | ¹⁶ | ³ |

6 | ⁶ | ² | ⁷ | ⁵ | ⁷ | ⁸ | ⁹ |

7 | ¹⁵ | ¹⁶ | ³ |

8 | ¹¹ | ² | ¹⁸ | ¹² | ¹ | ² | ³ | ⁴ | ⁵ |

WORDGAME 21

BEHEADED WORDS

If you 'behead' certain German words, i.e. take away their first letter, you are left with another German word. For example, if you behead 'Kleider' (— 'clothes'), you get 'leider' (— 'unfortunately'), and 'dort' (— 'there') gives 'Ort' (= 'place').

The following words have their heads chopped off, i.e. the first letter has been removed. Use your dictionary to help you form a new German word by adding one letter to the start of each word below. Write down the new German word and its meaning.

1. ragen (= to tower)
2. tollen (= to romp)
3. nie (= never)
4. Rand (= edge)
5. oben (= above)
6. ich (= I)
7. Rad (= wheel)
8. innen (= inside)
9. raten (= to guess)
10. indisch (= Indian)
11. eigen (= own)
12. eben (= level)
13. Ohr (= ear)
14. pur (= pure)

WORDGAME 22

CROSSWORD

Complete this crossword by looking up the words listed below in the English-German section of your dictionary. Remember to read through the entry carefully to find the word that will fit.

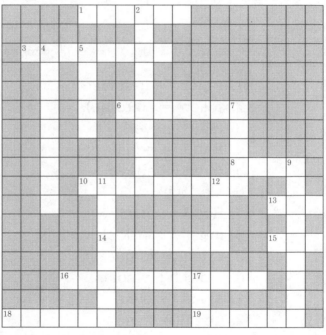

1.	Heavily	6.	Sad	11.	To start up	15.	Time
2.	Tearful	7.	Smooth		(a car)	16.	To dirty
3.	Meal	8.	Deaf	12.	Tap	17.	Day
4.	To record	9.	To reassure	13.	Place	18.	To fold
5.	Mood	10.	(A piece of) news	14.	To withdraw	19.	Profit

WORDGAME 23

There are twelve German words hidden in the grid below. Each word is made up of five letters but has been split into two parts.

Find the German words. Each group of letters can only be used once.

Use your dictionary to help you.

re	ten	cke	er	Lad	Na
rbe	Sch	tr	Sip	eh	wei
unt	en	He	am	ank	pe
ren	be	ne	cht	se	ben

WORDGAME 24

Here is a list of German words for things you will find in the kitchen. Unfortunately, they have all been jumbled up. Try to work out what each word is and put the word in the boxes on the right. You will see that there are six shaded boxes below. With the six letters in the shaded boxes make up <u>another</u> German word for an object you can find in the kitchen.

1 CSIHT Die Kinder decken den ____

2 DERH Die Kasserolle steht auf dem ____

3 RSNAHKC Ist die Kaffekanne in diesem ____ ?

4 SAETS Sie gießt den Tee in die ____

5 SRIGHCRE Das ____ liegt im Spülbecken

6 HKRÜHNSKCLA Hol die Milch aus dem ____ heraus

The word you are looking for is:

WORDGAME 25

Take the four letters given each time and put them in the four empty boxes in the centre of each grid. Arrange them in such a way that you form four six-letter words. Use your dictionary to check the words.

ANSWERS

WORDGAME 1

1	gekannt	6	zahle
2	Aktien	7	einschreiben
3	Kino	8	übel
4	kaufen	9	Ganz
5	Pudel	10	Tante

WORDGAME 2

1	gerecht	7	Wade
2	erreichen	8	Ort
3	erfahren	9	fassen
4	Herbst	10	Stelle
5	treffen	11	Gleis
6	schwer	12	Heim

WORDGAME 3

Morgenrock + Hausschuhe
Handtasche + Lederwaren
Bett + Decke
Kirchturm + Glockengeläut
Fisch + Schuppe
Nest + Elster
Diplom + Student
Buch + Regal

WORDGAME 4

1	Weise	6	berühmt
2	versuchen	7	Last
3	Brand	8	Karte
4	passieren	9	treffen
5	Uüberheblichkeit	10	Tendenz

WORDGAME 5

2 Nacht   5 Natur   6 neureich

WORDGAME 6

1	leugnen	6	Armut
2	verstecken	7	lärmend
3	schuldig	8	abreisen
4	verkaufen	9	tapfer
5	erlauben	10	sauber

WORDGAME 7

1	Frikadelle	6	nautisch
2	Spur	7	Gewölbe
3	fein	8	keuchen
4	Lüge	9	mögen
5	Stachel	10	glaubwürdig

WORDGAME 8

1 The sentence is much too long.
2 Underline every sentence which starts with a conjunction.
3 Everybody knows Pythagoras' theorem.
4 The orchestra performed the last movement really well.
5 Steffi Graf hasn't lost a set in the championships.
6 All the grounds were in the cup.
7 For deliveries abroad there is a different rate.
8 She jumped for joy.

WORDGAME 9

1	gestellt	7	gesprochen
2	Stelle	8	Sprachen
3	hoffentlich	9	Studium
4	hofft	10	studiert
5	betrügen	11	kürzlich
6	Betrüger	12	gekürzt

WORDGAME 11

1	adj	6	adv
2	noun	7	adj
3	noun	8	verb
4	verb	9	verb
5	adv	10	adj

WORDGAME 12

1 der/das
2 die/das
3 das (or ein)/der
4 der/das
5 der/der
6 ein/die

WORDGAME 13

1	englisch	7	alt
2	rot	8	schwarz
3	letzte(r,s)	9	groß
4	klein	10	heftig
5	lang	11	siebte(r,s)
6	gut	12	neu

WORDGAME 14

ich sah
du schläfst
ich bin
ich schlug
ich habe angerufen
er fährt ab
ich habe studiert
ich hatte
du fängst an
er wächst
ich wurde
ich habe genommen

WORDGAME 15

gesungen	gelegen
gebissen	gelogen
gebracht	geschnitten
gefroren	gekannt
gerieben	gemocht
gewonnen	gewußt
geholfen	gekonnt
geschehen	

WORDGAME 16

1	vergessen	9	fahren
2	anrufen	10	einladen
3	ankommen	11	bekommen
4	festhalten	12	lesen
5	sein	13	sterben
6	können	14	wegwerfen
7	fliegen	15	mitnehmen
8	werden		

WORDGAME 17

1	d	5	i	9	b
2	j	6	l	10	h
3	c	7	a	11	e
4	k	8	f	12	g

WORDGAME 18

1 health food shop
2 brochure
3 boss
4 crisps
5 dinner jacket
6 wants
7 pension
8 parliamentary party
9 foreign currency

WORDGAME 19

1 resigns
2 wealth
3 know
4 offer
5 service
6 bar
7 guesthouse
8 newspaper

WORDGAME 20

1 Wagen
2 Roller
3 Taxi
4 Omnibus
5 Flugzeug
6 Bahnhof
7 Zug
8 Lastwagen

WORDGAME 21

1 tragen (= to carry)
2 Stollen (= gallery)
3 Knie (= knee)
4 Brand (= fire)
5 loben (= to praise)
6 dich (= you);
sich (= oneself);
mich (= me)
7 Grad (= degree)
8 sinnen (= to ponder)
9 braten (= to roast)
10 kindisch (= childish)
11 zeigen (= to show);
neigen (= to incline)
12 geben (= to give);
leben (= to live);
neben (= next to)
13 Rohr (= pipe, tube)
14 Spur (= trace)

WORDGAME 22

1 schwer
2 weinerlich
3 Mahlzeit
4 aufnehmen
5 Laune
6 traurig
7 glatt
8 taub
9 beruhigen
10 Nachricht
11 anlassen
12 Hahn
13 Ort
14 abheben
15 Uhr
16 beschmutzen
17 Tag
18 falten
19 Gewinn

WORDGAME 23

1 recht
2 Laden
3 Hecke
4 ehren
5 beten
6 Narbe
7 neben
8 Sippe
9 unter
10 Scham
11 weise
12 trank

WORDGAME 24

1 Tisch   4 Tasse
2 Herd   5 Geschirr
3 Schrank 6 Kühlschrank

Hidden word — KESSEL

WORDGAME 25

1

2

3